The Waite Group's
Microsoft® C Bible
Second Edition

Nabajyoti Barkakati
Revised by Earl Young

SAMS
A Division of Macmillan Computer Publishing
11711 North College, Carmel, Indiana 46032 USA

To Leha, Ivy, and Emily

SECOND EDITION
FIRST PRINTING—1990

International Standard Book Number: 0-672-22736-3
Library of Congress catalog Card Number: 90-61918

From The Waite Group, Inc.
Development Editor: *Mitchell Waite*
Editorial Director, Second Edition: *Scott Calamar*
Editorial Director, First Edition: *James Stockford*
Content Editor: *Harry Henderson*
Technical Reviewer: *John Ferguson*
Assistant Editor, Second Edition: *Joel Fugazzotto*

From SAMS
Acquisitions Editor, Second Edition: *Richard K. Swadley*
Acquisitions Editor, First Edition: *James S. Hill*
Development Editor, Second Edition: *Gregory Croy*
Development Editor, First Edition: *James Rounds*
Manuscript Editor, Second Edition: *Denise Lohr, BooksCraft, Inc., Indianapolis*
Manuscript Editor, First Edition: *Don MacLaren, BooksCraft, Inc., Indianapolis*
Keyboarder: *Joyce Smith, Automated Business Services, Indianapolis*
Designer: *Glenn Santner*
Illustrator: *T.R. Emrick*
Cover Illustrator: *Kevin Caddell*
Production Coordinator: *Steve Noe*
Production: *Jerry Ellis, Marj Hopper, Chuck Hutchinson, Betty Kish, Bob LaRoche, Larry Lynch, Diana Moore, San Dee Phillips, Dennis Sheehan*
Indexer: *Lynn Brown, Brown Editorial Service*
Compositor: *Shepard Poorman Communications Corp., Indianapolis*

Printed in the United States of America

Thomas Healy

Contents

Preface

Microsoft C is a huge product, loaded with features, tools, aids, extensions, and manuals that no one book could ever fully describe. One of Microsoft C's greatest values is its huge library of C function calls. With more than 500 routines, requiring almost 1,000 manual pages to cover (counting the C language reference and the library reference), the Microsoft C library lets you do everything from calculating an arc sine to drawing a pie chart to performing a quicksort of an array of strings.

Much of this power remains untapped, however. The manuals provided by Microsoft are *so* extensive that they are hard to use for ready reference, yet not detailed enough to use for learning. Their emphasis is on providing an "official" description of every function and feature. My approach, on the other hand, is to write as a programmer for programmers, to put the information you need at your fingertips while at the same time providing you with the background, context, and practical tips you need to master the C library.

Frankly, I wrote *The Waite Group's Microsoft C Bible* because *I* wanted such a book at my elbow when I wrote my next big C program. This book is based on The Waite Group's "bible" model, which has been successful in both the MS-DOS and UNIX worlds. My goal was to make a reference book that would be handy for looking up functions and would provide a clear and concise tutorial.

The Waite Group's Microsoft C Bible describes each of the more than 500 functions in the Microsoft C library. Practical, real-world MS-DOS-based examples are provided for each function. The routines are divided into functional categories, with an intermediate-level tutorial preceding each category, followed by the reference entries in alphabetical order. Additionally, this book features:

- Two "quick start" tutorials: one is a refresher course on the basic elements of the C language and one is on running the Microsoft C compiler, including a survey of its main features and options

- Tutorials that detail how the functions in each category are related, how to pick the right function to do a given job, and cautions to observe
- Complete ANSI prototypes for each function
- More extensive (and, I hope, more interesting) program examples than those in the Microsoft manuals
- Tables that provide helpful, MS-DOS-specific information
- Check boxes that tell you at a glance whether a given function is compatible with earlier releases of the Microsoft C compiler, the new ANSI standard, the System V UNIX library, Xenix, QuickC, Turbo C, Turbo C++, and the DOS and OS/2 operating systems
- Quick access to any function through two "jump tables," one in alphabetical order and one grouped by functional category
- Suggestions for further reading on C in general, aspects of programming, and algorithms used by particular functions

Your use of this book can grow as your programming ability does. If you are new to programming, you can use this book as a learning resource, together with a good C primer such as those suggested in the *Further Reading* for the first tutorial. By reading the tutorials in order, you can ensure that you grasp all of the key ideas of C, move beyond the coverage of a "beginner's" book, and get a feel for the practical considerations involved in each area of programming. As you start to write programs you can study the various groups of functions in detail.

If you are an experienced programmer in languages other than C, this book can give you a fast start to learning C because its survey of C is complete but not condescending. Since you already know what programs have to do, you can quickly find out how they do it with Microsoft C. And if you are an experienced C programmer, you can jump to the second tutorial, quickly master the compiler, and then survey the functional areas to find out how Microsoft C deals with your areas of interest. This book will also help you port your applications to Microsoft C by enabling you to find equivalent functions quickly.

I hope you will be pleased with the convenience and utility of this book. If you have questions or suggestions, or would like to contribute to a future revision, please contact The Waite Group, 100 Shoreline Highway, Suite A-285, Mill Valley, CA 94941.

Acknowledgments

From the author:
I am grateful to Mitchell Waite for providing me with the opportunity to write this book and for his guidance throughout the project. I would like to thank Harry Henderson for his thorough editing, helpful suggestions, and thoughtful comments. Finally, a project of this magnitude requires the support of family and friends. This book would not be possible without the love and inspiration of my wife Leha and my daughters Ivy and Emily. Thanks for being there!

Nabajyoti Barkakati

From Mitchell Waite:
Every once in a great while a writer comes to us who is so special that we must stop and acknowledge how lucky we are to have met him or her. I first met Naba Barkakati when he wrote a chapter on serial communications for *The Waite Group's MS-DOS Papers.* His chapter was especially lucid and had absolutely great illustrations (something unusual for computer book authors). What really shocked us was that he delivered the chapter early (unheard of in this industry)! Obviously, we needed this author. From that start, Naba has gone on to write what we think is the most comprehensive C reference book available.

I would like to take this opportunity to thank Naba for his commitment to this massive project (well over 1,200 manuscript pages, 370 program examples, and 100 tables) and for his diligence and sensitivity to the subject. This is truly his magnum opus. I would like to offer thanks to Earl Young for the energy and attention to detail that he devoted to revising this book.

I would like to thank all the folks at Microsoft Corporation who have helped make this book possible, especially Todd Warren, who provided constant updates of the beta versions of the Microsoft C compiler and continuing support to our author.

Finally, I give my thanks to the people behind the scenes at SAMS, who took our manuscript and turned it into the marketable first edition that we are all proud of: to Jim Hill for his faith in the idea for a user-friendly C reference book; to Wendy Ford for skillfully managing a most complex production job; to Kevin Caddell for the book's great cover painting; to Jim Rounds for casting off this back-breaker of a manuscript; to Glenn Santner for bringing the vision of the cover to the artists; to Don MacLaren for editing the manuscript; to Jim Irizarry and his sales team for moving our titles into the book stores in ever increasing quantities; to Damon Davis and Tom Surber for steering SAMS so wisely over the years; and to all the other people at SAMS who in one way or another were involved with making *The Waite Group's Microsoft C Bible* a success.

I would like to thank Harry Henderson, editor of the Waite Group's UNIX and C series, for his meticulous editing of both editions, ideas for sample programs, sincere letters to the author, and perpetually cooperative spirit; Robert Lafore, for his warm-hearted assistance; Jim Stockford, for his management of the first edition of this book; and John Ferguson, for his technical review of the first edition. I would like to express my sincere appreciation to Scott Calamar, our second edition editorial director, who, enduring a difficult transition, never complained, while our author and editors struggled with complex compatibility issues; new, undocumented C 6.0 features; and other strange and hard-to-articulate events. Finally, thanks to Joel Fugazzotto for his assistance in delivering the manuscript.

Mitchell Waite

Trademarks

Introduction

Overall Organization

The book is organized into the following five parts.

PART I: THE C LANGUAGE AND MICROSOFT C

This part is a refresher on C and the features of Microsoft C suitable for beginning and intermediate C programmers. Chapter 1, "Overview of the C Language," provides a succinct discussion of the C programming language including references to the ANSI extensions. You can skip this section if you are already familiar with C. Chapter 2, "Microsoft C 6.0 Compiler Features and Options," discusses keywords and features of C programming that are specific to Microsoft C, including the new options, features, and utilities introduced with Microsoft C 6.0. For example, we describe the memory models offered by Microsoft C, and we detail the command-line options for the compiler program, CL.

PART II: PROCESS CONTROL AND MEMORY MANAGEMENT

Part II begins the tutorials and reference pages on the functions in the Microsoft C library. The common theme in this part is the management of processes, communication between functions, and memory management. This part includes the following categories of functions:

3. Process control
4. Variable-length argument lists
5. Memory allocation and management
6. Buffer manipulation

PART III: DATA PROCESSING

This part covers the routines that process, convert, calculate, and handle data. Such tasks as mathematical computations, searching, and sorting are discussed here. This part includes the categories:

7. Data conversion routines
8. Math routines
9. Character classification and conversion
10. String comparison and manipulation
11. Searching and sorting
12. Time and locale routines

PART IV: FILES AND I/O Part IV focusses on routines that manipulate files and perform Input and Output (I/O) operations. The MS-DOS and BIOS interface routines are covered in Chapter 16, "System Calls." These categories are included:

13. File manipulation
14. Directory manipulation
15. Input and output routines
16. System calls

PART V: GRAPHICS The three chapters in this part describe the graphics routines introduced in Microsoft C 5.0, 5.1, and 6.0. Chapter 17, "Graphics Modes, Coordinates, and Attributes," includes all the preliminary information you need to get started with graphics programming. Among the routines discussed are those that set colors, line styles, and fill masks and those that enable you to determine the status of parameters maintained internally by the graphics library. Chapter 18, "Drawing and Animation," covers the objects you can draw with the graphics routines, including point, line, rectangle, ellipse, arc, and pie. We also discuss how to perform animation and how to use the new presentation graphics and charting functions introduced with Microsoft C 6.0. Chapter 19, "Combining Graphics and Text," describes the text output routines and tells you how to control the appearance of text on the screen and confine text to a window.

Chapter Organization

Starting with Chapter 3, each chapter begins with a tutorial on the category of routines being discussed in that section. Each tutorial establishes the concepts necessary to understand and use that category of routines. In each category the routines are catalogued alphabetically and also grouped according to the tasks they perform. The tutorials show how the functions in a group are related, and details their similarities and differences so you will know which of many similarly named functions is appropriate for a given situation. They show you how to use the functions to perform commonly needed programming tasks and in many cases offer suggestions for further reading.

The tutorial is followed by the reference entries for the functions in that category, arranged alphabetically. The reference entries provide a structured guide to the purpose, syntax, and usage of the function and contain an example call and example program using the function. Each reference entry is presented as in Figure I-1.

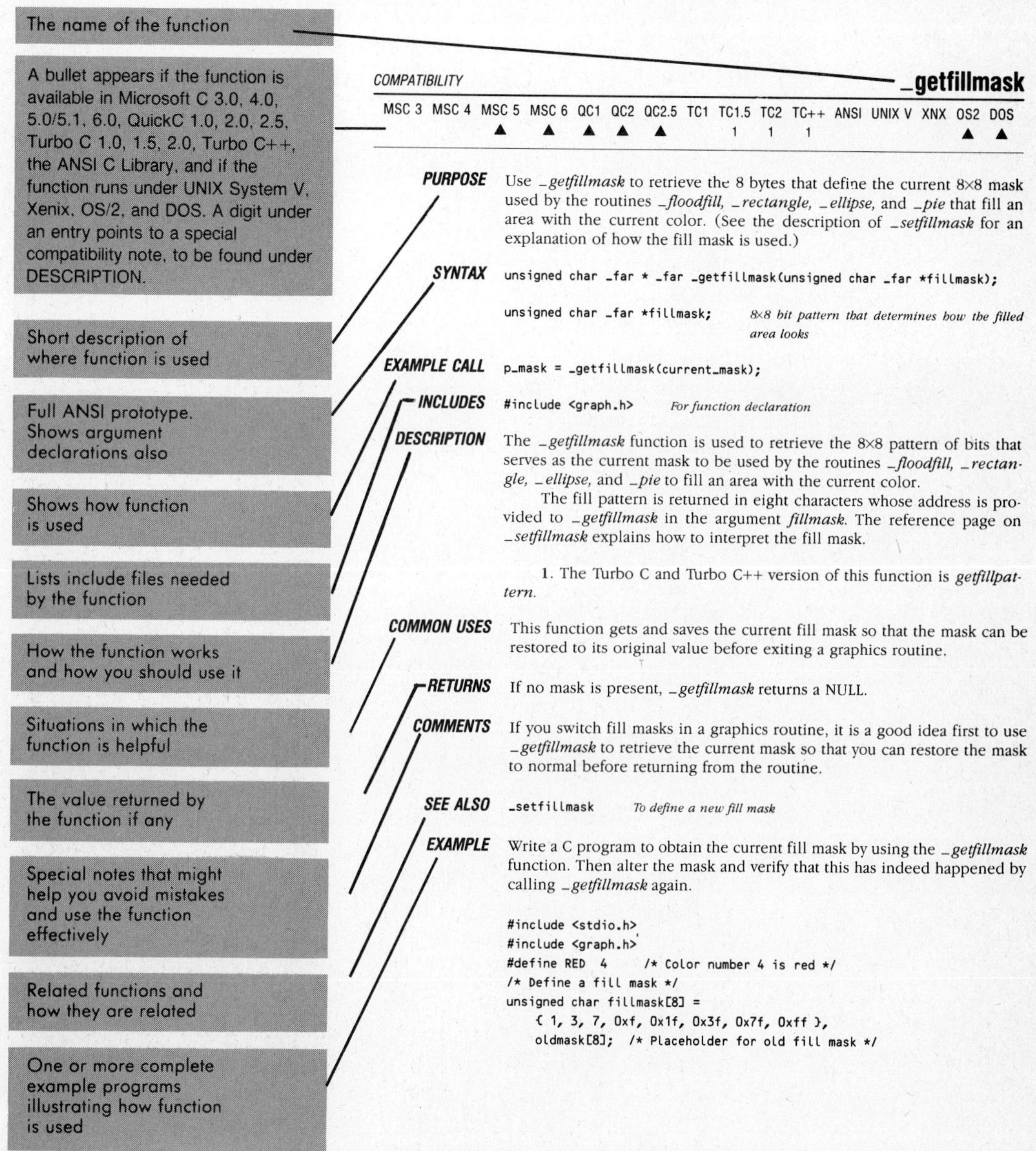

The name of the function
A bullet appears if the function is available in Microsoft C 3.0, 4.0, 5.0/5.1, 6.0, QuickC 1.0, 2.0, 2.5, Turbo C 1.0, 1.5, 2.0, Turbo C++, the ANSI C Library, and if the function runs under UNIX System V, Xenix, OS/2, and DOS. A digit under an entry points to a special compatibility note, to be found under DESCRIPTION.
Short description of where function is used
Full ANSI prototype. Shows argument declarations also
Shows how function is used
Lists include files needed by the function
How the function works and how you should use it
Situations in which the function is helpful
The value returned by the function if any
Special notes that might help you avoid mistakes and use the function effectively
Related functions and how they are related
One or more complete example programs illustrating how function is used
COMPATIBILITY
_getfillmask
MSC 3 MSC 4 MSC 5 MSC 6 QC1 QC2 QC2.5 TC1 TC1.5 TC2 TC++ ANSI UNIX V XNX OS2 DOS
▲ ▲ ▲ ▲ ▲ 1 1 1 ▲ ▲
PURPOSE
Use _getfillmask to retrieve the 8 bytes that define the current 8×8 mask used by the routines _floodfill, _rectangle, _ellipse, and _pie that fill an area with the current color. (See the description of _setfillmask for an explanation of how the fill mask is used.)
SYNTAX
unsigned char _far * _far _getfillmask(unsigned char _far *fillmask);
unsigned char _far *fillmask;
8×8 bit pattern that determines how the filled area looks
EXAMPLE CALL
p_mask = _getfillmask(current_mask);
INCLUDES
#include <graph.h>
For function declaration
DESCRIPTION
The _getfillmask function is used to retrieve the 8×8 pattern of bits that serves as the current mask to be used by the routines _floodfill, _rectangle, _ellipse, and _pie to fill an area with the current color.
The fill pattern is returned in eight characters whose address is provided to _getfillmask in the argument fillmask. The reference page on _setfillmask explains how to interpret the fill mask.
1. The Turbo C and Turbo C++ version of this function is getfillpattern.
COMMON USES
This function gets and saves the current fill mask so that the mask can be restored to its original value before exiting a graphics routine.
RETURNS
If no mask is present, _getfillmask returns a NULL.
COMMENTS
If you switch fill masks in a graphics routine, it is a good idea first to use _getfillmask to retrieve the current mask so that you can restore the mask to normal before returning from the routine.
SEE ALSO
_setfillmask
To define a new fill mask
EXAMPLE
Write a C program to obtain the current fill mask by using the _getfillmask function. Then alter the mask and verify that this has indeed happened by calling _getfillmask again.
#include <stdio.h>
#include <graph.h>
#define RED 4 /* Color number 4 is red */
/* Define a fill mask */
unsigned char fillmask[8] =
{ 1, 3, 7, 0xf, 0x1f, 0x3f, 0x7f, 0xff },
oldmask[8]; /* Placeholder for old fill mask */

Figure I-1. *Layout of reference entries*

A number of library functions come in "families" where essentially the same function has several variants based on memory model, data type, or graphics coordinate system used. For example, the general-purpose memory allocation routine *malloc* as the variant *_fmalloc* for use with far pointers, *_halloc* for the huge memory model, *_nmalloc* for near pointers, and *_bmalloc* for the "based pointers" introduced in Microsoft C 6.0. Since all of these functions have many things in common, this new edition of the *Microsoft C Bible* groups them into a single entry, placed alphabetically under *malloc.* The tables on the inside covers of the book list all of the functions individually, however, so you can still find the relevant entry at a glance.

When an entry covers more than one function, separate syntax definitions and example calls are given for each function. Some entries do not provide example programs; instead, they refer to example programs in other entries that also cover the function under discussion.

Note: Many times string constants (lines contained in double quotes) and the strings in *printf, outtext*, etc., statements are too long to fit on one line in the printed listings, so they have been broken. However, this will cause a "new line in string constant" compile error. Therefore, either these string constants should be typed on one line without a line break or the backslash (\) character should be typed before the line break. (The backslash tells the compiler to treat the whole string as one line.)

While this book is useful for in-depth study, we realize that you probably will use it most frequently as a ready reference resource. For this purpose, "jump tables" inside the front and back covers allow you to find any function by name or by category. The reference entries also refer back to the appropriate tutorials for further details.

And in Conclusion . . .

Now that you know more about the *The Waite Group's Microsoft C Bible*, it's time for you to jump in and use the book to explore the capabilities of Microsoft C 6.0. You may be pleasantly surprised by how helpful the library can be. I hope you will enjoy using this book as much as I have enjoyed writing it!

About the Author

Nabajyoti Barkakati works as an electronics engineer for a well-known research laboratory. He began his programming career in 1975 and he has worked extensively with FORTRAN, C, and several assembly languages. An avid programmer still, he is primarily interested in developing communications and graphics software on the IBM PC and Macintosh. He has a Ph.D. in electrical engineering from the University of Maryland at College Park. He is also the author of *The Waite Group's Turbo C++ Bible*, *The Waite Group's Microsoft Macro Assembler Bible*, and *The Essential Guides to Microsoft C*, *Turbo C*, and *ANSI C*.

I The C Language and Microsoft C

- ▶ Overview of the C Language
- ▶ Microsoft C 6.0 Compiler Features and Options

Chapter 1 Overview of the C Language

Introduction

The C language as defined by the ANSI standard consists of a basic core of keywords that provide control structures and definitions of data types. This core is accompanied by a standard library of functions for input and output (I/O), math calculations, string operations, and other generic computing tasks. Programs that confine themselves to these standard keywords and library functions are portable to other ANSI-standard compilers, even those running on a machine with a different processor and architecture, though the programmer must be aware of possible differences in the size of certain data types and in the order in which bytes are stored in memory.

Beyond the standard functions, modern C compilers specify many other functions that are designed to work with a particular system architecture (such as PC-compatible systems using the Intel 80x86 processors) or under particular operating systems (such as DOS or OS/2). Vendors of PC-compatible compilers, therefore, add many PC-specific functions for memory allocation, access to peripheral devices, calls to DOS and BIOS services, graphics, and other areas. This access to all parts of the system enables you to harness the system's full potential.

Over the years, Microsoft C has continually expanded and enhanced its support for the PC-compatible architecture by providing many new library functions beyond those required by the ANSI standard. Version 5.0 (introduced in 1987) enhanced the library, most notably in the area of system calls for accessing DOS and BIOS services and in improved graphics capabilities including support for VGA and other graphics standards. In 1988, version 5.1 was introduced. This update provided support for the OS/2 operating system. With it, it is possible to build programs that work with both OS/2 "protected" mode and "real" mode (which is functionally equivalent to DOS 3.x and 4.x). Overall, changes from version 5.0 to 5.1 were minor.

Version 6.0, released in 1990, added more than 150 functions, including a complete library of presentation graphics and charting routines, support for inline assembly language instructions, and expanded flexibility in dealing with pointers and memory models.

As the capabilities of the C library and the complexity of the programming environment have grown, the need for tools to help programmers manage this complexity has grown. To help answer these needs, Microsoft C 6.0 comes with the Programmer's WorkBench (PWB) software suite, NMAKE for automating recompilations, and the significantly enhanced CodeView symbolic debugger. With these developments, Microsoft C 6.0 offers one of the best environments for program development.

Now that the ANSI standard for C has been finalized, portability will be improved and sounder programming practices (such as the use of function prototypes) will help make programs easier to debug and to maintain. Microsoft C 6.0 presents a language implementation generally conforming to the ANSI standard for C. It also brings the compiler into compatibility with UNIX System V 3.4.

This chapter is designed to give you a refresher course in the C language itself, without regard to particular features of Microsoft C. It is not intended to be a complete tutorial, but we include a list of recommended books on C programming, in general, and in C programming for PC-compatible systems, in particular. Chapter 2 summarizes features specific to Microsoft C 6.0 and describes the compiler and the linker that you use to build your programs. In the following discussion of the basic features of C, we will point out how the ANSI standard for C affects a particular feature. For your convenience, these notes are marked with the symbol: ANSI

Structure of a C Program

As shown in Figure 1-1, a typical C program consists of preprocessor directives, declarations of functions and global variables, a *main* function, the body of the *main* function, and usually several other functions. The body of each function, including *main*, contains declarations for local variables as well as expressions and statements.

While a stand-alone C program must contain a *main* function, not every C source file will contain a *main* function. In many applications, already-tested functions in separate source files are combined with the main program using LINK or a similar utility. These additional files will not have a *main* function because *main* appears only once in a compiled C program. A C program always begins executing at the start of the definition for *main*.

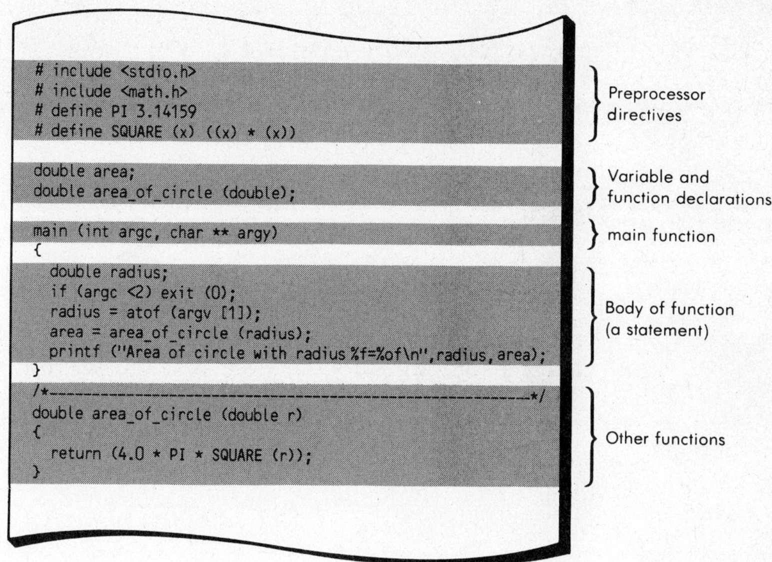

include <stdio.h>
include <math.h>
define PI 3.14159
define SQUARE (x) ((x) * (x))
double area;
double area_of_circle (double);
main (int argc, char ** argy)
{
double radius;
if (argc <2) exit (0);
radius = atof (argv [1]);
area = area_of_circle (radius);
printf ("Area of circle with radius %f=%of\n",radius,area);
}
/*--*/
double area_of_circle (double r)
{
return (4.0 * PI * SQUARE (r));
}
Preprocessor directives
Variable and function declarations
main function
Body of function (a statement)
Other functions

Figure 1-1. ***Structure of a C program***

Comments

As you can see, comments enclosed in the symbols /* and */ are liberally used to explain the parts of the program. A comment can appear entirely on one line, or it can spread across several lines:

```
/* The comment starts here
   and continues here
   and ends here */
```

Many languages allow comments to be nested, with comments appearing within comments. Since the material within a comment is ignored by the compiler, certain sections of code can be "commented out" during various phases of the construction of a program (for example, code that is not yet complete enough to run). C does not allow comment nesting, which means that using comments to hide code from the compiler is not possible if any of the hidden code is already commented. A way around this restriction is to use the *#if 0/#endif* statement, which we will describe later.

Starting with version 5.1, Microsoft C allows an alternative (but non-portable) method of identifying comments: starting them with a pair of slashes (//). This means anything from a // to the end of a line is a comment. For example:

```
printf ("CYR Associates");  // company name
```

or

```
printf ("Production Department Schedule");
// company name
```

In these cases, "// company name" is a comment identifying the title of a report—the second instance showing the // as a comment occupying the entire line. Versions 5.1 and 6.0 of Microsoft will accept either without giving a warning through level 3 of the warning messages. Version 6.0, which introduced a fourth level for warnings, will flag it on that level as a nonstandard C extension—thus allowing you to identify where the // convention is used. Since this comment convention is used with C++, it is likely to become more prevalent in the future.

Preprocessor Directives

The "preprocessor" is a facility unique to C. It processes the source file before compilation starts, performing tasks such as merging the contents of one or more other files into the C program (the *#include* directive) and replacing one string pattern with another throughout the program (the *#define* directive).

The preprocessor processes the source text of a program file and acts on commands, called "preprocessor directives," embedded in the text. These directives begin with the character #, and convention holds that such lines are not indented unless being nested within other preprocessor directives. There are twelve preprocessor directives in Microsoft C 6.0: *#define, #elif, #else, #endif, #error, #if, #ifdef, #ifndef, #include, #line, #pragma,* and *#undef.* Version 6.0 also has four preprocessor "operators" that can be used within certain directives: *token-pasting, stringizing, charizing,* and *defined.* Note that preprocessor commands, unlike actual program statements, do not end with a semicolon.

The compiler typically invokes the preprocessor before beginning compilation, but recent versions of Microsoft C allow you to run the preprocessor and perform the specified substitutions without actually compiling the program. The /E option writes preprocessed output to stdout and includes *#line* directives, /EP writes preprocessed output to stdout and strips the *#line* directives, /P writes preprocessed output to a file and appends an .I extension, and /C (legal only when used with /E, /P or /EP) preserves comments during preprocessing. These options can be useful for making sure that your preprocessor directives are having the intended effect.

The preprocessor provides three important services that enable users to make programs modular, more easily readable, and easier to "port" to different computers. You use *#include* to merge the contents of a file with a C source file. You can use *#define* to replace one string with another (also known as *token replacement* and *macro processing*). You can use *#ifdef*-type statements to allow compilation to be restricted to selected blocks of a source file (*conditional compilation*). For example, different files can be merged and compiled, based on whether the target system has a math coprocessor or on whether the program will be run under DOS or OS/2.

PREPROCESSOR DEFINITIONS

The program in Figure 1.1 uses two *#define* statements, one for a constant numeric value and one for a string. This usage is widely followed by C programmers and is a staple of many C books, but it has become largely obsolete with ANSI C. Current convention is to use the keyword *const* (an ANSI construct introduced in version 5.1) instead of *#define*. The *const* keyword identifies the data item as one that cannot be changed within the program—a constant value—and it can be used with assignments to create an initialization. For example, *const float PI = 3.14159F* serves the same purpose as *#define PI 3.14159F*.

Both statements include an "F" after the 3.14159 because unsuffixed floating-point constants have type *double*. If you leave out the F, the compiler will generate a "conversion between floating types" warning message (warning level 2 of version 5.1, warning level 4 of version 6.0) when PI or a similarly defined variable is used in calculations with a normal float variable. Thus, two changes should be made in the TYPICAL.C example program to avoid receiving warning messages:

```
#define PI 3.14159
```

should be changed to

```
const float PI = 3.14159F;
```

and

```
crcmfrnc = 2.0 * PI * radius;
```

should be changed to

```
crcmfrnc = 2.0F * PI * radius;
```

Equally important, use of *const* ensures that the compiler can perform full "type-checking" on constant values—for example, making sure that the values used to call a function match the types specified in the function's parameter list.

FILE INCLUSION The ability to include other files in the program being compiled provides for modularity, because tested, reliable code can be easily incorporated in the program being developed. This is especially important now because ANSI-usage calls for function prototypes. Declarations that are used repeatedly can be kept in a file and included where needed using *#include*. The *#include* statement has three formats:

```
#include <stdio.h>
#include "local.h"
#include "c:\test\specific.h"
```

The first format, which is the most common, tells the preprocessor to read the named file from the default *include* directory. In Microsoft C, the default *include* directory is specified either by the compiler option /I *directory* or by the environment variable INCLUDE. The angle brackets (< >) alert the preprocessor to look in the *include* directory. The search occurs first in the directories specified by the /I switch, and then, if necessary, in the directories specified by the INCLUDE variable. Our example asks for the *stdio.h* file, which is a standard C header file. It is one of over forty header files provided by Microsoft C version 6.0.

The second example specifies inclusion of the *"local.h"* file. The compiler recognizes the double quotation marks as requiring a search of the directory in which the source C file is located. If the file in which the *include* statement is located is itself an include file, the search continues recursively until the directory of the original C source file is searched. If the search of the C source directory fails to locate the appropriate file, the compiler defaults to the search path used in the previous example, using the /I directories and then, if necessary, those specified by the *include* statement.

The third example is the most restrictive. The only directory to be searched for the file will be *c:\test*. In general, remember that the compiler will not search in any directories that have not been specified using these rules. You can use the /X switch (explained in detail in the help files packaged with the Microsoft C 6.0 product) to override the standard directories of an include search.

The INCLUDE environment variable can contain several directories and refer to several drives. The following example specifies three different directories in which include files may be stored. The first two are on the D drive and the third is on the C drive.

```
INCLUDE=d:\MSC\MINC;d:\ZINC;c:\CTUL\TINC
```

Token Replacement and Macro Processing

A common preprocessor task is replacing all occurrences of a "string" (or "token") with a different string. This is done with the *#define* directive and is the C equivalent of the word processing search-and-replace command. A frequent use of this directive is to define a symbolic constant for a numeric one, and normally this greatly improves the readability of the source code. (As we explained earlier, this use of *#define* leads to occasional problems and is no longer recommended.) The *#define* directive comes in two forms, one of which takes optional parameters. Here is an example:

```
#define PI 3.14159F
#define SQUARE(x)   ((x)*(x))
```

The first *#define* directive, an example of obsolescent usage, stipulates that the string *3.14159* be substituted for every occurrence of the string *PI* in the source file. Before compilation begins, the preprocessor will search for this string and replace it with the specified literal value. The second line defines a macro with one parameter. "Macros," like functions, can have arguments (parameters) that are replaced by appropriate actual values. Here the macro definition would cause *SQUARE(2)* in your code to become *((2)*(2))* after the preprocessor has performed the replacement of *x* with the parameter 2. This macro is equivalent to a function that squares its arguments.

The parentheses in the definition of *SQUARE(x)* are absolutely necessary. Suppose the definition read *#define SQUARE(x) x*x*. If you used this version of the macro in the form *SQUARE(y+z)* to square the sum of two variables *y* and *z*, after the preprocessor makes the replacements, the macro reduces to *y+z*y+z* which is certainly not what you want. With the definition shown earlier, however, the macro would have generated *((y+z)*(y+z))*, which gives the correct result. Use parentheses liberally when defining macros with arguments that might be ambiguous.

Although a macro operates on its parameters like a function does, using a macro does not involve the overhead of making a function call. Rather, the macro substitutes the specified expression in the source file wherever the specified name occurs. When you use macros, you are trading the speed of execution for an increase in the size of the compiled program. You should also note that the compiler cannot perform type-checking on the arguments used in a macro, which can lead to hard-to-trace bugs.

TOKEN-PASTING OPERATOR

Starting with version 5.1, Microsoft C supports the ANSI standard preprocessor operators. The first one, called the "token-pasting" operator, enables you to join one token to another to create a third token. (A "token" is a symbol separated from adjacent symbols by whitespace.) The operator is a double pound sign (##) and is only used with macros. The syntax is

```
token##parameter
```

or

```
parameter##token
```

The actual argument is concatenated with the token on the other side of the ## when the macro is expanded if the ## operator precedes or follows a formal parameter in the macro definition. Here is an example:

```
#define MSC 5
#define MSC C 6
#define version(x) MSC##x
```

Thus, when the preprocessor checks *version(6)*, it first gets the string *MSC##6* and checks to see whether 6 is a valid value that can follow *MSC*. Since 6 is one of the defined values for the *MSC* token, the ## is deleted and the space closed up, resulting in the value of *version(6)* being *MSC 6*. (If an undefined value such as *version(4)* had been used, then no substitution would be made.) The stringizing facility, therefore, makes it easy to generate a variety of appropriate symbols according to the specified value.

STRINGIZING OPERATOR

The "stringizing" operator is a single pound sign (#), and it makes a string out of any operand with a # prefix. It works with macros only, and does this by putting the operand in double quotes. For example, if you defined and used a macro

```
#define value_now(x) printf (#x" = %d\n", x)
```

and later in your program used the *value_now (counter);* statement, the preprocessor generates the statement *printf ("counter"" = %d\n", counter);* as the replacement. Since the ANSI standard also stipulates that adjacent strings will be concatenated, this becomes equivalent to *printf ("counter = %d\n", counter);*. Indeed, the stringizing operator is most useful for generating complicated *printf* or *sprintf* statements automatically. Whitespace between tokens in the actual argument is ignored, and the operator automatically inserts the backslash in front of string characters that need it, such as the double quote and the backslash.

CHARIZING OPERATOR

The "charizing" preprocessor operator, a pound sign followed immediately by the "at" sign (#@), uses the syntax #@*parameter*. Like the token-pasting and stringizing operators, it is used only with arguments to macros. When the macro is expanded, its argument is enclosed in single quotes and expanded. (The charizing operator cannot handle the single-quote character.) For example:

```
#define quote(x)  #@x
```

causes the statement

```
a = quote(b);
```

to expand to

```
a = 'b';
```

Conditional Compilation

Conditional compilation lets you control which parts of a source file are compiled, depending on specified conditions. This capability enables you to maintain a single set of source files that can be compiled with different compilers and in different environments. Other forms of customization are also possible; for example, you may decide to insert *printf* statements for debugging that are compiled only if a symbol named DEBUG is defined.

The directives *#if, #elif, #else,* and *#endif* are the primary means of conditionally excluding portions of source text from use by the compiler. One use for them is to help you comment-out code that contains comments (as you have seen, nested comments aren't allowed by most compilers):

```
#if 0
printf ("%s", string);      /* print a string */
getch();                    /* await the user */
#endif
```

Here, *#if 0* and *#endif* have two commented lines of code between them. The *#if 0* will always evaluate false and will thus shift immediately to *#endif.* This means you can use the preprocessor to comment-out pieces of your code. To make a block of commented-out code executable again, either remove the *#if* and *#endif* statements or change the first statement to *#if 1.*

The *#ifdef* and *#ifndef* directives, special cases of the *#if* directive, are used more widely than the other conditional directives: they test whether a particular symbol had been defined earlier (with a *#define* directive). The first fragment in the following listing uses *#ifdef* to compile a *printf* statement only if the symbol DEBUG is defined. This can be called using the /D option to the CL command when you compile the file.

```
      :
      :

#ifdef DEBUG
      printf ("Count = %d\n", count);
#endif
```

The next example shows nested *#ifdef* statements. The first *#ifdef* statement tests whether the condition ANSI is true, and if so, nested statements check which compiler is to be used, including the appropriate system definitions file:

```
#ifdef ANSI
      #include <dos.h>
      #ifdef __TURBOC__
            #include <BSYS/STAT.H>
      #endif

      #ifdef __WATCOMC__
            #include <sys/stat.h>
      #else
            #ifdef M_I86
                  #include <MSYS/STAT.H>
            #endif
      #endif
#endif
```

You can write code that is quite portable if you accommodate compiler differences in this fashion. It will also work for differences between versions of a given compiler; for example, handling the logical graphics coordinates of Microsoft 5.1 that Microsoft 6.0 has abandoned in favor of viewport coordinates.

THE defined PREPROCESSOR OPERATOR

The *defined* preprocessor operator uses the syntax *defined (name)* or *!defined (name)*. It is used with the *#if* directive to test whether *name* is defined in the current program. It returns TRUE (nonzero) if *name* is defined, or FALSE (0) if not. By use of the logical NOT operator (!), the logic of the defined operator can be reversed. For example,

```
#if defined(MSC51)
```

is TRUE if the value MSC51 is defined, while:

```
#if defined(MSC6) && !defined(TURBOC)
```

is true if MSC6 is defined and TURBOC is not defined.

Here is a way to accommodate the different names that Borland and Microsoft give their graphics header file:

```
    :
    :
#ifdef (MSC)
    #include graph.h
#elif defined (TURBOC)
    #include graphics.h
#endif
```

Since only one of MSC or TURBOC should be defined, the statement checks first for MSC, and if that is not defined, it then checks whether TURBOC is defined.

Other Preprocessor Directives

There are other preprocessor directives. The *#undef* directive can be employed when you wish to undo the current definition of a symbol. For instance, the command *#undef DEBUG* removes the definition of DEBUG.

The Microsoft C compiler maintains two predefined preprocessor symbols, __FILE__ and __LINE__. The first refers to the name of the current input file, and the latter is a reference to the line number the compiler is processing. The *#line* preprocessor directive may be used to change the values of these two symbols. For example, *#line 20 "myprog.c"* causes the line number maintained by the compiler to be reset to 20 and the file name to be changed to *myprog.c*. This is useful when you write a translator that takes an input file in a language of your design (let us call it MY4GL, for "my 4th-generation language") and generates a C source file. You can insert *#line* directives in the source file that refer to the file name of the MY4GL file and the line number that you are translating. The __FILE__ and the __LINE__ can also be used in reporting errors. That way, the printed error messages make sense because they refer to the file name and line number of the original MY4GL file, instead of the file name and line number of the file into which they are being merged. (Version 5.1 of Microsoft C added predefined processor symbols, which are discussed in Chapter 2 and detailed in Table 2-4.)

You can use the *#pragma* directive to instruct the C compiler to turn certain features on or off. The pragmas supported vary from one compiler to another. Table 1-1 is a list of those used by Microsoft C, which includes the version in which they were introduced. (Please note the *data_seg* pragma was introduced in version 5.1 and removed from version 6.0.)

Table 1-1. *Microsoft C Pragmas*

#pragma alloc_text (text_segment, function1, function2 . . .)
(version 5.0) Places the _far functions (function1, function2 . . .) in *text_segment*, where the compiled code (the *code segment*) resides. This is useful for organizing the memory layout of the code.

#pragma check_pointer (on) or #pragma check_pointer (off)
(version 6.0) Tells the compiler to turn pointer checking on or off, depending upon the specification.

#pragma check_stack (on) or #pragma check_stack (off)
(version 4.0) Turns the generation of stack-checking code on or off. (Also see compiler option /Gs.)

#pragma comment (commenttype, [commentstring]) (version 5.1) Places a comment record of type *commenttype* in the object file. The optional parameter *commentstring* is used to add additional information to comment records. The following comment-record types are supported:

compiler	Places the name and the version number of the compiler in a comment record. Use of the *commentstring* parameter will cause a warning message to be generated. The linker ignores this comment record.
exestr	Places the string specified in *commentstring* in a comment record. The linker copies this string into the executable file but it does not load when the .EXE file loads. Finding the string requires a scan program such as *LIST* or Norton *TS*. Useful for including copyright notices, version numbers, serial numbers, and the like.
lib	Places the *commentstring* into a library search comment record. The linker searches the named library to resolve external references. The parameter *commentstring* should be the name of a library, including, if necessary, the complete pathname. A source file may have multiple "lib" references.
user	Places the *commentstring* into a general comment record that is ignored by the linker.

#pragma data_seg ([segmentname]) (version 5.1) When present, *segmentname* is used as the name of the data segment to be loaded by any subsequent function that will

Table 1-1. *(cont.)*

load its own data segment. **Support for this pragma was dropped starting with version 6.0 of Microsoft C.** The /ND compiler switch and/or use of _based data can accomplish the work of data-seg in Microsoft C 6.0.

#pragma function (name1, name2 . . .) (version 5.0) Tells the compiler to generate function calls instead of using the intrinsic forms of the functions *(name1, name2 . . .)*. Tends to generate smaller, but somewhat slower, code. See also the *intrinsic* pragma and the /Oi compile switch option, and check the documentation with your version of the compiler for a list of functions with intrinsic forms.

#pragma intrinsic (name1, name2 . . .) (version 5.0) Tells the compiler to use the intrinsic form of functions called "name1, name 2 . . . ." This form typically executes faster than the function call form. Check the documentation with your compiler version for the list of eligible functions and for comments on memory-model side effects. See also the /Oi compiler switch and the *function* pragma.

#pragma linesize ([numchars]) (version 5.1) Tells the compiler the line size to use when generating source listings. The value of *numchars* should be between 79 and 132. If you do not specify *numchars*, the value given by the /Sl option is used. If the /Sl option is not used, the line size defaults to 79 characters. Takes effect the line after it appears.

#pragma loop_opt (on) or #pragma loop_opt (off) (version 5.0) Turns optimization of loops on or off, depending on which form and which compiler switch is used. If *on* or *off* is not specified, defaults to *off* if the /Ox or /Ol options are not used, or to *on* if they are. Can be used more than once in a file.

#pragma message (messagestring) (version 5.1) Tells the compiler to display the string *messagestring* as it processes the line with this pragma.

#pragma optimize ([list], {off | on}) (version 6.0) The optimization pragma turns various optimizer routines on or off. The value of *list* is one or more of the characters *a, c, e, g, l, n, p, t, w,* which correspond to the /O compiler option.

#pragma pack ([boundary]) (version 5.0) Specifies the byte boundary for packing the members of C structures. The value for *boundary* must be either 1, 2, or 4. The default value is 2. The /Zp option may also be used for this purpose.

Table 1-1. *(cont.)*

#pragma page ([numpages]) (version 5.1) Asks the compiler to generate form feeds in the source listing at the line where it appears. The number of form feeds is specified by the parameter *numpages*. Legal values for *numpages* are 1 through 127. The default value is 1.

#pragma pagesize ([numlines]) (version 5.1) Specifies the number of lines per page for source listings. The parameter *numlines* must be between 15 and 255. If the *pagesize* pragma is used without an explicit *numlines* value, the compiler defaults to any value supplied by the /Sp option. If /Sp cannot be found, the default is 63.

#pragma same_seg (variable1, variable2 . . .) (version 5.0) Directs the compiler to assume that the external far variables named *variable1, variable2* . . . are all in the same segment. The option /ND must be used when compiling modules in which the variables are actually defined. See also pragma *alloc_text*.

#pragma skip ([numlines]) (version 5.1) Directs the compiler to skip *numlines* number of lines in the source listing. The value of *numlines* is any integer from 1 through 127. If no value is specified, the compiler defaults to 1 and 1 line is skipped.

#pragma subtitle (subtitlestring) (version 5.1) Tells the compiler to use the string *subtitlestring* as the subtitle for the rest of the pages in the source listing. The subtitle appears below the title on each page of the listing.

#pragma title (titlestring) (version 5.1) Tells the compiler to use the string *titlestring* as the title for the rest of the pages in the source listing. The title appears in the upper left corner of each listing page. A null *titlestring* erases any previous title.

Declarations in C

All variables and functions must be declared before use. The declaration of a variable specifies several important things: "Visibility" specifies the parts of the program that will have access to the variable. "Lifetime" specifies how long the value will be preserved. The variable's "type" determines what kind of numeric or character data can be stored in the variable. Finally, declarations can often specify an initial value for the variable.

MICROSOFT NAMING CONVENTIONS

The Microsoft C compiler reserves certain naming conventions for its own use. It is good practice to avoid names that begin with more than a single underscore, or names that end with the suffix QQ. No global name should begin with an underscore, as Microsoft uses the leading underscore to identify certain non-ANSI values, including the names of noncomplying functions.

DATA TYPES IN C

C uses seven keywords to specify data types: *int, long, short, unsigned, char, float,* and *double.* Four more keywords were added with ANSI C: *signed, void, const,* and *volatile.*

The storage sizes for floating-point types depend on the convention used to represent floating-point numbers in binary form on a particular machine. Microsoft uses the Institute of Electrical and Electronics Engineers (IEEE) format for floating-point numbers. A *char* takes a single byte while an *int* is the same size as a word on the underlying machine (for instance, 2 bytes on an IBM or compatible PC, and thus in MICROSOFT C, and 4 bytes on a DEC VAX). Here are some declarations using basic types:

```
char c;
int total, tax, x;
float tax_rate, loan_rate;
double x, y, z;
```

These four basic data types can be expanded into a much larger set with the use of the *long, short, unsigned,* and *signed* qualifiers as prefixes. The *long* and the *short* qualifiers are size modifiers. For example, a *long int* is 4 bytes long in Microsoft C, and is capable of holding a much larger value than an *int.* (In Chapter 2 [in Table 2-1] we list the sizes of data types in Microsoft C, and the range of values that each type can store.)

SIGNED

The *signed* prefix, added in ANSI C, explicitly identifies the variable as having a sign. The *unsigned* qualifier is for *int* and *char* types only. Normally, each of those can hold negative as well as positive values; this is the default *signed* form of these variable types. With the unsigned qualifier, you tell the compiler that the variable will hold positive values only, which allows the variable to hold maximum positive values that are twice as large as the maximum positive value of the signed variable. Here is a code fragment showing the use of the qualifiers:

```
unsigned char c;
short i, j, small_int;   /* shorthand for "short int" */
long large_int;          /* shorthand for "long int" */
unsigned count;          /* shorthand for "unsigned int" */
unsigned short ui, uj;
```

```
unsigned long ul;
long double xlarge;
```

Note that you can drop the *int* from the declaration when the *long, short,* and *unsigned* qualifiers are used with *int* types, though you may prefer to leave them in to make your code more easily understood. Among the floating-point types, only *double* takes the *long* qualifier.

ENUM

The ANSI standard introduced the type *enum*, which holds one integer value from a fixed set of named integer constants. An *enum* variable can be used anywhere an *int* type is used. The *enum* type can be used in such a situation as:

```
enum boolean {false = 0, true = 1, no = 0, yes = 1, off = 0, on = 1};
enum boolean flag = off;
```

The example shows several properties of *enum*. The first line defines *boolean* to be an enumerated type. The list within the braces shows the constants that are valid values of a *enum boolean* variable. Each constant can be initialized to a value of your choice, and several constants can use the same value. In our example, we have chosen the constants *false, no* and *off* to be 0 and *true, yes* and *on* to be 1. The second line shows the declaration of an enumerated variable of type *boolean*. Its name is *flag* and it is initially set to *off*. Note that *enum* does not introduce a new basic data type; it simply improves the readability of your programs.

The *long double* is another type of floating-point variable specified in the ANSI standard. Some older compilers recognize the type *long float*, which is no longer valid under the proposed standard.

ARRAYS

An "array" is a convenient way to organize a large number of identical data items. You can declare arrays of any type of data item, including structures and types defined by the *typedef* statement. Arrays can be single- or multi-dimensional. For example,

```
char    str[81];
int     id[100];
double  x[40], a[5][10];
:
str[0] = 'A';     /* Set the first character in str to 'A'  */
id[99] = -1;      /* The last element in array id is -1     */
a[4][9] = x[1]; /* Copy an element of x into another in a */
```

declares a character string, *str*, capable of holding 81 characters, an array of 100 integers named *id*, an array of 40 double variables *x*, and a 5×10 two-dimensional array of doubles, *a*. Using the syntax of the last three lines any element in an array can be referenced. Notice that while the dimension of an array shows the actual number of items, the index goes up from 0. So an array with 100 elements can have indices ranging from 0 to 99. Also, strings in C are always terminated by a byte containing a 0 (a "null character" denoted by \0). Thus, in our example, *str* can only hold 80 characters because the last space will be occupied by a null. A two-dimensional array represents a "matrix," such as a spreadsheet. Think of a *[5][10]* as a spreadsheet with 5 rows and 10 columns, capable of holding up to 50 elements. Since memory is not laid out like a spreadsheet, the actual storage is done by laying out one row after another in memory. In the notation shown above, the second dimension denotes the number of columns, or the number of elements along a row. Because C stores a matrix by row, it always needs the second dimension in the declaration of a matrix.

POINTERS A "pointer" is a variable that can hold the address of an object that can be either a variable or a function. If *px* is a pointer to an integer, you would declare and use it as

```
int *px, x;
:
px = &x;
```

The compiler will allocate storage space for an integer *x* and a *pointer to the integer px*. The number of bytes necessary to hold the address will depend on the machine's addressing scheme. Of course, you should not use *px* until it contains the address of a valid object. The last line shows *px* being initialized to the address of the integer variable *x* (the *&* operator extracts the address of *x*). Following this, you can refer to the value of *x* with **px* ("the contents of the object whose address is in *px*").

Pointers are useful in many situations. Consider, for example, dynamic allocation of memory. In C you can request a chunk of memory—enough to hold, say, 100 integers. Once the memory is reserved, you get back the starting address of the block. Since this address is the only way to reach that memory block, you must store it in a variable capable of holding the address of an integer, so you need a pointer to an integer. If you used *px* for this purpose, how could you access the integers in that block of memory? You would treat it like an "array" of 100 integers with the name *px*. So the last element in the array is referenced as

```
px[99]
```

which is equivalent to

```
*(px+99)
```

Similarly, the compiler treats the name of an array as a pointer to the first element of the array (element 0). The difference between the name of an array and a pointer variable is that the first is a "constant" lacking explicit storage necessary to hold the address of the array's first element, whereas the latter is actually a "storage bin" capable of holding the address of any data of a specific type.

Neither an array nor a function can be returned by a function. To circumvent this, you can give the address of the array or the function that you want as the return value. (We will discuss *pointers to functions* in a later section.)

STRUCTURES AND UNIONS

When organizing any type of data, it is preferable to group items in a way that makes sense. For example, when storing the names and addresses of acquaintances, we treat the name and the address of each person as a single data record. In C you can organize your data in this manner with "structures." The definition of a structure to hold names, addresses, and some other information might look like:

```
struct financial;
{
    double        annual_income;
    double        life_insurance;
    double        net_worth;
    unsigned char investment_strategy;
};

struct client_info
{
    char             name[80];
    char             company[80];
    char             mailstop[20];
    char             street[80];
    char             city[40];
    char             state[40];
    unsigned int     zipcode;
    struct financial details;
};

struct client_info client[100];
```

This is the data base of an investment counselor. First we define a structure called *financial* that contains information about the client's financial situation. Each of the data fields in the *financial* structure, such as *annual_income* and *life_insurance*, is called a "member" of the structure. Next we define the structure *client_info* that contains the name and address of the client as well as the *financial* structure embedded in it. The last line declares a 100-element array called *client* in which each element is a structure of type *client_info*. (The fields of a structure are accessed by the "member selection" operator, which we will discuss later.)

"Unions" are declared like structures, but they are used when you want to view the same data item in different ways. The header file *dos.h* in Microsoft C library includes an example. Each of the 8086 registers AX, BX, CX and DX is 16 bits in size, but each can also be thought of as two 8-bit registers; for example, the 16-bit AX comprises the 8-bit registers AH and AL. To use one storage area for these registers, but to refer to them in either manner, we first declare a structure, WORDREGS, containing the 16-bit registers:

```
struct WORDREGS
{
    unsigned int ax;
    unsigned int bx;
    unsigned int cx;
    unsigned int dx;
    unsigned int si;
    unsigned int di;
    unsigned int cflag;
};
```

Then we define another structure, BYTEREGS, using symbols for the 8-bit registers:

```
struct BYTEREGS
{
    unsigned char al, ah;
    unsigned char bl, bh;
    unsigned char cl, ch;
    unsigned char dl, dh;
};
```

Now a "union" of the two structures enables us to refer either to WORDREGS or BYTEREGS, accessing the registers as 16-bit or as 8-bit entities. The union that overlays the two structures is defined as:

```
union REGS
{
    struct WORDREGS x;
    struct BYTEREGS h;
};
```

Now if we declare *union REGS reg1* in the program, we can access the AH register using the name *reg1.h.ah*, and a reference such as *reg1.x.ax* gets the 16-bit AX register.

NAMING YOUR OWN DATA TYPES

Using the *typedef* facility, you can define names for your own data types. Here are some examples:

```
typedef unsigned char byte;
typedef struct POINT
{
    short x;
    short y;
} POINT;

typedef POINT *P_POINT;  /* Defines P_POINT as pointer to POINT */

byte   flag;
POINT  a, b;
P_POINT p_a = &a;
```

We have defined *byte*, POINT, and P_POINT as synonyms for other data types. The last three lines show the use of the new data types. Note that we first defined POINT and then used it in the definition of P_POINT. In this way, you can use *typedef* to declare complex data types.

Visibility and Lifetime of Variables

The "visibility" or the "scope" of a variable tells you which source file (also called a "module") of your program can use the variable without declaring it. For example, all variables that are declared outside the body of functions are global in nature; any module can use them. On the other hand, declarations within the function's body define variables that are visible only inside that function. Take, for example, the code:

```
:
int current_object_id;
:
:
main()
{
    int id;
    :
    :
```

```
    id = create_object();
    :
}
int create_object()
{
    int id;
    :
    :
    if(current_object_id == 0) ...
    :
    return(id);
}
```

The variable *current_object_id* is declared before any of the functions (including *main*), so it is visible in the entire source file. On the other hand, the variable *id* is local to *main( )* and to *create_object( )*. Each function has its own copy of *id*. Changes made to one copy do not affect any of the others.

The variable *current_object_id* is not only visible in its source file, it can even be referenced from any other file with the declaration

```
extern int current_object_id;
```

This is how global variables are used in C. Since the variable may be accessed at any time during the execution of the program, these variables are allocated storage for the life of the program and are said to have global "lifetimes."

The qualifier *static* also declares variables with global lifetimes, but it restricts the visibility of variables to a single source file. For example, you could define the variable *current_object_id* as

```
static int current_object_id = 0;
```

in a file and use it within the file without altering its globally visible counterpart with the same name. In other words, you have a separate storage location for the copy of *current_object_id* that is visible only in the file in which it is declared.

When a variable, such as *id* in our example, is defined within the body of a function, its storage remains allocated as long as that function is active. Such variables are said to have local lifetimes. You can also declare variables with local lifetimes by using the reserved words *auto* and *register*. Variables declared inside a function are by default of type *auto*. The *register* storage specifier is a hint to the compiler to place that variable in a register, if possible. You can use the *register* qualifier only for variables of type *int* or for pointers that can be stored in the same number of bytes as an *int.* Table 1-2 summarizes the information on the visibility and lifetime of declarations in C.

Table 1-2. ***Scope and Lifetime of C Declarations***

Where Declared	Keyword	Visibility	Lifetime
Before all functions in a file (may be initialized here)	None	Entire file plus other files where variable is declared extern	Until program ends (global)
Before all functions in a file (cannot be initialized here)	extern	Entire file plus other files where variable is declared	Global
Before all functions in a file	static	Only in that file	Global
Inside a function	None or auto	Only in that function	Until function returns
Inside a function	register	Only in that function	Until function returns
Inside a function	static	Only in that function	Global

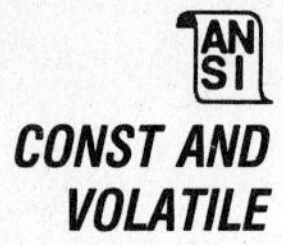

CONST AND VOLATILE

Two keywords, *const* and *volatile*, are ANSI Standard constructs introduced with the version 5.1 compiler. (We mentioned *const* earlier in this chapter in the discussion about the preprocessor directive *#define*.) You can use *const* as a modifier in a declaration to tell the compiler that the particular data object must not be modified by the program. This means the compiler must not generate code that might alter the contents of the location where that data item is stored. On the other hand, *volatile* specifies that the value of a variable may be changed by factors beyond the control of the program. You can use both keywords on a single data item to mean that while the item must not be modified by your program, it may be altered by some other process. The *const* and *volatile* keywords always modify the item immediately to their right. The information provided by *const* and the *volatile* helps the compiler optimize the code it generates. For example, if you declare and initialize the variable *x* as

```
const int x = 1024;
```

the compiler need not generate code to load the value of *x* from memory. Instead it can use the value 1024 wherever *x* is used. However, if you add *volatile*:

```
volatile const int x = 1024;
```

the compiler cannot optimize away any reference to *x* because its contents might be changed by an external process. This can happen when you declare a pointer to an I/O port or video memory in order to access them from your program.

A complete list of the keywords for version 6.0 of Microsoft C is provided in Table 1-3. The *_based, _segment, _segname,* and *_self* keywords were introduced in Microsoft C 6.0.

Table 1-3. ***Microsoft C 6.0 Keywords***

argc	else	int	_setenvp
argv	_emit	_interrupt	short
_asm	enum	_loadds	signed
auto	envp	long	sizeof
_based	_export	main	static
break	extern	_near	struct
case	_far	_pascal	switch
_cdecl	_fastcall	register	typedef
char	float	return	union
const	for	_saveregs	unsigned
continue	_fortran	_segment	void
default	goto	_segname	volatile
do	_huge	_self	while
double	if	_setargv	

FUNCTION DECLARATIONS

A function declaration tells the compiler the type of value the function returns and the number and type of arguments it takes. Most of us are used to declaring functions only when they return something other than an *int.* For example, a typical declaration would be

```
char *locate_char();
```

This changes under the ANSI standard for C.

PROTOTYPES

The introduction of *function prototypes* is probably the most significant feature of ANSI C. It requires you to declare the formal parameters that a function takes as well as the return value. If our sample function *locate_char( )* takes a string and an integer as an argument, the ANSI-style prototype for this function is

```
char *locate_char(char *, int);
```

with the formal argument list shown with the type of each parameter only. You may include an identifier for each formal parameter, such as

```
char *locate_char(char *str, int c);
```

In this case, the prototype can look exactly like the first line in the definition of the function, except that in the prototype you terminate the line with a semicolon.

Microsoft C provides a command-line switch /Zg that causes the compiler to generate prototypes for you, to help you bring old code up to ANSI standard. It reads the source file and constructs prototypes on the fly. The example CFNC.BAT file below creates a list of function prototypes and redirects them to a file that can be merged into the source code. The destination file has the .FNC extension, but that is a matter of personal preference and is not required by the compiler. It uses the Microsoft C /Zg option and does not compile the file. QuickC cannot be used. CFNC takes one command-line argument (the name of the C source file) and pushes it into the source.C and source.FNC file slots. The @ECHO OFF and ECHO commands assume DOS 3.3 or later, and are optional.

```
ECHO OFF
CLS
ECHO.
ECHO CFNC FILE <file_name> -- written for Microsoft C
ECHO "CL /Zg %1.C %1.FNC"
ECHO.
CL /Zg %1.C %1.FNC
ECHO.
```

What is the purpose of the prototype? It is mainly there to help the compiler check function arguments and to let it generate code that uses a faster mechanism to return from functions. Since the prototype tells the compiler the exact number and type of arguments to expect, it can catch any mistakes you might make when calling a function, such as passing the wrong number of arguments (when the function takes a fixed number of arguments), or passing the wrong type of argument to a function.

Prototypes also allow the C compiler to use a calling convention different from the usual one used by C. (See the tutorial in Part IV for a discussion of the ordinary argument-passing mechanism used by C.) The non-C convention, used by all other languages, involves placing the arguments on the stack in the order that they appear in the function call. In this case, the function knows the exact number of arguments placed on the stack and can clean up the stack with a single 8086 assembly language statement of the form *RET* <*n*> where <*n*> refers to the number of bytes to be discarded from the stack before returning. The usual C calling convention places arguments in the reverse order and does not require a fixed number of arguments in each call. Since the function does not know the number of arguments on the stack, only the calling program can clean up the stack by adjusting the stack pointer (SP). This is normally done with the assembly language instruction *ADD SP,<n>*. Not only is this instruction slower than *RET <n>* but it also makes the program larger because the *ADD SP,<n>* instruction appears wherever a function is called.

Microsoft provides a non-ANSI keyword *_cdecl* (there was no leading underscore before version 6.0), which specifies that the C calling convention must be used with any function with *_cdecl* in its declaration, and this means you cannot use the *_fastcall* convention.

What do you do when a function does not return anything or when it does not accept any parameters? To answer this, we have to describe a data type that is part of ANSI Standard C.

THE TYPE void

The ANSI standard adds to C the type *void*, which is useful for declaring functions and for describing pointers that can point to any type of data. If a function does not return anything, say the *exit* function in the library, it can be declared as

```
void exit(int);
```

If a function does not accept formal parameters, its list of arguments can be represented by the word *void*:

```
int getchar(void);
```

The use of a pointer to a *void* as a data type is appropriate for functions that manipulate contiguous arrays of bytes ("buffers") in memory. For example, when you request a certain number of bytes from the memory allocation routine *malloc*, you can use these locations to store any data that fits the space. In this case, the address of the first location of the allocated block of memory is returned as a pointer to a variable of type *void* with

```
void *malloc(size_t size);
```

as the prototype. By the way, *size_t* is a new standard data type in ANSI C. Microsoft C uses *typedef* to define *size_t* as an alias for *unsigned int*. Most library routines that require the size of a data item use the *size_t* type. The *sizeof* operator also returns a value of type *size_t* in ANSI C.

The ANSI standard for C states that a function declared with an empty argument list (nothing in the parentheses) is assumed to be taking an unspecified number of arguments with unspecified data types. The keyword *void* explicitly identifies the function as having no arguments, and its use may head off trouble if you move programs to a C++ environment. In C++, unlike C, empty parentheses are not an invitation to add arguments. Rather, they mean that no arguments are expected, which is what *void* tells C. Use of *void* in your C code will document your intentions and probably ease your porting problems if you move any of your programs to C++.

Expressions in C

An expression in C is a combination of variables, function calls, and operators with the result a single value. For example,

```
(strlen(my_string) * sizeof(char) + 1)
```

is an expression, which yields a value of type *size_t*, involving a function call, *strlen(my_string)*, and the operators *sizeof*, a multiplication (*) and an addition (+).

Since operators are at the heart of expressions, let us summarize the operators available in C. We do this in Table 1-4, where each operator is shown with an example and a short explanation of its usage.

Table 1-4. *Operators in C*

Operator	Name	Example	Explanation
		Arithmetic Operators	
*	Multiplication	x*y	Multiply x and y
/	Division	x/y	Divide x by y
%	Modulo	x%y	Divide remainder of x by y
+	Addition	x+y	Add x and y
–	Subtraction	x–y	Subtract y from x
++	Increment	x++	Increment x after use
––	Decrement	––x	Decrement x before use
–	Negation	–x	Negate the value of x
		Relational and Logical Operators	
>	Greater than	x>y	1 if x exceeds y, else 0
>=	Greater than or equal to	x>=y	1 if x is greater than or equal to y, else 0
<	Less than	x<y	1 if y exceeds x, else 0
<=	Less than or equal to	x<=y	1 if x is less than or equal to y, else 0
==	Equal to	x==y	1 if x equals y, else 0
!=	Not equal to	x!=y	1 if x and y unequal, else 0
!	Logical NOT	!x	1 if x is 0, else 0
&&	Logical AND	x&&y	0 if either x or y is 0
¦¦	Logical OR	x¦¦y	0 if both x and y are 0

Table 1-4. ***(cont.)***

Operator	Name	Example	Explanation
		Assignment Operators	
=	Assignment	x=y;	put value of y into x
0=	Compound assignment	x 0= y;	equivalent to x = x 0 y; where 0 is one of the operators: + – * / % << >> & ^ ¦
		Data Access and Size Operators	
[ ]	Array element	x[0]	first element of array x
.	Member selection	s.x	member x in structure s
→	Member selection	p→x	member named x in a structure that p points to
*	Indirection	*p	contents of location whose address is in p
&	Address of	&x	address of x
:>	Base operator	0xB800:>0010	base plus offset to form far pointer
sizeof	Size in bytes	sizeof(x)	size of x in bytes
		Bitwise Operators	
~	Bitwise complement	~X	flip 1 bits to 0 and 0 bits to 1
&	Bitwise AND	x&y	bitwise AND of x and y
¦	Bitwise OR	x¦y	bitwise OR of x and y
^	Bitwise exclusive OR	x^y	value with 1s at bits where corresponding bits of x and y differ
<<	Left shift	x << 4	x shifted to the left by 4 bit positions
>>	Right shift	x >> 4	x shifted to the right by 4 bit positions
		Miscellaneous Operators	
( )	Function	malloc(10)	call malloc with argument 10
(type)	Type cast	(double)i	i converted to a double
? :	Conditional	x1 ? x2 : x3	if x1 is not 0, x2 is evaluated, else x3 is evaluated
,	Sequential evaluation	i++, j++	first increment i, then increment j

Operator Precedence

Typically, you use several operands and operators in many statements of your program. For example, if you write

```
*ptr[2]
```

is the result the value to which ptr[2] points, or is it the third element from the location whose address is in *ptr*? To determine this, you need to know the order in which operators are applied. This is specified by operators' *precedence*, which is summarized in Table 1-5. Operators with highest precedence—those which are applied first—are shown first. The order in which operators at the same level get evaluated (associativity) is also shown. If you consult the table, you will find that the [] operator has precedence over the * operator. So in our example, ptr[2] will be evaluated first and then the "indirection" operator applied, resulting in the value whose address is in ptr[2].

Table 1-5. *Operator Precedence and Associativity in C*

Operator type	Operators	Associativity
Expression	( ) :> [ ] . →	Left to right
Unary	– ~ ! * & ++ –– sizeof (type)	Right to left
Multiplicative	* / %	Left to right
Additive	+ –	Left to right
Shift	<< >>	Left to right
Relational (inequality)	< <= > >=	Left to right
Relational (equality)	== !=	Left to right
Bitwise AND	&	Left to right
Bitwise XOR	^	Left to right
Bitwise OR	|	Left to right
Logical AND	&&	Left to right
Logical OR	| |	Left to right
Conditional	? :	Right to left
Assignment	= *= /= %= += –= <<= >>= &= |= ^=	Right to left
Sequential Evaluation	,	Left to right

Statements in C

Statements control the flow of execution of a C program. A "statement" consists of keywords, expressions, and other statements. Each statement ends with a semicolon. Here are some simple C statements:

```
;          /* a null statement */
x = y = 2;
x++;
if(y > 0) x /= y;
```

The body of a function that is enclosed in a pair of braces ({ . . . }) is considered a single statement. Known as "blocks," such compound statements can have local variable declarations and statements.

Here is a summary of C statements, in terms of keywords.

---

assignment statement Assigns a value of the expression on the right-hand side to the variable on the left-hand side of the equality (=).

Example:

```
pages = 800;
```

---

break; Ends the innermost do, for, switch, or while statement in which it appears.

Example:

```
while(i > 0)
{
    if(i < 10) break;
    /* Loop ends when i < 10 */
}
```

---

continue; Begins the next iteration of the innermost do, for, or while statement in which it appears, skipping the loop body.

Example:

```
for (1=0; i < 100; i++)
{
    if(i == 50) continue;
    /* Loop skipped for i=50 */
}
```

---

do-while loop Executes a block of statements until the expression in the while statement fails.

Example:

```
do   /* Copy y to x until i exceeds 10 */
{
    x[i] = y[i];
} while (++i < 10)
```

---

for loop For (*expr1*; *expr2*; *expr3*) <*statements*>

Evaluates *expr1* once. The <*statements*> are executed as long as *expr2* is true (nonzero). After each pass through the loop, *expr3* is evaluated. Loop stops when *expr2* becomes false (0).

Example:

```
for (i=0, sum=0; i < 11; i++) sum += i;
/* Computes sum of integers 0 through 10 */
```

---

goto statement Transfers control to statement designated LABEL.

Example:

```
if(i == 0) goto L1;
    a = x[i];
L1: x[i] = c;
```

---

if statement

if (*expr1*) *statement1* else *statement2* executes *statement1* if *expr1* is nonzero. Otherwise *expr2* is executed. The else clause is optional.

Example:

```
if (y !=0)
    x /= y;
else
    x = 0;
```

Null statement

Indicates, with a solitary semicolon, that nothing happens. Used, for example, when all processing is to be done in the loop expressions rather than the body of the loop.

Example:

```
for (i=0; str[i] != '\0'; i++)
    ;  /* Null statement */
```

---

return

Stops executing the current function and returns control to the calling function. A single value can be passed back.

Example:

```
return (answer);
```

---

switch

```
switch (expr)
{
    case value1: statement_block_1
    case value2: statement_block_2
    :
    :
    default: statement_default
}
```

If *expr* evaluates to *value1*, *statement_block_1* is executed. If it is equal to *value2*, *statement_2* is executed. If the value does not match any of the case statements, control passes to the block *statement_default*. Each statement block typically ends with a break statement.

Example:

```
switch (interrupt_id)
{
    case MDMSTATUS:   s_ms();
                      break;
    case TXREGEMPTY:  s_trmty();
                      break;
    case RXDATAREADY: s_rda();
```

```
                                break;
        case RLINESTATUS: s_rls();
                                break;
        default:
}
```

---

while loop

while *(expr) statement_block*

The *statement_block* is executed repeatedly as long as *expr* evaluates to a nonzero value.

Example:

```
while (i >= 0)  /* Copy one string onto
another */
{
   str1[i] = str2[i];
   i--;
}
```

Function Definitions

The building blocks of C programs, *functions* are independent collections of declarations and statements you mix and match to create stand-alone applications in C. Each C program has at least one function: the *main* function. The library supplied with the Microsoft C compiler consists mainly of functions (in addition to quite a few macros). For the most part, developing software in C is a matter of writing functions.

COMPLEX RETURN TYPES FOR FUNCTIONS

The definition of a C function starts with the type of value returned by the function; the function's name; and, in parentheses, the list of arguments the function accepts. For example, a function *getmax* that returns the larger of two *double* variables can be declared as:

```
double getmax( double a, double b)
{
    if ( a >= b)
        return (a);
    else
        return (b);
}
```

If you wanted the definition of this function to be localized to the source file in which it appears, you could use the keyword *static* as a prefix on the line declaring *getmax*. Without *static*, the function would be visible outside the source file.

Sometimes you need to return more complicated data types from your function. Normally, these would be pointers to one data type or another, but the ANSI standard lets you return a structure, directly. When declaring complex return types, you can use the *typedef* statement to your advantage. Suppose you want to write a function that accepts a pointer to an array of three double variables and its return value is of the same type. In notation cryptic enough to confuse even an expert, the function that we call *process3double* can be declared as

```
double (*process3double(double (*)[3]))[3];          /* Prototype */
:
:
double (*process3double(double (*x)[3]))[3]          /* Definition */
{
    return (x);
}
```

On the other hand, with a judicious use of *typedef*s you can rewrite the example as

```
typedef double DBL3[3];    /* DBL3 will mean array of 3 doubles */
typedef DBL3   *PDBL3;    /* PDBL3 will mean pointer to DBL3    */
PDBL3          process3double(PDBL3);              /* Prototype */
:
:
PDBL3 process3double(PDBL3 x)                      /* Definition */
{
    return (x);
}
```

The first approach takes less space, but the second method is certainly more readable than the first.

POINTERS TO FUNCTIONS

A function cannot return an array or another function directly. Also, an array cannot have functions among its elements. This is not a problem because you can always use pointers to functions in places where functions themselves are not allowed. Declaring a pointer to a function is similar to declaring a pointer to a variable. For example, you can declare a pointer to a function that accepts two *int* arguments and returns an *int* as

```
int (*p_func)(int, int)
```

Once *p_func* is initialized to point to the appropriate function, its invocation will look like the declaration above:

```
z = (*p_func)(x, y);
```

Again, the *typedef* keyword can come to your rescue when you have to declare something complicated, say an array of 5 functions, each like the *process3double* function of our earlier example. Using *typedef*, the declaration will be as simple as

```
/* First define a synonym for a pointer to this function */
typedef PDBL3  (*P_F_PDBL3)(PDBL3);

/* Now declare the array of functions */
P_F_DBL3   funclist[5];

funclist[0] = process3double;
```

In this example, we even initialized the first element of the array *funclist* to the function *process3double*, which we defined in our previous example.

Further Reading

If you are beginning to learn C on an IBM PC, Lafore's book[1] is an ideal place to start. An alternative is the latest fully ANSI- and Microsoft-compatible version of the best-selling *Waite Group's New C Primer Plus*[2]. You can follow up with the more advanced guide by Prata[3].

A more systematic, structured approach, especially good for classroom use has also been published by The Waite Group and Sams[4]. If you will be using QuickC and its integrated programming environment, a good tutorial is available from The Waite Group and Microsoft Press, covering QuickC through version 2.5[5].

A different, but very effective approach to learning C is offered by The Waite Group's *Master C*, which gives you an experienced "teacher on a disk." *Master C* automatically analyzes the student's strengths and weaknesses and provides reinforcement as needed.[6]

As you become more experienced you can explore the finer nuances of C syntax, programming "tricks," and pitfalls in the Koenig[7] and Jaeschke[8] books.

Once you feel comfortable with C, there are several resources that can help you learn more about using C effectively on the IBM PC. The books by Hansen[9], Biggerstaff[10], Campbell[11], and Rochkind[12] develop libraries of functions that show you how to use the DOS and BIOS services for file input/output (I/O) and fast screen updates.

If you wish to program the serial communications port or the graphics cards directly, another Campbell book[13] has all you need to know to access the serial port, and Johnson's book[14] shows examples of graphics programming for the EGA. The text by Lafore also shows how to program the graphics adapters.

On the MS-DOS front, Duncan[15] and The Waite Group[16] can advise you of the various services available. Another recent book by the Waite Group[17] is a collection of essays, each of which illustrates a specific aspect of the PC and MS-DOS. This can be a valuable source for ideas for your programs.

For information on the IBM PC and the PC-AT, the popular book by Norton[18] and the one by Smith[19] can provide all the information you need to get started.

1. Robert Lafore, The Waite Group, *Microsoft C Programming for the PC,* 2d ed., Howard W. Sams & Company, Carmel, IN, 1990, 768 pages.
2. Mitchell Waite and Stephen Prata, *The Waite Group's New C Primer Plus,* Howard W. Sams & Company, Carmel, IN, 1990, 731 pages.
3. Stephen Prata, The Waite Group, *Advanced C Primer++*, Howard W. Sams & Company, Carmel, IN, 1986, 502 pages.
4. Mitchell Waite, Stephen Prata, The Waite Group, *C: Step-by-Step.* Howard W. Sams & Company, Carmel, IN, 1989, 630 pages.
5. Mitchell Waite, Stephen Prata, Bryan Costales, Harry Henderson, The Waite Group, *The Waite Group's Microsoft QuickC Programming,* 2d ed., Microsoft Press, Redmond, WA, 1990, 640 pages.
6. Mitchell Waite, Stephen Prata, Rex Woollard, *Master C.* Waite Group Press, Mill Valley, CA, 1990, 240 pages.
7. Andrew Koenig, *C Traps and Pitfalls.* Addison-Wesley, Reading, MA, 1988, 147 pages.
8. Jaeschke, Rex, *Solutions in C.* Addison-Wesley, Reading, MA, 1986, 254 pages.
9. Augie Hansen, *Proficient C,* Microsoft Press, Redmond, WA, 1987, 492 pages.
10. Ted J. Biggerstaff, *Systems Software Tools,* Prentice-Hall, Englewood Cliffs, NJ, 1986, 317 pages.
11. Joe Campbell, *Crafting Tools for the IBM PCs,* Prentice-Hall, Englewood Cliffs, NJ, 1986, 434 pages.
12. Marc J. Rochkind, *Advanced C Programming for Displays,* Prentice-Hall, Englewood Cliffs, NJ, 1988, 331 pages.

13. Joe Campbell, *C Programmer's Guide to Serial Communications*, Howard W. Sams & Company, Carmel, IN, 1987, 655 pages.
14. Nelson Johnson, *Advanced Graphics in C*, Osborne McGraw-Hill, Berkeley, CA, 1987, 670 pages.
15. Ray Duncan, *Advanced MS-DOS*, Microsoft Press, Redmond, WA, 1986, 468 pages.
16. The Waite Group, *The Waite Group's MS-DOS Developer's Guide*, 2d ed., Howard W. Sams & Company, Carmel, IN, 1988, 783 pages.
17. The Waite Group, Ed., *MS-DOS Papers*, Howard W. Sams & Company, Carmel, IN, 1988, 608 pages.
18. Peter Norton, *The Peter Norton Programmer's Guide to the IBM PC*, Microsoft Press, Redmond, WA, 1985, 426 pages.
19. James T. Smith, *The IBM PC AT Programmer's Guide*, Prentice-Hall, New York, NY, 1986, 277 pages.

Chapter 2 Microsoft C 6.0 Compiler Features and Options

Implementation Notes

While the core of the C language and standard library are portable, Microsoft C adds many hardware-specific features that accommodate the needs of the 80x86 family of microprocessors used in IBM PC-compatible systems. This processor architecture affects the storage size of certain types of variables and requires the use of several "memory models" that specify how memory can be used for program code and data. Because of this, Microsoft C has a number of special-purpose keywords, predefined global variables, and preprocessor constants. We describe these in this chapter, and we also describe the options that can be used with the compiler (CL); ways to automate the process of compilation; and the MAKE, NMAKE, and LINK utilities.

STORAGE SIZE OF DATA ITEMS

Table 2-1 shows the basic data types in Microsoft C 6.0, their storage sizes, and the range of values they can hold.

MEMORY MODELS IN MICROSOFT C

The various versions of the Microsoft C compiler are designed to run on the Intel 80x86 family of microprocessors. A partial roster of the 80x86 family includes the 8086, 80186, 80286, 80386SX, 80386DX, 80386, and the 80486. It is common to use one of two shorthand names for the entire series—either "80x86" or "x86." It is also common to refer to individual models as "286," "386," and so forth. The 8086 and 286 use 16-bit data and 16-bit internal registers, while the 386DX and 486 use 32-bit data and 32-bit internal registers. The 80386SX uses 16-bit data registers and 32-bit internal registers.

The memory-addressing scheme used on the 80x86 family forces those who use 80x86-based compilers to learn about memory manage-

Table 2-1. *Data Types and Sizes in Microsoft C*

Type Name	Alternative Names	Size	Range of Values
char	signed char	1 byte	-128 to 127
int	signed, signed int	2 bytes	-32,768 to 32,767
short	short int, signed short, signed short int	2 bytes	-32,768 to 32,767
long	long int, signed long, signed long int	4 bytes	-2,147,483,648 to 2,147,483,647
unsigned char	n/a	1 byte	0 to 255
unsigned	unsigned int	2 bytes	0 to 65,535
unsigned short	unsigned short int	2 bytes	0 to 65,535
unsigned long	unsigned long int	4 bytes	0 to 4,294,967,295
_segment[1]	n/a	2 bytes	0 to 65,535
enum	n/a	2 bytes	-32,768 to 32,767
float	n/a	4 bytes	Approximately 1.2E-38 to 3.4E+38 with 7-digit precision[2]
double	n/a	8 bytes	Approximately 2.2E-308 to 1.8E+308 with 15-digit precision[2]
long double[3]	n/a	10 bytes	Approximately 3.4E-4932 to 1.2E+49320 with 19-digit precision[2]

1. The *_segment* type was added with Microsoft C 6.0.
2. Note that the on-line help from Microsoft C 6.0 gives incorrect values for *float*, *double*, and *long double*.
3. The *long double* type has 8 bits in Microsoft C 5.1, but in Microsoft C 6.0 it has 10 bits, using a format compatible with the 80x87 math coprocessors.

ment. Some of the decisions you make to accommodate the 80x86 scheme may reduce the portability of your software to other platforms and/or lead to hard-to-find bugs.

C programs compile into at least two parts—or "segments"—one of which is called *data* and the other is called *code*. The *data* portion contains the constants and variables for the program, and the *code* segment is used to store the function definitions. Some programs may have more than one code segment and/or more than one data segment. The concepts behind code and data are important to understand.

Executable C programs keep track of elements within the various code and data segments via their respective addresses. Such addresses are frequently stored in pointer variables that, depending on several factors, are either 16 bits or 32 bits in length.

A pointer variable needs 32 bits to fully specify a memory address. The first 16 bits identify the address of the segment, and the second 16 bits provide a 0-byte-based offset within that segment. Within the processor, the CS register stores the code segment address and the DS register stores the data segment address.

Memory addresses are manipulated in registers, and thus, the size of the largest possible memory address is limited by whatever can be stored in a register. Intel used 16-bit registers in early 80x86 models. Sixteen bits provide a maximum of 65,536 unique values, popularly known as "64 K," and thus, each segment (code or data) has a maximum size of 64 K.

There are 16 "segments" on an 8086 chip, each of which is 64-K bytes long. Ten of those 16 are available for routine programming tasks. Multiplying the 10 available segments by the 64-K size limit yields the 640-K memory limit against which large programs are constantly bumping. (While 80286 and later processors can directly address several megabytes of memory, DOS retains this 640-K limit.)

The segment and the offset addresses are combined to generate the final 20-bit "physical address" using the formula:

*Physical Address (20-bit) = Segment Address (16-bit) * 16 + Offset (16-bit)*

An advantage of this strategy is that if your data fits into a single 64-K segment, the 80x86 can set up the segment address in a segment register (specifically the DS register) and refer to data items using only the 16-bit offset. This results in faster code, because the code does not have to manipulate the segment portion of the address. The disadvantage is that any program that cannot be cleanly run in a single segment may fall prey to one or more of a host of memory management errors, and at any rate will be slowed by address-manipulation arithmetic.

A compiler for 80x86 machines will either force you to write programs that use only a single segment each of data and code or allow you to mix and match various segment and offset addressing schemes. Most modern compilers (including Microsoft C) take the latter course, and provide a rich collection of memory models and modifiers. These models are summarized in Table 2-2.

The six standard Microsoft memory models may be further modified by the keywords *_near, _far, _huge,* and *_based.* The *_based* keyword was introduced in version 6.0 of Microsoft C. The *_near, _far,* and *_huge* keywords were introduced in version 5.1, but in that version they did not have a leading underscore as a part of their name. (The leading underscore is an ANSI convention that identifies nonstandard and thus possibly nonportable items.) Version 6.0 accepts the "old" form as long as the /Za compiler option is not used.

It is good practice when using these four keywords to employ standard include files whenever possible in order to coerce pointer arguments to the correct type for your desired memory model.

These four keywords allow you to mix data items with an addressing scheme that differs from the defaults used by the selected standard model. These keywords can qualify the address of a data item as well as that of a function. Table 2-3 summarizes the meaning of these keywords.

Please remember that the concept of using memory models is not a part of the C language, but is instead mandated by characteristics of the Intel 80x86 family of microprocessors. This is important because the keywords *_near, _far, _huge,* and *_based* are not ANSI C items—they are Microsoft-specific accommodations to Intel chip designs. Their use makes your programs considerably less portable.

Table 2-2. *Microsoft C Compiler Memory Models*

Memory Model	Meaning
Tiny	Introduced in version 6.0. Code and data are all in one 64-K segment. Generates .COM files instead of .EXE files. DOS only. Compiler option: /AT
Small	All data and code addresses are 16-bit offsets. Program size limited to one segment of code and one segment of data. Compiler option: /AS
Medium	All data addresses are 16-bit offsets, but code addresses use explicit segments and offsets. A program can have a single segment of data, but many segments of code. Compiler option: /AM
Compact	Introduced in version 4.0. All code addresses are offset only, but data addresses use segments as well as offsets. Programs can have multiple data segments, but only one code segment. Compiler option: /AC
Large	All data and code addresses include explicit segments and offsets. Program size is limited only by available memory (which is limited by the 20-bit physical address in DOS), but a single data item cannot exceed a 64-K segment. Compiler option: /AL
Huge	Introduced in version 4.0. Same as the large model, but address arithmetic is performed in such a way that an array can span across multiple segments. Compiler option: /AH

Memory Model	Code Seg. Limit	Data Seg. Limit	Largest Data Object
Tiny	64 K (Code and Data combined)	—	64 K
Small	64 K	64 K	64 K
Medium	No limit[1]	64 K	64 K
Compact	64 K	No limit	64 K
Large	No limit	No limit	64 K
Huge	No limit	No limit	No limit

1. "No limit" actually means available memory.

Table 2-3. *The _near, _far, _huge, and _based Keywords in Microsoft C*

Keyword	When Used with Data	When Used with Function
_near	Data addresses are 16-bit offsets of the segment address of a default data segment. Data pointers and pointer arithmetic use 16 bits.	Function is assumed to be in the current code segment. Pointers to functions are 16 bits, and the pointer arithmetic is 16 bits.
_far	Full segment and offset addresses used. Data may be anywhere in memory. Uses 32 bits for addresses, but pointer arithmetic is 16 bits.	Referenced using full segment and offset address. Pointers to functions are 32 bits, but pointer arithmetic is 16 bits.
_huge	Full segment and offset addresses used. An array can be larger than a 64-K segment because 32-bit arithmetic is used on pointers.	Not applicable to functions.
_based	The data may be anywhere in memory and is not assumed to be in the current data segment. The 32-bit address scheme consists of a 16-bit address and a known base. Pointer arithmetic is 16 bits.	Not applicable to functions.

SEGMENT NAMES

The *_based* keyword needs to refer to a specific segment on which pointers will be based. Microsoft C, starting with version 6, provides the keyword *_segname*, which is used with four predefined segments to ease the task of declaring *_based* values. These segment names are summarized in Table 2-4.

Table 2-4. *The _CODE, _CONST, _DATA, and _STACK Segment Names in Microsoft C*

Segment	Name Description
_CODE	Default code segment
_CONST	Constant segment for strings such as "My name is Hal."
_DATA	Default data segment
_STACK	Stack segment

The *_segname* keyword identifies the name of a segment. It is always followed by parentheses and a string giving the segment name. A detailed description of *_segname* may be found in the Help files accompanying those Microsoft C versions equipped with the Programmer's WorkBench.

THE _ASM KEYWORD

Version 6 of the Microsoft C compiler allows you to include assembly language code in your C source files. You specify the start of a block of assembler instructions through use of the *_asm* keyword. The assembly language that Microsoft C 6.0 recognizes is a subset of the Microsoft Macro Assembler (MASM), version 5.1. The default instruction set is the 8086 and 8087, but it can be changed to the 80286 and 80287, if you use the /G2 option with the compiler.

The Microsoft C 6.0 in-line assembler does not recognize data directives and operators such as DB, DW, DUP, RECORD, or STRUCT. It does not process 80386, 80387, and 80486 specific instructions, nor does it handle equates, macros, and related directives and operators. The in-line assembler will also not work with calls and jumps to far labels or to segment directives and names.

An *_asm* block set up under Microsoft C 6.0 does allow you to mix many elements of the C language with the assembler code, including comments that follow either C convention or the Microsoft // practice, macros, preprocessor directives, type or typedef names (wherever a MASM type is legal), symbols (including labels, variables, and function names), and constants (including symbolic constants, enum members, and hex values).

The compiler identifies a block of inline assembly code through the use of the keyword *_asm*, which can be used with or without braces, as shown below:

```
_asm   assembler instruction
_asm   { assembler instructions}
...
```

The braces behave as they do in C, identifying that each line within them belongs to a set of lines that, in this instance, is being operated on by the *_asm* keyword. Absent the braces, the compiler treats the rest of the line with the *_asm* keyword as an assembly language statement.

An *_asm* block in a function disables automatic register variable storage, and it also inhibits the following optimizations for the entire function: global register allocation (/Oe), global optimizations and common subexpressions (/Og), and loop (/Ol).

The in-line assembler recognizes two MASM directives, EVEN and ALIGN. Certain conditions, which we will cover briefly, are applied to operators. A segment override must use a segment register (es:[bx]), and indexes within brackets are unscaled. The operators LENGTH, TYPE, and SIZE may be used with C arrays, and you may use the dollar sign ($) as the counter for the current location. You may use the SEG and OFFSET operators with C variable names (SEG i or OFFSET i).

Any C symbol in the scope where the block appears may be referred to by an *_asm* block, including variables such as arguments, local variables, static local variables, functions, and global values. Except in LENGTH, TYPE, and SIZE expressions, an assembly-language statement may not contain more than one C symbol. You must provide a previous prototype for any function that you plan to reference in an *_asm* block. Microsoft states that you should not use the *_fastcall* calling convention for functions with *_asm* blocks.

You do not need to preserve the AX, BX, CX, DX, or ES registers within a function, but you should preserve DI, SI, DS, SS, SP, and BP. An *_asm* block inherits the register values generated by the normal flow of control. Functions return integer and near pointers in AX and return long and far pointers in the AX and DX registers. (If your function changes the direction flag, you should restore it with CLD.)

You can use C macros in an *_asm* block by enclosing the *_asm* block in braces, typing the *_asm* keyword at the front of each assembly instruction, using the ANSI (non-Microsoft) form for comments, and using the backslash (\) to join statements into a single line. Examples of this construct may be found in the on-line Help files accompanying the Microsoft C 6.0 compiler.

THE _EMIT KEYWORD

The *_emit* keyword is used in an *_asm* block(*_asm _emit byte*, for example) to define an individual immediate byte to be compiled at the current location. It is a pseudoinstruction, and it is similar to the Microsoft Macro Assemble (MASM) DB directive.

The *_emit* keyword allows definition of a single byte (one byte at a time) at the current location of the current code (_TEXT) segment. The syntax is the same as that used for the INT instruction. It is one way to define 80386-specific instructions, which the in-line assembler does not support. The on-line Help files with the Microsoft C 6.0 product cover this usage of *_emit* and provide an example program with which you can work.

KEYWORDS CONTROLLING CODE GENERATION

Three keywords, *_export, _loadds,* and *_savregs,* were introduced in Microsoft C 5.1. Each modifies the code generated for a function in a Microsoft-specific fashion.

The *_export* keyword allows you to create functions that will reside in dynamic-link libraries. At great risk of over-simplifying, a dynamic-link library is essentially a library to which more than one program may be simultaneously linked. The *_export* usage will typically be with OS/2, but Windows developers will also find it of interest. The *_fastcall* convention may not be used with *_export.* The *_export* keyword and dynamic-link libraries keyword are described in detail in the on-line LINK help files of the Microsoft Programmer's WorkBench.

The *_loadds* (pronounced load-DS) keyword loads a specified segment value to the data-segment (DS) register when entering a specified function. This makes it easy for a function to work with a data segment outside of the current segment. The immediately previous DS value is restored when the function terminates. A function declared with *_loadds* causes the most recent data segment to load to DS. The segment value set by the /ND option is used. (In Microsoft C version 5.1 only, the *data_seg* pragma is used to specify the segment value loaded into DS. The pragma was not included in version 6.0. If there are no *data_seg* pragmas in a 5.1 program, the segment value set by the /ND option is used.) If there is no /ND switch, the compiler uses the default group DGROUP to derive the segment value. The *_loadds* keyword has the same effect as the /Au option, but on a function-by-function instead of program-by-program basis.

An example of *_loadds* using the Microsoft C 5.1 *data_seg* pragma appears below:

```
#pragma data_seg (MYSEG)
void _far _loadds myfunction (int command);
```

declares myfunction, in a version 5.1 program, as a function that loads the segment value MYSEG into the DS register upon entry.

Another example, without the pragma, has a *main*( ) function that contains a declaration of *staf_list*( ), a *_far* function that takes one argument (any type pointer) and has no return value. The function loads a new data segment at entry.

```
void _far _loadds staf_list(void *frst_nam); /* prototype */
main()
{
     char frst_nm[20];
     staf_list ((void *)frst_nam);  /* call the function */
}
```

The second file defines the function. The program is compiled with /ND:

```
void _far _loadds staf_list (void *frst_nam)
{
     :
}
```

The *_saveregs* keyword instructs the compiler to generate code to save all CPU registers upon entering the function and restore them when exiting it. The AX register (and DX in some cases) is not restored if the function returns a value. Use of *_saveregs* is indicated wherever you are uncertain as to what register conventions are in use by a calling program. If, for example, you are building a library that will link with products of other languages, using *_saveregs* provides independence from the calling convention used by Microsoft C. Do not declare a function with both *_saveregs* and *_interrupt* set. The *_fastcall* convention may not be used with *_saveregs*.

THE _INTERRUPT ATTRIBUTE

If you write C applications that require handling interrupts (for example, programming the serial communication ports for interrupt-driven I/O), you will find the *_interrupt* keyword useful. Introduced in Microsoft C 5.0, and given a leading underscore in version 6.0 (to indicate noncompliance with ANSI), this keyword serves as a qualifier for a function you want to install as the interrupt handler for a specific interrupt number. When the compiler translates a function with the *_interrupt* attribute, it generates code to push the registers AX, CX, DX, BX, BP, SP, SI, DI, DS, and ES. Then it sets up the DS register to point to the data segment of that function. Next, the code of the function is included. Finally, the compiler uses an IRET instruction (instead of a normal RET) to return from the function. IRET is a return from an interrupt handler.

A typical use of the *_interrupt* attribute, allowing reference of the various saved registers is:

```
void _interrupt _far int_hndlr (unsigned es, unsigned ds,
                                unsigned di, unsigned si,
                                unsigned bp, unsigned sp,
                                unsigned bx, unsigned dx,
                                unsigned cx, unsigned ax,
                                unsigned ip, unsigned cs,
                                unsigned flags)
{

/*  Place code to handle interrupt referring
    to registers by name when necessary.*/
}
```

Within the *_interrupt* handler, you can access the values of registers by referring to them by name. An *_interrupt* function must be *_far*. Compilations using the small or compact memory model require explicit *_far* function declarations. The small model is the default, unless otherwise specified with the /A switch to the compiler.

Precautions that apply to assembly language interrupt handlers also apply to the C function. For example, you should not call a library routine that calls a _dosxxx function or stream and low-level I/O routines, because they employ 21H or BIOS calls. On the other hand, routines in the string manipulation category are generally safe within interrupt handlers because they do not call 21H or BIOS. The *interupt* keyword is covered in detail in the on-line help provided with Microsoft C compilers version 6 and higher.

GLOBALS AND PREPROCESSOR CONSTANTS

Microsoft C includes a number of predefined global variables and preprocessor constants. Among other things, there are global variables that contain the DOS version number, last error number, and pointer to the process environment block. We refer to these global variables as predefined variables. Table 2-5 summarizes the predefined global variables and their purpose. The leading underscore identifies the variable (or function or macro, etc.) as not being ANSI-compliant: a convention Microsoft follows throughout its C products.

Table 2-5. ***Predefined Global Variables in Microsoft C 6.0***

Variable	Declaration and Purpose
_amblksiz	Declaration: unsigned _amblksiz; Declared in: malloc.h When the Microsoft C memory allocation routines have to allocate memory from the far heap, they first request memory from DOS in a big chunk, then they parcel out memory to satisfy calls made to *malloc* until the chunk is exhausted. The *_amblksiz* variable contains the size of a single chunk in bytes. The default value is 8,192 bytes (or 8K). The *halloc* and the *_malloc* routines do not use this variable.
_doserrno	Declaration: int _doserrno; Declared in: stdlib.h Contains the MS-DOS error code returned by the last MS-DOS system call.
_fmode	Declaration: int _fmode Declared in: stdlib.h Contains the default file translation mode. The default value is 0, which means files are translated in the text mode. (See File Manipulation routines for more details.)
_osmajor	Declaration: unsigned char _osmajor; Declared in: stdlib.h This is the major version number of MS-DOS. For example, the _osmajor value for DOS 3.10 is 3. The _osmajor value for DOS 4.0 is 4.
_osminor	Declaration: unsigned char _osminor; Declared in: stdlib.h This is the minor version number of MS-DOS. The _osminor value for DOS 3.10 is 10, for example, and the _osminor for DOS 3.30 is 30.
_osmode	Declaration: unsigned char _osmode Declared in: stdlib.h Indicates whether your program is running in the protected mode of OS/2 or the real mode of DOS. OS2_MODE is the constant it carries when in protected mode. The real mode value is DOS_MODE.
_osversion	Declaration: unsigned _osversion Declared in: dos.h Contains the complete DOS version number. The _osversion value for DOS 3.20 is 320.
_psp	Declaration: unsigned int _psp; Declared in: stdlib.h

Table 2-5. ***(cont.)***

Variable	Declaration and Purpose
	This variable contains the segment address of the program segment prefix (PSP) of the current process. The PSP contains information about the process, such as command-line arguments, pointer to the environment block, and return address. The PSP begins at offset 0 of the segment address contained in _psp.
daylight	Declaration: int daylight;
	Declared in: time.h
	The daylight variable is 1, if a daylight saving time zone is specified in the TZ environment variable. It is used when converting local time to Greenwich Mean Time. (See Time functions for details.)
environ	Declaration: char *environ[];
	Declared in: stdlib.h
	This is an array of pointers to strings where the strings are the values in the DOS environment passed to the process. This allows you to access the environment variables, such as the PATH for use by a particular program.
errno	Declaration: int errno;
	Declared in: stdlib.h
	Contains an error code corresponding to the last system call.
sys_errlist	Declaration: char *sys_errlist[];
	Declared in: stdlib.h
	This is an array of pointers to a set of strings each corresponding to a system error message.
sys_nerr	Declaration: int sys_nerr;
	Declared in: stdlib.h
	This is the total number of strings in the sys_errlist array.
timezone	Declaration: long timezone
	Declared in: time.h
	The timezone variable contains the difference in seconds between Greenwich Mean Time and the local time. (See Time functions for details.)
tzname	Declaration: char *txname[2];
	Declared in: time.h
	The value of tzname[0] is the name of the local time zone, such as EST or PST. The name of the daylight saving time zone is contained in tzname[1]. (See Time functions for details.)

Preprocessor constants are used extensively in the library routines to define values for specific parameters in a more readable fashion. A few of the preprocessor symbols are defined by the compiler itself. These predefined symbols, shown in Table 2-6, can help you write code that can be easily ported to other machines. For example, consider this fragment of code:

```
#ifdef MSDOS
     :
/* MSDOS specific code goes here */
     :
#endif

#ifdef vms
     :
/* DEC VAX/VMS specific code goes here */
     :
#endif
```

When this code is compiled with the Microsoft C compiler, the symbol MSDOS is predefined, so only the section of code appropriate for MS-DOS machines is processed. On the other hand, on a DEC VAX/VMS system, the symbol vms is predefined. So on a DEC VMS system we only get the part that applies to DEC VMS systems. Other examples of this usage are found in the Chapter 1 section on Conditional Compilation.

DISPLAYING DIAGNOSTIC MESSAGES

The ANSI-compatible *#error* directive was introduced in version 5.1 of the Microsoft compiler. The *#error* directive causes the compiler to display a specific diagnostic message during compilation. You can use the *#error*

Table 2-6. *Predefined Preprocessor Symbols in Microsoft C*

Symbol	Purpose
MSDOS	This symbol, which is always defined, indicates that the operating system is MS-DOS.
_MS_VER	Identifies which version of Microsoft C is in use. Always defined.
M_I86	This symbol, which is always defined, identifies the machine for which the compiler generates code as a member of the Intel 80x86 family.
M_I86xM	This symbol, which is always defined, is keyed by the value of x which identifies the memory model. The model symbols are M_I86TM for tiny, M_I86SM for small, M_I86CM for compact, M_I86MM for the medium model, and M_I86LM for large. Two symbols—M_I86LM and M_I86HM—are defined for the huge model. The small model is the default.
M_I8086	Identifies an 8088 or 8086 processor. It is the default or is used with the /G0 option.
M_I286	Identifies the 80286 processor. It is defined with the /G1 or /G2 options.
NO_EXT_KEYS	This symbol is defined when the /Za option is used to disable all of the Microsoft-specific (and hence, non-ANSI) extensions to C.
_CHAR_UNSIGNED	This symbol is defined when the /J option—which changes the default type of char variables from signed to unsigned—is in use.

directive to remind others; for example, to compile a program using a specific compiler option. The syntax of this directive is:

```
#error <message string>
```

in which *#error* prints the contents of the message. For instance, suppose you know that your source file contains nonstandard extensions to the C language. If the user wanted to compile with the /Za option enforcing strict ANSI compatibility, *#error* would remind the user to use the /Ze option (which enables the extensions) instead. Here's how:

```
#ifdef NO_EXT_KEYS
  #error Program uses nonstandard extensions. Recompile with /Ze
#endif
```

Since the NO_EXT_KEYS symbol is defined when the /Za option is used, the error message is displayed only when you turn off extensions.

Compiler Notes

Writing C code is only one aspect of developing software in Microsoft C. First, you compile the code, then link it with libraries to create the executable file, and then debug the program if it fails to work properly. The Microsoft C 6.0 compiler comes with a set of tools that help with one or more of these steps. Both the compiler and the linker are accessed via a command-line oriented program named CL.EXE, but the linker can also be invoked separately as LINK. Object modules are organized into libraries by the LIB utility. The NMAKE utility (starting with version 6, this replaces the MAKE program supplied with earlier releases of the compiler) lets you automate the steps involved in creating an executable file, helping you manage the "compile-link" cycle. Finally, the substantially improved CodeView debugger helps you locate the bugs in your program.

PROGRAMMER'S WORKBENCH

A major change between Microsoft C 6.0 and earlier versions of the Microsoft C compiler is the addition of the Programmer's WorkBench (PWB) to version 6.0. The PWB, portions of which (under another name) first appeared in QuickC version 2.0, gives you an "environment" within which to draft, edit, compile, and debug your programs.

The Programmer's WorkBench is invoked with the *PWB* command. The complete list of PWB options is not covered here, but we do provide a brief discussion of the PWB setup logic, a list of the main menus and their options, and a summary of PWB program development methodology. The on-line Help files should be your primary source for PWB information.

Customizing the PWB is largely a matter of setting PWB switches. A PWB switch is a variable that controls a specific PWB condition. There are three PWB switch types: Numeric, Text, and Boolean. The Editor Settings command on the *Options* menu is one way to set them, and the *Assign* function is another. An example of a PWB switch is "Height." The Height switch changes the number of lines in the editing window. The TOOLS.INI file, which is the initialization file for Programmer's WorkBench, provides a handy place to store your default switch settings.

In addition to the default switch values, TOOLS.INI also contains the macros used by PWB when it starts each editing session and the PWB functions used by the program. These are loaded when you type the *PWB* command. The Programmer's WorkBench uses "PWB functions" (not to be confused with C functions) to perform the various PWB tasks, such as managing files, editing files, building programs, changing option settings, and moving the cursor. Functions may be invoked directly—by pressing, for example, the key to which the function is assigned—or by calling a PWB macro. The subject of PWB functions is central to PWB usage, and there are numerous on-line help screens that cover this topic.

The main screen of the PWB displays an eight-option horizontal menu at the top of the screen. The eight menus and their commands are briefly covered to give you the flavor of the Programmer's WorkBench, but the on-line Help files provide much more thorough treatment. The main menu choices are *File, Edit, View, Search, Make, Run, Options,* and *Browse.*

File Menu

The File menu is used to create, load, and manage files. The PWB keeps track of the files you have recently accessed—the "file history"—so you can easily go back to a particular file or browse through the list. The following choices appear on the File menu of the PWB:

- *New* creates a new file.
- *Open* opens an existing file.
- *Merge* inserts one or more file(s) into a file.
- *Next* opens the next file from the command line.
- *Save* saves the current file.
- *Save As* saves the current file, but with new name.
- *Save All* saves all edited files in their current state.
- *Close* closes the current file and removes it from the history.
- *Print* prints a file.
- *DOS or OS/2 Shell* runs either a DOS or OS/2 shell.
- *Exit* exits from PWB—returning to the operating system.
- *File Name 1* lists the first file in the file history.

- *File Name 6* lists the first six files in the file history.
- *More Files* lists the entire file history.

Edit Menu

The PWB Edit menu allows you to revise and otherwise manipulate the text in the active window. The following are the Edit menu options:

- *Undo* reverses your last edit.
- *Redo* restores your last "undone" edit.
- *Repeat* repeats your last editing command.
- *Cut* moves selected text to the Clipboard.
- *Copy* copies the selected text to the Clipboard.
- *Paste* inserts the contents of the Clipboard into your file.
- *Clear* deletes (entirely) your selected text.
- *Set Anchor* saves current cursor position as an "anchor."
- *Select to Anchor* selects from the cursor to the anchor.
- *Box Mode* sets a selection mode for box, stream or line.
- *Read-Only* prohibits changes to a file.
- *Set Record* sets the name of the macro to record.
- *Record On* toggles "record" on or off.
- *Edit Macro* brings up the "record" pseudofile.

The cut and paste options allow you to cut or copy text from a window to a temporary storage area called the Clipboard. Text in the Clipboard may be pasted (inserted) in some other location.

Macro sequences are copied and read from a pseudofile, and they allow you to compress multiple keystrokes into a "fewer-key" sequence.

View Menu

Use the View menu to manipulate the size and number of windows open on the screen. The following are the View menu selections:

- *Split Horizontal* divides the editing window left-to-right.
- *Split Vertical* divides the editing window top-to-bottom.
- *Size Window* changes the size of the active window.
- *Maximize Window* toggles between two window sizes.
- *Close Window* closes the active window.
- *Compile Results* opens the error window.

The *Split Horizontal* command divides the active window into a top window and bottom window, splitting at the location of the cursor. The minimum window size is five lines, meaning the cursor must be five lines away from the top or bottom border of the active window or the split horizontal window command will not work.

Use the *Split Vertical* command to divide the active window into a left window and right window, splitting at the location of the cursor. The minimum vertical window size is 10 columns, meaning that the cursor must be 10 columns away from the left or right border of the active window for the command to be successful.

Search Menu

The Search menu is used to call various search routines. The menu prompts are presented below:

- *Find* searches the file in the active window for text.
- *Selected Text* searches the file for previously selected text.
- *Repeat Last Find* searches again for the same text.
- *Change* replaces old text with new text.
- *For File* searches for a file on the selected disk drive.
- *Next Error* finds the line with the next error.
- *Previous Error* finds the line with the previous error.
- *Set Error* finds the line that contains the error whose message is under the cursor.
- *Go to Mark* finds a predefined mark.
- *Define Mark* defines a mark position in the file.
- *Set Mark File* opens the file containing "bookmarks" that you have set.

Make Menu

The Make menu is used to call the routines that you use to compile programs and manage your various program lists. Microsoft made significant changes to the MAKE routines between versions 5.1 and 6.0. The seven PWB Make menu options are:

- *Compile File* compiles the file named on the menu.
- *Build* builds the program named on the menu.
- *Rebuild All* rebuilds the modules for the program list.
- *Build Target* builds the named "target" for the program list.
- *Set Program List* names the program list (or creates a new one).
- *Edit Program List* changes the contents of the program list.
- *Clear Program List* removes files from the program list.

Compile File is the command that compiles your current source file. It should be used with a single-module program or an individual module of a multimodule program. To compile all of the (changed) modules of a multimodule program, use the *Build* command on the *Make* menu. Running such a program after it has been (re)built requires a switch to the *Run* menu and selection of the *Execute* command. (The *Debug* command on *Run* invokes the debugger.) Use the *Build* command to compile and link all out-of-date (modified) files in a multimodule program and to create a single executable file.

A file is out of date if it has been edited since it was last compiled or compiled since it was last linked. A multimodule program uses a program list to manage the compilation process. The program list contains the names of all the files needed by the multimodule program (single file programs do not need a program list). The appropriate commands are *Set Program List* to create a program list or open a program list file, *Edit Program List* to add/delete files in your program list, and *Clear Program List* to remove all the files from the program list.

The *Rebuild All* command compiles and links all the files in a program—even those that have not changed—and creates a single, executable file.

Run Menu

The Run menu is used to execute or debug a program, or it can be used to call your own or third-party utilities accessible from within the PWB. The five *Run* prompts are:

- *Execute* executes the program most recently built.
- *Debug* debugs the current program.
- *Command Line* sets the command line for a program to execute or debug.
- *Run DOS or OS/2 Command* executes any DOS or OS/2 command.
- *Customize Menu* allows you to add items to the menu.

Options Menu

The items and display order of the choices on the Options menu will change, depending on which extensions are loaded and their location in the path. The on-line Help file describes the conditions under which such change occurs. The ten items on the Options menu are:

- *Environment* sets the various PWB environment variables.
- *Key Assignments* assigns commands to keys.
- *Editor Settings* changes switches for the editor.
- *Build Options* sets the options for the build process.
- *Browse Options* sets up a PWB Source Browser database.
- *C Compiler Options* allows you to choose C compiler options.

- *NMAKE Options* sets the command-line options for NMAKE.
- *LINK Options* sets the command-line options for LINK.
- *CodeView Options (DOS)* sets the DOS CodeView options.
- *CodeView Options (OS/2)* sets the CodeView options for OS/2.

The *Environment* command allows you to specify which directories should be searched for include files, libraries, and on-line Help. A location for each type of file may be specified in an environment variable, which, if not specified, is assumed to be the current directory. The Help search defaults to the Help-files environment variable.

The *CodeView* program, the options for which can be set from the Options menu, has been substantially changed for Microsoft C 6.0. The operation of the revised version of *CodeView* is beyond the scope of this book, but a complete set of on-line Help files is available for your use with the Microsoft C 6.0 compiler.

The *Options* menu commands typically correspond to switch values, and the switches always take the values that have been most recently assigned. Assignments may come from the Options menu, Assign function, or settings in the TOOLS.INI file.

Browse Menu

The items on the Browse menu of the Programmer's WorkBench are:

- *Goto Definition* finds the definition of a symbol.
- *Goto Reference* finds the reference for a symbol.
- *View Relationship* views symbol relationships.
- *List References* lists references to the variables in a program.
- *Call Tree* displays a call tree for a program.
- *Outline* displays an outline of a program.
- *Next* goes to the next definition or reference.
- *Previous* goes to the previous definition or reference.
- *Case Sensitive* makes a symbol search case sensitive.
- *Split Window* splits the screen for a Browse window.

The *Call Tree* routine appeared as a utility program named CALLTREE.EXE in the pre-6.0 versions of Microsoft C. If you have CALLTREE and wish to build tree diagrams without using the PWB environment, copy CALLTREE to your Microsoft C 6.0 environment and use it as a stand-alone routine from the command line.

The Browse system is one of the most exciting advantages of the Programmer's WorkBench. Browse allows you to track, automatically, the various dependencies and variable assignments generated by your program. It will help you find all instances of a call to a specified C function, for example, and list the values assigned to a specified variable.

The only wrinkle in the Browse routine is that it builds its database from compiled code, and thus, is of no value during the stages before your code is compiled successfully. One way to invoke the power of Browse on a large project is to begin compiling it in pieces, allowing the Browse database to grow as the number of compiled modules grows. The Browse routines can help identify problems, even within a project where all of the modules have not been compiled. The Browse options are explained in detail in the on-line Help files.

PWB PROGRAM DEVELOPMENT

An abbreviated plan for program development is presented below. It assumes that the code has already been entered into the edit window.

The first step within the PWB is to choose the *Set Program List* from the Make menu and enter the name of a new or existing .MAK file (the name of a non-PWB make file is preceded by an "at" (@) sign). The *Edit Program List* dialog box will appear if you are entering a new make file. If such is the case, select files for the program list and save it. The *Options Menu* is your next stop. Set the compiler options as you desire (see Figure 2-1). Then you switch to the Run menu and invoke the *Build* command, which will build an executable file, assuming that the compilation is successful. OS/2 users will need to explicitly invoke the *Compile Results* command to check the status of the build operation. The *Compile Results* routine opens automatically under DOS. The *Debug* command invokes the debugger, and the *Execute* command runs the program.

USING ON-LINE HELP

Help may be invoked from within the PWB by clicking the left mouse button twice or the right button once. Clicking the right mouse button when not over any particular item gives the general "Help on Help"

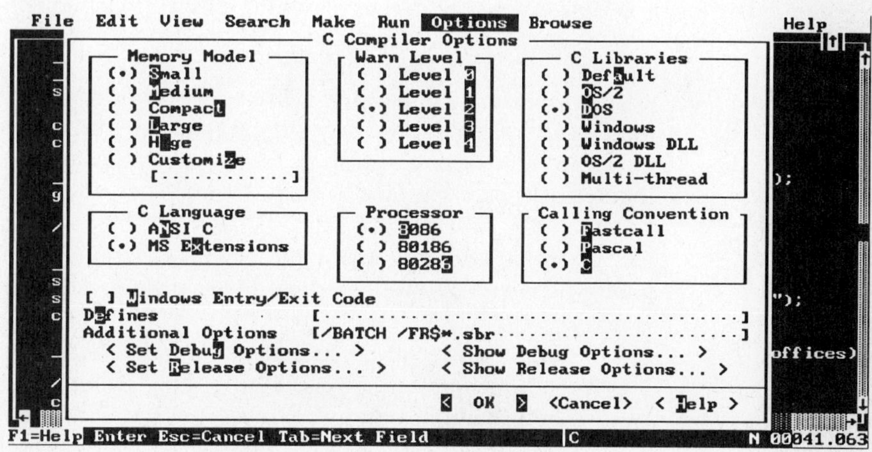

Figure 2-1. ***C Compiler Options Selection Box***

screen shown in Figure 2-2. (The behavior of the mouse buttons may be defined within the PWB.) There are several Help "selection" screens and a Help menu within the on-line Microsoft C Help files.

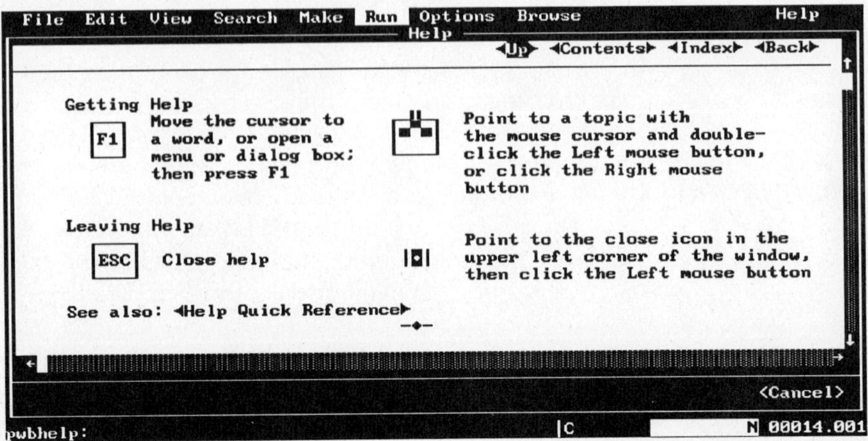

Figure 2-2. *General Help Screen*

The Help menu is a horizontal bar that displays at the top of the Help window as shown in Figure 2-2. Not all options are displayed on all screens. Clicking on the prompts yields the following:

- *Up* cycles the display to the next Help screen.
- *Contents* displays the Help table of contents.
- *Index* displays an alphabetic list of Help topics.
- *Back* cycles the display to the previous Help screen.

The *Index* command displays an alphabetic index of topics. You have three courses of action at this point: Type one of the displayed letters and click the right mouse button to see a list of Help entries starting with that letter, click the right mouse button while the cursor is on a specific word on the display for Help (if available) on the topic you have highlighted, or use the scroll bars and arrow keys to move through the list. You can also get help on currently selected menu items. Figure 2-3 shows a typical topic Help screen.

There is a special Help package available with the CL program. Typing *CL HELP* displays a Help menu for the CL software and allows you to receive help without being within the PWB environment.

There are additional steps you may take with the Microsoft C 6.0 Help files. One is to use the Microsoft C 6.0 *HELPMAKE* utility, with which you can decompile the Microsoft Help files into ASCII text files. The decom-

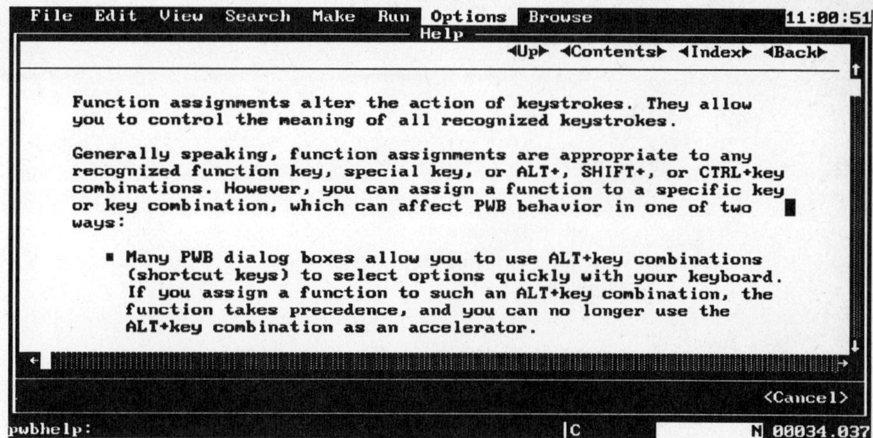

Figure 2-3. ***Topic Help Screen***

piled files may be edited and recompiled for use within PWB, adding, for instance, examples of local convention so that all the programmers on a project share the same style. You may also elect to leave the decompiled help files in ASCII, and view them with a file viewer such as the shareware program *LIST*. A file viewer is a better tool than a word processor for such work, because the viewers are typically smaller than a WP program and can thus be invoked while editing code (through a DOS exit), without consuming the remainder of the system's free memory. A batch file that allows you to view the Help routines might look like this:

```
ECHO OFF
REM - for calling LIST for the .OUT files in 6.0 Microsoft C C
CLS
DIR  C:\HLP_OUT\*.OUT /W
LIST C:\HLP_OUT\%1.OUT
```

This batch file example assumes that the Microsoft Help files are on drive C in a subdirectory named *C:\HLP_OUT* and have an ".OUT" file extension. The viewer program is named *LIST*, and it is called from within the batch file named *LST*. Typing *LST CLANG* will cause the contents of the *CLANG.OUT* file to be displayed. If *LST* is typed without an argument, the *DIR* command will display a directory of the *.OUT* files. (The directory is displayed with or without the argument, but is quickly erased when the appropriate *.OUT* file is displayed.)

CL: COMPILING AND LINKING

In many cases, you will find it more convenient to compile and link programs directly from PWB. Sometimes, however, the traditional command-line compilation is more appropriate—for example, if the program is large and there isn't enough memory for the PWB. From the DOS or OS/2 command line, CL is your gateway to both the compiler and the linker. CL is a small program with few modules, and it can be used to compile and link files as simply as

```
CL TEST.C REST.C
```

Using the small memory model as the default, CL will create the object files TEST.OBJ and REST.OBJ and invoke the linker to generate the executable TEST.EXE. The *main*( ) function can appear in either TEST.C or REST.C.

Using CL without options is suitable for small programs, but creating larger applications typically leads the programmer into the land of memory models, math coprocessors, third-party toolkits, debuggers, and assorted other development tools. The Microsoft C compiler provides dozens of ways to prepare for and use such tools. You specify your choices through command-line arguments to the CL program. For example, you can use the CL program to compile TEST.EXE for the large memory model while generating code for both an 80x87 math coprocessor and a debugger such as Microsoft CodeView. The command looks like this:

```
CL /AL /FPi87 /Zi TEST.C REST.C
```

Each option begins with a slash (/), though a dash (-) is also accepted. The letter after the slash identifies the type of the option for the Microsoft compiler. Subsequent characters and/or digits specify subclasses within a type.

In our TEST.EXE example above, the /AL option specified the large memory model. /FPi87 told the compiler to embed 80x87 math coprocessor code in the output. /Zi caused the generation of debug data of importance to CodeView. An alphabetic list of options for CL is shown in Table 2-7. The options are arranged according to their purpose in Table 2-8.

Some of the options are straightforward, but a few, such as the optimization options (the /O family), are difficult to use. The best approach is to begin by using only the simple options and add the complex ones as you go.

Table 2-7. ***List of Options for CL***

Option	Action by CL
/A <string>	Setup a custom memory model. The A /<string> command sets up a customized memory model. The <string> consists of three characters, one from each group:

Table 2-7. *(cont.)*

Option	Action by CL

Group	Letter	Interpretation	Pointer size
Code size	s	small	near (16-bit) code pointers
	l	large	far (32-bit) code pointers
Data size	n	near	near (16-bit) data pointers
	f	far	far (32-bit) data pointers
	n	huge	huge (32-bit) data pointers
Segments	d		SS is equal to DS.
	u		SS not same as DS. DS loaded in each module.
	w		SS not same as DS. DS remains fixed. Primarily for Microsoft Windows and DLL development.

Option	Action by CL
/AC	Selects compact memory model.
/AH	Selects huge memory model.
/AL	Selects large memory model.
/AM	Selects medium memory model.
/AS	Selects small memory model (default).
/AT	Selects tiny memory model. Introduced in version 6.0.
/B1 [path]	Calls C1L.EXE, an alternative preprocessor used when dealing with "compiler out of near heap" messages. The value for "path" is where C1L.EXE is kept . See also the switches /B2 and /B3. Introduced in version 6.0.
/B2 [path]	Calls C2L.EXE, an alternative pass two compiler. See also the switches /B1 and /B3. Introduced in version 6.0.
/B3 [path]	Calls C3L.EXE, an alternative pass three compiler. See also switches /B1 and /B2. Introduced in version 6.0.
/C	Retains comments when preprocessing a file. Valid only with /E, /P, or /EP.
/D <name> [=text]	Defines the macro with the text. The equal sign and the following text may be omitted.
/E	Preprocesses a file and sends the output (including #line directives) to stdout.
/EP	Same as option /E, but no line numbers are printed.
/F <hex_number>	Sets the stack size to the number of bytes specified by the hexadecimal number. This is the same as /link /STACK:number.
/FPa	Generates calls to an alternate math library for floating-point operations. Not valid with /qc option.
/FPc	Generates calls to an emulator library for floating-point operations. At run-time, uses the 80x87 coprocessor, if one is found. Not valid with /qc option.
/FPc87	Generates calls to an 80x87 library. Requires 80x87 coprocessor at run-time. Not valid with /qc option.

Table 2-7. ***(cont.)***

Option	Action by CL
/FPi	Generates in-line code that uses an emulator library. Uses 80x87 coprocessor at run-time, if one is found. This is the default /FP option.
/FPi87	Generates in-line instructions and selects an 80x87 library. The 80x87 library elements require an 80x87 coprocessor at run-time.
/FR [browse_file]	Generates an extended data base for the source browser. /FR defaults to *basename.*SBR if no *browse_file* is specified. Introduced in version 6.0.
/Fa <asm_file>	Sends assembly listing to *asm_file*. If *asm_file* is not specified, defaults to *source_file.*ASM. Not valid with /qc option.
/Fb [bound_file]	Creates a bound executable file for OS/2. Should only be used with the /Lp switch. Introduced in version 6.0.
/Fc [code_file]	Generates a combined source-assembly listing. Defaults to *source_file.*COD if *code_file* is not specified. Not valid with /qc option.
/Fe <exe_file>	Accepts the *exe_file* as the name of the executable file.
/Fl [list_file]	Generates an object code listing. If *list_file* is absent, defaults to *source_file.*COD. Not valid with /qc option.
/Fm [map_file]	Generates a linker map file. If *map_file* is not specified, /Fm defaults to *first_source_file.*MAP.
/Fo <filename>	Accepts *filename* as the name of the object file.
/Fr [browse_file]	Generates a standard source browser data base. If no *browse_file* is specified, the /Fr option defaults *basename.*SBR. Introduced in version 6.0.
/Fs [source_file]	Produces source listing. If *source_file* is not specified, defaults to *source_file.* LST. Not valid with /qc option.
/Fx <ref_file>	Specifies a name for a MASM cross-reference file. If no *ref_file* is specified, the /Fx default is *source_file.*CRF. Introduced in version 6.0.
/G0	Generates 8086/8088 instructions. The is the /G-series default.
/G1	Generates 80186 instructions.
/G2	Generates 80286 instructions.
/GW	Same as /Gw, but generates more efficient entry sequences.
/Gc	Uses Pascal-style function calls (arguments are pushed on stack in the order they appear in the function call and stack is cleaned up by the function before returning). Generates fast, compact code.
/Gd	Specifies standard C calling conventions (default), forcing the _cdecl style. Introduced in version 6.0.
/Ge	Enables calls to stack-checking routine (default).
/Gi	Compiles incrementally when used with /qc option. When used without /qc, /Gi incrementally links by padding object files. Implies /Li.
/Gm	Stores strings in the CONST segment, which is used for constants. Not valid with /qc option.

Table 2-7. *(cont.)*

Option	Action by CL
/Gr	Enables new _fastcall function. Helps speed some function calls. Introduced in version 6.0.
/Gs	Stack-checking calls are not generated.
/Gt [number]	Places data items larger than [*number*] bytes in a new data segment. (Default [*number*] is 256.)
/Gw	Generates entry/exit code for Windows.
/H <number>	Restricts significant characters in external names to the *number* length. The default is 31. Not valid with /qc option.
/HELP	In version 6.0, invokes the HELP system. In earlier versions, displays a list of CL options.
/I <pathname>	The *pathname* is added to the list of directories that are searched for #include files.
/J	Changes the default type of char to unsigned.
/Lc	Compiles for DOS "compatibility mode." Similar to /Lr.
/Li [number]	Invokes incremental linker ILINK instead of standard linker LINK. ILINK is faster than LINK, but creates larger files. The option *number* is the byte boundary to which all near functions are to be padded. Introduced in version 6.0.
/Lp	Compiles for OS/2 protected mode.
/Lr	Causes linker to generate a "real mode" executable.
/MA MASM_option	Passes specified option to MASM. MASM is automatically invoked for files listed on command line with extension .ASM.
/MD	Creates dynamically linked C run-time library for OS/2 only. Equivalent to /ALw/FPi/G2/DDLL/DMT. No library search record. Introduced in version 6.0.
/ML	Statically links C runtime library as part of dynamic link library. For OS/2 only. Equivalent to /ALw/FPa/G2/DMT. Library search record is changed to LLIBCDLL.LIB. Introduced in version 6.0.
/MT	Enables support for multithread OS/2 programs. Equivalent to /ALw /FPi /G2 /DMT. The library search record is changed to LLIBCMT.LIB. Introduced in version 6.0.
/ND <data_seg>	Sets the name of the data segment to <data_seg>.
/NM <module>	Sets the name of the module to <module>.
/NT <text_seg>	Sets the name of the code segment to <text_seg>.
/O	Enables optimization (same as /Ot).
/Oa	Ignores aliasing—multiple names for the same memory location.
/Oc	Enables default (block-level) local common expressions. Introduced in version 6.0.
/Od	Disables all optimizations.
/Oe	Enables global register allocation. Introduced in version 6.0.
/Og	Enables global optimizations and global common expressions. Introduced in version 6.0.
/Oi	Enables the use of intrinsic functions.

Table 2-7. *(cont.)*

Option	Action by CL
/Ol	Enables loop optimizations.
/On	Disables "unsafe" optimizations.
/Op	Enables precision optimizations on floating-point calculations.
/Or	Disables in-line return.
/Os	Optimizes for space.
/Ot	Optimizes for speed (default).
/Ow	Assumes no aliases except across function calls. Not valid with /qc option.
/Ox	Enables maximum optimization (same as /Oailt /Gs).
/Oz	Enables maximum loop and global-register-allocation optimization. Intrcduced in version 6.0.
/P	Preprocesses and sends output to the file with same name as source, but with the extension .I.
/Sl <line width>	Sets the characters per line in the source listings (should be between 79 and 132).
/Sp <page length>	Sets the page length in lines for source listings (should be between 15 and 255).
/Ss <subtitle>	Sets the subtitle string for source listings.
/St <title>	Sets the title string for source listings.
/ Ta <asm_srcfile>	Specifies that *asm_srcfile* is to be treated as an assembler source file, whether or not it has an .ASM extension. Introduced in version 6.0.
/ Tc <file_name>	Specifies a <file_name> without the .c extension.
/U <name>	Removes the definition of all predefined macros.
/V <string>	Puts a version string into the object file.
/ W <number>	Sets the level for compiler warning messages. The <number> is an integer from 0 through 4. The lowest level is set by 0—all warnings off—and 4 sets the highest level. Level 4 was introduced in version 6.0.
/WX	Makes all warnings fatal: no object code generated when a warning occurs. Introduced in version 6.0, serves essentially as the W5 warning level.
/X	Ignores the list of "standard places" when searching for #include files.
/Za	Enforces ANSI compatibility by disabling all Microsoft extensions to the language.
/Zc	Causes functions declared as _pascal to be treated without regard to case. Not valid with /qc option. Introduced in version 6.0.
/Zd	Generates line number information for the Microsoft SYMDEB symbolic debugger.
/Ze	Enables all features specific to Microsoft C (default).
/Zg	Generates function declarations without compiling program. The result is sent to standard output.

Table 2-7. *(cont.)*

Option	Action by CL
/Zi	Generates symbolic debugging information required by Microsoft CodeView, a window-oriented debugger.
/Zl	Removes default library information from the object files.
/Zp	Packs members of structures on *n* byte boundary, legal values of which are 1, 2, or 4.
/Zr	Generates code that checks for NULL pointers and out-of-range _far pointers. Use only with /qc as the normal CL command handles NULL checks by default.
/Zs <filename>	Performs a syntax check only of *filename*.
/c	Compiles without linking.
/link <options>	Passes the <options> to LINK.
/nologo	Suppresses display of sign-on banner. Introduced in version 6.0.
/qc	Invokes the quick compile command. Options /Fa, /Fc, /Fl, /FPa, /FPc, /FPc87, /Fs, /Gm, /H, /Ow, and /Zc may not be used with /qc.
/u	Removes (undefines) definitions of *all* predefined identifiers.
/w	Suppresses all compiler warning messages: the same as /W0.

CREATING OS/2 EXECUTABLES

The /L options, which tell the linker whether to compile the program for OS/2 protected mode (/Lp) or DOS real mode (/Lr) or (/Lc), were added in version 5.1. Before compiling OS/2 protected mode programs, you should use the Microsoft SETUP program to specify the mode-specific libraries you will need. The SETUP program is fully explained in the documentation that accompanies the Microsoft compiler.

Table 2-8. *Option Categories for CL*

Purpose of Option	Options
Selecting a memory model.	/AC, /AH, /AL, /AM, /AS, /AT, /A <string> Default: /AS
Developing assembler.	/MA MASM_option, / Ta <asm_srcfile>
Generating code for specific processor and mixed language calls.	/Gt [number], /G0, /G1, /G2, /Gc, /Gd, /Ge, /Gi, /Gm, /Gr, /Gs, /Gw, /GW Default: /G0
Supporting CodeView, error checking, and language extensions.	/Za, /Zc, /Zd, /Ze, /Zg, /Zi, /Zl, /Zp <n>, /Zr, /Zs <filename>, /WX, /W <number>, /w Default: /ZE
Controlling optimization.	/O, /Oa, /Oc, Od, /Oe, /Og, /Oi, /Ol, /On, /Op, /Or, /Os, /Ot, /Ox, /Ow, /Oz Default: /Ot

Table 2-8. *(cont.)*

Purpose of Option	Options
Controlling the preprocessor.	/C, /D <name> [=text], /E, /EP, /I <pathname>, /P, /u, /U <name>, /X
Creating listing, object, and executable files.	/Fa <asm_file>, /Fc [code_file], /Fe <exe_file>, /Fl [list_file], /Fm [map_file], /Fs [source_file], /Fb [bound_file], /Fr [browse_file], /FR [browse_file], /Fx <ref_file>, /Fo <obj_file>
Formatting source listings.	/Sp <page length>, /St <title>, /Ss <subtitle>, /Sl <line width>
Increasing compiler capacity.	/B1 [path], /B2 [path], /B3 [path]
Linking.	/link <options>, /F <hex_number>, /Li [number]
Miscellaneous.	/c, /H <number>, /Gm, /J, / Tc <file_name>, /ND <data_seg>, /NM <module>, /NT <text_seg>, /V <string>, /HELP, /nologo, /qc
OS/2 development.	/MD, /ML, /MT
Selecting a floating-point library.	/FPa, /FPc, /FPc87, /FPi, /FPi87 Default: /FPi
Specifying execution mode (real or OS/2 protected).	/Lc, /Lp, /Lr

USING BIND TO CREATE DUAL-MODE EXECUTABLES

Use the Microsoft BIND utility to create a single executable file that will run in both real (DOS) and protected (OS/2) mode. Before doing this, you should:

- Run the SETUP program to choose the appropriate default protected-mode libraries.
- Read about BIND and CodeView in the Microsoft documentation that accompanied your compiler.
- Read the on-line HELP files if you are using a version of Microsoft C that contains the Programmer's WorkBench (PWB).
- Check your distribution disks for README files. They may contain information that broke too late to be included in either the manuals or this book.

The easiest way to invoke BIND is to use the /Fb option with CL. This specifies that BIND will be invoked to create a bound (dual-mode) executable from the current program. If you want to use a program name other than the current one, give the name following the /Fb (without intervening space). For example, the CL command line:

```
CL /Lp /Fbtest
```

creates the dual-mode executable TEST.EXE<N> (the extension is supplied automatically). The /Lp option specifies that the protected-mode version of the library will be used; alternatively, you can specify protected-mode default libraries in the SETUP program.

COMMAND LINE SHORTCUTS

Identifying and typing the options to CL can be tedious work. You are limited to 128 characters on the command line. Many of the options look nearly alike—especially late at night—and that leads to errors. There are several ways to reduce the tedium and typos, three of which are using environment variables, using BATCH files, and/or using the MAKE/NMAKE utility. Each will be discussed in some detail.

Microsoft C recognizes a number of DOS environment variables, one of which is called CL after the executable program of the same name. The CL environment variable is used to store options (arguments) for the CL command. For example, a CL environment variable defined as follows

```
SET CL=/AS /Gs /Od /Zi /FPc
```

causes the Microsoft C compiler to read a CL <filename> command as though you typed CL /AS /Gs /Od /Zi /FPc<filename>. In this case, the program will be compiled and linked using the small model (/AS), without stack-checking calls (/Gs), without optimizations (/Od), with CodeView hooks (/Zi), and with calls to a floating-point emulator (/FPc).

Our second approach is to use a batch file. This example file uses the same options to CL as in the preceding example, and it takes the name of a source .C file as an argument.

```
ECHO OFF
IF NOT "%1" == "" GOTO run
:usage
ECHO ! usage: RUN filename
ECHO !      where filename is program you are testing
ECHO !           (do not include extension, .C assumed)
ECHO !
GOTO end
:run
IF EXIST %1.c GOTO filefound
ECHO !RUN: File %1.c not found.  Exiting...
GOTO end
:filefound
ECHO ! Now starting CL...
CL /AS /Gs /Od /Zi /FPc %1.c
:end
```

This example batch file is named RUNMS6.BAT. Compiling and linking a source file named TEST.C is done by typing *RUNMS6 TEST* where TEST is the argument to the batch name.

RUNMS6.BAT first checks whether an argument is present. If it finds one, it looks for a filename matching the argument. If it finds such a filename, RUNMS6.BAT invokes CL.

The third approach is use of a MAKE/NMAKE utility. MAKE routines are available from Microsoft and a number of third-party vendors. They help keep track of which files are used to build a given application (a major job on even a medium-scale project) and the date/time on which those files were last modified. Some MAKE packages ensure that only modules that have changed are recompiled along the way, and that can save a lot of time during development. Microsoft significantly improved its MAKE capability when it introduced NMAKE with the version 6.0 compiler. It replaces the MAKE utility of earlier releases.

The older MAKE utility generated a make file similar to the example below:

```
##################################################

# Makefile for Microsoft MAKE
# Comments start with '#'
#
# Model set to small

MODEL = S

# Compiler flags -- generate object code only (/c option)

CFLAGS=/A$(MODEL)   /Gs   /Od   /Zi   /FPc   /c
CL=cl $(CFLAGS)       # General inference rules

# Rule to make .OBJ files from .C files

.C.OBJ:
     $(CL) $*.C

# Compile the files

prog.obj: prog.c local.h common.h
file1.obj: file1.c common.h
file2.obj: file2.c local.h

# Make the executable
```

```
prog.exe:  prog.obj  file1.obj  file2.obj
        LINK $**, $@;
```

This older-version MAKE file builds a program named PROG.EXE that has three source files, PROG.C, FILE1.C, and FILE2.C, and two include files, LOCAL.H and COMMON.H. The MAKE commands are "dependency rules" showing, for each file, the other files on which it depends. The dependency list is followed by a line showing how to prepare the file. If a generic rule is defined (for example, "build an .OBJ file out of a .C file by using CL with the following options"), you do not have to state the command to build a file. In our sample MAKE file, PROG.OBJ depends on the source files PROG.C, COMMON.H, and LOCAL.H, and PROG.EXE depends on the object files PROG.OBJ, FILE1.OBJ, and FILE2.OBJ. The LINK command to build the executable is stated because we did not provide a rule to arrive at an executable from object modules.

The newer Microsoft NMAKE is invoked by the command *NMAKE <makefile>*, in which *<makefile>* is a file that contains commands for NMAKE. It may be called as a stand-alone program or from within the PWB environment. The specifics of Microsoft NMAKE are not within the scope of this book, and they are covered in detail in the manuals and the PWB Help files accompanying the compiler. The following make file fragments, taken from various places in an NMAKE file, are provided as a contrast with the older-format file displayed earlier.

```
PROJ = anul_rpt
BROWSE  = 0
PWBRMAKE  = pwbrMAKE
FLAGS_D  = /CO /INC /FAR /PACKC
CFLAGS_R  = /Ot /Oi /Ol /Oe /Og /Gs
OBJS  = ANUL_RPT.obj FIGUR_01.obj SALES_01.obj
ANUL_RPT.obj : ANUL_RPT.C C:\INC\stdlib.h C:\INC\stdio.h\
C:\INC\conio.h C:\INC\graph.h $(PROJ).bsc : $(SBRS)
$(PWBRMAKE) @<
),$@,NUL,$(LLIBS_G) $(LLIBS_R) $(LIBS),$(DEF_FILE) $(LFLAGS_G)
```

The NMAKE options are presented in Table 2-9. You can specify options in uppercase or lowercase. For example, /a and /A are equivalent.

LINK: THE LINKER

Although CL invokes the linker, you might want to invoke the linker alone, especially when no compilation is necessary. The /link option enables you to specify linker options. Table 2-10 describes the linker command-line options and their meaning.

Table 2-9. *NMAKE Options*

Option	Action by NMAKE
/A	Builds all targets.
/C	Suppresses messages.
/D	Displays modification dates.
/E	Overrides environment variables.
/F	Specifies description file.
/HELP	Displays Help suggestions.
/I	Ignores exit codes.
/N	Displays commands.
/NOLOGO	Suppresses sign-on banner.
/P	Prints macros/targets.
/Q	Returns exit code.
/R	Ignores TOOLS.INI file.
/S	Suppresses command display.
/ T	Changes target modification dates.
/X	Specifies standard error output.
/Z	(Internal PWB Option).
/?	Displays short Help.

Table 2-10. *LINK Options*

Option	Action by LINK
/?	Displays a short HELP screen at the operating system prompt. The /HELP option in Microsoft products equipped with PWB now calls an in-depth Help file.
/A[LIGNMENT]:size	Aligns .EXE segments along boundaries specified by <size>. The <size> value must be a power of 2. The default is 512.
/BA[TCH]	Disables prompting for pathname when library or object is not found. Primarily used from a batch or NMAKE description file.
/CO[DEVIEW]	Generates executable file with information needed by the Microsoft CodeView debugger.
/CP[ARMAXALLOC]:<num>	Sets the maximum number of 16-byte paragraphs needed by program to <num>. Valid range for <num> is 1 to 65,535 (though the top limit always exceeds the limits of DOS memory). Used only with DOS.
/DO[SSEG]	Forces segments to be arranged as follows: All code segments, _far data segments, _near data (DGROUP) segments. It is the default behavior of the linker.
/DS[ALLOCATE]	Forces loading of data at the high end of the data segment. *Use this option with assembly language real-mode programs only.*

Table 2-10. ***(cont.)***

Option	Action by LINK
/E[XEPACK] <exe> <pack>	Packs the executable <exe> during linking and places the result in <pack>. Typically removes sequences of repeated bytes such as NULLs. Strips debugger information.
/F[ARCALLTRANSLATION]	Converts _far calls within the same segment to _near calls. Speeds up protected mode programs and typically cuts loading time. There is an obscure bug when immediate data is stored in code segments.
/HE[LP]	Lists the LINK options in early versions. Displays the on-line HELP file when used with PWB-equipped versions.
/HI[GH]	Places the executable file as high as possible in memory. *Use this option with DOS assembly language routines, only.*
/INC[REMENTAL]	Prepare for incremental linking with ILINK. /INC and ILINK are not intended for typical DOS programs or for release versions. Typically used with /PADC and /PADD versions.
/INF[ORMATION]	Displays informative messages during linking.
/LI[NENUMBERS]	Shows the line numbers of source statements in the map file. Requires an object file(s) with line number information, which can be generated with the /Zd option on most Microsoft compilers. Creates a map file even if one was not explicitly requested.
/M[AP]:[number]	Generates a listing of all global symbols in the input modules. The [number] denotes the maximum number of symbols the linker can sort.
/NOD[EFAULTLIBRARYSEARCH]	Ignores default libraries when resolving external references. Can be combined with a *pathname* argument, causing LINK to ignore libraries only in *pathname*.
/NOE[XTDICTIONARY]	Disables the Extended Dictionary—generated by the LIB /NOE command—and must be used when LINK error L2044 is generated.
/NOF[ARCALLTRANSLATION]	Turns off the /FARCALLTRANSLATION option, which is the default behavior of the linker. Other routines may cause it to turn on, and this will issue a reset.
/NOG[ROUPASSOCIATION]	Causes the linker to ignore group associations. It is provided for compatibility with earlier versions of the linker (2.02 and before) and early Microsoft compilers.
/NOI[GNORECASE]	The default behavior of the linker is to ignore case differences. This changes that condition, causing lowercase and uppercase letters to be seen as different values.
/NOL[OGO]	Disables the LINK sign-on banner.

Table 2-10. ***(cont.)***

Option	Action by LINK
/NON[ULLSDOSSEG]	Similar to the /DO option except that it does not insert 16 null bytes at the start of any defined _TEXT segment. Takes precedence over /DO if both are used.
/NOP[ACKCODE]	Code segment packing is on by default. This turns it off.
/O[VERLAYINTERRUPT]:<num>	Sets up *<num>* as the interrupt number to be used when an overlay has to be loaded. The default is Hex 3F (Dec 63). Valid only with DOS real-mode programs.
/PACKC[ODE]:<num>	Packs adjacent code segments into 64-K chunks. Use with /F[ARCALLTRANSLATION]. The value for *<num>* is the maximum size of a code segment grouped by the option—the default is 65,530. Typically causes modest execution speedup, particularly in Windows and OS/2 programs.
/PACKD[ATA]:<num>	Groups neighboring data segments. Similar to /PACKC code segment pack option. The *<num>* value defaults to 65,536 if left blank, and it represents the maximum size of a data segment to be packed. Use with OS/2 and Windows software only.
/PADC[ODE]:<num>	Adds pad bytes to end of each module for use by ILINK. The *<num>*value may be in Hex, Octal, or Decimal, and it contains the number of bytes to append.
/PADD[ATA]:<num>	Adds fill bytes to end of each data module. Used with /ILINK. The *<num>*value is the number of bytes to add and can be expressed in Octal, Hex, or Decimal.
/PAU[SE]	Pauses before writing executable to disk, allowing you to swap diskettes.
/PM[TYPE]:<type>	Names the type of application being generated. Use with OS/2 and Windows programs only.
/Q[UICKLIB]	Produces a library for use with early versions of QuickBASIC or QuickC compilers by Microsoft. Quick libraries default to a .QLB extension.
/SE[GMENTS]:<number>	Sets *<number>* of logical segments a program may contain. The default is 128, but the legal range is 1 to 3,072.
/ST[ACK]:<number>	Sets the stack size to *<number>* bytes. The default is 2,048, and the top limit is 65,535.
/ T[INY]	Generate a .COM file instead of an .EXE file.
/W[ARNFIXUP]	Issues a "fixup" warning for each segment. Use with OS/2 and Windows routines only.

Note: the letters in square brackets ([ ]) are optional parts of the option name. Items in angle brackets (< >) are required items.

Microsoft C 6.0 changes how the /HELP command behaves in the link program by tying the HELP routines together under the rubric of the PWB. (The *LST* batch file shown earlier provides one way to get stand-alone LINK help.) Other link changes are the addition of several OS/2 and Window-specific link options and the capability of generating .COM files instead of the somewhat larger .EXE files.

MISCELLANEOUS COMMANDS

The Programmer's WorkBench also provides seven less important "miscellaneous" utility commands. Table 2-11 defines these commands. The online Help files of the PWB cover these commands in more detail.

Table 2-11. ***Miscellaneous PWB Commands***

Command	Action
CVPACK <command>	CVPACK compresses a .EXE file by reducing the size of the CodeView debugger information within the file. Options are /HELP to call the Help file and /P to pack the file to the smallest size possible.
EXEHDR <command>	Displays and allows modification of the header of an executable file. Works with DOS, Windows, and OS/2.
EXP <command>	PWB allows you to set up a hidden DELETED subdirectory where old, but perhaps still important, files may be kept out of your way. The EXP command deletes all files in this directory provided the PWB Backup switch is set to UNDEL. Options include /HELP, /R to operate recursively, and /Q to suppress display of erased files.
NMK <command>	The NMK command helps deal with real-mode memory limits on large projects. NMK is a MAKE utility, but should be used only when NMAKE runs into memory limits.
PWBRMAKE <command>	The PWB creates a Source Browser database, if you are so inclined, and the PWBRMAKE program converts the various source files into data that can be read into that database.
RM <command>	Moves a file to a hidden DELETED subdirectory (assuming you have set up for same). Options are /F for delete read-only files without a prompt, /HELP to access the Help file, /I to inquire before moving a file, /K to keep read-only files without a prompt, and /R to set up a recursive run. See also UNDEL.
UNDEL <command>	Moves a file from a hidden DELETED subdirectory to its parent directory. The only option is /HELP.

RUNNING FROM BATCH FILES

You may prefer to run the Microsoft C compiler from a batch file into which you have written the commands you use most frequently. The example below is a useful shell to which you can add whatever commands are of interest. It takes two arguments—the first a code you assign to a combination of CL options, and the second, the name of the file on which to work. This is easily modified to handle additional arguments.

The file automatically generates a Help screen whenever asked or whenever an error is discerned. Certain useful error tests have been left out (such as testing both upper- and lowercase commands) to save space.

```
ECHO OFF
CLS
IF %1 !==!        GOTO NO_ARG
IF %2 !==!        GOTO NO_SRC
IF %1==CW4        GOTO CW4
IF %1==CLPG       GOTO CLPG
IF %1==FNC        GOTO FNC
IF %1==?          GOTO HELP

GOTO ILLEGAL

:CW4
ECHO command = B CW4 [srce_file]
ECHO result  = CL /c /W4 %2.C
CL /c /W4 %2.C
GOTO FINISH

:CLPG
ECHO command = B CLPG [srce_file] -- defaults to SMALL
ECHO result  = CL /W4 %2.C /link GRAPHICS.LIB PGCHART.LIB
CL /W4 %2.C /link GRAPHICS.LIB PGCHART.LIB
GOTO FINISH

:FNC
ECHO command = B FNC [srce_file]
ECHO result  = CL /Zg %2.C (to) %2.FNC
CL /Zg %2.C  %2.FNC
GOTO FINISH

:NO_ARG
CLS
ECHO You did not supply any arguments. I cannot proceed.
GOTO HELP

:NO_SRC
CLS
ECHO You did not supply a source file name. I cannot proceed.
GOTO HELP

:MSNG_ARG
CLS
ECHO You did not supply a third argument - typically an object file
ECHO name.  I cannot proceed.
GOTO HELP
```

```
:ILLEGAL
CLS
ECHO Your argument(s) - "%1" "%2" - are not on my list.

:HELP
ECHO The following are the legal arguments.  The switch settings and
ECHO appropriate remarks are to the right. "#" is substituted for the
ECHO percent sign because percent is a batch command and thus won't show.
ECHO.


ECHO Argument        Microsoft C Switches                    Remarks

ECHO --------        -------------------------------  -----------------
ECHO CW4             /c /W4        #1.C               start with 6.0
ECHO CLPG               /W4        #1.C /link         GRAPHICS & PGCHART
ECHO FNC                /Zg        #1.C  (to) #1.FNC  funct.list only
PAUSE
:FINISH
```

Another useful batch file is one that will erase various work files from your programming subdirectories. The file MOPUP.BAT, shown below, is an example of such a file.

```
ECHO OFF
REM - MOPUP.BAT
REM - DELs files which match the argument list on the FOR/IN line.
REM - Works on current directory.
ECHO.
ECHO FOR a IN (*.ASM *.CRF *.CTR *.ERR *.FNC *.LNK *.LRF *.MAP *.OBJ *.OUT *.STS) DO DEL a

FOR %%a IN (*.ASM *.CRF *.CTR *.ERR *.FNC *.LNK *.LRF *.MAP *.OBJ *.OUT *.STS) DO DEL %%a

ECHO.
ECHO DEL *.~*
DEL *.~*
ECHO.

DIR /W
```

The file displays the list of commands it is going to run, and then it runs them. The *FOR/IN* logic repeats the DEL command on each file specification listed within the parentheses and thus can erase multiple specifications. The *DEL *.~** command erases backup files generated by a popular software editor. It is an example of erasing one file specification at a time.

II Process Control and Memory Management

- ▶ Process Control
- ▶ Variable-Length Argument List
- ▶ Memory Allocation and Management
- ▶ Buffer Manipulation

Chapter 3 Process Control

Introduction

Reusing existing code is increasingly important as software grows more complex. Microsoft has responded to this need by including the Programmer's Tool Kit starting with QuickC 2.0, and the Programmer's WorkBench starting with Microsoft C 6.0. Both of these contain several tools, including the HELPMAKE program, that allow you to keep track of what you've written and how it should behave. The compilers will even support routines written in other languages, enabling you to take advantage of a wider range of existing code resources.

Some of the code you may wish to reuse may be in the form of an "executable"—an MS-DOS .COM or .EXE file. These are freestanding programs in their own right and you may have no knowledge of what they call, how they were written, or what side effects they may generate. You need a way to control their execution from your program so that you can treat them as modules within your design.

Suppose you are developing an application that provides an electronic mail (e-mail) service. You want the user to be able to enter and edit a message that your application will then send over the network to another computer. An editor is ideal for entering and editing text, and nearly every PC has one. If you can invoke the editor of your choice from the mail program, prepare the text, and store it in a temporary file, you won't have to develop and debug an editor from scratch. Luckily, the Microsoft C library provides the facilities that let you run another program from your program. This is called "executing a child" process, or "spawning" or "launching" a child. The Microsoft C library contains a set of "process control" routines that help you launch a child process and control certain aspects of your own process. For our e-mail example, you could use the *spawnlp* function in the process control category to invoke an editor (you can ask the user to enter the name) in which the user can prepare the mail message. Use of the *spawn* functions is demonstrated in the reference pages.

We should note that the Microsoft C compiler, starting with version 5.1, supports OS/2. In version 6.0, many existing functions were changed to make them OS/2 compatible. OS/2 has a much more complex (and powerful) notion of processes and the environment. Although our discussion focuses on MS-DOS, we provide reference material on the various OS/2 items. If you are going to be programming in OS/2 protected mode, we recommend that you first read such books as Gordon Letwin's *Inside OS/2* (Microsoft Press, 1988).

Next, we examine what MS-DOS processes are, how they are started and terminated, and how error conditions (exceptions) are handled by processes.

Concepts: Process, Environment, and Signals

A "process" is an executable program in memory and its associated *environment.* You create a process any time you run a program. The environment of a program is automatically stored by DOS in the program's Program Segment Prefix (PSP) and contains information necessary to execute the program, including the locations of code and data in memory, and information about the files that are opened by the program. The PSP also includes the DOS environmental variables such as the PATH.

ENVIRONMENT OF A PROGRAM

The familiar *C>* prompt is evidence that you are talking to a process running the DOS command processor, a file named COMMAND.COM. In this case, the environment includes the DOS variables of PATH, COMSPEC, and PROMPT. Many programs, including the Microsoft C compiler, create their own environment variables. Microsoft C uses, depending on the version, some combination of variables named INCLUDE, LIB, TMP, HELPFILES, and INIT. The environment associated with a process in MS-DOS consists of an array of null-terminated strings, with each string defining a symbol in the format *VARIABLE=Value.* The MS-DOS command interpreter, COMMAND.COM, is located by DOS using the definition of an environment variable named COMSPEC. You can see a list of the current environment variables by typing SET at the DOS prompt. The results of typing SET might look like this:

```
COMSPEC=C:\COMMAND.COM
PATH=d:\BIN;d:\MSC;c:\UTL;c:\;d:\DBUG
INCLUDE=d:\MSC\MINC;d:\ZINC;c:\BLAZ
```

```
LIB=d:\MSC\MLIB
TMP=f:\
PROMPT=$_ $P$_ msc
```

This example shows files on two logical drives, C and D, which are used as part of a backup strategy that puts the files that do not change on logical drive D; and keeps the files that do change on drive C. Logical drive C may be backed up as frequently as twice a day during periods of intense program development. Drive D, on the other hand, will only be backed up if new files are added, because its files can be restored from the archive copies of the original disks. This procedure saves many hours of backup time.

Each symbol to the left of the equal sign is an *environment variable*. The string to the right of the equal sign is its value. As shown in Figure 3-1, the environment strings are laid out one after the other with a zero byte (a NULL value) separating the definition of one variable from the next. The end of the environment is marked by two consecutive null characters.

The example above sets the environment to deal with a Microsoft C compiler. The name of the INCLUDE subdirectory was truncated to *MINC* at time of installation because it is shorter and thus easier to type. Include files are found on drives C and D. The prompt has been customized with msc so that the user knows which set of environment variables are in use, as each compiler takes its own.

Passing Information via Environment Variables

The environment variables may be used to pass information to processes. When you type the command *CL*, for example, COMMAND.COM will search for an executable CL in the directories stored in the PATH environ-

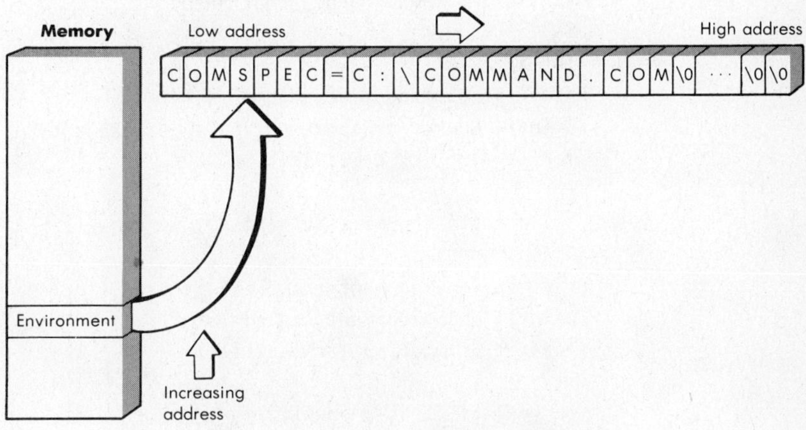

Figure 3-1. ***The MS-DOS environment***

ment variable. CL.EXE is the program that "drives" the compiler, based on command-line options you specify. It looks into C:–BIN by default, and that is where COMMAND.COM will normally find it. As noted above, some people put their unchanging files on one logical drive and their volatile files on another. The PATH examples in this section reflect such an arrangement, and COMMAND.COM will find the CL.EXE file in D:\BIN. Once found, CL.EXE will be loaded into memory and run. When DOS runs a program, CL.EXE in this case, it passes a copy of the parent environment to the child process. The environment variables that you saw when you typed SET are thus available to CL.EXE. The compiler needs them to find the include files, various libraries, and a destination for temporary files.

Using the Environment in Your Programs

The capability of accessing environment variables can be exploited by your C programs as well. For example, if you are developing an e-mail application, you can decide that you will send a copy of a mail message to all addresses listed in an environment variable DISTLIST. You can get at this environment variable via the library routine *getenv*. There is another routine named *putenv* which lets you add new definitions to your environment table. Keep in mind, however, that these definitions will vanish the moment your program exits because your program's environment table is only a copy of the parent's environment. Changes made to this copy will not affect the parent's table. A little later, we will describe another way of accessing the environment of your process.

CHILD PROCESS Suppose you wrote, compiled, and linked a small C program called TEST.EXE whose source file is

```
#include <stdio.h>
main(int argc, char **argv, char **envp)
{
    int i;
/* Print the command line arguments */
    printf("Number of command line arguments = %d\n", argc);
    for (i = 0; i < argc; i++)
    {
        printf("Argument %d = %s\n", i, argv[i]);
    }
/* Print the environment */
    printf("\nEnvironment contains:\n");
    for(i = 0; envp[i] != NULL; i++)
    {
        printf("%s\n", envp[i]);
    }
}
```

You run the program by typing *TEST One Two Three* at the DOS prompt. The *One Two Three* following the name of the program are called "command-line arguments." This mechanism is used to pass optional items to the program. As shown in Figure 3-2, COMMAND.COM will execute TEST.EXE as a child process. If the TEST.EXE file is in the C:\TEST directory, COMMAND.COM will find it (no matter the current directory) as long as PATH contains C:\TEST. For example, you may define PATH as PATH=C:\DOS; C:\BIN;C:\TEST. You may instead define PATH as D:\BIN;C:\TEST;D:\MSC; C:\UTL;C:\;D:\DBUG. It makes no difference as long as C:\TEST can be found. The child process running TEST.EXE also receives a copy of all the DOS environment variables.

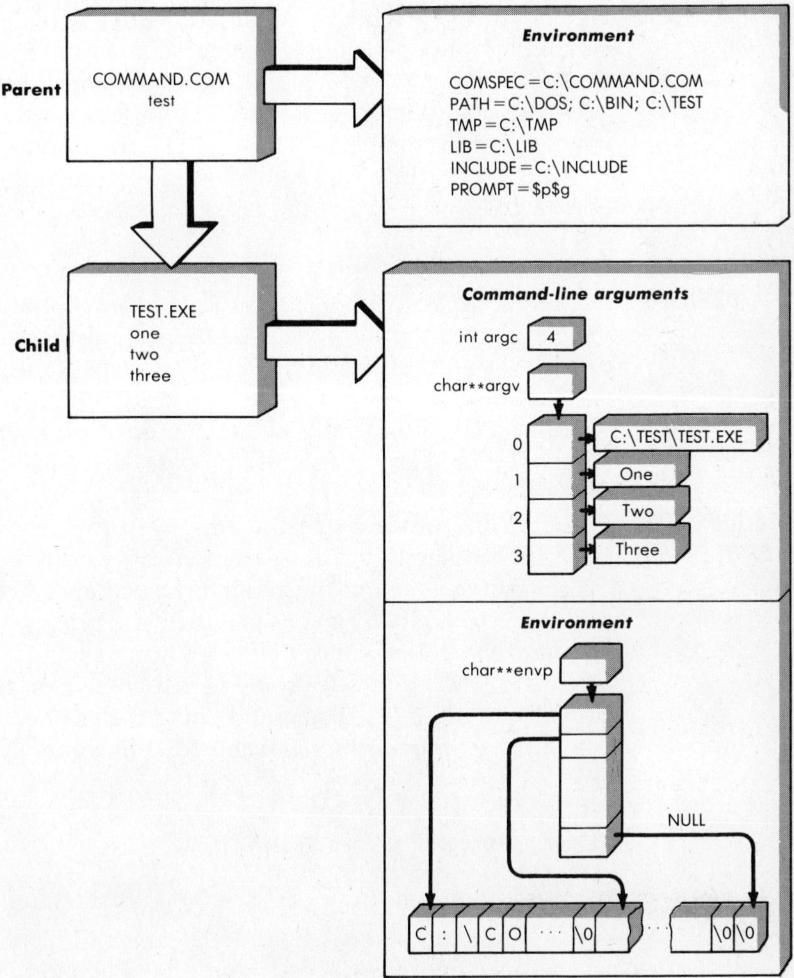

Figure 3-2. *Process running TEST.EXE under MS-DOS*

To the child process running TEST.EXE, COMMAND.COM is the parent. In this case, the parent waits until the child finishes its job. When TEST.EXE exits, the PC will run the parent process again and you will see the DOS prompt.

ACCESSING COMMAND-LINE ARGUMENTS AND ENVIRONMENT

Let's see how to access the command-line arguments and the environment in a Microsoft C program (this is the second method of accessing the environment, the first is to use the function *getenv*). Note that in the example program, the *main* function has three arguments. The first argument is an integer, *argc*, containing the number of command-line arguments. In MS-DOS versions 3.0 and later, the first argument is always the full pathname of the program. So *argc* will be 4 in our example. The argument *argv* is a pointer to an array of C strings (see Figure 3-2), each containing one command-line argument. In our example, argv[0] will be C:\TEST\TEST.EXE, which is the full pathname of the executable file.

The environment is passed to a process in the same manner as the command-line arguments. Thus, *envp* is also a pointer to an array of null-terminated C strings, each containing one environment setting. A NULL entry signifies the end of the environment table.

OS/2 PROCESSES

OS/2 goes beyond MS-DOS in supporting multiple concurrently executing processes. To accommodate OS/2, two new library routines were introduced in Microsoft C 5.1. These routines, *cwait* and *wait*, work in OS/2's protected mode only and are used to suspend a process until a certain child terminates or any of its child processes terminate. The *cwait* function waits for a specific child process whereas *wait* keeps the calling process suspended until any of its child processes terminate.

EXIT CODES FOR PROCESSES

When a child process exits, it returns an integer value, called the "exit code" to its parent just as a function call would return a value. The exit code signifies whether the program executed successfully. An exit code equal to zero normally means that the child process executed successfully. Nonzero exit codes indicate error. If you execute a program from a DOS batch file, the exit code from the program is available in a parameter named ERRORLEVEL. You could check for erroneous return from our example program by using the batch code fragment:

```
TEST One Two Three
if not ERRORLEVEL 0 echo TEST failed
```

SIGNALS

"Signals" are the operating system's way of interrupting a process when certain error conditions, also called "exceptions," occur. The signal mechanism is present in UNIX and is supported by most C libraries, Microsoft C included. Each recognized exception has a routine to handle the exception, and you can use the library routine *signal* to install your own routine to handle a particular signal. When a signal occurs, the appropriate handler is called. The *raise* function can be used to artificially generate a signal.

Constants are defined in the *signal.h* header file for each signal that your version of the Microsoft C compiler can handle. Version 5.0, for example, defined six signals. Version 5.1 defined ten, as did version 6.0. As indicated in Table 3-1, some of the signals are included strictly for ANSI compatibility and have no role on a DOS and/or OS/2 system.

SIGBREAK and SIGINT are likely to be the most frequently used signals in your programs. They are generated by users trying to get the attention of the computer by pressing Ctrl-Break or Ctrl-C respectively. Both default to ending the process, but can be changed in your code to do something else. There is an example of this on the reference page for *signal.*

Table 3-1. ***List of Signals in Microsoft C***

Signal	Exception Condition	Default Action
SIGABRT	Abnormal program termination.	Terminates calling program—exit code 3.
SIGBREAK	Generated when user types CTRL+BREAK.	Terminates calling program—exit code 3.
SIGFPE	Floating-point error, such as overflow, division by zero, etc.	Terminates calling program.
SIGILL	Illegal instruction. Not supported by OS/2 or DOS, but included because it is an ANSI signal.	Terminates calling program.
SIGINT	Generated when user types CTRL+C.	INT 23H generated.
SIGSEGV	Illegal memory access. Not supported by OS/2 or DOS, but included because it is an ANSI signal.	Terminates calling program.
SIGTERM	Termination request. Not supported by OS/2 or DOS, but included because it is an ANSI signal.	Ignored.
SIGUSR1	Defined by user.	Ignored.
SIGUSR2	Defined by user.	Ignored.
SIGUSR3	Defined by user.	Ignored.

NONLOCAL GOTOs IN C: LONGJMP AND SETJMP

Sometimes it is handy to be able to abort what you were doing and get back to where you started. For example, you may want to return to execute some code for error recovery no matter where an error is detected in your application. The *setjmp* and the *longjmp* functions provide the tools to accomplish this. The *setjmp* function saves the "state" or the "context" of the process and the *longjmp* uses the saved context to revert to a previous point in the program. What is the context of the process? In general, the context of a process refers to information that enables you to reconstruct exactly the way the process is at a particular point in its flow of execution. In C programs the relevant information includes quantities such as the address of the current instruction and of the registers SP, BP, SI, DI, DS, ES, and SS.

To understand the mechanics of *setjmp* and *longjmp*, look at the following code fragment:

```
#include <setjmp.h>
jmp_buf saved_context;

main()
{
    if (setjmp(saved_context) == 0)
    {
        do_something();
    }

    else
    {
/* This part executed when longjmp is called */
        handle_error();
    }
}

do_something()
{
    int something_wrong;
    :
    :
    if(something_wrong) longjmp(saved_context, 1);
}
```

Incidentally, the data type *jmp_buf* is defined in the header file *setjmp.h*. This is a system-dependent data type because different systems might require different amounts of information to capture the context of a process. In Microsoft C, *jmp_buf* is simply an array of nine 2-byte integers, as shown in Figure 3-3. Upon entry to *setjmp*, the stack contains the address of the buffer *saved_context* and the address of the *if* statement in the main function, to which *setjmp* will return. The *setjmp* function copies this return address (2 bytes of segment address and 2 bytes of offset) as well as the current values of the seven registers, SP, BP, SI, DI, DS, ES, and SS, into

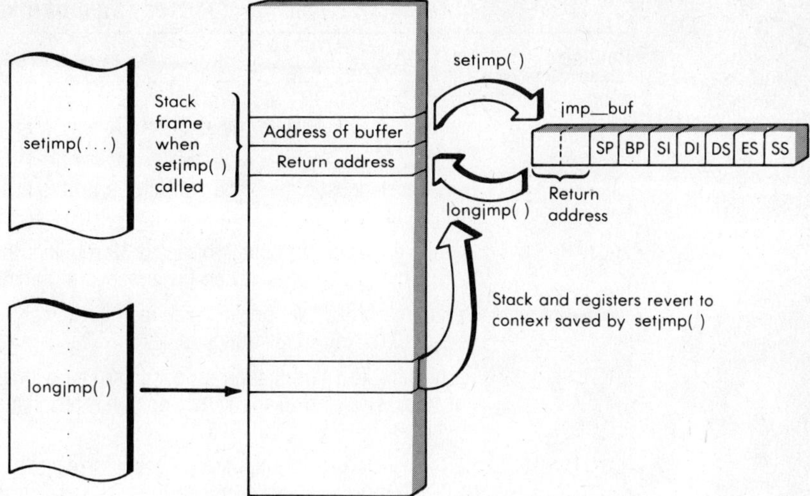

Figure 3-3. setjmp *and* longjmp *in action*

the buffer *saved_context*. Then *setjmp* returns with a zero. In this case, the *if* statement is satisfied and *do_something( )* is called.

When something goes wrong in *do_something( )* (indicated by the flag *something_wrong*), we call *longjmp* with two arguments: the first is the buffer that contains the context to which we will return. When the stack reverts back to this saved state, and the return statement in *longjmp* is executed, it will be as if we were returning from the call to *setjmp*, which originally saved the buffer *saved_context*. The second argument to *longjmp* specifies the return value to be used during this return. It should be other than zero so that in the *if* statement we can tell whether the return is induced by a *longjmp*.

The *setjmp/longjmp* combination enables you to jump unconditionally from one C function to another without using the conventional return statements. Essentially, *setjmp* marks the destination of the jump and *longjmp* is a nonlocal *goto* that executes the jump.

Notes on Process Control

The process control functions (see Table 3-2 for a complete catalog) can perform a variety of functions beyond the task of starting and stopping a process. Table 3-3 shows the process control routines listed by task. As you can see, many of the routines are for spawning or executing a child process.

Table 3-2. *Catalog of Process Control Routines*

Routine	Description
abort	Raises the SIGABRT signal after printing a message to *stderr.* The normal handler for SIGABRT terminates the process without flushing the file buffers.
assert	Prints a diagnostic message and aborts program if a given local message evaluates to false.
atexit	Installs a routine to a stack of up to 32 routines that will be called in last in-first out (LIFO) order when the process terminates.
_beginthread	Creates a thread that begins execution at start_address. Introduced in version 6.0. Not a DOS function.
_c_exit	Performs _exit termination procedures (i.e., without cleanup operations), but returns control to the caller; does not terminate the process. Introduced in version 6.0.
_cexit	Performs the exit termination procedures (e.g., flushing buffers) but returns to the caller; does not terminate the process. Introduced in version 6.0.
cwait	Suspends execution of the calling program until the specified child (or grandchild) process is terminated. OS/2 protected mode only.
_endthread	Terminates a thread created by _beginthread( ). Introduced in version 6.0. Not a DOS function.
execl	Executes a child process that overlays the parent in memory. Command-line arguments to the child are passed in a list terminated by a NULL and the child inherits the parent's environment.
execle	Executes a child process that overlays the parent in memory. Command-line arguments and a new environment are passed to the child in the form of a NULL-terminated list.
execlp	Executes a child process that overlays the parent in memory. Command-line arguments to the child are passed in a NULL-terminated list and the PATH environment variable is used to locate the file to be executed as a child.
execlpe	Executes a child process that overlays the parent in memory. The command-line arguments and a new environment are passed to the child in a NULL-terminated list and the PATH environment variable is used to find the file that is executed as a child.
execv	Executes a child process that overlays the parent in memory. A pointer to a variable-length array of command-line arguments is passed to the child. The child also receives a copy of the parent's environment.
execve	Executes a child process that overlays the parent in memory. Command-line arguments and a new environment are passed in variable-length arrays with NULLs indicating the end of each array.
execvp	Executes a child process that overlays the parent in memory. Command-line arguments are passed in a variable-length array that ends with a NULL. The child inherits a copy of the parent's environment and the PATH environment variable is used to locate the program executed as a child.
execvpe	Executes a child process that overlays the parent in memory. Command-line arguments for the child and a specified environment are passed via pointers to NULL-terminated variable-length arrays. The environment

Table 3-2. *(cont.)*

Routine	Description
	variable PATH specifies the directories in which the program to be executed as a child can reside.
exit	Calls the functions installed by *atexit* or *onexit*, flushes all buffers associated with files that are open for I/O, and terminates the process and returns the parent.
_exit	Terminates the process and immediately returns the parent without performing the services provided by *exit*.
getenv	Returns the definition of an environment variable from the environment of the process.
getpid	Returns a unique integer process identification number.
longjmp	Restores the context of a process, thus effecting an unconditional jump to the place where *setjmp* was called to save that context.
onexit	Installs a routine to a stack of up to 32 routines that are called in LIFO order when the process terminates.
_pclose	Closes stream and waits for the associated child command. Introduced in version 6.0. Not a DOS function.
perror	Prints an error message using your message and the system message corresponding to the value in the global variable *errno*.
_pipe	Creates a pipe for both reading and writing, generally in preparation for linking it to a child process. Introduced in version 6.0. Not a DOS function.
_popen	Creates a pipe and asynchronously executes a child copy of the command processor. Introduced in version 6.0. Not a DOS function.
putenv	Adds the definition of a new environment variable to the process environment table.
raise	Generates a signal (an exception).
setjmp	Saves the context of a process in a buffer that can be used by *longjmp* to jump back.
signal	Installs a function to handle a specific exception or signal.
spawnl	Executes a child process either by destroying the parent in memory or leaving it intact and returning to it when the child terminates. The command-line arguments to the child are passed in a NULL-terminated list, and the child receives a copy of the parent's environment.
spawnle	Behaves like *spawnl*, but a new environment is passed in a list that ends with a NULL.
spawnlp	Functions as *spawnl* does and also searches all directories named in the PATH environment variable to locate the program that is executed as a child.
spawnlpe	Behaves as *spawnle* does and also uses the setting of the PATH environment variable to locate the executable file to be run as a child.
spawnv	Executes a child process either by destroying the parent in memory or leaving it intact and returning to it when the child terminates. The command-line arguments to the child are passed as a pointer to a variable-length array the last element of which is a NULL. The child receives a copy of the parent's environment.

Table 3-2. *(cont.)*

Routine	Description
spawnve	Functions like *spawnv*, but a new environment is passed via a pointer to a variable-length array that ends with a NULL.
spawnvp	Functions as *spawnv* does and also searches all directories named in the PATH environment variable to locate the program that is executed as a child.
spawnvpe	Behaves as *spawnve* does and also uses the setting of the PATH environment variable to locate the executable file to be run as a child.
system	Executes an MS-DOS system command.
wait	Suspends execution of the calling program until any of its immediate child processes is terminated. OS/2 protected mode only.

Table 3-3. *Process Control Routines by Task*

Task	Name of Routines
Install the exception handler and generate an exception.	raise, signal
Execute an MS-DOS command.	system
Get identification number of process.	getpid
Get and set the environment.	getenv, putenv
Handle errors.	assert, perror
Launch a child process that destroys the parent in memory.	execl, execle, execlp, execlpe, execv, execve, execvp, execvpe
Launch a child process that optionally overlays the parent in memory or returns to the parent when it exits.	spawnl, spawnle, spawnlp, spawnlpe, spawnv, spawnve, spawnvp, spawnvpe
Make nonlocal jump from one function to another.	longjmp, setjmp
Wait for termination of all or selected OS/2 chile processes.	cwait, wait
Start or end an OS/2 thread.	_beginthread, _endthread
Open or close an OS/2 pipe.	_pclose, _pipe, _popen
Terminate a process.	abort, _c_exit, _cexit, exit, _exit
Install routines to be called when the process terminates.	atexit, onexit

SPAWN *AND* EXEC *FUNCTIONS*

Just as COMMAND.COM creates a child process and runs your program, the program can, in turn, execute a child of its own and run any other executable. The library routines in the process control category provide you with two choices: the *exec* routines or the *spawn* routines. Both sets of routines rely on the MS-DOS EXEC function to create a process, although they have slightly differing capabilities. The *exec* routines load the child into memory in the space previously used by the parent. Thus, the parent is "overlaid" by the child and destroyed. When the child ends, it returns to DOS. The *spawn* routines are more general. They offer you the choice of either overlaying the parent, in which case they behave exactly like their *exec* counterparts, or loading the child into a different place in memory. While the child executes, the parent waits and when the child terminates, the parent process resumes.

Versions of spawn *and* exec

The *exec* and *spawn* routines have eight versions each. This large assortment gives you control over how you pass the command-line arguments and the environment to the child process. It is easy enough to decide which routine to use once you know the naming scheme (see Figure 3-4).

The first part of a routine name is *exec* or *spawn*. The next character must be present. It can be either an "l" or a "v" to indicate how command-line arguments and environment (if a new one is provided) are passed. An "l" indicates that the command-line arguments (each a C string) are listed one after another with a NULL ending the list. This list appears in the call to the *spawn* or the *exec* function. You should use this form when the number of command-line arguments and entries in the environment table are fixed and known in advance. A "v" indicates that the strings that make up the command-line arguments and environment are placed in an array, and a pointer to this array is passed to the function. The last element in the array is a NULL pointer. Since this array can be constructed at run-time, this form of the routines is suitable when there is a variable number of command-line arguments to be passed to the child process.

The next letters, "p" or "e" or the pair "pe," are optional. Whenever a "p" is included in the name, the PATH environment variable of the parent process is used as the list of directories that will be searched when trying to locate the executable file that will be excuted as a child process. The "e" signifies that instead of inheriting the parent's environment, a new environment is being specified. The format used to specify the environment is the same as that for the command-line arguments and is determined by which of the letters "l" or "v" is present in the function's name.

Spawn or Exec: Which One to Use

The *spawn* and *exec* functions allow you to start a child process and execute another program. The choice of one over the other depends on your application. If you want to use a tool like an editor and return to your program, then one of the *spawn* functions will meet your needs. There are situations in which *exec* is more suitable. Suppose, your application can be broken up into three programs, MODULE1.EXE, MODULE2.EXE, and MODULE3.EXE, each independent of the other. You can run your application by first executing MODULE1.EXE in which you use *exec* to launch a child process, MODULE2.EXE. When MODULE2.EXE ends, you can

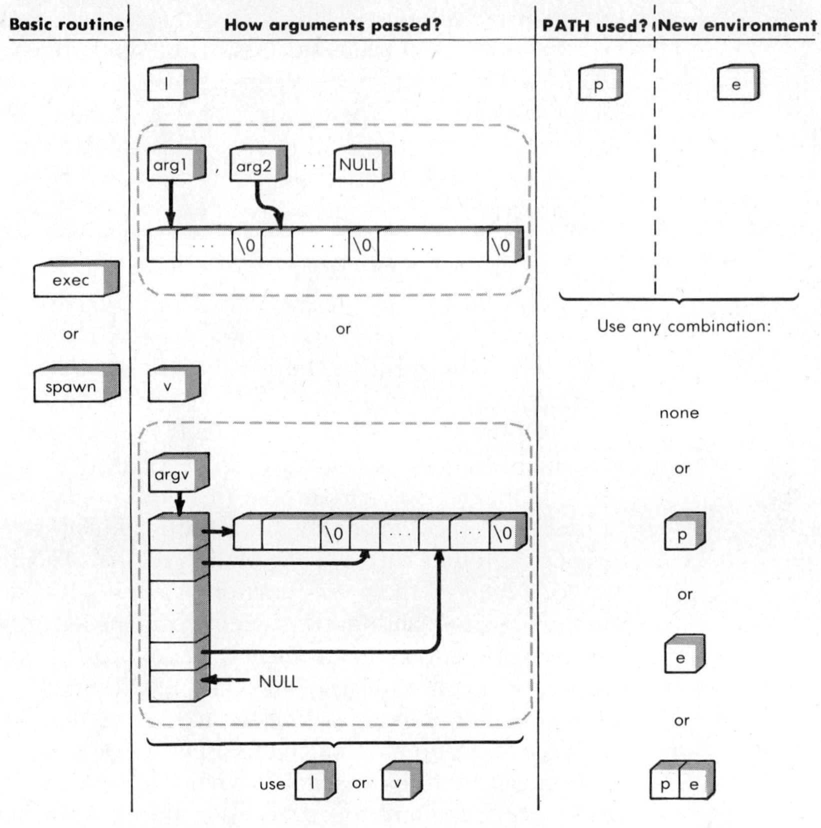

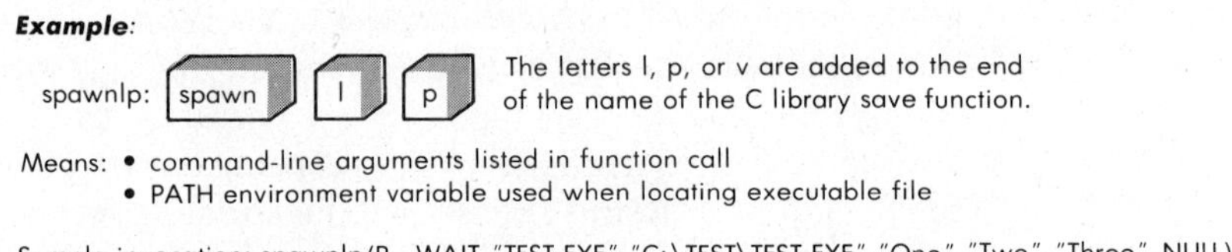

Figure 3-4. *Naming conventions and use of* exec *and* spawn *functions*

switch to MODULE3.EXE by another *exec* call. Thus you can chain from one program to another by using the *exec* functions. Despite this, you may decide to use *spawn* exclusively because the functionality of *exec* can be obtained by invoking the *spawn* functions with the execution mode P_OVERLAY.

EXECUTING DOS COMMANDS

What if you want to use an MS-DOS command, like DIR, from your C program? Since DOS commands are only understood by COMMAND.COM, the *exec* or *spawn* functions have to spawn a copy of COM-

MAND.COM to execute any DOS command. This task is made simple by the Microsoft C library routine *system*, which can accept and execute any MS-DOS command. The *system* function actually looks at the COMSPEC environment variable to locate a copy of COMMAND.COM to run as a child while your program waits. The PATH environment variable is used when executing the command that you provide to *system*.

TERMINATING A PROCESS

Three functions can terminate a process: *abort*, *_exit*, and *exit*. Of course any process terminates automatically when its body of code ends. When a C process terminates normally via a call to *exit* or when its execution is complete, several things happen. First a set of up to 32 routines (installed earlier by calls to *atexit* or *onexit*) will be called one after another in a last-in first-out (LIFO) manner. Then, all buffers associated with files open for buffered I/O will be "flushed," which involves writing out the contents of a buffer to its associated file. Finally, the process ends and returns to its parent.

The *abort* and *_exit* functions terminate a process without going through the niceties of normal termination. The buffers are not flushed (desirable when you know that the data in the buffers may be corrupted), nor do they call the routines that are supposed to be called upon program termination. The *abort* function even prints a message indicating that the program terminated abnormally.

Cautions

- When you use *exec* or *spawn* to launch a child process, the file translation mode (see the tutorial in Chapter 13) of open files is included in the environment that is passed to the child. Specifically, it is in the entry named ;C_FILE_INFO in the environment. The information on the translation mode is passed in binary form. Normally, when you invoke a C program, the "startup" code (that which is executed before your *main* function is called) reads this entry in the environment and removes it. If you run a non-C program (such as COMMAND.COM), this entry is left behind in the environment and you may see some "junk" when you print the environment in the child although normal functioning of the program should not be affected by this. To see this effect, try the following example program:

```
#include <stdlib.h>
main()
{
/* Execute the DOS command SET to see environment */
    system("set");
}
```

- The child process does not inherit the signal handlers you may have installed in the parent. All signal handlers revert to the default settings.
- The combined length of all the strings that form the command-line arguments to the child cannot exceed 128 bytes.
- You should be aware of some limits on the size of environment table. The total length of the entire environment cannot exceed 32 K and the size of individual definitions is limited to 128 bytes.

Further Reading

The use of the *exec* and the *spawn* functions as well as the handling of signals has been covered in Prata's text[1] and in Hansen's book[2].

1. Stephen Prata, The Waite Group, *Advanced C Primer++*, Howard W. Sams & Company, Carmel, IN, 1986, 502 pages.
2. Augie Hansen, *Proficient C*, Microsoft Press, Redmond, WA, 1987, 492 pages.

COMPATIBILITY

abort

MSC 3	MSC 4	MSC 5	MSC 6	QC1	QC2	QC2.5	TC1	TC1.5	TC2	TC++	ANSI	UNIX V	XNX	OS2	DOS
▲	▲	▲	▲	▲	▲	▲	▲	▲	▲	▲	▲	▲	▲	▲	▲

PURPOSE Use *abort* to exit your program abnormally.

SYNTAX

```
void abort(void);
```

EXAMPLE CALL

```
abort();
```

INCLUDES

```
#include <process.h>
```

For function declaration

or

```
#include <stdlib.h>
```

DESCRIPTION The *abort* function first prints the message *Abnormal program termination* to *stderr* and then calls *raise(SIGABRT)*. Subsequent processing depends on your arrangement for the signal SIGABRT. The default action on SIGABRT is to terminate the calling process with exit code 3 and return to the parent process or MS-DOS. Note that *abort*, unlike *exit*, will not flush the file buffers or call the routines set up by *atexit* or *onexit*. You can take care of these chores, however, by correctly setting up the processing for the SIGABRT signal.

RETURNS The default action of SIGABRT raised by *abort* is to terminate the process and return code 3 to the parent process.

COMMENTS In Microsoft C 4.0 *abort* prints the final message and terminates the process without raising the signal SIGABRT. Changed in Microsoft C 5.0 to raise (SIGABRT) instead of using the exit function.

SEE ALSO

`exit, _exit` *To terminate a process*

`raise, signal` *To generate and handle exceptions*

EXAMPLE Write a program that uses *abort* to exit when it is invoked without any command-line arguments. Otherwise, the program simply prints out the arguments.

```
#include <stdio.h>
#include <stdlib.h>
main(int argc, char **argv)
```

```
        int i;
        if(argc < 2)
        {
            printf("Not enough arguments!\n");
            abort();
        }
        for (i=0; i<argc; i++)
        {
            printf("Argument %d = %s\n", i+1, argv[i]);
        }
    }
```

assert

COMPATIBILITY

MSC 3	MSC 4	MSC 5	MSC 6	QC1	QC2	QC2.5	TC1	TC1.5	TC2	TC++	ANSI	UNIX V	XNX	OS2	DOS
▲	▲	▲	▲	▲	▲	▲	▲	▲	▲	▲	▲	▲	▲	▲	▲

PURPOSE Use *assert* to print an error message and abort the program if a specific assertion is false.

SYNTAX

```
void assert(<expression>);
```

`<expression>` *C statements specifying assertion being tested*

EXAMPLE CALL

```
assert(arg_value >= 0);
```

INCLUDES

`#include <stdio.h>` *For definition of stderr, used in definition of* assert

`#include <assert.h>` *For definition of* assert

DESCRIPTION The *assert* macro is defined in Microsoft C 5.0 and 5.1 in such a way that if the expression is false (i.e., evaluates to zero), it prints a diagnostic message of the form

```
Assertion failed: expression, file (filename), line (linenumber)
```

and calls *abort.* In the diagnostic message, *filename* is the name of the source file and *linenumber* is the line number where the *assert* macro appears in the source file. In Microsoft C 4.0 the diagnostic message does not include the *expression.* In Microsoft C 5.0, *assert* was changed to call *abort* instead of *exit.*

COMMON USES The *assert* macro identifies program errors during the debugging phase. After the program is debugged, you can disable all occurrences of the *assert* macro either by using the option /DNDEBUG=1 in the compiler's command line or by inserting a *#define NDEBUG 1* in the source file.

SEE ALSO `abort:` *To abort a program*

EXAMPLE This program considers it a fatal error if it is invoked without any argument on the command line. This test is implemented by *assert.* When invoked with one or more arguments, the program simply prints the arguments.

```
#include <stdio.h>
#include <assert.h>
main(int argc, char **argv)
{
    int i;
/* Make sure that there is more than one argument */
    assert(argc > 1);
/* Just print out the arguments */
    printf("Thanks for these \"arguments\"\n");
    for (i=0; i<argc; i++)
    {
        printf("Argument %d = %s\n", i+1, argv[i]);
    }
}
```

COMPATIBILITY

atexit

MSC 3	MSC 4	MSC 5	MSC 6	QC1	QC2	QC2.5	TC1	TC1.5	TC2	TC++	ANSI	UNIX V	XNX	OS2	DOS
		▲	▲	▲	▲	▲	▲	▲	▲	▲	▲			▲	▲

PURPOSE Use *atexit* to set up a stack of up to 32 functions that the system will call in a LIFO manner when your program terminates normally.

SYNTAX `int atexit(void (*func)(void));`

`void (*func)(void);` *Pointer to function to be called*

INCLUDES `#include <stdlib.h>` *For function declaration*

DESCRIPTION The *atexit* function places the function pointer *func* on a stack of functions to be called when the program terminates. (Note that the name of a function denotes a pointer to it.) Up to 32 functions can be specified with *atexit*. These are invoked in a LIFO manner when the calling program exits. (The function whose address you provide in the first call to *atexit* is called last.) Note that the functions passed to *atexit* cannot take any arguments.

COMMON USES The *atexit* and *onexit* functions allow you to set up "house cleaning" functions that should be performed when exiting your application program. These might include making sure all files are updated and saving the last setting of internal parameters to a disk file.

RETURNS The *atexit* function returns a 0 if successful. If you have already called *atexit* more than 32 times, the return value will be nonzero.

SEE ALSO `exit` *To terminate process (after calling functions installed by* atexit)

`onexit` *UNIX version of* atexit

EXAMPLE Demonstrate the use of *atexit* by calling it with three functions. Let each function print out an identifying message. Notice that the functions are called in the reverse order. Thus the first function "registered" with *atexit* gets called last.

```
#include <stdio.h>
#include <stdlib.h>
main(int argc, char **argv)
{
    void first(void), second(void), third(void);
    atexit(first);
    atexit(second);
    atexit(third);
    printf("Now exiting...\n");
}
/*-------------------------------------------------*/
void first(void)
{
    printf("Function number 1: called last\n");
}
/*-------------------------------------------------*/
void second(void)
{
    printf("Function number 2:\n");
}
/*-------------------------------------------------*/
void third(void)
{
```

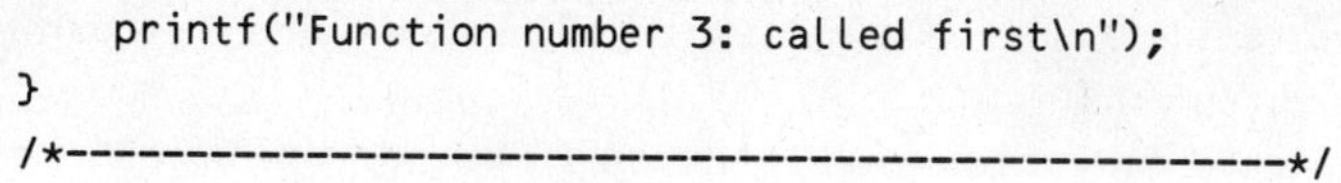

```
    printf("Function number 3: called first\n");
}
/*-----------------------------------------------------*/
```

COMPATIBILITY

_beginthread

MSC 3	MSC 4	MSC 5	MSC 6	QC1	QC2	QC2.5	TC1	TC1.5	TC2	TC++	ANSI	UNIX V	XNX	OS2	DOS
			▲											▲	

PURPOSE Use the *_beginthread* function to start the execution of an OS/2 routine.

SYNTAX

```
int _far _beginthread (void (_far *start_adrs) (void _far
*stack_bottom, unsigned stack_size, void _far *arg_lst);
```

`start_address`	*Address where execution begins*
`stack_bottom`	*Address of the thread stack (or NULL)*
`stack_size`	*Stack space to reserve*
`arg_lst`	*Address of data item to pass to new thread*

EXAMPLE CALL

```
_beginthread (srch_tag, NULL, STACK_SIZE, NULL);
```

INCLUDES

```
#include <process.h>

#include <stddef.h>
```

DESCRIPTION The _beginthread routine is used to create a thread that begins executing a far routine at the location specified by *start-adrs.* A returning thread is automatically terminated. (The *_endthread* function may be used for explicit thread termination.)

The thread stack address is passed by the *start_adrs* value, which, if set to NULL, alerts the run-time library to allocate and deallocate the thread stack on the fly. This is because the *_beginthread* function is aware of the current status of all thread IDs, and it can thus free and allocate stack space whenever a reused thread is encountered. If *start_adrs* is not NULL, the argument must specify a valid word address for a stack at least as long as the length specified by the *stack_size* argument. It must be even and not a zero and is typically a global array or a segment of memory returned by call to *malloc* (or in the far-pointered version, *_fmalloc*). The *stack_size* value identifies the size of the stack you wish to create. It is good practice to be generous with this value, assuming that adequate memory is available. The Microsoft recommendation is for a minimum of 2,048 (2K) bytes for the stack of a child thread from which C run-time calls are made. The 2K recommendation also holds for a call to any Applications Program Interface (API) function such as OS/2 system calls. The *arg_lst* argument, a parameter the size of a far pointer, is passed to the newly created thread. It is generally the address of a data item—for example, a character string—that is being passed to the new thread. You may use the value NULL for *arg_list* if nothing is being passed, but Microsoft recommends providing some value to pass to the child thread.

RETURNS A successful call to *_beginthread* returns the thread identification number of the new thread. A return of –1 indicates that an error was encountered (with errno set to either EAGAIN or EINVAL).

COMMENTS The *_beginthread* routine is not a DOS function. You should remember that the OS/2 system function *DosCreateThread*, which is similar to *_beginthread*, should not be directly called when you wish to create threads. That is because the initialization procedures required to safely call other C run-time library functions are built into *_beginthread*. The *_beginthread* function (and its companion, *_endthread*) cannot be accessed unless you are using the multithread libraries *LLIBCMT.LIB, LLIBCDLL.LIB,* and *CDLLOBJS.LIB.* You access these libraries via the CL option /MT.

All threads are terminated if any thread calls *abort, _exit, exit,* or *DosExit.* This means that your multithread programs should designate the first thread as the major thread of the program, and your main thread exit should await the termination of the other threads. The *_threadid* variable (an int defined in <stddef.h>) is a pointer to the ID of the current thread in what OS/2 calls its "local information segment." The *_threadid* value is checked in a multithread program to find the ID number of the current thread. Knowing the thread ID number is helpful when managing threads generated by *_beginthread.*

SEE ALSO `_endthread` *To terminate a thread*

EXAMPLE Use *_beginthread* to start a new thread. Have the original and new threads create some output, which will be mixed together on the screen as the threads run concurrently. Use *_endthread* to terminate the second thread when the user presses a key.

```
/* ezthread.c */
#define INCL_DOS                /* for DosSleep() */
#include <os2.h>
#include <process.h>            /* for _beginthread(), etc. */
#include <stddef.h>             /* for definitions, etc. */
#include <conio.h>              /* for kbhit() */
#define STACK_SIZE 1024
```

```
void thread2( void );
int stop_flag;

void main()
{
   stop_flag = FALSE;
   _beginthread( thread2, NULL, STACK_SIZE, NULL );

   while ( !kbhit() )     /* wait for first keystroke */
      {
      printf("---");      /* first thread prints this */
      DosSleep(200L);
      }
   getch();               /* eat the character */

   stop_flag = TRUE;      /* set flag for second thread */
                          /*  (could use semaphore) */
   while ( !kbhit() )     /* wait for second keystroke */
      {
      printf("+++");      /* first thread prints this */
      DosSleep(200L);
      }
   printf("\nThread 1 is terminated\n");
}

void thread2( void )
{
   while(1)
      {
      printf("222");           /* second thread prints this */
      DosSleep(300L);
      if( stop_flag==TRUE )    /* if flag set, */
         {
         printf("\nThread 2 is terminated\n");
         _endthread();         /* end this thread */
         }
      }
}
```

Sample output:

```
---222---222---222------222---222------222---222------222---222
---222------222---222------222---222------222---222+++
Thread 2 is terminated
++++++++++++++++++++++++++++++++++++++
Thread 1 is terminated
```

_cexit, _c_exit

COMPATIBILITY

MSC 3	MSC 4	MSC 5	MSC 6	QC1	QC2	QC2.5	TC1	TC1.5	TC2	TC++	ANSI	UNIX V	XNX	OS2	DOS
			▲			▲								▲	▲

PURPOSE Use the *_cexit* routine to exit a process after invoking normal library termination procedures but without terminating the process. Use the *_c_exit* routine to exit a process without invoking the normal library and cleanup routines (flushing the buffers, closing the files, etc.) or terminating the process.

SYNTAX

```
void _cexit  (void);

void _c_exit (void);
```

EXAMPLE CALL

```
_cexit (void);

_c_exit (void);
```

INCLUDES

```
#include <process.h>
```

DESCRIPTION The *_cexit* function calls, in LIFO order, any functions that have been tagged by the *atexit* and/or *onexit* routines. *_cexit* then flushes all I/O buffers and closes all open file handles before returning. It performs complete library termination procedures. The *_c_exit* function does not execute any *atexit* or *onexit* functions, nor does it flush any stream buffers. It merely returns to the calling process after performing minimum library termination procedures. Neither *_cexit* nor *_c_exit* terminate a process.

COMMON USES The *_cexit* and *_c_exit* functions are used to provide an orderly procedure for taking leave of a program.

RETURNS No return value.

SEE ALSO

`atexit`	*To specify one or more functions to be called at exit (ANSI-compatible)*
`onexit`	*To specify one or more functions to be called at exit (Microsoft extension)*
`exit`	*To call* atexit *and/or* onexit *functions, flush buffers, perform library terminate procedures, but not to terminate the process*
`_exit`	*To terminate the process without executing* onexitor atexit *functions and without flushing buffers*

EXAMPLE The example programs on the reference pages for *_exit* and *exit* show the usage of exit-specific functions.

COMPATIBILITY

cwait

MSC 3	MSC 4	MSC 5	MSC 6	QC1	QC2	QC2.5	TC1	TC1.5	TC2	TC++	ANSI	UNIX V	XNX	OS2	DOS
		1	▲	▲	▲	▲								▲	

PURPOSE Use *cwait* in OS/2's protected mode to wait until a specified child process terminates.

SYNTAX

```
int cwait(int *p_status, int proc_id, int action);
```

`int *p_status;` *Address of integer to hold the termination status code of child*

`int proc_id;` *Process identification number of the child*

`int action;` *Action code to indicate whether process waits for child alone or for all grandchildren too*

EXAMPLE CALL

```
pid = spawnv(P_NOWAIT, "child.exe", args);
if (cwait(&status, pid, WAIT_GRANDCHILD) == -1)
                                perror("cwait failed");
```

INCLUDES `#include <process.h>` *For function prototype and action codes*

DESCRIPTION Available in OS/2's protected mode only, the *cwait* function suspends the calling process until the child process specified by the identification number in the argument *proc_id* terminates. Depending on the value of the *action* argument, the parent process either waits only for the child or for all the grandchildren of that child. The *action* can be one of the two values shown in Table 3-4. These constants are defined in the include file *process.h*. When *cwait* returns, the integer at the address *p_status* contains a termination code that can be interpreted by consulting Table 3-5.

1. The *cwait* function was introduced in Microsoft C 5.1.

Table 3-4. ***Action Codes***

Action Code	Meaning
WAIT_CHILD	Parent process waits until the child process ends.
WAIT_GRANDCHILD	Parent waits until the specified child process and all grandchildren of that child terminate.

COMMON USES The *cwait* function synchronizes processes in OS/2's protected mode environment.

RETURNS When *cwait* returns after a normal termination of the child process, it returns the process identification of the child. In case of abnormal termination of the child, it returns −1 and sets the global variable *errno* to

Table 3-5. *Contents of the Status Word*

Byte	Contents	
Low order	Zero if child terminated normally. Otherwise, this byte contains the termination code from the service DOSCWAIT, to be interpreted as follows:	
	Content	**Meaning**
	1	Hard error abort
	2	Trap operation
	3	SIGTERM signal (asking child to terminate) was not intercepted
High order	When child returns normally, this contains the low-order byte of the result code that was passed by the child process to DOSEXIT.	

EINTR. For other types of errors, *cwait* returns –1 immediately and sets *errno* either to EINVAL to indicate an invalid action code or to ECHILD to signify that the child process specified by *proc_id* does not exist.

COMMENTS You should be familiar with the protected mode operation of the OS/2 operating system before using the *cwait* function.

SEE ALSO `spawn` *To launch a child process*

`wait` *To wait until any one of the child processes terminates*

_endthread

COMPATIBILITY

MSC 3	MSC 4	MSC 5	MSC 6	QC1	QC2	QC2.5	TC1	TC1.5	TC2	TC++	ANSI	UNIX V	XNX	OS2	DOS
			▲											▲	

PURPOSE Use the *_endthread* function to (conditionally) terminate a thread created by *_beginthread*.

SYNTAX
```
void _far _endthread (void);
```

EXAMPLE CALL
```
_endthread();
```

INCLUDES
```
#include <process.h>
```

DESCRIPTION The *_endthread* function is used to conditionally terminate a thread created by *_beginthread*. Since threads terminate automatically upon completion, the *_endthread* routine is not necessary under normal circumstances. It is useful, however, when you wish to terminate a thread earlier than normal.

RETURNS The *_endthread* routine generates no return value.

COMMENTS The *_endthread* routine is not a DOS function—it is used only with OS/2. It works only if the multithread libraries, *LLIBCMT.LIB, LLIBBCDLL.LIB,* and *CDLLOBJS.LIB,* are in use. There is an OS/2 function called *DosExit* which is used by some programmers to end a thread that was created by the Microsoft C *_beginthread* routine. Microsoft warns against this practice because the results are unpredictable.

SEE ALSO `_beginthread` *To begin an OS/2 thread*

EXAMPLE See the example in the reference page for *_beginthread.*

COMPATIBILITY

exec functions

MSC 3	MSC 4	MSC 5	MSC 6	QC1	QC2	QC2.5	TC1	TC1.5	TC2	TC++	ANSI	UNIX V	XNX	OS2	DOS
	▲	▲	▲	▲	▲	▲	▲	▲	▲	▲		▲	▲	▲	▲

PURPOSE Use one of the *exec* functions to load and execute a child process in the memory currently occupied by your program's code.

SYNTAX

```
int execl(char *path, char *arg0, char *arg1,..., NULL);

int execle(char *path, char *arg0, char *arg1,..., NULL,
           char *envp[]);

int execlp(char *path, char *arg0, char *arg1,..., NULL);

int execlpe(char *path, char *arg0, char *arg1,..., NULL,
            char *envp[]);

int execv(char *path, char *argv[]);

int execve(char *path, char *argv[], char *envp[]);

int execvp(char *path, char *argv[]);

int execvpe(char *path, char *argv[], char *envp[]);
```

`char *path;` *Pathname of file to be executed as a child process*

`char *arg0, *arg1, ..., NULL;` *Command-line arguments for the child process (ends with a NULL)*

`char *argv[];` *Array of command-line arguments for the child process*

`char *envp[];` *The environment parameter table*

EXAMPLE CALL `execv ("child.exe", argv);`

INCLUDES `#include <process.h>` *For function declaration*

DESCRIPTION The *exec* functions create a child process to load and execute the program specified by the argument *path*. In doing so, they destroy the calling process. The variations among the different forms of the *exec* functions are due to the way in which arguments and environment variables are passed to the child process. Table 3-6 uses the name of each function as a key to tabulate its action.

As you can see, the fifth letter of the name, "l" or "v," determines how command-line arguments are received by the child process. The next one or two letters indicate how environment variables are passed to the child process.

If the sixth letter of the name is a "p," then the PATH environment variable is used by COMMAND.COM to locate the executable program whose name you specify in the argument *path*. Otherwise, you must specify the full pathname of the file to be executed or specify a path beginning at the current working directory. If the *path* argument does not have an extension, the *exec* function first searches for a file without an extension. If none is found and *path* does not end with a period, it tries the extensions .COM and .EXE, in that order.

Note that the combined length of all the command-line argument strings, including a separating space between each adjoining argument, must not exceed 128 bytes. Although a different string will not produce any error, it is customary to provide the full pathname of the executable file as the first command-line argument to the child process.

The last two points to note are about files and signal handlers. In the child process, all signal handlers are reset to the default ones. Files that were open in the parent remain open in the child, but the translation modes (see *fopen*) in Chapter 13 of the open files are not preserved in the child. You must reset the translation modes by calling the *setmode* function.

COMMON USES The *exec* functions may be used to chain the execution from one program to another.

Table 3-6. exec *Functions*

Fifth Letter of Name	Meaning
l	Command-line arguments to the child process are listed on the statement that invokes the *exec* function. These forms are useful when the number of arguments is known in advance. The arguments, *arg0, arg1* . . . , are listed one after another with NULL marking the end.
v	Command-line arguments are passed in the form of a pointer to an array of argument strings. This is useful when the number of arguments is not known in advance. In this case, you prepare an array of NULL-terminated strings,

Table 3-6. *(cont.)*

Fifth Letter of Name	Meaning	
	each representing one command-line argument for the child program, put NULL to mark the end of the list, and pass the pointer to this array, *argv*, to the child process via the *exec* function.	
	Next Two Letters	**How Environment Variables Are Handled**
	none	Child process inherits parent's environment variables.
	p	PATH environment variable is used to locate the executable file. In this case, the *path* argument may specify a program name without any directory information and COMMAND.COM will locate the program if it is present in one of the directories included in your PATH environment variable.
	e	Child process receives a pointer *envp* to an array of environment strings. Each environment variable definition is of the form *NAME=value of variable*, and the end of the array is marked by NULL.
	pe	This is a combination of letters described above. The PATH environment variable is used and the child process gets a pointer to a table of environment variables that you prepare.

RETURNS If successful, the *exec* functions do not return to the parent. If an error occurs, the return value is −1 and the global variable *errno* is set to one of the constants shown in Table 3-7, indicating the cause of the error.

Table 3-7. *Error Codes Returned by* exec *Functions*

Error	Cause of Error
E2BIG	Either the total length of the command-line arguments exceeds 128 bytes, or the memory required for the environment variables exceeds 32 K.
EACCES	You are running MS-DOS 3.0 or higher with file-sharing enabled and the file specified in *path* is either locked or not set up for sharing.
EMFILE	COMMAND.COM has to open the specified file first to determine if it is executable. This error means there were already too many files open (20) to prevent COMMAND.COM from doing this.
ENOENT	Either the path or the file specified in the argument *path* was not found.
ENOEXEC	The specified file is not executable because its format does not match the DOS specification for an executable file.
ENOMEM	Either there is not enough memory to load and execute the child process or available memory is corrupted or an invalid block of memory was located, indicating that the parent process was incorrectly loaded.

COMMENTS Since the *exec* functions overwrite the parent in memory, they are good only for chaining one program to another. Use the *spawn* functions if you want to launch a program and return to the original program.

Microsoft warns that because of a bug in DOS versions 2.0 and 2.1, a child process launched by *exec* may cause fatal system errors when it exits. Use DOS versions 3.0 or higher for reliable operation when calling *exec*.

SEE ALSO `spawn functions` *To launch a program and return when it terminates*

EXAMPLE Demonstrate the use of the *exec* functions in a program that allows a child process to run using any one of the eight *exec* functions. Prepare data in a structure allocated in the parent program and pass the data to the child by encoding the address as a character string and using that string as a command-line argument. In the child program, print the command-line arguments and the environment passed to it. Then access the data structure using the address passed in the command line and display the various fields. *Note:* Remember to compile and link the child program first and save it in a file named *child.exe*.

```
/*====================== PARENT ======================*/
#include <stdio.h>
#include <process.h>
#include <malloc.h>
#include <string.h>
typedef struct TEST_DATA
{
    char name[20];
    int n;
    double x;
} TEST_DATA;
/* PARENT: Test the "exec" functions. Pass address of
 *         data in command line arguments as well as
 *         environment variables when appropriate.
 */
char *envp[] =
{
    "PARENT=EXEC FUNCTIONS",
    NULL
};
main()
{
    char *argv[4], buf[20], rname[40];
    TEST_DATA *pdata;
/* Set up a data structure and initialize it */
    if((pdata=(TEST_DATA *)
        malloc(sizeof(TEST_DATA))) == NULL) abort();
```

```
    strcpy(pdata->name, "PARENT");
    pdata->n = 100;
    pdata->x = 1000.99;
/* Set up the arguments for the child process */
    argv[0] = "child.exe",
    argv[1] = rname;
    sprintf(buf, "%p", (void far *)pdata);
    argv[2] = buf;
    argv[3] = NULL;
/* Ask user which "exec" routine to call */
    printf("Enter name of \"exec\" function to call:");
    gets(rname);
    strlwr(rname);
/* Call the "exec" function requested by the user */
    if(strcmp(rname, "execl") == 0)
    {
        execl("child.exe",
               "child.exe", "execl", buf, NULL);
    }
    if(strcmp(rname, "execle") == 0)
    {
        execle("child.exe",
        "child.exe", "execle", buf, NULL, envp);
    }
    if(strcmp(rname, "execlp") == 0)
    {
        execlp("child.exe",
               "child.exe", "execlp", buf, NULL);
    }
    if(strcmp(rname, "execlpe") == 0)
    {
        execlpe("child.exe",
        "child.exe", "execlpe", buf, NULL, envp);
    }
    if(strcmp(rname, "execv") == 0)
    {
        execv("child.exe", argv);
    }
    if(strcmp(rname, "execve") == 0)
    {
        execve("child.exe", argv, envp);
    }
    if(strcmp(rname, "execvp") == 0)
    {
        execvp("child.exe", argv);
```

```
    }
    if(strcmp(rname, "execvpe") == 0)
    {
        execvpe("child.exe", argv, envp);
    }
/* Check if we could call child or not */
    if(strcmp(pdata->name, "CHILD") == 0)
    {
        printf("Back from child: name = %s, n = %d, \
x= %f\n", pdata->name, pdata->n, pdata->x);
    }
    else
    {
         printf("Don't know: %s\n", rname);
     }
}
/*====================== CHILD ======================*/
/*     Must be in a file named:  CHILD.EXE           */
#include <stdio.h>
#include <dos.h>
#include <string.h>
typedef struct TEST_DATA
{
    char name[20];
    int n;
    double x;
} TEST_DATA;
/* Child: First argument is program name,
 *        Second one tells us how child was invoked
 *        Third argument is an address in the form
 *        SSSS:OOOO (segment:offset). This is the
 *        address of a data structure allocated in
 *        the parent.
 */
static char far cname[] = "CHILD";
main(int argc, char **argv, char **envp)
{
    char  **p_table;
    TEST_DATA far *pdata;
    void far *p_s1;
    void far *p_s2;
    printf("CHILD: received %d arguments\n", argc);
    if(argc < 3){
        printf("not enough arguments\n");
        exit(1);
```

```
    }
    printf("CHILD invoked by a %s call.\n", argv[1]);

/* Now print the environment passed to CHILD     */
    printf("==== CHILD: Environment contains ====\n");
    for(p_table = envp;
        *p_table != NULL;
        p_table++) printf("%s\n", *p_table);

/* Read in address of parent's data from argv[2] */
    sscanf(argv[2], "%p", (void far *)&pdata);
    printf("In child: name = %Fs, n = %d, x= %f\n",
           pdata->name, pdata->n, pdata->x);
/* Put new values in the data structure. If CHILD was
 * created by a "spawn" function call, this data will
 * be available to the parent when child exits.
 * Notice that we have to use "movedata" to copy
 * "far" data in small or medium model.
 */
    p_s1 = (void far *)cname;
    p_s2 = (void far *)pdata->name;
    movedata(FP_SEG(p_s1), FP_OFF(p_s1),
             FP_SEG(p_s2), FP_OFF(p_s2), 6);
    pdata->n = 101;
    pdata->x = 999.99;
    exit(0);
}
```

COMPATIBILITY **exit**

MSC 3	MSC 4	MSC 5	MSC 6	QC1	QC2	QC2.5	TC1	TC1.5	TC2	TC++	ANSI	UNIX V	XNX	OS2	DOS
▲	▲	▲	▲	▲	▲	▲	▲	▲	▲	▲	▲	▲	▲	▲	▲

PURPOSE Use *exit* to terminate your program normally by flushing file buffers, closing files, and invoking functions set up with *atexit* and *onexit.*

SYNTAX `void exit(int status);`

`intstatus;` *Exit status code*

EXAMPLE CALL `exit(0);`

INCLUDES `#include <stdlib.h>` *For function declaration*

or

```
#include <process.h>
```

DESCRIPTION The *exit* function flushes all buffers associated with files opened for buffered I/O, closes all files, and then invokes in LIFO order the functions set up by earlier calls to *atexit* and *onexit*. After the calls are complete, *exit* terminates the program and makes available to the parent process or DOS the low-order byte of the argument *status*. Ordinarily, a *status* of zero means normal exit, whereas nonzero values indicate errors. If the program was invoked from an MS-DOS batch file, the value of *status* can be checked from the batch file with the command IF_ERRORLEVEL. Starting with Microsoft C 5.1, *exit* terminates all threads of a program in OS/2's protected mode operation.

SEE ALSO

`_exit`	*To terminate process without performing the normal "housekeeping" chores*
`atexit, onexit`	*To set up functions called when a process terminates normally*

EXAMPLE Illustrate how file buffers are flushed when a program *exit*s by opening a file, writing a line to it, and using *exit* to terminate. The line appears in the file because *exit* flushed the buffer.

```
#include <stdio.h>
main()
{
    FILE *fp;
    char filename[40];
    printf("Enter name of a file to be opened \
for writing:");
    gets(filename);
    if((fp = fopen(filename, "w+")) == NULL)
    {
        perror("File open error");
        abort();
    }
    fprintf(fp, "If you use \"exit\", this line will \
appear in the file\nbecause it flushes buffers\n");
    printf("TYPE %s to see if buffers were flushed\n",
            filename);
    exit(0);
}
```

COMPATIBILITY

_exit

MSC 3	MSC 4	MSC 5	MSC 6	QC1	QC2	QC2.5	TC1	TC1.5	TC2	TC++	ANSI	UNIX V	XNX	OS2	DOS
▲	▲	▲	▲	▲	▲	▲	▲	▲	▲	▲				▲	▲

PURPOSE Use *_exit* to terminate your program immediately without flushing file buffers.

SYNTAX
```
void _exit(int status);

int  status;        _exit status code
```

EXAMPLE CALL
```
_exit(0);
```

INCLUDES
```
#include <stdlib.h>        For function declaration
```

or

```
#include <process.h>
```

DESCRIPTION The *_exit* function terminates the program immediately, without flushing the buffers associated with files opened for buffered I/O. The files are closed "as-is" and, after terminating the program, *_exit* makes available to the parent process or to DOS the low-order byte of the argument *status*. Ordinarily a *status* of zero means normal exit, whereas nonzero values indicate errors. If the program was invoked from an MS-DOS batch file, the value of *status* can be checked with the command IF_ERRORLEVEL. Starting with Microsoft C 5.1, *_exit* terminates all threads of a program in OS/2's protected mode operation.

SEE ALSO `exit` *To terminate process after performing "housekeeping" chores*

EXAMPLE Illustrate that file buffers are not flushed when a program *_exit*s by opening a file, writing a line to it and using *_exit* to terminate the program. Notice that the line does not appear in the file because *_exit* did not flush the buffer when exiting the program.

```
#include <stdio.h>
main()
{
    FILE *fp;
    char filename[40];
    printf("Enter name of a file to be opened \
for writing:");
```

```
    gets(filename);
    if((fp = fopen(filename, "w+")) == NULL)
    {
        perror("File open error");
        abort();
    }
    fprintf(fp, "If you use \"_exit\", this line will \
not appear in the file\nbecause buffers are not \
flushed\n");
    printf("TYPE %s to see if buffers were flushed\n",
            filename);
    _exit(0);
}
```

getenv

COMPATIBILITY

MSC 3	MSC 4	MSC 5	MSC 6	QC1	QC2	QC2.5	TC1	TC1.5	TC2	TC++	ANSI	UNIX V	XNX	OS2	DOS
▲	▲	▲	▲	▲	▲	▲	▲	▲	▲	▲	▲	▲	▲	▲	▲

PURPOSE Use *getenv* to get the definition of a variable from the environment table of the process.

SYNTAX

```
char *getenv(const char *varname);

const char *varname;
```

Name of environment variable to look for

EXAMPLE CALL

```
current_path = getenv("PATH");
```

INCLUDES

```
#include <stdlib.h>
```

For function declaration

DESCRIPTION The *getenv* function uses the global variable *environ* to locate the list of environment variables and then it searches the list for an entry for the variable named *varname.*

RETURNS If *varname* is found, *getenv* returns a pointer to the string value of *varname.* Thus if the environment variable LIB is defined as LIB=C:\LIB in the environment table, invoking *getenv* with LIB as *varname* returns a pointer to the string C:\LIB. If *varname* is undefined, *getenv* returns a NULL.

COMMENTS Under MS-DOS, the *main* function can get a pointer to the list of environment variables as a third argument, say, *envp.* The library routine *putenv* may alter the location of this list, however, and render *envp* useless. So, it is safer to use the functions *getenv* and *putenv*, respectively, to locate and modify the environment table.

SEE ALSO putenv — *To add the definition of a new variable to the environment table of the process*

EXAMPLE Prepare a small utility program that lets you see the setting of an environment variable. Assume that the name of the environment variable is given on the command line. Use *getenv* to get the value of that variable and print it.

```
#include <stdio.h>
#include <stdlib.h>
main(int argc, char **argv)
{
    char *value;
    if(argc < 2)
    {
        printf("Usage: %s <env_var_name>\n", argv[0]);
        exit(0);
    }
/* Get the value of the environment variable */
    strupr(argv[1]);
    if ((value = getenv(argv[1])) == NULL)
    {
        printf("%s <-- no such environment variable\n",
               argv[1]);
    }
    else
    {
        printf("%s=%s\n", argv[1], value);
    }
}
```

getpid

COMPATIBILITY

MSC 3	MSC 4	MSC 5	MSC 6	QC1	QC2	QC2.5	TC1	TC1.5	TC2	TC++	ANSI	UNIX V	XNX	OS2	DOS
▲	▲	▲	▲	▲	▲	▲						▲	▲	▲	▲

PURPOSE Use *getpid* to obtain the "process ID," an integer value that identifies the calling process to MS-DOS.

SYNTAX
```
int getpid(void);
```

INCLUDES `#include <process.h>` *For function declaration*

DESCRIPTION The *getpid* function returns an integer value, the process ID, that identifies the calling process. The process ID is also used by the *mktemp* function to generate temporary file names.

SEE ALSO `mktemp` *To generate temporary file name using process ID*

EXAMPLE Use *getpid* to get the identification number of the process and print it. A different number is returned every time you run the program.

```
#include <stdio.h>
#include <process.h>
main()
{
    int process_id;
    process_id = getpid();
    printf("The process ID is: %d\n", process_id);
}
```

longjmp

COMPATIBILITY

MSC 3	MSC 4	MSC 5	MSC 6	QC1	QC2	QC2.5	TC1	TC1.5	TC2	TC++	ANSI	UNIX V	XNX	OS2	DOS
▲	▲	▲	▲	▲	▲	▲	▲	▲	▲	▲	▲	▲	▲	▲	▲

PURPOSE Use *longjmp* to restore a stack environment that was saved by an earlier call to *setjmp*, thus restoring all local variables to their previous states and returning as if from the last call to *setjmp*.

SYNTAX `void longjmp(jmp_buf env, int value);`

`jmp_buf env;` *Data type in which the registers and a return address representing the stack environment are stored*

`int value;` *Value that appears to be returned by the earlier call to* setjmp

EXAMPLE CALL `longjmp(stack_env, 1);`

INCLUDES `#include <setjmp.h>` *For function declaration and definition of the data type* jmp_buf

DESCRIPTION The *longjmp* function restores the registers saved in *env* as part of the stack environment saved earlier by a call to *setjmp*. Then it jumps to the return address for *setjmp* which is also saved in *env*. This restores all stack-based local variables to their state when the *setjmp* function was called, making it appear as if *setjmp* returned again. The argument *value* is used in this "forced" return from *setjmp*. However, this process might not properly restore all register-based variables to the routine where the call to *setjmp* occurred. Since *longjmp* jumps to the return address of the corresponding call to *setjmp*, you must make sure that the call to *longjmp* occurs before the function in which you called *setjmp* has returned.

COMMON USES The *longjmp* function is used in conjunction with its companion *setjmp* to divert the flow of execution to error-recovery code without using the normal function call and return conventions. First a call to *setjmp* is necessary to set up the place to which *longjmp* can return control when called. After that, when the error condition occurs, you can call *longjmp* and jump to the point where the *setjmp* function would have returned.

COMMENTS It is a little difficult to understand the behavior of *setjmp* and *longjmp* but, essentially, they give you the flexibility of jumping to an arbitrary location from within C. This is akin to a "goto" statement which lets you jump from one function to another.

SEE ALSO `setjmp` *To save a stack environment to be used in a subsequent call to* longjmp

EXAMPLE The pair of *setjmp* and *longjmp* is ideal for error-handling or handling special conditions in a program. You call *setjmp* at a place where you have code that you may want to execute later. Then whenever the conditions are met, call *longjmp* with the stack environment variable saved earlier by *setjmp*. This places you where *setjmp* was called originally. It will appear as though the *setjmp* function returned a second time, this time with the value from the second argument to *longjmp*. Here is a small program to illustrate a way to use this versatile duo.

```
#include <stdio.h>
#include <setjmp.h>
static jmp_buf mark_place;
static void call_longjmp(void);
main()
{
    int rvalue;
    rvalue = setjmp(mark_place);
    if(rvalue != 0)
    {
        printf("Second return from \"setjmp\" induced \
by call to \"longjmp\"\n");
        printf("Return value = %d\n", rvalue);
```

```
        exit(rvalue);
    }
    printf("Calling \"longjmp\" next...\n");
    call_longjmp();
}
/*--------------------------------------------------------*/
static void call_longjmp(void)
{
    longjmp(mark_place, 3);
}
```

onexit

COMPATIBILITY

MSC 3	MSC 4	MSC 5	MSC 6	QC1	QC2	QC2.5	TC1	TC1.5	TC2	TC++	ANSI	UNIX V	XNX	OS2	DOS
	▲	▲	▲	▲	▲	▲						▲		▲	▲

PURPOSE Use *onexit* to set up a stack of as many as 32 functions that the system will call in a LIFO manner when your program terminates normally.

SYNTAX

```
onexit_t onexit(onexit_t (*func)(void));
```

`onexit_t (*func)(void);` *Pointer to function to be called*

INCLUDES `#include <stdlib.h>` *For function declaration and definition of* onexit_t

DESCRIPTION The *onexit* function places the function address *func* on a stack of functions to be called when the program terminates. (Note that in C the name of a function denotes a pointer to itself.) Up to 32 functions can be specified using *onexit.* These will be invoked in a LIFO manner when the calling program exits. Thus the function whose address you provide in the first call to *onexit* will actually be called last.

Note that the functions passed to *onexit* cannot take any arguments and it returns a value of type *onexit_*, a data type defined in *stdlib.h.* The *onexit* function is duplicated, starting with Microsoft C 5.0 with the ANSI-compatible name *atexit.*

COMMON USES The *onexit* and *atexit* functions allow your application program to "clean house" before returning to DOS.

RETURNS The *onexit* function returns a pointer *func* to the function if successful. If there is no more room in its stack for the function, *onexit* returns a NULL.

COMMENTS The *onexit* function is not a part of the ANSI definition. The *atexit* function

performs the same function and *is* a part of the ANSI definition. So if portability is a concern, you may want to use *atexit* instead of *onexit.*

SEE ALSO

exit — *To terminate process (after calling functions installed by* onexit*)*

atexit — *ANSI version of* onexit

EXAMPLE

Demonstrate the use of *onexit* by calling it with three different function addresses. Let each function print out an identifying message. Notice that the first function registered with *onexit* gets called last.

```
#include <stdio.h>
#include <stdlib.h>
main(int argc, char **argv)
{
    void first(void), second(void), third(void);
    onexit(first);
    onexit(second);
    onexit(third);
    printf("Now exiting...\n");
}
/*---------------------------------------------------*/
void first(void)
{
    printf("Function number 1: called last\n");
}
/*---------------------------------------------------*/
void second(void)
{
    printf("Function number 2:\n");
}
/*---------------------------------------------------*/
void third(void)
{
    printf("Function number 3: called first\n");
}
/*---------------------------------------------------*/
```

_pclose

COMPATIBILITY

MSC 3	MSC 4	MSC 5	MSC 6	QC1	QC2	QC2.5	TC1	TC1.5	TC2	TC++	ANSI	UNIX V	XNX	OS2	DOS
			▲											▲	

PURPOSE Use the *_pclose* function to close a pipe opened by a call to the *_popen* routine.

SYNTAX

```
int _pclose (FILE *strm_name);
```

strm_name *Return value from a previous call to* _popen

EXAMPLE CALL

```
printf ("\nThe process returned %d\n", _pclose (dir_srt));
```

INCLUDES

```
#include <stdio.h>
```

DESCRIPTION The *_pclose* routine waits for the termination of an associated child process (which was started by a call to *_popen*). Upon termination of that process, it closes the stream associated with either the standard input or output of the child process. Whether standard input or standard output is to be closed is determined by the arguments to the *_popen* call which initiated the process. The *_pclose* routine executes a *cwait* call on the child process and returns its exit status.

RETURNS The *_pclose* routine returns –1 if the call was not successful. A successful call returns the exit status of the child process, yielding low- and high-order bytes. The format of the return value is the same as that used by cwait, except that the low- and high-order bytes are reversed.

The high-order byte is equal to 0 upon normal termination.

The low-order byte is from the "result code" passed by the child to the OS/2 *DosExit* routine. If the child process returned from *main( )*, called either *_exit* or *exit*, or reached the end of *main( )*, the child calls *DosExit*. The resulting code's low byte is either the low-order byte of the return value from *main( )*, the low-order byte of the argument to *exit* or *_exit*, or a random value if the child process reached the end of *main( )*.

A child process that terminates without a call to *DosExit* generates a termination-status word, with a low-order value equal to 0. The high-order value is 1, if there is a hard-error; 2, which indicates a trap operation; and 3, to alert you that a SIGTERM signal was not intercepted.

COMMENTS The *DosExit* function of OS/2 allows the return of a 16-bit result code. The *wait* and *cwait* functions in Microsoft C (introduced in version 5.1) return only the low-order byte of that result code, and thus *_pclose* is also limited

to an 8-bit return code. Your *_pclose* return logic should be written to take this into account.

SEE ALSO _popen

EXAMPLE See the example program on the reference page for *_popen*.

COMPATIBILITY

perror

MSC 3	MSC 4	MSC 5	MSC 6	QC1	QC2	QC2.5	TC1	TC1.5	TC2	TC++	ANSI	UNIX V	XNX	OS2	DOS
▲	▲	▲	▲	▲	▲	▲	▲	▲	▲	▲	▲	▲	▲	▲	▲

PURPOSE Use *perror* to construct an error message by concatenating your message with that from the system which corresponds to the current value in the global variable *errno*. The message prints to *stderr*.

SYNTAX

```
void perror(const char *string);

const char *string;        Your part of the message
```

EXAMPLE CALL

```
perror("Error closing file");
```

INCLUDES

```
#include <stdio.h>        For function declaration
```

DESCRIPTION The *perror* function takes the message from the argument "string," appends a colon and a space, and concatenates to this the message from the system's error message table corresponding to the value in the global variable *errno*. The value in *errno* is the error number corresponding to the last error that occurred in a C library routine. All error messages are stored in a table of strings called *sys_errlist*. There is no need, however, to declare or to directly access these variables in your program.

COMMON USES When an error occurs in certain C library routines, the variable *errno* is set to a value that reflects the cause of the error. Typically, *perror* is called immediately after an error return from a library routine to print a message detailing the error. This message then prints to *stderr*.

COMMENTS Rather than access *errno* and the system error-message list *sys_errlist* directly, you should always use *perror* to print the error message when a library routine returns with an error. This approach is safer because it does not use error numbers, which very well can change during a later release of the compiler.

SEE ALSO `_strerror, strerror` *Alternate functions to prepare error messages*

EXAMPLE Demonstrate the use of *perror* by creating the error of closing a file with a bad handle and then printing an error message.

```
#include <stdio.h>
#include <io.h>
main()
{
    printf("We'll call \"close\" with an invalid file \
handle\n");
    if (close (100) == -1)
    {
/* Error occurred. Use perror to print error message */
        perror("Error closing file");
    }
}
```

_pipe

COMPATIBILITY

MSC 3	MSC 4	MSC 5	MSC 6	QC1	QC2	QC2.5	TC1	TC1.5	TC2	TC++	ANSI	UNIX V	XNX	OS2	DOS
			▲											▲	

PURPOSE Use the *pipe* routine to create a pipe. A pipe is a filelike I/O device with which your program can pass information to other programs.

SYNTAX `int _pipe (int *p_hndls, unsigned int pipe_siz, int text_mode);`

`p_hndls` *A pointer to read/write handles—p_hndls[0] and p_hndls[1].*

`pipe_siz` *Amount of memory, in bytes, reserved for the pipe.*

`text_mode` *The file mode to use—O_BINARY, O_TEXT*

EXAMPLE CALL `if (_pipe (cust_nams, 256, O_BINARY) == -1) exit (1);`

INCLUDES `#include <io.h>`

`#include <errno.h>`

`#include <fcntl.h>` *For O_BINARY and O_TEXT*

DESCRIPTION The *_pipe* function creates a pipe. A pipe, which is a staple of the UNIX world, is a "memory-based" file-like I/O channel that programs may use

to pass information to, and receive information from, other programs. The *_pipe* function is similar to *open* but opens the pipe for both reading and writing and thus returns two file handles, instead of just one.

The two handles returned by a call to *_pipe* are found in the *p_hndls* argument. The element *p_hndls[0]* contains the read handle, and *p_hndls[1]* contains the write handle. File handles for a pipe are used just like handles for ordinary files, and the low-level read and write functions can operate on a pipe. No locking is performed in multithread OS/2 programs. The returned handles should not be called by any thread until the call to *_pipe* is complete.

The *pipe_siz* argument specifies a requested size for the pipe buffer. The size of a pipe does not affect whether it will work, but it does affect the speed and efficiency with which it works. If the pipe is filled faster than it is emptied (and the pipe runs out of space), writing is suspended until more space is available in the pipe. All read and write operations on the pipe wait until there is enough data, or enough space, to complete the I/O request. The *pipe_siz* argument, then, is of interest to you when your attention turns toward optimizing pipe usage.

The *text_mode* argument specifies which text translation mode will be valid for the pipe. There is a manifest constant, O_TEXT, which specifies a text translation. Another constant, O_BINARY, specifies binary translation. If you specify a 0 for *text_mode* argument, the *_pipe* function defaults to the translation mode provided by the default-mode variable *_fmode*.

The manifest constants O_BINARY and O_TEXT determine the translation mode for files using *open* and *sopen* or the translation mode for streams opened with *setmode*. The O_TEXT constant sets a text (translated) mode. All carriage-return/line-feed (CR-LF) combinations are changed to a single line feed (LF) on input. The line-feed characters are changed into a CR-LF combinations on output.

The text mode also interprets a CTRL+Z as an end-of-file (EOF) character on input. The *fopen* routine checks files that are opened for reading and reading/writing to see if there is a CTRL+Z at the end of the file. It removes any CTZL-Z that it finds, if it is possible. (Removing the CTRL-Z is important because otherwise the *fseek* function may behave improperly near the end of the file.)

The O_BINARY constant sets a binary, or untranslated, mode. None of the CR-LF conversions are made.

There is a third constant, O_RAW, which behaves the same as O_BINARY. It is supported to stay compatible with the very early versions of Microsoft C.

An OS/2 pipe is destroyed when all of its handles have been closed. An error will be generated if your program tries to write to a pipe whose read handles have been closed. Pipe handles should be closed with the low-level *close* function.

COMMON USES A pipe is used to pass the results of one program to another. The dir command, for example, yields a list of files. That list can be "piped" into a sorting or a printing module for subsequent processing. The example program on the reference page for the *_popen* function shows just such a situation.

A pipe behaves a lot like a file. A pipe has a file pointer or a file descriptor (or both), and it can be read from or written to using the standard input and output functions of the Microsoft C library. A pipe is not, however, a specific device or file—but is instead temporary storage in memory. A pipe is controlled entirely by the operating system and is thus independent of the program's own memory.

A pipe (or pipes) may be used to pass information between separate programs. The command processor in OS/2, for instance, creates a pipe when executing a command such as:

```
PROG_1 ¦ PROG_2
```

The standard output handle of PROG_1 is attached to the write handle of the pipe, the end from which the pipe is filled. The standard input handle of PROG_2 is attached to the read handle of the pipe, which you might think of as the spigot of the pipe. This linkage means that you do not need to create a temporary file (consuming disk space and execution time in the process) to pass information to other programs. (Note that the "pipe" used in DOS commands, unlike that in OS/2, uses a temporary disk file.)

The *_pipe* routine normally opens a pipe in preparation for dealing with a child process. A parent, for instance, can open a pipe and send data to the write handle of that pipe. A child can receive the data through the read handle of that pipe. This means that the pipe handle opened by the parent needs to be available to the child, and this is usually done by passing the handle as an argument or storing it in shared memory.

There are circumstances where parent and child routines will both read and write data. While it is possible to synchronize the reading and writing on the same file handles between the two, Microsoft recommends that you open two sets of handles.

RETURNS The return value for the *_pipe* function is set to 0 if the call was a success. A –1 value indicates an error, and the errno variable is set to to either EMFILE or ENFILE.

COMMENTS The *_pipe* capability is an OS/2 function and does not work under DOS. Pipe routines are a staple of the UNIX environment, and most of the introductory UNIX texts go into the subject of pipes in some detail.

SEE ALSO _popen *To create a pipe and execute a specific command*

Process Control

`_pclose` *To close the pipe and get child's return status*

EXAMPLE This example uses two programs that should be compiled separately. The first program opens a pipe to the second program, which runs as a child process. The first (parent) program does arithmetic processing and sends the results as they are calculated to the second program via the pipe. The second program displays the results. In a real-world application the second program might be doing elaborate filtering or formatting of data being generated by the first program.

```
#include <io.h>
#include <fcntl.h>
#include <process.h>
#include <stdio.h>
#include <stdlib.h>
#define PIPE_SIZE 128
#define READ 0
#define WRITE 1
#define MAX_NUMB 100

void main ()
{
   int     handles[2], termstat, j, data;
   char    argument[20];

      /* open pipe */
      if ( _pipe (handles, PIPE_SIZE, O_BINARY) == -1 )
         { printf("Can't open pipe"); exit (1); }

      /* convert read handle from number to string */
      itoa( handles[READ], argument, 10 );

      /* spawn child, using read handle as argument */
      if( spawnl(P_NOWAIT, "pipe_ch.exe",
                          "pipe_ch.exe", argument, NULL)  == -1 )
         { printf( "Can't create child"); exit(1); }

      /* write data to pipe */
      for (j=0; j<MAX_NUMB; j++)
      {
         data = j*10 + 5;
         printf ("+%d+", data);
         write (handles[WRITE], (char *)&data, sizeof (int));
      }
```

```
      /* wait for child termination before closing pipe handles      */
      wait (&termstat);
      if (termstat & 0xff)
         { printf ("child failed\n"); exit(1); }
      close (handles[READ]);
      close (handles[WRITE]);
      printf("\nParent ending\n");
}

/* pipe_ch.c */
/* reads data from pipe and displays it */
#include <io.h>
#include <fcntl.h>
#include <stdio.h>
#include <stdlib.h>
#define MAX_NUMB 100

void main( int argc, char *argv[] )
{
   int handle, data, j;

   /* convert handle (passed as arg) from string to integer */
   handle = atoi (argv[1]);
   printf("\nChild beginning\n");

   /* read data from pipe and display it */
   for (j=0; j<MAX_NUMB; j++)
      {
      read( handle, (char *)&data, sizeof(int) );
      printf("-%d-", data);
      }
   printf("\nChild ending\n");
}
```

Sample output:

```
+5++15++25++35++45++55++65++75++85++95++105++115++125++135++145+
+155++165++175++185++195++205++215++225++235++245++255++265++275+
+285++295++305++315++325++335++345++355++365++375++385++395++405+
+415++425++435++445++455++465++475++485++495++505++515++525++535+
+545++555++565++575++585++595++605++615++625++635++645++655++665+
Child beginning
-5--15--25--35--45--55--65--75--85--95--105--115--125--135--145-
-155--165--175--185--195--205--215--225--235--245--255--265--275-
```

```
-285--295--305--315--325--335--345--355--365--375--385--395--405-
-415--425--435--445--455--465--475--485--495--505--515--525--535-
-545--555--565--575--585--595--605--615--625--635-+675++685++695+
+705++715++725++735++745++755++765++775++785++795++805++815++825+
+835++845++855++865++875++885++895++905++915++925++935++945++955+
+965++975++985++995+-645--655--665--675--685--695--705--715--725-
-735--745--755--765--775--785--795--805--815--825--835--845--855-
-865--875--885--895--905--915--925--935--945--955--965--975--985-
-995-
Child ending

Parent ending
```

COMPATIBILITY

_popen

MSC 3	MSC 4	MSC 5	MSC 6	QC1	QC2	QC2.5	TC1	TC1.5	TC2	TC++	ANSI	UNIX V	XNX	OS2	DOS
			▲											▲	

PURPOSE The *_popen* function creates a pipe and executes a command.

SYNTAX

```
FILE* _popen (char *cmnd_strng, char *mode_strng);
```

`cmnd_strng` *Command string*

`mode_strng` *Access permissions - "r", "rt", "rb", "w", "wt", "wb"*

EXAMPLE CALL

```
if ((chkdsk = _popen ("dir *.* | sort", "rt")) == NULL) exit(1);
```

INCLUDES

```
#include <stdio.h>
```

DESCRIPTION The *_popen* function executes, in an asynchronous fashion, a child copy of the OS/2 command processor, providing it with a specified command string. It opens a pipe that behaves either as the standard input or standard output of the child process. Using *_popen* is analagous to using the *system* and *_pipe* functions in combination.

The *cmnd_strng* portion of the arguments for *_popen* is a string specifying the command or program and the arguments to be processed by the child copy of CMD.EXE. The next argument, *mode_strng*, is a string specifying the type of access requested. The mode values "r, w, t, and b" are similar to those found in the file manipulation routines. An "r" means that a calling process can read the standard output data of the child process via any returned stream. A "w" means that the calling process has permission to write, via a returned stream, to the child command's standard input. The "t" value means that the pipe is opened in text mode, and the "b" indicates that the pipe is opened in binary mode. The *mode_strng* string should contain either "r" or "w". Conflicting characters, such as "rw" or "wr", are evaluated to the first character in the string. An "rw" command, for instance, will become an "r". The pipe should be closed with a call to *_pclose* when processing of the piped data is complete. This completion usually occurs when CMD.EXE terminates.

RETURNS A successful call to the *_popen* function returns a stream associated with one end of the pipe it created. The pipe's other end is associated with either standard output or as the standard input of a child command. A NULL is returned in the event of an error.

COMMENTS The *_popen* command is not a DOS function.

SEE ALSO `_pclose` *To terminate a child process and get its status*

EXAMPLE Use *_popen* to open a pipe and give it a directory, sort, and "more" (paging) command. When output has ended, close the pipe with *_pclose.*

```
#include <stdio.h>
#include <stdlib.h>
void main()
{
   char    bufr[128];
   FILE    *dir_srt;
   /* DIR_SRT writes its output to a pipe, and the pipe is opened
        with "read text" as the attribute so that it may be
        examined just as though it were a text file.
   */
   if ((dir_srt = _popen ("DIR *.* ¦ SORT ¦ MORE", "rt")) == NULL)
      exit (1);
   /* The pipe is being read until end-of-file (EOF) just as a
      text file would. The EOF indicates that the DIR_SRT pipe
      has closed the "standard out" with which it is associated.
      This is normally a sign that it has terminated.
   */
   while (!feof (dir_srt))
   {
       fgets  (bufr, 128, dir_srt);
       printf (bufr);
   }
   /* It is time to close the pipe (with a call to _pclose) and
        display the return value of the DIR_SORT pipe.
   */
   printf ("\nThe process returned %d\n", _pclose (dir_srt));
}
```

COMPATIBILITY

putenv

MSC 3	MSC 4	MSC 5	MSC 6	QC1	QC2	QC2.5	TC1	TC1.5	TC2	TC++	ANSI	UNIX V	XNX	OS2	DOS
▲	▲	▲	▲	▲	▲	▲	▲	▲	▲	▲		▲	▲	▲	▲

PURPOSE Use *putenv* to enter the definition of a new variable into the environment table of the process.

SYNTAX

```
int putenv(char *envstring);

char *envstring;        Definition of environment variable to be added
```

EXAMPLE CALL

```
putenv("TMP=c:\mydir\temp");
```

INCLUDES

```
#include <stdlib.h>        For function declaration
```

DESCRIPTION The *putenv* function uses the global variable *environ* to locate the copy of the environment table that the process inherits from the parent. To this table it adds the new definition specified in the argument *envstring*, which must be of the form:

```
VARNAME=definition
```

If the environment variable named VARNAME already exists, its definition is changed to the new definition. Otherwise, an entirely new definition is added to the environment table. Note that the environment table altered by *putenv* is only a copy. Once the process terminates, the environment definitions revert to the original ones under the parent process. Thus, you cannot use *putenv* in a program to alter the environment variable settings seen at DOS command level. Any process launched by your program via *exec* or *spawn* functions, however, gets a copy of the environment settings with all the alterations you made with *putenv*.

COMMON USES The *putenv* function is useful to add new application-specific definitions to the environment table, which revert to their original meanings once the program exits.

RETURNS The *putenv* function returns a 0 if successful. A return value of −1 indicates failure due to lack of memory in the environment space of the process.

COMMENTS Under MS-DOS, the *main* function can get a pointer to the list of environment variables as a third argument, for instance, *envp*. The library routine *putenv* may alter the location of this list, however, rendering *envp* useless.

So it is safer to use the functions *getenv* and *putenv*, respectively, to locate and modify the environment table.

SEE ALSO getenv *To get the definition of a variable from the environment table of the process*

EXAMPLE Write a program that enables you to define a new environment variable or redefine an existing one. Accept the definition on the command line and use *putenv* to add the definition to the list of current environment variables. Notice that anything you define is gone when you exit the program.

```
#include <stdio.h>
#include <stdlib.h>
main(int argc, char **argv)
{
    char *value;
    if(argc < 2)
    {
        printf("Usage: %s <env_var_def.>\n", argv[0]);
        exit(0);
    }
/* Add new definition to the environment table */
    strupr(argv[1]):
    if (putenv(argv[1]) == -1)
    {
        printf("Error adding the definition: %s\n",
                argv[1]);
    }
    else
    {
        printf("Added to environment table: %s\n",
                argv[1]);
        printf("This definition will be gone once the \
program exits.\n");
    }
}
```

COMPATIBILITY

raise

MSC 3	MSC 4	MSC 5	MSC 6	QC1	QC2	QC2.5	TC1	TC1.5	TC2	TC++	ANSI	UNIX V	XNX	OS2	DOS
		▲	▲	▲	▲	▲		▲	▲	▲	▲			▲	▲

PURPOSE Use *raise* to "raise a signal" that generates an exception, leading to special handling.

SYNTAX

```
int raise(int signum);

int signum;
```

Signal number to be raised

INCLUDES

```
#include <signal.h>
```

For function declaration

DESCRIPTION The *raise* function creates an exception condition corresponding to the number *signum*. The exception will be handled by invoking a routine that was set up earlier by calling the function *signal*. If this was not done, certain default actions are performed for that particular exception. Table 3-6 in the reference pages on *signal* shows the default action for each exception condition and the defined constants for signals used as arguments to *raise*. The *abort* function uses *raise* to create the exception SIGABRT to initiate actions to be taken when aborting a program.

RETURNS If successful, *raise* returns a zero. Otherwise, it returns a nonzero value.

SEE ALSO

abort *To terminate a program abnormally and raise the SIGABRT signal*

signal *To install exception handlers for signals*

EXAMPLE Demonstrate the use of *raise* by generating the signal SIGABRT, signifying "abnormal termination" of a process. This shows how the *abort* function works.

```
#include <stdio.h>
#include <signal.h>
main()
{
    printf("Raising SIGABRT...\n");
    raise(SIGABRT);
}
```

setjmp

COMPATIBILITY

MSC 3	MSC 4	MSC 5	MSC 6	QC1	QC2	QC2.5	TC1	TC1.5	TC2	TC++	ANSI	UNIX V	XNX	OS2	DOS
▲	▲	▲	▲	▲	▲	▲	▲	▲	▲	▲	▲	▲	▲	▲	▲

PURPOSE Use *setjmp* to save a stack environment before calling another function. This environment can be restored by a call to *longjmp*, achieving the effect of a nonlocal *goto*.

SYNTAX

```
int setjmp(jmp_buf env);
```

`jmp_buf env;` *Data type where the registers and a return address representing the stack environment are stored*

EXAMPLE CALL

```
if (setjmp(env) != 0) printf("Returned from longjmp\n");
```

INCLUDES `#include <setjmp.h>` *For function declaration and definition of the data type* jmp_buf

DESCRIPTION The *setjmp* function saves certain registers and its own return address in the argument *env*, which is of type *jmp_buf* as defined in *setjmp.h*. The saved values represent the stack environment at the statement where the call to *setjmp* occurred. When *longjmp* is later called with the saved stack environment, it restores all stack-based local variables in the routine to the values they had when *setjmp* was called and jumps to the return address that *setjmp* had saved. This will feel like a return, one more time, from the last call to *setjmp*. Note that this process does not guarantee the proper restoration of register-based variables.

COMMON USES The *setjmp* function is used in conjunction with *longjmp* to pass control of execution to error-recovery code without using the normal function call and return conventions.

RETURNS After saving the stack environment, *setjmp* returns a zero. When *longjmp* is called with the environment saved by this particular call to *setjmp*, the effect is the same as returning from *setjmp* again, this time with the second argument of *longjmp* as the return value.

COMMENTS It is a little difficult to understand the behavior of *setjmp* and *longjmp*. Essentially, these routines give you the flexibility of jumping to an arbitrary location from within C. This is akin to a "goto" statement that lets you jump from one function to another.

SEE ALSO `longjmp` *To jump back to where* setjmp *was called earlier*

EXAMPLE Demonstrate the functioning of *setjmp* in a program that sets up the stack environment and then calls a function that in turn calls *longjmp* with the environment saved earlier. Notice how the effect is one of returning twice from the first call to *setjmp*. The second return is with a different return value than the first one, so you can do some extra processing after *longjmp* is called. Note too that you can return from a function without using the normal *return* statement.

```
#include <stdio.h>
#include <setjmp.h>
static jmp_buf this_place;
static void fake_error(void);
main()
{
    int retval;
    retval = setjmp(this_place);
    if(retval == 0)
    {
        printf("First return from \"setjmp\"\n");
    }
    else
    {
        printf("Second return from \"setjmp\" induced \
by call to \"longjmp\"\n");


/* Do processing that's otherwise skipped. For example,
 * error recovery.
 */
        printf("There may be an error handler here.\n\
We simply exit.\n");
        exit(retval);
    }
/* Somewhere else, in another function call longjmp */
    printf("Everything seemed fine until suddenly...\n");
    fake_error();
}
/*--------------------------------------------------*/
static void fake_error(void)
{
    printf("Illegal instruction\n");
    printf("--- longjmp called ---\n");
    longjmp(this_place, 1);
}
```

signal

COMPATIBILITY

MSC 3	MSC 4	MSC 5	MSC 6	QC1	QC2	QC2.5	TC1	TC1.5	TC2	TC++	ANSI	UNIX V	XNX	OS2	DOS
▲	▲	▲	▲	▲	▲	▲		▲	▲	▲	▲	▲	▲	▲	▲

PURPOSE Use *signal* to define a function that handles an exception condition.

SYNTAX

```
void (*signal(int signum,
      void (*func)(int signum[, int subcode])))(int signum);
```

`int signum;` *Signal number for which a handler is being set up*

`void (*func)(int , int);` *Pointer to handler that can accept the signal number and an optional subcode as arguments*

INCLUDES `#include <signal.h>` *For function declaration*

DESCRIPTION The *signal* function sets up the routine *func* as the handler for the exception or signal number (*signum*). The handler is expected to accept the signal number and an optional error code as arguments. The signal number must be one of the constants shown in Table 3-8. These are defined in the include file *signal.h*. The default handling of each exception is also explained in Table 3-8. The argument *func* must be either the address of a C or assembly language routine or one of the constants SIG_DFL or SIG_IGN. Table 3-9 summarizes the action taken by these exception handlers. The *signal* function was changed in Microsoft C 5.1 to accommodate the user-defined flags SIGUSR1, SIGUSR2, and SIGUSR3 used with OS/2.

Table 3-8. *Exception Conditions*

Signal	Exception Condition	Default Action
SIGABRT	Abnormal termination of program	Terminate program with exit code 3.
SIGFPE	Floating-point error, such as overflow, division by zero, etc.	Terminate program.
SIGILL	Illegal instruction. This exception is not generated by MS-DOS, but is included for ANSI compatibility.	Not applicable in MS-DOS.
SIGINT	Generated when user hits Control-C.	Generate software interrupt number 23h.
SIGSEGV	Illegal memory access. This exception is not generated under MS-DOS, but is included for ANSI compatibility.	Not applicable in MS-DOS.

Table 3-8. *(cont.)*

Signal	Exception Condition	Default Action
SIGTERM	Termination request sent to the program. This is not generated in MS-DOS, but is included for ANSI compatibility.	Not applicable in MS-DOS.

Table 3-9. *Exception Handlers*

Handler	Action
SIG_DFL	This refers to the default handler. If the program is terminated, files will be closed, but buffers associated with files open for buffered I/O will not be flushed.
SIG_IGN	If you provide this as the handler, the exception condition will be ignored. This should not be used as the handler for the SIGFPE signal because this leaves the floating-point package unusable.
Function Address	The function will be called with the signal and an optional code as the arguments. The SIGINT and SIGFPE exceptions are handled differently. For the SIGINT exception, the handler will be called with SIGINT as the argument. At the same time, SIG_DFL is set up as the handler for subsequent SIGINT signals. Of course, you can reset the handler in the function called as a result of SIGINT. For SIGFPE exceptions, the installed handler will be called with the value SIGFPE and an integer code representing the floating-point error. This second argument is a constant of FPE_<code> where the constants are defined in the include file *float.h*. The handler for SIGFPE should call *_fpreset* to reset the floating-point package and clear the error condition.

RETURNS If successful, *signal* returns the pointer to the previous handler. In case of error, it returns the constant SIG_ERR and sets the global variable *errno* to EINVAL to indicate an invalid signal number.

SEE ALSO `raise` *To generate a signal*

EXAMPLE The SIGINT signal is generated when you hit Control-C. The default handler for this signal terminates the program. Use *signal* in a program to install your own handler for SIGINT. This way, instead of abruptly ending the program, the user has a chance to cancel the signal.

```
#include <stdio.h>
#include <signal.h>
int ctrlc_handler(int);
int back_again = 0;
main()
```

```
{
/* Take over the Control-C interrupt */
    if(signal(SIGINT, ctrlc_handler) == SIG_ERR)
    {
        perror("signal failed");
        exit(0);
    }
    printf("Installed SIGINT signal handler\n");
    printf("Hit Control-C to exit:");
    while(1)
    {
        kbhit();
        if(back_again != 0)
        {
            back_again = 0;
            printf("\nHit Control-C to exit:");
        }
    }
}
/*-----------------------------------------------------*/
int ctrlc_handler(int sig)
{
    int c;
/* First arrange to ignore further SIGINT */
    signal(SIGINT, SIG_IGN);
    printf("\nInterrupted. Quit?");
    c = getche();
    if(c == 'y' || c == 'Y') exit(0);
/* Reenable interrupt handler -- and return */
    back_again = 1;
    signal(SIGINT, ctrlc_handler);
}
```

Table 3-10 lists the four protected-mode only signals introduced in version 5.1.

Table 3-10. *Additional Microsoft C 5.1 Signals*

Constant	Meaning
SIGBREAK	Control-Break signal. Default action is to terminate the program.
SIGUSR1	OS/2 process flag A. Default action is to ignore the signal.
SIGUSR2	OS/2 process flag B. Default action is to ignore the signal.
SIGUSR3	OS/2 process flag C. Default action is to ignore the signal.

A new action code, SIG_ACK, is also available for use in OS/2. If a user-defined handler is installed, OS/2 sends no signals until a SIG_ACK acknowledgment is received for the last signal.

COMPATIBILITY

spawn functions

MSC 3	MSC 4	MSC 5	MSC 6	QC1	QC2	QC2.5	TC1	TC1.5	TC2	TC++	ANSI	UNIX V	XNX	OS2	DOS
	▲	▲	▲	▲	▲	▲	▲	▲	▲	▲				▲	▲

PURPOSE Use any one of the *spawn* functions to load and execute a child process and to return to your program when the child process terminates.

SYNTAX

```
int spawnl(int modeflag, char *path, char *arg0, char *arg1,...,
           NULL);

int spawnle(int modeflag, char *path, char *arg0, char *arg1,...,
            NULL, char *envp[]);

int spawnlp(int modeflag, char *path, char *arg0, char *arg1,...,
            NULL);

int spawnlpe(int modeflag, char *path, char *arg0, char *arg1,...,
             NULL, char *envp[]);

int spawnv(int modeflag, char *path, char *argv[]);

int spawnve(int modeflag, char *path, char *argv[], char *envp[]);

int spawnvp(int modeflag, char *path, char *argv[]);

int spawnvpe(int modeflag, char *path, char *argv[], char *envp[]);
```

`int  modeflag;` *Execution mode of calling process*

`char *path;` *Pathname of file to be executed as a child process*

`char *arg0, *arg1, . . . , NULL;` *Command-line arguments for the child process (ends with a NULL)*

`char *argv[];` *Array of command-line arguments for the child process*

`char *envp[];` *The environment parameter table*

INCLUDES `#include <process.h>` *For function declaration and definition of the constants P_WAIT, P_OVERLAY, and P_NOWAIT*

DESCRIPTION The *spawn* functions create a child process to load and execute the program specified by the argument *path*. The argument *modeflag* indicates how the parent process should be treated while the child is running. Under MS-DOS, this flag can take either of the values P_WAIT or P_OVERLAY. The P_WAIT flag indicates that the parent process should be suspended until the child finishes, whereas P_OVERLAY means that the child overwrites the parent in memory, destroying the parent. The P_OVERLAY mode has the same effect as the *exec* functions have. A third constant P_NOWAIT, is defined in *process.h* and is meant for concurrent execution of parent and child, but use of this mode under MS_DOS produces an error. This mode might be useful in a multitasking operating system of the future.

The variations among the *spawn* functions are reflections of the way in which arguments and environment variables are passed to the child process. Table 3-11 describes each function's action. The fifth letter of the name, "1" or "v," determines how command-line arguments are received by the child process. The next one or two letters indicate how environment variables are passed to the child process. If the sixth letter of the name is a "p," the PATH environment variable is used by COMMAND.COM to locate the executable program you specify in the argument *path*. Otherwise, you must specify the full pathname of the file to be executed or specify a path beginning at the current working directory. If the *path* argument does not have an extension, the *spawn* function first searches for a file without an extension. If none is found and *path* does not end with a period, it tries the extensions .COM and .EXE, in that order.

Table 3-11. ***The* spawn *Functions***

Fifth Letter of Name	Meaning
l	Command-line arguments to the child process are listed on the statement that invokes the *spawn* function. These forms are useful when the number of arguments is known in advance. The arguments *arg0, arg1 . . .* are listed one after another with a NULL marking the end.
v	Command-line arguments are passed in the form of a pointer to an array of argument strings. This is useful when the number of arguments is not known in advance. In this case, you prepare an array of null-terminated strings, each representing one command-line argument for the child program, put a NULL to mark the end of the list and pass the pointer to this array (*argv*) to the child process via the *spawn* function.

Two Letters	How Environment Variables Are Handled
none	Child process inherits parent's environment variables.
p	PATH environment variable is used to locate the executable file. In this case, the *path* argument may specify a program name without any directory information and COMMAND.COM

Table 3-11. *(cont.)*

Fifth Letter of Name	Meaning
	will locate the program, if present, in any one of the directories included in your PATH environment variable.
e	Child process receives a pointer *envp* to an array of environment strings. Each environment variable definition is of the form *NAME=value of variable*, and the end of the array is marked by a NULL.
pe	This is a combination of the letters described above. Thus, in this, the PATH environment variable is used and the child process gets a pointer to a table of environment variables that you prepare.

Note that the combined length of all the command-line argument strings, including a separating space between adjoining arguments, must not exceed 128 bytes. It is customary to provide the full pathname of the executable file as the first command-line argument to the child process, although using a different string will not produce an error.

In the child process, all signal handlers are reset to the default ones. Files that were open in the parent remain open in the child, and, unlike the *exec* functions, the translation modes of the open files (see *fopen*) are also preserved in the child process.

Starting with Microsoft C 5.1, under OS/2, the P_NOWAIT mode of execution implies that the child process runs concurrently with the parent. In this case, the return value is the identification number of the child. An additional P_NOWAITO flag allows execution of the parent while ignoring all *cwait* and *wait* calls against the child process.

The *spawn* functions in Microsoft C 6.0 will also search for files with the.BAT extension under DOS and the .CMD extension under the protected mode of OS/2. Microsoft C 6.0 also allows you to control whether the open file information of a process will be passed to a child process. The *_fileinfo* variable is used for this purpose.

The *_fileinfo* variable identifies whether the open file information of a process (stored in the _C_FILE_INFO environment variable) will be passed to a child process. A *_fileinfo* of 0 means that _C_FILE_INFO information is not passed to the child, while a nonzero value means that it is passed. The default value is 0. It may be changed either by linking FILEINFO.OBJ (a supplied file) into your program (using the /NOE option to avoid defining the symbol several times) or by setting the *_fileinfo* variable to nonzero from your C program.

COMMON USES The *spawn* functions are useful when you want to execute a separately compiled and linked application from your program and return to your main program when that process terminates. The example below illustrates how you can pass pointers to data areas for sharing between the two processes.

RETURNS When used with P_WAIT as *modeflags*, the *spawn* functions return the exit status of the child process to the parent. The return value for P_NOWAIT (when this mode becomes available) will be the process ID of the child process. In this case, if you want the exit code, you will have to call a routine to wait for it. If the child process cannot be started, the return value is –1 and *errno* is set to one of the constants shown in Table 3-12, indicating the cause of the error.

Table 3-12. *Error Codes Returned by* spawn *Functions*

Error	Cause of Error
E2BIG	Either the total length of the command-line arguments exceeds 128 bytes or the memory required for the environment variables exceeds 32 K.
EINVAL	The *modeflag* argument is invalid.
ENOENT	Either the path or the file specified in the argument *path* was not found.
ENOEXEC	The specified file is not executable because its format does not match the DOS specification for an executable file.
ENOMEM	There is not enough memory to load and execute the child process or available memory is corrupted or an invalid block of memory was located, indicating the parent process was incorrectly loaded.

COMMENTS The *spawn* functions provide a powerful mechanism to make your application versatile. Essentially, you can let programs that are "well-behaved" toward your application (in that they do not hinder its performance) run from the application, giving the functionality of terminate-but-stay-resident (TSR) utilities that are so prevalent in the MS-DOS world.

Microsoft warns that because of a bug in DOS versions 2.0 and 2.1, a child process launched by *spawn*, with the P_OVERLAY argument, may cause fatal system errors when it exits. Use DOS versions 3.0 or higher for reliable operation when calling *spawn* with P_OVERLAY.

The Microsoft C 6.0 versions of the *spawn* functions used with P_OVERLAY mode will not work in OS/2 DOS-compatibility mode if the program was bound with FAPI for execution with dual mode. You should not use either *setjmp* or *longjmp* to enter or exit an overlay routine, because they cannot guarantee that the overlays will be either properly initialized or terminated.

SEE ALSO `exec functions` *To launch a process that overlays its parent in memory*

EXAMPLE Demonstrate their use in a program that allows a child process to run using any one of the eight *spawn* functions. Prepare data in a structure allocated in the parent program and pass this data to the child by encoding the address as a character string and using that string as a command-line argument. In the child program, print the command-line arguments and the environment passed to it. Then, using the address passed in the command line, acces the data structure and display the various fields. Finally, make changes to the data structure and exit. In the parent program, print the values in the data structure to show that the changes made in the child came through. Note: Remember to compile and link the child program first and save it in a file named *child.exe.*

```
/*===================== PARENT =====================*/
#include <stdio.h>
#include <process.h>
#include <malloc.h>
#include <string.h>
typedef struct TEST_DATA
{
    char name[20];
    int n;
    double x;
} TEST_DATA;
/* PARENT: Test the "spawn" functions. Pass address of
 *         data in command line arguments as well as
 *         environment variables when appropriate.
 */
char *envp[] =
{
    "PARENT=SPAWN FUNCTIONS",
    NULL
};
main()
{
    char *argv[3], buf[20], rname[40];
    TEST_DATA *pdata;
/* Set up a data structure and initialize it */
    if((pdata=(TEST_DATA *)
        malloc(sizeof(TEST_DATA))) == NULL) abort();
    strcpy(pdata->name, "PARENT");
    pdata->n = 100;
    pdata->x = 1000.99;
/* Set up the arguments for the child process */
    argv[0] = "child.exe",
    argv[1] = rname;
```

```
    sprintf(buf, "%p", (void far *)pdata);
    argv[2] = buf;
    argv[3] = NULL;
/* Ask user which "spawn" routine to call */
    printf("Enter name of \"spawn\" function to call:");
    gets(rname);
    strlwr(rname);
/* Call the "spawn" function requested by the user */
    if(strcmp(rname, "spawnl") == 0)
    {
        spawnl(P_WAIT, "child.exe",
               "child.exe", "spawnl", buf, NULL);
    }
    if(strcmp(rname, "spawnle") == 0)
    {
        spawnle(P_WAIT, "child.exe",
        "child.exe", "spawnle", buf, NULL, envp);
    }
    if(strcmp(rname, "spawnlp") == 0)
    {
        spawnlp(P_WAIT, "child.exe",
               "child.exe", "spawnlp", buf, NULL);
    }
    if(strcmp(rname, "spawnlpe") == 0)
    {
        spawnlpe(P_WAIT, "child.exe",
        "child.exe", "spawnlpe", buf, NULL, envp);
    }
    if(strcmp(rname, "spawnv") == 0)
    {
        spawnv(P_WAIT, "child.exe", argv);
    }
    if(strcmp(rname, "spawnve") == 0)
    {
        spawnve(P_WAIT, "child.exe", argv, envp);
    }
    if(strcmp(rname, "spawnvp") == 0)
    {
        spawnvp(P_WAIT, "child.exe", argv);
    }
    if(strcmp(rname, "spawnvpe") == 0)
    {
        spawnvpe(P_WAIT, "child.exe", argv, envp);
    }
/* Check if we could call child or not */
```

```
    if(strcmp(pdata->name, "CHILD") == 0)
    {
        printf("Back from child: name = %s, n = %d, \
x= %f\n", pdata->name, pdata->n, pdata->x);
    }
    else
    {
        printf("Don't know: %s\n", rname);
     }
}
/*====================== CHILD =======================*/
/*     Must be in a file named:  CHILD.EXE             */
#include <stdio.h>
#include <dos.h>
#include <string.h>
typedef struct TEST_DATA
{
    char name[20];
    int n;
    double x;
} TEST_DATA;
/* Child: First argument is program name,
 *       Second one tells us how child was invoked
 *       Third argument is an address in the form
 *       SSSS:OOOO (segment:offset). This is the
 *       address of a data structure allocated in
 *       the parent.
 */
static char far cname[] = "CHILD";
main(int argc, char **argv, char **envp)
{
    char  **p_table;
    TEST_DATA far *pdata;
    void far *p_s1;
    void far *p_s2;
    printf("CHILD: received %d arguments\n", argc);
    if(argc < 3){
        printf("not enough arguments\n");
        exit(1);
    }
    printf("CHILD invoked by a %s call.\n", argv[1]);


/* Now print the environment passed to CHILD      */
    printf("==== CHILD: Environment contains ====\n");
    for(p_table = envp;
```

```
            *p_table != NULL;
            p_table++) printf("%s\n", *p_table);

/* Read in address of parent's data from argv[2] */
    sscanf(argv[2], "%p", (void far *)&pdata);
    printf("In child: name = %Fs, n = %d, x= %f\n",
           pdata->name, pdata->n, pdata->x);
/* Put new values in the data structure. If CHILD was
 * created by a "spawn" function call, this data will
 * be available to the parent when child exits.
 * Notice that we have to use "movedata" to copy
 * "far" data in small or medium model.
 */
    p_s1 = (void far *)cname;
    p_s2 = (void far *)pdata->name;
    movedata(FP_SEG(p_s1), FP_OFF(p_s1),
             FP_SEG(p_s2), FP_OFF(p_s2), 6);
    pdata->n = 101;
    pdata->x = 999.99;
    exit(0);
}
```

system

COMPATIBILITY

MSC 3	MSC 4	MSC 5	MSC 6	QC1	QC2	QC2.5	TC1	TC1.5	TC2	TC++	ANSI	UNIX V	XNX	OS2	DOS
▲	▲	▲	▲	▲	▲	▲	▲	▲	▲	▲	▲	▲	▲	▲	▲

PURPOSE Use *system* to execute an MS-DOS command from your program.

SYNTAX `int system(const char *string);`

`const char *string;` *MS-DOS command to be executed*

INCLUDES `#include <process.h>` *For function declaration*

or

`#include <stdlib.h>`

DESCRIPTION The *system* function uses the environment variable COMSPEC to locate a copy of COMMAND.COM and passes to it the argument *string* as a command to be executed. The environment variable PATH is used to locate any program whose execution may be specified in the command *string*. In Microsoft C 5.0, if *string* is NULL, *system* will only check to see if COMMAND.COM is present. In version 4.0, a NULL argument is not allowed. Starting with Microsoft C 5.1, in OS/2, *system* runs CMD.EXE to execute

the command string. Beginning in Microsoft C 5.0, this returns a 0 with a NULL pointer argument and changes the return under certain conditions.

RETURNS If *string* is not NULL, *system* returns 0 if the command was successfully executed. In case of error, *system* returns –1 and sets *errno* to one of the constants shown in Table 3-13 to indicate the cause of the error. In Microsoft C 5.0, if *string* is NULL and COMMAND.COM is found *system* returns a nonzero value. In case COMMAND.COM cannot be located using the environment variable COMSPEC, *system* will return a zero and set *errno* to ENOENT. Note that syntax errors in the specified command are not considered "errors"; only errors resulting in the inability to execute COMMAND.COM are returned.

Table 3-13. ***Error Codes Returned by*** **System**

Error	Cause of Error
E2BIG	Either the argument list for COMMAND.COM exceeds 128 bytes or the memory required for the environment variables exceeds 32 K.
ENOENT	COMMAND.COM not found.
ENOEXEC	The COMMAND.COM file is not executable because it has an invalid format.
ENOMEM	There is not enough memory to load COMMAND.COM and execute the command or available memory is corrupted or an invalid block of memory was located, indicating that the parent process was incorrectly loaded.

SEE ALSO `exec functions, spawn functions` *To launch a process*

EXAMPLE Write a program that lets you type a command and have it executed by a copy of COMMAND.COM that is launched by calling *system*.

```
#include <stdio.h>
#include <stdlib.h>
main()
{
    char command[80];
    while(1)
    {
        printf("Enter command (\"quit\" to exit):");
        gets(command);
        strlwr(command);
/* Exit if user typed "quit" */
        if(strcmp(command, "quit") == 0) exit(0);
/* Otherwise pass command to a copy of COMMAND.COM */
        if(system(command) == -1)
        {
```

```
                    perror("error in system");
                }
            }
        }
```

wait

COMPATIBILITY

MSC 3	MSC 4	MSC 5	MSC 6	QC1	QC2	QC2.5	TC1	TC1.5	TC2	TC++	ANSI	UNIX V	XNX	OS2	DOS
		1	▲	▲	▲							▲	▲	▲	

PURPOSE Use *wait* in OS/2's protected mode to wait until any one of your immediate child processes terminates.

SYNTAX

```
int wait(int *p_status);
```

`int *p_status;` *Address of integer to hold the termination status code*

EXAMPLE CALL

```
if(wait(&status) == -1) perror("wait failed");
```

INCLUDES `#include <process.h>` *For function prototype*

DESCRIPTION Available in OS/2's protected mode only, the *wait* function suspends the calling process until any one of the immediate child process of the calling process terminates. When *wait* returns, the integer at the address *p_status* will contain a termination code that can be interpreted by consulting Table 3-5.

1. The *wait* function was introduced in version 5.1.

COMMON USES The *wait* function synchronizes processes in OS/2's protected mode environment.

RETURNS When *wait* returns after a normal termination of the child process, it returns the process identification of the child. In case of abnormal termination of the child, it returns −1 and sets the global variable *errno* to EINTR. For other types of errors, *wait* returns −1 immediately and sets *errno* to ECHILD to indicate that no child processes exist for the calling process.

COMMENTS You should be familiar with the protected mode operation of the OS/2 operating system before using the *wait* function.

SEE ALSO

`spawn` *To launch a child process*

`cwait` *To wait for a specific child of the calling process*

Chapter 4 Variable-Length Argument List

Introduction

In writing C programs you encounter functions, such as *printf*, that can take a variable number of arguments. Take, for instance, a routine (*findmax*) that picks the largest integer from an array (*a,b,c,d*). If the routine can accept a variable number of arguments, you can use such calls as *findmax(1,2,3)* and *findmax(a,b,c,d)* to find the maximum of any number of arguments. Fortunately this can be done quite easily in C because of its convention of passing arguments on the stack. A set of macros in the Microsoft C library makes a straightforward task of handling a variable number of arguments. This section explains how this is done.

Concepts

The secret to handling a variable number of arguments in C lies in the way arguments are passed to a function. Figure 4-1 shows the contents of the state at the moment a C and a FORTRAN or a Pascal function are entered. When a function is called, the arguments followed by the return address (the place in the calling program to which the microprocessor will ultimately return) are placed on the stack.

THE STACK: C AND FORTRAN OR PASCAL

As you can see in Figure 4-1, in FORTRAN and Pascal the arguments of the function are placed on the stack in the order they appear in the function call, exactly the opposite of a C function call. The result is that the first argument in C is always at a fixed positive offset (the number of bytes needed to store the return address) from the stack pointer SP, so no matter how many arguments are passed to a C function, the first argument is always easily reachable. This is not true in FORTRAN and Pascal. In fact, in these, if you do not pass the required number of arguments, the addresses computed for each argument will be erroneous.

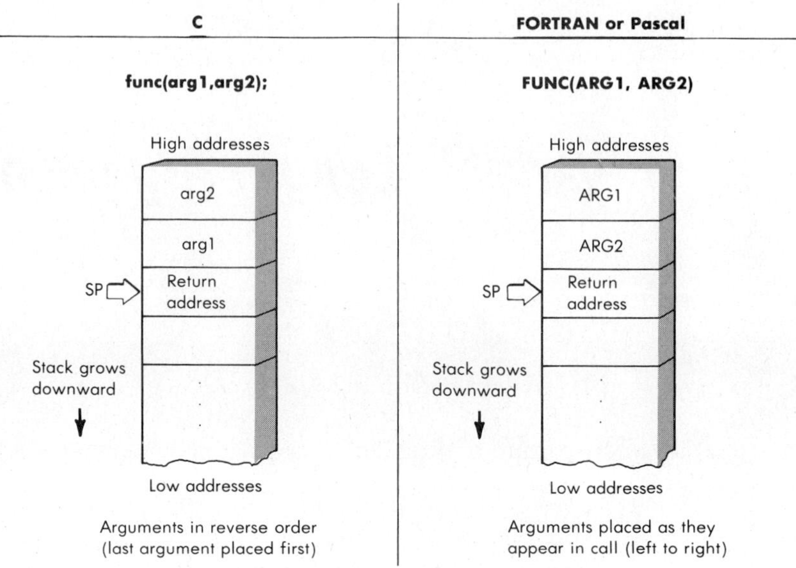

Figure 4-1. ***The stack upon entry to a function***

GETTING TO THE ARGUMENTS IN C

The parameter-passing conventions in C help us access a variable number of arguments. As shown in Figure 4-2, upon entry to the C function the first argument appears on the stack just above the return address (meaning it has the next higher address). Additional arguments have successively higher addresses. If you could get to the first argument on the stack and you knew the size of all other arguments you could retrieve the arguments one by one. This, respectively, is what the *va_start* and the *va_arg* macros do.

While the macros help us access the arguments on the stack, they cannot tell us when the argument list ends. In fact, the only way to find this is by adopting a convention. If each argument were a pointer, for example, you could mark the end of the argument list with a NULL value. To illustrate how the arguments are accessed using these macros, suppose we are writing the *findmax* function to accept a variable number of integers and return the largest of the arguments. Since we want positive numbers only, we assume that a value of –9999 indicates the end of the argument list. Here is one way to implement the *findmax* function, using the ANSI version of the macros:

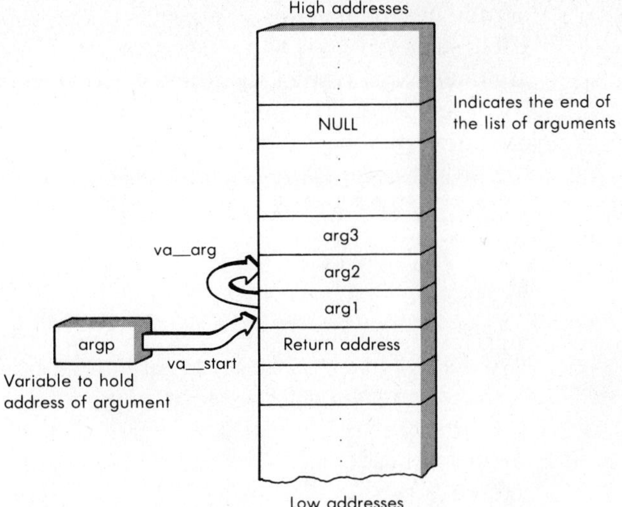

Figure 4-2. ***Accessing a variable number of arguments in C***

```
int findmax(int firstint, ...)
{
    int maxval = -9999, x = 0;
    va_list argp;
/* Get the first optional parameter using "va_start" */
    va_start(argp, firstint);
    x = firstint;
    while(x != -9999)  /* -9999 marks end of arguments */
    {
            if(maxval < x) maxval = x;
            x = va_arg(argp, int);
    }
    return (maxval);
}
```

The variable *argp* of type *va_list* is used to point to arguments. (In Microsoft C, *va_list* is defined to be a pointer to a character.) The first step in accessing the arguments is to use *va_start* to initialize *argp*. The ANSI standard requires that a function accepting a variable number of arguments must have at least one argument. The *va_start* macro uses the address of this compulsory first argument to set up *argp*. Once this is done, you can get subsequent arguments by repeatedly using the *va_arg* macro. (See the reference pages that follow for the UNIX version of these macros.) The UNIX System V and the ANSI approaches to accessing arguments are based on the stack layout shown in Figure 4-2. The function accepting variable-length arguments must declare a pointer to hold the address of the current argument. The macro *va_start* must be used first to initialize this pointer. Each successive use of the macro *va_arg* sets the pointer to the next argument. The type of variables on the stack must be given as an argument to these macros. The macro *va_end* is not needed because it sets the local argument pointer to NULL, which you can do yourself if you want to repeat the process. See Table 4-1 for a description of these macros.

Notes

Two sets of macros handle variable-length argument lists. One set conforms to the ANSI standard for C and is defined in the header file *stdarg.h*. The other set is for UNIX System V compatibility, and is defined in the *varargs.h* header file. The method for using each set is described in the reference pages.

Table 4-1. *Variable-Length Argument List Macros*

Macro	Description
va_arg	Gets the next argument from the stack.
va_end	Sets the argument pointer to NULL.
va_start	Initializes the argument pointer to the address of the first argument on the stack.

Cautions

- The UNIX version of the macros requires that you use a specific format in declaring the function that will accept variable-length arguments. Two macros appear in the declaration as shown in this sample:

```
int func(va_alist)
va_dcl
{
/* ... body of function ... */
}
```

  Note the use of macros *va_alist* in the argument list and *va_dcl* where you would normally declare the arguments. The second macro, *va_dcl*, must appear *without* a terminating semicolon.

ANSI version

COMPATIBILITY **va_arg, va_end, va_start**

MSC 3	MSC 4	MSC 5	MSC 6	QC1	QC2	QC2.5	TC1	TC1.5	TC2	TC++	ANSI	UNIX V	XNX	OS2	DOS
	▲	▲	▲	▲	▲	▲	▲	▲	▲	▲	▲			▲	▲

PURPOSE Use the *va_start, va_arg,* and *va_end* macros to access arguments in a function that accepts a variable number of arguments. This entry describes the ANSI-compatible version of the macros.

SYNTAX

```
void va_start(va_list arg_ptr, prev_param);

<type> va_arg(va_list arg_ptr, <type>);

void va_end(va_list arg_ptr);
```

va_list arg_ptr;	*Pointer to list of arguments*
prev_param	*Name of parameter preceding first optional argument*
<type>	*Type of argument to be retrieved*

INCLUDES #include <stdarg.h> *For macro declarations and definition of data type* va_list

DESCRIPTION The *va_start, va_arg,* and *va_end* macros provide an ANSI-compatible method for accessing the arguments of a function when the function takes a fixed number of required arguments followed by a variable number of optional arguments. The required arguments are in standard style and are accessed by parameter names. The optional arguments are accessed using the macros *va_start, va_arg,* and *va_end.* These, respectively, are used to initialize a pointer to the beginning of the list of optional arguments, to advance the pointer to the next argument of a particular type, and to reset the pointer to NULL when all the arguments are used. The procedure for accessing the optional arguments is outlined below:

1. Access the required arguments by name. These arguments are declared as parameters in the usual manner. Declare a variable *arg_ptr* of type *va_list.*
2. Use the *va_start* macro with *arg_ptr* and the name of the last required argument. This sets *arg_ptr* to the beginning of the list of optional arguments to the function. *Caution:* If the last required argument is declared with the *register* storage class, *va_start* will not work properly.

3. Use the *va_arg* macro to retrieve the next argument. This macro updates *arg_ptr* and returns a pointer to the argument being sought. Repeat this step until you have accessed all the arguments. You have to decide on a value that will mark the end of the list. For example, if you are accessing integer arguments, you might use a value of –1 to mark the end of the argument list.
4. Use the *va_end* macro to set *arg_ptr* to NULL.

Note that an identical set of macros with slightly different usage exists to access variable-length arguments as specified by the UNIX System V standard. These macros are defined in the header file *varargs.h* and are described under a separate heading.

COMMON USES These macros can be used in conjunction with the routines *vfprintf*, *vprintf*, and *vsprintf* to design error-handling routines that accept variable-length arguments.

RETURNS The *va_arg* macro returns a pointer to the next argument of a given type. The *va_start* macro sets a pointer to the beginning of the list of arguments; *va_end* resets this pointer to NULL.

SEE ALSO *Unix V version of* va_start, va_arg, va_end

EXAMPLE Demonstrate the use of ANSI-style variable-length argument processing by writing a function that accepts a variable number of integer arguments and returns the largest value. Assume that a value of –999 marks the end of the argument list. Write a main program that shows how the function is used.

```
#include <stdio.h>
#include <stdarg.h>
int findmax(int, ...);
main()
{
    int maxvalue;
/* The end of the list of integers is marked by -9999 */
    maxvalue = findmax(-1, 20, 30, 50, -9999);

    printf("findmax(-1, 20, 30, 50, -9999) returns: \
    %d\n", maxvalue);
    maxvalue = findmax(1, 2, 3, 4, 5, 6, 7, 8, -9999);
    printf("findmax(1, 2, 3, 4, 5, 6, 7, 8, -9999)\
returns: %d\n", maxvalue);
}
/*------------------------------------------------*/
/* The "findmax" finds the largest value in a list
 * of integers. It uses the "va..." macros to get
```

```
 * the arguments. This is the ANSI version.
 */
int findmax(int firstint, ...)
{
    int maxval = -9999, x = 0;
    va_list argp;
/* Get the first optional parameter using "va_start" */
    va_start(argp, firstint);
    x = firstint;
    while(x != -9999)
    {
            if(maxval < x) maxval = x;
            x = va_arg(argp, int);
    }
    return (maxval);
}
```

UNIX V version

COMPATIBILITY

va_arg, va_end, va_start

MSC 3	MSC 4	MSC 5	MSC 6	QC1	QC2	QC2.5	TC1	TC1.5	TC2	TC++	ANSI	UNIX V	XNX	OS2	DOS
	▲	▲	▲	▲	▲	▲						▲	▲		

PURPOSE Use the *va_start*, *va_arg*, and *va_end* macros to access arguments in a function that accepts a variable number of arguments. This entry describes the UNIX V version of the macros.

SYNTAX

```
void va_start(va_list arg_ptr);

<type> va_arg(arg_ptr, <type>);

void va_end(va_list arg_ptr);
```

`va_alist`	*Name that must appear at the end of all required arguments to the function*
`va_dcl`	*Declaration of* va_alist
`va_list arg_ptr;`	*Pointer to list of arguments*
`<type>`	*Type of argument to be retrieved*

INCLUDES `#include <varargs.h>` *For macro declarations and definition of data types* va_list, va_alist, *and* va_dcl

DESCRIPTION The *va_start, va_arg,* and *va_end* macros provide a UNIX System V-compatible method for accessing the arguments of a function when the function takes a fixed number of required arguments followed by a variable number of optional arguments. The required arguments are in standard style and are accessed by parameter names. The optional arguments are accessed using the macros *va_start, va_arg,* and *va_end.* These, respectively, are used to initialize a pointer to the beginning of the list of optional arguments, to advance the pointer to the next argument of a particular type, and to reset the pointer to NULL when all the arguments are used. The procedure for accessing the optional arguments is outlined below:

1. Declare the required arguments as parameters in the usual manner. End the list of parameters with the name *va_alist* which denotes all optional arguments to the function. Place the macro *va_dcl* (no semicolon at the end) between the function declaration and its definition. This declares the variable *va_alist.* In the function, declare a variable *arg_ptr* of type *va_list.*
2. Use the *va_start* macro with *arg_ptr* as the parameter. This sets *arg_ptr* to the beginning of the list of optional arguments to the function.
3. Use the *va_arg* macro to retrieve the next argument. This macro updates *arg_ptr* and returns a pointer to the argument being sought. Repeat this step until you have accessed all the arguments. You have to decide on a value that will mark the end of the list. For example, if you are accessing string arguments, you might use a value of NULL to mark the end of the argument list.
4. Use the *va_end* macro to set *arg_ptr* to NULL.

Note that an identical set of macros with slightly different usage exists to access variable-length arguments as specified by the ANSI C standard. These macros are defined in the header file *stdarg.h* and are described under a separate heading.

COMMON USES These macros can be used in conjunction with the routines *vfprintf, vprintf,* and *vsprintf* to implement error-handling routines that accept variable-length arguments.

RETURNS The *va_arg* macro returns a pointer to the next argument of a given type. The *va_start* macro sets a pointer to the beginning of the list of arguments; *va_end* resets this pointer to NULL.

SEE ALSO *ANSI version of* `va_start, va_arg, va_end`

EXAMPLE Demonstrate the use of UNIX-style variable-length argument processing by writing a function that accepts a variable number of character strings

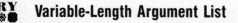

and returns the longest string. Assume that a NULL marks the end of the argument list. Write a main program that shows how the function is used.

```
#include <stdio.h>
#include <string.h>
#include <varargs.h>
char *findlong();
main()
{
    char *longest;
/* The end of the list of strings is marked by NULL */
    longest = findlong("Microsoft C", "Turbo C",
                       "QuickC",  NULL);
    printf("Longest of: Microsoft C Turbo C QuickC =\
    %s\n", longest);
    longest = findlong("a", "ab", "abc", "x",
                       "xy", NULL);
    printf("Longest of: a  ab  abc  x xy  = %s\n",
            longest);
}
/*-----------------------------------------------------*/
/* The "findlong" finds the longest string in a list
 * of strings. It uses the "va_..." macros to get
 * the arguments. This is the UNIX version.
 */
char *findlong(va_alist)    /* Note declaration      */
va_dcl        /* Macro must appear without semicolon */
{
    size_t length, maxlen = 0;
    char *longest = NULL, *str;
    va_list argp;
/* Get the first optional parameter using "va_start" */
    va_start(argp);

    while((str = va_arg(argp, char*)) != NULL)
    {
         length = strlen(str);
         if(maxlen < length)
        {
           maxlen = length;
           longest = str;
        }
    }
    return (longest);
}
```

Chapter **5** # Memory Allocation and Management

Introduction

Most computers, including PCs, operate from a basic concept: they store instructions and data in memory, and using a central processing unit or CPU—such as the 8086 microprocessor—they repeatedly retrieve instructions from memory and execute them. The operating system, which is itself a program residing in memory, takes care of loading other programs and executing them. The operating system manages the available memory for its own data and provides memory as requested by application programs, as well.

In older programming languages such as FORTRAN, there is no way to request memory at run-time. All data items and arrays must be declared before the program is compiled. You have to guess the maximum size of an array beforehand and you cannot change that size without recompiling the program. Locking in the program's maximum amount of memory is inefficient, therefore, because it may tie up memory that might be better used elsewhere. It is also inflexible, in that such a program cannot take advantage of memory that may become available later. We will look at how to reserve only the memory needed at each step in the program, thus preserving maximum flexibility.

C allows you to request and release blocks of memory during run-time. This permits your program to exploit all available memory in a system, including the extended megabytes above the 640-K limit in DOS (assuming an appropriate driver is available) and the multiple-megabytes of direct address memory in UNIX and OS/2.

C has routines that identify how much memory is available, and they allow a suitably written program to adjust its operation accordingly. The main benefit is speed of execution because additional memory typically means fewer trips to the disk drive to swap code or data in or out.

Disk drives—at least in computer terms—are slow. A program working on a 400,000- (400 K-) byte file on a machine with only 100 K bytes of free memory is faced with multiple disk calls. There isn't enough room in memory to store the entire file, so it has to go to the disk many times to get various pieces of the file. That same program on a machine with 500 K of free memory reads the disk just once, assuming an appropriate controller card. There is a point of diminishing returns, however, as managing added memory imposes overhead; but, generally, the larger the memory, the faster the program.

Like most other things in C, the memory-management capability comes in the form of library code, a set of functions known collectively as the "memory allocation" routines. The set that comes with the post-5.0 versions of Microsoft C compilers offers more such routines than are found on UNIX systems. We will now cover their salient features.

Concepts: Memory Layout and Addressing

First, we present concepts and terminology necessary for understanding memory allocation in Microsoft C under MS-DOS. The questions we answer here include: How is memory addressed in an 80x86 microprocessor? What is the layout of memory during the execution of a C program? How does DOS manage memory? How does Microsoft C add another level of management?

MEMORY ADDRESSING IN THE IBM PC

The 80x86 family of microprocessors uses a 20-bit address to access memory. This usually means that systems based on the 80x86 family can accommodate a maximum memory size of 1,024 K, or one megabyte (note that 1 K = 1,024 bytes). After deducting system overhead, the effective limit is 640 K. We said "usually" because it is possible to circumvent this limit with so-called "expanded memory" mechanisms, which swap blocks of memory in and out of areas within the 640 K space. Also, members of the 80x86 family (starting with the 80286) have larger memory address spaces which can be accessed as extended memory under the so-called "protected" mode. DOS cannot be used in the protected mode, so when these newer processors—the 286, 386, and 486—run under DOS in the "real" mode, the 640-K limit on memory size still applies.

Segments and Offsets

The Intel 80x86 microprocessor family has 16-bit internal registers through the 286 model. The 386 SX, 386 and 486 use 32-bit internal registers. (The 386 SX uses 32 bits internally, but 16 bits externally.) A 16-bit register cannot hold a 20-bit physical address, so the address is broken into two parts. The first part is called a segment, and the second is called an offset. There are 16 segments, each with an offset, and each segment and each offset is a 16-bit value. Understanding the use of segments is the key to understanding memory management.

In this model, as shown in Figure 5-1, we view the physical memory as a collection of segments. The segment address is the address of the first byte of a segment. The offset tells us the location of a specific byte with respect to the beginning of the segment. Together, segment and offset express the complete address of the byte. In hexadecimal (hex) notation, it is customary to denote the segment and offset addresses in the form *SSSS:OOOO* in which the two sets of hexadecimal digits are separated by a colon. With this scheme, two registers, one containing the segment address and the other the offset, can specify the address of one byte in memory.

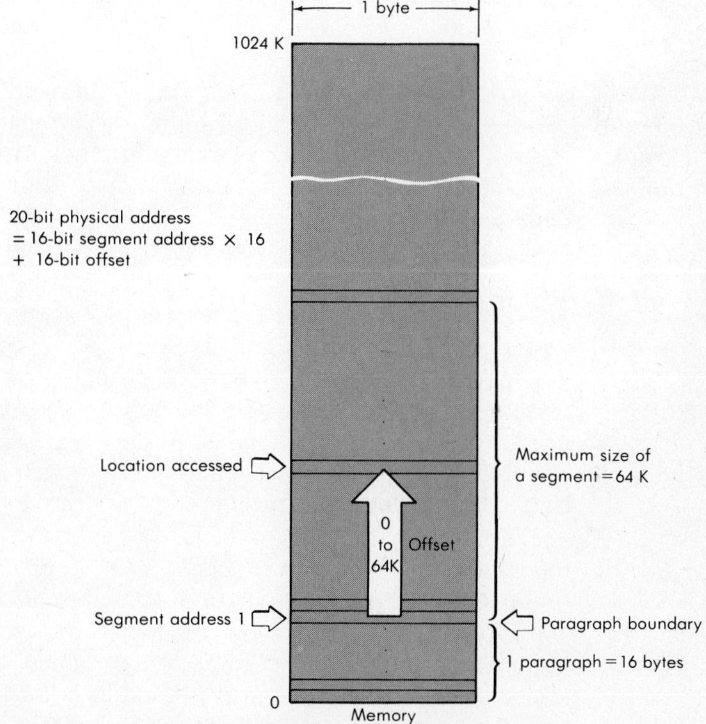

Figure 5-1. *Memory addressing in IBM PC*

Since both the segment address and the offset use a 16-bit representation, we can have at most 65,536 segments with each segment 64 K in size at most. Although this implementation of the addressing scheme implies a greater capacity for memory size than we previously claimed, the mapping of segment and offset addresses to a physical address explains the apparent discrepancy: the physical address is 20 bits, so the maximum number of bytes that can be addressed is 2^{20}, which is equal to 1,024 K or 1 megabyte (Mb). The physical address of a memory location is computed by shifting the segment address to the left by four bits and adding the offset to the result.

Paragraphs

Shifting the segment address to the left by four bits corresponds to multiplying it by 16 (which is the same as 10 hex). In fact, a group of 16 contiguous bytes has a special name in the PC: a "paragraph." This means that in the PC we can have, at most, 65,536 paragraphs. The address of a paragraph is that of the first byte in the paragraph. Since paragraphs are located at 16-byte boundaries, in terms of segment and offset notation, each paragraph address has a zero offset. Thus, when DOS allocates a certain number of paragraphs, it only returns the segment address.

MEMORY LAYOUT OF A TYPICAL C PROGRAM

Suppose you have written, compiled, and linked a C program into an executable file. Now you begin running the program. How are the different components of the program arranged in memory?

Code Segment

Let's take a snapshot of low memory at the time the program starts executing. All the instructions of your programs start at a paragraph boundary. This is the so-called "code" segment (see Figure 5-2). The code segment register (CS) holds the segment address of the code segment. The instruction pointer (IP) of the 80x86 chip keeps track of the location of the current instruction to execute by storing its offset to the CS segment address.

Data Segment and the Stack

At the next highest paragraph address after the program's code, you find the data for your program. This is called the "data segment," and its address is stored in the DS (Data Segment) register. After the data, a fixed size block (2 K by default) of memory is used for passing arguments during function calls and for storing local variables. This block is known as the "stack segment," or SS, and it is used as a last in-first out (LIFO) buffer. The 8086 microprocessor uses a "stack pointer" (SP) register to keep track of the current place in the stack. The segment address of the stack is kept in the "segment register" SS.

In 80x86 based computers, the stack always grows downward. This means that when placing an element on the stack, the stack pointer is first decremented and then the element is saved at the address SS:SP by default. Microsoft C programs begin the stack segment at the same place as the data

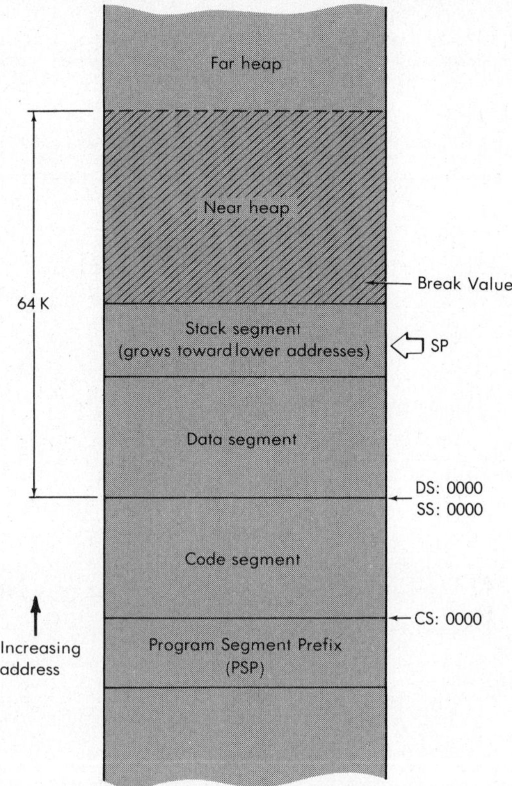

Figure 5-2. ***Memory layout of a Microsoft C program in IBM PC***

segment. You can use compiler options /Au or /Aw to tell the compiler to separate the stack and data segments, but you must create a customized library to support them.

The Break Value

The first address beyond the data segment of a program is called the *break value* of the process, and it identifies the boundary of the memory allocated to the process (see Figure 5-2). To alter the break value and enlarge the memory currently in use by your process in a Microsoft C program using the small or medium model and compiled with versions before 6.0, you can use the *sbrk* function from the library. The *sbrk* function is not ANSI-compliant and was dropped by Microsoft starting with version 6.0.

MEMORY MODELS IN MICROSOFT C

Because of the segment:offset addressing scheme in the PC, several "memory models" are available in the Microsoft C compiler. (Version 6.0 added a sixth model, tiny, discussed below.) For each item of code or data, the compiler can generate explicit segment and offset addresses, or it can use the offset alone with a default segment address. Each combination of code and data address generation defines a specific memory model.

Each model makes certain assumptions about the memory environment, and this will occasionally lead to inefficient code. On the other hand, specifying a memory model always makes the programs easier to write, because you only specify storage allocation once. You are also freed of the burden of explicitly declaring each variable as a "far" or a "near." Their biggest advantage, therefore, is portability: standard models do not require use of such Microsoft-specific keywords as *_far* and *_near* that complicate the task of moving your program to OS/2, UNIX, and other operating systems.

Near and Far Data

Data items are said to be *near* when an offset alone may be used to reach them. An offset, as you will recall, is a 16-bit value relative to the start of some segment, and "near data" is an offset to the data segment. The address of that segment is stored in the DS register, and data so addressed is called *near data.*

Near objects—code or data—may be accessed with 16-bit pointers because they are within a single 64-K segment. Pointers to objects within a segment are called "near pointers," and the process of accessing near objects is called "near addressing." Near addressing will work in any program that will run with 64 K or less for code, and 64 K or less for data.

Programs that need more than 64 K for code and/or data must specify the appropriate code and/or data segment as well as its offset. This means that addressing the "additional" memory requires 32-bit pointers instead of 16-bit pointers, with the extra 16-bits used for the segment address. Such addresses are called "far pointers" and the access process is "far addressing."

When explicit segment and offset addresses are generated for data items, they are called "far data." *Far data* items may be located anywhere in memory, and the compiler generates code that explicitly loads an 80x86 segment register, such as ES, to access them.

Segment:Offset or Offset Alone: Pros and Cons

The selection of a memory model also has other implications. For example, when offsets alone are used in addressing data or accessing instructions in the code segment, the code executes faster because the 80x86 processor does not have to spend cycles explicitly loading and manipulating a segment register. The tradeoff is that only 64 K of data is available. Instead of forcing you to deal with the various speed-vs-size issues, Microsoft C compilers provide a number of "standard" memory models—each of which exchanges execution speed for program size. The version 5.0 and 5.1 compilers provide five standard models, while the newer versions provide six. Additionally, the compilers allow the creation of up to seven additional "custom" models.

Note that on Microsoft C 6.0 leading underscores were added to the *near, far,* and *huge* keywords to identify them as non-ANSI compatible. Thus, you will generally see those keywords with underscores, but pointers, variables, and functions may still be seen without the underscore. The Microsoft C 6.0 compiler accepts both.

Tiny Model

The tiny model, introduced in version 6.0, allows a maximum of 64 K per program, which must include *both* the code and data. The tiny model is DOS-specific and cannot be used for OS/2 programs. The /AT compiler option invokes the tiny model, and generates an executable with the .COM extension instead of an .EXE.

Tiny model programs are the smallest that can be produced with the Microsoft C compiler, but they do not execute faster than small model programs. (They load faster than small model programs since .COM programs are not relocated by DOS.) Small and tiny share the top speed honors among the Microsoft standard memory models.

Small and Medium Models

The small and medium models allow only a single segment of data. The small model also limits code to a single segment, but the medium model allows multiple segments of code. Small shares with the tiny model the characteristic of generating the fastest executing code. As shown in Figure 5-3, all data addresses for the small and medium models use offsets to the segment address in the DS register. These models are most useful when the amount of data is expected to be limited. When program size is also small—but too large for the tiny model—select the small model; for lengthy programs the medium model is the best choice.

Compact and Large Models

In these two models, the compiler generates explicit segment and offset addresses for all data items. These models thus allow an unlimited amount of data with only one constraint: *no single data item can exceed 64 K.* The compact model allows only a single code segment, whereas the large model allows unlimited (subject to memory capacity) code and data, though each data item must fit into a single 64-K segment. Operating systems that support "virtual memory" allow code or data to be swapped out to disk when physical memory is exceeded, and take special advantage of the unlimited nature of the code and data size of the large model.

Although these two models allow multiple data segments, all initialized global and static data is still placed in a segment the address of which is in DS. This "default data segment" is present in each memory model, and the stack is normally located in it.

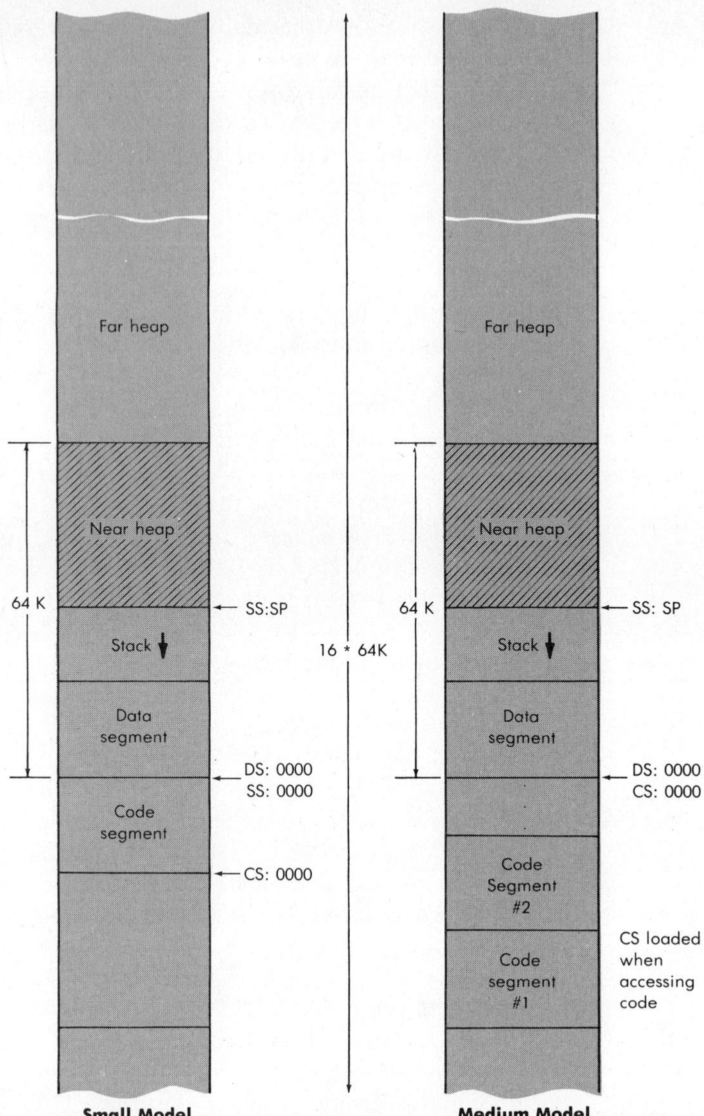

Figure 5-3. ***Memory layout for Microsoft C memory models***

Huge Memory Model

The *huge* memory model, which was introduced with version 4.0 of the Microsoft C compiler, removes the limitation that a single data item must be 64 K or smaller. It uses huge pointers that are 32 bits long, but these are available for data only, and not for code. The difference between *far* pointers and *huge* pointers is that with *huge* pointers all 32 bits are treated as the pointer address. The *far* process splits the bits into the segment:offset

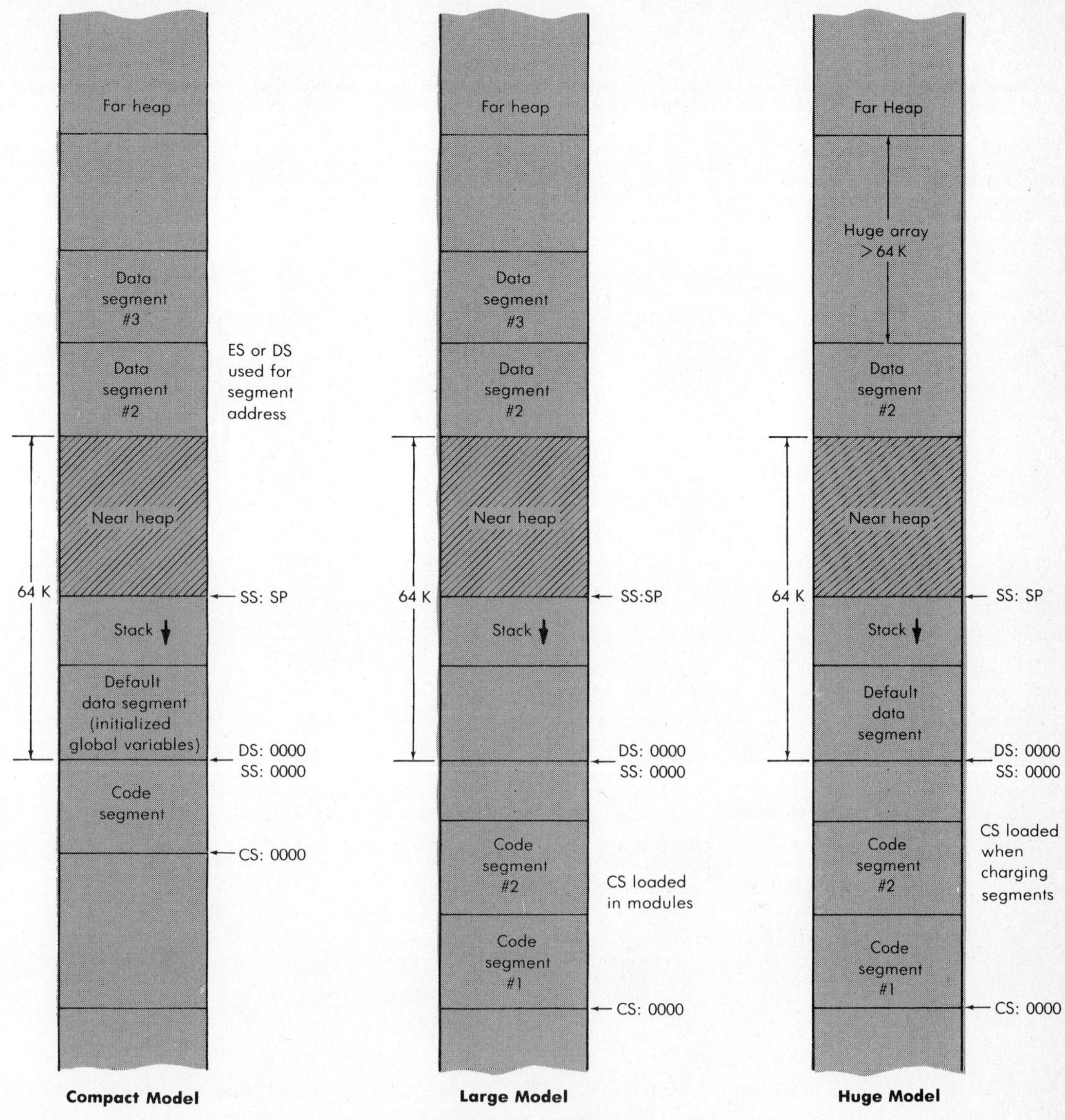

Figure 5-3. ***(Cont.)***

arrangement. The 32-bit pointer allows the pointer address to range through more than a single segment, but it also slows pointer arithmetic because twice as many bits are being manipulated.

The huge model has a couple of quirks. No single element of an array may be larger than 64 K, although the array itself may be larger. Any array larger than 128 K (two segments) must have elements all of which have sizes that are powers of 2: 2 bytes, 4 bytes, and 512 bytes are among the legal values. Care must also be taken with *prtdiff_t( )* and *sizeof( )* operations on huge pointers because they normally return type *signed int* and *unsigned int*, respectively, and thus must use the cast operator to deal with the *unsigned long* used for the huge pointer.

The huge model is otherwise identical to the large model. Address calculations are performed on the unsigned long integer in which the segment address is in the high-order bytes.

Custom Memory Models: *_near*, *_far*, *_huge*, and *_based* Keywords

The predefined memory models suffice for most operations, but occasionally you may want to address a *far* data item (for instance, to directly access video memory) in a small model, and the small model lacks that capability. The Microsoft C compiler allows you to mix and match an occasional data item of a type not available in the selected model through use of the *_near*, *_far*, *_huge*, and *_based* keywords. The *_based* keyword was introduced in version 6.0 of the Microsoft compiler. The other three were in previous editions, but without the leading underscore as a part of their name. (Recall that the leading underscore identifies a non-ANSI item. Version 6.0 will, however, recognize the old form.)

In the compact, large, and huge models, the keyword *_near* can be used to signify that certain pieces of data reside in the default data segment (one whose segment address is in the DS register). The small and medium memory models allow you to use the *_far* keyword to tell the compiler to use explicit segment and offset addresses when generating code that accesses a specific data item (the ES segment register is used to hold the segment addresses of such data items). The *_huge* keyword allows you to use a *huge* data item (size exceeding 64 K) in every memory model except tiny.

_based Keyword

The *_based* keyword allows you to specify exactly where in memory the data resides. The compiler handles pointer storage and memory allocation for far, near, and huge variables, but *based* turns the data location over to you.

The syntax for a *_based* command is *_based (base)<declarator>*. A data object resides in the segment named by *base*, and it is understood that it is not the current data segment. A based pointer is 16 bits long, and is added to the address of the base segment to create a 32-bit address.

Microsoft C, starting with version 6.0, predefines four segment constants to ease working with the *_based* keyword. They are *_CODE*, which is the default code segment; *_CONST*, which is the constant segment for strings such as *"His name is David"*; the *_DATA* segment, which is the default data segment; and *_STACK*, which is the stack segment.

A *_based* variable may be declared by giving it one of the predefined segment constants as a base. (These segment constants are defined in

C1.EXE, C3.EXE, and QCC.EXE of Microsoft C 6.0.) The keyword *_segname* identifies a segment name and is always followed by parentheses and a string. The following code fragment gives the flavor of the process:

```
#include <malloc.h>            /* standard header */
#include <stdio.h>             /* standard header */
char _based (_segname ("_CODE")) doctor[] = "Raymond";
```

The character array—a list of doctors—is based in the default code segment.

You may also declare based variables by providing a variable of type *_segment*. The *_segment* data type was introduced in version 6.0 of the Microsoft C compiler, and is very briefly discussed in the list of all active data types found in Figure 2-1 of Chapter 2. The keyword *_segment* is of the same type as *char* and *int*, uses the syntax *_segment declarator*, and is the data type used to store a segment address. It is used to declare a based variable. Consider the following example, in which the variable *intgr* is of type *int* and *pntr* is a pointer:

```
int intgr;
char *pntr;
double _based( ((_segment)&intgr) *bsd_adrs; /*address segment*/
char   _based( ((_segment)pntr)   *bsd_pntr; /*pointer segment*/
```

Intgr is an integer whose address can be cast to a segment and used as a base for *bsd_adrs*. The *pntr* variable, as an address, is cast to the type *_segment* and becomes the base for *bsd_pntr*.

A based pointer may be given no base at all. Pointer variables—and only pointer variables—may be based on *void*. A void pointer has no record about the object or function to which it currently points, and therefore cannot be dereferenced or have arithmetic operations done on it. (Knowledge of the underlying object type is required for those operations.) The keyword *void* in a based context creates a generic pointer which will act as an offset to a specified segment name. The segment and the offset are combined via the *base operator*, which Microsoft included, starting with version 6.0 of its C compiler. The base is a Level 1 operator—the highest precedence in C—with left-to-right associativity. The base operator is written with a colon followed immediately with a greater-than symbol. The operator looks like this—*:>*—and the command is *segment :> offset*. For example, in *trgt_sgmnt :> pntr* the pointer *pntr* acts as an offset into the segment specified by *trgt_sgmnt*.

The fourth way of declaring a based pointer is to use the *_self* keyword. The *_self* keyword is another item added to Microsoft C in version 6.0, and it is cast to a segment value.

```
typedef struct family FMLY;
struct FMLY
{
     int name;
     FMLY _based ((_segment) _self) *christopher;
     FMLY _based ((_segment) _self) *david;
};

main()
{
     FMLY _based (_segname("TESTSEG")) smith;
}
```

This example declares "smith" to be a structure of type name. The pointers in the structure point within the segment in which the structure is located is a process known as "self based" or "self basing." That means they have the size of near pointers and the "any segment" addressability of the far pointer. Performance of based pointers is faster than far pointers and marginally slower than near pointers. Programs with a lot of far pointers will greatly benefit from using based pointers, instead.

A major advantage of based pointers is their ability to directly access the "overhead" areas of PC memory—such as the video area.

THE HEAP: NEAR AND FAR

Now we are ready to identify the region of memory from which allocation normally takes place. Of the 64-K "default data segment," 2 K is used as a stack, and an indeterminate amount is used by the data and static variables of the program. The rest of the memory in the segment, in the region above the stack (see Figures 5-2 and 5-3), is known as the "heap"—or more accurately, the "near heap"—because all locations in this block are reached by an offset from the segment address in DS. When allocation of far data items is requested, an area beyond the default data segment is used and this pool is called the "far heap."

The heap is a bit more than simply a block of memory—it is partitioned into smaller blocks, some of which are in use and some, free. Also, there are links allowing the memory allocation routines to search for a free block and assign the block to a requesting function. These tasks fall under the category of memory management.

MEMORY MANAGEMENT: A TWO-STEP PROCESS

Memory management is done in two steps in programs compiled and linked with the Microsoft C memory allocation routines. As an operating system, MS-DOS has to keep track of the memory so that it can load and execute programs. Essentially, it keeps track of the first free paragraph address and provides a service that can dole out a specified number of paragraphs to a requesting process.

The steps involved in accessing the heap depend on the memory model. In the small and medium models, the memory remaining in the default data segment (near heap) after allocating the stack is used as a free pool.

In the compact and large models, which use far data, the Microsoft C allocation routine first gets a segment of a size equal to the value in the global variable *_amblksiz* (initially set to 8,192 bytes or 8 K) from MS-DOS. This segment becomes the far heap from which smaller blocks are handed out to satisfy calls made to *malloc* or *_fmalloc*. When the 8-K block is exhausted, the allocation routine gets another 8-K chunk from DOS. You can alter this block size of the far heap by setting *_amblksiz* (which is already declared in the header file *malloc.h*) to a value of your choice.

The allocation of huge data is handled differently. The Microsoft C routine *halloc* gets the requested memory directly from MS-DOS and when *hfree* is called to free this memory, it is returned to DOS.

Other than *halloc*, the allocation routines keep track of the memory pool in a linked list in which each entry contains the starting address of the block, the size of the block in bytes, and whether it is currently in use or not. Initially, the entire block, excluding the bytes needed to store a single list entry, is maintained as a contiguous free block. As blocks of memory get allocated and freed, the list grows.

The heap is the pool of memory together with the linked list data structure, which keeps track of which component blocks are free and which are in use. (See Figure 5-4.) When we refer to heap elements, we mean the entries in the linked list data structure. The "consistency of a heap" refers to the requirement that all entries in the heap's linked list data structure have reasonable values. For example, the address of a block, as it appears in an entry, must lie within the bounds of the heap. The Microsoft C library includes a set of routines that lets you verify the consistency of the heap as well as find out further information about each entry in the heap.

Notes

The memory allocation routines, cataloged in Table 5-1, give you all the memory management and debugging tools necessary for building complex applications that use the available memory intelligently. Note that many of these routines perform similar functions but for different heaps. See Table 5-2 for a breakdown of generic and heap-specific routines.

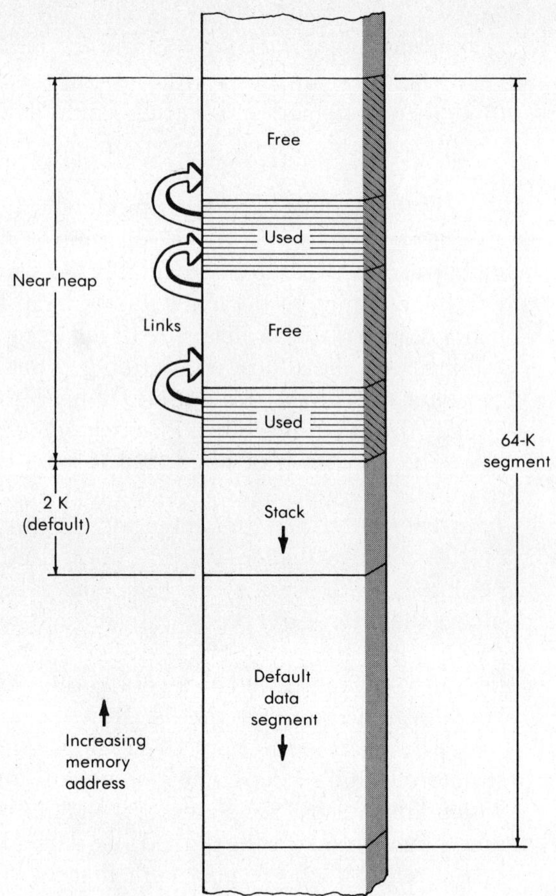

Figure 5-4. ***The heap in memory (the near heap is shown here)***

Table 5-1. ***Memory Allocation Routines***

Routine	Description
alloca	Allocates a number of bytes from the stack. Use of this function is not recommended.
_bcalloc	Allocates array storage on the specified based heap. Introduced in Microsoft C 6.0.
_bexpand	Changes the size of a block in the based heap. Introduced in Microsoft C 6.0.
_bfree	Frees a memory block in the based heap. Recommended to release blocks called by *_bcalloc, _bmal loc,* or *_brealloc*. Introduced in Microsoft C 6.0.
_bfreeseg	Frees a specified based heap segment. Introduced in Microsoft C 6.0.
_bheapadd	Adds an unused piece of memory to the specified based heap. Introduced in Microsoft C 6.0.

Table 5-1. ***(cont.)***

Routine	Description
_bheapchk	Checks for minimal consistency in the based heap specified by the selector value segment. Introduced in Microsoft C 6.0.
_bheapmin	Releases unused memory in the based heap, minimizing the heap. Introduced in Microsoft C 6.0.
_bheapseg	Allocates a based heap segment. Introduced in Microsoft C 6.0.
_bheapset	Checks for minimal consistency in the based heap segment specified by the selector value segment, then sets the heap's free entries with the fill value. Introduced in Microsoft C 6.0.
_bheapwalk	Walks through a specified based heap segment, (or all based heap segments if the specification is equal to _NULLSEG), one entry per call, returning a pointer to a _HEAPINFO structure that contains information about the next based heap entry. Introduced in Microsoft C 6.0.
_bmalloc	Allocates a memory block of the least sized bytes in a specified based heap segment. Introduced in Microsoft C 6.0.
_bmsize	Represents the size (in bytes) of the based heap memory block allocated by a call to *_balloc, _bmalloc,* or *_brealloc*. An unsigned integer. Introduced in Microsoft C 6.0.
_brealloc	Changes the size of previously allocated based memory block. It may possibly relocate it. Introduced in Microsoft C 6.0.
calloc	Allocates a number of bytes from the heap (near heap in tiny, small and medium models, far heap in large, compact, and huge models) and initializes them to zero.
_expand	Enlarges or shrinks a previously allocated block of memory without moving the block in the heap.
_fcalloc	Allocates storage space for an array in the far heap. Introduced in Microsoft C 6.0.
_fexpand	Changes the size of a block in the far heap. Introduced in version 6.0.
_ffree	Frees a memory block in the far heap. Recommended to release blocks called by *_fcalloc, _fmalloc,* or *_frealloc*.
_fheapchk	Tests the far heap for consistency.
_fheapmin	Releases unused memory in the far heap back to the operating system. Introduced in Microsoft C 6.0.
_fheapset	Sets all free far heap elements to a specified value.
_fheapwalk	Traverses the far heap and returns information on each block of memory.
_fmalloc	Allocates a number of bytes from the far heap.
_fmsize	Returns the size of a block allocated on the far heap (outside the default data segment) by *_fmalloc*.
_frealloc	Changes the size of a previously allocated far memory block, possibly moving it. Introduced in Microsoft C 6.0.
free	Frees a memory block. Recommended to release blocks allocated by *calloc, malloc,* or *realloc*. Works in near heap with tiny, small and medium models; or in far heap with large and compact.
_freect	Returns the approximate number of elements of a given size that can be allocated on the heap (near heap in tiny, small and medium models; far heap in large and compact models).

Table 5-1. *(cont.)*

Routine	Description
halloc	Allocates a huge array (size can exceed 64 K, but size of each element must be a power of 2 when it exceeds 128 K). No single member of an array may be larger than 64 K.
_heapadd	Adds an unused piece of memory to the heap. Introduced in version 6.0.
_heapchk	Checks heap for consistency (near heap in tiny, small and medium models; far heap in large and compact models).
_heapmin	Releases unused memory in the heap back to the operating system. Introduced in Microsoft C 6.0.
_heapset	Sets heap elements to specified value (near heap in tiny, small and medium models; far heap in large and compact models).
_heapwalk	Traverses heap entries and returns information on each entry (near heap in tiny, small and medium models; far heap in compact, large, and huge models).
hfree	Frees block of memory allocated by *halloc*.
malloc	Allocates a number of bytes from the heap (near heap in tiny, small and medium models; far heap in large, compact, and huge models).
_memavl	Returns approximate number of bytes available for allocation on the heap.
_memmax	Returns the largest number of contiguous bytes available for allocation on the near heap.
_msize	Returns the size of a memory block allocated earlier by *calloc, malloc,* or *realloc* . Near heap models—tiny, small, and medium—map to *_nmsize*. Far heap models—compact, large, and huge—map to *_fmsize*.
_ncalloc	Allocates storage for an array of "number" elements, each of length size bytes in the near heap. Storage is initialized to zero. Introduced in Microsoft C 6.0.
_nexpand	Changes the size of a previously allocated memory block by attempting to expand or contract the block without moving its location in the near heap. Introduced in Microsoft C 6.0.
_nfree	Frees a memory block in the near heap. Recommended to release blocks called by *_ncalloc, _nmalloc,* or *_nrealloc*.
_nheapchk	Checks the near heap consistency.
_nheapmin	Releases unused memory in the near heap back to the operating system. Introduced in Microsoft C 6.0.
_nheapset	Sets all free near heap elements to a specified value.
_nheapwalk	Traverses the near heap and returns information on each block of memory.
_nmalloc	Allocates a number of bytes from the near heap. (Tiny, small, and medium models.)
_nmsize	Returns the size of a block allocated on the default data segment by *_nmalloc*.
_nrealloc	Changes the size and possibly the location of a memory block in the near heap. Introduced in Microsoft C 6.0.
realloc	Enlarges or shrinks a previously allocated block of memory, moving the block in the heap, if necessary.
stackavail	Gets the amount of memory available in the stack.

THE MEMORY ALLOCATION ROUTINES BY TASK

Table 5-2 lists the memory allocation routines grouped according to the tasks they perform. The most important purpose of these routines is the allocation and the deallocation of memory from the heap, but they can also allocate memory from the stack. Another crucial task is obtaining size information about memory blocks: both allocated and available. Lastly, an entire subcategory of routines provides the capability of "snooping" around in the heap and helping debug problems related to the heap. Note that the routines marked generic call the routine for the appropriate heap dependent on the selected memory model of the program.

Table 5-2. ***Memory Allocation Routines by Task***

Task	Routines
Allocate the based heap.	_bheapseg
Alter the size of an allocated block.	_expand, _bexpand, _fexpand, _nexpand, realloc, _brealloc, _frealloc, _nrealloc
Determine the size of an allocated block.	_msize (generic), _bmsize (based heap), _fmsize (far heap), _nmsize (near heap)
Add to the size of an allocated block.	_heapadd (generic), _bheapadd (based heap)
Check the consistency of the heap.	_heapchk (generic), _bheapchk (based heap), _fheapchk (far heap), _nheapchk (near heap)
Fill the heap with a specified value.	_heapset (generic), _bheapset (based heap), _fheapset (far heap), _nheapset (near heap)
Free unused heap space.	_heapmin (generic), _bheapmin (based heap), _fheapmin (far heap), _nheapmin (near heap)
Determine the amount available in the near heap for allocation.	_freect, _memavl, _memmax
Step through elements in the heap.	_heapwalk (generic), _bheapwalk (based heap), _fheapwalk (far heap), _nheapwalk (near heap)
Allocate memory.	calloc (generic), _bcalloc (based heap), _fcalloc (far heap), _ncalloc (near heap), halloc, malloc (generic), _bmalloc (based heap), _fmalloc (far heap), _nmalloc (near heap)
Free unused memory.	_bfreeseg (based heap), free (generic), _bfree (based heap), _ffree (far heap), _nfree (near heap), hfree (huge data)
Allocate memory from the stack.	alloca (Microsoft recommends against its use)
Determine amount of memory available in the stack.	stackavail

TYPICAL USE OF MEMORY ALLOCATION

You need memory allocation capabilities when you cannot determine in advance the exact amount of space you will need to store the data used or generated in your program. If the data is generated during the course of the program, you may simply want to get space as and when needed. (You may also want to free memory when it is no longer needed.) Typically, the data elements are in the form of a C structure with a field containing pointers to the next element. This enables you to link one element to the next and keep them accessible via a single pointer to the beginning of the linked list. It is also common to want to allocate, at run-time, a number of data elements contiguously. Such a structure, called an "array," provides faster access to arbitrary data elements than linked lists because you do not have to start at the beginning and trace through the links. In either case, the allocation of memory proceeds as described below. (Huge arrays are handled differently and are described later.)

Heap Prefix

Starting with Microsoft C 6.0, many of the memory allocation functions come in four versions—*generic, _based, _far,* and *_near*. The *_based* version of a memory function typically has a *_b* prefix on the underlying generic name. The *_near* prefix is *_n*, and the *_far* prefix is *_f*. These prefixes are combined with the generic names *calloc, expand, free, heapchk, heapmin, heapset, heapwalk, malloc, msize,* and *realloc* to create *_based, _far,* and *_near* functions, respectively. The generics also appear as free-standing functions (six of which, *_expand, _heapchk, _heapmin, _heapset, _heapwalk,* and *_msize*, are not ANSI-compliant and, therefore, have a leading underscore in their name.) This naming convention makes it easier to remember the object of these functions. The near heap lies inside the default data segment. The far heap lies outside the default data segment. In the reference entries, all of the versions of each function are combined in a single entry alphabetically under the "root" name: for example, *malloc, _fmalloc, _halloc, _nmalloc,* and *_bmalloc* are all found in the *malloc* entry. If you have trouble finding a particular function, you can search for it in the jump tables, which list all of the variant functions, individually.

Default Function Mapping

The typical behavior of these functions is for the generic versions to map the large data memory models (the compact, large, and huge models) to the far heap versions. The near heap (*_n*) functions are normally mapped by the generic to the small data models, which are the tiny, small, and medium models. The based heap (*_b*) versions are directed to their specified segment. You may directly call the explicit version of each generic.

Requesting Memory

You may use *calloc* or *malloc* to get additional memory. The *malloc* function returns a block of memory of a specified size. The *calloc* routine allocates room for an array of a specified number of elements, each of a given size, and also initializes all the allocated bytes to zero. There are _far, _near, and _based versions available for these functions. Use the *sizeof* statement to get the size of a data element.

Whether you use *calloc* or *malloc*, the actual allocation portion of the work is invoked by calling *malloc*. In large data models (compact, large, and huge), the call to *malloc* is mapped to *_fmalloc*, the _far version of the *malloc* generic. In small data models (tiny, small, and medium), the *malloc* call is mapped to *_nmalloc* or the _near version of generic *malloc*. You may call the *_fmalloc* and *_nmalloc* routines explicitly when you allocate room for *_near* or *_far* data items.

Using the Allocated Block

The allocation routines return the address of the allocated block as a pointer to a *void* data item. This pointer *must* be cast into a pointer of the type of data for which you requested space. Engaging this pointer is absolutely the only way to gain access to the newly allocated block, and by assigning it to a pointer variable, you will ensure that it cannot be destroyed.

The return value for a failed memory allocation is NULL. It is always good practice to check for a returned NULL value, remembering that a returned NULL leads to a "Null pointer assignment" message when you exit your program.

Releasing Memory

The *free* routines are: *free, _bfree, _ffree,* and *_nfree*. They allow you to release a block of memory that was previously allocated by a call to *malloc* or *calloc*, or one that was reallocated by a call to *realloc*. The released block is returned to the appropriate heap for use by other routines. Of course, the size of the returned block matches what was specified in the original call to the allocation routine.

Choosing the correct version of *free* is easy—just match the heap prefix (*_b, _f* or *_n*) with the *calloc, malloc*, or *realloc* used to allocate the block. If you used the generic allocation routines—*calloc, malloc*, or *realloc*—then use the generic *free* to release the blocks. Otherwise, use *_bfree* to release from *_bcalloc, _bmalloc*, or *_brealloc*; *_ffree* to release from *_fcalloc, _fmalloc*, or *_frealloc*; and *_nfree* to release from *_ncalloc, _nmalloc*, or *_nrealloc*.

The *free* functions map large data (compact, large, and huge model) to *_ffree*, just as the *_far* prefix would lead you to believe. The *_nfree* function is mapped to small data models (tiny, small and medium) as indicated by the *_near* prefix.

Altering the Size of a Block

What if you allocate room for an array, only to discover that you need room for more elements? Fortunately, the C library includes routines that can enlarge or shrink the size of an allocated block. The *_expand* function tries to expand the block in its current position in the heap. It fails if there is not adequate adjacent free space. The *realloc* function actually relocates the block in the heap to satisfy the enlargement request. Both guarantee that the data taking space up to the old size of the block will remain intact. Both come with the full complement of *_b, _f,* and *_n* heap-sensitive versions.

Getting the Size Information

The library with Microsoft C includes several routines that let your program determine how much memory is left for allocation, and how much is allocated by a given call. The *_msize* generic and its three heap-explicit variants return the size of an allocated block in bytes. They take the pointer returned by the allocation routine as their argument. The *_msize* mapping behavior follows the default, and explicit versions should be matched by their heap prefix.

Three other routines return size information: *_freect, _memavl,* and *_memmax.* All deal exclusively with the near heap in the default data segment, so they work in tiny, small, and medium models or with any near data in the compact, large, and huge models. The *_freect* routine tells your program how many elements of a given size will fit into available near heap memory. The *_memavl* function returns the total number of bytes available for allocation in the near heap. A call to the *_memmax* function reveals the size (in bytes) of the largest contiguous block available for allocation within the near heap. A call to yield the largest contiguous block in the near heap is:

```
_nmalloc (_memmax() )
```

HUGE ARRAYS

The allocation and deallocation of huge arrays is handled by the *halloc* and *hfree* routines. As mentioned earlier in this chapter, the huge model has a couple of quirks. No single element of an array may be larger than 64 K, although the array itself may be larger. Any array larger than 128 K—two segments—must have elements all of which have sizes that are powers of 2: 2 bytes, 4 bytes, 8 bytes and 512 bytes are among the legal values.

The *halloc* function gets its memory directly from MS-DOS, and blocks are returned there by *hfree* using a DOS function call. There is no heap with which to deal, and these routines may be used either within a huge model or to allocate data item of type *_huge.* The returned pointer from *halloc* is of the *_huge* type—which, as we covered earlier, is a 32-bit pointer that does not follow default 16-bit offset:segment pairs.

ALLOCATING FROM THE STACK

Function arguments and local variable are stored on the stack. Running out of stack space (by trying to store too many local variables, for instance) is known as "stack overflow." One solution to this problem is dynamic local allocation where locals are allocated on a stack instead of being declared in a function. The function with which this is done is named *alloca*, but Microsoft in the documentation accompanying recent versions of its C compiler, recommends against this practice. The *alloca* routine is supported for compatibility with earlier releases and should be stripped from your programs as time permits.

The *alloca* function has an accompanying routine called *stackavail*, which is used to identify how much space may be allocated.

SNOOPING AROUND THE HEAP

Dynamic memory allocation can lead to hard-to-identify errors. You may, for example, allocate an array of 100 integers and write something beyond the last element position. You may get away with this the first six times you run the program, because the adjacent memory area was left unused. The seventh try, however, might trash something important because the memory next to your array was in use this time. The nature of dynamic allocation is that no two run-times generate the same memory map.

The *_heapchk* generic and its three associates, *_bheapchk, _fheapchk*, and *_nheapchk*, run checks of what is called "heap consistency" to ensure that entries have valid addresses for the blocks in use. They report any bad node entry they find. The *_heapset* generic and its *_b, _f*, and *_n* variants allows you to write a specified fill character to every byte in all free blocks in the heap. The *_heapwalk* routines, generic and *_b, _f*, and *_n*, let your program examine each entry in the linked list data structure of the heap.

These routines help isolate problems that are caused by damage to the heap. The generics follow default mapping convention, and care should be taken to keep the prefixes matched. The explicit versions may be called.

Cautions

- Do not mix the *halloc* and *hfree* functions with other routines for memory allocation and deallocation. The *halloc* and *hfree* functions deal with *_huge* items, real 32-bit pointers, and directly with DOS; the other routines do not.
- Always pass a valid pointer to the deallocation routine *free* (*hfree* for huge data, and the *_b, _f*, and *_n* explicits). Subsequent calls to memory allocation functions will produce errors if you pass a pointer that was not passed by the corresponding allocation routine.
- The *sbrk* function introduced in Microsoft C version 5.1 has been removed from the product starting with version 6.0. This routine should be edited from your programs.

Further Reading

Memory management is covered in most textbooks on operating systems. The book on XINU by Comer[1] and the book on MINIX by Tanenbaum[2] describe memory management from the point of view of an operating system. Each includes samples of C code that implement the memory management algorithms. Knuth's classic text[3] describes the basic algorithms used in deciding how to assign a particular block of memory to satisfy a request. For a more practical and relevant description of the C memory allocation routines and their usage, consult Prata's book[4].

1. Douglas Comer, *Operating System Design The XINU Approach*, Prentice-Hall, Inc. Englewood Cliffs, NJ, 1984, 486 pages.
2. Andrew S. Tanenbaum, *Operating Systems Design and Implementation*, Prentice-Hall, Inc. Englewood Cliffs, NJ, 1987, 719 pages.
3. Donald E. Knuth, *The Art of Computer Programming, Volume 1: Fundamental Algorithms*, Addison-Wesley, Reading, MA, 1968.
4. Stephen Prata, The Waite Group, *Advanced C Primer++*, Howard W. Sams & Company, Carmel, IN, 1986, 502 pages.

COMPATIBILITY

alloca

MSC 3	MSC 4	MSC 5	MSC 6	QC1	QC2	QC2.5	TC1	TC1.5	TC2	TC++	ANSI	UNIX V	XNX	OS2	DOS
	▲	▲	▲	▲	▲	▲						▲		▲	▲

PURPOSE Use *alloca* to obtain a specified amount of space in the program's stack for temporary use.

SYNTAX

```
void *alloca(size_t num_bytes);

size_t num_bytes;      Number of bytes to be allocated from the stack
```

EXAMPLE CALL

```
ptr = alloca(80);
```

INCLUDES

```
#include <malloc.h>      For function declaration and definition of data type size_t
```

DESCRIPTION The *alloca* function allocates the number of bytes specified in the argument *num_bytes* to the program's stack. Before calling *alloca* you should call *stackavail* to determine the amount of space available on the stack for allocation. The *alloca* function only creates room for local variables; it does not increase the size of a program's stack. The allocated bytes begin at an address that satisfies all requirements for storage of any C data type. There is no need to deallocate this memory from the stack because the space is freed as soon as the calling function returns.

COMMON USES The *alloca* function allocates temporary storage on the stack. In fact, all local variables in a function are allocated on the stack, but *alloca* enables us to get only as much space on the stack as we need, when we need it. For temporary needs, this is more efficient than allocating memory in the default segment with *malloc.*

RETURNS The return value from *alloca* is a pointer to a type *void*, representing the address of the first byte of the space allocated on the stack. If the function fails because of insufficient space on the stack, a NULL is returned.

COMMENTS Since the stack is used for passing parameters and storing return addresses during function calls, you cannot use *alloca* inside an argument to another function. Attempting to free the space by calling other memory deallocation functions such as *free* will most likely crash your program. Microsoft recommends against using the *alloca* function. Microsoft supports the function only to provide source compatibility with earlier versions of the C compiler. Routines using the *alloca* function should be compiled without any optimization, using the /Od option.

SEE ALSO

`stackavail`	*To determine the space available on the stack*
`malloc`	*To allocate memory from the heap*
`free`	*To release memory allocated earlier*

EXAMPLE Use *alloca* to allocate room for a buffer to hold 80 characters on the program's stack. Prompt the user for a string and store it in the buffer you allocate.

```
#include <stdio.h>
#include <malloc.h>
main()
{
    char *buffer;
/* Get 80 bytes from stack */
    buffer = (char *) alloca(80);
    if (buffer == NULL)
    {
        printf("alloca failed.\n");
        exit(0);
    }
    printf("Buffer allocated. Enter string to store: ");
    gets(buffer);
    printf("\nYou entered: %s\n",buffer);
}
```

_bfreeseg

COMPATIBILITY

MSC 3	MSC 4	MSC 5	MSC 6	QC1	QC2	QC2.5	TC1	TC1.5	TC2	TC++	ANSI	UNIX V	XNX	OS2	DOS
			▲			▲								▲	▲

PURPOSE Use the *_bfreeseg* function to free based heap memory in the specified based segment.

SYNTAX `int _bfreeseg (_segment seg_name);`

`seg_name` *The based heap segment selector*

EXAMPLE CALL `_bfreeseg (seg_name);`

INCLUDES `#include <malloc.h>` *For function declaration*

DESCRIPTION The *_bfreeseg* routine is used to free a based heap. The *seg_name* argument, which specifies the based heap to be freed, is a based heap returned by an earlier call to the *_bheapseg* function.

The *_bfreeseg* function frees the number of bytes specified when the block was originally allocated, and returns the freed heap to the pool available for allocation.

It is important to remember that you cannot free a based heap segment (unlinking it from the based heap list and returning it to the operating system) by a call to *_bheapmin*. You must use *_bfreeseg* to free the based heap.

RETURNS The *_bfreeseg* returns a 0 if the heap is successfully freed. An error is identified by the return of a –1 value.

COMMENTS Using *_based*, the syntax of which is *_based (base) vrbl_nam*, specifies that a data object resides in the segment identified by the *(base)* argument. (It is not assumed to reside in the current data segment.) Based pointers occupy 16 bits, and are added to the base to provide a 32-bit address range.

SEE ALSO `_bheapseg` *To allocate a based heap*

EXAMPLE See the example program on the reference page for *_bheapseg*.

COMPATIBILITY

_bheapseg

MSC 3	MSC 4	MSC 5	MSC 6	QC1	QC2	QC2.5	TC1	TC1.5	TC2	TC++	ANSI	UNIX V	XNX	OS2	DOS
			▲			▲								▲	▲

PURPOSE Use the *_bheapseg* function to allocate based heap memory.

SYNTAX

```
_segment _bheapseg (size_t num_bytes);
```

`num_bytes` *Size of the segment (in bytes) to allocate*

EXAMPLE CALL

```
if ((seg_name = _bheapseg (1000)) == _NULLSEG) exit(3);
```

INCLUDES `#include <malloc.h>` *For function declaration*

DESCRIPTION The *_bheapseg* function allocates a based heap segment of at least *num_bytes* in size. The allocated block may be larger than than the requested size because of the overhead required for maintenance and alignment. The *_bheapseg* function may be called repeatedly. The C library allocates a new based heap segment for each call.

RETURNS The *_bheapseg* function returns the allocated segment selector, which should be saved for use by subsequent based heap functions. A failed call is identified by a return value of –1. It is important to check the return—

especially when used in real mode—even if the amount of requested memory is small. A missed error can propagate errors throughout your program.

SEE ALSO `_bfreeseg` *To free memory from a based heap*

COMMENTS The keyword *_segname*, used in the command string *_segname ("segname")*, specifies the name of a segment of memory. You can declare a based variable in several ways, one of which is to give it a segment constant as a base. Microsoft C version 6.0 predefines four constants: *_CODE*, the default code segment; *_CONST*, the constant segment for strings such as *"His name is Michael"*; *_DATA*, which is the default data segment; and *_STACK*, which is the stack segment.

The *_segname* keyword identifies the name of a segment. It must be followed by parentheses and a string, for instance:

```
#include <stdio.h>
#include <malloc.h>

char _based (_segname ("_CODE")) b_strng[] = "Her name is
              Lynne.\n";
int  _based (_segname ("_CODE")) b_int = 9788;
       /* code-based int */

void main()
{
       printf ("%Fs %d", (char _far *) b_strng, b_int);
}
```

Note the character array variable *b_strng* and the *int* variable *b_int* are based in the code segment. The *_b_int* value is not a pointer. You also need to remember that the small model *printf* would treat *b_strng* as a near pointer. The format specifier *%Fs* forces the function to treat it as a far pointer and the *(char _far*)* cast coerces the address to four bytes.

You may, if you choose, name your own segments:

```
char _based (_segname ("OWN_SEG")) b_strng[] = "Los Gatos";
```

Here, the compiler creates a new segment called *OWN_SEG* and places the string *"Los Gatos"* in the segment.

EXAMPLE The following program sets up a based heap and uses it to store and reverse a string.

```
/* _based memory example program */

#include <malloc.h>
```

```
#include <stdio.h>
#include <stdlib.h>
#include <string.h>

void main(void)
{
   char     scratch[80];
   int      str_len;
   _segment  seg_nam;
   char     _based (seg_nam) *out_str, _based (seg_nam) *in_str;

   /* use gets() to accommodate any spaces */
   printf ("\ntype a string to reverse: ");
   gets (scratch);

   /* request based heap to show how it is done */
   if ((seg_nam = _bheapseg (2048)) == _NULLSEG) exit (1);

   /* allocate based memory for strings - remember terminating null */

   str_len = strlen (scratch);
   if (((in_str = _bmalloc (seg_nam, str_len + 1)) == _NULLOFF)
      ||
      ((out_str = _bmalloc (seg_nam, str_len + 1)) == _NULLOFF))

      exit (2);

   /* based memory is "far" when addressed as a whole
       copy and reverse + upper-case only the output string */

   _fstrcpy ((char _far *)in_str, (char _far *)scratch);
   _fstrcpy (out_str, in_str);
   _fstrupr (_fstrrev (out_str));

   /* display in and out (strings as a whole are "far") */

   printf ("in:  %Fs\n", (char _far *)in_str);
   printf ("out: %Fs\n", (char _far *)out_str);

   /* free the blocks, release the based heap */

   _bfree (seg_nam, in_str);
   _bfree (seg_nam, out_str);
   _bfreeseg (seg_nam);
   exit (8);
}
```

```
/* The results of a run are:
type a string to reverse: penn state

 in: penn state
out: ETATS NNEP  */
```

calloc, _bcalloc, _fcalloc, _ncalloc, halloc

COMPATIBILITY

MSC 3	MSC 4	MSC 5	MSC 6	QC1	QC2	QC2.5	TC1	TC1.5	TC2	TC++	ANSI	UNIX V	XNX	OS2	DOS
▲	▲	1	2	▲	▲	▲	3	3	3	3	▲	▲	▲	▲	▲

PURPOSE Use *calloc* and its variants to allocate memory for an array of a given number of elements, each having a specified size in bytes. All bytes of the allocated array will be initialized to zero. The compiler selects the appropriate variant for the memory model in use, as described below.

For an array whose size is greater than 64 K, use the *halloc* variant. Use *_bcalloc* to allocate memory for an array using a based heap.

SYNTAX

```
void *calloc(size_t num_elems, size_t elem_size);

void _far *_fcalloc (size_t num_elems, size_t elem_size);

void _near *_ncalloc (size_t num_elems, size_t elem_size);

void _based(void) *_bcalloc (_segment seg_name, size_t
num_elems, size_t elem_size);

void _huge *halloc(long num_elems, size_t elem_size);
```

`size_t num_elems`	*Number of elements*
`size_t elem_size`	*Length in bytes of each element*
`seg_name`	*The based heap segment selector (used with* _bcalloc*; see Comments below)*

EXAMPLE CALL

```
p_int = (int *) calloc(100, sizeof(int));
pf_int = (int far *) _fcalloc(500, sizeof(int));
pn_int = (int near *) _ncalloc(50, sizeof(int));
pb_int = (int _based *) _bcalloc(_DATA, 10, sizeof(int));
p_huge = (short huge *)halloc(100000, sizeof(short));
```

INCLUDES

`#include <malloc.h>`	*For function declaration and definition of data type* size_t
`#include <stdlib.h>`	*For ANSI-compatibility*

DESCRIPTION The *calloc* function first computes the total number of bytes that it must allocate by multiplying the number of elements *num_elems* by the size of each element *elem_size*. Then it calls *malloc* to allocate the memory. Finally, the *memset* function is called to set each byte of the allocated memory to zero.

The compiler maps the call to *calloc* to a routine appropriate for the memory model in use: in the compact, large, and huge models, *calloc* is mapped to *_fcalloc*. In the tiny, small, and medium models, *calloc* is mapped to *_ncalloc*. Thus *calloc* will work properly for all memory models except *huge*. To allocate huge (that is, longer than 64 K) arrays, use the *halloc* function. If you will be using near or far pointers not supported by the memory model in use, you can call *_fcalloc* for far pointers and *_ncalloc* for near pointers. The *_bcalloc* function allocates array storage on the specified based heap.

The *halloc* function allocates the memory necessary to hold the number of data elements specified in the argument *num_elems*, each of size *elem_size*, by calling the MS-DOS memory allocation function (function number 48H). Each byte in the allocated memory is set to 0. Similar to *calloc*, except that the size of *halloc's* block of memory can be huge—it can exceed 64 K. When allocating memory blocks larger than 128 K (131,072 bytes), the size of each data element must be a power of 2. You release the allocated memory by calling *hfree* before exiting the program.

1. The *calloc* function was changed in Microsoft C 5.0 to return a null instead of a zero-length heap item. 2. *_fcalloc, _ncalloc,* and *_bcalloc* were introduced in version 6.0. 3. The Turbo C equivalent for *_fcalloc* is *far calloc*.

COMMON USES The *calloc* function is used to create and initialize (to zero) arrays of data objects at run-time. This allows your application to get memory as needed instead of setting aside a fixed amount and running the risk of filling up the space with no way of getting additional room. You can use *calloc*, for example, to set aside memory for a 100 elements each 80 bytes long. Allocating based memory with *_bcalloc* is particularly useful for accessing specific far memory areas such as video memory.

RETURNS The return value from *calloc* and its variants is a pointer to a type *void*, representing the address of the allocated memory. For *halloc* this will be a huge object.

A successful call to the *_bcalloc* routine returns a based pointer to the allocated space. A failure yields a _NULLOFF if insufficient memory is available, if *num_elems* or *elem_size* is 0, or if the specified segment has not been initialized as part of the based heap. The *_fcalloc* and *_ncalloc* versions return a far or near pointer, respectively, if they are successful.

The storage locations are guaranteed to be able to hold data objects of any kind. If the memory allocation is unsuccessful because of insufficient space or bad values of the arguments, a NULL is returned.

COMMENTS In Microsoft C 4.0, you could get a valid pointer even if the element size was given as zero. This pointer could be used with the function *realloc* to enlarge the memory to a desired size. However, this is no longer true in Microsoft C 5.0 and beyond.

The *malloc* functions are the most general-purpose memory allocation routine in the Microsoft C run-time library. The *calloc* function merely computes the total memory requested in bytes and calls *malloc.*

When using *bcalloc,* you need to define or segment for the based pointer. The keyword *_segname* specifies the name of a segment of memory. Microsoft C 6.0 predefines four constants: *_CODE, _CONST, _DATA,* and *_STACK.* They are covered in the tutorial for this chapter. The *_segname* must be followed by parentheses and a string: for instance:

```
#include <stdio.h>
#include <malloc.h>

char _based (_segname ("_CODE")) b_strng[] = "His name is Larry.\n";
int  _based (_segname ("_CODE")) b_int = 8627;
/* code-based int */

void main()
{
    printf ("%Fs %d", (char _far *) b_strng, b_int);
}
```

Note the character array variable *b_strng* and the *int* variable *b_int* are based in the code segment. The *_b_int* value is not a pointer.

You may name your own segments, as in the example:

```
char _based (_segname ("STATE_SEG")) b_strng[] = "Virginia";
```

Here, the compiler creates a new segment called STATE_SEG and places the string "Virginia" in the segment.

SEE ALSO `malloc, _fmalloc, _nmalloc, _bmalloc:` *General purpose memory allocation routines*

`free, _ffree, _nfree, _bfree:` *To release memory allocated earlier*

EXAMPLES Use *calloc* to allocate room for a buffer to hold 100 lines of text, each line 80 characters long. Prompt the user for a string and store it in the buffer you allocated.

```
#include <stdio.h>
#include <stdlib.h>
#include <malloc.h>
unsigned char *buffer;
```

```
main()
{
    buffer = (char *) calloc(100, 80);
    if (buffer == NULL)
    {
         printf("Allocation Failed.\n");
           exit(0);
    }
    printf("Buffer allocated. Enter string to store: ");
    gets(buffer);
    printf("\nYou entered: %s\n",buffer);
}
```

Suppose you are developing a small data base of your client's vital statistics. You have grouped all information about a single client in a C data structure of type CLIENT_T with all the appropriate fields. Define this data type and use *calloc* to allocate enough memory for 100 clients.

```
#include <stdio.h>
#include <malloc.h>
#include <stdlib.h>
#define MAX_CHR     80
#define MAX_CLIENTS 100
typedef struct CLIENT_T     /* Define a data structure */
{
        char      name[MAX_CHR];
        unsigned  age;
        double    networth;
} CLIENT_T;

main()
{
    CLIENT_T *client_list;  /* Define pointer to data */
    if( (client_list =      /* Cast returned pointer  */
        (CLIENT_T *) calloc(MAX_CLIENTS,
                            sizeof(CLIENT_T))) == NULL)
    {
        fprintf(stderr,"No room for clients!\n");
    }
    else
    {
        printf("Client list allocated successfully.\n");
    }
/* The array of structures can now be accessed by using
 * the pointer "client_list". For example the net worth
```

```
 * of client number 10 is--client_list[10].networth
 */
}
```

Note that both of the preceding examples will work with *_fcalloc* if you use far pointers, and *_ncalloc* if near pointers are used. To use based pointers you must set up the desired segment as shown in the Comment above and declare based pointers for use with *_bcalloc*.

Use *halloc* to allocate room for a _huge array of 100,000 short integers and initialize each element to zero. Deallocate the array by calling *hfree* before exiting the program.

```
#include <stdio.h>
#include <stdlib.h>
#include <malloc.h>
#define MAX_SIZE 100000L
main()
{

    short _huge *larray;
/* Allocate room for string and check for NULL pointer*/
    if( (larray = (short_huge *)halloc(MAX_SIZE,
                                  sizeof(short)))  == NULL)
    {
        printf("Allocation by halloc Failed.\n");
        exit(0);
    }
    print("Array of 100,000 short ints allocated.\n");
/*  Free the array and exit */
    hfree((void huge *)larray);
    print("_Huge array deallocated\n");
}
```

_expand, _bexpand _fexpand, _nexpand

COMPATIBILITY

MSC 3	MSC 4	MSC 5	MSC 6	QC1	QC2	QC2.5	TC1	TC1.5	TC2	TC++	ANSI	UNIX V	XNX	OS2	DOS
	▲	▲	1	▲	▲	▲								▲	▲

PURPOSE Use the *_expand* function or its variants to enlarge or shrink a previously allocated block of memory, without moving the location of the block in the heap. The compiler automatically substitutes the appropriate variant depending on the memory model in use, as explained below.

SYNTAX

```
void *_expand(void *mem_address, size_t newsize);

void _far *_fexpand (void _far *mem_address, size_t newsize);

void _near *_nexpand (void _near *mem_address, size_t newsize);

void _based (void) *_bexpand (_segment seg_name, void _based
(void) *mem_address, size_t newsize);
```

`void *mem_address;` *Pointer to previously allocated block of memory*

`size_t newsize;` *Requested size of block in number of bytes*

`seg_name` *The based heap segment selector (used with* _bexpand*)*

EXAMPLE CALL

```
_expand(p_old_block, 2000*sizeof(int));
_fexpand(p_far_block, 5000*sizeof(int));
_nexpand(p_near_block, 50*sizeof(int));
_bexpand(_CODE, p_code_block, 100*sizeof(int));
```

INCLUDES

`#include <malloc.h>` *For function declaration and definition of data type* size_t

DESCRIPTION

The *_expand* function and its variants alter the size of a previously allocated block of memory to the number of bytes specified in the argument *newsize*. The address of the block is provided as a pointer to a *void* data type in the argument *mem_address*. For *_fexpand* this is a _far object, for *_nexpand* it is a _near object, and for *_bexpand* it is a _based object.

The argument *mem_address* is the pointer returned by an earlier call to one of the memory allocation routines such as *malloc, calloc,* or *realloc*. It can also be the address of a block of memory that was just freed, as long as there have been no calls to any memory allocation routine since the block had been freed.

Unlike *realloc*, which also provides the same services, *_expand* will not move the block of memory to another location in the heap in an attempt to satisfy the requested change in size.

In the compact, large, and huge models, the compiler maps *_expand* to *_fexpand*. In the tiny, small, and medium models, *_expand* is mapped to *_nexpand*.

In the large data models—compact, large, and huge—the *_expand* function defaults to *_fexpand*. The small data models—tiny, small, and medium—cause *_expand* to default to *_nexpand*.

The *_bexpand* version changes the size of a block in either the specified based heap; if no based heap is specified, all based heaps are affected.

You can also let the near heap borrow memory from any unused stack space by linking your code with the VARSTCK.ONJ file. That file allows the near memory allocation routines, of which *_nexpand* (in all models) and *_expand* (small and medium models, only) are part, to allocate items in unused stack space *if* they have run out of other memory. The stack cannot employ any unused heap space, or recover space that has been taken by the heap. The following command will link the object code of MEMORY.C with VARSTCK.OBJ:

```
CL MEMORY.C VARSTCK /link /NOE
```

1. The *_fexpand, _nexpand,* and *_bexpand* versions were introduced in Microsoft C version 6.0.

RETURNS The return value from *_expand* and its variants is a pointer to the block of memory whose size was altered. A successful call to the *_bexpand* version returns a based pointer to the resized memory block. The *_fexpand* function returns a far pointer to the resized memory block, if successful. The successful *_nexpand* routine returns a near pointer to the resized block. Thus, the *_expand* function group returns a void pointer to the reallocated memory block. You must type cast the return to coerce the pointer to a type other than *void.* The *_expand* functions, unlike *realloc,* cannot move a block in order to change its size.

Since *_expand* does not move the block around, the value returned upon a successful return is the same as the argument *mem_address.* The return value is NULL if there is not enough available memory to expand the block to the specified size without moving it. The *_bexpand* function (the based version) will return _NULLOFF if insufficient memory is available. This means that the item pointed to by the *_bexpand* argument will have been expanded as much as possible in its current location.

When the return points to the storage space, it is a guarantee that the space is now suitably aligned for the storage of any type of object. It is always a good practice to test whether you received the amount of memory that you requested, via a call to the *msize* function.

COMMENTS For normal allocation and reallocation needs, it is best to adhere to the portable routines, *malloc, calloc,* and *realloc.* Using *realloc* (and its variants) to enlarge the size of a block has the added advantage of having a greater possibility of success because *realloc* will move the block around in the heap in an attempt to find enough space. In fact, it is hard to find a situation where *realloc* won't do and *_expand* must be used, instead.

EXAMPLE The following program shows use of the allocation, expansion and reallocation routines. Five runs are documented, each of which involved changing among members of the heap-specific memory management function groups. (Use of an example with *_bexpand* requires the designation of segments and the use of based pointers as described in the tutorial.

```
/* Shows allocation, expansion and reallocation functions */

#include <stdio.h>
#include <malloc.h>
#include <stdlib.h>
```

```
char bnr1[] = "the buffer cannot be";
char bnr2[] = "the memory block was";
char bnr3[] = "bytes allocated at";

void main(void)
{
    int  *bfr_intg;
    char *bfr_char;

    printf ("\nallocating two 1024 element buffers\n\n");

/* allocate for a character and then for an integer buffer*/

    if ((bfr_char = (char *)calloc (1024, sizeof (char) )) == NULL)
        exit (1);

    printf ("%d %s %Fp\n", _msize (bfr_char), bnr3, (void _far *)
            bfr_char);

    if ((bfr_intg = (int *)calloc (1024, sizeof (int) )) == NULL)
        exit (1);

    printf ("%d %s %Fp\n", _msize (bfr_intg), bnr3, (void _far *)
           bfr_intg);

/* expand buffer one and reallocate the second. The expansion will fail
if
a buffer is in the way, because _expand does not relocate*/

     printf ("\n");

    if ((bfr_char = (char *)_expand (bfr_char, 1024)) == NULL)
       printf ("%s expanded", bnr1);
    else
       printf ("%s expanded\n    to %d bytes at %Fp\n", bnr2,
          _msize (bfr_char), (void _far *) bfr_char);

    if ((bfr_intg = (int *)realloc (bfr_intg, 1024 * sizeof (int)
       )) == NULL)

       printf ("%s reallocated\n", bnr1);
    else
       printf ("%s reallocated to %d bytes at %Fp\n", bnr2,
          _msize (bfr_intg), (void _far *) bfr_intg);
```

```
/* free the memory */
   free (bfr_intg);
   free (bfr_char);
   exit (4);
}
```

The following results were achieved in five runs in which various combinations of the function calls were changed. As written above, the first run yielded:

```
allocating two 1024 element buffers

1024 bytes allocated at 1841:1184
2048 bytes allocated at 1841:1586

the memory block was expanded    to 1024 bytes at 1841:1184
the memory block was reallocated to 2048 bytes at 1841:1586
```

When the calls to *_size* were both changed to *_fmsize*, the addresses changed as follows:

```
allocating two 1024 element buffers

1024 bytes allocated at 24DE:1184
2048 bytes allocated at 24DE:1586

the memory block was expanded    to 1024 bytes at 24DE:1184
the memory block was reallocated to 2048 bytes at 24DE:1586
```

When the call to *_expand* was changed to *_fexpand*, without revising the *calloc* to operate on the far heap, one warning message was generated and the following results were printed:

```
allocating two 1024 element buffers

1024 bytes allocated at 24E2:1194
2048 bytes allocated at 24E2:1596

the buffer cannot be expanded
the memory block was reallocated to 2048 bytes at 24E2:1596
```

Switching all the appropriate calls to *_f* (*far*) versions yielded four copies of the warning message:

```
     "Compiler warning (level 2) C4059
     segment lost in conversion
     The conversion of a far pointer (a full segmented address) or based
pointer to a near pointer (a segment offset) or based pointer
resulted in the loss of the segment address."
```

and the following results:

```
allocating two 1024 element buffers
26956 bytes allocated at 24E6:0016 11630 bytes allocated at 24E6:0418
the buffer cannot be expanded the buffer cannot be reallocated
```

Readjusting all of the *_f* functions to *_n* versions resulted in no warning messages and the following output:

```
allocating two 1024 element buffers

1024 bytes allocated at 24CC:1184 2048 bytes allocated at 24CC:1586
the memory block was expanded    to 1024 bytes at 24CC:1184 the memory
block was reallocated to 2048 bytes at 24CC:1586 */
```

Note that actual results will vary with machine configuration.

COMPATIBILITY

free, _bfree, _ffree, hfree, _nfree

MSC 3	MSC 4	MSC 5	MSC 6	QC1	QC2	QC2.5	TC1	TC1.5	TC2	TC++	ANSI	UNIX V	XNX	OS2	DOS
▲	▲	▲	1	▲	▲	▲	▲	▲	▲	▲	▲	▲	▲	▲	▲

PURPOSE Use the *free* function and its variants to release a previously allocated storage block to the pool of free memory. Only blocks allocated by *malloc, calloc,* and *realloc* can be safely deallocated by *free*. The compiler automatically selects the appropriate variant of *_free* for the current memory model, as described below. Memory allocated by *halloc* must be released by calling *hfree*. Use the *_bfree* version to free a memory block in the based heap.

SYNTAX

```
void free (void *mem_address)

void _ffree (void _far *mem_address);

void _nfree (void _near *mem_address);

void hfree (void _huge *mem_address);

void _bfree (_segment seg_name, void _based (void) *mem_address);
```

`seg_name` *The selected based segment (for _bfree)*

`mem_address` *The allocated memory block*

EXAMPLE CALL

```
free(buffer);

_ffree((void far *)buffer);

_nfree((void near *)near_buffer);

hfree((void  _huge *)big_buffer);

_bfree(_DATA, based_buffer);
```

INCLUDES

`#include <malloc.h>` *For function declaration*

`#include <stdlib.h>` *For ANSI-compatibility*

DESCRIPTION The functions in the *free* family deallocate a memory block, returning the memory to the pool of free memory. The *mem_address* argument points to a memory block previously allocated through a call to the *calloc, malloc,* or *realloc* function groups. A NULL pointer argument is ignored. The *free* functions release the same number of bytes specified when the block was allocated (or, in the case of *realloc*, reallocated). The freed block is available for allocation after the *free* call.

The Microsoft C compiler maps *free* to specific deallocation routines, depending on the memory model in use. In the small and medium models, where data addresses are all near pointers, the function maps to *_nfree.* It maps to *_ffree* in the large and compact models where the compiler uses *far* data pointers. If you are using far or near pointers not implicitly supported by the memory model in use, you can use *_ffree* and *_nfree* directly to free memory that was allocated with *_fmalloc* and *_nmalloc*, respectively. Note that huge objects allocated with *halloc* must be deallocated with *hfree.* (See the tutorial for a discussion of the characteristics of the various memory models.)

The *_bfree* version frees a memory block in the based heap. It is the recommended way to release blocks called by *_bcalloc, _bmalloc,* or *_brealloc.* The *seg_name* argument in the based call specifies the based heap containing the memory block to be released by the *_bfree* function.

You may generate a significant number of errors if you attempt to free an *invalid* pointer. That will likely affect subsequent allocations, and cause errors. *Memory block* pointers that were not allocated with the appropriate call are invalid.

There are certain restrictions to the use of the *free, _ffree,* and *_nfree* functions:

If you allocated with:	Release with:
`calloc, malloc, realloc`	`free`
`_bcalloc, _bmalloc, _brealloc`	`_bfree`
`_fcalloc, _fmalloc, _frealloc`	`_ffree`
`_ncalloc, _nmalloc, _nrealloc`	`_nfree`
`halloc`	`hfree`

Programs that use the large data models—compact, large, and huge—cause *free* to map to *_ffree.* The small data programs—using the tiny, small, or medium model—have *free* mapped to *_nfree.* Since the prefix indicates the heap with which the function works, the large data models map to far pointers and the small data models map to near pointers.

1. Like the rest of the _based memory routines, this was introduced in version 6.0.

COMMON USES The *free* function is used with *malloc, calloc,* and *realloc* to free up memory used by data objects that are no longer needed. The *_ffree* and *_nfree* functions perform the same service for memory that was allocated with far or near pointers respectively.

COMMENTS The *free* function should only be used with *malloc, calloc,* and *realloc.* If you use *free* with the model-specific allocation routines *_nmalloc* and *_fmalloc*, the Microsoft C heap management algorithm may not work properly during future allocation and deallocation requests.

Moreover, memory allocated by *halloc* must be released by calling *hfree* because instead of using the memory management facilities of Microsoft C, *halloc* fulfills memory requests by directly calling MS-DOS.

SEE ALSO

`malloc, _fmalloc, _nmalloc, _bmalloc:`	*To allocate a block of storage*
`calloc, _fcalloc, _ncalloc, _bcalloc:`	*To allocate and initialize an array*
`realloc, _frealloc, _nrealloc, _brealloc:`	*To alter size of previously allocated block of memory*
`free[r, _ffree, _nfree, _bfree]:`	*To release memory allocated earlier*

RETURNS The *free* family of routines have no return value.

EXAMPLE Use *malloc* to allocate room for a 80-character string. Prompt the user for a string and store it in the buffer you allocated. Print the string and then deallocate the buffer by calling *free*. This example will work with *_ffree* if the memory is allocated with *_fmalloc* with a far pointer to the buffer. Additionally, the example will work with *_nfree* if the memory is allocated with *_nmalloc* and a near pointer to the buffer. To use the example with *_bfree*, define a segment and a based pointer as shown in the tutorial.

```
#include <stdio.h>
#include <stdlib.h>
#include <malloc.h>
#define MAX_CHR 80
main()
{
    unsigned char *buffer;
/* Allocate room for string and check for NULL */
    if( (buffer = (char *)malloc(MAX_CHR)) == NULL)
    {
        printf("Allocation Failed.\n");
        exit(0);
    }
    printf("Buffer allocated. Enter string to store: ");
    gets(buffer);
    printf("\nYou entered: %s\n",buffer);
    free((void *)buffer);    /* Deallocate the memory */
    printf("Buffer deallocated.\n");
}
```

If you declare a huge pointer with *halloc* you can free it with *hfree* as follows:

```
#include <stdio.h>
#include <stdlib.h>
#include <malloc.h>
#define MAX_SIZE 65000L
main()
{
    char huge *bigbuf;
/* Allocate room for string and check for NULL */
    if( (bigbuf = (char huge *)halloc(MAX_SIZE,
                          sizeof(char))) == NULL)
    {
        printf("Allocation by halloc Failed.\n");
```

```
        exit(0);
    }
    printf("Array of 65,000 characters allocated.\n");
/* Free the array and exit */
    hfree((void huge *)bigbuf);
    printf("Huge array deallocated\n");
}
```

See the program on the reference page for *expand* and the program on the reference page for *_heapseg* for additional examples of the use of *free* and its variants.

COMPATIBILITY

_freect

MSC 3	MSC 4	MSC 5	MSC 6	QC1	QC2	QC2.5	TC1	TC1.5	TC2	TC++	ANSI	UNIX V	XNX	OS2	DOS
	▲	▲	1	▲	▲	▲								▲	▲

PURPOSE Use the *_freect* function to determine the approximate number of elements of a given size that can be allocated in the default data segment.

SYNTAX

```
unsigned int _freect(size_t elem_size);

size_t elem_size;        Size of each data element in bytes
```

EXAMPLE CALL

```
room_for_integers = _freect(sizeof(int));
```

INCLUDES

```
#include <malloc.h>        For function declaration and definition of data type size_t
```

DESCRIPTION The *_freect* function computes the total number of data elements, each of size *elem_size* bytes, that can fit into the free space in the default data segment. So it is usually called with the argument *sizeof* (type). In contrast to this, the *_memavl* function simply returns the total number of bytes available for allocation in the default data segment.

1. Changed in Microsoft C 6.0 to no longer call *malloc*.

RETURNS The *_freect* function returns an unsigned integer with the number of elements of the specified size that can fit into the available memory in the default data segment.

SEE ALSO `_memavl` *To determine the total bytes in the available memory in the default data segment*

EXAMPLE Call *_freect* in a small program to determine how many integers can fit into the free memory in the default data segment. Then call *malloc* to allocate 1,000 integers and repeat the call to *_freect* to see how many more integers will fit into the leftover space.

```
#include <stdio.h>
#include <malloc.h>
main()
{
    int *iarray;
    printf("There is room for %u integers in the free \
space\n", _freect(sizeof(int)) );    /* call _freect */
    printf("in default data segment\n");
/* Now allocate memory for 1000 integers */
    if( (iarray = (int *) malloc(1000) ) == NULL)
    {
        printf("Error allocating memory\n");
        exit(0);
    }
    printf("Room for %u integers left after allocating \
1000 integers\n",
   _freect(sizeof(int)) );    /* Call _freect again */
}
```

_heapadd, _bheapadd

COMPATIBILITY

MSC 3	MSC 4	MSC 5	MSC 6	QC1	QC2	QC2.5	TC1	TC1.5	TC2	TC++	ANSI	UNIX V	XNX	OS2	DOS
		▲	1			▲								▲	▲

PURPOSE Use the *_heapadd* function to add memory to the heap. Use the *_bheapadd* routine to add memory to a specified based heap.

SYNTAX

```
int _heapadd (void _far *mem_block, size_t mem_size);

int _bheapadd (_segment seg_name, void _based (void)
                *mem_address, size_t elem_size);
```

`mem_block` Far *pointer to heap memory*

`seg_name` *The based heap segment selector (for* _bheapadd*)*

`mem_address` *Pointer to based memory (for* _bheapadd*)*

`elem_size` *The size in bytes of memory to add*

INCLUDES `#include <malloc.h>` *For function declaration*

DESCRIPTION The *_heapadd* and *_bheapadd* functions add an unused area of memory to the heap. The *_bheapadd* routine adds the memory to the based heap specified by the *seg_name* argument. The *_heapadd* function looks at the segment value. If the segment value is DGROUP, the memory is added to the near heap. Any other value results in *_heapadd* putting the memory on the far heap.

1. Both functions were introduced in version 6.0.

RETURNS A segment selector is returned by the *_bheapadd* routine if the call is successful. A successful call by *_heapadd* yields a 0. Both generate a −1 if the call fails.

EXAMPLE

```
/* Illustrate the "add" and "min" memory management functions */

#include <conio.h>
#include <malloc.h>
#include <process.h>
#include <stdio.h>

void heap_look (char *banner);     /* Prototype */

char str_1[] = {"This is a list of some colleges.  Stanford,
                    Michigan,\n" };

char str_2[] = {"Navy, Penn State, Notre Dame, UCLA, Amherst,
                    Ohio U.\n\n" };

void main()
{ int *aray[3];

   int cntr;     /* a loop counter */

   printf ("%s%s", str_1, str_2);
   printf ("They are being written to the heap.");

   heap_look ("the heap as of the start");

   /* add the example strings to the heap */
   _heapadd (str_1, sizeof (str_1));
   _heapadd (str_2, sizeof (str_2));

   heap_look ("the strings have been added");

   /* allocate blocks */
```

```
    for (cntr = 0; cntr < 4; cntr++)
       if ((aray[cntr] = (int *)calloc (10 * (cntr + 1),
             sizeof (int))) == NULL)
       { --cntr;
          break;
       }

    heap_look ("memory has been allocated");

    /* free some of the blocks. */

    free (aray[1]);
    free (aray[2]);
    heap_look ("some memory has been freed");

    /* minimize the heap */
    _heapmin();
    heap_look ("the heap has been 'minimized'");

    printf ("\nthis concludes the test\n");
    exit (4);
}

/* walk through the heap */

void heap_look (char *banner)

{
    struct _heapinfo hep_inf;
    printf ("\n%s\n", banner);
    hep_inf._pentry = NULL;

    while (_heapwalk (&hep_inf) == _HEAPOK)
       {
       printf ("\t%s block at %Fp of size %u\t\n",
       hep_inf._useflag == _USEDENTRY ? "USED" : "FREE",
       hep_inf._pentry, hep_inf._size);
       getch();
       }
}
```

The results of the program are printed below. The actual block addresses will vary with machine configuration, as will the USED and FREE designations.

```
This is a list of some colleges.  Stanford, Michigan,
Navy, Penn State, Notre Dame, UCLA, Amherst, Ohio U.

They are being written to the heap.
the heap as of the start
     USED block at 4567:0EEC of size 100
     USED block at 4567:0F52 of size 8
     USED block at 4567:0F5C of size 512
     FREE block at 4567:115E of size 3744

the strings have been added

     USED block at 4567:0EEC of size 100
     USED block at 4567:0F52 of size 8
     USED block at 4567:0F5C of size 512
     FREE block at 4567:115E of size 3744

memory has been allocated

     USED block at 4567:0EEC of size 100
     USED block at 4567:0F52 of size 8
     USED block at 4567:0F5C of size 512
     USED block at 4567:115E of size 20
     USED block at 4567:1174 of size 40
     USED block at 4567:119E of size 60
     USED block at 4567:11DC of size 80
     FREE block at 4567:122E of size 3536

some memory has been freed

     USED block at 4567:0EEC of size 100
     USED block at 4567:0F52 of size 8
     USED block at 4567:0F5C of size 512
     USED block at 4567:115E of size 20
     FREE block at 4567:1174 of size 40
     FREE block at 4567:119E of size 60
     USED block at 4567:11DC of size 80
     FREE block at 4567:122E of size 3536

the heap has been 'minimized'

     USED block at 4567:0EEC of size 100
     USED block at 4567:0F52 of size 8
     USED block at 4567:0F5C of size 512
     USED block at 4567:115E of size 20
     FREE block at 4567:1174 of size 102
```

```
    USED block at 4567:11DC of size 80
    FREE block at 4567:122E of size 0
*/
```

Note: use of the example with *_bheapadd* would require the designation of a segment and the use of based pointers, as explained in the tutorial.

_heapchk, _bheapchk, _fheapchk, _nheapchk

COMPATIBILITY

MSC 3	MSC 4	MSC 5	MSC 6	QC1	QC2	QC2.5	TC1	TC1.5	TC2	TC++	ANSI	UNIX V	XNX	OS2	DOS
		▲	1	▲	▲	▲			2,3	2,3				▲	▲

PURPOSE Use *_heapchk* functions to check the consistency of the heap, or the linked list of memory blocks from which functions such as *malloc* allocate memory. They are debugging tools to pinpoint problems related to memory allocation from the heap. Use the *_fheapchk* routine to check the far heap, the *_nheapchk* version to check the near heap, and the *_bheapchk* version to check based-heap memory.

SYNTAX

```
int _heapchk (void);

int _fheapchk (void);

int _nheapchk (void);

int _bheapchk (_segment seg_name);
```

`seg_name` *The based-heap segment to check (or _NULLSEG, to check all based heap segments) for* _bheapchk

EXAMPLE CALL

```
/* Verify status of the heap */

heapstat  (_heapchk (void));

fheapstat (_fheapchk (void));

nheapstat (_nheapchk (void));

bheapstat (_bheapchk (special_seg));
```

INCLUDES `#include <malloc.h>` *For function declaration*

DESCRIPTION The *_heapchk* family of functions—*_heapchk, _bheapchk, _fheapchk,* and *_nheapchk*—help you to debug heap related problems by checking for minimal consistency of the heap area of the memory. Each of the versions checks a particular heap. The *_heapchk* function (generic version) checks on a heap that is determined by the memory model of the program. In the compact, large, and huge memory models, *_heapchk* maps to *_fheapchk*. It maps to *_nheapchk* in the tiny, small, and medium memory models.

The *_bheapchk* version checks the based heap specified by *seg_name* argument. The far heap (outside the default data segment for your program) is the province of *_fheapchk*, and the near heap (which is inside your default data segment) is tested by the *_nheapchk* function.

1. The far and near versions date from Microsoft C 5.0. The *_bheapchk* version was introduced in version 6.0. 2. The Turbo C version of *_heapchk* is *heapcheck*. 3. The Turbo C version of *_fheapchk* is *farheapchk*.

COMMON USES The *_heapchk* function is used with its companions *_heapset* and *_heapwalk* to pinpoint problems related to the heap; for example, overwriting allocated memory.

RETURNS All four of the *_heapchk* routines return an integer value that is one of the following manifest constants (as defined in MALLOC.H): _HEAPOK, _HEAPEMPTY, _HEAPBADBEGIN, _HEAPBADNODE. The return value from *_heapchk* and its variants should be interpreted by comparing it with the constants shown in Table 5-3 and defined in the include file *malloc.h*.

Table 5-3. *Meaning of* _heapchk *Return Codes*

Constants	Interpretation of the constant
_HEAPOK	All entries in the linked list that make up the heap appear to be consistent (all addresses are within the limits of the memory block assigned to the heap).
_HEAPEMPTY	The heap is probably not initialized. This means the "heap checking" utility routine could not find any linked list data structure that would indicate an existing heap. This is the condition before any of the allocation routines are called.
_HEAPBADBEGIN	The initial header information of the heap data structure could not be found.
_HEAPBADNODE	A node in the linked list data structure of the heap was found to be bad. This may indicate overwriting beyond the array limits in a dynamically allocated array.

COMMENTS Ten functions—*calloc, _expand, free, _heapchk, _heapmin, _heapset, _heapwalk, malloc, _msize,* and *realloc*—are supplied in generic, _based, _far and _near versions. The based functions are named with a *_b* prefix. A leading *_f* is used to identify the far versions, and the near versions are named with an *_n* prefix. The leading underscore identifies the function as being a Microsoft-specific routine (and therefore not ANSI-C compatible) and appears only once in the function name. Thus the based version of *calloc* is *_bcalloc*, and the based version of *_expand* is *_bexpand*. The majority of these functions, including all of the based versions, were introduced in Microsoft C 6.0.

Using *_based*, the syntax of which is *_based (base) vrbl_nam*, specifies that a data object resides in the segment identified by the *_(base)* argument. (It is not assumed to reside in the current data segment.) Based pointers occupy 16 bits and are added to the base to provide a 32-bit address range.

The keyword *_segname* specifies the name of a segment of memory. Microsoft C 6.0 predefines four constants: *_CODE*, the default code segment; *_CONST*, the constant segment for strings such as *"His name is Dragi"*; *_DATA*, which is the default data segment; and *_STACK*, which is the stack segment. You may also make up your own.

The *_segname* keyword identifies the name of a segment. It must be followed by parentheses and a string, for instance:

```
#include <stdio.h>
#include <malloc.h>

char _based (_segname ("_CODE")) b_strng[] = "Her name is Candy.\n";
int  _based (_segname ("_CODE")) b_int = 9539;
/* code-based int */

void main()
{
     printf ("%Fs %d", (char _far *) b_strng, b_int);
}
```

where the character array variable *b_strng* and the *int* variable *b_int* are based in the code segment. The *_b_int* value is not a pointer.

SEE ALSO

`_heapset, _fheapset, _nheapset, _bheapset`	*To fill all unallocated memory in the heap with a specified character*
`_heapwalk, _fheapwalk, _nheapwalk, _bheapwalk`	*To navigate through the heap's linked list data structure and check the size and status (free or used) of blocks*

EXAMPLE Use *malloc* and *free* to allocate and deallocate a few blocks of memory. Then call *_heapchk* to check if the heap is in good shape. Display the information returned by *_heapchk*.

```
#include <stdio.h>
#include <malloc.h>
main()
{
   char *buffer;
   int heapstatus;
/* Perform some allocations and deallocations */
   buffer = (char *) malloc(500);
   malloc(800);
   free((void *)buffer);
/* Now get the status of the heap by calling _heapchk */
   heapstatus = _heapchk();
   switch (heapstatus)
   {
       case _HEAPOK:        printf("Heap OK\n");
                            break;
       case _HEAPEMPTY:     printf("Heap not initialized\n");
                            break;
       case _HEAPBADBEGIN: printf("Heap header bad\n");
                            break;
       case _HEAPBADNODE:   printf("Heap has bad node/s\n");
                            break;
   }
}
```

For the far heap, the declarations would be:

```
   char _far *buffer;
   int heapstatus;
```

The allocations and deallocations would be:

```
   buffer = (char _far *) _fmalloc(500);
   _fmalloc(800);
   _ffree((void _far *)buffer);
```

The rest of the program would be the same except that the status would be returned as *heapstatus = _fheapchk( );*.

For the *near* heap, the declarations would be:

```
   char _near *buffer;
   int heapstatus;
```

The allocations and deallocations would be:

```
buffer = (char _near *) _nmalloc(500);
_nmalloc(800);
_nfree((void _near *)buffer);
```

The rest of the program would be the same except that the status would be returned as *heapstatus = _nheapchk( );*.

For an additional example, see the reference entry for *heapset.*

_heapmin, _bheapmin, _fheapmin, _nheapmin

COMPATIBILITY

MSC 3	MSC 4	MSC 5	MSC 6	QC1	QC2	QC2.5	TC1	TC1.5	TC2	TC++	ANSI	UNIX V	XNX	OS2	DOS
			▲			▲								▲	▲

PURPOSE Use the *_heapmin* functions to release unused heap memory to the operating system. Releasing memory in the based heap is the job of *_bheapmin.* The *_fheapmin* version is used to release memory in the far heap. Use *_nheapmin* to release near heap memory.

SYNTAX

```
int _heapmin (void);

int _bheapmin (segment seg_name);

int _fheapmin (void);

int _nheapmin (void);
```

`seg_name` *Based heap segments to minimize, or _NULLSEG for all based heap segments (for* _bheapmin)

EXAMPLE CALL

```
_heapmin  (void);

_bheapmin (exampl_sgmnt);

_fheapmin (void);

_nheapmin (void);
```

DESCRIPTION The *_heapmin* group of functions helps minimize memory consumption by releasing unused heap back to the operating system. The *_heapmin* function, as explained below, operates according to the data model of the program in which it is run. The *_bheapmin* function frees the based heap as specified by the segment value (_NULLSEG specifies all based heaps). The *_fheapmin* routine frees the far heap outside the default data segment, while *_nheapmin* works with the near heap. The near heap is inside the default data segment.

COMMON USES Conserving memory is a growing problem as applications become more complex. The various *_heapmin* functions allow your program to free the parts of the heap that it doesn't need.

RETURNS The *_heapmin* function family returns a −1 in the event of an error, and a value of 0 if the call was a success.

COMMENTS When used in large data models (compact, large, and huge) *_heapmin* defaults to *_fheapmin*. The small data models (tiny, small, and medium) cause *_heapmin* to map to *_nheapmin*. This is one of the ten memory management functions supplied in generic, based, far, and near versions. The other nine functions include *calloc, _expand, free, _heapchk, _heapset, _heapwalk, malloc, _msize,* and *realloc*. The *_based* functions are named with a *_b* prefix. A leading *_f* is used to identify the *_far* versions, and the *near* versions are named with an *_n* prefix. Therefore, the generic *heapmin* defaults to *near* behavior in smaller programs and *_far* behavior in larger ones—exactly as you would expect.

A based heap segment cannot be unlinked from the based heap list and released to the operating system by a *_bheapmin* call; instead, the release of based segments is accomplished through a call to *_bfreeseg*.

EXAMPLE See the program on the reference page for *_heapadd*.

COMPATIBILITY

_heapset, _bheapset, _fheapset, _nheapset

MSC 3	MSC 4	MSC 5	MSC 6	QC1	QC2	QC2.5	TC1	TC1.5	TC2	TC++	ANSI	UNIX V	XNX	OS2	DOS
		▲	1	▲	▲	▲				2,3				▲	▲

PURPOSE Use the *_heapset* family of functions to check for memory consistency followed by writing or "setting" a specified fill value to the memory area identified in the arguments. For example, you can use *_heapset* to fill all unallocated memory with a specific character (or byte value) so that you can later identify an area that was accidently overwritten.

SYNTAX

```
int _heapset (unsigned int fill_val);

int _fheapset (unsigned int fill_val);

int _nheapset (unsigned int fill_val);

int _bheapset (_segment seg_name, unsigned int fill_val);
```

`seg_name` *Based heap segment selector (or* _NULLSEG *for all based heap segments) for* _bheapset `fill_val` *The character or byte value with which to fill the unused memory locations in the specified heap*

EXAMPLE CALL

```
heapstatus = _heapset ('H');  /* fill generic with 'H' */

heapstatus = _fheapset ('F'); /* fill far with 'F' */

heapstatus = _nheapset ('N'); /* fill near with 'N' */

heapstatus = _bheapset (_sgmnt_nam, 'B'); /* fill based with 'B' */
```

INCLUDES `#include <malloc.h>` *For function declaration*

DESCRIPTION The *_heapset* functions help you identify heap related problems. They show you free memory locations and/or nodes that were unintentionally overwritten. First, the *_heapset* functions check the specified heap for minimal consistency, performing the work of the *_heapchk* function family. Then, upon completion of the consistency check, the *_heapset* routines set or write each byte of the free entries in the specified heap to the specified fill value, giving you a consistent value for all free memory. This consistency makes it easier to spot which memory areas are being used and which are lying fallow. You can examine the memory using various utility programs or the CodeView debugger, and thereby identify which locations of the heap contain free nodes or discover where data was unintentionally written to an area you believe should still contain free memory.

The *_heapset* function (generic version) checks on a heap that is determined by the memory model of the program. In the compact, large, and huge memory models, *_heapset* defaults to *_fheapset.* It maps to *_nheapset* in the tiny, small, and medium memory models.

The *_bheapset* version checks the based heap specified by *seg_name* argument. The far heap (outside the default data segment for your program) is the province of *_fheapset,* and the near heap (which is inside your default data segment) is tested by the *_nheapset* function.

1. The *_bheapset* version was introduced in version 6.0. The far and near versions date from Microsoft C 5.0. 2. The Turbo C++ equivalent for *_heapset* is *heapfillfrec.* 3. The Turbo C++ equivalent for *_fheapset* is *farheapfillfree.*

COMMON USES The *_heapset* function and its variants are used to locate errors in the program that may be overwriting dynamically allocated data in the heap. After filling the unused memory with a known character, you can determine overwritten locations by examining the range of heap locations. The *_heapwalk* function and its variants allow you to access each block of memory in the heap individually and examine it, if necessary.

RETURNS The four *_heapset* routines return an type of *int* whose value is a constant defined in MALLOC.H. A value of _HEAPBADBEGIN indicates that the header information was not found, or it was invalid. A return of _HEAPBADNODE is a warning that a bad node was found, or that the heap is damaged. The _HEAPEMPTY return means that the heap has not been initialized, and _HEAPOK is your signal that the heap is consistent and now ready for use.

COMMENTS The *_heapset* functions are members of a group of ten memory management functions supplied in generic, _based, _far, and _near versions. (The other nine functions in the group are *calloc, _expand, free, _heapchk, _heapmin, _heapwalk, malloc, _msize,* and *realloc.*) The *_based* functions are named with a *_b* prefix. A leading *_f* is used to identify the *far* versions, and the *near* versions are named with an *_n* prefix. The leading underscore identifies the function as being a Microsoft-specific routine (and therefore not ANSI-C compatible) and appears only once in the function name. Thus the *_based* version of *calloc* is *_bcalloc,* and the *_based* version of *_expand* is *_bexpand.* The majority of these functions, including all of the _based versions, were introduced in Microsoft C 6.0.

The *_heapset* function and its variants are meant for use with the appropriate *_heapwalk* variant to locate causes of program failure due to overwriting dynamically created data objects in the heap. While *_heapset* lets you fill the unused memory with a known character, *_heapwalk* allows you to access each block individually. These functions, used to manipulate the heap from C programs, were introduced in Microsoft C version 5.0 and are very helpful in debugging mishaps caused by inadvertent damage to the heap.

Call a memory allocation function before using *_heapset* so that the heap is initialized; otherwise there will not be any blocks, free or used, with which to work.

SEE ALSO

`_heapchk, _fheapchk, _nheapchk, _bheapchk`	*To check the heap's linked list data structure for consistency*
`_heapwalk, _fheapwalk, _nheapwalk, _bheapwalk`	*To traverse through the heap's linked list data structure and check the size and free or used status of blocks*

EXAMPLE The following program shows usage of the check, set, walk and size families of memory management functions.

```
#include <conio.h>
#include <malloc.h>
#include <stdio.h>
```

```
#include <stdlib.h>
#include <time.h>

void main     (void);                  /* prototypes */
void heap_look (char  fill);
void heap_stts (int   status);

/* macro to get random integer from within a range */
#define getrandom( min, max ) ((rand() % (int)(((max)+1) - (min))) +
(min))

void main (void)
{
   int *h_adrs[4] step;
   srand ((unsigned)time (NULL));  /* Seed with current time */

   /* chk status of heap */
   heap_stts (_heapchk());

   /* work with heap - allocating random-size blocks */

   for (step = 0; step < 3; step++)
   {
      if ((h_adrs[step] = (int *)calloc (getrandom (1, 6000),
            sizeof (int))) == NULL)
      {
         --step;
         break;
      }
      printf ("allocated %6u at address %Fp\n", _msize
            (h_adrs[step]),
            (void _far *)h_adrs[step]);
   }

   /* fill the free blocks with a specified character */
   heap_stts (_heapset (254));

   /* verify the status with heap_look */
   heap_look (254); /* Gives warning, but MSC converts */

   /* more heap manipulation */

   for (; step >= 0; step--)
   {
      free (h_adrs[step]);
```

```
      printf ("deallocated %6u at adrs %Fp\n",
             _msize (h_adrs[step]), (void _far *)h_adrs[step]);
   }

   /* verify the status with heap_look */
   heap_look (254);
}

/* look at each block in the heap */

void heap_look (char fill)
{
   struct _heapinfo hp_inf;
   int hep_stt, stpr;
   char _far *hp_lst;

   /* heapwalk, displaying results and checking the free blocks    */

   printf ("\nheap dump:\n");
   hp_inf._pentry = NULL;
   while ((hep_stt = _heapwalk (&hp_inf)) == _HEAPOK)
   {
      printf ("\n%s block at adrs %Fp of size %6u   ",
      hp_inf._useflag ==_USEDENTRY ? "USED" : "FREE",
            hp_inf._pentry, hp_inf._size);

   /* check each free byte to verify that it has only the fill     */

      if (hp_inf._useflag != _USEDENTRY)
      {
         for (hp_lst = (char _far *) hp_inf._pentry, stpr = 0;
                  stpr < hp_inf._size; hp_lst++, stpr++)
               if ((char)*hp_lst != fill) break;
            if (stpr == hp_inf._size) printf ("Not changed");
         else
            printf ("Changed");
      }
   }

   heap_stts (hep_stt);
}

/* status reports */

void heap_stts (int status)
```

```
        char bnr1[] = "OKAY, the heap is ";
        char bnr2[] = "ERROR, a bad ";
        char bnr3[]     = " to the heap";

        printf ("\n\nthe current status of the heap: ");

        switch (status)

        {

        case _HEAPBADPTR:

            printf ("%spointer%s", bnr2, bnr3);
            break;

        case _HEAPBADBEGIN:

            printf ("%sstart%s", bnr2, bnr3);
            break;

        case _HEAPBADNODE:

            printf ("%snode%s", bnr2, bnr3);

        case _HEAPOK:

            printf ("%sfine", bnr1);
            break;

        case _HEAPEMPTY:

            printf ("%sempty", bnr1);
            break;

        case _HEAPEND:

            printf ("%sat the end", bnr1);
            break;
    }
    printf ("\n\n");
}
```

The results of a run follow. Note that details will vary with system configuration.

```
the current status of the heap: OKAY, the heap is fine

allocated   6282 at address 3013:1354
allocated    544 at address 3013:2BE0
allocated   4334 at address 3013:2E02

the current status of the heap: OKAY, the heap is fine


heap dump:

USED block at adrs 3013:103C of size    256
USED block at adrs 3013:113E of size     18
USED block at adrs 3013:1152 of size    512
USED block at adrs 3013:1354 of size   6282
USED block at adrs 3013:2BE0 of size    544
USED block at adrs 3013:2E02 of size   4334
FREE block at adrs 3013:3EF2 of size    268  Not changed

the current status of the heap: OKAY, the heap is at the end

deallocated  24946 at adrs 3013:0019
deallocated   4334 at adrs 3013:2E02
deallocated    544 at adrs 3013:2BE0
deallocated   6282 at adrs 3013:1354

heap dump:

USED block at adrs 3013:103C of size    256
USED block at adrs 3013:113E of size     18
USED block at adrs 3013:1152 of size    512
FREE block at adrs 3013:1354 of size   6282   Changed
FREE block at adrs 3013:2BE0 of size    544   Changed
FREE block at adrs 3013:2E02 of size   4334   Changed
FREE block at adrs 3013:3EF2 of size    268   Not changed

the current status of the heap: OKAY, the heap is at the end
```

_heapwalk, _bheapwalk, _fheapwalk, _nheapwalk

COMPATIBILITY

MSC 3	MSC 4	MSC 5	MSC 6	QC1	QC2	QC2.5	TC1	TC1.5	TC2	TC++	ANSI	UNIX V	XNX	OS2	DOS
		▲	1	▲	▲	▲				2,3				▲	▲

PURPOSE Use the *_heapwalk* function and its variants to traverse through the entries in the linked list data structure that makes up the heap, or the pool of free memory blocks from which functions such as *malloc* allocate memory. Each call to *_heapwalk* returns a pointer to the next actual block of memory in the heap, determines its size, and decides whether it is free or in use. When you use *_heapwalk*, the compiler automatically selects the appropriate variant for the memory model in use, as described below. Use *_bheapwalk* to walk through the specified based heap segment.

SYNTAX

```
int _heapwalk (_HEAPINFO *heap_entry );

int _fheapwalk (_HEAPINFO *heap_entry);

int _nheapwalk (_HEAPINFO *heap_entry);

int _bheapwalk (_segment seg_name, _HEAPINFO *heap_entry);
```

`seg_name` *A* _based *heap selector (or* _NULLSEG *for all _based heap segments) For* _bheapwalk

`heap_entry` *A structure of type* _HEAPINFO, *defined in MALLOC.H, to contain information about the next heap*

EXAMPLE CALL

```
heapstatus = _heapwalk(&heapinfo);          /* regular heap */
heapstatus = _fheapwalk(&heapinfo);         /* far heap */
heapstatus = _nheapwalk(&heapinfo);         /* near heap */
heapstatus = _bheapwalk(_DATA, &heapinfo);/*based heap */
```

INCLUDES `#include <malloc.h>` *For function declaration and definition of structure* _heapinfo

DESCRIPTION The *_heapwalk* family of functions help you debug heap related problems in programs. They walk through the specified heap, traversing one entry per call, and return a pointer to a structure of type *_heapinfo* (defined in MALLOC.H) that contains information about the next heap entry. This structure is defined as follows:

```
struct _heapinfo
{
    int far *_pentry;        /* Pointer to next heap entry   */
    size_t  _size;           /* Size of this block of memory */
```

```
    int      _useflag;       /* Flag to indicate if block is "in use" */
};
```

A successful *_heapwalk* call will return _HEAPOK, store the size of the entry in the *_size* field, and set the *_useflag* field to either _FREEENTRY or _USEDENTRY (constants defined in MALLOC.H). You may get this information about the first entry in the heap by passing *_heapwalk* a pointer to a *_heapinfo* type structure where the *_heapinfo._pentry* field evaluates to a NULL.

Members of the *_heapwalk* family behave as follows: The *_heapwalk* version walks a heap that is determined by the memory model of the program in which it is running. This is true of all of the generic versions of the ten memory functions that appear in generic, _based, _far, and _near formats. When used in large data models (compact, large, and huge), *_heapwalk* defaults to *_fheapwalk*. The small data models (tiny, small, and medium) cause *_heapwalk* to map to *_nheapwalk*. The *_bheapwalk* version operates on the based heap specified by *seg_name* value, though a _NULLSEG specifies all based heaps. The near heap is walked by the *_nheapwalk* version, and the far heap (the area outside the default data segment) is the area of interest to the *_fheapwalk* function.

1. The *_bheapwalk* variant was added in Microsoft C 6.0. 2. The Turbo C equivalent for *_heapwalk* is *heapwalk*. 3. The Turbo C equivalent for *_fheapwalk* is *farheapwalk*.

COMMON USES The *_heapwalk* function and its variants are used to locate errors in the program that may be inadvertently overwriting dynamically allocated data in the heap. You can first call *_heapset* to fill all the free memory in the heap with a known character. Now you can determine overwritten locations by examining them. The *_heapwalk* function is used to step through the blocks in the heap and examine each one, if necessary.

RETURNS A call to a member of the *_heapwalk* family may yield a return value of _HEAPOK, _HEAPEMPTY, _HEAPBADPTR, _HEAPBADBEGIN, _HEAPBADNODE, or _HEAPEND. These values are further described in Table 5-4 accompanying the reference entry for *heapwalk*. There are two "status" constants posted to the *_useflag* field of the *_heapinfo* structure: _FREEENTRY and _USEDENTRY. These constants indicate the status of the heap entry.

Table 5-4. *Return Values from* _heapwalk

Constant	Interpretation
_HEAPOK	The entries of the heap are all right up to the current one. In this case, the *_heapinfo* structure contains information about the next entry in the heap's linked list data.

Table 5-4. *(cont.)*

Constant	Interpretation
_HEAPEMPTY	The heap is probably not initialized. This means no calls have been made to a memory allocation routine.
_HEAPBADPTR	The *_pentry* field in the *_heapinfo* data structure does not contain a valid pointer to an entry in the heap.
_HEAPBADBEGIN	The initial header information of the heap data structure could not be found.
_HEAPBADNODE	A node in the linked list data structure of the heap was found to be bad. This may indicate overwriting beyond the array limits in a dynamically allocated array.
_HEAPEND	The end of the heap was reached successfully.

COMMENTS The *_heapinfo* structure is defined in *malloc.h* as:

```
typedef struct _heapinfo { int _far * _pentry; size_t _size;
int _useflag; } _HEAPINFO;
```

SEE ALSO `_heapchk, _fheapchk, _nheapchk, _bheapchk` *To check the heap's linked list data structure for consistency*

`_heapwalk, _fheapwalk, _nheapwalk, _bheapwalk` *To navigate through the heap's linked list data structure and check the size and status (free or used) of blocks*

EXAMPLE The following program uses *_heapwalk* to traverse through all the entries of the heap and prints a short report about the entries. Test the routine by calling it from a main program where a number of allocation and deallocation operations are performed. Notice that the heap is uninitialized until the first call to a memory allocation function.

```
#include <stdio.h>
#include <malloc.h>
static void traverse_heap (void);
main()
{
    char *buffer;

    traverse_heap();            /* Uninitialized heap */
    buffer = (char *) malloc(80); /* Allocate a buffer*/
    traverse_heap();     /* Check heap entries now    */
    free(buffer);        /* Release the buffer        */
```

```
    traverse_heap();     /* Check heap entries again  */
}

static void traverse_heap(void)
{
    struct _heapinfo heapentry;
    int heapstatus;
/* Set _pentry field to NULL to begin at first entry */
    heapentry._pentry = NULL;
/* Now keep calling _heapwalk as long as return value
 * is _HEAPOK. Print information about entry from the
 * structure 'heapentry'
 */
    printf("-------- BEGIN HEAP TRAVERSAL ---------\n");
    while ( (heapstatus = _heapwalk(&heapentry)) ==
              _HEAPOK)
    {
       printf("Address: %p  Status: %6s  Size: %5u\n",
              heapentry._pentry, (heapentry._useflag ==
              _FREEENTRY ? "FREE" : "USED"),
              heapentry._size);
    }
    switch (heapstatus)  /* Print last status */
    {
       case _HEAPOK:       printf("Heap OK\n");
                           break;
       case _HEAPEMPTY:    printf("Heap not initialized\n");
                           break;
       case _HEAPBADBEGIN: printf("Heap header bad\n");
                            break;
       case _HEAPBADNODE: printf("Heap has bad node/s\n");
                           break;
    }
    printf("----------- END HEAP TRAVERSAL --------\n");
}
```

For the far heap, the declarations are:

```
    struct _heapinfo heapentry;
    char far *buffer;
```

The buffer allocation and heap status check is:

```
    buffer = (char far *) _fmalloc(80);
    _fmalloc(500);      /* Another one ...     */
    _ffree(buffer);     /* Free the first one */
```

```
heapentry._pentry = NULL;
printf("-------- BEGIN HEAP TRAVERSAL ---------\n");
while (  _fheapwalk(&heapentry) == _HEAPOK)
```

The rest of the program is the same as in the first example.

For the near heap, the declarations are:

```
struct _heapinfo heapentry;
char near *buffer;
```

The buffer allocation and heap status check is:

```
buffer = (char near *) _nmalloc(80);
_nmalloc(500);              /* Another one ...    */
_nfree(buffer);             /* Free the first one */

heapentry._pentry = NULL;
printf("-------- BEGIN HEAP TRAVERSAL ---------\n");
while (  _nheapwalk(&heapentry) == _HEAPOK)
```

The rest of the program is the same as in the first example. To use *_bheapwalk*, you must first designate a segment and create a based pointer as described in the tutorial.

See the example program on the reference page for *_heapset* for an additional example.

malloc, _bmalloc, _fmalloc, _nmalloc

COMPATIBILITY

MSC 3	MSC 4	MSC 5	MSC 6	QC1	QC2	QC2.5	TC1	TC1.5	TC2	TC++	ANSI	UNIX V	XNX	OS2	DOS
▲	▲	1	2	▲	▲	▲	▲	▲	▲	▲	▲	▲	▲	▲	▲

PURPOSE A call to a *_malloc* family function is used to allocate memory in a specified based segment. Note that *malloc* can only allocate memory for an array whose size is less than 64-K bytes. Use the *halloc* function to allocate arrays larger than 64 K.

SYNTAX

```
void *malloc (size_t elem_size);

void _far *_fmalloc (size_t elem_size);

void _near *_nmalloc (size_t elem_size);

void _based (void) *_bmalloc (_segment seg_name, size_t
                                    elem_size);
```

```
seg_name        The based heap segment selector (for _bmalloc)

elem_size       The number of bytes to allocate
```

EXAMPLE CALL

```
buffer = (char *)malloc(100*sizeof(char));     /* malloc */

far_int_buffer = (int _far *)_fmalloc(10000);  /* far items */

near_int_buffer = (int _near *)_nmalloc(100*sizeof(int));
                                                /* near items*/

based_buffer =(int _based *)_bmalloc(_DATA,100*sizeof(int));
                                                /*based pointer*/
```

INCLUDES

```
#include <malloc.h>     For function declaration and definition of data type size_t

#include <stdlib.h>     For ANSI-compatibility
```

DESCRIPTION The *malloc* group of functions allocates a memory block of at least *elem_size* bytes. The block may turn out to be larger than the value of *elem_size* bytes because of space required for maintenance data and for alignment. The *malloc* routine will allocate a zero-length item in the heap and return a *valid* pointer to any item specified as having a *elem_size* of zero.

The *malloc* functions guarantee that the storage space pointed to by the return value is appropriately aligned for storage of any type of object. A pointer to a type other than *void* may be returned if you use a type cast on the return value.

The generic *malloc* version follows the mapping rules we have identified for *_heapset, _heapchk,* and the other memory functions that are clustered into heap-specific versions: the compact, large, and huge model programs map to the _far version (*_fmalloc*); and the tiny, small, and medium models map to the _near version (*_nmalloc*).

The *_bmalloc* version allocates a memory block of at least *elem_size* bytes in the based heap segment specified by the selector *seg_name.* It was introduced in version 6.0. The *_fmalloc* version deals with the far heap, and it is called by three C run-time routines: *_frealloc, _fcalloc,* and *_fstrdup.* The *_nmalloc* version deals with the near heap and is also called by three run-time routines: *_nrealloc, _ncalloc,* and *_nstrdup.*

1. The *malloc* function was changed in Microsoft C 5.0 to return a NULL rather than a zero-length heap item. 2. The *_fmalloc* function was changed in Microsoft C 6.0 to return a NULL instead of retrying an allocation in a default data segment.

COMMON USES The *malloc* function and its variants are used to create room for arrays of data objects at run-time. This allows you to write programs without having to guess beforehand the total amount of storage that will be needed at run-time.

RETURNS The *malloc* function returns a pointer of type *void* to the allocated space. The *_nmalloc* version returns a pointer of *(void _near *)* type, and the *_fmalloc* routine returns a pointer of *(void _far *)*. The return from a *_bmalloc* call is *(void _based (void) *)*.

The *_malloc, _fmalloc,* and *_nmalloc* functions return NULL if there is insufficient memory available to allocate the desired space. The return from *_bmalloc* under that circumstance is _NULLOFF. Recommended practice is to always check the status of the return from one of the *malloc* functions because an error may affect most subsequent memory operations.

COMMENTS The *malloc* function is the basic memory allocation function in Microsoft C run-time library. The *calloc* function calls *malloc* to do the actual memory allocation.

Note that when using *malloc* to allocate storage for a specific data type, you should cast the returned *void* pointer to that type, as shown in the Example Calls.

Microsoft recommends that you bind with APILMR.OBJ as well as API.LIB and OS2.LIB whenever you create a program that runs in both real mode and protected mode. This shifts from a recommendation to a requirement for any program that uses the *_nmalloc* function.

The following routines call the *malloc* functions:

```
calloc      fgets       getc        puts        spawnve
execl       fprintf     getchar     putw        spawnvp
execle      fputc       getcwd      realloc     spawnvpe
execlp      fputchar    _getdcwd    scanf       strdup
execlpe     fputs       gets        _searchenv  system
execv       fread       getw        setvbuf     tempnam
execve      fscanf      _popen      spawnl      ungetc
execvp      fseek       printf      spawnle     vfprintf
execvpe     fsetpos     putc        spawnlp     vprintf
fgetc       _fullpath   putchar     spawnlpe
fgetchar    fwrite      putenv      spawnv
```

The following routines call *malloc* only in the OS/2 multithread run-time libraries (CDLLOBJS, LLIBCMT, LLIBCDLL), but not in the regular run-time DOS libraries:

asctime	localtime	_strerror
_beginthread	mktime	tmpfile
ctime	strerror	tmpnam
gmtime		

The *_fmalloc* version in Microsoft C 5.1 would retry allocating within the default data segment if sufficient memory was not available outside the default data segment. The Microsoft C 6.0 version of *_fmalloc* returns a NULL under these conditions.

The C start-up code uses *malloc* to allocate storage for the environ/envp[] and argv[] strings and arrays. In Microsoft C 5.1, the start-up code used *malloc* only if wild-card expansion was used. Another Microsoft C 5.1 item of which to be aware is that the 5.1 versions of *_freect*, *_memavl*, and *_memmax* called *malloc*, but the Microsoft C 6.0 versions do not.

SEE ALSO

calloc, _fcalloc, _ncalloc, _bcalloc:	*To allocate and initialize an array*
halloc:	*To allocate* _huge *(greater than 64KB) arrays*
realloc, _frealloc, _nrealloc, _brealloc:	*To alter size of previously allocated block of memory*
free, _ffree, _nfree, _bfree:	*To release memory allocated earlier*

EXAMPLE The following program using *malloc* allocates room for a 80-character string. It prompts the user for a string and stores it in the buffer you allocated.

```
#include <stdio.h>
#include <stdlib.h>
#include <malloc.h>
#define MAX_CHR 80
main()
{
```

```
    unsigned char *buffer;
/* Allocate room for string and check for NULL pointer*/
    if( (buffer = (char *)malloc(MAX_CHR)) == NULL)
    {
        printf("Allocation Failed.\n");
        exit(0);
    }
    printf("Buffer allocated. Enter string to store: ");
    gets(buffer);
    printf("\nYou entered: %s\n",buffer);
}
```

For *_fmalloc* the declaration and call would be:

```
    unsigned char far *buffer;
/* Allocate room for string and check for NULL pointer*/
    if( (buffer = (char far *)_fmalloc(MAX_CHR))
         == NULL)
    {
         printf("Allocation Failed.\n");
         exit(0);
    }
```

For *_nmalloc*, the declaration and call would be:

```
    unsigned char near *buffer;
/* Allocate room for string and check for NULL */
    if( (buffer = (char near *)_nmalloc(MAX_CHR))
         == NULL)
    {
         printf("Allocation Failed.\n");
         exit(0);
    }
```

The program in the reference entry for *_heapseg* shows usage of the *_bmalloc* function.

COMPATIBILITY

_memavl

MSC 3	MSC 4	MSC 5	MSC 6	QC1	QC2	QC2.5	TC1	TC1.5	TC2	TC++	ANSI	UNIX V	XNX	OS2	DOS
	▲	▲	1	▲	▲	▲								▲	▲

PURPOSE Use the *_memavl* function to determine the number of bytes available in the default data segment beyond the space already being used by the program's data. For example, you can use *_memavl* in small and medium models to determine memory available for allocation before calling *calloc* or *malloc*.

SYNTAX

```
size_t _memavl(void);
```

EXAMPLE CALL

```
available_memory = _memavl();
```

INCLUDES

```
#include <malloc.h>
```

For function declaration and definition of data type size_t

DESCRIPTION The *_memavl* function returns the number of bytes available in the default data segment from which *malloc*, *calloc*, and *realloc* allocate memory in the small and medium models. In *all* memory models the function *_nmalloc* can be used to allocate memory in the default data segment. You can use *_memavl* in all memory models to make sure enough memory is available before calling the allocation routine. Note, however, that the size returned by *_memavl* is not necesarily contiguous bytes. There is no guarantee, therefore, that a call to *_nmalloc* to allocate the entire amount will succeed. To find the largest block of contiguous bytes, you can use *_memmax*.

1. Changed in Microsoft C 6.0 to no longer call *malloc*.

RETURNS The return value from *_memavl* is an unsigned integer of type *size_t* containing the number of bytes available for allocation in the default data segment.

SEE ALSO

`malloc, calloc, realloc`	*To allocate memory from the heap*
`_nmalloc`	*Always allocates memory from the default data segment*
`free`	*To release memory allocated earlier*

EXAMPLE Call the *_memavl* function to determine the number of bytes available in the default data segment. Use *malloc* to allocate room for a buffer to hold 8,000 characters. Now call *_memavl* again to see how many bytes are available after allocating these 8,000 bytes. Compile and run the program in the small model, then in the large model, and note the difference. In the large model the amount of available memory remains unchanged because *malloc* allocates outside the default data segment.

```
#include <stdio.h>
#include <malloc.h>
main()
{
    size_t max_bytes;
    char *large_buffer;
/* Check how much room is available in the default data
 * segment
 */
    max_bytes = _memavl();
    printf("%u bytes available in the data segment\n",
           max_bytes);
/* Allocate 8000 bytes  */
    large_buffer = (char *) malloc(8000);
/* Check available memory again */
    max_bytes = _memavl();
    printf("%u bytes available after allocating 8000 \
bytes\n", max_bytes);
}
```

_memmax

COMPATIBILITY

MSC 3	MSC 4	MSC 5	MSC 6	QC1	QC2	QC2.5	TC1	TC1.5	TC2	TC++	ANSI	UNIX V	XNX	OS2	DOS
	▲	▲	1	▲	▲	▲								▲	▲

PURPOSE Use the *_memmax* function to determine the maximum number of *contiguous* bytes that can be allocated from the default data segment. Use *_memmax* in the small or the medium models, for example, to find the largest chunk of memory that you can allocate by using *malloc*.

SYNTAX

```
size_t _memmax(void);
```

EXAMPLE CALL

```
max_single_block_size = _memmax();
```

INCLUDES `#include <malloc.h>` *For function declaration and definition of data type* size_t

DESCRIPTION The *_memmax* function returns the size of the largest block of memory available in the default data segment. Use *_memavl* to determine the *total* amount of memory available, which together with *_memmax* suggests how many smaller sized blocks may be allocated. Note that since we want to use *printf( )* to print a message, we must call that function at least once before calling *memmax( )*. This ensures that the buffer that *printf( )* uses for formatting data will be set up before, not after, the call to *memmax( )*, and the latter will correctly reflect the amount of memory available for allocation.

1. Changed in MSC 6.0 to no longer call *malloc*.

COMMON USES In the small and medium memory models *malloc* allocates memory from the default data segment while *_nmalloc* allocates space from this segment in all memory models. Before calling the allocation routine, it is useful to call *_memmax* to determine the largest chunk of memory that can be allocated. A call of the form *malloc(_memsize( ))* can also be used to allocate the largest available block.

RETURNS The return value from *_memmax* is the size of the largest block of contiguous memory available for allocation in the default data segment.

SEE ALSO `_memavl` *To determine the total number of bytes available for allocation in the default data segment*

EXAMPLE Use *_memmax* with *_nmalloc* to allocate the largest chunk of contiguous memory from the default data segment.

```
#include <stdio.h>
#include <malloc.h>
main()
{
    char near *buffer;
    size_t max_bytes;
/* Find size of largest block */
    printf("Calling printf() to allocate
    buffer for formatting\n");
    max_bytes = _memmax();
    printf("%u bytes in largest contiguous block\n",
           max_bytes);
    if( (buffer = (char near *) _nmalloc(max_bytes) )
        == NULL)
    {
        printf("Error allocating buffer\n");
        exit(0);
    }
    printf("%u contiguous bytes allocated \
successfully\n", max_bytes);
}
```

_msize, _bmsize, _fmsize, _nmsize

COMPATIBILITY

MSC 3	MSC 4	MSC 5	MSC 6	QC1	QC2	QC2.5	TC1	TC1.5	TC2	TC++	ANSI	UNIX V	XNX	OS2	DOS
	▲	▲	1	▲	▲	▲								▲	▲

PURPOSE Use the *_msize* function family to determine the byte size of a block of memory that has been allocated or manipulated by the *malloc, calloc,* or *realloc* function groups.

SYNTAX

```
size_t _msize (void *mem_address);

size_t _fmsize (void _far *mem_address);

size_t _nmsize (void _near *mem_address);

size_t_bmsize (_segment seg_name, void _based (void)
                *mem_address);
```

`seg_name` *Based heap segment selector (for* _bmsize

`mem_address` *Pointer to an allocated memory block the size of which is to be determined*

EXAMPLE CALL

```
/* for regular pointer */
blocksize = _msize(p_block);

/* for _far pointer */
blocksize = _fmsize((void _far *)buffer);

/* for _near pointer */
bufsize = _nmsize(_near_buffer);

/* for _based pointer */
blocksize = _msize (mem_blk);
```

INCLUDES `#include <malloc.h>` *For function declaration and definition type* size_t

DESCRIPTION The family of *_msize* functions return the byte size of the memory block allocated by a call to the appropriate iteration of the *calloc, malloc,* or *realloc* function groups.

The *_bsize* routine returns the size of the specified based heap. The *_fsize* version finds the size of the far heap. The *_nsize* version discovers the size of the near heap. In all three cases, the function name prefix indicates the heap with which the function works. All three initialize the storage to zero.

As you read in the tutorial and may have seen in the reference pages for other heap-specific memory management functions, the generic version of each function family maps either to the far or near version, depending on the memory model of the program in which it runs. The *_msize* generic maps to *_fmsize* in a compact, large, or huge model program, and to *_nmsize* in programs compiled with a tiny, small or medium model. The *_bmsize* version measures the specified _based heap segment, the *_fmsize* routine measures the _far heap (outside default data segment), and the *_nmsize* function gives you the size of the default data segment (inside the _near heap).

1. The *_bmsize* function was introduced in version 6.0.

COMMON USES *_msize* can be used after a failed call to a routine such as *_expand* to determine the actual size of the block after a failed request to expand.

RETURNS The *_msize* routines return the size of the appropriate block expressed in number of bytes.

COMMENTS The *_msize* routine is part of a set of ten memory management functions supplied in generic, _based, _far, and _near versions. (The other nine functions include *calloc, _expand, free, _heapchk, _heapmin, _heapset, _heapwalk, malloc,* and *realloc.*) The *_based* functions are named with a *_b* prefix. A leading *_f* is used to identify the *_far* versions, and the *_near* versions are named with an *_n* prefix. The leading underscore identifies the function as a Microsoft-specific routine (and therefore not ANSI-C compatible), and appears only once in the function name. Therefore, the _based version of *_msize* is *_bmsize.* The majority of these functions, including all of the based versions, were introduced in Microsoft C 6.0.

The keyword *_segname,* used with the based versions of the heap-specific memory management functions, specifies the name of a segment of memory.

SEE ALSO

`malloc, _fmalloc, _nmalloc, _bmalloc`	*To allocate a block of memory*
`expand, _fexpand, _nexpand, _bexpand`	*To expand an existing block of memory*

EXAMPLE The following program allocates an 80-byte buffer using *malloc.* It then calls the *_expand* function to enlarge the size to a large number of bytes (for instance, 65,000 bytes), so that the function fails and enlarges the block to the maximum possible value. Finally, it uses *_msize* to check the size to which the buffer was enlarged.

The example will work with *_fmsize* if you use a far pointer for the buffer and allocate the memory with *_fmalloc.* Additionally, the example will work with *_nmsize* if you use near pointers and allocate the memory with *_nmalloc.*

```
#include <stdio.h>
#include <malloc.h>
main()
{
    size_t max_bytes = 65000;
    char *buffer;

    if( (buffer = (char *) malloc(80) ) == NULL)
    {
        printf("Error allocating buffer\n");
        exit(0);
    }
/* Now enlarge the buffer to maximum possible size */
    if( _expand((void *)buffer, max_bytes) == NULL)
    {
        printf("_expand failed. Buffer still usable\n");
    }
    max_bytes = _msize(buffer); /* Find size of block */
    printf("Buffer size was increased to: %u bytes\n",
            max_bytes);
}
```

See the example program on the reference page for *expand* for another example using *_msize*.

realloc, _brealloc, _frealloc, _nrealloc

COMPATIBILITY

MSC 3	MSC 4	MSC 5	MSC 6	QC1	QC2	QC2.5	TC1	TC1.5	TC2	TC++	ANSI	UNIX V	XNX	OS2	DOS
▲	▲	▲	1	▲	▲	▲	2	2	2	2	▲	▲	▲	▲	▲

PURPOSE Use *realloc* to adjust the size of a block of memory allocated by *malloc* or *calloc*. The *_frealloc* function performs the same task on a _far memory block, and the *_nrealloc* routine is used to change the size of an already allocated near memory block. The prefix character after the leading underscore identifies the area of memory upon which the function works.

SYNTAX

```
void *realloc (void *mem_address, size_t byt_size);

void _far *_frealloc (void _far *mem_address, size_t
                      byt_size);

void _near *_nrealloc (void _near *mem_address, size_t
                       byt_size);
```

```
void _based (void) *_brealloc (_segment seg_name, void
_based (void) *mem_address, size_t, byt_siz);
```

`seg_name`	*Based heap segment selector (for* _brealloc*)*
`mem_address`	*Pointer to a previously allocated memory block*
`byt_size`	*The new size in bytes*
`mem_address`	*Pointer to previously allocated far memory block*

EXAMPLE CALL

```
new_buffer = realloc(old_buffer, old_size+100);

new_fbuffer = _frealloc(far_buffer, old_size+1000);

new_nbuffer = _nrealloc(near_buffer, old_size+20);

new_basedbuffer = (int _based * ) _brealloc (_DATA,
                    video_buffer, 4000);
```

INCLUDES

`#include <realloc.h>`	*For function declaration*
`#include <stdlib.h>`	*For ANSI-compatibility and definition of data type* size_t

DESCRIPTION

The *realloc* functions change the size of a memory block that has been previously allocated. The *elem_size* argument points to the beginning of the specified memory block. If the value for *elem_size* is NULL, the *realloc* group behaves the same as *malloc* would and allocates a new block of *byt_size* bytes. A non-NULL *elem_size* argument should be a pointer returned by a call to one of the *calloc* or *malloc* family, or a prior call to to a member of the *realloc* group.

The argument *byt_size* provides the new size of the block, expressed in bytes. Block contents are unchanged up to the shorter of the old and new, although the new block may be moved to a different location in the memory. (The *_expand* function family should be used if you do not want to move the block.)

The *elem_size* argument can also point to a block that has been released a member of the *_free* function group, as long as there has been no intervening call to the corresponding *calloc, _expand, malloc,* or *realloc* function groups.

The *realloc* family shares the characteristic of default mapping with the other heap-specific memory management function groups. This means that the generic version *realloc* maps to the *_far* version (*_frealloc*) in compact, large, and huge model programs, and to the *_near* (*_nrealloc*) version in programs compiled with the tiny, small, or medium memory models.

The *_brealloc* version operates on a specified based heap, the *_frealloc* version operates on the far heap (outside the default data segment), and the *_nrealloc* interation works on the near heap (inside the default data segment).

1. The three variants (based, near, and far) may possibly move the block in order to find contiguous space, and were introduced in Microsoft C 6.0. 2. The Turbo C equivalent for *_frealloc* is *farrealloc.*

COMMON USES The *realloc* function is normally used to enlarge a block of memory as, and when, the need arises to store more data elements. This function allows you to write programs that work with variable size arrays—enlarging and shrinking as data is added or removed.

RETURNS The *realloc* function group returns a pointer of type *void* to the reallocated (and possibly moved) memory block. Use a type cast on the return value to get a pointer to a type other than *void.* The memory area pointed to by the return is guaranteed to be appropriately aligned for storage of any type of object.

A successful *_brealloc* call generates a *void _based* pointer to the reallocated memory block. The *_frealoc* version generates a far pointer to the reallocated block if it succeeds, and a successful call to *_nrealloc* generates a near pointer to the reallocated block. (The prefixes *_b, _f,* and *_n* tell you the kind of pointer that results from a successful call.)

The return value from the *realloc* family (except *_brealloc)* is NULL if the size is zero and the buffer argument is not a NULL. A NULL will also result if there is not enough memory available to expand the block to the requested size. In the first situation, the original memory block is freed, but the second leaves the original block is unchanged. A *_NULLOFF* is returned if the *_brealloc* call fails.

COMMENTS Ten functions are supplied in generic, _based, _far, and _near versions: *calloc, _expand, free, _heapchk, _heapmin, _heapset, _heapwalk, malloc, _msize,* and *realloc.* The *_based* functions are named with a *_b* prefix. A leading *_f* is used to identify the *_far* versions, and the *_near* versions are named with an *_n* prefix. The leading underscore identifies the function as being a Microsoft-specific routine (and therefore not ANSI-C compatible); this appears only once in the function name. Thus, the *_based* version of *realloc* is *_brealloc,* and the *_based* version of *_expand* is *_bexpand.* The majority of these functions, including all of the *_based* versions, were introduced in Microsoft C 6.0.

Using *_based,* the syntax of which is *_based (base) vrbl_nam,* specifies that a data object resides in the segment identified by the *(_base)* argument. (It is not assumed to reside in the current data segment.) _Based pointers occupy 16 bits, and are added to the base to provide a 32-bit address range.

SEE ALSO

calloc, _fcalloc, _ncalloc, _bcalloc: *To allocate and initialize an array*

malloc, _fmalloc, _nmalloc, _bmalloc: *To allocate a block of memory*

free, _ffree, _nfree, _bfree: *To release memory allocated earlier*

EXAMPLES

Use *malloc* to allocate room for 40 characters. Read in a short string and store in the allocated buffer. Now, enlarge the buffer to hold an 80-character string. Show the user the contents again to verify that the original string is still there. Note that a null character must be inserted to terminate the string after reallocation.

```
#include <stdio.h>
#include <stdlib.h>
#include <malloc.h>

main()
{
    unsigned char *buffer;
/* Allocate room for string and check for NULL */
    if( (buffer = (char *)malloc(40)) == NULL )
    {
         printf("Allocation Failed.\n");
         exit(0);
    }
    printf("Buffer allocated. Enter string to store: ");
    gets(buffer);  /* Enter up to 40 chars. */
    printf("\nYou entered: %s\n",buffer);
/* Now enlarge size of buffer and redisplay string */
    if( (buffer = (char *)realloc((void *)buffer, 80))
         == NULL )
    {
         printf("Reallocation Failed.\n");
         exit(0);
    }
    else
    {
    buffer[40] = NULL; /* Make sure there's a null to end string */
    printf("Buffer still contains: %s\n",buffer);
    }
}
```

You can substitute *_frealloc* or *_nrealloc* in the example, if you specify far or near pointers, respectively. To use *_brealloc*, you must set up a segment and a based pointer as described in the tutorial.

sbrk

COMPATIBILITY

MSC 3	MSC 4	MSC 5	MSC 6	QC1	QC2	QC2.5	TC1	TC1.5	TC2	TC++	ANSI	UNIX V	XNX	OS2	DOS
▲	▲	▲	1	▲	▲		▲	▲	▲	▲		▲			

PURPOSE Use *sbrk* in small and medium memory models to alter the break value of a process. The break value is the address of the first available byte in the default data segment beyond the memory already being used by the data in the process.

SYNTAX

```
void *sbrk(int change);

int change;        Number of bytes by which the break value is to be changed
```

EXAMPLE CALL

```
buffer = (char *) sbrk(80);
```

INCLUDES

```
#include <malloc.h>        For function declaration
```

DESCRIPTION The *sbrk* function adds the number of bytes specified in the argument *change* to the break value of the process from which *sbrk* is called. The break value indicates the number of bytes that the process is currently using in the default data segment. In fact, it is the offset at which the heap (the chunk of memory from which new blocks may be allocated) begins. Since *sbrk* adds the argument *change* to the current break value, specifying a negative value in *change* reduces the memory being used by the process.

Since all address specifications in this function work with the default data segment, only models using near data addresses—small and medium—can use the *sbrk* function.

1. The *sbrk* function was removed from the compiler starting with version 6.0.

COMMON USES The *sbrk* function is used in small and medium models as an alternate memory allocation routine.

RETURNS The return value from *sbrk* is a pointer to a type *void*, representing the address of the previous break value. If the break value could not be altered because of insufficient space or if the memory model is compact, large, or huge, a character pointer to a value of –1 is returned. See the example below for a sample error check.

COMMENTS The *sbrk* function provides compatibility with UNIX System V library. It is better to use *malloc* for memory allocation because it is portable, it conforms to the proposed ANSI standard, and it works in all memory models except the huge model. Use *halloc* in the huge model.

SEE ALSO

malloc — *Most general-purpose memory allocation routine*

halloc — *To allocate* huge *(greater than 64 K) arrays*

free — *To release memory allocated earlier*

EXAMPLE Use *sbrk* to allocate room for a buffer to hold 80 characters at the end of the default data segment in a small model program. Prompt the user for a string and store it in the buffer you allocated. Call *sbrk* with a negative argument to deallocate this memory.

```
#include <stdio.h>
#include <malloc.h>
unsigned char *buffer;
main()
{
/* Allocate a buffer by adding 80 to the break value */
     buffer = (char *) sbrk(80);
    if (buffer == -1)
    {
            printf("sbrk failed.\n");
            exit(0);
    }
    printf("Buffer allocated. Enter string to store: ");
    gets(buffer);
    printf("\nYou entered: %s\n",buffer);
    sbrk(-80);  /* Deallocate the buffer */
    printf("Buffer deallocated\n");
}
```

COMPATIBILITY

stackavail

MSC 3	MSC 4	MSC 5	MSC 6	QC1	QC2	QC2.5	TC1	TC1.5	TC2	TC++	ANSI	UNIX V	XNX	OS2	DOS
	▲	▲	▲	▲	▲	▲								▲	▲

PURPOSE Use *stackavail* before calling *alloca* to determine the approximate size in bytes of the space available on the stack for allocation.

SYNTAX `size_t stackavail(void);`

EXAMPLE CALL `room_in_stack = stackavail();`

INCLUDES `#include <malloc.h>` *For function declaration and definition of data type* size_t

DESCRIPTION The *stackavail* function returns the number of bytes available on the program's stack for allocation by the function *alloca*. This space can be used for storing temporary arrays or other data.

RETURNS The return value from *stackavail* is the approximate number of bytes available on the stack. The return value is of type *size_t*, which is defined in *malloc.h* as the type *unsigned int*.

COMMENTS Since function calls use the stack to hold arguments, it is important to leave some space on the stack rather than using all the space indicated by *stackavail*.

SEE ALSO

`alloca`	*To allocate space on the stack*
`malloc`	*To allocate memory from the heap*
`free`	*To release memory allocated earlier*

EXAMPLE Call the *stackavail* function to determine the number of bytes available on the stack. Use *alloca* to allocate room for a buffer to hold 80 characters on the program's stack. Call *stackavail* again to see how many bytes are available after allocating these 80 bytes. Don't be surprised if the numbers do not quite add up; each allocated chunk may be required to start at a specific address to meet the requirement that the space be suitable for storing any type of data.

```
#include <stdio.h>
#include <malloc.h>
main()
{
    size_t max_bytes;
    char *buffer;
/* Check how much room is available on the stack */
    max_bytes = stackavail();
    printf("%u bytes available on the stack\n",
           max_bytes);
/* Get 80 bytes from stack */
    buffer = (char *) alloca(80);
    max_bytes = stackavail();
    printf("%u bytes available after allocating 80 \
bytes\n", max_bytes);
}
```

Chapter 6 Buffer Manipulation

Introduction

Buffer manipulation routines manipulate groups of bytes in memory. You can use these routines to initialize a block of memory (setting every byte in that block to a specified value); to copy data from one memory area to another; to compare the contents of two buffers; or to search for the occurrence of a specific byte value, among other things. A common use for buffer manipulation is in screen capture programs that copy the contents of the video memory to a buffer for subsequent output to a file—perhaps for desktop publishing. File comparison is yet another application where the buffer manipulation routines can be useful. Assuming adequate memory is available, you can copy the contents of two files to memory and use the *memcmp* or *_fmemcmp* routines to compare them.

Concepts: Buffers, Pointers, and Byte Ordering

You need to be familiar with the concept of a buffer and its address in order to make effective use of the buffer manipulation routines. These routines are similar to the string manipulation routines discussed in Chapter 10.

BUFFERS A buffer is a contiguous set of bytes in memory. The contents of the buffer are frequently ASCII characters, but they can also be numeric (binary) values. Figure 6-1 shows that the buffer is accessed by a pointer to the first byte. The figure shows Buffer 2 with the string *Hello.* Buffers and strings are similar in C except that strings are terminated with a null character

(\0—a byte containing zero) while the routines that manipulate buffers require an argument which specifies the number of bytes on which you wish them to work. Many of the buffer routines have corresponding string versions and vice versa. It is typically easier, though, to use a string function than its buffer equivalent when working with strings.

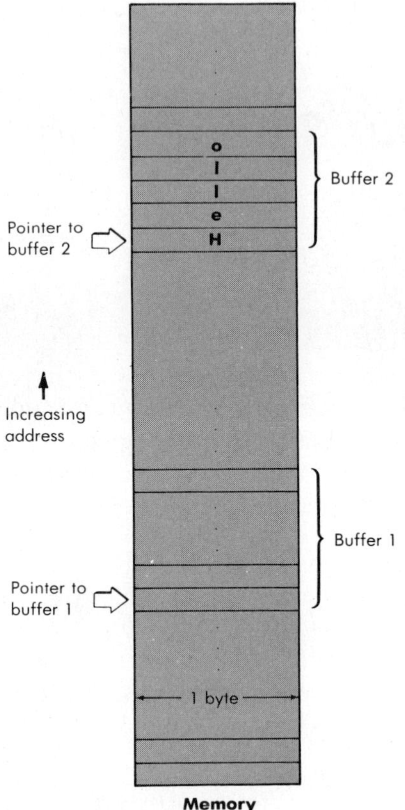

Figure 6-1. ***Buffers in memory***

BUFFER POINTERS: SEGMENTS AND OFFSETS

The pointer to the buffer is an address that consists of two 16-bit parts, a segment and an offset, as we explained in the tutorial in Chapter 5. The 20-bit physical address used by the 80x86 microprocessor family is constructed by shifting the segment address 4 bits to the left and adding the offset to the result. A buffer address is specified as "the name of an array" or as a "pointer variable." The segment and offset addresses are implicit in the memory model of the program. In the small and medium models, for example, all data is assumed to reside within a single 64-K segment of memory whose address is specified in the DS segment register (see Chapter 2). In this case, the pointer to a given buffer points to the 16-bit offset of the first byte of the buffer within that segment (which can be 64 K at most). Thus, in the small and the medium models, the buffers being manipulated (like all other data items) are confined to a single segment. The tiny model, introduced in version 6.0 of Microsoft C, allows the combined data and code to be within a single segment.

Pointers have full segment and offset addresses in the compact, large, and huge memory models. The buffers can be anywhere in memory with these models. Buffer size in compact and large models is limited to 64 K; only available memory limits buffer size with the huge model. The buffer manipulation routines *memccpy, memchr, memcmp, memcpy, memicmp, memmove,* and *memset* accept *_huge* pointers as arguments in the compact, large, and huge memory models.

MODEL-INDEPENDENT

Microsoft C 6.0 added model-independent (large model) forms for the *memccpy, memchr, memcmp, memcpy, memicmp, memmove,* and *memset.* The new forms adopt a prefix of *_f* where the leading underscore indicates noncompliance with ANSI, and the prefix character *_f* identifies them as handling far data. These additional functions are *_fmemccpy, _fmemchr, _fmemcmp, _fmemcpy, _fmemicmp, _fmemmove,* and *_fmemset* and they can be called from any point within a program. The behavior and return values of these new versions match their companion functions, except that both the arguments and the return values are far objects. This means they can be anywhere in memory, regardless of the memory model you are using. In the *_fstrcmp* function, for example, the *strcmp* version takes pointers as arguments, while *_fstrcmp* receives far pointers. The tutorial in Chapter 5 describes far objects.

BYTE ORDERING

The *swab* routine provides a special service: it swaps adjacent pairs of bytes in a buffer. This routine takes care of the "byte ordering" mismatch among different computer systems. *Byte ordering* is how the bytes of a 2- or 4-byte integer are arranged in memory. Consider, for example, a short integer variable *shortvar* that occupies 2 bytes in memory. We will store the hexadecimal value 0x0201 into this variable. What will be contained in the byte at the address of *shortvar*? What about the byte at the next higher address? In the 80x86 family, as shown in Figure 6-2, the least significant byte (01, in this case) is at the address of *shortvar*, while the most significant byte is at the next higher address.

If we load the value 0x04030201 into a long integer variable *longvar*, the ordering in the 80x86 would similarly start with the least significant byte at the lowest address with the bytes of higher significance placed at successively higher addresses (Figure 6-2). The order of bytes, therefore, is the same for both short and long integers in the 80x86 family of microprocessors. A common name for this arrangement is "little-endian" because the least significant byte is at the lowest address. Other processors—most notably the Motorola 680x0 family and those in the IBM 370—reverse this order. These are the "big-endian" systems because the most significant byte is at the lowest address.

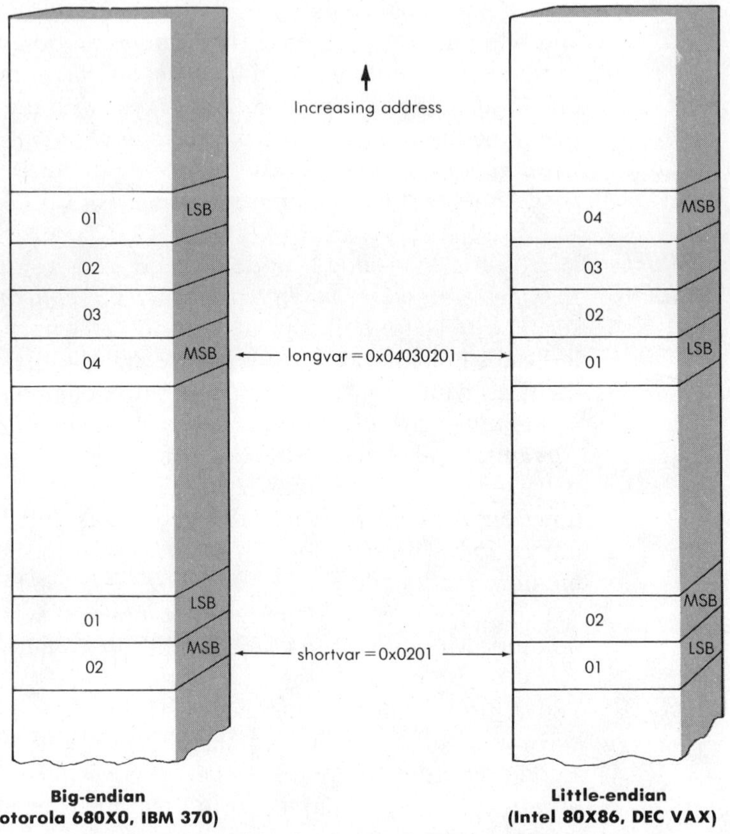

Figure 6-2. ***Byte ordering***

You will not need to worry about byte ordering unless you are writing programs that run on a network of different types of interconnected computers. Such mixed-architecture networks are a growing portion of the computer business. Byte ordering is important, for example, if you plan to transfer binary data between little-endian PCs and big-endian Macintosh machines. The *swab* function swaps adjacent bytes and can be used to convert short integers from one form of ordering to another.

Notes on Using the Buffer Routines

The buffer manipulation routines (see Table 6-1) are a more general form of the string manipulation routines that operate on strings in C. The operation of a buffer routine can be clarified by comparing it with its string counterpart. The difference between these two, as noted earlier in this chapter, is that the buffer routines always need a byte count, whereas the string routines determine the end of a string by searching for the null character. For example, *memchr* works like *strchr*; *memcmp* like *strcmp*; *memcpy* and *memmove* like *strcpy*; *memicmp* performs like *stricmp*; and *memset* like *strset*. These buffer routines have companion model-independent versions which use a *_f* prefix. The *memccpy* function works like the *memcpy* function, except that it takes an additional argument: a character that it uses as a marker. It copies the source buffer to the destination until either a specified number of bytes has been used, or until *memccpy* encounters the marker character in the source buffer. So the call

```
char title[81], this_book[] = "Microsoft C Bible";
memccpy (title, this_book, '\0', 81);
```

copies eighty-one characters or up to (and including) the null character, from *this_book* into *title*. The string *this_book* has a null character before the eighty-first position, so the entire string is copied to *title*.

The *movedata* function is a special-purpose routine for moving data between two buffers anywhere in memory. In the small and medium memory models, the buffers involved in the move must be in the same segment because all addresses are offsets of the segment address that is specified in the DS register. Thus, you cannot use the ordinary buffer copy routines, such as *memcpy*, to copy data in a small or medium model program to the video memory (treated as a buffer at a specified address) because the video memory is outside the data segment of your program. Since the *movedata* routine lets you specify the segment and offset addresses of the source and destination buffers explicitly, you can overcome the limitations of the memory model and copy between buffers in different segments.

A second solution is use of the *_based* keyword. The predefined memory models suffice for most operations, but in this instance you wish to address a far data item (video memory) in a small model—and the small model does not support that capability. Microsoft C allows you to mix and match an occasional data item of a type not available in the selected model through use of the *_near, _far, _huge,* and *_based* keywords. The *_based* keyword was new to version 6.0 and is discussed in Chapter 5.

A third alternative for use with those Microsoft C versions that predate the *_based* keyword is to select *segread* (see the chapter on System Calls) and the *FP_SEG* and *FP_OFF* macros to get the necessary values for your buffers. For example, in the CGA and the EGA in text mode, video memory begins at the address B800:0000.

You can view this block of memory as representing 25 rows by 80 columns of 2-byte data values, laid out by row, beginning at address B800:0000. The 2-byte values each correspond to a screen position with the high-order byte storing the attribute (such as normal, reverse video, blinking) and the other byte storing the actual character. If we have another buffer in memory with the same organization, we can prepare a screenful of text in this buffer and then display it by copying the buffer to the video memory. Here is an example:

```
    void far *address;
    short dispbuf [25][80];  /* the display buffer */
/* set all locations to zero */
    memset (dispbuf, '\0', sizeof(dispbuf));
/* get segment, offset of dispbuf */
    address = (void far *) dispbuf;
    bufseg = FP_SEG (address);
    bufoff = FP_OFF (address);
/* copy buffer into video memory -- clears screen */
    movedata (bufseg, bufoff, 0xb800, 0x0000, sizeof (dispbuf));
```

We set up a buffer, *dispbuf,* which is set to all zeroes by the call to *memset.* The segment and offset values are obtained via FP_SEG and FP_OFF, respectively. We have to copy the *dispbuf* address into a far pointer variable named *address* because FP_SEG and FP_OFF only work properly with far addresses. The last statement calls *movedata* to copy *dispbuf* to the video memory at B800:0000. The result is a cleared screen.

Table 6-2 summarizes the buffer manipulation routines by task. As you can see, the routines are primarily intended for copying, comparing, and initializing regions of memory.

Cautions

There are a few pitfalls you must be wary of when using the buffer manipulation routines:

- ▶ The *memcpy* routine in Microsoft C 4.0 properly handled, copying between overlapping source and destination values. This is not guaranteed with subsequent versions, which rely on *memmove* to perform this task. Programs that were developed with 4.0 should be checked for this overlap situation, and rewritten to use *memmove.*

- ▶ Source and destination buffers in the tiny, small, and medium memory models are both in the same data segment because addresses are offsets from the segment in the Data Segment (DS) register. The *movedata* function should be used to copy bytes between buffers in different segments because it accepts the explicit segment of the buffers being manipulated.

Table 6-1. *Buffer Manipulation Routines*

Routine	Description
_fmemccpy	Copies zero or more bytes of the source buffer to the destination buffer, copying up to, and including, the first occurrence of a specified character (or byte value), or until the specified number of bytes have been copied, whichever comes first. It is a model-independent version of *memccpy*, and was introduced in Microsoft C 6.0.
_fmemchr	Looks for the first occurrence of a specified character (or byte value) in the first specified number of bytes of a buffer. Model-independent version of *_memchr*. Introduced in Microsoft C 6.0.
_fmemcmp	Compares the specified number of bytes of two buffers and returns a value indicating their relationship. A model-independent version of *memcmp*, introduced in Microsoft C 6.0. See the tutorial for more information about far pointer functions.
_fmemcpy	Copies the specified number of bytes from the source to the destination buffer. A model-independent version of *memcpy*, it was introduced in Microsoft C 6.0.
_fmemicmp	Compares a specified number of characters from two buffers without regard to letter case. A model-independent version of *memicmp*, introduced in Microsoft C 6.0. See the tutorial for more information about far pointer functions.
_fmemmove	Copies a specified number of characters (or byte values) from a source to a destination buffer. It is a model-independent version of *memmove*, and was introduced in Microsoft C 6.0.
_fmemset	Sets the first specified number of bytes of the destination buffer to an identified character (or byte value). A model-independent version of *memset*, it was introduced in Microsoft C 6.0.
memccpy	Copies bytes from one buffer to another until a specific character (or byte value) is encountered, or until a specified number of bytes have been copied.
memchr	Searches for a specific character in a given number of bytes of the buffer.
memcmp	Compares a specified number of bytes of two buffers.
memcpy	Copies a specified number of bytes from one buffer to another (*not for overlapping source or destination*).
memicmp	Compares a specified number of bytes of two buffers without regard to the case of the characters in the buffers.

Table 6-1. ***(cont.)***

Routine	Description
memmove	Copies a specified number of bytes from one buffer to another (*handles overlapping source and destination*).
memset	Sets the specified number of bytes of a buffer to a given value.
movedata	Copies a specified number of bytes from one buffer to another; these buffers can be in different segments.
swab	Takes an array of bytes and swaps the contents of each pair of adjacent bytes.

Table 6-2. ***Buffer Manipulation Routines by Task***

Task	Routines
Compares two buffers.	memcmp, _fmemcmp, memicmp, _fmemicmp
Copies one buffer into another.	memccpy, _fmemccpy, memcpy, _fmemcpy, memmove, _fmemmove, movedata
Locates a specific character in a buffer.	memchr, _fmemchr
Initializes all bytes of a buffer.	memset, _fmemset
Swaps the contents of the high-order byte with that of the low-order one in a 2-byte word.	swab

COMPATIBILITY

memccpy, _fmemccpy

MSC 3	MSC 4	MSC 5	MSC 6	QC1	QC2	QC2.5	TC1	TC1.5	TC2	TC++	ANSI	UNIX V	XNX	OS2	DOS
▲	▲	▲	1	▲	▲	▲	▲	▲	▲	▲		▲		▲	▲

PURPOSE Use *memccpy* to copy bytes from one memory buffer to another. Copying continues until *memccpy* encounters a specified character or until a specified number of bytes have been copied, whichever happens first. Use the *_fmemccpy* routine when you wish to use a memory-model-independent version of *memccpy*.

SYNTAX

```
void *memccpy (void *dest, void *srce, int chr, unsigned int
              chr_count);

void _far *_far _fmemccpy (void _far *fr_dest, void _far *fr_src,
          int chr, unsigned int chr_count);
```

`void *dest;`	*Pointer to the buffer to which the data will be copied*
`void *srce;`	*Pointer to a buffer from which data will be copied*
`fr_dest`	*Far pointer to the destination buffer*
`fr_src`	*Far pointer to the source buffer*
`chr`	*Last character to be copied*
`chr_count`	*Maximum number of bytes to be copied*

EXAMPLE CALL

```
memccpy(dest_buf, inbuf, '\0', 81);

_fmemccpy (fr_dest, fr_srce, 'Y', 66);
```

INCLUDES `#include <memory.h>` *For function declaration*

or

`#include <string.h>`

DESCRIPTION The *memccpy* function copies bytes from the buffer at the *source* address to another buffer at *dest.* The copying starts at the first byte of the source and continues until one of two events occur: *memccpy* encounters a byte containing the character *c* in the source buffer or the total number of bytes copied from the source to *dest* equal the count specified in the argument *count.* When *memccpy* stops because of the first event, it copies the character *c* before returning.

Note that you are responsible for allocating enough space for the destination buffer. If you copy more bytes than the size allocated, *memccpy* may destroy other data and cause the program to fail in mysterious ways.

The *_fmemccpy* version is functionally identical to *memccpy* except that it returns far pointers. See the tutorial for more information about the far pointer functions.

1. The *_fmemccpy* routine is a model-independent version of *memccpy* and was introduced in version 6.0.

COMMON USES The *memccpy* and *_fmemccpy* functions, and their counterparts *memcpy, _fmemcpy, memmove, _fmemmove,* and *movedata*, are efficient tools for copying large blocks of data from one array to another. (There is no *far* version of the *movedata* function.)

RETURNS If the character *chr* is copied, both *memccpy* and *_fmemccpy* return a pointer (or far pointer) to the byte in the destination buffer that immediately follows the *chr* character. They both return a NULL if the *chr* is not copied.

COMMENTS Be sure that there is enough room in the destination buffer before calling any string or memory copy functions. This is a major source of error in C programs.

SEE ALSO

`memcpy, memmove`	*To copy one buffer to another*
`movedata`	*To copy buffers even if the source and destination are in different segments*

EXAMPLE Use *memccpy* to copy a string typed in by the user from an input buffer to an internal buffer. Copy until the null character (\0) is encountered or until 81 bytes are copied.

Use of the *_fmemccpy* function differs only in that the arguments are far pointers, as shown in the example calls above.

```
#include <stdio.h>
#include <memory.h>
static char dest[81];    /* Destination buffer */
main()
{
    char inbuf[81];
    printf("Enter a string: ");
    gets(inbuf);
    memccpy(dest, inbuf, '\0', 81);
    printf("Destination buffer has: %s\n", dest);
}
```

COMPATIBILITY

memchr, _fmemchr

MSC 3	MSC 4	MSC 5	MSC 6	QC1	QC2	QC2.5	TC1	TC1.5	TC2	TC++	ANSI	UNIX V	XNX	OS2	DOS
▲	▲	▲	1	▲	▲	▲	▲	▲	▲	▲	▲	▲	▲	▲	▲

PURPOSE Use the *memchr* function to search a memory buffer for a specific character. A memory model independent way to search for characters is provided by the *_fmemchr* function.

SYNTAX

```
void *memchr (const void *bufr, int chr, size_t chr_count);

void _far *_far _fmemchr (const void _far *f_bufr,
                          int chr, size_t chr_count);
```

`const void *bufr` *A pointer to the buffer in which the search takes place*

`chr` *The character for which to look*

`chr_count` *Maximum number of bytes to be examined*

`f_bufr` *A* _far *pointer to the searched buffer*

EXAMPLE CALL

```
/* Look for the first occurrence of 'I' in a 100 byte buffer */
    first_i = memchr(start_address, 'I', 100);

first_i = _fmemchr (start_address, 'I', 100);
```

INCLUDES `#include <memory.h>` *For function declaration and definition of* size_t

or

`#include <string.h>`

DESCRIPTION The *memchr* and *_fmemchr* routines look for the first occurrence of the character *chr* in the first *chr_count* bytes of the source buffer. They stop either when they find the target character or when they have examined the specified number of bytes. See the tutorial for more information about far pointer functions.

1. The *_fmemchr* version is the model-independent version of *_memchr* and was introduced in version 6.0.

RETURNS If *memchr* finds the character *c*, it returns a pointer to it. Otherwise, *memchr* returns a NULL. The *_fmemchr* function returns a far pointer, but is otherwise identical to *memchr*.

SEE ALSO memcmp, memicmp *To compare characters in two buffers*

EXAMPLE The listing of the ROM BIOS in the IBM PC Technical Reference manual shows that IBM's copyright notice appears at offset E000h in the BIOS segment F000h. Use *memchr* in a large memory model program to look for the I in IBM's copyright notice. If you do not have an IBM, substitute an appropriate character and address. On successful return, copy the next eight characters into a local buffer and print them out. To use the example with *_fmemchr*, change the pointers to *_far* pointers.

```
/* Use the the large memory model (-AL flag)          */
#include <stdio.h>
#include <memory.h>
/* Copyright notice begins at segment F000 and offset
 * E000
 */
#define  COPYRIGHT_NOTICE  0xf000e000L
static char dest[81];           /* Destination buffer */
main()
{
    void *copr_address, *first_i;
    copr_address = COPYRIGHT_NOTICE;
/* Look for the 'I' of IBM in the copyright notice    */
    if((first_i = memchr(copr_address, 'I', 24))
        == NULL)
    {
        printf("Search failed!\n");
    }
    else
    {
        printf("Found an 'I'at %p\n", first_i);
/* Copy next 8 characters into buffer 'dest' for
 * printing
 */
        memcpy(dest, first_i, 8);
        dest[8] = '\0';
        printf("The next 8 characters are: %s\n", dest);
    }
}
```

COMPATIBILITY

memcmp, _fmemcmp

MSC 3	MSC 4	MSC 5	MSC 6	QC1	QC2	QC2.5	TC1	TC1.5	TC2	TC++	ANSI	UNIX V	XNX	OS2	DOS
▲	▲	▲	1	▲	▲	▲	▲	▲	▲	▲	▲	▲	▲	▲	▲

PURPOSE Use *memcmp* to compare a number of bytes from one buffer with those in another. Use the *_fmemcmp* function when you need a memory-model-independent version of *memcmp*.

SYNTAX

```
int memcmp(const void *buffer1, const void *buffer2,
           size_t count);

int _far _fmemcmp (const void _far *f_buffer1, const
                   void _far *f_buffer2, size_t count);
```

`const void *buffer1;` *Pointer to first buffer*

`const void *buffer2;` *Pointer to second buffer*

`size_t count;` *Number of bytes to be compared*

`f_buffer1, f_buffer2` *Far pointers to the buffers you wish to compare*

EXAMPLE CALL

```
if (memcmp(buffer1, buffer2, sizeof(buffer1)) == 0)
                printf("The buffers are identical\n");

if (_fmemcmp (f_buffer1, f_buffer2, sizeof (f_buffer1)) == 0)
     printf ("The 'far' buffers are identical\n");
```

INCLUDES `#include <memory.h>` *For function declaration and definition of* size_t

`#include <string.h>`

DESCRIPTION The *memcmp* function compares the first *count* bytes of *buffer1* and *buffer2* and returns an integer value indicating the order in which these two sets of characters would have appeared in a dictionary.

The *_fmemcmp* version behaves identically except that it uses far pointers. See the tutorial for more information about far pointer functions.

1. *_fmemcmp* is a model-independent version of *memcmp*, and it was introduced in version 6.0.

COMMON USES Because the other string-comparison routine, *strcmp*, can be used only with null-terminated strings, the *memcmp* function is preferable for comparing portions of two strings.

RETURNS The integer values returned by *memcmp* have the following meanings:

Value	Interpretation
Less than 0	The first *count* characters in *buffer1* are less than those of *buffer2*, meaning *buffer1* would have appeared before *buffer2* if they were in a dictionary.
Equal to 0	The two buffers are equal up to the first *count* characters.
Greater than 0	*buffer1* is greater than *buffer2*.

The values returned by *_fmemcmp* are identical except for being far pointers.

COMMENTS The "intrinsic" form of the *memcmp* function does not support huge arrays in compact or large model programs. You have to use the huge memory model (with compiler option /AH) to get this support with the intrinsic version of *memcmp*.

SEE ALSO `memicmp` *To compare one buffer to another without regard to case of the characters*

EXAMPLE Use *memcmp* to compare two buffers. Let one be in uppercase and the other in lowercase. Notice that unlike *memicmp*, *memcmp* considers *buffer1* greater than *buffer2*. To use the example with *_fmemcmp*, change the pointers to far pointers.

```
#include <stdio.h>
#include <memory.h>
static char buffer1[81] = "Buffer 1",
            buffer2[81] = "BUFFER 1";
main()
{
    int result;
    printf("First buffer = %s\nSecond buffer = %s\n",
            buffer1, buffer2);
    result = memcmp(buffer1, buffer2, sizeof(buffer1));
    if(result == 0) printf("The buffers are equal.\n");
    if(result < 0) printf("%s less than %s\n", buffer1,
                          buffer2);
    if(result > 0) printf("%s greater than %s\n",
                           buffer1, buffer2);
}
```

memcpy, _fmemcpy

COMPATIBILITY

MSC 3	MSC 4	MSC 5	MSC 6	QC1	QC2	QC2.5	TC1	TC1.5	TC2	TC++	ANSI	UNIX V	XNX	OS2	DOS
▲	▲	1	2	▲	▲	▲	▲	▲	▲	▲	▲	▲	▲	▲	▲

PURPOSE Use *memcpy* to copy bytes from one memory buffer to another. Use *_fmemcpy* when you need a memory copy function that is independent of the memory model with which you are working.

SYNTAX

```
void *memcpy(void *dest, const void *source, size_t count);

void _far *_far _fmemcpy (void _far *f_dest, const
                          void _far *f_src, size_t count);
```

`void *dest;`	*Pointer to buffer to which data will be copied*
`const void *source;`	*Pointer to buffer from which data will be copied*
`size_t count;`	*Maximum number of bytes to be copied*
`f_dest`	*A far pointer to the destination buffer*
`f_src`	*A far pointer to the source buffer*

EXAMPLE CALL

```
memcpy (dest, src, 80); /* copy 80 bytes from src to dest */

_fmemcpy (f_dest, f_src, 66); /* copy 66 bytes from
f_src to f_dest */
```

INCLUDES `#include <memory.h>` *For function declaration and definition of* size_t

or

`#include <string.h>`

DESCRIPTION The *memcpy* function copies *count* bytes from the buffer at address *source* to another buffer at *dest.* This function can be used to copy a screen image from an offscreen buffer to the video memory. (This is true only in large data models; use *movedata* in small and medium models.) The *_fmemcpy* function behaves exactly like *memcpy* except that it operates with far pointers. See the tutorial for more information about the far pointer functions.

1. The *memcpy* function changed in Microsoft C 5.0 and is no longer guaranteed to handle overlapping regions; the *memmove* function is used in those instances. 2. The *_fmemcpy* function is a model-independent version of *memcpy* that was introduced in version 6.0.

RETURNS The *memcpy* function returns a pointer to the destination buffer *dest*. The *_fmemcpy* routine returns a pointer to the *far* destination buffer.

COMMENTS In Microsoft C 5.0 and 5.1, if some parts of the source and destination buffers overlap, *memcpy* does not ensure that the bytes in *source* are copied before being overwritten. This used to work correctly in version 4.0. In versions 5.0 and 5.1, the *memmove* function still handles copying between overlapping buffers properly so you should use *memmove* when you copy to and from overlapping buffers.

The intrinsic version of *memcpy* cannot handle huge arrays in compact or large memory model programs.

SEE ALSO

memccpy, memmove	*To copy one buffer to another*
movedata	*To copy buffers even if the source and destination are in different segments*

EXAMPLE Use *memcpy* to copy 80 bytes from one buffer to another. Print both buffers before and after the move to verify the results. The only change for use with *_fmemcpy* is turning the *memcpy (dest, src, 80)* call to *_fmemcpy (dest, src, 80)*.

```
#include <stdio.h>
#include <memory.h>
static char src[80]="This is the SOURCE buffer\n";
static char dest[80]="Destination\n";
main()
{
    printf("Before memcpy: Source = %s Destination \= %s", src, dest);
/* Copy from source to destination */
    memcpy(dest, src, 80);
    printf("After  memcpy: Source = %s Destination \
= %s", src, dest);
}
```

memicmp, _fmemicmp

COMPATIBILITY

MSC 3	MSC 4	MSC 5	MSC 6	QC1	QC2	QC2.5	TC1	TC1.5	TC2	TC++	ANSI	UNIX V	XNX	OS2	DOS
	▲	▲	1	▲	▲	▲	▲	▲	▲	▲		▲		▲	▲

PURPOSE Use *memicmp* to compare a number of bytes from one buffer with those in another without regard to the case of the letters in the two buffers. Use *_fmemicmp* when you need a memory-model-independent version of *memicmp*.

SYNTAX

```
int memicmp(void *buffer1, void *buffer2, unsigned count);

int _far _fmemicmp (void _far *buf_ptr1, void _far
                    *buf_ptr2, unsigned int count);
```

`void *buffer1;`	*Pointer to first buffer*
`void *buffer2;`	*Pointer to second buffer*
`unsigned count;`	*Number of bytes to be compared*
`buf_ptr1, buf_ptr2`	*Far pointers to the buffers being compared*

EXAMPLE CALL

```
if(memicmp(buffer1, buffer2, 10) == 0)
    puts("The buffers are equal up to the first 10 bytes\n");

if (_fmemicmp (buf_ptr1, buf_ptr2, 20) == 0) puts
   ("These far buffers are equal for the first 20 bytes\n");
```

INCLUDES `#include <memory.h>` *For function declaration*

or

`#include <string.h>`

DESCRIPTION The *memicmp* function converts the first *count* characters in *buffer1* and *buffer2* into lowercase letters. Then it compares the first *count* bytes of the two buffers and returns an integer value indicating the order in which these two sets of characters would have appeared in a dictionary.

The *_fmemicmp* version behaves in exactly the same fashion except that it operates on far pointers. See the tutorial for more information about far pointer functions.

1. The *_fmemicmp* function is the model-independent version of *memicmp* and was introduced in version 6.0.

RETURNS The integer values returned by *memicmp* have the following meanings:

Value	Interpretation
Less than 0	The first *count* characters in *buffer* are less than those of *buffer2*, meaning *buffer1* would have appeared before *buffer2* if they were in a dictionary.
Equal to 0	The two buffers are equal up to the first *count* characters.
Greater than 0	*buffer1* is greater than *buffer2*.

The *_fmemicmp* routine uses the same values for returns.

SEE ALSO `memcmp` *To compare one buffer to another (the case of letters matters)*

EXAMPLE Use *memicmp* to compare two buffers. Let one be in uppercase and the other in lowercase. Note that unlike *memcmp*, *memicmp* considers the buffers equal regardless of the case of the letters. This example works equally well with the *_fmemicmp* version.

```
#include <stdio.h>
#include <memory.h>
static char buffer1[81] = "Buffer 1",
            buffer2[81] = "BUFFER 1";
main()
{
    int result;
    printf("First buffer = %s\nSecond buffer = %s\n",
            buffer1, buffer2);
    result = memicmp(buffer1, buffer2, sizeof(buffer1));
    if(result == 0) printf("The buffers are equal.\n");
    if(result < 0) printf("%s less than %s\n", buffer1,
                          buffer2);
    if(result > 0) printf("%s greater than %s\n",
                          buffer1, buffer2);
}
```

memmove, _fmemmove

COMPATIBILITY

MSC 3	MSC 4	MSC 5	MSC 6	QC1	QC2	QC2.5	TC1	TC1.5	TC2	TC++	ANSI	UNIX V	XNX	OS2	DOS
▲	▲	▲	1	▲	▲	▲	▲	▲	▲	▲	▲			▲	▲

PURPOSE Use *memmove* to copy bytes from one memory buffer to another. The *memmove* function can correctly copy to and from overlapping buffers. Use the *_fmemmove* version when you need a buffer copy routine which operates independently of the memory model.

SYNTAX

```
void *memmove(void *dest, const void *source, size_t count);

void _far *_far _fmemmove (void _far *f_dest, const void
                          _far *f_src, size_t count);
```

`void *dest;`	*Pointer to buffer to which data will be copied*
`const void *source;`	*Pointer to buffer from which data will be copied*
`size_t count;`	*Maximum number of bytes to be copied*
`f_dest`	*Far pointer to the destination buffer*
`f_src`	*Far pointer to the source buffer*

EXAMPLE CALL

```
memmove(dest, src, sizeof(src));

_fmemmove (f_dest, f_src, sizeof (f_src));
```

INCLUDES `#include <string.h>` *For function declaration and definition of* size_t

DESCRIPTION The *memmove* function copies *count* bytes from the buffer at address *source* to another buffer at *dest.* The source and destination buffers may overlap. The *memmove* function handles *huge* pointers properly.

The *_fmemmove* routine works exactly the same as *memmove,* except that it uses far pointers. See the tutorial for more information about far pointer functions.

1. *_fmemmove* is the model-independent version of *memmove* and was introduced in version 6.0.

RETURNS The *memmove* function returns a pointer to *dest.* The *_fmemmove* function returns a pointer to a far buffer.

SEE ALSO

memccpy, memcpy — *To copy one buffer to another*

movedata — *To copy buffers even if the source and destination are in different segments*

EXAMPLE Use *memmove* to copy 80 bytes from one part of a buffer to another. Print the buffer before and after the move to verify that *memmove* can handle overlapping source and destination buffers properly. Substituting the function name *_fmemmove* for *memmove* will allow the example to work with far pointers. Since the functions are otherwise identical, their behavior is the same.

```
#include <stdio.h>
#include <string.h>
static char src[80]="FirstSecond";
main()
{
    printf("Before memmove:Source = %s\n", src);
/* Copy from source to itself */
    memmove(&src[5], src, sizeof(src));
    printf("After  memmove:Source = %s\n", src);
}
```

memset, _fmemset

COMPATIBILITY

MSC 3	MSC 4	MSC 5	MSC 6	QC1	QC2	QC2.5	TC1	TC1.5	TC2	TC++	ANSI	UNIX V	XNX	OS2	DOS
▲	▲	▲	1	▲	▲	▲	▲	▲	▲	▲	▲	▲	▲	▲	▲

PURPOSE Use *memset* to set a specified number of bytes in memory to a specific character. Use the *_fmemset* version when you need a memory-model-independent version of *memset.*

SYNTAX

```
void *memset(void *buffer, int c, size_t count);

void _far *_far _fmemset (void _far *f_dest, int
                                c, size_t count);
```

`void *buffer;` *Pointer to memory where bytes are to be set*

`int c;` *Each byte in buffer is set to this character*

`size_t count;` *Maximum number of bytes to be set*

`f_dest` *A far pointer to the buffer where bytes are to be set*

EXAMPLE CALL

```
memset(big_buffer, '\0', 2048);

_fmemset (far_bufr, 'A', 1024);
```

INCLUDES `#include <memory.h>` *For function declaration and definition of* size_t

or

`#include <string.h>`

DESCRIPTION The *memset* function sets the first *count* bytes in the buffer to the character *c*. The *_fmemset* function behaves in exactly the same way, except that it uses a far pointer. See the tutorial for more information about far pointer functions.

1. *_fmemset* is the model-independent version of *memset,* introduced in version 6.0.

COMMON USES The *memset* function is useful for initializing large chunks of memory. For example, *calloc* calls *memset* to set each byte of the allocated block of memory to zero.

RETURNS The *memset* function returns a pointer buffer to the buffer. The *_fmemset* routine returns a far pointer to a buffer, but is otherwise identical.

COMMENTS There is an intrinsic version of *memset* also, but that version cannot handle huge arrays in compact or large model programs.

SEE ALSO `memccpy, memcpy, memmove` *To copy one buffer to another*

EXAMPLE Set all bytes in a buffer to the letter Z, append a null character, and print the resulting C string. Changing the call from *memset* to *_fmemset* will yield exactly the same results, but to a buffer reached by a far pointer.

```
#include <stdio.h>
#include <memory.h>
static char buffer[41];     /* Destination buffer */
main()
{
    char *result;
    result = memset(buffer, 'Z', 40);
    buffer[40] = '\0';
    printf("The buffer now contains: %s\n", buffer);
}
```

COMPATIBILITY

movedata

MSC 3	MSC 4	MSC 5	MSC 6	QC1	QC2	QC2.5	TC1	TC1.5	TC2	TC++	ANSI	UNIX V	XNX	OS2	DOS
▲	▲	▲	▲	▲	▲	▲	▲	▲	▲	▲				▲	▲

PURPOSE Use the *movedata* function to copy a specified number of bytes from a source address to a destination address that can be in a different segment.

SYNTAX

```
void movedata(unsigned source_seg, unsigned source_off,
                   unsigned dest_seg, unsigned dest_off, unsigned count);
```

`unsigned source_seg;` *Segment address of source buffer*

`unsigned source_off;` *Offset address of source buffer*

`unsigned dest_seg;` *Segment address of destination*

`unsigned dest_off;` *Offset address of destination*

`unsigned count;` *Number of bytes to be copied*

EXAMPLE CALL `movedata(src_seg, src_off, dest_seg, dest_off, 4096);`

INCLUDES `#include <memory.h>` *For function declaration*

or

`#include <string.h>`

DESCRIPTION The *movedata* function copies *count* bytes from the source address given by *source_seg:source_off* to the destination address *dest_seg:dest_off*. Since the addresses are in segment and offset format, *movedata* can copy from one segment to another.

COMMON USES The *movedata* function is useful for moving data from one *far* array to another in small and medium memory models. It can also be used to copy data directly into the video memory.

COMMENTS In large and compact models, the *memcpy* and *memmove* functions perform the same as *movedata* because all data objects in these models are addressed using explicit segment and offset values.

SEE ALSO

`memcpy, memmove`	*To copy one buffer to another*
`segread`	*To get current values of the segment registers*
`FP_OFF, FP_SEG`	*Macros to determine segment and offset addresses of a* far *data item*

EXAMPLES Write a C program that calls *movedata* to copy the first 22 bytes from the address F000:E000 (in ROM BIOS) to a buffer in your program. Append a null character (\0) and print the resulting C string. On an IBM PC-AT this will print the IBM copyright notice.

```
#include <stdio.h>
#include <dos.h>          /* For FP_OFF and FP_SEG    */
#include <memory.h>
static char far buffer[41];   /* Destination buffer */
main()
{
    void far *address;
    unsigned bufseg, bufoff;
/* Get segment and offset address of buffer */
    address = (void far *)buffer;
    bufseg = FP_SEG(address);
    bufoff = FP_OFF(address);
    movedata(0xf000, 0xe000, bufseg, bufoff, 22);
    buffer[22] = '\0';
/* Use the 'F' address modifier when printing buffer */
    printf("The buffer now contains: %Fs\n", buffer);
}
```

In a Color Graphics Adapter (and EGA in text mode), the video memory starts at the address B800:0000. Prepare a buffer with 2,000 (25 rows by 80 columns) short integers. Initialize the entire buffer to zero (use *memset*). Now use *movedata* to copy the contents of the buffer into video memory.

The effect of setting the video memory to zeroes is to clear the display screen. This approach is used for preparing text output offscreen and for updating the display very rapidly.

```
#include <stdio.h>
#include <dos.h>
#include <memory.h>
static short dispbuf[25][80]; /* Display buffer */
main()
{
    void far *address;
    unsigned bufseg, bufoff;
/* Initialize display buffer to zero */
    memset(dispbuf, '\0', sizeof(dispbuf));
/* Get segment and offset address of buffer */
    address = (void far *)dispbuf;
    bufseg = FP_SEG(address);
    bufoff = FP_OFF(address);
/* Copy buffer into video memory -- clears screen */
    movedata( bufseg, bufoff, 0xb800, 0x0000,
              sizeof(dispbuf));
}
```

COMPATIBILITY

swab

MSC 3	MSC 4	MSC 5	MSC 6	QC1	QC2	QC2.5	TC1	TC1.5	TC2	TC++	ANSI	UNIX V	XNX	OS2	DOS
▲	▲	▲	▲	▲	▲	▲	▲	▲	▲	▲		▲	▲	▲	▲

PURPOSE Use *swab* to copy an even number of bytes from one location to another, at the same time swapping each pair of adjacent bytes.

SYNTAX

```
void swab(char *source, char *destination, int n);
```

`char *source;` *Data to be copied after byte swapping*

`char *destination;` *Buffer for byte-swapped data*

`int n;` *Number of bytes to copy (must be even)*

EXAMPLE CALL

```
swab("badc", result, 4); /* result will be "abcd" */
```

INCLUDES `#include <stdlib.h>` *For function definition*

DESCRIPTION The *swab* function copies *n* bytes of data from the buffer *source* to another buffer at *dest*, taking two adjacent bytes at a time and swapping their positions in *dest*. The number *n* should be even to allow *swab* to perform the byte swapping.

COMMON USES The byte-swapping capability afforded by *swab* is useful when preparing binary data to be read by a system in which the ordering of least significant and most significant bytes in a short integer is just the opposite of the order in the current system.

COMMENTS Although most computer systems today use the 8-bit byte as the smallest unit for data storage, there is no such standard for which byte is least significant and which most significant in multibyte data objects. Even in the simplest case of a short integer with 2 bytes in it you have two possibilities: the least significant byte is either the one at the lower address or the one at the higher memory address. The situation is more complicated in a network environment where machines with differing conventions may be connected together. In these situations you have to use such functions as *swab* to convert the byte ordering of one machine to the liking of another.

EXAMPLE Illustrate the use of *swab* in a program that takes a string on the command line (with no blanks embedded) and copies it into another buffer. Print the copy made by *swab*.

```
#include <stdio.h>
#include <stdlib.h>
#include <string.h>
main(int argc, char **argv)
{
    size_t len;
    char src[80], dst[80];
/* Make sure that there are at least 2 arguments */
    if(argc < 2)
    {
        printf("Usage: %s <string for \"swab\">\n",
                argv[0]);
        abort();
    }
/* Take an even no. of characters and feed it to swab */
    len = 2*(strlen(argv[1])/2);
    strncpy(src, argv[1], len);
/* Mark the end of string in both source and dest.    */
    src[len] = '\0';
    dst[len] = '\0';
/* Now copy after swapping adjacent bytes */
    swab(src, dst, len);
    printf("Input string to \"swab\" : %s\n\
Output string to \"swab\": %s\n", src, dst);
}
```

Buffer Manipulation

III Data Processing

- ► Data Conversion Routines
- ► Math Routines
- ► Character Classification and Conversion
- ► String Comparison and Manipulation
- ► Searching and Sorting
- ► Time and Locale Routines

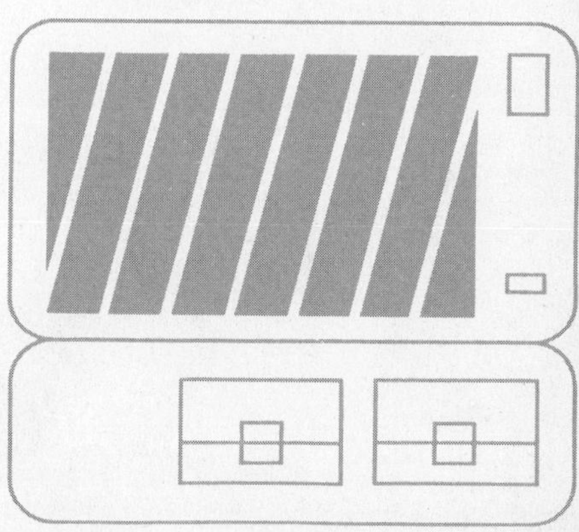

Chapter 7 Data Conversion Routines

Introduction

Information management with microcomputers frequently requires crunching numbers. These numbers are represented internally in several forms depending on the type of C variable in which the value is held. The Microsoft C data conversion routines allow us to convert back and forth between the internal form of a C variable and the character string representations that we can read.

Concepts: Internal Representations of Data

The data conversion routines rely on several internal representations of a number—as a series of bytes in memory containing a binary representation as well as in a character string (with the values expressed in decimal and hexadecimal, among other numbering systems).

NUMBERS IN MANY FORMS

All computers store numbers in binary representation in their memory locations. This is true of all types of numbers, floating point or integer. As illustrated in Figure 7-1, the character string representation of a value depends on the radix, or the base of the number system in which the value is being expressed. For example, decimal 100 is written as 64 in hexadecimal, 144 in octal, and 1100100 in binary. Figure 7-1 also shows the internal binary representations of the value 100 stored as a short integer and as an Institute of Electrical and Electronics Engineers (IEEE) format double-precision floating-point number. The character string, though, is the form we deal with to obtain numbers from the user or to format and print numbers calculated by the program.

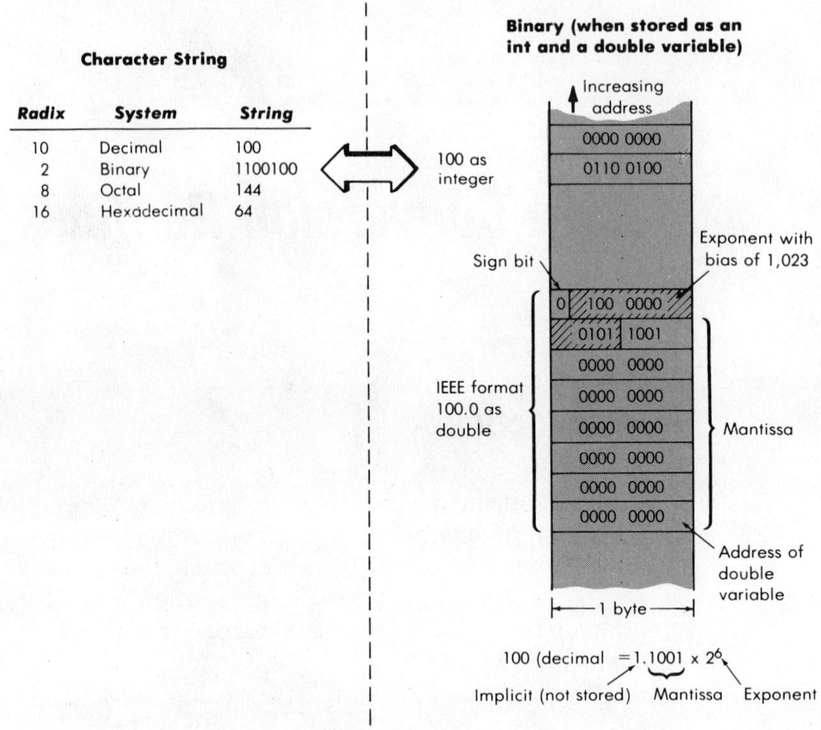

Figure 7-1. *Decimal 100 as a character string and in internal forms*

NUMBERS FOR THE MICROPROCESSORS

The pattern of bits that represents a value (such as decimal 100) in memory is determined by the type of C variable used to hold that value. If the variable type is *int*, which has a size of two bytes on the IBM PC, the value will be stored in binary in these two bytes (Figure 7-1). On the other hand, if we were to store 100 in a variable of type *double*, eight bytes will be used to hold the value and the bit pattern will depend on a format known as the IEEE format for double-precision numbers. Both the 8086 microprocessor and its "math whiz" companion 8087 store floating-point numbers in the IEEE format. See Chapter 6 of *The Waite Group's MS-DOS Developer's Guide*, 2d ed.,[1] for a detailed presentation of binary representation of floating-point numbers in the 8087 math coprocessor.

Notes on Using the Data Conversion Routines

The Microsoft C data conversion routines help us create a bridge between the two styles of representing numbers: the human readable text string and the machine readable binary form. Table 7-1 lists the routines at our disposal.

Table 7-1. ***Data Conversion Rountines***

Routine	Description
atof	Converts a string to a double-precision floating-point value.
atoi	Converts a string to an integer.
atol	Converts a string to a long integer.
_atold	Converts a character string to a long double-precision floating-point value. Introduced in Microsoft C 6.0.
ecvt	Converts a double-precision floating-point value into a string without an embedded decimal point (the sign of the value and the position of the decimal point are returned separately).
fcvt	Rounds the value to a specified number of digits; almost identical to *ecvt*.
gcvt	Converts a double-precision floating-point value into a string using a specified number of significant digits and having an extended decimal point.
itoa	Converts an integer value to a string.
ltoa	Converts a long integer value to a string.
strtod	Converts a string to a double-precision floating-point value.
strtol	Converts a string to a long integer.
_strtold	Converts a character string to a long double-precision floating-point value. Introduced in Microsoft C 6.0.
strtoul	Converts a string to an unsigned long integer.
ultoa	Converts an unsigned long integer value to a string.

The conversion routines are ideal for converting command-line arguments from their string representation into the internal format. For example, we may want the user to invoke a small calculator utility in the form

```
eval 4.5 + 2.3
```

where *eval* is the name of the program that accepts command-line arguments of the form <*value1*> <*operator*> <*value2*> and prints out the answer to the operation. In the sample invocation above, we get back 6.8 as the answer. When implementing the program *eval*, we can make use of the function *atof* to convert the second and the fourth command-line argument (the first argument is always the name of the program) to *double* variables. The code implementing the addition operator might be:

```
:
value1 = atof(argv[1]);
value2 = atof(argv[3]);
switch(argv[2][0])
{
:
    case '+': result = value1 + value2;
              break;
:
}
printf("%f", result);
```

In this example, we assumed a decimal calculator. If we want a hexadecimal calculator (so that all input and output is in hexadecimal), we can use *strtoul* to convert the input arguments to unsigned long integers. Use *ultoa* and specify a hexadecimal base to convert the result to a string.

Since the conversion routines are mostly used to read numerical values typed in by the user and to convert them to internal formats, you must consider the maximum values that each type of C variable can hold. Table 7-2 summarizes this information. Note that the range of values and the sizes shown in Table 7-2 apply only to Microsoft C on the IBM PC, XT, AT, and compatibles.

Table 7-2. *Limits of Values that Can Fit into C Variables*

Type	Bytes	Limits
double	8	15 significant digits, exponent ranging from –306 to 306
int	2	–32,767 to 32,767
long	4	–2,147,483,647 to 2,147,483,647
unsigned int	2	0 to 65,535
unsigned long	4	0 to 4,294,967,295

DATA CONVERSION ROUTINES BY TASK

The twelve data conversion routines perform two basic tasks: converting a C numerical value to a string or converting a string to a specific type of C variable. Table 7-3 shows the routines grouped by task.

OTHER DATA CONVERSION RESOURCES

A few other routines in the C library provide data conversion facilities. The *sprintf* and the *sscanf* functions in the I/O category convert internal values to strings and strings back to internal representations, respectively. The *sprintf* routine, however, lacks the ability to convert an integer to a string using an arbitrary radix—only decimal and hexadecimal formats are supported. To print a value in binary or octal you have to use such routines as *itoa, ltoa,* or *ultoa.*

Table 7-3. ***Data Conversion Routines by Task***

Task	Routines
Convert character string to a floating-point value.	atof, strtod
Convert floating-point values to a character string.	ecvt, fcvt, gcvt
Convert character string to an integer.	atoi
Convert integer value to a string.	itoa
Convert character string to a long integer.	atol, strtol
Convert long integer to a string.	ltoa
Convert character string to a long double.	_atold, _strtold
Convert unsigned long integer to a character string.	ultoa
Convert character string to an unsigned long integer.	strtoul

Further Reading

The Waite Group[1] devotes their Chapter 6 to the subject of writing programs for the 8087 math coprocessor. In that chapter they also describe the binary representation of floating-point numbers.

1. *The Waite Group's, MS-DOS Developer's Guide,* 2d Ed., Howard W. Sams & Company, Carmel, IN, 1989, 783 pages.

atof

COMPATIBILITY

MSC 3	MSC 4	MSC 5	MSC 6	QC1	QC2	QC2.5	TC1	TC1.5	TC2	TC++	ANSI	UNIX V	XNX	OS2	DOS
▲	▲	▲	▲	▲	▲	▲	▲	▲	▲	▲	▲	▲	▲	▲	▲

PURPOSE Use *atof* to convert a character string to a double-precision floating-point value.

SYNTAX

```
double atof(const char *string);

const char *string;        String to be converted
```

EXAMPLE CALL

```
dbl_value = atof(input_string);
```

INCLUDES

```
#include <math.h>        For function declaration
```

or

```
#include <stdlib.h>
```

DESCRIPTION The *atof* function converts the argument "string" into a double value. The string is expected to be of the form:

[whitespace][sign][digits.digits]
[exponent_letter][sign][digits]

The "whitespace" characters are optional blanks and tab characters, the "sign" is optional, and "digits" refer to decimal digits. The "exponent_letter" is either d, D, e, or E, marking the beginning of the exponent field (no matter which letter appears in the exponent field, the exponent always denotes a power of 10). If a decimal point appears without any digits preceding it, at least one digit must appear after the decimal point. The conversion of characters from the string continues until *atof* encounters a character it cannot handle (the null character will suffice).

In the compact and large memory models *atof* can only handle strings with a maximum length of 100 characters.

RETURNS The *atof* function returns the double-precision value after conversion. The return value is undefined if an overflow occurred during conversion.

SEE ALSO

`atoi, atol` *To convert strings to integers and long integer values*

`ecvt, fcvt, gcvt` *To convert floating-point values to strings*

EXAMPLE Write a program that accepts a floating-point number, uses *atof* to convert it to internal representation, and then prints that value.

```
#include <stdio.h>
#include <math.h>
main(int argc, char **argv)
{
    double value;
    if(argc < 2)
    {
        printf("Usage: %s <value>\n", argv[0]);
    }
    else
    {
        value = atof(argv[1]);
        printf("Value entered = %g\n", value);
    }
}
```

COMPATIBILITY **atoi**

MSC 3	MSC 4	MSC 5	MSC 6	QC1	QC2	QC2.5	TC1	TC1.5	TC2	TC++	ANSI	UNIX V	XNX	OS2	DOS
▲	▲	▲	▲	▲	▲	▲	▲	▲	▲	▲	▲	▲	▲	▲	▲

PURPOSE Use *atoi* to convert a character string to an *int* value.

SYNTAX

```
int atoi(const char *string);
```

`const char *string;` *String to be converted*

EXAMPLE CALL

```
int_value = atoi(input_string);
```

INCLUDES `#include stdlib.h>` *For function declaration*

DESCRIPTION The *atoi* function converts the argument *string* into an *int* value. The string is expected to be of the form:

[whitespace][sign][digits]

The "whitespace" characters are optional blanks and tab characters, the "sign" is optional, and "digits" refer to decimal digits. The conversion of characters from the string continues until *atoi* encounters a character it cannot handle (for example, a terminating null character, a decimal point, or a letter).

RETURNS The *atoi* function returns the integer value as an *int* variable. The return value is undefined if it is too large to fit an *int* variable.

SEE ALSO

atof	*To convert strings to floating-point values*
atol	*To convert strings to long integers*
itoa, ltoa, ultoa	*To convert integers to strings*

EXAMPLE Write a program that accepts a sequence of decimal integers, uses *atoi* to convert it to an integer, and then prints that integer.

```
#include <stdio.h>
#include <stdlib.h>
main(int argc, char **argv)
{
    int value;
    if(argc < 2)
    {
        printf("Usage: %s <value>\n", argv[0]);
    }
    else
    {
        value = atoi(argv[1]);
        printf("Value entered = %d\n", value);
    }
}
```

atol, _atold

COMPATIBILITY

MSC 3	MSC 4	MSC 5	MSC 6	QC1	QC2	QC2.5	TC1	TC1.5	TC2	TC++	ANSI	UNIX V	XNX	OS2	DOS
▲	▲	▲	1	▲	▲	▲	▲	▲	▲	▲	▲	▲	▲	▲	▲

PURPOSE Use *atol* to convert a character string to a long integer value. The *atold* function is the long double version of *atol.*

SYNTAX

```
int atol (const char *string);

long double_atold (const char *string);

const char *string;
```

String to be converted

EXAMPLE CALL

```
long_value = atol(input_string);
```

INCLUDES

```
#include <math.h>
```

For function declaration

```
#include <stdlib.h>
```

DESCRIPTION The *atol* function converts the argument *string* into a *long* integer value. The string is expected to be of the form:

[whitespace][sign][digits]

The "whitespace" characters are optional blanks and tab characters, the "sign" is optional, and "digits" refer to decimal digits. The conversion of characters from the string continues until *atol* encounters a character it cannot handle (for example, a terminating null character, a decimal point, or a letter). See the tutorial for more information about long double functions.

1. The *atold* version is a long double-precision version of *atol* and was introduced in version 6.0.

RETURNS The *atol* function returns the integer value as a *long* variable. The return value is undefined if it is too large to fit a *long* integer.

A successful call to the *atold* version returns the converted string. A 0 is returned if the string cannot be converted.

SEE ALSO

atof	*To convert strings to floating-point values*
atoi	*To convert strings to integers*
itoa, ltoa, ultoa	*To convert integers to strings*

EXAMPLE Write a program that accepts a sequence of decimal integers, uses *atol* to convert it to a long integer and then prints that long integer.

```
#include <stdio.h>
#include <stdlib.h>
main(int argc, char **argv)
{
    long value;
    if(argc < 2)
    {
        printf("Usage: %s <value>\n", argv[0]);
    }
    else
    {
        value = atol(argv[1]);
        printf("Value entered = %ld\n", value);
    }
}
```

ecvt

COMPATIBILITY

MSC 3	MSC 4	MSC 5	MSC 6	QC1	QC2	QC2.5	TC1	TC1.5	TC2	TC++	ANSI	UNIX V	XNX	OS2	DOS
▲	▲	▲	▲	▲	▲	▲	▲	▲	▲	▲		▲	▲	▲	▲

PURPOSE Use *ecvt* to convert a floating-point value to a character string.

SYNTAX

```
char *ecvt(double value, int count, int *dec, int *sign);
```

`double value;` *Floating-point value to be converted to string*

`int count;` *Number of digits to be stored*

`int *dec;` *Pointer to integer where position of decimal point is returned*

`int *sign;` *Pointer to integer where sign of the number is returned*

EXAMPLE CALL

```
string = ecvt(value, precision, &d_position, &sign);
```

INCLUDES `#include <stdlib.h>` *For function declaration*

DESCRIPTION The *ecvt* function converts the *double* argument *value* into a null-terminated character string with *count* digits. If the number of digits in *value* exceeds *count*, the last digit is rounded. On the other hand, if there are fewer than *count* digits, the string is padded with zeroes.

You must specify the addresses of integer variables *dec* and *sign*, which are used by *ecvt* to return the location of the decimal point from the beginning of the string and from the sign of the number, respectively. If *ecvt* returns a zero or a negative number in *dec*, the decimal point lies at the beginning of the string or to the left of the first digit. If the value in *sign* is zero, the number is positive. Otherwise, it is negative.

RETURNS The *ecvt* function returns a pointer to an internal string where the string of digits is stored. The next call to either *ecvt* or *fcvt* destroys the result.

SEE ALSO

`atof` *To convert strings to floating-point values*

`fcvt, gcvt` *To convert floating-point numbers to strings*

`itoa, ltoa, ultoa` *To convert integers to strings*

EXAMPLE Write a program that accepts a floating-point number, uses *atof* to convert it to internal form, and prepares a character string representing the value of that number by calling *ecvt* with a precision of 10 digits. Print the buffer prepared by *ecvt*, the location of the decimal point, and the value of the sign indicator.

```
#include <stdio.h>
#include <math.h>
#include <stdlib.h>
main(int argc, char **argv)
{
    int dec, sign, precision = 10;
    double value;
    char  *p_buffer;
    if(argc < 2)
    {
        printf("Usage: %s <value>\n", argv[0]);
    }
    else
    {
/* Convert the number to internal form. Then call ecvt */
        value = atof(argv[1]);
        p_buffer = ecvt(value, precision, &dec, &sign);
        printf("Buffer from ecvt contains: %s\n\
Location of decimal point: %d\n\
Sign (0 = pos, 1 = neg)   : %d\n", p_buffer, dec, sign);
    }
}
```

COMPATIBILITY

fcvt

MSC 3	MSC 4	MSC 5	MSC 6	QC1	QC2	QC2.5	TC1	TC1.5	TC2	TC++	ANSI	UNIX V	XNX	OS2	DOS
▲	▲	▲	▲	▲	▲	▲	▲	▲	▲	▲		▲	▲	▲	▲

PURPOSE Use *fcvt* to convert a floating-point value to a character string. The function of *fcvt* is similar to that of *ecvt* but *fcvt* rounds the number to a specified number of digits.

SYNTAX

```
char *fcvt(double value, int count, int *dec, int *sign);
```

`double value;` *Floating-point value to be converted to string*

`int count;` *Number of digits to be stored*

`int *dec;` *Pointer to integer where position of decimal point is returned*

`int *sign;` *Pointer to integer where sign of the number is returned*

EXAMPLE CALL `string = fcvt(value, precision, &d_position, &sign);`

INCLUDES `#include <stdlib.h>` *For function declaration*

DESCRIPTION Like *ecvt*, the *fcvt* function converts the *double* argument *value* into a character string with *count* digits. If the number of digits in *value* exceeds *count*, the excess digits are rounded off to *count* places. On the other hand, if there are fewer than *count* digits, the string is padded with zeroes. You must specify the addresses of integer variables *dec* and *sign*, which are used by *fcvt* to return the location of the decimal point from the beginning of the string and from the sign of the number, respectively. If *fcvt* returns a zero or a negative number in *dec*, the decimal point lies at the beginning of the string or to the left of the first digit. If the value in *sign* is zero, the number is positive. Otherwise, it is negative.

RETURNS The *fcvt* function returns a pointer to an internal string where the string of digits is stored. The next call to either *fcvt* or *ecvt* destroys the result.

SEE ALSO

`atof`	*To convert strings to floating-point values*
`ecvt, gcvt`	*To convert floating-point numbers to strings*
`itoa, ltoa, ultoa`	*To convert integers to strings*

EXAMPLE Write a program that accepts a floating-point number, uses *atof* to convert it to internal form, and prepares a character string representing the value of that number by calling *ecvt* with a precision of 10 digits. Print the buffer prepared by *fcvt*, the location of the decimal point, and the value of the sign indicator.

```
#include <stdio.h>
#include <math.h>
#include <stdlib.h>
main(int argc, char **argv)
{
    int dec, sign, precision = 10;
    double value;
    char  *p_buffer;

    if(argc < 2)
    {
        printf("Usage: %s <value>\n", argv[0]);
    }
    else
    {
```

```
/* Convert the number to internal form. Then call fcvt */
        value = atof(argv[1]);
        p_buffer = fcvt(value, precision, &dec, &sign);
        printf("Buffer from fcvt contains: %s\n\
Location of decimal point: %d\n\
Sign (0 = pos, 1 = neg)  : %d\n", p_buffer, dec, sign);
    }
}
```

gcvt

COMPATIBILITY

MSC 3	MSC 4	MSC 5	MSC 6	QC1	QC2	QC2.5	TC1	TC1.5	TC2	TC++	ANSI	UNIX V	XNX	OS2	DOS
▲	▲	▲	▲	▲	▲	▲	▲	▲	▲	▲		▲	▲	▲	▲

PURPOSE Use *gcvt* to convert a floating-point value to a character string. Unlike *ecvt* and *fcvt, gcvt* returns the results in a character buffer supplied by you.

SYNTAX

```
char *gcvt(double value, int digits, char *buffer);
```

`double value;` *Floating-point value to be converted to string*

`int digits;` *Number of significant digits to be stored*

`char *buffer;` *Pointer to character array where result is returned*

EXAMPLE CALL

```
gcvt(value, significant_digits, resulting_string);
```

INCLUDES `#include <stdlib.h>` *For function declaration*

DESCRIPTION The *gcvt* function converts the *double* argument *value* into a character string that it saves in the buffer whose address is given in the argument *buffer*. You must allocate enough room in the buffer to hold all digits of the converted string and the terminating null character (\0).

The argument *digits* specifies the number of significant digits that *gcvt* should produce in the character string. If *gcvt* cannot meet this requirement in normal decimal format, it generates a string in scientific notation using mantissa and exponent (e.g., 1.234e−7 as opposed to 0.0000001234).

RETURNS The *gcvt* function returns a pointer to the string of digits, i.e., it returns the argument *buffer*.

COMMENTS Unlike *ecvt* and *fcvt, gcvt* uses a string supplied by you and it includes the decimal point and the sign in the result.

SEE ALSO `atof` *To convert strings to floating-point values* `ecvt, fcvt` *To convert floating-point numbers to strings*

`itoa, ltoa, ultoa` *To convert integers to strings*

EXAMPLE Write a program that accepts a floating-point number, uses *atof* to convert it to internal form, and prepares a formatted representation of that number (with six significant digits) by calling *gcvt*. Print the resulting string.

```
#include <stdio.h>
#include <math.h>
#include <stdlib.h>
main(int argc, char **argv)
{
    int significant_digits = 6;
    double value;
    char  buffer[80];              /* Buffer for gcvt */
    if(argc < 2)
    {
        printf("Usage: %s <value>\n", argv[0]);
    }
    else
    {
/* Convert the number to internal form. Then call gcvt */
        value = atof(argv[1]);
        gcvt(value, significant_digits, buffer);
        printf("Buffer from gcvt contains: %s\n",
                buffer);
    }
}
```

itoa

COMPATIBILITY

MSC 3	MSC 4	MSC 5	MSC 6	QC1	QC2	QC2.5	TC1	TC1.5	TC2	TC++	ANSI	UNIX V	XNX	OS2	DOS
▲	▲	▲	▲	▲	▲	▲	▲	▲	▲	▲				▲	▲

PURPOSE Use *itoa* to convert an integer value to a null-terminated character string.

SYNTAX `char *itoa(int value, char *string, int radix);`

`int value;` *Integer value to be converted to string*

`char *string;` *Pointer to character array where result is returned*

`int radix;` *Radix in which the result is expressed (in the range 2–36)*

EXAMPLE CALL
```
itoa(32, buffer, 16); /* buffer will contain "20" */
```

INCLUDES `#include <stdlib.h>` *For function declaration*

DESCRIPTION The *itoa* function converts the *int* argument *value* into a null-terminated character string using the argument *radix* as the base of the number system. The resulting string with a length of up to 17 bytes is saved in the buffer whose address is given in the argument *string*. You must allocate enough room in the buffer to hold all digits of the converted string plus the terminating null character (\0). For radixes other than 10, the sign bit is not interpreted; instead, the bit pattern of *value* is simply expressed in the requested *radix*.

The argument *radix* specifies the base (between 2 and 36) of the number system in which the string representation of *value* is expressed. For example, using either 2, 8, 10, or 16 as *radix*, you can convert *value* into its binary, octal, decimal, or hexadecimal representation, respectively. When *radix* is 10 and the *value* is negative, the converted string will start with a minus sign.

RETURNS The *itoa* function returns the pointer to the string of digits (i.e., it returns the argument *string*).

SEE ALSO `ecvt, fcvt, gcvt` *To convert floating-point numbers to strings*

`ltoa, ultoa` *To convert long and unsigned long integers to strings*

EXAMPLE Write a program to print an integer value using a specified radix. Assume the program will be invoked with the decimal value and the radix on the command line. Use *itoa* to generate the formatted string.

```
#include <stdio.h>
#include <stdlib.h>
main(int argc, char **argv)
{
    char buffer[17];            /* Buffer for itoa  */
    int value, radix;
    if(argc < 3)
    {
        printf("Usage: %s <value> <radix>\n", argv[0]);
    }
    else
    {
        value = atoi(argv[1]);
        radix = atoi(argv[2]);
        itoa(value, buffer, radix);
```

```
        printf("%s in radix %s = %s\n", argv[1], argv[2],
                buffer);
    }
}
```

ltoa

COMPATIBILITY

MSC 3	MSC 4	MSC 5	MSC 6	QC1	QC2	QC2.5	TC1	TC1.5	TC2	TC++	ANSI	UNIX V	XNX	OS2	DOS
▲	▲	▲	▲	▲	▲	▲	▲	▲	▲	▲				▲	▲

PURPOSE Use *ltoa* to convert a *long* integer value to a null-terminated character string.

SYNTAX `char *ltoa(long value, char *string, int radix);`

`long value;` *Long integer value to be converted to string*

`char *string;` *Pointer to character array where result is returned*

`int radix;` *Radix in which the result is expressed (in the range 2–36)*

EXAMPLE CALL `ltoa(0x10000, string, 10); /* string = "65536"  */`

INCLUDES `#include <stdlib.h>` *For function declaration*

DESCRIPTION The *ltoa* function converts the *long* argument *value* into a character string using the argument *radix* as the base of the number system. A *long* integer has 32 bits when expressed in radix 2, so the string can occupy a maximum of 33 bytes with the terminating null character. The resulting string is returned in the buffer whose address is given in the argument *string*.

The argument *radix* specifies the base (between 2 and 36) of the number system in which the string representation of *value* is expressed. For example, using either 2, 8, 10, or 16 as *radix*, you can convert *value* into its binary, octal, decimal, or hexadecimal representation, respectively. When *radix* is 10 and the *value* is negative, the converted string will start with a minus sign.

RETURNS The *ltoa* function returns the pointer to the converted string (i.e., it returns the argument *string*).

SEE ALSO `ecvt, fcvt, gcvt` *To convert floating-point numbers to strings*

`itoa, ultoa` *To convert* int *and* unsigned long *integers to strings*

EXAMPLE Write a program that accepts a long integer value and a radix on the command line and then calls *ltoa* to prepare a character representation of that number in the specified radix and prints the string.

```
#include <stdio.h>
#include <stdlib.h>
main(int argc, char **argv)
{
    char buffer[17];           /* Buffer for ltoa  */
    int  radix;
    long value;
    if(argc < 3)
    {
        printf("Usage: %s <value> <radix>\n", argv[0]);
    }
    else
    {
        value = atol(argv[1]);
        radix = atoi(argv[2]);
        ltoa(value, buffer, radix);
        printf("%s in radix %s = %s\n", argv[1], argv[2],
                buffer);
    }
}
```

strtod

COMPATIBILITY

MSC 3	MSC 4	MSC 5	MSC 6	QC1	QC2	QC2.5	TC1	TC1.5	TC2	TC++	ANSI	UNIX V	XNX	OS2	DOS
	▲	▲	▲	▲	▲	▲	▲	▲	▲	▲	▲	▲	▲	▲	▲

PURPOSE Use *strtod* to convert a character string to a double-precision value.

SYNTAX `double strtod(const char *string, char **endptr);`

`const char  *string;` *Pointer to character array from which double-precision value is extracted*

`char **endptr;` *On return, points to character in* string *where conversion stopped*

EXAMPLE CALL `dbl_value = strtod(input_string, &endptr);`

INCLUDES `#include <stdlib.h>` *For function declaration*

`#include <float.h>` *For the definition of the constant HUGE_VAL*

`#include <math.h>` *For the definition of ERANGE*

DESCRIPTION The *strtod* function converts the *string* to a double-precision value. The string is expected to be of the form

[whitespace][sign][digits.digits][exponent_letter][sign][digits]

where "whitespace" refers to (optional) blanks and tab characters, "sign" is a + or a −, and the "digits" are decimal digits. The "exponent_letter" can be either d, D, e, or E (no matter which exponent letter is used, the exponent always denotes a power of 10). If there is a decimal point without a preceding digit, there must be at least one digit following it.

The *strtod* function begins the conversion process with the first character of *string* and continues until it finds a character that does not fit the above form. Then it sets *endptr* to point to the leftover string. In compact and large model programs *strtod* can only handle strings with a maximum length of 100 characters.

RETURNS The *strtod* function returns the double-precision value as long as it is not too large. If it is too large, an overflow occurs and the return value is the constant HUGE_VAL with the same sign as the number represented in *string*. Additionally, the global variable *errno* is set to the constant ERANGE.

COMMENTS The advantage of using *strtod* over *atof* is that *strtod* returns a pointer to the character where the conversion stopped, enabling you to handle the rest of the string any way you wish.

SEE ALSO `atof` *To convert strings to double-precision values*

`strtol, strtoul` *To convert strings to long and unsigned long integers*

EXAMPLE Prompt the user for a floating-point number followed by arbitrary characters. Then call *strtod* to convert the floating-point number to internal form. Print the number and the rest of the string, which in a more realistic program would be processed further.

```
#include <stdio.h>
#include <stdlib.h>
main()
{
    char input[80], *stop_at;
    double value;
    printf(
```

```
    "Enter a number followed by other characters:\n");
    gets(input);
/* Now convert the number to internal value */
     value = strtod(input, &stop_at);
     printf("Value = %g\n\
Stopped at: %s\n", value, stop_at);
}
```

COMPATIBILITY

strtol, _strtold

MSC 3	MSC 4	MSC 5	MSC 6	QC1	QC2	QC2.5	TC1	TC1.5	TC2	TC++	ANSI	UNIX V	XNX	OS2	DOS
▲	▲	1	▲	▲	▲	▲	▲	▲	▲	▲	▲	▲	▲	▲	

PURPOSE Use *strtol* to convert a character string to a long integer value. The *_strtold* routine should be used when you need a long-double method for converting a character string to a floating-point value.

SYNTAX `long strtol (const char *string, char **endptr, int radix);`

`long double _strtold (const char *string, char **endptr);`

`string` *A pointer to character array from which the arithmetic value is to be extracted*

`endptr` *Pointer to the character that causes the scan to end, and thus the character in* string *where the conversion stopped*

`int radix` *Radix in which the value in the string is expressed (the radix must be in the range of 2–36)*

EXAMPLE CALL `value = strtol(input, &endptr, radix);`

`value = strtold (input, &endptr);`

INCLUDES `#include <stdlib.h>` *For function declaration*

`#include <limits.h>` *For the definition of the constants LONG_MIN and LONG_MAX*

`#include <math.h>` *For the definition of ERANGE*

DESCRIPTION The *strtol* function converts the *string* to a long integer value. The string is expected to be of the form

[whitespace][sign][0][x or X][digits]

where "whitespace" refers to optional blanks and tab characters, "sign" is a + or a –, and the "digits" are decimal digits. The string is expected to contain a representation of the long integer using the argument *radix* as the base of the number system. If *radix* is given as zero, though, *strtol* will use the first character in *string* to determine the radix of the value. The rules are given in the table.

First Character	Next Character	Radix Selected
0	0–7	Radix 8 is used (octal digits expected)
0	x or X	Radix 16 (hexadecimal digits expected)
1–9	—	Radix 10 (decimal digits expected)

Of course, other radixes may be specified via the argument *radix*. The letters a through z (or A through Z) are assigned values of 10 through 35. For a specified radix, *strtol* expects only those letters whose assigned values are less than the *radix*.

The *strtol* function begins the conversion process with the first character of *string* and continues until it finds a character that meets the above requirements. Then, before returning, *strtol* sets *endptr* to point to that character.

The *_strtold* function converts a character string to a long double-precision floating-point value.

1. A long double version of *strtol, _strtold* ws introduced in version 6.0.

RETURNS The *strtol* function returns the long integer value except when it would cause an overflow. In which case, *strtol* sets *errno* to ERANGE and returns either LONG_MIN or LONG_MAX depending on whether the value was negative or positive.

The *_strtold* function returns the long double-precision value of the floating-point number, if successful. The error on overflow is LHUGE_VAL; a zero is generated for other errors.

COMMENTS The advantage of using *strtol* over *atol* is that *strtol* allows radix values other than 10 and it can determine the radix automatically based on the first two characters of the string. Unlike *atol, strtol* returns a pointer to the character where the conversion stopped, enabling you to handle the rest of the string any way you wish.

The *_strtold* function limits the maximum length of the string argument to 100 characters when used in a program with a compact, large, or huge memory model.

SEE ALSO `atol` *To convert strings to long integer values*

`ltoa`	*To convert long integers to strings*
`strtoul`	*To convert strings to unsigned long integers*

EXAMPLE Write a program that accepts on the command line a long integer value followed by the radix in which the value is represented. Use *strtol* with the radix to convert the representation of that number to an internal value. Print this value.

```
#include <stdio.h>
#include <stdlib.h>
main(int argc, char **argv)
{
    char *stop_at;    /* Marks where strtol stopped  */
    int  radix;
    long value;
    if(argc < 3)
    {
        printf("Usage: %s <value> <radix>\n", argv[0]);
    }
    else
    {
        radix = atoi(argv[2]);
        value = strtol(argv[1], &stop_at, radix);
        printf("Value read in radix %d = %ld\n\
Stopped at: %s\n", radix, value, stop_at);

    }
}
```

strtoul

COMPATIBILITY

MSC 3	MSC 4	MSC 5	MSC 6	QC1	QC2	QC2.5	TC1	TC1.5	TC2	TC++	ANSI	UNIX V	XNX	OS2	DOS
		▲	▲	▲	▲	▲		▲	▲	▲	▲			▲	▲

PURPOSE Use *strtoul* to convert a character string to an unsigned long integer.

SYNTAX `unsigned long strtoul(const char *string, char **endptr, int radix);`

`const char *string;`	*Pointer to character array from which the unsigned long value is extracted*
`char **endptr;`	*On return, points to character in* string *where conversion stopped*

`int radix;`	*Radix in which the value is expressed in the string (radix must be in the range 2–36)*

EXAMPLE CALL

```
value = strtoul(input_string, &stop_at, radix);
```

INCLUDES

`#include stdlib.h>`	*For function declaration*
`#include <limits.h>`	*For the definition of the constants LONG_MIN and LONG_MAX*
`#include <math.h>`	*For the definition of ERANGE*

DESCRIPTION The *strtoul* function converts the *string* to an unsigned long integer value. The string is expected to be of the form

[whitespace][0]x or X][digits]

where "whitespace" refers to optional blanks and tab characters, "sign" is a + or a −, and the "digits" are decimal digits. The string is expected to contain a representation of the unsigned long integer with the argument *radix* as the base of the number system. If *radix* is given as zero, however, *strtoul* uses the first character in *string* to determine the radix of the value. The rules are shown in the table.

First Character	Next Character	Radix Selected
0	0–7	Radix 8 is used (octal digits expected)
0	x or X	Radix 16 (hexadecimal digits expected)
1–9	—	Radix 10 (decimal digits expected)

Of course, other radix may be specified via the argument *radix*. The letters a through z (or A through Z) are assigned values 10 through 35. For a specified radix, *strtoul* expects only those letters whose assigned values are less than the *radix*.

The *strtoul* function begins the conversion process with the first character of *string* and continues until it finds a character that meets the above requirements. Then before returning, *strtoul* sets *endptr* to point to that character.

RETURNS The *strtoul* function returns the unsigned long integer value except when it will cause an overflow. In which case, *strtoul* sets *errno* to ERANGE and returns the value ULONG_MAX.

SEE ALSO

`atol`	*To convert strings to long integer values*
`ultoa`	*To convert unsigned long integers to strings*
`strtol`	*To convert strings to long integers*

EXAMPLE Write a program that accepts on the command line an unsigned long integer value followed by the radix in which the value is represented. Use *strtoul* with the radix to convert the representation of that number to an internal value. Print this value.

```
#include <stdio.h>
#include <stdlib.h>
main(int argc, char **argv)
{
    char *stop_at;    /* Marks where strtoul stopped */
    int  radix;
    unsigned long value;
    if(argc < 3)
    {
        printf("Usage: %s <value> <radix>\n", argv[0]);
    }
    else
    {
        radix = atoi(argv[2]);
        value = strtoul(argv[1], &stop_at, radix);
        printf("Value read in radix %d = %lu\n\
Stopped at: %s\n", radix, value, stop_at);

    }
}
```

COMPATIBILITY

ultoa

MSC 3	MSC 4	MSC 5	MSC 6	QC1	QC2	QC2.5	TC1	TC1.5	TC2	TC++	ANSI	UNIX V	XNX	OS2	DOS
▲	▲	▲	▲	▲	▲	▲	▲	▲	▲	▲				▲	▲

PURPOSE Use *ultoa* to convert an *unsigned long* integer value to a character string.

SYNTAX `char *ultoa(unsigned long value, char *string, int radix);`

`unsigned long value;` *Unsigned long integer value to be converted to string*

`char *string;` *Pointer to character array where result is returned*

`int radix;` *Radix in which the result is expressed (in the range 2–36)*

EXAMPLE CALL `ultoa(0x100000, string, 10); /* string = "131072"  */`

INCLUDES `#include <stdlib.h>` *For function declaration*

DESCRIPTION The *ultoa* function converts the *unsigned long* argument *value* into a null-terminated character string using the argument *radix* as the base of the number system. A *long* integer has 32 bits when expressed in radix 2, so the string can occupy a maximum of 33 bytes with the terminating null character. The resulting string is returned by *ultoa* in the buffer whose address is given in the argument *string*.

The argument *radix* specifies the base (between 2 and 36) of the number system in which the string representation of *value* is expressed. For example, using either 2, 8, 10, or 16 as *radix*, you can convert *value* into its binary, octal, decimal, or hexadecimal representation, respectively.

RETURNS The *ultoa* function returns the pointer to the converted string (i.e., it returns the argument *string*).

SEE ALSO `ecvt, fcvt, gcvt` *To convert floating-point numbers to strings*

`itoa, ltoa` *To convert* int *and* long *integers to strings*

EXAMPLE Write a program to print an unsigned long integer value in a specific radix. Assume that the program accepts the value followed by the radix on the command line. Use *ultoa* to prepare the character representation of the number in the radix.

```
#include <stdio.h>
#include <stdlib.h>

main(int argc, char **argv)
{
    char buffer[17];              /* Buffer for ultoa */
    int  radix;
    unsigned long value;
    if(argc < 3)
    {
        printf("Usage: %s <value> <radix>\n", argv[0]);
    }
    else
    {
        value = atol(argv[1]);
        radix = atoi(argv[2]);
        ultoa(value, buffer, radix);
        printf("%s in radix %s = %s\n", argv[1], argv[2],
                buffer);
    }
}
```

Chapter 8 Math Routines

Introduction

You often need computational capabilities beyond basic arithmetic operations. The 8086 family of microprocessors from Intel does not have machine instructions for directly performing such arithmetic operations as addition or multiplication of real or floating-point numbers. If your program will be performing floating-point calculations intensively and a math coprocessor will be available on the target machine, Microsoft C can be told to generate code for the 8087 family of math coprocessors. (Note that the new 80486 processor has a built-in coprocessor.) If floating-point hardware isn't available, you can by use Microsoft C's floating-point emulation library.

Microsoft C provides floating-point support through compiler options (FP followed by various arguments), which, in turn, cause the compiler either to generate code for an 8087 coprocessor or to use its software library to generate similar instructions using 8086 commands. The coprocessor code executes more quickly. The emulation is used by default if no floating-point option is specified. See Table 2-7 in Chapter 2 for a summary of the compiler options.

Microsoft C also includes a set of *math functions* to control the operational characteristics of the underlying floating-point package and to compute common mathematical functions such as the sine and the cosine. This tutorial provides a summary of the math library in Microsoft C.

Concepts: Floating-Point Operations

Most of the math functions operate on floating-point variables, therefore we'll begin by explaining how floating-point numbers are stored and manipulated in the PC.

FLOATING-POINT FORMATS

A *floating-point variable* holds a floating-point number, or a number with a fractional part. We usually use a decimal point when writing such numbers, as in the example, 1.2345×10^5. This format is called scientific or engineering notation. Any floating-point number can be represented in this form: a "mantissa" (the number's significant digits) multiplied by 10, raised to the power of an integer "exponent." The mantissa and exponent form is how floating-point numbers are represented in the PC, except that the exponent represents a base of 2 instead of base 10 because base 2 is the natural format for computers.

Precision: Single and Double

The number of bytes used to represent a floating-point number depends on the precision of the variable. The C variable type *float* is used to declare *single-precision* floating-point variables. The type *double* identifies *double-precision* values. Figure 8-1 shows that a single-precision *float* variable requires 4 bytes of storage while a *double* variable uses 8 bytes. The representation of the mantissa and the exponent in the variables is in accordance with the IEEE floating-point standards, is used in Microsoft C, and is understood by the 80x87 family of math coprocessors.

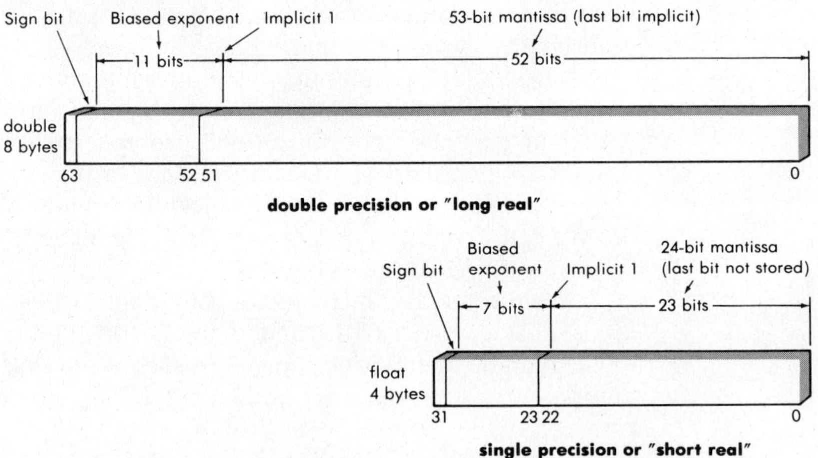

Figure 8-1. ***IEEE format for binary representation of floating-point numbers***

IEEE Format for Floating-Point Numbers

The IEEE format expresses a floating-point number in binary form known as "normalized." Normalization involves adjusting the exponent so that the "binary point" (the binary analog of the decimal point) in the mantissa always lies to the right of the most significant nonzero digit. In binary representation, this means that the most significant digit of the mantissa is always a 1. This property of the normalized representation is exploited by the IEEE format when storing the mantissa.

Consider an example of generating the normalized form of a floating-point number. Suppose, we want to represent the decimal number 5.375. Since this can be written as

$$4 + 1 + 1/4 + 1/8$$

the binary form will be

101.011

The normalized form is obtained by adjusting the exponent until the decimal point is to the right of the 1 in the most significant position. In this case, the result is

$$1.01011 \times 2^2$$

The IEEE format for floating-point storage uses a sign bit, a mantissa, and an exponent representing the power of 2. The "sign bit" denotes the sign of the number: a 0 represents a positive value and a 1 denotes a negative value. The mantissa is represented in binary. Constraining the floating-point number to be in normalized form results in a mantissa whose most significant binary digit is always 1. The IEEE format takes advantage of this by not storing this bit at all. The exponent is an integer stored in unsigned binary format after adding a positive integer "bias" to ensure that the stored exponent is always positive. The value of the bias depends upon the precision of the floating-point representation.

The single-precision *float* variable uses 4 bytes (32 bits) comprising 1 sign bit and 7 bits for the exponent and allows a 24-bit mantissa that can be stored in the rest of the 23 bits because the most significant bit is always 1 (Figure 8-1). The exponent is stored with a bias of 127. Thus, the smallest positive value you can store in a *float* variable is 2^{-126}, which is approximately 1.175×10^{-38}. The largest positive value is 2^{128}, which is about 3.4×10^{38}. About seven significant decimal digits can be handled in a *float* variable.

The double-precision *double* variable uses 8 bytes providing 64 bits of storage. As shown in Figure 8-1, the first bit is used for the sign bit, the next 11 bits hold the exponent, which has a bias of 1,023 added to it. The rest of the 52 bits contain the 53-bit mantissa. This representation allows about 15 significant decimal digits and the smallest positive value is 2^{-1022}, which is approximately 2.23×10^{-308}. The largest positive value that can be held in a *double* variable is 2^{1024}, which is approximately 1.8×10^{308}.

The IEEE format also specifies certain bit-patterns that represent such special conditions as infinite values or NANs (for "not a number"), but we will not go into the details here.

Other Formats: Microsoft Binary Format

The IEEE standard format for binary representation of floating-point numbers is a recent one. Prior to its development, Microsoft used its own binary representation of floating-point numbers in Microsoft BASIC. The single- and double-precision versions of the Microsoft formats use the same number of bytes for storage as the corresponding IEEE representation, but the meaning of the internal bits differ. If you need to pass floating-point data between Microsoft BASIC and Microsoft C, you can use the following library routines: *dieeetomsbin* for converting double-precision IEEE format to the corresponding Microsoft Binary format and *dmsbintoieee* for the reverse. For single-precision numbers, use the routines *fieeetomsbin* and *fmsbintoieee*, respectively.

COMPILER OPTIONS FOR THE FLOATING-POINT LIBRARY

If an 8087 math coprocessor is not present in your system, the Microsoft C library is equipped with alternatives to handle all floating-point calculations. Table 8-1 lists the compiler options providing an array of choices, from generating in-line 8087 instructions to using an alternate math library which is also supplied with Microsoft C. The options */FPc87* and */FPi87* require a math coprocessor at run-time and should not be used for applications that will be distributed widely. For such applications, the options */FPc* or */FPi* generate code that uses the 8087 if the PC has one, but also uses a software emulator.

Table 8-1. ***Compiler Options for Floating-Point Libraries***

Option	8087 or 80287 Required?	Description
/FPa	No	Generates function call to an alternate math library. Will not use an 8087 even if system has it. This alternate math library is provided with Microsoft C.
/FPc	No	Generates function calls and uses the math coprocessor if one is present (otherwise uses an emulator library).
/FPc87	Yes	Generates function calls to routines that use 8087 instructions.
/FPi	No	Generates in-line 8087 instructions that will use the 8087 if found. Otherwise, these instructions will be fielded by the emulator library. This is the default.
/FPi87	Yes	Generates in-line 8087 instructions that require the coprocessor at run-time.

THE FLOATING-POINT PACKAGE

The IEEE standard for binary floating-point arithmetic is used in the 8087 family of math coprocessors. The software implementation that emulates the 8087 when no coprocessor is present in the system also uses the IEEE standard. The routines that handle floating-point calculations are collectively called the "floating-point package."

You can control certain parameters of the floating-point package, such as precision of the calculations and method of rounding the numbers, with the library routines *_clear87*, *_control87*, and *_status87*. The floating-point package maintains two 16-bit registers, the control word and the status word, for this purpose. There are similarly named registers in the 8087 processors. As their names imply, the "status word" maintains the current status of the floating-point package and the "control word" lets you control the precision of the computations and decide how a floating-point result should be truncated to fit in the number of bits available for that precision. The alternate math library does not have these provisions; when you see the compiler option */FPa* these routines are not available. The entire floating-point package can be reset by the library routine *_fpreset*.

FLOATING-POINT EXCEPTIONS

When certain errors occur in the floating-point package, it raises the signal SIGFPE (see the tutorial in Chapter 3 for details on signals). The exceptional conditions, "exceptions" for short, that raise the signal can be controlled by setting bits in the control word with the function *_control87*. The floating-point package has six exceptions (as does the 8087): invalid operation, unnormalized operand, divide by zero, overflow, underflow, and loss of precision (inexact result).

Error Handling in the Floating-Point Package

When an error occurs in a math function, function *matherr* is called. A default, *matherr* is supplied in the Microsoft C library, but you can write your own version of *matherr* to handle errors differently. You have to use the linker option /NOE (see Chapter 2 for details) when adding your own version of *matherr*. Otherwise, the linker will complain when it finds another *matherr* in the library.

Notes

Table 8-2 catalogs the math functions available in the Microsoft C 6.0 library. Most of these routines are for computing specific functions, but a few are dedicated to other chores such as error handling, format conversion, and controlling the floating-point package. The most noteworthy change between version 5.1 and 6.0 is the addition of the *long double* functions which you can identify because of the *l* suffix on their root-name.

Table 8-2. *Library Math Functions*

Routine	Description
abs	Returns the absolute value of an integer argument.
acos	Computes the arc cosine of a value between –1 and 1 and returns an angle between 0 and π radian.
acosl	Returns the arc cosine of x in the range 0 to π radians. It is a long double-precision floating-point version of *acos* and was introduced in Microsoft C 6.0. See the tutorial for more information about the long double functions.
asin	Computes the arc sine of a value between –1 and 1 and returns an angle between $-\pi/2$ and $\pi/2$ radians.
asinl	Computes the arc sine of a value between –1 and 1 and returns an angle between $-\pi/2$ and $\pi/2$ radians. This long double-precision floating-point version of *asin* was introduced in Microsoft C 6.0.
atan	Computes the arc tangent of a value and returns an angle between $-\pi/2$ and $\pi/2$ radians.
atanl	Calculates the arc tangent of a value in the range $-\pi/2$ to $\pi/2$. *atanl* is a long double-precision floating-point version of *atan* and was introduced in Microsoft C 6.0.
atan2	Computes the arc tangent of one argument divided by the other and returns an angle between $-\pi$ and π radians.
atan2l	Calculates the arc tangent of *y/x* in the range $-\pi$ to π and is a long double-precision floating-point version of *atan2*. It was introduced in Microsoft C 6.0.
cabs	Computes the absolute value of a complex number.
cabsl	Calculates the absolute value of a complex number as a long double-precision floating-point version of *cabs*. The *cabsl* routine was introduced in Microsoft C 6.0.
ceil	Finds the smallest integer larger than, or equal to, the function's floating-point argument.
ceill	Returns a long double-precision floating-point value representing the smallest integer that is greater than, or equal to, the argument; introduced in Microsoft C 6.0.
_clear87	Clears the status word of the floating-point package (not available in the alternate math library used when compiler option /FPa is specified).
_control87	Gets and sets the control word of the floating-point package (not available in the alternate math library used when compiler option /FPa is specified).
cos	Evaluates the cosine of an angle in radians.
cosl	Calculates the cosine of an angle in radians. A long double-precision floating-point version of *cos*, it was introduced in Microsoft C 6.0.
cosh	Evaluates the hyperbolic cosine of its argument.
coshl	Calculates the hyperbolic cosine of its argument, which is potentially a large one because it is a long double-precision floating-point version of *cosh*. Introduced in Microsoft C 6.0.
dieeetomsbin	Converts a double-precision number from IEEE format to Microsoft Binary format (used in Microsoft BASIC until BASIC version 6.0).

Table 8-2. *(cont.)*

Routine	Description
div	Divides one integer by another and returns an integer quotient and an integer remainder.
dmsbintoieee	Converts a double-precision number from Microsoft Binary format (used in Microsoft BASIC until BASIC version 6.0) to IEEE format.
exp	Computes the exponential of a floating-point argument.
expl	Returns the exponential function of a floating-point argument. Long double-precision floating-point version of *exp* that was introduced in Microsoft C 6.0.
fabs	Returns the absolute value of a floating-point argument.
fabsl	Gets the absolute value of a double-precision floating-point value. Introduced in Microsoft C 6.0.
fieeetomsbin	Converts a single-precision number from IEEE format to Microsoft Binary format (used in Microsoft BASIC until Microsoft C BASIC 6.0).
floor	Finds the largest integer smaller than, or equal to, the function's floating-point argument.
floorl	Returns a long double-precision floating-point value representing the largest integer that is less than, or equal to, x. Introduced in Microsoft C 6.0.
fmod	Computes the floating-point remainder after dividing one floating-point value by another, so that the quotient is the largest possible integer for that division.
fmodl	Calculates the long double-precision floating-point remainder f of (x,y) such that $x = i * y + f$, where i is an integer, f has the same sign as x, and the absolute value of f is less than the absolute value of y. Long double-precision floating-point version of *fmod* and was introduced in Microsoft C 6.0.
fmsbintoieee	Converts a single-precision number from Microsoft Binary format used in Microsoft BASIC (until BASIC version 6.0) to IEEE format.
_fpreset	Reinitializes the floating-point match package.
frexp	Breaks down a floating-point value into a mantissa between 0.5 and 1 and an integer exponent so that the value is equal to the mantissa x 2 raised to the power of the exponent.
frexpl	Breaks down the long double-precision floating-point value (x) into a mantissa (m) and an exponent (n) such that the absolute value of m is greater than or equal to 0.5 and less than 1.0, and $x = m * 2^n$. Long double-precision floating-point version of *frexp*.
hypot	Computes the length of the hypotenuse of a right-angled triangle.
hypotl	Calculates the length of the hypotenuse of a right-angled triangle, given the length of the two sides x and y, using the long double-precision floating-point version of arguments and return values. Introduced in Microsoft C 6.0.
j0	Returns the Bessel function of the first kind (order 0).
_j0l	Returns the Bessel function of the first kind (order 0) and is a long double-precision floating-point version of *j0*. Introduced in Microsoft C 6.0.
j1	Returns the Bessel function of the first kind (order 1).

Table 8-2. *(cont.)*

Routine	Description
_j1l	Returns the Bessel function of the first kind (order 1); long double-precision floating-point version of j1. Introduced in Microsoft C 6.0.
jn	Returns the Bessel function of the first kind (order n).
_jnl	Returns the Bessel function of the first kind (order n); long double-precision floating-point version of *jn*. Introduced in Microsoft C 6.0.
labs	Returns the absolute value of a long integer argument.
ldexp	Computes a floating-point value equal to a mantissa x 2 raised to power of an integer exponent.
ldexpl	Converts the mantissa and exponent to a floating-point value. It is the long double-precision floating-point version of *ldexp* and was introduced in Microsoft C 6.0. (See the tutorial for more details about long double functions.)
ldiv	Divides one long integer by another and returns a long integer quotient and a long integer remainder.
log	Evaluates the natural logarithm of its floating-point argument.
logl	Calculates the natural logarithm of its floating-point argument. A long double-precision floating-point version of *log*, *logl* was introduced in Microsoft C 6.0.
log10	Evaluates the logarithm to the base 10 of its floating-point argument.
log10l	Calculates the base-10 logarithm of its argument. It is a long double-precision floating-point version of *log10* and was introduced in Microsoft C 6.0.
_lrotl	Rotates an unsigned long integer to the left by a given number of bits.
_lrotr	Rotates an unsigned long integer to the right by a given number of bits.
matherr	Handles error conditions occurring in the functions of the math library package.
_matherrl	Processes errors generated by the long double-precision functions of the math library. Introduced in Microsoft C 6.0.
max	A macro that returns the larger of two values.
min	A macro that returns the smaller of two values.
modf	Breaks down a floating-point value into its integer part and its fractional part.
modfl	Breaks down the long double-precision floating-point value of its argument into fractional and integer parts with the same sign as its argument. It was introduced in Microsoft C 6.0.
pow	Computes the value of one argument raised to the power of a second one.
powl	Computes the value of one argument raised to the power of a second argument. The *powl* version is a long double-precision floating-point iteration of *pow* that was introduced in Microsoft C 6.0.
rand	Returns a random integer between 0 and 32,767.
_rotl	Rotates an unsigned integer left by a given number of bits.
_rotr	Rotates an unsigned integer right by a given number of bits.
sin	Evaluates the sine of an angle in radians.

Table 8-2. ***(cont.)***

Routine	Description
sinl	Calculates the sine of an angle in radians. Long double-precision floating-point version of *sin*. Introduced in Microsoft C 6.0.
sinh	Evaluates the hyperbolic sine of its argument.
sinhl	Calculates the hyperbolic sine of its argument. Long double-precision floating-point version of *sinh*. Introduced in Microsoft C 6.0.
sqrt	Computes the square root of a positive floating-point number.
sqrtl	Calculates the square root of a positive value, and is a long double-precision floating-point version of *sqrt* that was introduced in Microsoft C 6.0.
srand	Sets the starting point for the sequence of random numbers generated by *rand*.
_status87	Gets the status word of the floating-point package (not available in the alternate math library used when compiler option /FPa is specified).
tan	Evaluates the tangent of an angle in radians.
tanl	Evaluates the tangent of an angle in radians. Long double-precision floating-point version of *tan*. Introduced in Microsoft C 6.0.
tanh	Evaluates the hyperbolic tangent of its argument.
tanhl	Calculates the hyperbolic tangent of its argument. A long double-precision floating-point version of tanh, the tanhl routine was introduced in Microsoft C 6.0.
y0	Returns the Bessel function of the second kind (order 0).
_y0l	Returns the Bessel function of the second kind (order 0). It is a long double-precision floating-point version of *y0*, introduced in Microsoft C 6.0.
y1	Returns the Bessel function of the second kind (order 1).
_y1l	Returns the Bessel function of the second kind (order 1), and is a long double-precision floating-point version of y1. It was introduced in Microsoft C 6.0.
yn	Returns the Bessel function of the second kind (order n).
_ynl	Returns the Bessel function of the second kind (order n). Long double-precision floating-point version of *yn*. Introduced in Microsoft C 6.0.

THE MATH FUNCTIONS BY TASK

When we categorize the math functions in terms of the tasks (Table 8-3), we discover that several important types of computation are supported in the library.

Table 8-3. ***Math Functions by Task***

Task	Routines
Compare two values for relative size.	max, min
Compute magnitudes and absolute values.	abs, cabs, cabsl, fabs, fabsl, hypot, hypotl
Compute square roots.	sqrt, sqrtl

Table 8-3. *(cont.)*

Task	Routines
Convert from one format to another.	dieeetomsbin, dmsbintoieee, fieeetomsbin, fmsbintoieee
Evaluate Bessel functions of first and second kind of integral orders.	j0, _j0l, j1, _j1l, jn, _jnl, y0, _y0l, y1, _y1l, yn, _ynl
Evaluate hyperbolic functions.	cosh, coshl, sinh, sinhl, tanh, tanhl
Evaluate powers and logarithms.	exp, expl, frexp, frexpl, ldexp, ldexpl, log10, log10l, log, logl, pow, powl
Evaluate trigonometric functions.	acos, acosl, asin, asinl, atan, atanl, atan2, atan2l, cos, cosl, sin, sinl, tan, tanl
Find integer limits (upper and lower) for floating-point numbers.	ceil, ceill, floor, floorl
Find floating-point remainder.	fmod, fmodl
Break down floating-point number into integer and fraction.	modf, modfl
Generate random numbers.	rand, srand
Handle errors.	matherr, _matherrl
Integer arithmetic.	abs, div, labs, ldiv
Manipulate floating-point package (status and control information).	_clear87, _control87, _fpreset, _status87
Rotate bits.	_rotl, _lrotl, _rotr, _lrotr

Basic Math Functions

The seven trigonometric functions *cos, sin, tan, acos, asin, atan,* and *atan2* respectively evaluate the cosines, sines, and tangents of any angle in radians and compute their particular inverses. You will find these routines useful for tasks such as changing from rectangular to polar coordinates, which often occur in graphics programs. Microsoft C 6.0 introduced long double versions of the trig routines. They are identified by a suffix *l* after the generic name: *cosl, sinl, tanl, acosl, asinl, atanl,* and *atan2l.*

The Bessel functions *j0, j1, jn, y0, y1,* and *yn* are not typically encountered in everyday programming, unless you are working with such phenomena as sound and radio reflection. Microsoft C 6.0 added six new Bessel routines, long double versions of the above, which have the following names: _j0l, _j1l, _jnl, _y0l, y1l, and _ynl. The long double versions use the 80-bit math routines. The j and _j prefixes identify Bessel functions of the so-called first kind, and the *y* and *_y* functions are Bessels of the second kind.

The hyperbolic functions *cosh, sinh,* and *tanh* are useful when calculating the hyperbolic cosine, hyperbolic sine, and hyperbolic tangent, respectively. They are joined in version 6.0 by long double versions named *coshl, sinhl,* and *tanhl.* The *l* suffix identifies the long double versions, and they work to 80-bit precision.

C, unlike FORTRAN, does not have built-in support for complex variables and exponentiation. You have to use C library routines for these tasks. The *pow* routine enables you to raise one number to the power of another. The *cabs* and the *hypot* functions can compute the magnitude of a complex number. Other commonly used functions include *sqrt* to compute square roots. The *log* and *log10* functions return the logarithm, natural, and to the base 10, respectively, of an argument. Exponentials (for example, *e 15*) can be computed by *exp*. The *abs* and *fabs* functions return the absolute value of an argument. The *ceil* and *floor* routines find the nearest integer, larger or smaller than a given floating-point number. These functions, with the exception of *abs*, have long double-precision equivalents that were introduced in Microsoft C 6.0. They can be identified by an *l* suffix, as in *cabsl* and *hypotl*, for example.

INTEGER ARITHMETIC

There are four routines that use integer arguments to handle arithmetic, and they are, therefore, not accompanied by long double versions. The routines *abs* and *labs* return the absolute value of an integer and a long integer, respectively. The *div* function divides one integer by another and returns the integer quotient and an integer remainder. The *ldiv* function operates similarly, but uses long integers as arguments.

ROTATING BITS

The bit shift operators are ideal for extracting a specified number of bits from an integer variable. You may, however, want to *rotate* the bits, rather than shift them. As shown in Figure 8-2, in a shift operation, one bit is discarded at one end while a zero bit is inserted at the other end at each step. Rotation is similar to shift except that the bit shifting out is brought into the other end. You can implement the byte-swapping capability of *swab*, for instance, by rotating the bits of each 2-byte integer 8 bits to the right.

The routines *_rotl* and *_lrotl* rotate an unsigned integer and an unsigned long integer, respectively, to the left by a specified number of bits. The corresponding routines for rotating to the right are *_rotr* and *_lrotr*.

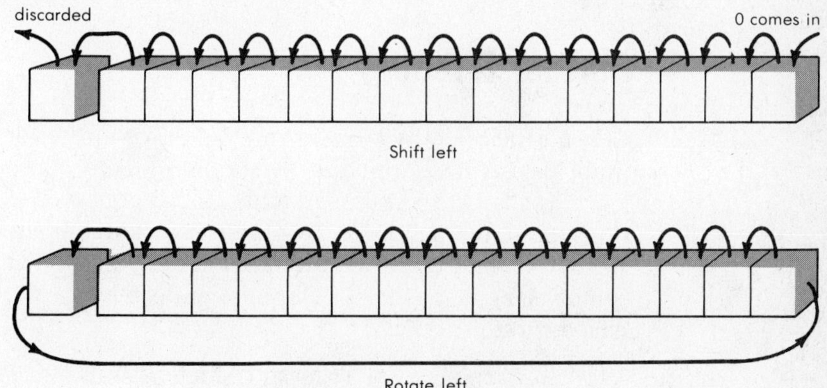

Figure 8-2. ***Shift vs rotate***

GENERATING RANDOM NUMBERS The Microsoft C library includes a *rand* routine that can generate a random positive integer in the range 0 through 32,767. Random numbers are useful for screen patterns, games, or statistical analysis, and using *rand* is akin to throwing a die with 32,768 faces. The generator uses an algorithm and always generates the same sequence of numbers from a given starting point, so it is considered a pseudorandom rather than a truly random sequence. If the generating algorithm is well designed, the ensuing sequence will not repeat itself too early and any of the legal values will appear with equal probability. The *srand* function sets the starting point of the random sequence. One way to increase the randomness of the numbers is to use the system time as a *srand* argument to establish a new random seed for *rand*.

Cautions

- The *_clear87, _control87,* and *_status87* functions should not be called in any program compiled using option */FPa* to select an alternate math library.
- If you install your own handler for the floating-point exception SIGFPE, your handler should call *_fpreset* to reset the floating-point package before returning.
- Use the linker option /NOE if you provide an alternate *matherr* routine to handle errors.
- The basic math functions without the leading underscore exist in ANSI-standard C libraries, but the floating-point functions are specific to MS-DOS.

Further Reading

Consult the book by Morgan and Waite[1] for further details on the floating-point data types supported by the 8087 math coprocessor (or, Numeric Data Processor). If you need to use the trigonometric and the Bessel functions often, the handbook by Abramowitz and Stegun[2] is a good reference. If you are interested in programming the 8087 math coprocessor in assembly language, the developer's guide by The Waite Group[3] devotes a chapter to this topic.

1. Christopher L. Morgan and Mitchell Waite, *8086/8088 16-bit Microprocessor Primer*, BYTE/McGraw-Hill, Peterborough, NH, 1982, 355 pages.

2. Milton Abramowitz and Irene A. Stegun, Eds., *Handbook of Mathematical Functions with Formulas, Graphs and Mathematical Tables*, Dover Publications, New York, NY, 1972, 1046 pages.
3. The Waite Group, *MS-DOS Developer's Guide*, 2d Ed., SAMS & Company, Carmel, IN, 1989, 783 pages.
4. Graham, Ronald L., Knuth, Donald E., and Patashnik, Oren, *Concrete Mathematics*, Addison-Wesley, Reading, MA, 1989, 638 pages.

abs

COMPATIBILITY

MSC 3	MSC 4	MSC 5	MSC 6	QC1	QC2	QC2.5	TC1	TC1.5	TC2	TC++	ANSI	UNIX V	XNX	OS2	DOS
▲	▲	▲	▲	▲	▲	▲		▲	▲	▲	▲	▲	▲	▲	▲

PURPOSE Use *abs* to get the absolute value of an integer.

SYNTAX

```
int abs(int n);
```

`int n;` *Integer whose absolute value is returned*

EXAMPLE CALL

```
x = abs(-5); /* x will be 5 now */
```

INCLUDES `#include <stdlib.h>` *For function declaration*

DESCRIPTION The *abs* function returns the absolute value of the integer argument *n*. Thus *abs (–10)* returns +10.

RETURNS The integer returned by *abs* is the absolute value of *n*.

SEE ALSO

`cabs` *To obtain the magnitude (or absolute value) of a complex number*

`fabs` *To get the absolute values of a floating-point number*

`labs` *To get the absolute values of a long integer*

EXAMPLE Write a program that reads an integer value as a command-line argument and prints its absolute value.

```
#include <stdio.h>
#include <stdlib.h>
main(int argc, char **argv)
{
    int value, result;
    if(argc < 2)
    {
        printf("Usage: %s <integer_value>\n", argv[0]);
    }
    else
    {
        value = atoi(argv[1]);
        result = abs(value);
        printf("Absolute value of %d = %d\n",
                value, result);
    }
}
```

COMPATIBILITY

acos, acosl

MSC 3	MSC 4	MSC 5	MSC 6	QC1	QC2	QC2.5	TC1	TC1.5	TC2	TC++	ANSI	UNIX V	XNX	OS2	DOS
▲	▲	▲	1	▲	▲	▲	▲	▲	▲	▲	2	2	2	▲	▲

PURPOSE Use *acos* to compute the arc cosine of a *double* variable whose value lies between −1 and 1. Use the *acosl* function when you need a long double floating-point version of *acos*.

SYNTAX

```
double acos (double x);

long double acosl (long double x);

x;          Argument whose arc cosine is to be computed
```

EXAMPLE CALL

```
angle = acos(0.5); /* angle is "pi"/3 */

angle_2 = acosl (0.6);
```

INCLUDES `#include <math.h>` *For function declaration and definition of constants EDOM and DOMAIN*

DESCRIPTION The *acos* function accepts an argument *x* whose value lies in the range −1 to 1 and computes its arc cosine. The result is an angle with value between 0 and π radians. The *acosl* version returns the arc cosine of *x* in the range 0 to π radians, and is a long double precision (80-bit) floating-point version of *acos( )*. See the tutorial for more information about the long double functions.

1. The *acosl* function was introduced in Microsoft C 6.0. 2. *acosl* is not compatible with ANSI, UNIX, or XENIX.

RETURNS When the value of the argument *x* is in the valid range of −1 to 1, *acos* returns the result. If the argument's value is outside the acceptable range, *acos* sets the global variable *errno* to the constant EDOM which is defined in *math.h*, prints a DOMAIN error message to *stderr*, and returns a value of 0. You can write your own error-handling routine with the name *matherr* to perform differently when an error occurs. The *acosl* version returns 0 if x is less than −1 or greater than 1.

SEE ALSO

`matherr` *To handle math errors (you can add your own)*

`cos` *To compute a cosine of an angle*

EXAMPLE Write a program that accepts a floating-point number on the command line and computes the arc cosine of that number if it lies between −1 and 1. The example program will work as written with the substitution of a call to *acosl* for the call to *acos*.

```
#include <stdio.h>
#include <math.h>
#include <stdlib.h>          /* errno is defined here */
#define  R_TO_D   57.29578 /* radians to degrees   */
main(int argc, char **argv)
{
    double result;
    if(argc < 2)
    {
        printf("Usage: %s <value>\n", argv[0]);
    }
    else
    {
        result = acos(atof(argv[1])) * R_TO_D;
        if(errno != EDOM)
        {
            printf("Arc cosine (%s) = %f deg.\n",
                    argv[1], result);
        }
    }
}
```

asin, asinl

COMPATIBILITY

MSC 3	MSC 4	MSC 5	MSC 6	QC1	QC2	QC2.5	TC1	TC1.5	TC2	TC++	ANSI	UNIX V	XNX	OS2	DOS
▲	▲	▲	1	▲	▲	▲	▲	▲	▲	▲	2	2	2	▲	▲

PURPOSE Use *asin* to compute the arc sine of a *double* variable whose value lies between −1 and 1. There is a long double version of this function: *asinl.*

SYNTAX

```
double asin (double x);

long double asinl (long double x);
```

`x;` *Argument whose arc sine is to be computed*

EXAMPLE CALL

```
angle = asin(0.707)  /* angle is roughly "pi"/4  */

angle = asinl (0.703)
```

INCLUDES `#include <math.h>` *For function declaration and definition of constants EDOM and DOMAIN*

DESCRIPTION The *asin* function computes the arc sine of the argument *x* provided its value lies in the range −1 to 1. The result is an angle with value between −π/2 and π/2 radians. The *asinl* function calculates the arcsine of a value in the range −π/2 to π/2 radians and is the long (80-bit) double-precision floating-point version of asin( ).

1. The *asinl* function was introduced in Microsoft C 6.0. 2. The *asinl* function is not compatible with ANSI, UNIX, or XENIX.

RETURNS For a valid argument *x* with values between −1 and 1, *asin* returns an angle whose sine is equal to *x*. If the argument's value lies outside the acceptable range, however, *asin* sets the global variable *errno* to the constant EDOM which is defined in *math.h*, prints a DOMAIN error message to *stderr*, and returns a value of 0. You can write your own error-handling routine with the name *matherr* to perform differently when an error occurs.

The *asinl* version returns 0 if *x* is less than −1 or greater than 1.

SEE ALSO `matherr` *To handle math errors (you can add your own)*

`sin` *To compute a sine of an angle*

EXAMPLE Write a program that computes and prints the arc sine of 10 numbers between −1 and 1, starting with −1 and advancing to 1 with a stepsize of 0.2. The example program will work as written if the call to *asin* is substituted by a call to *asinl* and the variables are declared as long doubles.

```
#include <stdio.h>
#include <math.h>
#include <stdlib.h>         /* errno is defined here */
#define  R_TO_D   57.29578 /* radians to degrees   */
main()
{
    double value, result;
    for (value = -1.0; value <= 1.0; value += 0.2)
    {
        result = asin(value) * R_TO_D;
        if(errno != EDOM)
        {
            printf("Arc sine (%f) = %f deg.\n",
                    value, result);
        }
    }
}
```

atan, atanl

COMPATIBILITY

MSC 3	MSC 4	MSC 5	MSC 6	QC1	QC2	QC2.5	TC1	TC1.5	TC2	TC++	ANSI	UNIX V	XNX	OS2	DOS
▲	▲	▲	1	▲	▲	▲	▲	▲	▲	▲	2	2	2	▲	▲

PURPOSE Use *atan* to compute the arc tangent of a variable. The *atanl* function is a long double version of *atan*.

SYNTAX

```
double atan (double x);

long double atanl (long double x);
```

`x;` *Value whose arc tangent is sought*

EXAMPLE CALL

```
angle = atan(1.0)  /* angle is "pi"/4  */

angle = atanl (1.0) /* angle is "pi"/4  */
```

INCLUDES `#include <math.h>` *For function declaration*

DESCRIPTION The *atan* function computes the arc tangent of the argument *x*. The result is an angle with value between $-\pi/2$ and $\pi/2$ radians. The *atanl* version calculates the arc tangent of *x* in the range $-\pi/2$ to $\pi/2$. It is a long double-precision (80-bit) floating-point version of *atan*.

1. The *atanl* function was introduced in Microsoft C 6.0. 2. The *atanl* function does not work under ANSI, UNIX, or XENIX.

RETURNS The *atan* function returns the angle in the range $-\pi/2$ and $\pi/2$ whose tangent is equal to *x*. The *atanl* version returns the arc tangent result, or, if the call fails, a zero if the value of *x* is zero.

COMMENTS When used with the *intrinsic* pragma (see Chapter 1), the convention of the argument calling for both the regular and long double versions is changed to pass the arguments on the floating-point chip.

SEE ALSO `atan2` *To compute arc tangent of the ratio of two arguments*

EXAMPLE Write a program that prompts for a floating-point number and then computes the arc tangent of that number. The example program will work with the newer long double version if the *atan* call is changed to *atanl* and the appropriate variables are declared as long doubles.

```
#include <stdio.h>
#include <math.h>
#include <stdlib.h>          /* errno is defined here */
#define  R_TO_D   57.29578 /* radians to degrees  */
main()
{
    double tanvalue, result;
    printf("Enter value whose arctangent you want \
to evaluate: ");
    scanf(" %le", &tanvalue);
    result = atan(tanvalue) * R_TO_D;
    if(errno != EDOM)
    {
        printf("Arc tangent (%f) = %f deg.\n",
                tanvalue, result);
    }
}
```

COMPATIBILITY

atan2, atan2l

MSC 3	MSC 4	MSC 5	MSC 6	QC1	QC2	QC2.5	TC1	TC1.5	TC2	TC++	ANSI	UNIX V	XNX	OS2	DOS
▲	▲	▲	1	▲	▲	▲	▲	▲	▲	▲	2	2	2	▲	▲

PURPOSE Use *atan2* to compute the arc tangent of the ratio of two nonzero variables. The *atan2l* function is a long double version of *atan2*.

SYNTAX

```
double atan2 (double y, double x);

long double atan2l (long double y, long double x);

double x, y;
```
The arc tangent of y/x *will be computed*

EXAMPLE CALL

```
angle = atan2(y, x);

angle = atan2l (y, x);
```

INCLUDES `#include <math.h>` *For function declaration and definition of constants EDOM and DOMAIN*

DESCRIPTION The *atan2* function computes the arc tangent of the ratio of the arguments *y/x*. The result is an angle with value between $-\pi$ and π radians. In contrast to *atan*, which takes a single argument, *atan2* can use the sign of its two arguments to determine the quadrant (a 90° sector in cartesian coordinates) in which the angle should lie. The *atan2l* routine calculates the arc tangent of y/x in the range $-\pi$ to π and is a long (80-bit) double-precision floating-point version of *atan2*. See the tutorial for more information about long double versions.

1. The *atan2l* function was introduced in Microsoft C 6.0. 2. *atanl* does not work under ANSI, UNIX, or XENIX.

RETURNS Provided both arguments x and y are nonzero, *atan2* returns an angle whose tangent is equal to x. If both arguments are zero, however, *atan2* sets the global variable *errno* to the constant EDOM, prints a DOMAIN error message to *stderr*, and returns a value of zero. You can write your own error-handling routine to perform differently when an error occurs with the name *matherr*.

The *atan2l* routine returns the arc tangent result if the call is a success, but will return a 0 if the value of either x or y is a 0.

COMMENTS When used with the *intrinsic* pragma (see Chapter 1), the convention of the argument calling for both the regular and long double versions is changed to pass the arguments on the floating-point chip.

SEE ALSO

`atan`	*To compute arc tangent of an argument*
`matherr`	*To handle math errors (you can add your own)*
`tan`	*To compute a tangent of an angle*

EXAMPLE Write a program that accepts two floating-point numbers y and x on the command line and computes the arc tangent of y/x. As is true with the other long double functions, the example program will work if the long double version of the function is substituted for the regular version, and the appropriate variables are declared as long doubles. In this case, the call to *atan2* would be changed to *atan2l*.

```
#include <stdio.h>
#include <math.h>
#include <stdlib.h>         /* errno is defined here */
#define  R_TO_D   57.29578 /* radians to degrees  */
main(int argc, char **argv)
{
    double result;
    if(argc < 3)
    {
        printf("Usage: %s <y> <x>\n", argv[0]);
    }
```

```
        else
        {

            result = atan2(atof(argv[1]),
                                atof(argv[2])) * R_TO_D;
            if(errno != EDOM)
            {
                printf("Arc tangent (%s/%s) = %f deg.\n",
                        argv[1], argv[2], result);
            }
        }
    }
```

COMPATIBILITY

Bessel functions

MSC 3	MSC 4	MSC 5	MSC 6	QC1	QC2	QC2.5	TC1	TC1.5	TC2	TC++	ANSI	UNIX V	XNX	OS2	DOS
▲	▲	▲	1	▲	▲	▲						2	2	▲	▲

PURPOSE Use the functions in this group to evaluate Bessel functions of first and second kind of any integer order for an argument. (For further details, see a reference book such as *Handbook of Mathematical Functions* by M. Abramowitz and I.A. Stegun, Dover, 1970.)

SYNTAX

```
double j0(double x);

double j1(double x);

double jn(int n, double x);

double y0(double x);

double y1(double x);

double yn(int n, double x);

long double _j01 (long double ldx);

long double _jnl (int numm, long double ldx);

long double _j1l (long double ldx);

long double _y0l (long double ldx);
```

```
long double _y1l (long double ldx);

long double _ynl (int numm, long double ldx);
```

`double x;`	*Positive argument for the Bessel function*
`int n;`	*Integer order of the Bessel function for* jn *and* yn
`ldx;`	*Long double-precision floating-point value*
`numm;`	*Integer order of the Bessel function for* _jnl *and* _ynl.

INCLUDES `#include <math.h>` *For function declaration and definition of constants EDOM, DOMAIN, and HUGE_VAL*

DESCRIPTION This group of functions evaluates the Bessel function of first and second kind of integer order at an argument *x*. The functions *jn* and *yn* also accept an integer *n* that denotes the order of the Bessel function being evaluated. The argument *x* must be positive when calling the functions *y0, y1* and *yn*, which compute Bessel functions of the second kind.

The *_j0l* routine is a long double-precision floating-point version of *j0* and returns the result of a Bessel function of *ldx*. The *_jnl* iteration returns the Bessel function of the first kind (order numm) and is the long double-precision floating-point version of *jn*. The *j1l* version returns the Bessel function of the first kind (order 1) and is a long (80-bit) double-precision floating-point version of *j1*.

The *_y0l* version returns the Bessel function of the second kind (order 0). It is a long double-precision floating-point version of *y0*. The *_y1l* routine returns the Bessel function of the second kind (order 1). It is a long (80-bit) double-precision floating-point version of *y1*. The *_ynl* version returns the Bessel function of the second kind (order n). It is a long double-precision floating-point version of *yn*.

1. Note that the six "leading underscore" Bessel functions were introduced in Microsoft C 6.0. **2**. These "leading underscore" functions are not compatible with UNIX or XENIX.

COMMON USES Bessel functions appear in mathematical theories of electromagnetic wave propagation. You may not need them for everyday programming, but they are available in the Microsoft C library if your application requires them.

RETURNS Normally, the functions return the value of the appropriate Bessel function at the specified argument *x*, and for the order *n* in the case of *jn* and *yn*. But if the Bessel functions of the second kind are called with a negative *x*, the routines return the value HUGE_VAL, set *errno* to the constant EDOM, and print a DOMAIN error message on *stderr*. Additional error handling can be provided by linking your version of the routine named *matherr*.

The return value of the newer "underscore" variants is identical to earlier versions except _LHUGE_VAL instead of HUGE_VAL is to be used if the value of *ldx* is negative.

SEE ALSO `matherr` *To handle math errors (you can add your own)*

EXAMPLE Write a program that accepts a command line of the form *bessel*<*j or y*><*n*><*x*> and computes the value of the appropriate Bessel function by calling *jn* or *yn* with argument *x*. Remember to handle the cases $n = 0$ and $n = 1$ separately. The long (80-bit) double versions of the Bessel routines will work in the example program if the Bessel function calls are changed to include the leading underscore and if the appropriate variables (*x* and *result*) are declared as long doubles instead of doubles.

```
#include <stdio.h>
#include <math.h>
#include <stdlib.h>   /* errno is declared here */
main(int argc, char **argv)
{
    int    n;
    double x, result;
    if(argc < 4)
    {
        printf("Usage: %s <j or y> <n> <x>\n",
                argv[0]);
    }
    else
    {
        n = atoi(argv[2]);
        x = atof(argv[3]);
        switch(argv[1][0])
        {
            case 'j':
            case 'J':
                if(n == 0) result = j0(x);
                if(n == 1) result = j1(x);
                if (n != 0 && n != 1) result = jn(n, x);
                break;
            case 'y':
            case 'Y':
                if(n == 0) result = y0(x);

                if(n == 1) result = y1(x);
```

```
                if (n != 0 && n != 1) result = yn(n, x);
                break;
            default:
                printf("Unknown function: %s\n", argv[1]);
                exit(0);
        }
        if (errno != EDOM)
            printf("%s %d (%f) = %f\n",
                    argv[1], n, x, result);
    }
}
```

cabs, cabsl

COMPATIBILITY

MSC 3	MSC 4	MSC 5	MSC 6	QC1	QC2	QC2.5	TC1	TC1.5	TC2	TC++	ANSI	UNIX V	XNX	OS2	DOS
▲	▲	▲	1	▲	▲	▲	▲	▲	▲	▲		2	2	▲	▲

PURPOSE Use *cabs* to compute the magnitude of a complex number stored in a structure of type *complex*. The *cabsl* routine is a long double version of *cabs*.

SYNTAX

```
double cabs (struct complex z);

long double cabsl (struct _complexl ldz);
```

`struct complex z;` *Structure containing the complex number whose magnitude is computed*

`struct _complexl ldz;` *Long double-precision complex number structure defined in MATH.H*

EXAMPLE CALL

```
magnitude = cabs(z);

magnitude - cabsl (y);
```

INCLUDES `#include <math.h>` *For function declaration and definition of the structure complex*

DESCRIPTION The *cabs* function computes the magnitude of a complex number *z* stored in a structure of type *complex* which is defined in *math.h* as follows:

```
struct complex
{
    double x;    /* Real part of the complex number      */
```

```
    double y;     /* Imaginary part of the complex number */
};
```

The magnitude of *z* is computed with the expression

```
magnitude = sqrt(z.x*z.x + z.y*z.y);
```

The *cabsl* function computes the absolute value of a complex number using a structure of type *_complexl*, which is defined in *math.h* as follows:

```
struct _complexl
    {
    long double x,y;     /* real and imaginary parts */
    } ;
```

It is a long double-precision (80-bit) floating-point version of *cabs*. See the tutorial for more information about the *long double* functions.

1. The *cabsl* function was introduced in Microsoft C 6.0. 2. *cabsl* does not work under UNIX or XENIX.

RETURNS If the magnitude of *z* is too large, *cabs* calls the routine *matherr* to handle the error. In this case, it returns a value HUGE_VAL defined in *math.h* and sets the variable *errno* to the constant ERANGE. If all goes well, *cabs* returns the magnitude of the complex number. Like the *cabs* version, *cabsl* returns the absolute value, if successful, but an overflow is returned by _LHUGE_VAL instead of HUGE_VAL.

SEE ALSO

`matherr`	*To handle math errors (you can add your own)*
`hypot`	*To compute the length of the hypotenuse of a right triangle*
`fabs`	*To compute the absolute value of a* double *variable*

EXAMPLE Write a program that accepts the real and the imaginary part of a complex number on the command line and computes the magnitude of the complex number by using *cabs*. The example program can be modified to run the *cabsl* version by ensuring that the *double* variables are declared as *long doubles*, and by avoiding the transmission of the 80-bit long double-precision floating-point values to functions that cannot handle them.

```
#include <stdio.h>
#include <math.h>
#include <stdlib.h>      /* errno is defined here */
main()
```

```
{
    struct complex z;
    double result;
    printf("Enter complex number in the form \
\"(real, imaginary)\":");
    scanf(" (%le , %le )", &z.x, &z.y);
    result = cabs(z);
    if(errno != ERANGE)
    {
        printf("Magnitude of (%f, %f) = %f\n",
                z.x, z.y, result);
    }
}
```

ceil, ceill

COMPATIBILITY

MSC 3	MSC 4	MSC 5	MSC 6	QC1	QC2	QC2.5	TC1	TC1.5	TC2	TC++	ANSI	UNIX V	XNX	OS2	DOS
▲	▲	▲	1	▲	▲	▲	▲	▲	▲	▲	2	2	2	▲	▲

PURPOSE Use *ceil* to compute the *ceiling*, the smallest integer value that is greater than or equal to a *double* variable. The *ceill* routine is a long double version of *ceill.*

SYNTAX

```
double ceil(double x);

long double ceill (long double ldx);
```

`double x;` *Variable whose "ceiling" is to be returned*

`ldx;` *Long double-precision floating-point value whose "ceiling" is to be returned*

EXAMPLE CALL

```
x_ceiling = ceil(4.1);  /* x_ceiling is 5.0 */

y_ceiling = ceill (6.1);  /* y_ceiling is 7.0 */
```

INCLUDES `#include <math.h>` *For function declaration*

DESCRIPTION The *ceil* function finds the ceiling of a *double* argument *x*. The ceiling is the smallest integral value that is equal to or that just exceeds *x*. This can be used in rounding a *double* value up to the next integer. The *ceill* version returns a long (80-bit) double-precision floating-point value representing the smallest integer that is greater than, or equal to, the argument.

1. The *ceill* function was introduced in Microsoft C 6.0. 2. *ceill* is not compatible with ANSI, UNIX, or XENIX.

RETURNS The return value is the ceiling of *x* expressed as a *double*. The *ceill* function returns a long double result, rounded up.

COMMENTS When used with the *intrinsic* pragma (see Chapter 1), the convention of the argument calling for both the regular and long double versions is changed to pass the arguments on the floating-point chip.

SEE ALSO `floor` *To determine the largest integer that is just less than a variable*

EXAMPLE Write a program that accepts a floating-point number on the command line and prints the ceiling of that number. The *ceill* function, the long double-precision version of *ceil*, will work in the example. Substitute the *ceill* call for the original *ceill* and declare the *result* variable as a long double instead of a regular double. The long double is an 80-bit number.

```
#include <stdio.h>
#include <math.h>
main(int argc, char **argv)
{
    double result;
    if(argc < 2)
    {
        printf("Usage: %s <value>\n", argv[0]);
    }
    else
    {
        result = ceil(atof(argv[1]));
        printf("ceil of %s = %f\n", argv[1], result);
    }
}
```

_clear87

COMPATIBILITY

MSC 3	MSC 4	MSC 5	MSC 6	QC1	QC2	QC2.5	TC1	TC1.5	TC2	TC++	ANSI	UNIX V	XNX	OS2	DOS
	▲	▲	▲	▲	▲	▲	▲	▲	▲	▲				▲	▲

PURPOSE Use *_clear87* to retrieve the current contents of the floating-point status word and reset all bits to zero.

SYNTAX `unsigned int _clear87(void);`

EXAMPLE CALL `status = _clear87();`

INCLUDES `#include <float.h>` *For function declaration and definition of constants denoting status-word bit settings*

DESCRIPTION The *_clear87* function retrieves the status word of the floating-point package of the C library and clears all its bits before returning. This status word is a composite of the status word of the 8087 math coprocessor and other conditions detected by the 8087 exception handler. (See the reference page on *_status87* for details on the bit settings of the status word.)

RETURNS The *_clear87* function returns the prior contents of the floating-point status word.

SEE ALSO `_status87` *To get the floating-point status word*

`_control87` *To alter bits in the floating-point control word*

EXAMPLE Copy a small *double* variable into a *float* variable and generate an underflow and an inexact result. Now call *_clear87* to clear the status word. The return value reflects the error that occurred, but if you read the status again with *_status87*, it will show a cleared status word.

```
#include <stdio.h>
#include <float.h>
main()
{
    float a;
    double b = 1.e-40;
    unsigned fpstatus;
/* Perform operation that produces underflow and
 * an inexact result
 */
    a = b;   /* This will produce inexact result */
    printf("After undeflow/inexact ");
```

```
/* Clear status word. It'll return prior status */
    fpstatus = _clear87();
    printf("status word was: %X\n", fpstatus);
    fpstatus = _status87();
    printf("After _clear87, status word is: %X\n",
                                            fpstatus);
}
```

COMPATIBILITY

_control87

MSC 3	MSC 4	MSC 5	MSC 6	QC1	QC2	QC2.5	TC1	TC1.5	TC2	TC++	ANSI	UNIX V	XNX	OS2	DOS
	▲	▲	▲	▲	▲	▲	▲	▲	▲	▲				▲	▲

PURPOSE Use *_control87* to get and set the floating-point control word. When an 8087 math coprocessor is being used, *_control87* sets its control word.

SYNTAX `unsigned int _control87(unsigned new, unsigned mask);`

`unsigned int new;` *New control word bit values*

`unsigned int mask;` *Mask to indicate which bits of control word to set*

EXAMPLE CALL `status = _control87(PC_24, MCW_PC); /* 24-bit precision */`

INCLUDES `#include <float.h>` *For function declaration and definition of constants denoting control-word bit settings*

DESCRIPTION The *_control87* function gets and sets the floating-point control word. The settings control the precision, the rounding, the infinity mode, and the exceptions that will be generated. The value of the argument *mask* determines which of these four categories is being changed. The possible values are shown in Table 8-4 in terms of constants defined in *float.h*. If the *mask* is zero, *_control87* simply returns the value of the status word. For any other mask setting from Table 8-4, you must specify the new value, given in the argument *new*, for that option from the list under that mask value. Thus, to set the precision to 24 bits, you need the call *_control87(PC_24, MCW_PC);*.

RETURNS The *_control87* function returns the floating-point control word (see Table 8-4).

SEE ALSO `_status87` *To get the floating-point status word*

`_clear87` *To get and clear the floating-point status word*

Table 8-4. *Floating-Point Control Word*

Mask Constant	Mask Meaning	Values	Meaning of Value
MCW_EM	Controls the conditions under which interrupts will be generated by the floating-point package. Choose from these values:	EM_INVALID	Exception on invalid operation
		EM_DENORMAL	Exception if denormalized argument
		EM_ZERODIVIDE	Exception on divide by zero
		EM_OVERFLOW	Exception on overflow
		EM_UNDERFLOW	Exception on underflow
		EM_INEXACT	Exception on loss of precision
MCW_IC	Controls the interpretation of "infinity" by the package.	IC_AFFine	Use"affine" infinity (affine infinity distinguishes between positive and negative infinity, "projective" infinity does not)
		IC_PROJECTIVE	Use "projective" infinity
MCW_RC	Controls the rounding options.	RC_CHOP	Round off results by chopping
		RC_UP	Round to next higher number
		RC_DOWN	Round to next lower number
		RC_NEAR	Round to nearest number
MCW_PC	Controls the level of precision of the results.	PC_24	24-bits precision
		PC_53	53-bits precision
		PC_64	64-bits precision

EXAMPLE Get and display the current contents of the floating-point control word. Now set the precision to 24 bits and compute the product of 0.1 with itself. Display the result and note the difference from 0.01. Use the constant CW_DEFAULT to set the control word back to its default. The precision will now be 64 bits. Repeat the previous computation and note the improvement in the accuracy of the results.

```
#include <stdio.h>
#include <float.h>
main()
{
```

```
    double a = 0.1;
/* Read current floating point control word       */
    printf("Current control word = %.4X\n",
            _control87(0,0));
/* Now lower the precision to 24 bits             */
    _control87(PC_24, MCW_PC);
/* Perform a math operation and see the result    */
    printf("0.1 x 0.1 = 0.01 in 24 bit precision\
 = %.15e\n", a*a);
/* Restore precision to default 64 bits and redo */
    _control87(CW_DEFAULT, 0xffff);
    printf("0.1 x 0.1 = 0.01 in 64 bit precision\
 = %.15e\n", a*a);
}
```

COMPATIBILITY

cos, cosl

MSC 3	MSC 4	MSC 5	MSC 6	QC1	QC2	QC2.5	TC1	TC1.5	TC2	TC++	ANSI	UNIX V	XNX	OS2	DOS
▲	▲	▲	1	▲	▲	▲	▲	▲	▲	▲	2	2	2	▲	▲

PURPOSE Use *cos* to compute the cosine of an angle whose value is given in radians. The *cosl* function is a long double version of *cos*.

SYNTAX

```
double cos (double x);

long double cosl (long double ldx);

double x;             Angle in radians whose cosine is to be computed

long double ldx;      Angle in radians whose cosine is to be computed
```

EXAMPLE CALL

```
cos_angle = cos(ang_radian);

cos_angle = cosl (ang_radian);
```

INCLUDES

```
#include <math.h>     For function declaration and definition of error constants
```

DESCRIPTION The *cos* function computes the cosine of *double* argument *x*. The *cosl* function calculates the cosine of *long double* argument ldx. It is a long double-precision floating-point version of *cos*.

1. The *cosl* function was introduced in Microsoft C 6.0. 2. *cosl* does not work with ANSI, UNIX, or XENIX.

RETURNS As long as the angle *x* is less than approximately 1.34×10^8 radians (this was found by experimentation), *cos* accurately computes and returns the cosine of *x*. If the value of *x* is large enough to cause a loss of significance (i.e., the result is correct up to a few digits only), *cos* will generate a PLOSS error to indicate "partial loss of precision." If the value is so large that the result is totally useless, a TLOSS error will be sent to *stderr* and the return value is zero and *errno* is set to the constant ERANGE.

The *cosl* function returns the cosine of *ldx* if the call is successful. A zero is returned if *ldx* is so large that significance is completely lost.

COMMENTS When used with the *intrinsic* pragma (see Chapter 1), the convention of the argument calling for both the regular and long-double versions is changed to pass the arguments on the floating-point chip.

SEE ALSO

`acos` *To compute the arc cosine of a variable*

`sin` *To compute the sine of an angle*

EXAMPLE Write a program that prints a table showing the cosine of the angles between 0 and 180° in steps of 10°. The example program can be modified to run the *cosl* version by ensuring that the *double* variables are declared as *long doubles* and by avoiding the transmission of the 80-bit long double-precision floating-point values to functions that cannot handle them.

```
#include <stdio.h>
#include <math.h>
#include <stdlib.h>       /* errno is defined here */
#define  R_TO_D   57.29578 /* radians to degrees   */
main()
{
    double angle, result;
    printf("------- Table of Cosines --------\n");
    printf("Angle\t\tCosine\n");
    for(angle = 0.0; angle <= 180.0; angle += 10.0)
    {
        result = cos(angle / R_TO_D);
        if(errno != ERANGE)
        {
            printf("%f deg.\t%f\n", angle, result);
        }
    }
}
```

COMPATIBILITY

cosh, coshl

MSC 3	MSC 4	MSC 5	MSC 6	QC1	QC2	QC2.5	TC1	TC1.5	TC2	TC++	ANSI	UNIX V	XNX	OS2	DOS
▲	▲	▲	1	▲	▲	▲	▲	▲	▲	▲	2	2	2	▲	▲

PURPOSE Use *cosh* to compute the hyperbolic cosine of a *double* variable. The *long double* version is *coshl.*

SYNTAX

```
double cosh(double x);

long double coshl (long double ldx);
```

`double x;` *Variable whose hyperbolic cosine is to be computed*

`long double ldx;` *Variable whose hyperbolic cosine is to be computed*

EXAMPLE CALL

```
result = cosh(x);

l_result = coshl (ldx);
```

INCLUDES `#include <math.h>` *For function declaration and definition of error constants*

DESCRIPTION The *cosh* function computes the hyperbolic cosine of the *double* variable *x*.

The *coshl* routine calculates the hyperbolic cosine of *x*, and is a long (80-bit) double-precision floating-point version of *cosh.*

1. The *coshl* function was introduced in Microsoft C 6.0. 2. *coshl* does not work with ANSI, UNIX, or XENIX.

RETURNS Normally, *cosh* returns the hyperbolic cosine of *x*. If the value of the result is too large (a *double* variable can be as large as 10^{308}), *cosh* returns the value HUGE_VAL and, at the same time, sets *errno* to the constant ERANGE.

The *coshl* routine, which behaves just like *cosh* except that it can work on 80-bit numbers, returns the hyperbolic cosine of *ldx*, if successful. A "too large" result returns _LHUGE_VAL, and a 0 comes back if *ldx* is so large that significance is completely lost.

COMMENTS When used with the *intrinsic* pragma (see Chapter 1), the convention of the argument calling for both the regular and long-double versions is changed to pass the arguments on the floating-point chip.

SEE ALSO `sinh` *To compute the hyperbolic sine of a variable*

EXAMPLE Write a program that accepts a floating-point number on the command line and computes its hyperbolic cosine.

This program may also be written to use the 80-bit version—*coshl*—by changing the declaration *double result* to *long double* result. The statement *result = cosh (atof (argv [1]));* may be rewritten as *result = coshl (atof (argv[1]));*, but the *atof* routine will have trouble with an 80-bit value. One defense against this would be to substitute the *_atold* function for *atof*, if possible.

```
#include <stdio.h>
#include <math.h>
#include <stdlib.h>      /* errno is defined here */
main(int argc, char **argv)
{
    double result;
    if(argc < 2)
    {
        printf("Usage: %s <value>\n", argv[0]);
    }
    else
    {
        result = cosh(atof(argv[1]));
        if(errno != ERANGE)
        {
            printf("Hyperbolic cosine of %s = %f\n",
                    argv[1], result);
        }
    }
}
```

dieeetomsbin

COMPATIBILITY

MSC 3	MSC 4	MSC 5	MSC 6	QC1	QC2	QC2.5	TC1	TC1.5	TC2	TC++	ANSI	UNIX V	XNX	OS2	DOS
	▲	▲	▲	▲	▲	▲								▲	▲

PURPOSE Use the *dieeetomsbin* function to convert a double-precision number from IEEE format to Microsoft Binary format.

SYNTAX

```
int dieeetomsbin(double *src8, double *dst8);
```

`double *src8;` *Pointer to* double *variable with value in IEEE format* `double *dst8;` *Pointer to* double *variable where Microsoft Binary representation is returned*

EXAMPLE CALL `dieeetomsbin(&d_ieee, &d_msbin);`

INCLUDES `#include <math.h>` *For function declaration*

DESCRIPTION The *dieeetomsbin* function converts the double-precision value in IEEE format stored at the address *src8* to Microsoft Binary format and returns this value at the address *dst8*. This routine can not handle IEEE NAN (not-a-number) and infinities. Also, IEEE "denormals" are treated as zeroes.

RETURNS The *dieeetomsbin* function returns a 0 if conversion is successful and a 1 if conversion caused an overflow.

COMMENTS In Microsoft C programs double-precision values are kept in the IEEE format, but Microsoft BASIC stores such values in the Microsoft Binary format. The *dieeetomsbin* function allows C programs to create data files that may be read by Microsoft BASIC.

SEE ALSO dmsbintoieee *To convert from Microsoft Binary format to IEEE format*

fieeetomsbin, fmsbintoieee *Conversion routines for single-precision* float *variables*

EXAMPLE Write a program that uses *dieeetomsbin* to convert some *double* values (by default in IEEE double-precision format) to Microsoft Binary format and saves the result in a binary file. In the example for *dmsbintoieee* we will use this data file as input.

```
#include <math.h>
#include <stdio.h>
double data[10] = {1.0, 2.0, 3.0, 4.0, 5.0, 6.0, 7.0,
                   8.0, 9.0, 10.0};
double conv[10];
main()
{
    int i;
    char filename[80];
    FILE *outfile;
/* Convert data to MS binary format */
    for(i=0; i<10; i++)
        dieeetomsbin(data+i, conv+i);
/* Save in a file */
    printf("Enter file name for MS binary data:");
```

```
    gets(filename);
    if ((outfile = fopen(filename, "wb")) == NULL)
    {
        printf("Error opening file: %s\n", filename);

        exit(0);
    }
    i = fwrite(conv, sizeof(double), 10, outfile);
    printf("Saved %d bytes in file: %s\n", i, filename);
}
```

div

COMPATIBILITY

MSC 3	MSC 4	MSC 5	MSC 6	QC1	QC2	QC2.5	TC1	TC1.5	TC2	TC++	ANSI	UNIX V	XNX	OS2	DOS
		▲	▲	▲	▲	▲	▲	▲	▲	▲	▲			▲	▲

PURPOSE Use *div* to divide one integer value by another and get the quotient and remainder in a structure of type *div_t*.

SYNTAX

```
div_t div(int numer, int denom);
```

`int numer;` *Numerator*

`int denom;` *Denominator*

EXAMPLE CALL

```
result = div(32, 5);
/* result.quot = 6 and result.rem = 2 */
```

INCLUDES `#include <stdlib.h>` *For function declaration and definition of structure* div_t

DESCRIPTION The *div* function divides the first integer *numer* by the second one *denom* and returns the resulting quotient and remainder packed in a structure of type *div_t*. The structure of type *div_t* is defined in *stdlib.h* as

```
typedef struct
{
    int quot;   /* The quotient  */
    int rem;    /* The remainder */
} div_t;
```

RETURNS The *div* function returns a structure of type *div_t* containing the quotient and remainder of the division.

SEE ALSO `ldiv` *To divide one long integer by another*

EXAMPLE Write a program that accepts a numerator and a denominator on the command line and uses *div* to compute the quotient and the remainder of the division.

```
#include <stdio.h>
#include <stdlib.h>
main(int argc, char **argv)
{
    int x, y;
    div_t result;
/* Make sure that there is at least 3 arguments */
    if(argc < 3)
    {
        printf("Usage: %s <int numerator> <int denom>\n",
                argv[0]);
        exit(0);
    }
/* Divide first integer by second and display
 * quotient and remainder
 */
    x = atoi(argv[1]);
    y = atoi(argv[2]);
    result = div(x,y);
    printf("Dividing %d by %d. Quotient = %d and \
remainder = %d\n", x, y, result.quot, result.rem);
}
```

COMPATIBILITY

dmsbintoieee

MSC 3	MSC 4	MSC 5	MSC 6	QC1	QC2	QC2.5	TC1	TC1.5	TC2	TC++	ANSI	UNIX V	XNX	OS2	DOS
	▲	▲	▲	▲	▲	▲								▲	▲

PURPOSE Use the *dmsbintoieee* function to convert a double-precision number from Microsoft Binary format to the IEEE format.

SYNTAX `int dmsbintoieee(double *src8, double *dst8);`

`double *src8;` *Pointer to* double *variable with value in Microsoft Binary format*

`double *dst8;` *Pointer to* double *variable where IEEE representation will be returned*

EXAMPLE CALL `dmsbintoieee(&d_msbin, &d_ieee);`

INCLUDES `#include <math.h>` *For function declaration*

DESCRIPTION The *dmsbintoieee* function converts the double-precision value in Microsoft Binary format stored at the address *src8* to IEEE format and returns this value at the address *dst8*.

RETURNS The *dmsbintoieee* function returns a 0 if conversion is successful and a 1 if conversion caused an overflow.

COMMENTS In Microsoft C programs double-precision values are kept in the IEEE format, but Microsoft BASIC stores such values in the Microsoft Binary format. The *dmsbintoieee* function allows C programs to read binary data files with double-precision values stored by Microsoft BASIC.

SEE ALSO `dieeetomsbin` *To convert from IEEE format to Microsoft Binary format*

`fieeetomsbin, fmsbintoieee` *Conversion routines for single-precision* float *variables*

EXAMPLE In the example for *dieeetomsbin* we wrote a binary file with 10 floating-point values in Microsoft Binary format. Now write a program that reads this data and converts it back to IEEE format using *dmsbintoieee*. Print the converted values.

```
#include <math.h>
#include <stdio.h>
double data[10], conv[10];
main()
{
    int i;
    char filename[80];
    FILE *infile;
/* Read data from binary file */
    printf("Enter file name for MS binary data:");
    gets(filename);
    if ((infile = fopen(filename, "rb")) == NULL)
    {
        printf("Error opening file: %s\n", filename);
        exit(0);
    }
    i = fread(data, sizeof(double), 10, infile);
    printf("Read %d bytes from file: %s\n", i, filename);
/* Convert from MS binary to IEEE format */
```

```
        printf("Values are: ");
        for(i=0; i<10; i++)
        {
            dmsbintoieee(data+i, conv+i);

            printf("%g ", *(conv+i));
        }
        printf("\n");
}
```

COMPATIBILITY

exp, expl

MSC 3	MSC 4	MSC 5	MSC 6	QC1	QC2	QC2.5	TC1	TC1.5	TC2	TC++	ANSI	UNIX V	XNX	OS2	DOS
▲	▲	▲	1	▲	▲	▲	▲	▲	▲	▲	2	2	2	▲	▲

PURPOSE Use *exp* to compute the exponential of a *double* variable. The *expl* version returns the exponential function of a floating-point argument.

SYNTAX

```
double exp (double x);

long double expl (long double ldx);
```

`double x;`	*Variable whose exponential is to be computed*
`long double ldx;`	*Long double-precision floating-point variable whose exponential is to be computed*

EXAMPLE CALL

```
y = exp(x);

c = expl (ldx);
```

INCLUDES `#include <math.h>` *For function declaration and definition of error constants*

DESCRIPTION The *exp* function computes the exponential of the *double* variable *x*. The exponential of a variable *x* is e^x where *e* is the base of natural logarithm ($e = 2.7182818$). The *expl* routine returns the exponential function of the floating-point argument *ldx*. It is a long double-precision floating-point version of *exp*.

1. The *expl* function was introduced in Microsoft C 6.0. **2**. *expl* does not work with ANSI, UNIX, or XENIX.

RETURNS Normally, *exp* returns the exponential of *x*. In case of overflow (the value of the result is too large), *exp* returns the value HUGE_VAL and sets *errno* to the constant ERANGE. On underflow, the return value will be zero, but *errno* is not set. The *expl* version behaves the same way, but sets _LHUGE_VAL instead of HUGE_VAL in the event of an overflow.

SEE ALSO

`log` *To compute the natural logarithm (the inverse of the exponential) of a variable*

`pow` *To raise* x *to the power* y

EXAMPLE Write a program that accepts a floating-point number on the command line and computes its exponential. The example program may be written to use the long double version by changing the declaration *double result* to *long double result* and the *exp* call to *result = expl (_atold (argv [1]));*.

```
#include <stdio.h>
#include <math.h>
#include <stdlib.h>  /* errno is declared here */
main(int argc, char **argv)
{
    double result;
    if(argc < 2)
    {
        printf("Usage: %s <value>\n", argv[0]);
    }
    else
    {
        result = exp(atof(argv[1]));
        if (errno != EDOM)
            printf("exp (%s) = %f\n", argv[1], result);
    }
}
```

fabs, fabsl

COMPATIBILITY

MSC 3	MSC 4	MSC 5	MSC 6	QC1	QC2	QC2.5	TC1	TC1.5	TC2	TC++	ANSI	UNIX V	XNX	OS2	DOS
▲	▲	▲	1	▲	▲	▲	▲	▲	▲	▲	2	2	2	▲	▲

PURPOSE Use *fabs* to compute the absolute value of a *double* variable. The *fabsl* function gets the absolute value of a float value.

SYNTAX

```
double fabs(double x);

long double fabsl (long double x_arg);
```

`double x;` *Variable whose absolute value is to be returned*

`long double x_arg;` *A floating-point value whose absolute value is to be returned*

EXAMPLE CALL

```
y = fabs(-5.15); /* y will be 5.15 */

g = fabsl (-6.06);
```

INCLUDES

`#include <math.h>` *For function declaration*

DESCRIPTION The *fabs* function returns the absolute value of its argument *x*. The *fabsl* version gets the absolute value of a double-precision floating-point value. The long double functions use an 80-bit, 10-byte coprocessor form for arguments and return values, but otherwise behave identically to their "root" versions.

1. The *fabsl* function was introduced in Microsoft C 6.0. 2. *fabsl* is not compatible with ANSI, UNIX, or XENIX.

RETURNS The return value is of type *double* with a positive value that is the absolute value of *x*. The *fabsl* routine returns the absolute value of its argument *x_arg*.

SEE ALSO `cabs` *To compute the magnitude of a complex variable*

EXAMPLE Write a program that accepts a floating-point number on the command line and computes the absolute value of the number by using *fabs*. The example program may be written to use the long double version by hanging the declaration *double result* to *long double result* and the *fabs* call to *result = fabsl (_atold (argv [1]));*.

```
#include <stdio.h>
#include <math.h>
main(int argc, char **argv)

{
    double result;
    if(argc < 2)
    {
        printf("Usage: %s <value>\n", argv[0]);
    }
    else
    {
        result = fabs(atof(argv[1]));
        printf("Absolute value of %s = %f\n",
                     argv[1], result);
    }
}
```

fieeetomsbin

COMPATIBILITY

MSC 3	MSC 4	MSC 5	MSC 6	QC1	QC2	QC2.5	TC1	TC1.5	TC2	TC++	ANSI	UNIX V	XNX	OS2	DOS
	▲	▲	▲	▲	▲	▲								▲	▲

PURPOSE Use the *fieeetomsbin* function to convert a single-precision number from IEEE format to Microsoft Binary format.

SYNTAX

```
int fieeetomsbin(float *src4, float *dst4);
```

`float *src4;` *Pointer to* float *variable with value in IEEE format*

`float *dst4;` *Pointer to* float *variable where Microsoft Binary representation is returned*

EXAMPLE CALL

```
fieeetomsbin(&f_ieee, &f_msbin);
```

INCLUDES `#include <math.h>` *For function declaration*

DESCRIPTION The *fieeetomsbin* function converts the single-precision value in IEEE format stored at the address *src4* to Microsoft Binary format and returns this value at the address *dst4*. This routine cannot handle IEEE NANs (not-a-number) and infinities. Also, IEEE "denormals" are treated as zeroes.

COMMON USES The *fieeetomsbin* function is useful in writing from C programs binary data files with single-precision values that can be read by Microsoft BASIC, which uses the Microsoft Binary format.

RETURNS The *fieeetomsbin* function returns a 0 if conversion is successful and a one if conversion caused an overflow.

SEE ALSO `fmsbintoieee` *To convert from Microsoft Binary format to IEEE format*

`dieeetomsbin, dmsbintoieee` *Conversion routines for double-precision* double *variables*

EXAMPLE Write a program that uses *fieeetomsbin* to convert some *float* values (by default in IEEE double-precision format) to Microsoft Binary format and saves the result in a binary file. In the example for *fmsbintoieee* we will use this data file as input.

```
#include <math.h>
#include <stdio.h>
float data[10] = {0.1, 0.2, 0.3, 0.4, 0.5, 0.6, 0.7,
                  0.8, 0.9, 1.0};
```

```
float conv[10];
main()
{
    int i;
    char filename[80];
    FILE *outfile;
/* Convert data to MS binary format */
    for(i=0; i<10; i++)
        fieeetomsbin(data+i, conv+i);
/* Save in a file */
    printf("Enter file name for MS binary data:");
    gets(filename);
    if ((outfile = fopen(filename, "wb")) == NULL)
    {
        printf("Error opening file: %s\n", filename);
        exit(0);
    }
    i = fwrite(conv, sizeof(float), 10, outfile);
    printf("Saved %d bytes in file: %s\n", i, filename);
}
```

floor, floorl

COMPATIBILITY

MSC 3	MSC 4	MSC 5	MSC 6	QC1	QC2	QC2.5	TC1	TC1.5	TC2	TC++	ANSI	UNIX V	XNX	OS2	DOS
▲	▲	▲	1	▲	▲	▲	▲	▲	▲	▲	2	2	2	▲	▲

PURPOSE Use *floor* to compute the "floor," the largest integer value that is less than or equal to a *double* variable. Use the *floorl* routine to compute that value in long double form.

SYNTAX

```
double floor(double x);

long double floorl (long double ldx);
```

`double x;` *Variable whose floor is to be returned*

`ldx;` *Long double-precision floating-point value whose floor is to be returned*

EXAMPLE CALL

```
x = floor(4.15);  /* x will be 4.0 */

ldx = floorl (9.78); /* ldx will be 9.0 */
```

INCLUDES `#include <math.h>` *For function declaration*

DESCRIPTION The *floor* function finds the floor of a *double* argument *x*. The floor is the largest integral value that is less than or equal to *x*. This can be used in rounding a *double* value *down* to the preceding integer.

The *floorl* function returns a long double-precision floating-point value representing the largest integer that is less than, or equal to, its argument, and except for the precision with which it works, behaves identically to floor.

1. The *floorl* function was introduced in Microsoft C 6.0. 2. The *floorl* function is incompatible with ANSI, UNIX, and XENIX.

COMMENTS When used with the *intrinsic* pragma (see Chapter 1), the convention of the argument calling for both the regular and long-double versions is changed to pass the arguments on the floating-point chip.

RETURNS The return value is the floor of *x* expressed as a *double*. The *floorl* version returns a long double-precision floating-point result, rounded down. See the tutorial for more information about long (80-bit) double functions.

SEE ALSO `ceil` *To determine the smallest integer that just exceeds a variable*

EXAMPLE Write a program that accepts a floating-point number on the command line and prints the floor of that number. The example will work with a call to *floorl* rather than *floor* if you use long double variables.

```
#include <stdio.h>
#include <math.h>
main(int argc, char **argv)
{
    double result;
    if(argc < 2)
    {
        printf("Usage: %s <value>\n", argv[0]);
    }
    else
    {
        result = floor(atof(argv[1]));
        printf("floor of %s = %f\n", argv[1], result);
    }
}
```

COMPATIBILITY

fmod, fmodl

MSC 3	MSC 4	MSC 5	MSC 6	QC1	QC2	QC2.5	TC1	TC1.5	TC2	TC++	ANSI	UNIX V	XNX	OS2	DOS
▲	▲	▲	1	▲	▲	▲	▲	▲	▲	▲	2	2	2	▲	▲

PURPOSE Use *fmod* to compute the floating-point remainder after dividing one floating-point number by another and ensuring that the quotient is the largest possible integer. Use the long double version *fmodl* to calculate long double remainders.

SYNTAX

```
double fmod(double x, double y);

long double fmodl (long double xx, long double yy);

double x, y;              The remainder after the division x/y is returned

long double xx, yy;       The remainder after the division xx/yy is returned
```

EXAMPLE CALL

```
rem = fmod(24.95, 5.5); /* rem will be 2.95 */

rem = fmodl(24.95, 5.5)  /* rem will be 2.95 */
```

INCLUDES

```
#include <math.h>        For function declaration
```

DESCRIPTION The *fmod* function divides x by y and finds the integral floor of the quotient, the largest integer that is less than or equal to the quotient. If this result is n, *fmod* returns the value r computed from the expression $r = x - n*y$. The entire operation is equivalent to

```
double n, r;
:
:
n = floor(x/y);
r = x - n*y;
```

The *fmodl* version calculates the long double-precision floating-point remainder f of (x,y) such that $x = i * y + f$, where i is an integer, f has the same sign as x, and the absolute value of f is less than the absolute value of y. See the tutorial for more information about the 80-bit long double functions.

1. The *fmodl* function is the long double-precision floating-point version of *fmod*, introduced in version 6.0. 2. *fmodl* is incompatible with ANSI, UNIX, and XENIX.

RETURNS When *y* is zero, *fmod* returns a zero. Otherwise, it returns the remainder computed as described above. The *fmodl* version returns the floating-point remainder.

COMMENTS When used with the *intrinsic* pragma (see Chapter 1), the convention of the argument calling for both the regular and long-double versions is changed to pass the arguments on the floating-point chip.

SEE ALSO `floor` *To find the largest integer that is less than or equal to a floating-point value*

EXAMPLE Write a program that takes two real numbers and computes the floating-point remainder after dividing the first number by the second and ensuring that the quotient is the largest integer possible. The example program will also work with the *fmodl* version. The declarations have to be changed from *double* to *long double*, and the call to *fmod* would be changed to *fmodl*. The long double versions of the math functions behave exactly like their less-precise cousins, except for taking and returning long double values.

```
#include <stdio.h>
#include <math.h>
#include <stdlib.h>      /* errno is defined here */
main(int argc, char **argv)
{
    double x, y, result;
    if(argc < 3)
    {
        printf("Usage: %s <x> <y>\n", argv[0]);
    }
    else
    {
        x = atof(argv[1]);

        y = atof(argv[2]);
        result = fmod(x,y);
        if(errno != ERANGE)
        {
            printf("fmod(%s, %s) = %f\n",
                    argv[1], argv[2], result);
        }
    }
}
```

COMPATIBILITY

fmsbintoieee

MSC 3	MSC 4	MSC 5	MSC 6	QC1	QC2	QC2.5	TC1	TC1.5	TC2	TC++	ANSI	UNIX V	XNX	OS2	DOS
	▲	▲	▲	▲	▲	▲								▲	▲

PURPOSE Use the *fmsbintoieee* function to convert a single-precision number from Microsoft Binary format to the IEEE format.

SYNTAX

```
int fmsbintoieee(float *src4, float *dst4);
```

`float *src4;` *Pointer to float variable with value in Microsoft Binary format*

`float *dst4;` *Pointer to float variable where IEEE representation is returned*

EXAMPLE CALL

```
fmsbintoieee(&f_msbin, &f_ieee);
```

INCLUDES `#include <math.h>` *For function declaration*

DESCRIPTION The *fmsbintoieee* function converts the single-precision value in Microsoft Binary format stored at the address *src4* to IEEE format and returns this result at the address *dst4*.

COMMON USES Since Microsoft C uses the IEEE format, the *fmsbintoieee* function is useful in reading binary data files with single-precision values in Microsoft Binary format that might have been created by Microsoft BASIC.

RETURNS The *fmsbintoieee* function returns a 0 if conversion is successful and a 1 if the conversion caused an overflow.

SEE ALSO

`fieeetomsbin` *To convert from IEEE format to Microsoft Binary format*

`dieeetomsbin, dmsbintoieee` *Conversion routines for double-precision variables*

EXAMPLE In the example for *fieeetomsbin* we wrote a binary file with 10 single-precision floating-point values in Microsoft Binary format. Write a program here that reads that data and uses *fmsbintoieee* to convert it back to IEEE format. Print the result. Compare these results with those in the example for *fieeetomsbin*.

```
#include <math.h>
#include <stdio.h>
float data[10], conv[10];
main()
```

```
{
    int i;
    char filename[80];
    FILE *infile;
/* Read data from binary file */
    printf("Enter file name for MS binary data:");
    gets(filename);
    if ((infile = fopen(filename, "rb")) == NULL)
    {
        printf("Error opening file: %s\n", filename);
        exit(0);
    }
    i = fread(data, sizeof(float), 10, infile);
    printf("Read %d bytes from file: %s\n", i, filename);
/* Convert from MS binary to IEEE format */
    printf("Values are: ");
    for(i=0; i<10; i++)
    {
        fmsbintoieee(data+i, conv+i);
        printf("%g ", *(conv+i));
    }
    printf("\n");
}
```

_fpreset

COMPATIBILITY

MSC 3	MSC 4	MSC 5	MSC 6	QC1	QC2	QC2.5	TC1	TC1.5	TC2	TC++	ANSI	UNIX V	XNX	OS2	DOS
	▲	▲	▲	▲	▲	▲	▲	▲	▲	▲				▲	▲

PURPOSE Use *_fpreset* to reinitialize the floating-point math package.

SYNTAX
```
void _fpreset(void);
```

EXAMPLE CALL
```
_fpreset();
```

INCLUDES `#include <float.h>` *For function declaration*

DESCRIPTION The *_fpreset* function reinitializes the floating-point math package. This function is provided so that you can begin with a clean floating-point system after using functions from the *system, signal* and *spawn, exec* families, which Microsoft suggests not be used within floating-point calculations. As an example, if you trap floating-point errors using *signal* with the constant

SIGFPE, the exception handler can safely recover from floating-point errors by calling *_fpreset* followed by a *longjmp*.

SEE ALSO `signal` *This can be used to trap floating-point exceptions*

EXAMPLE The *signal* function of the C library allows you to set up SIGFPE signals to handle floating-point errors. When a floating-point error occurs, the handler is invoked. As suggested above, inside the handler you should initialize the floating-point package before returning. Test the program by using *setjmp* and *longjmp* and a deliberate divide-by-zero error.

```
#include <stdio.h>
#include <float.h>
#include <setjmp.h>
#include <signal.h>
int myfphandler(int, int);
jmp_buf this_point;
main()
{
    double a = 1.0, b = 0.0, c;
/* Set up floating point error handler          */
    if(signal(SIGFPE, myfphandler) == SIG_ERR)
    {
        abort();
    }
/* Mark the place where we jump back after error */
    if(setjmp(this_point) == 0)
    {
/* Create a math error, divide by zero          */
        c = a/b;
    }
/* "longjmp" will get up here from "myfphandler" */
    printf("Recovered from floating point error\n");
}
/*-----------------------------------------------*/
int myfphandler(int sig, int num)
{
    printf("In handler: signal = %d, subcode = %d\n",
            sig, num);
/* As recommended, initialize floating point package */
    _fpreset();
/* Use "longjmp" to return                          */
    longjmp(this_point, -1);
}
```

frexp, frexpl

COMPATIBILITY

MSC 3	MSC 4	MSC 5	MSC 6	QC1	QC2	QC2.5	TC1	TC1.5	TC2	TC++	ANSI	UNIX V	XNX	OS2	DOS
▲	▲	▲	1	▲	▲	▲	▲	▲	▲	▲	2	2	2	▲	▲

PURPOSE Use *frexp* to compute a mantissa with an absolute value between 0.5 and 1.0 and an integer exponent such that the floating-point argument to *frexp* is equal to the mantissa $\times 2^n$. Use the *frexpl* routine when you need a long double mantissa.

SYNTAX

```
double frexp(double x, int *expptr);

long double frexpl (long double x_float, int *exp_ptr);
```

`double x;` *Floating-point argument to be decomposed*

`int *expptr;` *Pointer to an integer where the exponent is returned*

`x_float;` *A long double-precision floating-point value to be decomposed*

`exp_ptr;` *A pointer to an integer where the exponent is returned*

EXAMPLE CALL

```
mantissa = frexp(5.1, &exponent);

mantissa = frexpl(8.6, &exp_ptr);
```

INCLUDES `#include <math.h>` *For function declaration*

DESCRIPTION The *frexp* function breaks down the floating-point number *x* into a mantissa *m*, whose absolute value lies between 0.5 and 1.0, and an integer exponent *n*, so that $x = m \times 2^n$. The *frexpl* function breaks down the long double-precision floating-point value *(x_float)* into a mantissa *(m)* and an exponent *(n)* such that the absolute value of *m* is greater than or equal to 0.5 and less than 1.0, and *x_float = m * 2n*.

The exponent *n* is stored by *frexp* in the location whose address is given in the argument *expptr*. If *x* is zero, the exponent will also be zero.

1. The *frexpl* function is the long double-precision floating-point version of *frexp* and was introduced with Microsoft C 6.0. 2. *frexpl* is incompatible with ANSI, UNIX, and XENIX.

COMMON USES You can use *frexp* to generate the binary representation of a floating-point number. (The tutorial section explains how floating-point numbers are represented in binary form in computers.)

RETURNS Normally *frexp* returns the mantissa *m* computed as described above. When *x* is zero, *frexp* returns a zero as the mantissa. The *frexpl* routine returns the mantissa if it is successful and a 0 if the value of *x_float* is 0.

SEE ALSO

`dexp` *To reconstruct a floating-point number from mantissa and exponent, as computed by* frexp

`modf` *To decompose a floating-point number into its fractional and integral parts*

EXAMPLE Use *frexp* in a program to decompose a real value into a mantissa (between 0.5 and 1) and an exponent of 2. The long double functions behave exactly as their shorter counterparts, although care must be taken to ensure they do not send an 80-bit value at a function that is expecting an integer. The *frexpl* routine will work in the example if the *double* declarations for *x* and mantissa are changed to *long double.*

```
#include <stdio.h>
#include <math.h>
#include <stdlib.h>      /* errno is defined here */
main(int argc, char **argv)
{
    int exponent;
    double x, mantissa;
    if(argc < 2)
    {
        printf("Usage: %s <x>\n", argv[0]);
    }
    else
    {
        x = atof(argv[1]);
        mantissa = frexp(x, &exponent);
        printf("%s = %f times 2 raised to %d\n",
                    argv[1], mantissa, exponent);
    }
}
```

hypot, hypotl

COMPATIBILITY

MSC 3	MSC 4	MSC 5	MSC 6	QC1	QC2	QC2.5	TC1	TC1.5	TC2	TC++	ANSI	UNIX V	XNX	OS2	DOS
▲	▲	▲	1	▲	▲	▲	▲	▲	▲	▲		2	2	▲	▲

PURPOSE Use *hypot* to compute the length of the hypotenuse of a right triangle, given the length of the other two sides. Use *hypotl* when your needs call for greater precision and you need a long double result.

SYNTAX

```
double hypot(double x, double y);

long double hypotl (long double x_flt, long double y_flt);

double x, y;        sqrt(x*x + y*y) will be returned

x_flt, y_flt;       Long, double-precision floating-point values
```

EXAMPLE CALL

```
length = hypot(3.0, 4.0); /* length = 5.0 */

length = hypotl (3.0, 4.0); /* length = 5.0 */
```

INCLUDES `#include <math.h>` *For function declaration and definition of constants ERANGE and HUGE_VAL*

DESCRIPTION The *hypot* function computes the square root of the sum of the squares of the arguments *x* and *y*, giving the return value:

```
return_value = sqrt(x*x + y*y);
```

If *x* and *y* are the sides of a right triangle (i.e., these two sides met at a right angle), by the Pythagorean theorem the value returned by *hypot* corresponds to the length of the hypotenuse of the right triangle. If *x* and *y* represented the real and the imaginary parts of a complex number, respectively, the value returned by *hypot* is the magnitude (i.e., the absolute value) of the complex number represented by *x* and *y*. Thus *hypot* can be used to achieve the functionality of *cabs* as well.

The *hypotl* version calculates the length of the hypotenuse of a right triangle, given the length of the two sides *x* and *y*, using the long double-precision floating-point version of arguments and return values. (See the tutorial for more information about long (80-bit) double functions.)

1. The *hypotl* function was introduced in version 6.0. 2. *hypotl* is incompatible with UNIX and XENIX.

RETURNS The normal return value is the length of the hypotenuse as described above. If the result is too large, however, *hypot* returns the value HUGE_VAL and sets *errno* to the constant ERANGE.

The returns of a successful *hypotl* call match those of *hypot* except that _LHUGE_VAL is used instead of HUGE _VAL on overflow.

SEE ALSO `cabs` *To compute magnitude of a complex number*

EXAMPLE Write a program that computes the length of the hypotenuse of a right triangle whose sides are entered on the command line. The example program may be modified to run the *hypotl* version by ensuring that the *double* variables are declared as *long doubles*, and by avoiding the transmission of the 80-bit long double-precision floating-point values to functions that cannot handle them.

```
#include <stdio.h>
#include <math.h>
#include <stdlib.h>      /* errno is defined here */
main(int argc, char **argv)
{
    double x, y, result;
    if(argc < 3)
    {
        printf("Usage: %s <x> <y>\n", argv[0]);
    }
    else
    {
        x = atof(argv[1]);
        y = atof(argv[2]);
        result = hypot(x,y);
        if(errno != ERANGE)
        {
            printf("hypot(%s, %s) = %f\n",
                    argv[1], argv[2], result);
        }
    }
}
```

labs

COMPATIBILITY

MSC 3	MSC 4	MSC 5	MSC 6	QC1	QC2	QC2.5	TC1	TC1.5	TC2	TC++	ANSI	UNIX V	XNX	OS2	DOS
▲	▲	▲	▲	▲	▲	▲	▲	▲	▲	▲	▲			▲	▲

PURPOSE Use *labs* to get the absolute value of a long integer value.

SYNTAX

```
long labs(long n);
```

`long n;` *Long integer whose absolute value is returned*

EXAMPLE CALL

```
lresult = labs(-65540L); /* result will be 65540 */
```

INCLUDES

```
#include <stdlib.h>
```

For function declaration

DESCRIPTION The *labs* function returns the absolute value of the long integer argument *n*. For example, *labs(-999999L)* returns 999999.

RETURNS The long integer returned by *labs* is the absolute value of *n*.

SEE ALSO

`abs` *To get the absolute value of an integer*

`cabs` *To obtain the magnitude (or absolute value) of a complex number*

`fabs` *To get the absolute value of a floating-point number*

EXAMPLE Use *labs* to obtain the absolute value of a long integer entered as a command-line argument to a program.

```
#include <stdio.h>
#include <stdlib.h>
main(int argc, char **argv)
{
    long value, result;
    if(argc < 2)
    {
        printf("Usage: %s <long_integer_value>\n",
                argv[0]);
    }
    else
    {
        value = atol(argv[1]);
        result = labs(value);
        printf("Absolute value of %ld = %ld\n",
                value, result);
    }
}
```

ldexp, ldexpl

COMPATIBILITY

MSC 3	MSC 4	MSC 5	MSC 6	QC1	QC2	QC2.5	TC1	TC1.5	TC2	TC++	ANSI	UNIX V	XNX	OS2	DOS
▲	▲	▲	1	▲	▲	▲	▲	▲	▲	▲	2	2	2	▲	▲

PURPOSE Use *ldexp* to compute a floating-point number from a mantissa and an integer exponent such that the floating-point number is equal to the mantissa × 2^{exp}. Use the *ldexpl* version to compute a real number from the mantissa and exponent when you need 80-bit precision.

SYNTAX

```
double ldexp(double x, int exp);

long double ldexpl (double x_man, int exp);
```

`double x;` *Floating-point value of the mantissa*

`int exp;` *Integer exponent*

`x_man;` *A floating-point value for the mantissa*

EXAMPLE CALL

```
value = ldexp(mantissa, binary_exponent);

value = ldexpl (mantissa, binary_exponent);
```

INCLUDES `#include <math.h>` *For function declaration*

DESCRIPTION The *ldexp* function computes and returns the floating-point number equal to $x \times 2^{exp}$.

The *ldexpl* version converts the mantissa and exponent to a floating-point value. It is the long double-precision floating-point version of *ldexp*. See the tutorial for more detail about the long double functions.

1. The *ldexpl* version was introduced in Microsoft C 6.0. 2. *ldexpl* is incompatible with ANSI, UNIX, and XENIX.

COMMON USES The *ldexp* complements *frexp* by enabling you to determine the floating-point value corresponding to a binary representation in the mantissa-exponent form. (See the tutorial section for an explanation.)

RETURNS Normally *ldexp* returns the value computed as described above. When the result is too large, *ldexp* returns the value HUGE_VAL (with the sign of *x*) and sets *errno* to ERANGE. The *ldexpl* returns match those of the *ldexp* version.

SEE ALSO `frexp` *To decompose a floating-point number into a mantissa and an exponent as required by* ldexp

`modf` *To decompose a floating-point number into its fractional and integral parts*

EXAMPLE Write a program to accept a mantissa and an exponent of 2 and compute the number they represent. (The example program may be modified to run the *dexpl* version by ensuring that the *double* variables are declared as *long doubles* and by avoiding the transmission of the 80-bit long double-precision floating-point values to functions that cannot handle them.)

```
#include <stdio.h>
#include <math.h>
#include <stdlib.h>      /* errno is defined here */
main(int argc, char **argv)
{
    double mantissa, result;
    int    exponent;
    if(argc < 3)
    {
        printf("Usage: %s <mantissa> <exponent>\n",
                argv[0]);
    }
    else
    {
        mantissa = atof(argv[1]);
        exponent = atoi(argv[2]);
        result = ldexp(mantissa, exponent);
        if(errno != ERANGE)
        {
            printf("%s times 2 raised to %s = %f\n",
                    argv[1], argv[2], result);
        }
    }
}
```

COMPATIBILITY

ldiv

MSC 3	MSC 4	MSC 5	MSC 6	QC1	QC2	QC2.5	TC1	TC1.5	TC2	TC++	ANSI	UNIX V	XNX	OS2	DOS
		▲	▲	▲	▲	▲	▲	▲	▲	▲	▲			▲	▲

PURPOSE Use *ldiv* to divide one long integer value by another and get the quotient and remainder in a structure of type *ldiv_t.*

SYNTAX

```
ldiv_t ldiv(long numer, long denom);
```

`long numer;` *Numerator*

`long denom;` *Denominator*

EXAMPLE CALL

```
lresult = ldiv(65540L, 65536L);
/* lresult.quot = 1, lresult.rem = 4 */
```

INCLUDES `#include <stdlib.h>` *For function declaration and definition of structure* ldiv_t

DESCRIPTION The *ldiv* function divides the long integer *numer* by another long integer, *denom,* and returns the resulting quotient and remainder packed in a structure of type *ldiv_t.* The structure type *ldiv_t* is defined in *stdlib.h* as

```
typedef struct
{
    long quot;   /* The quotient  */
    long rem;    /* The remainder */
} ldiv_t;
```

RETURNS The *ldiv* function returns a structure of type *ldiv_t* containing the quotient and remainder of the division.

SEE ALSO `div` *To divide one integer by another*

EXAMPLE Write a program that accepts two long integers, a numerator and a denominator, on the command line and uses *ldiv* to compute the quotient and remainder of the division.

```
#include <stdio.h>
#include <stdlib.h>
main(int argc, char **argv)
{
    long int x, y;
    ldiv_t result;
```

```
/* Make sure that there is at least 3 arguments */
    if(argc < 3)
    {
        printf("Usage: %s <long numerator> <long denom>\n",
                argv[0]);
        exit(0);


    }
/* Divide first long integer by second and display
 * quotient and remainder
 */
    x = atol(argv[1]);
    y = atol(argv[2]);
    result = ldiv(x,y);
    printf("Dividing %ld by %ld. Quotient = %ld and \
remainder = %ld\n", x, y, result.quot, result.rem);
}
```

log, logl, log10, log10l

COMPATIBILITY

MSC 3	MSC 4	MSC 5	MSC 6	QC1	QC2	QC2.5	TC1	TC1.5	TC2	TC++	ANSI	UNIX V	XNX	OS2	DOS
▲	▲	1	2	▲	▲	▲	▲	▲	▲	▲	3	3	3	▲	▲

PURPOSE Use *log* and *log10* respectively to compute the natural logarithm and logarithm to the base 10 of a positive *double* variable. Use the *logl* function when you need to calculate the natural logarithm of *x* to long double floating-point precision. The *log10l* function is used when you want to calculate the base-10 logarithm of *x* with long double-precision.

SYNTAX

```
double log(double x);

double log10(double x);

long double logl (long double ldx);

long double log10l (long double ldx);
```

`double x;` *Variable whose logarithm is to be computed*

`ldx;` *Long double-precision floating-point value*

EXAMPLE CALL

```
a = log (w);

b = logl (x);

c = log10 (y);

d = log10l (z);
```

INCLUDES `#include <math.h>` *For function declaration and definition of error constants*

DESCRIPTION The *log* function computes the natural logarithm (base *e*) of the *double* variable *x* (i.e., the exponential of the result should be equal to *x*).

The *log10* function computes the logarithm of *x* with respect to base 10. Thus 10 raised to the power of the result should be *x*.

The *logl* function calculates the natural logarithm of its argument and is the long double-precision floating-point version of *log*. The *log10l* function calculates the base-10 logarithm of its argument. It is the long double-precision floating-point version of *log10*. (See the tutorial for more information about the numerous *long double* functions.)

1. *log* and *log10* changed in Microsoft C 5.0 to set *errno* to *ERANGE* rather than *EDOM*. 2. *Logl* and *Log10l* were introduced in Microsoft C 6.0. 3. Both *logl* and *log10l* are incompatible with ANSI, XENIX, or UNIX.

RETURNS Normally, *log* and *log10* return the logarithm of *x*. If *x* is negative, both functions return the value HUGE_VAL, print a DOMAIN error on *stderr*, and set *errno* to the constant EDOM. If *x* is zero, both functions will print a SING error message to indicate a singularity (a point where the function's value is infinity), return the value HUGE_VAL, and set *errno* to ERANGE.

Note that under Microsoft C 4.0 both *log* and *log10* set *errno* to EDOM when *x* was either zero or negative.

The *logl* version returns the natural logarithm of its argument. The base-10 logarithm of its argument results from a successful call to *log10l*.

COMMENTS When used with the *intrinsic* pragma (see Chapter 1), the convention of the argument calling for both the regular and long double versions is changed to pass the arguments on the floating-point chip.

SEE ALSO

`exp` *To compute the exponential (the inverse of the natural logarithm) of a variable*

`pow` *To compute the value of one variable raised to the power of another*

EXAMPLE Write a small program that accepts a number and computes its natural logarithm as well as its logarithm to the base 10. The example program may be modified to run the *logl* and *log10l* versions by ensuring that the appropriate variables are declared as *long doubles* and by avoiding the transmission of the 80-bit long double-precision floating-point values to functions that cannot handle them.

```
#include <stdio.h>
#include <math.h>
#include <stdlib.h>  /* errno is declared here */
main(int argc, char **argv)
{
    double result;
    if(argc < 2)
    {
        printf("Usage: %s <value>\n", argv[0]);
    }
    else
    {
/* Compute the natural logarithm                        */
        result = log(atof(argv[1]));
        if (errno != EDOM && errno != ERANGE)
            printf("log (%s) = %f\n", argv[1], result);

/* Now compute the logarithm to the base 10             */
        result = log10(atof(argv[1]));
        if (errno != EDOM && errno != ERANGE)
            printf("log10 (%s) = %f\n", argv[1], result);
    }
}
```

_lrotl

COMPATIBILITY

MSC 3	MSC 4	MSC 5	MSC 6	QC1	QC2	QC2.5	TC1	TC1.5	TC2	TC++	ANSI	UNIX V	XNX	OS2	DOS
		▲	▲	▲	▲	▲		▲	▲	▲				▲	▲

PURPOSE Use *_lrotl* to rotate to the left the bits in an unsigned long integer variable.

SYNTAX

```
unsigned long int _lrotl(unsigned long value, int shift);
```

`unsigned long value;` *Value to be rotated left*

`int shift;` *Number of bits to shift*

EXAMPLE CALL

```
result = _lrotl(0x0123454567L, 4) /* result is 0x12345670 */
```

INCLUDES `#include <stdlib.h>` *For function declaration*

DESCRIPTION The *_lrotl* function rotates to the left the bits in the unsigned long variable *value* by shifting bit positions. Bit rotation to the left by one position means that the leftmost bit is shifted out and inserted into the rightmost bit and all the other bits shift one step to the left.

RETURNS The unsigned long integer returned by *_lrotl* is the *value* rotated left.

SEE ALSO `_lrotr` *To rotate an unsigned long integer to the right*

`_rotl, _rotr` *To rotate unsigned integers*

EXAMPLE Write a program to illustrate the effect of rotating a long integer to the left. Ask the user for a value (up to eight digits) in hexadecimal. Use *_lrotl* to rotate the number to the left 32 times, printing the result in hexadecimal after each rotation.

```
#include <stdio.h>
#include <stdlib.h>
main()
{
    char input[80];
    int bits;
    unsigned long value;
    char **eptr;
    printf("Enter long integer to rotate (in hex): ");
    gets(input);
/* Convert string to unsigned long integer */
    value = strtoul(input, eptr, 16);
    for (bits = 1; bits < 33; bits++)
        printf(
        "%#8.8lx rotated left by %d bits = %#8.8lx\n",
        value, bits, _lrotl(value,bits));
}
```

COMPATIBILITY

_lrotr

MSC 3	MSC 4	MSC 5	MSC 6	QC1	QC2	QC2.5	TC1	TC1.5	TC2	TC++	ANSI	UNIX V	XNX	OS2	DOS
		▲	▲	▲	▲	▲		▲	▲	▲				▲	▲

PURPOSE Use *_lrotr* to rotate to the right the bits in an unsigned long integer variable.

SYNTAX `unsigned long int _lrotr(unsigned long value, int shift);`

`unsigned long value;` *Value to be rotated right*

`int shift;` *Number of bits to shift*

EXAMPLE CALL `result = _lrotr(0x0123454567L, 16) /* result is 0x45670123 */`

INCLUDES `#include <stdlib.h>` *For function declaration*

DESCRIPTION The *_lrotr* function rotates to the right the bits in the unsigned long variable *value* by shifting bit positions. Bit rotation to the right by one position means that the rightmost bit is shifted out and inserted into the leftmost bit and all the other bits shift one step to the right.

RETURNS The unsigned long integer returned by *_lrotr* is the *value* rotated right.

SEE ALSO `_lrotl` *To rotate an unsigned long integer to the left*

`_rotl, _rotr` *To rotate unsigned integers*

EXAMPLE Write a program to illustrate the effect of rotating a long integer to the right. Assume that the value (up to eight digits) in hexadecimal and the number of bits to rotate are entered on the command line. Use *_lrotr* to perform the rotation and then print the result. You can see the effect of rotation best if the number of bits to rotate is a multiple of 4.

```
#include <stdio.h>
#include <stdlib.h>
main(int argc, char **argv)
{
    int bits;
    unsigned long value;
    char **eptr;
    if(argc < 3)

    {
        printf("Usage: %s <hex value (max 8 digits)>\
<no. bits to rotate right>\n",
                argv[0]);
        exit(0);
    }
/* Convert argument to unsigned long integer */
    value = strtoul(argv[1], eptr, 16);
    bits = atoi(argv[2]);
    printf("%#8.8lx rotated right by %d bits = %#8.8lx\n",
            value, bits, _lrotr(value,bits));
}
```

COMPATIBILITY

matherr, _matherrl

MSC 3	MSC 4	MSC 5	MSC 6	QC1	QC2	QC2.5	TC1	TC1.5	TC2	TC++	ANSI	UNIX V	XNX	OS2	DOS
▲	▲	▲	1	▲	▲	▲	▲	▲	▲	▲		2	2	▲	▲

PURPOSE The default *matherr* function is called by a math function when an error occurs. You can develop your own version of *matherr* to customize error handling. The *_matherrl* version should be used to handle errors from the long double functions.

SYNTAX

```
int matherr(struct exception *error_info);

int _matherrl (struct exceptionl *exceptn);
```

`struct exception *error_info;` *Pointer to a structure that contains information about the error that just occurred*

`exceptn;` *Math exception information*

EXAMPLE CALL

```
int matherr (struct exception *uhoh);

int _matherrl (struct exceptionl *gooflist);
```

INCLUDES `#include <math.h>` *For function declaration*

DESCRIPTION The *matherr* function is called with a pointer to a structure of type *exception*, which is defined in *math.h* as follows:

```
struct exception
{
    int type;           /* exception type - see below          */
    char *name;         /* name of function where error occurred */
    double arg1;        /* first argument to function          */
    double arg2;        /* second argument (if any) to function */
    double retval;      /* value to be returned by function    */
} ;
```

The value put into *retval* by *matherr* is returned by the math function to its calling process.

A *matherr* is present in the library, but you can supply your own version as long as it conforms to the description provided here.

The *_matherrl* routine processes errors generated by the long double-precision functions of the math library.

1. The *matherrl* function was introduced in version 6.0. 2. *matherrl* is incompatible with UNIX and XENIX.

RETURNS The *matherr* function returns a zero to indicate an error and a nonzero to indicate successful corrective action. If *matherr* returns a zero the math function that called *matherr* displays an error message and sets *errno* to an appropriate value. Keep this in mind when writing your own *matherr* function.

A *_matherrl* call yields the same return values as a call to the *matherr*.

SEE ALSO `acos, asin, atan, atan2, bessel, cabs cos, cosh, exp, hypot, log, log10, pow, sin, sinh, sqrt, tan` — *How the math functions behave with the default* matherr

EXAMPLE As described above, you can write your own version of *matherr* to handle mathematical errors your way. As an example, write a *matherr* function that handles the DOMAIN error by returning the square root of the absolute value of a number when *sqrt* is called with a negative argument. You will have to use the linker option /NOE to stop LINK from complaining when it finds a duplicate *matherr* in the default library.

The example routine may be modified to handle the *_matherrl* long double version of *matherr*. Since the long double functions handle 80-bit values, it is important to make sure that the variables that the example defines as type *double* be changed to type *long double*.

```
/*  Use /NOE option with linker to use our copy of
 *  matherr error handler without complaining.
 */
#include <stdio.h>
#include <math.h>
#include <string.h>
main(int argc, char **argv)
{
    double result;
    if(argc < 2)
    {
        printf("Usage: %s <value>\n", argv[0]);
    }
    else
    {
        result = sqrt(atof(argv[1]));
        printf("sqrt (%s) = %f\n", argv[1], result);
    }
}
/*--------------------------------------------------*/
/*  Our own custom error handler. We will check if
 *  the function is "sqrt". If yes, and the error type
 *  is DOMAIN, we will return square root of the
 *  absolute value. Otherwise, our matherr will return
```

```
 *  zero to force the default actions.
 */
int matherr(struct exception *errorinfo)
{
    if(errorinfo->type == DOMAIN)
    {
        if(strcmp(errorinfo->name, "sqrt") == 0)

        {
          errorinfo->retval = sqrt(-(errorinfo->arg1));
          return(1);    /* return 1 == no more error  */
        }
    }
    return(0);  /* return 0 to indicate error        */
}
```

COMPATIBILITY **max**

MSC 3	MSC 4	MSC 5	MSC 6	QC1	QC2	QC2.5	TC1	TC1.5	TC2	TC++	ANSI	UNIX V	XNX	OS2	DOS
		▲	▲	▲	▲	▲	▲	▲	▲	▲				▲	▲

PURPOSE Use the *max* macro to obtain the larger of two values of any numerical data type, signed or unsigned.

SYNTAX

```
<type> max(<type> a, <type> b);
```

`<type> a, b;` *Values to be compared, <type> denotes any numerical data type*

EXAMPLE CALL

```
double dbl1, dbl2, dblmax;
int i1, i2, intmax;
dblmax = max(dbl1, dbl2);
intmax = max(i1, i2);
```

INCLUDES `#include <stdlib.h>` *For definition of the macro*

DESCRIPTION The *max* macro is defined in *stdlib.h*:

```
#define max(a,b)    (((a) > (b)) ? (a) : (b))
```

It accepts two values (constants or variables) of any numerical data type and returns the value of the larger of the two. For example, if a = 9 and b = 11, max(a,b) returns b.

RETURNS The *max* macro evaluates to the larger value of the two arguments *a* and *b*.

SEE ALSO `min` *Macro to get the smaller of two values*

EXAMPLE Write a utility program that accepts a single character to indicate the variable type (*i* for integer, *l* for long, and *d* for floating-point), followed by two values, and prints the maximum of the two values. Use *max* to obtain the larger of the two values.

```
#include <stdio.h>
#include <stdlib.h>
main(int.argc, char **argv)
{
    int    i1, i2, ir;
    long   l1, l2, lr;
    double d1, d2, dr;
    if(argc < 4)
    {
        printf("Usage: %s <type> <value1> <value2>\n",
               argv[0]);
    }
    else
    {
        switch(argv[1][0])
        {
            case 'i':
            case 'I':
                i1 = atoi(argv[2]);
                i2 = atoi(argv[3]);
                ir = max(i1, i2);
                printf("Larger of %d and %d = %d\n",
                        i1, i2, ir);
                break;
            case 'l':
            case 'L':
                l1 = atol(argv[2]);
                l2 = atol(argv[3]);
                lr = max(l1, l2);
                printf("Larger of %ld and %ld = %ld\n",
                        l1, l2, lr);
                break;
            case 'd':
            case 'D':
                d1 = atof(argv[2]);
                d2 = atof(argv[3]);
                dr = max(d1, d2);
                printf("Larger of %g and %g = %g\n",
                        d1, d2, dr);
                break;
```

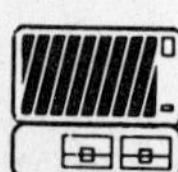

Math Routines

```
                    default:  printf("Don't know type: %c\n",
                                        argv[1][0]);
            }
        }
}
```

COMPATIBILITY

min

MSC 3	MSC 4	MSC 5	MSC 6	QC1	QC2	QC2.5	TC1	TC1.5	TC2	TC++	ANSI	UNIX V	XNX	OS2	DOS
		▲	▲	▲	▲	▲	▲	▲	▲	▲				▲	▲

PURPOSE Use the *min* macro to obtain the smaller of two values of any numerical data type, signed or unsigned.

SYNTAX

```
<type> min(<type> a, <type> b);
```

```
<type> a, b;
```
Values to be compared, <type> denotes any numerical data type

EXAMPLE CALL

```
double dbl1, dbl2, dblmin;
int i1, i2, intmin;
dblmin = min(dbl1, dbl2);
intmin = min(i1, i2);
```

INCLUDES

```
#include <stdlib.h>
```
For definition of the macro

DESCRIPTION The *min* macro is defined in *stdlib.h*:

```
#define min(a,b)     (((a) < (b)) ? (a) : (b))
```

It accepts two values (constants or variables) of any numerical data type and returns the smaller of the two. For example, if a = 9 and b = 11, min(a,b) returns *a*.

RETURNS The *min* macro evaluates to the smaller of the two arguments *a* and *b*.

SEE ALSO `max` *Macro to get the larger of two values*

EXAMPLE Write a program that accepts a single character to indicate the variable type (*i* for integer, *l* for long and *d* for floating-point), followed by two values, and prints the smaller of the two values. Use *min* to obtain the minimum of the two values.

```
#include <stdio.h>
#include <stdlib.h>
main(int argc, char **argv)
```

```
{
    int    i1, i2, ir;
    long   l1, l2, lr;
    double d1, d2, dr;
    if(argc < 4)
    {
        printf("Usage: %s <type> <value1> <value2>\n",
                argv[0]);
    }
    else
    {
        switch(argv[1][0])
        {
            case 'i':
            case 'I':
                i1 = atoi(argv[2]);
                i2 = atoi(argv[3]);
                ir = min(i1, i2);
                printf("Smaller of %d and %d = %d\n",
                        i1, i2, ir);
                break;
            case 'l':
            case 'L':
                l1 = atol(argv[2]);
                l2 = atol(argv[3]);
                lr = min(l1, l2);
                printf("Smaller of %ld and %ld = %ld\n",
                        l1, l2, lr);
                break;
            case 'd':
            case 'D':
                d1 = atof(argv[2]);
                d2 = atof(argv[3]);
                dr = min(d1, d2);
                printf("Smaller of %g and %g = %g\n",
                        d1, d2, dr);
                break;

            default:  printf("Don't know type: %c\n",
                              argv[1][0]);
        }
    }
}
```

Math Routines

COMPATIBILITY

modf, modfl

MSC 3	MSC 4	MSC 5	MSC 6	QC1	QC2	QC2.5	TC1	TC1.5	TC2	TC++	ANSI	UNIX V	XNX	OS2	DOS
▲	▲	▲	1	▲	▲	▲	▲	▲	▲	▲	2	2	2	▲	▲

PURPOSE Use *modf* to decompose a floating-point number into its fractional and integral parts. Use the *modfl* function when you need long double-precision for a *modf* call.

SYNTAX

```
double modf(double x, double *intptr);

long double modfl (long double ldx, long double *int_ptr);
```

`double x;` *Floating-point value to be decomposed*

`double *intptr;` *Integral part of* x *is returned here*

`ldx;` *Long double-precision floating-point value to be decomposed*

`int_ptr;` *The integral part of* ldx *is returned here*

EXAMPLE CALL

```
fraction = modf(24.95, &int_part); /* fraction is .95 */

fraction = modfl(862.7, &intgr_list) /* fraction is .7 */
```

INCLUDES `#include <math.h>` *For function declaration*

DESCRIPTION The *modf* function separates the floating-point number *x* into its fractional part and its integral part. The integer part is returned as a floating-point value in the location whose address is given in the argument *intptr*.

The *modfl* routine breaks down the long double-precision floating-point value of its first argument into fractional and integer parts with the same sign as the argument.

1. *modfl* was introduced in version 6.0 and is the long version of *modf*.
2. The *modfl* function is incompatible with ANSI, XENIX, and UNIX.

RETURNS The *modf* function returns the signed fractional part of *x*. The *modfl* routine returns the signed fractional portion of the first argument, and except for the precision with which it works, behaves exactly like *modf*.

SEE ALSO

`frexp` *To decompose a floating-point number into a mantissa and an exponent*

`ldexp` *To construct a floating-point number from its mantissa and exponent*

EXAMPLE Write a program that accepts a real number and decomposes it into its integral part and its fractional part.

The example program may be modified to run the *modfl* version by ensuring that the appropriate variables are declared as *long doubles* and by avoiding the transmission of the 80-bit long double-precision floating-point values to functions that cannot handle them.

```
#include <stdio.h>
#include <math.h>
#include <stdlib.h>      /* errno is defined here */
main(int argc, char **argv)
{
    double x, intpart, fract;
    if(argc < 2)
    {
        printf("Usage: %s <x>\n", argv[0]);
    }
    else
    {
        x = atof(argv[1]);
        fract = modf(x, &intpart);
        printf("Integer part of %s    = %f\n\
Fractional part of %s = %f\n", argv[1], intpart,
        argv[1], fract);
    }
}
```

pow, powl

COMPATIBILITY

MSC 3	MSC 4	MSC 5	MSC 6	QC1	QC2	QC2.5	TC1	TC1.5	TC2	TC++	ANSI	UNIX V	XNX	OS2	DOS
▲	▲	▲	1	▲	▲	▲	▲	▲	▲	▲	2	2	2	▲	▲

PURPOSE Use *pow* to compute the value of one argument raised to the power of another. Use the *powl* function when you need long double-precision for a call to *pow*.

SYNTAX

```
double pow(double x, double y);

long double powl (long double ldx, long double ldy);
```

`double x, y;`	*x raised to the power y is computed*
`ldx;`	*Number to be raised*
`ldy;`	*Power of ldx;*

EXAMPLE CALL

```
x = pow(2.0, 3.0); /* x will be 8.0 */

y = powl(20.0, 3.00);
```

INCLUDES

`#include <math.h>` *For function declaration and definition of constants EDOM, ERANGE, DOMAIN, and HUGE_VAL*

DESCRIPTION The *pow* function computes the value of *x* raised to the power *y*. Neither argument can be zero and when *x* is negative, *y* can only take integral values less than 2^{64}.

The *powl* function behaves exactly like the *pow* versions except that it deals with double-precision floating-point values.

1. *powl* is the long double-precision floating-point version of *pow* and was introduced in version 6.0. 2. The *powl* function is incompatible with ANSI, XENIX, and UNIX.

RETURNS When both *x* and *y* are nonzero positive numbers, *pow* returns the value *x* raised to the power *y*. If *x* is nonzero and *y* is zero, the return value is unity (one). When *x* is zero and *y* is negative, *pow* returns the value HUGE_VAL and sets *errno* to EDOM. If both *x* and *y* are zero or if *x* is negative and *y* is not an integral value, *pow* returns a zero, sets *errno* to EDOM, and prints a DOMAIN error message to *stderr*. If the result is too large, *pow* prints no message but returns the value HUGE_VAL.

The *powl* returns match those of *pow*, except that an overflow condition is identified by _LHUGE_VAL instead of HUGE_VAL.

SEE ALSO

`exp`	*To compute exponential*
`matherr`	*To handle math errors (you can add your own)*
`log, log10`	*To compute logarithms*
`sqrt`	*To compute square root*

EXAMPLE Write a program to accept floating-point numbers *x* and *y* on the command line and compute the value of *x* raised to the power *y*. (The *powl* function will work with the example program as long as the variable declarations are adjusted to long double from double.)

```
#include <stdio.h>
#include <math.h>
#include <stdlib.h>      /* errno is defined here */
main(int argc, char **argv)
{
    double x, y, result;
    if(argc < 3)
```

```
        {
            printf("Usage: %s <x> <y>\n", argv[0]);
        }
        else
        {
            x = atof(argv[1]);
            y = atof(argv[2]);
            result = pow(x,y);
            if(errno != ERANGE)
            {
                printf("%s raised to the power %s = %f\n",
                        argv[1], argv[2], result);
            }
        }
}
```

rand

COMPATIBILITY

MSC 3	MSC 4	MSC 5	MSC 6	QC1	QC2	QC2.5	TC1	TC1.5	TC2	TC++	ANSI	UNIX V	XNX	OS2	DOS
▲	▲	▲	▲	▲	▲	▲	▲	▲	▲	▲	▲	▲	▲	▲	▲

PURPOSE Use *rand* to generate a pseudorandom integer with a value in the range 0–32,767.

SYNTAX `int rand(void);`

EXAMPLE CALL `random_value = rand();`

INCLUDES `#include <stdlib.h>` *For function definition*

DESCRIPTION The *rand* function generates a pseudorandom integer with a value between 0 and 32,767. The starting point of the pseudorandom integers (the "seed") is set by calling *srand.*

RETURNS The *rand* function returns the pseudorandom integer it generates.

COMMENTS We say the integer returned by *rand* is pseudorandom, instead of random, because, given the seed, the sequence of numbers to be generated is predictable. After all, they are generated by a fixed algorithm. If the algorithm is well designed, though, the numbers within the sequence appear to be random.

Select a random seed each time you call *srand* to get a new sequence of numbers each time.

SEE ALSO `srand` *To set a new seed for the random number generator*

EXAMPLE Call *rand* and generate 20 pseudorandom integers. Print the integers and note that the same sequence is generated every time the program is run. A different sequence can be obtained by changing the starting seed.

```
#include <stdio.h>
#include <stdlib.h>
main()
{
    int i;
/* Generate and display 20 pseudorandom integers */
    printf("20 pseudorandom integers from \"rand\"\n");
    for(i=0; i<20; i++)
    {
        printf("%d\n", rand());
    }
}
```

COMPATIBILITY

_rotl

MSC 3	MSC 4	MSC 5	MSC 6	QC1	QC2	QC2.5	TC1	TC1.5	TC2	TC++	ANSI	UNIX V	XNX	OS2	DOS
		▲	▲	▲	▲	▲		▲	▲	▲				▲	▲

PURPOSE Use *_rotl* to rotate to the left the bits in an unsigned integer variable.

SYNTAX

```
unsigned _rotl(unsigned value, int shift);
```

`unsigned int value;` *Value to be rotated left*

`int shift;` *Number of bits to shift*

EXAMPLE CALL

```
new_pattern = _rotl(0x1234, 8); /* result is 3412h */
```

INCLUDES `#include <stdlib.h>` *For function declaration*

DESCRIPTION The *_rotl* function rotates to the left the bits in the *value* by shifting bit positions. Bit rotation to the left by one position means that the leftmost bit is shifted out and inserted into the rightmost bit and all the other bits shift one step to the left.

RETURNS The unsigned integer returned by *_rotl* is the *value* rotated left. For example, *_rotl(0x0123, 4* returns *0x1230.*

SEE ALSO `_lrotl, _lrotr` *To rotate unsigned long integers*

`_rotr` *To rotate an unsigned integer to the right*

EXAMPLE Write a program that accepts an integer value in hexadecimal form and the number of bits to rotate, uses *_rotl* to rotate that number to the left, and displays the result in hexadecimal. The effect of left rotation is most apparent if you run the program with shifts of 4 and 8.

```
#include <stdio.h>
#include <stdlib.h>
main(int argc, char **argv)
{
    int bits;
    unsigned value;
    if(argc < 3)
    {
        printf("Usage: %s <hex value (max 4 digits)>\
<no. bits to rotate left>\n",
                argv[0]);
        exit(0);
    }
/* Convert argument to unsigned long integer */
    sscanf(argv[1], "%4x", &value);
    bits = atoi(argv[2]);
    printf("%#4.4x rotated left by %d bits = %#4.4x\n",
            value, bits, _rotl(value,bits));
}
```

_rotr

COMPATIBILITY

MSC 3	MSC 4	MSC 5	MSC 6	QC1	QC2	QC2.5	TC1	TC1.5	TC2	TC++	ANSI	UNIX V	XNX	OS2	DOS
		▲	▲	▲	▲	▲		▲	▲	▲				▲	▲

PURPOSE Use *_rotr* to rotate to the right the bits in an unsigned integer variable.

SYNTAX `unsigned _rotr(unsigned value, int shift);`

`unsigned int value;` *Value to be rotated right*

`int shift;` *Number of bits to shift*

EXAMPLE CALL `rotated_value = _rotr(0x1234, 4); /* result is 4123h */`

INCLUDES #include <stdlib.h> *For function declaration*

DESCRIPTION The *_rotr* function rotates the bits in the *value* to the right by shifting bit positions. Bit rotation to the right by one position means that the rightmost bit is shifted out and inserted into the leftmost bit and all the other bits shift one step to the right.

RETURNS The unsigned integer returned by *_rotr* is the *value* rotated right. For example, *_rotr(0x0123, 4)* will return *0x2301*.

SEE ALSO `_lrotl, _lrotr` *To rotate unsigned long integers*

`_rotl` *To rotate an unsigned integer to the left*

EXAMPLE Write a program that accepts an integer value in hexadecimal form, uses *_rotl* to rotate that number 16 times to the right, and displays the result in hexadecimal at each step.

```
#include <stdio.h>
#include <stdlib.h>
main()
{
    int bits;
    unsigned value;
    printf("Enter a hexadecimal value to be rotated :");
    scanf("%4x", &value);
    for (bits = 1; bits < 17; bits++)
        printf(
        "%#4.4x rotated right by %d bits = %#4.4x\n",
        value, bits, _rotr(value,bits));
}
```

COMPATIBILITY

sin, sinl

MSC 3	MSC 4	MSC 5	MSC 6	QC1	QC2	QC2.5	TC1	TC1.5	TC2	TC++	ANSI	UNIX V	XNX	OS2	DOS
▲	▲	▲	1	▲	▲	▲	▲	▲	▲	▲	2	2	2	▲	▲

PURPOSE Use *sin* to compute the sine of an angle whose value is expressed in radians. Use *sinl* for double-precision sine calculations.

SYNTAX `double sin(double x);`

`long double sinl (long double ld_x);`

`double x;` *Angle in radians whose sine is to be computed*

`ld_x;` *Angle in radians whose sine is to be computed*

EXAMPLE CALL

```
y = sin(x)

c = sinl (d)
```

INCLUDES `#include <math.h>` *For function declaration and definition of error constants*

DESCRIPTION The *sin* function computes the sine of *double* argument *x*, which represents an angle in radians. The *sinl* function is used to calculate the sine of a long double argument—*ld_x* in the syntax example above.

1. The *sinl* function is the long double-precision floating-point version of *sin( )*, and it was introduced in version 6.0. 2. *sinl* is incompatible with ANSI, UNIX, and XENIX.

RETURNS As long as the angle *x* is less than approximately $1.34e^8$ radians (found by experimentation), *sin* computes and returns the sine of *x*. If the value of *x* is larger, a loss of significance (the result is correct up to a few digits only) occurs and *sin* generates a PLOSS error to indicate "partial loss of precision." If the value is so large that the result is totally useless, a TLOSS error is sent to *stderr*, the return value is zero, and *errno* is set to the constant ERANGE.

The *sinl* routine returns the sine of *ld_x*.

SEE ALSO

`asin` *To compute the arc sine of a variable*

`cos` *To compute cosine of an angle*

EXAMPLE Write a program that accepts an angle in degrees and prints its sine. The behavior of the *sinl* function exactly matches that of the *sin* function except that it passes and returns 80-bit long double values instead of double values. Modifying the example program to allow use of the *sinl* function is thus a matter of ensuring that the double variables are declared as *long doubles*, and that no function that expects an *int* receives a 10-byte *long double*, instead.

```
#include <stdio.h>
#include <math.h>
#include <stdlib.h>       /* errno is defined here */
#define  R_TO_D   57.29578 /* radians to degrees  */
main(int argc, char **argv)
{
    double result;
    if(argc < 2)
    {
```

```
        printf("Usage: %s <degrees>\n", argv[0]);
    }
    else
    {
        result = sin(atof(argv[1]) / R_TO_D);
        if(errno != ERANGE)
        {
            printf("Sine (%s deg.) = %f\n",
                    argv[1], result);
        }
    }
}
```

COMPATIBILITY

sinh, sinhl

MSC 3	MSC 4	MSC 5	MSC 6	QC1	QC2	QC2.5	TC1	TC1.5	TC2	TC++	ANSI	UNIX V	XNX	OS2	DOS
▲	▲	▲	1	▲	▲	▲	▲	▲	▲	▲	2	2	2	▲	▲

PURPOSE Use *sinh* to compute the hyperbolic sine of a *double* variable. The *sinhl* version provides a long double degree of precision.

SYNTAX

```
double sinh(double x);

long double sinhl (long double ld_x);
```

`double x;` *Variable whose hyperbolic sine is to be computed*

`ld_x;` *Variable whose hyperbolic sine is to be computed*

EXAMPLE CALL

```
a = sinh (b);

x = sinhl (y);
```

INCLUDES `#include <math.h>` *For function declaration and definition of error constants*

DESCRIPTION The *sinh* function computes the hyperbolic sine of the *double* variable *x*. The *sinhl* function calculates the hyperbolic sine of the long double variable *ld_x*.

1. *sinhl* is the long double-precision floating-point version of *sinh* and was introduced in version 6.0. 2. *sinhl* is incompatible with ANSI, UNIX, and XENIX.

RETURNS Normally, *sinh* returns the hyperbolic sine of *x*. If the result is too large (a *double* variable can be as large as approximately 10^{308}), *sinh* returns the value HUGE_VAL and sets *errno* to the constant ERANGE.

The *sinhl* returns match those of the *sinh* function, except that _LHUGE_VAL is used instead of HUGE_VAL to identify the overflow condition.

COMMENTS When used with the *intrinsic* pragma (see Chapter 1), the convention of the argument calling for both the regular and long-double versions is changed to pass the arguments on the floating-point chip.

SEE ALSO `cosh` *To compute the hyperbolic cosine of a variable*

EXAMPLE Write a program that accepts a floating-point number on the command line and computes its hyperbolic sine.

The example program may be modified to run the *sinhl* version by ensuring that the appropriate variables are declared as *long doubles* and by avoiding the transmission of the 80-bit long double-precision floating-point values to functions that cannot handle them.

```
#include <stdio.h>
#include <math.h>
#include <stdlib.h>       /* errno is defined here */
main(int argc, char **argv)
{
    double result;
    if(argc < 2)
    {
        printf("Usage: %s <value>\n", argv[0]);
    }
    else
    {
        result = sinh(atof(argv[1]));
        if(errno != ERANGE)
        {
            printf("Hyperbolic sine of %s = %f\n",
                    argv[1], result);
        }
    }
}
```

COMPATIBILITY

sqrt, sqrtl

MSC 3	MSC 4	MSC 5	MSC 6	QC1	QC2	QC2.5	TC1	TC1.5	TC2	TC++	ANSI	UNIX V	XNX	OS2	DOS
▲	▲	▲	1	▲	▲	▲	▲	▲	▲	▲	2	2	2	▲	▲

PURPOSE Use *sqrt* to compute the square root of a non-negative *double* variable. The *sqrtl* function is used when you need a double-precision version of *sqrt*.

SYNTAX

```
double sqrt (double x);

long double sqrtl (long double x);
```

`x;` *Variable whose square root is to be computed*

EXAMPLE CALL

```
sqrt_2 = sqrt(2.0); /* sqrt_2 = 1.414 */

sqrt_4 = sqrtl (8.2);
```

INCLUDES `#include <math.h>` *For function declaration*

DESCRIPTION The *sqrt* function computes the square root of the *double* variable *x*, provided *x* is not negative. The *sqrtl* function calculates the square root.

1. The *sqrtl* function was introduced in version 6.0 as the long double-precision floating-point version of *sqrt*. 2. *sqrtl* is incompatible with ANSI, UNIX, and XENIX.

RETURNS The *sqrt* function returns the square root of *x*. If *x* is negative, though, *sqrt* prints a DOMAIN error message to *stderr*, sets the global variable *errno* to EDOM, and returns a zero. The *sqrtl* function returns the square root of x if successful; zero if not.

SEE ALSO `pow` *To compute the value of one argument raised to the power of another*

EXAMPLE Write a program that accepts a number and computes its square root. The example program may be modified to run the *sqrtl* version by ensuring that the appropriate variables are declared as *long doubles* and by avoiding the transmission of the 80-bit long double-precision floating-point values to functions that cannot handle them.

```
#include <stdio.h>
#include <math.h>
#include <stdlib.h>  /* errno is declared here */
main(int argc, char **argv)
{
```

```
        double result;
        if(argc < 2)
        {
            printf("Usage: %s <value>\n", argv[0]);
        }
        else
        {
            result = sqrt(atof(argv[1]));
            if (errno != EDOM)
                printf("sqrt (%s) = %f\n", argv[1], result);
        }
    }
```

srand

COMPATIBILITY

MSC 3	MSC 4	MSC 5	MSC 6	QC1	QC2	QC2.5	TC1	TC1.5	TC2	TC++	ANSI	UNIX V	XNX	OS2	DOS
▲	▲	▲	▲	▲	▲	▲	▲	▲	▲	▲	▲	▲	▲	▲	▲

PURPOSE Use *srand* to set the starting value (seed) for generating a sequence of pseudorandom integer values.

SYNTAX `void srand(unsigned seed);`

`unsigned seed;` *Starting point for random number generator*

EXAMPLE CALL `srand(new_seed);`

INCLUDES `#include <stdlib.h>` *For function definition*

DESCRIPTION The *srand* function sets the seed of the random number generation algorithm used by the function *rand*.

If the seed is 1, the random number generator is initialized to its default starting point, generating the sequence that is produced when *rand* is called without prior calls to *srand*. Any other value for the seed sets a random starting point for the pseudorandom sequence to be generated by *rand*.

SEE ALSO `rand` *To obtain a random integer value*

EXAMPLE Write a program that uses *srand* to set the seed for a sequence of pseudorandom integers generated by *rand*. Notice that the same seed always generates the same sequence of numbers (instead of its being purely random).

That is why we call the sequence of numbers "pseudorandom" (instead of being purely random).

```
#include <stdio.h>
#include <stdlib.h>
main()
{
    int i;
    unsigned seed;
/* Ask user to enter a new seed */
    printf("Enter a seed: ");
    scanf(" %u", &seed);
/* Set new seed by calling "srand" */
    srand(seed);
/* Generate and display 20 pseudorandom integers */
    printf("20 pseudorandom integers from \"rand\"\n");
    for(i=0; i<20; i++)
    {
        printf("%d\n", rand());
    }
    printf("Try again with the same seed.\n\
You'll get the same sequence.\n");
}
```

COMPATIBILITY

_status87

MSC 3	MSC 4	MSC 5	MSC 6	QC1	QC2	QC2.5	TC1	TC1.5	TC2	TC++	ANSI	UNIX V	XNX	OS2	DOS
	▲	▲	▲	▲	▲	▲	▲	▲	▲	▲				▲	▲

PURPOSE Use *_status87* to get the contents of the floating-point status word, which is a combination of the 8087 math coprocessor status word and other conditions detected by the 8087 exception handler.

SYNTAX `unsigned int _status87(void);`

EXAMPLE CALL `if(_status87() & SW_ZERODIVIDE) puts("Zero divide error");`

INCLUDES `#include <float.h>` *For function declaration and definition of constants denoting status-word bit settings*

DESCRIPTION The *_status87* function returns the status word of the floating-point package. This status word is a composite of the status word of the 8087 math coprocessor and other conditions detected by the 8087 exception handler.

You can use the status word to detect error conditions in your own floating-point exception handler.

You should check the return value by performing a bitwise AND with the constant from Table 8-5 that matches the condition you are verifying and then comparing that result for equality with the constant itself. In other words, if the return value is *status*, checking for a loss of precision is done by the code fragment

```
    status = _status87();
    if ((status & SW_INEXACT) == SW_INEXACT)
    {
/* A loss of precision has occurred */
         :
         :
    }
```

RETURNS The bits in the value returned by *_status87* indicate the status of the floating-point package. Table 8-5 shows the constants defined in *float.h* to indicate specific conditions.

Table 8-5. *The Floating-Point Status Word*

Status Constant	Meaning
SW_INVALID	Invalid operation.
SW_DENORMAL	Operands are stored in a "normalized" form in in the 8087 math coprocessor. This bit indicates a denormalized operand.
SW_ZERODIVIDE	Divide-by-zero attempted.
SW_OVERFLOW	Floating-point overflow.
SW_UNDERFLOW	Floating-point underflow.
SW_INEXACT	Loss of precision in result.
SW_UNEMULATED	The floating-point package can use a library that emulates 8087 instructions. This bit indicates that an unemulated instruction was encountered. (SW_INVALID also set.)
SW_SQRTNEG	Computation of the square root of a negative number attempted. (SW_INVALID also set.)
SW_STACKOVERFLOW	Floating-point stack overflow. (SW_INVALID also set.)
SW_STACKUNDERFLOW	Floating-point stack underflow. (SW_INVALID also set.)

SEE ALSO `_clear87` *To reset the floating-point status word*

`_control87` *To alter bits in the floating-point control word*

EXAMPLE Read and display the current floating-point status word. Now copy a small double variable into a *float* one and create an underflow and an inexact result. Read and display the status word again; the new value reflects the error.

```
#include <stdio.h>
#include <float.h>
main()
{
    float a;
    double b = 1.e-40;
    unsigned fpstatus;
    printf("Before any computations ");
    fpstatus = _status87();
    printf("status word is: %X\n", fpstatus);
/* Perform operation that produces underflow and
 * an inexact result
 */
    a = b;   /* This will produce inexact result */
    printf("After undeflow/inexact ");
    fpstatus = _status87();
    printf("status word is: %X\n", fpstatus);
}
```

COMPATIBILITY

tan, tanl

MSC 3	MSC 4	MSC 5	MSC 6	QC1	QC2	QC2.5	TC1	TC1.5	TC2	TC++	ANSI	UNIX V	XNX	OS2	DOS
▲	▲	▲	1	▲	▲	▲	▲	▲	▲	▲	2	2	2	▲	▲

PURPOSE Use *tan* to compute the tangent of an angle whose value is expressed in radians. The *tanl* function is a long double version of *tan*.

SYNTAX

```
double tan(double x);

long double tanl (long double ld_x);
```

`double x;` *Angle in radians whose tangent is to be computed*

`ld_x;` *Angle in radians*

EXAMPLE CALL

```
y = tan(x);

e = tanl (y);
```

INCLUDES `#include <math.h>` *For function declaration and definition of error constants*

DESCRIPTION The *tan* function computes the tangent of *double* argument *x*, which represents an angle in radians. The *tanl* version calculates the tangent of *ld_x* as a long double-precision floating-point version of *tan*. (See the tutorial for more information about double-precision functions.)

1. The *tanl* function was introduced in version 6.0. 2. *tanl* does not work with ANSI, UNIX, or XENIX.

RETURNS As long as the angle *x* is less than approximately $1.34e^8$ radians (found by experimentation), *tan* correctly computes and returns the tangent of *x*. If the value of *x* is larger, a loss of precision results (the result is correct up to a few digits only) and *tan* generates a PLOSS error to indicate "partial loss of precision." If the value is so large that the result is totally void of precision, a TLOSS error is sent to *stderr* and the return value is zero. At the same time, *errno* is set to the constant ERANGE.

The *tanl* function returns the tangent of *ld_x* if the call was successful. A return value of zero signals an error.

COMMENTS When used with the *intrinsic* pragma (see Chapter 1), the convention of the argument calling for both the regular and long double versions is changed to pass the arguments on the floating-point chip.

SEE ALSO `atan` *To compute the arc tangent of a variable*

EXAMPLE Write a program that accepts an angle in degrees and prints its tangent.

The example program may be modified to run the *sqrtl* version by ensuring that the appropriate variables are declared as *long doubles* and by avoiding the transmission of the 80-bit long double-precision floating-point values to functions that cannot handle them.

```
#include <stdio.h>
#include <math.h>
#include <stdlib.h>        /* errno is defined here */
#define  R_TO_D   57.29578 /* radians to degrees   */
main(int argc, char **argv)
{
    double result;
    if(argc < 2)
    {
        printf("Usage: %s <degrees>\n", argv[0]);
    }
    else
    {
        result = tan(atof(argv[1]) / R_TO_D);
        if(errno != ERANGE)
        {
```

```
            printf("Tangent (%s deg.) = %f\n",
                    argv[1], result);
        }
    }
}
```

COMPATIBILITY

tanh, tanhl

MSC 3	MSC 4	MSC 5	MSC 6	QC1	QC2	QC2.5	TC1	TC1.5	TC2	TC++	ANSI	UNIX V	XNX	OS2	DOS
▲	▲	▲	1	▲	▲	▲	▲	▲	▲	▲	2	2	2	▲	▲

PURPOSE Use *tanh* to compute the hyperbolic tangent of a *double* variable. Use the *tanhl* version when you need an 80-bit degree of precision.

SYNTAX

```
double tanh(double x);

long double tanhl (long double ld_x);

double x;        Variable whose hyperbolic tangent is to be computed

ld_x;            An angle in radians
```

EXAMPLE CALL

```
a = tanh(b);

e = tanhl(y);
```

INCLUDES `#include <math.h>` *For function declaration*

DESCRIPTION The *tanh* function computes the hyperbolic tangent of the *double* variable *x*. The *tanhl* version calculates the tangent of *ld_x* as a long double-precision floating-point version of *tanh*. (See the tutorial for more information about double-precision functions.)

1. The *tanhl* function was introduced in version 6.0. 2. *tanhl* is incompatible with ANSI, UNIX, and XENIX.

RETURNS The *tanh* function returns the hyperbolic tangent of *x*. The *tanhl* returns match those of the *tanh* version, except that the values are 80-bit *long doubles*.

COMMENTS When used with the *intrinsic* pragma (see Chapter 1), the convention of the argument calling for both the regular and long double versions is changed to pass the arguments on the floating-point chip.

SEE ALSO `cosh, sinh` *To compute the hyperbolic cosine and hyperbolic sine of a variable*

EXAMPLE Write a program that accepts a floating-point number on the command line and computes its hyperbolic tangent.

The example program may be modified to run the *tanhl* version by ensuring that the appropriate variables are declared as *long doubles* and by avoiding the transmission of the 80-bit long double-precision floating-point values to functions that cannot handle them.

```
#include <stdio.h>
#include <math.h>
#include <stdlib.h>      /* errno is defined here */
main(int argc, char **argv)
{
    double result;
    if(argc < 2)
    {
        printf("Usage: %s <value>\n", argv[0]);
    }
    else
    {
        result = tanh(atof(argv[1]));
        if(errno != ERANGE)
        {
            printf("Hyperbolic tangent of %s = %f\n",
                    argv[1], result);
        }
    }
}
```

Chapter 9 Character Classification and Conversion

Introduction

C uses the American Standard Code for Information Interchange (ASCII) character set, which contains characters that can be printed as well as some that have special meanings and are not printable. Often you need to determine the category of a character or to convert a character from one case to another. The C library includes character classification macros for this purpose. (See Table 9-1.)

THE ASCII CHARACTER SET

The ASCII character set relies on a 7-bit code to represent all letters, numbers, punctuation symbols, and some special (unprintable) control characters. The 128 ASCII characters are shown in Figure 9-1. The single-

First hexadecimal digit	Second digit															
	0	**1**	**2**	**3**	**4**	**5**	**6**	**7**	**8**	**9**	**A**	**B**	**C**	**D**	**E**	**F**
0	NUL	SOH	STX	ETX	EOT	ENQ	ACK	BEL	BS	HT	LF	VT	FF	CR	SO	SI
1	DLE	DC1	DC2	DC3	DC4	NAK	SYN	ETB	CAN	EM	SUB	ESC	FS	GS	RS	US
2	SP	!	"	#	$	%	&	'	(	)	*	+	,	–	.	/
3	0	1	2	3	4	5	6	7	8	9	:	;	<	=	>	?
4	@	A	B	C	D	E	F	G	H	I	J	K	L	M	N	O
5	P	Q	R	S	T	U	V	W	X	Y	Z	[	\	]	^	_
6	`	a	b	c	d	e	f	g	h	i	j	k	l	m	n	o
7	p	q	r	s	t	u	v	w	x	y	z	{	|	}	~	DEL
	0	**1**	**2**	**3**	**4**	**5**	**6**	**7**	**8**	**9**	**A**	**B**	**C**	**D**	**E**	**F**

Figure 9-1. ***The ASCII character set***

character entries are printable. The two- and three-letter codes are unprintable (except SP which denotes a blank space).

Beyond the basic 128, the IBM PC also supports character codes from 128 through 255 that a single unsigned C character variable can represent. Often called the "IBM PC extended ASCII character set," these are a collection of Greek, accented, and graphical characters. In fact, even the nonprinting ASCII characters can be displayed on the IBM PC and some are useful for drawing borders of pop-up menus and windows in PC applications. Most printers meant for the IBM PC also support the extended character set. The Microsoft C character classification macros, however, work with the ASCII (128) character set only.

Notes on Character Classification and Conversion

Table 9-1 shows catalogs of the available character classification macros. The macros are defined in the header file *ctype.h* where you can examine them. Table 9-2 groups the macros by task.

Table 9-1. ***Character Classification Macros***

Macro	Description
isalnum	Tests if a character is alphanumeric.
isalpha	Tests if a character is alphabetic.
isascii	Tests if an integer value is a valid ASCII character.
iscntrl	Tests if a character belongs to the set of control characters.
isdigit	Tests if a character is a numerical digit.
isgraph	Tests if a character is printable (excluding the space character).
islower	Tests if a character is lowercase.
isprint	Tests if a character is printable (including the space character).
ispunct	Tests if a character belongs to the set of punctuation characters.
isspace	Tests if a character belongs to the set of whitespace characters.
isupper	Tests if a character is uppercase.
isxdigit	Tests if a character is a hexadecimal digit.
toascii	Converts an integer value to a valid ASCII character.
tolower	Converts a character to lowercase if that character is an uppercase letter.
_tolower	Converts a character to lowercase without checking if it is an uppercase letter.
toupper	Converts a character to uppercase if that character is a lowercase letter.
_toupper	Converts a character to uppercase without checking if it is a lowercase letter.

Table 9-2. *Character Classification Macros by Task*

Task	Macros
Classify a character.	isalnum, isalpha, isascii, iscntrl, isdigit, isgraph, islower, isprint, ispunct, isspace, isupper, isxdigit
Convert from uppercase to lowercase.	tolower, _tolower
Convert from lowercase to uppercase.	toupper, _toupper

CHARACTER CLASSIFICATION: BEHIND THE SCENES

The Microsoft C library maintains an array named *_ctype* containing unsigned characters and information that is used in the macro definitions to classify the characters. If 'c' is an ASCII character, the unsigned character _ctype [c+1] contains the classification information about that character. By testing the contents of _ctype[c+1], the macros determine whether 'c' belongs to a category (for example, uppercase letters). That information is encoded in the bits of the single byte in the array *_ctype* that corresponds to the character 'c'. For example, the uppercase 'c' has bit 0 of _ctype[c+1] set to 1. Thus 'c' is uppercase if

```
(_ctype[c+1] & 1)
```

is true (or 1). We could rewrite the test for uppercase letters to compare the ASCII code of the test character with the ASCII codes 'A' and 'Z' and to conclude that the character is uppercase if it satisfies

```
if(c >= 'A' && c <= 'Z') /* character is uppercase */
```

Both approaches work fine, but the library macros are faster because they use a single test while our method needs two logical tests.

The bit patterns in *_ctype* that determine the classification of characters comprise eight basic categories. These and the range of ASCII characters that belong to each are shown in Table 9-3.

Table 9-3. *Basic Categories of Character Classification*

Category	ASCII Characters
Uppercase letter	'A' through 'Z'
Lowercase letter	'a' through 'z'
Digit (0 through 9)	'0' through '9'
Whitespace	tab, line feed (newline), vertical feed, form feed and carriage return
Punctuation character	! " # $ % & ' ( ) * + , – . / : ; < = > ? @ [\ ] ^ _ ['] { | } ~
Control character	All characters with codes 0 through 1F and the final character 7F
Blank space	The blank space character
Hexadecimal digit	'0' through '9', 'A' through 'F' and 'a' through 'f'

All the macros are based on these basic classification categories. Table 9-4 summarizes the categories of characters that satisfy the classification macros.

Table 9-4. *Tests Performed by Classification Macros*

Macro	Test for Basic Categories
isalpha	Uppercase or lowercase letter
isupper	Uppercase letter
islower	Lowercase letter
isdigit	Digit
isxdigit	Hexadecimal digit
isspace	Whitespace
ispunct	Punctuation character
isalnum	Uppercase or lowercase letter or digit
isprint	Blank space or punctuation character or uppercase letter or lowercase letter or digit
isgraph	Punctuation character or uppercase letter or lowercase letter or digit
iscntrl	Control character
isascii	Value less than 80 hex

Cautions

- The possibility of "side effects" constitutes a common pitfall of using macros. This is best illustrated by an example. Consider the *tolower* macro, defined in *ctype.h* as

```
#define _tolower(c)      ( (c)-'A'+'a' )
#define tolower(c)       ( (isupper(c)) ? _tolower(c) : (c) )
```

which says you subtract the ASCII code of 'A' and add the ASCII equivalent of 'a' to get lowercase letters from uppercase ones. You can confirm the derivation of this formula with the ASCII codes shown in Figure 9-1. Now suppose you used the macro in your program as follows

```
int c;
c = tolower(getch());
```

hoping to get a single keystroke converted to lowercase when you press a key. Will this happen?

In the first step of the compilation process, the C preprocessor replaces *tolower* with its definition and produces

```
int c;
c = ( (isupper(getch())) ? ( (getch())-'A'+'a' ) : (getch()) );
```

Since the macro's argument is *getch( )*, that function call is inserted wherever *c* appears in the macro definition. Notice that *getch* is called three times in the expanded macro. Instead of processing a single keystroke, the statement consumes two characters from the keyboard; if the first is an uppercase character, the second is converted to a value by subtracting the value of 'A' and adding 'a'. For any other type of first keystroke, the second key hit at the keyboard will be copied to the variable *c* without any change.

All the extra function calls that occurred in this example are the side effects of using a macro. Because of this, you should avoid using as an argument to a macro any expression or function that when evaluated changes your program's behavior. If you use the conversion macros (with possible side effects), you might consider linking to the function versions of the *toupper* and *tolower* macros. You can do this by "undefining" the macros (use *#undef*) after the statement *#include <ctype.h>* in your program. Insert an *#include <stdlib.h>* after this to include the definition of the function versions.

▶ Although the macros *_tolower* and *_toupper* run faster because they do no checking of the characters, do not use them unless the character is known to be of the appropriate case. Otherwise, the character will be mapped to another, possibly invalid, value.

▶ Note that the *toascii* macro converts an integer value to ASCII by chopping off all high-order bits above the seventh one.

isalnum

COMPATIBILITY

MSC 3	MSC 4	MSC 5	MSC 6	QC1	QC2	QC2.5	TC1	TC1.5	TC2	TC++	ANSI	UNIX V	XNX	OS2	DOS
▲	▲	▲	▲	▲	▲	▲	▲	▲	▲	▲	▲	▲	▲	▲	▲

PURPOSE Use the *isalnum* macro to check whether an ASCII character is alphanumeric.

SYNTAX `int isalnum(int c);`

`int c;` *Integer with ASCII character*

EXAMPLE CALL `if(isalnum(c) != 0) printf("%c is alphanumeric\n", c);`

INCLUDES `#include <ctype.h>` *For macro definition*

DESCRIPTION The *isalnum* macro determines if the value in the integer argument *c* is one of the digits 0 to 9, a lowercase letter from a to z, or an uppercase letter from A to Z. The *isalnum* macro can only handle valid ASCII values (from 0 to 127) and the constant EOF, defined in *stdio.h*.

RETURNS The *isalnum* macro returns a nonzero value if the *c* is an alphanumeric character. Otherwise it returns a zero.

SEE ALSO `isascii` *To test if an arbitrary integer value is a valid ASCII character*

EXAMPLE Write a program that prints out the ASCII table with a special mark next to each character that satisfies *isalnum*.

```
#include <stdio.h>
#include <ctype.h>
main()
{
    int ch, count,
        mark = 0xdb; /* to mark characters */
/* Go over entire ASCII table and display the
 * alphanumeric ones.
 */
    printf(
    "Alphanumeric ones are marked with a %c\n",
            mark);
    for(count = 0, ch = 0; ch <= 0x7f; ch++)
    {
        printf("%#02x ", ch);
```

```
/* Print character -- if printable              */
        if(isprint(ch))
        {
            printf(" %c", ch);
        }
        else
        {
            printf("  ");
        }
/* Perform test and put a mark if test succeeds */
        if(isalnum(ch) != 0)
        {
            printf(" %c", mark);
        }
        else
        {
            printf("  ", ch);
        }
        count++;
        if(count == 8)
        {
            printf(" \n");
            count = 0;
        }
    }
}
```

COMPATIBILITY

isalpha

MSC 3	MSC 4	MSC 5	MSC 6	QC1	QC2	QC2.5	TC1	TC1.5	TC2	TC++	ANSI	UNIX V	XNX	OS2	DOS
▲	▲	▲	▲	▲	▲	▲	▲	▲	▲	▲	▲	▲	▲	▲	▲

PURPOSE Use the *isalpha* macro to check whether an ASCII character is alphabetic.

SYNTAX

```
int isalpha(int c);

int c;       Integer with ASCII character
```

EXAMPLE CALL

```
if(isalpha(c) != 0) printf("%c is letter\n", c);
```

INCLUDES

```
#include <ctype.h>       For macro definition
```

DESCRIPTION The *isalpha* macro determines if the value in the integer argument *c* is a lowercase letter from a to z or an uppercase letter from A to Z. The *isalpha* macro can only handle valid ASCII values (from 0 to 127) and the constant EOF, defined in *stdio.h*.

RETURNS The *isalpha* macro returns a nonzero value if the *c* is indeed a letter. Otherwise it returns a zero.

SEE ALSO isascii *To test whether an arbitrary integer value is a valid ASCII character*

EXAMPLE Write a program that prints out the ASCII table with a special mark next to each character that satisfies *isalpha*.

```
#include <stdio.h>
#include <ctype.h>
main()
{
    int ch, count,
        mark = 0xdb; /* to mark characters */
/* Go over entire ASCII table and display the
 * alphabetic ones.
 */
    printf(
    "Letters are marked with a %c\n", mark);
    for(count = 0, ch = 0; ch <= 0x7f; ch++)
    {
        printf("%#02x ", ch);
/* Print character -- if printable                */
        if(isprint(ch))
        {
            printf(" %c", ch);
        }
        else
        {
            printf("  ");
        }
/* Perform test and put a mark if test succeeds */
        if(isalpha(ch) != 0)
        {
            printf(" %c", mark);
        }
        else
        {
            printf("  ", ch);
        }
        count++;
        if(count == 8)
```

```
            {
                printf(" \n");
                count = 0;
            }
        }
}
```

COMPATIBILITY

isascii

MSC 3	MSC 4	MSC 5	MSC 6	QC1	QC2	QC2.5	TC1	TC1.5	TC2	TC++	ANSI	UNIX V	XNX	OS2	DOS
▲	▲	▲	▲	▲	▲	▲	▲	▲	▲	▲		▲	▲	▲	▲

PURPOSE Use the *isascii* macro to check whether an arbitrary integer value is a valid ASCII character.

SYNTAX `int isascii(int c);`

`int c;` *Integer value being checked*

EXAMPLE CALL `if(isascii(c) != 0) printf("%d - not ASCII value\n", c);`

INCLUDES `#include ctype.h>` *For macro definition*

DESCRIPTION The *isascii* macro determines if the value of the integer argument *c* is in the range 0–127 (the range of values that the ASCII character set occupies).

RETURNS The *isascii* macro returns a nonzero value if the *c* is a valid ASCII character. Otherwise it returns a zero.

COMMENTS The IBM PC supports extended ASCII characters (those with codes from 128 to 255). The *isascii* macro treats these as non-ASCII.

SEE ALSO `toascii` *To convert an arbitrary integer value to a valid ASCII character*

EXAMPLE Write a program that accepts an integer value on the command line and prints out a message indicating whether that value is an ASCII character. (This is true if the value is between 0 and 127.)

```
#include <stdio.h>
#include <ctype.h>
main(int argc, char **argv)
{
```

```
    int ch;
    if(argc < 2)
    {
        printf("Usage: %s <integer_value>\n",
                argv[0]);
    }
    else
    {
        if (isascii(ch = atoi(argv[1])) != 0)
        {
            printf("%s is an ASCII character\n\
It prints as %c on the IBM PC\n", argv[1],  ch);
        }
        else
        {
            printf("%s is not an ASCII char.\n",
                    argv[1]);
        }
    }
}
```

iscntrl, isdigit, isgraph, islower, isprint, ispunct, isspace, isupper, isxdigit

COMPATIBILITY

MSC 3	MSC 4	MSC 5	MSC 6	QC1	QC2	QC2.5	TC1	TC1.5	TC2	TC++	ANSI	UNIX V	XNX	OS2	DOS
▲	▲	▲	▲	▲	▲	▲	▲	▲	▲	▲	▲	▲	▲	▲	▲

PURPOSE Use this group of macros to determine specific properties of an ASCII character: whether it is a control character, a digit, a lowercase letter, printable, and so on.

SYNTAX

```
int iscntrl(int c);

int isdigit(int c);

int isgraph(int c);

int islower(int c);

int isprint(int c);

int ispunct(int c);

int isspace(int c);
```

```
int isupper(int c);

int isxdigit(int c);

int c;        Integer with ASCII character
```

EXAMPLE CALL

```
if(isprint(c) != 0) printf("%c is printable\n", c);
if(isdigit(c) != 0) printf("%c is a digit\n", c);
if(iscntrl(c) != 0) printf("%d is a control char\n", c);
```

INCLUDES

```
#include <ctype.h>        For macro definitions
```

DESCRIPTION This group of macros determines if the value in the integer argument *c* satisfies a specific condition. The macros can only handle valid ASCII values (from 0 to 127) and the constant EOF, defined in *stdio.h*. Table 9-5 shows the test performed by each of the macros.

Table 9-5. ***Character Classification Tests***

Macro	Tests for	Acceptable Values
iscntrl	Control character	7Fh or in the range 0 to 1Fh
isdigit	Decimal digit	'0' to '9'
isgraph	Printable character excluding the space	21h to 7Eh
islower	Lowercase character	'a' to 'z'
isprint	Printable character	'a' to 'z'
ispunct	Punctuation character	21h to 2Fh or 3Ah to 40h or 5Bh to 60h or 7Bh to 7Ch
isspace	Whitespace character	9h to Dh or 20h (space)
isupper	Uppercase character	'A' to 'Z'
isxdigit	Hexadecimal digit	'0' to '9' or 'A' to 'F' or 'a' to 'f'

RETURNS Each macro returns a nonzero value if the *c* satisfies the criteria for that macro. Otherwise it returns a 0.

COMMENTS You should use *isascii* first to verify that the integer value is indeed a valid ASCII character. Only then should you use any one of these macros to test for specific properties of that ASCII value.

The Microsoft C library maintains a list of characters classified according to these tests, allowing the macros to perform the tests swiftly. You can determine how these tests work by studying the file *ctype.h*. In particular, try printing out the external array *(_ctype+1)* for index 0 through 127. For example, each character code for which a 10 (which is equal to the defined constant _PUNCT in *ctype.h*) appears in the array is a punctuation character.

SEE ALSO `isascii` *To test whether an arbitrary integer value is a valid ASCII character*

EXAMPLE Write a program that accepts the name of one of the macros *iscntrl, isdigit, isgraph, islower, isprint, ispunct, isspace, isupper,* or *isxdigit* and prints the ASCII table with a mark next to each character that satisfies the test. This is a convenient tool. Figure 9-2 shows the output for the macro *ispunct.* See if your understanding of punctuation characters matches those of the C library.

Those marked with a ■ satisfy ispunct

00	0×01	0×02	0×03	0×04	0×05	0×06	0×07
0×08	0×09	0×0a	0×0b	0×0c	0×0d	0×0e	0×0f
0×10	0×11	0×12	0×13	0×14	0×15	0×16	0×17
0×18	0×19	0×1a	0×1b	0×1c	0×1d	0×1e	0×1f
0×20	0×21 ! ■	0×22 " ■	0×23 # ■	0×24 $ ■	0×25 % ■	0×26 & ■	0×27 ' ■
0×28 (■	0×29) ■	0×2a * ■	0×2b + ■	0×2c , ■	0×2d - ■	0×2e . ■	0×2f / ■
0×30 0	0×31 1	0×32 2	0×33 3	0×34 4	0×35 5	0×36 6	0×37 7
0×38 8	0×39 9	0×3a : ■	0×3b ; ■	0×3c < ■	0×3d = ■	0×3e > ■	0×3f ? ■
0×40 @ ■	0×41 A	0×42 B	0×43 C	0×44 D	0×45 E	0×46 F	0×47 G
0×48 H	0×49 I	0×4a J	0×4b K	0×4c L	0×4d M	0×4e N	0×4f O
0×50 P	0×51 Q	0×52 R	0×53 S	0×54 T	0×55 U	0×56 V	0×57 W
0×58 X	0×59 Y	0×5a Z	0×5b [■	0×5c \ ■	0×5d] ■	0×5e ^ ■	0×5f _ ■
0×60 ` ■	0×61 a	0×62 b	0×63 c	0×64 d	0×65 e	0×66 f	0×67 g
0×68 h	0×69 i	0×6a j	0×6b k	0×6c l	0×6d m	0×6e n	0×6f o
0×70 p	0×71 q	0×72 r	0×73 s	0×74 t	0×75 u	0×76 v	0×77 w
0×78 x	0×79 y	0×7a z	0×7b { ■	0×7c | ■	0×7d } ■	0×7e ~ ■	0×7f

Figure 9-2. *ASCII characters that satisfy the macro* ispunct

```
#include <stdio.h>
#include <string.h>
#include <ctype.h>
/* Define a table of function names and numbers */
typedef struct FUNC_TABLE
{
    char name[16];
    int  funcnum;
} FUNC_TABLE;
#define CNTRL  0
#define DIGIT  1
#define GRAPH  2
#define LOWER  3
#define PRINT  4
#define PUNCT  5
#define SPACE  6
#define UPPER  7
#define XDIGIT 8
/* Now declare the table and initialize it        */
static FUNC_TABLE isfuncs[9] =
```

```
{
    "iscntrl", CNTRL, "isdigit", DIGIT,
    "isgraph", GRAPH, "islower", LOWER,
    "isprint", PRINT, "ispunct", PUNCT,
    "isspace", SPACE, "isupper", UPPER,
    "isxdigit", XDIGIT
};
static int numfunc = sizeof(isfuncs)/sizeof(FUNC_TABLE);
main(int argc, char **argv)
{
    int ch, count, i, test_result,
        mark = 0xdb; /* to mark characters */
    if (argc < 2)
    {
        printf("Usage: %s <function_name>\n", argv[0]);
        exit(0);
    }
/* Search table for function name and pointer */
    for(i=0; i<numfunc; i++)
    {
        if (strcmp(argv[1], isfuncs[i].name) == 0)
            break;
    }
    if (i >= numfunc)
    {
        printf("Unknown function: %s\n", argv[1]);
        exit(0);
    }
/* Now go over entire ASCII table and mark the
 * characters that satisfy requested test.
 */
    printf(
    "Those marked with a %c satisfy %s\n",
          mark, argv[1]);
    for(count = 0, ch = 0; ch <= 0x7f; ch++)
    {
        printf("%#02x ", ch);
/* Print character -- if printable                */
        if(isprint(ch))
        {
            printf(" %c", ch);
        }
        else
        {
            printf("  ");
```

```
            }
/* Perform the test and put a mark if test succeeds */
            switch(isfuncs[i].funcnum)
            {
                case CNTRL: test_result = iscntrl(ch);
                            break;
                case DIGIT: test_result = isdigit(ch);
                            break;
                case GRAPH: test_result = isgraph(ch);
                            break;
                case LOWER: test_result = islower(ch);
                            break;
                case PRINT: test_result = isprint(ch);
                            break;
                case PUNCT: test_result = ispunct(ch);
                            break;
                case SPACE: test_result = isspace(ch);
                            break;
                case UPPER: test_result = isupper(ch);
                            break;
                case XDIGIT: test_result = isxdigit(ch);
                            break;
            }
            if(test_result != 0)
            {
                printf("%c ", mark);
            }
            else
            {
                printf("  ", ch);
            }
            count++;
            if(count == 8)
            {
                printf(" \n");
                count = 0;
            }
        }
}
```

Character Classification and Conversion

COMPATIBILITY

toascii

MSC 3	MSC 4	MSC 5	MSC 6	QC1	QC2	QC2.5	TC1	TC1.5	TC2	TC++	ANSI	UNIX V	XNX	OS2	DOS
▲	▲	▲	▲	▲	▲	▲	▲	▲	▲	▲		▲	▲	▲	▲

PURPOSE Use the *toascii* macro to convert an arbitrary integer value to a valid ASCII character.

SYNTAX `int toascii(int c);`

`int c;` *Integer to be converted*

EXAMPLE CALL `c = toascii(int_value);`

INCLUDES `#include <ctype.h>` *For macro definition*

DESCRIPTION The *toascii* macro sets all but the low-order seven bits of the integer *c* to zero so that the converted value represents a valid ASCII character. If *c* is already an ASCII character, it remains unchanged. As an example, this macro could be used to remove the high bit (the most significant bit) from characters in a WordStar document file. (WordStar uses the high bit to store formatting information.)

RETURNS The *toascii* macro returns the converted character.

SEE ALSO `isascii` *To test whether an arbitrary integer value is a valid ASCII character*

EXAMPLE Write a program to convert an integer value to an ASCII character.

```
#include <stdio.h>
#include <stdlib.h>
#include <ctype.h>
main(int argc, char **argv)
{
    int ch;
    if(argc < 2)
    {
        printf("Usage: %s <integer_value>\n",
                argv[0]);
    }
    else
    {
        ch = toascii(atoi(argv[1]));
        printf("%s converted to ASCII character = %#x\n\
```

```
It prints as %c on the IBM PC\n", argv[1], ch, ch);
    }
}
```

_tolower, tolower

COMPATIBILITY

MSC 3	MSC 4	MSC 5	MSC 6	QC1	QC2	QC2.5	TC1	TC1.5	TC2	TC++	ANSI	UNIX V	XNX	OS2	DOS
▲	▲	▲	▲	▲	▲	▲	▲	▲	▲	▲	1	▲	▲	▲	▲

PURPOSE Use the *_tolower* and *tolower* macros to convert an uppercase ASCII character to lowercase. Use *_tolower* only when you are sure that the character being converted is an uppercase letter.

SYNTAX

```
int _tolower(int c);

int tolower(int c);

int c;        ASCII character to be converted
```

EXAMPLE CALL

```
c = tolower('Q'); /* c will become 'q' */
```

INCLUDES `#include <ctype.h>` *For macro definition*

DESCRIPTION Both *_tolower* and *tolower* macros apply a formula to the ASCII character *c* that will convert it to lowercase if *c* is indeed an uppercase letter. Since *tolower* checks to see if *c* is actually an uppercase letter before making the conversion it is safer to use it than to take the risk with *_tolower*.

1. _tolower is not compatible with ANSI C.

RETURNS The *_tolower* and *tolower* macros return a lowercase character.

COMMENTS Since *tolower* is implemented as a macro, if you give it an integer expression with side effects, things may go awry. In such cases you may choose to use a version of *tolower* implemented as a function. The prototype for this version appears in *stdlib.h*, and you can use it either by "undefining" the macro with the *#undef* preprocessor directive or by simply not including *ctype.h*.

SEE ALSO

`isascii` *To test whether an arbitrary integer value is a valid ASCII character*

`_toupper, toupper` *To convert lowercase letters to uppercase*

EXAMPLE Write a program that accepts a string from the user and calls *tolower* to convert the characters to lowercase until a blank is encountered or the string ends. Print the results of the conversion.

```
#include <stdio.h>
#include <ctype.h>
main()
{
    int i, ch;
    char input[81];
    printf("Enter a string: ");
    gets(input);
    for(i=0; (input[i] != ' ') && (input[i] != '\0');
        i++)
    {
        input[i] = tolower(input[i]);
    }
    printf("Result: %s\n", input);
}
```

COMPATIBILITY

_toupper, toupper

MSC 3	MSC 4	MSC 5	MSC 6	QC1	QC2	QC2.5	TC1	TC1.5	TC2	TC++	ANSI	UNIX V	XNX	OS2	DOS
▲	▲	▲	▲	▲	▲	▲	▲	▲	▲	▲	1	▲	▲	▲	▲

PURPOSE Use the *_toupper* and *toupper* macros to convert a lowercase ASCII character to uppercase. Use the *_toupper* macro only when you are sure that the character being converted is a lowercase letter.

SYNTAX
```
int _toupper(int c);

int toupper(int c);

int c;        ASCII character to be converted
```

EXAMPLE CALL
```
c = toupper('q'); /* c will become 'Q' */
```

INCLUDES
```
#include <ctype.h>        For macro definition
```

DESCRIPTION The *_toupper* applies a formula to the ASCII character *c* that will convert it to uppercase if *c* is indeed a lowercase letter. Since *toupper* first checks to see if *c* is actually a lowercase letter before making the conversion it is safer to use it than *_toupper*.

1. _toupper is not compatible with ANSI C.

RETURNS Both *_toupper* and *toupper* macros return an uppercase character.

COMMENTS A version of *toupper* in the Microsoft C library is implemented as a function. The prototype for this version appears in *stdlib.h*, and you can use it either by "undefining" the macro with the *#undef* preprocessor directive or by simply not including *ctype.h*. This is sometimes necessary because when you feed a macro an integer expression with side effects, things may go awry.

SEE ALSO

`isascii`	*To test whether an arbitrary integer value is a valid ASCII character*
`_tolower, tolower`	*To convert uppercase letters to lowercase*

EXAMPLE Write a program that accepts a string from the user and calls *toupper* to convert the characters to uppercase until a blank is encountered or the string ends. Print the results of the conversion.

```
#include <stdio.h>
#include <ctype.h>
main()
{
    int i, ch;
    char input[81];
    printf("Enter a string: ");
    gets(input);
    for(i=0; (input[i] != ' ') && (input[i] != '\0');
        i++)
    {
        input[i] = toupper(input[i]);
    }
    printf("Result: %s\n", input);
}
```

Chapter 10 String Comparison and Manipulation

Introduction

Text manipulation is a significant part of many computer applications. Its importance within the industry is growing as text-retrieval systems are developed that scan thousands of documents searching for key words and phrases. Text manipulation might also involve text editing and word processing; capture and interpretation of user commands; creation of multifield sort tags for databases; and preparation of files for desktop publishing.

Consider, for example, processing user commands in a program. Your program will typically read a single line of command(s) into a C string and interpret it. Depending on the syntax of your application's command set, the interpretation may include such tasks as extracting the command and parameters from the string, comparing the command against entries in a stored table, or copying the parameters to separate strings for use later. An example of this process is the Microsoft C compiler itself and the various compiler options you can use in program development. The command-line options (see Chapter 2) are separated, tested for validity against a table, and copied for subsequent use as the linker and other programs are invoked. Although C has no built-in operators for handling strings, the Microsoft C library has a set of string manipulation routines that provides many capabilities for processing strings.

Concepts: Strings in C

C has no basic data type for strings. Strings are instead treated as arrays of characters, each of which occupies a byte. The end of a C string is marked by a byte containing the null character (\0). C strings are therefore known either as null-terminated strings or ASCIIZ (ASCII characters with a zero marking the end) strings.

DECLARING STRINGS IN C Since strings are treated as an array of characters, they can be declared in your program by such a statement as:

```
char str1[81], str2[] = "A string";
```

Here, *str1* is declared as an array with room for 81 characters, of which the last should always be a terminating null. That leaves room for 80 characters. (It must be stressed that all string arrays must be declared to be one character longer than the longest string being stored in order to leave room for the terminating null.) The second string, *str2,* does not show a size, but the compiler can guess its size since it is being initialized to a value. In this case, *str2* takes nine bytes including the terminating null (see Figure 10-1). You can declare a local string inside a function but you cannot initialize a local string. You have to declare a string outside the function definitions to initialize it.

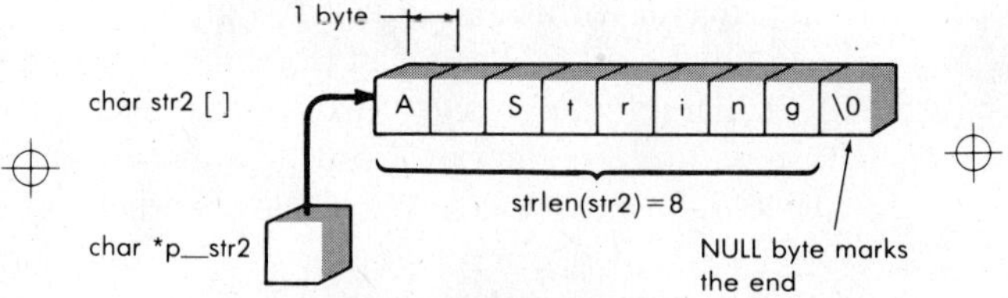

Figure 10-1. ***Strings in C***

Another way of accessing a string is through a pointer, which can hold the address of a variable (see Chapter 1). If you wanted to access the string *str2* using a pointer named *ptr_str2,* you could use the code fragment below:

```
char str2[] = "A string";
char *ptr_str2;
ptr_str2 = str2;
```

Once *ptr_str2* is initialized, it can be used to access the string in the same manner *str2* is used (see Figure 10-1). The pointer, of course, requires some additional storage space.

You can declare and initialize a string at the same time with the code fragment *char *ptr_str= "A string";*, in which the character pointer *ptr_str* is initialized to the address of a string constant *A string.*

MIXED MODELS IN MICROSOFT C 6.0

You may find it advantageous to use a mixed-model memory layout in a text program. Your code may be used to access source documents from a wide variety of vendors, and it may require pointer addressing that is beyond the reach of one of the six Microsoft default memory models. Microsoft C 6.0 added 24 functions to support such mixed-model programming. All but one of the new functions use far pointers, so they have a prefix *f*. They are not ANSI-compliant, so they have a leading underscore in their name. Consequently, the *_f* functions may be identified as version 6.0 model-independent, far-pointered string functions. (There is one *_n* function among the new routines: *_nstrdup*, and it uses near pointers). All 24 of these functions are covered in the reference pages and in Tables 10-1 and 10-2.

LEXICOGRAPHIC ORDERING

The string comparison routines compare and order strings as they would appear in a dictionary. The comparison is based on the ASCII value of the characters in corresponding bytes of the two strings, but the order of the ASCII codes is such that the collating sequence of the letters correspond to their pace in the lexicon. Thus, the ordering is known as "lexicographic" ordering.

Notes on String Manipulation

The string manipulation routines provide a host of capabilities (see Table 10-1 for a catalog). Major categories include copying one specified string into another, comparing two specified strings, and searching for the occurrence of any ASCII value in a specified string. Table 10-2 presents a list of the Microsoft C string functions organized by task.

Table 10-1. ***String Manipulation Routines***

Routine	Description
_fstrcat	Appends *string2* to *string1*. It is a model-independent version of *strcat* and was introduced in Microsoft C 6.0.
_fstrchr	Searches for the first occurrence of a specified character in a specified string. The *_fstrchr* routine is a model-independent version of *strchr* and was introduced in Microsoft C 6.0.
_fstrcmp	Compares two identified strings. It is a model-independent version of *strcmp*, and was introduced in Microsoft C 6.0.
_fstrcpy	Copies specified *string2* to *string1*. It is a model-independent version of *strcpy*. Introduced in Microsoft C 6.0.
_fstrcspn	Finds first substring in a specified *string1* consisting of characters not in a specified *string2*. A model-independent version of *strcspn*, it was introduced in Microsoft C 6.0.

Table 10-1. ***(cont.)***

Routine	Description
_fstrdup	Duplicates a specified string, copying it to memory allocated by a call to *_fmalloc*. The *_fstrdup* function is one of two model-independent versions of *strdup* (the other is *_nstrdup*) introduced in Microsoft C 6.0. The *_fmalloc* function is a far-pointered version of *malloc* and was also introduced in Microsoft C 6.0.
_fstricmp	Compares two identified strings without regard to case. A model-independent version of *stricmp*, it was introduced in Microsoft C 6.0.
_fstrlen	Finds the length of a specified string. It is a model-independent version of *strlen* and was introduced in Microsoft C 6.0.
_fstrlwr	Converts any uppercase letters in the given null-terminated string to lowercase; other characters are unaffected. This model-independent version of *strlwr* was introduced in Microsoft C 6.0.
_fstrncat	Appends, at most, the first specified number of characters (or byte values) of *string2* to *string1* and terminates the resulting string with a null character (*0*). It is a model-independent version of *strncat*, introduced in Microsoft C 6.0.
_fstrncmp	Compares, at most, the specified number of characters (or byte values) at the beginning of specified *string1* and *string2*, and it is case sensitive. This is the model-independent version of *strncmp* and was introduced in version 6.0.
_fstrncpy	Copies exactly the specified number of characters (or byte values) of *string2* to *string1*. It was introduced in Microsoft C 6.0 as a model-independent version of *strncpy*.
_fstrnicmp	Compares, at most, the specified number of characters (or byte values) at the beginning of specified *string1* and *string2*, without regard to letter case. A model-independent version of *strnicmp*, it was introduced in Microsoft C 6.0.
_fstrnset	Sets, at most, the specified number of characters (or byte values) of a specified string to a specified character (or byte value). A model-independent version of *strnset* introduced in version Microsoft C 6.0.
_fstrpbrk	Finds the first occurrence of a character from one specified string that appears in another specified string. It is a model-independent version of *strpbrk* and was introduced in Microsoft C 6.0.
_fstrrchr	Finds the last occurrence of a given character in a string. A model-independent version of *strrchr*, it was introduced in Microsoft C 6.0.
_fstrrev	Reverses the order of the characters in a specified string. The terminating null character (*0*) remains in place. A model-independent version of *strrev*, it was introduced in Microsoft C 6.0.
_fstrset	Sets all of the bytes in a specified string to a specified value, except that the terminating null (*0*) of the target string is left in place. It is a model-independent version of *strset* and was introduced in Microsoft C 6.0.
_fstrspn	Returns the index (the location within the string) of the first character in a specified *string1* that does not belong to the set of characters specified by *string2*. This value is equivalent to the length of the initial substring of *string1* that consists entirely of characters from *string2*. It is a model-independent version of *strspn* and was introduced in Microsoft C 6.0.
_fstrstr	Finds the first occurrence of a given string in another specified string. It is

Table 10-1. ***(cont.)***

Routine	Description
	a model-independent version of *strstr*, and it was introduced in Microsoft C 6.0.
_fstrtok	Reads specified *string1* as a series of zero or more tokens as separated by the set of delimiter characters specified in *string2*, It is a model-independent version of *strtok*, introduced in Microsoft C 6.0.
_fstrupr	Converts any lowercase letters in a specified string to uppercase. Other characters are not affected. A model-independent version of *strupr*, it was introduced in Microsoft C 6.0.
_nstrdup	Duplicates a specified string, copying it to memory allocated by *_nmalloc*. The *_nmalloc* function, introduced in Microsoft C 6.0, is the near-pointered version of *malloc*. The *_nstrdup* function is one of two model-independent versions of *strdup* introduced in Microsoft C 6.0. (The other was *_fstrdup*.) It returns a near pointer.
strcat	Appends one specified string to another.
strchr	Locates the first occurrence of a character in a specified string.
strcmp	Compares one specified string to another and differentiates between lowercase and uppercase letters.
strcmpi	Compares one specified string to another without regard to case of the letters. Identical to *stricmp*. There is no model-independent version of this function.
strcpy	Copies one specified string to another.
strcspn	Returns the position in the specified string of the first character that belongs to a given set of characters.
strdup	Allocates memory and makes a duplicate copy of a specified string.
strerror	Returns a string containing the system error message corresponding to a specified error number.
_strerror	Returns a string constructed out of a user-supplied message concatenated to the system error message for the last error in a library routine.
stricmp	Compares one specified string to another without regard to the case of the letter. Functionally identical to *strcmpi*.
strlen	Returns the length of a specified string as the number of bytes in the string, excluding the terminating NULL (*0*).
strlwr	Converts all characters in a given string to lowercase.
strncat	Appends a specified number of characters (or byte values) of one specified string to another.
strncmp	Compares a specified number of characters (or byte values) of two identified strings while maintaining the distinction between lowercase and uppercase letters.
strncpy	Copies a specified number of characters (or byte values) from one identified string to another. (Note that the resulting string will not automatically have a null character appended.)
strnicmp	Compares a specified number of characters (or byte values) of two specified strings without regard to the case of letter values.
strnset	Copies the same character (or byte value) into a specified number of positions in a string.

Table 10-1. ***(cont.)***

Routine	Description
strpbrk	Locates the first occurrence of any character from one specified string in another specified string.
strrchr	Locates the last occurrence of a character in a string.
strrev	Reverses the character order in a specified string.
strset	Copies the same character to every position in a string, leaving the terminating null of the destination string in place.
strspn	Returns the position in the string of the first character that does not belong to a given set of characters.
strstr	Locates the first occurrence of one string in another.
strtok	Returns the next token in a string with the token delimiters specified in a string.
strupr	Converts all characters in a string to uppercase.

LENGTH OF A STRING

The length of a string in C is determined by the number of bytes in the string exclusive of the terminating null byte. The string *str2* in our Figure 10-1 example is eight bytes long, for instance, but nine bytes are needed to store the string because of the terminating byte.

Table 10-2. ***String Manipulation Routines by Task***

Task	Routines
Convert a string from uppercase to lowercase and back.	strlwr, _fstrlwr (far), strupr, _fstrupr (far)
Compare two strings, lexicographically.	strcmp, _fstrcmp (far), strcmpi, stricmp, _fstricmp (far), strncmp, _fstrncmp (far), strnicmp, _fstrnicmp (far)
Copy, append, and duplicate.	strcat, _fstrcat (far), strcpy, _fstrcpy (far), strdup, _fstrdup (far), _nstrdup (near), strncat, _fstrncat (far), strncpy, _fstrncpy (far)
Prepare error message in a string.	strerror, _strerror
Extract tokens from a string.	strtok, _fstrtok (far)
Find the length of a string.	strlen, _fstrlen (far)
Reverse a string.	strrev, _fstrrev (far)
Load the same character into every position in a string.	strnset, _fstrnset (far), strset, _fstrset (far)
Search for a character or a substring.	strchr, _fstrchr (far), strcspn, _fstrcspn (far), strpbrk, _fstrpbrk (far), strrchr, _fstrrchr (far), strspn, _fstrspn (far), strstr, _fstrstr (far)

COMPARING C STRINGS

There are five library functions that compare two strings: *strcmp, strcmpi, stricmp, strncmp,* and *strnicmp*. Each returns a 0 when the strings match. A negative value indicates that the first string is lexicographically less than the second, which means that it appears before the second one in a dictionary. A positive return value indicates that the first string is lexicographically greater than the second. The model-independent versions introduced in Microsoft C 6.0 are called *_fstrcmp, _fstricmp, _fstrncmp,* and *_fstrnicmp*. There is no new version for *strcmpi*, for reasons that will be explained later.

The routine *strcmp* compares the entire length of two strings, and it differentiates between lowercase and uppercase letters. The *strncmp* function is like *strcmp*, however it only compares a specified number of characters from the beginning of each string.

The *strcmpi* and *stricmp* functions are identical in function and perform like *strcmp* except that they are case insensitive; that is, they ignore the case of letters when comparing between strings. (The likelihood is that one of these duplicates will be retired, and Microsoft seems to be voting to keep *stricmp*: they added a model-independent version of *stricmp* while apparently ignoring *strcmpi*.) The *strnicmp* function is a case-insensitive version of *strncmp*. If we compare the two strings *Microsoft* and *MICROSOFT* using *strcmp*, for example, the return would show *MICROSOFT* is less than *Microsoft* because capital letters appear before the lowercase in the ASCII code sequence. The case-insensitive functions *strcmpi* and *stricmp*, because they do not look for case, would find the strings equal and thus return a 0.

COPYING, APPENDING, AND DUPLICATING

The *strcat, strcpy, strdup, strncat,* and *strncpy* functions are for copying, concatenating, and duplicating strings. The model-independent versions introduced in Microsoft C 6.0 are *_fstrcat, _fstrcpy, _fstrdup, _fstrncat,* and *_fstrncpy*.

The *strcat* function appends the second string argument to the first one, producing a null-terminated string as the result. The *strncat* function is a version of *strcat* that copies only a specified number of characters from the second string to the first.

The *strcpy* (or *_fstrcpy*) function copies the whole second string argument to the first string while *strncpy* copies only a specified number of bytes from the second to the first. When *strncpy* does not copy the entire string, it does not automatically append a null to the result. Understandably, this can cause problems. You can avoid these concerns by declaring an array of characters or by allocating memory at run-time, making sure that there is enough room in the first string to hold the contents of the second string. The *strdup* (or *_fstrdup*) is handy because it performs those steps for you. It allocates memory to hold a string and then copies the string into the newly-allocated memory.

Taking Care with the Terminating Null

One characteristic of an overwritten terminating null is that a shorter string suddenly, and intermittently, becomes longer. Consider a program with two string variables, each 10 bytes long, that happen to be stored next to each other in memory. If a copy routine writes eleven bytes of data to the address specified by the name of the first string, the terminating null may be erased. (If the eleventh character is a null, the null would have been moved instead of erased.)

The next reference to the first string will retrieve every byte between the first address and the terminating null. If the eleventh character of our example is a null, the result will be eleven characters instead of ten. (A call to the second variable would return only the null, since the first character of the second variable occupies the same memory space as the last character of our accidently expanded first string.) It is possible that the call for the first string would return up to twenty characters (stopping only at the null at the end of the second string), if the eleventh character in the original copying operation was not a null.

This kind of error becomes either more or less obvious, depending on how memory is arranged at run-time. The memory assigned to *string2* may be empty the first several times your program accesses *string1*, but once written, the value of *string2* may be appended to *string1* and begin wreaking havoc. You will, of course, wonder why code that has "worked all morning" is suddenly failing. Verifying that the length of your string declarations allows room for the terminating null, and routinely verifying the length of returned values with *strlen* calls is one way to avoid this kind of problem.

PARSING A COMMAND LINE: EXTRACTING TOKENS

The need to interpret application commands was discussed at the start of this chapter. We considered how the CL program needs to break the command line into individual instructions in order to compile and link a program. CL and many other programs use a command syntax of the form:

```
<COMMAND> <PARAMETER_1> <PARAMETER_2>
```

which shows a command word (typically the name of the executable file) followed by two parameters. The elements of this command-line are separated by whitespace (tabs, spaces): a common convention that requires you to use quotes around arguments that contain whitespace. Now read a command line of the form,

```
CL /c TEST.C
```

which means run the CL executable with */c* and *TEST.C* as arguments. In Microsoft C versions since 5.0, this command would compile—but not link—the source file *TEST.C*. The component parts of this command are:

```
<COMMAND> = CL

<PARAMETER_1> = /c

<PARAMETER_2> = TEST.C
```

The process of separating the command line into parts is known as "parsing." Each part is called a token.

Extracting Tokens

There are routines in the C library which help your program parse a string. The *strtok* function can get the tokens one by one. You may choose to use the *strcspn* and *strspn* routines to construct your own parser, especially if your command language is very complicated. The *strcspn* function returns the index of the first character (its location in the array) that matches one of the characters in a second string, while *strspn* does just the opposite: returning the first character that does not belong in the second string. The model-independent versions are *_fstrtok, _fstrcspn, _fstrspn,* respectively.

The *strpbrk* routine works the same as *strcspn*, but returns a pointer to the matched character instead of returning an aray index. Finding an occurrence of one string in another is the province of the *strstr* routine. Locating a single character in a string is the task for which *strchr* and *strrchr* were written, *strchr* looking from the beginning of a string and *strrchr* searching from the end. The *_fstrpbrk, _fstrstr, _fstrchr,* and *_fstrrchr* are the versions introduced in version 6.0.

Converting Case

Once you parse the command line and get the first token—*CL* in the example above—you can compare the token with entries in an internal string array in which valid entries are stored. Before doing so, you can choose to use *strlwr* or *strupr* to convert the entire command line into lowercase or uppercase, respectively. You can then use *strcmp* to see if the command matches any in your stored table. Alternatively, you can run your comparison through the case-insensitive function *stricmp* to avoid having to convert the command-line into consistent case. All three of these have model-independent equivalents.

MISCELLANEOUS UTILITIES

Some of the string manipulation routines are difficult to categorize. The *strnset, strset, _fstrnset,* and *_fstrset* functions let you set all positions in a string to the same character; *strnset* sets only a specified number of characters, while *strset* works on the whole string. The *strrev* (or *_fstrrev*) function reverses the characters in a string and *strerror* returns a string containing an error message corresponding to an error number. The function *_strerror* is the renamed version 4.0 function *strerror*; renamed, so that an ANSI-compliant *strerror* could be introduced in Microsoft C 5.0.

Microsoft recommends against using *_strerror* where portability is desired.

THE BUFFER MANIPULATION CATEGORY

A string is really a special kind of buffer. That means that buffer manipulation routines (see Chapter 6) can also be used to manipulate strings. The reverse is normally impossible, or impractical, because most string manipulation functions look for a null byte as the marker indicating the end of a string buffer. String routines with a *strn* prefix are exceptions, because they take a character count as an argument. In general, buffer routines are the most efficient way to deal with buffers and string routines are the most efficient way to deal with strings.

Cautions

- Remember to account for the terminating null character when allocating memory for a string. Consider an example where you are allocating memory to hold a copy of a specific string named *strng_copy*. Compute the number of bytes you need by adding one to the return value of *strlen (strng_copy)*. Forgetting the null can lead to having the contents of one string written into the memory space occupied by another, often causing significant trouble.
- When copying one string to another, you must make sure that the destination string has enough room to hold the incoming characters. You will not receive a warning or error message if the copy continues beyond the last character of the destination string. There is no way to tell what values will be stepped on in such circumstances, but it is highly likely that such an overwrite will lead to unusual and intermittent failures.
- Use of *strncpy* to copy a specific number of bytes fewer than the length of the source string (copying, say, 10 bytes from a string that is 30 bytes long) will result in a destination string that does not have a null appended. There are times, though, when this is exactly what you want: when copying several data fields into a single combined field, for instance; but a null must be appended before the destination can become a valid C string.

COMPATIBILITY

strcat, _fstrcat

MSC 3	MSC 4	MSC 5	MSC 6	QC1	QC2	QC2.5	TC1	TC1.5	TC2	TC++	ANSI	UNIX V	XNX	OS2	DOS
▲	▲	▲	1	▲	▲	▲	▲	▲	▲	▲	2	2	2	▲	▲

PURPOSE Use *strcat* to concatenate (append) one string to another. The *_fstrcat* function should be used when you need a memory-model independent version of *strcat.*

SYNTAX

```
char *strcat(char *string1, const char *string2);

char _far *_far _fstrcat (char _far *f_string1,
const char _far *f_string2);
```

`char *string1;` *Destination string*

`const char *string2;` *String to be appended to the first one*

`f_string1` *Far pointer to destination string*

`f_string2` *Far pointer to the string to be appended*

EXAMPLE CALL

```
char metoo[7] = "Me ";
strcat(metoo, "too"); /* Result is "Me too" */

_fstrcat (name_lst, "Lee");
```

INCLUDES `#include <string.h>` *For function declaration*

DESCRIPTION The *strcat* function accepts the C strings *string1* and *string2* as arguments. It appends the second string to the first one, terminating the resulting string with a null character (\0). The terminating NULL of the first string is removed and *string1* becomes the concatenation of the old *string1* and *string2.* Note that you are responsible for allocating enough space for the destination string *string1.* If, after appending *string2* to *string1,* the length of the resulting string exceeds the allocated size of *string1, strcat* may destroy other data and cause the program to fail.

The *_fstrcat* routine appends specified *f_string2* to *f_string1,* and, except for the form of its arguments, behaves exactly as *strcat.* The *_f* versions of the string functions are large model forms that use *_far* string arguments and return values. They can be called from anywhere within your program.

1. *_fstrcat* is a model-independent version of *strcat* introduced in version 6.0. 2. The *_fstrcat* function is incompatible with ANSI C, UNIX, and XENIX.

RETURNS The *strcat* function returns a pointer to the concatenated string (i.e., it returns *string1*). A *_fstrcat* call yields a far pointer to the concatenated string.

SEE ALSO

strncat	*To concatenate a specified number of characters of one string to another*
strcpy, strncpy	*To copy one string into another*
strdup	*To allocate storage and create a duplicate of a string*

EXAMPLE Write a program that prompts the user for first name, last name, and middle initial. Then use *strcat* to construct the full name. The *_f* version of *strcat* behaves exactly as the root version, except that the arguments and return values take the form of *far.*

```
#include <stdio.h>
#include <string.h>
main()
{
    char fullname[80], last[40], middle[10];
    printf("Enter your first name: ");
    gets(fullname);
    printf("Last name: ");
    gets(last);
    printf("Middle initial: ");
    gets(middle);
/* Append the parts together to get full name */
    strcat(fullname," ");
    strcat(fullname, middle);
    strcat(fullname," ");
    strcat(fullname, last);
    printf("Greetings! %s\n", fullname);
}
```

COMPATIBILITY

strchr, _fstrchr

MSC 3	MSC 4	MSC 5	MSC 6	QC1	QC2	QC2.5	TC1	TC1.5	TC2	TC++	ANSI	UNIX V	XNX	OS2	DOS
▲	▲	▲	1	▲	▲	▲	▲	▲	▲	▲	2	2	2	▲	▲

PURPOSE Use *strchr* to find the first occurrence of a particular character in a given string. The *_fstrchr* function is a model-independent alternative to the *strchr* function.

SYNTAX

```
char *strchr(const char *string, int c);

char _far *_far _fstrchr (const char _far *f_string, int c);
```

`const char *string;` *String to be searched*

`int c;` *Character to be located*

`f_string` *Far pointer to the source string*

EXAMPLE CALL

```
cost_is = strchr("Estimated cost = $120", '$');
/* Now cost_is will be the C string "$120"  */
part_no = _fstrchr ("Ship 500 of #332", '#');
/* String is in far memory */
/* Now part_no will be the C string "#332" */
```

INCLUDES `#include <string.h>` *For function declaration*

DESCRIPTION The *strchr* function searches for the first occurrence of the character *c* in the C string *string*. The terminating null character is included in the search; it can also be the character to be located.

The *_fstrchr* function searches for the first occurrence of the character *C* in *f_string*. The *_f* versions of the string functions are large model forms that use *far* string arguments and return values. They can be called from anywhere within your program. See the tutorial for more information about far pointer functions.

1. *_fstrchr* is a model-independent version of *strchr* introduced in version 6.0. 2. The *_fstrchr* function does not work under ANSI C, UNIX, or XENIX.

RETURNS If the character *c* is found, *strchr* returns a pointer to the first occurrence of *c* in *string1*. For example,

```
printf("%s", strchr("Annual salary = $35,750", '$'));
```

will print *$35,750.* If the search fails, *strchr* returns a NULL.

The *_fstrchr* function also returns a far pointer to the first occurence of the identified character (*C,* in the examples above) in the target string.

SEE ALSO

`strrchr`	*To locate the last occurrence of a character in a string*
`strcspn, strpbrk`	*To locate the first character in a string that matches one of the characters in another*
`strstr`	*To locate the occurrence of one string in another*

EXAMPLE Prompt the user for a string and a character whose first occurrence in the string will be found by using *strchr.* Display the result of the search. The *_f* version of *strchr* behaves exactly as the root version, except that the arguments and return values take the form of *far.*

```
#include <stdio.h>
#include <conio.h>
#include <string.h>
main()
{
    int c;
    char buf[80], *result;
    printf("Enter a string: ");
    gets(buf);
    printf(
"Enter character to be located (first occurrence):");
    c = getche();
    if ((result = strchr(buf, c)) == NULL)
    {
        printf("\n'%c' <-- not in \"%s\"\n", c, buf);
    }
    else
    {
        printf("\n'%c' first occurs at: %s\n",
                                        c, result);
    }
}
```

String Comparison and Manipulation

COMPATIBILITY

strcmp, _fstrcmp

MSC 3	MSC 4	MSC 5	MSC 6	QC1	QC2	QC2.5	TC1	TC1.5	TC2	TC++	ANSI	UNIX V	XNX	OS2	DOS
▲	▲	▲	1	▲	▲	▲	▲	▲	▲	▲	2	2	2	▲	▲

PURPOSE Use *strcmp* to compare one string to another. The comparison is case sensitive. Use the *_fstrcmp* function when you need a model-independent version of *strcmp*.

SYNTAX

```
int strcmp(const char *string1, const char *string2);

int _far _fstrcmp (const char _far *f_string1,
const char _far *f_string2);
```

`const char *string1;` *First string*

`const char *string2;` *Second string*

`f_string1, f_string2` *Far pointers to the strings to be compared*

EXAMPLE CALL

```
if( strcmp(username, "sysmgr") != 0 ) exit(0);

if (_fstrcmp (actn_list, "failed") == 0) exit (14);
```

INCLUDES `#include <string.h>` *For function declaration*

DESCRIPTION The *strcmp* function accepts the C strings *string1* and *string2* as arguments. It compares the two strings lexicographically and returns an integer value indicating the lexicographic order of *string1* with respect to *string2*. Note that unlike *strcmpi* and *stricmp*, *strcmp* is case sensitive.

The *_fstrcmp* function compares two strings using the same logic as *strcmp*, of which it is a model-independent version. The *_f* versions of the string functions are large model forms that use *far* string arguments and return values. They can be called from anywhere within your program. See the tutorial for more information about far pointer functions.

1. *_fstrcmp* was introduced in version 6.0. 2. The *_fstrcmp* function does not work with ANSI C, UNIX, or XENIX.

RETURNS The *strcmp* function returns an integer indicating the lexicographic ordering of *string1* with respect to *string2*. The return value is 0 if the two strings are identical. If *string1* is less than *string2*, the return value is less than 0. When *string1* is greater than *string2*, *strcmp* returns an integer greater than 0. For example,

```
result = strcmp("ABC", "abc"); /* result less than 0    */
result = strcmp("abc", "abc"); /* result equal to  0    */
result = strcmp("xy",  "abc"); /* result greater than 0 */
```

The *_fstrcmp* routine returns a value less than 0 if *f_string1* < *f_string2*; 0 if *f_string1* = *f_string2*; a value greater than 0 if *f_string1* > *f_string2*. This is the same pattern followed by the root *strcmp* function.

SEE ALSO

strncmp	*To compare a specified number of characters of two strings*
strcmpi, stricmp, strnicmp	*To compare two strings regardless of the case of the characters*

EXAMPLE Write a program that uses *strcmp* to compare two strings typed by the user and display the result. The *_f* version of *strcmp* behaves exactly as the root version, except that the arguments and return values take the form of *far*.

```
#include <stdio.h>
#include <string.h>
main()
{
    int result;
    char str1[80], str2[80];
    printf("Enter a string: ");
    gets(str1);
    printf("Enter string to compare with first: ");
    gets(str2);
    printf("Case sensitive comparison shows that\n");
    result = strcmp(str1, str2);
    if(result == 0)
    {
        printf("\"%s\" == \"%s\"\n", str1, str2);
    }
    if(result < 0)
    {
        printf("\"%s\" < \"%s\"\n", str1, str2);
    }
    if(result > 0)
    {
        printf("\"%s\" > \"%s\"\n", str1, str2);
    }
}
```

COMPATIBILITY

strcmpi

MSC 3	MSC 4	MSC 5	MSC 6	QC1	QC2	QC2.5	TC1	TC1.5	TC2	TC++	ANSI	UNIX V	XNX	OS2	DOS
▲	▲	▲		▲	▲			▲	▲	▲					

PURPOSE Use *strcmpi* to compare one string to another without regard to case.

SYNTAX

```
int strcmpi(const char *string1, const char *string2);
```

`const char *string1;` *First string*

`const char *string2;` *Second string*

EXAMPLE CALL

```
if( strcmpi(command, "delete") == 0 ) do_delete();
```

INCLUDES `#include <string.h>` *For function declaration*

DESCRIPTION The *strcmpi* function first converts all alphabetic characters in strings *string1* and *string2* to lowercase. Then it compares the two strings and returns an integer value indicating the lexicographic order of *string1* with respect to *string2*.

RETURNS The *strcmpi* function returns a 0 if the two strings are identical. If *string1* is less than *string2*, the return value is less than 0. When *string1* is greater than *string2*, *strcmpi* returns an integer greater than 0. Thus *strcmpi ("XYZ", "xyz");* returns 0.

SEE ALSO

`strnicmp` *Same as* strcmpi, *but only compares a specified number of characters of the two strings*

`strcmp, strncmp` *To compare two strings (case sensitive)*

`stricmp` *Identical to* strcmpi

EXAMPLE Demonstrate the use of *strcmpi* by comparing two strings entered by user.

```
#include <stdio.h>
#include <string.h>
main()
{
    int result;
    char str1[80], str2[80];
    printf("Enter a string: ");
    gets(str1);
```

```
        printf("Enter string to compare with first: ");
        gets(str2);
        printf("Case insensitive comparison shows that\n");
        result = strcmpi(str1, str2);
        if(result == 0)
        {
            printf("\"%s\" == \"%s\"\n", str1, str2);
        }
        if(result < 0)
        {
            printf("\"%s\" < \"%s\"\n", str1, str2);
        }
        if(result > 0)
        {
            printf("\"%s\" > \"%s\"\n", str1, str2);
        }
    }
```

strcpy, _fstrcpy

COMPATIBILITY

MSC 3	MSC 4	MSC 5	MSC 6	QC1	QC2	QC2.5	TC1	TC1.5	TC2	TC++	ANSI	UNIX V	XNX	OS2	DOS
▲	▲	▲	1	▲	▲	▲	▲	▲	▲	▲	2	2	2	▲	▲

PURPOSE Use *strcpy* to copy one string to another. Use the *_fstrcpy* function when you need a memory-model-independent routine with which to copy strings.

SYNTAX

```
char *strcpy(char *string1, const char *string2);

char _far *_far _fstrcpy (char _far *f_dest_str,
const char _far *f_src_str);
```

`char *string1;`	*Destination string*
`const char *string2;`	*String to be copied to the first one*
`f_dest_str`	Far *pointer to the destination string*
`f_src_str`	Far *pointer to the source string*

EXAMPLE CALL

```
strcpy(dos_command, "DIR");

_fstrcpy (team_roster, "Stephen, 3rd base");
```

INCLUDES `#include <string.h>` *For function declaration*

DESCRIPTION The *strcpy* function copies the string *string2* to the buffer whose address is given by *string1*. The terminating null character of the second string is also copied so *string1* becomes an exact copy of *string2*.

The *_fstrcpy* function copies the source string to the destination string (argument *two* to argument *one*). The *_f* versions of the string functions are large model forms that use *far* string arguments and return values. They can be called from anywhere within your program. See the tutorial for more information about far pointer functions.

1. *_fstrcpy* is the model-independent version of *strcpy* introduced in version 6.0. 2. *_fstrcpy* does not work under ANSI C, UNIX, or XENIX.

RETURNS The *strcpy* function returns a pointer to the copied string (i.e., it returns *string1*). The *_fstrcpy* routine also returns a pointer to the copied (destination) string.

COMMENTS The string manipulation routines *strcpy* and *strncpy* can be harmful to your program if you forget to allocate enough room in the buffer *string1* for the entire destination string, including the terminating null character. If, after appending *string2* to *string1*, the length of the resulting string exceeds the allocated size of *string1*, *strcpy* may destroy other data and cause the program to fail.

SEE ALSO

`strcat, strncat`	*To concatenate one string to another*
`strncpy`	*To copy a specified number of characters of one string into another*
`strdup`	*To allocate storage and create a duplicate copy of a string*

EXAMPLE Write a program to accept a string and use *strcpy* to copy it into another internal buffer. The *_f* version of *strcpy* behaves exactly as the root version, except that the arguments and return values take the form of *_far*.

```
#include <stdio.h>
#include <string.h>
main()
{
    char str1[80], str2[80];
    printf("Enter a string: ");
    gets(str2);
    strcpy(str1, str2);
    printf("String copied. Result is: %s\n", str1);
}
```

strcspn, _fstrcspn

COMPATIBILITY

MSC 3	MSC 4	MSC 5	MSC 6	QC1	QC2	QC2.5	TC1	TC1.5	TC2	TC++	ANSI	UNIX V	XNX	OS2	DOS
▲	▲	▲	1	▲	▲	▲	▲	▲	▲	▲	2	2	2	▲	▲

PURPOSE Use *strcspn* to locate the position of the first occurrence in a string of any character from another. The *_fstrcspn* function should be used when you need a memory-model-independent version of *strcspn*.

SYNTAX

```
size_t strcspn(const char *string1, const char *string2);

size_t _far _fstrcspn (const char _far *f_src_str,
const char _far *f_chrset_str);
```

`const char *string1;` *String to be searched*

`const char *string2;` *String describing set of characters to be located*

`f_src_str` *Far pointer to source string to be searched*

`f_chrset_str` *Far pointer to the character set to be located*

EXAMPLE CALL

```
first_q = strcspn("soliloquy", "q"); /* first_q = 6 */

second_q = _fstrcspn ("Variable List", "b"); /* secondq = 5 */
```

INCLUDES `#include <string.h>` *For function declaration*

DESCRIPTION The *strcspn* function locates the first occurrence in *string1* of any character other than the terminating null in *string2*.

The *_fstrcspn* function finds the first substring in *f_src_str* consisting of characters that are not in the *f_chrset_str* string. The *_f* versions of the string functions are large model forms that use *far* string arguments and return values. They can be called from anywhere within your program.

1. *_fstrcspn* was introduced in version 6.0 and is the model-independent version of *strcspn*. 2. The *_fstrcspn* function does not work under ANSI C, UNIX, or XENIX.

RETURNS If successful, the *strcspn* function returns the index of the first character in *string1* that belongs to the set of characters *string2*. Thus this value is the length of the initial substring of *string1* that consists of characters *not* in *string2* (i.e., the substring that does not "span" the character set *string2*).

If *string1* begins with a character from *string2*, the return value is zero. If *string1* is devoid of characters from *string2*, *strcspn* returns the length of *string1*.

The *_fstrcspn* routine returns the index (the location in the array) of the first character in *src_str* that belongs to the set of characters specified by the string named *chrset_str*.

SEE ALSO

strpbrk — *To search for the first occurrence of any character from one string in another*

strspn — *To find the length of the initial substring made up entirely of characters in another string*

EXAMPLE Prompt the user for a string with some numeric values followed by other characters. Then use *strcspn* to locate the first occurrence of a non-numeric character in the string. This can be used to catch input errors when only numeric values are expected. The *_f* version of *strcspn* behaves exactly as the root version, except that the arguments and return values take the form of *far*.

```
#include <stdio.h>
#include <string.h>
char *digits = "0123456789";
main()
{
    int loc;
    char str1[80];
    printf("Enter a number followed by other \
characters: ");
    gets(str1);
    loc = strcspn(str1, digits);
    printf("First non-numeric character in \
\n%s\nis at location %d\n", str1, loc);
}
```

COMPATIBILITY

strdup, _fstrdup, _nstrdup

MSC 3	MSC 4	MSC 5	MSC 6	QC1	QC2	QC2.5	TC1	TC1.5	TC2	TC++	ANSI	UNIX V	XNX	OS2	DOS
▲	▲	▲	1	▲	▲	▲	▲	▲	▲	▲	2	2	2	▲	▲

PURPOSE Use *strdup* to allocate memory and copy a given string into that space. Use the *_fstrdup* or *_nstrdup* function for a memory-model-independent method of duplicating a string to a far or near pointer, respectively.

SYNTAX

```
char *strdup(const char *string);
```

```
char _far *_far _fstrdup (const char _far *f_src_str);

char _near *_far _nstrdup (const char _far *n_src_str);

const char *string;      String to be duplicated

f_src_str                Far pointer to the string to be duplicated

n_src_str                Near pointer to the string to be duplicated
```

EXAMPLE CALL

```
saved_command = strdup(command);

vessel_crew = _fstrdup ("Captain Picard");

vessel_list = _nstrdup ("USS Enterprise");
```

INCLUDES

```
#include <string.h>      For function declaration
```

DESCRIPTION The *strdup* function first calls *malloc* to allocate enough memory to hold *string*. It then copies the string into the newly allocated buffer.

The *_fstrdup* function duplicates the specified string (*f_src_str* in the example above), copying it to memory allocated by *_fmalloc*, and is a model-independent version of *strdup*. The *_nstrdup* function duplicates a string (*n_src_str*, above) copying it to memory allocated by *_nmalloc*, and is also a model-independent version of *strdup*. See the tutorial for more information about memory-model-independent functions.

1. The *_fstrdup* and *_nstrdup* functions were introduced in version 6.0. 2. Neither new function works under ANSI C, XENIX, or UNIX.

RETURNS If the *strdup* function succeeds, it returns a pointer to the new copy of the string. If memory allocation fails, *strdup* returns a NULL.

The *_fstrdup* function returns a far pointer to the storage space containing the duplicate string. The *_nstrdup* function returns a near pointer to the storage space containing the duplicate string. A NULL is returned if the memory allocation fails.

SEE ALSO

strcat, strncat	*To concatenate one string to another*
strcpy, strncpy	*To copy one string into another*

EXAMPLE Read in a string and make a duplicate by calling the function *strdup*. The *_f* and *_n* versions of *strdup* behave exactly as the root version, except that the arguments and return values take the form of *far* and *near*, respectively.

```
#include <stdio.h>
#include <string.h>
main()
{
    char str1[80], *str1_copy;
    printf("Enter a string: ");
    gets(str1);
    str1_copy = strdup(str1);
    printf("String duplicated. Result is: %s\n",
           str1_copy);
}
```

COMPATIBILITY

strerror

MSC 3	MSC 4	MSC 5	MSC 6	QC1	QC2	QC2.5	TC1	TC1.5	TC2	TC++	ANSI	UNIX V	XNX	OS2	DOS
	▲	1	▲	▲	▲	▲		▲	▲	▲	▲			▲	

PURPOSE Use *strerror* to retrieve an error message corresponding to an error number.

SYNTAX

```
char *strerror(int errnum);

int errnum;        Error number
```

EXAMPLE CALL

```
error_message = strerror(errno);
```

INCLUDES

```
#include <string.h>     For function declaration
```

DESCRIPTION The *strerror* function finds the system error message corresponding to the error number given in the argument *errnum*. The *strerror* function gets the system error message by using the value in the global variable *errno* as the index of a table of error messages called *sys_errlist*, which is declared in the header file *stdlib.h*. In a typical use, you should call *strerror* immediately after an error return from a library routine and provide the value of *errno* as the argument. Note that *strerror* only returns the error message; printing the message is up to you.

1. Changed in Microsoft C 5.0 to a new name, *_strerror*, but the old version remains for compatibility with older code.

RETURNS The *strerror* function returns a pointer to the error message from the table *sys_errlist.*

COMMENTS The *strerror* function of Microsoft C 4.0 is called *_strerror* in versions 5.0, 5.1, and 6.0. The new *strerror* is a version conforming to ANSI standards.

SEE ALSO

`_strerror`	*To construct an error message by appending the system message to one supplied by you*
`perror`	*To print an error message*

EXAMPLE Write a program in which you create an error by attempting to close a nonexistent file handle (say, 100). Once the error occurs, call *strerror* with *errno* as argument and print the error message returned by *strerror.* Note that *stdlib.h* is included to provide the appropriate declaration of *errno.*

```
#include <stdio.h>
#include <stdlib.h>
#include <io.h>
#include <string.h>
main()
{
    int handle=100;
    char *errmsg;
/* Generate an error condition by closing a
 * file with non-existent handle 100
 */
    if(close(handle) == -1)
    {
        errmsg = strerror(errno);
        printf("Error closing file: %s", errmsg);
    }
}
```

_strerror

COMPATIBILITY

MSC 3	MSC 4	MSC 5	MSC 6	QC1	QC2	QC2.5	TC1	TC1.5	TC2	TC++	ANSI	UNIX V	XNX	OS2	DOS
		▲	▲	▲	▲	▲		▲	▲	▲				▲	▲

PURPOSE Use *_strerror* to construct an error message consisting of your message concatenated with a system message corresponding to the last error that occurred in a library routine.

SYNTAX

```
char *_strerror(char *string);

char *string;        String containing user-supplied error message
```

EXAMPLE CALL

```
error_message = _strerror("Error opening file");
```

INCLUDES

```
#include <string.h>      For function declaration
```

DESCRIPTION The *_strerror* function constructs an error message by appending a colon to the contents of *string* and appending a system message that corresponds to the last error occurring in a library routine. The length of *string* can be at most 94 bytes. If *string* is NULL, the message constructed by *_strerror* only contains the system message. The message always has a newline character (\n) at the end.

The *_strerror* function gets the system error message by using the value in the global variable *errno* as the index of a table of error messages called *sys_errlist.* You should call *_strerror* immediately after a library routine returns with an error. Otherwise, subsequent calls to other routines may overwrite the value of *errno.* Note that *_strerror* only prepares the error message; printing the message is up to you.

RETURNS The *_strerror* function returns a pointer to the error message it constructed.

COMMENTS The *_strerror* function of Microsoft C 5.0, 5.1, and 6.0 is identical to the *strerror* function of version 4.0. The name was changed in Microsoft C 5.0 so that Microsoft could include an ANSI version of the *strerror* function.

SEE ALSO

```
strerror      To get system message corresponding to error number (ANSI version)

perror        To print an error message
```

EXAMPLE Write a program that illustrates the use of *_strerror* to construct error messages. Generate an error by attempting to duplicate the file handle 100 (a file not yet open). Display the error message returned by *_strerror.*

```
#include <stdio.h>
#include <io.h>
#include <string.h>
main()
{
    int handle=100;
    char *errmsg;
/* Generate an error condition by attempting to
 * duplicate a unused file handle (100)
```

```
*/
    if(dup(handle) == -1)
    {
        errmsg = _strerror("Error duplicating handle");
        printf(errmsg);
    }
}
```

stricmp, _fstricmp

COMPATIBILITY

MSC 3	MSC 4	MSC 5	MSC 6	QC1	QC2	QC2.5	TC1	TC1.5	TC2	TC++	ANSI	UNIX V	XNX	OS2	DOS
	▲	▲	1	▲	▲	▲	▲	▲	▲	▲					

PURPOSE Use *stricmp* to compare one string to another without regard to the case of the letters. Use the *_fstricmp* function as a memory-model-independent way to compare strings without regard to the case of the characters contained in the strings.

SYNTAX

```
int stricmp(const char *string1, const char *string2);

int _far _fstricmp (const char _far *f_string1,
const char _far *f_string2);
```

`const char *string1;` *First string*

`const char *string2;` *Second string*

`f_string1, f_string2` *Far pointers to the strings you wish to compare*

EXAMPLE CALL

```
if( stricmp(answer, "yes") == 0 ) delete_file(fname);

if (_fstricmp (answer, "no") == 0) exit (12);
```

INCLUDES `#include <string.h>` *For function declaration*

DESCRIPTION The *stricmp* function converts all alphabetic characters in *string1* and *string2* to lowercase. Then it compares the two strings and returns an integer value indicating the lexicographic order of *string1* with respect to *string2*.

Like *stricmp*, the *_fstricmp* function compares two strings without regard to case. The *_f* versions of the string functions are large model forms that use *_far* string arguments and return values. They can be called from anywhere within your program.

1. *_fstricmp* is a model-independent version of *stricmp* and was introduced in version 6.0.

RETURNS The *stricmp* function returns an integer indicating the lexicographic ordering of *string1* with respect to *string2* after all alphabetic characters have been converted to lowercase. The return value is 0 if the two strings are identical. If *string1* is less than *string2*, the return value is less than 0. When *string1* is greater than *string2*, *stricmp* returns an integer greater than 0.

The *_fstricmp* function returns a value less than 0 if *f_string1* < *f_string2*; 0 if *f_string1* = *f_string2*; a value greater than 0 if *f_string1* > *f_string2*. This is the same pattern followed by the root *stricmp* function.

SEE ALSO

`strnicmp`	*Same as* stricmp, *but only compares a specified number of characters of the two strings*
`strcmp, strncmp`	*To compare two strings (case sensitive)*
`strcmpi`	*Identical to* stricmp

EXAMPLE Write a program that uses *stricmp* to perform a comparison of two strings, regardless of cases. The *_f* version of *stricmp* behaves exactly as the root version, except that the arguments and return values take the form of *far*.

```
#include <stdio.h>
#include <string.h>
main()
{
    int result;
    char str1[80], str2[80];
    printf("Enter a string: ");
    gets(str1);
    printf("Enter string to compare with first: ");
    gets(str2);
    printf("Case insensitive comparison shows that\n");
    result = stricmp(str1, str2);
    if(result == 0)
    {
        printf("\"%s\" == \"%s\"\n", str1, str2);
    }
    if(result < 0)
    {
        printf("\"%s\" < \"%s\"\n", str1, str2);
    }
    if(result > 0)
```

```
        {
            printf("\"%s\" > \"%s\"\n", str1, str2);
        }
}
```

strlen, _fstrlen

COMPATIBILITY

MSC 3	MSC 4	MSC 5	MSC 6	QC1	QC2	QC2.5	TC1	TC1.5	TC2	TC++	ANSI	UNIX V	XNX	OS2	DOS
▲	▲	▲	1	▲	▲	▲	▲	▲	▲	▲	2	2	2	▲	▲

PURPOSE Use *strlen* to find the length of a string in bytes, not counting the terminating null character. The *_fstrlen* function provides you with a memory-model-independent manner to find the length of a string.

SYNTAX

```
size_t strlen(const char *string);

size_t _fstrlen (const char_far *f_string);
```

`const char *string;` *String whose length is to be returned*

`f_string` *Far pointer to the string whose length is to be returned*

EXAMPLE CALL

```
length = strlen(name);

length = _fstrlen (_far_name);
```

INCLUDES `#include <string.h>` *For function declaration*

DESCRIPTION The *strlen* function counts the number of bytes in *string*, not including the terminating null character.

The *_fstrlen* function also finds the length of the target string identified in the argument. The *_f* versions of the string functions are large model forms that use *far* string arguments and return values. They can be called from anywhere within your program. See the tutorial for more information about memory-model-independent routines.

1. *_fstrlen* is a model-independent version of *strlen* introduced in Microsoft C 6.0. 2. The *_fstrlen* function does not work under ANSI C, UNIX, or XENIX.

RETURNS The *strlen* function returns the length in bytes of *string*.The *_fstrlen* function returns the length in bytes of the target string, not including the terminating null character (\0).

EXAMPLE Use *strlen* to determine and print the length of a string. The *_f* version of *strlen* behaves exactly as the root version, except that the arguments and return values take the form of *_far*.

```
#include <stdio.h>
#include <string.h>
main()
{
    size_t len;
    char buf[80];
    printf("Enter a string: ");
    gets(buf);
    len = strlen(buf);
    printf("The length of the string is: %u\n", len);
}
```

COMPATIBILITY

strlwr, _fstrlwr

MSC 3	MSC 4	MSC 5	MSC 6	QC1	QC2	QC2.5	TC1	TC1.5	TC2	TC++	ANSI	UNIX V	XNX	OS2	DOS
▲	▲	▲	1	▲	▲	▲	▲	▲	▲	▲		▲	▲		

PURPOSE Use *strlwr* to convert any uppercase letters in a string to lowercase. The *_fstrlwr* function affords you a way to use a memory-model-independent routine to convert uppercase characters in a specified string to lowercase characters.

SYNTAX

```
char *strlwr(char *string);

char _far *_far _fstrlwr (char _far *f_string);
```

`char *string;` *String to be converted to lowercase*

`f_string` *Far pointer to the string to be converted*

EXAMPLE CALL

```
char command[] = "QUIT";
strlwr(command); /* Now command = "quit" */

char food[] = "RICE";
_fstrlwr (food); /* Now food = "rice" */
```

INCLUDES `#include <string.h>` *For function declaration*

DESCRIPTION The *strlwr* function converts any uppercase letters in the *string* to lowercase. Other characters in the string are unaffected.

The *_fstrlwr* function also converts any uppercase letters in the given null-terminated string to lowercase. Other characters are not affected. The *_f* versions of the string functions are large model forms that use *_far* string arguments and return values. They can be called from anywhere within your program. See the tutorial for more information about memory-model-independent functions.

1. *_fstrlwr* is a model-independent version of *strlwr* introduced in version 6.0.

RETURNS The *strlwr* function returns a pointer to the converted string, (i.e., it returns *string*). The *_fstrlwr* function returns a far pointer to the converted string.

COMMENTS The *strlwr* routine and its companion *strupr* are not part of the proposed ANSI definition. You can implement your own versions of these using the macros *tolower* and *toupper*, respectively.

SEE ALSO `strupr` *To convert a string to uppercase*

`tolower` *To convert a single uppercase letter to lowercase*

EXAMPLE Use *strlwr* to convert a string to lowercase. The *_f* version of *strlwr* behaves exactly as the root version, except that the arguments and return values take the form of *far*.

```
#include <stdio.h>
#include <string.h>
main()
{
    char buf[80];
    printf("Enter a string with uppercase letters: ");
    gets(buf);
    strlwr(buf);
    printf("The string in lowercase is:\n%s\n", buf);
}
```

String Comparison and Manipulation

COMPATIBILITY

strncat, _fstrncat

MSC 3	MSC 4	MSC 5	MSC 6	QC1	QC2	QC2.5	TC1	TC1.5	TC2	TC++	ANSI	UNIX V	XNX	OS2	DOS
▲	▲	▲	1	▲	▲	▲	▲	▲	▲	▲	2	2	2	▲	▲

PURPOSE Use *strncat* to concatenate a specified number of characters of one string to another. The *_fstrncat* function provides you with a memory-model-independent way to append characters from one string to another.

SYNTAX

```
char *strncat(char *string1, const char *string2, size_t n);

char _far *_far _fstrncat (char _far *f_string1,
const char _far *f_string2, size_t n);
```

`char *string1;`	*Destination string*
`const char *string2;`	*String whose first* n *characters are to be appended to the destination string*
`size_t n;`	*Number of characters of* string2 *to be appended to* string1
`f_string1`	*A far pointer to destination string*
`f_string2`	*A far pointer to source string*

EXAMPLE CALL

```
char id[16] = "ID = ";
strncat(id, name, 10); /* id is first 10 char of name */

_fstrncat (id, name, 10); /* id is first 10 char of name */
```

INCLUDES `#include <string.h>` *For function declaration*

DESCRIPTION The *strncat* function appends the first *n* characters of *string2* to *string1* and terminates the resulting string with a null character. The terminating null of the first string is removed and *string1* becomes the resulting concatenation. If *n* is larger than the length of *string2*, the entire second string is appended to *string1*.

The *_fstrncat* function also appends, at most, the first *n* number of characters of *f_string2* to *f_string1*, and terminates the resulting string with a null character (\0). The *_f* versions of the string functions are large model forms that use *_far* string arguments and return values. They can be called from anywhere within your program. See the tutorial for more information about memory-model-independent routines.

1. *_fstrncat* is a model-independent version of *strncat* introduced in version 6.0. 2. The *_fstrncat* function does not work under ANSI C, UNIX, and XENIX.

RETURNS The *strncat* function returns a pointer to the concatenated string (i.e., it returns *string1*). The *_fstrncat* function returns a far pointer to the concatenated string.

SEE ALSO

`strcat`	*To concatenate one string to another*
`strcpy, strncpy`	*To copy one string into another*
`strdup`	*To allocate storage and create a duplicate a string*

EXAMPLE Use *strncat* to generate and print the sequence of the following strings:

```
a
ab
abc
abcd
...
...
abcdefghijklmnopqrstuvwxyz
```

The *_f* version of *strncat* behaves exactly as the root version, except that the arguments and return values take the form of *_far*.

```
#include <stdio.h>
#include <string.h>
char result[40] = "a";
char rest[] = "bcdefghijklmnopqrstuvwxyz";
unsigned length = sizeof(rest)/sizeof(char);
main()
{
    unsigned i;
    for(i = 0; i<length; i++, result[1]='\0')
    {
        strncat(result, rest, i);
/* Show the current result */
        printf("%s\n", result);
    }
}
```

String Comparison and Manipulation

COMPATIBILITY

strncmp, _fstrncmp

MSC 3	MSC 4	MSC 5	MSC 6	QC1	QC2	QC2.5	TC1	TC1.5	TC2	TC++	ANSI	UNIX V	XNX	OS2	DOS
▲	▲	▲	1	▲	▲	▲	▲	▲	▲	▲	2	2	2	▲	▲

PURPOSE Use *strncmp* to compare a specified number of characters of two strings to one another. The comparison is case sensitive. The *_fstrncmp* function gives you a memory-model-independent method of using *strncmp* to compare strings.

SYNTAX

```
int strncmp(const char *string1, const char *string2, size_t n);

int _far _fstrncmp (const char _far *f_string1,
const char _far *f_string2, size_t n);
```

`const char *string1;`	*First string*
`const char *string2;`	*Second string*
`size_t n;`	*Number of characters of strings to be compared*
`f_string1, f_string2`	Far *pointers to strings to compare.*

EXAMPLE CALL

```
if(strncmp(command, "quit", 2) == 0) quit_program();

if (_fstrncmp (mountain, "Nittany", 4) != 0) exit (8);
```

INCLUDES `#include <string.h>` *For function declaration*

DESCRIPTION The *strncmp* function compares the first *n* characters of *string1* and *string2*. The result of the case-sensitive comparison is returned as an integer value indicating the lexicographic order of the first *n* characters of *string1* with respect to the same part of *string2*.

The *_fstrncmp* function also compares, at most, the first *n* number of characters in *f_string1* and *f_string2*. The *_f* versions of the string functions are large model forms that use *_far* string arguments and return values. They can be called from anywhere within your program. See the tutorial for more information about memory-model independence.

1. *_fstrncmp* is the model-independent version of *strncmp* introduced in version 6.0. 2. The *_fstrncmp* function does not work under ANSI C, UNIX, or XENIX.

RETURNS The *strncmp* function returns an integer indicating the lexicographic ordering of the first *n* characters of *string1* with respect to the same part of *string2.* The return value will be 0 if the two substrings are identical. If *substring1* is less than *substring2,* the return value is less than 0. When *substring1* is greater than *substring2, strncmp* returns an integer greater than 0.

The *_fstrncmp* function returns a value less than 0 if *f_string1* < *f_string2*; 0 if *f_string1* = *f_string2*; a value greater than 0 if *f_string1* > *f_string2.* This is the same pattern followed by the root *strncmp* function.

SEE ALSO

`strcmp`	*To compare two strings*
`strncmpi, stricmp, strnicmp`	*To compare two strings disregarding the case of the characters*

EXAMPLE Write a program that accepts two strings and specifies the number of characters that are to be compared. Use *strncmp* to perform the comparison and then display the result. The *_f* version of *strncmp* behaves exactly as the root version, except that the arguments and return values take the form of *_far.*

```
#include <stdio.h>
#include <string.h>
main()
{
    int len, result;
    char str1[80], str2[80];
    printf("Enter a string: ");
    gets(str1);
    printf("Enter string to compare with first: ");
    gets(str2);
    printf("How many characters to compare:");
    scanf(" %d", &len);
    printf("Based on case sensitive comparison of \
the first %d characters\n", len);
    result = strncmp(str1, str2, len);
    if(result == 0)
    {
        printf("\"%s\" == \"%s\"\n", str1, str2);
    }
    if(result < 0)
    {
        printf("\"%s\" < \"%s\"\n", str1, str2);
    }
    if(result > 0)
    {
        printf("\"%s\" > \"%s\"\n", str1, str2);
    }
}
```

String Comparison and Manipulation

COMPATIBILITY

strncpy, _fstrncpy

MSC 3	MSC 4	MSC 5	MSC 6	QC1	QC2	QC2.5	TC1	TC1.5	TC2	TC++	ANSI	UNIX V	XNX	OS2	DOS
▲	▲	▲	1	▲	▲	▲	▲	▲	▲	▲	2	2	2	▲	▲

PURPOSE Use *strncpy* to copy a specified number of characters of one string to another. Use the *_fstrncpy* routine when you need a memory-model-independent way to copy characters from one string to another.

SYNTAX

```
char *strncpy(char *string1, const char *string2, size_t n);

char _far *_far _fstrncpy (char _far *f_string1,
const char _far *f_string2, size_t n);
```

`char *string1;`	*Destination string*
`const char *string2;`	*String whose first* n *characters are to be copied to the destination string*
`size_t n;`	*Number of characters to be copied*
`f_string1`	*Far pointer to destination string*
`f_string2`	*Far pointer to source string*

EXAMPLE CALL

```
strncpy(fname, "tmp12345678", 8); /* fname = "tmp12345" */

_fstrncpy (city, "San Francisco", 8); /* city = "San Fran" */
```

INCLUDES `#include <string.h>` *For function declaration*

DESCRIPTION The *strncpy* function copies the first *n* characters of *string2* to the buffer whose address is given by *string1*. The copy is placed starting at the first character position of *string1*. If *n* is less than the length of *string2*, no terminating null character is appended to *string1*. If *n* exceeds the length of *string2*, however, *string1* is padded with null characters until it is *n* bytes long.

You should avoid situations where the *n* bytes following *string1* overlap *string2* because the behavior of *strcpy* with such arguments is not guaranteed to be correct.

The *_fstrncpy* function copies exactly *chr_cnt* number of characters of *f_string2* to *f_string1*. The *_f* versions of the string functions are large model forms that use *far* string arguments and return values. They can be called from anywhere within your program.

1. *_fstrncpy* was introduced in version 6.0 and is a model-independent version of *strncpy*. 2. The *_fstrncpy* function does not function under ANSI C, XENIX, or UNIX.

RETURNS The *strncpy* function returns a pointer to the copied string (i.e., it returns *string1*). The *_fstrncpy* function returns *f_string1*.

SEE ALSO

strcat, strncat	*To concatenate one string to another*
strcpy	*To copy one string into another*
strdup	*To allocate storage and create a duplicate of a string*

EXAMPLE Read in a string and copy the first half into another buffer using *strncat*. Note that no null character is appended to the copied string so you have to add one if you want to use it as a C string (for example, when you print it using *printf*). The *_f* version of *strncpy* behaves exactly as the root version, except that the arguments and return values take the form of *_far*.

```
#include <stdio.h>
#include <string.h>
main()
{
    size_t len;
    char str1[80], str2[80];
    printf("Enter a string: ");
    gets(str2);
    len = strlen(str2)/2;
    strncpy(str1, str2, len);
/* Since '\0' is not appended automatically, we have
 * to do so before printing string
 */
    str1[len] = '\0';
    printf("Half the length of string copied. Result:\
 %s\n", str1);
}
```

COMPATIBILITY

strnicmp, _fstrnicmp

MSC 3	MSC 4	MSC 5	MSC 6	QC1	QC2	QC2.5	TC1	TC1.5	TC2	TC++	ANSI	UNIX V	XNX	OS2	DOS
	▲	▲	1	▲	▲	▲	▲	▲	▲	▲				▲	▲

PURPOSE Use *strnicmp* to compare a specified number of characters of two strings without regard to case. The *_fstrnicmp* function should be used when you need a memory-model-independent routine for case-insensitive string comparison.

SYNTAX

```
int strnicmp(const char *string1, const char *string2, size_t n);

int _far _fstrnicmp (const char _far *f_string1,
const char _far *f_string2, size_t n);
```

`const char *string1;` *First string*

`const char *string2;` *Second string*

`size_t n;` *Number of characters of strings to be compared*

`f_string1, f_string2` *Far pointers to strings to be compared*

EXAMPLE CALL

```
if (strnicmp(command, "exit", 2) == 0) exit_program();

if (_fstrnicmp (college, "Miami", 4) == 0) quit_s (6);
```

INCLUDES `#include <string.h>` *For function declaration*

DESCRIPTION The *strnicmp* function compares the first *n* characters of *string1* with the corresponding ones in *string2*, but during the comparison it converts each uppercase letter to lowercase. The result of this comparison is returned as an integer value indicating the lexicographic ordering of the first *n* characters of *string1* with respect to *string2*.

The *_fstrnicmp* function also compares, at most, the first *n* number of characters of *f_string1* and *f_string2*, without regard to letter case. The *_f* versions of the string functions are large model forms that use *_far* string arguments and return values. They can be called from anywhere within your program.

1. *_fstrnicmp* is a model-independent version of *strnicmp* and was introduced in version 6.0.

RETURNS The *strnicmp* function returns 0 if the two substrings are identical. If *substring1* is less than *substring2*, the return value is less than 0. When *substring1* is greater than *substring2*, *strnicmp* returns an integer greater than 0.

The *_fstrnicmp* function returns a value less than 0 if *f_string1* < *f_string2*; 0 if *f_string1* = *f_string2*; a value greater than 0 if *f_string1* > *f_string2*. This pattern matches that of the *strnicmp* function.

SEE ALSO

`strcmpi, stricmp`	*To compare two strings (case sensitive)*
`strcmp, strncmp`	*To compare two strings (case sensitive)*

EXAMPLE Use *strnicmp* in a program that compares two strings without regard to case. Let the program accept two strings and the number of characters to compare and then display the result of the comparison. The *_f* version of *strnicmp* behaves exactly as the root version, except that the arguments and return values take the form of *_far*.

```
#include <stdio.h>
#include <string.h>
main()
{
    int len, result;
    char str1[80], str2[80];
    printf("Enter a string: ");
    gets(str1);
    printf("Enter string to compare with first: ");
    gets(str2);
    printf("How many characters to compare:");
    scanf(" %d", &len);
    printf("Based on case insensitive comparison of \
the first %d characters\n", len);
    result = strnicmp(str1, str2, len);
    if(result == 0)
    {
        printf("\"%s\" == \"%s\"\n", str1, str2);
    }
    if(result < 0)
    {
        printf("\"%s\" < \"%s\"\n", str1, str2);
    }
    if(result > 0)
    {
        printf("\"%s\" > \"%s\"\n", str1, str2);
    }
}
```

COMPATIBILITY

strnset, _fstrnset

MSC 3	MSC 4	MSC 5	MSC 6	QC1	QC2	QC2.5	TC1	TC1.5	TC2	TC++	ANSI	UNIX V	XNX	OS2	DOS
▲	▲	▲	1	▲	▲	▲	▲	▲	▲	▲				▲	▲

PURPOSE Use *strnset* to set a specified number of characters in a string, excluding the terminating null, to a specific character value. Use the *_fstrnset* routine when you need a memory-model-independent function to set a character in a string.

SYNTAX

```
char *strnset(char *string, int c, size_t n);

char _far *_far _fstrnset (char _far *f_string, int chr, size_t n);
```

`char *string;` *String whose first* n *characters are to be set to* c

`int c;` *Value to be copied into first* n *character positions of* string

`size_t n;` *Number of characters to be set*

`f_string` *Far pointer to the string to be initialized*

EXAMPLE CALL

```
strnset(all_zzz, 'z', 40);

_fstrnset (all_yyy, 'y', 40);
```

INCLUDES `#include <string.h>` *For function declaration*

DESCRIPTION The *strnset* function copies the character in the integer *c* to the first *n* character positions in *string*. If *n* exceeds the length of the string, all character positions, except the last one (the terminating null character), are set.

The *_fstrnset* function sets, at most, the first *n* number of characters of the string argument to the character *chr*. Though many think of it as a way to write several copies of the same character to a string, it will work with one character at a time. The *_f* versions of the string functions are large model forms that use *_far* string arguments and return values. They can be called from anywhere within your program. See the tutorial for more information about memory-model independence.

1. *_fstrnset* is a model-independent version of *strnset* and was introduced in version 6.0.

RETURNS The *strnset* function returns a pointer to the altered string (i.e., it returns *string*). The *_fstrnset* function returns a *far* pointer to the altered string.

SEE ALSO `strset` *To set all characters of a string to a specific character value*

EXAMPLE Use *strnset* to fill the first half of a string entered by the user with a character also entered by the user. The *_f* version of *strnset* behaves exactly as the root version, except that the arguments and return values take the form of *_far*.

```
#include <stdio.h>
#include <conio.h>
#include <string.h>
main()
{
    int c;
    size_t len;
    char buf[80];

    printf("Enter a string: ");
    gets(buf);
    printf(
"Enter character you want half the string set to:");
    c = getche();
    len = strlen(buf)/2;
/* Set first half of string to character in c */
    strnset(buf, c, len);
    printf("\nString is now: %s\n", buf);
}
```

strpbrk, _fstrpbrk

COMPATIBILITY

MSC 3	MSC 4	MSC 5	MSC 6	QC1	QC2	QC2.5	TC1	TC1.5	TC2	TC++	ANSI	UNIX V	XNX	OS2	DOS
▲	▲	▲	1	▲	▲	▲	▲	▲	▲	▲	2	2	2	▲	▲

PURPOSE Use *strpbrk* to locate the first occurrence of any of the characters from one string in another string. The *_fstrpbrk* function is a memory-model-independent way to find the first occurrence of a specific character in a string.

SYNTAX

```
char *strpbrk(const char *string1, const char *string2);

char _far *_far _fstrpbrk (const char _far *f_string1,
const char _far *f_string2);
```

`const char *string1;` *String to be searched*

`const char *string2;`	*String describing set of characters to be located*
`f_string1`	*Far pointer to source string*
`f_string2`	*Far pointer to character set*

EXAMPLE CALL

```
first_vowel = strpbrk(word, "aeiou");

second_vowel = _fstrpbrk (word, "aeiou");
```

INCLUDES `#include <string.h>` *For function declaration*

DESCRIPTION The *strpbrk* function searches for the first occurrence in *string1* of any of the characters from *string2.* The terminating null is not included in the search.

The *_fstrpbrk* function finds the first occurrence of a character from one string in another. The *_f* versions of the string functions are large model forms that use *_far* string arguments and return values. They can be called from anywhere within your program.

1. *_fstrpbrk* is a model-independent version of *strpbrk* introduced in version 6.0. 2. The *_fstrpbrk* function does not function under ANSI C, UNIX, or XENIX.

RETURNS If successful, the *strpbrk* function returns a pointer to the first occurrence of any character from *string2* in *string1.* If the search fails, *strpbrk* returns a NULL. Failure implies that *string1* and *string2* have no characters in common. The *_fstrbrk* function returns a far pointer to the first occurrence of any character from *f_string2* in *f_string1.*

SEE ALSO

`strchr`	*To search for the first occurrence of a character in a string*
`strcspn`	*To locate the first character in a string that matches one of the characters in another*

EXAMPLE Use *strpbrk* to locate the first occurrence of a vowel in a word and print the word up to and including the vowel (this will tend to extract the first syllable from the word). The *_f* version of *strbrk* behaves exactly as the root version, except that the arguments and return values take the form of *_far.*

```
#include <stdio.h>
#include <string.h>
char *vowels = "aeiou";
main()
{
    char str1[80], *result;
```

```
    printf("Enter a word: ");
    gets(str1);
    if ((result = strpbrk(str1, vowels)) == NULL)
    {
        printf("No vowels in word\n");
    }
    else
    {
        printf("First syllable in %s ", str1);
/* Put a null character just after the first vowel */
        result++;
        *result = '\0';
        printf("is: %s\n", str1);
    }
}
```

strrchr, _fstrrchr

COMPATIBILITY

MSC 3	MSC 4	MSC 5	MSC 6	QC1	QC2	QC2.5	TC1	TC1.5	TC2	TC++	ANSI	UNIX V	XNX	OS2	DOS
▲	▲	▲	1	▲	▲	▲	▲	▲	▲	▲	2	2	2	▲	▲

PURPOSE Use *strrchr* to find the last occurrence of a particular character in a given string. The *_fstrrchr* function is a memory-model-independent way to find the last occurrence of a target character in a string.

SYNTAX

```
char *strrchr(const char *string, int c);

char _far *_far _fstrrchr (const char _far *f_string, int c);
```

`const char *string;` *String to be searched*

`int c;` *Character to be located*

`f_string` *Far pointer to searched string*

EXAMPLE CALL

```
char line_cost[] = "10 units at $1.20 ea. = $12.00";
total_cost = strrchr(line_cost, '$');
/* Now total_cost will be the string "$12.00" */

total_cost = _fstrrchr (line_codt, '$');
```

INCLUDES `#include <string.h>` *For function declaration*

DESCRIPTION The *strrchr* function searches for the last occurrence of the character *c* in *string.* The terminating null character is included in the search and can be the character to be located.

The *_fstrrchr* function finds the last occurrence of a given character in a string. The *_f* versions of the string functions are large model forms that use *_far* string arguments and return values. They can be called from anywhere within your program. See the tutorial for more information about memory-model independence.

1. The *_fstrrchr* function is a model-independent version of *strrchr* introduced in version 6.0. 2. The *_fstrrchr* function does not function under ANSI C, UNIX, or XENIX.

RETURNS If the character *c* is found, *strrchr* returns a pointer to the last occurrence of *c* in *string.* If the search fails, *strrchr* returns a NULL. The *_fstrrchr* function returns a far pointer to the last occurrence of the character *chr* in a string.

SEE ALSO strchr *To locate the first occurrence of a character in a string*

EXAMPLE Write a program that accepts a date in the form "MM/DD/YY" and uses *strrchr* to locate the last occurrence of the / character and print the returned string as a year. The *_f* version of *strrchr* behaves exactly as the root version, except that the arguments and return values take the form of *_far.*

```
#include <stdio.h>
#include <string.h>
main()
{
    char buf[80], *result;
    printf("Enter date: ");
    gets(buf);
    if ((result = strrchr(buf, '/')) == NULL)
    {
        printf("%s <-- not a date!\n", buf);
    }
    else
    {
        result++;    /* Skip the '/' */
        printf("The year is: 19%s\n", result);
    }
}
```

strrev, _fstrrev

COMPATIBILITY

MSC 3	MSC 4	MSC 5	MSC 6	QC1	QC2	QC2.5	TC1	TC1.5	TC2	TC++	ANSI	UNIX V	XNX	OS2	DOS
▲	▲	▲	1	▲	▲	▲	▲	▲	▲	▲				▲	▲

PURPOSE Use *strrev* to reverse the order of characters in a string. Use the *_fstrrev* function for a memory-model-independent routine that allows you to reverse the order of the characters specified in a string.

SYNTAX

```
char *strrev(char *string);

char _far *_far _fstrrev (char _far *f_string);
```

`char *string;` *String to be reversed*

`f_string` *Far pointer to string to be reversed*

EXAMPLE CALL

```
strrev(input_string);

printf ("%s", _fstrrev ("Pennsylvania"));

/* yields "ainavlysnneP" */
```

INCLUDES `#include <string.h>` *For function declaration*

DESCRIPTION The *strrev* function reverses the order of the characters in *string*. The terminating null character remains at the same place.

The *_fstrrev* function also reverses the order of the characters in a specified string. The terminating null character (\0) remains in place. The *_f* versions of the string functions are large model forms that use *_far* string arguments and return values. They can be called from anywhere within your program. See the tutorial for more information about memory-model independence.

1. *_fstrrev* is a model-independent version of *strrev* and was introduced in version 6.0.

RETURNS The *strrev* function returns a pointer to the reversed string (it returns the argument *string*). The *_fstrrev* function returns a far pointer to the altered string.

SEE ALSO `strcpy, strncpy` *To copy one string to another*

EXAMPLE Use *strrev* to reverse a string typed at the keyboard and print the result. One use of this program is to check whether a string is a "palindrome," that is, whether it reads the same backward and forward.

The _f version of *strrev* behaves exactly as the root version, except that the arguments and return values take the form of _*far*.

```
#include <stdio.h>
#include <string.h>
main()
{
    char buf[80];
    printf("Enter a string: ");
    gets(buf);
    strrev(buf);
    printf("Reversed string is:\n%s\n", buf);
}
```

COMPATIBILITY

strset, _fstrset

MSC 3	MSC 4	MSC 5	MSC 6	QC1	QC2	QC2.5	TC1	TC1.5	TC2	TC++	ANSI	UNIX V	XNX	OS2	DOS
▲	▲	▲	1	▲	▲	▲	▲	▲	▲	▲				▲	▲

PURPOSE Use *strset* to set all characters in a string, excluding the terminating null, to a specific character value. The _*fstrset* function allows you to set all the characters in a string to the value of a specified character. It is memory-model independent.

SYNTAX

```
char *strset(char *string, int c);

char _far *_far _fstrset (char _far *f_string, int c);
```

`char *string;` *String to be set to* c

`int c;` *Value to be copied into each character position of* string

`f_string` *Far pointer to string to be set*

EXAMPLE CALL

```
char password[16];
strset(password, 'x'); /* Set password to all 'x' */

_fstrset (password, 'H'); /* Set password to all 'H' */
```

INCLUDES `#include <string.h>` *For function declaration*

DESCRIPTION The *strset* function copies the character in the integer *c* to every character position in *string*, except the terminating null character. This is useful for setting a string to blanks or other default values.

The *_fstrset* function sets all of the characters of string to the value of *chr*, except the terminating null (\0). The *_f* versions of the string functions are large model forms that use *far* string arguments and return values. They can be called from anywhere within your program. See the tutorial for more information about memory-model independence.

1. *_fstrset* is a memory-model-independent version of *strset* and was introduced in version 6.0. 2. The *_fstrset* function does not work under ANSI C, UNIX, or XENIX.

RETURNS The *strset* function returns a pointer to the altered string (i.e, it returns *string*). The *_fstrset* function returns a *_far* pointer to the altered string.

SEE ALSO `strnset` *To set a specified number of characters of a string to a specific character value*

EXAMPLE Write a C program that reads in a string from the keyboard, prompts for a fill character, and uses *strset* to set the entire string to that character. Then the program displays the result.

The *_f* version of *strset* behaves exactly as the root version, except that the arguments and return values take the form of *_far*.

```
#include <stdio.h>
#include <conio.h>
#include <string.h>
main()
{
    int c;
    char buf[80];
    printf("Enter a string: ");
    gets(buf);
    printf(
"Enter character you want entire string set to:");
    c = getche();
    strset(buf, c);
    printf("\nString is now: %s\n", buf);
}
```

COMPATIBILITY

strspn, _fstrspn

MSC 3	MSC 4	MSC 5	MSC 6	QC1	QC2	QC2.5	TC1	TC1.5	TC2	TC++	ANSI	UNIX V	XNX	OS2	DOS
▲	▲	▲	1	▲	▲	▲	▲	▲	▲	▲	2	2	2	▲	▲

PURPOSE Use *strspn* to locate the position of the first character in a string that does not belong to the set of characters in another. The *_fstrspn* function is a memory-model-independent way to identify the first character in a string that does not match one of the characters in a specified set.

SYNTAX

```
size_t strspn(const char *string1, const char *string2);

size_t _far _fstrspn (const char _far *f_string1,
const char _far *f_string2);
```

`const char *string1;`	*String to be searched*
`const char *string2;`	*String describing set of characters*
`f_string1`	*Far pointer to searched string*
`f_string2`	*Far pointer to source character set*

EXAMPLE CALL

```
char *input = "28OZX";
first_nondigit_at = strspn(input, "1234567890");
/* first_nondigit_at will be  3 */

char _far *input = "386SX"
answer = _fstrspn (input, "1234567890");
/* answer will be 3 */
```

INCLUDES `#include <string.h>` *For function declaration*

DESCRIPTION The *strspn* function locates the first character in *string1* that is not present in *string2*. The terminating null is not included in the search.

The *_fstrspn* function returns the index (the location of the character in the string) of the first character in *f_string1* that does not belong to the set of characters specified by *f_string2*. This value is equivalent to the length of the initial substring of *f_string1* that consists entirely of characters from *f_string2*. The *_f* versions of the string functions are large model forms that use *_far* string arguments and return values. They can be called from anywhere within your program. See the tutorial for more information about memory-model independence.

1. *_fstrspn* is a memory-model-independent version of *strspn* and was introduced in version 6.0. 2. The *_fstrspn* function does not work under ANSI C, UNIX, or XENIX.

RETURNS If successful, the *strspn* function returns the index of the first character in *string1* that does not belong to the set of characters *string2*. Thus, this value is the length of the initial substring of *string1* that consists entirely of characters in *string2*, i.e., the substring that spans the character set in *string2*.

If *string1* begins with a character that does not appear in *string2*, the return value is 0. On the other hand, if *string1* only contains characters from *string2*, *strspn* returns the length of *string1*.

The *_fstrspn* function returns an integer value specifying the length of the segment in *f_string1* consisting entirely of characters in *f_string2*.

SEE ALSO

`strpbrk`	*To search for the first occurrence of any of the characters from one string in another string*
`strcspn`	*To find the length of the initial substring that is made up entirely of characters not in another string*

EXAMPLE Read in a string and use *strspn* to locate the first nonwhitespace character in the string. The *_f* version of *strspn* behaves exactly as the root version, except that the arguments and return values take the form of *_far*.

```
#include <stdio.h>
#include <string.h>
/*space, tab and newline are the whitespace characters */
char *whitespace = " \t\n";
main()
{
    int loc;
    char str1[80];
    printf("Enter a string with preceding blanks: ");
    gets(str1);
    loc = strspn(str1, whitespace);
    printf("First nonwhitespace character in\
\n%s\nis at location %d\n", str1, loc);
}
```

COMPATIBILITY

strstr, _fstrstr

MSC 3	MSC 4	MSC 5	MSC 6	QC1	QC2	QC2.5	TC1	TC1.5	TC2	TC++	ANSI	UNIX V	XNX	OS2	DOS
▲	▲	▲	1	▲	▲	▲	▲	▲	▲	▲	2			▲	▲

PURPOSE Use *strstr* to locate the first occurrence of one string in another. Use the *_fstrstr* version when you need a memory-model-independent version of a function to search for a string.

SYNTAX

```
char *strstr(const char *string1, const char *string2);

char _far *_far _fstrstr (const char _far *f_string1,
const char _far *f_string2);
```

`const char *string1;` *String to be searched*

`const char *string2;` *String to be located*

`f_string1` *Far pointer to the searched string*

`f_string2` *Far pointer to string for which to search*

EXAMPLE CALL

```
char input[]="The account number is MSCB-87-08-01";
acc_no = strstr(input, "MSCB");
/* Now the string acc_no will be "MSCB-87-08-01" */

acc_no = _fstrstr (input, "MSCB");
```

INCLUDES `#include <string.h>` *For function declaration*

DESCRIPTION The *strstr* function searches for the first occurrence of *string2* in *string1*.

The *_fstrstr* function finds the first occurrence of a given string in another string. The *_f* versions of the string functions are large model forms that use *_far* string arguments and return values. They can be called from anywhere within your program. See the tutorial for more information about memory-model independence.

1. *_fstrstr* is a memory-model-independent version of *strstr* and was introduced in version 6.0. 2. The *_fstrstr* function does not work under ANSI, although *strstr* does.

RETURNS If successful, the *strstr* function returns a pointer to the first occurrence of *string2* as a substring in *string1*. If the search fails, *strstr* returns a NULL. The *_fstrstr* function returns a far pointer to the first occurrence of *f_string2* in *f_string1*.

SEE ALSO

`strchr` — *To search for the first occurrence of a character in a string*

`strcspn, strpbrk` — *To locate the first character in a string that matches one of the characters in another string*

EXAMPLE Read in a string and then a substring that you want to find in the first string. Use *strstr* to perform the search. Display the results of the search. The *_f* version of *strstr* behaves exactly as the root version, except that the arguments and return values take the form of *_far*.

```
#include <stdio.h>
#include <string.h>
main()
{
    char str1[80], str2[80], *result;
    printf("Enter a string: ");
    gets(str1);
    printf("Enter string to locate in the first: ");
    gets(str2);
    if((result = strstr(str1, str2)) == NULL)
    {
        printf("\"%s\" NOT IN \"%s\"\n", str2, str1);
    }
    else
    {
        printf("\"%s\" FOUND.\n\Rest of string: %s\n",
               str2, result);
    }
}
```

strtok, _fstrtok

COMPATIBILITY

MSC 3	MSC 4	MSC 5	MSC 6	QC1	QC2	QC2.5	TC1	TC1.5	TC2	TC++	ANSI	UNIX V	XNX	OS2	DOS
▲	▲	▲	1	▲	▲			▲	▲	▲	2	2			

PURPOSE Use *strtok* to get the next token, or substring, in a string delimited by any character from a second string. The *_fstrtok* function provides a memory-model-independent manner for parsing tokens.

SYNTAX

```
char *strtok(char *string1, const char *string2);

char _far *_far _fstrtok *char _far (f_string1,
const char _far *f_string2);
```

`char *string1;` — *String from which tokens are returned*

```
const char *string2;
```
String describing set of characters that delimit tokens

`f_string1` *Far pointer to string containing token(s)*

`f_string2` *Far pointer to set of delimiter characters*

EXAMPLE CALL

```
next_token = strtok(input, "\t, ");

next_token = _fstrtok (input, "\t, ");
```

INCLUDES `#include <string.h>` *For function declaration*

DESCRIPTION The *strtok* function isolates a token, or substring, from *string1.* The token is marked by delimiting characters given in the second string argument *string2.* All tokens in a particular string *string1* can be extracted through successive calls to *strtok* in the following way. Make the first call to *strtok* with the string to be "tokenized" as the first argument. Provide as the second argument a C string composed from the delimiting characters. After that, call *strtok* with a NULL as the first argument and the delimiting characters appropriate for that token in the second string. This tells *strtok* to continue returning tokens from the old *string1.* The example below illustrates how this is done.

Note that the set of delimiters can change in each call to *strtok.* In the process of separating tokens, *strtok* modifies the string *string1.* It inserts null characters in place of delimiters to convert tokens to C strings.

The *_fstrtok* function reads *f_string1* as a series of zero or more tokens and *f_string2* as the set of characters serving as delimiters of the tokens in *f_string1.* The *_f* versions of the string functions are large model forms that use *_far* string arguments and return values. They can be called from anywhere within your program. See the tutorial for more information about memory-model independence.

1. *_fstrtok* is a model-independent version of *strtok* that was introduced in version 6.0. 2. The *_fstrtok* function does not work under ANSI C, UNIX, or XENIX.

COMMON USES The *strtok* function is handy when you are developing an application in which the user enters commands using a specified syntax. The routine that parses the command lines can use *strtok* to isolate the tokens. Quite complex syntax can be accommodated by using a different set of delimiters for each token.

RETURNS The first call to *strtok* with the argument *string1* returns a pointer to the first token. Subsequent calls with a NULL as the first argument will return the next tokens. When there are no tokens left, *strtok* returns a NULL.

The *_fstrtok* function returns a far pointer to the first token in *f_string1*; successive calls against the same string return the subsequent tokens in the string.

SEE ALSO

`strpbrk, strcspn`	*To search for the first occurrence of any character from one string in another*
`strspn`	*To find the first occurrence of a character in a string that does not belong to another string*

EXAMPLE Write a C program that reads a string and separates it into tokens. The tokens are separated by blank spaces, tabs, or commas. This process of converting input strings to tokens is known as "parsing" and is one of the first things any command interpreter or compiler has to do. The *_f* version of *strtok* behaves exactly as the root version, except that the arguments and return values take the form of *_far*.

```
#include <stdio.h>
#include <string.h>
char tokensep[] = " \t,";
main()
{
    int i = 0;
    char buf[80], *token;
    printf("Enter a string of tokens separated by comma\
 or blank:");
    gets(buf);
/* Call strtok once to get first token and initialize it */
    token = strtok(buf, tokensep);
/* Keep calling strtok to get all tokens                 */
    while(token != NULL)
    {
        i++;
        printf("Token %d = %s\n", i, token);
        token = strtok(NULL, tokensep);
    }
}
```

COMPATIBILITY

strupr, _fstrupr

MSC 3	MSC 4	MSC 5	MSC 6	QC1	QC2	QC2.5	TC1	TC1.5	TC2	TC++	ANSI	UNIX V	XNX	OS2	DOS
▲	▲	▲	1	▲	▲	▲	▲	▲	▲	▲				▲	▲

PURPOSE Use *strupr* to convert any lowercase letters in a string to uppercase. Use the *_fstrupr* function for a memory-model-independent routine that converts lowercase characters to uppercase characters.

SYNTAX

```
char *strupr(char *string);

char _far *_far _fstrupr (char _far *trgt_str);
```

`char *string;` *String to be converted to uppercase*

`trgt_str` *Far pointer to string to be capitalized*

EXAMPLE CALL

```
strupr("help"); /* converts it to "HELP" */

_fstrupr ("state college"); /* becomes "STATE COLLEGE" */
```

INCLUDES `#include <string.h>` *For function declaration*

DESCRIPTION The *strupr* function converts any lowercase letters in the *string* to uppercase. Other characters in the string are unaffected.

The *_fstrupr* routine converts any lowercase letters in a specified string (*trgt_str* in the syntax example above) to uppercase. Other characters are not affected. The *_f* versions of the string functions are large model forms that use *_far* string arguments and return values. They can be called from anywhere within your program. See the tutorial for more information about memory-model independence.

1. *_fstrupr* is a memory-model-independent version of *strupr* and was introduced in version 6.0.

RETURNS The *strupr* function returns a pointer to the converted string (i.e., it returns "string"). The *_fstrupr* routine returns a far pointer to the converted string.

COMMENTS The *strupr* routine and its companion *strlwr* are not part of the proposed ANSI definition. Using the macros *toupper* and *tolower*, respectively, you can implement your own versions.

SEE ALSO

`strlwr` *To convert a string to lowercase*

`toupper` *To convert a single lowercase letter to uppercase*

EXAMPLE Write a program that reads a string from the keyboard and converts the entire screen to uppercase by calling the function *strupr*. The *_f* version of *strupr* behaves exactly as the root version, except that the arguments and return values take the form of *_far*.

```
#include <stdio.h>
#include <string.h>
main()
{
    char buf[80];
    printf("Enter a string with lowercase letters: ");
    gets(buf);
    strupr(buf);
    printf("The string in uppercase is:\n%s\n", buf);
}
```

String Comparison and Manipulation

Chapter 11 Searching and Sorting

Introduction

Searching and *sorting* are commonplace in business applications of the PC. All commercial data base programs have these capabilities. If you implement your own data base program tailored to your specific requirements, you invariably need search and sort capabilities. For example, if your data base contains the names and addresses of the customers of your company, you may want to search the list for information about a certain customer. And for mailings, you might want to print labels for all entries in your data base, sorted by zip code.

If you are developing your data base in C, Microsoft C makes your job easier by providing four library routines for sorting and searching lists in memory. We describe these routines in this section.

Concepts

Many algorithms are used for searching and sorting, some meant for arrays that fit into memory and others that can handle files much too large to fit into the memory of the PC. The sort and search functions in the Microsoft C library are for in-memory operations only.

SORTING The typical sort operation involves a data layout like that shown in Figure 11-1. You have an array of pointers each of which contains the address of a data structure (for example, a structure with fields that contain the name, address, and zip code for a customer). Sorting is done not by rearranging the data records themselves, which would be inefficient, but by rearranging the pointers to cause a particular field in the data structure (the "key" for the sort) to appear in ascendant or descendant position. In Figure 11-1 we show the original list and the list after it was sorted with the ZIP code (the key field) ascendant. Notice that only the pointers were rearranged; the data structures stayed put. This improves sorting speed because the pointers are much smaller than the structures themselves, but the pointers require extra storage space.

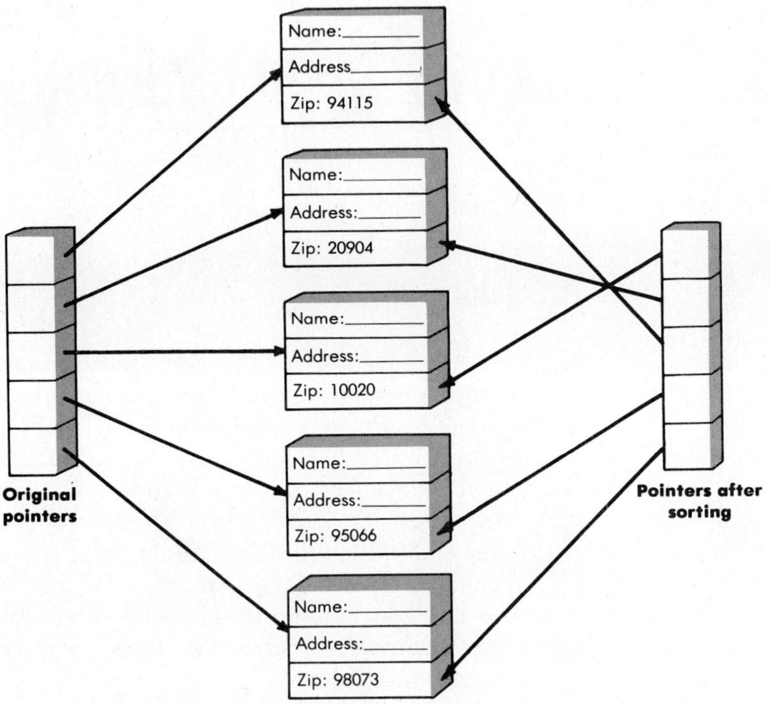

Figure 11-1. *Sorting*

In its sort and search routines the Microsoft C library supplies the basic algorithms but you supply the starting address of the array, the number of elements in it, the size (in bytes) of each element, and a pointer to a function that performs the comparison of two elements.

You write the function that compares two elements from the array. The function receives the pointers to the two elements and returns an integer value. A positive return value signifies that the first element is "greater than" the second one. A zero signifies equality, and a negative number means that the first element is "less than" the second one. You define what less than and greater than mean. In the name and address data base example, you could compare the zip code field of the two structures and return a value based on which zip is higher. If you wanted to sort by the name field, you could compare the names alphabetically. With your definition, the Microsoft *qsort* function sorts the array in ascending order. You can change the order by reversing the less than and greater than definitions in the function performing the comparison.

The Quicksort Algorithm

The only sort routine in the library, *qsort*, is based on the well-known "quicksort" algorithm. This popular, general-purpose sort algorithm was invented by C. A. R. Hoare in 1962. The quicksort algorithm is based on the principle of divide and conquer. The array being sorted is partitioned into two parts and the algorithm is applied to each part. The algorithm can be implemented with the following recursive program:

```
quicksort(lower_bound, upper_bound)
int lower_bound, upper_bound;
{
    int i;
    if (upper_bound > lower_bound)
    {
        i = partition_array(upper_bound, lower_bound);
        quicksort(lower_bound, i);
        quicksort(i+1, upper_bound);
    }
}
```

The *upper_bound* and *lower_bound* are the array indices describing a particular partition. As you can see from the code, the *partitioning of the array* is at the heart of the quicksort algorithm. The partitioning algorithm must satisfy three conditions. First, after the partitioning is complete, one element we'll call X must move to its final position in the sorted array. Second, all elements in the lower half of the new partition must be less than X. Third, all elements in the upper half must be greater than X.

One way to implement the partitioning is to arbitrarily select the element X, at the *upper_bound*, as the one to move into its final place in the sorted array. Then we scan the array from bottom to top until we find an element greater than X, and we also scan it from top to bottom until we find an element less than X. Next we exchange these two elements with one another. This step is repeated until the partitioning is complete, which is indicated by the condition that the scan from top down crosses the one from bottom up. The C code fragment below illustrates this partitioning algorithm (for simplicity, we assume that the array is named *array* and that it contains integer values only):

```
int partition_array(lower_bound, upper_bound)
int lower_bound, upper_bound;
{
    int i, j, X, temp;

    X = array[upper_bound];
    i = lower_bound - 1;
    j = upper_bound;
    while(j <= i)          /* Till partitioning is done */
    {
        while(a[i] >= X) i++;          /* Scan array */
        while(a[j] <= X) j--;          /* Scan array */
/* Exchange elements */
        temp = a[i];
        a[i] = a[j];
        a[j] = temp;
    }
    return(i); /* Return index to indicate partition */
}
```

SEARCHING

The Microsoft C library includes two searching algorithms: the linear search and the binary search.

The Linear Search Algorithm

The linear search is the simpler method of searching: we look through the array sequentially until the specific element is found or, if the array ends before the element is found, the search fails. The *lfind* routine implements this search.

The Binary Search Algorithm

The binary search algorithm is implemented by the function *bsearch*. Like quicksort, binary search uses a divide and conquer approach to find an element in an array. This approach is analogous to searching for a word in the dictionary. You flip to a page around the middle of the dictionary and if the words on that page occur later in alphabetic order than the word you are looking for, you repeat the search in the first half of the dictionary. This method works because the dictionary is already sorted in a particular order.

The array also must be sorted in ascending order. On such a sorted array, the binary search proceeds as follows. The value of the key field in the middle entry of the array is compared with the value being sought. If the entry has a value either too high or too low, this search step is repeated on the upper half or lower half of the array, respectively. Thus at every step of the search you reduce the length of the array to be searched by half, allowing even a large array to be searched very quickly.

General Usage

Microsoft provides four sort and search routines (see Table 11-1). One, *qsort*, is meant for sorting an array of elements. The others, *bsearch, lfind*, and *1search* are for searching an array of elements for a given value. These routines are designed to be used in a standard way. Figure 11-2 shows the arguments that you pass to the routines. These include the starting address of the array; the number of elements in it; the size (in bytes) of each element, and a pointer to a function, *compare( )*, that performs the comparison of two elements. Figure 11-2 shows sorting or searching the command-line arguments that are passed to the *main* function in your program. For a declaration of the form *main(int argc, char **argv)*, the number of arguments is in *argc* (the standard way a program accesses its command-line arguments) and the starting address of the array is *argv*. Each element is a pointer to a C string, so the size of each element is given by *sizeof(char *)*. The comparison function is called as *compare(char **elem1, char **elem2)* with two arguments, each a pointer to a variable that points to a string. We can use a string comparison routine such as *strcmp* to perform the comparison inside *compare( )*.

Table 11-1. *Search and Sort Routines*

Routine	Description
bsearch	Performs binary search for an element in a sorted array.
lfind	Performs linear search for an element in an array. The array need not be sorted.
lsearch	Performs linear search like *lfind*, but appends the value being searched to the array if the value is not found.
qsort	Sorts an array of elements using the "quicksort" algorithm.

The Routines

The sorting routine is named *qsort* and it uses the quicksort algorithm. The other three routines, *bsearch, lfind*, and *lsearch*, are for searching. The *bsearch* function performs binary search on a sorted array. You can use *qsort* to perform the sorting before calling *bsearch*. The *lfind* and *lsearch* routines implement a linear search technique, but *lsearch* also provides the additional service of inserting the element into the array if it is not found during the search.

Further Reading

Search and sort algorithms are covered in every computer science text on data structures and algorithms. An entire volume by Knuth[1] deals with sort

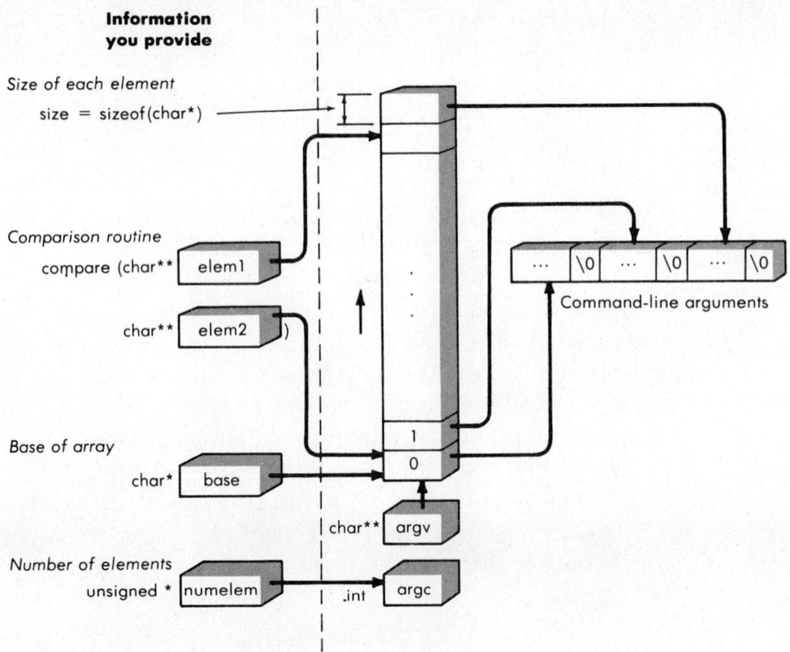

Figure 11-2. *Sorting and searching command-line arguments*

and search algorithms alone. For a shorter introduction to these algorithms, you can consult the books by Sedgewick[2] and Tremblay and Sorenson[3].

1. Donald E. Knuth, *The Art of Computer Programming, Volume 3: Sorting and Searching*, Addison-Wesley Publishing Co., Reading, MA, 1973.
2. Robert Sedgewick, *Algorithms*, Addison-Wesley Publishing Co., Reading, MA, 1983, 551 pages.
3. Jean-Paul Tremblay and Paul G. Sorenson, *An Introduction to Data Structures with Applications*, Second Edition, McGraw-Hill, Inc., New York, NY, 1984, 861 pages.

COMPATIBILITY

bsearch

MSC 3	MSC 4	MSC 5	MSC 6	QC1	QC2	QC2.5	TC1	TC1.5	TC2	TC++	ANSI	UNIX V	XNX	OS2	DOS
▲	▲	▲	▲	▲	▲	▲	▲	▲	▲	▲	▲	▲	▲	▲	▲

PURPOSE Use *bsearch* to perform a binary search of a sorted array with a specific number of elements, each a fixed number of bytes long.

SYNTAX

```
void *bsearch(const void *key, const void *base, size_t num,
              size_t width,
              int (*compare)(const void *elem1, const void *elem2));
```

`const void *key;` *Pointer to element value being searched for*

`const void *base;` *Pointer to beginning of array being searched*

`size_t num;` *Number of elements in array*

`size_t width;` *Size of each element in bytes*

`int (*compare)(const void *elem1, const void *elem2);`
Pointer to a function that compares two elements, elem1 *and* elem2, *each of type* const void *

EXAMPLE CALL

```
int mycompare(const void *, const void *);
result = (char **) bsearch((const void *)keyword,
                           (const void *)envp,
                           (size_t)count,
                           (size_t)sizeof(char *),
                           mycompare);
```

INCLUDES `#include <search.h>` *For function declaration and definition of* size_t

or

`#include <stdlib.h>` *For function declaration, definition of* size_t *and for ANSI compatibility*

DESCRIPTION The *bsearch* function performs a binary search (see the tutorial section) of a sorted array, beginning at the address *base* and comprising *num* elements, each of size *width* bytes. The argument *key* points to the value being sought.

In the argument *compare*, you supply the address of a routine which should accept two arguments *elem1* and *elem2*, each a pointer to an element in the array. The *bsearch* function calls your routine when it has to compare two elements of the array, passing the address of the array elements as arguments. Your routine should compare the two elements and return one of the values shown in the table (for strings, "greater than" and "less than" usually refer to alphabetic order).

Return Value	To Indicate
Negative	First element is less than the second one
Zero	The two elements are identical to each other
Positive	First element is greater than the second one

Note that you can use the *qsort* routine to sort the array before calling *bsearch*.

RETURNS The *bsearch* function returns a pointer to the first occurrence of the value *key* in the array. If the value is not found, *bsearch* returns a NULL.

SEE ALSO `lfind, lsearch` *To perform a linear search*

`qsort` *To sort an array using the "quick sort" algorithm*

EXAMPLE In Microsoft C under MS-DOS, the *main* function is invoked with three arguments: the number of strings in the command line, the command line itself, and the MS-DOS environment table, which is also an array of strings. Write a program that accepts a keyword on the command line and uses *bsearch* to search the environment table for the string beginning with this keyword. First it sorts the environment table using *qsort*, prints it, and then calls *bsearch* to perform the search. Count the number of entries in the table, noting that the end of the environment table is marked by a NULL.

```
#include <stdio.h>
#include <string.h>
#include <search.h>
int mycompare(const void *, const void *);
main(int argc, char **argv, char **envp)
{
    unsigned int i, count;
    char **p_table, **result;
    if(argc < 2)
    {
        printf("Usage: %s <KEYWORD>\n", argv[0]);
        exit(0);
    }
```

```
/* Find length of environment table                      */
    for(count = 0, p_table = envp;
        *p_table != NULL;
        p_table++, count++);        /* a null loop   */
/* Sort the environment table using "qsort"              */
    qsort((void *) envp, (size_t)count,
          (size_t)sizeof(char *), mycompare);
/* Print sorted environment table                        */
    printf("===== Sorted environment table =====\n");
    for(i = 0, p_table = envp; i < count; i++)
    {
        printf("%s\n", *p_table);
        p_table++;
    }
/* Search for the KEY variable in the environment   */
    result = (char **) bsearch((const void *)&argv[1],
                               (const void *)envp,
                               (size_t)count,
                               (size_t)sizeof(char *),
                               mycompare);
    if(result != NULL)
    {
        printf("\nFound %s in\n%s\n", argv[1], *result);
    }
    else
    {
        printf("\n%s not found.\
Try with uppercase keyword\n", argv[1]);
    }
}
/*--------------------------------------------------*/
int mycompare(char **arg1, char **arg2)
{
/* Compare two strings up to the length of the key    */
    return(strncmp(*arg1, *arg2, strlen(*arg1)));
}
```

lfind

COMPATIBILITY

MSC 3	MSC 4	MSC 5	MSC 6	QC1	QC2	QC2.5	TC1	TC1.5	TC2	TC++	ANSI	UNIX V	XNX	OS2	DOS
	▲	▲	▲	▲	▲	▲	▲	▲	▲	▲		▲	▲	▲	▲

PURPOSE Use *lfind* to make a linear search through an array with a specific number of elements, each a fixed number of bytes long.

SYNTAX

```
char *lfind(char *key, char *base, unsigned *num, unsigned width,
            int (*compare)(const void *elem1, const void *elem2));
```

`char *key;` *Pointer to element value being searched for*

`char *base;` *Pointer to beginning of array being searched*

`unsigned *num;` *Number of elements in array*

`unsigned width;` *Size of each element in bytes*

`int (*compare)(const void *elem1, const void *elem2);`
Pointer to a function that compares two elements, elem1 *and* elem2, *each of type* const void *

EXAMPLE CALL

```
int mycompare(void *, void *);
result = (char **)lfind((char *)keyword,
                        (char *)envp,
                        &count,
                        sizeof(char *),
                        mycompare);
```

INCLUDES #include <search.h> *For function declaration*

or

#include <stdlib.h> *For function declaration and ANSI compatibility*

DESCRIPTION The *lfind* function makes a linear search through an array that begins at the address *base* and consists of *num* elements, each of size *width* bytes. The argument *key* points to the value being sought.

In the argument *compare*, *lfind* expects the address of a routine to compare a pair of elements from the array. This routine should accept arguments *elem1* and *elem2*, each a pointer to an element in the array. The *lfind* function calls this routine with the address of two array elements as

arguments. The routine compares the two elements and returns a 0 if the elements are identical. Otherwise, it returns a nonzero value.

RETURNS If the value *key* is found, *lfind* returns a pointer to its first occurrence in the array. If it is not found, *lfind* returns a NULL.

SEE ALSO `lsearch` *To perform a linear search of an array*

`bsearch` *To perform a binary search of a sorted array*

EXAMPLE Write a program that accepts a keyword on the command line and uses *lfind* to find the first occurrence in the process environment table of a string that begins with the keyword. Note that the environment table is automatically the third parameter in the *main* function with Microsoft C on an MS-DOS system.

```
#include <stdio.h>
#include <stdlib.h>
#include <string.h>
#include <search.h>
int mycompare(void *, void *);
main(int argc, char **argv, char **envp)
{
    unsigned int count;
    char **p_table, **result;
    if(argc < 2)
    {
        printf("Usage: %s <KEYWORD>\n", argv[0]);
        exit(0);
    }
/* Find length of environment table and print it    */
    printf("==== Environment table contains ====\n");
    for(count = 0, p_table = envp;
        *p_table != NULL;
        p_table++, count++) printf("%s\n", *p_table);
/* Search for the KEY variable in the environment   */
    result = (char **)lfind((char *)&argv[1],
                            (char *)envp,
                            &count,
                            sizeof(char *),
                            mycompare);
    if(result != NULL)
    {
        printf("\nFound %s in\n%s\n", argv[1], *result);
    }
```

```
    else
    {
        printf("\n%s not found.\
Try with uppercase keyword\n", argv[1]);
    }
}
/*-----------------------------------------------------*/
int mycompare(char **arg1, char **arg2)
{
    return(strncmp(*arg1, *arg2, strlen(*arg1)));
}
```

lsearch

COMPATIBILITY

MSC 3	MSC 4	MSC 5	MSC 6	QC1	QC2	QC2.5	TC1	TC1.5	TC2	TC++	ANSI	UNIX V	XNX	OS2	DOS
	▲	▲	▲	▲	▲	▲	▲	▲	▲	▲		▲	▲	▲	▲

PURPOSE Use *lsearch* to perform a linear search of an array with a specified number of elements, each a fixed number of bytes long. The value being sought is added to the array if it is not found.

SYNTAX

```
char *lsearch(char *key, char *base, unsigned *num, unsigned width,
              int (*compare)(const void *elem1, const void *elem2));
```

`char *key;` *Pointer to element value being searched for*

`char *base;` *Pointer to beginning of array being searched*

`unsigned *num;` *Pointer to number of elements in array*

`unsigned width;` *Size of each element in bytes*

`int (*compare)(const void *elem1, const void *elem2);`
Pointer to a function that compares two elements, elem1 *and* elem2, *each of type* const void *

EXAMPLE CALL

```
int client_compare(void *, void *);
result = (char **) lsearch((char *)client_name,
                           (char *)client_table,
                           &count,
                           sizeof(char *),
                           client_compare);
```

INCLUDES `#include <search.h>` *For function declaration*

or

`#include <stdlib.h>` *For function declaration and ANSI compatibility*

DESCRIPTION The *lsearch* function performs a linear search (see the tutorial section) of an array beginning at the address *base* and comprising *num* elements, each of size *width* bytes. The argument *key* points to the value being sought.

The *lsearch* function needs a routine that it can call or compare a pair of elements from the array. It should find the address of such a routine in the argument *compare*. You should write this routine to accept arguments *elem1* and *elem2*, each a pointer to an element in the array. The *lsearch* function calls this routine with the address of two array elements as arguments. The routine compares the elements and returns a zero if the elements are identical. Otherwise, the routine returns a nonzero value.

RETURNS The *lsearch* function returns a pointer to the first occurrence of the value *key* in the array. If the value is not found, *lsearch* adds the element at the end of the array, updates the value in *num*, and returns a pointer to the newly added item. If you don't want to add missing items to the array, use *lfind* instead.

SEE ALSO `lfind` *To perform a linear search without adding element to array*

`bsearch` *To perform a binary search of a sorted array*

EXAMPLE Write a program using *lsearch* to search in a small table of C strings for an entry beginning with a keyword entered on the command line. When the entry is not found, *lsearch* inserts the entry into the array and updates the element count. You can verify this by providing a keyword you know is not in the table.

```
#include <stdio.h>
#include <string.h>
#include <search.h>
int mycompare(void *, void *);
char *our_table[20] =
{
        "Microsoft C 6.0",
        "QuickC 2.5",
        "Turbo C 2.0",
        NULL
};
```

```
main(int argc, char **argv)
{
    unsigned int i, count, oldcount;
    char **p_table, **result;
    if(argc < 2)
    {
        printf("Usage: %s <KEYWORD>\n", argv[0]);
        exit(0);
    }
/* Find length of our table  and print it   */
    printf("==== Our table contains ====\n");
    for(count = 0, p_table = our_table;
        *p_table != NULL;
        p_table++, count++) printf("%s\n", *p_table);
    oldcount = count;
/* Search for the PATH variable in the environment   */
    result = (char **) lsearch((char *)&argv[1],
                               (char *)our_table,
                               &count,
                               sizeof(char *),
                               mycompare);
    if(count == oldcount)
    {
        printf("\nFound %s in\n%s\n", argv[1], *result);
    }
    else
    {
        printf("\n%s was added to table\n", argv[1]);
/* Print table again */

        printf("==== Now table contains ====\n");
        for(i=0; i<count; i++)
            printf("%s\n", our_table[i]);
    }
}
/*-------------------------------------------------*/
int mycompare(char **arg1, char **arg2)
{
/* Compare two strings up to the length of the key    */
    return(strncmp(*arg1, *arg2, strlen(*arg1)));
}
```

COMPATIBILITY **qsort**

MSC 3	MSC 4	MSC 5	MSC 6	QC1	QC2	QC2.5	TC1	TC1.5	TC2	TC++	ANSI	UNIX V	XNX	OS2	DOS
▲	▲	▲	▲	▲	▲	▲	▲	▲	▲	▲	▲	▲	▲	▲	▲

PURPOSE Use *qsort* to sort an array having a given number of elements, each a fixed number of bytes long.

SYNTAX

```
void qsort(void *base, size_t num, size_t width,
           int (*compare)(const void *elem1, const void *elem2));
```

`const void *base;` *Pointer to beginning of array being sorted*

`size_t num;` *Number of elements in array*

`size_t width;` *Size of each element in bytes*

`int (*compare)(const void *elem1, const void *elem2);`
Pointer to a function that compares two elements, elem1 *and* elem2*, each of type* const void *

EXAMPLE CALL

```
int compare(const void *, const void *);
qsort((void *) envp, (size_t)count,
      (size_t)sizeof(char *), compare);
```

INCLUDES `#include <search.h>` *For function declaration and definition of* size_t

or

`#include <stdlib.h>` *For function declaration and definition of* size_t *and for ANSI compatibility*

DESCRIPTION The *qsort* function uses the *quicksort* algorithm (see the tutorial section) to sort an array beginning at the address *base* and comprising *num* elements, each of size *width* bytes.

During the sort, *qsort* compares pairs of elements from the array by calling a routine whose address you provide in the argument *compare.* This function should accept arguments *elem1* and *elem2*, each a pointer to an element in the array. The *qsort* function calls this routine using the address of two array elements as arguments. Your routine should compare the two elements and return one of the values shown in the table (for strings, "greater than" and "less than" usually refer to alphabetic order):

Return Value	To Indicate
Negative	First element is less than the second one.
Zero	The two elements are identical to each other.
Positive	First element is greater than the second one.

On the basis of these values, the array is sorted in ascending order of element values, but you can reverse the order by changing the return value of the greater than and less than tests in the function that compares elements from the array.

SEE ALSO `find, lsearch` *To perform a linear search*

`bsearch` *To perform a binary search on a sorted array*

EXAMPLE Illustrate the use of *qsort* by sorting the environment table (an array of strings with a NULL string at the end) that is the third argument in the *main* function with Microsoft C under MS-DOS.

```
#include <stdio.h>
#include <string.h>
#include <search.h>
int mycompare(const void *, const void *);
main(int argc, char **argv, char **envp)
{
    unsigned int i, count;
    char **p_table, **result;
/* Find length of environment table and print it     */
    printf("==== Unsorted environment table ====\n");
    for(count = 0, p_table = envp;
        *p_table != NULL;
        p_table++, count++) printf("%s\n", *p_table);
/* Sort the environment table using "qsort"          */
    qsort((void *) envp, (size_t)count,
          (size_t)sizeof(char *), mycompare);
/* Print sorted environment table                    */
    printf("===== Sorted environment table =====\n");
    for(i = 0, p_table = envp; i < count; i++)
    {
        printf("%s\n", *p_table);
        p_table++;
    }
```

```
}
/*--------------------------------------------------------*/
int mycompare(char **arg1, char **arg2)
{
/* Compare two strings up to the length of the key    */
    return(strncmp(*arg1, *arg2, strlen(*arg1)));
}
```

Chapter 12 Time and Locale Routines

Introduction

Time is of the essence in a computer. The processor executes instructions at a steady rate, once every clock tick—and the clock ticks very fast, indeed. One million ticks per second translates to 1 megahertz (MHz). The MHz rate is sometimes called the "clock rate" and the clock rate for PCs has climbed steadily from 4 MHz in the early 1980s to 33 MHz by the beginning of the 1990s. Rates of 50 and 60 MHz are on the horizon.

Time, in hours, minutes, and seconds, is also important and is used by the operating system (such as MS-DOS, OS/2, or UNIX) for a variety of tasks. One example is the date and time *stamp* on each file in the system, used to record when a file was created and when it was last modified. You see this information when you list the directory with a DIR command (*ls –al* in UNIX) at the operating system prompt.

The international use of PCs has increased within the last decade. Time, date, currency, and other formats vary from nation to nation, and Microsoft C 6.0 has introduced the *locale*, a data structure that C programs can use to set up the appropriate formats for a particular country. This chapter covers the various time functions, and also suggests how to go about internationalizing your programs.

Your C programs may use the date and time information as well. If, for example, you develop a graphical user interface and you wish to display current date and time in a corner of the screen, the Microsoft C library includes routines for just this kind of task. In fact, it contains many different routines, giving you a choice of getting the date and time information in a variety of formats, each suitable for a specific job.

Concepts: Time in MS-DOS Systems

The 8086 microprocessor uses a *system clock* which ticks several million times a second to execute its instructions. The hardware requires this fast clock, but humans prefer a slower pace. So the PC provides circuitry to generate an interrupt at the rate of 18.2 times a second and includes code in the ROM BIOS (see the tutorial in Chapter 16) to handle these interrupts. The interrupt handler updates a count of such interrupts since the PC was last turned on. In the early days of the IBM PC, if you knew the time when the PC was turned on, these tick counts could be used to compute the current time. This is why MS-DOS always asks for the date and time when you power up your PC. Now, however, most PCs have a "clock/calendar" card or, in the case of the PC-AT and PS/2, a built-in "real-time clock." These are similar to digital clocks and they can keep running even when your PC is off because they use a battery as a backup power supply. The PC-AT and PS/2 get the system date and time at power-up from the real-time clock, so the user is not asked for it by MS-DOS.

THE CLOCK DRIVER

MS-DOS uses device drivers to communicate with peripheral devices and it uses a special driver, identified by a particular bit in the attribute word in the driver's header, to get or set the date and the time. As shown in Figure 12-1, this CLOCK driver, maintains the current time and date as a 6-byte sequence. The time is expressed in hours, minutes, seconds, and hundredths of seconds and the date is expressed as the number of days elapsed since January 1, 1980. In fact, none of the time routines understands any date prior to January 1, 1980, since that's when time began for MS-DOS. The CLOCK driver marks directory entries with date and time stamps and provides date and time services to application programs (via DOS functions numbered 2Ah through 2Dh). The fact that MS-DOS uses a driver for those functions made it easy to add a clock/calendar board to the original PC. You just popped the board into your system and loaded the CLOCK driver by placing a statement like *DEVICE=<path name of driver>* in your CONFIG.SYS file.

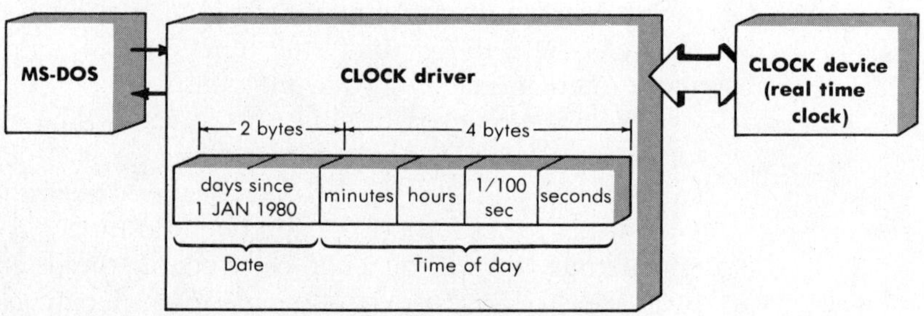

Figure 12-1. ***Time in MS-DOS***

TIME IN UNIX AND IN MICROSOFT C

You need not worry about the CLOCK driver when using the time functions in the Microsoft C library, but you do need to know how time is maintained in UNIX systems. This is because Microsoft C has maintained a high degree of compatibility with UNIX, helping to ensure portability.

In UNIX, and in Microsoft C, the date and the time are expressed jointly by the number of seconds elapsed since 00:00:00 hours Greenwich Mean Time (GMT) on January 1, 1970. This is a more universal representation than in MS-DOS because it uses the same reference (GMT) at any location in the world. How is this universal time derived from the local time kept by MS-DOS? Here is the scheme used by Microsoft C.

The TZ Environment Variable

An environment variable (see Chapter 3) named TZ defines the time zone (for example, PST, MST, EST), the difference between the local time and GMT in hours, and whether daylight saving time is honored. You can use the DOS command SET to define the environment variable TZ. For a PC in the Eastern Standard Time with daylight saving honored, for example, the definition of TZ will be *TZ=EST5EDT* because there is a difference of 5 hours between EST and GMT. If TZ is not defined, a default of *TZ=PST8PDT* is assumed.

Global Variables: *daylight, timezone,* and *tzname*

Three global variables store time zone information that is used by several time functions for their operation. The library function *tzset* sets these variables from the setting of the environment variable TZ.

The variable *daylight* is an integer that contains either a 1 or a 0 depending on whether the daylight saving is honored in this time zone. The long integer variable *timezone* contains the number of seconds to be added to the local time to get GMT when both are expressed as seconds elapsed since 00:00:00 hour, January 1, 1970. The *tzname* variable is an array of two strings, the first containing the name of the time zone and the second, the corresponding daylight-saving time zone (for example, EST and EDT).

Conversion from Local Time to GMT

Figure 12-2 illustrates the conversion of local time from MS-DOS to the format used in Microsoft C. The date and time from MS-DOS are converted to seconds elapsed since the 00:00:00 hour, January 1, 1970, and the value of *timezone* is added to this number. If daylight savings is honored and on at that time, the value is further modified. The result is what the function *time* returns: the current date and time expressed as seconds elapsed since 00:00:00 hours GMT, 1970.

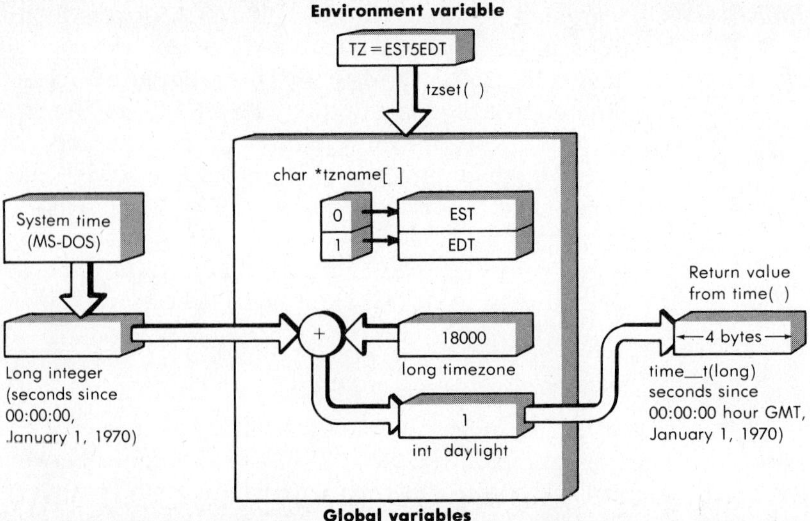

Figure 12-2. ***Time in Microsoft C***

TIME IN MANY FORMS The main function of the time routines is to get the current date and time in various formats and to convert from one format to another. A list of the functions is given in Table 12-1 and the functions are classified by task in Table 12-2.

Table 12-1. ***Time Routines***

Routine	Description
asctime	Converts time from a structure of type *tm* to a string.
clock	Returns the elapsed processor time in number of ticks.
ctime	Converts time from a value of type *time_t* to a string.
difftime	Computes the difference of two values of type *time_t*.
ftime	Returns the current time in a structure of type *timeb*.
gmtime	Converts time from a value of type *time_t* to a structure of type *tm* that corresponds to GMT.
localeconv	Gets detailed information on locale settings. Introduced in Microsoft C 6.0.
localtime	Converts time from a value of type *time_t* to a structure of type *tm* that corresponds to the local time.
mktime	Converts the local time from a structure of type *tm* to a value of type *time_t*.
setlocale	Sets categories specified for a certain location.
strcoll	Compares two strings for locale-specific collating sequences.
_strdate	Returns the current date as an eight-character string of the form *11/26/87*.
strftime	Copies text into a string related to date and time values from a *tm* structure and specified by format. Introduced in Microsoft C 6.0.
_strtime	Returns the current time as an eight-character string of the form *17:09:35*.

Table 12-1. *(cont.)*

Routine	Description
strxfrm	Transforms the string pointed to by *string2* into a new form, based on locale-specific information and stores the result in *string1*. Introduced in Microsoft C 6.0.
time	Returns the seconds elapsed since 00:00:00 hour, GMT, January 1, 1970, as a value of type *time_t*.
tzset	Assigns values to the global variables *timezone, daylight,* and *tzname* based on the time zone specified in the environment variable *TZ*.
utime	Sets the "last modified" time stamp of a file to which you have write access.

Table 12-2. *Time Routines by Task*

Task	Routines
Get current date and time.	ftime, _strdate, _strtime, time
Convert time from one form to another.	asctime, ctime, gmtime, localtime, mktime
Compute elapsed time.	clock, difftime
Set file modification time.	utime
Load environment variable setting into internal variables.	tzset
Internationalization functions.	localeconv, setlocale, strcoll, strftime, strxfrm

Figure 12-3 depicts the different formats of date and time and conversion among them. The basic function *time* returns a value of type *time_t*, which is defined to be a long integer in the *time.h* header file. This long integer value is converted to a structure named *tm* (defined in the *time.h* header file) by the *gmtime* and *localtime* routines. The *gmtime* function sets all fields in the *tm* structure to correspond to GMT while *localtime* sets them to the local time. The *mktime* function converts time back from structure *tm* to a value of type *time_t*.

A different structure, *timeb*, defined in the file *sys\timeb.h*, is used by the *ftime* function to return the current date and time. The field *time* in the *timeb* structure is identical to the value returned by the *time* function.

Printing Date and Time

The *asctime* function converts the value in a structure of type *tm* to a C string that you can print. The *ctime* function converts the output of *time* directly to a string. The functions *_strdate* and *_strtime* return in printable strings the date and the time, respectively.

ELAPSED TIME Sometimes you have to compute the time elapsed between two events. The *difftime* function returns the difference of two values of type *time_t* in

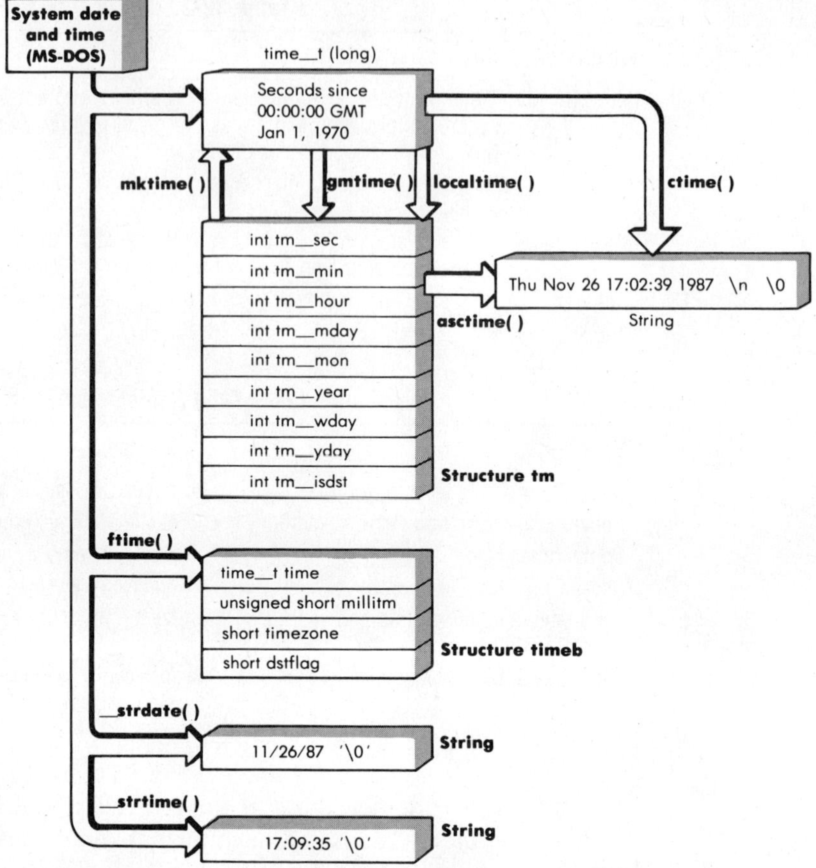

Figure 12-3. ***Conversion among different forms of date and time***

seconds. The *clock* function returns the number of *clock ticks* used by the process so far. The number of ticks per second is defined in the constant CLK_TCK (in file *time.h*) to be 1,000 (see the example program in the *clock* reference page). Although this implies an accuracy of a millisecond, it is misleading for the PC because the actual updating of the clock happens only 18.2 times a second or approximately once every 55 milliseconds.

Internationalizing

There are five functions that help you prepare software for international markets: *localeconv, setlocale, strcoll, strftime,* and *strxfrm.* The purpose of the internationalizing functions is to allow you to make your programs more portable—but not portable in the sense in which it is typically used in the computer business. Portability is generally defined as being able to move from one platform to another, although in this section it can also mean moving from one country (and that country's customs and practices) to another. (An alternative term for this process is "localization.") The tutorial briefly covers the *generic* characteristics of these functions, followed by a more detailed presentation in the reference pages.

The file *locale.h* defines many of the characteristics of the so-called internationalization functions.

LOCALE CATEGORIES

The *locale.h* file defines eight manifest constants for use by the five internationalization functions: *LC_ALL, LC_COLLATE, LC_CTYPE, LC_MAX, LC_MIN, LC_MONETARY, LC_NUMERIC,* and *LC_TIME.* They are known collectively as *locale categories* and work with the *localeconv, setlocale, strcoll, strftime,* and *strxfrm* functions.

These constants are used by the localization routines to specify which portion of a program's locale information will be used. "Locale" refers to the locality or nation for which various aspects of your program may be customized. The formatting of dates or the display format for monetary values are the primary focus of the current localization routines.

The *LC_ALL* constant affects all locale-specific behavior in all categories. The *LC_COLLATE* constant modifies the behavior of the *strcoll* and *strxfrm* functions by affecting the collating sequence, or the order in which characters are sorted. The character-handling functions (except *isdigit* and *isxdigit*) are modified by *LC_CTYPE.* The *LC_MAX* value is the same as *LC_TIME* and the *LC_MIN* value is the same as *LC_ALL.* Monetary formatting information returned by the *localeconv* function is in the purview of *LC_MONETARY.*

The last two constants are *LC_NUMERIC* and *LC_TIME.* The *LC_NUMERIC* value is the decimal-point character for the various formatted output routines such as *printf* for the data conversion routines and for the nonmonetary formatting information returned by the *localeconv* routine. *LC_TIME* helps modify the behavior of the *strftime* function.

Perhaps the most important of the definitions in *locale.h* is the *lconv* structure. It is presented below:

```
struct lconv
{
   char * decimal_point;      /* Nonmonetary dec-point character */
   char * thousands_sep;      /* Nonmonetary digit-group separator */
   char * grouping;           /* Nonmonetary digit-group size */
   char * int_curr_symbol;    /* International currency symbol */
   char * currency_symbol;    /* Current locale currency symbol */
   char * mon_decimal_point; /* Monetary decimal-point character */
   char * mon_thousands_sep; /* Monetary digit-group separator */
```

```
    char * mon_grouping;        /* Monetary digit-group size */
    char * positive_sign;       /* Non-negative monetary sign */
    char * negative_sign;       /* Negative monetary sign */
    char int_frac_digits;       /* Int'l monetary fract'l digits */
    char frac_digits;           /* Monetary fractional digits */
    char p_cs_precedes;         /* Non-negative currency-symbol
                                   placement */
    char p_sep_by_space;        /* Non-negative currency-symbol
                                   separator */
    char n_cs_precedes;         /* Negative currency-symbol placement */
    char n_sep_by_space;        /* Negative currency-symbol
                                   separator */
    char p_sign_posn;           /* Sign placement/nonneg monetary val */
    char n_sign_posn;           /* Sign placement/neg monetary value*/
};
```

Various values in the structure are broken out according to a set of rules discussed below.

Grouping and *mon_grouping* values are interpreted according to rules. (A group is, for example, three digits separated by commas in ordinary American numeric usage: for instance 1,000,500.) Three values serve as identifiers: *CHAR_MAX, 0,* and *n*. The *CHAR_MAX* value means that no further grouping is to be performed; a *0* means that the previous element is to be repeatedly used for the rest of the digits; and an *n* indicates that the integer value specified by *n* is the number of digits that make up the current group. The next element is subsequently examined to determine the size of the next group of digits before the current group.

The values for *int_curr_symbol* (international currency symbol) are identified in accordance with the following procedures: Characters *1, 2,* and *3* specify the alphabetic international currency symbol (as defined in the ISO 4217 Codes for the Representation of Currency and Funds standard). Character *4* (which immediately precedes the NULL character) is used to separate the international currency symbol from the monetary quantity.

The *p_sep_by_space* and *n_sep_by_space* values are processed as follows (*n_sep_by_space* logic is in parentheses): A *0* means that the currency symbol is separated from the monetary value by a space for a non-negative (negative) formatted monetary value. There is no space separation between the currency symbol and the value for a non-negative (negative) formatted monetary value if the value of this characteristic is set to a *1*.

The *p_sign_posn* and *n_sign_posn* values are interpreted according to the following logic: A value of *0* identifies that parentheses should surround the quantity and currency symbol. The sign string should precede the quantity and currency symbol if the value is *1*, and follow the quantity and currency symbol if the value evaluates to *2*. Value *3* means that the sign string immediately precedes the currency symbol, and a value of *4* means that the sign string immediately follows the currency symbol.

There are two values for *p_cs_precedes* and *n_cs_precedes*. With *n_cs_precedes* logic in parentheses, they are: *0*, which means that the currency symbol follows the value for a non-negative (negative) formatted monetary value, and *1*, which states that the currency symbol precedes the value for a non-negative (negative) formatted monetary value.

Cautions

- ▶ If the TZ environment variable is not set on your system, the GMT will be computed wrongly. Since everything in MS-DOS is done in local time, this is important only if you need an accurate universal time. The default settings of TZ imply that local time is Pacific Standard Time.
- ▶ The functions *gmtime* and *localtime* use a single structure of type *tm* to store the time. Each call to either function overwrites the result of the previous call.
- ▶ The *ctime* and *asctime* functions also use a single character string to store results. Thus any call to one overwrites the result of the previous call.

Further Reading

The time functions have not received much attention in books about C programming on the PC. One exception is Hansen's book[1], which includes a detailed discussion of the time routines in the Microsoft C 4.0 library. Consult Duncan's book[2] on MS-DOS for further information on the CLOCK driver, and on drivers in general, in MS-DOS.

1. Augie Hansen, *Proficient C*, Microsoft Press, Redmond, WA, 1987, 492 pages.
2. Ray Duncan, *Advanced MS-DOS*, 2d Ed., Microsoft Press, Redmond, WA, 1988, 669 pages.

asctime

COMPATIBILITY

MSC 3	MSC 4	MSC 5	MSC 6	QC1	QC2	QC2.5	TC1	TC1.5	TC2	TC++	ANSI	UNIX V	XNX	OS2	DOS
▲	▲	▲	▲	▲	▲	▲	▲	▲	▲	▲	▲	▲	▲	▲	▲

PURPOSE Use *asctime* to convert a time stored in a structure of type *tm* to a character string.

SYNTAX

```
char *asctime(const struct tm *time);
```

`const struct tm *time;` *Pointer to a structure containing time to be converted to a string*

EXAMPLE CALL

```
printf("The time is %s\n", asctime(&timedata));
```

INCLUDES `#include <time.h>` *For function declaration and definition of structure* tm

DESCRIPTION The *asctime* function converts to a character string the value of a time stored in the structure of type *tm* at the address *time*. The value is set up by an earlier call to *gmtime* or *localtime*, both of which accept a long integer value for the time, prepare the fields of a structure of type *tm*, and return a pointer to that structure. The structure *tm* is defined in *time.h* as follows:

```
struct tm
{
    int tm_sec;        /* seconds after the minute - [0,59] */
    int tm_min;        /* minutes after the hour - [0,59]   */
    int tm_hour;       /* hours since midnight - [0,23]     */
    int tm_mday;       /* day of the month - [1,31]         */
    int tm_mon;        /* months since January - [0,11]     */
    int tm_year;       /* years since 1900                  */
    int tm_wday;       /* days since Sunday - [0,6]         */
    int tm_yday;       /* days since January 1 - [0,365]    */
    int tm_isdst;      /* daylight savings time flag        */
};
```

The string prepared by *asctime* is 26 characters long, counting the null character at the end, and has the form:

```
Thu Nov 26 17:02:39 1990\n\0
```

As the definition shows, a 24-hour clock is used for the time.

RETURNS The *asctime* function returns a pointer to the data area where the string is stored.

COMMENTS To prepare the time for printing, the *asctime* and *ctime* functions use a single static string so it will be destroyed by subsequent calls to these routines.

SEE ALSO `ctime, gmtime, localtime, time`

EXAMPLE Use *asctime* to get and display the local time.

```
#include <stdio.h>
#include <time.h>
main()
{
    struct tm *curtime;
    time_t bintime;
/* Get time in seconds since 00:00:00 GMT, 1/1/70 */
    time(&bintime);
/* Convert time to local time (default is PST)    */
    curtime = localtime(&bintime);
/* Use asctime to print the date and time         */
    printf("Current time: %s\n", asctime(curtime));
}
```

COMPATIBILITY

clock

MSC 3	MSC 4	MSC 5	MSC 6	QC1	QC2	QC2.5	TC1	TC1.5	TC2	TC++	ANSI	UNIX V	XNX	OS2	DOS
		▲	▲	▲	▲	▲	▲	▲	▲	▲	▲			▲	▲

PURPOSE Use *clock* to obtain in number of ticks the amount of processor time used by the current process.

SYNTAX `clock_t clock(void);`

EXAMPLE CALL `ticks_now = clock();`

INCLUDES `#include <time.h>` *For function declaration and definition of type* clock_t

DESCRIPTION The *clock* function tells how much processor time has been used by the calling process. The value is expressed as the number of ticks. The constant CLK_TCK, defined in *time.h*, is the number of ticks per second, so the value returned by *clock* should be divided by CLK_TCK to get the elapsed processor time in seconds.

RETURNS If processor time is available to *clock*, it returns the current time in ticks, cast as a value of type *clock_t* which is defined in *time.h*. Otherwise, it returns the value −1, cast as *clock_t*.

SEE ALSO

`difftime` *To get the difference of two time values*

`time` *To get the current time as a long integer*

EXAMPLE Use *clock* to determine and display the processor time used in a program that performs a computational loop 10,000 times.

```
#include <stdio.h>
#include <time.h>
main()
{
    unsigned i, tused, count=10000;
    double a, b, c, d;
    clock_t ticksnow;
    for(i=0; i<count; i++)
    {
        a = (double)(i-1);
        b = (double)(i+1);
        c = (double)(i*i);
        d = a*b - c;
    }
/* Get current clock ticks by calling "clock"     */
    if((ticksnow = clock()) == (clock_t)-1)
    {
        printf("Processor time not available!\n");
        abort();
    }
/* Convert processor time to seconds. Use CLK_TCK  */
    tused = (unsigned)ticksnow/CLK_TCK;
    printf("10,000 loops ran for %u seconds\n", tused);
}
```

COMPATIBILITY **ctime**

MSC 3	MSC 4	MSC 5	MSC 6	QC1	QC2	QC2.5	TC1	TC1.5	TC2	TC++	ANSI	UNIX V	XNX	OS2	DOS
▲	▲	▲	▲	▲	▲	▲	▲	▲	▲	▲	▲	▲	▲	▲	▲

PURPOSE Use *ctime* to convert to a character string a time stored as a value of type *time_t*.

SYNTAX

```
char *ctime(const time_t *time);
```

`const time_t *time;` *Pointer to variable containing time to be converted to a string*

EXAMPLE CALL

```
printf("Current time = %s\n", ctime(&bintime));
```

INCLUDES `#include <time.h>` *For function declaration and definition of* time_t

DESCRIPTION The *ctime* function converts to a character string the value of time stored in the variable of type *time_t* at the address *time*. This value is obtained by an earlier call to the function *time*, which returns the number of seconds elapsed since 00:00:00 hours GMT, January 1, 1970. The string prepared by *ctime* is 26 characters long, counting the null character at the end, and has the form:

```
Thu Nov 26 17:02:39 1990\n\0
```

As the preceding example shows, a 24-hour clock is used for the time.

RETURNS As long as the value in *time* represents a date on or after the year 1980, *ctime* returns a pointer to the data area where the character string is stored. If the value in *time* represents a date prior to 1980, *ctime* returns a NULL in Microsoft C 5.0 and later versions. Under similar circumstances in version 4.0, *ctime* returns the date and time of January 1, 1980, and 00:00:00 hours.

COMMENTS To prepare the time for printing, the *ctime* and *asctime* functions use a single static string so it will be destroyed by subsequent calls to these routines.

SEE ALSO

`asctime` *To convert time from a* tm *structure into a character string*

`time` *To get the current time as a long integer value*

EXAMPLE Use *ctime* to prepare a string version of the value returned by a call to *time* and print this string.

```
#include <stdio.h>
#include <time.h>
main()
{
    time_t bintime;
/* Get time in seconds since 00:00:00 GMT, 1/1/70 */
    time(&bintime);
/* Use ctime to print the date and time           */
    printf("Current time: %s\n", ctime(&bintime));
}
```

difftime

COMPATIBILITY

MSC 3	MSC 4	MSC 5	MSC 6	QC1	QC2	QC2.5	TC1	TC1.5	TC2	TC++	ANSI	UNIX V	XNX	OS2	DOS
	▲	▲	▲	▲	▲	▲	▲	▲	▲	▲	▲	▲	▲	▲	▲

PURPOSE Use *difftime* to obtain the difference of two time values, each of type *time_t*.

SYNTAX `double difftime(time_t time2, time_t time1);`

`time_t time2;` *Value of time from which* time1 *will be subtracted*

`time_t time1;` *Value of time to be subtracted from* time2

EXAMPLE CALL `seconds_used = difftime(oldtime, newtime);`

INCLUDES `#include <time.h>` *For function declaration definition of* time_t

DESCRIPTION The *difftime* function computes the difference between time values *time2* and *time1*. These times are obtained by calling *time*, which returns the current time in seconds since 00:00:00 hours GMT, January 1, 1970. This function is useful for computing elapsed time between arbitrary events. Use *clock* for determining how long the current program has been running.

RETURNS The *difftime* function returns the elapsed time, *time2 – time1*, in seconds as a double-precision number.

SEE ALSO `time` *To get current time in seconds since 00:00:00 hours GMT, January 1, 1970*

EXAMPLE Use *difftime* to determine the time it takes to perform a computational loop a specified number of times.

```
#include <stdio.h>
#include <time.h>
main()
{
    unsigned long i, count;
    double a, b, c, d, tused, tperstep;
    time_t tstart, tstop;
/* Ask user number of times "multiply" to be done */
    printf("Enter number of times loop is run:");
    scanf(" %lu", &count);
/* Get current time by calling "time"            */
    time(&tstart);
    for(i=0; i<count; i++)
    {
        a = (double)(i-1);
        b = (double)(i+1);
        c = (double)(i*i);
        d = a*b - c;
    }
/* Get time again and print time used.           */
    time(&tstop);
    tused = difftime(tstop, tstart);  /* in sec   */
    tperstep = tused/(double)count;
    printf("Total time = %f seconds\n\
Time per iteration: %f milliseconds\n", tused,
           tperstep*1000.0);
}
```

ftime

COMPATIBILITY

MSC 3	MSC 4	MSC 5	MSC 6	QC1	QC2	QC2.5	TC1	TC1.5	TC2	TC++	ANSI	UNIX V	XNX	OS2	DOS
▲	▲	▲	▲	▲	▲	▲		▲	▲	▲		▲	▲	▲	▲

PURPOSE Use *ftime* to get the current time and store it in a structure of type *timeb*.

SYNTAX `void ftime(struct timeb *timeptr);`

`struct timeb *timeptr;` *Pointer to structure of type* timeb *to which time is returned*

EXAMPLE CALL `ftime(&time_buffer);`

INCLUDES `#include <sys\timeb.h>` *For function declaration and definition of structure* timeb

DESCRIPTION The *ftime* function gets the current time and stores it in a structure of type *timeb* that you allocate and whose address you provide in the argument *timeptr*. The fields in the structure at *timeptr* are set to appropriate values by *ftime*. The *timeb* structure is defined in the include file *sys\timeb.h* as:

```
struct timeb
{
    time_t         time;     /* Time in seconds since 00:00:00
                                GMT, January 1, 1970          */
    unsigned short millitm;  /* Fraction of a second in milli-
                                seconds                       */
    short          timezone; /* Difference in minutes moving
                                westward, between GMT and local
                                time                          */
    short          dstflag;  /* Nonzero if daylight saving is
                                in effect in the local time zone*/
};
```

The *ftime* function uses the settings of the global variables *timezone* and *daylight* in setting the values of the fields *timezone* and *dstflag* in the *timeb* structure. These variables are set by calling *tzset* and using the environment variable TZ. (See the reference page on *tzset* for more details.)

SEE ALSO

`time`	*To get current time as a long integer value*
`tzset`	*To set environment variables that indicate time zones and enable daylight saving hours*

EXAMPLE Use *ftime* to get the current time. Use *ctime* to display the *time* field of the *timeb* structure.

```
#include <stdio.h>
#include <sys\types.h>
#include <sys\timeb.h>
#include <time.h>
main()
{
    struct timeb time_buffer;
    char *date_time;
/* Use "ftime" to get current time into time_buffer */
    ftime(&time_buffer);
/* Convert "time" field to a string and print it    */
    printf("Time = %s", ctime(&time_buffer.time));
}
```

COMPATIBILITY

gmtime

MSC 3	MSC 4	MSC 5	MSC 6	QC1	QC2	QC2.5	TC1	TC1.5	TC2	TC++	ANSI	UNIX V	XNX	OS2	DOS
▲	▲	▲	▲	▲	▲	▲	▲	▲	▲	▲	▲	▲	▲	▲	▲

PURPOSE Use *gmtime* to separate a time value of type *time_t* into fields of a structure of type *tm*. This results in values that represent the GMT relative to the time zone specified in the environment variable TZ.

SYNTAX

```
struct tm *gmtime(const time_t *time);
```

`const time_t *time;` *Pointer to stored time in seconds elapsed since 00:00:00 GMT, January 1, 1970*

EXAMPLE CALL

```
t_gmt = gmtime(&bintime);
```

INCLUDES `#include <time.h>` *For function declaration and definition of structure* tm *and data type* time_t

DESCRIPTION The *gmtime* function breaks down a time value, stored at the location *time*, to year, month, day, hour, minutes, seconds, and several other fields that it saves in a structure of type *tm*. The value at *time* is the number of seconds elapsed from 00:00:00 hours GMT, January 1, 1970, to a time obtained by calling the function *time*. The structure *tm* is defined in *time.h* as follows:

```
struct tm
{
    int tm_sec;       /* seconds after the minute - [0,59] */
    int tm_min;       /* minutes after the hour - [0,59]   */
    int tm_hour;      /* hours since midnight - [0,23]     */
    int tm_mday;      /* day of the month - [1,31]         */
    int tm_mon;       /* months since January - [0,11]     */
    int tm_year;      /* years since 1900                  */
    int tm_wday;      /* days since Sunday - [0,6]         */
    int tm_yday;      /* days since January 1 - [0,365]    */
    int tm_isdst;     /* daylight savings time flag, nonzero
                         if enabled                        */
};
```

The fields set up by *gmtime* correspond to GMT as dictated by the environment variable TZ, which indicates the time zone and the daylight saving zone for use in converting from local time to GMT. TZ must be set to a three-letter time zone name (such as PST, EST, etc.), followed by a signed number giving the difference between GMT and the local time zone (a positive sign can be omitted). An optional three-letter daylight saving zone name can be added to the setting. The *gmtime* function uses this information to convert the local time to GMT based on the time zone and the daylight saving season. If TZ is not defined, a default setting of PST8PDT is used. Note that TZ is not a part of the proposed ANSI definition; it is a Microsoft extension.

RETURNS Provided the value in *time* does not represent a date prior to 1980, *gmtime* returns a pointer to the structure where the converted time is stored. Otherwise, in Microsoft C 5.0 and later, it returns a NULL and in version 4.0, it returns the date and time: January 1, 1980, 00:00:00 hours.

COMMENTS MS-DOS does not understand dates prior to 1980, so time values provided to the library routines *gmtime* and *localtime* must be later than 1980. Note that *gmtime* uses the static structure of type *tm* to return the result so each call to this routine destroys the result of the preceding call.

SEE ALSO

`asctime`	*To convert time from a structure of type* tm *into a character string*
`localtime`	*To convert from GMT to local time*
`time`	*To get current time in seconds elapsed since 00:00:00 hours GMT, January 1, 1970*

EXAMPLE Get the current time using *time*, convert it to GMT using *gmtime*, and display this latter time.

```
#include <stdio.h>
#include <time.h>
main()
{
    time_t tnow;
    struct tm *tmnow;
/* Get the time in seconds since 0 hrs GMT, 1/1/70  */
    time(&tnow);
/* Convert it to string showing Greenwich Mean Time */
    tmnow = gmtime(&tnow);
    printf("Greenwich Mean Time = %s\n",
            asctime(tmnow));
}
```

COMPATIBILITY

localeconv

MSC 3	MSC 4	MSC 5	MSC 6	QC1	QC2	QC2.5	TC1	TC1.5	TC2	TC++	ANSI	UNIX V	XNX	OS2	DOS
			▲			▲				▲	▲			▲	▲

PURPOSE Use the *localeconv* function to get detailed information on locale settings, or country-specific formats for numbers and currency.

SYNTAX

```
struct lconv *localeconv (void);
```

EXAMPLE CALL

```
localeconv ();
```

INCLUDES `#include <locale.h>` *For function declaration*

DESCRIPTION The *localeconv* function retrieves information about a specific locale from a structure of type *lconv*. This structure is defined in the *locale.h* file, and was discussed in the tutorial. Among the items identified by an *lconv* structure is the character used to separate groups of digits (American usage is a comma); the local currency symbol (the English use the pound sign); and a flag that explains which side of an amount gets a currency symbol.

COMMON USES This function is one of a group of ANSI-compatible routines that make it easier to "internationalize" your software. Others in the same subcategory include *setlocale, strcoll, strftime,* and *strxfrm.* Their use reduces the burden of making your programs work in countries where particulars such as currency symbols and decimal placements differ from American practice.

RETURNS The *localeconv* function returns a pointer to a structure of type *lconv.* You can overwrite the values in this structure by calling the *setlocale* routine and passing category values o*f LC_ALL (1), LC_MONETARY (3),* or *LC_NUMERIC (4).*

SEE ALSO `setlocale` *To select national formats*

EXAMPLE See the entry for *setlocale* for an example program that also uses *localeconv.*

localtime

COMPATIBILITY

MSC 3	MSC 4	MSC 5	MSC 6	QC1	QC2	QC2.5	TC1	TC1.5	TC2	TC++	ANSI	UNIX V	XNX	OS2	DOS
▲	▲	▲	▲	▲	▲	▲	▲	▲	▲	▲	▲	▲	▲	▲	▲

PURPOSE Use *localtime* to separate a time value of type *time_t* into various fields of a structure of type *tm*.

SYNTAX

```
struct tm *localtime(const time_t *time);
```

`const time_t *time;` *Pointer to stored time in seconds elapsed since 00:00:00 hours GMT, January 1, 1970*

EXAMPLE CALL

```
t_local = localtime(&bintime);
```

INCLUDES `#include <time.h>` *For function declaration and definition of structure* tm *and data type* time_t

DESCRIPTION The *localtime* function breaks down the time value, stored at the location *time*, to year, month, day, hour, minutes, seconds, and several other fields that it saves in a structure of type *tm*. The fields set up by *localtime* correspond to local time. The value at *time* is the number of seconds elapsed from 00:00:00 hours GMT, January 1, 1970, to a time obtained by calling the function *time*. The structure *tm* is defined in *time.h* as shown in the reference pages on *gmtime*.

RETURNS Provided the value in *time* does not represent a date prior to 1980, *localtime* returns a pointer to the structure where the converted time is stored. Otherwise, in Microsoft C 5.0 and later, it returns a NULL and in version 4.0, it returns the date and time: January 1, 1980, 00:00:00 hours.

COMMENTS MS-DOS does not understand dates prior to 1980, so time values provided to the library routines *localtime* and *gmtime* must be later than 1980. Note that *localtime* uses the static structure of type *tm* to return the result so each call to this routine destroys the result of the preceding call.

SEE ALSO

`asctime` *To convert time from a structure of type* tm *into a character string*

`gmtime` *To convert from local time to GMT*

`time` *To get current time in seconds elapsed since 00:00:00 hours GMT, January 1, 1970*

EXAMPLE Use *time* to get the current time. Convert it to a detailed representation of the local date and time by using *localtime*. Use *asctime* to print the date and time.

```
#include <stdio.h>
#include <time.h>
main()
{
    time_t tnow;
    struct tm *tmnow;
/* Get the time in seconds since 0 hrs GMT, 1/1/70  */
    time(&tnow);
/* Convert it to string showing local time. Use the
 * environment variable TZ and the function "tzset"
 * to set the timezone appropriately.
 * Default time is PST.
 */
    tmnow = localtime(&tnow);
    printf("Local Time = %s\n", asctime(tmnow));
}
```

COMPATIBILITY

mktime

MSC 3	MSC 4	MSC 5	MSC 6	QC1	QC2	QC2.5	TC1	TC1.5	TC2	TC++	ANSI	UNIX V	XNX	OS2	DOS
		▲	▲	▲	▲	▲					▲			▲	▲

PURPOSE Use *mktime* to convert the local time from a structure of type *tm* into a value of type *time_t*.

SYNTAX `time_t mktime(struct tm *timeptr);`

`struct tm *timeptr;` *Pointer to structure of type* tm *where local time is stored*

EXAMPLE CALL `bintime = mktime(&timebuf);`

INCLUDES `#include <time.h>` *For function declaration and definition of structure* tm

DESCRIPTION The *mktime* function converts the local time currently at the address *timeptr* from the form of year, month, day, and so on, to the number of seconds elapsed since 00:00:00 hours GMT, January 1, 1970. This is the same format in which *time* returns the current time and is the format used in the argument to the functions *ctime*, *difftime*, and *localtime*.

Two fields in the structure of type *tm* are ignored by *mktime*: *tm_wday* and *tm_yday*, denoting the day of the week and day of the year, respectively. The *mktime* function sets the fields in the *tm* structure to appropriate values before returning.

RETURNS If successful, *mktime* returns the contents of *timeptr* as a value of type *time_t.* If the local time in *timeptr* cannot be handled by *mktime* (e.g., the date is prior to 1980), the return value will be a –1 cast to the type *time_t.*

SEE ALSO

`asctime` *To convert time from a structure of type* tm *into a character string*

`time` *To get current time in seconds elapsed since 00:00:00 hours GMT, January 1, 1970*

EXAMPLE Note that *mktime* adjusts if the fields in the *tm* data structure are not within a valid range. For instance, you could set the number of days since the first of the month to 45 and *mktime* would alter other fields (such as making it the next month) to bring all entries to valid ranges. This feature is useful for setting up a utility program that prints the date a specified number of days from today. Write a program that accepts as a command-line argument the number of days to look ahead.

```
#include <stdio.h>
#include <time.h>
main(int argc, char **argv)
{
    time_t    tresult, tnow;
    struct tm *tmnow;
    if(argc<2)
    {
        printf("Usage: %s <number of days>\n", argv[0]);
        exit(0);
    }
/* Get todays's date and convert it to a "tm" structure */
    time(&tnow);
    tmnow = localtime(&tnow);
/* Adjust the number of days */
    tmnow->tm_mday += atoi(argv[1]);
/* Now call "mktime" to set everything in tmnow */
    if((tresult = mktime(tmnow)) == (time_t)-1)
    {
        printf("mktime failed\n");
    }
    else
    {
        printf("%d days from now it'll be %s\n",
                  atoi(argv[1]), ctime(&tresult));
/*                atoi(argv[1]), asctime(tmnow)); */
    }
}
```

Time and Locale Routines

COMPATIBILITY **setlocale**

MSC 3	MSC 4	MSC 5	MSC 6	QC1	QC2	QC2.5	TC1	TC1.5	TC2	TC++	ANSI	UNIX V	XNX	OS2	DOS
			▲			▲				▲	▲			▲	▲

PURPOSE Use the *setlocale* function to set numeric, currency, and other formats specified for a certain location in a structure of type *lconv*.

SYNTAX

```
char *setlocale (int locale_ctgry, const char *new_locale);
```

`locale_ctgry`

`LC_ALL, LC_COLLATE, LC_TYPE, LC_MONETARY, LC_NUMERIC,`
`LC_TIME, NULL` *Categories of locale information*

`new_locale` *Pointer to a string that specifies the name of the locale; the only locale currently supported is* C.

EXAMPLE CALL

```
setlocale (LC_ALL, current_locale)
```

INCLUDES `#include <locale.h>` *For function declaration*

DESCRIPTION The *setlocale* function sets specified categories (by the *locale_ctgry* argument in the syntax example above) to the new locale specified by the *new_locale* argument. The term locale refers to a locality—typically a country—for which your program can be tailored. The *locale_ctgry* argument specifies which groups of functions are affected, and the *new_locale* argument identifies the location whose characteristics are being selected.

The *locale_ctgry* argument must be one of the following manifest constants, as defined in the *locale.h* file, and explained in the tutorial accompanying this chapter:

0 = *LC_ALL*	3 = *LC_MONETARY*
1 = *LC_COLLATE*	4 = *LC_NUMERIC*
2 = *LC_CTYPE*	5 = *LC_TIME*

The *new_locale* argument is a pointer to a string. The string identifies the name of the locale. If the *new_locale* string is empty, the locale defaults to the native environment as defined by the implementation. The minimal ANSI-conforming environment for C translation is specified with a locale value of *C*, and *C* is the only locale supported by Microsoft C 6.0.

If a NULL pointer is used for the *new_locale* argument, *setlocale* will return a pointer to the string associated with the category of the program's locale and will not change the locale setting of the program.

COMMON USES This function is one of a group of ANSI-compatible routines that make it easier to internationalize your software. Others in the same subcategory include *localeconv, strcoll, strftime,* and *strxfrm.* Their use reduces the burden of making your programs work in countries where particulars such as currency symbols and decimal placements differ from American practice.

RETURNS If valid arguments are given for the *new_locale* and the *locale_ctgry*, the *setlocale* routine returns a pointer to the string associated with the specified *locale_ctgry* for the new locale. If *locale_ctgry* or *new_locale* arguments are invalid, *setlocale* returns a NULL pointer, and the program's current locale settings are left unchanged.

The string pointer returned by *setlocale* can be referenced by subsequent calls to restore that part of the locale information of the program. Later calls to *setlocale* will cause the string to be overwritten.

SEE ALSO `localeconv` *To get national format information*

EXAMPLE The following program sets the current locale to *locale 3* (*C*) and gets formatting information. (Note that your results may differ.)

```
/*Note that the minimal locale currently in use */
/*has values for only a few of the structure members */

#include <locale.h>
#include <stdio.h>

void main (void)
{
     struct lconv locale_val;
     struct lconv *locale_ptr = &locale_val;
     setlocale (LC_ALL, "C");
     locale_ptr = localeconv();

     /* Display the locale structure */
     printf("Decimal point value: ");
     printf ("%s\n", locale_ptr->decimal_point);

     printf("Character used to separate thousands");
     printf ("%s\n", locale_ptr->thousands_sep);

     printf("Value grouping: ");
     printf ("%s\n", locale_ptr->grouping);

     printf("International currency symbol: ");
```

```
        printf ("%s\n", locale_ptr->int_curr_symbol);

        printf("Local currency symbol: ");
        printf ("%s\n", locale_ptr->currency_symbol);

        printf("Monetary decimal point symbol: ");
        printf ("%s\n", locale_ptr->mon_decimal_point);

        printf("Monetary thousands separator: ");
        printf ("%s\n, locale_ptr->mon_thousands_sep);

        printf("Monetary grouping separator: ");
        printf ("%s\n", locale_ptr->mon_grouping);

        printf("Positive sign: ");
        printf ("%s\n", locale_ptr->positive_sign);

        printf("Negative sign: ");
        printf ("%s\n", locale_ptr->negative_sign);

        printf("International fraction digits; ");
        printf ("%d\n", locale_ptr->int_frac_digits);

        printf("Local fraction digits: ");
        printf ("%d\n", locale_ptr->frac_digits);

        printf("Positive $ symbol precedes: ");
        printf ("%d\n", locale_ptr->p_cs_precedes);

        printf("Positive sign space separation: ");
        printf ("%d\n", locale_ptr->p_sep_by_space);

        printf("Negative $ symbol precedes: ");
        printf ("%d\n", locale_ptr->n_cs_precedes);

        printf("Negative sign space separation: ");
        printf ("%d\n", locale_ptr->n_sep_by_space);

        printf("Positive sign position: ");
        printf ("%d\n", locale_ptr->p_sign_posn);

        printf("Negative sign position: ");
        printf ("%d\n", locale_ptr->n_sign_posn);
}
```

setlocale

```
/****************** The results are:

[774]
[760]

  15284  8653  6003  -30013  -6140   5484   -32557      0  32750
 -32557   -53     0      -2      0      0        0     25      0

*************************************/
```

strcoll

COMPATIBILITY

MSC 3	MSC 4	MSC 5	MSC 6	QC1	QC2	QC2.5	TC1	TC1.5	TC2	TC++	ANSI	UNIX V	XNX	OS2	DOS
			▲			▲				▲	▲			▲	▲

PURPOSE Use the *strcoll* function to compare two strings for locale-specific collating sequences.

SYNTAX

```
int strcoll (const char *string1, const char *string2);
```

`string1, string2;` *Strings you wish to compare*

EXAMPLE CALL

```
if strcoll(string1, string2)
```

INCLUDES `#include <string.h>` *For function declaration*

DESCRIPTION The *strcoll* routine lexicographically compares *string1* with *string2* in the same manner as the *strcmp* function, but it differs from *strcmp* in that it uses locale information to build locale-specific collating sequences. This allows local usage to be honored without programs having to be altered.

The *strcoll* function compares two null-terminated strings. Currently, only the *C* locale is supported by Microsoft C 6.0, thus rendering *strcoll* and *strcmp* identical.

COMMON USES This function is one of a group of ANSI-compatible routines that make it easier to "internationalize" your software. Others in the same subcategory include *localeconv, setlocale, strftime,* and *strxfrm.* Their use reduces the burden of making your programs work in countries where particulars such as currency symbols and decimal placements differ from American practice.

RETURNS The *strcoll* function returns a value less than, equal to, or greater than 0, depending on whether the string pointed to by *string1* is less than, equal to, or greater than the string pointed to by *string2.* A value of < 0 means that *string1* is less than *string2*; a value of 0 means that the two strings are identical; and a return of > 0 means that *string1* is greater than *string2*.

COMMENTS Since Microsoft C 6.0 supports only the *C* locale, the *strcoll* and *strcmp* functions behave identically.

SEE ALSO

`strcmp` *To compare two strings, locale-independent*

`localeconv` *To get detailed locale information*

EXAMPLE See the entry for *strxfrm* for a program that also demonstrates *strcoll*.

_strdate

COMPATIBILITY

MSC 3	MSC 4	MSC 5	MSC 6	QC1	QC2	QC2.5	TC1	TC1.5	TC2	TC++	ANSI	UNIX V	XNX	OS2	DOS
		▲	▲	▲	▲	▲				▲				▲	▲

PURPOSE Use *_strdate* to obtain the current date as an eight-character string of the form *11/26/90*.

SYNTAX

```
char *_strdate(char *date);
```

`char *date;` *Current date in the form MM/DD/YY returned by* _strdate

EXAMPLE CALL

```
_strdate(date_buffer);
```

INCLUDES `#include <time.h>` *For function declaration*

DESCRIPTION The *_strdate* function gets the current date, formats it into an eight-character string of the form MM/DD/YY, and copies it into a nine-character buffer that you allocate and whose address you provide in the argument *date*. For example, November 26, 1990 is returned by *_strdate* as 11/26/90 with a null at the end.

RETURNS The *_strdate* function returns the argument *date*.

SEE ALSO

`ctime, time` *To get and convert date and time into a string*

`_strtime` *To get current time in a string*

EXAMPLE Use *_strdate* to convert today's date to a string and then print the string.

```
#include <stdio.h>
```

```
#include <time.h>
main()
{
    char date_buffer[9];
    _strdate(date_buffer);
    printf("Today is: %s\n", date_buffer);
}
```

strftime

COMPATIBILITY

MSC 3	MSC 4	MSC 5	MSC 6	QC1	QC2	QC2.5	TC1	TC1.5	TC2	TC++	ANSI	UNIX V	XNX	OS2	DOS
			▲			▲					▲			▲	▲

PURPOSE Use the *strftime* routine to format a time value according to a specifed national format.

SYNTAX

```
size_t strftime (char *time_strng, size_t max_len, const char
                 *format, const struct tm *time_ptr);
```

`time_strng` *Output string*

`max_len` *Maximum length of the string*

`format` *A format-control string*

`time_ptr` *A structure of type* tm

EXAMPLE CALL

```
strftime (scratch, 128,"today is %A, day %d of %B of %Y.\n", today);
```

INCLUDES `#include <time.h>` *For function declaration*

DESCRIPTION The function *strftime* formats the time value stored in a structure of type *tm* according to directions specified by the format control argument. The result, to a maximum of *max_len* number of characters, is written to the *time_strng* buffer.

The layout of the format control argument is similar to that used by the *printf* function family. A format code is preceded by a % sign, and any character that is not preceded by a % sign is copied unchanged to the destination string. The output format of *strftime* is determined by the *LC_TIME (5)* category of the current locale. The codes are as follows:

%%	Percent sign
%a	Abbreviated name of weekday
%A	Full name of weekday
%b	Abbreviated name of month
%B	Full name of month
%c	Date and time representation appropriate for locale
%d	Decimal day of the month (01-31)
%H	Hour in 24-hour format (00-23)
%I	Hour in 12-hour format (01-12)
%j	Decimal day of the year (001-366)
%m	Decimal month (01-12)
%M	Decimal minute (00-59)
%p	Current locale's AM/PM indicator for a 12-hour clock
%S	Decimal second (00-59)
%U	Decimal week of the year; Sunday is first day of week (00-51)
%w	Weekday as a decimal number (0-6; Sunday is 0)
%W	Decimal week of the year; Monday is first day of week (00-51)
%x	Date representation for current locale
%X	Time representation for current locale
%y	Decimal year without century (00-99)
%Y	Year with the century as a decimal number
%z	Time zone name or abbreviation; nothing if time zone unknown

COMMON USES This function is one of a group of ANSI-compatible routines that make it easier to internationalize your software. Others in the same subcategory include *localeconv, setlocale, strcoll,* and *strxfrm*. Their use reduces the burden of making your programs work in countries where particulars such as currency symbols and decimal placements differ from American practice.

RETURNS The *strftime* function will return the number of characters in the string if the total number, including the terminating null character, is less than the value for the *max_len* argument. Otherwise a 0 is returned.

SEE ALSO `setlocale` *To select a national format*

EXAMPLE The following program shows the time and date and then builds a custom format line, which it also displays. The format line shows only one of dozens of possible ways that the *strftime* format attributes can be combined.

```
#include <time.h>
#include <stdio.h>
#include <string.h>
#include <sys\timeb.h>

void main()
{
   time_t lcl_time;
   struct tm *today;
   struct timeb tstruct;
   char scratch[128], ampm[] = "AM";
   tzset(); /* get time zone */

   /* display date and time */
   _strtime (scratch);
   printf ("time: %s\n", scratch);

   _strdate (scratch);
   printf ("date: %s\n", scratch);
   time (&lcl_time);

   /* convert to time structure (PM adjust if needed) */

   today = localtime (&lcl_time);
   if (today->tm_hour > 12)
   {
      strcpy (ampm, "PM");
      today->tm_hour -= 12;
   }
      ftime (&tstruct);

   /* use time structure and build special time string */

   today = localtime (&lcl_time);
   strftime (scratch, 128,"today is %A, day %d of %B of %Y.\n",
             today);

   printf (scratch);
}
```

A run of the program yields:

time: 13:32:12
date: 10/11/90
today is Thursday, day 11 of October of 1990.

Time and Locale Routines

COMPATIBILITY

_strtime

MSC 3	MSC 4	MSC 5	MSC 6	QC1	QC2	QC2.5	TC1	TC1.5	TC2	TC++	ANSI	UNIX V	XNX	OS2	DOS
		▲	▲	▲	▲	▲								▲	▲

PURPOSE Use *_strtime* to obtain the current time as an eight-character string of the form *17:09:35*.

SYNTAX

```
char *_strtime(char *time);
```

`char *time;` *Current time in the form HH:MM:SS returned by* _strtime

EXAMPLE CALL

```
_strtime(time_buffer);
```

INCLUDES `#include <time.h>` *For function declaration*

DESCRIPTION The *_strtime* function gets the current time, formats it into an eight-character string of the form HH:MM:SS, and copies it into a nine-character buffer that you allocate and whose address you provide in the argument *time*. For example, the current time of 9 minutes and 35 seconds past 5 pm, returns as 17:09:35 with a null at the end.

RETURNS The *_strtime* function returns the argument *time*.

SEE ALSO `ctime, time` *To get and convert date and time into a string*

`_strdate` *To get current date in a string*

EXAMPLE Use *_strtime* to convert the current time to a C string and then print the string.

```
#include <stdio.h>
#include <time.h>
main()
{
    char time_buffer[9];
    _strtime(time_buffer);
    printf("Time now: %s\n", time_buffer);
}
```

strxfrm

COMPATIBILITY

MSC 3	MSC 4	MSC 5	MSC 6	QC1	QC2	QC2.5	TC1	TC1.5	TC2	TC++	ANSI	UNIX V	XNX	OS2	DOS
			▲			▲				▲	▲			▲	▲

PURPOSE Use *strxfrm* to transform a string based on locale-specific information.

SYNTAX

```
size_t strxfrm (char *string1, const char *string2,
                size_t byt_cnt);
```

`string1` *The destination string*

`string2` *The source string*

`byt_cnt` *The number of characters transformed*

EXAMPLE CALL

```
str_len = strxfrm(NULL, orig_string, 0
```

INCLUDES `#include <string.h>` *For function declaration*

DESCRIPTION The *strxfrm* function transforms the string pointed to by *string2* into a new form, based on locale-specific information, and stores the result in *string1*. A call to *strcmp* with two transformed strings yields a result identical to a *strcoll* call applied to the original two strings. No more than *byt_cnt* number of characters—including the terminating null—are transformed and placed into the destination string.

The value of this expression is the size of the array needed to hold the transformed source string: *1 + strxfrm (NULL, string_2, 0)*. Since the Microsoft C 6.0 compiler only supports one locale, *C*, a call to *strxfrm* is identical to:

```
strncpy (string1, string2, byt_cnt);
return (strlen (string2));
```

COMMON USES This function is one of a group of ANSI-compatible routines that make it easier to internationalize your software. Others in the same subcategory include *localeconv, strcoll, setlocale,* and *strftime*. Their use reduces the burden of making your programs work in countries where particulars such as currency symbols and decimal placements differ from American practice.

RETURNS The *strxfrm* routine returns the length of the transformed string (without the terminating null character). If the return value is greater than or equal to the value in the *byt_cnt* argument, you may have an error because the contents of *string1* are considered unpredictable.

COMMENTS The Microsoft C 6.0 compiler only supports one locale, *C*. Therefore, at this time, *strxfrm* merely copies the specified string to the destination and returns the (unchanged) length of the string.

SEE ALSO `setlocale` *To select a national format*

EXAMPLE The following program "transforms" a string using the *C* locale and compares the two strings, which are the same.

```
#include <string.h>
char orig_string [40] = "Able, Charlie 334-9954, $545.00";
/* original string */

char xfrm_string [40]; /* string for transformed copy */
size_t charcount;

void main()
{
     charcount = strlen(orig_string);
     strxfrm(xfrm_string, orig_string, charcount);
     printf("\nTransformed string is: %s:\n", xfrm_string);

     if (strcoll (orig_string, xfrm_string) == 0
     printf("The strings are the same.\n");
}
```

COMPATIBILITY

time

MSC 3	MSC 4	MSC 5	MSC 6	QC1	QC2	QC2.5	TC1	TC1.5	TC2	TC++	ANSI	UNIX V	XNX	OS2	DOS
▲	▲	▲	▲	▲	▲	▲	▲	▲	▲	▲	▲	▲	▲	▲	▲

PURPOSE Use *time* to obtain the number of seconds elapsed since 00:00:00 hours, GMT, January 1, 1970.

SYNTAX `time_t time(time_t *timeptr);`

`time_t *timeptr;` *Pointer to variable where result is returned*

EXAMPLE CALL `time(&bintime);`

INCLUDES `#include <time.h>` *For function declaration and definition of* time_t

DESCRIPTION The *time* function gets the current time and adjusts it according to the value in the global variable *_timezone* which is set by the function *tzset*). Then it computes the number of seconds elapsed since 00:00:00 hour GMT, January 1, 1970, till the adjusted current time. The result is stored as a variable of type *time_t* at the location *timeptr*. If *timeptr* is NULL, the result is not stored.

RETURNS The *time* function returns the number of elapsed seconds.

COMMENTS The value obtained from *time* can be converted to a string by calling *ctime* and the fields of the date and time can be separated by calling *gmtime* or *localtime*.

SEE ALSO `ctime` *To convert time into a string*

`gmtime, localtime` *To convert time into a* tm *structure*

`tzset` *To set environment variables that indicate the local time zone*

EXAMPLE Get and display the current time.

```
#include <stdio.h>
#include <time.h>
main()
{
    time_t tnow;
/* Get the time in seconds since 0 hrs GMT, 1/1/70 */
    time(&tnow);
/* Convert the time to a string and print it. This
 * will be your local time provided you have set the
 * environment variable TZ to your time zone. The
 * default is PST with daylight saving enabled.
 * See "tzset" for details.
 */
    printf("Current time = %s\n", ctime(&tnow));
}
```

COMPATIBILITY

tzset

MSC 3	MSC 4	MSC 5	MSC 6	QC1	QC2	QC2.5	TC1	TC1.5	TC2	TC++	ANSI	UNIX V	XNX	OS2	DOS
▲	▲	▲	▲	▲	▲	▲	▲	▲	▲	▲		▲	▲	▲	▲

PURPOSE Use *tzset* to assign values to the global variables *timezone, daylight* and *tzname* based on the time zone specified in the environment variable TZ.

SYNTAX

```
void tzset(void);
```

INCLUDES `#include <time.h>` *For function declaration and declaration of the global variables*

DESCRIPTION The *tzset* function uses the current setting of the environment variable TZ to assign appropriate values to the global variables shown in Table 12-3. TZ indicates the time zone and the daylight saving zone for use in converting from GMT to local time. TZ must be set to a three-letter time zone name (PST, EST, etc.), followed by a signed number giving the difference between GMT and the local time zone (a positive sign can be omitted). An optional three-letter daylight saving zone name can be added to the setting. The *tzset* function uses this information to compute and save the values of the global variables shown in Table 12-3. If TZ is not defined, a default setting of PST8PDT is used. TZ and *tzset* are not part of the proposed ANSI definition; they are Microsoft extensions.

Table 12-3. ***Global Variables for Time Zone and Daylight Saving***

Variable	Type and Value
timezone	Long integer. The difference in seconds between GMT and local time. Default value is 28800 (this means that the local time is Pacific Standard Time which is 28,800 seconds or 8 hours later than GMT).
daylight	Integer. Nonzero if a daylight saving time zone is specified TZ. Otherwise it is 0. Default value is 1.
tzname[0]	Character string. Three-letter time zone name from TZ. Default is PST.
tzname[1]	Character string. Three-letter daylight saving time zone name from TZ, or an empty string if omitted from TZ. Default is PDT.

COMMENTS The functions *ftime* and *localtime* use the global variables as set by *tzset.*

SEE ALSO `ftime, localtime, time` *Functions that use the environment variables set up by* tzset

EXAMPLE Use *putenv* to set the environment variable TZ to the value EST5EDT. Then call *tzset* and print the values of the global variables *timezone* and *daylight* and the strings in the array *tz.*

```
#include <stdio.h>
#include <stdlib.h>
#include <time.h>
main()
{
    time_t tnow;
/* Set the environment variable TZ to Eastern Standard
 * Time with daylight saving enabled. See text for
 * information on defining TZ.
 */
    if(putenv("TZ=EST5EDT") == -1)
    {
        printf("Error defining TZ\n");
        exit(1);
    }
/* Now call "tzset" to set up internal global variables */
    tzset();
/* Print the current values of the global variables     */
    printf("timezone = %ld, daylight = %d,\n\
tzname[0] = %s\ntzname[1] = %s\n", timezone, daylight,
           tzname[0], tzname[1]);
/* Get and display current local time -- should be EDT   */
    time(&tnow);
    printf("Local time = %s", ctime(&tnow));
}
```

utime

COMPATIBILITY

MSC 3	MSC 4	MSC 5	MSC 6	QC1	QC2	QC2.5	TC1	TC1.5	TC2	TC++	ANSI	UNIX V	XNX	OS2	DOS
▲	▲	▲	▲	▲	▲	▲						▲	▲	▲	▲

PURPOSE Use *utime* to change the "last modified" time stamp of a file to which you have write access.

SYNTAX

```
int utime(char *path, struct utimbuf *timeptr);
```

`char *path;` *Pathname of file whose last modified time is set*

`struct utimbuf *timeptr;` *Pointer to a structure through which the modification time is specified*

EXAMPLE CALL

```
/* Set modification time of file to current time */
    utime(file_name, NULL);
```

INCLUDES `#include <sys\utime.h>` *For function declaration and definition of structure* utimbuf

DESCRIPTION The *utime* function sets the last modified time of the file specified by the pathname *path* to the value provided in the *modtime* field of a structure of type *utimbuf* whose address is given in the argument *timeptr*. The structure *utimbuf* is defined in the include file *sys\utime.h*, as shown below. Under MS-DOS, only the modification time is significant. If the second argument to *utime* is NULL, the modification time of the file is set to the current time.

```
struct utimbuf
{
    time_t actime;        /* access time       */
    time_t modtime;       /* modification time */
};
```

For *utime* to succeed, you must have write access to *path*.

RETURNS If *utime* is successful, it returns a 0. In case of an error, it returns a –1 and sets *errno* to one of the constants shown in the table.

Error	Cause of Error
EACCES	File cannot be accessed. This means the file specified by *path* is either a directory or a read-only file.
EINVAL	The structure *timesptr* has invalid values.
EMFILE	The file has to be opened by *utime* before it can change the modification time. This means there are too many files open to allow *utime* to perform this step.
ENOENT	File specified by *path* not found or the pathname includes nonexistent directory names.

SEE ALSO `time` *To get current time in seconds elapsed since 00:00:00 hours GMT, January 1, 1970*

EXAMPLE Utilities such as MAKE use the modification times of files to decide whether, for example, a recompilation or relinking is necessary. Often a utility called TOUCH is available to update the modification time of a file. Use *utime* to write such a program. The program should accept a file name as an argument and set the file's modification time to the current time. Try the program on a file and see if it works.

```
/* Utility to update the modification time of a file */
#include <stdio.h>
```

```
#include <sys\types.h>
#include <sys\utime.h>
main(int argc, char **argv)
{
    if(argc < 2)
    {
        printf("Usage: %s <file_name>\n", argv[0]);
        exit(0);
    }
/* Use "utime" to set modification time of file to
 * current time.
 */
    if(utime(argv[1], NULL) == -1)
    {
        perror("\"utime\" failed");
    }
    else
    {
        printf("%s: mod time changed\n", argv[1]);
    }
}
```

Time and Locale Routines

IV Files and I/O

- File Manipulation
- Directory Manipulation
- Input and Output Routines
- System Calls

Chapter 13 File Manipulation

Introduction

The file system is a key system component of the PC. All applications and data reside in files. If you develop an application, it is likely to use files for temporary storage of its data and results so that they can be reused at a later date. We cover reading from and writing to files in the I/O discussion in Chapter 15. File manipulation covers routines that enable us to determine status of a file and to perform certain housekeeping chores to keep the files in order.

Concepts

The concepts of file system and of mechanisms used to access files are central to file manipulation.

HIERARCHICAL FILE SYSTEM IN MS-DOS

The file system describes the way files are organized under an operating system. MS-DOS uses a hierarchical file system, which refers to its tree-like structure. As illustrated in Figure 13-1, that file system has a root directory under which there are directories and files. Each directory can have more files and directories under it.

PATHNAMES TO ACCESS FILES

Files under MS-DOS can be specified by their pathnames. This is a string (see Figure 13-2) with four major components: the drive letter, the directory names, the file name, and the extension. The drive letter is a single letter followed by a colon specifying the disk drive in which the file resides. Each directory name starts with the root directory (indicated by a \) followed by

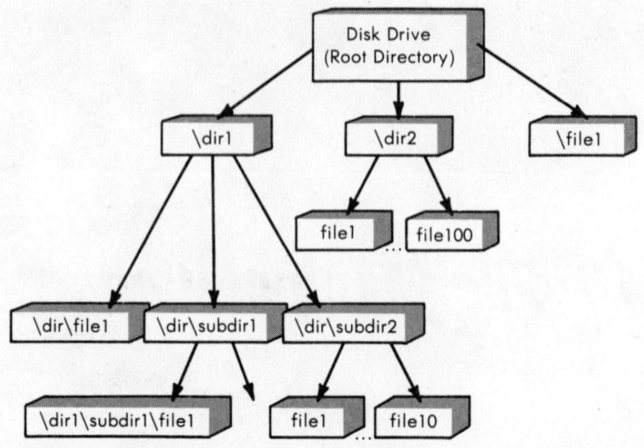

Figure 13-1. *MS-DOS hierarchical file system*

all its subdirectories, each separated from the previous one by a \. The last directory name is followed by a \ and then a file name with up to eight characters and, optionally, a three-letter extension. A period separates the extension from the file name. Files can be renamed with the Microsoft C routine *rename*. The *_makepath* and *_splitpath* routines, respectively, let you combine and take apart a pathname by its component parts.

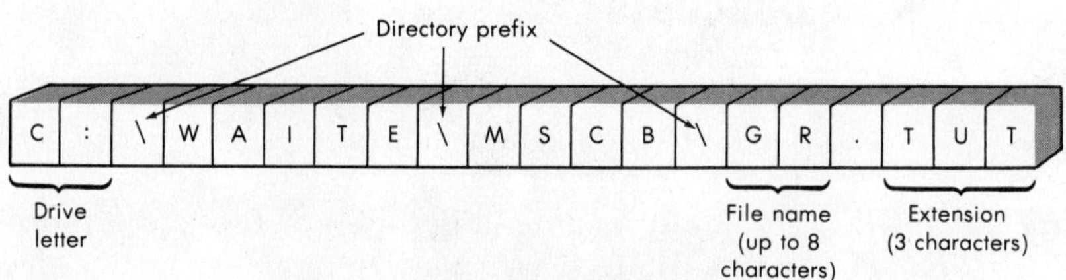

Figure 13-2. *Pathname of a file in MS-DOS*

FILE HANDLES The pathname of a file is one way of identifying it, but there is another way to reach a file. When you create or open a file using the functions *open, sopen* or *creat*, an integer identifier, called the "handle" of the file, is returned. The handle is used by the system to access a structure where certain pertinent information about the open file is stored. When you query the system about an open file, its handle suffices as an identifier.

PERTINENT FILE INFORMATION

To manipulate files, certain pieces of information are crucial to your application, among them permission and permission mask settings, file size and status, and translation mode.

Permission Settings

Normally, you can read from and write to a file. You may not want to allow others to read from a file, however, if the data is confidential. You may also want certain files to be "read only" because you don't want others to overwrite the data in these files inadvertently. Each operating system provides a means to control access to a file. In MS-DOS certain "permission settings" are associated with a file. If you think of the read and write access to a file as one-way doors, the permission settings indicate which of these doors are open. As shown in Figure 13-3, for example, in a read-only file, only the read door is open and the write door is locked.

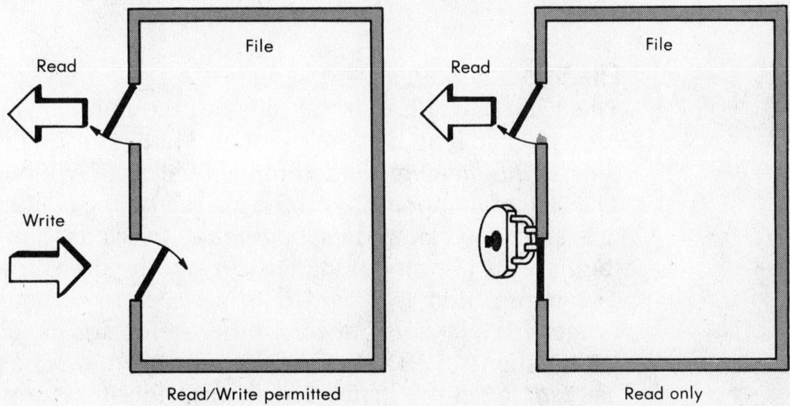

Figure 13-3. *Permission settings of a file*

There are three types of permission settings. In Microsoft C the include file *sys\stat.h* contains the constants S_IREAD and S_IWRITE which denote read and write permissions, respectively. When both reading and writing are permitted, permission is set to the bitwise-OR of the two, S_IREAD¦S_IWRITE. Under MS-DOS reading and writing are allowed on all directories. Also, all files are always readable under MS-DOS. Thus a file's permission setting to S_IWRITE is equivalent to the Microsoft setting S_IREAD¦S_IWRITE.

The *access* function lets you check the permission settings of a file while *chmod* lets you alter the permission setting of an open file.

Permission Mask

The "permission mask" is not associated with individual files, but is a bit pattern used by the file creation routines to determine the permission settings of a newly created file. You specify the permission mask with the same permission constants, S_IREAD and S_IWRITE, but their interpretation is different. If the permission mask is S_IREAD, reading from the file is not allowed, so the file will be write only. (This is ignored in MS-DOS, but included for compatibility with UNIX System V). On the other hand, a permission mask of S_IWRITE implies the file will be read only. You use the routine *umask* to specify the default permission mask.

The permission mask is applied in the following manner. When you create a file by a call to *creat, open* or *sopen*, you specify the desired permission setting for the new file. If necessary, the file creation routines use the current value of the permission mask to override the requested permission setting. For example, if the mask says that all files should be read only (remember, you cannot have a write-only file in MS-DOS), a request for a permission setting of S_IREAD¦S_IWRITE is changed to S_IREAD.

File Size and Status

The size or length of a file refers to the number of bytes in the file. For example, the length of the file shown in Figure 13-4 is 8 bytes. You can use the routine *filelength* to determine the length of a file that is already open. The size of an open file can be altered by the routine *chsize*. If the file is not open, you can find its length from its status. The status includes when the file was last modified, its size, and the disk drive where it is located. The information is provided in a structure of type *stat* defined in the header file *sys\stat.h*. Several other fields are included for compatibility with System V UNIX, but they are not used in MS-DOS. For an open file, use *fstat* to get the status. The *stat* provides the same information for a file specified by its pathname.

Translation Mode

In Chapter 15 we discuss the way the contents of a file can be interpreted when reading from or writing to the file under MS-DOS. The interpretation depends on which of the two "translation modes" is associated with the open file: text or binary. "Text mode" is useful for reading to and writing from ASCII text files. "Binary mode" is used to read data files.

In binary mode each byte in the file is treated as a value with no special significance, as shown in Figure 13-4. Since the number of bytes in the file is known, the end-of-file is encountered when all the bytes have been read; there is no specific end-of-file value in the binary mode.

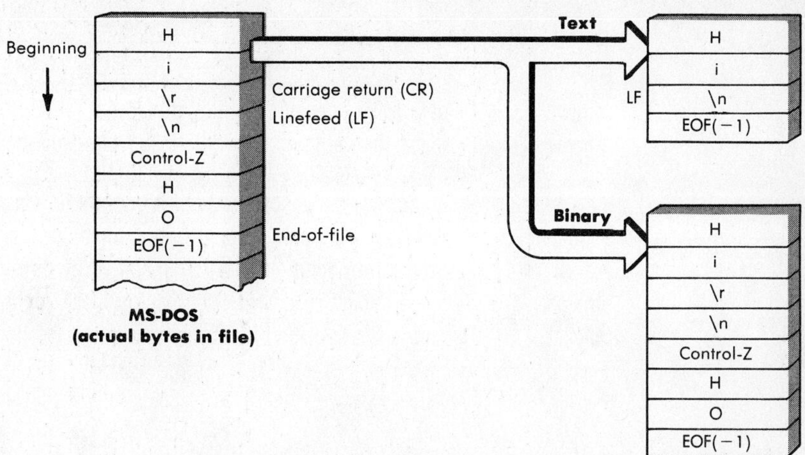

Figure 13-4. ***Text and binary translation modes***

In text mode, a carriage return (\r) followed by a linefeed, or newline \n, is translated to a single newline. Also, as soon as a Control-Z is encountered, the file is considered to have ended. Thus anything after a Control-Z cannot be read in this mode.

Figure 13-4 illustrates how the contents of a file are treated when opened in both modes. In text mode, the contents of the file are checked to see if a Control-Z or a carriage return is encountered, but in binary mode, the file's contents are taken literally, without any translation. Use the function *setmode* if you want to change the translation mode of a file that is already open.

Table 13-1 details the routines for file manipulation. Next we explain some of the capabilities described.

Table 13-1. ***File Manipulation Routines***

Routine	Description
access	Checks for existence as well as read/write permission settings of a file.
chmod	Changes the read/write permission settings of a file.
chsize	Extends or truncates a file.
filelength	Returns length of a file in bytes.
fstat	Returns information about an open file specified by handle.
_fullpath	Expands the pathname fragment to form a fully qualified path that is stored in buffer. Introduced in Microsoft C 6.0.
isatty	Checks if a file handle refers to a character device.
locking	When file-sharing is enabled (MS-DOS 3.0 and higher), locks or unlocks a specified number of bytes in an open file.
_makepath	Constructs a DOS pathname out of component parts.
mktemp	Generates a unique file name by use of a template.

Table 13-1. ***(cont.)***

Routine	Description
remove	Deletes a file specified by its pathname.
rename	Changes the pathname of a file to a new value (can be used to move file to new directory).
setmode	Changes the translation mode of an open file specified by its handle.
_splitpath	Separates a DOS pathname into its component parts.
stat	Returns information about a file specified by its pathname.
umask	Sets the default read/write permission mask for the current process.
unlink	Deletes a file specified by its pathname.

FILE MANIPULATION BY TASK

The file manipulation routines let you modify and obtain certain information about MS-DOS files. They also allow you to delete files (using *remove* and *unlink*) and perform certain utility functions such as generating temporary file names (with *mktemp*) and locking certain parts of a file that has been opened for sharing. Table 13-2 shows the routines grouped by task.

File or Device

In MS-DOS, devices are opened like files and I/O with devices can be done using a common set of routines. For each open file, the system maintains information to tell devices apart from disk files. The *isatty* function lets you determine if a file handle refers to a device or to a disk file. For example, the preopened files *stdin* and *stdout* are initially connected to the keyboard and the monitor, which are *devices*. If either of these are redirected to a disk file, MS-DOS will mark the handles as such. You can use the *isatty* function to determine whether a handle refers to a disk file or a device.

Table 13-2. ***File Manipulation Routines by Task***

task	Routines
Delete a file.	remove, unlink
Alter and set permission setting.	access, chmod, umask
Get status information of a file.	fstat, stat
Name file.	mktemp, rename
Change or check file size.	chsize, filelength
Check if file is a character device.	isatty
Set translation mode (text or binary).	setmode
Lock/unlock portions of a file.	locking
Assemble and disassemble MS-DOS pathnames.	_makepath, _splitpath, _fullpath

File-Sharing

Under MS-DOS 3.0 and higher, the command SHARE installs the file-sharing option that allows multiple processes to open and access a file. After opening a file for sharing (with *sopen*), the actual sharing is achieved by a mechanism (the *locking* function) that enables you to lock and unlock specific portions of the file.

Cautions

- File-sharing is not available in MS-DOS versions below 3.0 because the *locking* function does not work in those versions.
- Note that several functions require the file handle as an input parameter. If you open the file using a higher-level stream I/O routine (see Chapter 15), use *fileno* to get the handle.
- Remember that MS-DOS imposes a limit of 20 open files per process. You can change this under DOS 3.3 by following instructions included in the README.DOC file of the Microsoft C 5.1 distribution disk.

Further Reading

Consult Prata's book[1] for a detailed exposition of the file manipulation routines. Permission settings and translation modes are also explained.

1. Stephen Prata, The Waite Group, *Advanced C Primer++*, Howard W. Sams & Company, Carmel, IN, 1986, 502 pages.

access

COMPATIBILITY

MSC 3	MSC 4	MSC 5	MSC 6	QC1	QC2	QC2.5	TC1	TC1.5	TC2	TC++	ANSI	UNIX V*	XNX	OS2	DOS
▲	▲	▲	▲	▲	▲	▲	▲	▲	▲	▲		▲	▲	▲	▲

PURPOSE Use *access* to check whether a file exists and if so, whether read and/or write operations are permitted.

SYNTAX

```
int access(char *path, int mode);
```

`char *path;` *Pathname of file being checked*

`int mode;` *Integer denoting permission setting being checked*

EXAMPLE CALL

```
if(access("temp.dat", 4) == 0) puts("Data file exists");
```

INCLUDES `#include <io.h>` *For function declaration*

DESCRIPTION The *access* function determines whether the file specified by the pathname *path* exists and whether the permission setting of the file allows the operation indicated by the argument *mode*. Use one of the values shown in the table for the argument *mode*. If the pathname *path* specifies a directory, *access* only verifies whether the directory exists. Under MS-DOS all directories have both read and write permissions, and all files have read permission.

Value of *mode*	Interpretation
00	Only existence of file will be checked.
02	Check if file has write permission.
04	Check if file has read permission.
06	Check if file has read and write permission.

RETURNS If *access* finds that the file or directory specified by *path* exists and allows the access specified by *mode*, it returns a 0. If the pathname does not exist or is not accessible in the specified *mode*, the return value is −1 and the global variable *errno* is set to ENOENT to indicate that the specified pathname is invalid or to EACCES to denote that the requested type of access is not allowed.

SEE ALSO

`chmod` *To alter the permission setting of a file*

`fstat, stat` *To find information about an open file, including permission settings*

File Manipulation

EXAMPLE Using *access*, write a program that checks the existence of the file CONFIG.SYS in the root directory of drive C. If the file exists and has read permission, open it with *fopen* and display its contents.

```
#include <stdio.h>
#include <io.h>
char filename[] = "c:\\config.sys";
main()
{
        FILE *infile;
        char buffer[80];
/* Check if the file exists. Note that we need two '\'*/
        if(access(filename, 4) == -1)
        {
            perror("access failed");
            exit(1);
        }
        if ( (infile = fopen(filename, "r")) == NULL)
        {
            perror("fopen failed");
            exit(1);
        }
        printf("Contents of %s\n", filename);
        while ( fgets(buffer, 80, infile) != NULL)
        {
            printf(buffer);
        }
}
```

COMPATIBILITY

chmod

MSC 3	MSC 4	MSC 5	MSC 6	QC1	QC2	QC2.5	TC1	TC1.5	TC2	TC++	ANSI	UNIX V	XNX	OS2	DOS
▲	▲	▲	▲	▲	▲	▲	▲	▲	▲	▲		▲	▲	▲	▲

PURPOSE Use *chmod* to alter the read/write permission settings of a file.

SYNTAX

```
int chmod(char *path, int pmode);
```

`char *path;` *Pathname of file whose permission is being changed*

`int pmode;` *Integer denoting new permission setting for the file*

EXAMPLE CALL

```
chmod("inventory.lis", S_IWRITE);
```

INCLUDES `#include <io.h>` *For function declaration*

`#include <sys\types.h>` *Required by <sys\stat.h>*

`#include <sys\stat.h>` *For definition of constants denoting permission settings*

DESCRIPTION The *chmod* function sets the read/write permission setting of the file whose pathname is given in the argument *path* to the new setting specified in the integer *pmode*. The permission settings are specified in terms of constants defined in the include file *sys\stat.h*. The table below shows the possible combinations of the permission settings and their meanings. Under MS-DOS all files are readable, so it is not possible to give write-only permission to a file.

Constant	Interpretation
S_IWRITE	Both reading and writing permitted.
S_IREAD	Only reading permitted.
S_IREAD ¦ S_IWRITE	Both reading and writing permitted.

RETURNS If *chmod* successfully changes the permission setting to *pmode*, it returns a 0. In case of error, the return value is −1 and the global variable *errno* is set to ENOENT to indicate that the specified pathname is invalid.

SEE ALSO `access` *To check if read/write operations are permitted on a file*

`fstat, stat` *To find information about an open file, including permission settings*

EXAMPLE Write a small utility program using *chmod* to enable the user to change the read/write permission of a file. Assume that the command-line syntax is: "CHMOD <pathname><permission>" in which "permission" is a single character R (for read-only) or W (both read and write).

```
#include <stdio.h>
#include <sys\types.h>

#include <sys\stat.h>
#include <io.h>
main(int argc, char **argv)
{
    int pmode=-999;
    if(argc < 3)
    {
        printf(
```

```
                "Usage: %s <pathname> <R|W>\n", argv[0]);
        }
        else
        {
/* Convert last argument to permission code           */
            if(argv[2][0]=='R') pmode = S_IREAD;
            if(argv[2][0]=='W') pmode = S_IREAD|S_IWRITE;
            if(pmode==-999)
            {
                    printf("Unknown permission: %s\n",
                            argv[2]);
                    exit(1);
            }
            if(chmod(argv[1], pmode) == -1)
            {
                perror("Error in \"chmod\"");
            }
        }
}
```

COMPATIBILITY

chsize

MSC 3	MSC 4	MSC 5	MSC 6	QC1	QC2	QC2.5	TC1	TC1.5	TC2	TC++	ANSI	UNIX V	XNX	OS2	DOS
▲	▲	▲	▲	▲	▲	▲	▲	▲	▲	▲		▲	▲	▲	▲

PURPOSE Use *chsize* to extend or truncate a file open for unbuffered, unformatted write operations.

SYNTAX

```
int chsize(int handle, int size);
```

`int handle;` *Handle of file whose size is being changed*

`long size;` *New length of file in bytes*

EXAMPLE CALL

```
chsize(filehandle, 0L);  /* Truncate file to zero length */
```

INCLUDES `#include <io.h>` *For function declaration*

DESCRIPTION The *chsize* function truncates or extends the file specified by the argument *handle* to match the new length in bytes given in the argument *size*. When the file is extended, null characters are appended to the file. When the file is truncated, all data beyond the new *size* is lost.

RETURNS The *chsize* returns a 0 to indicate success. In case of error, the return value is –1 and the global variable *errno* is set to one of the constants shown in Table 13-3.

Table 13-3. *Values of* errno *on Return from* chsize

Error Constant	Interpretation of Error Code
EACCES	Access to file was denied. For DOS 3.0 and above this means the file is locked against writing.
EBADF	File is read only or the handle does not refer to an open file.
ENOSPC	No more space left on the device where the file is stored. This can occur when trying to extend a file on a nearly full disk.

SEE ALSO `access` *To check if read/write operations are permitted on a file*

`chmod` *To change read/write permissions of a file*

`fstat, stat` *To find information about an open file, including permission settings*

EXAMPLE Prompt the user for the name of an existing file to open and truncate to size zero.

```
#include <stdio.h>
#include <fcntl.h>
#include <io.h>
main()
{
    int  filehandle, answer = 0;
    char filename[80];
    printf("Enter name of file to truncate: ");
    gets(filename);
    if((filehandle = open(filename, O_RDWR)) == -1)
    {
        perror("open failed");
        exit(1);
    }
/* Now give user a warning and a chance to abort     */
    while(answer != 'N' && answer != 'Y')

    {
        printf("Truncate %s to size zero? (Y or N)",
               filename);
        scanf(" %1s", &answer);
        answer = toupper(answer);
```

```
        }
        if(answer == 'Y')
        {
            if(chsize(filehandle, 0L) == -1)
            {
                perror("chsize failed");
            }
            else
            {
                printf("%s successfully truncated.\n",
                       filename);
            }
        }
    }
```

COMPATIBILITY

filelength

MSC 3	MSC 4	MSC 5	MSC 6	QC1	QC2	QC2.5	TC1	TC1.5	TC2	TC++	ANSI	UNIX V	XNX	OS2	DOS
	▲	▲	▲	▲	▲	▲	▲	▲	▲	▲				▲	▲

PURPOSE Use the *filelength* function to determine the length of a file in bytes. To use this function, you have to specify the file handle (see the tutorial).

SYNTAX

```
long filelength(int file_handle);
```

`int file_handle;` *Handle of file whose length is to be returned*

EXAMPLE CALL

```
filesize = filelength(filehandle);
```

INCLUDES `#include <stdio.h>` *For function declaration*

DESCRIPTION The *filelength* function returns the size in number of bytes of the file whose handle is specified in the argument *file_handle*. To get the handle of a file opened by *fopen*, you use *fileno* and then use *filelength* to get its length.

RETURNS The long integer value returned by *filelength* is the size of the file in number of bytes. If an error occurs, the return value is –1L. If the error is due to an invalid handle, the global variable *errno* is set to constant EBADF.

SEE ALSO

`fileno` *To obtain the handle of a file whose pointer to the associated FILE data structure is known*

EXAMPLE Ask the user for a file name. Open the file with *fopen* for read only. Now call *filelength* to determine the size of the file. Use *fileno* to get the handle for the file.

```
#include <stdio.h>
main()
{
        char filename[80];
        FILE *infile;
        long filesize;
        printf("Enter the name of an existing file: ");
        gets(filename);
/* Open the file */
        if ( (infile = fopen(filename, "r")) == NULL)
        {
            printf("fopen failed to open: %s\n", filename);
            exit(0);
        }
  /* Get file size and display it. Use fileno to get the handle. */
        if( (filesize = filelength(fileno(infile))) != -1L)
        {
            printf("Size of %s = %ld bytes\n", filename, filesize);
        }
        else
        {
            printf("Error getting file size\n");
        }
}
```

fstat

COMPATIBILITY

MSC 3	MSC 4	MSC 5	MSC 6	QC1	QC2	QC2.5	TC1	TC1.5	TC2	TC++	ANSI	UNIX V	XNX	OS2	DOS
▲	▲	▲	▲	▲	▲	▲	▲	▲	▲	▲		▲	▲	▲	▲

PURPOSE Use the *fstat* function to retrieve information about a file that has been opened for unbuffered, unformatted I/O.

SYNTAX `int fstat(int handle, struct stat *buffer);`

`int handle;` *Handle of file whose "vital statistics" will be returned*

`struct stat *buffer;` *Pointer to structure where result will be returned*

EXAMPLE CALL `fstat(filehandle, &stat_buffer);`

INCLUDES `#include <sys\types.h>` *Required by <sys\stat.h>*

`#include <sys\stat.h>` *For function declaration and definition of structure* stat

DESCRIPTION The *fstat* function returns information about the file specified by the argument *handle*. You must allocate a structure of type *stat* and provide a pointer to this structure in the argument *buffer*. After *fstat* returns successfully, this structure contains the information about the file. The structure *stat* is defined in <sys\stat.h> and a commented version of its declaration is shown below. Several fields in the *stat* structure are used in UNIX but not in MS-DOS and are included here for compatibility.

```
struct stat
{
    dev_t          st_dev;   /* Drive number of disk or handle of
                                device containing the file       */
    ino_t          st_ino;   /* Unused in MS-DOS. The "i-node"
                                number of file in UNIX           */
    unsigned short st_mode;  /* Bit mask of file's mode          */
    short          st_nlink; /* Always set to 1 under MS-DOS     */
    short          st_uid;   /* Unused in MS-DOS. For "user-id"
                                under UNIX                       */
    short          st_gid;   /* Unused in MS-DOS. For "group-id"
                                under UNIX                       */
    dev_t          st_rdev;  /* Same as the field st_dev         */
    off_t          st_size;  /* Size of file in bytes            */
    time_t         st_atime; /* Time of last modification        */
    time_t         st_mtime; /* Same as st_atime                 */
    time_t         st_ctime; /* Same as st_atime                 */
};
```

RETURNS Note that *fstat* was changed in Microsoft C 5.1 to give undefined values for *st_dev* and *st_rdev* in protected mode. If *fstat* is successful in obtaining the information about the file, it returns a 0. In case of error, the return value is −1 and the global variable *errno* is set to the constant EBADF to indicate that the specified handle is invalid.

SEE ALSO `access` *To check if read/write operations are permitted on a file*

`chmod` *To change read/write permissions for a file*

`stat` *To find information about a file specified by a pathname*

EXAMPLE Use *fstat* to display information about the standard output file *stdout* (you can get its handle by using *fileno*).

```
#include <stdio.h>
#include <sys\types.h>
#include <sys\stat.h>
#include <io.h>
main()
{
    struct stat info;
    if (fstat(fileno(stdout), &info) != 0)
    {
        perror("fstat failed");
        exit(1);
    }
    if ((info.st_mode & S_IFCHR) == S_IFCHR)
    {
        printf("stdout is a device\n");
    }
    if ((info.st_mode & S_IFREG) == S_IFREG)
    {
/* This means stdout has been redirected to a file */
        printf("stdout is a regular file on drive %c\n",
            info.st_dev+65);
    }
}
{
    struct stat info;
    if (fstat(fileno(stdout), &info) != 0)
    {
        perror("fstat failed");
        exit(1);
    }
    if ((info.st_mode & S_IFCHR) == S_IFCHR)
    {
        printf("stdout is a device\n");
    }
    if ((info.st_mode & S_IFREG) == S_IFREG)
    {
/* This means stdout has been redirected to a file */
        printf("stdout is a regular file on drive %c\n",
                info.st_dev+65);
    }
}
```

File Manipulation

COMPATIBILITY

_fullpath

MSC 3	MSC 4	MSC 5	MSC 6	QC1	QC2	QC2.5	TC1	TC1.5	TC2	TC++	ANSI	UNIX V	XNX	OS2	DOS
			▲			▲								▲	▲

PURPOSE Use the *_fullpath* function when you need to expand a pathname fragment into a fully qualified path.

SYNTAX

```
char *_fullpath (char *pth_bufr, const char *pth_nam,
                 size_t max_len);
```

`pth_bufr;` *A pointer to the user pathname buffer*

`pth_nam;` *A pointer to a pathname fragment*

`max_len;` *The maximum length of the buffer*

EXAMPLE CALL

```
if (_fullpath (ful_path, prtl_path, _MAX_PATH) != NULL)
```

INCLUDES `direct.h` *For function declaration*

DESCRIPTION The *_fullpath* function expands a pathname fragment (*pth_nam* in the example above) to form a fully qualified path (a path with the full list of directories from root to the file in question). The fully qualified path is then stored in a buffer. The *_fullpath* function was introduced in version 6.0.

RETURNS The *_fullpath* routine returns a pointer to the absolute path in the buffer if the call is successful. A function failure yields a NULL.

EXAMPLE The sample program below reads a directory name supplied via keyboard entry and sends that to the *fullpath* function.

```
/* FULLPATH.C */
#include <stdio.h>
#include <stdlib.h>
#include <direct.h>

char ful_path[_MAX_PATH], prtl_path[_MAX_PATH];
void main()

{
   printf ("Type a path segment (ENTER quits)");
   gets (prtl_path);
   if (_fullpath (ful_path, prtl_path, _MAX_PATH) != NULL)
      printf ("The full path is: %s\n", ful_path);
   else
      printf ("You typed an invalid path\n");
}
```

isatty

COMPATIBILITY

MSC 3	MSC 4	MSC 5	MSC 6	QC1	QC2	QC2.5	TC1	TC1.5	TC2	TC++	ANSI	UNIX V	XNX	OS2	DOS
▲	▲	▲	▲	▲	▲	▲	▲	▲	▲	▲		▲	▲	▲	▲

PURPOSE Use the *isatty* function to determine whether a particular file handle refers to a "character device" which, under MS-DOS, means the console, printer, or a serial port.

SYNTAX

```
int isatty(int handle);
```

`int handle;` *Handle about which this query is being made*

EXAMPLE CALL

```
if(isatty(fileno(stdout)) != 0) puts("stdout is console");
```

INCLUDES `#include <io.h>` *For function declaration*

DESCRIPTION The *isatty* function determines whether a specified handle refers to a character device.

COMMON USES The *isatty* function provides a way to determine if I/O redirection is in effect (the return value is zero when the I/O stream is redirected to a file). Knowing that it is might cause you to do things differently in your program. For example, when your application, XYZ, is executed with a command like XYZ>OUTFILE (meaning output from the program XYZ goes to the file OUTFILE), you might not want to make any calls to graphics functions because the user would not be expecting any output on the screen.

RETURNS The *isatty* function returns a nonzero value if the handle refers to a character device. If not, it returns a 0.

EXAMPLE Write a program using *isatty* that determines whether *stdout* is a character device or not. If it is a device, the program must run in interactive mode, in which characters are sent to the display rather than a file.

```
#include <stdio.h>
#include <io.h>
main()
{
   if(!isatty(fileno(stdout)))
   {
        printf("stdout redirected to a file\n");
   }
   else
```

```
    {
        printf("Executing in interactive mode\n");
    }
}
```

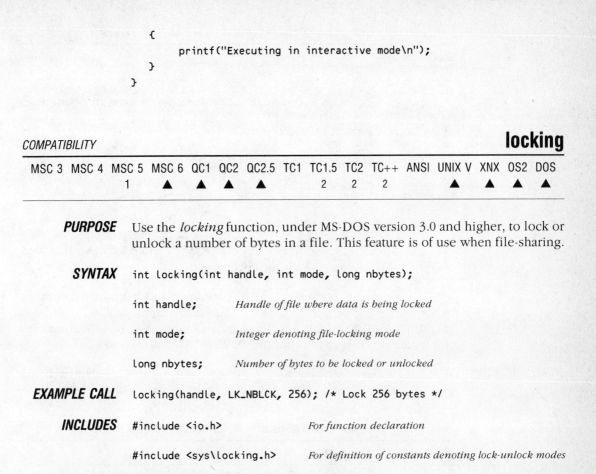

COMPATIBILITY

locking

MSC 3	MSC 4	MSC 5	MSC 6	QC1	QC2	QC2.5	TC1	TC1.5	TC2	TC++	ANSI	UNIX V	XNX	OS2	DOS
		1	▲	▲	▲	▲		2	2	2		▲	▲	▲	▲

PURPOSE Use the *locking* function, under MS-DOS version 3.0 and higher, to lock or unlock a number of bytes in a file. This feature is of use when file-sharing.

SYNTAX

```
int locking(int handle, int mode, long nbytes);
```

`int handle;` *Handle of file where data is being locked*

`int mode;` *Integer denoting file-locking mode*

`long nbytes;` *Number of bytes to be locked or unlocked*

EXAMPLE CALL

```
locking(handle, LK_NBLCK, 256); /* Lock 256 bytes */
```

INCLUDES

`#include <io.h>` *For function declaration*

`#include <sys\locking.h>` *For definition of constants denoting lock-unlock modes*

DESCRIPTION The *locking* function is for use when file-sharing is enabled by executing the MS-DOS command SHARE. Because earlier versions of DOS do not have the SHARE command the *locking* function should be used only under MS-DOS versions 3.0 and later. Starting with Microsoft C 5.1, under OS/2, *locking* can be used to coordinate file-sharing even when SHARE.COM or SHARE.EXE is not installed.

When called, *locking* performs the lock or unlock action requested by the argument *mode* on the file specified by the handle. The action affects the file's next *n* bytes (or to the end-of-file) from its current position. The argument *mode* must be specified by one of the constants shown in Table 13-4. These constants are defined in the include file *sys\locking.h*.

Locking a number of bytes (a region) prevents further reading and writing of those bytes by any process. Unlocking removes this restriction, but each region that is locked must be unlocked individually, even if two locked regions are adjacent to each other. Many separate regions in a file can be locked simultaneously, but no two regions can overlap. Finally, all locked regions must be unlocked before closing the file or exiting the

Table 13-4. *Constants Denoting File-Locking Modes*

Locking-Mode Constant	Interpretation
LK_LOCK	Locks the specified bytes. If they cannot be locked, *locking* retries every second, up to a maximum of 10 attempts. It returns error if it fails even after these attempts.
LK_RLCK	Performs same function as LK_LOCK.
LK_NBLCK	Locks the specified bytes and returns an error immediately if it fails.
LK_NBRLCK	Performs same function as LK_NBLCK.
LK_UNLCK	Unlocks previously locked bytes.

program. Microsoft warns that under MS-DOS 3.0 and 3.1 locked files may become unlocked when a child process exits.

1. Changed in Microsoft C 5.1 to coordinate file sharing on a network under DOS 3.x after SHARE.COM or SHARE.EXE are installed. 2. Turbo C and Turbo C++ equivalent functions are *lock* and *unlock* for Microsoft C 5 and 6 and QuickC. They do not work with Microsoft C 3 or 4.

RETURNS If *locking* succeeds, it returns a 0. Otherwise, it returns a –1 and sets the global variable *errno* to one of the constants shown in Table 13-5.

Table 13-5. *Values of* errno *on Return from* locking

Error Constant	Interpretation
EACCES	Access to file was denied. File is already locked or unlocked.
EBADF	The handle does not refer to an open file.
EDEADLOCK	This code is set if the mode is set to LK_LOCK or LK_RLCK and the file could not be locked even after 10 retries at 1-second intervals.
EINVAL	Either *mode* or *nbytes* is invalid. This error means the argument values are erroneous.

COMMENTS Under MS-DOS versions earlier than 3.0, the *locking* function does not operate.

SEE ALSO sopen *To open with various file-sharing options*

EXAMPLE Assuming that you are writing an application to be used in a networked environment with file-sharing under DOS, write a sample program that locks a part of the file using *locking* (presumably it updates that portion of the file) and then unlocks it for use by other processes. Remember to run SHARE before executing the program.

```
#include <stdio.h>
#include <io.h>
#include <fcntl.h>
#include <sys\locking.h>
main()
{
    long curpos;
    int filehandle;


    char filename[80], buffer[80];
    printf("Enter name of file to test with:");
    gets(filename);
    if ((filehandle = open(filename, O_RDONLY)) == -1)
    {
        perror("open failed");
        exit(1);
    }
/* Read 80 characters from the file                    */
    if (read(filehandle, buffer, 80) == -1)
    {
        perror("read error");
        exit(1);
    }
/* Get and save current position                       */
    curpos = tell(filehandle);
/* Now go to beginning of file and lock 80 bytes       */
    lseek(filehandle, 0L, SEEK_SET);
    if (locking(filehandle, LK_NBLCK, curpos) == -1)
    {
        perror("locking failed");
    }
    else
    {
        printf("First %ld bytes of file %s locked\n",
               curpos, filename);
/* In an actual program, you would make changes and
 * write these bytes back to the file before unlocking
 */
        lseek(filehandle, 0L, SEEK_SET);
        if (locking(filehandle, LK_UNLCK, curpos)
             == -1)
        {
            perror("unlocking failed");
        }
        else
```

```
            {
                printf("File unlocked\n");
            }
        }
    }
```

_makepath

COMPATIBILITY

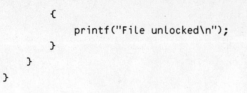

MSC 3	MSC 4	MSC 5	MSC 6	QC1	QC2	QC2.5	TC1	TC1.5	TC2	TC++	ANSI	UNIX V	XNX	OS2	DOS
		▲	▲	▲	▲	▲		1	1	1				▲	▲

PURPOSE Use *_makepath* to create a full pathname composed of a drive letter, directory path, file name, and file extension.

SYNTAX

```
void _makepath(char *path, char *drive, char *dir,
               char *fname, char *ext);
```

`char *path;` *Pointer to buffer where full pathname will be returned*

`char *drive;` *Drive letter*

`char *dir;` *Directory path*

`char *fname;` *File name*

`char *ext;` *File extension*

EXAMPLE CALL

```
_makepath(pathname, "c", "temp", "result", "dat");
/* pathname will be "c:\temp\result.dat"  */
```

INCLUDES `#include <stdlib.h>` *For function declaration and definition of the constant _MAX_PATH*

DESCRIPTION The *_makepath* function combines the strings *drive, dir, fname*, and *ext* to construct a full pathname and store it in the buffer *path*. You must allocate enough room in the buffer to hold the complete pathname, but the individual strings may be of any length. The constant _MAX_PATH, defined in *stdlib.h*, describes the maximum-length pathname that MS-DOS can handle so a size of _MAX_PATH for *path* is a safe choice, assuming that the combined length of the strings does not exceed _MAX_PATH. The arguments *drive, dir, fname*, and *ext* are described in Table 13-6.

1. The equivalent Turbo C and Turbo C++ function is *fnmerge*.

Table 13-6. *Components of Pathname*

Argument	Description
drive	Contains the drive letter (A, B, C, etc.) followed by an optional colon. If the colon is missing, *_makepath* inserts it automatically in the pathname. If this string is empty, no drive letter and colon appear in the pathname.
dir	Contains the path of directories, excluding the drive letter and the actual file name. Either forward (/) or backward (\) slashes may be used as separators in directory names and the trailing slash is optional. A trailing slash is automatically added after *dir*. If *dir* is an empty string, nothing is inserted in this position in the complete pathname. Remember that to get a single backslash character, you must have two backslashes in the string.
fname	Contains the file name without the extension.
ext	This is the file's extension with or without a leading period (.); *_makepath* automatically inserts a period. If this string is empty, no extension appears in the pathname.

SEE ALSO `_splitpath` *To separate a pathname into its components*

EXAMPLE Illustrate the use of *_makepath* by constructing a complete pathname out of component strings entered by the user.

```
#include <stdio.h>
#include <stdlib.h>
main()
{
    char pathname[_MAX_PATH], drive[_MAX_DRIVE],
         dir[_MAX_DIR], filename[_MAX_FNAME],
         ext[_MAX_EXT];
/* Prompt user for various components                  */
    printf("Enter drive letter:");
    gets(drive);
    printf("      directory path (%d characters max):",
            _MAX_DIR-1);
    gets(dir);
    printf("      filename (%d characters max):",
            _MAX_FNAME-1);
    gets(filename);
    printf("      extension (up to 3 letters):");
    gets(ext);
/*  Construct the complete path name and display it  */
    _makepath(pathname, drive, dir, filename, ext);
    printf("Path name is:  %s\n", pathname);
}
```

mktemp

COMPATIBILITY

MSC 3	MSC 4	MSC 5	MSC 6	QC1	QC2	QC2.5	TC1	TC1.5	TC2	TC++	ANSI	UNIX V	XNX	OS2	DOS
▲	▲	▲	▲	▲	▲	▲	▲	▲	▲	▲		▲	▲	▲	▲

PURPOSE Use the *mktemp* function to generate unique file names by modifying a given template for the names.

SYNTAX

```
char *mktemp(char *template);

char *template;        Pattern string to be used in constructing file names
```

EXAMPLE CALL

```
char tfilename = "mscbXXXXXX";
mktemp(tfilename);
```

INCLUDES

```
#include <io.h>        For function declaration
```

DESCRIPTION The *mktemp* function uses the string *template* and modifies a portion of it to generate unique file names. The *template* string must be of the form: baseXXXXXX. The "base" of the template consists of one or more characters that appear in every file name. The Xs are treated as place holders to be replaced by a single alphanumeric character followed by five digits, which is a unique number identifying the calling process (no attention is paid to the eight-character limit on DOS file names). For the alphanumeric digit, *mktemp* starts with 0 and goes on to the lowercase alphabet, a through z. Before returning a file name, *mktemp* checks that no file with that name exists in the working directory. Note that *mktemp* is not creating or opening a file, only creating a file name.

COMMON USES If your program creates many temporary files, *mktemp* relieves you of the responsibility of coming up with unique file names.

RETURNS The *mktemp* function returns a pointer to the modified template. In case of an error, for example, when no more unique file names can be created out of a given template, the return value will be NULL.

SEE ALSO

`tempnam, tmpnam` *Other routines to create temporary file names*

`tmpfile` *To open an unnamed temporary file that is deleted when closed*

EXAMPLE Use *mktemp* to get a unique file name with the prefix "naba" and open the file. The file name returned by *mktemp* will be 10 characters long, if you check the directory (using the DIR command), you will find that the newly created file uses only the first eight characters of the name.

```
#include <stdio.h>
#include <io.h>
static char *our_template = "nabaXXXXXX";
main()
{
    char unique_name[9];
/* First copy template into placeholder for name      */
    strcpy(unique_name, our_template);
    if(mktemp(unique_name) == NULL)
    {
        printf("Could not create unique file name!\n");
    }
    else
    {
        fopen(unique_name, "w");
        printf("File %s opened\n", unique_name);
    }
}
```

COMPATIBILITY

remove

MSC 3	MSC 4	MSC 5	MSC 6	QC1	QC2	QC2.5	TC1	TC1.5	TC2	TC++	ANSI	UNIX V	XNX	OS2	DOS
▲	▲	▲	▲	▲	▲	▲	▲	▲	▲	▲	▲			▲	▲

PURPOSE Use *remove* to delete a file specified by its pathname.

SYNTAX

```
int remove(const char *path);

const char *path;        Pathname of file to be deleted
```

EXAMPLE CALL

```
remove("c:\\tmp\\tmp01234"); /* Delete temporary file */
```

INCLUDES

```
#include <io.h>       For function declaration
```

or

```
#include <stdio.h>
```

DESCRIPTION The *remove* function deletes the file specified by *path*.

RETURNS If *remove* successfully deletes the specified file, it returns a 0. Otherwise, the return value is −1 and the global variable *errno* is set to either ENOENT if the pathname is not found or to EACCES if the pathname is that of a directory or a read-only file.

SEE ALSO `unlink` *Also deletes a file*

EXAMPLE Write a utility program that uses *remove* to delete a file. Assume that the program will be invoked with a command of the form "rm <filename>" where "rm.exe" is the program name.

```
#include <stdio.h>
#include <io.h>
main(int argc, char **argv)
{
    if(argc < 2)
    {
        printf("Usage: %s <pathname>\n", argv[0]);
    }
    else
    {
        printf("File %s ", argv[1]);
        if(remove(argv[1]) != 0)
        {
            perror("remove failed");
        }
        else
        {
            printf("deleted\n");
        }
    }
}
```

rename

COMPATIBILITY

MSC 3	MSC 4	MSC 5	MSC 6	QC1	QC2	QC2.5	TC1	TC1.5	TC2	TC++	ANSI	UNIX V	XNX	OS2	DOS
▲	▲	▲	▲	▲	▲	▲	▲	▲	▲	▲	▲			▲	▲

PURPOSE Use *rename* to change the name of a file or directory specified by its pathname. For example, you can use *rename* to write a program that provides the function of the UNIX command *mv* (to move a file from one directory to another).

SYNTAX

```
int rename(const char *oldname, const char *newname);
```

`const char *oldname;` *Current pathname of file or directory*

`const char *newname;` *New pathname*

EXAMPLE CALL

```
/* Copy "text.exe" from c:\tmp to c:\bin and give it a new name */
    rename("c:\\tmp\\test.exe", "c:\\bin\\grview.exe");
```

INCLUDES

`#include <io.h>` *For function declaration*

or

`#include <stdio.h>`

DESCRIPTION The *rename* function changes the name of a file or directory from *oldname* to *newname*. Use *rename* to move a file from one directory to another, but only in the same device. Directories cannot be moved.

Note that *rename* was changed in Microsoft C 4.0 from earlier versions to revise the order of arguments to agree with ANSI practice.

RETURNS If *rename* is successful, it returns a zero. In case of an error, it returns a nonzero value and the global variable *errno* contains further information. This variable equals the constant EACCES if a file or directory called *newname* exists, if a file with *newname* could not be created, or if *oldname* is a directory and *newname* specifies a different directory path. Attempting to specify a different drive letter results in *errno* set to EXDEV or to ENOENT if the pathname *oldname* does not refer to an existing file or directory.

SEE ALSO `creat, fopen, open` *To create and open a file*

EXAMPLE Write a program using *rename* that mimics the UNIX command *mv*.

```
#include <stdio.h>
#include <io.h>
main(int argc, char **argv)
{
    if(argc < 3)
    {
        printf("Usage: %s <oldname> <newname>\n",
                argv[0]);
    }
    else
    {
        printf("File %s ", argv[1]);
        if(rename(argv[1], argv[2]) != 0)
        {
            perror("rename failed");
        }
        else
        {
```

```
                printf("renamed to %s\n", argv[2]);
            }
        }
    }
```

setmode

COMPATIBILITY

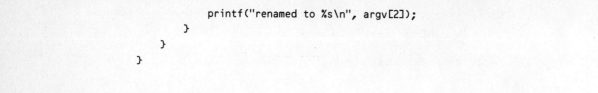

MSC 3	MSC 4	MSC 5	MSC 6	QC1	QC2	QC2.5	TC1	TC1.5	TC2	TC++	ANSI	UNIX V	XNX	OS2	DOS
▲	▲	▲	▲	▲	▲	▲	▲	▲	▲	▲				▲	▲

PURPOSE Use the *setmode* function to set the translation mode (see the tutorial section) of a file opened for unbuffered, unformatted I/O.

SYNTAX

```
int setmode(int handle, int mode);
```

`int handle;` *Handle of open file*

`int mode;` *Integer denoting new translation mode*

EXAMPLE CALL

```
setmode(filehandle, O_BINARY); /* Set file mode to binary */
```

INCLUDES `#include <io.h>` *For function declaration*

`#include <fcntl.h>` *For definition of constants that are used to specify translation modes*

DESCRIPTION The *setmode* function changes to *mode* the translation mode of the file specified by *handle*. The translation mode specifies how carriage return-linefeed pairs are treated during file I/O. The value of the argument *mode* is either the constant 0_TEXT to open in text, or translated, mode or 0_BINARY to open in binary, or untranslated, mode. These are both defined in *fcntl.h*.

COMMON USES Typically, the *setmode* is used to change the default translation modes associated with the files *stdin, stdout, stderr, stdaux*, and *stdprn*. For other files, you can specify the translation mode when opening the file with *open* or *fopen*.

RETURNS When there are no errors, *setmode* returns the previous value of the translation mode. Otherwise, it returns a –1 and sets the global variable *errno* to EBADF if the file handle is invalid or to EINVAL if the value given for the argument *mode* is not equal to one of the constants O_TEXT or O_BINARY.

SEE ALSO `fopen, open` *To open a file and specify a translation mode*

EXAMPLE Use *setmode* to write a program that changes the translation mode of *stdout* from its default "text" to "binary." Now print a string with a newline (\n). You will see that only a single linefeed appears (instead of the normal carriage return-linefeed pair).

```
#include <stdio.h>
#include <io.h>
#include <fcntl.h>
main()
{
/* Set mode of stdout to O_BINARY (binary mode) */
    if(setmode(fileno(stdout), O_BINARY) == -1)
    {
        perror("setmode failed");
    }
    else
    {
        printf("stdout is in binary mode now.\n");
        printf("Notice how this output looks\n");
    }
}
```

COMPATIBILITY

_splitpath

MSC 3	MSC 4	MSC 5	MSC 6	QC1	QC2	QC2.5	TC1	TC1.5	TC2	TC++	ANSI	UNIX V	XNX	OS2	DOS
		▲	▲	▲	▲	▲	1	1	1	1				▲	▲

PURPOSE Use *_splitpath* to separate a full pathname into its components: drive letter, directory path, file name, and file extension.

SYNTAX

```
void _splitpath(char *path, char *drive, char *dir,
                char *fname, char *ext);
```

`char *path;` *Pointer to buffer where full pathname is stored*

`char *drive;` *Drive letter*

`char *dir;` *Directory path*

`char *fname;` *File name*

`char *ext;` *File extension*

EXAMPLE CALL `_splitpath(pathname, drive, dir, filename, extension);`

INCLUDES `#include <stdlib.h>` *For function declaration and definition of the constants _MAX_DRIVE, _MAX_DIR, _MAX_FNAME, and _MAX_EXT*

DESCRIPTION The *_splitpath* function splits the full pathname given in the argument *path* into its component substrings, which are returned in the strings *drive, dir, fname,* and *ext.* You must allocate enough room for each of these strings. The constants _MAX_DRIVE, _MAX_DIR, _MAX_FNAME, and _MAX_EXT, defined in *stdlib.h,* denote the maximum lengths of the strings *drive, dir, fname,* and *ext,* respectively, and should be used to declare the strings.

When *_splitpath* returns, *drive* contains the drive letter followed by a colon; *dir* has the directory path with either forward or backward slashes as separators; *fname* is the file name; and *ext,* is the extension with a leading period. If a component is absent in the argument *path,* the corresponding string will be empty (it contains a single null character (\0).

1. The equivalent Turbo C and Turbo C++ function is *fnsplit.*

SEE ALSO `_makepath` *To construct a pathname from its components*

EXAMPLE Write a program that uses *_splitpath* to parse a complete pathname entered by the user.

```
#include <stdio.h>
#include <stdlib.h>
main()
{
    char pathname[_MAX_PATH], drive[_MAX_DRIVE],
         dir[_MAX_DIR], filename[_MAX_FNAME],
         ext[_MAX_EXT];
/* Prompt user for a complete path name              */
    printf("Enter complete path name to parse:\n");
    gets(pathname);
/*  Decompose complete path name and display result  */
   _splitpath(pathname, drive, dir, filename, ext);
   printf("Drive         : %s\n", drive);
   printf("Directory path: %s\n", dir);
   printf("Filename      : %s\n", filename);
   printf("Extension     : %s\n", ext);
}
```

stat

COMPATIBILITY

MSC 3	MSC 4	MSC 5	MSC 6	QC1	QC2	QC2.5	TC1	TC1.5	TC2	TC++	ANSI	UNIX V	XNX	OS2	DOS
▲	▲	▲	▲	▲	▲	▲	▲	▲	▲	▲		▲	▲	▲	▲

PURPOSE Use the *stat* function to obtain information about an existing file specified by its pathname.

SYNTAX

```
int stat(char *path, struct stat *buffer);

char *path;              Pathname of file whose "vital statistics" will be returned

struct stat *buffer;     Pointer to structure where result will be returned
```

EXAMPLE CALL

```
stat("result.dat", &stat_buffer);
```

INCLUDES

```
#include <sys\types.h>      Required by <sys\stat.h>

#include <sys\stat.h>       For function declaration and definition of structure stat
```

DESCRIPTION The *stat* function returns certain information about the file or directory specified by the pathname in the argument *path*. The information is stored by *stat* in a structure of type *stat*. A pointer to an allocated structure of this type must be provided in the argument *buffer*. The structure *stat* is defined in <sys\stat.h> and its declaration is of the form:

```
struct stat
{
    dev_t          st_dev;   /* Drive number of disk or handle of
                                device containing the file      */
    ino_t          st_ino;   /* Unused in MS-DOS. The "i-node"
                                number of file in UNIX           */
    unsigned short st_mode;  /* Bit mask of file's mode          */
    short          st_nlink; /* Always set to 1 under MS-DOS     */
    short          st_uid;   /* Unused in MS-DOS. For "user-id"
                                under UNIX                       */
    short          st_gid;   /* Unused in MS-DOS. For "group-id"
                                under UNIX                       */
    dev_t          st_rdev;  /* Same as the field st_dev         */
    off_t          st_size;  /* Size of file in bytes            */
    time_t         st_atime; /* Time of last modification        */
    time_t         st_mtime; /* Same as st_atime                 */
    time_t         st_ctime; /* Same as st_atime                 */
};
```

If the pathname refers to a directory, the field *st_mode* has the bit corresponding to the constant S_IFDIR set. For a file, on the other hand, the bit corresponding to the value S_IFREG is set. Other bits in this field indicate read/write permissions and whether the *path* refers to a device. When it refers to a device, the values in the time and size fields are meaningless.

RETURNS The *stat* function returns 0 to indicate its success in obtaining the information about the file. Otherwise, the return value is –1 and the global variable *errno* is set to the constant ENOENT, indicating that no file, directory, or device exists by the specified pathname.

SEE ALSO

`access`	*To check if read/write operations are permitted on a file*
`chmod`	*To change read/write permissions of a file*
`fstat`	*To find information about a file specified by a valid handle*

EXAMPLE Use *stat* to write a utility program that prints useful information about a file.

```
#include <stdio.h>
#include <sys\types.h>
#include <sys\stat.h>
#include <time.h>
main(int argc, char **argv)
{
    struct stat info;
    if(argc < 2)
    {
        printf("Usage: %s <pathname>\n", argv[0]);
    }
    else
    {
        if(stat(argv[1], &info) != 0)
        {
            perror("Error in \"stat\"");
            exit(1);
        }
/* Print out information about the file              */
        printf("File: %s\n\
Drive        :  %c\n\
Size         :  %ld bytes,\n\
Last modified:  %s\n",  argv[1], info.st_dev+65,
                info.st_size, ctime(&info.st_atime));
    }
}
```

COMPATIBILITY

umask

MSC 3	MSC 4	MSC 5	MSC 6	QC1	QC2	QC2.5	TC1	TC1.5	TC2	TC++	ANSI	UNIX V	XNX	OS2	DOS
▲	▲	▲	▲	▲	▲	▲	▲	▲	▲	▲		▲	▲	▲	▲

PURPOSE Use the *umask* function to set the read/write permission mask that modifies the read/write permission settings of subsequent files created by this process.

SYNTAX

```
int umask(int pmode);

int pmode;        Permission mask to be used in all subsequent new files
```

EXAMPLE CALL

```
/* Make all future files read-only */
    oldmask = umask(S_IWRITE);
```

INCLUDES

```
#include <io.h>              For function declaration

#include <sys\types.h>       For definition of data types used in <sys\stat.h>

#include <sys\stat.h>        For definition of constants to specify permission settings of a file
```

DESCRIPTION The *umask* function accepts a read/write permission setting mask (see the tutorial) in the integer argument *pmode*. The mask modifies the permission settings for new files created by calls to *creat*, *open*, or *sopen*.

The mask *pmode* is interpreted as follows. If a particular bit is set to 1, the corresponding bit in the file's permission setting is 0 (which means that operation will not be allowed). On the other hand, a 0 in a particular bit of *pmode* implies that the corresponding bit in the permission setting is left unchanged.

The *pmode* argument can take one of the values shown in Table 13-7 expressed in terms of constants that are defined in the include file *sys\stat.h*.

Because MS-DOS always allows reading from a file, only the S_IWRITE setting has use in an MS-DOS system.

Table 13-7. *Possible Values of Permission Mask in* umask

Constant	Interpretation
S_IWRITE	Writing is not allowed.
S_IREAD	Reading is not allowed (that is ignored in MS-DOS).
S_IREAD ¦ S_IWRITE	Both reading and writing disallowed (reading is always allowed in MS-DOS).

RETURNS The *umask* function returns the previous value of the permission mask.

SEE ALSO `creat, open, sopen` *To create and open new files for unformatted I/O*

EXAMPLE Write a program to set the permission mask so that future files are read only. Display the previous value of the mask.

```
#include <stdio.h>
#include <sys\types.h>
#include <sys\stat.h>
#include <io.h>

main()
{
    int oldmask;
/* Make all future files read-only */
    oldmask = umask(S_IWRITE);
    printf("Previous value of permission mask was %X\n",
            oldmask);
}
```

unlink

COMPATIBILITY

MSC 3	MSC 4	MSC 5	MSC 6	QC1	QC2	QC2.5	TC1	TC1.5	TC2	TC++	ANSI	UNIX V	XNX	OS2	DOS
▲	▲	▲	▲	▲	▲	▲	▲	▲	▲	▲		▲	▲	▲	▲

PURPOSE Use *unlink* to delete a file specified by its pathname.

SYNTAX `int unlink(const char *path);`

`const char *path;` *Pathname of file to be deleted*

EXAMPLE CALL `unlink("old.dat");`

INCLUDES `#include <io.h>` *For function declaration*

or

`#include <stdio.h>`

DESCRIPTION The *unlink* function deletes the file specified by the pathname *path*. (This function is more useful under UNIX, in which a file can be linked to multiple directories.)

RETURNS If *unlink* successfully deletes the specified file, it returns a 0. A return value of −1 indicates error. If *unlink* cannot find the file specified by the pathname, the global variable *errno* is set to ENOENT. If the file is read only or if it is a directory, *errno* is set to EACCES.

SEE ALSO `remove` *Also deletes a file*

EXAMPLE Use *unlink* in a program that deletes a file chosen by the user.

```
#include <stdio.h>
#include <io.h>
main(int argc, char **argv)
{
    if(argc < 2)
    {
        printf("Usage: %s <pathname>\n", argv[0]);
    }
    else
    {
        printf("File %s ", argv[1]);
        if(unlink(argv[1]) != 0)
        {
            perror("unlink failed");
        }
        else
        {
            printf("deleted\n");
        }
    }
}
```

Chapter 14 Directory Manipulation

Introduction

MS-DOS is an operating system with a file system that takes care of the details of physical storage of data and lets you work with files at a high level.

MS-DOS, like UNIX, uses a hierarchical filing system enabling you to organize your files in directories and subdirectories. The Microsoft directory manipulation routines provide the basic tools to create, modify, and remove directories from within your C program. These routines are distinct from the routines discussed in Chapter 13, which work with files rather than directories.

Concepts

You need to understand the MS-DOS file system before you can make appropriate use of the Microsoft C directory manipulation routines.

DOS FILE SYSTEM As you saw in Figure 13-1, DOS—like many other operating systems—uses a hierarchical file system. Each disk consists of a root directory under which there are typically additional directories and files. Each of these directories may have additional directories, to a depth of 32 levels from the root. A directory in this model is just a file capable of storing data (such as name, address, and size) about other files. The *pathname* of a file is constructed by concatenating the drive name to a list of directory names ending with the name of the file, as was illustrated in Figure 13-2. Although this conceptual model is similar to that used in most other file systems, the naming conventions and the way data is stored on the physical media (hard disk, floppy disk, CD-ROM, etc.) normally varies from one operating system to another. See the discussion of pathnames on pages 501–2.

Notes

MS-DOS includes such commands as *MKDIR (MD), RMDIR (RD),* and *CHDIR (CD)* which allow you to create a directory, remove a directory, or change the current working directory. Both the five-character version and the shorter version in parentheses are legal commands. The directory manipulation routines in the Microsoft C compiler allow you to accomplish these tasks from within your C program, however, the full name of the routine (for example, *mkdir*) rather than an abbreviation must be used. Version 5.1 of the compiler provided five directory functions, and three routines were added by Microsoft C 6.0. The routines are summarized in Table 14-1.

One function of special interest is *_searchenv*, with which your program can search for a particular file in a list of directories (including the current working directory) that are specified in an environment variable such as PATH. You can, for example, use *_searchenv* to locate the file *AUTOEXEC.BAT* in the directories defined in the PATH environment variable by using the call

```
_searchenv ("autoexec.bat", "PATH", buffer);
```

where *buffer* is a character array in which *_searchenv* places the full pathname of the file for which it is looking. In this example, the return from *_searchenv* will load the variable *buffer* with the string *C:\AUTOEXEC.BAT* if the file is found on the root directory of drive C.

Table 14-1. *Directory Manipulation Routines*

Routine	Description
chdir	Changes the current working directory.
_chdrive	Changes the current working drive from your program. The argument uses an integer to identify the drive, where 1 = A, 2 = B, and so on. This does not change the current working directory. When writing in protected mode in OS/2, remember that the working drive is a process resource, and is reset to its earlier state upon process termination.
getcwd	Returns the current working directory.
_getdrive	Returns the name of the current working drive. It uses an integer to identify which drive, with 1 = A, 2 = B, and so on. There is no error return because a working drive is an assumed condition of the system.

Table 14-1. *(cont.)*

Routine	Description
_getdcwd	Inserts the full pathname (including the disk drive specification) of the current working directory on a drive to a storage buffer. The maximum length for the pathname is specified in an argument.
mkdir	Creates a new directory.
rmdir	Deletes a directory, provided it is empty.
_searchenv	Searches for a file in directories listed in a specified environment variable.

Cautions

- The directory manipulation routines did not allow you to switch to a different drive until Microsoft C version 6.0.
- The C language and a DOS pathname both use the backslash (\) character for "control" purposes, and thus you must isolate pathname backslashes from your C program. A newline character in C, for example, is represented by *n*, and a bell is denoted by *a*. Since *n* and *a* and the other C backslash commands could also be legal names for a directory, you must add a second backslash when you want to prevent C from interpreting a backslash from indicating a control character. For example: *chdir (\\dos)*.
- MS-DOS assigns less space for entries in the root directory than it does to any of the other directories. A 9-track double-sided double-density floppy, for example, can store 112 files in the root directory; a high-density 5 1/4 floppy can hold 512. No other directories have such low limits; their constraint is simply the amount of available storage space.

Further Reading

One aspect of the DOS file system we did not discuss is the physical storage of files. The developer's guide by The Waite Group[1] devotes a chapter to the physical layout files on disks in MS-DOS. Duncan's book[2] is another source for such information.

1. The Waite Group, *MS-DOS Developer's Guide* 2d Ed., Howard W. Sams & Company, Carmel, IN, 1989, 723 pages.
2. Ray Duncan, *Advanced MS-DOS*, Microsoft Press, Redmond, WA, 1986, 468 pages.

chdir

COMPATIBILITY

MSC 3	MSC 4	MSC 5	MSC 6	QC1	QC2	QC2.5	TC1	TC1.5	TC2	TC++	ANSI	UNIX V	XNX	OS2	DOS
▲	▲	▲	▲	▲	▲	▲	▲	▲	▲	▲		▲	▲	▲	▲

PURPOSE Use *chdir* to change the current working directory. The *chdir* function works exactly like the MS-DOS command CD.

SYNTAX

```
int chdir(char *path);

char *path;        Pathname of new working directory
```

EXAMPLE CALL

```
chdir("c:\\bin\\sample");
```

INCLUDES

```
#include <direct.h>        For function declaration
```

DESCRIPTION The *chdir* function changes the current working directory to the one specified by the argument *path*. As with the MS-DOS command, CD, you cannot change the default drive. Use the *_dos_setdrive* function to change the drive.

COMMON USES The *chdir* function allows you to change working directories while in your application program.

RETURNS When *chdir* succeeds in changing the current directory, it returns a 0. In case of error, it returns a −1 and sets the global variable *errno* to ENOENT to indicate that the specified pathname is invalid.

COMMENTS A call to *chdir* with a pathname that includes a drive specification sets the current working directory to the one on that drive, but the drive name remains unchanged. To use that directory, set the default drive with a call to the DOS function *_dos_setdrive* or with the use of *system*.

SEE ALSO

`mkdir, rmdir` — *Other functions to manipulate directories*

`_dos_setdrive` — *To change the default drive*

`system` — *To execute an MS-DOS command from a program*

EXAMPLE Write a program using *chdir* that provides the functionality of the MS-DOS command CD.

```
#include <stdio.h>
#include <direct.h>
```

```
main(int argc, char **argv)
{
    if(argc < 2)
    {
        printf("Usage: %s <pathname>\n", argv[0]);
    }
    else
    {
        if(chdir(argv[1]) != 0)
        {
            perror("Error in \"chdir\"");
        }
    }
}
```

COMPATIBILITY

_chdrive

MSC 3	MSC 4	MSC 5	MSC 6	QC1	QC2	QC2.5	TC1	TC1.5	TC2	TC++	ANSI	UNIX V	XNX	OS2	DOS
			▲			▲								▲	▲

PURPOSE Use the *_chdrive* function to change the current working drive from your program.

SYNTAX

```
int _chdrive (int dsk_drv);
```

`dsk_drv` *The number of a new working drive (A:= 1, B:= 2, etc.)*

EXAMPLE CALL

```
if (! _chdrive (drive)) printf ("\nThis is a test.");
```

INCLUDES `#include <direct.h>` *For function declaration*

DESCRIPTION Use the *_chdrive* function to change the current working drive from within your program. The argument uses an integer to identify the drive, where 1 = A, 2 = B, and so on. This does not change the current working directory.

RETURNS The *_chdrive* function returns a 0 if the working drive is successfully changed. A failed call yields a nonzero value.

COMMENTS When writing in protected mode under OS/2, remember that the working drive is a process resource, and it is reset to its earlier state upon process termination. The original drive in a DOS environment must be explicitly reset if it is something to which you wish your program to return.

SEE ALSO `_dos_setdrive` *DOS system service to set default drive*

`_getdrive` *To get current working drive*

EXAMPLE The example program assumes a development system on which two 40-megabyte physical drives (for a combined 80 megabytes) are broken into logical drives *C:* through *I:*. This layout makes it possible to easily segregate projects from each other. Backup copies of work in progress are made from one physical disk to the other, and two smaller disks are used instead of one larger disk, so that a given hard disk failure only traps one copy of the data. It is important, however, to keep track of which disk and which subdirectory are current.

The program displays the list of legal logical drive names, and —upon request—the current directory of a selected drive. (It can be easily modified to show the current directories, automatically.)

```
#include <conio.h >
#include <direct.h>
#include <stdio.h >
#include <stdlib.h>

void main ()
{
  int chk_byt, orig_drv, next_drv;
  static char path[_MAX_PATH];
  /* save current drive - restore it at program end */

  orig_drv = _getdrive ();
  printf ("The drives on your system are: \n");

  /* cycle through the alphabet looking for drives */
  for (next_drv = 1; next_drv <= 26; next_drv++)
     if (!_chdrive (next_drv)) printf ("\\%c: ", next_drv +
         'A'-1);
         printf ("\nLook for the current directory on the
                    valid drives:\n");
   while(1)
   {
      printf ("\nEnter a valid drive letter (ESC = quit): ");
      chk_byt = getch ();

      if (chk_byt == 27) break;

      if (_getdcwd (toupper (chk_byt) - 'A'+1, path, _MAX_PATH)
         != NULL)
```

```
            printf ("\nThe directory for the drive is %s\n", path);
        }

        /* restore the original drive */

        _chdrive (orig_drv);
}
```

Sample output:

```
The drives on your system are:
\A: \B: \C: \D: \E: \F: \G: \H: \I:
Look for the current directory on the valid drives:
Enter a valid drive letter (ESC = quit): G
The directory for the drive is G:\C600\BIN
Enter a valid drive letter (ESC = quit): C
The directory for the drive is C:\TYPESET\C\REFS
```

COMPATIBILITY

getcwd

MSC 3	MSC 4	MSC 5	MSC 6	QC1	QC2	QC2.5	TC1	TC1.5	TC2	TC++	ANSI	UNIX V	XNX	OS2	DOS
▲	▲	▲	▲	▲	▲	▲	▲	▲	▲	▲		▲	▲	▲	▲

PURPOSE Use *getcwd* to get the full pathname of the current working directory, including the drive name.

SYNTAX

```
char *getcwd(char *path, int numchars);
```

`char *path;` *Buffer where pathname of current working directory is returned*

`int numchars;` *Number of bytes available in the buffer for pathname*

EXAMPLE CALL `getcwd(path_buffer, 80);`

INCLUDES `#include <direct.h>` *For function declaration*

DESCRIPTION The *getcwd* function gets the pathname of the current working directory, including the drive specification, and stores it in the buffer specified by the argument *path*. The integer argument *numchars* tells *getcwd* the maximum number of characters the buffer *path* can hold. If the *path* argument is NULL, *getcwd* allocates *numchars* bytes using *malloc* and stores the pathname in this space. When you no longer need the space, you can free it by calling *free* with the pointer returned by *getcwd* as argument.

COMMON USES The *getcwd* function is useful for getting the current directory name and saving it. If your program changes working directories during its execution, it can use the saved name to restore the original working directory before exiting.

RETURNS The *getcwd* function returns a pointer to the buffer in which the pathname is stored. If *path* is not NULL, the return value is equal to *path* or a pointer to the buffer allocated to hold the pathname. A return value of NULL indicates an error. The global variable *errno* is set to ENOMEM if the *path* argument is NULL and *getcwd* fails when allocating a buffer. If the pathname has more characters than *numchars*, *errno* is set to ERANGE.

SEE ALSO `chdir` *To change current working directory*

EXAMPLE Use *getcwd* to get the pathname of the current working directory and display it.

```
#include <stdio.h>
#include <direct.h>
main()
{
    char pathname[81];
    if (getcwd(pathname, 80) == NULL)
    {
        perror("Error in getcwd");
    }
    else
    {
        printf("Current directory: %s\n", pathname);
    }
}
```

_getdcwd

COMPATIBILITY

MSC 3	MSC 4	MSC 5	MSC 6	QC1	QC2	QC2.5	TC1	TC1.5	TC2	TC++	ANSI	UNIX V	XNX	OS2	DOS
			▲			▲								▲	▲

PURPOSE Use the *_getdcwd* function when you need the full pathname *and* the disk drive specification of the current working directory on a drive. The related *getcwd* function does not provide the drive name.

SYNTAX `char *_getdcwd (int drv_num, char *pth_bufr, int max_len)`

`drv_num` *An integer value for a disk drive (1 = A; 2 = B)*

`pth_bufr` *Storage location for the fully qualified pathname*

`max_len` *The maximum length of the pathname*

EXAMPLE CALL

```
if(_getcwd (toupper(ch) - 'A' + 1, path, _MAX_PATH) !=NULL)
```

INCLUDES `#include <direct.h>` *For function declaration*

`#include <errno.h>`

DESCRIPTION The *_getdcwd* routine stores the full path in the specified buffer. The maximum length for the pathname is carried in the *max_len* argument; be forewarned: error will result if the limit is exceeded. The value of the _MAX_PATH constant is defined in *stdlib.h.*

A *NULL* argument for the buffer is legal; in that case the *_getdcwd* function will make a call to *malloc* to reserve a buffer of at least size *max_len*. If your application is running short on space, the buffer can be subsequently returned to the system with a call to *free*.

RETURNS The *_getdcwd* function returns the buffer with the pathname after a successful call. A failed call generates a NULL. The values to *errno* are ENOMEM and ERANGE.

SEE ALSO

`chdir` *To change working directory*

`getcwd` *To get current working directory*

`_getdrive` *To get current drive*

EXAMPLE See the example program on the reference page for *_chdrive*.

COMPATIBILITY

_getdrive

MSC 3	MSC 4	MSC 5	MSC 6	QC1	QC2	QC2.5	TC1	TC1.5	TC2	TC++	ANSI	UNIX V	XNX	OS2	DOS
			▲			▲								▲	▲

PURPOSE Use the *_getdrive* function when you need the name of the current working drive.

SYNTAX

```
int _getdrive (void)
```

EXAMPLE CALL

```
orig_drv = _getdrive (); /* saving the current drive id */
```

INCLUDES `#include <direct.h>` *For function declaration*

DESCRIPTION The *_getdrive* function uses an integer to identify a drive, with the pattern being 1 = A, 2 = B, and so on.

RETURNS The integer indicating the current working drive (1 = A:, 2 = B:). There is no error return because a working drive is an assumed condition of the system.

SEE ALSO `getcwd` *To get current working directory*

`_getdcwd` *To get drive and working directory*

EXAMPLE See the example program on the reference page for *_chdrive*.

mkdir

COMPATIBILITY

MSC 3	MSC 4	MSC 5	MSC 6	QC1	QC2	QC2.5	TC1	TC1.5	TC2	TC++	ANSI	UNIX V	XNX	OS2	DOS
▲	▲	▲	▲	▲	▲	▲	▲	▲	▲	▲				▲	▲

PURPOSE Use *mkdir* to create a new directory with a specified pathname.

SYNTAX `int mkdir(char *path);`

`char *path;` *Pathname of new directory*

EXAMPLE CALL
```
mkdir("c:\\waite\\mscb"); /* c:\waite must already exist */
```

INCLUDES `#include <direct.h>` *For function declaration*

DESCRIPTION The *mkdir* function creates a new directory with the pathname *path*. The pathname can include drive specification and directory/subdirectory names, but because *mkdir* can only create one directory at a time all but the last subdirectory must already exist. For example, if you have an existing directory named TEMP in the root directory of drive C, you can create a new directory with the pathname *C:\TEMP\NEW_1*, but *C:\TEMP\NEW_1\NEW_2* is illegal because it requires the creation of two directories.

COMMON USES The *mkdir* function is convenient in "setup" programs that you might distribute with your application. It can be used to implement, for example, the setup program provided with Microsoft C 5.1 for installing the compiler. Essentially, *mkdir* lets you create new directories from your program.

RETURNS When *mkdir* succeeds in creating the directory, it returns a 0. In case of error, it returns a −1 and sets the global variable *errno* to ENOENT, indicating that the specified pathname is invalid, or to EACCES, indicating that that pathname is that of a drive or an existing file or directory.

SEE ALSO `rmdir` *To delete a directory*

`chdir` *To change the current working directory*

EXAMPLE Write a program using *mkdir* that provides the functionality of the MS-DOS command *md.*

```
#include <stdio.h>
#include <direct.h>
main(int argc, char **argv)
{
    if(argc < 2)
    {
        printf("Usage: %s <pathname>\n", argv[0]);
    }

    else
    {
        if(mkdir(argv[1]) != 0)
        {
            perror("Error in \"mkdir\"");
        }
    }
}
```

COMPATIBILITY **rmdir**

MSC 3	MSC 4	MSC 5	MSC 6	QC1	QC2	QC2.5	TC1	TC1.5	TC2	TC++	ANSI	UNIX V	XNX	OS2	DOS
▲	▲	▲	▲	▲	▲	▲	▲	▲	▲	▲				▲	▲

PURPOSE Use *rmdir* to delete an existing directory with a specified pathname.

SYNTAX `int rmdir(char *path);`

`char *path;` *Pathname of directory to delete*

EXAMPLE CALL `rmdir("c:\\temp\\last"); /* c:\temp\last must be empty */`

INCLUDES `#include <direct.h>` *For function declaration*

DESCRIPTION The *rmdir* function deletes an existing directory with the pathname *path*. The pathname can include drive specification, directory, and subdirectory names. As with the MS-DOS command RD, the directory must be empty before it can be deleted. For example, if you have an existing directory named TEMP in the root directory of drive C, provided it is empty, you can use *rmdir("c:\\temp")* to delete it.

RETURNS If *rmdir* successfully deletes the directory, it returns a 0. In case of error, it returns a −1 and sets the global variable *errno* to ENOENT if the specified pathname is invalid or to EACCES if the pathname is that of a drive or an existing file, if the directory is not empty, or if the specified directory is the root directory or the current working directory.

SEE ALSO `mkdir` *To create a new directory*

`chdir` *To change the current working directory*

EXAMPLE Write a program using *rmdir* that provides the functionality of the MS-DOS command *rd.*

```
#include <stdio.h>
#include <direct.h>
main(int argc, char **argv)
{
    if(argc < 2)
    {
        printf("Usage: %s <pathname>\n", argv[0]);
    }
    else
    {
        if(rmdir(argv[1]) != 0)
        {
            perror("Error in \"rmdir\"");
        }
    }
}
```

COMPATIBILITY

_searchenv

MSC 3	MSC 4	MSC 5	MSC 6	QC1	QC2	QC2.5	TC1	TC1.5	TC2	TC++	ANSI	UNIX V	XNX	OS2	DOS
		▲	▲	▲	▲	▲		1	1	1				▲	▲

PURPOSE Use *_searchenv* to search for a particular file in a list of directories, including the current working directory and those defined in a specific environment variable.

SYNTAX

```
void _searchenv(char *name, char *env_var, char *path);
```

`char *name;` *Name of file to find*

`char *env_var;` *Environment variable that defines directories to search through*

`char *path;` *Buffer you supply to hold the full pathname of the file if it is found*

EXAMPLE CALL

```
_searchenv(fname, "PATH", buffer);
```

INCLUDES `#include <stdlib.h>` *For function declaration*

DESCRIPTION The *_searchenv* function first searches in the current working directory for the file whose name is given in the argument *name*. If the file is not found in the current directory, *_searchenv* continues the search in each directory path specified in the definition of the environment variable *env_var*. The definition of this variable is of the same form as that of the DOS environment variable PATH in that the directory names are separated by semicolons. If the file is found, *_searchenv* copies the file's pathname into the buffer at address *path* which must be large enough to hold the full pathname. If *_searchenv* fails to locate the file, *path* will contain a single null character.

1. The equivalent Turbo C and Turbo C++ function is *searchpath*. It is compatible with Microsoft C 5 and 6, but incompatible with versions 3 and 4.

SEE ALSO `getenv, putenv` *To access and alter the environment table*

EXAMPLE Write a utility that accepts a file name and searches for that file in all directories listed in the PATH environment variable. If found, print the full pathname of the file. Use *_searchenv* to locate the file.

```
#include <stdio.h>
#include <stdlib.h>
main(int argc, char **argv)
```

```
{
    char path_buffer[80];
    printf("This program searches for a file in all\n\
the directories specified in the PATH \n\
environment variable\n");
    if(argc < 2)
    {
        printf("Usage: %s <filename>\n", argv[0]);
        exit(0);
    }
/* Use "_searchenv" to locate the file */
    _searchenv(argv[1], "PATH", path_buffer);
    if(path_buffer[0] == '\0')
    {
        printf("File: %s not found\n", argv[1]);
    }
    else
    {
        printf("Found as: %s\n", path_buffer);
    }
}
```

Directory Manipulation

Chapter 15 Input and Output Routines

Introduction

Input and output (I/O) make computers useful as information processing tools. I/O can involve reading from and writing to files in the disk or reading input from the keyboard and sending output to the display screen or sending commands to peripherals. The Microsoft C library provides a large assortment of I/O routines for each of these tasks. We will discuss the salient features of the Microsoft C I/O routines here.

The C programming language has no built-in capability to perform I/O. This is the responsibility of the library accompanying your C compiler. The Microsoft C library includes the ANSI standard I/O library along with a group of I/O routines that provide access to hardware in the PC. The Microsoft C library also includes a UNIX C library core of routines that was the de facto standard before the official adoption of the ANSI standard in 1989.

We will describe the available file types in MS-DOS and the types of I/O necessary to access all IBM PC hardware features. The I/O categories include file I/O and I/O operations with registers in peripheral devices. Then we will describe all Microsoft C I/O routines, grouping them by common function, and finally we provide some cautions that should help you use these routines properly.

Concepts of File and Other I/O

The concept of a "file" is universal to almost all I/O in MS-DOS and Microsoft C, with the exception of reading or writing to *port* addresses in the peripheral devices attached to the 8086 microprocessor. You can think of a file as a sequence of bytes of data stored on a diskette, a RAM disk, CD ROM, or some external media. A file must be able to receive or impart a stream of bytes; physical storage need not underlie a file, as is shown in Figure 15-1A. Thought of in this manner, the keyboard, the serial communications port, and the display screen are all files—precisely the model used by the file I/O routines in Microsoft C.

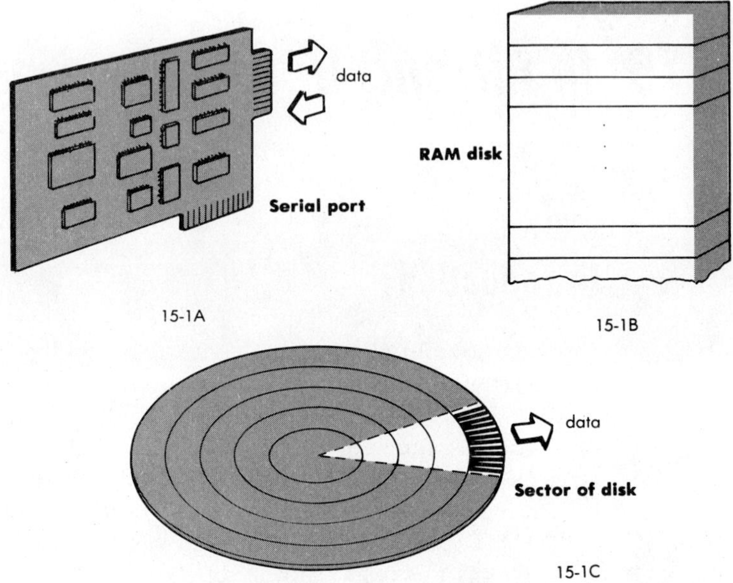

Figure 15-1. *Files in Microsoft C*

TEXT AND BINARY FILES

In addition to this abstract view of a file as a stream of bytes, C programmers have to remember another distinction among files: how the constituent bytes are interpreted. Under MS-DOS, a file can be either text or binary.

In "text" files, each byte is interpreted as an ASCII character with a Control-Z representing the end of the file. In C (and in UNIX), a newline character (\n) signifies the end of a line (newline is an ASCII 10). In an MS-DOS text file, however, the end of a line of text is marked by a pair of characters: a carriage return (CR) followed by a linefeed (LF). We call this pair the CR-LF. By the way, CR and LF are represented in C by \r and \n, respectively. This end-of-line difference between C and MS-DOS can be a problem during file I/O.

Microsoft C solves this problem by allowing the file I/O routines to perform some translation when interacting with a text file. A Control-Z character in an MS-DOS file opened in text mode signifies the end of that file (even if there is more data after the character). When reading from the file, a CR-LF pair is translated by the C I/O routines to LF (which is the newline character \n in C). When writing to the file using the C I/O routines, a single LF causes a CR-LF pair to be written, allowing proper formatting under MS-DOS. This approach keeps the model of text files fixed in your C program whether it is running under UNIX or MS-DOS. There is little impact on your programming because the translation takes place automatically whenever you open an MS-DOS file in the text mode.

In reading and writing "binary" files using C I/O routines, the bytes are not interpreted in any manner. To understand and use the contents of a binary file you must know what was stored there in the first place. After all, a 4-byte value in the file could be a long integer, a *float* variable, or even two short integers. When you know how the binary file was written, reading from it is straightforward. For example, if you write 1,000 short integer values to a binary file from a 2,000-byte buffer in memory, each two-byte value you later read from the file represents a short integer—a perfect match.

Binary files are ideal for storing numeric data because of the efficient manner of storage. To represent an integer value, say 32,767, in a text file, you would need 5 bytes to store the ASCII representation of the five digits. In binary form, 2 bytes are enough to hold this number. So if you had two files full of such data, the binary one would be 2.5 times smaller than the ASCII counterpart. Note, however, that the binary file would not be readable by a word processor or a text editor.

TYPES OF I/O ROUTINES IN MICROSOFT C

The Microsoft C library has three types of I/O routine: the stream routines, followed by the low-level file I/O routines, and finally the console and port I/O routines.

The "stream" routines refer to I/O performed using the model of files as a stream of bytes together with a buffer associated with a file. The "buffer" is a temporary storage area for the stream of bytes being read from or written to the file. The "low-level" routines are similar except that they do not use a buffer. "Console and port I/O" is meant for direct input and output from the keyboard, the monitor, and any peripheral devices (such as the serial adapter) attached to the PC.

Buffered Stream I/O

The stream I/O routines use a buffer to hold data in transit to and from a file. In a buffered read operation from a disk file, as Figure 15-2 illustrates, a fixed chunk of bytes is read from the disk into a buffer of the same size. The routines requesting data from the file actually read from the buffer. When the buffer has no characters left, it is automatically refilled by a disk read operation. A similar sequence occurs when writing to a file.

The use of a buffer leads to efficient I/O on disk files because there are fewer disk accesses which are much slower than reading from a buffer

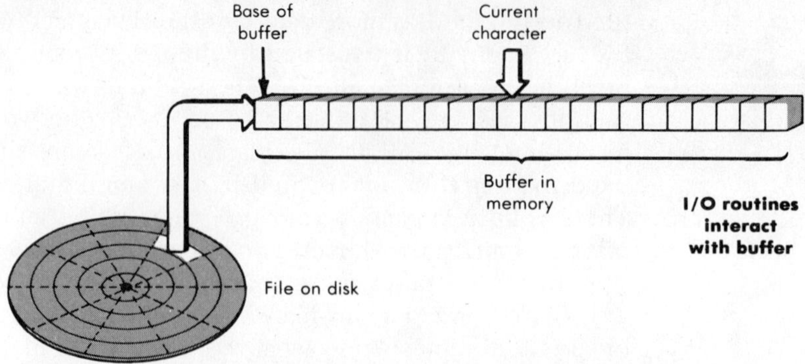

Figure 15-2. *Buffered file I/O*

in memory. There is only one drawback of the buffered approach to I/O; data written to a buffer do not actually appear in the disk file until the buffer is written out. This is "flushing" the buffer, a housekeeping chore normally handled automatically in C programs. In certain cases, however, the buffers are not flushed. These include ending the program abnormally because of a fatal error, exiting a C program with a call to the *_exit* function, or a hardware error occurring.

The Microsoft C stream I/O functions use an internal data structure to maintain information about the file being accessed. The data structure, named FILE, is defined in the include file *stdio.h*. As shown in Figure 15-3, the FILE structure has room for information about the current buffer, including an identifying number for the file (known as the file's "handle") and a single byte flag to indicate such status and control information as whether an end-of-file occurred during a read operation or an error occurred during I/O. When a file is opened by a stream I/O routine such as *fopen*, a pointer to a FILE structure is returned to the calling program. Subsequent stream I/O operations identify the file by the pointer to the associated FILE data structure. In fact, this pointer to the FILE data structure is commonly referred to as the *stream*. Thus, when we say read from the stream *stdin*, we mean read from the file whose associated FILE structure's address is in *stdin*. Incidentally, *stdin* is a stream that refers to the keyboard and it is already open when a C program begins running.

Another important feature of the stream I/O routines is *formatting I/O*, the process of converting internal binary values of variables to character strings that can be written out to a file. For example, suppose a single byte contains the bit pattern: 01100100 (which is a binary representation of the decimal value 100). Converting this binary pattern into three ASCII characters in the string *100* involves formatting. Thus formatting is the step that makes the binary representations printable. Not all stream I/O routines are meant for formatted I/O; the *fread* and *fwrite* routines are for reading and writing unformatted binary data.

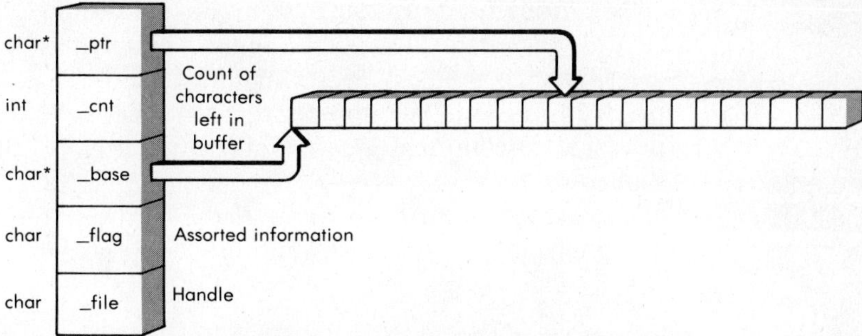

Figure 15-3. ***FILE data structure***

Unbuffered Low-Level I/O

Low-level I/O refers to unbuffered I/O, thus no buffer holds data read from the disk. Instead, each read request results in accessing the disk (or the device the file refers to) to fetch a requested number of bytes. Since disk accesses are time-consuming, the low-level routines are meant for reading or writing a significant number of bytes at a time.

The low-level I/O routines include no formatting capability. Since formatting is necessary when reading and writing text files (because we have to convert from character strings to internal representations), the low-level I/O routines are not suitable for performing I/O with text files. Binary files, on the other hand, do not require formatting during read/write operations so the low-level routines are ideal for I/O with binary files.

Like the buffered stream I/O routines, the low-level routines maintain data structures that contain such information as the current read/write position in the file and the permission settings for the file. Instead of the FILE pointer used by the stream routines, the low-level routines use the handle, a unique number, to identify each file. A stream file, with its associated FILE data structure, can also be accessed by a handle, which you can get by using the Microsoft C library function *fileno.* Similarly, a buffer may be associated with a file opened by a low-level call so that high-level stream I/O routines can be used on that file. This is accomplished by the library routine *fdopen.*

Console and Port I/O

This last category of I/O is not related to file I/O. Instead, these routines are meant for direct access to the keyboard, the screen, and any I/O port in the PC. Note that the keyboard and the monitor together are called the "console." Access to the keyboard and screen using the console I/O routines is similar to using BIOS calls (described in Chapter 16). There is no buffering of any sort and you do not have to formally open the device to perform these I/O operations.

Various hardware subsystems in the IBM PC can be controlled by sending commands to specific registers known as "ports." These registers are similar to memory locations, but they are accessed by an addressing mechanism in the 8086 microprocessor that is separate from the one used to reach conventional memory and video memory. Thus these ports have their own address space—the I/O address space. The port I/O routines allow you to read from and write to the hardware registers using the assembly language instructions IN and OUT, respectively.

Communications and the Serial Port

The *serial port* on the PC is an example of peripheral hardware that can be programmed by reading from and writing to I/O ports. The serial port on the PC is used for communicating with other computers and on-line services such as CompuServe, BIX, Genie, or your local bulletin board system. A plug-in card that fits into a slot in your PC, the serial port has an RS 232C serial adapter for sending data out. In the typical arrangement, shown in Figure 15-4, individual bytes from the computer are converted into an on-off, or digital, signal by a Universal Asynchronous Receiver Transmitter (UART) on the serial adapter. This signal goes out through the serial port into a "modem," which converts the signals into a continuously variable form ("analog" signal) suitable for transmission over telephone lines. At the receiving end, another modem converts the signal back into digital form and finally another UART at the receiving end packs the individual bits from the digital signal into bytes. The UART is controlled by writing to or reading from a set of internal registers which can be accessed via port addresses. Because the port addresses are assigned sequentially, it is enough to know the address of the first port, commonly known as the "base address," of the serial adapter. In the IBM PC, the two serial ports COM1 and COM2 are assigned base port addresses 3F8h and 2F8h, respectively. Thus for the serial adapter COM1, the first register is at 3F8h, the next at 3F9h, and so on.

We will not discuss the function of each register in the UART, except to say that they allow you to control all parameters necessary for communicating data (such as baud rate and word length) and to enable hardware "interrupts" to be generated when certain events occur (such as an incoming byte being ready at the UART or the UART being free to send a byte out). The programming of the registers in the UART can be done by using the Microsoft C I/O functions *inp* and *outp*.

We discuss the concept of interrupts in the section on *System Calls* (Chapter 16). To handle the physical interrupts, you must also program another device—the Intel 8259A Programmable Interrupt Controller in your PC. This device acts as a gatekeeper deciding which device can interrupt the 8086 microprocessor and which ones cannot. The 8259A is also programmed by sending commands to its registers accessible via I/O port

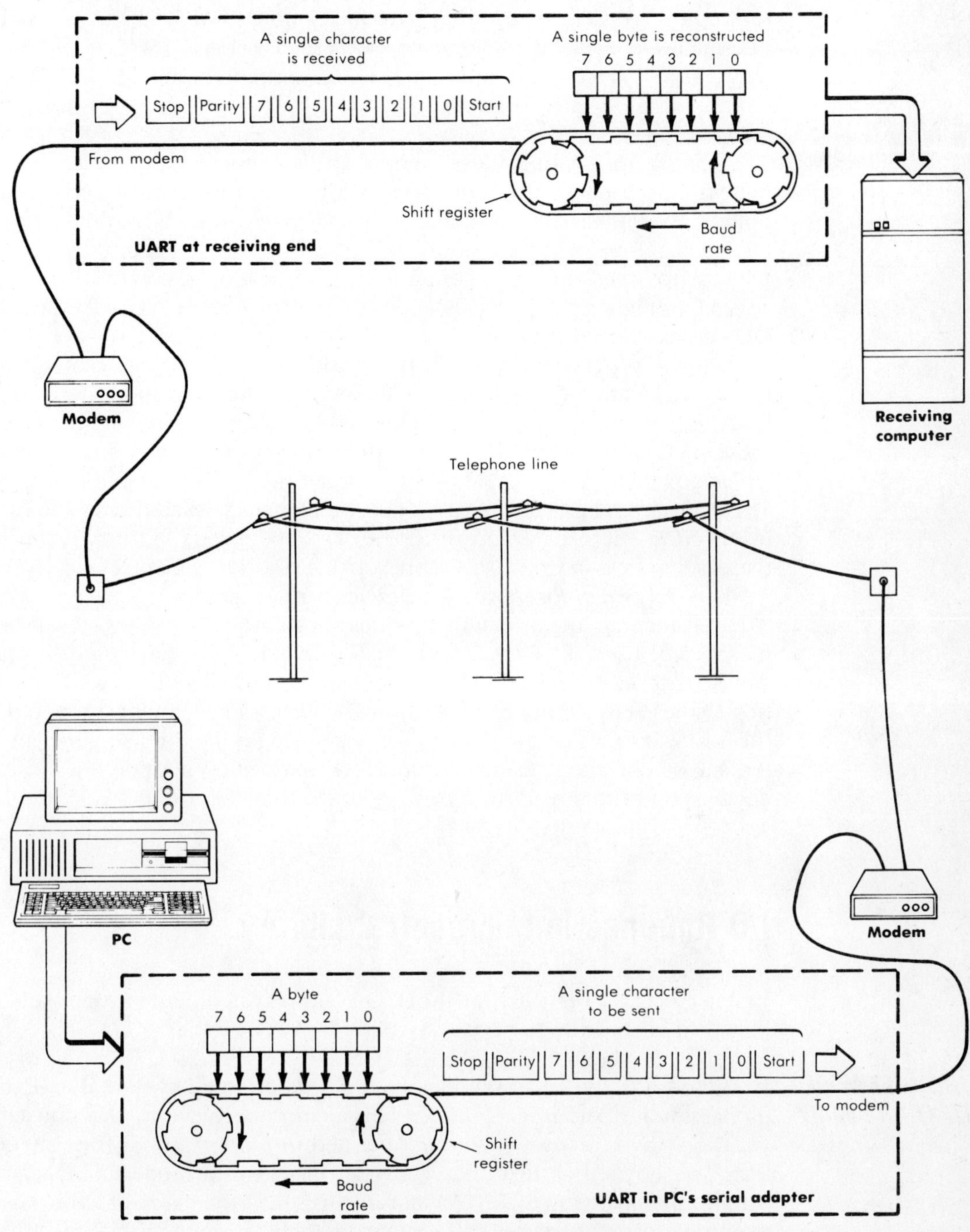

Figure 15-4. ***Communicating via the serial port in the IBM PC***

addresses (20h and 21h). If your interest is piqued by this summary description of *communications programming* on the PC, you can get more information in Chapter 13 of the *MS-DOS Papers* (Howard W. Sams & Company, 1988), a compendium on MS-DOS programming by The Waite Group.

FILE-SHARING The concept of sharing files is important because computers are being increasingly connected in networks so users can reach across and create, open, or modify files in another PC. MS-DOS version 3.0 introduced certain mechanisms to allow multiple processes on different computers in the network to access files at a common node. If you are using MS-DOS version 3.0 or higher, you can enable this file-sharing capability by issuing the DOS command SHARE.

At the programmer's level, file-sharing is achieved by opening the file with a call to the *sopen* library function with the exact mode of sharing specified with flags. Then you use the Microsoft C function *locking* to lock those parts of the file that you want to work on. When you are finished, *unlocking* them makes these portions of the file again available to others. There are several other MS-DOS services that manage shared access to files in MS-NET, Microsoft's network for PCs. Since a detailed discussion of these services is beyond the scope of this tutorial, we refer you to the *MS-DOS Technical Reference Manual* for further details.

In general, the file I/O routines, both stream and low-level, are meant to be used as follows: open the file (where a file can be a device as well), perform the read and write operations, and close the file. In addition to these tasks other routines allow I/O from a specific position in the file, or format a value for printing, or read a single line or a single character, and so on. The console and port I/O routines do not open or close a device; you simply read from or write to the console or the I/O port.

I/O Routines in Microsoft C Library

In this section we describe the I/O routines included in Microsoft C library to enable you to use these routines effectively.

DEFAULT MODE: TEXT OR BINARY In Microsoft C, the default mode of a file is determined by the value of the global integer variable *_fmode*. This is normally set to the constant O_TEXT (a preprocessor constant defined in *fcntl.h*), so all files, by default, are opened as text files. You can change the mode to binary by setting *_fmode* to O_BINARY. You can also select the mode of a file when opening it or you can use the *setmode* library function to change the translation mode of a file that is already open.

FILES ALREADY OPENED FOR YOUR CONVENIENCE

When your C program starts up, the five files shown in Table 15-1 are opened for you by Microsoft C. These may be called as streams or by handles. The first three files, *stdin, stdout,* and *stderr*, get input from the user, display the output, and display error messages, respectively. From DOS, you can redirect *stdin* and *stdout* to other files.

Table 15-1. *Preopened Files in Microsoft C*

File	Stream Name	Handle Number	Connected to/Mode
Standard input	stdin	0	Console (keyboard)/Text mode
Standard output	stdout	1	Console (display screen)/Text mode
Standard error	stderr	2	Console (display screen)/Text mode
Standard auxliary	stdaux	3	Cannot be connected/Binary mode
Standard print	stdprn	4	Printer port on PC/Binary mode

OPEN FILE LIMIT IN MS-DOS

MS-DOS imposes a limit of 20 open files per process (processes are defined in Chapter 11). Since 5 files are already opened, your program can open 15 files. Files opened for buffered as well as unbuffered I/O count towards this limit.

The number of open streams that use pointers to FILE data structures remains fixed at 20 at all times. But in MS-DOS 3.3, the number of open file handles for the low-level I/O routines such as *open, read, write,* and *lseek* can be made larger. Increasing the number of open file handles involves changing an assembly language file named CRTODAT.ASM, which is distributed with Microsoft C 5.0 and up. This file contains code that runs at the beginning and end of every C program. At the beginning of the file you will find the line

```
_NFILE_ = 20 ; Maximum number of file handles
```

which initializes the symbol *_NFILE_* to 20. By editing this line and changing 20 to a higher value you alter the upper limit on the number of file handles. Assemble this file using Microsoft Macro Assembler MASM version 4.0 or later. If you link the new object file CRT0DAT.OBJ explicitly with your program, the new maximum takes effect. You can make the change permanent by replacing the CRT0DAT.OBJ module in the C runtime library for the memory model you plan to use.

GLOBAL VARIABLES AND CONSTANTS THAT MATTER

The I/O routines are affected by certain global variables and preprocessor constants defined by the Microsoft C library. (We have already mentioned one of the variables, *_fmode*, which determines the default translation mode of a file.) Table 15-2 lists the most important of these as they relate to the I/O routines. Many more predefined constants are significant to individual I/O routines, but these are described in the reference pages for the relevant I/O routines.

Table 15-2. ***Certain Constants and Global Variables Relevant to I/O Routines***

Name	Meaning and Default Value
BUFSIZ	Defines the size of each buffer associated with a stream. Constant is defined in *stdio.h* to be equal to 512.
EOF	Denotes end-of-file. Constant is defined in *stdio.h* as –1.
_fmode	Controls the translation modes (text or binary) of files opened in the program. Global integer's default setting is O_TEXT.
NFILE	Denotes the maximum number of files that can be opened by a process. Constant is defined in *stdio.h* to 20 and can be redefined under MS-DOS 3.3.
NULL	Signifies error returns defined in *stdio.h* to 0 (or 0L for compact, large, and huge memory models).

THE I/O ROUTINES

Table 15-3 catalogs the I/O routines. Since the number of routines in the entire I/O category is quite large, in addition to listing the routines alphabetically, in Table 15-4 we group them according to the specific tasks they perform. In listing the I/O routines by function, we start with the ones that perform file I/O. This group also includes routines that perform I/O with the preopened streams: *stdin* and *stdout.*

Table 15-3. ***I/O Library Routines***

Routine	Description
	Stream Routines
clearerr	Clears the error indicator of a stream.
fclose	Closes a stream.
fcloseall	Closes all streams that are currently open.
fdopen	Associates a stream with a file already opened by a low-level call.
feof	Returns a nonzero value if current position in a stream is at the end of file.
ferror	Returns a nonzero value if an error had occurred during read/write operations on a stream.
fflush	Writes to the file the contents of the buffer associated with a stream.
fgetc	Reads a character from a stream.
fgetchar	Reads a character from the stream *stdin*.
fgetpos	Returns current position of a stream in an internal format suitable for use by *fsetpos*.
fgets	Reads a line (up to and including the first newline character) from a stream.
fileno	Returns the file handle associated with a stream.
flushall	Flushes all buffers of all open streams to the respective files.

Table 15-3. *(cont.)*

Routine	Description
fopen	Opens a named file as a buffered stream (includes options for selecting translation modes and access types).
fprintf	Performs formatted output to a stream.
fputc	Writes a character to a stream.
fputchar	Writes a character to the stream *stdout*.
fputs	Writes a string of characters to a stream.
fread	Reads a specified amount of binary data from a stream.
freopen	Closes a stream and reassigns it to a new file.
fscanf	Performs formatted input from a stream.
fseek	Sets current position to a specific location in the file.
_fsopen	Opens a file as a stream and prepares it for reading and writing. It was introduced in Microsoft C 6.0.
fsetpos	Sets current position of a stream using value returned by an earlier call to *fgetpos*.
ftell	Returns the current position in the file associated with a stream.
fwrite	Writes a specified number of bytes of binary data to a stream.
getc	Reads a character from a stream.
getchar	Reads a character from the stream *stdin*.
gets	Reads a string up to a newline character from the stream *stdin*.
getw	Reads two bytes of binary data from a stream.
printf	Performs formatted output to the stream *stdout*.
putc	Writes a character to a stream.
putchar	Writes a character to the stream *stdout*.
puts	Writes a C string to the stream *stdout*.
putw	Writes two bytes of binary data to a stream.
rewind	Sets the current position to the beginning of the file associated with a stream.
rmtmp	Deletes all files created by *tmpfile*.
scanf	Performs formatted input from the stream *stdin*.
setbuf	Assigns a fixed-length user-defined buffer to an open stream.
setvbuf	Assigns a variable-length user-defined buffer to an open stream.
sprintf	Performs formatted output to a buffer.
sscanf	Performs formatted input from a buffer.
tempnam	Generates a temporary file name with arbitrary directory name.
tmpfile	Creates a temporary file open for buffered stream I/O.
tmpnam	Generates a temporary file name with the directory name specified by the constant *P_tmpdir*.
ungetc	Pushes a character back into the buffer associated with a stream.
vfprintf	Version of *fprintf* that accepts a pointer to a list of arguments and performs formatted output to a stream.
vprintf	Version of *printf* that accepts a pointer to a list of arguments and performs formatted output to the stream *stdout*.
vsprintf	Version of *sprintf* that accepts a pointer to a list of arguments and performs formatted output to a buffer.

Table 15-3. *(cont.)*

Routine	Description
	Low-Level Routines
close	Closes a file using its handle.
creat	Creates a new file, opens it, and returns its handle.
dup	Creates a second handle given an existing handle associated with an open file.
dup2	Assigns a specified second handle to an existing handle so that both handles refer to the same file.
eof	Checks for end-of-file condition of a file specified by a handle.
lseek	Sets the current position in a file referenced by a handle.
open	Opens a file for low-level I/O and returns a handle.
read	Reads a specified number of bytes of binary data from a file open for low-level I/O.
sopen	Opens a file for shared low-level I/O and returns a handle.
tell	Returns the current position in a file referenced by a handle.
write	Writes a specified number of bytes of binary data to a file open for low-level I/O.
	Console and Port Routines
cgets	Reads a string of characters from the console.
cprintf	Performs formatted output to the console.
cputs	Writes a string to the console.
cscanf	Performs formatted input from the console.
getch	Reads (without echoing) a single unbuffered character from the console.
getche	Reads and echoes a single unbuffered character from the console.
inp	Reads a single byte from a specified I/O port address.
inpw	Reads two contiguous bytes from a specified I/O port address.
kbhit	Tests whether there are any keystrokes waiting to be read.
outp	Writes a single byte to a specified I/O port address.
outpw	Writes two bytes to a specified I/O port address.
putch	Writes a single unbuffered character to the console.
ungetch	Pushes a character back to the console.

Table 15-4. *Library Routines by Task*

I/O Task	Stream I/O	Low-level I/O
Create a file	fopen	creat, open, sopen
Open a file	fopen, freopen, _fsopen	open, sopen
Close a File	fclose, fcloseall	close
Formatted read	fscanf, scanf	—
Formatted write	fprintf, printf, vfprintf, vprintf	—
Read a character	fgetc, fgetchar, getc, getchar	—
Write a character	fputc, fputchar, putc, putchar	—

Table 15-4. ***(cont.)***

I/O Task	Stream I/O	Low-level I/O
Read a line	fgets, gets	—
Write a line	fputs, puts	—
Set read/write position	fseek, fsetpos, rewind	lseek
Get read/write position	fgetpos, ftell	tell
Binary read	fread, getw	read
Binary write	fwrite, putw	write
Flush buffer	fflush, flushall	—
Get handle of a stream	fileno	—
Assign buffer to a handle	fdopen	—
Duplicate a handle	—	dup, dup2
Check error/eof	clearerr, feof, ferror	eof
Manage temporary files	rmtmp, tempnam, tmpfile, tmpnam	—
Control buffering	setbuf, setvbuf	—
Push character to buffer	ungetc	—

String I/O

If you think of files as a stream of bytes, the data sources or destinations do not have to be disk files or devices; they can also be buffers in memory. A group of Microsoft C I/O routines provides the capability to read from and write to arrays of characters ("strings"). These routines allow you to format data and place the result in a string or get characters from a string and convert the characters to internal values. This is often convenient because you can prepare a string that can be output by routines that do not have any formatting capability (for example, the *_outtext* routine in the Graphics category). Table 15-5 lists the three string I/O routines according to the task they perform.

Table 15-5. ***String I/O Routines by Task***

I/O Task	Routines
Format input from a string	sscanf
Format output to a string	sprintf, vsprintf

Console and Port I/O Routines by Task

Table 15-6 shows the console and port I/O routines that interact with the keyboard and the screen, grouped by task. As you can see, the console I/O routines also support formatting. The formatting capabilities are identical to those supported by *printf* and *scanf* which we describe next.

Table 15-6. *Console and Port I/O Routines Grouped by Task*

I/O Task	Routines
Read from an I/O port address	inp, inpw
Write to an I/O port address	outp, outpw
Read character from console	getch, getche
Write character to console	putch
Check for waiting keystrokes	kbhit
Push a character back to console	ungetch
Read a string from console	cgets
Write a string to console	cputs
Format input from the console	cscanf
Format output to the console	cprintf

FORMATTED I/O: PRINT *AND* SCANF

The formatting I/O capabilities of *printf* and *scanf* deserve special attention because they are widely used in C programs and a large number of formatting options are available under each function. Many other functions, such as *cprintf, cscanf, fprintf, fscanf, sprintf,* and *sscanf,* provide identical formatting options. Thus understanding *printf* and *scanf* should help you use all the formatted I/O routines in the Microsoft C library.

Formatting involves converting internal representation of a variable into a character string that humans can understand. To interpret the contents of a set of memory locations you must know the type of C variable being stored there. For example, a set of four bytes can hold a long integer and it can also hold a single-precision floating-point number. The *printf* and *scanf* functions, responsible for formatting the data, have to be told how the contents of these bytes are to be interpreted. This is done by embedding formatting commands in the arguments passed to *printf* and *scanf.*

Formatted Output with printf

In the simplest case, when printing out values of variables, you can use *printf* with a minimal amount of formatting code:

```
float   floatvar = 24.95;
double  dblvar = 99.95;
int     intvar = 100;
char    string[] = "Microsoft C 6.0";
:
:
printf("Float = %f, Double = %f, Integer = %d,\nString = %s\n",
        floatvar, dblvar, intvar, string);
```

In this case, each formatting command consists of a percent sign (%) followed by a single letter that indicates the type of the variable. The format codes are embedded in a string and each command appears exactly where you want the variable to be printed. The string with the formatting codes is followed by the variables that you want printed. Here's what you get if you embed the code fragment above in a C program and execute it.

```
Float = 24.950001, Double = 99.950000, Integer = 100, String =
Microsoft C 6.0
```

You may have noticed the discrepancy between the assigned value of the *float* variable and the value shown by *printf.* The single-precision *float* variables are accurate to 7 significant digits. When we used the %f format to print the value, *printf* used more than 7 significant digits (by default it used 6 digits following the decimal point). Since the stored value is only accurate to 7 significant digits, the value prints as *24.950001* instead of the expected *24.950000.* This illustrates an important point about formatted output: you can only print results that can have at best the accuracy present in the stored value. Since a *float* variable is accurate to 7 digits, you cannot expect to get a more accurate value just by asking *printf* to use a formatting option that requires the use of, say, 15 significant digits.

Notice too that both *float* and *double* floating-point values are printed with six digits after the decimal place. The integer value is printed without any leading blanks and the string is printed in its entirety. These are the default settings of the respective formats: %f, %d, and %s. Additional qualifiers can be placed between the percent sign and the type letter to indicate options, such as the number of digits after the decimal point or a fixed size of field within which to print a value.

Other data types can also be printed out, including the *long* and *unsigned* forms of integers as well as single characters and addresses of variables in hexadecimal format. See the reference pages on *printf* for complete coverage of the formatting options and commands. We will not repeat the information here except to note that while *printf* is meant for writing to the stream *stdout*, *fprintf* performs the same operation to a file and *sprintf* writes formatted output to a string. There is even a formatted console output routine named *cprintf.* Each of these accepts the same formatting commands as *printf.*

Formatted Input with scanf

The *scanf* function is meant for formatting input, which involves reading characters and converting groups of them into internal representation of C variables. Like *printf,* a string with embedded format codes specifies how the input characters are to be treated during the conversion process. In fact, a call to *scanf* looks like a call to *printf,* except that the argument list has addresses of the variables into which *scanf* loads the values converted from the input string. If we were reading a *float*, a *double*, and an integer, the call might look like:

```
float   floatvar;
double  dblvar;
int     intvar;
:
:
scanf(" %f %lf %d", &floatvar, &dblvar, &intvar);
```

This formatted read statement reads the three values with any number of blank spaces between them. Note that the format code meant for the *float* variable is different from that for the *double*. The %f code tells *scanf* to convert the string into the internal representation of a *float* variable. The qualifier l between the % and the f tells *scanf* to use the internal representation of a *double* instead of a *float*.

Like *printf*, *scanf* is used with formatted input from the stream *stdin*. The Microsoft C I/O library also includes *fscanf* for formatted reading from a file and *sscanf* for formatted input from a string. Lastly, there is a formatted input routine for the console called *cscanf*. All of these routines use the same formatting commands as *scanf*. The reference page on *scanf* gives a detailed discussion of the formatting options available to you as a programmer.

Cautions

- Do not mix low-level I/O read and write routines with the buffered stream routines because the two sets are not compatible.
- Remember that the translation mode O_TEXT causes interpretation of the bytes in a file and the number of bytes read or written does not correspond to the number in the file. This means that you cannot rely on absolute byte positions when accessing a file in the text mode.
- Single keystrokes from the console cannot be read by *getchar* (it waits until a carriage return is hit). Use the console routines *getch* or *getche* for this purpose. For example, if you wanted to end a program when the user presses any key, you could use

```
{
    :
    :
    printf("Press any key to exit:");
    getch()  /* Read a keystroke and exit */
}
```

If you use *getchar*, the function does not return immediately after a key is pressed. It waits until a carriage return to end the read operation.

- When using the buffered I/O routines, the buffers sometimes have to be explicitly written out (flushed) with the library routines *fflush* or *flushall* before output data actually appears in a file. Normally, buffers are flushed during program termination, but not when a program ends with a call to *_exit*.
- The formatting options available in the *printf* and the *scanf* family are quite extensive and several format codes are specific to Microsoft C 5 and above. When portability is a concern, check the appropriate reference pages carefully before using a particular format code.
- Note that file-sharing is supported only under MS-DOS 3.0 and higher.

Further Reading

The standard I/O routines are covered in almost every book on C. Prata's book[1] provides a gentle introduction to these functions, yet includes a detailed exposition of the concepts behind the C I/O library. The basic file I/O routines are also carefully explained in Lafore's text on C[2].

Chapter 13 of the *MS-DOS Papers*[3] covers in detail how you can program the serial port of a PC in Microsoft C, and it includes an example program illustrating the use of the port I/O routines *inp* and *outp*.

1. Stephen Prata, The Waite Group, *Advanced C Primer++*, Howard W. Sams & Company, Carmel, IN, 1986, 502 pages.
2. Robert Lafore, *The Waite Group's Microsoft C Programming for the PC*, 2d Ed., Howard W. Sams & Company, Carmel, IN, 1990, 816 pages.
3. The Waite Group, *MS-DOS Papers*, Howard W. Sams & Company, Carmel, IN, 1988, 608 pages.

Stream I/O

clearerr

COMPATIBILITY

MSC 3	MSC 4	MSC 5	MSC 6	QC1	QC2	QC2.5	TC1	TC1.5	TC2	TC++	ANSI	UNIX V	XNX	OS2	DOS
▲	▲	▲	▲	▲	▲	▲	▲	▲	▲	▲	▲	▲	▲	▲	▲

PURPOSE Use the *clearerr* function to reset the error and end-of-file indicators of a file specified by a file pointer (i.e., a pointer to the associated FILE data structure).

SYNTAX

```
void clearerr(FILE *file_pointer);
```

`FILE *file_pointer;` *Pointer to FILE data structure associated with the file whose error flag is being cleared*

EXAMPLE CALL

```
clearerr(outfile);
```

INCLUDES `#include <stdio.h>` *For function declaration and definition of the FILE data type*

DESCRIPTION The *clearerr* function sets to zero a flag in the FILE data structure associated with the file specified by the argument *file_pointer*. This flag has a nonzero value after an error or an end-of-file condition occurs. The error indicator for the file remains set until cleared by calling *clearerr*. These conditions may be verified by calling *ferror* and *feof*, respectively.

SEE ALSO `ferror` *To detect an error condition of a file*

`feof` *To determine an end-of-file condition*

EXAMPLE Write a C program that prompts the user for a file name. Open the file with *fopen* for read operations only. Then create an error condition by trying to write to the file. Call *ferror* to detect the error and call *clearerr* to reset the error flag.

```
#include <stdio.h>
main()
{
    char filename[81];
    FILE *infile;
    long filesize;
    printf("Enter the name of an existing file: ");
    gets(filename);
/* Open the file */
    if ( (infile = fopen(filename, "r")) == NULL)
```

```
    {
        printf("fopen failed to open: %s\n", filename);
        exit(0);
    }
    fprintf(infile, "Test..."); /* Try to read a line*/
    if (ferror(infile) != 0)   /* Check for the error*/
    {
        printf("Error detected\n");
        clearerr(infile);       /* Now clear the error */
        printf("Error cleared\n");
    }
}
```

Stream I/O

COMPATIBILITY

fclose

MSC 3	MSC 4	MSC 5	MSC 6	QC1	QC2	QC2.5	TC1	TC1.5	TC2	TC++	ANSI	UNIX V	XNX	OS2	DOS
▲	▲	1	▲	▲	▲	▲	▲	▲	▲	▲	▲	▲	▲	▲	▲

PURPOSE Use *fclose* to close a file opened earlier for buffered input and output using *fopen*.

SYNTAX

```
int fclose(FILE *file_pointer);
```

`FILE *file_pointer;` *Pointer to file to be closed*

EXAMPLE CALL

```
fclose(infile);
```

INCLUDES `#include <stdio.h>` *For function declaration and definition of FILE data type*

DESCRIPTION The *fclose* function closes the file specified by the argument *file_pointer*. This pointer must have been one returned earlier when the file was opened by *fopen*. If the file is open for writing, the contents of the buffer associated with the file are flushed before the file is closed. The buffer is then released.

1. Beginning in Microsoft C 5.0 *fclose* automatically deletes any file created by the *tmpfile* function.

COMMON USES To ensure that all buffers get flushed and freed for reuse and that the file is properly closed, use *fclose* for files that you no longer intend to use in your program.

RETURNS If the file is successfully closed, *fclose* returns a zero. In case of an error, the return value is equal to the constant EOF defined in *stdio.h*.

COMMENTS You can use the *fcloseall* function to close all open files at the same time. Since only 20 files opened by *fopen* can be present at the same time, however, for file-intensive applications you may find it necessary to close files with *fclose* when you are done with a file.

SEE ALSO

`fopen` *To open a file for buffered I/O*

`fcloseall` *To close all open files at the same time*

EXAMPLE Use *fopen* to open a file specified by the user. Read and display the file's contents. Close the file by calling *fclose* and then exit.

```
#include <stdio.h>
char filename[80],      /* Name of file to open        */
     line[81];          /* For lines from the file     */
FILE *inputfile;        /* File pointer to opened file */
main()
{
    printf("Enter name of file to open: ");
    gets(filename);
/* Open the file */
    if ((inputfile = fopen(filename,"r")) == NULL)
    {
        printf("Error opening file: %s\n", filename);
        exit(0);
    }
    printf("==== Contents of input file ====\n");
    while(fgets(line, 80, inputfile) != NULL)
    {
        printf(line);
    }
/* Now close the file and exit */
    fclose(inputfile);
}
```

COMPATIBILITY

fcloseall

MSC 3	MSC 4	MSC 5	MSC 6	QC1	QC2	QC2.5	TC1	TC1.5	TC2	TC++	ANSI	UNIX V	XNX	OS2	DOS
▲	▲	1	▲	▲	▲	▲	▲	▲	▲	▲				▲	▲

PURPOSE Use *fcloseall* to close all files opened for buffered input and output with *fopen* or *tmpfile*, respectively.

SYNTAX

```
int fcloseall(void);
```

EXAMPLE CALL

```
number_closed = fcloseall();
```

INCLUDES

```
#include <stdio.h>
```
For function declaration

DESCRIPTION The *fcloseall* function closes all files that have been opened by *fopen* or *tmpfile* for buffered I/O. Buffers associated with files opened for writing are written out to the corresponding file before closing.

Note that *fcloseall* does not close the five I/O *streams* (*stdin, stdout, stderr, stdaux,* and *stdprn*) that are preopened by the system (see the tutorial section).

1. Beginning in Microsoft C 5.0 *fclosall* automatically deletes any file created by the *tmpfile* functions.

COMMON USES You can use *fcloseall* to close, in a single stroke, all files opened by your program.

RETURNS If files are successfully closed, *fcloseall* returns the number closed. In case of an error, the return value is equal to the constant EOF defined in *stdio.h.*

SEE ALSO

`fopen` *To open a file for buffered I/O*

`fclose` *To close a single file*

EXAMPLE We'll illustrate two features of the file I/O routines with this example. The function *tmpfile* enables you to create a temporary file. Write a sample C program in which you attempt to open 20 temporary files. Since MS-DOS allows only 20 files (for buffered I/O) and 5 are already open, the *tmpfile* call will fail after 15 files are open. Now call *fcloseall* to close them all at once. Print the number returned by *fcloseall* to verify that it's 15.

```
#include <stdio.h>
main()
```

```
{
    int i;
/* Try opening 20 temporary files -- we'll just throw
 * away the returned pointers because we are not going

 * to use these files. The file open will fail after 15
 * files are opened. So the number of closed files
 * should be 15.
 */
    for (i=0; i<20; i++)
    {
        if (tmpfile() == NULL)
            printf("Error opening file # %d\n", i);
        else
            printf("Temporary file #%d opened\n", i);
    }
/* Now close all the files and inform user how many were
 * closed
 */
    i = fcloseall();
    printf("%d files were closed -- should be 15\n", i);
}
```

Stream I/O

fdopen

COMPATIBILITY

MSC 3	MSC 4	MSC 5	MSC 6	QC1	QC2	QC2.5	TC1	TC1.5	TC2	TC++	ANSI	UNIX V	XNX	OS2	DOS
▲	▲	▲	▲	▲	▲	▲	▲	▲	▲	▲		▲	▲	▲	▲

PURPOSE Use *fdopen* to associate a buffer with a file that has been opened for unbuffered, unformatted I/O. This allows subsequent buffered, formatted read/write operations with the file.

SYNTAX `FILE *fdopen(int handle, char *access_mode);`

`int handle;` *Handle of open file being upgraded for buffered I/O*

`char *access_mode;` *A character string denoting whether file is being opened for read/write.*

EXAMPLE CALL `p_datafile = fdopen(handle, "rb");`

INCLUDES `#include <stdio.h>` *For function declaration and definition of FILE data type*

DESCRIPTION The *fdopen* function associates a FILE data structure with the file specified by the argument *handle*. The *handle* is an integer returned by low-level I/O routines such as *open, creat*, and *sopen* that originally opened the file. Once buffered I/O becomes permissible, the type of operations you intend to perform on the file must be indicated by the argument *access_mode*. Table 15-7 lists the possible values of *access_mode* and their meanings.

Table 15-7. *Access Modes When Opening Files for Buffered I/O*

Access Mode String	Interpretation
r	Opens file for read operations only. The *fopen* function fails if the file does not exist.
w	Opens a new file for writing. If the file exists, its contents are destroyed.
a	Opens file for appending. A new file is created if the file does not exist.
r+	Opens an existing file for both read and write operations. Error is returned if file does not exist.
w+	Creates a file and opens it for both reading and writing. If file exists, current contents are destroyed.
a+	Opens file for reading and appending. Creates a new file if one does not exist.

In addition to the basic access modes shown in Table 15-7, one of the characters shown in Table 15-8 can be appended to each of the strings in Table 15-7 to specify how the contents of the file are to be translated. Note that the character denoting the translation mode (see the tutorial section) can come before or after the + in the strings above. For example, *w+b* is considered the same as *wb+* and means "open the file for reading and writing in the binary mode." If no translation mode is specified, the default mode is determined by the global variable *_fmode*, which is declared in the header file *stdio.h*. When a file is opened for appending with the *a* or *a+* access mode, existing data can never be destroyed because the *file pointer* is moved to the end of the file before writing occurs. This pointer keeps track of the current position where writing occurs. When a file is opened for updating, using the *r+*, *w+* or *a+* access modes, you must call one of the functions *fsetpos, fseek*, or *rewind* when switching between read and write operations. These calls serve to set the file pointer properly before the operation. You can also call *fsetpos* or *fseek* and set the file pointer to the current position.

COMMON USES The *fdopen* function is used to enable buffered, formatted I/O on a file that was originally opened for unbuffered, unformatted I/O.

Table 15-8. ***File Translation Modes for Buffered I/O***

Translation Mode	Interpretation
b	Opens file in untranslated or binary mode. Every character in the file is read as is without the changes described below.
t	Opens file in translated mode. This is a Microsoft C extension and not an ANSI standard mode. Its purpose is to accommodate MS-DOS file conventions. In this mode, the following interpretations will be in effect: (1) Carriage Return-Line Feed (CR-LF) combinations on input are translated to single linefeeds. During output, single linefeed characters are translated to CR-LF pairs. (2) During input, the Control-Z character is interpreted as the end-of-file character.

RETURNS If successful, *fdopen* returns a pointer to the FILE structure that is associated with the file. In case of an error, *fdopen* returns a NULL. See below for an example of checking for error return from *fdopen*.

COMMENTS The *access-mode* specified in the call to *fdopen* must be compatible with the access and sharing modes used when the file was first opened by *open, creat,* or *sopen*. Microsoft warns against using *fdopen* with a file that was opened with *sopen* and file-sharing enabled. The buffered operations are inherently incompatible with the concept of file-sharing because the file is not up to date and ready for sharing as long as some of the data resides in the buffer.

SEE ALSO

`fclose` *To close a file opened by* fdopen

`open` *To open a file using a handle, a lower-level routine*

EXAMPLE Use *open* to open a file, say, *autoexec.bat* (this is one file every PC has) in the root directory of your current drive, say, drive C. Now call *fdopen* to allow buffered I/O on the file. Read and display all lines in the file.

```
#include <stdio.h>
#include <io.h>
#include <fcntl.h>

main()
{
        int handle;
        FILE *infile;
        char buffer[80];
/* Open the file. Note that we need two '\'  */
        if ( (handle = open("c:\\autoexec.bat",
```

```
                O_RDONLY)) == -1)
        {
            perror("open failed");
            exit(1);
        }
/* Use fdopen to assign a FILE data structure to file */
        if ((infile = fdopen(handle, "r")) == NULL)
        {
              perror("fdopen failed");
              exit(1);
          }
/* All's well. Read and print the contents of the file*/
          printf("Contents of c:autoexec.bat:\n");
          while ( fgets(buffer, 80, infile) != NULL)
          {
              printf(buffer);
          }
}
```

Stream I/O

COMPATIBILITY

feof

MSC 3	MSC 4	MSC 5	MSC 6	QC1	QC2	QC2.5	TC1	TC1.5	TC2	TC++	ANSI	UNIX V	XNX	OS2	DOS
▲	▲	▲	▲	▲	▲	▲	▲	▲	▲	▲	▲	▲	▲	▲	▲

PURPOSE Use the *feof* macro, defined in *stdio.h*, to determine whether the end of a file has been reached.

SYNTAX `int feof(FILE *file_pointer);`

`FILE *file_pointer;` *Pointer to FILE data structure associated with the file whose status is being checked*

EXAMPLE CALL `if (feof(infile) != 0) printf("File ended\n");`

INCLUDES `#include <stdio.h>` *For function declaration and definition of the FILE data type*

DESCRIPTION The *feof* macro returns a value indicating whether the file specified by the argument *file_pointer* has reached its end.

COMMON USES When you get an error return from a read operation, you can call *feof* to determine if the error occurred because you tried to read past the end-of-file.

RETURNS If the end of the file is reached, *feof* returns a nonzero value after the first read operation beyond the end-of-file. Otherwise, it returns a 0.

COMMENTS Since *feof* is implemented as a macro, checking for end-of-file with *feof* does not involve the overhead of calling a function.

SEE ALSO

`clearerr` *To reset the end-of-file and error indicator of a file*

`rewind` *To move the file pointer to the beginning of a file*

`fclose` *To close a single file*

EXAMPLE Use *fopen* to open the file *autoexec.bat* for buffered read operations. Read and display each line until an error is returned by the read routine *fgets*. Then call *feof* to check whether end-of-file is reached. If not, there is another error in reading from the file.

```
#include <stdio.h>
main()
{
        FILE *infile;
        unsigned char buffer[81];
/* Open the file "c:\autoexec.bat". We need two '\'  */
        if ( (infile = fopen("c:\\autoexec.bat", "r"))
             == NULL)
        {
            printf("fopen failed.\n");
            exit(0);
        }
        printf("Contents of c:autoexec.bat:\n");
        while ( fgets(buffer, 80, infile) != NULL)
        {
            printf(buffer);
        }
        if (feof(infile) != 0) /* Check end-of-file */
        {
            printf("*** End-of-file reached ***");
        }
        else
        {
            printf("ERROR: reading from file!\n");
        }
}
```

Stream I/O

COMPATIBILITY

ferror

MSC 3	MSC 4	MSC 5	MSC 6	QC1	QC2	QC2.5	TC1	TC1.5	TC2	TC++	ANSI	UNIX V	XNX	OS2	DOS
▲	▲	▲	▲	▲	▲	▲	▲	▲	▲	▲	▲	▲	▲	▲	▲

PURPOSE Use the *ferror* macro, defined in *stdio.h*, to determine if an error has occurred during a previous read or write operation on a file that had been opened for buffered I/O.

SYNTAX

```
int ferror(FILE *file_pointer);
```

`FILE *file_pointer;` *Pointer to FILE data structure associated with the file whose status is being checked*

EXAMPLE CALL

```
if (ferror(infile) != 0) printf("Error detected\n");
```

INCLUDES `#include <stdio.h>` *For function declaration and definition of the FILE data type*

DESCRIPTION The *ferror* macro returns a value indicating whether there has been an error during a prior read/write operation on the file specified by the argument *file_pointer*. The FILE data structure associated with the file has a flag field that holds the information about the end-of-file and error conditions during read or write operations. The *ferror* macro checks whether the flag equals a predefined constant that indicates an error condition.

COMMON USES If you have not checked for error returns from read/write operations, you can check after the fact by calling *ferror*. If there was an error, you can call *clearerr* to clear the error flag. Rewinding the file also clears the error flag.

RETURNS If an error has occurred during a read or a write operation on the file, *ferror* returns a nonzero value. Otherwise, it returns a 0.

COMMENTS Since *ferror* is implemented as a macro, checking for errors with it does not involve calling a function. On the other hand, it may be best to check for error returns during calls to read and write routines *fprintf*, *fgets*, and *fscanf*.

SEE ALSO `clearerr` *To clear the error condition of a file*

EXAMPLE Use *fopen* to open the file *autoexec.bat* for buffered read operations only. Now create an error condition by attempting to write a line to it. Call *ferror* to confirm that there was an error and then call *clearerr* to clear the error condition.

```
#include <stdio.h>
char buffer[81] = "This will not be written";
main()
{
        FILE *infile;
/* Open the file "c:\autoexec.bat". Note the two '\'  */
        if ( (infile = fopen("c:\\autoexec.bat", "r"))
              == NULL)
        {
           printf("fopen failed.\n");
           exit(0);
        }
        fprintf(infile, "%s\n", buffer);
        if (ferror(infile) != 0)    /* Check for error */
        {
           printf("Error detected\n");
           clearerr(infile);        /* Now clear the error */
           printf("Error cleared\n");
        }
}
```

Stream I/O

fflush

COMPATIBILITY

MSC 3	MSC 4	MSC 5	MSC 6	QC1	QC2	QC2.5	TC1	TC1.5	TC2	TC++	ANSI	UNIX V	XNX	OS2	DOS
▲	▲	▲	▲	▲	▲	▲	▲	▲	▲	▲	▲	▲	▲	▲	▲

PURPOSE Use the *fflush* function to process the current contents of the buffer associated with a file opened for buffered I/O (see the tutorial section).

SYNTAX

```
int fflush(FILE *file_pointer);
```

`FILE *file_pointer;` *Pointer to FILE data structure associated with the file whose buffer is being flushed*

EXAMPLE CALL

```
fflush(stdin);
```

INCLUDES `#include <stdio.h>` *For function declaration and definition of the FILE data type*

DESCRIPTION The *fflush* function flushes the buffer associated with the file specified by the argument *file_pointer*. This pointer to the FILE data structure is the value returned by an earlier call to *fopen*. If the file is open for write operations, the flushing involves writing the contents of the buffer to the file. Otherwise, the buffer is cleared.

COMMON USES You can use *fflush* to ignore and discard data read from a file opened for buffered read operations. For a file opened for write or update operations, you can call *fflush* to ensure that the contents of the buffer are written without waiting for the buffer to get full. This may be necessary when launching a child process (see Chapter 11) to ensure that a file is up to date before the child process uses it.

RETURNS If the buffer is successfully flushed, *fflush* returns a 0. In case of an error, the return value is the constant EOF defined in *stdio.h*.

COMMENTS During buffered I/O from files, the actual read or write operation is performed only when the buffer associated with the file becomes full, the file is closed, or the program exits normally. In most cases, you never have to explicitly call *fflush*. But if you must ensure that when you say "write" you mean write to the file and not hold in a buffer, you can insert a call to *fflush* to accomplish this. This helps ensure data integrity at the cost of some loss in efficiency.

SEE ALSO

`fopen` *To open a file for buffered I/O*

`fclose` *To close a single file*

EXAMPLE Use *fopen* to open the file *autoexec.bat* for buffered read operations. Read the first 5 characters with calls to *fgetc* and save them in an array called *line*. Flush the buffer by using *fflush*. Continue reading with *fgetc* until you reach the end of the line or until you have read 80 characters. Now display the array—it should have the first 5 characters of the first line in your *autoexec.bat*, but the rest will be missing because we flushed the buffer after reading those characters.

```
#include <stdio.h>
main()
{

       int i;
       char line[81];
       FILE *infile;
/* Open the file. Note that we need two '\'  */
        if ( (infile = fopen("c:\\autoexec.bat", "r"))
               == NULL)
        {
           printf("fopen failed.\n");
```

```
                exit(0);
            }
/* Now read characters using fgetc */
            for (i=0; i<80; i++)
            {
                line[i] = fgetc(infile);
                if (i==4) fflush(infile); /* Flush buffer */
                if(line[i] == '\n') break;
            }
            line[i+1] = '\0';        /* Mark end of string */
/* Now print the line and see how it looks */
            printf("The line is: %s", line);
}
```

Stream I/O

fgetc

COMPATIBILITY

MSC 3	MSC 4	MSC 5	MSC 6	QC1	QC2	QC2.5	TC1	TC1.5	TC2	TC++	ANSI	UNIX V	XNX	OS2	DOS
▲	▲	▲	▲	▲	▲	▲	▲	▲	▲	▲	▲	▲	▲	▲	▲

PURPOSE Use *fgetc* to read a single character from a file opened for buffered input.

SYNTAX

```
int fgetc(FILE *file_pointer);
```

`FILE *file_pointer;` *Pointer to FILE data structure associated with the file from which a character is to be read*

EXAMPLE CALL

```
char_read = fgetc(infile);
```

INCLUDES `#include <stdio.h>` *For function declaration and definition of FILE data type*

DESCRIPTION The *fgetc* function reads a character from the current position of the file specified by the argument *file_pointer* and then increments this position. The character is returned as an integer. Note that *getc*, defined in *stdio.h* as a macro, also reads a character from a file.

RETURNS If there are no errors, *fgetc* returns the character read. Otherwise, it returns the constant EOF. Call *ferror* and *feof* to determine if there was an error or the file simply reached its end.

SEE ALSO

`getc` *Macro to read a character from a file*

`fgetchar` *Function to read a character from* stdin

fputc, fputchar, putc, putchar	*To write a character to a file*

EXAMPLE Use *fgetc* to read a line (maximum length of 80 characters or to the newline character \n) from the file *autoexec.bat* and display the line on the screen using *printf.*

```
#include <stdio.h>
main()
{
        FILE *infile;
        char buffer[81];
        int i, c;
/* Open the file. */
        if ( (infile = fopen("c:\\autoexec.bat", "r"))
              == NULL)
        {
            printf("fopen failed.\n");
            exit(0);
        }
        c = fgetc(infile);
        for(i=0; (i<80) && (feof(infile) == 0) &&
                         (c != '\n'); i++)
        {
            buffer[i] = c;
            c = fgetc(infile);
        }
        buffer[i] = '\0';  /* make a C-style string */
        printf("First line of c:autoexec.bat: %s\n",
                buffer);
}
```

Stream I/O

fgetchar

COMPATIBILITY

MSC 3	MSC 4	MSC 5	MSC 6	QC1	QC2	QC2.5	TC1	TC1.5	TC2	TC++	ANSI	UNIX V	XNX	OS2	DOS
▲	▲	▲	▲	▲	▲	▲	▲	▲	▲	▲				▲	▲

PURPOSE Use *fgetchar* to read a single character from the file *stdin,* normally the keyboard.

SYNTAX `int fgetchar(void);`

EXAMPLE CALL `c = fgetchar();`

INCLUDES `#include <stdio.h>` *For function declaration*

DESCRIPTION The *fgetchar* function reads a character from the file *stdin*. This function is equivalent to *fgetc(stdin)*.

RETURNS If there are no errors, *fgetchar* returns the character read. Otherwise, it returns the constant EOF.

SEE ALSO `fgetc` *General function to read a character from a file*

`fputc, fputchar, putc, putchar` *To write a character to a file*

EXAMPLE Use *fgetchar* to read a line (maximum length of 80 characters or up to the newline character \n) from the keyboard and display the line on the screen using *printf*. Even if you wanted to read only one character, because of the buffered input mechanism, the input does not end until you hit the carriage return key.

```
#include <stdio.h>
main()
{
        char buffer[81];
        int i, c;
        printf("Enter a line (end with a return):\n");
        c = fgetchar();
        for(i=0; (i<80) && (c != '\n'); i++)
        {
            buffer[i] = c;
            c = fgetchar();
        }
        buffer[i] = '\0';  /* make a C-style string */
        printf("You entered: %s\n", buffer);
}
```

Stream I/O

COMPATIBILITY

fgetpos

MSC 3	MSC 4	MSC 5	MSC 6	QC1	QC2	QC2.5	TC1	TC1.5	TC2	TC++	ANSI	UNIX V	XNX	OS2	DOS
		▲	▲	▲	▲	▲	▲	▲	▲	▲				▲	▲

PURPOSE Use *fgetpos* to get and save the current position where reading or writing occurs in a file opened for buffered I/O.

SYNTAX

```
int fgetpos(FILE *file_pointer, fpos_t *current_pos);
```

`FILE *file_pointer;` *Pointer to FILE data structure associated with file whose current position is requested*

`fpos_t *current_pos;` *Pointer to location where file's current position is returned*

EXAMPLE CALL

```
fgetpos(infile, &curpos);
```

INCLUDES #include <stdio.h> *For function declaration and definition of FILE and* fpos_t *data types*

DESCRIPTION The *fgetpos* function gets the current read or write position of the file specified by the argument *file_pointer*, which is a pointer to the FILE data structure associated with a file that is already open. Next *fgetpos* saves this position in a location specified by the pointer *current_pos*. This location is of type *fpos_t*, which is defined in *stdio.h* to be a *long* integer.

COMMON USES The *fgetpos* function is used with its counterpart *fsetpos* to remember a location in the file and return to it at a later time.

RETURNS The *fgetpos* returns a zero when successful. In case of error, the return value is nonzero and the global variable *errno* is set to the constant EINVAL if the *file_pointer* is invalid or to EBADF if *file_pointer* does not point to a file or if it points to an inaccessible file.

COMMENTS The value of the current read/write position in the file is meaningful only to the buffered input and output routines. Although you can access this value, you should not interpret it in any way. Thus the retrieved file position should be used only as an input argument to *fsetpos*. Use *ftell* if you want the position expressed in terms of byte offsets from the beginning of the file.

SEE ALSO `fsetpos` *To change the current position indicator of a file*

EXAMPLE Open a file using *fopen* for reading. Read 10 characters into a buffer and save the current position by calling *fgetpos*. Now read in 10 more characters and call *fsetpos* to return to the position saved earlier. Read in another 10 characters. Print the buffer out and note that the last 10 characters are the same as the 10 read earlier.

```
#include <stdio.h>
void read10char(FILE *, char *);
main()
{
        fpos_t curpos;
        FILE *infile;
        char filename[81], buffer[40];
        printf("Enter name of a text file: ");
        gets(filename);
/* Open the file for reading */
        if ( (infile = fopen(filename, "r")) == NULL)
        {
            printf("fopen failed.\n");
            exit(0);
        }
        read10char(infile, buffer);
/* Save current position */
        if (fgetpos(infile, &curpos) != 0)
            perror("fgetpos failed!");
/* Read another 10 characters */
        read10char(infile, &buffer[11]);
/* Reset to previous position in file */
        if (fsetpos(infile, &curpos) != 0)
            perror("fsetpos failed!");
/* Read another 10 characters -- these should be same
 * as last 10.
 */
        read10char(infile, &buffer[21]);
        buffer[32] = '\0';    /* Convert to C string */
        printf("Buffer now has:\n%s", buffer);
}
/*---------------------------------------------------*/
void read10char(FILE *infile, char *buffer)
{
        int i;
        for(i=0; i<10; i++)

        {
            if((*buffer = fgetc(infile)) == EOF)
```

```
        {
            printf("file ended. buffer so far has: \
%s\n", buffer);
            exit(0);
        }
        buffer++;
    }
    *buffer = '\n';
}
```

Stream I/O

COMPATIBILITY

fgets

MSC 3	MSC 4	MSC 5	MSC 6	QC1	QC2	QC2.5	TC1	TC1.5	TC2	TC++	ANSI	UNIX V	XNX	OS2	DOS
▲	▲	▲	▲	▲	▲	▲	▲	▲	▲	▲	▲	▲	▲	▲	▲

PURPOSE Use the *fgets* function to read a line from a file opened for buffered input. The line is read until a newline (\n) character is encountered or until the number of characters reaches a specified maximum.

SYNTAX

```
char *fgets(char *string, int maxchar, FILE *file_pointer);
```

`char *string;` *Pointer to buffer where characters are stored*

`int maxchar;` *Maximum number of characters that can be stored*

`FILE *file_pointer;` *Pointer to FILE data structure associated with file from which a line is read*

EXAMPLE CALL

```
fgets(buffer, 80, infile);
```

INCLUDES `#include <stdio.h>` *For function declaration and definition of FILE data type*

DESCRIPTION The *fgets* function reads a line from the file specified by the argument *file_pointer* and stores the characters in the buffer whose address is given in the argument *string*. Characters are read until a newline (\n) character is encountered or until the total number of characters read is one less than the number specified in *maxchar*. The buffer is converted to a C string by storing a null character (\0) after the last character stored in the buffer. Any newline characters are also included in the string.

Note that *gets* performs similarly but, unlike *fgets*, it reads up to the newline character and then replaces the newline character with a null character (thus the resulting string does not include a newline).

RETURNS If there are no errors, *fgets* returns the argument *string*. Otherwise, it returns a NULL. You can call *ferror* and *feof* to determine whether the error is genuine or if it occurred because the file reached its end.

SEE ALSO

`gets` *To read a line from* stdin

`fputs` *To write a string to a file*

`puts` *To write a string to* stdout

EXAMPLE Use *fgets* to read lines (maximum length, 80 characters) from the file *autoexec.bat* and display the lines on the screen using *fputs* with the file *stdout*.

```
#include <stdio.h>
main()
{
        FILE *infile;
        char string[81];
/* Open the file. Because of the special significance
 * of '\' in C, we need two of them in the path name for
 * autoexec.bat
 */
        if ( (infile = fopen("c:\\autoexec.bat", "r"))
              == NULL)
        {
            printf("fopen failed.\n");
            exit(0);
        }
        printf("Contents of c:autoexec.bat:\n");
        while ( fgets(string, 80, infile) != NULL)
        {
            fputs(string,stdout);
        }
}
```

Stream I/O

COMPATIBILITY

fileno

MSC 3	MSC 4	MSC 5	MSC 6	QC1	QC2	QC2.5	TC1	TC1.5	TC2	TC++	ANSI	UNIX V	XNX	OS2	DOS
▲	▲	▲	▲	▲	▲	▲	▲	▲	▲	▲		▲	▲	▲	▲

PURPOSE Use the *fileno* macro, defined in *stdio.h*, to obtain the handle of the file currently associated with a specified file pointer. You must have the file handle in order to use some file I/O routines in the run-time library.

SYNTAX

```
int fileno(FILE *file_pointer);
```

`FILE *file_pointer;` *Pointer to FILE data structure associated with the file whose handle is to be returned*

EXAMPLE CALL

```
handle = fileno(file_pointer);
```

INCLUDES `#include <stdio.h>` *For function declaration and definition of the FILE data type*

DESCRIPTION The *fileno* macro returns an integer which constitutes the handle for the file specified by the argument *file_pointer*.

The FILE data structure associated with the file has a field that includes the handle for the file. A call to *fileno* returns this handle. Handles are necessary when performing lower-level, unbuffered I/O using calls to such routines as *read* or *write*.

RETURNS The integer value returned by *fileno* is the handle of the specified file. The return value is undefined if the argument *file_pointer* does not correspond to an open file.

SEE ALSO `fopen` *To open a file for buffered I/O*

EXAMPLE Use *fileno* to get and display the handles for the five files, *stdin, stdout, stderr, stdaux*, and *stdprn*, which are already open in your program.

```
#include <stdio.h>
main()
{
    printf("Handle for stdin: %d\n", fileno(stdin));
    printf("Handle for stdout: %d\n", fileno(stdout));
    printf("Handle for stderr: %d\n", fileno(stderr));
    printf("Handle for stdaux: %d\n", fileno(stdaux));
    printf("Handle for stdprn: %d\n", fileno(stdprn));
}
```

Stream I/O

flushall

COMPATIBILITY

MSC 3	MSC 4	MSC 5	MSC 6	QC1	QC2	QC2.5	TC1	TC1.5	TC2	TC++	ANSI	UNIX V	XNX	OS2	DOS
▲	▲	▲	▲	▲	▲	▲	▲	▲	▲	▲				▲	▲

PURPOSE Use the *flushall* function to flush all buffers associated with files opened for buffered I/O, including those that are opened as soon as your program begins executing: *stdin, stdout, stderr, stdaux*, and *stdprn*.

SYNTAX

```
int flushall(void);
```

EXAMPLE CALL

```
flushall();
```

INCLUDES `#include <stdio.h>` *For function declaration*

DESCRIPTION The *flushall* function flushes all buffers associated with files opened for buffered I/O. This includes the five files already open when you start up your program: *stdin, stdout, stderr, stdaux*, and *stdprn*. If the file is open for write operations, the flushing involves writing the contents of the buffer to the file. Otherwise, the buffer is cleared.

Note that buffers are automatically flushed when they are full, when a file is closed, or when the program terminates normally.

RETURNS The *flushall* function returns the number of buffers it has flushed, which should match the total number of files currently open for input and output.

SEE ALSO

`fflush` *To flush the buffer of a single file*

`fclose` *To close a single file*

EXAMPLE Call *flushall* in a program and print the number of buffers that were flushed. The number should be 5, corresponding to the preopened files.

```
#include <stdio.h>
main()
{
       int files_open;
/* Flush all buffers */
        files_open = flushall();
/* Now print the total number of buffers flushed */
        printf("%d buffers flushed. So this many files \
are open now.\n", files_open);
}
```

Stream I/O

COMPATIBILITY

fopen

MSC 3	MSC 4	MSC 5	MSC 6	QC1	QC2	QC2.5	TC1	TC1.5	TC2	TC++	ANSI	UNIX V	XNX	OS2	DOS
▲	▲	▲	▲	▲	▲	▲	▲	▲	▲	▲	▲	▲	▲	▲	▲

PURPOSE Use *fopen* to open a file for buffered input and output operations.

SYNTAX

```
FILE *fopen(const char *filename, const char *access_mode);
```

`const char *filename;` *Name of file to be opened including drive and directory specification*

`const char *access_mode;` *Character string denoting whether file is being opened for reading or writing, or both*

EXAMPLE CALL

```
input_file = fopen("data.in", "rb");
```

INCLUDES `#include <stdio.h>` *For function declaration and definition of FILE data type*

DESCRIPTION The *fopen* function opens the file specified in the argument *filename*. The type of operations you intend to perform on the file must be given in the argument *access_mode*. Table 15-7 explains the values that the *access_mode* string can take.

In addition to the basic access modes shown in Table 15-7, one of the characters from Table 15-8 can be appended to each of the strings in Table 15-7 to specify how the contents of the file are to be translated. Note that the character denoting the translation mode can come before or after the + in the strings above. For example, *w+b* is considered the same as *wb+* and means "create the file and open it for reading and writing in binary mode." If no translation mode is specified, the default mode is determined by the global variable *_fmode*, which is declared in the header file *stdio.h*. When a file is opened for appending with the *a* or *a+* access mode, existing data can never be destroyed because the *file pointer* is moved to the end of the file before writing occurs. This pointer keeps track of the current position where writing occurs.

When a file is opened for updating, using the *r+*, *w+*, or *a+* access modes, you must call one of the functions *fsetpos, fseek*, or *rewind* when switching between read and write operations. These calls serve to set the file pointer properly before the operation. You can also call *fsetpos* or *fseek* and set the file pointer to the current position.

COMMON USES The *fopen* function is used to open a file before performing buffered I/O operations on it. You must open a file with *fopen* before performing any read or write operations. You can, for example, use *fopen* to open the file *c:\autoexec.bat* and read its contents by calling *fgets*.

RETURNS If the file is opened successfully, *fopen* returns a pointer to the file. Actually, this is a pointer to a structure of type FILE, which is defined in the header file *stdio.h*. The actual structure is allocated elsewhere and you do not have to allocate it. In case of an error, *fopen* returns a NULL. See below for an example of checking for an error return from *fopen*.

COMMENTS A maximum of 20 files may be opened by a single process for buffered I/O in MS-DOS. Of these, 5 are already open when the program begins running: *stdin, stdout, stderr, stdprn,* and *stdaux*. This leaves 15 files that your program can simultaneously open with the function *fopen*.

SEE ALSO

fclose	*To close a file opened by* fopen
open	*To open a file using a handle (a lower-level routine)*
setmode, fdopen, freopen, fileno, ferror, fcloseall	*Other functions related to opening files*

EXAMPLES Use *fopen* to open the file *autoexec.bat* for read operations only in the root directory of your current drive, say, drive C. Now read each line and display it on the screen. Use *fclose* to close the file before exiting.

```
#include <stdio.h>
main()
{
        FILE *infile;
        unsigned char buffer[81];
/* Open the file. Note that we need two '\' because
 * backslash denotes the beginning of a C escape
 * sequence.
 */
        if ( (infile = fopen("c:\\autoexec.bat", "r"))
              == NULL)
        {
            printf("fopen failed.\n");
            exit(0);
        }
        printf("Contents of c:autoexec.bat:\n");
        while ( fgets(buffer, 80, infile) != NULL)
        {
            printf(buffer);
        }
        fclose(infile); /* Close file before exiting */
}
```

Write a C program to save lines typed by the user. Prompt the user for a file name, then open the file for reading and appending in the translation mode (access mode is a+). Next, ask the user to enter lines that you will save in this file. Finally, rewind the file, read it, and display its contents.

```
#include <stdio.h>
char filename[81],      /* Name of file to open        */
     input[80] = "xx"; /* To hold user's input lines  */
FILE *scriptfile;       /* File pointer to opened file */
main()
{
    printf("Enter name of file to save your input: ");
    gets(filename);
/* Open the file where we will save the user's input */
    if ((scriptfile = fopen(filename,"a+")) == NULL)
    {
        printf("Error opening file: %s\n", filename);
        exit(0);
    }
/* Accept input lines and save them in the file */
    printf("Enter lines. Hit 'q' to stop.\n");
    while(input[0] != 'q' || input[1] !='\0')
    {
        gets(input);                /* Read a line   */
        fprintf(scriptfile, "%s\n", /* Write to file */
                input);
    }
/* Now rewind file, read each line and display it */
    rewind(scriptfile);
    printf("==== Contents of script file ====\n");
    while(fgets(input, 80, scriptfile) != NULL)
    {
        printf(input);
    }
/* Now close the file and exit */
    fclose(scriptfile);
}
```

Stream I/O

fprintf

COMPATIBILITY

MSC 3	MSC 4	MSC 5	MSC 6	QC1	QC2	QC2.5	TC1	TC1.5	TC2	TC++	ANSI	UNIX V	XNX	OS2	DOS
▲	▲	1	▲	▲	▲	▲	▲	▲	▲	▲	▲	▲	▲	▲	▲

PURPOSE Use the *fprintf* function to format and write character strings and values of C variables to a specified file opened for buffered output.

SYNTAX

```
int fprintf(FILE *file_pointer, const char *format_string,...);
```

`FILE *file_pointer;` *Pointer to FILE data structure of the file to which the output goes*

`const char *format_string;` *Character string that describes the format to be used*

`...` *Variable number of arguments depending on the number of items being printed*

EXAMPLE CALL

```
fprintf(resultfile, "The result is %f\n", result);
```

INCLUDES `#include <stdio.h>` *For function declaration*

DESCRIPTION Like *printf, fprintf* accepts a variable number of arguments and prints them out to the file specified in the argument *file_pointer* which must be open for buffered output operations. Although *printf* is more widely used and better known, *fprintf* is more general because it can write formatted output to any file, whereas *printf* can send output to *stdout* only. The values of the arguments are printed in the format specified by *format_string*, an array of characters with embedded formatting commands. The formatting commands begin with a percentage sign (%) and *fprintf* accepts the same formatting commands as *printf* does. By the way, use two percentage signs together to actually print a % to the file. The description of the formats is too long to display here; see Tables 15-9, 15-10, 15-11, and 15-12 in the reference pages on *printf* for more detail.

1. Beginning in Microsoft C 5.0 *fprintf* supports *L* format and allows negative precision and width arguments.

COMMON USES Although *fprint* can be used in every situation where *printf* is used, one of its common uses is to print error messages to the file *stderr*.

RETURNS The *fprintf* function returns the number of characters it has printed.

SEE ALSO

printf — *For printing to* stdout *and for detailed information on formats*

vfprintf, vprintf — *For formatted printing to a file using a pointer to a list of arguments*

sprintf, vsprintf — *For formatted printing to a string*

EXAMPLE Ask the user for a file to open for writing. After opening the file with *fopen*, use *fprintf* to send output to the file. Later, use the DOS TYPE command to see how *fprintf* worked.

```
#include <stdio.h>
char    str[] = "Testing fprintf...";
char    c     = '\n';
int     i     = 100;
double  x     = 1.23456;
main()
{
    FILE *outfile;
    char filename[81];
    printf("Enter name of a file to open for WRITING:");
    gets(filename);
/* Open the file for reading */
    if ( (outfile = fopen(filename, "w")) == NULL)
    {
        printf("fopen failed.\n");
        exit(0);
    }
/* Write to this file ... */
    fprintf(outfile, "%s writing to file %s%c", str,
            filename, c);
    fprintf(outfile, "Integer: decimal = %d, \
octal = %o, hex = %X\n", i, i, i);
    fprintf(outfile, "Double: %f(in default f format)\n",
            x);
    fprintf(outfile, "        %.2f(in .2f format)\n",
            x);
    fprintf(outfile, "        %g(in default g format)\n",
            x);
/* Tell user to type file to see results */
    fprintf(stdout,
           "Use the command 'TYPE %s' to see results\n",
            filename);
}
```

Here is how the contents of the file should look:

```
Testing fprintf... writing to file junk1
Integer: decimal = 100, octal = 144, hex = 64
Double: 1.234560(in default f format)
        1.23(in .2f format)
        1.23456(in default g format)
```

Stream I/O

fputc

COMPATIBILITY

MSC 3	MSC 4	MSC 5	MSC 6	QC1	QC2	QC2.5	TC1	TC1.5	TC2	TC++	ANSI	UNIX V	XNX	OS2	DOS
▲	▲	▲	▲	▲	▲	▲	▲	▲	▲	▲	▲	▲	▲	▲	▲

PURPOSE Use *fputc* to write a single character to a file opened for buffered output.

SYNTAX `int fputc(int c, FILE *file_pointer);`

`int c;` *Character to be written*

`FILE *file_pointer;` *Pointer to FILE data structure associated with file to which the character is to be written*

EXAMPLE CALL `fputc('X', p_datafile);`

INCLUDES `#include <stdio.h>` *For function declaration and definition of FILE data type*

DESCRIPTION The *fputc* function writes a character given in the integer argument *c* to the file specified by the argument *file_pointer*. It writes to the current position of the file and increments this position after writing the character. Note that the *putc* macro, defined in *stdio.h*, also writes a character to a file.

RETURNS If there are no errors, *fputc* returns the character written. Otherwise, it returns the constant EOF. You should call *ferror* to determine whether there was an error or the integer argument *c* just happened to be equal to EOF.

SEE ALSO `putc` *Macro to write a character to a file*

`fputchar` *Function to write a character to* stdout

`fgetc, fgetchar, getc, getchar` *To read a character from a file*

EXAMPLE Use *fputc* to write a line (maximum length of 80 characters or up to the null character \0) to *stdout*.

```
#include <stdio.h>
char buffer[81] = "Testing fputc on stdout...\n";
main()
{
    int i;
/* A for loop that uses fputc to print to stdout */
    for(i=0; (i<81) &&
        (fputc(buffer[i], stdout) != EOF);
        i++);
}
```

Stream I/O

COMPATIBILITY

fputchar

MSC 3	MSC 4	MSC 5	MSC 6	QC1	QC2	QC2.5	TC1	TC1.5	TC2	TC++	ANSI	UNIX V	XNX	OS2	DOS
▲	▲	▲	▲	▲	▲	▲	▲	▲	▲	▲				▲	▲

PURPOSE Use *fputchar* to write a single character to the file *stdout*, which is connected to the display on program startup. The *fputchar* function is equivalent to using *fputc* with *stdout* as the argument.

SYNTAX `int fputchar(int c);`

`int c;` *Character to be written to* stdout

EXAMPLE CALL `fputchar('q');`

INCLUDES `#include <stdio.h>` *For function declaration*

DESCRIPTION The *fputchar* function writes a character to the file *stdout*. This function is equivalent to *fputc(stdout)*.

RETURNS If there are no errors, *fputchar* returns the character written. Otherwise, it returns the constant EOF.

SEE ALSO `fputc` *General function to write a character to a file*

`fgetc, fgetchar,`
`getc, getchar` *To read a character from a file*

EXAMPLE Use *fputchar* to write a line (maximum length of 80 characters or up to the null character \0) to *stdout.*

```
#include <stdio.h>
char buffer[81] = "Testing fputchar...\n";
main()
{
    int i;
/* A for loop that uses fputchar to print to stdout */
    for(i=0; (i<81) && (fputchar(buffer[i]) != EOF);
        i++);
}
```

Stream I/O

fputs

COMPATIBILITY

MSC 3	MSC 4	MSC 5	MSC 6	QC1	QC2	QC2.5	TC1	TC1.5	TC2	TC++	ANSI	UNIX V	XNX	OS2	DOS
▲	▲	▲	▲	▲	▲	▲	▲	▲	▲	▲	▲	▲	▲	▲	▲

PURPOSE Use the *fputs* function to write a C string (an array of characters ending with a null character, \0) to a file opened for buffered output.

SYNTAX `int fputs(char *string, FILE *file_pointer);`

`char *string;` *Null-terminated character string to be output*

`FILE *file_pointer;` *Pointer to FILE data structure associated with file to which string is output*

EXAMPLE CALL `fputs("Sample Input Data", p_datafile);`

INCLUDES `#include <stdio.h>` *For function declaration and definition of FILE data type*

DESCRIPTION The *fputs* function writes the C string given in the argument "string" to the file specified by the argument *file_pointer*, which is a pointer to the FILE data structure associated with a file that has been opened for write operations.

RETURNS In Microsoft C 6.0 the *fputs* function returns a nonnegative value if successful; if unsuccessful, the EOF constant is returned. In versions 5.0 and 5.1, the *fputs* function returns a 0 if it completes its task successfully. Otherwise it returns a nonzero value. In earlier versions, *fputs* returns the last character printed when all goes well. In case of error, it returns the constant EOF.

SEE ALSO

`fgets` *To read in a line from a file*

`puts` *To write a string to the display*

`gets` *To read a line from the console*

EXAMPLE Write a program using *fputs* to print a string to the display (which corresponds to the preopened file *stdout*).

```
#include <stdio.h>
char string[81] =
    "Using fputs with stdout is equivalent to puts\n";
main()
{
        fputs(string, stdout);
}
```

Stream I/O

COMPATIBILITY

fread

MSC 3	MSC 4	MSC 5	MSC 6	QC1	QC2	QC2.5	TC1	TC1.5	TC2	TC++	ANSI	UNIX V	XNX	OS2	DOS
▲	▲	▲	▲	▲	▲	▲	▲	▲	▲	▲	▲	▲	▲	▲	▲

PURPOSE Use the *fread* function to read a specified number of data items, each of a given size, from the current position in a file opened for buffered input. The current position is updated after the read.

SYNTAX

```
size_t fread(void *buffer, size_t size, size_t count,
                                      FILE *file_pointer);
```

`void *buffer;` *Pointer to memory where* fread *stores the bytes it reads*

`size_t size;` *Size in bytes of each data item*

`size_t count;` *Maximum number of items to be read*

`FILE *file_pointer;` *Pointer to FILE data structure associated with file from which data items are read*

EXAMPLE CALL `numread = fread(buffer, sizeof(char), 80, infile);`

INCLUDES `#include <stdio.h>` *For function declaration and definition of FILE and* size_t

DESCRIPTION The *fread* function reads *count* data items, each of *size* bytes, starting at the current read position of the file specified by the argument *file_pointer*. After the read is complete, the current position is updated.

You must allocate storage for a buffer to hold the number of bytes that you expect to read. The address of this buffer, in the form of a pointer to a *void* data type, is given in the argument *buffer*. The data items read are saved in this buffer.

COMMON USES The common use of *fread* is to read binary data files. As an example, if you devise a scheme for storing images to a file, you would probably use *fwrite* to write the file and *fread* to read the images back.

RETURNS The *fread* function returns the number of items it successfully read. If the return value is less than you expected, you can call *ferror* and *feof* to determine if a read error has occurred or if end-of-file has been reached.

COMMENTS When *fread* is used on a file opened in the text mode, the CR-LF pairs are translated to single-line feeds.

SEE ALSO

`fwrite` *To write data items from a buffer to a file*

`read` *Same function as* fread, *but uses file number or handle*

EXAMPLE Open a file using *fopen* for binary read operations (mode *rb*). Read 80 characters, and then display the buffer and the number of data items that *fread* says it read.

```
#include <stdio.h>
main()
{
    int numread;
    FILE *infile;
    char filename[80], buffer[80];
    printf("Enter name of a text file: ");
    gets(filename);
/* Open the file for reading */
    if ( (infile = fopen(filename, "rb")) == NULL)
    {
        printf("fopen failed.\n");
        exit(0);
    }
/* Read 80 characters and display the buffer */
    numread = fread((void *)buffer, sizeof(char), 80,
                    infile);
    printf("Read these %d characters:\n %s\n",
            numread, buffer);
}
```

COMPATIBILITY

freopen

MSC 3	MSC 4	MSC 5	MSC 6	QC1	QC2	QC2.5	TC1	TC1.5	TC2	TC++	ANSI	UNIX V	XNX	OS2	DOS
▲	▲	▲	▲	▲	▲	▲	▲	▲	▲	▲	▲	▲	▲	▲	▲

PURPOSE Use *freopen* to close a file and open another file with the same file pointer. For example, you can use *freopen* to redirect I/O from the preopened file *stdout* to a file of your choice.

SYNTAX

```
FILE *freopen(const char *filename, const char *access_mode,
                                         FILE *file_pointer);
```

`const char *filename;` *Name of file to be reopened, including drive and directory specification*

`const char *access_mode;` *Character string denoting whether file is being reopened for read/write*

`FILE *file_pointer;` *Pointer to FILE data structure associated with file being closed*

EXAMPLE CALL

```
freopen("output.txt", "w", stdout);
```

INCLUDES `#include <stdio.h>` *For function declaration and definition of FILE data type*

DESCRIPTION The *freopen* function closes the file specified by the argument *file_pointer*, a pointer to the FILE data structure associated with an open file. Next *freopen* opens a new file with the name specified in the argument *filename* and associates the old file pointer with this new file. Use the argument *access_mode* to indicate the type of operations you intend to perform on the file. Tables 15-6 and 15-7 explain the various values that the *access_mode* string can take.

COMMON USES The *freopen* function is often used to redirect input and output for the preopened files *stdin* and *stdout.*

RETURNS If all goes well, *freopen* returns a pointer to the newly opened file. This pointer is the same as the argument *file_pointer.* In case of error, a NULL is returned. See below for an example of checking for an error return from *freopen.*

SEE ALSO `fopen` *To open a file*

`fclose` *To close a file opened by* fopen *or* freopen

EXAMPLE Use *freopen* to redirect *stdout* to a file instead of the monitor. Prompt the user for the file name. Use *printf* to print a few lines that go to the file and do not appear on your screen. Exit and observe the contents of the file with the DOS TYPE <filename> command.

```
#include <stdio.h>
main()
{
    char filename[81];
    printf("Enter file name where output should go: ");
    gets(filename);
    printf("If all goes well, use TYPE %s to see \
result.\n", filename);
/* Redirect stdout to this file */
    if ( freopen(filename, "w", stdout) == NULL)
    {
        printf("freopen failed.\n");
        exit(0);
    }
/* Print some lines ... */
    printf("Redirecting stdout to the file %s\n",
            filename);
    printf("All output will be in this file.\n");
}
```

Stream I/O

fscanf

COMPATIBILITY

MSC 3	MSC 4	MSC 5	MSC 6	QC1	QC2	QC2.5	TC1	TC1.5	TC2	TC++	ANSI	UNIX V	XNX	OS2	DOS
▲	▲	1	▲	▲	▲	▲	▲	▲	▲	▲	▲	▲	▲	▲	▲

PURPOSE Use the *fscanf* function to read characters from a file that has been opened for buffered I/O and to convert the strings to values of C variables according to specified formats.

SYNTAX

```
int fscanf(FILE *file_pointer, const char *format_string,...);
```

`FILE *file_pointer;` *Pointer to the FILE data structure of file from which reading occurs*

`const char *format_string;` *Character string that describes the format to be used*

`...` *Variable number of arguments representing addresses of variables whose values are being read*

EXAMPLE CALL `fscanf(infile, "Date: %d/%d/%d", &month, &day, &year);`

INCLUDES `#include <stdio.h>` *For function declaration and definition of the FILE data structure*

DESCRIPTION The *fscanf* function reads a stream of characters from the file specified by the argument *file_pointer*, converts the characters to values according to format specifications embedded in the argument *format_string*, and stores the values into C variables whose addresses are provided in the variable length argument list.

Each optional argument indicating a value to be read has a corresponding format specification in the argument *format_string*. The format specification begins with a percentage sign and the formatting commands are identical to the ones used with the function *scanf*. A list of the formats is provided in the reference pages on *scanf*.

1. Beginning in Microsoft C 5.0 *fscanf* supports the *L* modifier and the *g*, *E*, and *G* format specifiers.

RETURNS The *fscanf* function returns the number of input items that were successfully read, converted, and saved in variables. If an end-of-file is encountered during the read, the return value will be equal to the constant EOF (defined in *stdio.h*).

COMMENTS The *fscanf* function is used more generally than *scanf*. You can read from any file using *fscanf* and the functions of *scanf* can be duplicated by using the file *stdin* as an argument to *fscanf*. It is customary in C reference books, including ours, however, to describe the format specifications in detail under *scanf*.

SEE ALSO

`scanf` *Formatted reading from* stdin

`sscanf` *For formatted reading from a string*

`cscanf` *Formatted, unbuffered input from console*

EXAMPLE The %s format reads strings separated by blanks, tabs, or newline characters. Open the file *autoexec.bat* for buffered I/O and then use *fscanf* to read and display the first 10 tokens, character sequences separated by blanks and newlines.

```
#include <stdio.h>
main()
{
    int i;
    FILE *infile;
```

```
    char token[80];
/* Open the file. Note that we need two '\'  */
    if ( (infile = fopen("c:\\autoexec.bat", "r"))
         == NULL)
    {
        perror("fopen failed");
        exit(1);
    }
    printf("First 10 blank separated strings in \
c:\\autoexec.bat:\n");
    for(i=0; i<10; i++)
    {
        if( fscanf(infile, " %s", token) == EOF)
        {
            printf("File ended!\n");
            break;
        }
        else
        {
            printf("Token %d = \"%s\"\n", i, token);
        }
    }
}
```

Stream I/O

fseek

COMPATIBILITY

MSC 3	MSC 4	MSC 5	MSC 6	QC1	QC2	QC2.5	TC1	TC1.5	TC2	TC++	ANSI	UNIX V	XNX	OS2	DOS
▲	▲	▲	▲	▲	▲	▲	▲	▲	▲	▲	▲	▲	▲	▲	▲

PURPOSE Use the *fseek* function to move to a new position in a file opened for buffered I/O.

SYNTAX `int fseek(FILE *file_pointer, long offset, int origin);`

`FILE *file_pointer;` *Pointer to FILE data structure associated with file whose current position is to be set*

`long offset;` *Offset of new position (in bytes) from origin*

`int origin;` *Constant indicating the position from which to offset*

EXAMPLE CALL `fseek(infile, 0L, SEEK_SET); /* Go to the beginning */`

INCLUDES `#include <stdio.h>` *For function declaration and definition of FILE*

DESCRIPTION The *fseek* function sets the current read or write position of the file specified by the argument *file_pointer* to a new value indicated by the arguments "offset" and "origin." The "offset" is a long integer indicating how far away the new position is from a specific location given in "origin." One of the constants, defined in *stdio.h* and shown in the table below, *must* be the "origin."

Origin	Interpretation
SEEK_SET	Beginning of file
SEEK_CUR	Current position in the file
SEEK_END	End of file

COMMON USES The *fseek* function is commonly used when reading data from a file in the binary read mode. For example, an application may create a data file with a specific format, say, a header of 512 bytes followed by actual data. When reading from such a file you can use *fseek* to skip over the header and move around in the file to retrieve specific pieces of information with *fread*.

RETURNS When successful, *fseek* returns a zero. In case of error, for example when attempting to set a position before the beginning of the file, *fseek* returns a nonzero value. If the file is associated with a device where setting the current position does not make sense (such as a printer), the return value is meaningless.

COMMENTS You should be aware of a few nuances of *fseek*.

- In text mode (see the tutorial section), you may not be able to give a proper value for offset because of the translation of CR-LF combinations. So only these arguments are guaranteed to work when using *fseek* in the text mode: (1) an offset of OL from any of the origins, and (2) an offset returned by *ftell* with an origin of SEEK_SET.
- In append mode, the current position is determined solely by the last I/O operation. Even if you move around in the file, the writing always takes place at the end of the file opened for appending.

SEE ALSO `ftell` *To get the offset of the current position in number of bytes from the beginning*

`lseek` *Same function as* fseek, *but works with file handles*

EXAMPLE Open a file using *fopen* for reading. Read and display a line. Now call *fseek* to go back to the beginning and read a line again. The two lines should be identical.

```
#include <stdio.h>
main()
{
    FILE *infile;
    char filename[80], buffer[81];
    printf("Enter name of a text file: ");
    gets(filename);
/* Open the file for reading */
    if ( (infile = fopen(filename, "r")) == NULL)
    {
        printf("fopen failed.\n");
        exit(0);
    }
/* Read and display a line */
    fgets(buffer, 80, infile);
    printf("Line read (before fseek): %s", buffer);
/* Move to beginning using fseek and read a line again */
    if (fseek(infile, 0L, SEEK_SET) != 0)
    {
        perror("fseek failed!");
    }
    else
    {
        fgets(buffer, 80, infile);
        printf("Line read (after fseek) : %s", buffer);
    }
}
```

Stream I/O

fsetpos

COMPATIBILITY

MSC 3	MSC 4	MSC 5	MSC 6	QC1	QC2	QC2.5	TC1	TC1.5	TC2	TC++	ANSI	UNIX V	XNX	OS2	DOS
		▲	▲	▲	▲	▲	▲	▲	▲	▲	▲			▲	▲

PURPOSE Use *fsetpos* to set the position where reading or writing can take place in a file opened for buffered I/O.

SYNTAX `int fsetpos(FILE *file_pointer, const fpos_t *current_pos);`

`FILE *file_pointer;` *Pointer to FILE data structure associated with file whose current position is to be set*

`const fpos_t *current_pos;` *Pointer to location containing new value of file position*

EXAMPLE CALL `fsetpos(infile, &curpos);`

INCLUDES `#include <stdio.h>` *For function declaration and definition of FILE and* fpos_t *data types*

DESCRIPTION The *fsetpos* function sets to a new value the current read or write position of the file specified by the argument *file_pointer*. The new value is given in a location whose address is in the argument *current_pos*. The data type of this variable is *fpos_t*, which is defined in the include file *stdio.h* to be a *long*.

COMMON USES The *fsetpos* function resets the file position to a value obtained by an earlier call to its counterpart *fgetpos*.

RETURNS If successful, *fsetpos* returns a zero. Otherwise, the return value will be nonzero, and the global variable *errno* is set to the constant EINVAL if the value of the argument *file_pointer* is invalid or to EBADF if the file is not accessible or if the object to which *file_pointer* points is not a file.

COMMENTS Since the value of the current read/write position in the file is meaningful only to the buffered input and output routines, you should always use *fsetpos* with a position obtained by an earlier call to *fgetpos*. You can use *fseek* if you want to set the position to a value expressed in terms of byte offsets from specific locations in the file.

SEE ALSO `fgetpos` *To retrieve the current position indicator of a file*

EXAMPLE Open a file using *fopen* for reading. Call *fgetpos* and remember the current position. Read 10 characters into a buffer and return to the saved position by calling *fsetpos*. Now read in 10 more characters. Display the buffer and note that the first 10 characters are the same as the last 10.

```
#include <stdio.h>
main()
{
    fpos_t curpos;
    FILE *infile;
    char filename[81], buffer1[20], buffer2[20];
    printf("Enter name of a text file: ");
    gets(filename);
/* Open the file for reading */
    if ( (infile = fopen(filename, "r")) == NULL)
    {
        printf("fopen failed.\n");
        exit(0);
```

```
    }
/* Save current position */
    if (fgetpos(infile, &curpos) != 0)
                   perror("fgetpos failed!");
/* Read 10 characters */
    if (fgets(buffer1, 10, infile) == NULL)
                  perror("fgets failed");
/* Reset to previous position in file */
    if (fsetpos(infile, &curpos) != 0)
                   perror("fsetpos failed!");
/* Read another 10 characters --
 * these should be same as last 10.
 */
    if (fgets(buffer2, 10, infile) == NULL)
                      perror("fgets failed");
    printf("We read:\n");
    puts(buffer1);
    puts(buffer2);
}
```

_fsopen

COMPATIBILITY

MSC 3	MSC 4	MSC 5	MSC 6	QC1	QC2	QC2.5	TC1	TC1.5	TC2	TC++	ANSI	UNIX V	XNX	OS2	DOS
			▲			▲								▲	▲

PURPOSE The *_fsopen* function opens a stream with file sharing.

SYNTAX

```
FILE *_fsopen (const char *file_name, const char *mode,
               int shr_flag);
```

`file_name;` *File pathname*

`mode;` *Access permissions—r, w, a, b, and t in various combinations*

`shr_flag;` *The share flag values SH_COMPAT, SH_DENYRW, SH_DENYWR, SH_DENYRD, SH_DENYNO*

EXAMPLE CALL

```
if ((out_file = _fsopen (file_name, "wb", SH_DENYWR)) == NULL)
```

INCLUDES `#include <stdio.h>` *For function declaration*

`#include <share.h>`

DESCRIPTION The *_fsopen* function opens the file identified by *file_name* as a stream and prepares it for shared reading and writing in accordance with the mode and *shr_flag* arguments. Valid mode types are *r* (read), *w* (write), and *a* (append), any of which may be followed by a + sign which indicates that both read and write operations are granted. The "normal" translation mode for line feeds may be specified by adding a *b* (for binary) or *t* (for text) to the argument.

The *shr_flg* argument identifies which permissions are assigned to the file, and it is expressed as one of the constants listed above. The *share flag* argument determines sharing mode, and that is made up of one of the following manifest constants. (These are sometimes combined when used by *_dos_open*, but not when used with *_fsopen*.)

The constants and their meanings are:

SH_COMPAT	**Sets the compatibility mode**
SH_DENYRW	**Denies both read and write access to the file**
SH_DENYWR	**Denies write access to the file**
SH_DENYRD	**Denies read access to the file**
SH_DENYNO	**Permits both read and write access to the file**

RETURNS The *_fsopen* function returns a pointer to the stream if the opening is successful. A failed call returns a NULL.

SEE ALSO `fopen` *To open an ordinary (nonshared) file*

COMMENTS File sharing is valid under OS/2, DOS 3.0 and later versions. Normal file closing routines work with shared files; there is no "shared" version of *fclose*, for example.

EXAMPLE The example program edits certain characteristics of a text file that was used in preparing this book. It opens two files with a call to *_fsopen*; calls which could easily be replaced with the more familiar *fopen* function. This shows the relationship between the new function and the old. The additional arguments of *_fsopen*, however, provide a great deal of control over the file that is denied you with the *fopen* routine, such as determining who on a network can access and edit the text files.

```
#include <ctype.h>
#include <share.h>
#include <stdio.h>
#include <stdlib.h>
#include <string.h>

extern void main      (void);
extern void read_rcrd (void);
```

```
unsigned int loop_cnt;  /*LOOP control*/
char srce_string [200]; /*entry string*/
char out_string [200];  /* exit string*/

FILE *FP_srce;
FILE *FP_out;

void main()
{
   FP_srce = _fsopen ("REFS.IN", "r", SH_DENYWR);
   FP_out = _fsopen ("REFS.OUT", "w+", SH_DENYNO);
   {
   printf ("\nAdds LFs if '@' is [0] so Ventura can load
           ASCII.\n");
        read_rcrd();
   }
   fcloseall();
   exit(16);
}

void read_rcrd() /*READ THE RECORDS */

{
   int flushall (void); /* FLUSH all buffers*/
   while (fgets (srce_string, 200, FP_srce) != NULL)
   {
      if (strlen (srce_string) > 4)
          {
          if (srce_string [0] == '@')
               {
               loop_cnt ++;
               printf ("\r %6u %4d", loop_cnt, strlen
                        (srce_string));
               fputs ("\n", FP_out);
               }
               /* adjust status tag for COMPATIBILITY 'y'
                  statements */

               if ((strncmp (srce_string,"", 8) == 0))
                    srce_string[8] = '.';
               fputs (srce_string, FP_out);
          }
   }
}
```

Input and Output Routines

COMPATIBILITY

ftell

MSC 3	MSC 4	MSC 5	MSC 6	QC1	QC2	QC2.5	TC1	TC1.5	TC2	TC++	ANSI	UNIX V	XNX	OS2	DOS
▲	▲	▲	▲	▲	▲	▲	▲	▲	▲	▲	▲	▲	▲	▲	▲

PURPOSE Use *ftell* to obtain the current position in a file opened for buffered I/O. The position is expressed as a byte offset from the beginning of the file.

SYNTAX

```
long ftell(FILE *file_pointer);
```

`FILE *file_pointer;` *Pointer to FILE data structure associated with file whose current position is to be returned*

EXAMPLE CALL

```
curpos = ftell(infile));
```

INCLUDES `#include <stdio.h>` *For function declaration and definition of FILE*

DESCRIPTION The *ftell* function returns the current read or write position of the file specified by the argument *file_pointer*.

RETURNS When successful, *ftell* returns a long integer containing the number of bytes the current position is offset from the beginning of the file. In case of error, *ftell* returns –1L. Also, the global variable *errno* is set to EINVAL if the *file_pointer* argument is invalid or to EBADF if the *file_pointer* does not point to a valid open file. The return value is undefined if the *file_pointer* is associated with a device (such as the keyboard) it would not make any sense to move to a new position in the file.

COMMENTS When *ftell* is used on a file opened in the text mode, the physical byte offset in the file may not be the same as the value reported by *ftell*. This is due to the translation of the CR-LF pairs in this mode. Everything works correctly, however, if you use *fseek* in combination with *ftell* to return to a specific position in a file opened in text mode.

SEE ALSO

`fseek` *To set the current position in a file*

`tell` *Same function as* ftell, *but uses file handles*

EXAMPLE Use *fopen* to open a file for binary read operations (mode *rb*). Read 80 characters and display the buffer. Now call *ftell* and print the value it returns.

```
#include <stdio.h>
main()
```

```
{
    long curpos;
    FILE *infile;
    char filename[80], buffer[80];
    printf("Enter name of a text file: ");
    gets(filename);
/* Open the file for reading */
    if ( (infile = fopen(filename, "rb")) == NULL)
    {
        printf("fopen failed.");
        exit(0);
    }
/* Read 80 characters and display the buffer */
    fread(buffer, sizeof(char), 80, infile);
    printf("Read these 80 characters:\n %s\n", buffer);
/* Get and display current position */
    if ((curpos = ftell(infile)) == -1L)
    {
        perror("ftell failed!");
    }
    else
    {
        printf("Currently at %ld bytes from beginning \
of file\n", curpos);
    }
}
```

Stream I/O

fwrite

COMPATIBILITY

MSC 3	MSC 4	MSC 5	MSC 6	QC1	QC2	QC2.5	TC1	TC1.5	TC2	TC++	ANSI	UNIX V	XNX	OS2	DOS
▲	▲	▲	▲	▲	▲	▲	▲	▲	▲	▲	▲	▲	▲	▲	▲

PURPOSE Use the *fwrite* function to write a specified number of data items, each of a given size, from a buffer to the current position in a file opened for buffered output. The current position is updated after the write.

SYNTAX

```
size_t fwrite(const void *buffer, size_t size, size_t count,
                                           FILE *file_pointer);
```

`const void *buffer;` *Pointer to buffer in memory from which* fwrite *will get the bytes it writes*

`size_t size;`	*Size in bytes of each data item*
`size_t count;`	*Maximum number of items to be written*
`FILE *file_pointer;`	*Pointer to FILE data structure associated with file to which the data items are to be written*

EXAMPLE CALL `numwrite = fwrite(buffer, sizeof(char), 80, outfile);`

INCLUDES `#include <stdio.h>` *For function declaration and definition of FILE and* size_t

DESCRIPTION The *fwrite* function writes *count* data items, each of *size* bytes, to the file specified by the argument *file_pointer*, starting at the current position. After the write operation is complete, the current position is updated. The data to be written is in the buffer whose address is passed to *fwrite* in the argument *buffer*.

COMMON USES The most common use of *fwrite* is to write binary data files. For example, if you want to save the current status of your application, you can save the values of all the key variables into a file using *fwrite*. Later, you can read these back with the function *fread*.

RETURNS The *fwrite* function returns the number of items it actually wrote. If that value is less than you expected, an error may have occurred.

COMMENTS If *fwrite* is used on a file opened in the text mode, each carriage return is replaced by a CR-LF pair.

SEE ALSO

`fread`	*To read data items from a file to a buffer*
`write`	*Same function as* fwrite, *but uses file number, or handle*

EXAMPLE Open a file using *fopen* for binary write operations (mode *wb*). Write 80 characters and display the number of data items that *fwrite* says it wrote. Type out the file to verify that the write worked.

```
#include <stdio.h>
char buffer[80] = "Testing fwrite\n\
This is the second line.\n";
main()
{
    int numwrite;
    FILE *infile;
    char filename[80];
    printf("Enter name of a file to write to: ");
```

```
    gets(filename);
/* Open the file for writing */
    if ( (infile = fopen(filename, "wb")) == NULL)
    {
        printf("fopen failed.\n");
        exit(0);
    }
/* write 80 characters and display the buffer */
    numwrite = fwrite((void *)buffer, sizeof(char), 80,
                       infile);
    printf("%d characters written to file %s\n",
        numwrite, filename);
    printf("Use 'TYPE %s' to see if it worked\n",
            filename);
}
```

Stream I/O

getc

COMPATIBILITY

MSC 3	MSC 4	MSC 5	MSC 6	QC1	QC2	QC2.5	TC1	TC1.5	TC2	TC++	ANSI	UNIX V	XNX	OS2	DOS
▲	▲	▲	▲	▲	▲	▲	▲	▲	▲	▲	▲	▲	▲	▲	▲

PURPOSE Use the *getc* macro to read a single character from a file opened for buffered input.

SYNTAX `int getc(FILE *file_pointer);`

`FILE *file_pointer;` *Pointer to file from which a character is to read*

EXAMPLE CALL `in_char = getc(p_txtfile);`

INCLUDES `#include <stdio.h>` *For function declaration and definition of FILE data structure*

DESCRIPTION The *getc* macro reads a character from the file specified by the argument *file_pointer*. The character is read from the current position in the file, and the current position then is advanced to the next character. The *file_pointer* must be a pointer returned earlier by an *fopen* or a *freopen* function call. Note that *fgetc* performs the same as *getc*, but *fgetc* is implemented as a function.

RETURNS The *getc* macro returns the character read as an integer value. A return value of EOF indicates an error. In that case, call the *ferror* and *feof* functions to determine if there was an error or if the file ended.

SEE ALSO

getchar	*Macro to read a character from* stdin
fgetc	*Function to read a character from a file*
fputc, fputchar, putc, putchar	*To write a character to a file*

EXAMPLE Use *getc* to read a line (maximum length of 80 characters or up to the newline character) from the file *config.sys* and display the line on the screen using *printf*.

```
#include <stdio.h>
main()
{
    FILE *infile;
    char buffer[81];
    int i, c;
/* Open the file -- assuming its at the root directory
 * of drive C:
 */
    if ( (infile = fopen("c:\\config.sys", "r"))
         == NULL)
    {
        printf("fopen failed.\n");
        exit(0);
    }
    c = getc(infile);
    for(i=0; (i<80) && (feof(infile) == 0) &&
                 (c != '\n'); i++)
    {
        buffer[i] = c;
        c = getc(infile);
    }
    buffer[i] = '\0';  /* to make a C-style string */
    printf("First line of c:config.sys: %s\n",
           buffer);
}
```

Stream I/O

getchar

COMPATIBILITY

MSC 3	MSC 4	MSC 5	MSC 6	QC1	QC2	QC2.5	TC1	TC1.5	TC2	TC++	ANSI	UNIX V	XNX	OS2	DOS
▲	▲	▲	▲	▲	▲	▲	▲	▲	▲	▲	▲	▲	▲	▲	▲

PURPOSE Use the *getchar* macro to read a single character from the preopened file *stdin*, which is normally connected to your keyboard input.

SYNTAX `int getchar(void);`

EXAMPLE CALL `c = getchar();`

INCLUDES `#include <stdio.h>` *For function declaration*

DESCRIPTION The *getchar* macro reads a character from *stdin* and is equivalent to the use *getc(stdin)*. Note that *getchar* is the macro equivalent of the *fgetchar* function.

RETURNS The *getchar* macro returns the character read from *stdin* as an integer value. In case of an error, the return value is equal to the constant EOF (defined in *stdio.h*).

COMMENTS You cannot use *getchar* to read a single character from the console because a carriage return must be entered to complete a single buffered read from the keyboard. Use *getch* or *getche* for unbuffered input from the keyboard.

SEE ALSO

`getc`	*Macro to read a character from a file*
`fgetc, fgetchar`	*To read a character from a file*
`fputc, fputchar,` `putc, putchar`	*To write a character to a file*

EXAMPLE Use *getchar* to read a line (maximum 80 characters) from the standard input. Call *printf* to display the line.

```
#include <stdio.h>
main()
{
    int i, c;
    char buffer[81];
    printf("Enter a line (end with a return):\n");
    c = getchar();
```

```
    for(i=0; (i<80) && (c != '\n'); i++)
    {
        buffer[i] = c;
        c = getchar();
    }
    buffer[i] = '\0';  /* to make a C-style string */
    printf("You entered: %s\n", buffer);
}
```

Stream I/O

COMPATIBILITY

gets

MSC 3	MSC 4	MSC 5	MSC 6	QC1	QC2	QC2.5	TC1	TC1.5	TC2	TC++	ANSI	UNIX V	XNX	OS2	DOS
▲	▲	▲	▲	▲	▲	▲	▲	▲	▲	▲	▲	▲	▲	▲	▲

PURPOSE Use *gets* to read a line from the standard input file *stdin*, by default, the keyboard.

SYNTAX

```
char *gets(char *buffer);
```

`char *buffer;` *Buffer where string will be stored*

EXAMPLE CALL `gets(command_line);`

INCLUDES `#include <stdio.h>` *For function declaration*

DESCRIPTION Until it encounters a newline character, the *gets* function reads and stores characters in the *buffer* from the standard input file *stdin*. When it does, it replaces the newline character with a null character and creates a C string. You must allocate room for the buffer in which the characters will be stored. Note that while *fgets* performs like *gets*, unlike *gets*, it retains the newline character in the final string.

RETURNS If there is no error, *gets* returns its argument. Otherwise, it returns a NULL. Call *ferror* and *feof* to determine whether the error is a read error or if it occurred because the file reached its end.

SEE ALSO `fgets` *To read a line from a file*

`fputs` *To write a string to a file*

`puts` *To write a string to the display*

EXAMPLE Use *gets* to read a line to the standard input. Call *printf* to display the line.

```
#include <stdio.h>
main()
{
    char string[81];
    printf("Enter a line: ");
    gets(string);
    printf("You entered: %s\n", string);
}
```

Stream I/O

getw

COMPATIBILITY

MSC 3	MSC 4	MSC 5	MSC 6	QC1	QC2	QC2.5	TC1	TC1.5	TC2	TC++	ANSI	UNIX V	XNX	OS2	DOS
▲	▲	▲	▲	▲	▲	▲	▲	▲	▲	▲		▲	▲	▲	▲

PURPOSE Use *getw* to read a word (two bytes) from a file that has been opened for buffered binary read operations.

SYNTAX

```
int getw(FILE *file_pointer);
```

`FILE *file_pointer;` *Pointer to FILE data structure associated with file from which a word is read*

EXAMPLE CALL

```
word = getw(infile);
```

INCLUDES `#include <stdio.h>` *For function declaration and definition of FILE*

DESCRIPTION The *getw* function reads a word from the current position of the file specified by the argument *file_pointer*. The current position is incremented by the size of an *int* (2 bytes).

RETURNS If successful, *getw* returns the integer value it read. Otherwise, the return value is the constant EOF (defined in *stdio.h*). Since EOF is also a legitimate integer value, you should call *feof* and *ferror* to determine if the end-of-file was reached or if an error occurred.

COMMENTS The *getw* function is provided only for compatibility with previous Microsoft C libraries. Do not use this function in new programs because the differences in size of words and arrangement of bytes (which one is most significant and which one is least significant) among microprocessors may cause problems when you move your program from one computer to another.

SEE ALSO `putw` *To write a word into a file*

EXAMPLE Use *fopen* to open a file for reading in the binary mode. Use *getw* to read the first word and print its value in hexadecimal. To get a feeling for byte ordering, give the name of a text file when running the program. Consult the ASCII code table to see which characters the hexadecimal value printed by the program represents. Use DOS TYPE to print the file out and compare the first two characters with the printed value.

```
#include <stdio.h>
main()
{
    int word1;
    FILE *infile;
    char filename[81];
    printf("Enter name of a file to read from: ");
    gets(filename);
/* Open the file for reading */
    if ( (infile = fopen(filename, "rb")) == NULL)
    {
        printf("fopen failed.\n");
            exit(0);
    }
/* Get first word from file */
    if( (word1 = getw(infile)) == EOF)
    {
/* Check if there was a real error */
        if(feof(infile) != 0)
        {
            printf("File: %s at EOF\n", filename);
            exit(0);
        }
        if(ferror(infile) != 0)
        {
            printf("File: %s Read error\n", filename);
            exit(0);
        }
    }
/* Print out the first word in hexadecimal */
    printf("The first word in file %s is: %X\n",
            filename, word1);

    printf("Use 'TYPE %s' to confirm this.\n", filename);
}
```

Stream I/O

printf

COMPATIBILITY

MSC 3	MSC 4	MSC 5	MSC 6	QC1	QC2	QC2.5	TC1	TC1.5	TC2	TC++	ANSI	UNIX V	XNX	OS2	DOS
▲	▲	▲	▲	▲	▲	▲	▲	▲	▲	▲	▲	▲	▲	▲	▲

PURPOSE Use *printf* to write character strings and values of C variables, formatted in a specified manner, to the standard output file *stdout* (normally the screen).

SYNTAX

```
int printf(const char *format_string,...);
```

`const char *format_string;` *Character string that describes the format to be used*

`...` *Variable number of arguments depending on the number of items being printed*

EXAMPLE CALL

```
printf("The product of %d and %d is %d\n", x, y, x*y);
```

INCLUDES `#include <stdio.h>` *For function declaration*

DESCRIPTION The *printf* function accepts a variable number of arguments and prints them out to the standard output file *stdout.* The value of each argument is formatted according to the codes embedded in the format specification *format_string.* The first argument must be present in a call to *printf.* Calling *printf* is equivalent to using *fprintf* with the file *stdin.*

If the *format_string* does not contain a % character (except for the pair %%, which appears as a single % in the output), no argument is expected and the *format_string* is written out to *stdout.* For example,

```
printf("Hello there!\n");
```

prints "Hello there!" on the screen and skips to the next line because of the newline (\n) in the string. In fact, the *format_string* may contain commonly accepted special characters with a "backslash" as prefix, such as \n (newline), \t (tab), \a (alert or bell), or an ASCII character in octal notation (such as \004, which prints as a diamond in the IBM PC). You can use these characters to align the printed values properly. For example, *printf("Name\t\tPhone Number\n");* will print "Name" and "Phone Number" separated by two tabs.

To print the values of C variables, a format specification must be embedded in the *format_string* for each variable listed in the argument list to *printf.* For most routine printing chores, you can use the formatting commands in their simplest form:

```
int    ivalue = 100;
double dvalue = 95.5;
char   name = "Microsoft C";
:
printf("Integer = %d, Double = %f, String = %s\n", ivalue,
                dvalue, name);
```

Here we are printing out the values of an *int*, a *double*, and a character string. The formatting command for each variable consists of a percent sign, followed by a single letter denoting the type of variable being printed.

When you need fine control over the appearance of the printed values, *printf* provides it in the form of optional characters between the % and the character denoting the type of C variable being printed. The complete format specification accepted by the *printf* function in Microsoft C has the following form:

Print Format Specification in Microsoft C

%[Flags][Width].[Precision][Addressing_mode][Size][Type]

Table 15-9 summarizes the purpose of each field in the format specification. Additional details for each field are given in Tables 15-10, 15-11, and 15-12.

Table 15-9. *Fields in a Format Specification for* printf

Field	Explanation
Flags (Optional)	One or more of the –, +, # characters or a blank space specifies justification, and the appearance of plus/minus signs and the decimal point in the values printed (see Table 15-11).
Width (Optional)	A number that indicates how many characters, at a minimum, must be used to print the value (see Table 15-12).
Precision (Optional)	A number that specifies how many characters, at maximum, can be used to print the value. When printing integer variables, this is the minimum number of digits used (see Table 15-12).
Addressing_mode (Optional)	This field is specific to Microsoft C 5.0 and 5.1. F (for "far") or N (for "near") can be used to override the default addressing mode of the memory model. Use this field only when the variable being passed to *printf* is a pointer (for example, when printing a string or the value of a pointer). As an example, use F in this field when printing a far string in the small memory model.
Size (Optional)	A character that modifies the *Type* field which comes next. One of the characters h, l, or L appears in this field to differentiate between short

Table 15-9. *(cont.)*

Field	Explanation
	and long integers and between float and double. Shown below is a summary of this field:

Prefix	When to Use
h	Use when printing integers using *Type* d, i, o, x, or X to indicate that the argument is a short integer. Also, use with *Type* u to indicate that the variable being printed is an unsigned short integer.
l	Use when printing integers or unsigned integers with a *Type* field of d, i, o, x, X, or u to specify that the variable to be printed is a long integer. Also use with floating-point variables (when the *Type* field is e, E, g, or G) to specify a double, rather than a float.
L	Use when the floating-point variable being printed is a long double and the *Type* specifier is one of e, E, f, g, or G.

Field	Explanation
Type (Required)	A letter that indicates the type of variable being printed. Table 15-10 lists the characters and their meanings.

The most important among these fields is the *Type* field which tells *printf* the type of C variable it has to convert to characters and print. Table 15-10 lists the characters that can appear in this field and the kind of C variable each signifies.

Table 15-10. Type *Field in Format Specification for* printf

Type	Type in C	Resulting Output Format
c	char	Single character. *printf("%c", 'Z');* prints a *Z*.
d	int	Signed decimal integer as a sequence of digits with or without a sign depending on the flags used. *printf("%d", 95);"* prints *95*.
e	double or float	Signed value in the scientific format. *double* x = –123.4567 printf("%e", x); prints –1.234567e+002.
E	double or float	Signed value in the scientific format, the above example prints *–1.234567E+002* if the %E format is used.
f	double or float	Signed value in the format, (sign)(digits).(digits), the example for *Type* e will print *–123.456700* if the %f format is used. The number of digits before the decimal point depends on the magnitude of the variable, and the number of digits that comes after the decimal point depends on the *Precision* field in the format specification. The default precision is 6. Thus a %f format alone always produces 6 digits after the decimal point, but a %.3f prints the value *–123.457* which is *–123.4567* rounded off to three decimal places.

Table 15-10. *(cont.)*

Type	Type in C	Resulting Output Format
g	double or float	Signed value printed using either the e or f format. The format that generates the most compact output, for the given *Precision* and value, is selected. The e format is used only when the exponent is less than –4 or when it is greater than the value of the *Precision* field. Printing the value *–123.4567* using a %g format results in *–123.457* because the g format rounds off the number.
G	double or float	Signed value printed using the g format, with the letter G in place of e when exponents are printed.
i	int	Signed decimal integer as a sequence of digits with or without a sign depending on the *Flags* field. For example, *printf("%d %+d", x, x);* prints as *123 + 123* when the *int* variable *x* has the value 123.
n	Pointer to int	This is not really a printing format. The argument corresponding to this format is a pointer to an integer. Before returning, the *printf* function stores in this integer the total number of characters it has printed to the output file or to the file's buffer. The EXAMPLES section illustrates the use of the n format.
o	unsigned	Octal digits without any sign.
p	far pointer to void	The address is printed in the form *SSSS:OOOO* where *SSSS* denotes the segment address and *OOOO* is the offset. In small and medium memory models, the argument should be cast as (void far *). If the *Flag* character N is used, as in %Np, only the offset of the address is printed. This format is only available in Microsoft C versions 4.0 and above under MS-DOS.
u	unsigned	Unsigned decimal integer as a sequence of digits.
x	unsigned	Hexadecimal digits using lowercase letters, abcdef.
X	unsigned	Hexadecimal digits using uppercase letters, ABCDEF.

Now we'll examine the rest of the components of the format specification and tabulate the choices. First comes the *Flags* field. One or more of the characters shown in Table 15-11 can appear in the *Flags* field. The Default column in Table 15-11 shows what happens when you do not include this optional field in the format specification.

The *Width* field, if present, should be a non-negative decimal number indicating the minimum number of characters output when printing the value to which the format specification applies. If the value being printed does not occupy the entire *Width*, blanks are added to the left or to the right depending on the justification indicated by the *Flags* field. When the *Width* is prefixed with a zero, all numbers being output are padded with zeroes instead of blanks. Note that specifying a *Width* does not imply that the value being printed will be truncated; this is determined by the *Precision* field.

An asterisk in the *Width* field indicates that an integer variable appearing in the argument list contains the value of width to be used for this format. This integer variable has to precede the actual variable to be printed. This is useful because you can compute the width at run-time and generate appropriately tabulated results.

The *Precision* field is separated from the *Width* field by a decimal point that is present only when *Precision* is explicitly specified. This field must be a non-negative decimal number that, as shown in Table 15-12, is interpreted by *printf* differently for each type of variable. The Default column in Table 15-12 indicates what *printf* does when *Precision* is not specified.

Table 15-11. Flags *Field in Format Specification for* printf

Flag	Meaning	Default
–	Left justify output value within a field wide enough to hold the specified maximum number of characters that can be used for this value.	Right justification.
+	If the output value is a numerical one, print a + or a – according to the sign of the value.	A negative sign is printed for negative numerical values.
blank	Positive numerical values are prefixed with blank spaces. This flag is ignored if the + flag also appears.	No blanks are printed.
#	When used in printing variables of type o, x, or X (i.e., octal or hexadecimal), nonzero output values are prefixed with 0, 0x, or 0X, respectively.	No special prefix appears.
	When the *Type* field in the format specification is e, E, or f, this flag forces the printing of a decimal point.	Decimal point appears only when digits follow it.
	For a g or a G in the *Type* field, the # flag prints a decimal point and all trailing zeroes.	Trailing zeroes are truncated and decimal point appears only when digits follow.

Table 15-12. *Interpretation of* Precision *for* Type *Fields*

Type	Meaning	Default
c	*Precision* is ignored.	A single character is printed.
d u i o x X	The *Precision* specifies the minimum number of digits to be printed. When the value occupies fewer characters than the *Precision*, the output is padded on the left with zeroes. The value	If *Precision* is not specified, or if it is 0 or just a decimal point without a number after it, a value of 1 is used for the *Precision*.

Table 15-12. *(cont.)*

Type	Meaning	Default
	is always expressed fully, even if it requires more characters than the *Precision*, *printf* will not truncate it.	
e E	The *Precision* tells *printf* the number of digits it should print after the decimal point.	*Precision* is 6. If the decimal point appears with 0 or no number after it, the decimal point is not printed.
f	*Precision* specifies the number of digits to be printed after the decimal point. If a decimal point is printed, at least one digit appears before it.	Default is 6. When *Precision* is explicitly given as 0, no decimal point is printed.
g G	The *Precision* specifies the maximum number of significant digits to be printed.	Default is to print all significant digits.
s	The *Precision* indicates the maximum number of characters to be printed. In this case, *printf* truncates the string and prints only up to *Precision* characters.	The character string is printed until a null character is encountered.

COMMON USES The *printf* function is one of the most commonly used functions in any C run-time library. It is rare that anyone uses all the possible fields in the format specifications, but when your application needs them the choices are available.

RETURNS The *printf* function returns the number of characters it has printed.

COMMENTS Use two percentage signs when you need to print a percentage sign. In fact, if *printf* finds a character after the % character, it simply prints the character.

Note that several features of *printf* in Microsoft C library are nonstandard extensions. In particular, should you want your application program to be portable across multiple systems, avoid the N and F addressing mode modifiers and the p and n formats for printing pointers.

SEE ALSO

`vprintf` *Another routine for printing to* stdout

`fprintf, vfprintf` *For formatted printing to a file*

`sprintf, vsprintf` *For formatted printing to a string*

```
cprintf
```
Formatted, unbuffered output to console

EXAMPLES Use *printf* to prompt the user for a string. Print it out, together with a count of characters printed during the first prompt.

```
#include <stdio.h>
main()
{
    int numprint;
    char inbuf[81];
    numprint = printf("Enter a string: ");
    gets(inbuf);
    printf("I printed %d characters and \
You entered:\n%s\n", numprint, inbuf);
}
```

Using the formatting capabilities of *printf*, print a table showing the numbers from 1 to 10 with their squares.

```
#include <stdio.h>
main()
{
    int i;
    printf("Table of squares\n");
    for (i=1; i<=10; i++)
    {
        printf("%4d\t%6d\n", i, i*i);
    }
}
```

Write a small C program to illustrate some of the special features of *printf*. Show the addressing mode modifiers, printing values of pointers, and width and precision fields of a format at run-time.

```
#include <stdio.h>
char far  strf[] = "Far string...";
char near strn[] = "Near string...";
char *var_name[] = {"long_name_variable",
                    "shorter_var", "short"};
double values[] = { 1.23,  3.4567, 9.87654321};
unsigned int num_vars = sizeof(values)/sizeof(double);
main()
{
    int i, j, numprint, chcount, width, precision=0;
```

```
    numprint = printf("Some special features of \
printf\n%n", &chcount);
    printf("printf returned %d and character count in \
variable is %d\n", numprint, chcount);
/* Use of addressing mode modifiers */
    printf("\nYou can print 'near' and 'far' data \
items properly:\n");
    printf("Example: %Fs (far),\n%Ns (near) will print \
in any model\n", strf, strn);
/* Printing addresses of variables */
    printf("\nYou can even print the addresses:\n");
    printf("Item            Segment:Offset\n");
    printf("'far'  string:    %4p\n", (void far *)strf);
    printf("'near' string:    %4p\n", (void far *)strn);

/*  Width and precision can be decided at run-time */
    printf("\nThe format can even be decided \
at run-time\n");
    for(i = 0; i < num_vars; i++)

    {
/* Find maximum length of variable names */
        if( (j = strlen(var_name[i])) > precision)
            precision = j;
    }
/* Make the width 4 characters longer and print names
 * left justified
 */
    width = precision + 4;
    printf("--- Table of Variables ---\n");
    for(i = 0; i < num_vars; i++)
    {
        printf("%-*.*s  %12.8f\n", width, precision,
                              var_name[i], values[i]);
    }
}
```

This example program produces the following listing (the addresses printed using the p format differ according to machine).

```
Some special features of printf
printf returned 32 and character count in variable is 32

You can print 'near' and 'far' data items properly:
Example: Far string... (far),
```

```
Near string... (near) will print in any model

You can even print the addresses:
Item          Segment:Offset
'far'  string:    2A4D:0000
'near' string:    2A64:0042

The format can even be decided at run-time
--- Table of Variables ---
long_name_variable       1.23000000
shorter_var              3.45670000
short                    9.87654321
```

Stream I/O

putc

COMPATIBILITY

MSC 3	MSC 4	MSC 5	MSC 6	QC1	QC2	QC2.5	TC1	TC1.5	TC2	TC++	ANSI	UNIX V	XNX	OS2	DOS
▲	▲	▲	▲	▲	▲	▲	▲	▲	▲	▲	▲	▲	▲	▲	▲

PURPOSE Use the *putc* macro to write a single character to a file opened for buffered output.

SYNTAX

```
int putc(int c, FILE *file_pointer);
int c;                    Character to be written

FILE *file_pointer;       Pointer to file to which the character is written
```

EXAMPLE CALL `putc('*', outfile);`

INCLUDES `#include <stdio.h>` *For function declaration and definition of FILE data structure*

DESCRIPTION The *putc* macro writes the character *c* to the current position of the file specified by the argument *file_pointer*. After writing the character, the current position is advanced to the next character. The *file_pointer* must be a pointer returned earlier by an *fopen* or a *freopen* function call or it can be one of the preopened files such as *stdout* or *stderr* for which writing a character makes sense.

Note that *fputc* performs in the same manner as *putc*, except that *fputc* is implemented as a function.

RETURNS The *putc* macro returns the character it wrote as an integer value. A return value of EOF indicates either an error or end-of-file condition. The *ferror* function should be called to determine if there was an error.

SEE ALSO

putchar — *Macro to write a character to* stdout

fputc — *Function to write a character to a file*

fgetc, fgetchar, getc, getchar — *To read a character from a file*

EXAMPLE Use *putc* to write a line (maximum length of 80 characters or up to the null character) to *stdout*.

```
#include <stdio.h>
char buffer[81] = "Testing putc on stdout...\n";
main()
{
    int i;
/* An empty for loop that uses putc to print to stdout */
    for(i=0; (i<81) && (putc(buffer[i],stdout) != EOF);
        i++);
}
```

Stream I/O

putchar

COMPATIBILITY

MSC 3	MSC 4	MSC 5	MSC 6	QC1	QC2	QC2.5	TC1	TC1.5	TC2	TC++	ANSI	UNIX V	XNX	OS2	DOS
▲	▲	▲	▲	▲	▲	▲	▲	▲	▲	▲	▲	▲	▲	▲	▲

PURPOSE Use the *putchar* macro to write a single character to the preopened file *stdout*, which is initially connected to your display.

SYNTAX

```
int putchar(int c);
```

int c; *Character to be written*

EXAMPLE CALL

```
putchar('?');
```

INCLUDES `#include <stdio.h>` *For function declaration*

DESCRIPTION The *putchar* macro writes the character *c* to *stdout* and is equivalent to the use *putc(stdout)*. Note that *putchar* is the macro equivalent of the *fputchar* function.

RETURNS The *putchar* macro returns the character written to *stdout*. In case of any error, the return value is equal to the constant EOF (defined in *stdio.h*).

COMMENTS Note that you cannot use *putchar* to write a single character to the console because a carriage return must be entered to complete a single buffered write to the keyboard. Use *putch* or *putche* for unbuffered output to the keyboard.

SEE ALSO

`putc`	*Macro to write a character to a file*
`fputc, fputchar`	*To write a character to a file*
`fputc, fputchar, putc, putchar`	*To write a character to a file*

EXAMPLE Use *putchar* to write a line (maximum length of 80 characters) to *stdout.*

```
#include <stdio.h>
char buffer[81] = "Testing putchar...\n";
main()
{
    int i;
/* A for loop that uses putchar to print to stdout */
    for(i=0; (i<81) && (putchar(buffer[i]) != EOF);
        i++);
}
```

Stream I/O

puts

COMPATIBILITY

MSC 3	MSC 4	MSC 5	MSC 6	QC1	QC2	QC2.5	TC1	TC1.5	TC2	TC++	ANSI	UNIX V	XNX	OS2	DOS
▲	▲	▲	▲	▲	▲	▲	▲	▲	▲	▲	▲	▲	▲	▲	▲

PURPOSE Use *puts* to output a string to the standard output file *stdout.*

SYNTAX `int puts(const char *string);`

`const char *string;` *String to be output*

EXAMPLE CALL `puts("Do you really want to quit? ");`

INCLUDES `#include <stdio.h>` *For function declaration*

DESCRIPTION The *puts* function writes the string specified in the argument *string* to the standard output file *stdout*—by default, the screen. The string's terminating null character is replaced by a newline (\n) in the output.

RETURNS In Microsoft C 5.0 and 5.1, *puts* returns a 0 if successful. In case of an error, it returns a nonzero value. In earlier versions, when all is well, *puts* returns the last character it wrote. Otherwise, it returns EOF to indicate error.

SEE ALSO

`fgets`	*To read a line from a file*
`fputs`	*To write a string to a file*
`gets`	*To read a line from the standard input,* stdin

EXAMPLE Use *puts* to write a message to the screen, assuming that *stdout* has not been redirected.

```
#include <stdio.h>
char message[81] =
        "Failure reading drive C\nAbort, Retry, Fail?";
main()
{
    puts(message);
}
```

Stream I/O

COMPATIBILITY

putw

MSC 3	MSC 4	MSC 5	MSC 6	QC1	QC2	QC2.5	TC1	TC1.5	TC2	TC++	ANSI	UNIX V	XNX	OS2	DOS
▲	▲	▲	▲	▲	▲	▲	▲	▲	▲	▲		▲	▲	▲	▲

PURPOSE Use *putw* to write a word (a binary value of type *int*) into a file opened for buffered binary writing.

SYNTAX `int putw(int intval, FILE *file_pointer);`

`int intval;`	*Integer value to be written to file*
`FILE *file_pointer;`	*Pointer to FILE data structure associated with file from which a word is read*

EXAMPLE CALL `putw(int_value, outfile);`

INCLUDES `#include <stdio.h>` *For function declaration and definition of FILE*

DESCRIPTION The *putw* function writes the binary value of the integer argument *intval* at the current position in the file specified by the argument *file_pointer*. As this is a 2-byte value on most MS-DOS machines the file pointer is updated accordingly.

RETURNS The *putw* function returns the integer value it wrote. A return value equal to the constant EOF defined in *stdio.h* may indicate an error. However, since EOF is also a valid integer, you should call *ferror* to determine if an error had actually occurred.

COMMENTS The *putw* function is provided only for compatibility with previous Microsoft C libraries. A program that uses this function may have problems when ported to a new system, because the size of integers and the ordering of the bytes within it (which one is most significant and which is least significant) vary among microprocessors.

SEE ALSO `getw` *To read a word from a file*

EXAMPLE Open a file in the binary write (*wb*) mode. Use *putw* to write some words to the file. Since the words are hexadecimal representations of a string, you can use the DOS TYPE command on the file to see how this works.

```
#include <stdio.h>
/* The string "Hi There\n" in hexadecimal. Because of
 * byte-ordering conventions they may not look obvious.
 * By the way, here are the ASCII codes:
 *  H = 48, i = 69, blank = 20, T = 54, h = 68, e = 65,
 *    and r = 72
 */
int words[] = {0x6948, 0x5420, 0x6568, 0x6572, 0x0A0D};
int numw = sizeof(words)/sizeof(int);
main()
{
    int i;
    FILE *infile;
    char filename[81];
    printf("Enter name of a file to write to: ");
    gets(filename);
/* Open the file for reading */
    if ( (infile = fopen(filename, "wb")) == NULL)
    {
        printf("fopen failed.\n");
        exit(0);
    }
/* Write the words to the file */
    for (i=0; i<numw; i++)
    {
```

```
            if( putw(words[i], infile) == EOF)
            {
/* Check if there was a real error */
                if(ferror(infile) != 0)
                {
                    printf("File: %s write error\n",
                           filename);
                    exit(0);
                }
            }
        }
/* Ask user to type file out and check */
    printf("To see results use 'TYPE %s'\n", filename);
}
```

Stream I/O

rewind

COMPATIBILITY

MSC 3	MSC 4	MSC 5	MSC 6	QC1	QC2	QC2.5	TC1	TC1.5	TC2	TC++	ANSI	UNIX V	XNX	OS2	DOS
▲	▲	▲	▲	▲	▲	▲	▲	▲	▲	▲	▲	▲	▲	▲	▲

PURPOSE Use the *rewind* function to set the current read or write position associated with a file opened for buffered I/O to the beginning of the file.

SYNTAX `void rewind(FILE *file_pointer);`

`FILE *file_pointer;` *Pointer to FILE data structure associated with file whose current position is to be set to the beginning of the file*

EXAMPLE CALL `rewind(input_file);`

INCLUDES `#include <stdio.h>` *For function declaration and definition of FILE*

DESCRIPTION The *rewind* function sets the current read or write position of the file specified by the argument *file_pointer* to the beginning of the file and clears the end-of-file or error indicator.

COMMON USES The *rewind* function is used to go to the beginning of a file which can also be achieved by calling *fseek* with the proper arguments. However, *fseek* will not clear the error indicator.

SEE ALSO `fseek` *To set the current position indicator of a file*

EXAMPLE Open a file using *fopen* for reading. Read and display a line. Now call *rewind* to go back to the beginning and read a line again. The two lines should be identical.

```
#include <stdio.h>
main()
{
    FILE *infile;
    char filename[80], buffer[81];
    printf("Enter name of a text file: ");
    gets(filename);
/* Open the file for reading */
    if ( (infile = fopen(filename, "r")) == NULL)
    {
        printf("fopen failed.\n");
        exit(0);
    }
/* Read and display a line */
    fgets(buffer, 80, infile);
    printf("Line read (before rewind): %s", buffer);
/* Rewind and read a line again */
    rewind(infile);
    fgets(buffer, 80, infile);
    printf("Line read (after rewind) : %s", buffer);
}
```

Stream I/O

rmtmp

COMPATIBILITY

MSC 3	MSC 4	MSC 5	MSC 6	QC1	QC2	QC2.5	TC1	TC1.5	TC2	TC++	ANSI	UNIX V	XNX	OS2	DOS
	▲	▲	▲	▲	▲	▲						▲	▲	▲	▲

PURPOSE Use *rmtmp* to close all temporary files created by *tmpfile* and delete them from the current working directory.

SYNTAX `int rmtmp(void);`

EXAMPLE CALL `number_removed = rmtmp();`

INCLUDES `#include <stdio.h>` *For function declaration*

DESCRIPTION The *rmtmp* function first looks for all temporary files in the current working directory that were created earlier by *tmpfile*. It then closes and deletes each file.

RETURNS The *rmtmp* function returns the total number of temporary files it closed and deleted.

COMMENTS If you change the current working directory (for example, by calling the DOS function 3Bh via *intdosx*) after calling *tmpfile*, *rmtmp* will not be able to delete the temporary file created in the previous directory. Even those files, however, are automatically deleted when the program terminates normally.

SEE ALSO `tmpfile` *To open a temporary file in the current working directory*

EXAMPLE Call *rmtmp* to open three temporary files and then call *rmtmp* to close and delete them. Display the number reported by *rmtmp* to confirm that three files were removed.

```
#include <stdio.h>
main()
{
    int i, numrm;
    FILE *tfile;
    for(i=0; i<3; i++)
    {
        if ((tfile = tmpfile()) == NULL)
            perror("rmtmp failed");
        else printf("Temp file %d created\n", i+1);
    }
/* Now remove these files */
    numrm = rmtmp();
    printf("%d files removed by rmtmp\n", numrm);
}
```

Stream I/O

COMPATIBILITY

scanf

MSC 3	MSC 4	MSC 5	MSC 6	QC1	QC2	QC2.5	TC1	TC1.5	TC2	TC++	ANSI	UNIX V	XNX	OS2	DOS
▲	▲	▲	▲	▲	▲	▲	▲	▲	▲	▲	▲	▲	▲	▲	▲

PURPOSE Use *scanf* to read character strings from the standard input file *stdin* and convert the strings to values of C variables according to specified formats. As an example, you can use *scanf* to read a value into a short integer from the standard input.

SYNTAX

```
int scanf(const char *format_string,...);
```

`const char *format_string;` *Character string that describes the format to be used*

`...`	*Variable number of arguments representing addresses of variables whose values are being read*

EXAMPLE CALL `scanf(" %d:%d:%d", &hour, &minute, &second);`

INCLUDES `#include <stdio.h>` *For function declaration*

DESCRIPTION The *scanf* function accepts a variable number of arguments, which it interprets as addresses of C variables, and reads character strings from *stdin,* representing their values. It converts them to their internal representations using formatting commands embedded in the argument *format_string* which must be present in a call to *scanf.*

The interpretation of the variables depends on the *format_string.* The formatting command for each variable begins with a percentage sign and can contain other characters as well. A whitespace character (a blank space, a tab, or a newline) may cause *scanf* to ignore whitespace characters from *stdin.* Other nonwhitespace characters, excluding the percentage sign, cause *scanf* to ignore each matching character from the input. It begins to interpret the first nonmatching character as the value of a variable that is being read.

For each C variable whose address is included in the argument list to *scanf,* there must be a format specification embedded in the *format_string.* The format specification for each variable has the following form:

Format Specification for *scanf* in Microsoft C

%[*][Width][Addressing_mode][Size][Type]

Table 15-13 summarizes the purpose of each field in the format specification used by *scanf.* Further details are provided in Table 15-14.

Table 15-13. *Fields in a Format Specification for* scanf

Field	Explanation
% (Required)	Indicates the beginning of a format specification. Use %% to read a percentage sign from the input.
* (Optional)	The characters representing the value are read according to the format specification, but the value is not stored. It is not necessary to give an argument corresponding to this format specification.
Width (Optional)	A positive value specifying the maximum number of characters to be read for the value of this variable.

Table 15-13. ***(cont.)***

Field	Explanation
Addressing_mode (Optional)	This field is specific to Microsoft C 4.0 and above. Either F (for "far") or N (for "near") can be used here to override the default addressing mode of the memory model being used. As an example, use F in this field when reading the value of a far integer in a small memory model program.
Size (Optional)	A character that modifies the *Type* field which comes next. One of the characters h, l, or L appears in this field to differentiate between short and long integers and between float and double. Shown below is a sumary of this field:

Prefix	When to Use
h	Use when reading integers using *Type* d, i, o, x, or X to indicate that the argument is a short integer. Also, use with *Type* u to indicate that the variable being read is an unsigned short integer.
l	Use when reading integers or unsigned integers with a *Type* field of d, i, o, x, X, or u to specify that the variable to be read is a long integer. Also use with floating-point variables (when the *Type* field is e, E, g, or G) to specify a double, rather than a float.

Field	Explanation
Type (Required)	A letter that indicates the type of variable being read. Table 15-14 lists the characters and their meanings.

The most important among these fields is the *Type* field which tells *scanf* the type of C variable into which it must convert the input characters. Table 15-14 lists the characters that can appear in the *Type* field and the kind of C variable each one signifies.

Table 15-14. Type *Field in Format Specification for* scanf

Type	Expected Input	Type of Argument
c	Single character. Whitespace characters (space, tab, or newline) will be read in this format.	Pointer to char
d	Decimal integer.	Pointer to int
D	Decimal integer.	Pointer to long
e E f g G	Signed value in the scientific format, for example, –1.234567e+002 and 9.876543e–002 or in the format (sign)(digits).(digits), for example, –1.234567 and 9.876543.	Pointer to float
i	Decimal, hexadecimal, or octal integer.	Pointer to int
I	Decimal, hexadecimal, or octal integer.	Pointer to long

Table 15-14. *(cont.)*

Type	Expected Input	Type of Argument
n	This is not really a reading format. The argument corresponding to this format is a pointer to an integer. Before returning, the *scanf* function stores in this integer the total number of characters it has read from the input file or the input file's buffer in this integer.	
o	Octal digits without any sign.	Pointer to int
O	Octal digits without any sign.	Pointer to long
p	Hexadecimal digits in the form *SSSS:OOOO* using uppercase letters. This format is only available in Microsoft C versions 4.0 and 5.0 under MS-DOS.	
s	Character string.	Pointer to an array of characters large enough to hold input string plus a terminating null
u	Unsigned decimal integer.	Pointer to unsigned int
U	Unsigned decimal integer.	Pointer to unsigned long
x	Hexadecimal digits.	Pointer to int
X	Hexadecimal digits.	Pointer to long

Normally, strings read using the %s format are assumed to be delimited by blank spaces. When you want to read a string delimited by any character other than those in a specific set, you can specify the set of characters within brackets and use this in place of the s in the format specification. If the first character inside the brackets is a caret (^), the set shows the characters that terminate the string. Thus, for example, %[^'\"] reads a string delimited by single or double quote characters.

Strings can be read and stored without the terminating null character by using the %[decimal number]c format in which the *decimal number* denotes the number of characters being read into the character string.

RETURNS The *scanf* function returns the number of input items that were successfully read, converted, and saved in variables. A return value equal to the constant EOF (defined in *stdio.h*) means that an end-of-file was encountered during the read operation.

COMMENTS Use two signs when you need to read a percentage sign. Note that several features of *scanf* in Microsoft C library are nonstandard extensions. In particular, should you want your application program to be portable across multiple systems, avoid the N and F addressing mode modifiers and the p and n formats for reading pointers.

SEE ALSO

`fscanf`	*Formatted read from any buffered file*
`sscanf`	*For formatted reading from a string*
`cscanf`	*Formatted, unbuffered input from console*

EXAMPLE Write a C program that reads the amount of principal, the interest rate, and the number of months to maturity of a certificate of deposit. Use *scanf* to read in the values. Now compute the amount at maturity and print it out.

```
#include <stdio.h>
#include <math.h>
main()
{
    int num_months;
    double interest_rate, principal, final_amount;
/* Ask user to enter all necessary amounts */
    printf("Enter amount of principal, annual interest \
rate:");
    scanf(" %lf %lf", &principal, &interest_rate);
    printf("Enter number of months before deposit \
matures:");
    scanf(" %d", &num_months);
/* Compute amount at maturity and print value */
    final_amount = principal *
                   pow((1.0 + interest_rate/12.0/100.0),
                         (double)num_months);
        printf("$%.2f @%.2f%% annual rate yields $%.2f \
after %d months\n", principal, interest_rate,
               final_amount, num_months);
}
```

Stream I/O

setbuf

COMPATIBILITY

MSC 3	MSC 4	MSC 5	MSC 6	QC1	QC2	QC2.5	TC1	TC1.5	TC2	TC++	ANSI	UNIX V	XNX	OS2	DOS
▲	▲	▲	▲	▲	▲	▲	▲	▲	▲	▲	▲	▲	▲	▲	▲

PURPOSE Use the *setbuf* function to assign your own buffer instead of the system-allocated one for use by a file that has been opened for buffered I/O.

SYNTAX

```
void setbuf(FILE *file_pointer, char *buffer);
```

`FILE *file_pointer;` *Pointer to FILE data structure associated with file whose buffer is being set*

`char *buffer;` *Pointer to buffer (or NULL if no buffering is to be done)*

EXAMPLE CALL

```
setbuf(infile, mybuffer);
```

INCLUDES `#include <stdio.h>` *For function declaration and definition of FILE*

DESCRIPTION The *setbuf* function sets the buffer to be used during I/O involving the file specified by the argument *file_pointer* which must have been returned earlier by *fopen*. If the pointer to buffer given in the argument *buffer* is NULL, *setbuf* turns off buffering for that file. If the pointer is not NULL, it should point to an allocated array of characters BUFSIZ bytes long, where BUFSIZ is a constant defined in *stdio.h* (the declared value is 512). This buffer is used for all subsequent I/O operations with the file specified by the argument *file_pointer*.

COMMENTS While *setbuf* merely lets you switch the buffer used for file I/O to one allocated by you, the companion function *setvbuf* enables you to control the size of the buffer and the level of buffering as well. For example, you would use *setvbuf* if you wanted to read data in chunks larger than the default 512-byte size of the buffer normally used by Microsoft C.

SEE ALSO `setvbuf` *To assign your own buffer with specific size and to control level of buffering during I/O to a file*

EXAMPLE Use *setbuf* to assign your own buffer, at least BUFSIZ characters long, to a file that you have opened with *fopen* for read operations. Now read a character using *fgetc* to initiate a read operation and fill the buffer. Print the buffer to see the effect.

```
#include <stdio.h>
main()
{
```

```
    FILE *infile;
    char filename[81], buffer[BUFSIZ+1];
    printf("Enter name of a text file: ");
    gets(filename);
/* Open the file for reading */
    if ( (infile = fopen(filename, "r")) == NULL)
    {
        printf("fopen failed.\n");
        exit(0);
    }
/* Set up a new buffer for the file */
    setbuf(infile, buffer);
/* Now read in a single character -- this should fill
 * up the buffer
 */
    fgetc(infile);
    buffer[BUFSIZ] = '\0';   /* Make it a C string */
    printf("After reading one character from file \
buffer has:\n%s\n", buffer);
}
```

Stream I/O

COMPATIBILITY

setvbuf

MSC 3	MSC 4	MSC 5	MSC 6	QC1	QC2	QC2.5	TC1	TC1.5	TC2	TC++	ANSI	UNIX V	XNX	OS2	DOS
▲	▲	1	▲	▲	▲	▲	▲	▲	▲	▲	▲	▲	▲	▲	▲

PURPOSE Use the *setvbuf* function to assign a buffer of a specific size to a file open for buffered I/O. You can also control the type of buffering to be used or turn off buffering for the specified file.

SYNTAX

```
int setvbuf(FILE *file_pointer, char *buffer, int buf_type,
                                          size_t buf_size);
```

`FILE *file_pointer;` *Pointer to FILE data structure associated with file whose buffer is being set*

`char *buffer;` *Pointer to buffer (or NULL if no buffering requested)*

`int buf_type;` *Type of buffering desired (see table below for values)*

`size_t buf_size;` *Size of buffer in bytes, if any assigned*

EXAMPLE CALL

```
setvbuf(infile, buffer, _IOFBF, 120);
```

INCLUDES

`#include <stdio.h>` *For function declaration and definition of FILE and* size_t *data types*

DESCRIPTION

The *setvbuf* function sets the buffer and the level of buffering for the file specified by the argument *file_pointer* which must have been returned earlier by *fopen*.

First *setvbuf* checks the argument *buf_type* to see the type of buffering requested. This argument can have one of the values shown in the table, each of which indicates a level of buffering.

Type	Interpretation
_IOFBF	Bytes will be read until buffer is completely filled. This is called "full buffering."
_IOLBF	Each line read from the input stream is buffered. In this "line buffering" mode the reading stops when a whole line has been read.
_IONBF	No buffering is done.

If the argument *buf_type* is _IONBF, the other arguments are ignored and the internal flags are set so that no buffering is done for the file indicated by *file_pointer*. If the argument *buf_type* is either _IOFBF or _IOLBF, the buffering option is first saved internally. Then *setvbuf* checks if the pointer to the buffer specified in the argument *buffer* is a NULL. If it is, *setvbuf* turns off buffering in version 4.0 of Microsoft C, but in versions 5.0, 5.1, and 6.0 it allocates a buffer using the size specified in the argument *buf_size*. (To turn off buffering in 5.0, 5.1, and 6.0 use buffer type _IONBF.) If the argument *buffer* is not NULL, it should be a buffer of size *buf_size* bytes allocated by you. This is set by *setvbuf* as the buffer for the specified file.

1. *setvbuf* was changed in Microsoft C 5.0 to use an allocated buffer if a NULL is passed as the buffer pointer and *_IOFBF* or *IOLBF* are used.

COMMON USES

The *setvbuf* function gives you control over the amount of buffering and the actual buffer to be used by a file.

RETURNS

If successful, *setvbuf* returns a zero. In cases of bad parameters or other errors, the return value is nonzero.

COMMENTS

If you only want to switch to a buffer of your own and not to change any other features of buffered I/O, *setbuf* is a much simpler function to use.

SEE ALSO `setbuf` *To assign your own buffer of fixed size to a file*

EXAMPLE Open a file using *fopen* for reading. Use *setvbuf* to assign a 120-byte buffer for the file and to specify buffer type _IOFBF. Now read a character from the file using *fgetc*, and print the buffer out using *putchar*. You will notice that because of buffering during read, the first 120 characters of the file are now in the buffer, even though you only read a single character.

```
#include <stdio.h>
main()
{
    FILE *infile;
    char filename[81], buffer[121];
    printf("Enter name of a text file: ");
    gets(filename);
/* Open the file for reading */
    if ( (infile = fopen(filename, "r")) == NULL)
    {
        printf("fopen failed.\n");
        exit(0);
    }
/* Set up a new buffer for the file */
    if (setvbuf(infile, buffer, _IOFBF, 120) != 0)
    {
        perror("setvbuf failed");
    }
    else
    {
        fgetc(infile);
        buffer[120] = '\0';
        printf("After reading one character buffer \
has:\n%s\n", buffer);
    }
}
```

Stream I/O

sprintf

COMPATIBILITY

MSC 3	MSC 4	MSC 5	MSC 6	QC1	QC2	QC2.5	TC1	TC1.5	TC2	TC++	ANSI	UNIX V	XNX	OS2	DOS
▲	▲	1	▲	▲	▲	▲	▲	▲	▲	▲	▲	▲	▲	▲	▲

PURPOSE Use the *sprintf* function to format and write the values of C variables to a string.

SYNTAX

```
int sprintf(char *p_string, const char *format_string,...);
```

`char *p_string;` *Pointer to an array of characters where* sprintf *sends its formatted output*

`const char *format_string;` *Character string that describes the format to be used*

`...` *Variable number of arguments depending on the number of items being printed*

EXAMPLE CALL

```
sprintf(buffer, "FY 88 Profit = %.2f\n", profit);
```

INCLUDES `#include <stdio.h>` *For function declaration*

DESCRIPTION The *sprintf* function accepts a variable number of arguments, converts their values to characters, and stores these characters in the buffer whose address is specified in the argument *p_string*. The performance of *sprintf* is identical to that of *fprintf* and *printf* except that *sprintf* sends its output to a character buffer instead of a file. After formatting and storing the characters in the buffer *p_string*, *sprintf* appends a null character to make the buffer a C string.

As in *printf*, the conversion of values of variables to character strings is done according to formatting commands given in a character string *format_string*. The available formatting commands and options are described in detail in the reference pages on *printf*. In particular, Tables 15-9, 15-10, 15-11, and 15-12 tabulate the characters that appear in the format commands (which always begin with the character %). By the way, to actually print a percent sign (instead of having it interpreted as a formatting command), use two percent signs in a row.

1. Starting in Microsoft C 5.0 this function supports *L* format and allows negative precision and width arguments.

COMMON USES A common use of *sprintf* is to prepare formatted strings for use by such other output routines as *_outtext* in the graphics library that do not have any formatting capabilities.

RETURNS The *sprintf* function returns the number of characters it has stored in the buffer, excluding the terminating null character.

SEE ALSO

`printf`	*For printing to* stdout *and for detailed information on formats*
`vprintf`	*Printing to* stdout *using a pointer to a list of arguments*
`fprintf, vfprintf`	*For formatted printing to a file*
`vsprintf`	*Another routine for formatted output to a string*

EXAMPLE Use *fprintf* to prepare a formatted string showing the value of a C variable. Display the string with *printf.*

```
#include <stdio.h>
int     i     = 100;
double  x     = 1.23456;
main()
{
    int numout;
    char outbuf[81];
    numout = sprintf(outbuf, "The value of i = %d and \
the value of x = %g\n", i, x);
    printf("sprintf wrote %d characters and the buffer \
contains:\n%s", numout, outbuf);
}
```

Stream I/O

COMPATIBILITY

sscanf

MSC 3	MSC 4	MSC 5	MSC 6	QC1	QC2	QC2.5	TC1	TC1.5	TC2	TC++	ANSI	UNIX V	XNX	OS2	DOS
▲	▲	1	▲	▲	▲	▲	▲	▲	▲	▲	▲	▲	▲	▲	▲

PURPOSE Use *sscanf* to read characters from a buffer and to convert and store them in C variables according to specified formats.

SYNTAX `int sscanf(const char *buffer, const char *format_string,...);`

`const char *buffer;`	*Pointer to buffer from which characters will be read and converted to values of variables*
`const char *format_string;`	*Character string that describes the format to be used*
`...`	*Variable number of arguments representing addresses of variables whose values are being read*

EXAMPLE CALL `sscanf(buffer, "Name: %s Age: %d", name, &age);`

INCLUDES `#include <stdio.h>` *For function declaration*

DESCRIPTION The *sscanf* function reads a stream of characters from the buffer specified in the argument *buffer* and converts them to values according to format specifications embedded in the argument *format_string*. It then stores the values in C variables whose addresses are provided in the variable length argument list.

The optional arguments following the *format_string* are addresses of C variables whose values are being read. Each address has a corresponding format specification in the argument *format_string*. The format specification always begins with a percent sign, and the formatting commands are identical to the ones used with the function *scanf*. A detailed list of the formats is provided in the reference pages on *scanf*.

1. Starting in Microsoft C 5.0 this function supports the *L* modifier and the *g*, *E*, and *G* format specifiers.

COMMON USES The *sscanf* function is handy for in-memory conversion of characters to values. You may often find it convenient to read in strings using either *gets* or *fgets* and then extract values from the string by using *sscanf*.

RETURNS The *sscanf* function returns the number of fields that were successfully read, converted, and assigned to variables. If the string ends before completing the read operation, the return value is the constant EOF, defined in the include file *stdio.h*.

SEE ALSO

`scanf`	*Formatted reading from* stdin
`fscanf`	*For formatted, buffered reading from a file*
`cscanf`	*Formatted, unbuffered input from console*

EXAMPLE Suppose you have a program that lets the user set the value of a variable by a command of the form "name = value" (i.e., the name is separated from the value by one or more blanks surrounding an equal sign). One way to implement this is to read the entire line into an internal buffer using *gets*. You can then use *sscanf* to separate the variable name and its value. As you can see from the example below, the features of *sscanf* provide easy ways of implementing such user-friendly features as this.

```
#include <stdio.h>
main()
{
```

```
    double value;
    char buffer[81], name[81];
    printf("Enter value of variable as \
\"name=<value>\":");
    gets(buffer);
/* Now use sscanf to separate name and value */
    sscanf(buffer, " %[^=] = %lf", name, &value);
/* Display result to user */
    printf("Value of variable named %s is set to %f\n",
            name, value);
}
```

Stream I/O

COMPATIBILITY

tempnam

MSC 3	MSC 4	MSC 5	MSC 6	QC1	QC2	QC2.5	TC1	TC1.5	TC2	TC++	ANSI	UNIX V	XNX	OS2	DOS
	▲	▲	▲	▲	▲	▲					▲	▲	▲	▲	▲

PURPOSE Use the *tempnam* function to generate a temporary file name for your application. The file name uses the default directory name from the MS-DOS environment variable TMP, if it is defined, and has a specified prefix.

SYNTAX

```
char *tempnam(char *dir_name, char *file_prefix);
```

`char *dir_name;` *Pointer to string with the directory name to be used if environment variable TMP is undefined*

`char *file_prefix;` *Pointer to string with prefix characters for the file name*

EXAMPLE CALL

```
tfilename = tempnam(NULL, "mscb");
```

INCLUDES `#include <stdio.h>` *For function declaration*

DESCRIPTION The *tempnam* function generates a file name in the following manner. It first checks if the MS-DOS environment variable TMP is defined. If TMP is defined, *tempnam* uses that as the directory portion of the file name. If TMP is undefined, and the argument *dir_name* is not NULL, the string from this argument is chosen as the directory name. If none of this works, the defined constant *P_tmpdir* in the include file *stdio.h* provides the directory name. If the directory name cannot be derived from any of these sources, the file name will not have a specific directory name, which means that when you create the file, it will be in the current working directory.

Following this process, *tempnam* creates the rest of the file name by appending up to five digits having a maximum value of 65,535 to the prefix provided in the argument *file_prefix.* (The prefix together with the digits may not exceed eight characters in length.) If a file with that name already exists, *tempnam* creates another name by incrementing the last digit in the file name. It continues this until a unique file name is found or until no more file names can be generated.

The *tempnam* function actually allocates the storage necessary to hold the file name it generates. You must deallocate the space by calling *free.*

COMMON USES The *tempnam* function is a handy tool, similar to *tmpnam*, for constructing temporary file names. It is more useful than the latter because of its increased control over generation of parts of the file name.

RETURNS The *tempnam* function returns a pointer to the name generated. If the generated name is not unique or if a file name could not be created with the specified prefix (for example, when a file with the same name already exists), *tempnam* returns a NULL.

COMMENTS If you do not care about the file name and simply want to open a temporary file for storing transient data in your application, you may be able to get by with *tmpfile*. Remember that when using *tmpnam* or *tempnam*, you have to explicitly open the temporary file (and delete it, too).

Note that *tempnam* accepts a prefix whose length is more than the number of characters allowed in an MS-DOS file name (11 characters including extension) and returns it as a name; the burden is on you to ensure that the file name meets MS-DOS requirements.

SEE ALSO

`tempnam`	*To create a temporary file name with a prefix in a different directory*
`tempfile`	*To open a temporary file in current working directory*

EXAMPLE Call *tempnam* to generate a temporary file name and print the name. Allow the user to enter the prefix. You will see that *tempnam* accepts a prefix much longer than a valid MS-DOS file name.

```
#include <stdio.h>
main()
{
    char *tfilename, prefix[80];
    printf("Enter a prefix for the file name: ");
    tfilename = tempnam(NULL, prefix);
    if (tfilename == NULL)
    {
```

```
        perror("tempnam failed");
    }
    else
    {
        printf("Temporary file name: %s\n", tfilename);
    }
}
```

Stream I/O

COMPATIBILITY

tmpfile

MSC 3	MSC 4	MSC 5	MSC 6	QC1	QC2	QC2.5	TC1	TC1.5	TC2	TC++	ANSI	UNIX V	XNX	OS2	DOS
	▲	1	▲	▲	▲	▲		▲	▲	▲	▲	▲	▲	▲	▲

PURPOSE Use *tmpfile* to open a temporary file in the current directory for buffered binary read/write operations.

SYNTAX `FILE *tmpfile(void);`

EXAMPLE CALL `p_tfile = tmpfile();`

INCLUDES `#include <stdio.h>` *For function declaration and definition of FILE data type*

DESCRIPTION The *tmpfile* function opens a temporary file in the current working directory. The file is opened in the mode *w+b* which means binary read and write operations can be performed on this file. You have no access to the name of the file that is created nor is the file available to you after a normal exit from the program. The file is automatically deleted when your program terminates normally or when you close the file. You can delete all such files by calling *rmtmp.*

1. Beginning in Microsoft C 5.0 *tmpfile* opens the temporary file in *default wb+* mode instead of *w+*.

COMMON USES The *tmpfile* function is a convenient way of opening temporary work files in an application.

RETURNS The *tmpfile* function returns a pointer to the FILE data structure of the temporary file it opens. In case of error, the return pointer will be NULL.

COMMENTS Unlike *tmpnam* and *tempnam,* which simply generate the file name, a file is opened by *tmpfile* and the file is truly temporary because it is deleted when the program ends.

SEE ALSO `rmtmp` *To delete all temporary files in current working directory*

EXAMPLE Call *tmpfile* to open a temporary file and write the contents of a buffer to the file. Unfortunately, the file will be gone when you exit the program, so there will be no evidence of the temporary file. Nor is the file name available for printing.

```
#include <stdio.h>
char   message[80] = "Testing tmpfile.... ";
main()
{
    FILE *tfile;
    if ((tfile = tmpfile()) == NULL)
    {
        perror("tmpfile failed");
    }
    else
    {
        printf("Temporary file successfully opened.\n");
        printf("Wrote %d characters to file\n",
               fwrite((void *)message, sizeof(char), 80,
               tfile));
        printf("File will be gone when you exit.\n");
    }
}
```

Stream I/O

tmpnam

COMPATIBILITY

MSC 3	MSC 4	MSC 5	MSC 6	QC1	QC2	QC2.5	TC1	TC1.5	TC2	TC++	ANSI	UNIX V	XNX	OS2	DOS
	▲	▲	▲	▲	▲	▲		▲	▲	▲	▲	▲	▲	▲	▲

PURPOSE Use the *tmpnam* function to generate a temporary file name for your application.

SYNTAX `char *tmpnam(char *file_name);`

`char *file_name;` *Pointer to string where file name will be returned*

EXAMPLE CALL `tmpnam(tfilename);`

INCLUDES `#include <stdio.h>` *For function declaration*

DESCRIPTION The *tmpnam* function generates a file name by appending six digits to the directory name defined by the constant *P_tmpdir* in the include file *stdio.h*. This null-terminated file name is returned in a buffer, which must be allocated by you and whose address must be passed to *tmpnam* in the argument *file_name*. The size of the buffer that holds the file name must be at least equal to the constant *L_tmpnam*, which is defined in *stdio.h* to be eight digits plus the length of the directory name *P_tmpdir*. The default directory name is set to "\\", (i.e., all temporary files will be at the root directory). You should call *tempnam* if you want to generate arbitrary file names in a separate directory and with specific prefix characters of your choice. You can generate up to *TMP_MAX* (defined in *stdio.h* to be 32,767) unique file names with *tmpnam*.

If the argument *file_name* is NULL, the generated file name is stored internally by *tmpnam* and a pointer to this name is returned by *tmpnam*. This name is preserved until another call is made to this function. So you can get by with a NULL argument to *tmpnam* and simply use the pointer returned by it as long as you use this name before the next call to *tmpnam*.

COMMON USES The *tmpnam* function is a handy tool if your application generates temporary files.

RETURNS The *tmpnam* function returns a pointer to the name generated. If the generated name is not unique, it returns a NULL.

COMMENTS You are responsible for opening the file using the file name generated by *tmpnam*. You can use *tmpfile* to directly open a temporary file.

SEE ALSO

`tempnam`	*To create a temporary file name with a prefix in a different directory*
`tmpfile`	*To open a temporary file in the current working directory*

EXAMPLE Call *tmpnam* to generate a temporary file name and print this name. Note that we do not allocate any storage for the string itself; we use the pointer returned by *tmpnam*.

```
#include <stdio.h>
main()
{
    char *tfilename;
    tfilename = tmpnam(NULL);
    if (tfilename == NULL)
    {
        perror("tmpnam failed");
    }
    else
```

```
        {
            printf("Temporary file name: %s\n", tfilename);
        }
    }
```

Stream I/O

ungetc

COMPATIBILITY

MSC 3	MSC 4	MSC 5	MSC 6	QC1	QC2	QC2.5	TC1	TC1.5	TC2	TC++	ANSI	UNIX V	XNX	OS2	DOS
▲	▲	▲	▲	▲	▲	▲	▲	▲	▲	▲	▲	▲	▲	▲	▲

PURPOSE Use *ungetc* to place any character, except the constant EOF, in the buffer associated with a file opened for buffered input.

SYNTAX `int ungetc(int c, FILE *file_pointer);`

`int c;` *Character to be placed in the file's buffer*

`FILE *file_pointer;` *Pointer to FILE data structure associated with file in whose buffer the character is placed*

EXAMPLE CALL `ungetc(last_char, infile);`

INCLUDES `#include <stdio.h>` *For function declaration and definition of FILE data type*

DESCRIPTION The *ungetc* function places the character given in the integer argument *c* in the buffer associated with the file specified by the argument *file_pointer* so that the next read operation on that file starts with that character. You must read at least once before attempting to place a character in a file's buffer; otherwise, the buffer is not in a usable state. Also, *ungetc* ignores any attempt to push the constant EOF.

Since *ungetc* places the character in the file's buffer, any operation that tampers with the buffer or the file's current position (for example, *fflush, fseek, fsetpos* or *rewind*) may erase the character.

The *ungetc* function affects the file's current position differently for different translation modes. In the text mode the current position remains as it was before the call to *ungetc*. Thus the file's position is undefined until the pushed character is read back or discarded. In the binary mode the file's position is decremented after each call to *ungetc*. Once the file's position reaches zero, however, the value becomes undefined after calls to *ungetc*.

COMMON USES The *ungetc* function is used to reject an invalid character that has just been read. The character can be placed back in the input buffer and then displayed by an error-reporting routine.

RETURNS If there are no errors, *ungetc* returns the character it pushed back. Otherwise, it returns the constant EOF to indicate an error.

SEE ALSO

`getc`	*Macro to read a character from a file*
`getchar`	*Function to read a character from* stdin
`fputc, fputchar, putc, putchar`	*To write a character to a file*

EXAMPLE Write a program that asks the user to enter an integer. Use *getchar* to read the digits and accumulate them into an integer. Once a nondigit is reached (use the macro *isdigit* to check), put that character back in the buffer by calling *ungetc*. Now print a message showing the integer value and indicating the first noninteger character that the user typed. This is a classic use of *ungetc*.

```
#include <stdio.h>
#include <ctype.h>       /* For the macro isdigit() */
main()
{
    int intval = 0, c;
    char buff[81];
/* Ask user to type in an integer */
    printf("Enter an integer followed by some other \
characters:");
    while ( (c = getchar()) != EOF && isdigit(c) )
    {
        intval = 10*intval + c - 48; /* 0 is ASCII 48 */
    }
/* Push back the first non-digit read from stdin */
    if (c != EOF) ungetc(c, stdin);
/* Print message to user */
    printf("Integer you entered = %d.\n\
Rest of the string beginning at the first non-integer \
in buffer: %s\n", intval, gets(buff));
}
```

Stream I/O

vfprintf

COMPATIBILITY

MSC 3	MSC 4	MSC 5	MSC 6	QC1	QC2	QC2.5	TC1	TC1.5	TC2	TC++	ANSI	UNIX V	XNX	OS2	DOS
	▲	▲	▲	▲	▲	▲	▲	▲	▲	▲	▲	▲	▲	▲	▲

PURPOSE Use *vfprintf* to write formatted output to a file, just as *fprintf* does, except that *vfprintf* accepts a pointer to the list of variables rather than the variables themselves, allowing a number of items to be printed.

SYNTAX

```
int vfprintf(FILE *file_pointer, const char *format_string,
                                  va_list arg_pointer);
```

FILE *file_pointer;	*Pointer to FILE data structure of the file to which the output goes*
const char *format_string;	*Character string that describes the format to be used*
va_list arg_pointer;	*Pointer to a list containing a variable number of arguments being printed*

EXAMPLE CALL

```
vfprintf(stderr, p_format, p_arg);
```

INCLUDES

#include <stdio.h>	*For function declaration*
#include <stdarg.h>	*When writing for ANSI compatibility (defines va_list)*
#include <varargs.h>	*When writing for UNIX System V compatibility (defines va_list)*

DESCRIPTION The *vfprintf* function accepts a pointer to a list of a number of arguments in *arg_pointer*, converts their values to characters, and writes them to the file specified by the argument *file_pointer*.

The only difference between *fprintf* and *vfprintf* is that *fprintf* accepts its arguments directly, whereas *vfprintf* accepts a pointer to a list of a variable number of arguments. The format used to print the variables is given in the argument *format_string*, a character string with embedded format commands that begin with a percent sign. Detailed information on the format specification appears in the reference pages on *printf* (see Tables 15-9, 15-10, 15-11, and 15-12).

COMMON USES The *vfprintf* is useful for printing values of arguments in routines that accept arguments of varying length. An example would be a customized error handler that accepts a list of arguments and prints them out.

RETURNS The *vfprintf* function returns the number of characters it has printed, excluding the terminating null character.

SEE ALSO

`printf`	*For printing to* stdout *and for detailed information on formats*
`vprintf`	*Printing to* stdout *using a pointer to a list of arguments*
`fprintf`	*For formatted printing to a file*
`sprintf, vsprintf`	*For formatted output to a string*
`va_start, va_arg, va_end`	*Macros for accessing variable-length argument lists*

EXAMPLE Write a routine to send error messages to *stderr*. The routine should accept a variable number of arguments, the first of which is a format string followed by one or more arguments, just like *fprintf* accepts. The routine, which in this example conforms to the UNIX System V standard of handling variable arguments, prints the arguments using the given format. Test the routine using a simple main program.

```
#include <stdio.h>
#include <varargs.h>      /* UNIX Sys V standard */
char filename[80] = "EXAMPLE.EXE";
main()
{
        int line_no = 131;
/* Call the error handler to print an error message.
 * First just a single line. Then a more detailed
 * message with more arguments.
 */
        my_errmsg("Syntax error\n");

        my_errmsg("File: %s at line_no %d\n", filename,
                    line_no);
}
/*-----------------------------------------------------*/
/*  my_errmsg: accepts variable number of arguments
 *             and prints their values to stderr
 */
my_errmsg(va_alist)
va_dcl
{
    char *p_format;
    va_list p_arg;
```

```
/* Use va_start followed by va_arg macros to get to the
 * start of the variable number of arguments. This will
 * alter the pointer p_arg to point to the list of
 * variables to be printed.
 */
    va_start(p_arg);
    p_format = va_arg(p_arg, char*);
    vfprintf(stderr, p_format, p_arg);
/* Use the va_end macro to reset the p_arg to NULL */
    va_end(p_arg);
}
```

Stream I/O

vprintf

COMPATIBILITY

MSC 3	MSC 4	MSC 5	MSC 6	QC1	QC2	QC2.5	TC1	TC1.5	TC2	TC++	ANSI	UNIX V	XNX	OS2	DOS
	▲	▲	▲	▲	▲	▲	▲	▲	▲	▲	▲	▲	▲	▲	▲

PURPOSE Use *vprintf* to write formatted output to *stdout* (that is, perform the same functions as *printf*) when you have only a pointer to the list of variables to be printed, rather than the variables themselves. This allows a variable number of arguments to be printed.

SYNTAX

```
int vprintf(const char *format_string, va_list arg_pointer);
```

`const char *format_string;`	*Character string that describes the format to be used*
`va_list arg_pointer;`	*Pointer to a list containing a variable number of arguments that are being printed*

EXAMPLE CALL

```
vprintf(p_format, p_arg);
```

INCLUDES

`#include <stdio.h>`	*For function declaration*
`#include <stdarg.h>`	*When writing for ANSI compatibility (defines va_list)*
`#include <varargs.h>`	*When writing for UNIX System V compatibility (defines va_list)*

DESCRIPTION The *vprintf* function accepts a pointer to a list of a variable number of arguments in *arg_pointer*, converts their values to characters, and writes them to the preopened file *stdout*. Except for accepting a pointer to a list of arguments rather than using the arguments themselves, *vprintf* works as *fprintf* and *printf* do. The argument *format_string* is a character string with embedded format commands that begin with a percent sign. Their meaning is explained in the reference pages on *printf* (see Tables 15-9, 15-10, 15-11, and 15-12).

COMMON USES The *vprintf* is necessary when you have a list of arguments available and want to print them out. A common example is a customized error handler that accepts a list of arguments.

RETURNS The *vprintf* function returns the number of characters it has printed, excluding the terminating null character.

SEE ALSO

`printf`	*For printing to* stdout *and for detailed information on formats*
`fprintf, vfprintf`	*For formatted printing to a file*
`sprintf, vsprintf`	*For formatted output to a string*
`va_start, va_arg, va_end`	*Macros for accessing variable-length argument lists*

EXAMPLE Write an error-handling routine, conforming to the proposed ANSI C standards, that takes a variable number of arguments and prints an error message that includes the values of the passed parameters. Use *vprintf* to do the printing in the error handler. Write a sample main program to demonstrate the use of the error handler.

```
#include <stdio.h>
#include <stdarg.h>      /* ANSI C compatible */
void error_handler(char *,...);
char filename[80] = "COMMAND.COM";
main()
{
    int offset = 0x232A;
/* Call the error handler to print an error message.
 * First just a single line. Then a more detailed
 * message with more arguments.
 */
    error_handler("System error\n");
    error_handler("File %s at offset %X\n",
                  filename, offset);
}
/*--------------------------------------------------*/
/*  error_handler: accepts variable number of arguments
 *                 and prints messages
 */
void error_handler(char *my_format,...)
{
```

```
    va_list arg_pointer;
/* Use va_start macro to get to the start of the
 * variable number of arguments. This will alter the
 * pointer arg_pointer to point to the list of
 * variables to be printed.
 */
    va_start(arg_pointer, my_format);
    vprintf(my_format, arg_pointer);
/* Use the va_end macro to reset the arg_pointer */
    va_end(arg_pointer);
}
```

Stream I/O

vsprintf

COMPATIBILITY

MSC 3	MSC 4	MSC 5	MSC 6	QC1	QC2	QC2.5	TC1	TC1.5	TC2	TC++	ANSI	UNIX V	XNX	OS2	DOS
	▲	▲	▲	▲	▲	▲	▲	▲	▲	▲	▲	▲	▲	▲	▲

PURPOSE Use *vsprintf* to write formatted output to a string (that is, perform the same function as *sprintf*), except that *vsprintf* uses a pointer to a list of variables rather than the variables themselves. Thus a variable number of arguments can be formatted.

SYNTAX

```
int vsprintf(char *p_string, const char *format_string,
                                     va_list arg_pointer);
```

`char *p_string;` *Pointer to an array of characters where* vsprintf *sends its formatted output*

`const char *format_string;` *Character string that describes the format to be used*

`va_list arg_pointer;` *Pointer to a list containing a variable number of arguments that are being printed*

EXAMPLE CALL `vsprintf(err_msg, p_format, p_arg);`

INCLUDES

`#include <stdio.h>` *For function declaration*

`#include <stdarg.h>` *When writing for ANSI compatibility (defines va_list)*

`#include <varargs.h>` *When writing for UNIX System V compatibility (defines va_list)*

DESCRIPTION The *vsprintf* function accepts a pointer to a list of a variable number of arguments in *arg_pointer*, prepares a formatted character string, and saves the string in the area of memory whose address is given in the argument *p_string*. In so doing, it functions exactly as *sprintf* does, except that *vsprintf* accepts a pointer. The conversion of a variable's value to a character string is done according to the format string in the argument *format_string*, which is an ordinary text string containing embedded format commands beginning with a percent sign. Detailed information on format specification appears in the reference pages on *printf* (see Tables 15-9, 15-10, 15-11, and 15-12). On return from *vsprintf*, the *p_string* will be a standard C string.

COMMON USES The *vsprintf* function is useful in preparing a string with the values of the arguments in routines that accept variable-length arguments. This string may be used by other output routines (such as *_outtext* in the graphics library, which does not have any formatting capability). An example of such a routine would be an error handler that accepts a list of arguments and prints them out in the graphics mode using *_outtext*.

RETURNS The *vsprintf* function returns the number of characters it has printed, excluding the terminating null character.

SEE ALSO

`printf`	*For printing to* stdout *and for detailed information on formats*
`vprintf`	*For printing to* stdout *using a pointer to a list of arguments*
`fprintf, vfprintf`	*For formatted printing to a file*
`sprintf`	*For formatted output to a string*
`va_start, va_arg, va_end`	*Macros for accessing variable-length argument lists*

EXAMPLE Write an error handler, conforming to the ANSI C standard, to display error messages in a graphics display using *_outtext*. The routine should accept a variable number of arguments, the first of which is a format string followed by one or more arguments, as would be used with *printf*. The routine should then use *vsprintf* to prepare a string with the values of the arguments in the given format. Test the routine with a simple main program.

```
#include <stdio.h>
#include <stdarg.h>              /* ANSI C compatible  */
#include <graph.h>
#define RED    4L  /* "long" constant for _setbkcolor */
#define YELLOW 14  /* Text color number 14 is yellow  */
```

```
void error_handler(char *,...);
char filename[80] = "COMMAND.COM";
main()
{
    int offset = 0x232A;
/* Assume we are already in text mode                    */
    _clearscreen(_GCLEARSCREEN);     /* Clear  screen */
    _settextwindow(10,10,15,70); /* Define text window*/
    _setbkcolor(RED);      /* Set background to red    */
    _clearscreen(_GWINDOW); /* clear out text window  */


/* Once a text window is defined all text positions are
 * relative to upper left corner of the window. Notice
 * that this can be used for pop-up menus.
 */
    _settextposition(1,1);      /* Set text position   */
    _settextcolor(YELLOW);       /* Set text color     */
/* Call the error handler to print an error message.
 * First just a single line. Then a more detailed
 * message with more arguments.
 */
    error_handler("System error\n");
    error_handler("File %s at offset %X\n", filename,
                   offset);
}
/*-----------------------------------------------------*/
/*  error_handler: accepts variable number of arguments
 *                 and prints messages
 */
void error_handler(char *my_format,...)
{
    va_list arg_pointer;
    char buffer[80];    /* Buffer for text string */
/* Use va_start macro to get to the start of the
 * variable number of arguments. This will alter the
 * pointer arg_pointer to point to the list of
 * variables to be printed.
 */
    va_start(arg_pointer, my_format);
    vsprintf(buffer, my_format, arg_pointer);
/* Now display the message by calling _outtext   */
    _outtext(buffer);
/* Use the va_end macro to reset the arg_pointer */
    va_end(arg_pointer);
}
```

Input and Output Routines

Low-level I/O

close

COMPATIBILITY

MSC 3	MSC 4	MSC 5	MSC 6	QC1	QC2	QC2.5	TC1	TC1.5	TC2	TC++	ANSI	UNIX V	XNX	OS2	DOS
▲	▲	▲	▲	▲	▲	▲	▲	▲	▲	▲		▲	▲	▲	▲

PURPOSE Use *close* to close a file specified by a valid handle, an integer returned by a prior call to *open*.

SYNTAX

```
int close(int handle);

int handle;      Handle of an open file
```

EXAMPLE CALL

```
close(handle);
```

INCLUDES

```
#include <io.h>      For function declaration
```

DESCRIPTION The *close* function closes the file specified by the argument *handle*. The *handle* must be the integer returned by a previous call to the function *open* or *creat*.

RETURNS If the file is successfully closed, *close* returns a 0. Otherwise, it returns a value of –1 to indicate error and sets the global variable *errno* to the constant EBADF, indicating an invalid file handle.

SEE ALSO

open — *To open a file for unformatted, unbuffered I/O*

fopen, fclose — *File opening and closing for buffered I/O*

EXAMPLE Illustrate the use of *close* by attempting to close a file that is not open. Use *perror* to print the error message returned by the system.

```
#include <stdio.h>
#include <io.h>
main()
{
/* Call close with an invalid file handle. Handles 0
 * thru 4 are in use by stdin, stdout, stderr, stdaux
 * and stdprn. So, let's use handle 5.
 */
    printf("Attempting to close file handle 5...\n");
    if (close(5) != 0)
    {
        perror("Close failed");
    }
}
```

Low-level I/O

creat

COMPATIBILITY

MSC 3	MSC 4	MSC 5	MSC 6	QC1	QC2	QC2.5	TC1	TC1.5	TC2	TC++	ANSI	UNIX V	XNX	OS2	DOS
▲	▲	▲	▲	▲	▲	▲	▲	▲	▲	▲		▲	▲	▲	▲

PURPOSE Use *creat* to make a new file or truncate an existing file. The file is specified by its name which may include a path specification.

SYNTAX

```
int creat(char *filename, int pmode);
```

`char *filename;`	*File name and path specification*
`int pmode;`	*Permission settings for the file, indicating whether reading, writing, or both are permitted*

EXAMPLE CALL

```
handle = creat("temp.dat", S_IREAD|S_IWRITE);
```

INCLUDES

`#include <io.h>`	*For function declaration*
`#include <sys\types.h>`	*For definition of data types used in <sys\stat.h>*
`#include <sys\stat.h>`	*For definition of constants to specify permission settings of a file*

DESCRIPTION The *creat* function first checks whether the file named *filename* exists. If it does, the file is truncated, opened for writing and the previous contents of the file are destroyed. If the file does not exist, a new one is created. The argument *filename* includes the directory specification as well as the name of the file. If no directory specification is present, the file is created in the current working directory. Thus if the *filename* is *"c:\\temp\\test.dat"* the file is created in directory \TEMP of drive C, even if the current directory is something else.

The integer argument *pmode* specifies the newly created file's permission setting, which is applied to the file when it is closed. The permission setting is given in terms of predefined constants. The permission settings given in *pmode* are validated against the current default settings defined by *umask*. Consult the reference pages on *umask* for this validation process. The possible values of *pmode* are given in Table 15-16.

RETURNS If the file is successfully created (or truncated), *creat* returns a valid handle to the file. In case of error, it returns a −1 and sets the global variable *errno* to one of the constants defined in the file *errno.h*. These are defined in the table below.

Error Constant	Meaning
EACCES	Cannot access file. This means the given file name refers to a directory, or the file is read only, or file-sharing is enabled and sharing mode does not allow the operation being attempted.
EMFILE	No more file handles available. This means you have hit the MS-DOS enforced limit of 20 files that a single process can open simultaneously.
ENOENT	File was not found or a directory corresponding to the path specification in the file name is nonexistent.

COMMENTS The *creat* function is included to preserve compatibility with libraries in earlier versions of Microsoft C. The function of *creat* is provided by *open* with the flags O_CREAT and O_TRUNC. Microsoft recommends that you use *open* to create files, instead of *creat*.

SEE ALSO open *To open a file for unformatted, unbuffered I/O*

umask *To specify default permission setting*

EXAMPLE Write a C program that prompts the user for a file name and then uses *creat* to open that file with both read and write permission settings. Use *perror* to inform the user of errors.

```
#include <stdio.h>
#include <sys\types.h>
#include <sys\stat.h>
#include <io.h>

main()
{
    int handle;
    unsigned char filename[81];

/* Ask user for file name */
    printf("Enter name of file to be created: ");
    gets(filename);
    if ( (handle = creat(filename, S_IREAD|S_IWRITE))
         == -1)
    {
        perror("Error creating file!");
    }
    else
    {
        printf("\nFile %s created\n", filename);
    }
}
```

Low-level I/O

dup

COMPATIBILITY

MSC 3	MSC 4	MSC 5	MSC 6	QC1	QC2	QC2.5	TC1	TC1.5	TC2	TC++	ANSI	UNIX V	XNX	OS2	DOS
▲	▲	▲	▲	▲	▲	▲	▲	▲	▲	▲		▲	▲	▲	▲

PURPOSE Use *dup* to create a second handle for a file that is already open and has a valid handle.

SYNTAX

```
int dup(int handle);
```

`int handle;` *Handle of an open file*

EXAMPLE CALL

```
new_handle = dup(old_handle);
```

INCLUDES `#include <io.h>` *For function declaration*

DESCRIPTION The *dup* function assigns another handle to a file that is already open and has a valid handlc. Thc current handle must be given in the argument *handle.* The creation of a duplicate handle counts as a new open file and is subject to the 20-file limit imposed by MS-DOS.

COMMON USES In UNIX systems, *dup* is used to perform I/O with an interprocess communication mechanism called "pipes."

RETURNS If a new handle is successfully created, *dup* returns the duplicate handie. Otherwise, it returns a value of –1 to indicate error and sets the global variable *errno* to either EMFILE if no more file handles are possible or to EBADF, indicating that the argument *handle* is not a valid file handle.

SEE ALSO `open` *To open a file for unformatted, unbuffered I/O*

`creat` *To create a new file and open it for unformatted, unbuffered I/O*

EXAMPLE Create a new handle for *stdout* that is assigned the handle 1 when the program starts running. Write a string to the new handle to show that indeed the new handle refers to stdout.

```
#include <stdio.h>
#include <io.h>
char message[] =
"Testing dup. This should appear on stdout\n";
main()
{
```

```
    int newhandle;
/* By default, stdout has handle 1.
 * create another handle for stdout
 */
    if((newhandle = dup(1)) == -1)
    {
            perror("dup on handle 1 failed!");
    }
    else
    {
            printf("New handle for stdout is %d\n", newhandle);
            write(newhandle, message, sizeof(message));
    }
}
```

Low-level I/O

COMPATIBILITY

dup2

MSC 3	MSC 4	MSC 5	MSC 6	QC1	QC2	QC2.5	TC1	TC1.5	TC2	TC++	ANSI	UNIX V	XNX	OS2	DOS
▲	▲	▲	▲	▲	▲	▲	▲	▲	▲	▲		▲	▲	▲	▲

PURPOSE Use *dup2* to force a second file handle to refer to the same file as a first one. The first handle must be a valid one, associated with a file that is already open.

SYNTAX `int dup2(int handle1, int handle2);`

`int handle1;` *Handle of an open file*

`int handle2;` *Another handle that will become associated with the same file as* handle1

EXAMPLE CALL `dup2(oldhandle, newhandle);`

INCLUDES `#include <io.h>` *For function declaration*

DESCRIPTION The *dup2* function forces *handle2* to refer to the same file as *handle1,* a valid handle to a file that is currently open. If *handle2* also refers to an open file, that file is closed and *handle2* is then assigned to the file associated with *handle1.* After successful return from *dup2,* either handle may be used to refer to the file.

COMMON USES The *dup2* function is used to redirect the standard input and output streams, *stdin* and *stdout.*

RETURNS If *handle2* is successfully assigned to the file associated with *handle1*, *dup2* returns a 0. Otherwise, it returns a −1 to indicate error and sets the global variable *errno* to either EMFILE if no more file handles are possible or to the constant EBADF, indicating that *handle1* is not a valid file handle.

SEE ALSO

open	*To open a file for unformatted, unbuffered I/O*
creat	*To create a new file and open it for unformatted, unbuffered I/O*

EXAMPLE Use *dup2* to write a program that redirects *stdout* to a file of your choice. Open a file and use *dup2* to assign *handle1* (the usual handle for *stdout*) to the newly opened file (use the macro *fileno* to find this). Now write some messages to *stdout* and they should go to the file. Remember to flush the buffers, close the file, and reassign handle 1 to *stdout.*

```
#include <stdio.h>
#include <io.h>
main()
{
    int saved_handle;
    char filename[81];
    FILE *new_stdout;
/* Ask for filename to which stdout will be assigned */
    printf("Enter filename to which stdout will be \
assigned:");

    gets(filename);
    if((new_stdout = fopen(filename, "w")) == NULL)
    {
            perror("fopen failed");
            exit(1);
    }
/* First duplicate the handle for stdout so that we can
 * reset things at the end
 */
    if((saved_handle = dup(1)) == -1)
    {
            perror("dup failed on handle 1!");
            exit(1);
    }
/* Get the handle of the new file using 'fileno' and
 * assign handle 1 (stdout) to it by calling dup2
 */
    if(dup2(fileno(new_stdout), 1) == -1)
    {
```

```
                perror("dup2 failed to assign handle 1!");
    }
    else
    {
                printf("New handle for stdout is %d\n",
                    fileno(new_stdout));
            printf("Testing dup2. \
This should be in file: %s\n", filename);
/* Flush to send output to open file */
            fflush(stdout);
/* Reassign stdout to handle 1 before exiting */
            fclose(new_stdout);
            dup2(saved_handle, 1);
            printf("Enter 'TYPE %s' to see result\n",
                    filename);
    }
}
```

Low-level I/O

COMPATIBILITY

eof

MSC 3	MSC 4	MSC 5	MSC 6	QC1	QC2	QC2.5	TC1	TC1.5	TC2	TC++	ANSI	UNIX V	XNX	OS2	DOS
▲	▲	▲	▲	▲	▲	▲	▲	▲	▲	▲				▲	▲

PURPOSE Use the *eof* function to determine whether end-of-file has been reached in a file specified by its handle.

SYNTAX

```
int eof(int handle);

int handle;      Handle of an open file
```

EXAMPLE CALL

```
if(eof(handle) != 0) printf("File ended!\n");
```

INCLUDES

```
#include <io.h>       For function declaration
```

DESCRIPTION The *eof* function checks whether the file specified by the argument *handle* is at the end-of-file. The analogous function for stream I/O is *feof.* Many low-level I/O routines return a –1 to indicate an error. Since low-level I/O routines are used primarily to read binary data and a data byte could very well contain a –1 (FF in hexadecimal), a function such as *eof* is necessary to determine if the file actually ended or you simply read a byte containing the value –1.

RETURNS For a valid file handle, *eof* returns a 1 to indicate an end-of-file and a 0 when not. If the specified file handle is invalid, it returns a −1 and sets the global variable *errno* to the constant EBADF.

SEE ALSO `feof, ferror` *To determine end-of-file and error conditions for files opened for buffered I/O*

EXAMPLE Write a program that opens up the file *autoexec.bat* in the root directory of drive C and reads it, 80 bytes at a time, until end-of-file is reached. Use the *eof* function to test for end-of-file. Display the data read.

```
#include <stdio.h>
#include <io.h>
#include <fcntl.h>
main()
{
    int fhandle, total=0, count;
    unsigned char buffer[80];
/* Open the file "autoexec.bat." Note the two '\'  */
    if ( (fhandle = open("c:\\autoexec.bat",
                         O_RDONLY)) == -1)
    {
           printf("open failed");
                  exit(1);
    }
    printf("Contents of c:autoexec.bat:\n");
    while ( !eof(fhandle))          /* Read until EOF */
    {
           if ((count = read(fhandle, buffer, 80)) == -1)
           {
               perror("read error");
               break;    /* exit from while loop */
           }
           total += count;
           write(1, buffer, count);
    }
    printf("=== %d bytes read ===\n", total);
}
```

Low-level I/O

COMPATIBILITY

lseek

MSC 3	MSC 4	MSC 5	MSC 6	QC1	QC2	QC2.5	TC1	TC1.5	TC2	TC++	ANSI	UNIX V	XNX	OS2	DOS
▲	▲	▲	▲	▲	▲	▲	▲	▲	▲	▲		▲	▲	▲	▲

PURPOSE Use the *lseek* function to move to a new position in a file opened for unbuffered and unformatted I/O.

SYNTAX

```
long lseek(int handle, long offset, int origin);
```

`int handle;` *Handle associated with file whose current position is to be set*

`long offset;` *Offset of new position (in bytes) from origin*

`int origin;` *Constant indicating the position from which to offset*

EXAMPLE CALL

```
lseek(fhandle, 512L, SEEK_SET); /* Skip 512 bytes */
```

INCLUDES

`#include <stdio.h>` *For definition of constants used to specify "origin"*

`#include <io.h>` *For function declaration*

DESCRIPTION The *lseek* function sets the current read or write position of the file specified by the argument *handle* to a new value indicated by the arguments *offset* and *origin*. The *offset* is a long integer indicating how far away the new position is from a specific location given in *origin*. The *origin*, defined in *stdio.h*, must be one of the constants shown in the table.

Origin	Interpretation
SEEK_SET	Beginning of file
SEEK_CUR	Current position in the file
SEEK_END	End of file

The file position may be set anywhere in the file except before the beginning of the file.

COMMON USES The *lseek* function is used when reading unformatted data from files in a random manner. For example, an application may create a data file with a specific format, say, a header of 512 bytes followed by actual data. When reading from such a file, you can use *lseek* to jump over the header and retrieve specific pieces of information with *read*.

RETURNS When successful, *lseek* returns the offset of the current position from the beginning of the file. In case of error, the return value is −1 and the global variable *errno* is set to either EBADF, indicating that the file handle is invalid, or to EINVAL if an attempt is made to set position before the beginning of the file. If the handle is associated with a device for which setting the current position does not make sense, the return value is meaningless.

SEE ALSO

`tell` *To get the offset of the current position in a file in number of bytes from the beginning*

`fseek` *Counterpart of* lseek *for files opened for buffered I/O*

EXAMPLE Open a file, *autoexec.bat*, in your system and go to the end of the file using *lseek* with SEEK_END as origin. Report the value returned by *lseek*. This is the size of the file in bytes. Now move back 20 bytes and read the last 20 bytes in the file. Display the characters read.

```
#include <stdio.h>
#include <io.h>
#include <fcntl.h>
main()
{
    int fhandle, count;
    long curpos;
    unsigned char buffer[20];
/* Open the file "autoexec.bat." */
    if ( (fhandle = open("c:\\autoexec.bat",
                    O_RDONLY)) == -1)
    {
           printf("open failed");
                      exit(1);
    }
/* Go to end of file using "lseek" and SEEK_END */
    curpos = lseek(fhandle, 0L, SEEK_END);
    printf("End of file in 'autoexec.bat' is %ld bytes \
from beginning\n", curpos);
/* Move back 20 bytes, read the last 20 bytes
 * and print the characters that were read in.
 */
    lseek(fhandle, -20L, SEEK_CUR);
    if ((count = read(fhandle, buffer, 20)) == -1)
    {
           perror("read error");
           exit(1);
```

```
    }
    printf("The last 20 characters in 'autoexec.bat' are:\n");
    write(1, buffer, count);
}
```

Low-level I/O

COMPATIBILITY **open**

MSC 3	MSC 4	MSC 5	MSC 6	QC1	QC2	QC2.5	TC1	TC1.5	TC2	TC++	ANSI	UNIX V	XNX	OS2	DOS
▲	▲	▲	▲	▲	▲	▲	▲	▲	▲	▲		▲	▲	▲	▲

PURPOSE Before performing any read or write operations, use *open* to open a file for unbuffered and unformatted I/O operations.

SYNTAX

```
int open(char *filename, int oflag [, int pmode]);
```

`char *filename;` *Name of file to be opened, including drive and directory specification*

`int oflag;` *Integer formed by bitwise OR of predefined constants that indicate the types of operations allowed on that file*

`int pmode;` *Optional argument to specify whether reading, writing, or both are permitted*

EXAMPLE CALL

```
filehandle = open("temp.dat", O_WRONLY|O_CREAT, S_IWRITE);
```

INCLUDES

`#include <io.h>` *For function declaration*

`#include <fcntl.h>` *For definition of constants to indicate valid operations*

`#include <sys\types.h>` *For definition of data types used in <sys\stat.h>*

`#include <sys\stat.h>` *For definition of constants to specify permission settings of a file*

DESCRIPTION The *open* function opens the file specified in the argument *filename*. The type of operations you intend to perform on the file once it is opened must be indicated by the argument *oflag*. This is an integer formed by the bitwise OR of the constants shown in Table 15-15. The constants are defined in the include file *fcntl.h*.

The third argument to *open*, *pmode*, you only need it when requesting the creation of a new file by using the flag O_CREAT. If the file does

Table 15-15. *Constants Indicating Type of Operations Allowed on File*

Constant	Interpretation
O_APPEND	Writing always occurs at the end of the file.
O_BINARY	File is opened in the binary, or untranslated, mode. This is the same binary mode used with *fopen*; see its reference pages for more explanation.
O_CREAT	Creates and opens a file for writing if the named file does not exist.
O_EXCL	Returns an error value if file already exists and O_CREAT was specified.
O_RDONLY	File is opened for reading only. When O_RDONLY is given, O_WRONLY and O_RDWR are disallowed.
O_RDWR	File is opened for both reading and writing. When O_RDWR is given, O_RDONLY and O_WRONLY are disallowed.
O_TEXT	File is opened in text, or translated, mode. This is the same text mode used with *fopen*; see its reference pages for elaboration.
O_TRUNC	Opens an existing file and truncates it to zero length, destroying its current contents. The file must have write permission for this to succeed.
O_WRONLY	File is opened for writing only. When O_WRONLY is used, O_RDONLY and O_RDWR are not allowed.

not exist, the value of *pmode* is used to set the permission of the newly created file. Table 15-16 shows the possible values of the argument *pmode*. These constants are defined in the header file *sys\stat.h*. As you can see in the table, a file in MS-DOS always has read permission. The permission setting indicated by the *pmode* argument is modified by the permission mask that you can set with *umask*. Consult its reference pages to see how this is done.

Table 15-16. *Permission Settings for Newly Created Files*

Constant	Interpretation
S_IWRITE	Both reading and writing permitted.
S_IREAD	Only reading permitted.
S_IREAD ¦ S_IWRITE	Both reading and writing permitted.

Microsoft warns users of a bug under MS-DOS versions 3.0 and above that can occur when file-sharing is enabled. The sharing is enabled by executing SHARE.EXE, which comes with these versions of MS-DOS. Once this is done and a file is opened with *oflag* set to O_CREAT¦O_READONLY or O_CREAT¦O_WRONLY, DOS prematurely closes the file during any system calls made within *open*. The suggested remedy is to open the file with *pmode* equal to S_IWRITE. Then, after closing the file you can call *chmod* to change the permission back to

S_IREAD. Another remedy is to open the file with *pmode* set to S_IREAD and *oflag* equal to O_CREAT¦O_RDWR.

COMMON USES The *open* function is used to open a file before performing any unbuffered and unformatted I/O (see the tutorial section) operations on it.

RETURNS If the file is successfully opened, *open* returns the file handle, an integer to be used in subsequent I/O operations on the file using the functions *read* and *write.* In case of an error, *open* returns a −1. At the same time, the global variable *errno* is set to one of the constants shown in Table 15-17 and defined in *errno.h.*

Table 15-17. *Error Codes Returned by* open

Error Constant	Meaning of Error Value
EACCES	Cannot access file. This means the file name refers to a directory, or an attempt was made to open a read-only file for write operations, or file-sharing is enabled and sharing mode does not allow the operation being attempted.
EINVAL	Invalid or conflicting open mode and permission setting.
EEXIST	This error is returned when the flags O_CREAT and O_EXCL are specified but the file already exists.
EMFILE	No more file handles available. This means you have hit the MS-DOS 20-file limit that a single process can open simultaneously.
ENOENT	File was not found or a directory corresponding to the path specification in the file name is nonexistent.

SEE ALSO

`close` *To close a file opened by* open

`fopen` *To open a file for buffered I/O*

EXAMPLE Write a program that prompts for a file name and opens that file for write operations. Use the O_CREAT and the O_EXCL operation flags to ensure that an existing file is not destroyed.

```
#include <stdio.h>
#include <io.h>
#include <fcntl.h>
#include <sys\types.h>
#include <sys\stat.h>

main()
{
    int handle;
```

```
    char filename[81];
    printf("Enter name of a file to open: ");
    gets(filename);
/* Open the file for write operations.
 * Don't overwrite existing file.
 */
    if ((handle = open(filename, O_WRONLY|O_CREAT|O_EXCL,
                   S_IREAD|S_IWRITE))  == -1)
    {
/* Use perror to print the message so that we also see
 * the error message corresponding to the value of
 * 'errno'
 */
            perror("Open failed! ");
    }
    else
    {
            printf("File %s opened successfully\n",filename);
/* In an actual program we will use the file for I/O.
 * Here we simply exit.
 */
    }
}
```

Low-level I/O

read

COMPATIBILITY

MSC 3	MSC 4	MSC 5	MSC 6	QC1	QC2	QC2.5	TC1	TC1.5	TC2	TC++	ANSI	UNIX V	XNX	OS2	DOS
▲	▲	▲	▲	▲	▲	▲	▲	▲	▲	▲		▲	▲	▲	▲

PURPOSE Use *read* to retrieve a specified number of bytes of data, without any formatting, from the current position in a file that has been opened for unformatted I/O.

SYNTAX
```
int read(int handle, char *buffer, unsigned count);
```

`int handle;` *Handle of file from which data will be read*

`char *buffer;` *Pointer to buffer into which data will be copied*

`unsigned count;` *Number of bytes to be read*

EXAMPLE CALL
```
if ((bytes_read = read(fhandle, bigbuffer, 60000)) == -1)
                  perror("read error");
```

INCLUDES `#include <io.h>` *For function declaration*

DESCRIPTION The *read* function copies the number of bytes specified in the argument *count* from the file whose handle is in the integer argument *handle* to the array of characters, *buffer*. Reading starts at the current position, which is incremented when the operation is completed. If the file is opened in the text mode, each CR-LF pair read from the file is replaced by a newline character in the *buffer*, and a Control-Z character is interpreted as end-of-file.

RETURNS The *read* function returns the number of bytes actually read from the file. In case of an error, *read* returns –1 and sets *errno* to EBADF to indicate an invalid file handle or that the file was not opened for writing. In MS-DOS 3.0 and higher, read errors may occur due to a locked file.

COMMENTS Since *read* returns a signed integer, the return value should be converted to *unsigned int* when reading more than 32 K of data from a file or the return value will be negative. Because the number of bytes to be read is specified in an unsigned integer argument, you could theoretically read 65,535 bytes at a time. But, 65,535 (or FFFFh) also means –1 in signed representation so when reading 65,535 bytes the return value indicates an error. The practical maximum then is 65,534.

SEE ALSO

`creat, open, sopen` *To create and open new files for unformatted I/O*

`write` *To write a specified number of bytes to a file*

EXAMPLE Write a program that opens a file, say, "autoexec.bat," in the root directory of drive C, reads 60,000 bytes from it, and displays the number of bytes read.

```
#include <stdio.h>
#include <io.h>
#include <fcntl.h>
static char bigbuffer[60000];
main()
{
        int fhandle, total=0;
        unsigned int bytes_read;

/* Open the file "autoexec.bat." Note that we need two '\'  */
        if ( (fhandle = open("c:autoexec.bat",
                            O_RDONLY)) == -1)
        {
            printf("open failed");
            exit(1);
```

```
            }
            printf(
            "Attempting to read 60000 bytes from c:autoexec.bat:\n");
            if ((bytes_read = read(fhandle, bigbuffer, 60000)) == -1)
            {
                perror("read error");
                exit(1);
            }
            printf("Only %u bytes read. Here's what was read:\n",
                    bytes_read);
            write(1, bigbuffer, bytes_read);
}
```

Low-level I/O

sopen

COMPATIBILITY

MSC 3	MSC 4	MSC 5	MSC 6	QC1	QC2	QC2.5	TC1	TC1.5	TC2	TC++	ANSI	UNIX V	XNX	OS2	DOS
▲	▲	▲	▲	▲	▲	▲	▲	▲	▲	▲				▲	▲

PURPOSE Use *sopen* to open a file for shared, unbuffered, and unformatted I/O operations. File-sharing is ignored if SHARE.EXE has not been run. Note that SHARE.EXE (or SHARE.COM), commands that facilitate use of MS-DOS systems in local area networks, is present only in MS-DOS versions 3.0 and higher.

SYNTAX

```
int sopen(char *filename, int oflag, int shflag [, int pmode]);
```

`char *filename;` *Name of file to be opened, including drive and directory specification*

`int oflag;` *Integer formed by bitwise OR of predefined constants that indicate the types of operations allowed on file being opened*

`int shflag;` *Integer formed by bitwise OR of predefined constants that indicate the modes of sharing to be enabled*

`int pmode;` *Optional argument to specify whether reading, writing, or both are permitted*

EXAMPLE CALL

```
fhandle = sopen("c:\\autoexec.bat", O_RDONLY, SH_DENYRW);
```

INCLUDES

`#include <io.h>` *For function declaration*

`#include <share.h>` *For definition of constants to indicate modes of sharing*

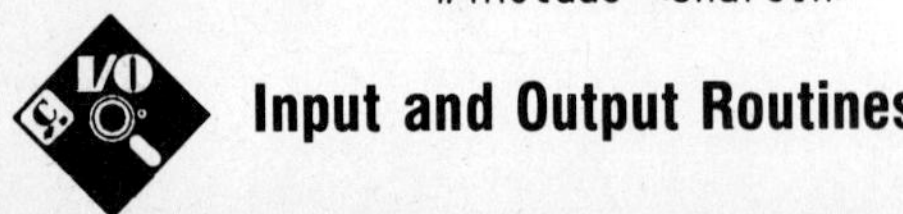

```
#include <fcntl.h>
```
For definition of constants to indicate valid operations

```
#include <sys\types.h>
```
For definition of data types used in <sys\stat.h>

```
#include <sys\stat.h>
```
For definition of constants to specify permission settings of a file

DESCRIPTION The *sopen* function opens the file specified in the argument *filename*. The type of operations you intend to perform on the file once it is opened must be indicated by the argument *oflag*, an integer formed by the bitwise OR of constants shown in Table 15-15. The constants are defined in the include file *fcntl.h*.

The argument *shflag* is used to specify the level of sharing enabled. It is specified by bitwise OR of an appropriate combination of constants defined in the file *share.h* and shown in Table 15-18. The argument is ignored if you have not enabled file-sharing by running SHARE.EXE (or SHARE.COM).

Table 15-18. *Constants that Indicate Level of File-Sharing*

Constant	Interpretation
SH_COMPAT	No other process is allowed to access the file. This is called the "compatibility mode" and the same process can open the file any number of times in this mode. This is how DOS normally operates, hence the name.
SH_DENYRW	A single process has exclusive read and write access to the file. The process must close the file before opening it again.
SH_DENYWR	No other process can access the file for writing.
SH_DENYRD	No other process can access the file for reading.
SH_DENYNO	Any process may access the file for both reading and for writing.

The last argument to *sopen*, *pmode*, is necessary only when requesting the creation of a new file by the flag O_CREAT. If the file does not already exist, the value of *pmode* is used to set the permission of the newly created file. Table 15-16 shows the various values of the argument *pmode*. As you can see in Table 15-16, an MS-DOS file always has read permission. The permission setting indicated by the *pmode* argument is modified by the permission mask set by calling *umask*. Consult the reference pages on *umask* to see how this is done. These *pmode* constants are defined in the header file *sys\stat.h*.

Microsoft warns users of a bug under MS-DOS versions 3.0 and above that can occur when opening a file with *sopen* with file-sharing enabled. File-sharing is enabled by executing SHARE.EXE which comes with these versions of MS-DOS. Once this is done and a file is opened with *oflag* set to O_CREAT¦O_READONLY or O_CREAT¦O_WRONLY and *sh_flag* set to SH_COMPAT, DOS prematurely closes the file during any system calls made within *sopen* or it will generate a "sharing violation" interrupt (number 24h). The suggested remedy is to sopen the file with *pmode* set to S_IWRITE. Then, after closing the file you can call *chmod* to change the permission back to S_IREAD. Another remedy is to sopen the file with *pmode* set to S_IREAD and *oflag* equal to O_CREAT¦O_RDWR and *shflag* set to SH_COMPAT. Starting with Microsoft C 5.1, under OS/2, *sopen* enables you to open files for sharing by multiple processes.

COMMON USES The *sopen* function is used to open files for sharing in networks. It works in the same way as *open* except that it can also specify the level of file-sharing allowed.

RETURNS If the file is successfully opened, *sopen* returns the file handle, an integer to be used in subsequent I/O operations on the file using the functions *read* and *write*. In case of an error, *sopen* returns a –1. At the same time, the global variable *errno* is set to one of the constants shown in Table 15-17 and defined in *errno.h*:

COMMENTS File-sharing modes work properly only with unbuffered files. So you should not call *fdopen* to associate a FILE data structure and enable buffering for a file opened by *sopen*.

SEE ALSO

`close`	*To close a file opened by* sopen
`fopen`	*To open a file for buffered I/O*

EXAMPLE If you are running MS-DOS version 3.0 or higher, install file-sharing by typing SHARE to run the program SHARE.EXE distributed with DOS. Now open a file, *autoexec.bat*, by calling *sopen* with the "share flag" equal to SH_DENYRW. Try to open the file once more. If it fails, you have not installed file-sharing. On the other hand, if SHARE has been run, this second call will fail because the file is already open and no one has permission to read or write (not even the same process!).

```
#include <stdio.h>
#include <io.h>
#include <fcntl.h>
#include <share.h>
main()
{
    int fhandle1, fhandle2;
```

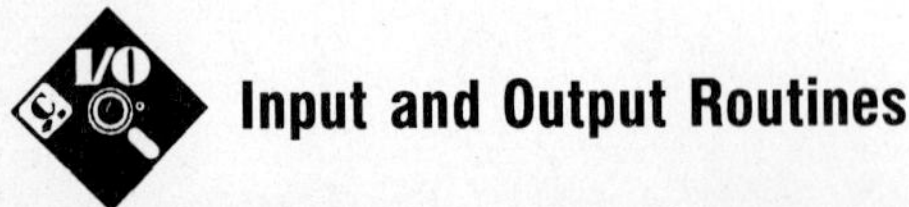

```
/* Open the file "autoexec.bat." */
    if ( (fhandle1 = sopen("c:\\autoexec.bat",
                     O_RDONLY, SH_DENYRW)) == -1)
    {
           perror("open failed");
           exit(1);
    }
    printf("AUTOEXEC.BAT opened once. Handle = %d\n",
              fhandle1);
/* Now open again */
    if ( (fhandle2 = sopen("c:autoexec.bat",
                     O_RDONLY, SH_DENYRW)) == -1)
    {
           perror("open failed");
           printf("SHARE installed\n");
           exit(1);
    }
    printf("AUTOEXEC.BAT opened again. Handle = %d\n",
              fhandle2);

    printf("SHARE has not been installed\n");
}
```

Low-level I/O

tell

COMPATIBILITY

MSC 3	MSC 4	MSC 5	MSC 6	QC1	QC2	QC2.5	TC1	TC1.5	TC2	TC++	ANSI	UNIX V	XNX	OS2	DOS
▲	▲	▲	▲	▲	▲	▲	▲	▲	▲	▲				▲	▲

PURPOSE Use *tell* to determine the current position in a file specified by its handle.

SYNTAX

```
long tell(int handle);

int handle;        Handle of an open file
```

EXAMPLE CALL

```
curpos = tell(filehandle);
```

INCLUDES

```
#include <io.h>        For function declaration
```

DESCRIPTION The *tell* function returns the current position in the file specified by the argument *handle*. The position is returned as the number of bytes from the beginning of the file.

RETURNS For a valid file handle, *tell* returns the current position as a long integer value containing the byte offset of the current location in the file from its beginning. If the specified file handle is invalid, it returns a −1 and sets the global variable *errno* to the constant EBADF. If the handle refers to a device for which the file position cannot be set arbitrarily, the value returned by *tell* is meaningless.

SEE ALSO

`lseek` *To set the current position in a file opened for unformatted I/O*

`ftell` *Counterpart of* tell *for files opened for buffered I/O*

EXAMPLE Write a program that opens a file and uses *tell* to report the current position in the file. Now read 80 bytes from the file using *read*. Check and report the position again after the read.

```
#include <stdio.h>
#include <io.h>
#include <fcntl.h>
main()
{
    int fhandle, count;
    long curpos;
    unsigned char buffer[80];
/* Open the file "autoexec.bat." */
    if ( (fhandle = open("c:\\autoexec.bat",
                                    O_RDONLY)) == -1)
    {
            printf("open failed");
            exit(1);
    }
/* Display current position using "tell" */
    curpos = tell(fhandle);
    printf("Currently at position %ld \
in 'autoexec.bat'\n", curpos);
/* Now read 80 bytes and check position again */
    if ((count = read(fhandle, buffer, 80)) == -1)
    {
            perror("read error");
            exit(1);
    }
    printf("Read following 80 characters:\n");
    write(1, buffer, count);
    curpos = tell(fhandle);
    printf("\nNow at position: %ld bytes from beginning\n",
            curpos);
}
```

Low-level I/O

COMPATIBILITY

write

MSC 3	MSC 4	MSC 5	MSC 6	QC1	QC2	QC2.5	TC1	TC1.5	TC2	TC++	ANSI	UNIX V	XNX	OS2	DOS
▲	▲	▲	▲	▲	▲	▲	▲	▲	▲	▲		▲	▲	▲	▲

PURPOSE Use *write* to save a specified number of bytes of data, without any formatting, at the current position in a file opened for unformatted I/O.

SYNTAX

```
int write(int handle, char *buffer, unsigned count);
```

`int handle;`	*Handle of file to which data will be written*
`char *buffer;`	*Pointer to array of characters representing data to be written*
`unsigned count;`	*Number of bytes to be written*

EXAMPLE CALL

```
write(handle, data_buffer, 1024);
```

INCLUDES #include <io.h> *For function declaration*

DESCRIPTION In a file opened by a call to *open* for writing or appending, the *write* function copies the number of bytes specified in the argument *count* from the array at *buffer* to the file whose handle is in the integer argument *handle*. The writing of the data begins at the current position in the file and the current position is appropriately incremented after writing out the data. If the file is opened for appending, the writing will always take place at the end of the file.

If the file is opened in text mode, each newline character in the data is replaced by a CR-LF pair in the file. Note that *write* treats a Control-Z character as the logical end-of-file.

RETURNS The *write* function returns the number of bytes actually written to the file. If, for example, the disk space runs out before all the data is written, the return value may be something less than *count*. A return value of –1 indicates an error. The value in the global variable *errno* will contain an error code; if it is equal to the constant EBADF, the error was caused by giving either an invalid file handle or one for a file not opened for writing. If the system runs out of disk space, *errno* is set to the constant ENOSPC.

COMMENTS When writing more than 32 K of data to a file, you receive the value returned by *write* in an *unsigned int* variable; otherwise an *int* shows a negative value. A consequence of returning a –1 to indicate error is that you can write no more than 65,534 bytes to a file at a time and still be able to tell if an error has occurred because 65,535 (or FFFF in hexadecimal) is also the representation of –1 in the microprocessor.

SEE ALSO

`creat, open, sopen`	*To create and open new files for unformatted I/O*
`read`	*To read a specified number of bytes from a file*

EXAMPLE Open a file for write operations and write a large number of bytes to the file. Report the value returned by *write*. Initialize the buffer to be written with a test message that ends with a Control-Z (\032) so you can type the file with the TYPE command and have the printing stop after that because it interprets Control-Z as the end-of-file.

```
#include <stdio.h>
#include <sys\types.h>
#include <sys\stat.h>
#include <fcntl.h>
#include <io.h>
/* Initialize array with a string plus Control-Z to
 * mark end of file.
 */
static char bigbuffer[60000]="Testing write\n\032";
main()
{
    unsigned bytes_written;
    int filehandle;
    char filename[81];
    printf("Enter name of file to be opened for \
writing:");
    gets(filename);
/* Open the file for write operations.
 * Don't overwrite existing file.
 */
    if ((filehandle = open(filename,
    O_WRONLY|O_CREAT|O_EXCL, S_IREAD|S_IWRITE))  == -1)
    {
        perror("Open failed! ");
        exit(1);
    }
/* Now write out 60,000 bytes of data.
 * Most of it'll be junk.
 */
    if((bytes_written = write(filehandle, bigbuffer,
                                60000)) == -1)
    {
```

```
        perror("write failed");
    }
    else
    {
        printf("%u bytes written to file: %s\n",
                bytes_written,  filename);
        printf("Use 'TYPE %s' to see result\n",
                filename);
    }
}
```

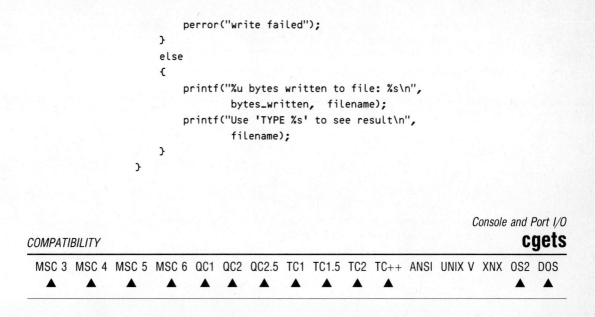

Console and Port I/O

COMPATIBILITY

cgets

MSC 3	MSC 4	MSC 5	MSC 6	QC1	QC2	QC2.5	TC1	TC1.5	TC2	TC++	ANSI	UNIX V	XNX	OS2	DOS
▲	▲	▲	▲	▲	▲	▲	▲	▲	▲	▲				▲	▲

PURPOSE Use *cgets* to read a string of characters from the keyboard. The line is read until a newline character is reached and replaced by a null character, which generates a C string. You must allocate the buffer in which the string is stored. Store as the first byte the maximum number of characters to be read.

SYNTAX `char *cgets(char *buffer);`

`char *buffer;` *Buffer where string will be stored*

EXAMPLE CALL `cgets(user_input);`

INCLUDES `#include <conio.h>` *For function declaration*

DESCRIPTION The *cgets* function begins by reading the value in the first character of the buffer whose address is given in the argument *buffer*. The function uses that as the maximum number of characters to be read. It accepts keystrokes and stores them in *buffer* starting at the third location (i.e., *buffer2*). The reading from the keyboard continues until a newline character is encountered or until the specified maximum number of characters has been read. Then *cgets* replaces the newline character with a null character and returns after storing in *buffer1* the number of characters it read. Note that the buffer whose address is given in the argument *buffer* must have enough room to hold all the characters, including the null character and the additional two bytes used to store the two lengths.

RETURNS The *cgets* function returns a pointer to the beginning of the string (i.e., the location *buffer2*).

SEE ALSO `cputs` *To write a string to the console*

EXAMPLE Use *cgets* to read a line from the console. Display the line using *cprintf.*

```
#include <conio.h>
main()
{
    int numread;
    char string[82], *input;
    string[0] = 80;        /* Max no. of characters */
    cprintf("Enter a line: ");
    input = cgets(string);
    numread = string[1];    /* Number of chars read*/
    cprintf("\nYou entered: %d characters. \
The string is \r\n%s\r\n",  numread, input);
}
```

Console and Port I/O

cprintf

COMPATIBILITY

MSC 3	MSC 4	MSC 5	MSC 6	QC1	QC2	QC2.5	TC1	TC1.5	TC2	TC++	ANSI	UNIX V	XNX	OS2	DOS
▲	▲	1	▲	▲	▲	▲	▲	▲	▲	▲				▲	▲

PURPOSE Use *cprintf* to convert the values of C variables into a character string according to specified formats and print the string on the display. This function provides the function of *printf* for console output operations.

SYNTAX `int cprintf(char *format_string, ...);`

`char *format_string;` *Character string that describes the format to be used*

`...` *Variable number of arguments depending on the number of items being printed*

EXAMPLE CALL `cprintf("File %s has %d bytes of data\n", fname, size);`

INCLUDES `#include <conio.h>` *For function declaration*

DESCRIPTION The *cprintf* function accepts a variable number of arguments and formats and prints them to the console. The format to be used for each variable is specified in *format_string*, an array of characters with embedded formatting commands that start with a percentage sign. The reference pages on *printf* describe in detail the formatting options available.

Note that *cprintf* does not translate the newline character (\n) to a CR-LF combination, instead \n is interpreted as a linefeed and \r should be used to indicate a carriage return.

1. Beginning with Microsoft C 5.0, *cprintf* supports *L* format and allows negative precision and width arguments.

RETURNS The *cprintf* function returns the number of characters it has printed on the console.

SEE ALSO `printf` *For printing to* stdout *and for detailed information on formats*

EXAMPLE Use *cprintf* to display a formatted table of the cubes of the numbers from 1 to 10 on the screen.

```
#include <conio.h>
main()
{
    int i;
    cprintf("Table of cubes\r\n");
    for(i=1; i<11; i++)
    {
        cprintf("The cube of %2d is %4d\r\n", i, i*i*i);
    }
}
```

Console and Port I/O

COMPATIBILITY

cputs

MSC 3	MSC 4	MSC 5	MSC 6	QC1	QC2	QC2.5	TC1	TC1.5	TC2	TC++	ANSI	UNIX V	XNX	OS2	DOS
▲	▲	▲	▲	▲	▲	▲	▲	▲	▲	▲				▲	▲

PURPOSE Use *cputs* to write a string to the display. No newline character is sent after the string.

SYNTAX `int cputs(char *string);`

`char *string;` *String to be output*

EXAMPLE CALL `cputs("Are you sure (Y/N)? ");`

INCLUDES `#include <conio.h>` *For function declaration*

DESCRIPTION The *cputs* function writes the string specified in the argument *string* to the display. Unlike *puts*, *cputs* does not automatically send a newline character after writing the string to the display.

RETURNS In Microsoft C version 5.0, and above, *cputs* returns a 0 if successful and a nonzero value in case of error. In earlier versions, *cputs* has no return value.

SEE ALSO `cgets` *To read a line from the console*

EXAMPLE Use *cputs* to write a message to the screen.

```
#include <stdio.h>
char message[81] =
        "Insert the 'Upgrade 1.1' disk into drive A:\n";
main()
{
    cputs(message);
}
```

Console and Port I/O

COMPATIBILITY

cscanf

MSC 3	MSC 4	MSC 5	MSC 6	QC1	QC2	QC2.5	TC1	TC1.5	TC2	TC++	ANSI	UNIX V	XNX	OS2	DOS
▲	▲	1	▲	▲	▲	▲	▲	▲	▲	▲				▲	▲

PURPOSE Use *cscanf* to read characters directly from the keyboard, convert them into values using specified formats, and store the values in C variables.

SYNTAX `int cscanf(char *format_string,...);`

`char *format_string;` *Character string that describes the format to be used*

`...` *Variable number of arguments representing addresses of variables whose values are being read*

EXAMPLE CALL `cscanf(" %d/%d/%d", &month, &day, &year);`

INCLUDES `#include <conio.h>` *For function declaration*

DESCRIPTION The *cscanf* function reads an unbuffered stream of characters directly from the keyboard and converts them to values according to the format specifications embedded in the argument *format_string*. It then stores the values in C variables whose addresses are provided in the rest of the variable-length argument list. Each variable must have a corresponding formatting command in *format_string*. The format specification for a variable always begins with a percentage sign and the formatting options are the same as the ones available with the function *scanf*. (See its reference pages for a detailed list of the specifications.)

1. Beginning in Microsoft C 5.0 the *cscanf* function supports the *L* modifier and the *g*, *E*, and *G* format specifiers.

RETURNS The *cscanf* function returns the number of fields that were successfully read, converted, and assigned to variables. The count excludes items that were read but not assigned to any variable. The constant EOF is returned in case of an end-of-file during the read.

SEE ALSO

`scanf`	*Formatted reading from* stdin
`fscanf`	*For formatted, buffered reading from a file*
`sscanf`	*Formatted reading from a string*

EXAMPLE Use *cscanf* with the %p format to read a memory address from the keyboard. The address is of the form *SSSS:OOOO* in which the S and O are uppercase hexadecimal digits. Now dump out, as ASCII characters, the values in the 25 bytes following that memory address. Try the address *F000:E000* for an interesting result. (How about extending this to a small tool to examine memory in various formats—say, hexadecimal digits or integers?)

```
#include <conio.h>
main()
{
    int i;
    char far *far_ptr;
    cprintf("Enter memory address to dump in the form \
SSSS:OOOO\r\n(Try F000:E000)   ");
    cscanf(" %p", &far_ptr);
    cprintf("Dump of 25 bytes at %p\r\n", far_ptr);
    for(i=0; i<25; i++)
    {
            cprintf("%Fc", *(far_ptr+i));
    }
}
```

Console and Port I/O

getch

COMPATIBILITY

MSC 3	MSC 4	MSC 5	MSC 6	QC1	QC2	QC2.5	TC1	TC1.5	TC2	TC++	ANSI	UNIX V	XNX	OS2	DOS
▲	▲	▲	▲	▲	▲	▲	▲	▲	▲	▲				▲	▲

PURPOSE Use the *getch* function to read a character from the keyboard without echoing it to the display.

SYNTAX
```
int getch(void);
```

EXAMPLE CALL
```
in_char = getch();
```

INCLUDES `#include <conio.h>` *For function declaration*

DESCRIPTION The *getch* function reads a character from the console without any buffering and the character is not echoed to the screen. Typing CONTROL-C during a call to *getch* generates the 8086 software interrupt number 23h.

COMMON USES The *getch* function is useful in implementing user interfaces in which the user hits a single key to indicate a choice and the choice is acted on as soon as the key is pressed.

RETURNS The *getch* function returns the character read from the keyboard.

SEE ALSO `getche` *To read a keystroke and echo it to the display*

`getchar` *For buffered read from* stdin

EXAMPLE Write a small C program enabling the user to hit any key to exit. Use *getch* to read the keystroke and exit as soon as it's done.

```
#include <stdio.h>
#include <conio.h>

main()
{
    printf("Hit any character to exit:");
    getch();  /* Ignore character being read */
}
```

COMPATIBILITY

getche

MSC 3	MSC 4	MSC 5	MSC 6	QC1	QC2	QC2.5	TC1	TC1.5	TC2	TC++	ANSI	UNIX V	XNX	OS2	DOS
▲	▲	▲	▲	▲	▲	▲	▲	▲	▲	▲				▲	▲

PURPOSE Use the *getche* function to read a character from the keyboard and echo it to the display.

SYNTAX

```
int getche(void);
```

EXAMPLE CALL

```
in_char = getche();
```

INCLUDES `#include <conio.h>` *For function declaration*

DESCRIPTION The *getche* function reads a character from the keyboard without any buffering and echoes the character to the screen. Typing CONTROL-C during a call to *getche* generates software interrupt number 23h.

RETURNS The *getche* function returns the character read from the keyboard.

SEE ALSO `getch` *To read a keystroke without echoing it to the display*

`getchear` *For buffered read from* stdin

EXAMPLE Write a program to read characters from the keyboard until a carriage return or until 80 characters have been read. Convert uppercase letters to lowercase and print the string entered. Note that you have to compare the value returned by *getche* with \r to confirm that it is a carriage return (comparing it with \n will not work).

```
#include <conio.h>

main()
{
    int i, c;
    char buffer[81];
    cprintf("Enter a line:");
    for(i=0; i<80; i++)
    {
        if((buffer[i] = tolower(getche())) == '\r')
            break;
    }
    buffer[i] = '\0';
    cprintf("\nYou entered: %s", buffer);
}
```

Console and Port I/O

inp

COMPATIBILITY

MSC 3	MSC 4	MSC 5	MSC 6	QC1	QC2	QC2.5	TC1	TC1.5	TC2	TC++	ANSI	UNIX V	XNX	OS2	DOS
▲	▲	▲	▲	▲	▲	▲		1	1	1				▲	▲

PURPOSE Use *inp* to read a byte from a specific I/O port whose address you provide as an argument. For example, you can use *inp* read from port 21h to determine which interrupt numbers are currently acknowledged by the 8259A programmable interrupt controller.

SYNTAX

```
int inp(unsigned port);
```

`unsigned port;` *Address of the port from which a byte is to be read*

EXAMPLE CALL

```
byte_read = inp(0x3f8);
```

INCLUDES `#include <conio.h>` *For function declaration*

DESCRIPTION The *inp* function uses the assembly language instruction IN to read a byte of data from the port address specified in the argument *port.*

1. The Turbo C and Turbo C++ version of this function is *inportb.*

COMMON USES The *inp* function is used to control input/output devices. The control circuitry of these devices has registers which are accessible through the IN and OUT instructions of the 8086 microprocessor family. The *inp* function is a C language interface to the IN instruction.

RETURNS The *inp* function returns the byte read from the port.

COMMENTS Everyone knows that in the IBM PC world, we are supposed to use DOS or BIOS to talk to the I/O devices (keyboard, video display, etc.). DOS and BIOS lack adequate support, however, for several important peripherals including the serial port and the speaker. In these cases you must access the device's registers using appropriate port addresses and the functions *inp* and *outp* come in handy.

SEE ALSO

`inpw` *To read a word from a port address*

`outp, outpw` *To write to an I/O port*

EXAMPLE The PC's peripheral devices get the microprocessor's attention by generating interrupts that are fielded by an integrated circuit (the Intel 8259A programmable interrupt controller). The 8259A looks at the bits in a register, reached via port number 21h, to decide which interrupts go on to the

CPU. Read the contents of this register using the *inp* function and display the contents in hexadecimal format.

```
#include <stdio.h>
#include <conio.h>
#define PORT_8259   0x21

main()
{
    int int_ack_status;
/* Read 8259's status */
    int_ack_status = inp(PORT_8259);
    printf("Current contents of register at \
port 21h: %X\n", int_ack_status);
}
```

Console and Port I/O

inpw

COMPATIBILITY

MSC 3	MSC 4	MSC 5	MSC 6	QC1	QC2	QC2.5	TC1	TC1.5	TC2	TC++	ANSI	UNIX V	XNX	OS2	DOS
		▲	▲	▲	▲	▲		1	1	1				▲	▲

PURPOSE Use *inpw* to read a 16-bit word from a specific I/O port. For example, you can use *inpw* to read two adjacent ports at once.

SYNTAX

```
unsigned int inpw(unsigned port);

unsigned port;
```

Address of the port from which a word is to be read

EXAMPLE CALL

```
word_8259 = inpw(0x20);
```

INCLUDES

```
#include <conio.h>
```

For function declaration

DESCRIPTION The *inpw* function uses the assembly language instruction IN to read a word (2 bytes) of data from the port address specified in the argument *port.*

1. The Turbo C and Turbo C++ version of this function is *inport.*

COMMON USES The *inpw* function is useful in reading two adjacent ports at once.

RETURNS The *inpw* function returns an unsigned integer containing the 16-bit word it read from the port address.

SEE ALSO

inp	*To read a byte from a port address*
outp, outpw	*To write to an I/O port*

EXAMPLE The Intel 8259A Programmable Interrupt Controller schedules and sometimes blocks interrupt signals generated by peripheral devices and meant for the microprocessor. The 8259A is programmed through two registers at port addresses 20h and 21h. Use *inp* to read the contents of each register and display them. Then, using the *inpw* function, read both registers simultaneously and display the contents in hexadecimal format. Compare these with the values you read individually.

```
#include <stdio.h>
#include <conio.h>
#define PORT_8259_20    0x20
#define PORT_8259_21    0x21

main()
{
    unsigned int word_8259;
    int p20, p21;
/* Read both ports of the 8259A */
    word_8259 = inpw(PORT_8259_20);
/* Now read them individually */
    p20 = inp(PORT_8259_20);
    p21 = inp(PORT_8259_21);
    printf("Current contents of register \
at port 20h: %X\n", p20);
    printf("Current contents of register \
at port 21h: %X\n", p21);
    printf("Result of reading with inpw at \
port 20h:  %X\n", word_8259);
}
```

Console and Port I/O

kbhit

COMPATIBILITY

MSC 3	MSC 4	MSC 5	MSC 6	QC1	QC2	QC2.5	TC1	TC1.5	TC2	TC++	ANSI	UNIX V	XNX	OS2	DOS
▲	▲	▲	▲	▲	▲	▲	▲	▲	▲	▲				▲	▲

PURPOSE Use the console I/O function *kbhit* to check whether any keystrokes are waiting to be read. Since *kbhit* does not wait for a key to be pressed, it is ideal for applications in which you can continue with your normal processing until the user interrupts by hitting a key.

SYNTAX

```
int kbhit(void);
```

EXAMPLE CALL

```
/* Do your thing until user presses a key */
    while( !kbhit() ) do_your_thing();
```

INCLUDES

```
#include <conio.h>        For function declaration
```

DESCRIPTION The *kbhit* function checks if any keystrokes are in the keyboard buffer waiting to be read.

COMMON USES The *kbhit* function is useful in writing applications where you can continue doing whatever your program is meant to do until the user actually hits a key. All you have to do is keep checking for any keystroke using *kbhit* every so often (such as at the beginning of an outer loop) and perform a read only when a keystroke is waiting.

RETURNS If a key was pressed, *kbhit* returns a nonzero value. Otherwise, it returns a 0.

COMMENTS The *kbhit* function is one function in the Microsoft C library that you cannot do without if you want to develop an event-driven application. Consider for example, an application such as a "terminal emulator." This will have a main loop where you must respond to two types of events (at least): characters arriving from the serial port and characters being entered from the keyboard. If you attempted to handle the keyboard events by using a function such as *getch*, you would soon discover that the program will keep waiting in that function until a character is actually entered and other events, such as serial input, would be lost. With *kbhit*, however, you are able to check and move on if nothing was hit on the keyboard.

EXAMPLE The graphics function *_putimage* can be used to perform rudimentary animation. Modify the example shown in the reference pages on *_putimage* to move the small stick figure on the screen continuously until the user hits a key. Use *kbhit* in an endless loop to achieve this.

```
#include <stdio.h>
#include <malloc.h>
#include <graph.h>
#define YELLOW 14
main()
{
    char far *image;           /* Storage for image */
    char buffer[80];
    short x=0, y=0;
    unsigned numbytes, c = 0;
```

```
/* Assume EGA. Put in high-resolution graphics mode */
    if (_setvideomode(_ERESCOLOR) == 0)
    {
/* Error setting mode */
        printf("Not EGA hardware\n");
        exit(0);
    }
/* Draw a small stick figure to save */
    _setcolor(YELLOW);
    _ellipse(_GFILLINTERIOR,0,0,10,10);
    _moveto(5,10);
    _lineto(5,20);
    _lineto(0,30);
    _moveto(10,30);
    _lineto(5,20);
    _moveto(0,15);
    _lineto(0,10);
    _lineto(10,15);
/* Determine storage needed for entire screen and
 * display result.
 */
    numbytes = (unsigned int)_imagesize(0,0,10,30);
/* Allocate buffer for image */
    if ((image = (char far *) malloc(numbytes))
        == (char far *)NULL)
    {
        _setvideomode(_DEFAULTMODE);
        printf("Not enough memory for image storage\n");
        exit(0);
    }
    _getimage(x,y,10,30,image); /* Save the image */
/* Now clear screen and draw saved image at several
 * screen locations.
 */
    _clearscreen(_GCLEARSCREEN);
    _settextposition(1,1);
    _outtext("Demonstrating animation with _putimage");
    _settextposition(20,1);
    _outtext("Hit any key to exit:");
    _setlogorg(320,175);
    _putimage(x,y,image,_GXOR);
/* Using kbhit and _putimage, perform animation
 * until user hits a key.
 */
    while( !kbhit() )
```

```
    {
/* Erase at last position */
        _putimage(x,y,image,_GXOR);
        y += 2;
        x += 2;
        if(x > 300) x = -300;
        if(y > 200) y = -100;
/* Redraw at new position */
        _putimage(x,y,image,_GXOR);
    }
/* Restore original mode  */
    _setvideomode(_DEFAULTMODE);
}
```

Console and Port I/O

outp

COMPATIBILITY

MSC 3	MSC 4	MSC 5	MSC 6	QC1	QC2	QC2.5	TC1	TC1.5	TC2	TC++	ANSI	UNIX V	XNX	OS2	DOS
▲	▲	▲	▲	▲	▲	▲		1	1	1				▲	▲

PURPOSE Use *outp* to write a byte to a specified I/O port. For example, you can use *outp* to generate sound on the IBM PC by sending appropriate data to the Intel 8255 programmable peripheral interface chip via port address 61h.

SYNTAX

```
int outp(unsigned port, int byte);
```

`unsigned port;` *Address of the port to which the byte is sent*

`int byte;` *Byte to be written to the port*

EXAMPLE CALL

```
outp(0x43, 0xb6);
```

INCLUDES `#include <conio.h>` *For function declaration*

DESCRIPTION The *outp* function uses the assembly language instruction OUT to send a byte of data from the argument *byte* to the port address specified in the argument *port.*

1. The Turbo C and Turbo C++ version of this function is *outportb.*

COMMON USES Use the *outp* function in conjunction with *inp* to access registers in input/output devices. The *outp* function is a C language interface to the OUT instruction.

RETURNS The *outp* function returns the byte it sent to the port.

COMMENTS Some peripheral devices such as the speaker and the serial ports are not adequately supported in the IBM PC's BIOS. In particular, the speaker is accessible only through the IN and OUT instructions; the Microsoft C library functions *inp* and *outp* are invaluable in such a situation.

SEE ALSO

`outpw` *To write a 16-bit word to a port address*

`inp, inpw` *To read from an I/O port*

EXAMPLE The IBM PC's speaker can be used to generate a tone by programming it via the 8255 chip at port address 61h and using the system timer (Intel 8254 chip) to control the speaker. Here is how it works. First you will set up the timer as an oscillator by sending the data byte B6h to the port 43h. Then you compute the ratio of the frequency of sound you want and the frequency of the timer's clock frequency (1.19 MHz). Write this value to port 42h. Tell the 8255 chip to drive the speaker under the control of the timer by reading the port 61h and writing the value back with the first two bits set to 1 (perform a logical OR with 3). This gets the sound going. Let the sound continue as long as you wish. Shut the speaker off by reading port 61h again and setting bits 0 and 1 to 0.

```
#include <conio.h>

#define TIMER_FREQ      1193180L /* Timer freq = 1.19 MHz */
#define TIMER_COUNT     0x42     /* 8253 timer -- count       */
#define TIMER_MODE      0x43     /* 8253 timer control port   */
#define TIMER_OSC       0xb6     /*To use timer as oscillator */
#define OUT_8255        0x61     /* 8255 PPI output port adrs */
#define SPKRON          3        /* Bit 0 = control spkr by timer*/
                                 /* Bit 1 = speaker on/off       */

main()
{
        unsigned freq, status, ratio, part_ratio;
        char input[81];
        cprintf("Enter frequency in Hz \
(between 100 and 15000):");
        cscanf("%hu", &freq);
/* First read and save status of the 8255 chip */
        status = inp (OUT_8255);
/* Put timer in oscillator mode */
        outp (TIMER_MODE, TIMER_OSC);
        ratio = (unsigned)(TIMER_FREQ/freq);
        part_ratio = ratio & 0xff; /* low byte of ratio   */
```

```
        outp(TIMER_COUNT, part_ratio);
        part_ratio = (ratio >> 8) & 0xff; /* high byte    */
        outp(TIMER_COUNT, part_ratio);
/* Finally turn on speaker */
        outp (OUT_8255, (status | SPKRON));

/* Ask user to indicate when to stop the
 * annoying tone...
 */
        cprintf("\nHit return to exit:");
        cgets(input);

/* Now turn off speaker */
        status = inp (OUT_8255); /* get current status */
/* Turn speaker off */
        outp (OUT_8255, (status & ~SPKRON));
}
```

Console and Port I/O

outpw

COMPATIBILITY

MSC 3	MSC 4	MSC 5	MSC 6	QC1	QC2	QC2.5	TC1	TC1.5	TC2	TC++	ANSI	UNIX V	XNX	OS2	DOS
		▲	▲	▲	▲	▲	1	1	1					▲	▲

PURPOSE Use the *outpw* function to write a 16-bit word to a specified I/O port address. For example, you can use *outpw* to send 2-bytes simultaneously to the control registers in your enhanced graphics adapter when programming it directly for graphics.

SYNTAX

```
int outpw(unsigned port, unsigned word);
```

`unsigned port;` *Address of the port to which the word is sent*

`unsigned word;` *Word to be written to the port*

EXAMPLE CALL

```
outpw(0x3ce, (2<<8) | 0x5);  /* Put EGA in write mode 2 */
```

INCLUDES

```
#include <conio.h>
```
For function declaration

DESCRIPTION The *outpw* function uses the assembly language instruction OUT to send a 16-bit word given in the argument *word* to the port address specified by the argument *port.*

1. The Turbo C and Turbo C++ version of this function is *outport.*

COMMON USES The *outpw* function, introduced in Microsoft C 5.0, allows you to send 2 bytes of data to two adjacent I/O ports by a single function call. As shown in the example, this comes in handy when programming the EGA.

RETURNS The *outpw* function returns the word it sent to the port.

COMMENTS Each I/O address on the IBM PC provides access to an 8-bit register. If you use *outpw* to send 2 bytes to, say, I/O address 3CEh, the first byte goes to the register at 3CEh and the second byte goes to the adjoining register at 3CFh. Thus when programming a peripheral such as the EGA, to which you often send specific data to two registers with addresses next to each other, it's advantageous to use *outpw*.

SEE ALSO `outp` *To write a byte to a port address*

`inp, inpw` *To read from an I/O port*

EXAMPLE The EGA can be programmed in its 640×350 high-resolution mode by manipulating the registers directly and sending data to its video memory. The programming involves sending a "register select" command to an I/O port followed by the register number to the next port. This can be achieved by a single call to *outpw*. The example below, meant to draw a rectangle filled with color, illustrates this.

```
#include <stdio.h>
#include <dos.h>

#define EGA_RAM ((unsigned char far *)0xA0000000)
#define MAX_GR_COLS  640
#define MAX_GR_ROWS  350
#define MAX_COL_BYTES (MAX_GR_COLS/8)

#define BIOS_VIDEO 0x10
#define SETMODE    0    /* BIOS Service: set video mode*/
#define EGAMODE    16   /* EGA mode for high resolution*/

#define EGA_GR12 0x3ce  /* Port to select register     */
#define EGA_GR_MODE 0x5 /* Register no. for write mode*/

/* The box size and the color */
#define XSTART  120
#define YSTART  120
#define XSIZE   280
#define YSIZE   200
#define COLOR   2
```

```
static union REGS xr, yr;
static char far *videoram;

main()
{
    int ynum, bytecount, startadrs, startbyte, stopbyte,
        horbytes, skipbytes;
    unsigned temp, egacommand;

/* Use BIOS to put EGA in high-res graphics mode */
    xr.h.ah = SETMODE;
    xr.h.al = EGAMODE;
    int86 (BIOS_VIDEO, &xr, &yr);

/* Compute starting address */
    startbyte = XSTART/8;
    startadrs = 80*YSTART + startbyte;
    videoram = EGA_RAM + startadrs;
    skipbytes = MAX_COL_BYTES;

/* Put EGA in write mode 2. Use outpw. The following
 * code is  equivalent to 2 lines:
 *          outp (EGA_GR12, EGA_GR_MODE);
 *          outp (EGA_GR_PORT, 2);
 */
    egacommand = (2<<8) | EGA_GR_MODE;
    outpw(EGA_GR12, egacommand);

    stopbyte = (XSTART + XSIZE - 1)/8;
    horbytes = stopbyte - startbyte;
    skipbytes = MAX_COL_BYTES - horbytes;

/* We already have the proper graphics mode settings */
        for (ynum = 0; ynum < YSIZE; ynum++)
        {
            for (bytecount = 0; bytecount < horbytes;
                  bytecount++)
            {
/* Fill in 8 bits at a time.
 * First read to latch in bytes.
 */
                temp = *videoram;
/* Now write out pixel value to all 8 bits at once */
                *videoram = COLOR;
```

```
                        videoram++;
                    }
/* Skip to next row */
                    videoram += skipbytes;
                }

/* Reset graphics environment back to BIOS standard */
    egacommand = EGA_GR_MODE;
    outpw(EGA_GR12, egacommand);
}
```

Console and Port I/O

putch

COMPATIBILITY

MSC 3	MSC 4	MSC 5	MSC 6	QC1	QC2	QC2.5	TC1	TC1.5	TC2	TC++	ANSI	UNIX V	XNX	OS2	DOS
▲	▲	▲	▲	▲	▲	▲	▲	▲	▲	▲				▲	▲

PURPOSE Use the *putch* function to write a single character to the display without intermediate buffering.

SYNTAX

```
int putch(int c);
```

`int c;` *Character to be written*

EXAMPLE CALL

```
putch('>');
```

INCLUDES `#include <conio.h>` *For function declaration*

DESCRIPTION The *putch* function writes the character *c* to the display.

RETURNS In Microsoft C versions 5.0 and above, *putch*, when successful, returns the character it wrote. Otherwise it returns the constant EOF (defined in *stdio.h*).

SEE ALSO `getch, getche` *For unbuffered read from the keyboard*

EXAMPLE Use *putch* to write a line (maximum length of 80 characters) to the standard output.

```
#include <stdio.h>
char buffer[81] = "Testing putch...\n";
main()
{
```

```
    int i;
/* Write characters to display until we reach the null */
    for(i=0; i<81 && buffer[i] != '\0'; i++)
    {
        putch(buffer[i]);
    }
}
```

Console and Port I/O

COMPATIBILITY

ungetch

MSC 3	MSC 4	MSC 5	MSC 6	QC1	QC2	QC2.5	TC1	TC1.5	TC2	TC++	ANSI	UNIX V	XNX	OS2	DOS
▲	▲	▲	▲	▲	▲	▲	▲	▲	▲	▲				▲	▲

PURPOSE Use the *ungetch* function to place a single character in the keyboard buffer so that it is the next character read from the console. You cannot place more than one character before the next read.

SYNTAX `int ungetch(int c);`

`int c;` *Character to be placed in the keyboard buffer*

EXAMPLE CALL `ungetch(last_char);`

INCLUDES `#include <conio.h>` *For function declaration*

DESCRIPTION The *ungetch* function places the character given in the integer argument *c* into the keyboard buffer so that the next console read operation returns that character. You can place only one character in the buffer before reading and the character must not be equal to the constant EOF defined in *stdio.h*.

RETURNS If there are no errors, *ungetch* returns the character it pushed back. Otherwise, it returns the constant EOF to indicate an error—which is why you should not try to push back EOF.

SEE ALSO `getch, getche` *To read a character from the console*

EXAMPLE Write a program that asks the user to enter an integer. Use *getche* to read the digits and accumulate them into an integer. Once you reach a nondigit (use the macro *isdigit* to check), put that character back into the console by calling *ungetch*. Now print a message showing the integer value and indicating the first noninteger character typed.

```
#include <stdio.h>
#include <conio.h>
#include <ctype.h>  /* For the macro isdigit() */
main()
{
    int intval = 0, c;
    char buff[81];
/* Ask user to type in an integer */
    printf("Enter an integer followed by some other \
characters:");
    while ( (c = getche()) != EOF && isdigit(c) )
    {
        intval = 10*intval + c - 48; /* 0 is ASCII 48 */
    }
/* Push back the first non-digit read from stdin */
    if (c != EOF) ungetch(c);
/* Print message to user */
    printf("\nInteger you entered = %d.\n\
First non-integer encountered: %c\n", intval, getch());
}
```

Chapter 16 System Calls

Introduction

All IBM-compatible MS-DOS machines come with a basic input/output system (BIOS) built into the read-only memory (ROM). This is a set of rudimentary I/O routines for accessing peripheral devices such as the keyboard, display, printer, serial port, and floppy or hard disk, among many others. In addition to the built-in ROM BIOS, MS-DOS itself has a host of standard utility functions that also perform I/O and provide access to the DOS file system. Essentially, you can count on both of these sets of services being present on every IBM PC or compatible that uses MS-DOS as its operating system. The DOS services are more portable than the BIOS ones because the BIOS code in PC-compatibles is only a functional copy of the original IBM BIOS, whereas the MS-DOS routines are part of the operating system software which is consistent across all machines. In general, however, programs that use DOS or BIOS calls to perform various I/O functions are likely to work properly in all IBM-compatible computers. Programs that directly access hardware using I/O port addresses or video memory addresses obtain the greatest processing speed, but may not work on all PC compatibles. Thus it is advantageous to be able to use these portable DOS and BIOS services in your programs whenever there are no overriding performance considerations.

The Microsoft C library includes a set of functions that provide access to the BIOS and DOS services from your C programs. These functions for making *system calls* enable you to harness the full potential of the PC without having to write, in most cases, even a single line of code in 8086 assembly language.

The *system calls* routines, with names prefixed by "_dos_" and "_bios_" were introduced in Microsoft C 5.0 and are specific to Microsoft

C. Unfortunately, every C compiler for the IBM PC has a different name for each of these routines. However, the basic set of *int86, int86x, intdos*, and *intdosx* appear to be present in most C compilers for the IBM PC.

We should also point out that many of the services offered by the system calls category are duplicated elsewhere in the Microsoft C library. Entire categories of portable routines exist for memory allocation, file I/O, and date/time information. For these tasks, you are better off using the standard library routines because they are much more portable than the DOS and BIOS calls. In general, use the most portable routine that provides acceptable performance.

Concepts: Basics of BIOS and DOS Interface

C programmers are familiar with the concept of compiling groups of functions to generate object code and using the linker to construct an executable file. In such a situation, you normally invoke a routine's code by a C function call. The parameters that you pass to the function are transferred via the stack.

Now consider the case of BIOS and DOS functions. These routines are also in compiled object code form, but you cannot link with them because the addresses of the routines are not known to you. (Even if they were, it would pose a problem if they changed in future revisions of the BIOS and DOS.) A more fundamental access mechanism is needed, a method that can be counted on to work on every PC irrespective of where the actual object code of the BIOS and DOS functions reside. The assembly language instruction INT which generates a software interrupt on an 8086 microprocessor provides the solution.

SOFTWARE INTERRUPTS ON 8086 MICROPROCESSORS

In a PC, an "interrupt" refers to a mechanism that hardware devices use to get the attention of the microprocessor that they service. The 8086 microprocessor keeps a table of function addresses called an "interrupt vector table" in the memory. When the microprocessor receives an interrupt signal, it first saves the contents of the internal registers and the address of the code it was executing at that moment. Next it determines the interrupt number from the interrupt signal and locates that entry in the interrupt vector table. Then it jumps to that function address and begins executing the code there, which presumably satisfies the needs of the device that generated the interrupt signal in the first place. The microprocessor returns to the code it was executing when it was interrupted as soon as it executes the assembly language instruction IRET. Thus the function that handles or services the interrupt must end with an IRET (see Figure 16-1).

Software interrupts behave in the same way as hardware interrupts, except that they are generated by an assembly language of the form *INT*

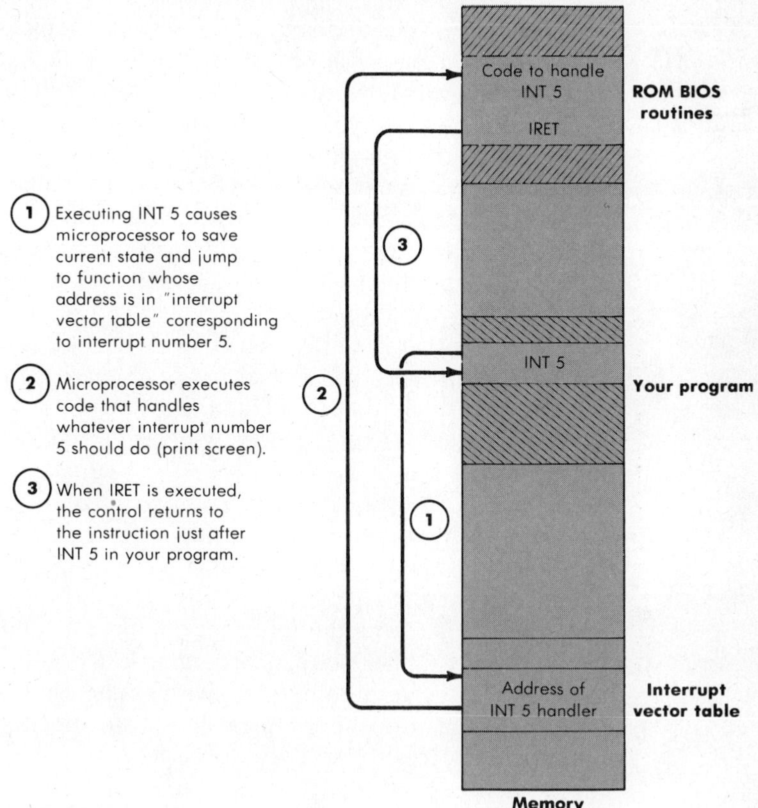

Figure 16-1. *Accessing BIOS and DOS functions via software interrupts*

<int_number> where *<int_number>* is the interrupt number we want generated. If we write a routine to perform a task, end it with an IRET instruction, and place its address in the entry corresponding to the *<int_number>* in the interrupt vector table, the routine can be invoked by executing the instruction *INT <int_number>*, which is precisely how the BIOS and DOS functions are made available to assembly language programmers. Parameters are passed from C to these routines by placing them in the microprocessor's registers, and results are returned through the registers also. Since the routines in the system calls category allow us to make software interrupts, they allow access to the BIOS and DOS functions.

Typically, a single interrupt number provides access to an entire category of service, with the specific service selected by a value in a register. For example, interrupt number 21h provides access to almost a hundred functions embedded in MS-DOS. The exact function to be invoked is specified by a function number placed in the AH register.

SOFTWARE INTERRUPTS FROM MICROSOFT C

Microsoft C provides the routines *int86* and *int86x* for generating arbitrary software interrupts. These routines accept the register settings in a "union" (see Chapter 1) named REGS, which is defined in the include file *dos.h* and is the overlay of two structures, one named *x* of type WORDREGS and the other named *h* of type BYTEREGS (see Figure 16-2). This arrangement means that the member *x* in the "union" REGS provides access to the 16-bit word registers AX, BX, CX, and DX, while the member *h* is used for accessing the corresponding 8-bit halves, AH, AL, BH, BL, CH, CL, DH, and DL. The segment registers ES, CS, SS, and DS are passed via a "structure" named SREGS, which is also defined in *dos.h*.

To pass register values you have to declare data items of type REGS and SREGS and set the internal fields of these structures to the desired register values. The interface routine in the C library loads the registers from these data structures before generating the software interrupt necessary to access the desired BIOS or DOS service. Upon return from the interrupt, the interface routine copies the register values into another structure which you also allocate and whose address you pass to the routine. This allows the program to obtain the results or error codes returned by the service called.

Table 16-1 shows the interrupt numbers for the BIOS services. Table 16-2 lists the DOS services according to function number. The DOS services all use interrupt number 21h, with a function number specified in the AH register. Each of these tables shows the specific Microsoft C routines that provide access to a particular service. For more information on a particular routine, consult the appropriate reference page. If no special Microsoft C routine exists, you can use the general-purpose interrupt routines *int86x* or *intdosx* to access the service. In this case, you can find further details in reference books on MS-DOS (Duncan[3]) and IBM PC (Norton[5], Smith[6]) listed under *Further Reading*.

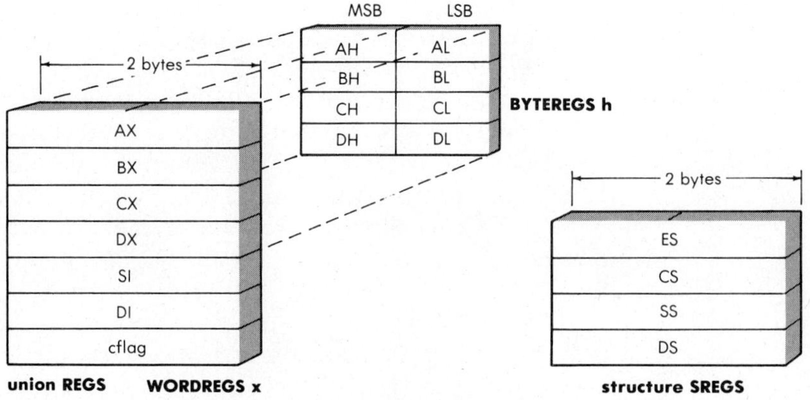

Figure 16-2. ***Union REGS and structure SREGS***

Table 16-1. *Interrupts to Access ROM BIOS Routines*

Interrupt Number (Hex)	Purpose	Microsoft C 6.0 Interface Routine
05	Print screen	N/A
10	Video I/O	N/A
11	Equipment determination	_bios_equiplist
12	Memory size determination	_bios_memsize
13	Diskette I/O (and hard disk I/O on AT, XT and PS/2)	_bios_disk
14	I/O with RS-232C serial communications port	_bios_serialcom
15	Cassette I/O (and system services on AT, XT, and PS/2)	N/A
16	Keyboard I/O	_bios_keybrd
17	Printer I/O	_bios_printer
18	Access ROM-resident BASIC	N/A
19	Bootstrap loader to load operating system from disk	N/A
1A	Time of day	_bios_timeofday
1B	Keyboard break address	N/A
1C	Timer tick	N/A

Table 16-2. *MS-DOS Interface Routines*

Function Number (Hex)	Action	Microsoft C 6.0 DOS Interface
00	Terminates program and returns to DOS.	
01	Reads a character from keyboard (AL has character).	
02	Displays character in DL on screen.	
03	Reads character from AUX into AL.	
04	Writes character in DL to AUX.	
05	Sends character in DL to printer port.	
06	Performs direct console I/O (DL=FF means input).	
07	Directly inputs a character from STDIN.	
08	Reads a character from keyboard without echoing it.	
09	Prints a string ending in a $.	
0A	Reads characters from keyboard into a buffer.	
0B	Checks status of STDIN.	
0C	Clears keyboard buffer.	
0D	Resets disk and flushes all disk buffers.	
0E	Sets the default disk drive.	
0F	Opens a disk file (requires File Control Block *[FCB]*).	
10	Closes a disk file (specified by FCB).	
11	Searches for first occurrence of a file using FCB.	

Table 16-2. *(cont.)*

Function Number (Hex)	Action	Microsoft C 6.0 DOS Interface
12	Searches for next occurrence of a file using FCB.	
13	Deletes file specified by an FCB.	
14	Reads a disk file sequentially.	
15	Writes sequentially to a disk file.	
16	Creates a disk file.	
17	Renames a disk file.	
18	Reserved.	
19	Returns default disk drive number in AL.	_dos_getdrive
1A	Sets up a disk transfer area (DTA) address.	
1B	Returns allocation information about default disk drive.	
1C	Returns allocation information of a specific drive.	
1D	Reserved.	
1E	Reserved.	
1F	Reserved.	
20	Reserved.	
21	Reads a record from disk (random access).	
22	Writes a record to disk (random access).	
23	Returns file size in FCB, if file found.	
24	Sets up record number for random access read/write.	
25	Sets up a new interrupt vector.	_dos_setvect
26	Creates a Program Segment Prefix (PSP).	
27	Reads a block of records from disk (random access).	
28	Writes a block of records to disk (random access).	
29	Parses a file name.	
2A	Returns current date (DL=day, DH=month, CX=year).	_dos_getdate
2B	Sets the current date.	_dos_setdate
2C	Returns the current time.ta_dos_gettime	
2D	Sets the current time.	_dos_settime
2E	Sets verify flag on or off.	
2F	Returns the address of disk transfer area (DTA).	
30	Returns version of DOS.	
31	Terminates program but leaves it intact in memory.	_dos_keep
32	Used internally by DOS to get drive parameter block.	
33	Gets or sets Control-Break flag.	
34	Used internally by DOS to get a pointer to a byte that indicates when DOS is in a "critical section" (when flag is set, it is not safe to call DOS functions; this	

Table 16-2. *(cont.)*

Function Number (Hex)	Action	Microsoft C 6.0 DOS Interface
	feature is used by many TSR utilities). This is not officially documented by Microsoft.	
35	Returns the interrupt vector for a specific interrupt.	_dos_getvect
36	Returns information about total and unused space on a specified disk drive.	_dos_getdiskfree
37	Used internally (switch character and device availability). This is not officially documented by Microsoft.	
38	Gets or sets country-dependent information.	
39	Creates a subdirectory.	
3A	Removes a subdirectory.	
3B	Changes the current directory.	
3C	Creates a named disk file and returns handle in AX.	_dos_creat
3D	Opens a named disk file and returns handle in AX.	_dos_open
3E	Closes a file specified by a handle.	_dos_close
3F	Reads a number of bytes from a disk file specified by a handle.	_dos_read
40	Writes a number of bytes to a disk file specified by a handle.	_dos_write
41	Deletes a named disk file.	
42	Moves the read/write pointer of a file specified by a handle.	
43	Gets or sets the attributes of a file. (Attributes determine if a file is hidden, read-only, and so on.)	_dos_getfileattr
44	Provides device driver control (IOCTL).	
45	Creates a duplicate file handle.	
46	Forces a new file handle to point to the same file as an existing handle.	
47	Returns current directory name.	
48	Allocates a specified number of paragraphs of memory and returns the segment address of the allocated memory.	_dos_allocmem
49	Releases a previously allocated block of memory.	_dos_freemem
4A	Adjusts the size of a previously allocated block of memory.	
4B	Loads and/or executes a program.	
4C	Terminates a program and returns an exit code.	
4D	Returns exit code of a subprogram.	
4E	Searches for first occurrence of a named file.	_dos_findfirst
4F	Searches for next occurrence of a named file.	_dos_findnext

Table 16-2. *(cont.)*

Function Number (Hex)	Action	Microsoft C 6.0 DOS Interface
50	Used internally to set new PSP segment.	
51	Used internally to get current PSP segment.	
52	Used internally by DOS to get list of disks.	
53	Used internally by DOS to translate the BIOS parameter block.	
54	Returns the verify flag in AH.	
55	Used internally by DOS to create a PSP.	
56	Renames a file.	
57	Gets or sets the modification time and date of a disk file specified by its handle.	_dos_getftime
58	Gets or sets the memory allocation strategy to be used by DOS. (*DOS 3.X and above only*).	
59	Returns extended error information (*DOS 3.X and above only*).	dosexterr
5A	Creates a temporary file (*DOS 3.X and above only*).	
5B	Creates a new file (*DOS 3.X and above only*).	_dos_creatnew
5C	Locks or unlocks a file for shared access (*DOS 3.X and above only*).	
5D	Used internally by DOS.	
5E	Returns machine name and printer set up (*DOS 3.X and above only*).	
5F	Gets list of device redirections in Microsoft network (*DOS 3.X and above only*).	
60	Used internally by DOS.	
61	Reserved.	
62	Returns the PSP (Program Segment Address) (*DOS 3.X and above only*).	
63	Returns lead byte table (*DOS 2.25 only*).	
64	Reserved.	
65	Returns extended country information (*DOS 3.3 and above only*).	
66	Gets or sets global page table (*DOS 3.3 and above only*).	
67	Sets the maximum number of file handles (must be less than 255). This breaks the "20 open file per process" limit of DOS 3.2 and lower. (*DOS 3.3 and above only*).	
68	Writes all buffered data meant for a file to the disk (*DOS 3.3 and above only*).	

Notes on BIOS and DOS Services

The functions in the system calls category allow you to use virtually all routines in the IBM PC ROM BIOS as well as all functions in DOS that are accessible via interrupt number 21h. Table 16-3 lists the Microsoft C routines that provide access to the system services, grouped according to the tasks they perform. The BIOS routines are not listed because each one performs a distinct task. Table 16-4 shows the routines that are part of the BIOS interface.

Table 16-3. ***Microsoft C 6.0 System Interface Routines by Task***

Task	Routines
Generate 8086 software interrupt	int86, int86x
Call any DOS function	bdos, intdos, intdosx
Get segment and offset addresses	FP_OFF, FP_SEG, segread
Perform file I/O using DOS(see I/O routines in Chapter 15)	_dos_close, _dos_creat, _dos_creatnew, _dos_open, _dos_read, _dos_write
Find and alter file information	_dos_findfirst, _dos_findnext, _dos_getdiskfree, _dos_getdrive, _dos_getfileattr, _dos_getftime, _dos_setfileattr, _dos_setftime
Handle interrupts	_chain_intr, _disable, _dos_getvect, _dos_setvect, _enable
Allocate and free memory (see Chapter 5 for others)	_dos_allocmem, _dos_freemem, _dos_setblock
Get or set date and time (see Chapter 12)	_dos_getdate, _dos_gettime, _dos_setdate, _dos_settime
Handle hardware and other errors	dosexterr, _harderr, _hardresume, _hardretn

MICROSOFT C INTERFACE TO DOS AND BIOS SERVICES

Microsoft C provides three ways to access the DOS services (see Figure 16-3). The first approach is to use the general software interrupts, *int86* and *int86x*, and call DOS directly using interrupt number 21h. The second method uses the generic DOS interrupt routines *bdos*, *intdos*, and *intdosx*. The third method is to use the specific DOS system calls (the routines in Table 16-5 whose names begin with *_dos_*).

BIOS services are accessed by two methods: via the general-purpose interrupt routines or by calling a specific BIOS interface routine listed in Table 16-4.

To call a DOS or BIOS service using the general-purpose interrupt routine, you set up the registers by using a "union" REGS data type and then provide the interrupt number to *int86* (or *int86x* if the service requires the use of the DS and ES registers). For DOS, the interrupt number

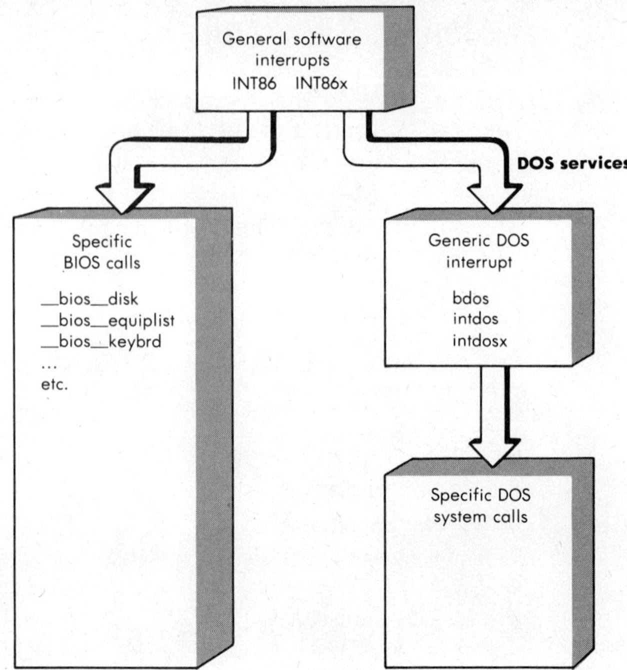

Figure 16-3. ***Microsoft C Interface for BIOS and DOS services***

Table 16-4. ***BIOS Interface Routines in Microsoft C 6.0***

Routine	Interrupt Number (Hex)	Purpose of Routine
_bios_disk	13	Access physical sectors in floppy and hard disk (hard disk only on XT, AT, and PS/2)
_bios_equiplist	11	Obtain a list of peripherals attached to the PC
_bios_keybrd	16	Read character from keyboard and query the status of function, Alt and Shift keys
_bios_memsize	12	Determine amount of memory in the system
_bios_printer	17	Send character to parallel printer port and determine status of printer
_bios_serialcom	14	Perform I/O with RS-232C serial port (initialize port, send and receive a character)
_bios_timeofday	1A	Read and set current clock setting (also, access the real-time clock in AT, XT, and PS/2)

is always 21h. Different services are accessed by placing the DOS function number in the AH register. Other register values depend on the DOS function being called. For example, the DOS time function (number 2Ch) may be called as follows:

```
#include <stdio.h>
#include <dos.h>
#define DOS_GETTIME 0x2c
main()
{
    union REGS xr, yr;
    xr.h.ah = DOS_GETTIME;
    int86(0x21, &xr, &yr);
    printf("Current time is %.2d:%.2d:%.2d\n",
           yr.h.ch, yr.h.cl, yr.h.dh);
}
```

The *dos.h* include file is necessary for the definition of the union REGS. If we were to use the *intdos* interface (we do not have to use *intdosx* because the service does not need anything in the segment registers), the line containing the call to *int86* in our example would be replaced by:

```
intdos(&xr, &yr);
```

Lastly, if we make use of the interface routine *_dos_gettime* provided specifically for accessing the system time, the example becomes:

```
#include <stdio.h>
#include <dos.h>
main()
{
    struct dostime_t time;
    _dos_gettime(&time);
    printf("Current time: %d:%d:%d.%d\n", time.hour,
            time.minute, time.second, time.hsecond);
}
```

This use of the function is more natural to C programmers because it does not involve the use of the 8086 specific data structures (REGS and SREGS).

The general-purpose interrupt routines, *int86* and *int86x*, are important because they enable you to generate *any* software interrupt on the PC. Consequently, every BIOS and DOS function shown in Tables 16-1 and 16-2 can be invoked with one of these two routines. The difference between them is that plain *int86* allows you to set all registers except the segment registers while *int86x* also lets you specify new values for the segment registers (only the DS and ES segment registers can be set to new values because CS contains the segment address of our code while SS holds the current stack segment address).

Despite their versatility, there is one drawback to the *int86* and *int86x* functions. To use them effectively, you have to know what each interrupt number accesses and its relevant register settings. The *intdos* and *intdosx* are versions of *int86* and *int86x* that are set to generate interrupt number 21h. Thus these two routines can access any one of the hundred or so DOS functions. Like the *int86* pair, *intdosx* enables you to specify new values for the segment registers DS and ES and *intdos* uses the default settings of DS and ES.

Many DOS and BIOS functions require that you specify both the segment address and the offset of a data item. You can get these values by using the macros FP_SEG and FP_OFF, respectively. The function *segread* lets you get the current values of the segment registers DS, ES, CS, and SS.

ACCESSING THE BIOS SERVICES

The BIOS has a relatively small number of functions that provide access to the following peripherals:

- disk (hard disk and diskette)
- keyboard
- video
- printer
- serial communications port
- system timer

Table 16-1 lists interrupt numbers that are used with the INT instruction to invoke the BIOS services. The Microsoft C 6.0 library provides interface routines for most of these interrupts. These interface routines are included in the table. Each routine is described in detail in its reference page and is also summarized in Table 16-4. Note in Table 16-1 that no explicit interface is included for the video services accessed via interrupt number 10h. This is not applicable in versions 5.0 and later of Microsoft C because there is an entire category of graphics routines (see Chapters 17, 18, and 19) available. You can still use *int86* to call the BIOS video routines.

Specific Interface Routines for BIOS

Table 16-4 summarizes the routines that call BIOS functions. In Table 16-1, we listed the interrupt numbers used to access the ROM BIOS services. Accessing the services through the interrupt number however, requires you to set up the registers using the REGS and SREGS data structures and then use either *int86* or *int86x* to generate the interrupt. The BIOS interface routines listed in Table 16-4 simplify the task. They are easier to use because they accept normal C arguments and return values normally rather than use the REGS and SREGS structures. They also have descriptive names. Table 16-4 also shows the interrupt number to which the function provides an interface. The interrupt numbers are provided as cross references to entries in Table 16-1.

ACCESSING THE DOS SERVICES

Compared to the BIOS, MS-DOS services are far more numerous. They generally affect the file system, memory management, process management, and input and output functions. Unlike the BIOS, all MS-DOS functions are accessible via the *INT 21h* instruction with the exact function specified in the AH register. In Table 16-2 we list the most common DOS functions. The function number shown in the table has to be put in the AH register before generating interrupt 21h. In certain cases, Microsoft C 6.0 provides a special purpose routine for accessing that DOS function and these are also listed in the table. Consult the reference page for specific routines for further information. Table 16-3 also summarizes all the DOS interface routines in Microsoft C 6.0. Short summaries of some important DOS services follow.

Access to the MS-DOS File System

A large percentage of the DOS interface routines provide access to the MS-DOS file system. You can find substitutes for each of the routines for performing file I/O. These substitutes are more portable and are described in Chapter 15. There is, however, no substitutes for the routines that allow you to get and set file attributes and let you search for files in the directory (*_dos_findfirst* and *_dos_findnext*). For these tasks, the DOS interface is very useful.

Servicing Interrupts

When we discussed hardware interrupts we mentioned installing a function in the interrupt vector table to process whatever a particular hardware interrupt requires. There are a few hidden treasures in Microsoft C 6.0 and its library that can help you write an interrupt handler entirely in C. The first of these is the newly introduced *interrupt* attribute for functions (see Chapter 1 for details) which causes the compiler to push all registers upon entry to the function and to use an IRET instruction for exiting the function. The other treasures are the library routines *_disable* and *_enable*, which are C equivalents of the assembly language instructions CLI and STI, respectively. Last but not least are the routines *_dos_getvect* and *_dos_setvect* for retrieving and setting particular entries in the interrupt vector table. Using these new features, you can write routines that, as an example, can perform interrupt-driven I/O with the serial port on the PC.

Memory Allocation and Time

You also get to access the DOS functions for memory allocation and for getting or setting the date and the time. These routines are redundant, though, because there is an assortment of memory allocation (Chapter 5) and time (Chapter 12) routines in the Microsoft C library.

Error Handling

Hardware errors on the PC cause an interrupt 24h to be generated. There are three routines, *_harderr*, *_hardresume*, and *_hardretn*, to help you set up an appropriate handler for this interrupt. By the way, the normal handler for this interrupt is the originator of the infamous message, "Abort, Retry, Ignore?"

Specific Interface Routines for DOS

Table 16-5 lists the Microsoft C 6.0 routines that are meant as gateways to a few selected DOS functions. These *DOS interface* routines make it easier to pass arguments and receive return values. Each routine in Table 16-5 also has an entry showing the DOS function number for which the routine serves as an interface. If you have the need to use one of the DOS functions listed in Table 16-2 for which no simple interface routine exists, you can access the function using the *intdos* and *intdosx* routines. The function number to be placed in the AH register (of a REGS structure) and you have to consult a DOS manual for details on the input and output parameters for the DOS function you want to call.

Table 16-5. ***MS-DOS Interface Routines in Microsoft C 6.0***

Routine	DOS Function Number (Hex)	Purpose of Routine
bdos	—	Access any DOS function that makes use of only AL and DX registers.
_dos_allocmem	48	Allocate a specified number of paragraphs of memory.
_dos_close	3E	Close a file specified by a handle.
_dos_creat	3C	Create and truncate a file of given name (a string) and get a handle back (deletes existing file of same name).
_dos_creatnew	5B	Like _dos_creat, but _dos_creatnew fails if named file already exists.
_dos_findfirst	4E	Find the first occurrence of a named file (a string). Requires a disk transfer area (DTA) which can be set up by function 1Ah.
_dos_findnext	4F	For a file name containing wildcard characters (* or ?), finds the next occurrence of a file of that name. Assumes _dos_findfirst was called and it found a file.
_dos_freemem	49	Free a block of memory.
_dos_getdate	2A	Get the current date (day, month, and year)
_dos_getdiskfree	36	Get the total number of clusters and the number available for use on a disk drive. The number of bytes per cluster is also returned. So the total storage capacity of a disk and the amount free can be computed easily.
_dos_getdrive	19	Get the current drive (0 means A, 1 means B, and so on).
_dos_getfileattr	43	Get the attribute of a file. This tells us if the file is

Table 16-5. ***(cont.)***

Routine	DOS Function Number (Hex)	Purpose of Routine
		read only, hidden, a system file, a volume label, a subdirectory, or changed since last backup.
_dos_getftime	57	Get the time and date a file was last modified (file specified by handle).
_dos_gettime	2C	Get the current time in hours, minutes, seconds, and hundredths of a second. (Note that system time is updated 18.2 times a second.)
_dos_getvect	35	Get the contents of the interrupt vector table for a specified interrupt number.
_dos_keep	31	Terminate current program but leave it intact in memory (used to install the "terminate-but-stay-resident" or TSR utilities).
_dos_open	3D	Open a named file for a specific type of access and obtain a 16-bit handle to uniquely identify the open file.
_dos_read	3F	Read a specified number of bytes from a file into a buffer in memory.
_dos_setblock	4A	Change the size of a previously allocated block of memory.
_dos_setdate	2B	Set the system date.
_dos_setdrive	0E	Set the default disk drive (specified by a number, 0 means A, 1 means B, and so on).
_dos_setfileattr	43	Alter the current attribute of a file (see _dos_getfileattr).
_dos_setftime	57	Set the modification time of a file (file specified by handle).
_dos_settime	2D	Set the current system time.
_dos_setvect	25	Set the entry in the interrupt vector table corresponding to a given interrupt number. The new value should be the address of a routine designed to handle that interrupt number.
_dos_write	40	Write a specified number of bytes from a buffer to an open file (need handle).
dosexterr	59	Get detailed error information about the last error that occurred during an "INT 21h" instruction. The information is returned in the registers and you will have to consult a DOS reference guide for exact meaning of the values that are returned.
intdos	any	Call any DOS function by placing function number in AH (using the REGS union). Not useful for those functions that require the use of DS and ES segment registers.
intdosx	any	Used to call any DOS function including those requiring the use of DS and ES segment registers.

MISCELLANEOUS INTERFACE ROUTINES

In addition to the BIOS and DOS interface routines, the system calls category of the Microsoft C 6.0 library also includes routines for obtaining register values of the 8086 microprocessor, handling hardware errors in the MS-DOS system, enabling and disabling interrupts, and installing interrupt handlers. We discussed these features in our overview of the system call routines. They are detailed in Table 16-6. Note that *int86* and *int86x* are considered basic system interface routines because their primary purpose is to generate software interrupts in the 8086 microprocessor. Thus, all the ROM BIOS and DOS functions can be accessed using the *int86* and *int86x* routines.

Cautions

- The system calls category of the Microsoft C 6.0 library contains routines that allow you to perform tasks that are often intimately tied to

Table 16-6. ***Interface Routines in Microsoft C 6.0***

Routine	Interrupt Number (Hex)	Purpose of Routine
_chain_intr	none	Chain one interrupt handler to another, allowing you to jump unconditionally to a function.
_disable	none	Execute a CLI instruction thus disabling all interrupts.
_enable	none	Execute an STI instruction to enable interrupts again.
FP_OFF	none	Return the offset address of a far pointer (see Chapter 2).
FP_SEG	none	Return the segment address of a far pointer (see Chapter 2).
_harderr	24	This does not generate the interrupt number 24h; rather this function sets the interrupt vector entry for 24h to a given function address. Since the system generates an interrupt 24h when a hardware error occurs, this function is meant to handle fatal hardware errors. Can you guess what the default function does? (Hint: Type DIR A: without placing a diskette in drive A.)
_hardresume	none	Return to MS-DOS after a hardware error (or interrupt 24h).
_hardretn	none	Return to application where hardware error (or interrupt 24h) occurred.
int86	any	Call any function accessible by a software interrupt. Not useful for those functions that require the use of DS and ES segment registers.
int86x	any	Used to call any function, including those requiring the use of DS and ES segment registers.
segread	none	Obtain the current contents of the segment registers CS, DS, ES, and SS.

hardware. To use these functions effectively, it is necessary to understand the basic operation of the IBM PC hardware as well as that of MS-DOS.

- Programs that depend on the system calls functions run on MS-DOS machines only and are not portable to other systems.
- If you are not familiar with the interrupt concept, the physical layout of a diskette, or the DOS file system, consult the references suggested at the end of this tutorial.
- Note that the Microsoft C library has other file I/O routines that use handles to access files. Although they may seem similar, you should not mix the DOS file I/O calls with those from the Input and Output category (see Chapter 15). In fact, there is no reason to use the file I/O routines in this section because the regular C library I/O routines are more functional than those in the system calls category. Besides, the I/O routines listed in Chapter 15 are portable because many of them are part of the proposed ANSI standard definition of C.

Further Reading

The number of system features and peripherals that you can access and manipulate using the system call routines is quite large. Although a detailed discussion of all the things you can do with these interface routines is beyond the scope of this book, there are quite a few resources that can help you.

The recent book by Lafore[1] is an excellent book for anyone learning C on the IBM PC. In the course of teaching the language, it also goes over the basics of the ROM BIOS routines. Prata's book[2] covers the same ground in a more advanced manner. For detailed information on MS-DOS, the book by Duncan[3] is ideal. The developer's guide by The Waite Group[4] has an excellent discussion of the physical layout of diskettes and of the DOS file system. The ROM BIOS functions are discussed in depth by Norton[5] and information specific to the IBM PC/AT appears in Smith's book[6].

1. Robert Lafore, The Waite Group, *Microsoft C Programming for the PC,* 2d Ed., Howard W. Sams & Company, Carmel, IN, 1990, 816 pages.
2. Stephen Prata, The Waite Group, *Advanced C Primer++*, Howard W. Sams & Company, Carmel, IN, 1986, 502 pages.
3. Ray Duncan, *Advanced MS-DOS*, Microsoft Press, Redmond, WA, 1986, 468 pages.
4. The Waite Group, *The Waite Group's MS-DOS Developer's Guide*, 2d Ed., Howard W. Sams & Company, Carmel, IN, 1989, 783 pages.

5. Peter Norton, *The Peter Norton Programmer's Guide to the IBM PC*, Microsoft Press, Redmond, WA, 1985, 426 pages.
6. James T. Smith, *The IBM PC AT Programmer's Guide*, Prentice-Hall, New York, NY, 1986, 277 pages.

COMPATIBILITY

bdos

MSC 3	MSC 4	MSC 5	MSC 6	QC1	QC2	QC2.5	TC1	TC1.5	TC2	TC++	ANSI	UNIX V	XNX	OS2	DOS
▲	▲	▲	▲	▲	▲	▲	▲	▲	▲	▲					▲

PURPOSE Use the *bdos* function to call a subset of the DOS functions that can be invoked by an INT 21h instruction. You can use *bdos* to call only those DOS functions that require no arguments or that take arguments in the *DX* and the *AL* registers only. For example, you can use *bdos* with function number 1 to read a character from the keyboard. The returned character will be in the low-order byte of the return value. In contrast to the more general-purpose *intdos* and *intdosx*, the *bdos* function is a simplified way to access a small set of DOS functions.

SYNTAX

```
int bdos (int funcno, unsigned dx_val, unsigned al_val);
```

`int funcno;` *DOS function number*

`unsigned dx_val;` *DX register value*

`unsigned al_val;` *AL register value*

EXAMPLE CALL

```
bdos(2, q', 0);  /* Use DOS function 2 to display 'q' */
```

INCLUDES #include <dos.h> *For function declaration*

DESCRIPTION The function *bdos* provides simplified access by an INT 21h instruction to the set of DOS functions requiring no arguments or taking arguments in the *DX* and *AL* registers only. This function first copies the values from the unsigned integer arguments *dx_val* and *al_val* into the system's *DX* and *AL* registers, respectively. Then it invokes the DOS function number *funcno* with an *INT 21h* instruction. At the end of the DOS call, *bdos* returns the contents of the *AX* register. The meaning of this value depends on the DOS service requested in *funcno* (see the tutorial section).

COMMON USES The *bdos* function is used to read characters from the keyboard and write characters to the screen using the MS-DOS interface. The advantage of using these services is that your programs will be compatible with all MS-DOS computers.

The *intdos* and *intdosx* functions are more general gateways to the DOS functions, but *bdos* is simpler to use. Of course, you cannot use *dos* if the function being called requires that you provide arguments in registers other than DX and AL.

RETURNS The return value is the content of the *AX* register at the end of the DOS call. For example, if the DOS call returns a value in *AL*, you can get this value by ignoring the high-order byte of the return value.

COMMENTS Note that the *intdosx* function provides a more versatile gateway to the DOS functions because it enables you to set up all register values before calling DOS via INT 21h. You should use *bdos* only when the specific conditions described above are met.

SEE ALSO

`intdosx, intdos`	*More general mechanism to access DOS functions*
`Table 16-5`	*Simplified access to several DOS functions*

EXAMPLES Read a character from the keyboard using DOS function 1. The character is returned in the *AL* register. Remember that *bdos* returns the value of the *AX* register.

```
#include <stdio.h>
#include <dos.h>
/* DOS function to read from keyboard */
#define DOS_KBDIN 1
main()
{
    unsigned int ch_read;
/* Nothing needs to be specified for DX and AL. Use 0's
 * Also, zero out the high-order byte by bitwise AND
 * with FFh
 */
    ch_read = bdos(DOS_KBDIN, 0, 0) & 0xff;
    printf("\nCharacter read = %c\n", ch_read);
}
```

Use DOS function number 2 to display on your monitor a character placed in the *DL* register (perhaps a character you just read from the keyboard). The return value has no meaning in this case.

```
#include <stdio.h>
#include <dos.h>
#define DOS_KBDIN    1
#define DOS_DISPCHAR 2
main()
{
    unsigned int ch_read;
/* First read a character. (see previous example) */
    ch_read = bdos(DOS_KBDIN, 0, 0) & 0xff;
```

```
/* Now display the character. DX is the character.
 * Nothing is needed in AL.
 */
    printf("\nHere's what you typed: ");
    bdos(DOS_DISPCHAR, ch_read, 0);
}
```

COMPATIBILITY

_bios_disk

MSC 3	MSC 4	MSC 5	MSC 6	QC1	QC2	QC2.5	TC1	TC1.5	TC2	TC++	ANSI	UNIX V	XNX	OS2	DOS
		▲	▲	▲	▲	▲		1	1	1					▲

PURPOSE Use the *_bios_disk* function to perform *raw* disk I/O operations on the PC's 5¼-inch disk drive by using BIOS. For example, you can use *_bios_disk* to read and write physical sectors from the disk, to determine the status of the floppy disk drive, and even format a disk (if you are writing an alternative to the DOS FORMAT command).

Since this function allows you to perform low-level disk I/O directly, you should use it with caution because it can destroy data and damage the existing MS-DOS file system on your disk.

SYNTAX

```
unsigned _bios_disk (unsigned service, struct diskinfo_t *info);

unsigned service;              Service code

struct diskinfo_t *info;       Disk information
```

EXAMPLE CALL

```
_bios_disk(_DISK_READ, &info);
```

INCLUDES

```
#include <bios.h>       For service codes and definition of structure diskinfo_t
```

DESCRIPTION The *_bios_disk* function, introduced in version 5.0 of Microsoft C, is a gateway to a set of ROM BIOS routines that provide access to the PC's disk drive via software interrupt number 13h. It provides a cleaner calling convention than is achieved by generating an INT 13h using the *int86x* function. The *_bios_disk* function performs the task requested in the argument *service code*. It expects information about the disk drive (for example, the head number, track number, etc.) in a C structure whose address must be provided in the argument *diskinfo*.

This structure data type, named *diskinfo_t*, having the layout shown below, is declared in the *include* file *bios.h*.

```
struct diskinfo_t
{
    unsigned drive;    /* Drive number (0 or 1)                    */
    unsigned head;     /* Head number (0 or 1) or which side?      */
    unsigned track;    /* Track number                             */
    unsigned sector;   /* Start sector number                      */
    unsigned nsectors; /* Number of sectors for which requested */
                       /* service is to be performed               */
    void far *buffer;  /* Pointer to buffer in memory for use      */
                       /* during requested service                 */
};
```

As shown in Table 16-7, the valid range of values for number of sectors and tracks depends on the type of disk.

Table 16-7. *Tracks and Sectors of Various Disks*

5¼-Inch Disks			
Disk Capacity	Drive Capacity	Valid Track Number	Valid Sector Number
320 K	320/360 K	0 through 39	1 through 8
360 K	320/360 K	0 through 39	1 through 9
320 K	1.2 Mb (AT)	0 through 39	1 through 8
360 K	1.2 Mb (AT)	0 through 39	1 through 9
1.2 Mb	1.2 Mb (AT)	0 through 79	1 through 15
3½-Inch Disks (AT and PS/2)			
Disk Capacity	Drive Capacity	Valid Track Number	Valid Sector Number
720 K	720 K	0 through 79	1 through 9
1.44 M	1.44 M	0 through 79	1 through 18

Enough memory must be allocated for the buffer used by *_bios_disk*. For example, since a single sector in an IBM PC disk can hold 512 bytes, to read *n* sectors the buffer size must be at least $n \times 512$ bytes.

The service requested from *_bios_disk* can be specified by using the mnemonic service names for the six services defined in the *bios.h* header file. These are summarized in Table 16-8.

1. The Turbo C and Turbo C++ version of this function is *biosdisk*.

COMMON USES This function is useful for developing disk utilities that allow the user to read and examine individual sectors and format disks, perhaps providing an alternative to the DOS FORMAT command with a nicer user interface.

Table 16-8. ***Disk Service Codes Accepted by _bios_***

Service	Function Performed	Fields of diskinfo_t Used
_DISK_RESET	Resets the floppy disk controller, so that status is set to zero to indicate that no error has occurred. Useful for resetting after an error.	None
_DISK_STATUS	Gets status of last disk operation. See description of *Returns* below for details of the status code.	
_DISK_READ	Reads specified number of sectors into buffer in memory. Return value indicates error, if any.	drive, head, track, sector, nsectors, buffer
_DISK_WRITE	Writes data from the memory buffer to specified number of sectors on the disk. This is the reverse of the _DISK_READ service.	drive, head, track, sector, nsectors, buffer
_DISK_VERIFY	First verifies that specified sectors exist and can be read. Then a cyclic redundancy check (CRC) is performed to verify that data in these sectors is correct. Since the stored data includes a CRC value it is possible to tell if any data has been corrupted. This service is similar to _DISK_READ except that the memory buffer is not used. Return value indicates error, if any.	drive, head, track, sector, nsectors
_DISK_FORMAT	Formats one track on one side (head) of the disk. This is similar to _DISK_WRITE except that sector information is not used. For proper formatting, the buffer pointer must point to a data area that contains four byte codes that describe the layout and the size of the sectors in that track.	

There are several commercial utility packages that allow you to "unerase" files and change file attributes, for example, to let you mark a file "hidden" so that it does not show up on directory listings. You can develop a similar function on your own by using the *_bios_disk* function.

RETURNS The *_bios_disk* function returns the contents of the *AX* register at the end of the call. Since it uses an INT 13h call, after a read, write, or verify operation, *AL* contains the total number of sectors for which the operation was to have been performed, while an 8-bit status code indicating success or cause of failure is returned in *AH*. When the operation is completed successfully, *AH* is zero. Thus, a good way to tell whether there has been an error is to compare the value returned by *_bios_disk* with the *nsectors* field of the *info* data structure. If they are equal, the operation went well. Otherwise the high-order byte of the return value contains the error code. The error codes are summarized in Table 16-9 (these error codes are also defined in the BIOS listings in the *IBM PC Technical Reference Manual*).

Table 16-9. ***Error Codes Returned by _bios_disk***

Contents of the High-Order Byte of Return Value (Hex)	Meaning of Error Code
01	Command not known to disk I/O system.
02	Could not find address marks that identify the side, track, sector, and sector size on soft-sectored disks.
03	Could not write because disk is write-protected.
04	Could not find specified sector.
05	Reset failed.
08	Data transfers can occur directly between the disk and the PC's memory in an interrupt-driven approach. This is known as Direct Memory Access (DMA) and there are DMA controller chips on the PC to perform this task. This error code means that some data was lost during a DMA transfer.
09	DMA transfers (see error code 8) are not allowed to write to memory across a 64-K boundary. This error indicates that there was an attempt to do this.
10	The disk controller stores a cyclic redundancy check (CRC) value for each sector of data. During a read operation it can compute the CRC value again and conclude whether the data has been corrupted. This error code tells us that the CRC check indicates an error.
20	Disk controller failed.
40	Could not move to requested track.
80	Disk drive timed out or failed to respond because the door is open or the drive motor has not come up to speed yet. A retry is recommended.

COMMENTS To make effective use of this function, you need a good understanding of how the MS-DOS file system is related to the physical tracks and sectors. Its use also calls for some care since the capability of formatting and writing data directly to sectors of a disk makes it possible to inadvertently damage existing files and, worse, destroy crucial sectors with information about how the sectors are allocated to files (e.g., the File Allocation Table [FAT]). Consult a book such as *MS-DOS Developer's Guide* by The Waite Group for detailed information on these topics.

SEE ALSO `int86x` *More general mechanism to access BIOS functions*

EXAMPLE Under MS-DOS, on double-sided double-density (9-track, 40-sector, 360-K) disks the directory entries begin at Track 0, Sector 6. A 512-byte sector has 16 directory entries, each 32 bytes long. The first 11 bytes of a directory entry contain the name of the file (8-character name followed by 3-character extension). Use *_bios_disk* to read the first directory sector from this disk and display the first 10 names found in it. By the way, if you have erased files or the disk is newly formatted, you may see some strange file names—this is perfectly normal. Also, if your disk has a volume name, it will be the first file name displayed.

```
#include <stdio.h>
#include <dos.h>
#include <bios.h>
#define DOS_DISPCHAR 2
main()
{
    int i, j, retry, strt;
    unsigned ch_out, status = 0;
    char buf[512];
    void far *pbuf;
    struct diskinfo_t info;

/* Set up diskette information and buffer pointer */
    pbuf = (void far *)(&buf[0]);
    info.buffer = pbuf;
    info.drive = 0;  /* Drive A, use 1 for drive B */
    info.head = 0;
    info.track = 0;
    info.sector = 6;  /* Location of first directory
                         entry for DSDD diskettes */
    info.nsectors = 1;

/* Read sector making up to 3 retries. Retries are
 * necessary to make sure that any error is not due to
 * motor start-up delay. See explanation for error code
 * 80h above.
 */
    for (retry = 0; retry <= 3; retry++)
    {
        if ((status = _bios_disk(_DISK_READ, &info))
            == info.nsectors)
        {
            printf("Read OK.\n");
            printf("First 10 directory entries are:\n");
            for (i=0; i<10; i++)
            {
                strt = 32*i; /* Each entry is 32-bytes */
                /* Each name is 11 bytes */
                for (j=0; j<11; j++)
                {
```

```
                    ch_out = buf[strt+j];
                    bdos(DOS_DISPCHAR, ch_out, 0);
                }
                printf("\n");
            }
            exit(0);
        }
    }

    /* Read failed despite 3 retries. Report error */
        printf("Error reading from diskette! status=%x\n",
            status);
    }
```

_bios_equiplist

COMPATIBILITY

MSC 3	MSC 4	MSC 5	MSC 6	QC1	QC2	QC2.5	TC1	TC1.5	TC2	TC++	ANSI	UNIX V	XNX	OS2	DOS
		▲	▲	▲	▲	▲		1	1	1					▲

PURPOSE Use *_bios_equiplist* to get information about the hardware and peripherals in the user's PC. The list of equipment is returned in coded form in a single unsigned integer, whose bit values are shown in Table 16-10.

SYNTAX
```
unsigned _bios_equiplist (void);
```

EXAMPLE CALL
```
equip_flag = _bios_equiplist();
```

INCLUDES `#include <bios.h>` *For declaration of function*

DESCRIPTION The *_bios_equiplist* function uses the BIOS interrupt 11h to get a list of hardware and peripherals currently installed in the PC. The combination of bits in the return value indicates the presence or absence of the hardware and peripherals specified in Table 16-10.

1. The Turbo C and Turbo C++ version of this function is *biosequip*.

RETURNS This function returns the contents of the *AX* register of BIOS interrupt 11h. The bits of the return value are interpreted as shown in Table 16-10. Note that bit 0 is the least significant bit.

COMMENTS This function is of limited usefulness. For example, bits 4 and 5 indicate the initial video mode, but not the current mode. The function does, however, provide such basic information as the number of RS232 serial ports, the number of disk drives, and the number of printers attached to the PC.

Table 16-10. *Meaning of Bits in Value Returned by _bios_equiplist*

Bits	Meaning
0	1 = one or more disk drives attached, 0 means no disk drives.
1	1 = a math coprocessor is present.
2–3	Size of system memory in units of 4 K.
4–5	Initial video mode (00 = unused, 01 = 40×25 black and white text with color card, 10 = 80×25 black and white text with color card, 11 = 80×25 text on monochrome card).
6–7	Number of disk drives installed (00 = 1, 01 = 2). Only floppy disk drives are reported.
8	Set to 0 only if a Direct Memory Access (DMA) chip is present.
9–11	Number of RS 232C serial ports in the system.
12	1 = a game adapter is installed.
13	1 = a serial printer is attached.
14–15	Number of printers attached to system.

SEE ALSO `int86` *For another way of generating BIOS interrupt 11h*

EXAMPLE Use the *_bios_equiplist* to obtain the number of disk drives, the number of serial ports, and the number of printers on the user's system and to determine if a math coprocessor is available. This approach can be used to ensure that the user's system has the minimal configuration necessary to run a program or to allow a program to use optional hardware.

```
#include <stdio.h>
#include <bios.h>
main()
{
    unsigned elist, d_drives=0, s_ports=0, printers=0;
    elist = _bios_equiplist();
/* Extract each item from the return value */
    if(elist & 0x0001)
    {
        d_drives = ((elist & 0x00c0) >> 6) + 1;
    }
    s_ports = (elist & 0x0e00) >> 9;
    printers = (elist & 0xc000) >> 14;
    printf("This system ");
    if((elist & 0x0002)>>1)
    {
        printf("has a math co-processor, ");
    }
```

```
        printf("%d diskette drives,\n", d_drives);
        printf("%d serial ports and %d printers\n",
                s_ports, printers);
}
```

_bios_keybrd

COMPATIBILITY

MSC 3	MSC 4	MSC 5	MSC 6	QC1	QC2	QC2.5	TC1	TC1.5	TC2	TC++	ANSI	UNIX V	XNX	OS2	DOS
		▲	▲	▲	▲	▲		1	1	1					▲

PURPOSE Use *_bios_keybrd* to access the BIOS routines for keyboard I/O. You can use it to read the next available character, to check if a character is waiting to be read, and to check if the special keys such as ALT, CTRL, and SHIFT are being pressed.

SYNTAX

```
unsigned _bios_keybrd (unsigned service);

unsigned service;       Keyboard function requested
```

EXAMPLE CALL

```
ch_read = _bios_keybrd(_KEYBRD_READ) & 0xff;
```

INCLUDES

```
#include <bios.h>       For definition of function and service codes
```

DESCRIPTION The *_bios_keybrd* routine accesses the BIOS keyboard services by generating 8086 interrupt number 16h. The service to be performed is specified by one of the mnemonic constants that are defined in *bios.h*. The service names and the tasks they perform are summarized in Table 16-11.

1. The Turbo C and Turbo C++ version of this function is *bioskey*.

Table 16-11. *Services Offered by* _bios_keybrd

Name	Service Performed
_KEYBRD_READ	Reads next available character from the keyboard buffer. Waits for a character if necessary. (See *Returns* for more information.)
_KEYBRD_READY	Checks the keyboard buffer for characters waiting to be read. (See *Returns* for explanation.)
_KEYBRD_SHIFTSTATUS	Returns current status of the SHIFT, CTRL, and ALT keys and indicates whether the SCROLL LOCK, NUM LOCK, and CAPS LOCK indicators are on.

RETURNS After the call *_bios_keybrd(_KEYBRD_READ)*, the low-order byte of the return value contains the ASCII code of the character just read, and the high-order byte has the *scan code*—a unique byte generated by the keyboard when a key is either pressed or released. (See the *IBM PC Technical Reference Manual* for a list of the scan codes for its keyboard.) The character read is removed from the buffer.

The *_KEYBRD_READY* service returns a 0 if the keyboard buffer is empty. Otherwise it returns the character in the same way that *_KEYBRD_READ* does, but it does not remove the character from the buffer.

The *_KEYBRD_SHIFTSTATUS* service returns in the low-order byte of the return value the current settings of the three LED indicators (CAPS LOCK, NUM LOCK, and SCROLL LOCK) and whether any of the SHIFT, ALT, or CTRL keys are being pressed. As shown in Table 16-12, one bit is used to represent each status.

Table 16-12. ***Interpreting SHIFT Status Byte Returned by _bios_keybrd***

Bit	Interpretation When Bit Is a 1
0	Right SHIFT key pressed.
1	Left SHIFT key pressed.
2	CTRL key pressed.
3	ALT key pressed.
4	Scroll Lock indicator is ON.
5	Num Lock indicator is ON.
6	Caps Lock indicator is ON.
7	In INSERT mode.

COMMENTS The *_KEYBRD_READY* service is very helpful when you want to continue doing something until the user presses a key. You can do your work in a loop, using this service to see if a key has been pressed. Since this service does not wait for a character to be typed, you can continue the work but respond quickly to the user's keystrokes. The *kbhit* function also provides this service and is easier to use.

SEE ALSO `int86` *Alternate ways to access BIOS keyboard functions using interrupt 16h*

`kbhit` *Another way to check for a keypress*

EXAMPLE Use the *_KEYBRD_READY* service to check if a key has been pressed. If not, keep updating a count until a key is pressed or the count is 50000.

```
#include <stdio.h>
#include <bios.h>

main()
{
    unsigned count=0, ch_hit=0;
    while(count<50000)
    {
        if(_bios_keybrd(_KEYBRD_READY))
        {
/* Read the keystroke and mask out the high byte */
            ch_hit = _bios_keybrd(_KEYBRD_READ) & 0xff;
            printf("You entered: %c\n", ch_hit);
        }
        count++;
    }
    printf("Count is %d\n", count);
}
```

_bios_memsize

COMPATIBILITY

MSC 3	MSC 4	MSC 5	MSC 6	QC1	QC2	QC2.5	TC1	TC1.5	TC2	TC++	ANSI	UNIX V	XNX	OS2	DOS
		▲	▲	▲	▲	▲		1	1	1					▲

PURPOSE Use *_bios_memsize* to determine the amount of memory in the PC. A program can use this to check if there is enough memory for it to run.

SYNTAX `unsigned _bios_memsize (void);`

EXAMPLE CALL `total_kilobytes = _bios_memsize();`

INCLUDES `#include <bios.h>` *For declaration of function*

DESCRIPTION This function gets the amount of memory in the system by using BIOS interrupt 12h.

1. The Turbo C and Turbo C++ version of this function is *biosmemory*.

RETURNS The return value is the total memory in the system in 1-K (1,024 bytes) blocks.

EXAMPLE Check the amount of memory on the system using *_bios_memsize*.

```
#include <bios.h>
main()
{
    unsigned memsize;
    memsize = _bios_memsize();
    printf("This system has %dK memory.\n", memsize);
}
```

COMPATIBILITY

_bios_printer

MSC 3	MSC 4	MSC 5	MSC 6	QC1	QC2	QC2.5	TC1	TC1.5	TC2	TC++	ANSI	UNIX V	XNX	OS2	DOS
		▲	▲	▲	▲	▲		1	1	1					▲

PURPOSE Use *_bios_printer* to initialize the printer, determine its status, and send characters to it.

SYNTAX

```
unsigned _bios_printer (unsigned service,
                        unsigned printer, unsigned data);
```

`unsigned service;` *Printer function requested*

`unsigned printer;` *Printer port, 0=LPT1 and 1=LPT2*

`unsigned data;` *Character being sent to printer*

EXAMPLE CALL `_bios_printer(_PRINTER_WRITE, LPT1, 'x');`

INCLUDES `#include <bios.h>` *For definition of function codes*

DESCRIPTION The *_bios_printer* function is an interface to the BIOS printer routines accessible through software interrupt 17h. The routine performs the service indicated by the argument *service* on the printer port selected by the argument *printer*, using the *data* where needed. Request the service by using the constants that are defined in *bios.h*. Table 16-13 shows these service codes.

1. The Turbo C and Turbo C++ version of this function is *biosprint*.

RETURNS The low-order byte of the return value represents the status of the printer. The meanings of the bits are shown in Table 16-14.

SEE ALSO `int86` *For another way to access the BIOS printer services*

Table 16-13. ***Service Codes for _bios_printer***

Name	Service Performed
_PRINTER_STATUS	Returns status of the printer. (See *Returns* for meaning.)
_PRINTER_INIT	Initializes printer connected to specified port. Note that *printer* = 0 means LPT1 and 1 means LPT2 and so on. The value of *data* is ignored. The status is returned.
_PRINTER_WRITE	Sends the low-order byte of *data* to the printer and returns the status after the operation.

EXAMPLE Use *_bios_printer* to initialize a printer at port LPT1 and print a line if the printer is ready.

```
#include <stdio.h>
#include <bios.h>
#define LPT1 0
char str[] = "\rTesting BIOS priniting routine\n\r";
main()
{
    unsigned status, data;
    int i;
    status = _bios_printer(_PRINTER_INIT, LPT1, data);
    for (i=0; str[i] != '\0'; i++)
    {
        data = str[i];
        _bios_printer(_PRINTER_WRITE, LPT1, data);
    }
}
```

Table 16-14. ***Interpreting Status Byte of Printer***

Bit	Interpretation when Bit Is a 1
0	Printer has timed out.
1	Not used.
2	Not used.
3	I/O error has occurred.
4	Printer is selected for output.
5	Printer is out of paper.
6	Acknowledgment from printer.
7	Printer not busy (if bit is 0, printer is busy).

COMPATIBILITY

_bios_serialcom

MSC 3	MSC 4	MSC 5	MSC 6	QC1	QC2	QC2.5	TC1	TC1.5	TC2	TC++	ANSI	UNIX V	XNX	OS2	DOS
		▲	▲	▲	▲	▲		1	1	1					▲

PURPOSE Use *_bios_serialcom* to access the RS232 serial ports (either COM1 or COM2) of the PC. You can use this function to perform "polled" I/O, set communications parameters (for example, baud rate, parity, etc.), and check the status of the port.

SYNTAX

```
unsigned _bios_serialcom (unsigned service, unsigned port,
                                            unsigned data);
```

`unsigned service;` *Service requested*

`unsigned port;` *Serial port number, 0=COM1 and 1=COM2*

`unsigned data;` *Character to be sent or communications parameters*

EXAMPLE CALL

```
ch_rcvd = 0xff & _bios_serialcom(_COM_RECEIVE, COM1, 0);
```

INCLUDES `#include <bios.h` *For definition of function codes*

DESCRIPTION This function lets you use the services offered by the BIOS routines normally accessible by interrupt number 14h. Only the ports COM1 and COM2 can be handled by this routine. The argument *port* specifies the port number: a 0 means COM1 and a 1 indicates COM2. The function performs the service requested in the argument *service* using the *data* where necessary. The service codes, defined in *bios.h*, are shown in Table 16-15. They can be used as the *service* argument.

Table 16-15. *Service Codes for* _bios_serialcom

Name	Service Performed
_COM_INIT	Initializes the serial port using the communications parameters given in *data*. (See Table 16-16 for the parameters.)
_COM_SEND	Sends the character in the low-order byte of *data* over the serial port *port*.
_COM_RECEIVE	Receives a character from *port* and returns it in the low-order byte of the return value.
_COM_STATUS	Returns the current status of the port. (See *Returns* for more details.)

Several communications parameters must be initialized before using the serial port: word length; number of bits that make one character; number of stop bits, indicating the end of a character; parity to be used; and baud rate, indicating how fast the port sends the bits that make up a single character. The *_bios_serialcom* function makes specifying the parameters simple: pick a constant from each of the four categories shown in Table 16-16 and logically OR them together to construct the unsigned argument *data*. For example, if you select an 8-bit word length, 1 stop bit, no parity, and a baud rate of 300 baud, you would use

```
(_COM_CHR8 | _COM_STOP1 | _COM_NOPARITY | _COM_300)
```

as the *data* argument with the service code _COM_INIT (the bar separating the values is the bitwise OR operator).

1. The Turbo C and Turbo C++ version of this function is *bioscom*.

Table 16-16. *Constants for Selecting Communications Parameters*

Category Name	List of Constants	Communications Parameter Setting
Word length	_COM_CHR7	7 bits per character
	_COM_CHR8	8 bits per character
Stop bits	_COM_STOP1	1 stop bit
	_COM_STOP2	2 stop bits
Parity	_COM_NOPARITY	No parity bit
	_COM_EVENPARITY	Even parity—parity bit is such that total number of 1s is even
	_COM_ODDPARITY	Odd parity—parity bit is such that total number of 1s is odd
Baud rate	_COM_110	110 baud
	_COM_150	150 baud
	_COM_300	300 baud
	_COM_600	600 baud
	_COM_1200	1200 baud
	_COM_2400	2400 baud
	_COM_4800	4800 baud
	_COM_9600	9600 baud

COMMON USES The *_bios_serialcom* function is useful for simple polled I/O from the serial port at baud rates of up to 300 baud. Beyond this rate, the characters arrive so fast that your program cannot keep up. For higher performance, it is necessary to use an interrupt-driven approach in which the serial port invokes an interrupt handler when it needs attention. (See Chapter 13 of *MS-DOS Papers* by The Waite Group for an example of an interrupt-driven serial I/O package.)

System Calls

RETURNS The high-order byte of the return value represents the status of the communications port. The meanings of the specific bits are shown in Table 16-17. For the _COM_SEND service, the low-order byte of the return value should contain the character just sent out. As is shown in the table, if bit 15 is set, the character was not sent because the port was not ready within a specified period of time. When reading a character from the serial port using the _COM_RECEIVE service, the low-order byte of the return value is the character just read, provided none of the bits in the high-order byte is set. If any bit in the high-order byte is set, an error has occurred and the cause of the error is indicated by the bit that is set.

Table 16-17. ***Interpreting Status of Serial Port***

Bit	Interpretation when Bit Is a 1
8	Received data is ready.
9	Data overrun error occurred (a character was received before the last one was read).
10	Parity error occurred.
11	Framing error occurred (the end of a character was not recognized properly).
12	"Break" signal was detected (meaning that the signal on the receive line went dead for a while).
13	Register that holds a character to be transmitted is empty.
14	Shift register that moves the character out for transmission is empty.
15	Serial port has timed out.

For the _COM_INIT and _COM_STATUS services the low-order byte contains the status of the modem. The meanings of the bits in this case are shown in Table 16-18.

Table 16-18. ***Modem Status***

Bit	Interpretation when Bit Is a 1
0	Change in "Clear To Send" signal (see bit 4).
1	Change in "Data Set Ready" signal (see bit 5).
2	Trailing edge ring indicator.
3	Change detected in quality of signal in the receive line.
4	Clear To Send (meaning modem is ready to receive data from the serial port).
5	Data Set Ready (meaning modem is connected to phone line).
6	Modem is receiving a "ring" voltage (meaning an incoming telephone call is detected).
7	Signal detected in the receive line.

SEE ALSO `int86` *For access to the BIOS serial I/O services through 8086 software interrupt number 14h*

EXAMPLE Use *_bios_serialcom* to set up the serial port at 300 baud, 8-bit word length, 1 stop bit, and no parity. If you have a Hayes-compatible modem connected, once you have set the port, you can try conversing with it. For example, if you type AT, the modem should answer back with an OK (if there is no response try typing ATE1V1 to set up the modem properly). Assume that you are using the COM1 port.

```
#include <stdio.h>
#include <bios.h>
#define COM1 0
main()
{
    int ch_hit;
    unsigned service, data, status;
    data = (_COM_CHR8 | _COM_STOP1 |_COM_NOPARITY |
            _COM_300);
    _bios_serialcom(_COM_INIT, COM1, data);
    printf("Connecting to serial port 1. \
Type 'q' to exit\n");

    while(1)
    {
/* First see if "DATA READY" flag is set. If yes read
 * character from serial port.
 */
        status = 0x100 &
                 _bios_serialcom(_COM_STATUS, COM1, 0);
        if (status == 0x100)
        {
/* If there is a character, get it and display it */
            ch_hit = 0xff &
                _bios_serialcom(_COM_RECEIVE, COM1, 0);
            printf("%c", ch_hit);
        }

/* Now check if any key has been pressed */
        if(_bios_keybrd(_KEYBRD_READY))
        {
/* If yes, read the keyboard buffer */
            ch_hit = _bios_keybrd(_KEYBRD_READ) & 0xff;
            if((ch_hit == 'q') || (ch_hit == 'Q'))
            {
```

```
/* Exit if it's a 'q' or a 'Q' */
                printf("Exiting...\n");
                exit(0);
            }

/* Else, wait until "transmit holding register empty"
 * flag is set. Once it's set, send out character to
 * serial port.
 */
            status = 0x2000 &
                _bios_serialcom(_COM_STATUS, COM1, 0);
            while (status != 0x2000)
            {
                status = 0x2000 &
                _bios_serialcom(_COM_STATUS, COM1, 0);
            }
            _bios_serialcom(_COM_SEND, COM1, ch_hit);
            if ((status & 0x8000) == 0x8000)
            {
                printf("Error sending: %c\n", ch_hit);
            }
        }
    }
}
```

COMPATIBILITY

_bios_timeofday

MSC 3	MSC 4	MSC 5	MSC 6	QC1	QC2	QC2.5	TC1	TC1.5	TC2	TC++	ANSI	UNIX V	XNX	OS2	DOS
		▲	▲	▲	▲	▲		1	1	1					▲

PURPOSE Use the *_bios_timeofday* function to retrieve or set the current system clock count on the PC. The clock count is incremented 18.2 times a second, so you can use this function to wait for a specified number of seconds, albeit with a resolution of 1/18.2 second (or about 55 milliseconds) only.

SYNTAX

```
unsigned _bios_timeofday (unsigned service, long *clockcount);
```

`unsigned service;` *Service requested*

`long *clockcount;` *Timer clock counts*

EXAMPLE CALL

```
_bios_timeofday(_TIME_GETCLOCK, &clock_count);
```

INCLUDES `#include <bios.h>` *For definition of service codes*

DESCRIPTION The *_bios_timeofday* function invokes the ROM BIOS time-of-day interrupt (number 1Ah) to get the current clock count or to reset the clock count to a new value. Incremented 18.2 times a second, the count can serve as a timer with a resolution of 1/18.2 second (or 55 milliseconds). The service requested is specified by using a constant defined in *bios.h*. Table 16-19 explains the use of the service codes.

Table 16-19. *Service Codes for* _bios_timeofday

Name	Service Performed
_TIME_GETCLOCK	Copies the current value of the clock count into the long integer that *clockcount* points to. The function returns 1 if midnight has passed since the clock was last read or set; otherwise the return value is 0.
_TIME_SETCLOCK	Sets the current system clock count to the value specified in the long integer that *clockcount* points to. The return value is unspecified.

1. The Turbo C and Turbo C++ version of this function is *biostime*.

COMMON USES This function is useful in writing delay routines that wait for a specified number of seconds before returning.

RETURNS The return value is defined only when *service* is _TIME_GETCLOCK. In this case, a return value of 1 indicates that midnight has passed since the last time the clock was read.

COMMENTS One drawback of using *_bios_timeofday* as a timer is the coarseness of the clock counts which are updated once every 55 milliseconds only.

SEE ALSO `int86` *For general purpose access to BIOS INT 1Ah services*

EXAMPLE Write a routine that uses *_bios_timeofday* to wait for a specified number of seconds before exiting.

```
#include <stdio.h>
#include <bios.h>

main()
{
    long oldcount, newcount;
    int ticks;
    printf("How many seconds to wait? ");
```

```
        scanf("%d", &ticks);
        ticks *= 18.2;
        _bios_timeofday(_TIME_GETCLOCK, &oldcount);
        newcount =oldcount;
        while ((newcount-oldcount) < ticks)
        {
            _bios_timeofday(_TIME_GETCLOCK, &newcount);
        }
        printf("\nWaited for %d clock ticks\n", ticks);
}
```

COMPATIBILITY

_chain_intr

MSC 3	MSC 4	MSC 5	MSC 6	QC1	QC2	QC2.5	TC1	TC1.5	TC2	TC++	ANSI	UNIX V	XNX	OS2	DOS
		▲	▲	▲	▲	▲									▲

PURPOSE Use *_chain_intr* to jump from one interrupt handler to another. For example, you can write your own interrupt handler for a particular interrupt and after performing the tasks you want done, you can call *_chain_intr* to jump to the interrupt handler originally installed.

SYNTAX

```
void _chain_intr (void (interrupt _far *handler)());

interrupt _far *handler;
```

Far pointer to the handler, a function of type interrupt

EXAMPLE CALL

```
void (interrupt _far *old_handler)();
_chain_intr(old_handler);
```

INCLUDES

```
#include <dos.h>
```

For declaration of function

DESCRIPTION The *_chain_intr* function simply jumps to the address of the interrupt handler specified in the argument *handler*, which is a far pointer to an interrupt handler. The handler is a function of type *interrupt*, a keyword introduced in version 5.0 to allow writing interrupt handlers in C. (See Chapter 1 for more information on the *interrupt* attribute.)

If you want to chain the existing interrupt handler to the one you are writing, you can first get the address of the old handler by calling the function *_dos_getvect*. Then in your own interrupt handler, after completing all processing, you can perform the chaining by invoking *_chain_intr* with the old handler's address as the argument.

COMMON USES This function is useful in writing interrupt handlers in Microsoft C 5.0 and later. When you want something extra done during a certain interrupt and yet want to retain all the old functions, you can install your own interrupt handler for that interrupt only and chain to the old interrupt vector from within your handler.

COMMENTS You need an understanding of the 8086 interrupt mechanism before you can make effective use of this function. See the tutorial section for some background information and further references.

SEE ALSO

`_dos_getvect` *To get the address of the current interrupt handler for an interrupt*

`_dos_setvect` *To install a new interrupt vector*

`_dos_keep` *To install "terminate and stay resident" programs*

EXAMPLE Use the *_dos_getvect* function to get and save the current address of the interrupt handler for the BIOS video interrupts (number 10h). Now install your own interrupt handler using *_dos_setvect.* In your interrupt handler, chain to the old handler by using the *_chain_intr* function. Try something with the video interrupt to see if this scheme works. For example, you can use the function that allows you to change the cursor shape and see if everything works. Before exiting, reset the interrupt vector to its original state. (Notice the use of the *_disable* and *_enable* pair to ensure that nothing goes wrong while we are taking over an interrupt vector.)

```
#include <stdio.h>
#include <dos.h>
#define BIOS_VIDEO 0x10
void interrupt far vio_handler(void);
void (interrupt far *old_handler)();
main()
{
    union REGS xr, yr;
    unsigned c;
    unsigned intno = BIOS_VIDEO;
    old_handler = _dos_getvect(intno);
/* Print out address of old handler using %p format */
    printf("\nThe address of the old handler is : %p\n",
           old_handler);
/* Install the new handler named vio_handler
 * Disable interrupts when changing handler
 */
    _disable();
    _dos_setvect(intno, vio_handler);
    _enable();
    printf("Installed new handler: %p\n", vio_handler);
```

```
/* Do some video I/O -- change cursor to a solid block*/
    xr.h.ah = 1;
    xr.h.ch = 0;
    xr.h.cl = 8;
    int86(BIOS_VIDEO, &xr, &yr);
/* Quit when user says so */
    printf("Hit q to quit: ");
    while ((c=getch()) != 'q'); /* Keep looping till 'q'*/
/* Reset vector. Disable interrupts when doing this      */
    _disable();
    _dos_setvect(intno, old_handler);
    _enable();
}
/*----------------------------------------------------*/
void interrupt far vio_handler()
{
/* Our handler simply chains to the old_handler using
 * the library routine _chain_intr.
 */
    _chain_intr(old_handler);
}
```

COMPATIBILITY

_disable

MSC 3	MSC 4	MSC 5	MSC 6	QC1	QC2	QC2.5	TC1	TC1.5	TC2	TC++	ANSI	UNIX V	XNX	OS2	DOS
		▲	▲	▲	▲	▲		1	1	1					▲

PURPOSE Use the *_disable* function to turn off interrupts on the 8086 microprocessor by a *CLI* instruction. You may, for example, want to turn off interrupts when installing a new handler for an interrupt. Remember to call *_enable* to turn interrupts back on as soon as possible.

SYNTAX `void_disable(void);`

EXAMPLE CALL `_disable();`

INCLUDES `#include <dos.h>` *For function declaration*

DESCRIPTION The *_disable* function executes an 8086 *CLI* instruction.

1. The Turbo C and Turbo C++ version of this function is *disable.*

COMMON USES The *_disable* function is useful when interrupts have to be turned off in critical sections of a program. Such cases typically arise in programs that install or remove interrupt handlers (see the tutorial section).

COMMENTS The *_disable* function was not present in earlier versions of Microsoft C (3.0 or 4.0). The addition of this function greatly enhances your capability to write software with interrupt handlers almost entirely in C, but you must be careful because of its intimate ties to the hardware. You should understand the interrupt mechanism of the 8086 microprocessor before using this function. In particular, the system clock is updated by interrupts so disabling interrupts for long periods of time interferes with the time-keeping. This function is a good example of the low-level access to hardware afforded by Microsoft C on the IBM PC.

SEE ALSO `_enable` *To enable 8086 interrupts*

EXAMPLE See the example in the reference page on *_dos_setvect* for a sample usage of *_disable.*

_dos_allocmem

COMPATIBILITY

MSC 3	MSC 4	MSC 5	MSC 6	QC1	QC2	QC2.5	TC1	TC1.5	TC2	TC++	ANSI	UNIX V	XNX	OS2	DOS
		▲	▲	▲	▲	▲		1	1	1					▲

PURPOSE Use *_dos_allocmem* to allocate memory in 16-byte chunks (called "paragraphs") from a pool maintained by DOS. Remember to free the memory using the companion function *_dos_freemem* when you no longer need it.

SYNTAX

```
unsigned _dos_allocmem (unsigned npara, unsigned *segadd);
```

`unsigned npara;` *Number of 16-byte paragraphs to be allocated*

`unsigned *segadd;` *Segment address of allocated memory*

INCLUDES `#include <dos.h>` *For declaration of function*

DESCRIPTION The *_dos_allocmem* function calls the DOS function 48h to allocate the paragraphs of memory requested in the argument *npara* and return the segment address of the block through the unsigned integer to which the argument *segadd* points. If the requested amount of memory could not be allocated, *_dos_allocmen* sets **segadd* to the maximum available memory size (in paragraphs). The offset is always zero. The address of the allocated memory should be saved for use in freeing the block later with *_dos_freemem.*

1. The Turbo C and Turbo C++ version of this function is *allocmem.*

RETURNS This function returns 0 if memory was successfully allocated. If unsuccessful, the return value is an MS-DOS error code (see the reference page on *dosexterr* for a list of codes) and the global variable *errno* is set to the constant ENOMEM, indicating that not enough memory is available.

COMMENTS The *_dos_allocmem* and *_dos_freemem* functions are MS-DOS specific. Other memory allocation functions (for example, *malloc, calloc, free*) are more portable (for example, when moving your program to UNIX). It is interesting to note that the standard allocation routines use a memory pool that the Microsoft C startup routine gets by requesting a chuck of memory from DOS using the same DOS function that *_dos_allocmem* invokes.

SEE ALSO

`_dos_freemem`	*To free up memory allocated by* _dos_allocmem
`_dos_setblock`	*To alter the size of the chunk allocated by* _dos_allocmem
`alloca, calloc, halloc, malloc`	*Other memory allocation routines*

EXAMPLE Use the *_dos_allocmem* to allocate 5 paragraphs of memory, enough to hold 80 characters. Store a string in the allocated buffer, print the string, and free the allocated buffer.

```
#include <stdio.h>
#include <dos.h>
#include <memory.h>
#define DOS_PRTSTR 0x09
char str[80]="Testing _dos_allocmem...\n$";
main()
{
    union REGS xr;
    struct SREGS sr;
    char far *stradd;
    unsigned int segadd;
    stradd = (char far *)(&str[0]);
    if (_dos_allocmem(5, &segadd) != 0)
    {
        printf("Memory allocation failed!\n");
        exit(0);
    }
/* Copy string into allocated memory using movedata */
    movedata(FP_SEG(stradd),FP_OFF(stradd),
             segadd, 0, 80);
    sr.ds = segadd;
```

```
        xr.x.dx = 0;
        xr.h.ah = DOS_PRTSTR;
        intdosx(&xr, &xr, &sr);

    /* Free memory before exiting */
        _dos_freemem(segadd);
    }
```

_dos_close

COMPATIBILITY

MSC 3	MSC 4	MSC 5	MSC 6	QC1	QC2	QC2.5	TC1	TC1.5	TC2	TC++	ANSI	UNIX V	XNX	OS2	DOS
		▲	▲	▲	▲	▲		1	1	1					▲

PURPOSE Use *_dos_close* to close a file that you opened by calling *_dos_open* or that you created by using *_dos_creat* or *_dos_creatnew.*

SYNTAX

```
unsigned _dos_close (int filehandle);

int filehandle;       The file handle or identifier
```

EXAMPLE CALL

```
_dos_close(handle);
```

INCLUDES `#include <dos.h>` *For declaration of function*

DESCRIPTION The *_dos_close* function calls DOS function 3Eh to close the file specified by the identifying number, or handle, in the argument *filehandle.* The file handle must be the one returned when the file was opened by *_dos_open* or created by *_dos_creat* or *_dos_creatnew.* The *_dos_close* operation involves flushing (writing) to the disk internal MS-DOS buffers associated with that file, closing the file, and releasing the handle for reuse. The date stamp, the time stamp, and the file size are also updated.

1. The Turbo C and Turbo C++ version of this function is *_close.*

RETURNS This function returns 0 if successful; otherwise, it returns the MS-DOS error code and sets the global variable *errno* to the constant EBADF, indicating that the file handle is invalid.

COMMENTS The functions *open* and *close* offer a more portable means of achieving the same result as this DOS-specific function.

SEE ALSO `_dos_open` *To open an existing file using a DOS call*

`_dos_creat,` `_dos_creatnew`	*To create a new file*
`open, close`	*Portable versions of similar file opening and closing functions*

EXAMPLE Use *_dos_close* to close a file opened by *_dos_open*.

```
#include <stdio.h>
#include <fcntl.h>
#include <dos.h>
main()
{
    char fname[40], *p_fname;
    int filehandle;

    printf("Enter name of file to open using \
_dos_open: ");
    p_fname = gets(fname);

/* Open the file using _dos_open */
    if (_dos_open(p_fname, O_RDONLY, &filehandle) != 0)
    {
        printf("Error opening file: %s\n", fname);
        exit(0);
    }
    printf("File %s opened.\n", fname);

/* Now close file */
    if (_dos_close(filehandle) != 0)
    {
        perror("Error closing file with _dos_close");
        exit(0);
    }
    printf("File %s closed.\n", fname);
}
```

_dos_creat

COMPATIBILITY

MSC 3	MSC 4	MSC 5	MSC 6	QC1	QC2	QC2.5	TC1	TC1.5	TC2	TC++	ANSI	UNIX V	XNX	OS2	DOS
		▲	▲	▲	▲	▲		1	1	1					▲

PURPOSE Use *_dos_creat* to create a new file or to truncate an existing file to zero length.

SYNTAX

```
unsigned _dos_creat (char *filename, unsigned attribute,
                                     int *filehandle);
```

`char *filename;` *File name, including path*

`unsigned attribute;` *Attributes of the file*

`int *filehandle;` *Pointer to location where the handle, or identifier, is returned*

EXAMPLE CALL

```
_dos_creat("c:\\tmptmp001", _A_NORMAL, &filehandle);
```

INCLUDES `#include <dos.h>` *For declaration of function and definition of attribute names*

DESCRIPTION The *_dos_creat* function calls the DOS function 3Ch to create the file whose name (including the DOS pathname) is specified by the argument *filename* and whose attributes are in the argument *attribute*. If the file already exists, it is truncated to zero length and its old attributes are retained.

The attribute indicates whether a file is read-only, whether it is hidden, and so on. You specify the attribute by using the bitwise OR of attribute names picked from Table 16-20. The attribute constants are defined in *dos.h*. Once the file is successfully opened, an identifying number, or handle, is returned in the location whose address is specified in the argument *filehandle*.

Table 16-20. *Interpretation of File Attribute Constants*

Name	Interpretation of Attribute
_A_NORMAL	Normal file without any read or write restrictions.
_A_RDONLY	File cannot be opened for write operations.
_A_HIDDEN	File will not show up on directory search.
_A_SYSTEM	File is marked as a system file and will be excluded from normal directory searches.
_A_VOLID	Volume name; can exist only in root directory.
_A_SUBDIR	Subdirectory name (meaning the file is a subdirectory).

Table 16-20. ***(cont.)***

Name	Interpretation of Attribute
_A_ARCH	If set, file will be archived by MS-DOS *BACKUP* command. This attribute is set after any changes to the file.

1. The Turbo C and Turbo C++ version of this function is *_creat.*

RETURNS This function returns 0 if successful; otherwise, it returns the MS-DOS error code and sets the global variable *errno* to one of the constants shown in Table 16-21.

Table 16-21. ***Error Codes Returned by*** **_dos_creat**

Error Code	Interpretation
ENOENT	Path not found.
EMFILE	Too many files open (limit is 20 for a process).
EACCES	Access denied. (For example, the file exists and cannot be overwritten or the root directory is full.)

COMMENTS The *creat* function provides a more portable means of achieving the same result as does this DOS-specific function.

Under MS-DOS, the maximum number of concurrently open files for a single process is 20.

SEE ALSO

`_dos_close` *To close a file*

`_dos_creatnew` *To create a new file but not overwrite existing ones*

`creat` *Portable versions of similar file creation function*

EXAMPLE Use *_dos_creat* to create a file. Close the file by calling *_dos_close.*

```
#include <stdio.h>
#include <dos.h>
main()
{
    char fname[40], *p_fname;
    int filehandle;

    printf("Enter name of file to create using \
_dos_creat: ");
    p_fname = gets(fname);
```

```
/* Create the file using _dos_creat */
    if (_dos_creat(p_fname, _A_NORMAL,
                            &filehandle) != 0)
    {
        perror("Error creating file");
        exit(0);
    }
    printf("File %s created.\n", fname);

/* Now close file */
    if (_dos_close(filehandle) != 0)
    {
        perror("Error closing file with _dos_close");
        exit(0);
    }
    printf("File %s closed.\n", fname);
}
```

_dos_creatnew

COMPATIBILITY

MSC 3	MSC 4	MSC 5	MSC 6	QC1	QC2	QC2.5	TC1	TC1.5	TC2	TC++	ANSI	UNIX V	XNX	OS2	DOS
		▲	▲	▲	▲	▲		1	1	1					▲

PURPOSE Use *_dos_creatnew* to create a new file. Unlike *_dos_creat*, this function does not overwrite an existing file.

SYNTAX

```
unsigned _dos_creatnew (char *filename, unsigned attribute,
                                        int *filehandle);
```

`char *filename;` *File name, including path*

`unsigned attribute;` *Attributes of the file*

`int *filehandle;` *Pointer to location where the handle, or identifier, is returned*

EXAMPLE CALL

```
_dos_creatnew("c:\\mscb\\toc.1", _A_NORMAL, &filehandle);
```

INCLUDES `#include <dos.h>` *For declaration of function and definition of attribute names*

DESCRIPTION The *_dos_creatnew* function calls the DOS function 5Bh to create the file whose name (including the full DOS pathname) is specified by the argu-

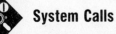

ment *filename* and whose attributes are in the argument *attribute*. This function fails if the file already exists.

The attribute indicates whether a file is read-only, hidden, and so on. You can specify the attribute by using the bitwise OR of attribute names picked from Table 16-21. The attribute constants are defined in *dos.h*.

Once the file is successfully opened, an identifying number, or handle, is returned in the location whose address is specified in the argument *filehandle*.

1. The Turbo C and Turbo C++ version of this function is *creatnew*.

RETURNS This function returns 0 if successful, otherwise, it returns the MS-DOS error code and sets the global variable *errno* to one of the constants shown in Table 16-22.

Table 16-22. ***Error Codes Returned by*** **_dos_creatnew**

Error Code	Interpretation
ENOENT	Path not found.
EMFILE	Too many files open (limit is 20 for a process).
EACCES	Access denied (for example, an attempt to create a file in a full root directory).
EEXIST	File already exists.

SEE ALSO

`_dos_close`	*To close a file*
`_dos_creat`	*To create a new file or to overwrite existing ones*
`creat`	*Portable versions of similar file creation function*

EXAMPLE Use *_dos_creatnew* to create a new file. Close the file by calling *_dos_close*.

```
#include <stdio.h>
#include <dos.h>
main()
{
    char fname[40], *p_fname;
    unsigned status;
    int filehandle;

    printf("Enter name of file to create: ");
    p_fname = gets(fname);
```

```
/* Create the file using _dos_creat */
    if((status = _dos_creatnew(p_fname, _A_NORMAL,
       &filehandle) != 0))
    {
        printf("Error creating file: %s\n", fname);
        if(status == EEXIST)
                printf("File already exists!\n");
        exit(0);
    }
    printf("File %s created.\n", fname);

/* Now close file */
    if (_dos_close(filehandle) != 0)
    {
        printf("Error closing file with _dos_close\n");
        exit(0);
    }
    printf("File %s closed.\n", fname);
}
```

_dos_findfirst

COMPATIBILITY

MSC 3	MSC 4	MSC 5	MSC 6	QC1	QC2	QC2.5	TC1	TC1.5	TC2	TC++	ANSI	UNIX V	XNX	OS2	DOS
		▲	▲	▲	▲	▲		1	1	1					▲

PURPOSE Use *_dos_findfirst* to find the first file whose name and attributes match the specified values. Since the specified name can have wildcard characters (* and ?), this function can find, for example, the first file with a *.C* extension by searching for all **.C* files.

SYNTAX

```
unsigned _dos_findfirst(char *filename, unsigned attribute,
                                        struct find_t *fileinfo);
```

`char *filename;` *File name to search for including path*

`unsigned attribute;` *File attributes to match*

`struct find_t *fileinfo;` *Structure to hold results of search*

EXAMPLE CALL

```
/* Search volume name */
_dos_findfirst("\*.*", _A_VOLID, &fileinfo);
```

INCLUDES `#include <dos.h>` *For declaration of function and definition of attribute names*

DESCRIPTION The *_dos_findfirst* function calls the DOS function 4Eh to get the information about the first file whose name matches the one in the character string *filename* and whose attributes are identical to those given in the argument *attribute*. The file name can have the * and *?* wildcard characters.

Specify the attribute to be matched by using a value created by the bitwise OR of attribute names picked from Table 16-21. These attribute constants are defined in *dos.h*.

The results of the search are returned in a structure of type *find_t*, which is defined in *dos.h*. A pointer to one structure must be provided in the argument *fileinfo*. The layout and C declaration of *dos.h* are shown below.

```
struct find_t
{
    char     reserved[21];  /* Reserved for use by MS-DOS */
    char     attrib;        /* Attribute byte of file     */
    unsigned wr_time;       /* Time of last file update   */
    unsigned wr_date;       /* Date of last file update   */
    long     size;          /* File's length in bytes     */
    char     name[13];      /* Null-terminated file name  */
};
```

After the function returns successfully, the field *name* contains the null-terminated name (not the entire path, just the file name and extension) of the first file that met the search criteria. The attribute of this file is copied into the field *attrib*. The date and time of last write to this file are in *wr_date* and *wr_time*. Finally, the long integer field *size* contains the length of the file in bytes.

1. The Turbo C and Turbo C++ version of this function is *findfirst*.

COMMON USES This function is commonly used with its companion *_dos_findnext* to find all occurrences of a file name with a wildcard specification such as all **.C* files.

RETURNS The function returns 0 if successful; otherwise, it returns the MS-DOS error code and sets the global variable *errno* to the constant ENOENT, indicating that the file could not be found.

SEE ALSO `_dos_findnext` *To get the next file that also meets search criteria*

EXAMPLE Use *_dos_findfirst* to find the volume name. You have to specify a search name *.* and an attribute of _A_VOLID to do this.

```
#include <stdio.h>
#include <dos.h>
main()
{
    struct find_t fileinfo;

    if (_dos_findfirst("\*.*", _A_VOLID,
                              &fileinfo) != 0)
    {
        printf("Unsuccessful _dos_findfirst call!\n");
        exit(0);
    }
    printf("The volume name is: %s\n",
            fileinfo.name);
}
```

_dos_findnext

COMPATIBILITY

MSC 3	MSC 4	MSC 5	MSC 6	QC1	QC2	QC2.5	TC1	TC1.5	TC2	TC++	ANSI	UNIX V	XNX	OS2	DOS
		▲	▲	▲	▲	▲		1	1	1					▲

PURPOSE Use *_dos_findnext* right after *_dos_findfirst* to find the remaining instances of files whose names and attributes match the values used during the *_dos_findfirst* call. You call *_dos_findnext* only if the file name specified in the call to *_dos_findfirst* contained one or more wildcard characters (* and ?). You can use this function to find, for example, all the files with a .C extension by searching for all **.C* files.

SYNTAX

```
unsigned _dos_findnext(struct find_t *fileinfo);

struct find_t *fileinfo;        Structure to hold results of search
```

EXAMPLE CALL

```
_dos_findnext(&fileinfo);
```

INCLUDES

```
#include <dos.h>        For declaration of function
```

DESCRIPTION The *_dos_findnext* function calls the DOS function 4Fh to find the next file whose name and attributes are identical to those given in the call to the *_dos_findfirst* function. The results of the search by *_dos_findnext* are returned in a structure of type *find_t*. You provide a pointer to a structure of this type in the argument *fileinfo* when calling *_dos_findnext*. The structure *find_t* is defined in *dos.h*; its layout and C declaration are shown in the description of the companion function *_dos_findfirst*.

After the function returns successfully, the field *name* contains the null-terminated name (not the entire path, just file name and extension) of the next file that met the search criteria. The attribute of this file is copied into the field *attrib* of the *find_t* structure. The date and time of the last write operation on this file are in *wr_date* and *wr_time*. Finally, *size* contains the length of the file in bytes.

1. The Turbo C and Turbo C++ version of this function is *findnext.*

COMMON USES This function is called in a loop right after *_dos_findfirst* to find the remaining occurrences of a file with a wildcard specification such as all **.C* files.

RETURNS The function returns zero if successful; otherwise, it returns the MS-DOS error code and sets the global variable *errno* to the constant ENOENT indicating that the search failed.

SEE ALSO `_dos_findfirst` *To begin the search and find the first file that meets the search criteria*

EXAMPLE Use *_dos_findnext* to find all files with a *.C* extension. You need to call *_dos_findfirst* to set up the search and get the first file that matches the specified name and attribute.

```
#include <stdio.h>
#include <dos.h>
main()
{
    int count;
    long totalsize;
    struct find_t fileinfo;
    if (_dos_findfirst("*.c", _A_NORMAL, &fileinfo)
        != 0)
    {
        printf("Unsuccessful _dos_findnext call!\n");
        exit(0);
    }
    printf("Listing of *.c files:\n");
    printf("%s    %d bytes\n", fileinfo.name,
                                fileinfo.size);
    count = 1;
    totalsize = fileinfo.size;
    while (_dos_findnext(&fileinfo) == 0)
    {
        count++;
        totalsize += fileinfo.size;
```

```
/* Now print the name and size of each matching file */
        printf("%s    %d bytes\n",
                fileinfo.name, fileinfo.size);
    }
    printf("\n%d files %d bytes.\n", count, totalsize);
}
```

_dos_freemem

COMPATIBILITY

MSC 3	MSC 4	MSC 5	MSC 6	QC1	QC2	QC2.5	TC1	TC1.5	TC2	TC++	ANSI	UNIX V	XNX	OS2	DOS
		▲	▲	▲	▲	▲		1	1	1					▲

PURPOSE Use *_dos_freemem* to free memory allocated with the *_dos_allocmem* function. Use the segment address returned by *_dos_allocmem* to indicate which chunk of memory you are freeing.

SYNTAX

```
unsigned _dos_freemem (unsigned segadd);

unsigned segadd;        Segment address of allocated memory
```

EXAMPLE CALL

```
_dos_freemem(segment);
```

INCLUDES `#include <dos.h>` *For declaration of function*

DESCRIPTION The *_dos_freemem* function calls DOS function 49h to free memory allocated with the *_dos_allocmem* function. The segment address of the block freed is specified through the unsigned integer *segadd*. The offset is always zero. This should be the same segment address that was returned by *_dos_allocmem* when the memory was allocated.

1. The Turbo C and Turbo C++ version of this function is *freemem.*

RETURNS This function returns 0 if memory was successfully released. Otherwise, the return value is the MS-DOS error code and the global variable *errno* is set to the constant ENOMEM, indicating a bad segment value.

SEE ALSO

`_dos_allocmem`	*The corresponding routine to allocate memory; also shows how to use* _dos_freemem
`_dos_setblock`	*To alter the size of the chunk allocated by* _dos_allocmem
`ffree, free, hfree, nfree`	*Other routines that release memory*

EXAMPLE Use *_dos_allocmem* to allocate 10 paragraphs of memory. Next call *_dos_freemem* to free this block of memory.

```
#include <stdio.h>
#include <dos.h>
main()
{
    unsigned segadd;
    if (_dos_allocmem(10, &segadd) != 0)
    {
        perror("Memory allocation failed");
        exit(0);
    }
    printf("10 paragraphs of memory allocated \n\
at segment address: %u\n", segadd);
/* Free memory before exiting */
    if(_dos_freemem(segadd) != 0)
    {
        perror("_dos_freemem failed");
    }
    else
    {
        printf("The memory is released now.\n");
    }
}
```

_dos_getdate

COMPATIBILITY

MSC 3	MSC 4	MSC 5	MSC 6	QC1	QC2	QC2.5	TC1	TC1.5	TC2	TC++	ANSI	UNIX V	XNX	OS2	DOS
		▲	▲	▲	▲	▲		1	1	1					▲

PURPOSE Use *_dos_getdate* to get the current system date, as maintained by DOS.

SYNTAX `void _dos_getdate (struct dosdate_t *date);`

`struct dosdate_t *date;` *Pointer to a structure that holds the components of date*

EXAMPLE CALL `_dos_getdate(&date);`

INCLUDES `#include <dos.h>` *For definition of the structure* dosdate_t

DESCRIPTION The *_dos_getdate* function calls DOS function 2Ah to get the current system date. The components of the date—the day, month, year, and day of the week—are stored in fields of the structure type *dosdate_t*, which is defined in *dos.h*. The layout of this structure and its C declaration are shown below.

```
struct dosdate_t
{
    unsigned char day;          /* day of the month (range 1-31) */
    unsigned char month;        /* month (range 1-12)            */
    unsigned int year;          /* year (range 1980-2099)        */
    unsigned char dayofweek;    /* Day of the week 0-6, 0=Sunday */
};
```

1. The Turbo C and Turbo C++ version of this function is *getdate*.

SEE ALSO

`_dos_setdate`	*The corresponding routine that sets the system date*
`_dos_gettime, _dos_settime`	*To get and set the system time*
`_strdate, _strtime, gmtime, localtime, mktime, time`	*Other date and time services*

EXAMPLE Use the *_dos_getdate* to get and display the current system date.

```
#include <stdio.h>
#include <dos.h>
main()
{
    struct dosdate_t date;
    _dos_getdate(&date);
    printf("Date: %d/%d/%d\n", date.month, date.day,
            date.year -1900);
}
```

_dos_getdiskfree

COMPATIBILITY

MSC 3	MSC 4	MSC 5	MSC 6	QC1	QC2	QC2.5	TC1	TC1.5	TC2	TC++	ANSI	UNIX V	XNX	OS2	DOS
		▲	▲	▲	▲	▲		1	1	1					▲

PURPOSE Use *_dos_getdiskfree* to determine the total capacity of a disk, as well as the amount of free space.

SYNTAX

```
unsigned _dos_getdiskfree(unsigned drive, struct diskfree_t *dfinfo);
```

```
unsigned drive;                  Drive number: 0=default, 1=A, 2=B

struct diskfree_t *dfinfo;       Structure to hold information on disk space
```

EXAMPLE CALL

```
_dos_getdiskfree (0, &dfinfo);
```

INCLUDES `#include <dos.h>` *For declaration of structure* diskfree_t

DESCRIPTION The *_dos_getdiskfree* function calls the DOS function 36h to retrieve information on the total and free disk space available on the drive specified by the argument *drive.* If the argument is a zero, information about the current default drive is returned; a value of 1 means drive A, 2 means B, and so on.

The requested information is returned in a structure of type *diskfree_t* whose address is specified in the argument *dfinfo.* The data structure is declared in *dos.h.* Its layout and C declaration are shown below.

```
struct diskfree_t
{
    unsigned total_clusters;
    unsigned avail_clusters;
    unsigned sectors_per_cluster;
    unsigned bytes_per_sector;
};
```

The information about disk space is returned as number of "clusters" on the disk and the number not in use. These values are in the fields *total_clusters* and *avail_clusters.* Since a cluster is a collection of sectors, by using the value given in *sectors_per_cluster* and the value from the field *bytes_per _sector,* we can compute in bytes the total disk space and the unused amount.

1. The Turbo C and Turbo C++ version of this function is *getdfree.*

COMMON USES This function can be used to verify that there is enough free space on the current disk before attempting a critical operation such as saving a file.

RETURNS The function returns a 0 if successful. In case of an error, it returns a nonzero and the global variable *errno* is set to EINVAL, indicating an invalid drive number.

SEE ALSO `_dos_getdrive, _dos_setdrive` *To get information about the current default drive or to change the current default*

EXAMPLE Use *_dos_getdiskfree* to display the total capacity of your drive in bytes and the amount not in use.

```
#include <stdio.h>
#include <dos.h>
main()
{
    unsigned long total_space, free_space,
                  bytes_per_cluster;
    struct diskfree_t dfinfo;
    if(_dos_getdiskfree (0, &dfinfo) !=0)
    {
        printf("Error in _dos_getdiskfree\n");
        exit(0);
    }
    bytes_per_cluster = dfinfo.sectors_per_cluster *
                        dfinfo.bytes_per_sector;
    total_space = dfinfo.total_clusters *
                  bytes_per_cluster;
    free_space = dfinfo.avail_clusters *
                 bytes_per_cluster;
    printf ("%ld bytes free out of %ld bytes of total \
space.\n", free_space, total_space);
}
```

_dos_getdrive

COMPATIBILITY

MSC 3	MSC 4	MSC 5	MSC 6	QC1	QC2	QC2.5	TC1	TC1.5	TC2	TC++	ANSI	UNIX V	XNX	OS2	DOS
		▲	▲	▲	▲	▲		1	1	1					▲

PURPOSE Use *_dos_getdrive* to determine the current default drive number.

SYNTAX `void _dos_getdrive (unsigned *driveno);`

`unsigned *driveno;` *Pointer to location where current default drive number is to be returned*

EXAMPLE CALL `_dos_getdrive(&drive_number);`

INCLUDES `#include <dos.h>` *For declaration of function*

DESCRIPTION The *_dos_getdrive* function calls the DOS function 19h to get the current default drive number. Before returning, it loads the drive number into the location whose address is in the argument *driveno*. The returned drive number is interpreted as follows: a 1 means drive A, a 2 means drive B, and so on.

1. The Turbo C and Turbo C++ version of this function is *getdisk*.

COMMON USES When you create a file or perform file I/O, DOS assumes you are referring to the file on the current default drive if a drive is not explicitly specified. The drive number returned by *_dos_getdrive* gives this default drive.

SEE ALSO _dos_setdrive *To change the current default drive number*

EXAMPLE Use *_dos_getdrive* to show the current default drive number.

```
#include <stdio.h>
#include <dos.h>
main()
{
    unsigned drive;
    _dos_getdrive(&drive);
    printf ("The current drive is: %c\n", drive+'A'-1);
}
```

COMPATIBILITY

_dos_getfileattr

MSC 3	MSC 4	MSC 5	MSC 6	QC1	QC2	QC2.5	TC1	TC1.5	TC2	TC++	ANSI	UNIX V	XNX	OS2	DOS
		▲	▲	▲	▲	▲		1	1	1					▲

PURPOSE Use *_dos_getfileattr* to get the attributes of a file. For example, you can determine if a file is a normal file or a subdirectory by using this function.

SYNTAX

```
unsigned _dos_getfileattr(char *filename, unsigned *attribute);
```

char *filename; *File name, including path*

unsigned *attribute; *Location to store attributes*

EXAMPLE CALL

```
_dos_getfileattr("c:\\autoexec.bat", &attribute);
```

INCLUDES #include <dos.h> *For declaration of function and definition of attribute names*

DESCRIPTION The *_dos_getfileattr* function calls DOS function 43h to get the attributes of the file whose name is in the character string *filename*. The argument *attribute* points to an unsigned integer whose low-order byte contains the attribute upon return.

The attribute indicates whether a file is read only, whether it is a subdirectory, and so on. You can test for an exact combination of attributes by comparing the returned attribute with the bitwise OR of attribute names picked from Table 16-20. The attribute constants are defined in *dos.h.*

Sometimes it is necessary to check only if a file has a certain attribute set. For example, if you want to determine whether a file has the archive attribute (_A_ARCH) set, you can do so by first performing a bitwise AND of the returned attribute value with _A_ARCH and comparing the result for equality with _A_ARCH. If the test succeeds, the attribute is set.

1. The Turbo C and Turbo C++ version of this function is *_chmod.*

RETURNS The function returns 0 if successful; otherwise, it returns the MS-DOS error code and sets the global variable *errno* to the constant ENOENT indicating that the file could not be found.

SEE ALSO `_dos_setfileattr` *To change the attributes of a file*

EXAMPLE Use *_dos_getfileattr* to check if a file whose name is provided by the user is a subdirectory.

```
#include <stdio.h>
#include <dos.h>
main()
{
    unsigned attribute;
    char filename[80], *p_fname;
    printf("Enter filename: ");
    p_fname = gets(filename);
    if (_dos_getfileattr(p_fname, &attribute) != 0)
    {
        printf("Error in _dos_getfileattr call!\n");
        exit(0);
    }
    if ( (attribute & _A_SUBDIR) == _A_SUBDIR )
    {
        printf("%s is a subdirectory.\n", filename);
    }
    else
    {
        printf("%s is NOT a subdirectory.\n", filename);
    }
}
```

COMPATIBILITY

_dos_getftime

MSC 3	MSC 4	MSC 5	MSC 6	QC1	QC2	QC2.5	TC1	TC1.5	TC2	TC++	ANSI	UNIX V	XNX	OS2	DOS
		▲	▲	▲	▲	▲		1	1	1					▲

PURPOSE Use *_dos_getftime* to get the date and time a file was last modified. To request this information, you need a handle returned by a function such as *_dos_open* or *_dos_creat.*

SYNTAX

```
unsigned _dos_getftime(int filehandle, unsigned *date,
                                          unsigned *time);
```

`int filehandle;` *The file handle, or identifier*

`unsigned *date;` *Pointer to location to hold date information*

`unsigned *time;` *Pointer to location to hold time information*

EXAMPLE CALL `_dos_getftime(handle, &date, &time);`

INCLUDES `#include <dos.h>` *For declaration of function*

DESCRIPTION For each file, DOS records the time and date the file was last modified: the information you get when you type the DIR command. The information is maintained in coded form. The date is stored in a 16-bit word whose bits are interpreted as follows:

Bits	Contents
0–4	Day of the month (value between 1 and 31).
5–8	Month (value between 1 and 12).
9–15	Years since 1980 (for example, 1988 is stored as 8).

The last update time of the file is also maintained in a 16-bit word:

Bits	Contents
0–4	Number of 2-second increments (value between 0 and 29).
5–10	Minutes (value between 0 and 59).
11–15	Hours (value between 0 and 23).

The *_dos_getftime* function calls the DOS function 57h to return the date and time information of the file specified by the identifying number, or handle, in the argument *filehandle.* The date and time information is returned in locations whose addresses are given in the arguments *date* and *time.* The file handle must be one returned when the file was opened by *_dos_open* or created by *_dos_creat* or *_dos_creatnew.*

1. The Turbo C and Turbo C++ version of this function is *getftime.*

RETURNS This function returns 0 if successful; otherwise, it returns the MS-DOS error code and sets the global variable *errno* to the constant EBADF, indicating that the file handle is invalid.

SEE ALSO

`_dos_setftime`	*To change the date and time stamp of a file*
`_dos_open`	*To open an existing file using a DOS call*
`_dos_creat, _dos_creatnew`	*To create a new file*

EXAMPLE Use *_dos_open* to open a file and then call *_dos_getftime* to display its date and time stamp.

```
#include <stdio.h>
#include <fcntl.h>
#include <dos.h>
main()
{
    char fname[40], *p_fname;
    int filehandle;
    unsigned date, time, day, month, year,
             hour, minute, second;

    printf("Enter name of an existing file: ");
    p_fname = gets(fname);

/* Open the file using _dos_open */
    if (_dos_open(p_fname, O_RDONLY, &filehandle) != 0)
    {
        printf("Error opening file: %s\n", fname);
        exit(0);
    }
    printf("File %s opened.\n", fname);

/* Get file's date and time stamp */
    _dos_getftime(filehandle, &date, &time);
```

```
/* Now decipher the return values */
    second = 2 * (time & 0x1f);
    minute = (time >> 5) & 0x3f;
    hour = (time >> 11) & 0x1f;
    day = date & 0x1f;
    month = (date >> 5) & 0xf;
/* NOTE: year is relative to 1980.
 * So we are adding 80.
 */
    year = ((date >> 9) & 0x7f) + 80;
    printf("File: %s  Date: %d-%d-%d Time: %.2d:%.2d:\
%.2d\n", fname, month, day, year, hour, minute, second);

/* Now close file */
    if (_dos_close(filehandle) != 0)
    {
        printf("Error closing file with _dos_close\n");
        exit(0);
    }
    printf("File %s closed.\n", fname);
}
```

COMPATIBILITY

_dos_gettime

MSC 3	MSC 4	MSC 5	MSC 6	QC1	QC2	QC2.5	TC1	TC1.5	TC2	TC++	ANSI	UNIX V	XNX	OS2	DOS
		▲	▲	▲	▲	▲		1	1	1					▲

PURPOSE Use *_dos_gettime* to get the current system time.

SYNTAX `void _dos_gettime (struct dostime_t *time);`

`struct dostime_t *time;` *Pointer to a structure that holds the components of time*

EXAMPLE CALL `_dos_gettime(&time_info);`

INCLUDES `#include <dos.h>` *For definition of the structure* dostime_t

DESCRIPTION The *_dos_gettime* function calls DOS function 2Ch to get the system time whose components—the hour, minute, second, and hundredth of a second—are stored in fields of the structure type *dostime_t*, which is defined in *dos.h*. The layout and C declaration of the structure *dostime_t* are shown below.

```
struct dostime_t
{
    unsigned char hour;     /* Hour (range 0-23)                   */
    unsigned char minute;   /* Minutes (range 0-59)                */
    unsigned char second;   /* Seconds (range 0-59)                */
    unsigned char hsecond;  /* Hundredth of a second (range 0-99) */
};
```

1. The Turbo C and Turbo C++ version of this function is *gettime.*

SEE ALSO

`_dos_settime`	*The corresponding routine that sets the system time*
`_dos_getdate,` `_dos_setdate`	*To get and set the system date*
`_strdate, _strtime,` `gmtime, localtime,` `mktime, time`	*Other date and time services*

EXAMPLE Use *_dos_gettime* to display the current system time.

```
#include <stdio.h>
#include <dos.h>
main()
{
    struct dostime_t time;
    _dos_gettime(&time);
    printf("Current time: %d:%d:%d.%d\n", time.hour,
            time.minute, time.second, time.hsecond);
}
```

_dos_getvect

COMPATIBILITY

MSC 3	MSC 4	MSC 5	MSC 6	QC1	QC2	QC2.5	TC1	TC1.5	TC2	TC++	ANSI	UNIX V	XNX	OS2	DOS
		▲	▲	▲	▲	▲		1	1	1					▲

PURPOSE Use *_dos_getvect* to get the current value of the interrupt vector for a specific interrupt number. The interrupt vector is the address of the routine that is invoked when the interrupt occurs.

SYNTAX

```
void (interrupt far *_dos_getvect (unsigned intno))();
```

`unsigned intno;` *Interrupt number whose handler's address is returned*

EXAMPLE CALL

```
void (interrupt far *int_handler)();
int_handler = _dos_getvect(int_number);
```

INCLUDES

`#include <dos.h>` *For declaration of function*

DESCRIPTION The *_dos_getvect* function calls the DOS function 35h to retrieve the address of the current interrupt handler for the interrupt specified in the argument *intno.*

1. The Turbo C and Turbo C++ version of this function is *getvect.*

COMMON USES This function is commonly used to get the address of the interrupt handler before setting it to a new value by calling the companion function *_dos_setvect.* Another use of this function is to get the address of certain tables that BIOS and DOS lets you access via interrupt vectors.

RETURNS The return value is a _far pointer to the interrupt handler, which is a function of type *interrupt,* a keyword introduced in version 5.0 to allow writing interrupt handlers in C (see Chapter 1 for more details).

SEE ALSO

`_dos_setvect` *To install a new interrupt handler*

EXAMPLE Use the *_dos_getvect* function to report the current interrupt vector corresponding to an interrupt number entered by the user. Try the interrupt number 18 (the vector to ROM-resident BASIC. On a PC-AT the vector should be F600:0000. On other machines, the technical reference guide may list the vector for resident BASIC.)

```
#include <stdio.h>
#include <dos.h>

main()
{
    void (interrupt _far *int_handler)();
    unsigned intno;
    printf("Enter interrupt number in hexadecimal \
format: ");
    scanf(" %x", &intno);
    int_handler = _dos_getvect(intno);
/* Print out address of handler using the %p format */
    printf("\nThe address of the handler is : %p\n",
            int_handler);
}
```

_dos_keep

COMPATIBILITY

MSC 3	MSC 4	MSC 5	MSC 6	QC1	QC2	QC2.5	TC1	TC1.5	TC2	TC++	ANSI	UNIX V	XNX	OS2	DOS
		▲	▲	▲	▲	▲		1	1	1					▲

PURPOSE Use *_dos_keep* to install "terminate-and-stay-resident" (TSR) programs.

SYNTAX

```
void _dos_keep(unsigned status, unsigned memsize);
```

`unsigned status;` *Status code to be returned to calling process*

`unsigned memsize;` *Size of memory needed by TSR program, in 16-byte paragraphs*

EXAMPLE CALL

```
_dos_keep(0, programsize_in_paragraphs);
```

INCLUDES `#include <dos.h>` *For declaration of function*

DESCRIPTION The *_dos_keep* function calls DOS function 31h to install the current program in memory, reserving the number of paragraphs specified in the argument *memsize*. Then it exits the program, returning the value specified in *status* to its parent (normally DOS). The return code is analogous to the code used with the *exit* routine. As in *exit*, a *status* equal to 0 means there were no errors. Other values signify errors.

1. The Turbo C and Turbo C++ version of this function is *keep*.

COMMON USES This function can be used to install your own memory-resident interrupt handler in the system.

COMMENTS It is not clear how you can set the argument *memsize* in the call to *_dos_keep*. One approach is to use your knowledge of the layout of the program in memory. The global variable *_psp* provides the segment address of the *program segment prefix*, which is where the program starts. The end of the program is the top of the stack. We can get the stack segment address (SS) by using *segread*. If we can also get the current stack pointer (SP), a good estimate of the program's size is:

```
prog_size = SS + (SP + safety_margin)/16 - _psp;
```

where *safety_margin* is a small number of bytes (around 100) to account for uncertainties in our estimate. The division by 16 is necessary to convert the stack pointer to paragraphs. One way to get the stack pointer is to use *alloca* to allocate some memory from the stack. The returned pointer, cast as an unsigned integer, can serve as SP in our formula for the program size.

You should gain some familiarity with the concepts of "terminate-and-stay-resident" programs before using the *_dos_keep* function.

SEE ALSO `_dos_getvect, _dos_setvect` *To retrieve current interrupt vector and install a new one*

`_chain_intr` *To jump from one interrupt handler to another*

EXAMPLE See the March 1988 issue of *Computer Language* (pp. 67–76) for an article by Al Stevens, "Writing Terminate-and-Stay-Resident Programs, Part II: Microsoft C and QuickC," in which he shows how to use *_dos_keep* to write a TSR utility entirely in Microsoft C.

COMPATIBILITY

_dos_open

MSC 3	MSC 4	MSC 5	MSC 6	QC1	QC2	QC2.5	TC1	TC1.5	TC2	TC++	ANSI	UNIX V	XNX	OS2	DOS
		▲	▲	▲	▲	▲		1	1	1					▲

PURPOSE Use *_dos_open* to open an existing file.

SYNTAX
```
unsigned _dos_open (char *filename, unsigned mode,
                    int *filehandle);
```

`char *filename;` *File name, including path*

`unsigned mode;` *Permissions for operations to be performed on the file*

`int *filehandle;` *Pointer to location where the file handle, or identifier, is returned*

EXAMPLE CALL
```
_dos_open(fname, SH_COMPAT|O_RDONLY, &filehandle);
```

INCLUDES `#include <dos.h>` *For declaration of function*

`#include <fcntl.h>` *For definition of permission mode names*

DESCRIPTION The *_dos_open* function calls DOS function 3Dh to open the file whose name (including the pathname) is specified by the argument *filename*. The operations that can be performed on the file are indicated by the argument *mode*: how the file can be accessed, how much sharing is allowed, and whether the file can be inherited by a child process. The argument is specified by a value created by the bitwise OR of mode names picked from Table 16-23. At most, you should pick one name from each category. These names are defined in the include file *fcntl.h*.

Table 16-23. *Modes in which Files Can Be Opened*

Category Name	Mode Name	Interpretation
Access	O_RDONLY	Only reading allowed.
	O_WRONLY	Only writing allowed.
	O_RDWR	Both reading and writing allowed.
Sharing	SH_COMPAT	No other process can access the file. This is called the "compatibilty mode" and the same process can open the file any number of times. This is how DOS normally operates.
	SH_DENYRW	No one else can read from or write to this file.
	SH_DENYWR	No one else can write to this file.
	SH_DENYRD	No one else can read from this file.
	SH_DENYNONE	File is completely shareable.
Inheritance	O_NOINHERIT	File will not be inherited by any child process.

Once the file is successfully opened, an identifying number, or handle, is returned in the location whose address is specified in the argument *file-handle*.

1. The Turbo C and Turbo C++ version of this function is *_open*.

RETURNS This function returns 0 if successful; otherwise, it returns the MS-DOS error code (see *dosexterr*) and sets the global variable *errno* to one of the constants shown in Table 16-24.

Table 16-24. *Error Codes Set by* _dos_open

Error Code	Interpretation
EINVAL	Either access mode value is invalid or a sharing mode value is specified when file-sharing routines are not loaded.
ENOENT	File not found.
EMFILE	Too many files open (limit is 20 for a process).
EACCES	Access was denied (for example, trying to open a read-only file for writing).

COMMENTS The functions *open* and *close* offer a more portable means of achieving the same result as this DOS-specific function.

Under MS-DOS, the maximum number of open files for a single process is 20.

SEE ALSO `_dos_close` *To close a file opened by* _dos_open

_dos_creat, _dos_creatnew	*To create a new file*
open, close	*Portable versions of similar file opening and closing functions*

EXAMPLE Use *_dos_open* to open a file. Close the file by calling *_dos_close*.

```
#include <stdio.h>
#include <fcntl.h>
#include <dos.h>
main()
{
    char fname[40], *p_fname;
    int filehandle;

    printf("Enter name of file to open using \
_dos_open: ");
    p_fname = gets(fname);

/* Open the file in "compatibilty mode" and for reading
 *  only
 */
    if (_dos_open(p_fname, SH_COMPAT¦O_RDONLY,
        &filehandle) != 0)
    {
        printf("Error opening file: %s\n", fname);
        exit(0);
    }
    printf("File %s opened.\n", fname);

/* Now close file */
    if (_dos_close(filehandle) != 0)
    {
        printf("Error closing file with _dos_close\n");
        exit(0);
    }
    printf("File %s closed.\n", fname);
}
```

_dos_read

COMPATIBILITY

MSC 3	MSC 4	MSC 5	MSC 6	QC1	QC2	QC2.5	TC1	TC1.5	TC2	TC++	ANSI	UNIX V	XNX	OS2	DOS
		▲	▲	▲	▲	▲		1	1	1					▲

PURPOSE Use *_dos_read* to read a specified number of bytes from a file into a buffer. To call this function, you need a handle returned by a function such as *_dos_open* or *_dos_creat* or *_dos_creatnew*.

SYNTAX

```
unsigned _dos_read(int filehandle, void _far *buffer,
                   unsigned readcount, unsigned *bytes_read);
```

`int filehandle;`	*The file handle or identifier*
`void _far *buffer;`	*Pointer to buffer where the data read from the file is stored*
`unsigned readcount;`	*Number of bytes to be read*
`unsigned *bytes_read;`	*Pointer to location that contains the number of bytes read*

EXAMPLE CALL `_dos_read(filehandle, pbuf, 80, &bytes_read);`

INCLUDES `#include <dos.h>` *For declaration of function*

DESCRIPTION The *_dos_read* function calls DOS function 3Fh to transfer the number of bytes requested in the argument *readcount* from the current position in the file to the locations accessed through the pointer *buffer*. Upon return, the location, whose address is in *bytes_read*, contains the number of bytes read. The file from which you want to read is specified by the identifying number, or handle, in the argument *filehandle*.

1. The Turbo C and Turbo C++ version of this function is *_read*.

RETURNS This function returns 0 if successful. Otherwise, it returns the MS-DOS error code and sets the global variable *errno* either to the constant EBADF, indicating that the file handle is invalid, or to EACCES, indicating that access was denied (the file probably is not open for read access).

COMMENTS The function *read* offers a more portable means of achieving the same result as this DOS-specific function.

SEE ALSO

`_dos_write`	*To write a buffer to a file*
`read, write`	*Portable versions of similar read and write functions*

_dos_open	*To open an existing file using a DOS call*
_dos_close	*To close a file*
_dos_creat, _dos_creatnew	*To create a new file*

EXAMPLE Use *_dos_open* to open an existing text file and then call *_dos_read* to read the first 80 characters into a buffer. Display the contents of the buffer. Finally, close the file using *_dos_close*.

```
#include <stdio.h>
#include <fcntl.h>
#include <dos.h>
main()
{
    char fname[40], *p_fname;
    char buffer[80];
    void _far *pbuf;
    int filehandle;
    unsigned bytes_read;
    pbuf = (void _far *)(&buffer[0]);
    printf("Enter name of an existing file: ");
    p_fname = gets(fname);

/* Open the file using _dos_open */
    if (_dos_open(p_fname, O_RDONLY, &filehandle) != 0)
    {
        printf("Error opening file: %s\n", fname);
        exit(0);
    }
    printf("File %s opened.\n", fname);

/* Now read the first 80 bytes */
    if (_dos_read(filehandle, pbuf, 80, &bytes_read)
        == 0)
    {
        printf("%d bytes read\n", bytes_read);
        printf("The bytes read are:\n%s\n", buffer);
    }

/* Now close file */
    if (_dos_close(filehandle) != 0)
    {
        printf("Error closing file with _dos_close\n");
```

```
        exit(0);
    }
    printf("File %s closed.\n", fname);
}
```

_dos_setblock

COMPATIBILITY

MSC 3	MSC 4	MSC 5	MSC 6	QC1	QC2	QC2.5	TC1	TC1.5	TC2	TC++	ANSI	UNIX V	XNX	OS2	DOS
		▲	▲	▲	▲	▲		1	1	1					▲

PURPOSE Use *_dos_setblock* to adjust the size of a block of memory allocated by *_dos_allocmem.*

SYNTAX

```
unsigned _dos_setblock (unsigned newsize, unsigned segadd,
                        unsigned *maxavail);
```

`unsigned newsize;` *New size of block in units of 16-byte paragraphs*

`unsigned segadd;` *Segment address of block*

`unsigned *maxavail;` *Pointer to location that upon failure is set to the maximum number of paragraphs available*

EXAMPLE CALL `_dos_setblock (5, segadd, &maxsize);`

INCLUDES `#include <dos.h>` *For declaration of function*

DESCRIPTION The *_dos_setblock* function calls DOS function 4Ah to enlarge the size of a block of memory allocated by *_dos_allocmem.* The argument *newsize* specifies the desired size of the block in paragraph (16-byte) units, *segadd* (segment address of the block previously returned by *_dos_allocmem*), and *maxavail* (pointer to an unsigned integer that, in case of failure, contains the maximum number of paragraphs available).

1. The Turbo C and Turbo C++ version of this function is *setblock.*

RETURNS This function returns 0 if memory was successfully allocated. Otherwise, the return value is the MS-DOS error code and the global variable *errno* is set to the constant ENOMEM, indicating that the segment address of the block was not valid.

If the MS-DOS error code returned by *_dos_setblock* is 8, insufficient memory was available to satisfy the request. In this case, the maximum

available block size (in paragraphs) is returned in the location whose address is in the argument *maxavail.*

COMMENTS The *_dos_setblock* function is analogous to the standard library routine *realloc.* Of course, *_dos_setblock* must be used only to enlarge or shrink blocks allocated by its counterpart, *_dos_allocmem.*

SEE ALSO

`_dos_allocmem`	*The corresponding routine that allocated the memory in the first place*
`_dos_freemem`	*To free memory allocated by* _dos_allocmem
`realloc`	*Other memory block resizing routines*

EXAMPLE Use *_dos_allocmem* to allocate 1 paragraph of memory. Now use *_dos_setblock* to enlarge the block size to 5 paragraphs in order to store 80 characters. Store a string in the new buffer and print the string out. Finally, free the allocated buffer.

```
#include <stdio.h>
#include <dos.h>
#include <memory.h>
char str[80]="Testing _dos_allocmem...\n$";
main()
{
    union REGS xr;
    struct SREGS sr;
    char _far *stradd;
    unsigned int segadd, maxsize;
    stradd = (char _far *)(&str[0]);
    if (_dos_allocmem(1, &segadd) != 0)
    {
        printf("Memory allocation failed!\n");
        exit(0);
    }

    if (_dos_setblock (5, segadd, &maxsize) != 0)
    {
        printf("_dos_setblock failed!\n");
        printf("Maximum size possible = %d \
paragraphs\n", maxsize);
        exit(0);
    }
/* Use movedata to copy the string to allocated memory*/
    movedata(FP_SEG(stradd),FP_OFF(stradd), segadd,
```

```
                0, 80);
    sr.ds = segadd;
    xr.x.dx = 0;
    xr.h.ah = DOS_PRTSTR;
    intdosx(&xr, &xr, &sr);

/* Free memory before exiting */
    _dos_freemem(segadd);
}
```

_dos_setdate

COMPATIBILITY

MSC 3	MSC 4	MSC 5	MSC 6	QC1	QC2	QC2.5	TC1	TC1.5	TC2	TC++	ANSI	UNIX V	XNX	OS2	DOS
		▲	▲	▲	▲	▲		1	1	1					▲

PURPOSE Use *_dos_setdate* to change the current system date.

SYNTAX `unsigned _dos_setdate (struct dosdate_t *date);`

`struct dosdate_t *date;` *Pointer to a structure that holds the components of date*

EXAMPLE CALL `_dos_setdate(&date_info);`

INCLUDES `#include <dos.h>` *For definition of the structure* dosdate_t

DESCRIPTION The *_dos_setdate* function calls DOS function 2Bh to set the system date whose components—the day, month, year, and day of the week—should be specified by placing appropriate values in fields of the structure type *dosdate_t*, which is defined in *dos.h*. The C declaration of the structure is shown below.

```
struct dosdate_t
{
    unsigned char day;          /* day of the month (range 1-31) */
    unsigned char month;        /* month (range 1-12)            */
    unsigned int year;          /* year (range 1980-2099)        */
    unsigned char dayofweek;    /* Day of the week 0-6, 0=Sunday */
};
```

1. The Turbo C and Turbo C++ version of this function is *setdate*.

RETURNS This function returns a 0 if the operation is successful. Otherwise, it returns a nonzero value and sets the global variable *errno* to the constant EINVAL, which means an invalid value was specified.

SEE ALSO

`_dos_getdate`	*The corresponding routine that returns the system date*
`_dos_gettime, _dos_settime`	*To get and set the system time*
`_strdate, _strtime, gmtime, localtime, mktime, time`	*Other date and time services*

EXAMPLE Use *_dos_setdate* to change the system date.

```
#include <stdio.h>
#include <dos.h>
main()
{
    unsigned month, day, year;
    struct dosdate_t date;
    printf ("Enter new date in the form MM/DD/YY:");
    scanf("%d/%d/&d", &month, &day, &year);
    date.day = day;
    date.month = month;
    date.year = year + 1900;
    if (_dos_setdate(&date) != 0)
    {
        printf("Error setting date!\n");
    }
    else
    {
        printf("New date: %d/%d/%d\n", date.month,
            date.day, date.year -1900);
    }
}
```

_dos_setdrive

COMPATIBILITY

MSC 3	MSC 4	MSC 5	MSC 6	QC1	QC2	QC2.5	TC1	TC1.5	TC2	TC++	ANSI	UNIX V	XNX	OS2	DOS
		▲	▲	▲	▲	▲		1	1	1					▲

PURPOSE Use *_dos_setdrive* to change to a new default drive number. For example, you can use this function to make drive A the default drive after starting your program from drive C.

SYNTAX

```
void _dos_setdrive (unsigned driveno, unsigned *maxdrives);
```

`unsigned driveno;` *New default drive number*

`unsigned *maxdrives;` *Total number of logical drives*

EXAMPLE CALL

```
_dos_setdrive(1, &maxdrives); /* New drive is A: */
```

INCLUDES #include <dos.h> *For declaration of function*

DESCRIPTION The *_dos_setdrive* function calls DOS function 0Eh to set the current default drive to one specified by the argument *driveno*, interpreted as follows: 1 means drive A, 2 means drive B, and so on.

The total number of logical drives in the system is returned in the unsigned integer variable whose address is in the argument *maxdrives*.

1. The Turbo C and Turbo C++ version of this function is *setdisk*.

COMMON USES MS-DOS uses the concept of "current default drive" when locating files. If all of your file I/O will be from a certain disk drive, you can use the *_dos_setdrive* function to set the default drive before performing any file I/O.

COMMENTS There is no return value, so the only way of knowing that this function worked is to call *_dos_getdrive* immediately afterwards to verify that the current default drive has indeed been changed.

SEE ALSO `_dos_getdrive` *To get the number of the current default drive*

EXAMPLE Use *_dos_setdrive* to change the default drive number to one requested by the user. Call *_dos_getdrive* to verify that the new default is in effect.

```
#include <stdio.h>
#include <ctype.h>
#include <dos.h>
```

```
main()
{
    char ch_in;
    unsigned drive, maxdrives;
    printf("Enter new drive name (A, B etc):";
    scanf("%c", ch_in);
/* Convert the letter into a number, 0 for A, 1 for B */
    drive = toupper(ch_in) - 'A' + 1;
    _dos_setdrive(drive, &maxdrives);
    _dos_getdrive(&drive);
    printf ("The current drive is: %c\n", drive+'A'-1);
    printf ("There are %d logical drives on the \
system\n", maxdrives);
}
```

COMPATIBILITY

_dos_setfileattr

MSC 3	MSC 4	MSC 5	MSC 6	QC1	QC2	QC2.5	TC1	TC1.5	TC2	TC++	ANSI	UNIX V	XNX	OS2	DOS
		▲	▲	▲	▲	▲		1	1	1					▲

PURPOSE Use *_dos_setfileattr* to change the attributes of a file. For example, you can hide a file so that it does not show up on a MS-DOS DIR command.

SYNTAX `unsigned _dos_setfileattr(char *filename, unsigned attribute);`

`char *filename;` *File name, including path*

`unsigned attribute;` *New attributes*

EXAMPLE CALL `_dos_setfileattr("secret.dat", _A_HIDDEN); /* Hide file */`

INCLUDES #include <dos.h> *For declaration of function and definition of attribute names*

DESCRIPTION The *_dos_setfileattr* function calls DOS function 43h to alter the attributes of the file whose name is in the character string *filename*. The new attributes for the file are specified in the argument *attribute*. You can select a combination of attributes by specifying a value created by the bitwise OR of attribute names picked from Table 16-20. These attribute constants are defined in *dos.h*.

1. The Turbo C and Turbo C++ version of this function is *_chmod*.

RETURNS The return value is 0 if successful. Otherwise, the function returns the

MS-DOS error code and sets the global variable *errno* to the constant ENOENT, indicating that the file could not be found.

SEE ALSO `_dos_getfileattr` *To determine the current attributes of a file*

EXAMPLE Use *_dos_setfileattr* to hide a file whose name is provided by the user. (You can write a similar program to make the file appear again).

```
#include <stdio.h>
#include <dos.h>
main()
{
    char filename[80], *p_fname;
    printf("Enter name of file to hide: ");
    p_fname = gets(filename);
    if (_dos_setfileattr(p_fname, _A_HIDDEN) != 0)
    {
        printf("Error in _dos_setfileattr call!\n");
        exit(0);
    }
    printf("%s is now hidden. Try DIR to verify.\n",
           filename);
}
```

_dos_setftime

COMPATIBILITY

MSC 3	MSC 4	MSC 5	MSC 6	QC1	QC2	QC2.5	TC1	TC1.5	TC2	TC++	ANSI	UNIX V	XNX	OS2	DOS
		▲	▲	▲	▲	▲		1	1	1					▲

PURPOSE Use *_dos_setftime* to change the date and time stamp of a file. Before calling this function, you need a handle returned by a function such as *_dos_open* or *_dos_creat.*

SYNTAX

```
unsigned _dos_setftime(int filehandle, unsigned date,
                       unsigned time);
```

`int filehandle;` *The file handle, or identifier*

`unsigned date;` *Date information in packed form*

`unsigned time;` *Time information in packed form*

EXAMPLE CALL `_dos_setftime(filehandle, date, time);`

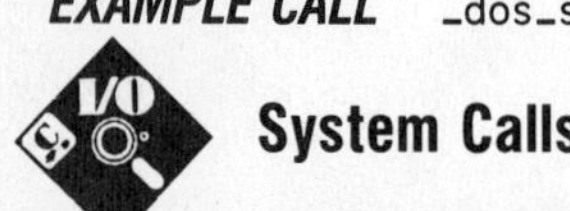

INCLUDES `#include <dos.h>` *For declaration of function*

DESCRIPTION The *_dos_setftime* function calls DOS function 57h to change the date and time stamp of the file specified by the identifying number, or handle, in the argument *filehandle*. The date and time information is entered in the arguments *date* and *time*. The handle must be one returned when the file was opened by *_dos_open* or created by *_dos_creat* or *_dos_creatnew*.

The date and time stamps indicate when the file was last modified. You can decode the stamps by consulting the figure shown in the description of *_dos_getftime*. The example below illustrates how you can prepare the date and time information for this function. Note that the value stored in the year field should be relative to 1980 (i.e., it is the current year minus 1980).

1. The Turbo C and Turbo C++ version of this function is *setftime*.

RETURNS This function returns 0 if successful; otherwise, it returns the MS-DOS error code and sets the global variable *errno* to the constant EBADF, indicating that the file handle is invalid.

SEE ALSO

`_dos_getftime`	*To get the date and time stamp of a file*
`_dos_open`	*To open an existing file using a DOS call*
`_dos_creat, _dos_creatnew`	*To create a new file*

EXAMPLE Use *_dos_open* to open a file and then call *_dos_setftime* to store a new date and time stamp. Use *_dos_getftime* to verify that the date and time stamps have indeed changed.

```
#include <stdio.h>
#include <fcntl.h>
#include <dos.h>
main()
{
    char fname[40], *p_fname;
    int filehandle;
    unsigned date, time, day, month, year,
             hour, minute, second;

    printf("Enter name of an existing file: ");
    p_fname = gets(fname);

/* Open the file using _dos_open */
    if (_dos_open(p_fname, O_RDONLY, &filehandle) != 0)
```

```
    {
        printf("Error opening file: %s\n", fname);
        exit(0);
    }
    printf("File %s opened.\n", fname);

/* Ask for new date and time stamp: */
    printf("Enter new date in the format MM-DD-YY:");
    scanf("%u-%u-%u", &month, &day, &year);
    printf("Enter new time in the format HH:MM:SS ");
    scanf("%u:%u:%u", &hour, &minute, &second);

/* Pack date and time information into single words */
    date = (((year - 80) << 9) | (date << 5)) | day;
    time = ((hour << 11) | (minute << 5)) | second;

/* Set the date and time stamp */
    _dos_setftime(filehandle, date, time);

/* Get file's date and time stamp to verify the new
 * date and time
 */
    _dos_getftime(filehandle, &date, &time);

/* Now decipher the return values */
    second = time & 0x1f;
    minute = (time >> 5) & 0x3f;
    hour = (time >> 11) & 0x1f;
    day = date & 0x1f;
    month = (date >> 5) & 0xf;
/* NOTE: year is relative to 1980. So we are adding 80*/
    year = ((date >> 9) & 0x7f) + 80;
    printf("File: %s  Date: %d-%d-%d Time: %.2d:%.2d:\
%.2d\n", fname, month, day, year, hour, minute, second);

/* Now close file */
    if (_dos_close(filehandle) != 0)
    {
        printf("Error closing file with _dos_close\n");
        exit(0);
    }
    printf("File %s closed.\n", fname);
}
```

System Calls

COMPATIBILITY

_dos_settime

MSC 3	MSC 4	MSC 5	MSC 6	QC1	QC2	QC2.5	TC1	TC1.5	TC2	TC++	ANSI	UNIX V	XNX	OS2	DOS
		▲	▲	▲	▲	▲		1	1	1					▲

PURPOSE Use *_dos_settime* to change the current system time.

SYNTAX

```
unsigned _dos_settime (struct dostime_t *time);
```

`struct dostime_t *time;` *Pointer to a structure that holds the components of time*

EXAMPLE CALL

```
_dos_settime(&time_info);
```

INCLUDES `#include <dos.h>` *For definition of the structure* dostime_t

DESCRIPTION The *_dos_settime* function calls DOS function 2Dh to set the current system time whose components—the hour, minutes, seconds, and hundredths of a second—are loaded in appropriate fields of the structure type *dostime_t, which is defined in dos.h.* The layout of this structure along with the C declaration of the internal fields are shown below:

```
struct dostime_t
{
    unsigned char hour;     /* Hour (range 0---23)                     */
    unsigned char minute;   /* Minutes (range 0---59)                  */
    unsigned char second;   /* Seconds (range 0---59)                  */
    unsigned char hsecond;  /* Hundredths of a second (range 0---99) */
};
```

1. The Turbo C and Turbo C++ version of this function is *settime.*

RETURNS This function returns a 0 if the operation is successful. Otherwise, it returns a nonzero value and sets the global variable *errno* to the constant EINVAL, which means an invalid value was specified.

SEE ALSO

`_dos_gettime` *The corresponding routine that returns the system time*

`_dos_getdate,`
`_dos_setdate` *To get and set the system date*

`_strdate, _strtime,`
`gmtime, localtime,`
`mktime, time` *Other date and time services*

EXAMPLE Use the *_dos_settime* to change the current system time.

```
#include <stdio.h>
#include <dos.h>
main()
{
    unsigned hour, minute, second;
    struct dostime_t time;
    printf ("Enter new time in the form HH:MM:SS:");
    scanf("%d:%d:&d", &hour, &minute, &second);
    time.hour = hour;
    time.minute = minute;
    time.second = second;
    if (_dos_settime(&time) != 0)
    {
        printf("Error setting time!\n");
    }
    else
    {
        printf("New time: %d:%d:%d.%d\n", time.hour,
            time.minute, time.second, time.hsecond);
    }
}
```

_dos_setvect

COMPATIBILITY

MSC 3	MSC 4	MSC 5	MSC 6	QC1	QC2	QC2.5	TC1	TC1.5	TC2	TC++	ANSI	UNIX V	XNX	OS2	DOS
		▲	▲	▲	▲	▲		1	1	1					▲

PURPOSE Use *_dos_setvect* to install a new interrupt vector for a specific interrupt number. The interrupt vector is the address of the routine that is invoked when the interrupt occurs.

SYNTAX

```
void _dos_setvect (unsigned intno,
                   void(interrupt _far *handler)());
```

`unsigned intno;` *Interrupt number whose vector is being set*

`interrupt _far *handler;` *Far pointer to the new handler, a function of type* interrupt

EXAMPLE CALL

```
void interrupt _far our_handler(void);
_dos_setvect(int_number, our_handler);
```

INCLUDES `#include <dos.h>` *For declaration of function*

DESCRIPTION The *_dos_setvect* function calls the DOS function 25h to install the address of the interrupt handler specified in the argument *handler* as the new vector for the interrupt number specified in the argument *intno*. The argument *handler* is a far pointer to the interrupt handler, a function of type *interrupt*, which is a keyword introduced in version 5.0 to allow writing interrupt handlers in C (see Chapter 1 for a discussion of the *interrupt* keyword).

1. The Turbo C and Turbo C++ version of this function is *setvect*.

COMMON USES This function is often used to install a new interrupt handler. For example, if you were writing an interrupt-driven I/O routine for the serial port you could use this routine to install your handler in place of the default handler.

COMMENTS It is good practice to save the interrupt vector before installing a new one. That way you can restore the system to its original status when your program exits.

SEE ALSO `_dos_getvect` *To get the address of the current interrupt handler*

EXAMPLE In the IBM PC, interrupt 1Ch is generated at every clock tick. These clock ticks occur about 18.2 times a second and are used to maintain the time in the system. You can hook your routine onto this interrupt and have the routine executed at every clock tick. Write a routine using *_dos_getvect* and *_dos_setvect* to install your own interrupt handler for interrupt 1Ch. You can increment a counter in the interrupt handler to show that the program worked.

```
#include <stdio.h>
#include <dos.h>
#define TIMER_TICK 0x1c
unsigned long tickcount = 0;
void interrupt _far our_handler(void);
main()
{
    unsigned c;
    void (interrupt _far *old_handler)();
    unsigned intno = TIMER_TICK;
    old_handler = _dos_getvect(intno);
/* Print out address of old handler using the %p
 * format
 */
```

```
    printf("\nThe address of the old handler is : %p\n",
            old_handler);
/* Install the new handler named our_handler
 * Disable interrupts when changing handler
 */
    _disable();
    _dos_setvect(intno, our_handler);
    _enable();
    printf("Installed new handler: %p\n", our_handler);
    printf("Hit q to quit: ");
    while ((c=getch()) != 'q'); /* Keep looping till 'q'*/
/* Reset vector and print the tickcount. Again disable
 * interrupts when doing this.
 */
    _disable();
    _dos_setvect(intno, old_handler);
    _enable();
    printf("The tick counter is now: %ld\n", tickcount);
}
/*------------------------------------------------------*/
void interrupt far our_handler()
{
/* Our handler simply increments a counter. But this
 * will be proof enough that the handler works because
 * we are not calling it explicitly in the main program
 * and the only way it gets called is via INT 1Ch.
 */
    tickcount++;
}
```

_dos_write

COMPATIBILITY

MSC 3	MSC 4	MSC 5	MSC 6	QC1	QC2	QC2.5	TC1	TC1.5	TC2	TC++	ANSI	UNIX V	XNX	OS2	DOS
		▲	▲	▲	▲	▲		1	1	1					▲

PURPOSE Use *_dos_write* to write a specified number of bytes from a buffer into a file at its current location. Before calling this function, you need a handle returned by a function such as *_dos_open* or *_dos_creatnew* or *_dos_creat*. DOS function 42h can be used to move the current location in a file.

SYNTAX

```
unsigned _dos_write(int filehandle, void _far *buffer,
                    unsigned writecount, unsigned *bytes_written);
```

`int filehandle;`	*The file handle, or identifier*
`void _far *buffer;`	*Pointer to buffer where the data read from the file is stored*
`unsigned writecount;`	*Number of bytes to be written*
`unsigned *bytes_written;`	*Pointer to location that contains the actual number of bytes written*

EXAMPLE CALL

```
_dos_write(filehandle, pbuf, 80, &bytes_written);
```

INCLUDES `#include <dos.h>` *For declaration of function*

DESCRIPTION The *_dos_write* function calls DOS function 40h to transfer the number of bytes specified in the argument *writecount* from the memory locations accessed through the pointer *buffer* into the file whose handle, or identifying number, is given in the argument *filehandle*. The data is written at the current position of the file pointer, which is updated when the writing is complete. Upon return, the location whose address is in *bytes_written* contains the number of bytes written to the file.

1. The Turbo C and Turbo C++ version of this function is *_write*.

RETURNS This function returns 0 if successful. Otherwise, it returns the MS-DOS error code and sets the global variable *errno* either to the constant EBADF, indicating that the file handle is invalid, or to EACCES, indicating that access was denied (the file probably is not open for write access).

COMMENTS The function *write* offers a more portable means of achieving the same result as this DOS-specific function.

SEE ALSO

`_dos_read`	*To read from a file*
`read, write`	*Portable versions of similar read and write functions*
`_dos_open`	*To open an existing file using a DOS call*
`_dos_close`	*To close a file*
`_dos_creat, _dos_creatnew`	*To create a new file*

EXAMPLE Use *_dos_open* to open an existing text file. Use *_dos_write* to write an extra line at the beginning of the file. Finally, close the file using *_dos_close*.

```
#include <stdio.h>
#include <fcntl.h>
#include <dos.h>
char buffer[80] = "Testing _dos_write ........ ";
main()
{
    char fname[40], *p_fname;
    void _far *pbuf;
    int filehandle;
    unsigned bytes;
    pbuf = (void _far *)(&buffer[0]);
    printf("Enter name of an existing file: ");
    p_fname = gets(fname);

/* Open the file using _dos_open */
    if (_dos_open(p_fname, O_RDWR, &filehandle) != 0)
    {
        printf("Error opening file: %s\n", fname);
        exit(0);
    }
    printf("File %s opened.\n", fname);

/* Now write out buffer */
    if (_dos_write(filehandle, pbuf, 80, &bytes) == 0)
    {
        printf("%d bytes written\n", bytes);
    }

/* Now close file */
    if (_dos_close(filehandle) != 0)
    {
        printf("Error closing file with _dos_close\n");
        exit(0);
    }
    printf("File %s closed.\n", fname);
}
```

System Calls

COMPATIBILITY

dosexterr

MSC 3	MSC 4	MSC 5	MSC 6	QC1	QC2	QC2.5	TC1	TC1.5	TC2	TC++	ANSI	UNIX V	XNX	OS2	DOS
▲	▲	▲	▲	▲	▲	▲	▲	▲	▲	▲					▲

PURPOSE On MS-DOS 3.0 or higher, use *dosexterr* after an error return from a DOS function call to obtain detailed information on the cause of error and possible remedial action.

SYNTAX

```
int dosexterr (struct DOSERROR *errbuf);
```

`struct DOSERROR *errbuf;` *Pointer to structure that contains information on return*

EXAMPLE CALL

```
dosexterr(&errbuf);
```

INCLUDES `#include <dos.h>` *For declaration of function and declaration of the structure type DOSERROR*

DESCRIPTION The *dosexterr* function calls DOS function 59h to get detailed information on the cause of an unsuccessful call to a DOS function (INT 21h). The information about the error is returned in a structure of type DOSERROR, and a pointer to one such structure must be passed in the argument *errbuf*. The DOSERROR structure is defined in *dos.h* and its C declaration is shown below.

```
struct DOSERROR
{
    int  exterror;  /* Extended error code */
    char class;     /* Error class         */
    char action;    /* Recommended action  */
    char locus;     /* Error locus -- device
                       where it occurred   */
};
```

The interpretation of the *exterror* field in this structure is given in Table 16-25. For more detailed information on this and the other fields consult the *Microsoft MS-DOS Programmer's Reference Manual* available from Microsoft Corporation.

Table 16-25. *Extended Error Codes from* dosexterr

Value of *exterror* (hex)	Interpretation
0	No error in previous DOS function call
1	Invalid function number
2	File not found

Table 16-25. ***(cont.)***

Value of *exterror* (hex)	Interpretation
3	Path not found (bad drive or directory name)
4	Too many open files
5	Access denied
6	Invalid file handle
7	Memory control blocks destroyed
8	Insufficient memory
9	Invalid memory block address
A	Invalid environment
B	Invalid format
C	Invalid access code
D	Invalid data
E	— Reserved —
F	Invalid disk drive
10	Attempt to remove current directory
11	Not the same device
12	No more files
13	Disk write protected
14	Unknown unit
15	Drive not ready
16	Unknown command
17	CRC error in data
18	Bad request structure length
19	Seek error
1A	Unknown medium
1B	Sector not found
1C	Printer out of paper
1D	Write fault
1E	Read fault
1F	General failure
20	Sharing violation
21	Lock violation
22	Invalid disk change
23	File Control Block (FCB) unavailable
24-4F	— Reserved —
50	File already exists
51	— Reserved —
52	Cannot make directory
53	Failed during critical error interrupt (INT 24h)

RETURNS The return value is identical to the field *exterror* which is the value of the *AX* register.

SEE ALSO perror *To print an error message*

EXAMPLE Try to close a nonexistent file using a DOS function call. Then call *dosexterr* to get the error code. You should get a report that *exterror* is 6, which means the file handle is invalid.

```
#include <stdio.h>
#include <dos.h>

main()
{

    struct DOSERROR errbuf;
/* Try closing a non-existent file */
    if (_dos_close(1000) != 0)
    {
        printf("Error closing file.\n");
        dosexterr(&errbuf);
        printf("exterror=%x, class=%x, action=%x, \
locus=%x\n", errbuf.exterror, errbuf.class,
        errbuf.action, errbuf.locus);
    }
}
```

_enable

COMPATIBILITY

MSC 3	MSC 4	MSC 5	MSC 6	QC1	QC2	QC2.5	TC1	TC1.5	TC2	TC++	ANSI	UNIX V	XNX	OS2	DOS
▲	▲	▲	▲	▲	▲	▲		1	1	1					▲

PURPOSE Use *_enable* to allow the 8086 microprocessor to acknowledge interrupts. Call *_enable* after turning off interrupts by calling *_disable.*

SYNTAX `void _enable(void);`

EXAMPLE CALL `_enable();`

INCLUDES #include <dos.h> *For declaration of function*

DESCRIPTION The *_enable* function executes an 8086 *STI* instruction.

1. The Turbo C and Turbo C++ version of this function, compatible with Microsoft 5.0 and 6.0, is *enable*.

COMMON USES The *_enable* function is used in conjunction with *_disable* to protect a section of code from being interrupted. You do not need the *_enable* function for routine programming chores, but its availability enables you to write such exotic programs as interrupt handlers in Microsoft C (see the tutorial section for a description of interrupt handlers).

SEE ALSO `_disable` *To disable 8086 interrupts*

EXAMPLE See the example in the reference page on *_dos_setvect* for sample usage.

FP_OFF

COMPATIBILITY

MSC 3	MSC 4	MSC 5	MSC 6	QC1	QC2	QC2.5	TC1	TC1.5	TC2	TC++	ANSI	UNIX V	XNX	OS2	DOS
▲	▲	▲	▲	▲	▲	▲	▲	▲	▲	▲				▲	▲

PURPOSE *FP_OFF* is a C macro to get the 16-bit offset portion of the address of any data element. The macro expects a long (32-bit) pointer to a memory location, such as the beginning of an array or a C structure. For example, you can see *FP_OFF* to get the offset of a string that you want to display using the DOS function 9h. Using the *FP_OFF* macro is the only way to get the offset of a data element in a C program.

SYNTAX
```
unsigned int FP_OFF(char _far *address);
```

`char _far *address;` *Long pointer to memory location*

EXAMPLE CALL
```
offset_buf = FP_OFF(p_buf); /* p_buf is a far pointer */
```

INCLUDES `#include <dos.h>` *For definition of the macro*

DESCRIPTION The *FP_OFF* function, implemented as a macro, accepts a 2-bit pointer as an argument and returns the 16-bit offset portion of the pointer. When using *FP_OFF*, the argument *address* must be of type *(char _far *)*.

COMMON USES *FP_OFF* is commonly used with its counterpart *FP_SEG* to generate 16-bit offset and segment addresses of strings and functions for use in DOS function calls.

RETURNS *FP_OFF* returns the offset as an unsigned 16-bit integer.

SEE ALSO `FP_SEG` *For segment address*

EXAMPLE Use *FP_OFF* to get the offset of a string. You'll need this, for example, when printing a string using DOS function 9h so that you can pass the offset address to the print function.

```
#include <stdio.h>
#include <dos.h>
char sample[] = "Test string";
main()
{
    char _far *ps;
    unsigned off_sample;
/* Cast the address of the first character as a far
 * pointer
 */
    ps = (char _far *)&sample[0];
    off_sample = FP_OFF(ps);
    printf("The offset of the string is: %d\n",
           off_sample);
}
```

COMPATIBILITY

FP_SEG

MSC 3	MSC 4	MSC 5	MSC 6	QC1	QC2	QC2.5	TC1	TC1.5	TC2	TC++	ANSI	UNIX V	XNX	OS2	DOS
▲	▲	▲	▲	▲	▲	▲	▲	▲	▲	▲				▲	▲

PURPOSE Use the *FP_SEG* macro to get the segment address of a memory location. The macro expects a long (32-bit) pointer to a memory location. For example, you can use *FP_SEG* to get the segment address of a string that you want to display using the DOS function 9h. You must use *FP_SEG* whenever a BIOS or DOS call requires the segment address of a data element.

SYNTAX `unsigned FP_SEG(char _far *address);`

`char _far *address;` *Long pointer to memory location*

EXAMPLE CALL `segadd_buf = FP_SEG(p_buf); /* p_buf is a far pointer */`

INCLUDES `#include <dos.h>` *For definition of the macro*

DESCRIPTION The *FP_SEG* function, implemented as a macro, accepts a 32-bit pointer as an argument and returns the segment address of the pointer. When using *FP_OFF*, the argument *address* must be of type *(char _far *)*.

COMMON USES *FP_SEG* is commonly used with its counterpart *FP_OFF* to generate segment and offset addresses of strings and functions for use in DOS function calls.

RETURNS *FP_SEG* returns the offset as an unsigned 16-bit integer.

SEE ALSO `FP_OFF` *For the offset address*

EXAMPLE Use *FP_SEG* to get the segment address of a string. For example, if you want to print the string using DOS function 9h, you will need to specify the offset and the segment address of the string. You can use the *FP_SEG* macro in this case.

```
#include <stdio.h>
#include <dos.h>
char sample[] = "Test string";
main()
{
    char _far *ps;
    unsigned seg_sample;
/* Cast the address of the first character as a _far
 * pointer
 */
    ps = (char _far *)&sample[0];
    seg_sample = FP_SEG(ps);
    printf("The segment address of the string is: %d\n",
                                    seg_sample);
}
```

_harderr

COMPATIBILITY

MSC 3	MSC 4	MSC 5	MSC 6	QC1	QC2	QC2.5	TC1	TC1.5	TC2	TC++	ANSI	UNIX V	XNX	OS2	DOS
		▲	▲	▲	▲	▲		1	1	1					▲

PURPOSE Use *_harderr* to install a new handler for interrupt 24h (critical error) to call a routine whose address you will pass to *_harderr* as an argument. This interrupt occurs on hardware errors during such I/O operations as trying to read from a disk with the drive door open.

SYNTAX `void _harderr (void (_far *funcptr)());`

```
void (_far *funcptr)();
```
Far pointer to the function that will be called by the new INT 24h handler

EXAMPLE CALL

```
void _far harderror_handler(unsigned, unsigned,
                                      unsigned _far *);
_harderr(harderror_handler);
```

INCLUDES

```
#include <dos.h>
```
For declaration of function

DESCRIPTION

The *_harderr* function installs a new handler for interrupt 24h to handle a critical error, which usually occurs when hardware malfunctions. The address of the routine to be called is specified in the argument *funcptr*. The installed handler will call the specified function with three arguments in the following manner:

```
(* funcptr)(unsigned deverror, unsigned errcode,
                                      unsigned _far *devhdr);
```

where *deverror* and *errcode* are unsigned integers containing, respectively, the *AX* and *DI* register values that MS-DOS passes to the INT 24h handler. The *devhdr* argument is a far pointer to a "device header" structure containing descriptive information about the device on which the error occurred. The routine you want called should not alter anything in this device header.

The value in the low-order byte of the argument *errcode* indicates the type of error that occurred. Table 16-26 shows the interpretation of the error code.

If the error occurred during disk I/O, bit 15 (the most significant bit) of the *deverror* argument is set to 0 and the *deverror* provides detailed information about the disk error. The bits and their meanings are shown in Table 16-27. The low-order byte of *deverror* contains the drive number where the error occurred. A 0 indicates drive A, a 1 means drive B, and so on.

If bit 15 of *deverror* is a 1, the error did not occur during disk I/O, and you have to look elsewhere to find the cause. A word located at offset 4 in the device header contains further information about where the error occurred. Access it as an unsigned integer at the address *devhdr+4*. Table 16-28 tells you how to interpret the source of the error in this case.

In the function, whose pointer you are specifying in the argument *funcptr*, you can also make certain MS-DOS function calls. Specifically, you can issue calls to DOS functions 01 through 0Ch and function 59h. Note, however, that many C library routines cannot be used within this function because they call MS-DOS functions to do their job.

If you want to return to MS-DOS, end this function with a *return* or a

Table 16-26. ***Error Codes Indicated by Low Byte of* errcode**

Error Code (hexadecimal)	Meaning
0	Attempted to write to a write-protected disk
1	Unknown unit (source of error not known)
2	Drive not ready
3	Unknown command
4	Cyclic Redundancy Check (CRC) indicates error in data
5	Length of "drive request structure" is bad
6	Seek error
7	Unknown media type
8	Sector not found
9	Printer out of paper
A	Write fault
B	Read fault
C	General failure

call to *_hardresume*. You can return to the program where the error occurred by issuing a call to *_hardretn*.

1. The Turbo C and Turbo C++ version of this function is *harderr*.

COMMON USES This function, introduced in Microsoft C 5.0, is useful in writing robust application programs in which user mistakes do not require aborting from the application.

Table 16-27. ***Disk Error Information in Critical Error Handler***

Bit	Meaning
15	If 0, it's a disk error. IGNORE rest if this bit is 1.
14	— Not used —
13	If 0, "Ignore" response is not allowed.
12	If 0, "Retry" response is not allowed,
11	If 0, "Abort" response is not allowed.
9–10	Indicates area where error occurred: 00 MS-DOS 01 File Allocation Table (FAT) 10 Directory 11 Data area
8	If 1, it's a write error. 0 means read error.

Table 16-28. *Source of Nondisk I/O Error*

Bits of the Word at (devhdr+4)	Source of Error
15	0 = Bad memory image of FAT.
	1 = Error in a character device, interpret error source from bits 0 through 3 of word at address *devhdr*.
	0001 = Error in standard input.
	0010 = Error in standard output.
	0100 = Error in null device.
	1000 = Error in clock device.

COMMENTS It is a good idea to install your own critical error handler; the default MS-DOS handler is somewhat crude and often causes the current application to abort. The availability of this function makes it easy to develop the error handler entirely in C.

SEE ALSO

`_hardresume`	*To return to DOS from the error handler*
`_hardretn`	*To return to the program where the error originally occurred*
`_dos_getvect`	*To retrieve an existing interrupt vector*
`_dos_setvect`	*To install a new interrupt vector*
`_chain_intr`	*To jump from one interrupt handler to another*
`_dos_keep`	*To install "terminate and stay resident" programs*

EXAMPLE Write a critical error handler that checks for a "drive not ready" error that occurs, for example, when you try to find the disk space on drive A when the drive is empty. Let the handler print a message asking the user to insert a disk and continue when the user strikes an appropriate key. Assume that current default drive is not A. Notice the global flag indicating when a critical error occurs so that we can tell when the call to *_dos_getdiskfree* fails because of a "drive not ready" error.

```
#include <stdio.h>
#include <dos.h>
/* Prototype of our critical error handler */
void _far harderror_handler(unsigned, unsigned,
                            unsigned _far *);
unsigned char _far error_flag = 0;
main()
{
```

```
    unsigned drivea =1;
    unsigned long total_space, free_space,
                  bytes_per_cluster;
    struct diskfree_t dfinfo;
/* Install our critical error handler */
    _harderr(harderror_handler);
    printf("We will check our critical error handler.\n\
Make sure drive A: is empty. Hit any key to continue: ");
    getch();
/* Try an operation on drive A: */
    _dos_getdiskfree (drivea, &dfinfo);

/* If error_flag is set call _dos_getdiskfree again */
    if(error_flag) _dos_getdiskfree(drivea, &dfinfo);

/* Compute space statistics and display result */
    bytes_per_cluster = dfinfo.sectors_per_cluster *
                        dfinfo.bytes_per_sector;
    total_space = dfinfo.total_clusters *
                  bytes_per_cluster;
    free_space = dfinfo.avail_clusters *

                 bytes_per_cluster;
    printf ("\n%ld bytes free out of %ld bytes of \
total space.\n", free_space, total_space);
}
/*-----------------------------------------------------*/
#define DRIVE_NOT_READY 2
void far harderror_handler(unsigned deverror,
                           unsigned errorcode,
                           unsigned far *devhdr)
{
    char dletter;
/* Set a flag to let our program know about the error */
    error_flag = 1;
/* Check if this is a "drive not ready" error */
    if ((errorcode & 0xff) == DRIVE_NOT_READY)
    {
/* Find out which drive, it's in low byte of deverror */
        dletter = 'A' + (deverror & 0xff);
/* Ask user to insert a diskette into the drive */
        printf("\nDrive %c is not ready.\n\
Please insert a diskette and hit any key to continue:",
               dletter);
        getch();  /* Read key before returning */
/* Use _hardretn to go back to your program    */
```

```
            _hardretn(-1);
        }
        else
        {
/* Unknown error, print message and abort program */
            printf("Unknown critical error. Aborting...\n");
            _hardresume(_HARDERR_ABORT);
        }
}
```

COMPATIBILITY

_hardresume

MSC 3	MSC 4	MSC 5	MSC 6	QC1	QC2	QC2.5	TC1	TC1.5	TC2	TC++	ANSI	UNIX V	XNX	OS2	DOS
		▲	▲	▲	▲	▲		1	1	1					▲

PURPOSE Use *_hardresume* to return to MS-DOS from your own critical error handler, which can be installed by calling the function *_harderr*.

SYNTAX `void _hardresume (int returncode);`

`int returncode;` *Tells DOS how the handler is returning*

EXAMPLE CALL `_hardresume(_HARDERR_ABORT);`

INCLUDES `#include <dos.h>` *For declaration of function and for return code constants*

DESCRIPTION The *_hardresume* function is used to return to DOS from a routine that you install to process interrupt 24h, which is triggered by critical hardware errors that might occur during an I/O request. The installation of the handler is done by passing its address to the function *_harderr*.

The argument *returncode* tells *_hardresume* what to do upon returning to DOS. Use one of the predefined constants given in Table 16-29 to specify the action. These constants are defined in *dos.h*.

Table 16-29. ***Error Codes Used by* _hardresume**

Return Code Constant	Action Taken by MS-DOS
_HARDERR_IGNORE	Ignores the error.
_HARDERR_RETRY	Retries the operation that caused the error.
_HARDERR_ABORT	Aborts the program by invoking INT 23h.
_HARDERR_FAIL	Causes the MS-DOS system call in progress to fail (only under MS-DOS 3.0 and higher).

1. The Turbo C and Turbo C++ version of this function is *hardresume*.

COMMENTS This function, introduced in Microsoft C 5.0, is used only in a user-installed critical error handler and is not intended for any other use.

SEE ALSO `_hardretn` *To return to the application program from the error handler*

`_chain_intr` *To jump from one interrupt handler to another*

EXAMPLE The example of the use of *_harderr* also includes the use of *_hardresume*.

_hardretn

COMPATIBILITY

MSC 3	MSC 4	MSC 5	MSC 6	QC1	QC2	QC2.5	TC1	TC1.5	TC2	TC++	ANSI	UNIX V	XNX	OS2	DOS
		▲	▲	▲	▲	▲		1	1	1					▲

PURPOSE Use *_hardretn* to return to the application program from your own critical error handler, which can be installed by calling the function *_harderr*.

SYNTAX `void _hardretn (int errorcode);`

`int errorcode;` *MS-DOS error code returned to application program*

EXAMPLE CALL `_hardretn(-1);`

INCLUDES `#include <dos.h>` *For declaration of function*

DESCRIPTION The *_hardretn* function is used to return directly to an application program from an error-handling routine designed to process critical hardware errors that might occur during an I/O request. This routine should be installed as the handler for interrupt 24h by passing its address to the function *_harderr*.

A call to *_hardretn* forces a return to the application program just past the point where the erroneous I/O request occurred. When invoking *_hardretn*, the argument *errorcode* should be an MS-DOS error code appropriate for the I/O operation during which the error occurred. The application program should have code to deal with a returned error condition.

If the number of the DOS function during which the error occurred is 38h or higher, the *_hardretn* function loads AX with the value of *errorcode* before forcing the return. Since integer and unsigned return values from C functions are passed in the AX register, this fools the application program into thinking that a DOS error occurred (instead of a hardware error).

If the hardware error occurred during a DOS I/O function numbered 37h or lower, the return value seen by the application program is FFh. No error code is returned to the application if the error occurs during a DOS function that does not have a way of returning an error condition. In these cases the argument *errorcode* is ignored.

1. The Turbo C and Turbo C++ version of this function is *hardretn*.

COMMENTS This function, introduced in Microsoft C 5.0, is used only in a user-installed critical error handler and is not intended for any other use.

SEE ALSO `_hardresume` *To return to DOS from the error handler*

`_chain_intr` *To jump from one interrupt handler to another*

EXAMPLE The example of the use of *_harderr* also shows how *_hardretn* is used.

COMPATIBILITY

int86

MSC 3	MSC 4	MSC 5	MSC 6	QC1	QC2	QC2.5	TC1	TC1.5	TC2	TC++	ANSI	UNIX V	XNX	OS2	DOS
▲	▲	▲	▲	▲	▲	▲	▲	▲	▲	▲					▲

PURPOSE Use the *int86* function to invoke any BIOS and DOS service routines that can be accessed by generating an 86 software interrupt of specified number. Use *int86* when the function you are calling via interrupt does not require that you pass an argument through the segment registers DS and ES or when you are using a memory model that does not require that you specify the segment registers to access data. For example, you can use *int86* to call the ROM BIOS video function to position the cursor on the screen. The *int86* function uses the REGS data structure to pass register values back and forth (see the tutorial section).

SYNTAX

```
int int86( int intno, union REGS *inregs, union REGS *outregs);
```

`int intno;` *Interrupt number*

`union REGS * inregs;` *Input registers*

`union REGS * outregs;` *Output registers*

EXAMPLE CALL

```
int86(0x10, &inregs, &outregs);
```

INCLUDES `#include <dos.h>` *For definition of REGS*

DESCRIPTION The *int86* function first copies the values for the registers from the C structure *inregs* into the corresponding registers in the microprocessor. Then it generates the software interrupt number *intno* via the INT instruction. After returning from the interrupt, the function copies the contents of the 8086 registers and the system carry flag into corresponding elements in the C structure *outregs*.

The arguments *inregs* and *outregs* are the union of two structures and are defined in the include file *dos.h* (see the tutorial section). Examples below illustrate how the register values are specified.

COMMON USES Prior to Microsoft C 5.0, the most common use of the *int86* function was to access the BIOS functions on the PC, enabling you to move the cursor, read the keyboard, perform screen I/O, and so on. In versions 5.0 and up of the compiler, however, a number of simpler routines are set up to access individual BIOS and DOS functions. Still, the *int86* function has its place. Since its underlying function is to generate software interrupts, you can use it to initiate any interrupt you want and consequently access any function that can be invoked by an interrupt. See Tables 16-1 and 16-2 for a list of all BIOS and DOS functions that can be called by software interrupts.

RETURNS The AX register contains the return value after the interrupt return. An error is indicated by a nonzero value in *outregs.cflag*. The global variable *_doserrno* is set to an error code that tells you what caused the error. See Table 16-25 for list of error codes.

COMMENTS The arguments required by the actual DOS or BIOS function invoked by the interrupt determine whether the segment registers DS and ES need to be loaded before executing the interrupt. For example, if register DX is supposed to contain the offset of a data element and you are using the large model, you can set the data segment register DS to point to your data area. In this case, you would use the *int86x* function for the interrupt because it allows you to load the DS register with a new value before making the software interrupt.

SEE ALSO

`int86x`	*For software interrupts that require that you set up segment registers DS and ES*
`bdos, intdos, intdosx`	*To make a MS-DOS system call with an INT 21H instruction*
Table 16-4	*Simplified access to several BIOS functions*
Table 16-5	*Simplified access to specific MS-DOS functions*

EXAMPLES Write a routine that uses the BIOS video services to position the cursor at column "col" and row number "row" on the screen. Note that (0,0) is the upper left corner of the screen.

```
#include <dos.h>
#define BIOS_VIDEO 0x10

void putcursor(row, col)
int row, col;
{
    union REGS xr;

    xr.h.ah = 2;    /* Function number to set cursor */
    xr.h.dh = row;
    xr.h.dl = col;

    xr.h.bh = 0;    /* Assume video page 0          */
                    /* Use xr for both input/output  */
    int86(BIOS_VIDEO, &xr, &xr);
}
```

On an IBM PC, when you press the SHIFT and PrtSc keys together, the keyboard generates interrupt 5. The BIOS already includes a routine to print the screen when this interrupt occurs. Use *int86* to print the screen by initiating interrupt 5.

```
#include <stdio.h>
#include <dos.h>
#define BIOS_PRNTSCR  5

union REGS xr;
main()
{
    printf("Test: Printing screen\n");
    int86(BIOS_PRNTSCR, &xr, &xr);
}
```

A large number of DOS functions are available via 8086 interrupt 21h. By specifying function 2Ah in AH, you can get the current date with the day in DL, month in DH, and year in CX. The program below shows how:

```
#include <stdio.h>
#include <dos.h>

#define DOS_GETDATE 0x2a
#define DOS_INT     0x21
```

```
static char *months[] = { "---", "JAN", "FEB", "MAR", "APR",
     "MAY", "JUN", "JUL", "AUG", "SEP", "OCT", "NOV", "DEC"};

main()
{
    union REGS xr, yr;
    xr.h.ah = DOS_GETDATE;
    int86 (DOS_INT, &xr, &yr);
    printf("Today's date is: %.2d-%s-%.4d\n",
           yr.h.dl, months[yr.h.dh], yr.x.cx);
}
```

If you have an Enhanced Graphics Adapter (EGA), the BIOS video interrupt (interrupt 10h with AH = 12h and BL = 10h) lets you find out how much physical memory is available on the graphics adapter and which video mode it is in. Write a routine using *int86* to get this information about the EGA.

```
#include <stdio.h>
#include <dos.h>
static union REGS xr, yr;
#define BIOS_VIDEO 0x10
main()
{
/* Set up registers as needed by BIOS video function. */
    xr.h.ah = 0x12;
    xr.h.bl = 0x10;
    int86 (BIOS_VIDEO, &xr, &yr);

/* Upon return values are in structure yr */
    if (yr.h.bh == 0) printf("EGA in color mode\n");
    if (yr.h.bh == 1) printf("EGA in mono mode\n");
    printf("Memory size: ");
    switch (yr.h.bl)
    {
        case 0: printf("64K\n");
                break;
        case 1: printf("128K\n");
                break;
        case 2: printf("192K\n");
                break;
        case 3: printf("256K\n");
                break;
    }
}
```

COMPATIBILITY **int86x**

MSC 3	MSC 4	MSC 5	MSC 6	QC1	QC2	QC2.5	TC1	TC1.5	TC2	TC++	ANSI	UNIX V	XNX	OS2	DOS
▲	▲	▲	▲	▲	▲	▲	▲	▲	▲	▲					▲

PURPOSE Use the *int86x* function to generate an 8086 software interrupt of specified number. Use *int86x* when the function called by the interrupt requires arguments placed in the segment registers DS and ES or when you are using a memory model that requires that you specify the segment registers to access data. For example, you can use *int86x* with interrupt 21h to access the MS-DOS function 3Bh, which allows you to change the current directory from your program. The *int86x* function uses the REGS and SREGS structures as shown below.

SYNTAX

```
int int86x(int intno, union REGS *inr, union REGS *outr,
           struct SREGS *segr);
```

`int intno;` Interrupt number

`union REGS *inr;` *Input registers*

`union REGS *outr;` *Output registers*

`struct SREGS *segr;` *Segment registers*

EXAMPLE CALL `int86x(0x21, &inregs, &outregs, &segregs);`

INCLUDES `#include <dos.h>` *For definition of REGS and SREGS*

DESCRIPTION The *int86x* function first copies the values of the registers from the C structure *inr* into the corresponding registers in the microprocessor. It saves the DS register and then copies new values from the *segr* structure into DS and ES. After that, it generates the software interrupt *intno* via the INT instruction. After returning from the interrupt, *int86x* copies the contents of the 8086 registers and the system carry flag into corresponding elements in the C structure *outr*. It also restores the DS register before returning.

The arguments *inr* and *outr* are the union of two structures. This and the structure SREGS are defined in the include file *dos.h* (see the tutorial section). The examples below illustrate how the register values are specified.

COMMON USES The most common use of the *int86x* function is to access the MS-DOS and BIOS functions on the PC, especially those that either accept arguments or return values via the segment registers DS and ES. The BIOS and DOS functions, for example, allow you to read from the floppy disk, change current directory, and print a string. Since the underlying function of *int86x* is to make software interrupts, you can use it to initiate any interrupt you want and consequently access anything on the PC that is reached by an interrupt. This includes all DOS services as well. See Tables 16-1 and 16-2 for a list of all significant DOS and BIOS functions invoked by software interrupts.

RETURNS The register AX contains the return value after the interrupt return. An error is indicated by a nonzero value in *outr.cflag*. The global variable *_doserrno* is set to an error code that tells you what caused the error. See Table 16-25 for a list of error codes.

COMMENTS The arguments required by the actual function invoked by the interrupt determine whether the segment registers DS and ES need to be loaded before executing the interrupt. You must use *int86x* whenever arguments have to be passed through DS and ES.

The *int86x* function is the most general interface to the BIOS and MS-DOS services. The Microsoft C run-time library includes several special functions designed as gateways to specific DOS and BIOS calls. Note, however, that *every* interrupt service on the PC is accessible via *int86x*.

SEE ALSO

`int86`	*For software interrupts that do not require that you set up segment registers DS and ES*
`bdos, intdos, intdosx`	*To make an MS-DOS system call with an INT 21H instruction*
Table 16-4	*Simplified access to several BIOS functions*
Table 16-5	*Simplified access to specific MS-DOS functions*

EXAMPLES Change the current directory by calling DOS function 3Bh with *int86x*. Use the *FP_OFF* and *FP_SEG* macros to find offset and segment addresses of strings that have to be passed to the DOS function 3Bh.

```
#include <stdio.h>
#include <dos.h>
/* Interrupt number for DOS functions */
#define DOS_INT 0x21
/* DOS "change directory" function    */
#define DOS_CHDIR 0x3b
/* Buffer to hold path name           */
static char buff[80];
main()
{
/* _Far pointer to directory name string*/
```

```
    char far *dirname;
/* Set up the structure for registers  */
    union REGS xr;
    struct SREGS sr;
    printf("Enter pathname: ");
    gets(buff);
 /* Set up _far pointer to name*/
    dirname = &buff[0];
    xr.h.ah = DOS_CHDIR;
/* Offset of string to DX    */
    xr.x.dx = FP_OFF(dirname);
/* Segment of string to DS   */
    sr.ds = FP_SEG(dirname);
    int86x(DOS_INT, &xr, &xr, &sr);
}
```

Use *int86x* to access the MS-DOS function 9h, accessible via interrupt 21h, to print a string terminated with a $. Use the *FP_SEG* and *FP_OFF* functions to get the segment and offset addresses of the string to be printed.

```
#include <dos.h>
#define DOS_INT     0x21
/* DOS "print string" function */
#define DOS_PRTSTR  0x9

char str[]="Testing String Print Function$";
main()
{
    union  REGS  xr;
    struct SREGS sr;

    xr.h.ah = DOS_PRTSTR;
/* Offset string to DX        */
    xr.x.dx = FP_OFF(str);
/* Segment of string to DS    */
    sr.ds = FP_SEG(str);
    int86x(DOS_INT, &xr, &xr, &sr);
}
```

intdos

COMPATIBILITY

MSC 3	MSC 4	MSC 5	MSC 6	QC1	QC2	QC2.5	TC1	TC1.5	TC2	TC++	ANSI	UNIX V	XNX	OS2	DOS
▲	▲	▲	▲	▲	▲	▲	▲	▲	▲	▲					▲

PURPOSE Use the *intdos* function to access the popular set of MS-DOS system utility routines that are normally called via 8086 software interrupt 21h. Use *intdos* when the DOS function does not require that you exchange any arguments through the segment registers DS and ES or when you are using a memory model that does not require that you specify the segment registers to access data. For example, you can use *intdos* with function 19h to get the current disk drive number.

Since the *int86* function can generate any software interrupt, you can duplicate the effect of *intdos* by calling *int86* with interrupt 21h. The only advantage of the *intdos* function is its shorter list of arguments.

SYNTAX

```
int intdos( union REGS *inregs, union REGS *outregs);

union REGS *inregs;        Input registers

union REGS *outregs;       Output registers
```

EXAMPLE CALL

```
intdos(&inregs, &outregs);
```

INCLUDES

```
#include <dos.h>      For definition of REGS
```

DESCRIPTION The *intdos* function first copies the values of the registers from the C structure *inregs* into the corresponding registers in the microprocessor. Then it generates the software interrupt 21h to access the MS-DOS system functions. After returning from the interrupt, *intdos* copies the contents of the 8086 registers and the system carry flag into corresponding elements in the C structure *outregs*. The task performed by DOS depends on the function number specified in the AH register.

The arguments *inregs* and *outregs* are the union of two structures and are defined in the include file *dos.h* (see the tutorial section). The examples below illustrate how the register values are specified.

COMMON USES The *intdos* function is used to access the MS-DOS system routines that are accessible through an INT 21h instruction. These routines, for example, allow you to read the keyboard, write to the screen, and manipulate DOS directories and files. Table 16-2 gives a complete list of all DOS functions.

RETURNS The register AX contains the return value after the interrupt return. An error is indicated by a nonzero value in the *outregs* field *.cflag*. The global variable *_doserrno* is set to an error code that tells you what caused the error. See Table 16-25 for a list of error codes.

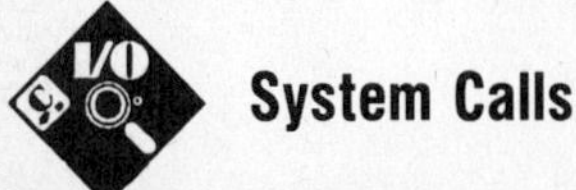

COMMENTS The arguments required by the MS-DOS function invoked by *intdos* determine whether the segment registers DS and ES need to be loaded before calling this function. For example if register DX is supposed to contain the offset of a data element and you are using the large model, you can set the data segment register DS to point to your data area. In this case, you would use the *intdosx* function because it allows you to load the DS register with a new value before invoking the DOS function.

SEE ALSO

`int86, int86x`	*For other software interrupts*
`intdosx`	*To access MS-DOS functions that require arguments in segment registers DS and ES*
`bdos`	*To access those MS-DOS routines that take arguments in the DX and AL registers only*

Table 16-5 *These functions provide simplified access to specific MS-DOS services*

EXAMPLES MS-DOS function 19h returns the default drive number in the *AL* register. Access this function via *intdos* and get the current drive number (0 means A, 1 means B, 2 means C, and so on).

```
#include <stdio.h>
#include <dos.h>
#define DOS_GETDRIVE 0x19
union REGS xr;
main()
{
    xr.h.ah = DOS_GETDRIVE;
    intdos(&xr, &xr);

/* Adding 65 to the value gives us the drive letter */
    printf("Current drive: %c\n", xr.h.al+65);
}
```

DOS function 2Ch returns the current time with the hours in *CH*, minutes in *CL*, and the seconds in *DH*. Use *intdos* to get the current time and display it.

```
#include <stdio.h>
#include <dos.h>
#define DOS_GETTIME 0x2c
main()
{
    union REGS xr, yr;
    xr.h.ah = DOS_GETTIME;
```

```
        intdos(&xr, &yr);
        printf("Current time is %.2d:%.2d:%.2d\n",
               yr.h.ch, yr.h.cl, yr.h.dh);
    }
```

intdosx

COMPATIBILITY

MSC 3	MSC 4	MSC 5	MSC 6	QC1	QC2	QC2.5	TC1	TC1.5	TC2	TC++	ANSI	UNIX V	XNX	OS2	DOS
▲	▲	▲	▲	▲	▲	▲	▲	▲	▲	▲					▲

PURPOSE Use the *intdosx* function to access any MS-DOS system function, even those that require arguments in the segment registers DS and ES (*intdos* cannot handle these cases). You must use *intdosx* when the DOS function requires arguments exchanged through the segment registers DS and ES or when you are using a memory model that requires that you specify the segment registers in order to access data. For example, you can use *intdosx* with function 39h to create a subdirectory.

SYNTAX

```
int intdosx(union  REGS *inr, union  REGS *outr,
            struct SREGS *segr);
```

`union  REGS  *inr;` *Input registers*

`union  REGS  *outr;` *Output registers*

`struct SREGS *segr;` *Segment registers*

EXAMPLE CALL `intdosx(&inregs, &outregs, &segregs);`

INCLUDES `#include <dos.h>` *For definition of REGS and SREGS*

DESCRIPTION The *intdosx* function copies the values of the registers from the C structure *inr* into the corresponding registers in the microprocessor. It saves the DS register and then copies new values from *segr* into DS and ES. After that, it calls DOS by an INT 21h instruction. After returning from DOS, *intdosx* copies the contents of the 8086 registers and the system carry flag into corresponding elements in the C structure *outr*. It also restores the DS register before returning. The actions performed by DOS depend on the function number specified in the AH register.

The arguments *inr* and *outr* are the union of two structures. This and the structure SREGS are defined in the include file *dos.h* (see the tutorial section). The examples below illustrate how the register values are specified.

COMMON USES The *intdosx* function is used to call MS-DOS functions on the PC, espe-

cially those that either accept arguments or return values via the segment registers DS and ES. The DOS functions, for example, allow you to read from the floppy disk, change the current directory, and create a subdirectory. See Table 16-2 for a list of all DOS functions that can be called by software interrupts.

RETURNS The register AX contains the return value after the interrupt return. An error is indicated by a nonzero value in *outr.cflag*. The global variable *_doserrno* is set to an error code that tells you what caused the error. See Table 16-25 for a list of error codes.

COMMENTS The arguments required by the DOS function invoked by *intdosx* determine whether the segment registers DS and ES need to be loaded before calling *intdosx*. You must use *intdosx* whenever parameters are exchanged through the segment registers DS and ES.

The *intdosx* function is a general interface to the MS-DOS functions. The Microsoft C run-time library includes several special functions designed as gateways to specific DOS calls. Note, however, that every DOS function on the PC is accessible via *intdosx*.

SEE ALSO

int86, int86x	*To generate any 8086 software interrupt*
intdos	*For MS-DOS calls that do not require that you set up segment registers DS and ES*
bdos	*To access those MS-DOS routines that take arguments in the DX and AL registers only*

Table 16-5 *These functions provide simplified access to specific MS-DOS services*

EXAMPLES Use the MS-DOS function 39h to create a subdirectory in the current directory. The segment and offset of the subdirectory name should be specified via the registers DS and DX, respectively.

```
#include <stdio.h>
#include <dos.h>

#define  DOS_MAKEDIR 0x39

union REGS xr;
struct SREGS sr;

main()
{
    char pathname[80];
```

```
    printf("Enter name of subdirectory: ");
    gets(pathname);

    xr.h.ah = DOS_MAKEDIR;
    sr.ds = FP_SEG(pathname);
    xr.x.dx = FP_OFF(pathname);
    intdosx(&xr, &xr, &sr);

    if (xr.x.cflag == 1)
    {
        printf("\nError creating subdirectory\n");
    }
}
```

Use DOS function Ah to read a line from the keyboard up to and including a carriage return. The line is stored in a buffer whose segment address must be in DS and the offset in DX. The first byte of the buffer contains the maximum number of characters to be read. On return, the second byte has the number of characters read.

```
#include <stdio.h>
#include <dos.h>
#define DOS_BUFIN 0x0a
static char buffer[82] = {80, 0};
main()
{
    union REGS xr;
    struct SREGS sr;
    int numchars;
    char _far *pbuf;
    pbuf = (char _far *)(&buffer[0]);
    printf("Enter a line: ");
    sr.ds = FP_SEG(pbuf);
    xr.h.ah = DOS_BUFIN;
    xr.x.dx = FP_OFF(pbuf);
    intdosx(&xr, &xr, &sr);
/* The number of characters not counting the carriage
 * return
 */
    numchars = buffer[1];
/* Make it an ASCIIZ string by adding a 0 at the end*/
    buffer[numchars+2] = '\0';
    printf("\nYou typed %d characters\n", numchars);
    printf("The string is: %s", buffer+2);
}
```

System Calls

V Graphics

- Graphics Modes, Coordinates, and Attributes
- Drawing and Animation
- Combining Graphics and Text

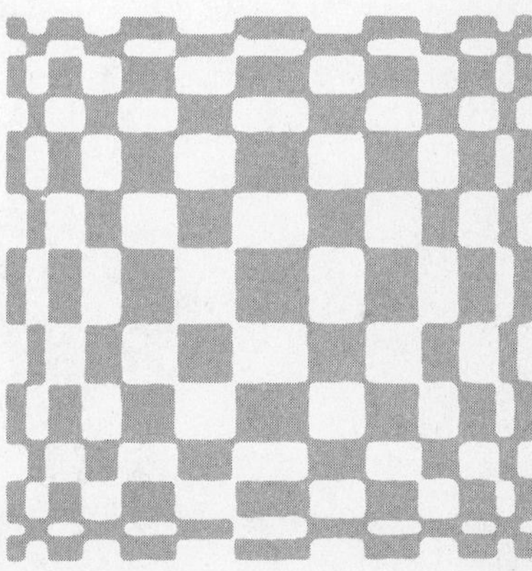

COMPATIBILITY

segread

MSC 3	MSC 4	MSC 5	MSC 6	QC1	QC2	QC2.5	TC1	TC1.5	TC2	TC++	ANSI	UNIX V	XNX	OS2	DOS
▲	▲	▲	▲	▲	▲	▲	▲	▲	▲	▲				▲	▲

PURPOSE Use the *segread* function to retrieve the values of the 8086 segment registers CS, DS, ES, and SS from C programs. For example, you may want to read and save the value of ES before it is altered during a call to *int86x* or *intdosx* or you may want to check the segment register values to debug your C program.

SYNTAX

```
void segread (struct SREGS *segregs);

struct SREGS *segregs;
```

C structure to hold segment registers

EXAMPLE CALL

```
segread(&segregs);
```

INCLUDES

```
#include <dos.h>
```

For definition of SREGS

DESCRIPTION The *segread* function copies the current values of the 8086 segment registers into the C structure *segregs* which has one unsigned integer variable for each segment register. These variables are named *cs, ds, es,* and *ss.* Starting with Microsoft C 5.1, under OS/2, the segment register values are selector values (see *Inside OS/2* by Gordon Letwin, Microsoft Press, 1988, for OS/2 terminology and features).

COMMON USES This function is commonly used to save the value of ES before calling *int86x* or *intdosx* since ES is frequently used by BIOS routines.

COMMENTS The segment register values are usually of no concern to C programmers except when accessing system-level functions.

SEE ALSO int86x, intdosx — *For 8086 software interrupts that may require you to set up segment registers DS and ES*

EXAMPLE Use the *segread* function to display the values of the 8086 segment registers.

```
#include <stdio.h>
#include <dos.h>
struct SREGS sr;

main()
{
    segread(&sr);
    printf("Currently cs = %x, ds = %x, es = %x, ss = %x\n",
            sr.cs, sr.ds, sr.es, sr.ss);
}
```

Chapter 17 Graphics Modes, Coordinates, and Attributes

Introduction

Graphic user interfaces are increasingly the norm for PC-based applications. Older text-based software, written when DOS ran on slower chips and only 512 K of memory, is now giving way to packages that take advantage of faster chips and additional memory. OS/2, with its promise of a bit-mapped window-oriented interface, is the focus of much attention. For DOS systems, Microsoft Windows is among the most popular of the packages that provide a Graphical User Interface (GUI).

Even though we recognize the need to build an easy-to-use interface, the task of programming good graphics and text capabilities remains a particularly complicated business in the PC world. The list of graphics adapters and the various displays that can be used with those adapters seems to grow each month. Adding to this complexity is the IBM PC's limited support for video I/O in the ROM BIOS (see Chapter 16). Until recently, maintaining an acceptable response time meant writing a significant amount of the program with assembly language. This is no longer true.

The Microsoft C 5.x versions introduced 43 graphics routines to the Microsoft library. The routines made the task of creating graphics-based programs much simpler by providing basic capabilities to determine what video hardware was installed and when to set an appropriate video mode. The 5.1 routines allowed you to select colors, line styles, and fill patterns; draw primitive shapes such as straight lines, rectangles, arcs, and ellipses; mix text and graphics on the screen; and perform moderately successful animation by saving and restoring screen images.

Many additional capabilities were added to version 6.0 of Microsoft C, including a number of new general graphics functions, support for Olivetti versions of video palettes, and more than 20 presentation graphics functions and font-management routines. (Some, but not all, of these new functions were actually introduced earlier with Quick C 2.0.)

We describe the Microsoft graphics library routines in the next three chapters of the book. This chapter presents the information you need to get started with the Microsoft C graphics library. In Chapter 18, we describe the drawing, animation, and presentation graphics routines. In Chapter 19, we cover the routines for text output in graphics mode.

We will start with a discussion of the options available for graphics programming on the PC, the video modes in which the common graphics adapters operate, and the coordinate systems used in the Microsoft C graphics library. We will then describe the library routines that let you control the modes and attributes of the Microsoft C graphics programming model. We will limit discussion of the graphics hardware to those aspects that directly affect graphics programming, so we will present information on the number of colors and resolutions, for example, but skip details such as scan rate of monitors and screen sizes.

Basics of PC Graphics

In the IBM PC (and compatibles), screen output relies on two components: the display adapter (popularly known as the graphics card) and the display monitor. As shown in Figure 17-1, the "adapter" is a card that you

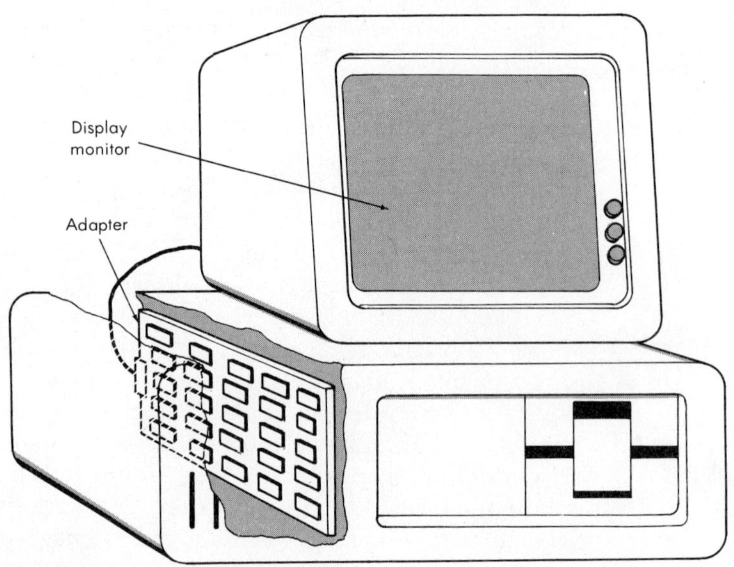

Figure 17-1. ***Display hardware in IBM PC***

plug into one of the slots inside the PC and the "monitor" is the display screen where the actual characters and graphics appear.

Whether we can display a particular format of graphics on a monitor depends on the adapter, although the resolution of the actual image also depends on the monitor. A monitor displays dots (each of which is known as a "pixel") in one of two formats. The first format is called "text," and the second is called "graphics." Text modes display preformed patterns of pixels which are normally in the shape of characters, numbers, and punctuation. Graphics modes let you turn the pixels on (and off) one-by-one, creating whatever shapes you wish. You may choose to build character patterns in a graphics mode (there are Microsoft library functions that help you generate fonts) but you can also draw lines, circles, pictures of a Space Shuttle, or any other shape you choose. Since the graphics adapter is the key piece of hardware, let's look at what is available.

ADAPTERS AND MONITORS FOR THE IBM PC

There are six popular display adapters defined in the *graph.h* file of the Microsoft 5.1 and 6.0 packages. They are Monochrome Display Adapter (MDA), Color Graphics Adapter (CGA), Enhanced Graphics Adapter (EGA), Hercules Graphics Card (HGC), Multicolor Graphics Array (MCGA), and Video Graphics Array (VGA). Version 6.0 also supports Olivetti versions of the CGA, EGA, and VGA modes. The *graph.h* file defines six types of monitors: Monochrome, Color, Enhanced Color, Analog Monochrome, Analog Color, and Analog Mono/Color. The analog units are of recent vintage, offering sharper resolution than earlier screens, and in some cases they are multisynchronous (accommodating a variety of display frequencies). Generally these units are found on PS/2 and high-end AT machines.

The MDA is the display used in the original IBM PC. It can display 80 characters (columns) by 25 lines (rows) of text output on the monochrome display, but the MDA does not have a graphics-display capability. The HGC displays text like the MDA, however, it will also display graphics on the monochrome monitor at a resolution of 720 pixels horizontally and 348 pixels vertically. (Another way of saying this is that the HGC has a resolution of 720x348: the nomenclature we will henceforth use to describe screen resolution.)

The CGA can display text as well as graphics, and will do so in color on a color monitor. The CGA can display text using a combination of any 1 of 16 foreground colors (8 colors with 2 levels of brightness) and 1 of 8 background colors. The "foreground" refers to the characters being displayed, and "background" refers to the color you see on an otherwise blank screen. CGA Graphics can be displayed in 4 colors with 320x200 resolution. If you choose 2-color (black and white) graphics, the resolution goes up to 640x200. We will explain the trade-off between number of colors and resolution, later.

The EGA, introduced by IBM in 1984, added higher resolution and more colors. It displays text and graphics in color on an enhanced color display monitor. To retain compatibility with earlier hardware, the EGA is provided with operational modes in which it can display text on a monochrome monitor or emulate a CGA. In its highest resolution mode, the EGA can generate 640x350 graphics output with 16 different colors.

VIDEO GRAPHICS ARRAY (VGA)

IBM introduced two adapters with its line of PS/2 machines: the Multi Color Graphics Array (MCGA) and the Video Graphics Array (VGA). The VGA is a successor to the EGA, and appropriate hardware is available from a variety of vendors for AT and PS/2 class machines. In one video mode (mode 12h), the VGA offers 640x480 resolution graphics with 16 colors out of a possible 256 simultaneous colors. The VGA can also provide 320x200 resolution graphics with 256 colors (mode 13h). VGA adapters can display all EGA and CGA modes. The MCGA is similar to the CGA, but has a 2-color 640x480 mode (rather than the 16 colors of the VGA in this mode).

The standard VGA adapters are designed to drive an "analog monitor," as opposed to the "digital" ones that are used with MDA, CGA, and EGA on the PC. As its name implies, a digital monitor uses a fixed number of on/off signals. For example, the enhanced color display monitor accepts the 6 on/off signals: red, green, and blue and intensified versions of each, so it is capable of displaying 64 distinct colors ($2^6 = 64$). It is, however, limited to 16 colors at once because there are only 4 bits of storage for each pixel on the display adapter. In an analog monitor, the red, green, and blue signals can vary constantly, instead of being on or off. This allows continuously varying shades of colors. Inside the MCGA and VGA adapters, the colors are still represented digitally. For example, in MCGA, red, green, and blue are each represented by 6-bit values. A Digital-to-Analog Converter (DAC) converts these digital values to analog signals before they are fed to the monitor. The potential number of colors is thus determined by the range of color values that can be represented digitally in the adapter.

HIGHER RESOLUTIONS

The IBM model 8514/A is a PC graphics board that provides hardware coprocessing to accelerate signal processing. The standard 8514/A offers a resolution of 1,024x1,024; clone versions of the chipset offer resolutions of up to 2,560x2,048. In between the 8514/A and standard VGA resolution of 640x480 are the so-called Super VGA resolutions of 800x600 and 1,024x768, each with 16 colors. The increasing popularity of higher resolutions makes relying on EGA quality images a bad idea for those who write commercial software.

You have to deal with quite a few combinations of adapters and monitors when working with DOS and OS/2-based machines. Fortunately, the graphics library in Microsoft C offers you a lot of help.

PROGRAMMING THE DISPLAY ADAPTERS

Like most peripheral devices in the IBM and compatible PCs and PS/2s, most graphics cards (display adapters) are programmed via 8-bit registers that are accessible by input port addresses (see the tutorial in Chapter 15 for a description of port I/O routines in Microsoft C). Some newer cards use 16- or 32-bit registers for certain tasks; this can greatly increase their speed. All PC display adapters share one common property: they are "memory-mapped." Each pixel on the display screen corresponds to one or more bits in a memory location in the graphics card accessible, just like the rest of the memory locations in the system. This "video memory," or video RAM, is physically present on the display adapter but it has addresses up to 256 K that map into the normal address space of the microprocessor. Microsoft C 6.0 introduced *_based* memory addressing (described in Chapter 5), which is very helpful in reaching these addresses.

The circuitry in the display adapter reads values from the video RAM and displays the pixels on the monitor. This allows you to display text and graphics on the monitor by directly manipulating the video RAM, provided you know how this memory is organized. The method of storing information in the video memory depends on whether text or graphics is being displayed.

In text display modes, a rectangular grid of pixels is used to display one character. Each character is stored using 2 bytes: the low-order byte for the 8-bit ASCII code for the character and the high-order byte to store the display attributes for that character. These attributes determine such characteristics as the colors of the character and of the background pixels and whether the character is blinking. The exact pattern of pixels necessary to draw each character is stored in a separate table in memory. These patterns are referred to as "fonts." (The default font is stored in ROM and read into memory at startup.)

In graphics modes, the number of bits necessary to represent a pixel depends on the number of colors to be displayed. For a black and white monitor, each pixel is either on or off, so a single bit is enough to store all the information necessary to display a pixel. By the same token, we need 4 bits of storage per pixel to display 16 colors. The maximum number of colors that can be displayed is given by 2 to the nth, where n is the number of bits per pixel. Since the maximum amount of memory on the adapter is fixed at 256 K, there is always a trade-off between the number of on-screen pixels and the number of colors.

The physical organization of the video RAM varies quite a bit from one adapter to another, and the details (especially in EGA and VGA) can be overwhelming—even for a simple program. Fortunately, the Microsoft C graphics routines eliminate the need to learn the detailed organization of the video memory and display adapters for most applications.

BIOS VIDEO ROUTINES

The BIOS routines which reside in the read-only memory (ROM) of every PC provide a portable way to program DOS and OS/2 video adapters. Using software interrupt 10h (see the tutorial in Chapter 16), you can invoke a set of functions that allow setting the video mode, and reading and writing pixel values. Several video modes for text or graphics output are available in the BIOS video routines, each of which is suitable for a specific monitor if that adapter supports multiple monitor types. In a text mode you can write a character to the screen with an associated attribute to control its appearance. In a graphics mode, you are limited to either writing a pixel or reading the value of a pixel. The BIOS is adequate for basic display programming, however, it is relatively slow. Fast-screen drawing, especially in graphics modes, normally requires that you write directly to the video memory. The BIOS trades its slower performance for portability. The procedures for direct-memory writes may vary between hardware manufacturers, and thus such programs are considerably less portable than their BIOS counterparts; for example, they often do not run well under MS Windows. Software using only BIOS calls is said to be graphically "well behaved."

THE MICROSOFT C SOLUTION

Where does the Microsoft C graphics library fit in this picture? The Microsoft graphics routines perform better than the BIOS video routines and they provide many more basic capabilities than does BIOS interrupt 10h. Additionally, the Microsoft C graphics library routines are much easier to use than the BIOS routines, which must be invoked via software interrupts. To use the graphics library, you do not have to know the implementation details of the routines, but you do have to understand the graphics "model" used by Microsoft.

The Microsoft C Graphics Model

The Microsoft C graphics model is the collection of such concepts as coordinates, colors, palettes, line styles, fill masks, and primitive shapes that the library uses. Many of the ideas have their roots in the hardware, and we will make these connections clear as the concepts are discussed.

DISPLAY SCREEN AND THE COORDINATE SYSTEMS

In text modes, as shown in Figure 17-2, the entire screen is viewed as a grid of cells that is usually 25 rows by 80 columns (though EGA can support 43 rows, and VGA 43 or 50). Each cell can hold a character with certain foreground and background colors, if the monitor is capable of displaying colors. A location on the screen is expressed in terms of rows and columns with the upper-left corner corresponding to (1,1). The row numbers increase from top to bottom and the column numbers increase from left to right. A typical text screen has a grid location of (1,1) at the top left and (25,80) at the bottom right. Remember that the numbering starts with 1 (not 0) and that the row is always listed before the column.

In graphics modes, the screen is seen as a matrix of individual pixels. Depending on the graphics mode and graphics card (or display adapter), the width and height of this matrix (measured in pixels) can be one of the following: 320x200, 640x200, 640x350, 640x400, 640x480, or 720x348.

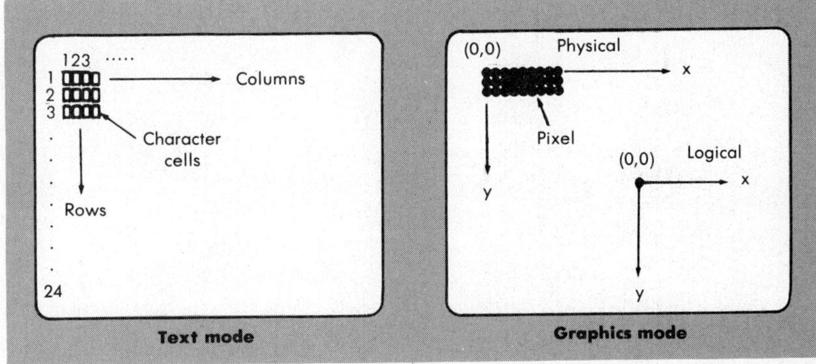

Figure 17-2. ***Coordinate frames in text and graphics modes***

There are other adapters on the horizon which offer greater resolution, but these are the adapters with which Microsoft C deals. Table 17-1 describes which mode attains which resolution.

Each pixel has a specific location. The differences between describing a graphic (pixel) location and a text location are important: graphic numbering starts at 0 (instead of the 1 used for text mode) and columns are listed before rows with graphic addresses instead of the row before column arrangement of text addresses.

The Microsoft C graphics library was introduced in version 5.0. The 5.0 and 5.1 products used two graphics coordinate systems: one "physical" and the other "logical." Both coordinate systems originate at the upper-left corner of the physical screen. The *x*-axis is a positive value on a row of pixels increasing from left-to-right. The *y*-axis is a positive value on a column of pixels and grows from top-to-bottom. This pattern is shown in Figure 17-2.

All graphics functions in the 5.0 and 5.1 graphics library work with logical graphics coordinates so the graphics output can be easily translated or shifted on the screen by redefining the logical origin. A call that draws a rectangle with its upper-left corner at logical (0,0) will be drawn at a new location on the screen if you move the logical origin to, say, (150,90) using *_setlogorg*, and issue the call to draw the rectangle again.

Microsoft C compiler versions after 5.1 (including Quick C 2.0 and 2.5) use three low-level graphics coordinate systems, two of which were not available in 5.0 or 5.1. The three coordinates were originally presented in Quick C 2.0 and are called "physical," "viewport," and "window." The "logical" coordinate system is no longer in use, and its functions *_setlogorg* and *_getlogcoord* are #defined to *_setvieworg* and *_getviewcoord* in the 6.0 *graph.h* file.

The first of the current coordinate systems for low-level graphics is the physical coordinate system. These coordinates are based on the

320x200, 640x200, 640x350, 640x400, 640x480, or 720x348 resolution models, and they are used in only five functions: *_setcliprgn, _setvieworg, _setviewport, _getviewcoord,* and *_getphyscoord.* The numbering starts in the upper-left corner with (0,0). The column numbers grow larger from top-to-bottom and the row numbers grow larger from left-to-right. Since the numbering starts at zero, the greatest physical-graphic pixel coordinate is one less than the number of pixels in either the column or the row. Thus the largest physical-graphics coordinate on a 640x480 screen would be (639,479) in the *(x,y)* format used to express physical coordinates.

The second of the current coordinate systems for low-level graphics is the viewport (sometimes called view) system. (A viewport is a clipping region whose coordinate system has its origin at its upper-left corner.) This is similar to the now-superseded logical coordinate system introduced in Microsoft 5.0. The default viewport is the physical screen. A new one may be defined with *_setviewport,* and an origin may be specified with *_setvieworg.* Viewport functions do not have a suffix in their name—a condition whose significance will be explained, momentarily—and they use coordinate arguments that are of type *short int.*

The third current coordinate system for low-level graphics is the window system. The window graphics coordinate system turns the current viewport into a window. The library functions ending in *_w* use window coordinates and their coordinate arguments are *doubles.* Those functions with *_wxy* suffixes take *_wxycoord* structures as arguments. That structure is defined in *graph.h.*

The *_getwindowcoord* (new to Microsoft C 6.0), *_getviewcoord,* and *_getphyscoord* functions help you translate between the various coordinate systems for the low-level graphics. They are covered in the reference pages. We will now turn our attention to a brief description of how the various coordinate systems work.

USING THE COORDINATES

Assume you have made a call in your program to the *_setvideomode* function, asking it to set the system to _MRES16COLOR. That will yield a physical coordinate system—essentially the physical screen—with a *(x,y)* resolution of 320x200. The 320 identifies the number of pixels in each row and 200 identifies the number of pixels in each column. This means that there are 320 columns and 200 rows. Columns are the *x* value and rows are the *y*, and graphics coordinates under Microsoft C always follow *(x,y)* order.

As shown in Figure 17-3, the origin (0,0) is the upper-left corner of a graphics screen. The physical columns (*x*) are numbered 0 through 319 and the physical rows (*y*) are numbered 0 through 199. If you were to change the mode to _VRES2COLOR, which generates a 640x480 screen, the columns would be numbered zero through 639 and the rows 0 through 479. (Remember that pixel numbering starts at 0 on a graphics screen and thus the highest number of *x* and *y* is one less than the resolution number. Numbering starts at 1 on a text screen.)

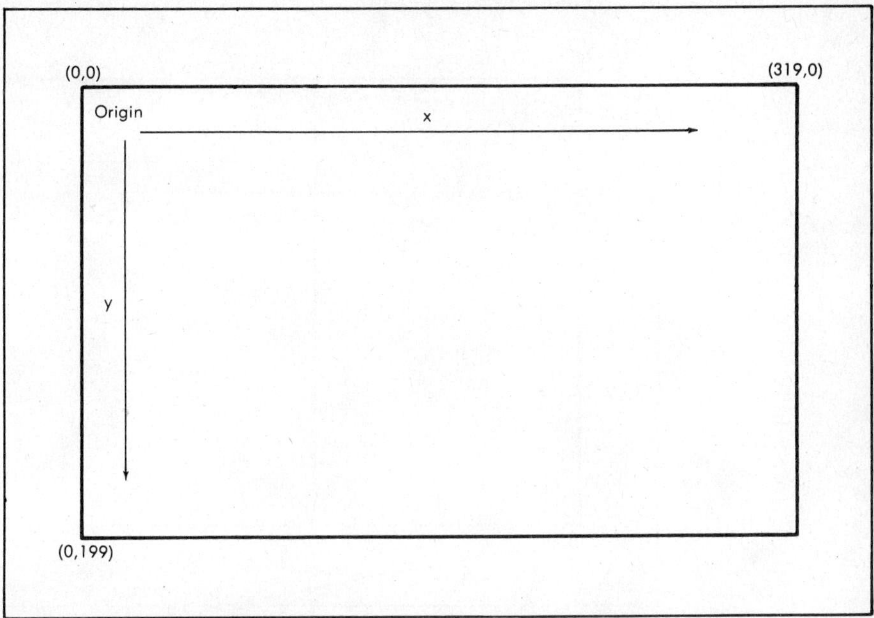

Figure 17-3. ***Origin is the upper-left corner of the graphics screen***

The viewport is an important concept to understand. The default viewport is the same size as the physical screen when the graphics mode is initialized, but it can be moved around with calls to the *_setvieworg* function. The viewpoint does not cause the number of pixels to change (they remain at 320x200 in our _MRES16COLOR example), however, it will change the meaning of the coordinates.

Suppose that your program makes a call to *_setvieworg* with integer arguments of 120 and 50. The *_setvieworg* function moves the view coordinate origin (the (0,0) point in the upper-left corner of the viewport) to the physical point (120,50). All other view-coordinate points will move the same direction and distance. The *_setvieworg* function replaced the *_setlogorg* function used in Microsoft C versions 5.0 and 5.1.

The viewport creates an area within the physical screen inside which subsequent graphics are placed by default. Coordinate addresses within the viewport have positive values, while coordinate addresses outside the viewport (but still within the physical screen) have negative values. Our example creates a viewport at (120,50) on a 320x200 _MRES16COLOR physical screen.

The "post-viewport" value for physical columns goes from 0 through 319 to −120 through 199. The similar value for rows goes from 0 through 199 to −50 through 149. This is shown in Figure 17-4. The effect of the viewport is to have moved the origin of the screen from (0,0) to (120,50). The (120,50) intersection is assigned the value of (0,0). Every point be-

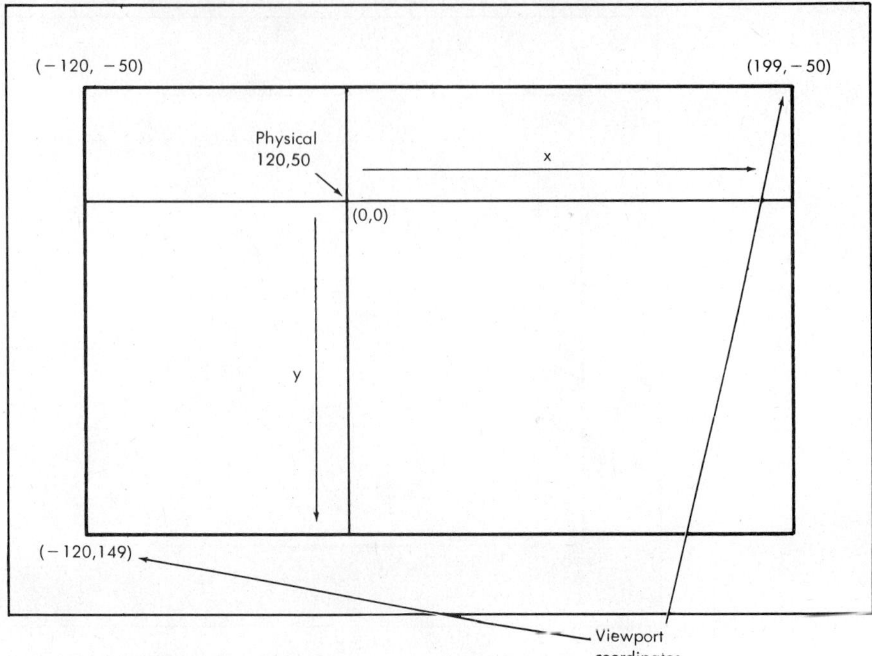

Figure 17-4. ***A viewport defined on the physical screen***

tween the new (0,0) and the old one is expressed in negative integers, whereas every point within the viewport is a positive number. The total number of pixels does not change. Once you have set a viewport, all of the standard graphics functions operate with the new coordinate values.

The *_setvieworg* function does not increment. You cannot, for example, move to (140,60) with successive commands such as:

```
_setvieworg (120,50);
_setvieworg (20,10);
```

In this case, the viewport would end up at (20,10). The base against which *_setvieworg* acts is always the border of the physical screen, and associated graphics move when the viewport moves.

The *_setviewport* and *_setcliprgn* functions both establish a clip region. A clip region is an invisible rectangular area on the screen, the boundaries of which are given by the calling function. Nothing can be drawn outside of the clip region, and even though two different functions are capable of creating a clip region, the procedures they use are identical. After setting a clip region, however, *_setviewport* sets the view coordinate of the viewport to the (0,0) area of the clip region while *_setcliprgn* does not change the coordinates. The *_setviewport*, then, behaves the same as would a call to *_setvieworg* followed by a call to *_setcliprgn*.

We have identified three ways of establishing a viewport: The first is the default, in which the viewport and the physical screen match as the graphics system is initialized. The second technique is to use the *_setvieworg* function. The third method requires the use of *_setviewport* to establish a clip region, and thereafter, setting the view coordinate origin—the (0,0) of the viewport—to the (0,0) of the clip region.

Window Coordinate System

The third current coordinate system for low-level graphics is the window coordinate system. The window system appears inside a viewport (remember that a viewport can encompass the entire screen), and it is a region created with a call to the *_setwindow* function. The window routines use functions that have a *_w* suffix on their name. Viewport graphics functions take integers as arguments, but window graphics functions take double-precision, floating-point arguments. This adds processing overhead to handle the math, but provides enormous flexibility for your drawings. The precision will allow for such effects as panning an image, for instance, with scaling possibilities from ranges that are quite large—such as −30,000 to 75,000—to quite small—such as 166.30 to 166.48. You may have several windows in a viewport.

SCREEN POSITIONS

There are two "addresses" (horizontal and vertical) to a screen coordinate. We noted earlier that *x* is the column value and *y* is the row. Passing one variable instead of two is possible, however, through the use of one of the two screen-coordinate structures defined in the *graph.h* file of version 6.0 and later. The first is *xycoord*, and it contains two short integers for use in viewport graphics. The second is *_wxycoord*, and it contains two doubles called *wx* and *wy*. It is used with window coordinate graphics. The *_wxycoord* structures are used with the functions that have a *_wxy* suffix in their name.

The following example program draws four boxes (each of a different shape) and places a filled graphic inside of each. Figure 17-5 shows the four window graphics drawn by the program. First, the window and graphic in the upper left is drawn, and after the user presses a key, the one in the lower right (or, the ellipse) is drawn. Graphic shapes 3 and 4 were not separated by a *getch* statement, so they display together. The intention of this program is to show that shapes change as the arguments to the calling functions change and that the border and placement of a shape may be "hard coded," or discerned, through reading the video status for number of available pixels, and then dividing that number by some constant.

```
#include <stdlib.h>
#include <conio.h>
#include <graph.h>
```

```
void main(void)

{

     short x_one, y_one, x_two, y_two;
     struct _wxycoord top_lft, btm_rgt;
     struct videoconfig vdocnfg;

      /**** GET MODE ****/

      if(!_setvideomode (_MAXRESMODE)) exit(1);

     _getvideoconfig(&vdocnfg);
     x_one = vdocnfg.numxpixels/3;
     y_one = vdocnfg.numypixels/2;
     x_two = x_one/3;
     y_two = y_one/2;

    /**** WINDOW ONE ****/

     _setviewport (0, 0, x_one -1, y_one -1);
     _setcolor (1);
     _rectangle (_GBORDER, 0,  0, x_one -1, y_one -1);
     _setcolor (2);
     _rectangle (_GFILLINTERIOR, x_two/2, y_two/2,
                 x_one - (x_two/6), y_one - (y_two/6));
     getch();
     _rectangle (_GBORDER, 0,  0, x_one -1, y_one -1);

     /**** WINDOW TWO ****/

     _setviewport(x_one, y_one, vdocnfg.numxpixels -1,
                  vdocnfg.numypixels -1);
     _setwindow (0, -4.0, -5.0, 4.0, 5.0);
     _setcolor (3);
     _rectangle_w (_GBORDER, -4.0, -5.0, 4.0, 5.0);
     _setcolor (4);
     _ellipse_w (_GFILLINTERIOR, -2.0, -2.5, 2.0, 2.5);
     getch();
     _rectangle_w (_GBORDER, -4.0, -5.0, 4.0, 5.0);

     /**** WINDOW THREE ****/

     _setcliprgn (x_one, 0, vdocnfg.numxpixels, y_one);
     _setvieworg (x_one + x_two -1,  y_two -1);
     _setcolor (6);
```

```
    _rectangle (_GBORDER, -x_two +4, -y_two +4, x_two, y_two);
    _setcolor (7);
    _rectangle (_GFILLINTERIOR, (-x_two * 2)/4, (-y_two * 2)/4,
                (x_two * 2)/4, (y_two * 2)/4);
    _rectangle (_GBORDER, -x_two +1, -y_two +1, x_two, y_two);

    /**** WINDOW FOUR ****/

    _setviewport (0, y_one, x_one -1, vdocnfg.numypixels -1);
    _setwindow(0, -5.0, -6.0, 4.0, 6.0);
    top_lft.wx = -4.0;
    top_lft.wy = -5.0;
    btm_rgt.wx = 4.0;
    btm_rgt.wy = 5.0;
    _setcolor (10);
    _rectangle_wxy (_GBORDER, &top_lft, &btm_rgt);
    top_lft.wx = -3.0;
    top_lft.wy = -3.5;
    btm_rgt.wx = 2.0;
    btm_rgt.wy = 2.5;
    _setcolor (12);
    _ellipse_wxy (_GFILLINTERIOR, &top_lft, &btm_rgt);
    getch();
    _setvideomode (_DEFAULTMODE);
}
```

VIDEO MODES

The video modes used in the Microsoft graphics library are directly linked to the BIOS video function modes. Video modes determine whether the hardware should be configured for text output only or for both graphics and text output. The mode also specifies the number of colors and the graphics resolution of the screen.

Table 17-1 shows the video mode constants known to the Microsoft graphics library. _MAXCOLORMODE and _MAXRESMODE are recent additions (introduced in Microsoft C 6.0) that will cause trouble if used with earlier versions of the compiler. For the same reason, _HERCMONO and _ORESCOLOR (both introduced in Quick C 2.0) should be avoided if an early compiler version is used. The adapter that supports each video mode is listed in the table. Mode constants are defined in the header file *graph.h*. You use these constants when selecting a video mode with a call to *_setvideomode*.

SELECTING A VIDEO MODE

As mentioned earlier, one of the problems in developing graphics software for the IBM PC is the diversity of hardware configurations that your software encounters once it is out of your hands. One common trend among developers has been to use a "least common denominator" approach and

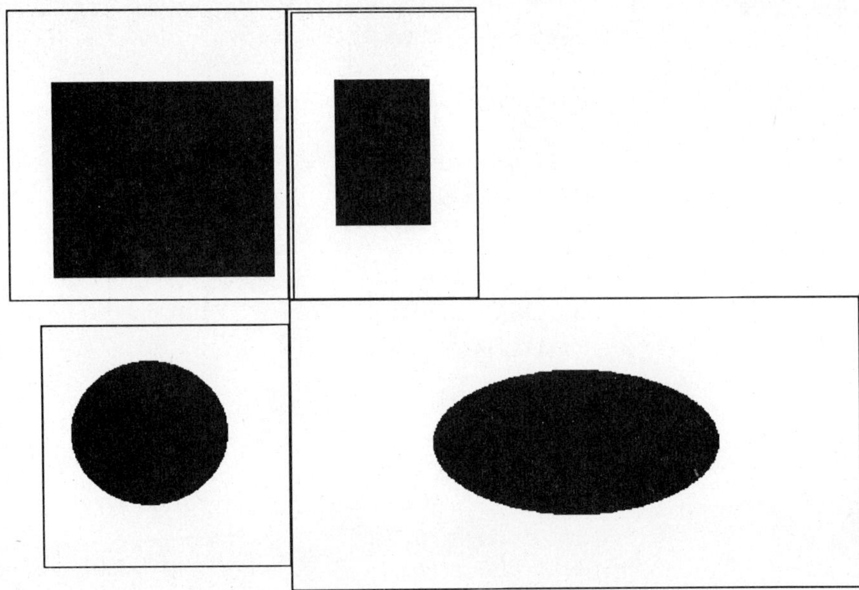

Figure 17-5. ***Output of example window program***

use the lowest resolution video mode (usually a CGA mode) that is guaranteed to be emulated on most other adapters. Naturally, this is commercially risky. EGA has supplanted CGA as the "baseline" mode, and lots of otherwise capable software is being ignored because a CGA-based display looks unprofessional to the users. The shift to VGA from EGA—and to Super VGA from VGA—threatens to leave EGA-only packages behind. You can avoid putting your software in this position by writing it to take advantage of whatever hardware it finds—assuming, of course, that your application can run on lower resolution modes. The Microsoft C graphics library allows you to use the best video mode the hardware can support. Follow this procedure:

First, call *_getvideoconfig* to check the adapter and monitor installed on the system. Your program can use that information to choose the video mode that best suits your application. For example, if you find an EGA with 128 K or more video memory attached to an enhanced color display, you can choose the _ERESCOLOR mode, which allows 16 color graphics with 640x350 resolution. On the other hand, with a CGA, you might settle for the 640x200 black and white model (_HRESBW). If your program must operate in a graphics mode and the *_getvideoconfig* routine reports a mode such as MDA which cannot display graphics, you can print an error message and exit.

Once a mode has been decided, a call to *_setvideomode* will put the graphics card (display adapter) in that mode. Call *_getvideoconfig* again to

Table 17-1. *Video Modes in Microsoft C Graphics Library*

Mode Constant	Interpretation	Adapter
_MAXCOLORMODE	Graphics mode with the most colors	All
_MAXRESMODE	Graphics mode with the highest resolution	All
_DEFAULTMODE	Default mode for current hardware configuration	All
_TEXTBW40	40x25 text in 16 shades of gray	CGA
_TEXTC40	40x25 text in 8 or 16 colors	CGA
_TEXTBW80	80x25 text in 16 shades of gray	CGA
_TEXTC80	80x25 text in 8 or 16 colors	CGA
_MRES4COLOR	320x200 graphics in 4 colors	CGA
_MRESNOCOLOR	320x200 graphics in 4 shades of gray	CGA
_HRESBW	640x200 graphics in black and white	CGA
_MRES16COLOR	320x200 graphics in 16 colors	EGA
_HRES16COLOR	640x200 graphics in 16 colors	EGA
_ERESNOCOLOR	640x350 graphics in black and white	EGA
_ERESCOLOR	640x350 graphics in 4 or 16 colors	EGA
_HERCMONO	720x348 graphics in black and white	HGC
_TEXTMONO	80x25 text in black and white	Monochrome Adapter
_ORESCOLOR	640x400 graphics; 1 of 16 possible colors	Olivetti
_VRES2COLOR	640x480 graphics in black and white	VGA
_VRES16COLOR	640x480 graphics in 16 colors	VGA
_MRES256COLOR	320x200 graphics in 256 colors	VGA

get such details as screen resolution, number of colors, and number of video pages available for this mode. The *videoconfig* structure is displayed below:

```
struct videoconfig {
      short numxpixels;     /* number of pixels on X axis       */
      short numypixels;     /* number of pixels on Y axis       */
      short numtextcols;    /* number of text columns available */
      short numtextrows;    /* number of text rows available    */
      short numcolors;      /* number of actual colors          */
      short bitsperpixel;   /* number of bits per pixel         */
      short numvideopages;  /* number of available video pages */
      short mode;           /* current video mode               */
      short adapter;        /* active display adapter           */
      short monitor;        /* active display monitor           */
      short memory;         /* adapter video memory in K bytes  */
};
```

At this point, your application can display graphics and text output. Consider the parameters such as graphics position, text position, line style, fill mask, and others that the graphics library uses during its operation (these are discussed later in this tutorial). Set these to appropriate values before calling graphics or text output routines.

When your application is ready to exit, call *_setvideomode* with the argument *_DEFAULTMODE.* This restores the hardware to its initial configuration. To summarize, three steps to displaying graphics with Microsoft C are (1) use *_getvideoconfig* to determine which graphic card (adapter) is installed, (2) use *_setvideomode* to set the desired mode, and (3) begin the graphics.

Here is how the skeleton of a graphics application looks; compare it with the example window graphics program that was presented earlier:

```
#include <graph.h>   /* Graphics programs always need this */
    :
    :
    struct videoconfig video_info;
    short videomode = _HRESBW;
    :
    :
    _getvideoconfig(&video_info);  /* Call to find adapter */
    switch (video_info.adapter)
    {
        case _MDPA:
            printf("This program needs a graphics adapter.\n");
            exit(0);

        case _CGA:
            videomode = _HRESBW;     /* 2 color 640x200 CGA mode */
            break;

        case _EGA:
            videomode = _ERESCOLOR;  /* 16 color 640x350 EGA mode */
            break;

        case _VGA:
            videomode = _VRES16COLOR; /* 16 color 640x480 VGA mode */
            break;
    }
/* Set adapter to selected mode */
    _setvideomode(videomode);
/* Call _getvideoconfig again to find resolution and colors of
 * this mode.
 */
```

```
    _getvideoconfig(&video_info);
/* Set color, line style, fill mask and draw the graphics you want */
    :
    :
/* Restore original mode */
    _setvideomode(_DEFAULTMODE);
    :
    :
```

COLORS AND PALETTES

Any color can be represented by a combination of the primary colors: red (R), green (G), and blue (B). In a digital scheme, a fixed number of bits are used to represent the permissible levels in each component of the RGB signal: a total of 2^6 (each combination of R, G, and B is a color). Even though an analog monitor has an infinite number of possible colors, we do not have an infinite number of levels in the RGB signal. In the VGA, for example, each component of RGB is represented by an 8-bit value of which the two high-order bits are always zero. Thus each component has a 6-bit value or 64 levels. This means we can have a total of $64 \times 64 \times 64$ = 262,144 (or 256 K) possible colors in the VGA. Although an adapter may be able to "understand" 256-K color values, we will need a lot of video memory to display these colors because, with 6 bits per primary color, the RGB value at each pixel will require at least 18 bits (3×6 bits) of storage.

With 4 bits of storage for each pixel (as in EGA and VGA mode 12h), the value stored at each video memory location corresponding to a pixel can be any value from 0 to 15 ($2^4 - 1$). Suppose the monitor is capable of accepting 64 (a 6-bit value) different colors and the display adapter is designed to generate the 6-bit value. How should the 4-bit value in a pixel be mapped into a 6-bit value sent to the monitor? The solution is to use a "palette," a table with as many entries as there are possible pixel values (16) and each pixel value has an entry showing one of the possible colors (a number from 0 to 63). The adapter uses the pixel value to look up the color it must send to the monitor. Figure 17-6 illustrates the concept of pixel values mapped to colors via the palette. Figure 17-6 also shows the video memory organized as four bit planes.

The color index (or "pixel value") refers to the contents of the bits in the video memory corresponding to a pixel. The color index is the digital signal that causes a monitor to display a specific color from the current palette, or set of colors (even an analog monitor receives a digital signal which is converted to analog using a DAC, or Digital-to-Analog Converter). The color index is stored at a memory location corresponding to a pixel. The color value denotes an RGB signal level that causes the monitor to display a specific color by use of the palette.

The color index (pixel value) of 0 is of special significance to display adapters, and current adapters treat pixels containing a 0 as part of the background. Many adapters, such as EGA and VGA, allow the current pal-

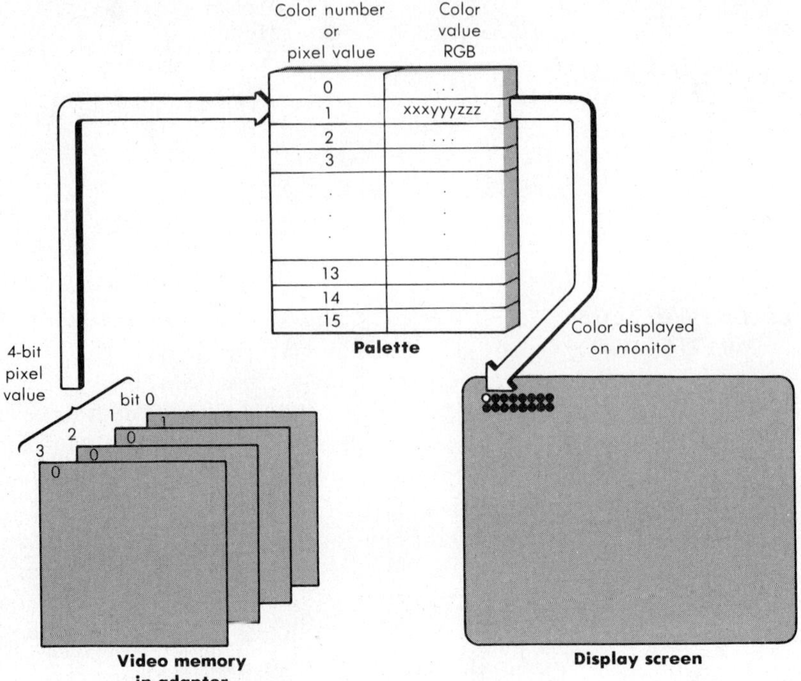

Figure 17-6. ***Colors and palettes***

ette to be redefined. The background will change colors with such cards when you change the mapping of pixel value 0 in the palette. For example, the statement *_remappalette(0, _BLUE)* will change the background to blue. A list of constants for the common color values appears in the *graph.h* file of the compiler and here in Table 17-2.

Palettes in CGA

The palettes are predefined in CGA. When operated in the text modes _TEXTC40 and _TEXTC80, CGA hardware allows up to 16 colors to be displayed. The colors are listed in Table 17-3. The two graphics modes, _MRES4COLOR and _MRESNOCOLOR, both have a resolution of 320x200. The _MRES4COLOR mode is designed for use with color monitors and provides four predefined palettes of four colors each. Color 0 of each palette is the background color and may be selected separately. Colors 1, 2, and 3 are shown in Table 17-4.

Color values are used by *_remappalette*, *_remapallpalette*, and the graphics-mode versions of *_setbkcolor*. It is important to remember the difference between color index and color value. A color index is always a short integer and a color value is always a long *int*—except that *_setbkcolor* uses a color index cast to a long *int* in text and CGA modes.

Table 17-2. ***Color Constants and Their Values***

Color Constant	Hexadecimal Value	Color Index
_BLACK	0x000000L	0
_BLUE	0x2A0000L	1
_GREEN	0x002A00L	2
_CYAN	0x2A2A00L	3
_RED	0x00002AL	4
_MAGENTA	0x2A002AL	5
_BROWN	0x00152AL	6
_WHITE	0x2A2A2AL	7
_GRAY	0x151515L	8
_LIGHTBLUE	0x3F1515L	9
_LIGHTGREEN	0x153F15L	10
_LIGHTCYAN	0x3F3F15L	11
_LIGHTRED	0x15153FL	12
_LIGHTMAGENTA	0x3F153FL	13
_YELLOW	0x153F3FL	14
_BRIGHTWHITE	0x3F3F3FL	15

Table 17-3. ***CGA Palette in Text Modes***

Pixel Value	Maps to Color
0	Black
1	Blue
2	Green
3	Cyan
4	Red
5	Magenta
6	Brown
7	White
8	Dark gray
9	Light blue
10	Light green
11	Light cyan
12	Light red
13	Light magenta
14	Yellow
15	Bright white

Table 17-4. _MRES4COLOR under CGA and EGA

Palette No.	Color Index (Pixel Value)		
	1	**2**	**3**
0	Green	Red	Brown
1	Cyan	Magenta	Light Gray
2	Light Green	Light Red	Yellow
3	Light Cyan	Light Magenta	White

_MRESNOCOLOR under CGA

Palette No.	Color Index (Pixel Value)		
	1	2	3
0	Blue	Red	Light Gray
1	Light Blue	Light Red	White

_MRESNOCOLOR under EGA

Palette No	Color Index (Pixel Value)		
	1	2	3
0	Green	Red	Brown
1	Light Green	Light Red	Yellow
2	Light Cyan	Light Red	Yellow

Earlier versions (5.1 and before) of the Microsoft C compiler refer to _YELLOW as _LIGHTYELLOW. Version 6.0 and later #define references to _LIGHTYELLOW as _YELLOW in *graph.h*.

The _MRESNOCOLOR mode is meant for use with monochrome displays that can produce shades of gray (or green, or amber); these displays are sometimes called "grayscale" monitors. On these monitors, _MRESNOCOLOR uses the same four palettes as _MRES4COLOR, only the "colors" are various shades of gray. The _MRESNOCOLOR mode can be used with a color monitor, but in CGA it generates only two-color palettes instead of the four palettes of the _MRESNOCOLOR with monochrome. Under EGA, three-color palettes are available with _MRESNOCOLOR. The palettes for the _MRES4COLOR and _MRESNOCOLOR modes are shown in Table 17-4. Understandably, palettes may differ on some clone PCs because of differences in emulating the CGA modes in EGA hardware.

The *_selectpalette* function is used to choose a CGA palette. For example, *_selectpalette(0)* selects palette *0*. The *_selectpalette* function is only used with CGA calls; it has no role with EGA or VGA.

Palettes in EGA and VGA

Palettes with EGA, VGA, and MCGA adapters may be redefined to your taste. There are 16 CGA-color indexes (also called "pixel values") listed in Table 17-2, and each can be remapped to a color value that describes the color you wish to represent. This process is normally known as "color mixing."

VGA makes a total of 262,144 (256 K) colors available, from which (depending on mode) 2, 16, or 256 may be active at one time. A VGA color value looks like this:

```
MSB                                  LSB

zzzzzzzz zzBBBBBB zzGGGGGG zzRRRRRR
```

(Remember that color values are 4 bytes long and are not to be confused with color indexes.) Note that the most-significant byte stays at 0, as do the two most-significant bits of the remaining 3 bytes. The least-significant 6 bits of those 3 bytes are used to signal an intensity level for their associated primary color (blue, green, or red). Six bits allows for 64 unique combinations ($2^6 = 64$) for each color so there are 64 possible levels of intensity for each VGA primary color. Three primary colors times 64 intensities each (64 x 64 x 64) yields the 262,144 number of colors available with VGA equipment.

VGA color mixing is accomplished by adjusting intensity levels. For example, a shade of very light red may be created by mixing a high red with low green and low blue in a bit pattern like this:

```
00000000 00100000 00100000 00111111
```

If the color is not exactly what you want, you may decide to turn blue and red down and turn green up, yielding the following color value:

```
00000000 00010000 00111000 00111000
```

Mixing colors in EGA is similar to the VGA process; however, it has been adjusted dramatically, due to the fact that EGA does not offer as many intensities. In 64-color mode, 2 bits are available to signal intensities and that means only four intensity levels are available.

The *_remapallpalette* function will redefine pixel values (color indexes) on EGA and VGA cards. A single pixel can be mapped to a new color with a call to *_remappalette*. For example, *_remappalette(1, _RED)* will map pixel value *1* to the color red.

VIDEO PAGES Although all PC displays are memory-mapped, the actual amount of video memory necessary for all pixels depends on the video mode. In some modes, there is enough video memory for all the screen pixels several times over. This allows multiple "video pages"; each area of memory sufficient to hold a full screen is a page. Only one page is displayed, but the adapter allows switching from one page to another. Since this "flipping of the video page" happens very fast, it can be used to your advantage in your programs to provide very fast screen updates. The trick is to prepare the entire screen in a video page that is not being shown and then switch to that video page to display its contents on the screen.

The number of video pages available in an adapter depends on the amount of video memory on the adapter and the mode in which the adapter is being operated. For example, the CGA with 16 K of video RAM supports up to four video pages in the text mode _TEXTC80. On the other hand, an EGA with 256 K of video RAM can have two video pages even in the high-resolution graphics mode _ERESCOLOR (see the reference pages on *_setactivepage* for an example program showing page flipping on the EGA in the 640×350 16-color mode).

The video pages are numbered starting at 0 and initially both active and visual pages are 0. You can select a new active page by calling *_setactivepage* and display another page with the call *_setvisualpage.* For example, *_setvisualpage(1)* will begin displaying video page 1 on the screen.

CURRENT POSITIONS, LINE STYLES, AND FILL MASKS

The drawing and text output routines in the graphics library rely on several internally maintained attributes and parameters. Table 17-5 summarizes these parameters, including the name of the relevant functions in the library. The functions themselves are further categorized in the next section and are described in detail in the reference pages that follow this tutorial.

Table 17-5. *Parameters Maintained by the Graphics Library Routines*

Parameter	Meaning
Active Page	When there is enough memory for more than one video page, the active page denotes the portion of video memory where all current graphics and text output goes. The *_getactivepage* function was new to Microsoft C 6.0. TO SET: _setactivepage TO GET: _getactivepage
Background Color	This is the color that fills an otherwise blank screen. It is specified by a color index in text mode. In graphics mode it is a color value specified by redefining color 0 in the palette. The color index is normally a short integer. A color value is normally a long integer. The _setbkcolor routine provides the only exception. It casts the color index to a long integer when used with text and CGA modes. TO SET: _setbkcolor TO GET: _getbkcolor
Clipping Region	This appears as a rectangle on the screen. It is specified by upper-left

Table 17-5. ***(cont.)***

Parameter	Meaning
	and lower-right coordinates. Any graphics output (but not text) that falls outside this rectangle is said to be "clipped" and will not show on the display. TO SET: _setcliprgn TO GET: cannot get
Cursor Shape	This sets and reads the shape of the text cursor. It is new to Microsoft 6.0. TO SET: _settextcursor TO GET: _gettextcursor
Fill Mask	The fill mask determines the pattern used in a fill operation, which fills an area with a color. It is specified by an 8-byte bit pattern (as shown in Figure 17-7) and it is viewed as an 8x8 array of bits. The area being filled is subdivided into 8x8 blocks of pixels. The fill mask is applied to each 8x8 block with a 1 in the mask setting a corresponding pixel in the block to the current graphics color; a 0 in the mask leaves the corresponding screen pixel unchanged. TO SET: _setfillmask TO GET: _getfillmask
Font Index	The font index reveals the identity of one of the fonts from the set of registered fonts that matches certain selection criteria. TO SET: _setfont TO GET: cannot get
Font Orientation	This is the current orientation for font text output; it ignores (0,0). TO SET: _setgtextvector TO GET: _getgtextvector
Graphics Color	The color index (also known as a "pixel value") is to be used for all subsequent color graphics output, employing functions such as *_lineto*. This default value remains until changed. TO SET: _setcolor TO GET: _getcolor
Graphics Position	This is a logical pixel position (x,y) coordinates—that represents the starting coordinates for subsequent graphics output. The appropriate graphics functions update this value. Microsoft 6.0 introduced the *_getcurrentposition_w* function. TO SET: _moveto TO GET: _getcurrentposition _getcurrentposition_w
Line Style	The line style determines the appearance of a line on the screen being drawn in graphics mode. As shown in Figure 17-7, it is a 16-bit unsigned integer viewed as an array of 16 bits. The line being drawn is divided into chunks of 16 pixels each. If a line style bit is set to 1, a corresponding screen pixel is set to the current color. The pixel is left unchanged if the bit is 0. This behavior matches that of the fill mask.

Table 17-5. *(cont.)*

Parameter	Meaning
	TO SET: _setlinestyle TO GET: _getlinestyle
Logical Origin	The physical coordinates are where the logical coordinate axes are currently located. The logical origin is used only in graphics mode and is replaced in 6.0 with the *_setvieworg* function. The 6.0 and later versions of Microsoft have abandoned the concept of logical coordinates in favor of viewports. TO SET: _setlogorg (before 6.0) _setvieworg (6.0/after) TO GET: _getphyscoord(0,0)
Pixel Color	This is a pixel value—also known as a color index—of a pixel. The versions with the *_w* suffix work in the Microsoft Windows environment, and were introduced in Microsoft 6.0. TO SET: _setpixel (before 6.0) _setpixel_w TO GET: _getpixel (before 6.0) _getpixel_w
Text Color	A color index (or pixel value) is used by the *_outtext* function to signify the color of the text being sent to the monitor. TO SET: _settextcolor TO GET: _gettextcolor
Text Position	This is a character position that uses (row, column) coordinates. It represents the screen address where subsequent text output will start. The *_outtext* function updates this value as it writes to the screen. TO SET: _settextposition TO GET: _gettextposition
Text Rows	This sets the number of display rows to be used in text modes. Typical values are 25 for CGA, 43 for EGA, and 50 for VGA. The *_settextrows* function was introduced in Microsoft 6.0. TO SET: _settextrows TO GET: cannot get
Text Window	This is a rectangular region, the boundaries of which are specified in the (row and column) nomenclature of the text coordinates. The values represent the upper-left and lower-right corners. All text output is confined in this window. The *_gettextwindow* function was introduced in Microsoft 6.0. TO SET: _settextwindow TO GET: _gettextwindow
Video Mode	This is the current video mode. TO SET: _setvideomode TO GET: _getvideomode
View Window	This is a rectangular region defined as a virtual window. The boundaries are specified coordinates within the current viewport. The *_setwindow* function is new to Microsoft 6.0. TO SET: _setwindow TO GET: cannot get

Table 17-5. *(cont.)*

Parameter	Meaning
Visual Page	When the adapter has enough display memory for more than one page, this denotes the portion of video memory currently being mapped to the display screen. The *_getvisualpage* function was introduced in Microsoft C 6.0. OS/2 supports only one visual page. TO SET: _setvisualpage TO GET: _getvisualpage

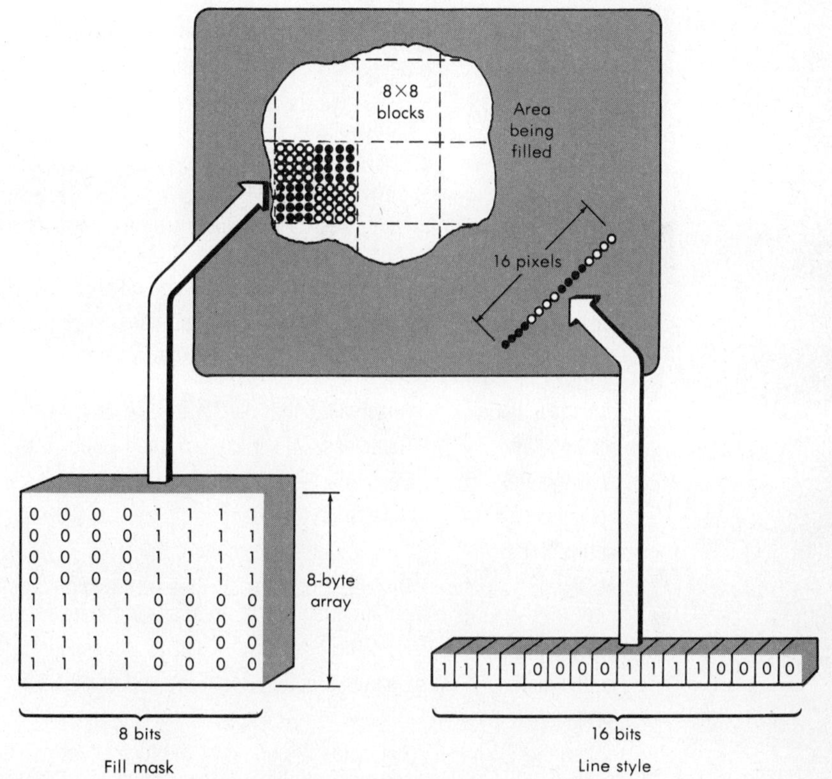

Figure 17-7. *Fill mask and line style*

ROUTINES TO CONTROL MODES AND ATTRIBUTES

The routines in the graphics library are useful for setting modes and attributes as well as getting their current values. Table 17-6 is an alphabetical list describing these routines, whereas Table 17-7 organizes the routines according to the attributes each one controls.

Table 17-6. *Mode and Attribute Control Routines*

Routine	Description
_displaycursor	Turns cursor on or off in graphics mode.
_getactivepage	Determines the current active graphics page. Introduced in Microsoft C 6.0.
_getbkcolor	Gets current background color.
_getcolor	Gets current color for graphics output.
_getfillmask	Gets current fill mask.
_getlinestyle	Gets current line style.
_getlogcoord	Converts physical coordinates to logical ones in Microsoft C 5.1 only. Subsequent versions switched from logical to viewport coordinates.
_getphyscoord	Converts logical coordinates to physical ones.
_getvideoconfig	Gets information about the current video configuration.
_getviewcoord	Translates the specified physical coordinates to view coordinates. Introduced in Microsoft C 6.0.
_getviewcoord_w	Translates the specified window coordinates to view coordinates. Introduced in Microsoft C 6.0.
_getviewcoord_wxy	Translates the specified window coordinate structure to view coordinates. Introduced in Microsoft C 6.0.
_getvisualpage	Gets the current visual page number. Introduced in Microsoft C 6.0.
_getwindowcoord	Translates the view coordinates (*x, y*) to window coordinates and returns them in an *_wxycoord* structure. Introduced in Microsoft C 6.0.
_remapallpalette	Redefines entire palette in EGA or VGA.
_remappalette	Redefines a pixel value in the palette (EGA or VGA only).
_selectpalette	Selects a predefined CGA palette.
_setactivepage	Selects a video page to be the page where all current output goes.
_setbkcolor	Sets a new background color.
_setcliprgn	Defines a rectangular area of the screen as the clipping region; output outside this area is not displayed.
_setcolor	Sets the color to be used by subsequent graphics output.
_setfillmask	Defines a new fill pattern used when filling a region.
_setlinestyle	Defines a new line style.
_setlogorg	Relocates the origin of the logical coordinate system on the screen. Valid in version 5.1 only. Replaced starting with Microsoft C 6.0 by the *_setvieworg* function.
_setvideomode	Selects a video mode.
_setvideomoderows	Selects a screen mode for a particular hardware/display combination, and requests the number of text rows to be used. Only text modes are available in OS/2. Introduced in Microsoft C 6.0.
_setvieworg	Moves the viewpoint origin (0,0) to the physical point (*x, y*). (All other view coordinate points move the same direction and distance.) Introduced in Microsoft C 6.0.

Table 17-6. ***(cont.)***

Routine	Description
_setviewport	Sets up a rectangular clipping region and moves the logical origin to the upper-left corner of the region. The concept of a logical origin was changed in Microsoft C 6.0 to a viewport/window orientation.
_setvisualpage	Selects a video page as the one to be displayed on the screen.
_setwindow	Defines a window coordinate system.

Table 17-7. ***Mode and Attribute Control Routines by Task***

Task	Routines
Control low-level graphics colors and palettes.	_getbkcolor, _getcolor, _remapallpalette, _remappalette, _selectpalette, _setbkcolor, _setcolor
Control video pages.	_getactivepage, _setactivepage, _getvisualpage, _setvisualpage
Control cursor in graphics mode.	_displaycursor
Determine available display hardware, the current video mode, and its capabilities.	_getvideoconfig
Control fill pattern and line style.	_getfillmask, _setfillmask, _getlinestyle, _setlinestyle
Manipulate coordinate systems (the logical coordinate system was replaced starting in Microsoft C 6.0).	_getlogcoord, _getphyscoord, _getviewcoord, _getviewcoord_w, _getviewcoord_wxy, _getwindowcoord, _setlogorg, _setvieworg
Set up a clip region.	_setcliprgn, _setviewport, _setwindow
Set the video mode.	_setvideomode, _setvideomoderows

MAX CONSTANTS

_MAXRESMODE and _MAXCOLORMODE are two symbolic constants introduced by Microsoft in version 6.0. The _MAXRESMODE function selects the highest possible resolution for the graphics monitor and adapter currently in use. The second function selects the greatest number of colors. These two constants work with all the adapters except the MDPA. Table 17-8 shows the relationship between these constants and various graphics formats. The GRPHCS.C program shown earlier in the tutorial showed a call using _MAXRESMODE.

Table 17-8. ***Maximum Modes Supported by Hardware***

Adapter/Monitor	_MAXRESMODE	_MAXCOLORMODE
VGA/OVGA	_VRES16COLOR	_MRES256COLOR
OEGA color	_ORESCOLOR (Olivetti only)	_ERESCOLOR

Table 17-8. *(cont.)*

Adapter/Monitor	_MAXRESMODE	_MAXCOLORMODE
OCGA	_ORESCOLOR (Olivetti only)	_MRES4COLOR
MDPA	n/a	n/a
MCGA	_VRES2COLOR	_MRES256COLOR
HGC	_HERCMONO	_HERCMONO
EGA mono	_ERESNOCOLOR	_ERESNOCOLOR
EGA 256 K	_ERESCOLOR	_ERESCOLOR
EGA 64 K	_ERESCOLOR	_HRES16COLOR
EGA	_HRES16COLOR	_HRES16COLOR
CGA	_HRESBW	_MRES4COLOR

Further Reading

Although a graphics library hides much of the detail of the display hardware, it is necessary to know about the inner working of the adapter in order to make the graphics application work right. Here are some references that can help you get familiar with PC graphics.

Norton's guide[1] discusses the basics of video and gives details of the CGA, MDA, EGA, and VGA. Coverage in popular journals[2] remains a good source for information on these adapters.) The recent book by Wilton[3] is an excellent reference on PC and PS/2 video programming, complete with sample assembly language routines that can be called from Microsoft C. Kliewer's book[4] can also serve as an EGA/VGA programmer's reference, although it does not have the depth and details of Wilton's text. Also, Lafore[6] covers CGA and EGA programming in his book.

Ferraro's book[5] is written especially for programmers & hardware designers and it covers all the most recent BIOS calls and display modes. There are program examples for each chip set.

Hansen's book[7] shows the development of a library of utility functions, including a set for screen display. He also shows several tricks used to determine the display hardware in a system and a way to write to the CGA memory without generating "snow" on the screen.

The book by Rochkind[8], the author of the PC editor EDIX, is devoted solely to the subject of developing a portable text-oriented display package. It has an excellent presentation of the gradual development of a modular display library that can help you manage any types of displays effectively.

On the graphics side, Johnson[9] presents the development of an EGA-based graphics package with complete source listings.

1. Peter Norton and Richard Wilton, *The New Peter Norton Programmer's Guide to the IBM PC & PS/2*, Microsoft Press, Redmond, WA, 1989, 528 pages.
2. Charles Petzold, "Exploring the EGA, Part I and II," *PC Magazine*, August 1986, 367–384 and September 1986, 287–313.
3. Richard Wilton, *Programmer's Guide to PC & PS/2 Video Systems*, Microsoft Press, Redmond, WA, 1987, 531 pages.
4. Bradley D. Kliewer, *EGA/VGA A Programmer's Reference Guide*, Intertext Publications, Inc., New York, NY, 1988, 269 pages.
5. Richard F. Ferraro, *Programmer's Guide to the EGA and VGA Cards*, Addison-Wesley, Reading, MA, 1990, 768 pages.
6. Robert Lafore, The Waite Group, *Microsoft C Programming for the PC*, 2d Ed., Howard W. Sams & Company, Indianapolis, IN, 1990, 780 pages.
7. Augie Hansen, *Proficient C*, Microsoft Press, Redmond, WA, 1987, 492 pages.
8. Marc J. Rochkind, *Advanced C Programming for Displays*, Prentice-Hall, Englewood Cliffs, NJ, 1988, 331 pages.
9. Nelson Johnson, *Advanced Graphics in C*, Osborne McGraw-Hill, Berkeley, CA, 1987, 670 pages.

_displaycursor

COMPATIBILITY

MSC 3	MSC 4	MSC 5	MSC 6	QC1	QC2	QC2.5	TC1	TC1.5	TC2	TC++	ANSI	UNIX V	XNX	OS2	DOS
		▲	1	▲	▲	▲								▲	▲

PURPOSE Use *_displaycursor* to turn the solid cursor on or off while in the graphics mode.

SYNTAX

```
short _far _displaycursor(short on_off);
```

```
short on_off;
```
Selected display mode of cursor

EXAMPLE CALL

```
_displaycursor(_GCURSOROFF);
```

INCLUDES

```
#include <graph.h>
```
For function declaration and definition of mode names

DESCRIPTION The *_displaycursor* function allows you to turn a solid cursor on or off during the graphics mode. By default, this cursor is not displayed when you first enter a graphics mode. The cursor state is specified in the short integer argument *on_off*. You can specify one of the following constants as the value of *on_off*.

_GCURSORON Turn cursor on.

_GCURSOROFF Turn cursor off.

These constants are defined in the header file *graph.h*.

1. Changed in Microsoft C 6.0 to provide OS/2 capability.

RETURNS The return value is the previous value of the cursor state (i.e., it is either _GCURSOROFF or _GCURSORON depending on whether the cursor was off or on before calling this function).

COMMENTS In the graphics mode, when text is printed using the routine *_outtext*, you may sometimes wish to turn the cursor on. When prompting for some input, for example, you can get the user's attention to the prompt by having the cursor on.

EXAMPLE If you have an EGA with an enhanced color monitor, write a C program using *_setvideomode* to put the adapter in the graphics mode and then turn the cursor on and off to illustrate the effect.

```
#include <stdio.h>
#include <graph.h>
main()
```

```
{
    char str[80];
    _setvideomode(_ERESCOLOR);
    _displaycursor(_GCURSORON);
    _settextposition(1,1);
    _outtext("Cursor is on now. \
Enter a string and see how it feels:");
    gets(str);
    _displaycursor(_GCURSOROFF);
    _settextposition(2,1);
    _outtext("Now the cursor is off. \
Type a string to see the difference.");
    gets(str);
    _settextposition(3,1);
    _outtext("Hit any key to reset to original mode:");
    getch();
    _setvideomode(_DEFAULTMODE);
}
```

COMPATIBILITY

_getactivepage

MSC 3	MSC 4	MSC 5	MSC 6	QC1	QC2	QC2.5	TC1	TC1.5	TC2	TC++	ANSI	UNIX V	XNX	OS2	DOS
			▲		▲	▲								▲	▲

PURPOSE Use the *_getactivepage* routine to identify the active graphics page to your program. The active page is the area of graphics memory to which all graphics output will go.

SYNTAX `short _far _getactivepage (void);`

EXAMPLE CALL `getactivepage();`

INCLUDES `#include <graph.h>` *For function declaration*

DESCRIPTION All hardware combinations support at least one active page. All graphics output is placed in the active page. The *_getactivepage* function identifies which page is current. Page numbering starts with 0.

The visual page, which is the area of graphics memory currently displayed on the screen, need not be the same as the active page. One way to provide simple animation is to prepare graphics on an active page while showing another visual page; then make the active page visual.

RETURNS The *_getactivepage* routine returns the number of the current active page.

The function cannot return an error because the system is presumed to have at least one active page, and thus the *_grstatus* message returned from this function is *_GROK*.

COMMENTS Only one page, page 0, is available in OS/2.

SEE ALSO

`_setactivepage`	*To specify the active graphics page*
`_getvisualpage`	*To get the current visual page*
`_setvisualpage`	*To specify the current visual page*

EXAMPLE The following program draws several nonsensical figures to the screen, switching back and forth between video pages to present the effect of animation. It shows, among others, the *_getactivepage* and *_getvisualpage* functions.

```
#include <conio.h>
#include <graph.h>
#include <stdlib.h>
#include <time.h>

void  main  (void);         /* prototypes */
char *grfc[3][3] = {{{"<x>"}, {" y "}, {"> <"}},
                    {{"-x-"}, {" Y "}, {"==="}},
                    {{"bxd"}, {"<Y>"}, {">+<"}}};

void main()
{
   short orig_vispg, orig_actpg, page, row, clm, line;
   struct videoconfig vdo_cfg;
  _getvideoconfig (&vdo_cfg);
   if (vdo_cfg.numvideopages < 4) exit (4); /* OS/2 or mono fails
                                                               */

   orig_actpg  = _getactivepage();
   orig_vispg  = _getvisualpage();
   if (!_setvideomoderows (_TEXTBW40, 25)) exit (6); /* no 40
                                                          colm */
   _displaycursor (_GCURSOROFF);

   /* set image on each page */
   for (page = 0; page < 4; page++)
   {
      _setactivepage (page);
```

```
        for (row = 1; row < 23; row += 10)
        {
            for (clm = 1; clm < 37; clm += 10)
            {
                for (line = 0; line < 3; line++)
                {
                    _settextposition (row + line, clm);
                    _outtext (grfc[line]);
                }
            }
        }
    }

    while (!kbhit())       /* walk through pages 0, 1 & 2 */
        for (page = 0; page <= 2; page++) _setvisualpage (page);

    getch();

    _setvideomode (_DEFAULTMODE);  /* restore original settings */
    _setactivepage (orig_actpg);
    _setvisualpage (orig_vispg);
}
```

COMPATIBILITY

_getbkcolor

MSC 3	MSC 4	MSC 5	MSC 6	QC1	QC2	QC2.5	TC1	TC1.5	TC2	TC++	ANSI	UNIX V	XNX	OS2	DOS
		▲	1	▲	▲	▲		2	2	2				▲	▲

PURPOSE Use the *_getbkcolor* function to get the value of the current background color. The meaning of the returned value depends on the current video mode.

SYNTAX `long _far _getbkcolor(void);`

EXAMPLE CALL `bcolor = _getbkcolor();    /* Retrieve background color */`

INCLUDES `#include <graph.h>`   *For function declaration*

DESCRIPTION The *_getbkcolor* function returns the pixel value for those pixels that are part of the background. The return value is interpreted according to the current video mode. In text modes, the background pixels contain a color number from the current palette. In graphics modes, the background pixels always contain a 0. For example, in the EGA, color number 4 in the default palette is red. So when the EGA is in text mode, the form *_setbkcolor(4L)* followed by a call to *_clearscreen* sets the screen background to red (see the example below). If you call *_getbkcolor* after this, the return value will be 4.

On the other hand, in the graphics mode, to set the background to red, we have to make a call of the form *_setbkcolor(_RED)*, where _RED is a predefined constant value (see the reference pages on *_setbkcolor*). The background immediately becomes red. A call to *_getbkcolor*, however, will not return the value of the constant _RED. It will, instead, return 0.

1. Changed in Microsoft C 6.0 to provide OS/2 capability. 2. The Turbo C and Turbo C++ function is *getbkcolor*.

COMMON USES The *_getbkcolor* function is useful in determining the background color number in text modes.

RETURNS The *_getbkcolor* function returns a long integer that has the value of background pixels.

SEE ALSO `_setbkcolor` *To change the current background color*

EXAMPLES Suppose you are in a text mode. Set a new background color by calling *_setbkcolor* and make it visible by calling *_clearscreen*. Now call *_getbkcolor* to check the current background color.

```
#include <stdio.h>
#include <graph.h>
/* Need a "long" constant for _setbkcolor   */
#define RED 4L
main()
{
    long bcolor;     /* for current background color */
    _setbkcolor(RED); /* Set background color to red */
    _clearscreen(_GCLEARSCREEN); /* make it effective*/
    bcolor = _getbkcolor(); /* Retrieve backgnd color*/
    printf("Current background color is: %d\n\n",
            bcolor);
    printf("Use the DOS command MODE CO80 to reset \
display\n");
}
```

Assuming an EGA environment, enter a high-resolution graphics mode and change the background color to blue by calling *_setbkcolor* (use the predefined _BLUE). Now call *_getbkcolor* to get the value and show it to the user. You will see that it is 0.

Graphics Modes, Coordinates, and Attributes

```
#include <stdio.h>
#include <graph.h>
main()
{
    long bcolor;
    char buffer[80];
/* Enter hi-resolution graphics mode on EGA */
    if (_setvideomode(_ERESCOLOR) == 0)
    {
/* Error setting mode */
        printf("Mode not supported by hardware\n");
        exit(0);
    }
/* Set background to _BLUE, then get value */
    _setbkcolor(_BLUE);
    bcolor = _getbkcolor();
    _settextposition(1,1);
    _outtext("Demonstrating _getbkcolor\n");
    sprintf(buffer,"Current background color is: %d",
            bcolor);
    _settextposition(2,1);
    _outtext(buffer);

/* Restore original mode */
/* Give user a chance to see the result */
    _settextposition(40,1);
    _outtext("Hit any key to exit:");
    getch();
    _setvideomode(_DEFAULTMODE);
}
```

COMPATIBILITY **_getcolor**

MSC 3	MSC 4	MSC 5	MSC 6	QC1	QC2	QC2.5	TC1	TC1.5	TC2	TC++	ANSI	UNIX V	XNX	OS2	DOS
		▲	▲	▲	▲	▲		1	1	1					▲

PURPOSE Use the *_getcolor* function to obtain the current color number. The current color can be set by calling *_setcolor*.

SYNTAX `short _far _getcolor(void);`

EXAMPLE CALL `current_color = _getcolor();`

INCLUDES `#include <graph.h>` *For function declaration*

DESCRIPTION The *_getcolor* function is used to get back the current color number used by all line-drawing and fill routines. Until a color is set, the default value is the highest numbered color from the current palette (see the tutorial for an explanation of palettes).

1. The Turbo C and Turbo C++ version of this function is *getcolor.*

COMMON USES The *_getcolor* function gets the current color value and saves it so that it may be restored to its original value before exiting the program.

RETURNS The *_getcolor* function returns the current color number.

SEE ALSO `_setcolor` *To change to a new color*

EXAMPLE Get the current color and draw a line to show what color it is. Then change to a new color and verify that the change occurred by calling *_getcolor.*

```
#include <stdio.h>
#include <graph.h>
#define RED  4      /* Color number 4 is red  */

main()
{
    int i;
    short y = 60;
    char buffer[80];
/* Enter hi-resolution graphics mode on EGA */
    if (_setvideomode(_ERESCOLOR) != 0)
    {
        _settextposition(1,1);
        _outtext("Demonstrating _getcolor");
/* Get current color number */
         sprintf(buffer,"Current color: %d",
                 _getcolor());
         _settextposition(2,1);
         _outtext(buffer);
         _moveto(0,y);
         _lineto(500,y);
         y += 40;
/* Select a new color and verify by calling _getcolor */
        _setcolor(RED);
         sprintf(buffer,"New color: %d (should be 4)",
                 _getcolor());
         _settextposition(6,1);
         _outtext(buffer);
```

```
        _moveto(0,y);
        _lineto(500,y);
/* Restore original mode */
/* Give user a chance to see the result */
        _settextposition(40,1);
        _outtext("Hit any key to exit:");
        getch();
        _setvideomode(_DEFAULTMODE);
    }
    else
    {
/* Error setting mode */
        printf("Mode not supported by hardware\n");
    }
}
```

COMPATIBILITY

_getfillmask

MSC 3	MSC 4	MSC 5	MSC 6	QC1	QC2	QC2.5	TC1	TC1.5	TC2	TC++	ANSI	UNIX V	XNX	OS2	DOS
		▲	▲	▲	▲	▲		1	1	1				▲	▲

PURPOSE Use *_getfillmask* to retrieve the 8 bytes that define the current 8×8 mask used by the routines *_floodfill, _rectangle, _ellipse,* and *_pie* that fill an area with the current color. (See the description of *_setfillmask* for an explanation of how the fill mask is used.)

SYNTAX

```
unsigned char _far * _far _getfillmask(unsigned char _far *fillmask);

unsigned char _far *fillmask;
```
8×8 bit pattern that determines how the filled area looks

EXAMPLE CALL

```
p_mask = _getfillmask(current_mask);
```

INCLUDES

```
#include <graph.h>
```
For function declaration

DESCRIPTION The *_getfillmask* function is used to retrieve the 8×8 pattern of bits that serves as the current mask to be used by the routines *_floodfill, _rectangle, _ellipse,* and *_pie* to fill an area with the current color.

The fill pattern is returned in eight characters whose address is provided to *_getfillmask* in the argument *fillmask.* The reference page on *_setfillmask* explains how to interpret the fill mask.

1. The Turbo C and Turbo C++ version of this function is *getfillpattern.*

COMMON USES This function gets and saves the current fill mask so that the mask can be restored to its original value before exiting a graphics routine.

RETURNS If no mask is present, *_getfillmask* returns a NULL.

COMMENTS If you switch fill masks in a graphics routine, it is a good idea first to use *_getfillmask* to retrieve the current mask so that you can restore the mask to normal before returning from the routine.

SEE ALSO `_setfillmask` *To define a new fill mask*

EXAMPLE Write a C program to obtain the current fill mask by using the *_getfillmask* function. Then alter the mask and verify that this has indeed happened by calling *_getfillmask* again.

```
#include <stdio.h>
#include <graph.h>
#define RED  4      /* Color number 4 is red */
/* Define a fill mask */
unsigned char fillmask[8] =
    { 1, 3, 7, 0xf, 0x1f, 0x3f, 0x7f, 0xff },
    oldmask[8];  /* Placeholder for old fill mask */
main()
{
    unsigned char _far *p_mask;
    char buffer[80];
    int i;
    short color=0, x1=0, y1=60;
/* Assuming a system with EGA, enter hi-resolution
 * graphics mode
 */
    if (_setvideomode(_ERESCOLOR) != 0)
    {
       _setcolor(RED);
       _settextposition(1,1);
       _outtext("Illustrating _getfillmask:");
/* Get current fill mask */
       p_mask = _getfillmask(oldmask);
       if (p_mask == NULL)
       {
           _settextposition(2,1);
           _outtext("No fill mask defined");
       }
/* Define a new mask */
        _setfillmask(fillmask);
```

```
            p_mask = _getfillmask(oldmask);
            sprintf(buffer,
            "Current fill mask is: %x %x %x %x %x %x %x %x",
               oldmask[0],oldmask[1],oldmask[2],oldmask[3],
               oldmask[4],oldmask[5],oldmask[6],oldmask[7]);
           _settextposition(3,1);
           _outtext(buffer);
           _settextposition(4,1);
           _outtext("Here is how it looks:");
/* Draw filled rectangle with new fill style */
            _rectangle(_GFILLINTERIOR, x1, y1,
                       x1+100, y1+60);
/* Restore original mode */
/* Give user a chance to see the result */
            _settextposition(40,1);
            _outtext("Hit any key to exit:");
            getch();
            _setvideomode(_DEFAULTMODE);
      }
      else
      {
/* Error setting mode */
            printf("Mode not supported by hardware\n");
      }
}
```

COMPATIBILITY

_getlinestyle

MSC 3	MSC 4	MSC 5	MSC 6	QC1	QC2	QC2.5	TC1	TC1.5	TC2	TC++	ANSI	UNIX V	XNX	OS2	DOS
		▲	▲	▲	▲	▲		1	1	1				▲	▲

PURPOSE Use *_getlinestyle* to retrieve the 16-bit mask used by the routines *_lineto* and *_rectangle* when drawing straight lines. The mask controls how the line looks.

SYNTAX `unsigned short _far _getlinestyle(void);`

EXAMPLE CALL `line_style = _getlinestyle();`

INCLUDES `#include <graph.h>` *For function declaration*

DESCRIPTION The *_getlinestyle* function is used to get back the 16-bit unsigned integer that determines the appearance of lines drawn by the routines *_lineto* and *_rectangle*. The line style represented by the mask determines whether the line is solid or dashed and if dashed, what the pattern of the dashes is. The reference page on *_setlinestyle* explains how the mask is used.

1. The Turbo C and Turbo C++ version of this function is *getlinesettings.*

COMMON USES The *_getlinestyle* function gets the current mask used by line-drawing routines and saves it before setting up a new mask. In that way, before exiting, the line style can be reset to its original value.

SEE ALSO `_setlinestyle` *To change to a new line style*

EXAMPLE Get the current line style and draw a line to show how it looks. Then change to a new line style, and verify that the change occurred by calling *_getlinestyle.*

```
#include <stdio.h>
#include <graph.h>
#define RED  4      /* Color number 4 is red */

main()
{
        int i;
        short y = 60, linemask = 0x3f;
        char buffer[80];
/* Enter hi-resolution graphics mode on EGA */
        if (_setvideomode(_ERESCOLOR) != 0)
        {
           _settextposition(1,1);
           _outtext("Demonstrating _getlinestyle");
/* Set up red as the current color */
           _setcolor(RED);
/* Get current line style */
           sprintf(buffer,"Current line style: %x", _getlinestyle());
           _settextposition(2,1);
           _outtext(buffer);
           _moveto(0,y);
           _lineto(500,y);
           y += 40;
/* Select a new line style and verify by calling _getlinestyle */
           _setlinestyle(linemask);
           sprintf(buffer,"New line style: %x", _getlinestyle());
           _settextposition(6,1);
           _outtext(buffer);
           _moveto(0,y);
```

```
                _lineto(500,y);
/* Restore original mode */
/* Give user a chance to see the result */
                _settextposition(40,1);
                _outtext("Hit any key to exit:");
                getch();
                _setvideomode(_DEFAULTMODE);
        }
        else
        {
/* Error setting mode */
                printf("Specified mode not supported by hardware\n");
        }
}
```

COMPATIBILITY

_getlogcoord

MSC 3	MSC 4	MSC 5	MSC 6	QC1	QC2	QC2.5	TC1	TC1.5	TC2	TC++	ANSI	UNIX V	XNX	OS2	DOS
		▲	1	▲											

PURPOSE Use *_getlogcoord* to convert from physical coordinates to logical ones.

SYNTAX `struct xycoord _far _getlogcoord(short x, short y);`

`short x, y;` *The physical x and y coordinates of the point on the screen whose location in the logical coordinate system is returned*

EXAMPLE CALL `xy_logical = _getlogcoord(x_physical, y_physical);`

INCLUDES #include <graph.h> *For function declaration and definition of the structure* xycoord

DESCRIPTION The *_getlogcoord* function returns the logical coordinates of the pixel whose physical location is at (*x,y*). See *_setlogorg* for a brief description of physical and logical coordinates.

1. Not used in Microsoft C 6.0 or QuickC 2.5; replaced by *_getviewcoord.*

COMMON USES The drawing routines in the graphics package, such as *_moveto, _lineto, _arc, _ellipse, _pie,* and *_rectangle,* accept arguments in logical coordinates. You can use *_getlogcoord* to find the logical equivalent of a physical coordinate so that you can pass the coordinates to one of the drawing routines.

RETURNS The *_getlogcoord* function returns the logical coordinates of the specified pixel in a structure of type *xycoord*, which is declared in the header file *graph.h* as shown below.

```
struct xycoord       /* Structure for pixel coordinates */
{
    short xcoord;    /* x-coordinate */
    short ycoord;    /* y-coordinate */
};
```

COMMENTS The logical coordinate system used in Microsoft C 5.0 and 5.1 has been replaced starting in Microsoft C 6.0. Microsoft C compiler versions after 5.1 (including Quick C 2.0) use three low-level graphics coordinate systems, two of which were not in 5.0 or 5.1. The three coordinates were originally presented in Quick C 2.0 and are called "physical," "viewport," and "window." The logical coordinate system is no longer in use, and its functions *_setlogorg* and *_getlogcoord* are #defined to *_setvieworg* and *_getviewcord* in the Microsoft C 6.0 *graph.h* file.

The graphics functions without a *_w* or *_wxy* suffix use the view coordinate system, and take short *ints* for coordinate arguments. Graphics functions with a *_w* suffix use window coordinates and take *doubles* for their coordinate arguments. The graphics functions that end with a *_wxy* suffix take *_wxycoord* structures as arguments.

SEE ALSO

`_getviewcoord` *Replaces* _getlogcoord *in Microsoft C 6.0*

`_getphyscoord` *To convert logical coordinates to physical*

EXAMPLE In a graphics mode, call *_setlogorg* to move the logical origin to the physical point (75,50). Then call *_getlogcoord* for the same physical point, and verify that the returned logical coordinates are indeed (0,0). You may also want to check that the logical coordinates of the physical point (0,0) are now (–75,–50).

```
#include <stdio.h>
#include <graph.h>
/* Yellow is 14 in EGA's default palette */
#define YELLOW 14
main()
{
    char buffer[80];
    struct xycoord logcoord;
/* Assume an EGA environment */
    if (_setvideomode(_ERESCOLOR) == 0)
    {
        printf("Not EGA environment\n");
```

```
        exit(0);
    }
    _settextposition(1,1);
    _outtext("Demonstrating _getlogcoord");
    _setlogorg(75,50);
    _setcolor(YELLOW);
    _setpixel(0,0);   /* Highlight new logical origin */
/* Verify that physical point (75,50) is logical (0,0)*/
    logcoord = _getlogcoord(75,50);
    sprintf(buffer,"Physical point (75,50) is logical \
(%d,%d)", logcoord.xcoord, logcoord.ycoord);
    _settextposition(2,1);
    _outtext(buffer);
/* Also, physical (0,0) is at logical (-75,-50) */
    logcoord = _getlogcoord(0,0);
    sprintf(buffer,"Physical point (0,0) is logical \
(%d,%d)", logcoord.xcoord, logcoord.ycoord);
    _settextposition(3,1);
    _outtext(buffer);
/* Wait for user to hit a key, then reset everything */
    _settextposition(25,1);
    _outtext("Hit any key to reset mode and exit:");
    getch();
    _setvideomode(_DEFAULTMODE);
}
```

COMPATIBILITY

_getphyscoord

MSC 3	MSC 4	MSC 5	MSC 6	QC1	QC2	QC2.5	TC1	TC1.5	TC2	TC++	ANSI	UNIX V	XNX	OS2	DOS
		▲	1	▲	▲	▲									▲

PURPOSE Use *_getphyscoord* to convert from logical coordinates to physical ones in Microsoft C 5.1. The logical coordinate system was dropped in later versions.

SYNTAX `struct xycoord _far _getphyscoord(short x, short y);`

`short x, y;` *The logical* x *and* y *coordinates of the point on the screen whose location in the physical coordinate system is returned*

EXAMPLE CALL `xy_physical = _getphyscoord(x_logical, y_logical);`

INCLUDES `#include <graph.h>` *For function declaration and definition of the structure* xycoord

DESCRIPTION The *_getphyscoord* function returns the physical coordinates of the pixel that is at the point (*x,y*) in the logical coordinate system.

The physical coordinate axes (with the origin at the upper left corner, the x-axis extending to the right and the y-axis going down) are fixed on the display screen, whereas the origin of the logical coordinate system can be moved around by calling *_setlogorg.*

1. This logical coordinate system was dropped as of Microsoft C 6.0, but this function remains.

COMMON USES The drawing routines *_moveto, _lineto, _arc, _ellipse, _pie,* and *_rectangle* accept arguments in logical coordinates. The origin of the logical coordinate system is, however, specified in physical coordinates. If you want to set the origin of the logical coordinate system to the upper-left corner of a rectangle, you first have to get the physical coordinate of that point by using *_getphyscoord.*

RETURNS The *_getphyscoord* function returns the physical coordinates of the specified pixel in a structure of type *xycoord,* which is declared in the header file *graph.h* as shown below.

```
struct xycoord        /* Structure for pixel coordinates */
{
    short xcoord;     /* x-coordinate */
    short ycoord;     /* y-coordinate */
};
```

COMMENTS As noted in more detail in the tutorial and on the reference page for the *_getviewcoord* function, Microsoft C 6.0 employs three coordinate systems for the low-level graphics functions. (The logical coordinate system of version 5.1 was left out of the later versions; see the tutorial for more information.) They are the physical coordinate system, the viewport (or view) coordinate system, and the window coordinate system. The window coordinate system is also referred to as being "real valued." The graphics functions without a *_w* or *_wxy* suffix use the view coordinate system, and take short *ints* for coordinate arguments. Graphics functions with a *_w* suffix use window coordinates and take *doubles* for their coordinate arguments. The graphics functions that end with a *_wxy* suffix take *_wxycoord* structures as arguments.

The only functions that use physical coordinates are *_setcliprgn, _setviewport, _setvieworg, _getviewcoord,* and *_getphyscoord.* You can translate values back and forth between the coordinate systems using the *_getphyscoord, _getviewcoord,* and *_getwindowcoord* function families.

SEE ALSO `_getlogcoord` *To convert physical coordinates to logical*

Graphics Modes, Coordinates, and Attributes

EXAMPLE If you have display hardware that can support graphics, set the video mode to graphics and relocate the logical origin to the physical point (75,50) by calling *_setlogorg*. Then call *_getphyscoord* for the logical origin (0,0), and verify that the returned logical coordinates are indeed (75,50).

```
#include <stdio.h>
#include <graph.h>
/* Yellow is 14 in EGA's default palette */
#define YELLOW 14
main()
{
    char buffer[80];
    struct xycoord physcoord;
/* Assume an EGA environment */
    if (_setvideomode(_ERESCOLOR) == 0)
    {
        printf("Not EGA environment\n");
        exit(0);
    }
    _settextposition(1,1);
    _outtext("Demonstrating _getphyscoord");
    _setlogorg(75,50);
    _setcolor(YELLOW);
    _setpixel(0,0); /* Highlight new logical origin */
/* Verify that logical origin is physical (75,50)   */
    physcoord = _getphyscoord(0,0);
    sprintf(buffer,"Logical (0,0) is physical (%d,%d)",
            physcoord.xcoord, physcoord.ycoord);
    _settextposition(2,1);
    _outtext(buffer);
    _settextposition(3,1);
    _outtext("It should be (75,50)");
/* Wait for user to hit a key, then reset everything */
    _settextposition(25,1);
    _outtext("Hit any key to reset mode and exit:");
    getch();
    _setvideomode(_DEFAULTMODE);
}
```

_getvideoconfig

COMPATIBILITY

MSC 3	MSC 4	MSC 5	MSC 6	QC1	QC2	QC2.5	TC1	TC1.5	TC2	TC++	ANSI	UNIX V	XNX	OS2	DOS
		▲	1	▲	▲	▲		2	2	2					

PURPOSE Use *_getvideoconfig* to get information about the current graphics environment. Values of parameters such as maximum number of pixels along *x* and *y* directions and number of colors, are returned in a structure of type *videoconfig*, which is defined in the file *graph.h*. When writing a graphics application, you can call *_getvideoconfig* to determine, for example, the number of columns and rows of text that the monitor can support in its text mode.

SYNTAX

```
struct videoconfig _far * _far _getvideoconfig(struct
                                        videoconfig _far *gr_info);
```

```
struct videoconfig _far *gr_info;
```

Pointer to structure that holds the information about the graphics environment

EXAMPLE CALL

```
_getvideoconfig(&gr_info);
```

INCLUDES

```
#include <graph.h>
```

For function declaration and definition of the structure of type videoconfig

DESCRIPTION The *_getvideoconfig* function returns information about the graphics environment in a structure of type *videoconfig*. The C declaration shown below describes the layout of this structure and identifies the pieces of information returned by *_getvideoconfig*.

```
struct videoconfig {
    short numxpixels;    /* number of pixels along X axis    */
    short numypixels;    /* number of pixels along Y axis    */
    short numtextcols;   /* number of text columns available */
    short numtextrows;   /* number of text rows available    */
    short numcolors;     /* number of actual colors          */
    short bitsperpixel;  /* number of bits per pixel         */
    short numvideopages;/* number of available video pages  */
    short mode;          /* current video mode               */
    short adapter;       /* active display adapter           */
    short monitor;       /* active display monitor           */
    short memory;        /* adapter video memory in K bytes  */

};
```

You are responsible for declaring this structure in your program (so that storage is allocated for the structure) and for providing a 32-bit far pointer to the structure as the argument *gr_info*.

For most of the fields in the structure, their meaning is obvious from the comments in the declaration of the structure. The value of the fields *adapter*, *mode*, and *monitor* can be intrepreted by comparing each with the mnemonic constants shown in Table 17-1 and in Tables 17-9 and 17-10 below.

Table 17-9. *Interpreting Adapter Value*

Adapter	Interpretation
_MDPA	Monochrome Display Adapter
_CGA	Color Graphics Adapter
_EGA	Enhanced Graphics Adapter
_MCGA	MultiColor Graphics Array
_VGA	Video Graphics Array
_HGC	Hercules Graphics Card

Table 17-10. *Interpreting Monitor Value*

Monitor	Interpretation
_MONO	Monochrome monitor
_COLOR	Color monitor (or Enhanced monitor in CGA mode)
_ENHCOLOR	Enhanced color monitor
_ANALOG	Analog monitor

1. Changed in Microsoft C 6.0 to provide OS/2 capability. 2. The Turbo C and Turbo C++ version of this function is *detectgraph*.

COMMON USES This function is useful when writing a robust graphics application program. By using *_getvideoconfig* you can get several crucial details about the graphics card and the monitor and use this information to automatically configure your application. Otherwise, your program has to ask the user to enter the information in some way or, worse, you have to assume default values for them.

RETURNS The return value is the pointer to the structure of type *videoconfig* that contains the return information. This is the pointer you supplied in the argument *gr_info*.

SEE ALSO `_setvideomode` *To select a particular video mode*

EXAMPLE Use *_getvideoconfig* to determine the current display adapter and monitor present on the PC.

```
#include <stdio.h>
#include <graph.h>
main()
{
    struct videoconfig gr_info, far *p_gr;
/* Get the current video configuration. */
    p_gr = _getvideoconfig(&gr_info);
    printf("This PC has:\n");
/* You can access the structure using the returned
 * pointer
 */
    switch(p_gr->adapter)
    {
      case _MDPA: printf("Monochrome Display Adapter");
                  break;
      case _CGA:  printf("Color Graphics Adapter");
                  break;
      case _EGA:  printf("Enhanced Graphics Adapter");
                  break;
      case _MCGA: printf("Multicolor Graphics Array");
                  break;
      case _VGA:  printf("Video Graphics Array");
                  break;
    }
    printf(" and ");
/* Or, you can access the structure directly */
    switch(gr_info.monitor)
    {
      case _MONO:      printf("Monochrome Monitor\n");
                       break;
      case _COLOR:     printf(
   "Color Monitor (or Enhanced monitor in CGA mode)\n");
                       break;
      case _ENHCOLOR:  printf("Enhanced Color Monitor\n");
                       break;
      case _ANALOG:    printf("Analog Monitor\n");
                       break;
    }
}
```

Graphics Modes, Coordinates, and Attributes

COMPATIBILITY

_getviewcoord, _getviewcoord_w, _getviewcoord_wxy

MSC 3	MSC 4	MSC 5	MSC 6	QC1	QC2	QC2.5	TC1	TC1.5	TC2	TC++	ANSI	UNIX V	XNX	OS2	DOS
			▲		▲	▲									▲

PURPOSE Use the *_getviewcoord* function to translate specified physical coordinates to view coordinates; the *_getviewcoord_w* version to translate window coordinates to view coordinates; and the *_getviewcoord_wxy* version to translate a specified window coordinate structure to view coordinates.

SYNTAX

```
struct xycoord _far _getviewcoord (short x, short y);

struct xycoord _getviewcoord_w (double wx, double wy);

struct xycoord _far _getviewcoord_wxy (struct _wxycoord _far *pwxy1);
```

`x, y` *Physical coordinates to translate*

`wx, wy` *Window coordinates to translate*

`pwxy1` *Window coordinates to translate*

EXAMPLE CALL

```
new_view = _getviewcoord_wxy (&new_wndw);
```

INCLUDES `#include <graph.h>` *For function definition*

DESCRIPTION The *_getviewcoord* function translates physical coordinates (*x, y*) to view coordinates. The *_getviewcoord_w* routine translates window coordinates (*wx, wy*) to view coordinates. The third function in this group, *_getviewcoord_wxy*, translates a window coordinates structure (*pwxy1*) to view coordinates. The *_getviewcoord_w* and *_getviewcoord_wxy* routines are implemented as macros. See the tutorial for more information about coordinate systems.

The declaration for a window coordinate pair in *graph.h* looks like this:

```
/* structure for window coordinate pair */

struct _wxycoord {
     double wx;      /* window x coordinate */
     double wy;      /* window y coordinate */
};
```

The declaration of the *_w* and *_wxy* macro versions in the GRAPH.H file is as follows:

```
/* convert from window to view coordinates */

struct xycoord _far _cdecl _getviewcoord_w(double,double);
struct xycoord _far _cdecl _getviewcoord_wxy(const struct
                                   _wxycoord _far *);
```

RETURNS All three functions return the view coordinates in an *xycoord* structure defined in *graph.h* as follows:

```
struct xycoord {
     short xcoord;
     short ycoord;
};
```

There is no error return.

COMMENTS In Microsoft C version 5.1, the *_getviewcoord* function is named *_getlogcoord.* Microsoft C 6.0 employs three coordinate systems for the low-level graphics functions. The physical screen coordinate system is the first, and the origin (0,0) is located at the upper-left corner of the screen. Coordinates increase downward and to the right, and the coordinates must be integral values. Physical coordinates are used only by the *_setcliprgn, _setviewport, _setvieworg, _getviewcoord,* and *_getphyscoord* routines.

The second of the three coordinate systems is the viewport (or view) coordinate system. A graphics viewport in Microsoft C is a clipping region whose coordinate system origin is at its upper-left corner. The default viewport is the physical screen, and will remain so until an explicit view defined using the *_setviewport* function. The viewport origin may be reset with a call to *_setvieworg.* Like coordinate system 1 (physical coordinates), the viewport coordinates must be integral values. The graphics functions without a *_w* or *_wxy* suffix use the view coordinate system, and take short *ints* for coordinate arguments.

The window coordinate system is the third of the three coordinate systems. The current graphics viewport is changed into a window by mapping a real valued coordinate system onto the viewport via a call to the *_setwindow* function. Each coordinate may have an arbitrary range as specified by arguments to the *_setwindow* routine. The value for the *y* coordinate may increase downward or upward. Graphics functions with a *_w* suffix use window coordinates and take *doubles* for their coordinate arguments. The graphics functions that end with a *_wxy* suffix take *_wxycoord* structures as arguments.

You may translate values back and forth between the coordinate sys-

tems using the *_getphyscoord*, *_getviewcoord*, and *_getwindowcoord* function families.

SEE ALSO

`_getphyscoord;` *To get physical coordinates from logical coordinates in Microsoft C 5.1*

`_getwindowcoord;` *To get window coordinates*

EXAMPLE The example program *1814.C* shows the translation of physical coordinates to view coordinates, checks to see if we are still on the physical screen, and draws a rectangle. It shows the usage of the *_getviewcoord* and the *_getwindowcoord* functions.

```
#include <conio.h>
#include <graph.h>
#include <stdlib.h>

void main()

{
   struct   xycoord view_crd, phys_crd;
   struct _wxycoord old_wndw, new_wndw;
   struct videoconfig vdo_cfg;

   if (!_setvideomode (_MAXRESMODE)) exit (1);

   _getvideoconfig (&vdo_cfg);

   /* build a window */
   _setwindow (1, -100.0, -125.0, 100.0, 125.0);

   /* figure coordinates */
   new_wndw = _getwindowcoord (2, 2);
   old_wndw = _getwindowcoord (1, 1);
   new_wndw = old_wndw = _getcurrentposition_w();
   view_crd = _getviewcoord_wxy (&new_wndw);
   phys_crd = _getphyscoord (view_crd.xcoord, view_crd.ycoord);

   /* have we fallen off the screen? */
   if ((phys_crd.xcoord >= 0)  &&
        (phys_crd.xcoord < vdo_cfg.numxpixels) &&
        (phys_crd.ycoord >= 0) &&
        (phys_crd.ycoord < vdo_cfg.numypixels))
   {
     _setcolor (4);
```

```
      _rectangle (_GBORDER,        -75, -125, 100, 125);
      _rectangle (_GFILLINTERIOR, -75, -125, 100, 125);
    }

    getch ();

      _setvideomode (_DEFAULTMODE);
}
```

_getvisualpage

COMPATIBILITY

MSC 3	MSC 4	MSC 5	MSC 6	QC1	QC2	QC2.5	TC1	TC1.5	TC2	TC++	ANSI	UNIX V	XNX	OS2	DOS
			▲		▲	▲								▲	▲

PURPOSE The *_getvisualpage* function lets you get the number of the current visual page of video memory. The visual page is the area of graphics memory currently being displayed on the screen.

SYNTAX `short _far _getvisualpage (void);`

EXAMPLE CALL `orig_vispg = _getvisualpage();`

INCLUDES `#include <graph.h>` *For function declaration*

DESCRIPTION All hardware combinations support at least one video page. The *_getvisualpage* function identifies which page is current. Page numbering starts with 0. The visual page (the one being shown) can be different from the active page (the page that gets current graphics output). See the entry for *_getactivepage* for a discussion of visual versus active graphics pages.

RETURNS The number of the current visual page.

COMMENTS Only one page, page 0, is available in OS/2.

SEE ALSO `_setvisualpage` *To select the visual page*

`_getactivepage` *To get the active page*

`_setactivepage` *To set the active page*

EXAMPLE See the program on the reference page for *_getactivepage*.

Graphics Modes, Coordinates, and Attributes

COMPATIBILITY

_getwindowcoord

MSC 3	MSC 4	MSC 5	MSC 6	QC1	QC2	QC2.5	TC1	TC1.5	TC2	TC++	ANSI	UNIX V	XNX	OS2	DOS
			▲		▲	▲									▲

PURPOSE Use the *_getwindowcoord* routine to translate the view coordinates (in [*x,y*] format) to window coordinates.

SYNTAX

```
struct _wxycoord _far _getwindowcoord (short x, short y);
```

`x, y` *The view coordinates you wish to translate*

EXAMPLE CALL

```
_getwindowcoord (120, 300);
```

INCLUDES `#include <graph.h>` *For function declaration*

DESCRIPTION The *_getwindowcoord* function translates the view coordinates (*x, y*) into window coordinates and returns them in a structure (defined in *graph.h*) of type *_wxycoord.*

RETURNS The *_getwindowcoord* function returns coordinates in a *_wxycoord* structure (as defined in *graph.h*). There is no error return.

COMMENTS As noted in more detail in the tutorial and on the reference page for the *_getviewcoord* function, Microsoft C 6.0 employs three coordinate systems for the low-level graphics functions. They are the physical coordinate system, the viewport (or view) coordinate system, and the window coordinate system. The window coordinate system is also referred to as being "real valued." The graphics functions without a *_w* or *_wxy* suffix use the view coordinate system, and take short *ints* for coordinate arguments.

Graphics functions with a *_w* suffix use window coordinates and take *doubles* for their coordinate arguments. The graphics functions that end with a *_wxy* suffix take *_wxycoord* structures as arguments.

You may translate values back and forth between the coordinate systems using the *_getphyscoord, _getviewcoord,* and *_getwindowcoord* function families.

SEE ALSO

`_getviewcoord;` *To translate specified coordinates to view coordinates*

`_getphyscoord;` *To translate view coordinates to physical coordinates (Microsoft C 5.1)*

EXAMPLE The example program in the reference entry for *_getviewcoord* also illustrates the use of *_getphyscoord.*

_remapallpalette

COMPATIBILITY

MSC 3	MSC 4	MSC 5	MSC 6	QC1	QC2	QC2.5	TC1	TC1.5	TC2	TC++	ANSI	UNIX V	XNX	OS2	DOS
		▲	▲	▲	▲	▲		1	1	1					▲

PURPOSE Use *_remapallpalette* in an EGA or VGA environment to redefine how the values that a pixel can take are associated with colors displayed on the screen. Thus, this function redefines the entire EGA or VGA palette. Once the pixel values are redefined, all existing text and graphics will change to the new colors immediately.

SYNTAX

```
short _far _remapallpalette(long far *colors);
```

`long _far *color;` *Array of colors to be assigned sequentially to the pixel values (use predefined constants)*

EXAMPLE CALL

```
_remapallpalette(&new_color_table);
```

INCLUDES `#include <graph.h>` *For function declaration and the definition of color constants*

DESCRIPTION Applicable only in EGA and VGA environments, the *_remapallpalette* associates the colors specified in the array of long integers *colors* with pixel values. The colors are assigned to the pixel values sequentially, starting with the pixel value 0 and continuing to the maximum value a pixel can take in that graphics mode. Thus, the array of long integers must have at least as many elements as the number of colors that can be simultaneously displayed on the hardware in the current graphics mode. For example, on the 16-color graphics mode on the VGA or the EGA, there must be 16 colors in the array specified by the argument *colors*.

The Microsoft C 5.1 graphics library expects the colors stored in the long integer array *colors* to be of a specific form (see the tutorial section). A set of predefined constants for the colors (see Table 17-2) appears in the header file *graph.h*. Their use is illustrated in the example below.

1. The Turbo C and Turbo C++ version of this function is *setallpalette*.

COMMON USES The *_remapallpalette* and its companion *_remappalette* functions are useful on EGA and VGA systems for designing user interfaces that can take advantage of the ability to quickly swap colors. For example, you can highlight selected menu items by redefining the displayed color from one that is subdued to one that really catches the eye.

RETURNS If the hardware is EGA or VGA, the *_remapallpalette* function returns a 0. Otherwise, it returns a –1 indicating an error.

SEE ALSO `_remappalette` *To redefine a single pixel value*

EXAMPLE If you have EGA or VGA hardware, set the display to a graphics mode. Display 16 rectangles, each filled with a color from the current palette, to illustrate the meaning of each pixel value in the default palette (black for 0, blue for 1, and so on). When the user hits a key, call *_remapallpalette* to redefine the entire palette. Exchange the positions of cyan and black, and red and blue. The background immediately becomes cyan (because pixel value 0 is always background) and the red rectangle swaps places with the blue one.

```
#include <stdio.h>
#include <graph.h>
/* Define new color map using defined constants from
 * graph.h. Notice that we have swapped red with blue
 * and cyan with black. So the background will become
 * cyan now.
 */
long newcolormap[] =
    {_CYAN, _RED, _GREEN, _BLACK, _BLUE, _MAGENTA,
     _BROWN, _WHITE, _GRAY, _LIGHTBLUE, _LIGHTGREEN,
     _LIGHTCYAN, _LIGHTRED, _LIGHTMAGENTA,
     _LIGHTYELLOW, _BRIGHTWHITE};
main()
{
    int i;
    short color=0, x1=0, y1=60, x2=100, y2=70;
/* Enter hi-resolution graphics mode on EGA */
    if (_setvideomode(_ERESCOLOR) == 0)
    {
/* Error setting mode */
        printf("Not EGA hardware\n");
        exit(0);
    }
/* Display rectangles filled with colors from current
 * palette
 */
     _settextposition(1,1);
    _outtext(
"Remapping the color palette using _remappalette");
/* Draw the filled rectangles */
    for (i=1; i<=8; i++)
    {
        color = 2*i-1;
        _setcolor(color);
```

```
            _rectangle(_GFILLINTERIOR, x1, y1, x2, y2);
            _setcolor(color+1);
            _rectangle(_GFILLINTERIOR,
                        x1+150, y1, x2+150, y2);
            y1 += 20;
            y2 += 20;
        }
/* Now remap entire palette -- swap red with blue, cyan
 * with black
 */
    _settextposition(3,1);
    _outtext(
      "Hit any key to remap the entire palette:");
    getch();
/* Display changes immediately */
    _remapallpalette(newcolormap);
/* Restore original mode */
/* Give user a chance to see the result */
    _settextposition(24,1);
    _outtext("Hit any key to exit:");
    getch();
    _setvideomode(_DEFAULTMODE);
}
```

_remappalette

COMPATIBILITY

MSC 3	MSC 4	MSC 5	MSC 6	QC1	QC2	QC2.5	TC1	TC1.5	TC2	TC++	ANSI	UNIX V	XNX	OS2	DOS
		▲	▲	▲	▲			1	1	1					▲

PURPOSE Use *_remappalette* in an EGA or VGA environment to redefine how a specific value contained in a pixel is associated with a color displayed on the screen. Thus this function redefines a single pixel value in EGA or VGA palette. For example, since a pixel value of 0 always signifies background, you can change the background color by calling *_remappalette* to redefine color number 0 (see the example below).

SYNTAX
```
long _far _remappalette(short pixel_value, long color);
```

`short pixel_value;` *Pixel value to be redefined*

`long color;` *Color to be associated with the pixel value (use predefined constants)*

EXAMPLE CALL

```
_remappalette(0, _CYAN);    /* Alter pixel value 0 to cyan */
```

INCLUDES

```
#include <graph.h>
```
For function declaration and the definition of color constants

DESCRIPTION The *_remappalette* function, available only in EGA and VGA environments, associates the color specified in the long integer argument *color* with the pixel value *pixel_value*. The maximum possible value of the argument *pixel_value* depends on the number of colors that can be simultaneously displayed in the current graphics mode. For example, on the 16-color graphics mode on the VGA or the EGA, the pixel value can be from 0 to 15.

The Microsoft C graphics library requires the color given in *color* to be of a specific form. Each color is defined by three bytes: the least significant byte contains the intensity of the red component, the next byte has the intensity of green, and the most significant byte is for the intensity of blue. A set of predefined constants (see Table 17-2) are given in the header file *graph.h*.

When a pixel value is redefined, existing text and graphics that are using the pixel value show the new color immediately.

1. The Turbo C and Turbo C++ version of this function is *setpalette*.

COMMON USES The *_remappalette* and its companion *_remapallpalette* are useful on EGA and VGA systems for special effects.

RETURNS If the hardware is EGA or VGA, the *_remappalette* function returns a long integer containing the previous color associated with the redefined pixel value. If the hardware is of the wrong type, *_remappalette* returns a –1, indicating an error.

SEE ALSO `_remapallpalette` *To redefine all possible pixel values in the current palette*

EXAMPLE If you have either EGA or VGA hardware, set the display to a graphics mode. Set the text color to 1 and display some text. Now change the background and the text colors by redefining pixel values 0 and 1 by calling *_remappalette*.

```
#include <stdio.h>
#include <graph.h>
#define BLUE 1  /* Blue is 1 in EGA's default palette */
/* Define array of colors using defined constants from
 * graph.h
 */
long colors[] =
    {_BLACK, _BLUE, _GREEN, _CYAN, _RED, _MAGENTA,
```

```
    _BROWN, _WHITE, _GRAY, _LIGHTBLUE, _LIGHTGREEN,
    _LIGHTCYAN, _LIGHTRED, _LIGHTMAGENTA, _LIGHTYELLOW,
    _BRIGHTWHITE};
main()
{
    char buffer[80];
    int i=0;
/* Assume an EGA environment */
    if (_setvideomode(_ERESCOLOR) == 0)
    {
        printf("Not EGA environment\n");
        exit(0);
    }
    _settextcolor(1);
    _settextposition(1,1);
    _outtext("Demonstrating _remappalette");
/* Loop through several colors for pixel
 * values 0 and 1
 */
    _settextposition(2,1);
    _outtext("Hit any key to go on, 'q' to exit");
    while(1)
    {
        if (getch() == 'q')
        {
/* Reset environment */
            _setvideomode(_DEFAULTMODE);
            exit(0);
        }
/* Alter pixel value 0 and 1 */
        _remappalette(0, colors[i%16]);
        _remappalette(1, colors[(i+2)%16]);
/* Select next color from array */
        i++;
    }
}
```

Graphics Modes, Coordinates, and Attributes

COMPATIBILITY

_selectpalette

MSC 3	MSC 4	MSC 5	MSC 6	QC1	QC2	QC2.5	TC1	TC1.5	TC2	TC++	ANSI	UNIX V	XNX	OS2	DOS
		▲	▲	▲	▲	▲									▲

PURPOSE Use the *_selectpalette* function to activate one of up to four predefined palettes when using the CGA or the EGA in _MRES4COLOR and _MRESNOCOLOR video modes (see the tutorial section).

SYNTAX

```
short _far _selectpalette(short palette_number);

short palette_number;      Palette number being selected
```

EXAMPLE CALL

```
_selectpalette(0);         /* Select CGA palette 0 */
```

INCLUDES

```
#include <graph.h>      For function declaration
```

DESCRIPTION Applicable only in the _MRES4COLOR and _MRESNOCOLOR video modes, the *_selectpalette* function selects the predefined palette number specified in the argument *palette_number* as the current palette from which colors are displayed. When a new palette is selected, all text and graphics change to the colors in that palette immediately.

The video modes _MRES4COLOR and _MRESNOCOLOR are supported by the CGA and the EGA. Use _MRES4COLOR with color displays. It provides four palettes, each with four colors (color number 0 in each palette is the background color and can be separately selected). Colors 1 through 3 of these four palettes are shown in Table 17-4. Use _MRESNOCOLOR with monochrome displays to produce shades of gray. When used with color displays this mode also allows a set of palettes. With an IBM EGA and an enhanced color display, both _MRES4COLOR and _MRESNOCOLOR modes provide the same palettes as the ones shown in Table 17-4. The palettes may differ on EGA clones, however, because of the differences in emulating the CGA modes in the EGA ROM.

RETURNS The *_selectpalette* function returns the previous palette number.

SEE ALSO `_setvideomode` *To set the display hardware to a specific mode*

EXAMPLE If you have either CGA or EGA hardware, set the display to the graphics mode _MRES4COLOR. Display three rectangles each filled with colors 1 through 3 from palette 0. Now cycle through the palettes by calling *_selectpalette*, letting the user see the color selections from each palette displayed on the screen. Exit when the user hits a 'q'.

```
#include <stdio.h>
#include <graph.h>
main()
{
        int i;
        short palette=0;
        short x1=0, y1=60, x2=100, y2=70;
/* Enter medium resolution graphics in EGA (emulating CGA) */
        if (_setvideomode(_MRES4COLOR) == 0)
        {
            printf("Not appropriate hardware\n"); /* Error setting mode
*/
            exit(0);
        }
/* Display rectangles filled with colors from current palette */
        _settextposition(1,1);
        _outtext("Color palettes using _selectpalette");
        _selectpalette(0);              /* Use palette 0 first */
        for (i=1; i<=3; i++)  /* Draw three filled rectangles */
        {
            _setcolor(i);
            _rectangle(_GFILLINTERIOR, x1, y1, x2, y2);
            y1 += 20;
            y2 += 20;
        }
/* Let user go through the palettes and see the effect */
        _settextposition(3,1);
        _outtext("Hit 'q' to exit, else change palette:");
        while(1)
        {
            if(getch() == 'q')
            {
                _setvideomode(_DEFAULTMODE);   /* Restore mode */
                exit(0);
            }
            palette++;
            _selectpalette(palette % 4);  /* Palettes in 0 to 3 */
        }
}
```

Graphics Modes, Coordinates, and Attributes

COMPATIBILITY **_setactivepage**

MSC 3	MSC 4	MSC 5	MSC 6	QC1	QC2	QC2.5	TC1	TC1.5	TC2	TC++	ANSI	UNIX V	XNX	OS2	DOS
		▲	▲	▲	▲	▲		1	1	1				▲	▲

PURPOSE Use the *_setactivepage* function in EGA or VGA graphics modes and in the text modes to select the current page or portion of display memory where graphics and text operations are performed. This function only works when the adapter has enough video memory to support multiple pages.

SYNTAX

```
short _far _setactivepage(short page_number);
```

```
short page_number;
```
The page number to be used for all further text and graphics operations

EXAMPLE CALL

```
_setactivepage(1);
```

INCLUDES #include <graph.h> *For function declaration*

DESCRIPTION The *_setactivepage* function selects the page specified in the argument *page_number* as the current active page. This determines the section of video memory where text and graphics operations will be performed.

In this context, a page is a chunk of storage in the video memory that can hold the contents of a screenful in the current video mode. For example, if the video adapter has enough memory to hold eight screensful of text, you can have eight pages in the text mode. In the graphics mode, on the other hand, the same adapter might have only enough memory for two screensful, giving two graphics pages. While most adapters provide for multiple pages in text modes, only EGA and VGA with 256 K of video memory support two pages in the high-resolution graphics modes.

Just as the current active page determines the portion of video memory where results of text and graphics operations are stored, the current "visual" page determines the portion of video memory that is actually mapped to the display screen. Use *_setvisualpage* to select the page being displayed. By default, page 0 is used as both active and visual page.

The number of video pages available in the current mode can be determined by calling *_getvideoconfig.*

1. The Turbo C and Turbo C++ version of this function is *setactivepage.*

COMMON USES Provided you have enough video memory for multiple pages, the *_setactivepage* function is useful for preparing a page in display memory while another is shown to the user. This can speed up the display or allow for smoother animation.

RETURNS The *_setactivepage* function returns the page number of the previous active page. If it fails, it returns a negative value.

SEE ALSO `_setvisualpage` *To select the page being displayed*

EXAMPLE If you have an EGA with 256 K of graphics memory, you can have two graphics pages, each capable of storing one 640×350, 16-color display screen. Set the adapter to the high-resolution graphics mode. Then draw a red rectangle on page 0, and while this is displayed, use *_setactivepage* to select page 1 and draw a yellow ellipse on the page. Next, let the user flip through the two pages (use the *_setvisualpage* function).

```
#include <stdio.h>
#include <graph.h>
#define RED    4
#define YELLOW 14
main()
{
    int i;
    short page = 0;
/* Assuming EGA with 256 KB graphics mèmory, enter
 * high-resolution mode
 */
    if (_setvideomode(_ERESCOLOR) == 0)
    {
/* Error setting mode */
        printf("Not appropriate hardware\n");
        exit(0);
    }
/* Default active page is page 0. Draw a red rectangle
 * in page 0.
 */
    _settextposition(1,1);
    _outtext("This is page 0");
    _setcolor(RED);
    _rectangle(_GFILLINTERIOR, 20, 50, 120, 100);
/* Now set active page to 1 and draw an ellipse there*/
    if(_setactivepage(1) < 0)
    {
        _setvideomode(_DEFAULTMODE);
        printf("Cannot support multiple pages\n");
        exit(0);
    }
/* Draw a yellow ellipse on this page */
    _settextposition(1,1);
    _outtext("This is page 1");
    _setcolor(YELLOW);
    _ellipse(_GFILLINTERIOR, 20, 50, 120, 100);
```

```
    _setactivepage(0);
/* Let user alternate between the two pages and see the
 * effect
 */
    while(1)
    {
        _settextposition(3,1);
        _outtext(
    "Hit 'q' to exit, any other key to change page:");

        if(getch() == 'q')
        {
/* Restore mode */
            _setvideomode(_DEFAULTMODE);
            exit(0);
        }
        page++;
/* Select the other page as the visual page */
/* Page number must be between 0 and 1      */
        _setvisualpage(page & 1);
        _setactivepage(page & 1);
    }
}
```

COMPATIBILITY

_setbkcolor

MSC 3	MSC 4	MSC 5	MSC 6	QC1	QC2	QC2.5	TC1	TC1.5	TC2	TC++	ANSI	UNIX V	XNX	OS2	DOS
		▲	1	▲	▲	▲		2	2	2				▲	▲

PURPOSE Use the *_setbkcolor* function to select a new background color.

SYNTAX

```
long _far _setbkcolor(long color);
```

`long color;` *New color value*

EXAMPLE CALL

```
_setbkcolor(4L);    /* Red background in text mode     */
_setbkcolor(_RED); /* Red background in graphics mode */
```

INCLUDES `#include <graph.h>` *For function declaration and definition of color constants*

DESCRIPTION The *_setbkcolor* function is used to set the current background color to the value given in the long integer argument *color*. In the graphics mode the change is visible immediately. In other modes, it is necessary to clear the screen (see *_clearscreen*) to see the new background color. The method of specifying the color depends on the video mode.

In text modes, the background color is specified by a number from the current palette. In the EGA, for example, color number 4 in the default palette is red. So when the EGA is in text mode, a call of the form *_setbkcolor(4L)* followed by a call to *_clearscreen* sets the screen to red (see the example below). The method of specifying the new background color is different in graphics modes. In this case, a predefined mnemonic constant specifies the color. These constants are defined in *graph.h*, and listed in Table 17-2. Each color consists of 3 bytes. These bytes, from the least significant (rightmost) to the most significant (leftmost), represent the intensity of the red, green, and blue components of that color. Microsoft's graphics library takes care of displaying the background color properly for your graphics environment.

1. Changed in Microsoft C 6.0 to provide OS/2 capability. 2. The Turbo C and Turbo C++ version of this function is *setbkcolor.*

COMMON USES The *_setbkcolor* function sets a new background color. In text modes, this color is also used by the *_clearscreen* function to clear the screen and fill it with the background color.

RETURNS The *_setbkcolor* function returns a long integer that has the value of the previous background color.

COMMENTS When the video adapter is in a graphics mode, the pixels in the graphics memory that are supposed to have the background color always contain zeroes—so the background color number is 0. But this pixel value is mapped to a specific color via the current palette. Some hardware, such as EGA and VGA, allows remapping of palettes, meaning that although black is the default color associated with a pixel value of zero, you could set any color to correspond to a zero pixel value. So during EGA and VGA graphics, you can change the background color by using the *_remappalette* function to redefine the meaning of a zero pixel value. See the description of *_remappalette* for an explanation of remapping of palettes. The entire palette can be remapped by *_remapallpalette.*

SEE ALSO

`_getbkcolor` *To retrieve the value of the current background color*

`_remappalette` *Another way of altering background color in EGA and VGA environments*

`_selectpalette` *To set background color in the _MRES4COLOR and _MRESNOCOLOR video modes (see* _setvideomode*)*

Graphics Modes, Coordinates, and Attributes

EXAMPLE In EGA's text mode, call *_setbkcolor* to set the background to red (color number 4 in the default palette). Call *_clearscreen* after setting the background color so that you can see the effect.

```
#include <stdio.h>
#include <graph.h>
/* Need a "long" constant for _setbkcolor */
#define RED 4L
main()
{
/* Set background color to red */
    _setbkcolor(RED);
    _clearscreen(_GCLEARSCREEN);
/* The screen should be red now */
    printf(
"Use the DOS command MODE CO80 to reset display\n");
}
```

Assuming an EGA environment, enter the high-resolution graphics mode and change the background color to blue by calling *_setbkcolor*.

```
#include <stdio.h>
#include <graph.h>

main()
{
  long lastcolor;
    char buffer[80];
/* Enter hi-resolution graphics mode on EGA */
    if (_setvideomode(_ERESCOLOR) != 0)
    {
/* First set background to _RED */
        _setbkcolor(_RED);
        _settextposition(1,1);
        _outtext("Hit a key to continue");
        getch();          /* Read a key -- to pause */
/* Now set background to _BLUE and get last color   */
        lastcolor = _setbkcolor(_BLUE);
        _settextposition(1,1);
       _outtext("Demonstrating _setbkcolor\n");
/* Report previous value so that we can check against
 * table in graph.h
 */
        sprintf(buffer,"Previous background color was: \
%d", lastcolor);
```

```
            _settextposition(2,1);
            _outtext(buffer);

/* Restore original mode */
/* Give user a chance to see the result */
            _settextposition(40,1);
            _outtext("Hit any key to exit:");
            getch();
            _setvideomode(_DEFAULTMODE);
        }
        else

        {
/* Error setting mode */
            printf("Mode not supported by hardware\n");
        }
}
```

_setcliprgn

COMPATIBILITY

MSC 3	MSC 4	MSC 5	MSC 6	QC1	QC2	QC2.5	TC1	TC1.5	TC2	TC++	ANSI	UNIX V	XNX	OS2	DOS
		▲	▲	▲	▲	▲									▲

PURPOSE Use *_setcliprgn* to define a rectangular region of the screen as the clipping region for graphics (i.e., any graphics falling outside this region will be cut off).

SYNTAX

```
void _far _setcliprgn(short x1, short y1, short x2, short y2);
```

`short x1, y1;` *Upper-left corner of clipping region in physical coordinates*

`short x2, y2;` *Lower-right corner of clipping region in physical coordinates*

EXAMPLE CALL

```
_setcliprgn(100, 50, 300, 150);
```

INCLUDES `#include <graph.h>` *For function declaration*

DESCRIPTION The *_setcliprgn* function defines an area of the screen as the clipping region for all graphics operations. The area is specified in terms of the physical coordinates (see the tutorial section) of the upper-left hand corner (*x1, y1*) and that of the lower-right corner (*x2, y2*). Unlike *_setviewport*, the *_setcliprgn* function leaves the logical coordinate system unchanged.

COMMON USES The *_setcliprgn* function can be used to ensure that graphics output is confined to a fixed area of the screen.

COMMENTS The *_setviewport* function also defines a clipping region for graphics. In addition to this, *_setviewport* also moves the origin of the logical coordinate system to the upper left corner of the clipping rectangle.

Use *_textwindow* to limit text output to a predefined area.

SEE ALSO

`_setlogorg`	*To define a new logical origin*
`_setviewport`	*To define a clipping region and relocate the origin of the logical coordinate system at the same time*
`_settextwindow`	*Analogous operation for text output*

EXAMPLE Put your graphics hardware into an appropriate mode, define a clipping region, and draw a filled ellipse to illustrate the clipping. Remember, unlike *_setviewport*, *_setcliprgn* does not alter the origin of the logical coordinate system.

```
 #include <stdio.h>
#include <graph.h>
#define RED  4  /* For defining the current color */
main()
{
    if (_setvideomode(_ERESCOLOR) == 0)
    {
        printf("EGA hi-res mode not supported\n");
        exit(0);
    }
    _settextposition(1,1);
    _outtext("Demonstration of _setcliprgn:");
    _setcolor(RED); /* Set current color to red    */
/* Dashed lines for boundary */
    _setlinestyle(0xf0f);
/* A 200 x 200 clip region */
    _setcliprgn(0, 100, 200, 300);
/* Show boundary of region, compare with example
 * for_setviewport
 */
    _rectangle(_GBORDER,0,100,200,300);
/* Now draw an ellipse filled with current color     */
    _ellipse(_GFILLINTERIOR, 50, 150, 450, 550);
/* NOTE: when tested, ellipse didn't get filled!     */
/* Return to default mode when user strikes any key */
```

```
        _settextposition(4,1);
        _outtext(
          "Press any key to return to original mode:");
        getch();  /* A do-nothing read */
        _setvideomode(_DEFAULTMODE);
    }
```

_setcolor

COMPATIBILITY

MSC 3	MSC 4	MSC 5	MSC 6	QC1	QC2	QC2.5	TC1	TC1.5	TC2	TC++	ANSI	UNIX V	XNX	OS2	DOS
		▲	▲	▲	▲	▲		1	1	1					▲

PURPOSE Use *_setcolor* to select the default color to be used by all future calls to the drawing functions *_arc, _ellipse, _lineto, _pie, _rectangle,* and *_setpixel.*

SYNTAX

```
short _far _setcolor(short color);
```

`short color;` *Selected color number*

EXAMPLE CALL

```
_setcolor(4);
```

INCLUDES `#include <graph.h>` *For function declaration and definition of mode names*

DESCRIPTION The *_setcolor* routine sets up the current color to the color number specified in the argument *color.* This color number is used as the default color by the *_arc, _ellipse, _lineto, _pie, _rectangle,* and *_setpixel* routines. The actual color displayed depends on the current palette.

Until a color has been set, these routines use the highest color number in the current palette (see *_selectpalette* and *_remapallpalette* to set the color palette).

There is no return value, but if the color number *color* specifies is out of the range of values allowed by the current palette, *_setcolor* sets the current color to the highest numbered color in the palette.

1. The Turbo C and Turbo C++ version of this function is *setcolor.*

SEE ALSO

`_remapallpalette` *To set up a color palette*

`_selectpalette` *To use a predefined palette*

EXAMPLE For a system with an EGA and an enhanced color monitor, write a C program that displays 16 rectangles, each filled with 1 color out of the 16

available for display. The lower 8 rectangles will be intensified versions of the upper 8.

```
#include <stdio.h>
#include <graph.h>
main()
{
    int i;
    short color=0, x1=0, y1=40, x2=100, y2=50;
/* Enter hi-resolution graphics mode on EGA */
    if (_setvideomode(_ERESCOLOR) != 0)
    {

/* Error setting mode */
        printf("Mode not supported by hardware\n");
        exit(0);
    }
    _settextposition(1,1);
    _outtext(
     "16 colors in 640x350 color graphics mode");
/* Draw a filled rectangle */
    for (i=1; i<=8; i++)
    {
        color = 2*i-1;
        _setcolor(color);
        _rectangle(_GFILLINTERIOR, x1, y1, x2, y2);
        _setcolor(color+1);
        _rectangle(_GFILLINTERIOR,
                       x1+150, y1, x2+150, y2);
        y1 += 20;
        y2 += 20;
    }
/* Restore original mode */
/* Give user a chance to see the result */
    _settextposition(2,1);
    _outtext("Hit any key to exit:");
    getch();
    _setvideomode(_DEFAULTMODE);
}
```

_setfillmask

COMPATIBILITY

MSC 3	MSC 4	MSC 5	MSC 6	QC1	QC2	QC2.5	TC1	TC1.5	TC2	TC++	ANSI	UNIX V	XNX	OS2	DOS
		▲	▲	▲	▲	▲		1	1	1				▲	▲

PURPOSE Use *_setfillmask* to define a pattern that will be used as a mask by the *_floodfill, _rectangle, _ellipse,* and *_pie* routines, which fill an area with the current color. Until you define a fill mask, a solid fill pattern is used.

SYNTAX

```
void _far _setfillmask(unsigned char _far *fillmask);
```

`unsigned char _far *fillmask;` *8×8 bit pattern that determines how the filled area looks*

EXAMPLE CALL

```
unsigned char _far mask1[] = {1, 3, 7, 0xf, 0x1f, 0x3f, 0x7f, 0xff};
_setfillmask(mask1);
```

INCLUDES `#include <graph.h>` *For function declaration*

DESCRIPTION The *_setfillmask* function defines an 8×8 pattern of bits as the current mask to be used by the routines *_floodfill, _rectangle, _ellipse,* and *_pie.*

The fill pattern is specified by the argument *fillmask*, which is a far pointer to an array of eight characters. Since each character has 8 bits, you can think of this array of bits as a model of an area on the screen, 8 pixels wide and 8 pixels tall, with the first character representing the first row of the area. When filling an 8×8 area using the mask, those pixels that correspond to 0 bits are left untouched while the rest are filled with the current color. For areas larger than 8×8 pixels, the fill operation uses the mask on successive 8×8 blocks until the entire screen is covered. Thus a solid fill is specified when all eight characters contain the value FFh. This is the default value of the fill style in the graphics package. See the example below on how to specify other fill masks using this method.

1. The Turbo C and Turbo C++ version of this function is *setfillpattern.*

COMMON USES This function is used to select different fill styles so that objects, such as slices of a pie chart, can be distinguished from one another.

COMMENTS If you switch fill masks in a graphics routine, it is a good idea first to retrieve the current mask with *_getfillmask* so that you can restore the style to normal before returning from the routine.

SEE ALSO `_getfillmask` *To determine the current fill mask*

Graphics Modes, Coordinates, and Attributes

EXAMPLE Write a C program to illustrate some of the fill styles that can be created using the *_setfillmask* function. Since this is a self-contained program, there is no need to save and restore the old fill mask.

```
#include <stdio.h>
#include <graph.h>
#define RED  4      /* Color number 4 is red */
/* Define the fill style masks */
unsigned char fillmask[4][8] =
{
/* First mask */
    1, 3, 7, 0xf, 0x1f, 0x3f, 0x7f, 0xff,
/* Mask 2     */
    0xf0, 0xf0, 0xf0, 0xf0, 0xf, 0xf, 0xf, 0xf,
/* Mask 3     */
    0xcc, 0x33, 0xcc, 0x33, 0xcc, 0x33, 0xcc, 0x33,
/* Mask 4     */
    0xc3, 0xc3, 0xc,  0xc,  0x30, 0x30, 0xc3, 0xc3
};
main()
{
    int i;
    short color=0, x1=0, y1=40;
/* Enter hi-resolution graphics mode on EGA */
    if (_setvideomode(_ERESCOLOR) != 0)
    {
       _setcolor(RED);
       _settextposition(1,1);
       _outtext("Illustrating different fill styles:");
/* Draw filled rectangle with different fill styles */
        for (i=1; i<=2; i++)
        {
            _setfillmask(fillmask[2*i-2]);
            _rectangle(_GFILLINTERIOR,
                       x1, y1, x1+100, y1+60);
            _setfillmask(fillmask[2*i-1]);
            _rectangle(_GFILLINTERIOR,
                       x1+150, y1, x1+250, y1+60);
            y1 += 100;
        }
/* Restore original video mode          */
/* Give user a chance to see the result */
        _settextposition(40,1);
        _outtext("Hit any key to exit:");
        getch();
```

```
            _setvideomode(_DEFAULTMODE);
    }
    else
    {
/* Error setting mode */
            printf("Mode not supported by hardware\n");
    }
}
```

_setlinestyle

COMPATIBILITY

MSC 3	MSC 4	MSC 5	MSC 6	QC1	QC2	QC2.5	TC1	TC1.5	TC2	TC++	ANSI	UNIX V	XNX	OS2	DOS
		▲	▲	▲	▲	▲		1	1	1				▲	▲

PURPOSE Use *_setlinestyle* to define a 16-bit mask that controls how dashed lines look. The mask is used by the routines *_lineto* and *_rectangle.*

SYNTAX

```
void _far _setlinestyle(unsigned short linemask);

unsigned short linemask;
```

Bit pattern that determines how the line looks

EXAMPLE CALL

```
_setlinestyle(0x3ff);
```

INCLUDES

```
#include <graph.h>
```

For function declaration

DESCRIPTION The *_setlinestyle* function is used to define the style of lines to be drawn by the routines *_lineto* and *_rectangle.* The style determines whether the line is solid or dashed and, if dashed, determines the pattern of the dashes.

The 16-bit argument *linemask* specifies the pattern to be repeated when drawing a line. Think of this mask as one representing a line segment 16 pixels long. If a bit in *linemask* is a 1, the corresponding pixel in that line gets painted with the current color (see *_setcolor*). If a bit is 0, the corresponding pixel is untouched. Note that a value of FFFFh for *linemask* means a solid line. This is the default value of the line style in the graphics package. The example below shows how to specify other line styles with this method.

1. The Turbo C and Turbo C++ version of this function is *setlinestyle.*

COMMON USES This function is used to select different line styles so that overlapping graphs can be distinguished from one another.

COMMENTS If you switch line styles in a graphics routine, it is a good idea first to retrieve the current style using *_getlinestyle* so that you can restore the style to normal before returning from the routine.

SEE ALSO `_getlinestyle` *To determine the current line style*

EXAMPLE Write a C program to illustrate some of the line styles that can be created using the *_setlinestyle* function. Since this is a self-contained program, there is no need to save and restore the old line style.

```
#include <stdio.h>
#include <graph.h>
#define RED  4      /* Color number 4 is red */
/* Define the line style masks */
short linemask[16] =
{1, 3, 7, 0xf, 0x1f, 0x3f, 0x7f, 0xff,
 0x1ff, 0x3ff, 0x7ff, 0xfff, 0x1fff, 0x3fff, 0x7fff,
 0xffff};
main()
{
    int i;
    short y = 30;
/* Enter hi-resolution graphics mode on EGA */
    if (_setvideomode(_ERESCOLOR) != 0)
    {
       _settextposition(1,1);
       _outtext("Demonstrating different line styles:");
/* Set up red as the current color */
        _setcolor(RED);
        for (i=0; i<16; i++)
        {
/* Select a line style from the array of style masks */
            _setlinestyle(linemask[i]);
            _moveto(0,y);
            _lineto(500,y);
            y += 10;
        }
/* Restore original mode */
/* Give user a chance to see the result */
        _settextposition(40,1);
        _outtext("Hit any key to exit:");
        getch();
        _setvideomode(_DEFAULTMODE);
    }
    else
    {
```

```
/* Error setting mode */
        printf("Mode not supported by hardware\n");
    }
}
```

_setlogorg

COMPATIBILITY

MSC 3	MSC 4	MSC 5	MSC 6	QC1	QC2	QC2.5	TC1	TC1.5	TC2	TC++	ANSI	UNIX V	XNX	OS2	DOS
		▲	1	▲	▲										

PURPOSE Use *_setlogorg* to move the origin (the point 0,0) of the logical coordinate system used for graphics to a specific physical pixel location on the display screen. (Not used by Microsoft C 6.0).

SYNTAX

```
struct xycoord far _setlogorg(short x, short y);
```

`short x, y;` *The physical* x *and* y *coordinates of the point on the screen that becomes the new origin of the logical coordinate system*

EXAMPLE CALL

```
_setlogorg(100, 100);
```

INCLUDES `#include <graph.h>` *For function declaration and definition of the structure* xycoord

DESCRIPTION The *_setlogorg* function sets the origin of the logical coordinate system to the physical point (*x,y*). From then on, the point (0,0) in logical coordinates corresponds to the pixel at (*x,y*).

The graphics library maintains two coordinate systems: one physical and the other logical (see Figure 17-2). The physical coordinate axes are fixed, with the origin (0,0) at the upper-left corner of the screen, with the x-axis extending horizontally to the right and the y-axis going downwards. The logical coordinate system's x and y axes are parallel to their physical counterparts. Its default origin corresponds to the physical coordinates (0,0) but with *_setlogorg* the origin can be relocated to any physical point. This allows you to translate or shift objects on the screen.

1. Replaced in Microsoft C 6.0 by *_setvieworg*.

COMMON USES The *_setlogorg* function is used for translations (shifts) of graphical objects. For example, to draw two identical rectangles, one translated from the other, you draw the first rectangle, use *_setlogorg* to move the logical origin, and repeat the call to draw the next rectangle (see the example below).

RETURNS The *_setlogorg* function returns the coordinates of the previous logical origin in a structure of type *xycoord*, which is declared as shown below in the header file *graph.h*.

```
struct xycoord        /* Structure for pixel coordinates */
{
    short xcoord;     /* x-coordinate */
    short ycoord;     /* y-coordinate */
};
```

COMMENTS As covered in the tutorial, the logical coordinate system is not used in Microsoft C after version 5.1. The *_setlogorg* function is #defined to *_setvieworg* starting with Microsoft C 6.0.

SEE ALSO

`_setviewport`	*To define a limited area of the screen as the clipping region and move the logical origin to the upper left corner of this region*
`_getlogcoord`	*To convert physical coordinates to logical*
`_getphyscoord`	*To convert logical coordinates to physical*

EXAMPLE If you have graphics capability, set the adapter to a graphics mode. Draw two identical filled rectangles, one shifted diagonally from the other by some amount. Use two calls to *_rectangle* with a call to *_setlogorg* in between to achieve the shift.

```
#include <stdio.h>
#include <graph.h>
#define BLUE 1 /* In EGA's default palette, BLUE is 1 */
#define RED  4 /* and RED is 4                        */
main()
{
/* Assume an EGA environment */
    if (_setvideomode(_ERESCOLOR) == 0)
    {
        printf("Not EGA environment\n");
        exit(0);
    }
    _settextposition(1,1);
    _outtext("Shift rectangles with _setlogorg");
/* Set current color to RED and draw filled rectangle */
    _setcolor(RED);
    _rectangle(_GFILLINTERIOR,10,40,110,90);
/* Now set new logical origin and make identical call */
    _setlogorg(70,30);
```

```
    _setcolor(BLUE);
    _rectangle(_GFILLINTERIOR,10,40,110,90);

/* Wait for user to hit a key, then reset everything  */
    _settextposition(25,1);
    _outtext("Hit any key to reset mode and exit:");
    getch();
    _setvideomode(_DEFAULTMODE);
}
```

_setvideomode

COMPATIBILITY

MSC 3	MSC 4	MSC 5	MSC 6	QC1	QC2	QC2.5	TC1	TC1.5	TC2	TC++	ANSI	UNIX V	XNX	OS2	DOS
		▲	1	▲	▲	▲		2	2	2				▲	▲

PURPOSE Use *_setvideomode* to set a display mode appropriate for a certain combination of adapter and display. For example, if you have an EGA with an enhanced color monitor you can select a 640×350 pixel graphics mode with up to 16 colors.

SYNTAX

```
short _far _setvideomode(short mode);

short mode;        Selected mode
```

EXAMPLE CALL

```
_setvideomode(_HRES16COLOR); /* 640 x 200, 16 color mode */
```

INCLUDES `#include <graph.h>` *For function declaration and definition of mode names*

DESCRIPTION The *_setvideomode* function sets up the graphics hardware to work in the mode specified in the argument *mode*. The value specified for the mode can be any one of the constants shown in Table 17-1 and defined in the include file *graph.h*.

1. Changed in Microsoft C 6.0 to provide OS/2 capability. 2. The Turbo C and Turbo C++ version of this function is *setgraphmode*.

COMMON USES This function is used to set up the graphics environment in an application program. For example, for graphics operation, you first choose a mode appropriate for your hardware, call *_setvideomode* to enter this mode, and proceed with the graphics operations.

RETURNS The return value is nonzero if everything went well. If the specified mode is not supported by the hardware configuration, *_setvideomode* returns a 0.

COMMENTS In a graphics program, setting the mode is one of the first things you do. In many cases you will want to use the highest resolution mode supported by the installed graphics hardware. Before exiting from the graphics application, you should return back to the original mode by using *_setvideomode* again with the mode constant _DEFAULTMODE.

SEE ALSO `_getvideoconfig` *To determine the hardware configuration*

EXAMPLE If you have an EGA with an enhanced color monitor, write a C program using *_setvideomode* to set up the hardware for 640×350 graphics and perform some sample graphics operations. Then restore everything to normal and exit.

```
#include <stdio.h>
#include <graph.h>
#define RED 4      /* Color number 4 is red */
main()
{
/* Enter hi-resolution graphics mode on EGA */
    if (_setvideomode(_ERESCOLOR) != 0)
    {
        _settextposition(1,1);
        _outtext("Now in 640x350 color graphics mode");
/* Draw a filled rectangle */
        _setcolor(RED);
        if(_rectangle(_GFILLINTERIOR,
                      200, 100, 400, 200) == 0)
        {
            _settextposition(2,1);
            _outtext("Error drawing filled rectangle!");
        }
/* Restore original mode */
/* Give user a chance to see the result */
        _settextposition(2,1);
        _outtext("Hit any key to exit:");
        getch();
        _setvideomode(_DEFAULTMODE);
    }
    else
    {
/* Error setting mode */
        printf("Mode not supported by hardware\n");
    }
}
```

_setvideomoderows

COMPATIBILITY

MSC 3	MSC 4	MSC 5	MSC 6	QC1	QC2	QC2.5	TC1	TC1.5	TC2	TC++	ANSI	UNIX V	XNX	OS2	DOS
			▲		▲	▲								▲	▲

PURPOSE Use the *_setvideomoderows* function to set the video mode and the number of text rows on the display.

SYNTAX

```
short _far _setvideomoderows (short mode, short rows);
```

`mode` *_MAXRESMODE, _MAXCOLORMODE, _DEFAULTMODE, _TEXTBW40, _TEXTC40, _TEXTBW80, _TEXTC80, _MRES4COLOR, _MRESNOCOLOR, _HRESBW, _TEXTMONO, _HERCMONO, _ERESNOCOLOR, _ERESCOLOR, _VRES2COLOR, _VRES16COLOR, _MRES256COLOR, _MRES16COLOR, _ERES16COLOR, _ORESCOLOR (Olivetti systems)*

`rows` *The number of rows requested*

EXAMPLE CALL

```
_setvideomoderows (_VRES16COLOR, 25);
```

INCLUDES `#include <graph.h>` *For function declaration*

DESCRIPTION The *_setvideomoderows* function selects a screen mode for a particular combination of a graphics card (display adapter) and a monitor, and it requests the number of text rows to be used. The details of the constants used to identify video modes appear in the tutorial.

The constant _MAXTEXTROWS may be specified for the *rows* argument. It will result in the maximum number of rows available, which in text modes is 50 on the VGA, 43 on EGA, and 25 on others. Some graphics modes support either 30 or 60 rows, and _MAXTEXTROWS chooses the 60-row value.

RETURNS The number of rows actually set if successful; 0 if not.

COMMENTS Only text modes are available in OS/2.

SEE ALSO `_setvideomode`

EXAMPLE This program shows the *_setvideomoderows* function switching between modes of 25 and 43 rows. Another example may be seen in the program on the reference page for *_getactivepage*.

```
#include <conio.h>
#include <stdio.h>
#include <graph.h>
```

```
short vd_mds[] = {_TEXTBW40,  _TEXTC40,  _TEXTBW80,  _TEXTC80};
char *vd_lbl[] = {"TEXTBW40", "TEXTC40", "TEXTBW80", "TEXTC80"};

short no_rows[]= { 43, 25 };  /* number of rows  */

void main()
{
   short cntr1, cntr2, row, y, w, x, num =
       sizeof(vd_mds)/sizeof(vd_mds[0]);

   struct videoconfig vdo_cfg;

   char scratch [512];          /* scratch buffer */
    _displaycursor (_GCURSOROFF);

   /* try each mode */
   for (cntr1 = 0; cntr1 <= num; cntr1++)
   {
      for (cntr2 = 0; cntr2 < 5; cntr2++)
      {
         /* try both row values */
         row = _setvideomoderows (vd_mds[cntr1], no_rows[cntr2]);
         if ((!row) || (no_rows[cntr2] != row))
            continue;
         else
         {
            _getvideoconfig (&vdo_cfg);
            x = (vdo_cfg.numtextcols - 25) / 2;
            y = (vdo_cfg.numtextrows - 12) / 2;

            /* set data to a string */
            w  = sprintf (scratch,   "mode: %s\n",
                          vd_lbl[cntr1]);

            w += sprintf (scratch+w, "rows: %d\n",
                          vdo_cfg.numtextrows);

            w += sprintf (scratch+w, "mntr: %d\n",
                          vdo_cfg.monitor);

            w += sprintf (scratch+w, "mmry: %d",
                          vdo_cfg.memory);

            _outtext (scratch);      /* display string */
            getch();
```

```
            }
        }
    }

    _displaycursor (_GCURSORON);
    _setvideomode  (_DEFAULTMODE);
}
```

_setvieworg

COMPATIBILITY

MSC 3	MSC 4	MSC 5	MSC 6	QC1	QC2	QC2.5	TC1	TC1.5	TC2	TC++	ANSI	UNIX V	XNX	OS2	DOS
			▲		▲	▲									▲

PURPOSE Use the *_setvieworg* function when you need to change the point of origin for a viewport. This function replaces *_setlogorg* starting with Microsoft C 6.0.

SYNTAX

```
struct xycoord _far _setvieworg (short x, short y);
```

`x, y` *New origin point for a graphic viewport*

EXAMPLE CALL

```
_setvieworg (120,50);
```

INCLUDES `#include <graph.h>` *For function declaration*

DESCRIPTION The *_setvieworg* function moves the viewpoint (or view, or view coordinate) origin (0,0) to the physical point (*x, y*). Suppose that your program makes a call to *_setvieworg* with integer arguments of 120 and 50. The *_setvieworg* function moves the view coordinate origin—the (0,0) point in the upper-left corner of the viewport—to the physical point (120,50). All other view coordinate points will move the same direction and distance. The *_setvieworg* function replaces the *_setlogorg* function used in Microsoft C versions 5.0 and 5.1.

COMMON USES The *_setvieworg* function is used to generate a new starting point for a graphic. In the example program GRPHCS.C in the tutorial, the *_setvieworg* function was called during the construction of window 3.

RETURNS The *_setvieworg* function returns the physical coordinates of the previous view origin in an *xycoord* structure. Structures of that type are defined in *graph.h*.

COMMENTS As covered in the tutorial, the logical coordinate system is not used in

Microsoft C after version 5.1. The *_setlogorg* function is #defined to *_setwieworg* starting with Microsoft C 6.0.

Microsoft C 6.0 employs three coordinate systems for the low-level graphics functions. They are the physical coordinate system, the viewport (or view) coordinate system, and the window coordinate system. The window coordinate system is also referred to as being "real-valued." The graphics functions without a *_w* or *_wxy* suffix use the view coordinate system, and take short *ints* for coordinate arguments. Graphics functions with a *_w* suffix use window coordinates and take *doubles* for their coordinate arguments. The graphics functions that end with a *_wxy* suffix take *_wxycoord* structures as arguments.

EXAMPLE See the program beginning on page 825 for an example of the *_setvieworg* function.

COMPATIBILITY

_setviewport

MSC 3	MSC 4	MSC 5	MSC 6	QC1	QC2	QC2.5	TC1	TC1.5	TC2	TC++	ANSI	UNIX V	XNX	OS2	DOS
		▲	▲	▲	▲	▲		1	1	1					▲

PURPOSE Use *_setviewport* to define a rectangular region of the screen as the clipping region for graphics (i.e., anything outside this region will be cut off). You can get the same effect by calling *_setcliprgn*, but *_setviewport* also sets the origin of the logical coordinate system (see the tutorial section) at the upper-left corner of the viewport.

SYNTAX

```
void _far _setviewport(short x1, short y1, short x2, short y2);
```

`short x1, y1;` *Upper left corner of clipping region in physical coordinates*

`short x2, y2;` *Lower right corner of clipping region in physical coordinates*

EXAMPLE CALL

```
_setviewport(150, 50, 350, 150);
```

INCLUDES `#include <graph.h>` *For function declaration*

DESCRIPTION The *_setviewport* function defines an area of the screen (the "viewport") as the current clipping region for all graphics operations. The area is specified in terms of the physical coordinates of the upper left-hand corner (*x1, y1*) and that of the lower-right corner (*x2, y2*). After setting the clipping region, *_setviewport* also moves the origin of the logical coordinates to the upper-left corner of the viewport.

1. The Turbo C and Turbo C++ version of this function is *setviewport.*

COMMON USES The *_setviewport* function maintains multiple "virtual" graphics screens, each with its own coordinate system.

COMMENTS The effect of *_setviewport* is identical to that of calling *_setcliprgn* to define the clipping region, followed by a call to *_setlogorg* to move the logical origin to the upper-left corner of the clipping region.

SEE ALSO

`_setlogorg`	*To define a new logical origin*
`_setcliprgn`	*To define a limited area of the screen as the region beyond which all graphics output will be clipped*
`_settextwindow`	*Analogous operation for text output*

EXAMPLE If you have an EGA environment, put the EGA into a graphics mode, call *_setviewport* to define a viewport, and draw a filled ellipse in it. Then define a second viewport and repeat the same call to *_ellipse*. Each ellipse appears in its own viewport and each is clipped according to the size of the viewport. This illustrates the idea of using viewports to maintain multiple virtual graphics screens.

```
#include <stdio.h>
#include <graph.h>
#define RED  4      /* Red is 4 in default palette */
main()
{
    if (_setvideomode(_ERESCOLOR) == 0)
    {
        printf("EGA hi-res mode not supported\n");
        exit(0);
    }
    _settextposition(1,1);
    _outtext(
    "Demonstration of _setviewport with 2 viewports");
/* Set current color to red   */
    _setcolor(RED);
/* Dashed lines for boundaries */
    _setlinestyle(0xf0f);
/* Set a 200 x 200 viewport */
    _setviewport(0,100, 200, 300);
/* Show boundary of viewport */
    _rectangle(_GBORDER,0,0,200,200);
/* Now draw an ellipse, remember the bounding rectangle
 * is specified in logical coordinates and the origin
 * is at upper left corner of viewport.
```

```
 */
    _ellipse(_GFILLINTERIOR, 50, 50, 250, 250);
/* Now set another viewport, and redraw same ellipse */
/* This is a 150 x 150 viewport                      */
    _setviewport(240,100,390,250);
/* Again show boundary of the viewport */
    _rectangle(_GBORDER, 0,0,150,150);
    _setfillmask(NULL);
/* Draw the same ellipse again. (NOTE: When tested,
 * this ellipse didn't get filled! Is it a bug?)
 */
    _ellipse(_GFILLINTERIOR, 50, 50, 250, 250);

/* Return to default mode when user strikes any key */
    _settextposition(4,1);
    _outtext(
      "Press any key to return to original settings:");
    getch();  /* A do-nothing read */
    _setvideomode(_DEFAULTMODE);
}
```

COMPATIBILITY

_setvisualpage

MSC 3	MSC 4	MSC 5	MSC 6	QC1	QC2	QC2.5	TC1	TC1.5	TC2	TC++	ANSI	UNIX V	XNX	OS2	DOS
		▲	▲	▲	▲	▲		1	1	1				▲	▲

PURPOSE Use the *_setvisualpage* function in EGA or VGA graphics modes and in the text modes to select the current page or the portion of display memory that is mapped to the screen and displayed. This function only works when the adapter has enough video memory to support multiple pages.

SYNTAX

```
short _far _setvisualpage(short page_number);
```

`short page_number;` *The page number being displayed*

EXAMPLE CALL

```
_setvisualpage(1);
```

INCLUDES `#include <graph.h>` *For function declaration*

DESCRIPTION The *_setvisualpage* function selects the page specified in the argument *page_number* as the current page being displayed on the screen, which is the portion of video memory that is used for the memory-mapped display operation. See the description of the function *_setactivepage* for more details on pages and on setting the active page for current text and graphics output.

The page where text and graphics output is stored is selected by the *_setactivepage* function and this need not be the same as the page currently being displayed. By default, page 0 is used as both visual and active page.

The number of video pages available in the current mode can be determined by calling *_getvideoconfig*.

1. The Turbo C and Turbo C++ version of this function is *setvisualpage*.

COMMON USES The *_setvisualpage* function is used together with its counterpart *_setactivepage* to prepare complex graphics on one page while the user is viewing what was drawn earlier on another page. This provides for fast updating of the display and can be used for smoother animation.

RETURNS The *_setvisualpage* function returns the page number of the previous visual page. If it is not possible to have multiple pages or if the page number is beyond the valid range, *_setvisualpage* returns a negative value.

SEE ALSO `_setactivepage` *To select the page for current text and graphics output*

EXAMPLE If you have hardware with enough memory to display multiple text pages, display a message to the user to wait while you prepare the other pages. Let the user select a page to look at, and make that page visible by calling *_setvisualpage*.

```
#include <stdio.h>
#include <graph.h>
#define YELLOW       14
#define BLINKING_RED 20
main()
{
    struct videoconfig config;
    char buffer[80];
    short page = 0;
/* Assuming EGA with 256 KB graphics memory, we can
 * have 8 text pages
 */
   _clearscreen(_GCLEARSCREEN);  /* Clear the screen */
   _getvideoconfig(&config);
/* Default visual page is page 0. Display a message on
 * this page
 */
```

```
        _settextposition(1,1);
        sprintf(buffer,
        "This is page 0. There are %d pages possible.\n",
                 config.numvideopages);
        _outtext(buffer);
        _settextcolor(BLINKING_RED);
        _outtext("...Wait while the other pages are being \
prepared...");
        for(page = 1; page < config.numvideopages; page++)
        {
            _setactivepage(page);
            _settextcolor(page);
            _settextposition(1,1);
            sprintf(buffer,
        "Page: %d. Drawn in color number %d\n", page, page);
            _outtext(buffer);
            _settextcolor(YELLOW);
            sprintf(buffer,
            "Hit 'q' to exit or other key to go to page %d",
                            (page+1) % config.numvideopages);
            _outtext(buffer);
        }
        _settextcolor(YELLOW);
        _settextposition(2,1);
        _setactivepage(0);
/* Let user cycle through the pages and see the effect*/
        _settextposition(3,1);
        _outtext(
        "Hit 'q' to exit, any other key to go to page 1:");
        while(1)
        {
            if(getch() == 'q')
            {
/* Restore mode */
                _setvideomode(_DEFAULTMODE);
                exit(0);
            }
            page++;
/* Select the other page as the visual page */
            _setvisualpage(page % config.numvideopages);
        }
}
```

_setwindow

COMPATIBILITY

MSC 3	MSC 4	MSC 5	MSC 6	QC1	QC2	QC2.5	TC1	TC1.5	TC2	TC++	ANSI	UNIX V	XNX	OS2	DOS
			▲		▲	▲									▲

PURPOSE Use the *_setwindow* function to define a window coordinate system. Window coordinates can be used for fine control of graphics placement.

SYNTAX

```
short _far _setwindow (short flg_invert, double wx1, double wy1,
                       double wx2, double wy2);
```

`flg_invert` *Invert flag*

`wx1, wy1` *Upper-left corner of window*

`wx2, wy2` *Lower-right corner of window*

EXAMPLE CALL `_setwindow (0, 20, 20, 200, 200);`

INCLUDES `#include <graph.h>` *For function declaration*

DESCRIPTION The *_setwindow* routine defines a window the boundaries of which are identified by the specified coordinates. The upper-left corner is the (*wx1,wy1*) argument, and the lower-right is the (*wx2,wy2*) argument. The invert flag, specified above by *flg_invert*, causes the *y* axis to grow from the screen bottom to the top when TRUE. That method is known as Cartesian coordinates. Another pattern, screen coordinates, has the *y* axis increasing from screen top to bottom, and that is active when the invert flag yields FALSE.

RETURNS The function returns a nonzero value, if successful. The *_setwindow* function will fail if the *wx1* argument equals the *wx2* argument, or if the *wy1* argument equals the *wy2* argument. It will also fail if it is not run in a graphics mode. Failures return a 0.

COMMENTS A window transformation done with the *_setwindow* routine applies only to the viewport, not to the entire screen. The function does not affect the output of the font-display routine *_outgtext* or the output of presentation graphics text such as labels or axis marks, because those items are defined separately by their own appropriate function.

SEE ALSO `_setviewport` *To define a graphics viewport*

EXAMPLE See the program beginning on page 825 for an example of the *_setwindow* function.

Chapter 18 Drawing and Animation

Introduction

The Microsoft graphics library includes a set of routines to draw basic shapes and manipulate color bit-mapped images. The library currently has provisions for drawing arcs, ellipses, pie wedges, and rectangles; each can be filled with the current color using the current fill mask (see the tutorial in Chapter 17). The drawing routines are the building blocks for graphics applications. With the basic shapes and the ability to draw pixels of any color, you can draw quite complicated images on the screen. This chapter describes the use of the basic drawing routines.

The image manipulation routines from the library are capable of saving a rectangular area of the screen in a buffer and restoring the image from the buffer at a specified screen coordinate. The image manipulation functions can be used to achieve "animation," or the process of creating the visual effect of motion of an object on the screen.

This chapter also covers the presentation graphics routines introduced in Microsoft C 6.0. These functions allow creation of various graphs and charts.

Notes on Drawing and Animation

Fourteen drawing and image manipulation routines were provided in the Microsoft C library for version 5.1. Many additional routines (including 22 for presentation graphics) were added to version 6.0. It is important to remember that one of the coordinate systems from versions 5.0 and 5.1 (the logical coordinate system) was replaced starting in version 6.0 with two other coordinate systems: "viewport" (or "view") and "window." This changes the way some of the routines work in Microsoft C 6.0. Table 18-1 explains the purpose of each routine and Table 18-2 categorizes them by task. Before using these drawing routines you set the graphics adapter to a graphics mode using *_setvideomode* (see Chapter 17 for modes).

PARAMETERS AND ATTRIBUTES THAT AFFECT DRAWING

All the drawing routines expect logical coordinates in versions 5.0 and 5.1, and viewpoint coordinates in later versions. Both kinds of coordinates were explained in the tutorial in Chapter 17. Physical coordinates, also described in Chapter 17, are only used in five functions: *_setcliprgn, _setvieworg, _setviewport, _getviewcoord,* and *_getphyscoord.* You set the origin of the logical coordinate system (in 5.0 and 5.1) anywhere on the screen by using *_setlogorg.* The *_setviewport* or *_setvieworg* functions perform the analagous task in version 6.0 and later.

The current position, current color, line style, and fill mask are some of the parameters of the Microsoft C graphics model that affect the drawing routines. The graphics model and parameters were described in the tutorial in Chapter 17.

Table 18-1. *Drawing and Animation Routines*

Routine	Purpose
_arc	Draws a segment of an ellipse (arc) using the current color.
_arc_w	Draws elliptical arc using window coordinate system.
_arc_wxy	Draws an elliptical arc using the window coordinate system. A *_wxycoord* structure version of *_arc*. Introduced in Microsoft C 6.0. See the Chapter 17 tutorial for more information about coordinate systems.
_clearscreen	Clears the screen and fills it with the current background color.
_ellipse	Draws an ellipse (optionally filled).
_ellipse_w	Draws an ellipse using window coordinates. Introduced in version 6.0. See the Chapter 17 tutorial for more information about the window coordinate systems. A double float version of *_ellipse*.
_ellipse_wxy	Draws an ellipse using window coordinates. Introduced in version 6.0. A *_wxycoord* structure version of *_ellipse*.
_floodfill	Fills an area of screen with the current color.
_floodfill_w	Fills an area of the window using the current color and fill mask. A double float version of *_floodfill*. Introduced in Microsoft C 6.0. See the Chapter 17 tutorial for more information about coordinate systems.
_getcurrentposition	Gets the logical coordinates of the current graphics position. Logical coordinates were replaced in Microsoft C 6.0 with the viewport/window coordinate systems.
_getcurrentposition_w	Gets the current graphics output position in window coordinates. Introduced in Microsoft C 6.0. A double float version of the *_getcurrentposition* function. See the Chapter 17 tutorial for more information about coordinate systems.

Table 18-1. ***(cont.)***

Routine	Purpose
_getarcinfo	Finds the endpoints in viewport coordinates of the arc most recently drawn by *_arc* or *_pie*. Introduced in Microsoft C 6.0.
_getimage	Saves a screen in off-screen memory.
_getimage_w	Stores the screen image defined by a specified bounding rectangle into the buffer image. Defines the bounding rectangle with the window coordinates (*wx1, wy1*) and (*wx2, wy2*). Introduced in Microsoft C 6.0 as a double float version of *_getimage*.
_getimage_wxy	Stores the screen image defined by a specified bounding rectangle into the buffer image. Defines the bounding rectangle with the window coordinate pairs *pwxy1* and *pwxy2*. Introduced in Microsoft C 6.0 as a *_wxycoord* structure version of *_getimage*.
_getpixel	Returns the value of a specific pixel.
_getpixel_w	Determines the pixel value at the location specified in the window coordinates. Introduced in Microsoft C 6.0, it is a double float version of *_getpixel*.
_getwritemode	Returns the current logical write mode used by *_lineto, _rectangle,* and *_polygon*. Introduced in Microsoft C 6.0.
_grstatus	Determines whether errors or warnings were generated by the most recently called graphics function. Should be used immediately following a call to test for errors. Introduced in Microsoft C 6.0.
_imagesize	Returns size of memory (in bytes) needed to save a particular rectangular region of screen.
_imagesize_w	Calculates the number of bytes needed to store the image defined by the bounding rectangle specified by the window coordinates (*wx1, wy1*) and (*wxy, wy2*). Introduced in Microsoft C 6.0. A *_wxycoord* structure version of *_imagesize*.
_imagesize_wxy	Calculates the number of bytes meeded to store the image defined by the bounding rectangle specified by the window coordinate pairs *pwxy1* and *pwxy2*. Introduced in Microsoft C 6.0. A *_wxycoord* structure version of *_imagesize*.
_lineto	Draws a line in current color and using current line style from current graphics position to a specified point.
_lineto_w	Draws a line from the current position up to and including the window coordinate (*wx, wy*). Introduced in Microsoft C 6.0. A double float version of *_lineto*. See the Chapter 17 tutorial for more information about coordinate systems.
_moveto	Sets current graphics position to a specified point.
_moveto_w	Moves the current graphics output position to the specified window coordinates. Introduced in Microsoft C 6.0. A double float version of *_moveto*. See the Chapter 17 tutorial for more information about coordinate systems.
_pie	Draws a wedge from an ellipse; optionally filled with current color using the current fill mask.

Table 18-1. *(cont.)*

Routine	Purpose
_pie_w	Draws a pie-shaped wedge through process of drawing an elliptical arc, the center and two endpoints of which are joined by lines. Introduced in Microsoft C 6.0. A double float version of *_pie*. See the Chapter 17 tutorial for more information about coordinate systems.
_pie_wxy	Draws a pie-shaped wedge by drawing an elliptical arc whose center and two endpoints are joined by lines. Points are defined using the window coordinate system. Introduced in Microsoft C 6.0. A *_wxycoord* structure version of *_pie*.
_pg_analyzechart	Analyzes a single series of data and fills the chart environment with default values for a single series bar, column, or line chart, depending on the type specified in the function call. The Boolean flags in the chart environment (such as legend) should be set to TRUE so that defaults are calculated.
_pg_analyzechartms	Analyzes a multiple series of data and fills the chart environment with default values for a multiseries bar, column, or line chart, depending on which type is specified in the function call. The "ms" suffix means "multiple series."
_pg_analyzepie	Analyzes a single series of data and fills the chart environment for a pie chart using the data contained in the array values. It does not actually display the data. The function fills the environment for a pie chart using information read from the *values* array.
_pg_analyzescatter	Analyzes a single series of data and fills the chart environment for a single series scatter diagram.
_pg_analyzescatterms	Analyzes a multiple series of data and fills the chart environment for a multiseries scatter diagram. (The "ms" suffix means "multiseries.")
_pg_chart	Displays a single-series bar, column, or line chart, depending on the type specified in the chart environment variable. The *values* array is two-dimensional and contains every value to be plotted on the chart.
_pg_chartms	Displays a multiseries bar, column, or line chart, depending on the type specified in the chart environment. The multiseries nature of the function is identified by the "ms" suffix. Values for the desired chart are maintained in the two dimensional array *values*.
_pg_chartpie	Displays a pie chart for the data contained in the array values. Pie charts are formed from a single series of data, so there is no multiseries version of them. Other chart types do have multiseries versions.
_pg_chartscatter	Displays a scatter diagram for a single series of data. The *x* and *y* arguments are arrays, two-dimensional in nature, which contain data for the axes. Each column in the array contains plot data for an individual series.
_pg_chartscatterms	Displays a scatter diagram for more than one series of data. The two-dimensional arrays that serve as *x* and *y* arguments contain

Table 18-1. ***(cont.)***

Routine	Purpose
	the values for the plot. One column of the array is used for each series of data; "five series" means an array of five columns.
_pg_defaultchart	Initializes all necessary variables in the chart environment for the type of chart specified by the *charttype* variable. The title fields are initialized and they should be set after a call to *_pg_defaultchart*.
_pg_initchart	Initializes the presentation graphics package. Initializes the color and style pools, resets the chartline styleset, builds default palette modes, and reads the presentation graphics character font definition from the disk. This function is required in all programs that use presentation graphics.
_pg_getpalette	Retrieves palette colors, line styles, fill patterns, and plot characters for all palettes. The pointer *palette* points to an array of palette structures that will contain the desired palette values. The presentation graphics palette is different from the palette used by the low-level graphics routines.
_pg_getchardef	Retrieves the current 8x8 pixel map for the character with the value that matches the ASCII number *charnum*. The *chardef* array is used to store the bitmap.
_pg_getstyleset	Retrieves the contents of the current styleset.
_pg_hlabelchart	Writes text horizontally on the screen. The arguments are pixel coordinates for the beginning location of text relative to the upper-left corner of the chart window.
_pg_resetpalette	Sets the palette colors, line styles, fill patterns, and plot characters for the palette to the default for the current screen mode. The presentation graphics palette is separate from the palette used by the low-level graphics functions.
_pg_resetstyleset	Reinitializes the styleset to the default values for the current screen mode.
_pg_setpalette	Sets palette colors, line styles, fill patterns, and plot characters for all palettes. The pointer palette points to an array of palette structures that contains the desired palette values, but this is not the same palette used in the low-level graphics routines.
_pg_setchardef	Sets the 8x8 pixel bit map for the character with the ASCII number *charnum*. The bit map is stored in the array named *chardef*.
_pg_setstyleset	Sets the current styleset.
_pg_vlabelchart	Writes text vertically on the screen. The arguments *x* and *y* are pixel coordinates for the starting location of text relative to the upper-left corner of the chart window.
_polygon	Draws or scan-fills a polygon, using the view coordinate system. Introduced in Microsoft C 6.0.
_polygon_w	Draws or scan-fills a polygon, using the window coordinate system. Introduced in Microsoft C 6.0. A double float version of *_polygon*. See the Chapter 17 tutorial for more information about coordinate systems.

Table 18-1. *(cont.)*

Routine	Purpose
_polygon_wxy	Draws or scan-fills a polygon, using the window coordinate system. Introduced in Microsoft C 6.0. A *_wxycoord* structure version of *_polygon*.
_putimage	Restores an image from off-screen memory and displays it on the screen in a specified manner.
_putimage_w	Transfers to the screen the image stored in the buffer image, placing the upper-left corner of the image at the window coordinate (*wx, wy*). Introduced in Microsoft C 6.0 as a double float version of *_putimage*. There is no *_wxycoord* structure version of this function.
_rectangle	Draws an optionally filled rectangle.
_rectangle_w	Draws a rectangle with the current color, line style, and write mode, using the window coordinate system. Introduced in Microsoft C 6.0 as a double float version of *_rectangle*. See the Chapter 17 tutorial for more information about coordinate systems.
_rectangle_wxy	Draws a rectangle with the current color, line style, and write mode, using the window coordinate system. Introduced in Microsoft C 6.0. A *_wxycoord* structure version of *_rectangle*.
_setpixel	Sets a pixel to a specific value.
_setpixel_w	Sets a pixel at the specified window coordinate location to the current color. Introduced in Microsoft C 6.0. A double float version of *_setpixel*. See the Chapter 17 tutorial for more information about coordinate systems.
_setwritemode	Helps to set the current logical write mode used when you draw lines with the *_lineto*, *_rectangle*, and *_polygon* functions. Introduced in Microsoft C 6.0.

Table 18-2. ***Drawing and Animation Routines by Task***

Task	Routines
Clear a selected area of the screen.	_clearscreen
Draw basic shapes.	_arc, _arc_w, _arc_wxy, _ellipse, _ellipse_w, _ellipse_wxy, _pie, _pie_w, _pie_wxy, _polygon, _polygon_w, _polygon_wxy, _rectangle, _rectangle_w, _rectangle_wxy
Draw a single point.	_getcurrentposition, _getcurrentposition_w, _getpixel, _getpixel_w, _setpixel, _setpixel_w
Draw a straight line.	_lineto, _lineto_w, _moveto, _moveto_w
Fill a region with color.	_floodfill, _floodfill_w
Analysis and error status.	_getarcinfo, _grstatus, _pg_analyzechart, _pg_analyzechartms, _pg_analyzepie, _pg_analyzescatter, _pg_analyzescatterms

Table 18-2. *(cont.)*

Task	Routines
Get/set the writemode.	_getwritemode, _setwritemode
Display presentation graphics.	_pg_chart, _pg_chartms, _pg_chartpie, _pg_chartscatter, _pg_chartscatterms, _pg_defaultchart, _pg_initchart
Manipulate presentation graphics.	_pg_getchardef, _pg_getpalette, _pg_getstyleset, _pg_hlabelchart, _pg_resetpalette, _pg_resetstyleset, _pg_setchardef, _pg_setpalette, _pg_setstyleset, _pg_vlabelchart
Save and restore images.	_getimage, _getimage_w, _getimage_wxy, _imagesize, _imagesize_w, _imagesize_wxy, _putimage, _putimage_w

DRAWING A SINGLE POINT

A basic operation in graphics is to set an arbitrary point on the screen to a selected color, or in other words, to "draw" it on the screen. This involves setting the current color and then setting the selected point to the current color. You can do this with the Microsoft C compiler (versions 5.0 and later) as follows:

```
_setcolor(1);           /* Normally blue */
_setpixel(100,50);      /* Set pixel to current color */
```

which will set the point at coordinate (100,50) to blue.

You can also "clear" a point, which means that you set that point to the background color which has the effect of making it invisible. Color index 0 is always the background color. Thus the coordinate (100,50) can be set to background by

```
_setcolor(0);           /* Normally black */
_setpixel(100,50);      /* Set pixel to current color */
```

Version 6.0 added the *_setpixel_w* function to set the color of a pixel within a window.

DRAWING LINES

Drawing lines is another capability of the graphics library. The *_lineto* function (*_lineto_w* when writing within the windows coordinate system) draws a line from the current position to the specified point and it updates the current position upon completion. It uses the current color to set the color of the line and the current line style to determine the appearance of the line. For example,

```
/* Draw a dashed line from (10,10) to (100,100) */
   _setcolor (4);           /* normally a red */
```

```
_setlinestyle (0xff00); /* dashed line */
moveto (10,10);         /* move to (10,10) */
_lineto (100,100);      /* draw the line */
```

draws a red dashed line from viewpoint coordinate (10,10) to the point (100,100). At the end of the drawing the current point will be (100,100) and another call such as *_lineto(200,100)* will draw a line joining (100,100) to (200,100).

LINE STYLE In the line drawing example above, the *_setlinestyle* function is used to set up a dashed line. The argument to *_setlinestyle* is a 16-bit mask that specifies the pattern to be repeated when drawing a line. Think of this mask as representing a line segment 16 pixels long. If a bit in the mask is a 1, the corresponding pixel in that line is painted with the current color (see *_setcolor*). If a bit is 0, the corresponding pixel is untouched. Note that a value of FFh for *linemask* means a solid line. This is the default value of the line style in the graphics package.

BASIC SHAPES The rectangle, ellipse, arc, and wedge (also called the "pie") are the four basic shapes supported in the graphics library. The ellipse forms the basis of the arc and the pie because these two shapes are part of an ellipse (see Figure 18-1).

Rectangle

A rectangle is specified by *(x,y)* coordinates of its upper-left and lower-right corners. It is optional whether it will be drawn filled with the current color or with a border in the current color and current line style. For example, you can draw a 20x20 rectangle with the upper-left corner located at (10,30) and filled with the current color by

```
_rectangle (_GFILLINTERIOR, 10, 30, 30, 50);
```

The first argument _GFILLINTERIOR is the fill flag, which, in this case, specifies that the inside of the rectangle be filled. A fill flag of _GBORDER means only a border will be drawn. The *_rectangle* function also comes in *_rectangle_w* form for use in the window coordinate mode and in *rectangle_wxy* form for use with *_wxycoord* structures within window coordinates.

Ellipse, Arc, and Pie

The specification of the arc, the ellipse, and the pie as shown in Figure 18-1 involves the concept of the "bounding rectangle," which is the smallest rectangle that completely encloses the figure you are drawing. You must specify the bounding rectangle of an ellipse because the arc and the pie are parts of an ellipse. Both bounding rectangle and basic rectangle

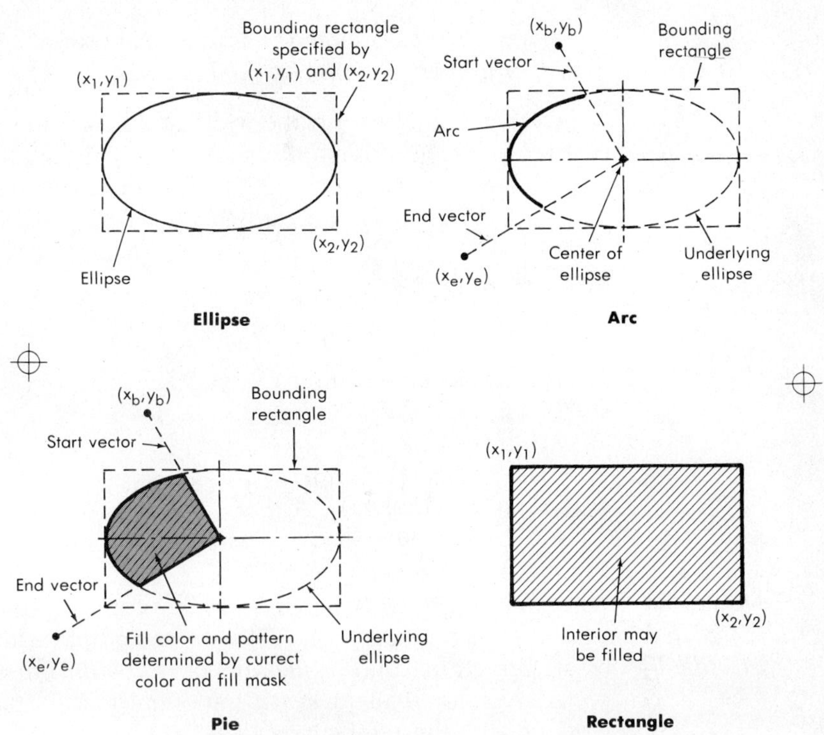

Figure 18-1. ***Specifications for ellipse, arc, pie, and rectangle***

shapes are specified by coordinates of their upper-left and lower-right corners. The location is called a logical coordinate in versions 5.0 and 5.1, but version 6.0 and later refers to them as viewports.

The elliptic segment of an arc or a pie is built from a line drawn from the center of the ellipse to a point specified as the beginning point. The various *_pie* and *_arc* functions begin drawing the curved line edge at the point where that line intersects the ellipse. The functions trace over the underlying ellipse, using current color, in a counter-clockwise direction until reaching the point where a line is drawn from the center to a specified endpoint cuts the ellipse (see Figure 18-1). Curved lines are always drawn in solid-line style. Thus, the ellipse and the pie can only have a solid boundary. Their interiors can be filled as though they were rectangles.

ASPECT RATIO

Being aware of the "aspect ratio" of a monitor is important if your application has to produce a truthful rendition of all geometric figures. The aspect ratio is the number of pixels along a vertical line on the screen to that along a horizontal line of the same length. Multiply the *y*-axis or vertical dimensions of the objects by the *aspect ratio* for a properly proportioned drawing. You compute the aspect ratio using the formula:

aspect ratio = (screen_width/screen_height)
** (number_of_ypixels/number_of_xpixels)*

Although you must supply the width and height of the screen, you can rely on the *_getvideoconfig* function to supply the number of *x* and *y* pixels. Here is how you can compute the aspect ratio of a screen that is 10 inches wide and 6.5 inches high:

```
#include <graph.h>
     :
     :
struct videoconfig vdocnfg;
double aspect_ratio
     :
_getvideoconfig (&vdocnfg);
aspect_ratio = (double)
               (10 * vdocnfg.numxpixels) / (6.5 * vdocnfg.numxpixels);
```

FILLING AN AREA WITH A COLOR

You can use *_floodfill* (or, in a window coordinate, *_floodfill_w*) to fill an area within a boundary. The fill starts at a point inside the area and spreads in all directions until *_floodfill* or *_floodfill_w* encounters a specific boundary color. This makes it important to have a solid boundary when working with these functions.

The floodfill functions apply a mask that is defined by the *_setfillmask* function (covered in Chapter 17). The fill mask is also used when filling shapes such as the rectangle, the ellipse, and the pie. Here is a code fragment that shows how to fill an area:

```
unsigned char far mask[ ] =
{0x0f, 0x0f, 0x0f, 0x0f, 0xf0, 0xf0, 0xf0, 0xf0};
          :
     _setfillmask(mask);          /* set up fill mask    */
     _setcolor(4);                /* set border color    */
     _rectangle (_GBORDER, 10, 10, 110, 110);
     _setcolor(1);                /* set new fill color */
     _floodfill (50, 50, 4);      /* stop at color 4     */
```

We set up a fill mask first and draw a rectangle with a border in color index 4, which is typically a red. Next, we switch the current color to index 1 (a blue) and call *_floodfill* to fill the rectangle. The function *_floodfill_w*, introduced in version 6.0, handles this task within the windows coordinate system.

FILL MASK

The *setfillmask* functions are used to define a pattern of bits as the current mask to be used by *_floodfill*, *_rectangle*, *_ellipse*, and *_pie* to fill an area with the current color. This pattern is called a fill mask. The fill pattern is specified by an 8-byte bit pattern (as shown in Figure 17-7) and is viewed as an 8x8 array of bits. The area being filled is subdivided into 8x8 blocks of pixels. The fill mask is applied to each 8x8 block with mask 1 setting the corresponding pixel to the current graphics color and mask 0 leaving the corresponding pixel unchanged. This behavior matches that of the line-style functions. Areas larger than 8x8 are filled by using the mask on successive 8x8 blocks until the entire area is covered. A solid fill is specified when all 8 characters contain the graphics package default value of FFh. Figure 18-1 illustrates this concept.

IMAGE SAVE AND RESTORE

The graphics library also includes provisions for saving a graphics image (*_getimage*) in a memory buffer, restoring the image (*_putimage*), and determining the size of memory needed to store an image (*_imagesize*).

Saving an image is straightforward. You call *_getimage* (or the windows version of the function, *_getimage_w* and *_getimage_wxy*) with the coordinates of the upper-left and lower-right corners of a rectangle on the screen and the address of the buffer to which you wish to save the image of that area of the screen. You can use *malloc* to allocate the buffer before saving the image. When doing so, you need to determine the size of the image; this can be found by calling *_imagesize* with the same rectangle as input. The function comes in windows versions *_imagesize_w* and *_imagesize_wxy*. For example, you can save a 20x20 rectangular image by:

```
char _far *buffer
    :
    buffer = (char _far *) malloc ((size_t) _imagesize (0, 0, 20, 20);
    _getimage (0, 0, 20, 20, buffer);
```

The image can be restored elsewhere on the screen by calling *_putimage*. The function comes in one windows version, *_putimage_w*. You only need to specify the point on the screen where the upper-left corner of the saved image will be placed. For instance, we can re-create the saved image at (100,100) by

```
_putimage (100, 100, buffer, _GPSET);
```

As you can see, restoring the image involves specifying how the image is to be reconstructed on the screen. In the example above, the constant _GPSET specifies that the pixel values (color indexes) in the image should be copied into the pixels in the new area. Other options include using logical OR, AND, or exclusive OR with existing pixel values. The reference pages for *_putimage* further explain the meaning of this argument.

ANIMATION USING _GETIMAGE AND _PUTIMAGE

The ability to save and restore images can be exploited to make an object appear to move on the display screen. First, draw the object and save it to a buffer. Restore it at the old location with the last argument of *_putimage* set to _GXOR. The exclusive OR clears the old image. Another call to *_putimage* for a new location should be followed by a restore with _GXOR. Putting this logic in a loop makes the image appear to move around on the screen. Here is how the loop might look:

```
/* Draw image */
_putimage (x, y, image, _GXOR);
     /* perform some animation */
     while (!kbhit())
     {
     /* First erase at last position */
          _putimage (x, y, image, _GXOR);
          x += 10;
          y += 5;
          if (x = numxpixels) x = 0;
          if (y = numxpixels) y = 0;
/* Redraw at new position */
     _putimage (x, y, image, _GXOR);
}
```

In this example, the image is drawn and saved in the buffer named *image.* Then the *while* animates the figure until the user presses a key. The example in the reference pages on *_putimage* shows a complete animation program.

ANIMATION BY FLIPPING VIDEO PAGE

If your graphics adapter has enough memory to support at least two pages in graphics mode, you can use the *_setactivepage* and the *_setvisualpage* functions (see Chapter 17 for a discussion of video pages) to perform some animation. The *_setactivepage* sets the area of video memory to which all graphics go. The page being displayed is set by *_setvisualpage.* The idea is to draw the next stage of an image on the active page while the user is watching the current visual page and then swap the two pages. Now you can clear out the old image and prepare the next frame of animation and repeat the cycle to achieve the effect of movement.

The EGA with 256 K of video memory can support two pages of graphics and this can be exploited for animation. The example in the reference pages on *_setactivepage* shows the swapping of graphics pages on an EGA.

ERROR STATUS

The *_grstatus* function was introduced in Microsoft C 6.0 and helps you identify why certain graphics functions do not behave as you expect. The return values from *_grstatus* are defined in *graph.h* as follows:

```
/* Successful Operation */

#define _GROK                        0

/* Error Values */

#define _GRERROR                    (-1)
#define _GRMODENOTSUPPORTED         (-2)
#define _GRNOTINPROPERMODE          (-3)
#define _GRINVALIDPARAMETER         (-4)
#define _GRFONTFILENOTFOUND         (-5)
#define _GRINVALIDFONTFILE          (-6)
#define _GRCORRUPTEDFONTFILE        (-7)
#define _GRINSUFFICIENTMEMORY       (-8)
#define _GRINVALIDIMAGEBUFFER       (-9)

/* Warning Values  */

#define _GRNOOUTPUT                  1
#define _GRCLIPPED                   2
#define _GRPARAMETERALTERED          3
```

The following functions cannot return errors: *_displaycursor*, *_getactivepage*, *_getgtextvector*, *_gettextcolor*, *_gettextposition*, *_gettextwindow*, *_getvideoconfig*, *_getvisualpage*, *_outmem*, *_outtext*, *_unregisterfonts*, and *_wrapon*.

PRESENTATION GRAPHICS

Version 6.0 of the Microsoft C compiler introduced 22 presentation graphics functions. They are included in the listing in Table 18-1 (these functions actually appeared first in version 2.0 of the Quick C compiler). The presentation graphics functions allow you to display data as a variety of graphs such as bar and column charts, line graphs, scatter diagrams, and pie charts.

Table 18-3 gives the possible errors and warnings that can be generated by each of the groups of graphics functions. Table 18-4 defines presentation graphics terms. Table 18-5 breaks down presentation graphics program structure.

Table 18-3. ***Graphics Functions That Can Generate Errors***

Function	Possible Errors Generated	Possible Warnings Generated
_arc functions	_GRNOTINPROPERMODE, _GRINVALIDPARAMETER	_GRNNOOUTPUT, _GRCLIPPED
_clearscreen	_GRNOTINPROPERMODE, _GRINVALIDPARAMETER	n/a
_ellipse functions	_GRNOTINPROPERMODE, _GRINVALIDPARAMETER, _GRINSUFFICIENTMEMORY	_GRNOOUTPUT, _GRCLIPPED

Table 18-3. ***(cont.)***

Function	Possible Errors Generated	Possible Warnings Generated
_getarcinfo	_GRNOTINPROPERMODE	n/a
_getcurrentposition functions	_GRNOTINPROPERMODE	n/a
_getfontinfo	_GRERROR	n/a
_getgtextextent	_GRERROR	n/a
_getgtextvector	_GRPARAMETERALTERED	n/a
_getimage	_GRNOTINPROPERMODE	_GRPARAMETERALTERED
_getphyscoord	_GRNOTINPROPERMODE	n/a
_getpixel	_GRNOTINPROPERMODE	n/a
_gettextcursor	_GRNOTINPROPERMODE	n/a
_getviewcoord functions	_GRNOTINPROPERMODE	n/a
_getwindowcoord	_GRNOTINPROPERMODE	n/a
_getwritemode	_GRNOTINPROPERMODE	n/a
_imagesize functions	_GRNOTINPROPERMODE	n/a
_lineto functions	_GRNOTINPROPERMODE	_GRNOOUTPUT, _GRCLIPPED
_moveto functions	_GRNOTINPROPERMODE	n/a
_outgtext	_GRNOTINPROPERMODE	_GRCLIPPED, _GRNOOUTPUT
_pie functions	_GRNOTINPROPERMODE, _GRINVALIDPARAMETER, _GRINSUFFICIENTMEMORY	_GRNOOUTPUT, _GRCLIPPED
_polygon functions	_GRNOTINPROPERMODE, _GRINVALIDPARAMETER, _GRINSUFFICIENTMEMORY	_GRNOOUTPUT, _GRCLIPPED
_putimage functions	_GRERROR, _GRNOTINPROPERMODE, _GRINVALIDPARAMETER, _GRINVALIDIMAGEBUFFER	_GRPARAMATERALTERED, _GRNOOUTPUT
_rectangle functions	_GRNOTINPROPERMODE, _GRINVALIDPARAMETER, _GRINSUFFICIENTMEMORY	_GRNOOUTPUT, _GRCLIPPED
_registerfonts	_GRCORRUPTEDFONTFILE, _GRFONTFILENOTFOUND, _GRINSUFFICIENTMEMORY, _GRINVALIDFONTFILE	n/a
_scrolltextwindow	n/a	_GRNOOUTPUT
_selectpallette	_GRNOTINPROPERMODE, _GRINVALIDPARAMETER	n/a
_setactivepage	_GRINVALIDPARAMETER	n/a
_setbkcolor	_GRINVALIDPARAMETER	_GRPARAMETERALTERED
_setcliprgn	_GRNOTINPROPERMODE	_GRPARAMETERALTERED
_setcolor	_GRNOTINPROPERMODE	_GRPARAMETERALTERED
_setfont	_GRERROR, _GRFONTFILENOTFOUND, _GRINSUFFICIENTMEMORY	_GRPARAMETERALTERED
_setgtextvector	n/a	_GRPARAMETERALTERED

Table 18-3. *(cont.)*

Function	Possible Errors Generated	Possible Warnings Generated
_settextcolor	n/a	_GRPARAMETERALTERED
_settextcursor	_GRNOTINPROPERMODE	n/a
_settextposition	n/a	_GRPARAMETERALTERED
_settextrows	_GRINVALIDPARAMETER	_GRPARAMETERALTERED
_settextwindow	n/a	_GRPARAMETERALTERED
_setvideomode	_GRERROR, _GRMODENOTSUPPORTED, _GRINVALIDPARAMETER	n/a
_setvideomoderows	_GRERROR, _GRMODENOTSUPPORTED, _GRINVALIDPARAMETER	n/a
_setvieworg	_GRNOTINPROPERMODE	n/a
_setviewport	_GRNOTINPROPERMODE	_GRPARAMETERALTERED
_setvisualpage	_GRINVALIDPARAMETER	n/a
_setwindow	_GRNOTINPROPERMODE, _GRINVALIDPARAMETER	_GRPARAMETERALTERED
_setwritemode	_GRNOTINPROPERMODE, _GRINVALIDPARAMETER	n/a

Table 18-4. *Presentation Graphics Terms*

Term	Definition
Axes	All charts created with presentation graphics functions (with the exception of pie charts) are displayed with perpendicular reference lines known as "axes." The *y* axis is vertical and runs top to bottom on the left side of the screen. The *x* axis is horizontal and runs left to right across the bottom of the screen. Two terms to keep in mind are "value axis" and "category axis." The type of chart determines which axis is used to show categories and which axis shows values. The *x* axis is the value axis for bar charts and the category axis for line and column charts. The *y* axis is the category axis for bar charts and the value axis for line and column charts.
Bar and Column	A bar chart uses horizontal bars to represent data. A column chart uses vertical bars. The value axis of a bar chart is *x* and the category axis is *y*. The column chart uses *x* for a value axis and *y* for a category axis.
Categories	Categories are non-numeric data that provide a reference against which numeric data can be plotted. Numeric data is called "values" and is covered later in this table. Days of the week, for example, are categories against which a chart of factory production can be shown. Financial data is frequently subtotalled on spreadsheets and other report formats. Items within the subtotal area are typically totalled at the end of the reports. A category, on the other hand, covers a set of data that is meaningful only within that particular category.
Chart Styles	Microsoft C compilers versions 6.0 and later provide five types of charts: pie, bar, column, line, and scatter. There are two "styles" of each chart type, although a column chart or bar chart with only a single

Table 18-4. *(cont.)*

Term	Definition
	data series has only one style because you need at least two values to go side-by-side or stacked.

Chart Type	Style One	Style Two
Pie	Show percentages	No percentages
Bar	Side-by-side	Stacked
Column	Side-by-side	Stacked
Line	Points with lines	Points without lines
Scatter	Points with lines	Points without lines

Term	Definition
Chart Windows	The part of the screen on which a chart is drawn is called a "chart window." The chart window is frequently the entire screen, but smaller sections can be defined so that either multiple charts can appear on the same screen, or so that a smaller chart can be displayed with a lot of text. The chart window defines the entire graph including axes and labels.
Data Series	A data series is data that is related by a common theme or purpose. The daily closing price of the New York Stock Exchange over a one month period, for example, constitutes a data series. That same data over a period of a year would also constitute a data series. Additional data series over the same period of time could be created from the opening price and the price at noon. The Microsoft presentation graphics functions allow you to plot multiple-data series on a single chart. Memory limitation is one factor that restricts the number of data series that may be presented on a chart. Other factors are monitor quality and the type of video adapter on your system. Colors are helpful in keeping data visually separate, and each data series should use a different combination of color and line style in order to be visually distinct. A CGA system offers only 3 foreground colors while some of the EGA and VGA modes boast 16 colors. Obviously the 16-color mode offers advantages in showing charts with several data series. Charts that will be displayed on CGA screens thus need to be less complex than those running on the newer display adapters.
Data Windows	The "data window" defines only the plotting area of the chart. The data window appears to the right of the *y* axis and above the *x* axis. The size of the data window is determined by the size of the chart window, and it is not something over which the programmer has specific control.
Line Graphs	Line graphs are normally used to show data points connected by lines. One example is the stock-price chart which appears in many newspapers. A new point is plotted each business day, and the peaks and valleys are easily visualized. Microsoft C allows you to connect the points with lines or to leave them as separate dots.
Pie Charts	A pie chart is the only type of chart that does not plot data with *x* and *y* axes. Pie charts show the relationship of each part of data to all the data. A chart of weather over a period of a month, for example, could show three groups: one each for rain days, snow days, and sunny days.

Table 18-4. ***(cont.)***

Term	Definition
	Microsoft C allows you to choose from two types of pie charts, enclosed and exploded. The enclosed chart shows all pieces within a circle. The exploded chart has one or more pieces separated for emphasis. Optional labels can be generated for each piece.
Scatter Diagrams	A scatter diagram plots points, and it is the only chart type in Microsoft C that compares values with values. An example of a scatter diagram is the comparison of current sales against the sales of a previous year, or perhaps current rainfall against the rainfall of some other period.
Values	Values are numeric data; they are plotted against categories and other numeric data. Typical kinds of numeric data are monthly and quarterly sales, annual profits, average temperatures, and grade point averages. Microsoft C allows you to overlay multiple sets of values on a single chart. As noted in the section on data series, there are both hardware and visual clutter limits on the number of values that can be plotted on a single chart.

Table 18-5. ***Structure of a Presentation Graphics Program***

Step	Comments
#include header files	The GRAPH.H and PGCHART.H files must be #included along with other header files.
Set video to graphics	The program must set the system to graphics mode from the current graphics or text mode. This is explained in Chapter 17.
Initialize the chart environment	Chart parameters are defined in a data structure. A default set of values is established at the initialization; this, however, can be changed as explained elsewhere in this chapter.
Assemble plot data	Data used in the charts is stored in arrays read by the various presentation graphics functions.
Call functions	Display the chart. A delay mechanism (typically, awaiting a return from the keyboard) allows the user to read the chart.
Reset video	The system should be reset to the original video mode.

A compiled presentation graphics program must be linked with PGCHART.LIB and GRAPHICS.LIB.

Palettes

It is important to remember that a palette for a presentation graphics function is not the same as the adapter display (graphics card) palette. The adapter display palette contains register values used by the video controller. The function *_selectpalette* works with adapter displays and has no role in presentation graphics functions.

Each presentation graphics data series is different. A separate palette is defined for every data series in a chart. These palettes consist of entries that determine color, fill pattern, line style, and point character used to graph the series. Palettes are maintained as an array of structures defined in *pgchart.h*. The definition appears below:

```
    typedef struct {
    unsigned short color;
    unsigned short style;
    fillmap        fill;
    char           plotchar;
} paletteentry;
```

Color Pool

All chart colors in presentation graphics are organized into a "color pool." The color pool consists of the pixel values (also called color indexes) that are valid for the current graphics mode. Color codes that refer to the color pool are maintained in the palette structures. The color code for each palette determines the color used to graph any data series with which the palette is associated. Colors of axes, labels, legends, and titles are also controlled by color pool contents.

Zero is always the first element of a color pool. It is the pixel value for the background color. Element 2 is always the highest pixel value available for the particular graphics mode. Repeating sequences of available color indexes, starting with 1, make up the remaining elements.

The first member of a palette structure is:

```
unsigned short color;
```

It is a variable that defines the color code for the data series associated with the palette. The color code is an index number to the color pool and is neither a color index nor a display attribute.

We'll assume you have written a program that calls graphics mode _MRES4COLOR, which generates a 320x200 resolution. It provides four displayable colors numbered 0 through 3. As shown in Table 18-6, the four colors are set in a repeating pattern to create the color pool.

As you can see, following black, the first data series would be displayed in brown. Series 2 would be displayed in green. The third series rounds out the available list of different colors (it will be displayed in red), and all subsequent series will repeat the brown-green-red pattern. Understandably, use of a graphics mode that supports more than four colors (_VRES16COLOR, for example) will allow more series to be plotted before a repeating color is encountered.

Table 18-6. *Colors and the Color Pool*

Color Pool	Color Index	Color
0	0	Black
1	3	Brown
2	1	Green
3	2	Red
4	3	Brown
5	1	Green
6	2	Red
7	3	Brown

Style Pool

The collection of available line styles is stored in a "style pool." Style pool entries define the appearance of grids, axes, and other lines. Lines may be dotted, dashed, solid, or some combination of these characteristics.

The style code is the second member of the presentation graphics palette structure. It is defined as follows:

```
unsigned short style;
```

The style code in each palette refers to a style pool entry. The style code value applies only to lined scatter diagrams and line graphs, and it determines the appearance of a line drawn between points. The style code is particularly useful when you have more lines to chart than unique colors with which to chart them. The _MRES4COLOR mode discussed earlier provides one background and three foreground colors, possibly making a graph with 12 lines confusing to read. The style code will allow each repetition of the foreground colors to present a unique pattern, and that may help avoid confusion.

Pattern Pool

The "pattern pool" is the third member of a palette structure and determines the fill design for bar, column, and pie charts. It is defined as an array:

```
fillmap fill;
```

where fillmap is typed defined as:

```
typedef unsigned char fillmap[8];
```

The fill pattern array is an 8x8 bit map that behaves similarly to the fill procedures covered earlier in this chapter. The array is loaded with 8-bit values where 0 is off and 1 is on.

Character Pool

The character pool is the last member of a palette structure. It is an index number in a pool of ASCII characters, declared as follows:

```
char plotchar;
```

The plotchar member represents plot points on scatter diagrams and line graphs. Each of your palettes will use a different character to distinguish the various plot points between data series.

CUSTOMIZING PRESENTATION GRAPHICS

Many of the Microsoft presentation graphics routines are driven from default values, but they can be changed to suit your needs. We will discuss how such changes are made.

The "chart environment" variables are defined in the *pgchart.h* file as a structure of type *chartenv*. A chart may be thought of as having two major components: the data being charted and the chart environment. The chart environment determines how the chart looks. The structure looks like this:

```
typedef struct {
     short charttype;          /* _PG_BAR, _PG_COLUMN,
                                  _PG_LINE,_PG_SCATTER, _PG_PIE */
     short chartstyle;         /* style for selected chart type */
     windowtype chartwindow;   /* chartwindow definition */
     windowtype datawindow;    /* datawindow definition */
     titletype maintitle;      /* main chart title */
     titletype subtitle;       /* chart sub-title */
     axistype xaxis;           /* x-axis definition */
     axistype yaxis;           /* y-axis definition */
     legendtype legend;        /* legend definition */
} chartenv;
```

The individual variables are explained in Table 18-7.

The default values are loaded with a call to *_pg_defaultchart*. We will assume a program where a structure named *grafcs* (the name has no special significance) of type *chartenv* is used to store environment data for presentation graphics. Loading a title to *grafcs* is done like this:

```
strcpy (grafcs.maintitle.title, "Barbara's Fabrics Inc.");
```

Some of the environment variables set line styles or colors. The variable *gridstyle* is an example. This kind of variable is an index number that corresponds to a presentation graphics palette. They do not directly access

Table 18-7. *Variables for the* chartenv *Structure*

charttype	Integer that determines chart type to display. The legal values (in parentheses), as defined in *PGCHART.H*, are _PG_BARCHART (1), _PG_COLUMNCHART (2), _PG_LINECHART (3), _PG_SCATTERCHART (4), or_PG_PIECHART (5). This variable is the second argument to the *_pg_defaultchart* function.
chartstyle	Integer that determines chart style. Values for chartstyle (in parentheses) are _PG_PERCENT (1) and _PG_NOPERCENT (2) for pie charts;_PG_PLAINBARS (1) and _PG_STACKEDBARS (2) for bar and column charts; _PG_POINTANDLINE (1) and _PG_POINTONLY (2) for scatter diagrams and line graphs. These correspond to Style 1 and Style 2 as shown in Table 18-4. This is the third argument to the *_pg_defaultchart* function.
chartwindow	A structure of type *windowtype*, detailed in Table 18-11, which defines the appearance of the chart window.
datawindow	A structure of type *windowtype*, detailed in Table 18-11, which defines the appearance of the data window. The data window is a component of the chart window.
maintitle	A structure of type *titletype*, detailed in Table 18-10, which defines the appearance of the main title of the chart.
subtitle	A structure of type *titletype*, detailed in Table 18-10, which defines the appearance of the subtitle of the chart.
xaxis	A structure of type *axistype*, detailed in Table 18-8, which defines (except in pie charts) the appearance of the *x* axis.
yaxis	A structure of type *axistype*, detailed in Table 18-8, which defines (except in pie charts) the appearance of the *y* axis.
legend	A structure of type *legendtype*, detailed in Table 18-9, which defines the appearance of the legend window.

the color pool or the style (line) pool. It is important to remember that a variable that references palette 3, for example, will behave as palette 3 says to behave. Thus a change of a color or a line style or both in palette 3 will show up in your chart.

There are four secondary structures in a structure of type *chartenv*. As defined in *pgchart.h*, they are: *axistype*, *legendtype*, *titletype*, and *windowtype*.

Type *axistype* Structure

The structure of type *axistype* contains variables that affect the drawing of axes. Color, grid style, and tickmarks are among the items defined. The structure is defined as:

```
typedef struct {
  short     grid;        /* TRUE=lines drawn; FALSE=no */
  short     gridstyle;   /* No. from style pool for lines */
```

```
    titletype axistitle;   /* Title definition for axis */
    short     axiscolor    /* Color for axis */
    short     labeled;     /* TRUE=tic marks and titles drawn */
    short     rangetype;   /*_PG_LINEARAXIS, _PG_LOGAXIS */
    float     logbase;     /* Base used if log axis */
    short     autoscale;   /* TRUE=next 7 values calculated by
                              system */
    float     scalemin;    /* Minimum value of scale */
    float     scalemax;    /* Maximum value of scale */
    float     scalefactor; /* Scale factor  data on this axis */
    titletype scaletitle;  /* Title def'n for scaling factor */
    float     ticinterval; /* Dist. between tic marks */
    short     ticformat;   /* _PG_EXPFORMAT or _PG_DECFORMAT
    short     ticdecimals; /* No. dcmls for tic labels(max=9) */
} axistype;
```

The individual variables are discussed in Table 18-8.

Table 18-8. *Variables in the* axistype *Structure*

grid	A true/false value (Boolean) that determines whether grid lines are drawn for an associated axis. The grid lines span the data window, and they are perpendicular to the appropriate axis.
gridstyle	Integer value between 1 and the current value of _PG_PALLETLEN (_PG_PALLETLEN is the total number of active palettes for the chart). It specifies the line style for the grid line. The default value is 1, and lines can be solid, dotted, dashed, or some combination. Line color is determined by the color of the parallel axis. The *x* axis grid color matches the *y* axis, and the *y* axis grid color matches the *x* axis.
axistitle	A structure of type *titletype* which defines the title of an associated axis. The *y* axis title displays vertically to the left of the *y* axis. The *x* axis title displays horizontally underneath the *x* axis.
axiscolor	An integer between 1 and the current value of _PG_PALLETLEN. It specifies the color for the axis and parallel grid lines. This color has nothing to do with the color of the title of the axis.
labeled	A value (Boolean) that identifies whether tick marks and labels are to be drawn on the axis. An axis label is different from an axis title.
rangetype	An integer of use only with value data (as opposed to category data) that identifies whether the scale of the axis is linear or logarithmic. A linear scale is specified with _PG_LINEARAXIS, while a logarithmic scale is specified with _PG_LOGAXIS.
logbase	The logbase determines the log base used to scale the axis for logarithmic axes. The default value is 10.
autoscale	A variable (Boolean) with a true/false value. A value of true tells the presentation graphics functions to automatically determine the values for *scalemin, scalemax, scalefactor, scaletitle, ticinterval, ticformat,* and *ticdecimals*. A value of false means you have to specify values for these variables in your program.

Table 18-8. *(cont.)*

scalemin	Lowest value represented by the axis.
scalemax	Highest value represented by the axis.
scalefactor	Dividing each value by the *scalefactor* yields the scale for numeric data. This variable is figured automatically when the scalefactor evaluates to true.
scaletitle	A structure of type *titletype* which defines a string of text that describes the scalefactor value. This is prepared automatically when scalefactor evaluates to true. An example of a *scaletitle* is "times 10 million persons."
ticinterval	Sets the interval between tick marks on the axis. The interval is measured with the same units as the underlying data, so if there are 3 tick marks for data between 100 and 300, the interval between them is 100. The marks would appear at 100, 200, and 300. This is only valid with value data; it has no role with category data.
ticformat	An integer that identifies the label format assigned to each tick mark. The value _PG_DECFORMAT (1) is for decimal format and is the default value. _PG_EXPFORMAT (2) is for exponential formats. Both are defined in PGCHART.H. This is only valid with value data.
ticdecimals	Number of digits displayed after a decimal point in a tick label. The maximum value is 9. This is only valid with value data. Category data ignores it.

Type *legendtype* Structure

A structure of type *legendtype* stores the data that identifies the location, size, and colors of the chart legend. The structure is defined in the PGCHART.H file as:

```
typedef struct {
  short      legend;        /* TRUE=draw lgnd; FALSE=no */
  short      place;         /* _PG_RIGHT, _PG_BOTTOM,
                               _PG_OVERLAY */
  short      textcolor;     /* Intrnl palette clr for text */
  short      autosize;      /* TRUE=system calculates size */
  windowtype legendwindow;  /* Wndw def'n for legend */
} legendtype;
```

The individual variables are discussed in Table 18-9.

Table 18-9. *Variables in the* legendtype *Structure*

legend	A true/false (Boolean) value that identifies whether the chart will have a legend. Single series charts do not have legends and thus ignore this value.
place	An integer that specifies legend location relative to the data window. Positioning values defined in PGCHART.H of version 6.0 are _PG_LEFT (1), _PG_CENTER (2), _PG_RIGHT (3), _PG_BOTTOM (4), and _PG_OVERLAY (5). If place == 3, the legend is to the right of the

Table 18-9. ***(cont.)***

	data window. If place == 5, the legend is positioned within the data window. All values except 5 (_PG_OVERLAY) cause the presentation graphics functions to automatically size the data window to accommodate the legend. The data window is sized without regard to the legend when place evaluates to _PG_OVERLAY.
textcolor	An integer between 1 and _PG_PALLETLEN that specifies text color within a legend window.
autosize	A true/false variable (Boolean) that identifies whether the size of the legend window will be sized automatically. A false means that the legend window is specified by a structure of type *legendwindow*.
legendwindow	A structure of type *windowtype* is used to define a legend window. It contains values for background color, border frame, and positioning coordinates. The coordinates are ignored if autosize is true.

Type *titletype* Structure

A structure of type *titletype* determines the placement, text, and color of titles appearing in your graphs. The structure is defined in PGCHART.H as follows:

```
   typedef   struct {
     char    title[_PG_TITLELEN];  /* Title text */
     short   titlecolor; /* Intrnl palette clr for title text */
     short   justify;    /* _PG_LEFT, _PG_CENTER, _PG_RIGHT */
} titletype;
```

The individual variables are discussed in Table 18-10.

Table 18-10. ***Variables in the* titletype *Structure***

title [len]	The value for [len] is the variable _PG_TITLELEN. The title variable is a character array which contains the text of the title. If *grafcs* is a structure of type *chartenv*, then: `strcpy (grafcs.maintitle.title, "CW's Air Sales");` holds the character string used for the main title for the chart. The length of the text must be one less than the value of_PG_TITLELEN in order to accommodate the trailing null.
titlecolor	An integer between 1 and _PALETTLEN that identifies the color of the title. The default is 1.
justify	An integer identifying how the title is justified within a chart window. Three variables are defined in PGCHART.H for this purpose: _PG_LEFT (1), _PG_CENTER (2), and _PG_RIGHT (3).

Type *windowtype* Structure

The type *windowtype* structure contains color codes, locations, and sizes for the three types of windows generated by Microsoft C presentation graphics: chart windows, data windows, and legend windows. The chart window is the most significant.

Windows are addresses relative to some starting point (it is the logical address in Quick C 2.0 and the viewport address in Microsoft C 6.0 and later) and moving the starting point moves the entire chart. The *windowtype* structure is defined in the *PGCHART.H* file as below:

```
typedef  struct {
    short   x1;           /* Left edge of window in pixels */
    short   y1;           /* Top edge of window in pixels */
    short   x2;           /* Right edge of window in pixels */
    short   y2;           /* Bottom edge of window in pixels */
    short   border;       /* TRUE for border, FALSE otherwise */
    short   background;   /* Intrnl palette color-wndw bckgrnd */
    short   borderstyle;  /* Style bytes for window border */
    short   bordercolor;  /* Intrnl palette color-wndw border */
} windowtype;
```

The individual variables are discussed in Table 18-11.

Table 18-11. ***Variables in the*** **windowtype** ***Structure***

x1, y1, x2, y2	Window coordinates expressed in pixels. The pair (*x1, y1*) locates the upper-left corner and the pair (*x2, y2*) identifies the bottom-right corner. The reference (starting) point for the coordinates varies according to window type. The chart window is located relative to a logical point in Quick C 2.0 and 2.5 and to a viewport in version 6.0 and later of the Microsoft C compiler. Data and legend windows are located relative to (0,0) of the chart window. As explained in Table 18-9, the coordinates are ignored when a *windowtype* structure is used in *legendwindow* of *legendtype* when the autosize of *legendtype* evaluates to true.
border	A Boolean value that identifies whether a border frame is drawn around a window.
background	An integer between 1 and _PG_PALLETLEN that identifies the background color of a window. The default is 1.
borderstyle	An integer between 1 and _PG_PALLETLEN that identifies the border style of a window. The default is 1.
bordercolor	An integer between 1 and _PG_PALLETLEN that identifies the color of a border frame of a window. The default is 1.

TYING IT TOGETHER The following program draws three charts (column, pie, and bar) representing hypothetical results for five airframe manufacturers. The examples are single series for clarity.

```
#include <conio.h>
#include <stdlib.h>
#include <graph.h>
#include <string.h>
#include <pgchart.h>

#define FIRMS 5

float _far value    [FIRMS] = {37.5F,  11.3F, 42.2F, 18.3F,
                               32.6F};

char  _far *category[FIRMS] = {"CWG Ind.", "Lockheed", "BTY
                                Corp.", "MLY Assoc.", "Boeing"};

short _far explode  [FIRMS] = {1, 1, 0, 0, 1};

void main()

{

     chartenv airfrm;
     if (!_setvideomode (_MAXRESMODE)) exit (5);
     _pg_initchart();   /* Initialize chart system */

/* column chart */

     _pg_defaultchart (&airfrm, _PG_COLUMNCHART, _PG_PLAINBARS);
     strcpy (airfrm.maintitle.title, "Airframe Production");
     _pg_chart (&airfrm, category, value, FIRMS);
     getch();
     _clearscreen (_GCLEARSCREEN);

/* pie chart */

     _pg_defaultchart (&airfrm, _PG_PIECHART, _PG_PERCENT);
     strcpy (airfrm.maintitle.title, "Airframe Production");
     _pg_chartpie (&airfrm, category, value, explode, FIRMS);
     getch();
     _clearscreen (_GCLEARSCREEN);

/* bar chart */
```

```
    _pg_defaultchart (&airfrm, _PG_BARCHART, _PG_PLAINBARS);
    strcpy (airfrm.maintitle.title, "Airframe Production");
    _pg_chart (&airfrm, category, value, FIRMS);
    getch();
    _setvideomode (_DEFAULTMODE);

}
```

The output is shown in Figures 18-2, 18-3, and 18-4.

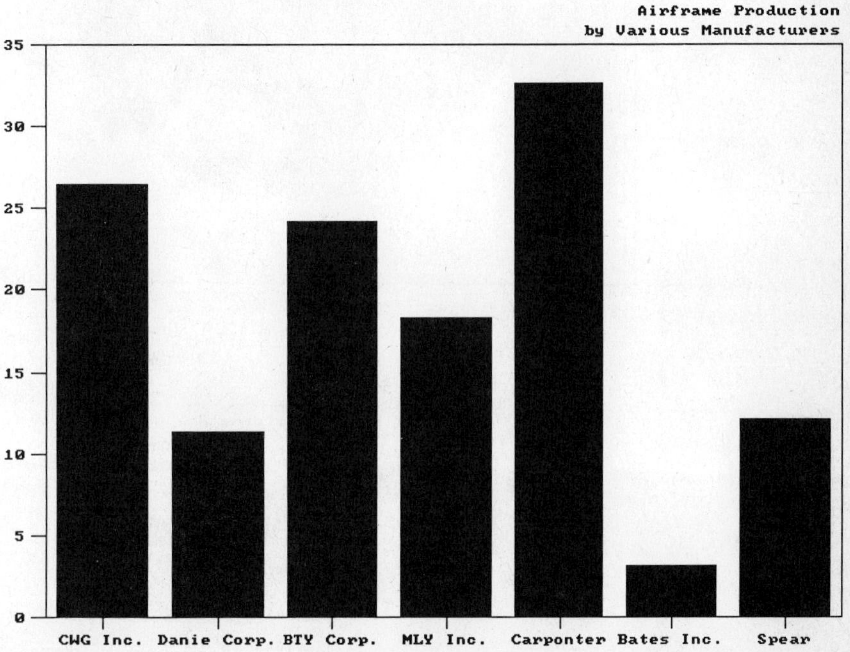

Figure 18-2. ***Column chart***

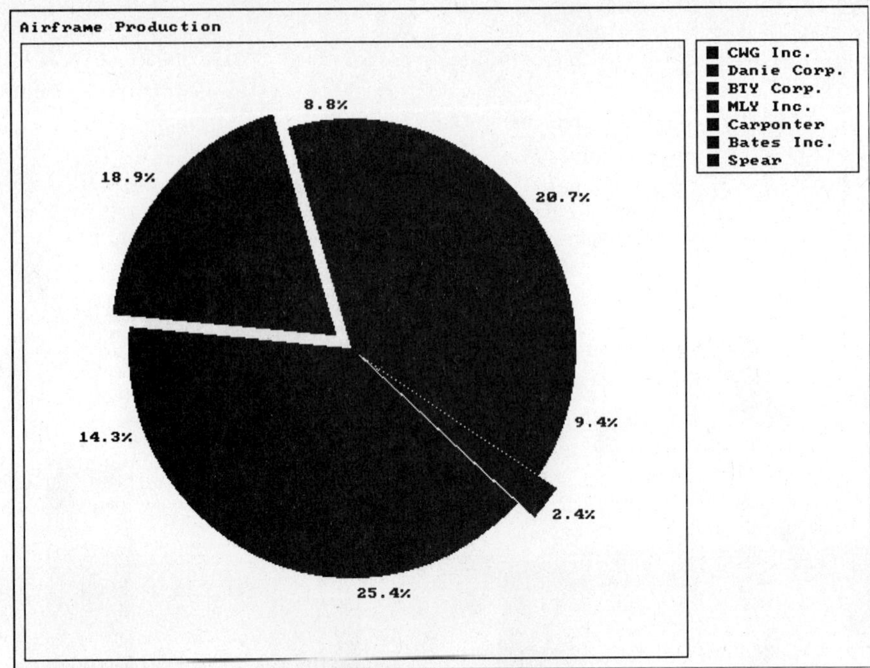

Figure 18-3. *Pie chart*

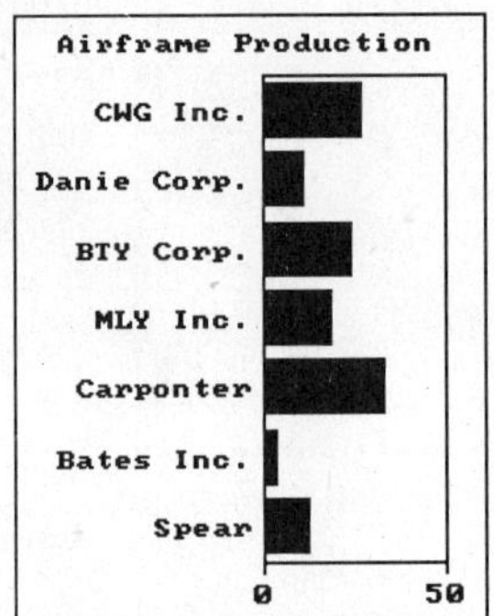

Figure 18-4. *Bar chart*

COMPATIBILITY

_arc, _arc_w, _arc_wxy

MSC 3	MSC 4	MSC 5	MSC 6	QC1	QC2	QC2.5	TC1	TC1.5	TC2	TC++	ANSI	UNIX V	XNX	OS2	DOS
		▲	1	▲	▲	▲		2	2	2					▲

PURPOSE Use the *_arc* family of functions when you wish to draw elliptical arcs. Use the *_arc_wxy* version when using window coordinates. The method of specifying the arc is described below.

SYNTAX

```
short _far _arc (short x1, short y1, short x2, short y2, short x3,
                short y3, short x4, short y4);

short _far _arc_w (double x1, double y1, double x2, double y2,
                  double x3, double y3, double x4, double y4);

short _far _far_wxy (struct _wxycoord _far *pwxy1,
                    struct _wxycoord _far
*pwxy2, struct _wxycoord _far *pwxy3, struct _wxycoord _far *pwxy4);
```

`x1, y1` *Upper-left corner of bounding rectangle*

`x2, y2` *Lower-right corner of bounding rectangle*

`x3, y3` *Second point of starting vector (remember that the center of the bounding rectangle is the first point of the start vector)*

`x4, y4` *Second point of end vector (remember that the center of the bounding rectangle is the first point of the end vector)*

`pwxy1` *Upper-left corner of bounding rectangle*

`pwxy2` *Lower-right corner of bounding rectangle*

`pwxy3` *Second point of starting vector (remember that the center of the bounding rectangle is the first point of the start vector)*

`pwxy4` *Second point of end vector (remember that the center of the bounding rectangle is the first point of the end vector)*

EXAMPLE CALL

```
_arc (x +20, y +20, x, y, x +43, y +38, x, y);
```

INCLUDES `#include <graph.h>` *For function declaration*

DESCRIPTION Drawing elliptical arcs requires understanding the concept of a "bounding rectangle." The bounding rectangle is an imaginary shape that surrounds the graphic shape you wish to draw. The size and location of the bounding rectangle depends on the size and location of the graphic shape it surrounds.

The center of an elliptical arc is the center of the bounding rectangle. It is defined by points (*x1, y1*) and (*x2, y2*) for the *_arc* and *_arc_w* routines. The *_arc_wxy* routine, which uses the *_wxy* structure to pass arguments, sets the center with pwxy1 and pwxy2.

The arc drawing starts where it intersects an imaginary line that extends from the arc's center through (*x3, y3*) for the *_arc* and *_arc_w* functions. The *_arc_wxy* macro uses pwxy3 for the (*x3, y3*) equivalent. The arc is drawn counter-clockwise about the arc's center. The end of the arc is an imaginary line that extends from the arc's center through the (*x4, y4*) or pwxy4 point.

The *_arc_w* and *_arc_wxy* versions—which are implemented as macros—use the so-called "real-world" (also called real-valued) window coordinate system. They are identical to the *_arc* routine in all other respects. An arc does not define a closed area, so it cannot be filled. The arcs generated by the three *_arc* functions are drawn in the current color.

1. The *_arc_w* and *_arc_wxy* routines were introduced in Microsoft C 6.0. 2. The Turbo C and Turbo C++ version of these functions is *arc*.

COMMON USES This function is useful in constructing line drawings that include curved sections. Several arcs can be pieced together to form a curved section.

RETURNS The *_arc*, *_arc_w*, and *_arc_wxy* routines return a nonzero value if the arc is successfully drawn. If nothing is drawn, they return a value of 0.

COMMENTS It is somewhat complicated to specify the arc to be drawn. For example, in most applications we know the beginning and end points of the curved line segment. These coordinates can be used directly as the arguments *xb, yb* and *xe, ye*. The complicated part is to specify the bounding rectangle for the ellipse of which the yet-to-be-drawn arc is a segment.

The logical coordinate system used in Microsoft C 5.0 and 5.1 has been replaced starting in Microsoft C 6.0.

Microsoft C compiler versions after 5.1 (including Quick C 2) use three low-level graphics coordinate systems, two of which were not in 5.0 or 5.1. The three coordinates were originally presented in Quick C 2.0 and are called "physical," "viewport," and "window." The logical coordinate system is no longer in use.

The graphics functions without a *_w* or *_wxy* suffix use the view coordinate system, and take short *ints* for coordinate arguments. Graphics functions with a *_w* suffix use window coordinates and take *doubles* for their coordinate arguments. The graphics functions that end with a *_wxy* suffix, such as *_arc_wxy*, take *_wxycoord* structures as arguments.

Drawing and Animation

SEE ALSO `_setcolor` *To set the current color*

EXAMPLE Write a C program to illustrate how arcs can be drawn using *_arc*. Show the bounding rectangle and the lines that determine the beginning and the end point of the arc being drawn. The only difference between the *_arc*, *_arc_w*, and *_arc_wxy* versions are the type of arguments. The example program will thus work equally well with all three versions.

```
#include <stdio.h>
#include <graph.h>
#define BLUE  1
#define GREEN 2
#define RED   4       /* Color number 4 is red */

main()
{
           /* bounding rectangle */
    short x1=100, y1=50, x2=250, y2=100,
           /* begin, end points  */
          xb=0, yb=50, xe=250, ye=100;
/* Enter hi-resolution graphics mode on EGA */
    if (_setvideomode(_ERESCOLOR) != 0)
    {
       _settextposition(1,1);
       _outtext("Demonstrating _arc");
       _settextposition(2,1);
       _outtext(
"Drawn counterclockwise from blue line to green");
/* Set up red as the current color */
       _setcolor(RED);
/* Select a dashed line style for the lines */
       _setlinestyle(0xff);
/* Draw the bounding rectangle -- with a border*/
       _rectangle(_GBORDER, x1, y1, x2, y2);
/* Draw the arc next */
       _arc(x1, y1, x2, y2, xb, yb, xe, ye);
/* Now show the line that determines the beginning of
 * the arc
 */
       _setcolor(BLUE);
/* Move to the center of the bounding rectangle */
       _moveto((x1+x2)/2, (y1+y2)/2);
       _lineto(xb, yb);
/* Next show the line that determines the end point of
 * the arc
```

```
*/
        _setcolor(GREEN);
        _moveto((x1+x2)/2, (y1+y2)/2);
        _lineto(xe, ye);

/* Restore original mode */
/* Give user a chance to see the result */
         _settextposition(40,1);
         _outtext("Hit any key to exit:");
         getch();
         _setvideomode(_DEFAULTMODE);
    }
    else
    {
/* Error setting mode */
         printf("Mode not supported by hardware\n");
    }
}
```

_clearscreen

COMPATIBILITY

MSC 3	MSC 4	MSC 5	MSC 6	QC1	QC2	QC2.5	TC1	TC1.5	TC2	TC++	ANSI	UNIX V	XNX	OS2	DOS
		▲	1	▲	▲	▲		2	2	2				▲	▲

PURPOSE Use *_clearscreen* to clear an area of the screen and fill it with the current background color.

SYNTAX

```
void _far _clearscreen(short area);

short area;
```

`short area;` *Constant indicating area to be cleared*

EXAMPLE CALL

```
_clearscreen(_GCLEARSCREEN); /* Clear the entire screen */
```

INCLUDES `#include <graph.h>` *For function declaration and definition of names for area*

DESCRIPTION The *_clearscreen* function clears out an area of the screen and fills that area with the background color. The background color may be altered by calling *_setbkcolor*. The area to be cleared is indicated by the parameter *area*, which should be set to one of the constants shown in Table 18-12. These constants are defined in the include file *graph.h*.

1. Changed in Microsoft C 6.0 to provide OS/2 capability. 2. The equivalent Turbo C and Turbo C++ functions are *cleardevice*, *clearviewport*, and *clrscr*.

Drawing and Animation

COMMON USES The *_clearscreen* function can be used with _GWINDOW as the argument to create pop-up menus.

Table 18-12. *Interpreting Area Constants*

Constant	Interpretation
_GCLEARSCREEN	Entire screen is cleared and filled.
_GVIEWPORT	Only current viewport is cleared and filled (see *_setviewport*).
_GWINDOW	Only current text window is cleared and filled (see *_settextwindow*).

SEE ALSO

`_setbkcolor` *To change the current background color*

`_setviewport` *To define a limited area of the screen as a viewport*

`_settextwindow` *To define a window within which text is output*

EXAMPLE From a text mode, define a window for text by calling *_settextwindow*. Next set a new background color by calling *_setbkcolor*. Now call *_clearscreen* to clear the text window and fill it with the new background color.

```
#include <stdio.h>
#include <graph.h>
/* Need a "long" constant for _setbkcolor   */
#define RED 4L
main()
{
/* Specify a text window using coordinates of upper
 * left and lower right corners
 */
    _settextwindow(10,10,15,70);
    _setbkcolor(RED);  /* Set background color to red */
    _clearscreen(_GWINDOW);      /* clear text window */

/* Once a text window is defined all text positions are
 * relative to upper left corner of the window. This
 * can be used for pop-up menus.
 */
    _settextposition(1,10);     /* Display a message */
    _outtext("_clearscreen on a text window");
}
```

_ellipse, _ellipse_w, _ellipse_wxy

COMPATIBILITY

MSC 3	MSC 4	MSC 5	MSC 6	QC1	QC2	QC2.5	TC1	TC1.5	TC2	TC++	ANSI	UNIX V	XNX	OS2	DOS
		▲	1	▲	▲	▲		2	2	2					▲

PURPOSE Use the *_ellipse* functions to draw a filled or bordered circle or ellipse that you specify by the corners of the bounding rectangle.

SYNTAX

```
short _ellipse (short control, short x1, short y1, short x2, short y2);

short _far_ellipse_w (short control, double wxl, double wyl,
                      double wx2, double wy2);

short _far _ellipse_wxy (short control, struct _wxycoord_far*pwxy1,
                         struct _wxycoord _far*pwxy2);
```

`control`	*To fill or draw a border (_GFILLINTERIOR, _GBORDER)*
`wx1, wy1`	*Upper-left corner of bounding rectangle*
`wx2, wy2`	*Lower-right corner of bounding rectangle*
`pwxy1`	*Upper-left corner of bounding rectangle*
`pwxy2`	*Lower-right corner of bounding rectangle*
`short x1, y1;`	*Coordinates of upper-left corner of rectangle circumscribing the ellipse*
`short x2, y2;`	*Coordinates of lower-right corner of rectangle circumscribing the ellipse*

EXAMPLE CALL

```
_ellipse (_GFILLINTERIOR, 100, 100, 200, 300);
_ellipse_w (_GFILLINTERIOR, -2.0, -2.5, 2.0, 2.5);
_ellipse_wxy (_GFILLINTERIOR, &upp_lft, &btm_rgt);
```

INCLUDES #include <graph.h> *For function declaration and definition of fill flag constants*

DESCRIPTION The *_ellipse* function family draw circles or ellipses (see Figure 18-1). The borders or the circle or the ellipse are drawn in the current color.

The center of an ellipse drawn by the *_ellipse* version is the center of the bounding rectangle defined by the view coordinate points (*x1, y1*) and (*x2, y2*).

The *_ellipse_w* routine, which is implemented as a macro, finds the center of the ellipse is the center of the bounding rectangle defined by the window coordinate points (*wx1, wy1*) and (*wx2, wy2*). It is a double float

version of *_ellipse*, and it was introduced in Microsoft C 6.0. See the tutorial for more information about the window coordinate systems.

The third member of the family, *_ellipse_wxy*, is also implemented as a macro. It is the *wxycoord* version of the *_ellipse* function. The center of the ellipse is the center of the bounding rectangle defined by the window coordinate pairs (*pwxy1, pwxy2*). It was introduced in Microsoft C 6.0.

The *control* argument may be one of two manifest constants: _GBORDER or _GFILLINTERIOR. The _GFILLINTERIOR option is equivalent to a call to *_floodfill* using the center of the ellipse as the starting point and the current color (set by the *_setcolor* routine) as the boundary color. If the arguments for the bounding rectangle define a point or a vertical or horizontal line, the functions will not draw a figure.

The *_setcolor* and *_setfillmask* routines should be run prior to a call to the *_ellipse* family so that the current color and fill style are set.

1. The *_ellipse_w* and *_ellipse_wxy* routines were introduced in Microsoft C 6.0. 2. The Turbo C and Turbo C++ versions of this function are *ellipse* and *fillellipse*.

COMMON USES This function can be used as a primitive object for building more complex graphical objects.

RETURNS The *_ellipse* group return a nonzero value if the drawing is constructed successfully. Otherwise, they return 0. The potential *_grstatus* codes are given in Table 18-3 in the tutorial.

COMMENTS The logical coordinate system used in Microsoft C 5.0 and 5.1 has been replaced beginning with Microsoft C 6.0.

Microsoft C compiler versions after 5.1 (including Quick C 2.0 and 2.5) use three low-level graphics coordinate systems, two of which were not in 5.0 or 5.1. The three coordinates were originally presented in Quick C 2.0 and are called "physical," "viewport," and "window." The logical coordinate system is no longer in use.

The graphics functions without a *_w* or *_wxy* suffix use the view coordinate system, and take short *ints* for coordinate arguments. Graphics functions with a *_w* suffix, such as *_ellipse_w*, use window coordinates and take *doubles* for their coordinate arguments. The graphics functions that end with a *_wxy* suffix, such as *_ellipse_wxy*, take *_wxycoord* structures as arguments.

If you want an ellipse with a border color different from that used to fill the interior, you can first draw the ellipse with a border, select a new color, and then fill the ellipse by calling the *_floodfill* function.

Table 18-13. ***Interpreting the Fill Flag***

Flag Constant	Interpretation
_GFILLINTERIOR	Fills the ellipse using the current color (see *_setcolor*). If a fill mask has been defined, the filling is done as if by painting over a stencil made out of a repeated pattern specified by the fill mask, with 1s being "holes" in the stencil (meaning the color passes through). See *_setfillmask* for more details.
_GBORDER	Only the outline of the ellipse is shown with solid lines drawn in the current color (contrast this with the border drawn by *_rectangle*).

SEE ALSO

`_setcolor` *To set the current color*

`_setfillmask` *To set the current fill mask*

`_floodfill` *To fill a bordered ellipse with color*

EXAMPLE Using a graphics mode appropriate for your graphics hardware, write a C program to draw two ellipses, one bordered and one filled, on the screen.

```
#include <stdio.h>
#include <graph.h>
#define BLUE 1     /* Color number 1 is blue */
#define RED  4      /* Color number 4 is red */
main()
{
/* Enter hi-resolution graphics mode on EGA */
    if (_setvideomode(_ERESCOLOR) != 0)
    {
/* Draw a filled rectangle */
        _settextposition(1,1);
        _outtext("A bordered ellipse:");
        _setlinestyle(0xff);
        _lineto(600,10);
        _setcolor(BLUE);
        _ellipse(_GBORDER, 0, 50, 150, 100);
/* Draw a filled ellipse */
        _settextposition(10,1);
        _outtext("A filled ellipse:");
        _setcolor(RED);
        _ellipse(_GFILLINTERIOR, 0, 150, 150, 200);

/* Restore original mode */
/* Give user a chance to see the result */
        _settextposition(20,1);
```

```
        _outttext("Hit any key to exit:");
        getch();
        _setvideomode(_DEFAULTMODE);
    }
    else
    {
/* Error setting mode */
         printf("Mode not supported by hardware\n");
    }
}
```

The following code fragment, from the program in the tutorial for Chapter 17, shows usage of *_ellipse_w* and *_ellipse_wxy*.

```
#include <stdlib.h>
#include <conio.h>
#include <graph.h>

void main(void)

{

   short x_one, y_one, x_two, y_two;
   struct _wxycoord upp_lft, btm_rgt;
   struct videoconfig vdocfg;

   if (!_setvideomode (_MAXRESMODE)) /**** GET VIDEO MODE ****/

      exit (1);

   _getvideoconfig (&vdocfg);

   x_one = vdocfg.numxpixels/3;
   y_one = vdocfg.numypixels/2;
   x_two = x_one/3;
   y_two = y_one/2;

   /**** WINDOW TWO ****/

   _setviewport (x_one, y_one, vdocfg.numxpixels -1,
                 vdocfg.numypixels -1);

   _setwindow (0, -4.0, -5.0, 4.0, 5.0);
   _setcolor (3);
   _rectangle_w (_GBORDER, -4.0, -5.0, 4.0, 5.0);
```

```
    _setcolor (4);

    _ellipse_w (_GFILLINTERIOR, -2.0, -2.5, 2.0, 2.5);
    getch();

    _rectangle_w (_GBORDER, -4.0, -5.0, 4.0, 5.0);

    /**** WINDOW FOUR ****/

    _setviewport (0, y_one, x_one -1, vdocfg.numypixels -1);
    _setwindow (0, -5.0, -6.0, 4.0, 6.0);
    upp_lft.wx = -4.0;
    upp_lft.wy = -5.0;
    btm_rgt.wx = 4.0;
    btm_rgt.wy = 5.0;
    _setcolor (10);

    _ellipse_wxy (_GFILLINTERIOR, &upp_lft, &btm_rgt);
    getch();

    _setvideomode (_DEFAULTMODE);
}
```

_floodfill, _floodfill_w

COMPATIBILITY

MSC 3	MSC 4	MSC 5	MSC 6	QC1	QC2	QC2.5	TC1	TC1.5	TC2	TC++	ANSI	UNIX V	XNX	OS2	DOS
		▲	1	▲	▲	▲		2	2	2					▲

PURPOSE Use the *_floodfill* function to fill an area of the screen with the current color (see *_setcolor*) using the current fill mask (see *_setfillmask*). Use the *_floodfill_w* version when you want a double version of *_floodfill.*

SYNTAX

```
short _far _floodfill(short x, short y, short boundary_color);

short _far _floodfill_w (double wx, double wy, short
                        (boundary_color);
```

`short x, y;` *Position of starting point in logical coordinates*

`short boundary_color;` *Color number of the boundary at which filling should stop*

`wx, wy` *Position of starting point*

EXAMPLE CALL

```
_floodfill(25, 75, 4);

_floodfill_w (x, y, trgt_clr);
```

INCLUDES `#include <graph.h>` *For function declaration*

DESCRIPTION The *_floodfill* function uses a well-known graphics algorithm of the same name to fill either the inside or the outside of a solid curve whose color is given in the argument *boundary_color*. The fill operation begins at the point whose logical coordinates are specified provided in the arguments *x* and *y*.

The region that gets filled depends on the starting "seed" point. If this point is inside the curve, the inside is filled. If it is outside, the region outside the curve gets filled. If you specify a point exactly on the boundary, the fill is not done. The filling begins at the seed point and spreads in all directions until *_floodfill* encounters a pixel of a border color that must be different from the fill color to prevent the whole screen from being filled.

The *_floodfill_w* version fills an area of the window using the current color and fill mask and is a double float version of *_floodfill*. It was introduced in version 6.0. See the tutorial for more information about coordinate systems.

1. *_floodfill_w* was introduced in Microsoft C 6.0. 2. The Turbo C and Turbo C++ version of this function is *floodfill*.

RETURNS The *_floodfill* function returns a nonzero value if the fill is successful. If there is an error, it returns a 0. The causes of error include specifying a seed point that lies on the boundary or outside the current clipping region (see *_setcliprgn*). The *_floodfill_w* routine returns a nonzero if successful; 0 if the starting point lies outside the clipping region, the fill could not be completed, or the starting point lies on the boundary color.

COMMENTS Since the filling algorithm colors all pixels on each row of pixels until it meets a pixel of color *boundary_color*, it is important to have a solid boundary for a proper fill. (In the example, we attempt to fill a rectangle with a boundary drawn in dashed line style.)

The logical coordinate system used in Microsoft C 5.0 and 5.1 has been replaced, beginning with Microsoft C 6.0.

Microsoft C compiler versions after 5.1 (including Quick C 2.0 and 2.5) use three low-level graphics coordinate systems, two of which were not in 5.0 or 5.1. The three coordinates that were originally presented in Quick C 2.0 are called "physical," "viewport," and "window." The logical coordinate system is no longer in use, and its functions *_setlogorg* and *_getlogcoord* are #defined to *_setvieworg* and *_getviewcord* in the

Microsoft C 6.0 *graph.h* file. The *_ellipse* function thus no longer takes logical coordinates in Microsoft C 6.0 and later.

The graphics functions without a *_w* or *_wxy* suffix use the view coordinate system, and take short *ints* for coordinate arguments. Graphics functions with a *_w* suffix use window coordinates and take *doubles* for their coordinate arguments. The graphics functions that end with a *_wxy* suffix take *_wxycoord* structures as arguments.

SEE ALSO

`_setcolor`	*To define the current color*
`_setfillmask`	*To define a pattern for the fill*

EXAMPLES If you have an EGA with enhanced color monitor, use the *_floodfill* function to fill a red rectangle with blue color. Draw the rectangle by calling *_rectangle*.

```
#include <stdio.h>
#include <graph.h>
#define BLUE 1      /* Color number 1 is blue  */
#define RED  4      /* Color number 4 is red   */

main()
{

    int i;
    char buffer[80];
    struct xycoord lastpos;
/* Enter hi-resolution graphics mode on EGA */
    if (_setvideomode(_ERESCOLOR) != 0)
    {
        _settextposition(1,1);
        _outtext("Demonstrating _floodfill:");
/* First draw a rectangle with a red border.
 * Use a solid line style.
 */
        _setlinestyle(0xffff);
        _setcolor(RED);
        _rectangle(_GBORDER, 0, 50, 100, 100);
/* Now use _floodfill to fill the interior with blue*/
        _setcolor(BLUE);
        _floodfill(25, 75, RED);
/* Restore original mode */
/* Give user a chance to see the result */
        _settextposition(20,1);
        _outtext("Hit any key to exit:");
```

```
        getch();
        _setvideomode(_DEFAULTMODE);
    }
    else
    {
/* Error setting mode */
        printf("Mode not supported by hardware\n");
    }
}
```

If the boundary of a region being filled is not solid, the *_floodfill* function leaks colors through the holes in the boundary. Demonstrate this effect by drawing a rectangle with a boundary in dashed line style and attempting to fill its inside. This example also works for the *_floodfill_w* version, except, of course, that the *shorts* used as arguments by the *_floodfill* function become *doubles* for the *_floodfill_w* routine. An example of explicit *_floodfill_w* usage can be found in the *1805.C* program on the reference page for *_getwritemode.*

```
#include <stdio.h>
#include <graph.h>
#define BLUE 1      /* Color number 1 is blue  */
#define RED  4      /* Color number 4 is red   */

main()
{
    int i;
    char buffer[80];
    struct xycoord lastpos;
/* Enter hi-resolution graphics mode on EGA */
    if (_setvideomode(_ERESCOLOR) != 0)
    {
        _settextposition(1,1);
        _outtext("_floodfill needs solid boundary");
/* First draw a rectangle with a blue border.
 * Use a solid line style.
 */
        _setlinestyle(0xf0f0);
        _setcolor(BLUE);
        _rectangle(_GBORDER, 0, 50, 100, 100);
/* Now use _floodfill to fill the interior with red */
        _setcolor(RED);
        _floodfill(25, 50, BLUE);
/* Restore original mode */
/* Give user a chance to see the result */
```

```
        _settextposition(20,1);
        _outtext("Hit any key to exit:");
        getch();
        _setvideomode(_DEFAULTMODE);
    }
    else
    {
/* Error setting mode */
        printf("Mode not supported by hardware\n");
    }
}
```

_getarcinfo

COMPATIBILITY

MSC 3	MSC 4	MSC 5	MSC 6	QC1	QC2	QC2.5	TC1	TC1.5	TC2	TC++	ANSI	UNIX V	XNX	OS2	DOS
			▲			▲									▲

PURPOSE Use the *_getarcinfo* function to find the endpoints in viewport coordinates of the arc most recently drawn by *_arc* or *_pie*.

SYNTAX

```
short _far _getarcinfo (struct xycoord _far *start, struct
xycoord _far *end, struct xycoord _far *fillpoint);
```

`start` *Starting point of an arc*

`end` *Ending point of an arc*

`fillpoint` *Point at which to begin filling the pie*

EXAMPLE CALL

```
_getarcinfo (&xy_start, &xy_end, &xy_fill);
```

INCLUDES `#include <graph.h>` *For function declaration*

DESCRIPTION The *_getarcinfo* function updates the value of the *start* and *end xycoord* structures (defined in *graph.h*) upon a successful return.

COMMON USES The *fillpoint* value specifies a point from which a pie graphic can be filled, allowing the use of one color for the border and another for the interior of the shape. An appropriate call to *_setcolor* will yield a color change, and the new color and the *fillpoint* coordinates can be sent to *floodfill* to effect the change.

RETURNS The *_getarcinfo* routine returns a nonzero value if it is successful. A value of 0 indicates that the call failed.

SEE ALSO

`_arc`	*To draw an arc*
`_getvideoconfig`	*To get video characteristics*
`_grstatus`	*To check result of graphics call*

EXAMPLE Write a program that draws arcs and uses *_getarcinfo* to find the endpoints of the arcs.

```
#include <conio.h>
#include <graph.h>
#include <stdlib.h>

void main (void)

{

   struct xycoord xy_strt, xy_endd, xy_fill;
   short x, y;

   /* find graphics mode - exit if cannot */
     if (!_setvideomode (_MAXRESMODE)) exit (7);

   x = 210; y = 70;                              /* rectangles */
   _rectangle (_GBORDER,        x - 44, y - 44, x, y);
   _rectangle (_GFILLINTERIOR, x + 44, y + 44, x, y);

   x = 330;                                      /* arcs       */
   _arc (x - 44, y - 44, x, y, x - 10, y - 44, x - 44, y - 10);
   _arc (x + 44, y + 44, x, y, x,      y + 10, x + 10, y);

   /* get arc endpoints & enclose and fill it */
   _getarcinfo (&xy_strt, &xy_endd, &xy_fill);

   if (_grstatus < _GROK) exit (14);  /* then handle error */
   _moveto     (xy_strt.xcoord, xy_strt.ycoord);
   _lineto     (xy_endd.xcoord, xy_endd.ycoord);
   _floodfill  (xy_fill.xcoord, xy_fill.ycoord, _getcolor());
    getch();

   _setvideomode (_DEFAULTMODE);

}
```

_getcurrentposition, _getcurrentposition_w

COMPATIBILITY

MSC 3	MSC 4	MSC 5	MSC 6	QC1	QC2	QC2.5	TC1	TC1.5	TC2	TC++	ANSI	UNIX V	XNX	OS2	DOS
		▲	1	▲	▲	▲		2	2	2					▲

PURPOSE Use *_getcurrentposition* to obtain the coordinates of the current graphics position, which is maintained internally by the graphics library routines. The *_getcurrentposition_w* version works with the window coordinate system.

SYNTAX

```
struct xycoord _far _getcurrentposition(void);

struct _wxycoord _far _getcurrentposition_w (void);
```

EXAMPLE CALL

```
curpos = _getcurrentposition();

_getcurrentposition_w (void);
```

INCLUDES `#include <graph.h>` *For function declaration and definition of the structure* xycoord

DESCRIPTION The *_getcurrentposition* function returns the coordinates of the current graphics position. This point is used by the function *_lineto* as the starting point of the line it draws. A new current position can be specified by calling *_moveto* and updated by the drawing routines *_arc* and *_lineto.*

An analogous concept is the current text position set by *_settextposition* and used during text output by *_outtext.*

The *_getcurrentposition_w* version gets the current graphics output position in window coordinates. It is the double float version of the *_getcurrentposition* function. See the tutorial for more information about coordinate systems.

The logical coordinate system mentioned earlier in the description is valid only with Microsoft C 5.0 and 5.1. As mentioned throughout the graphics chapters, the logical coordinate system has been replaced with the view and window coordinate systems.

1. The *_getcurrentposition_w* routine was introduced in Microsoft C 6.0. 2. The Turbo C and Turbo C++ equivalent to *_getcurrentposition* is found in two separate functions, *getx* and *gety.*

RETURNS The *_getcurrentposition* function returns the coordinates of the current graphics position in a structure of type *xycoord,* which is declared as shown below in the header file *graph.h.*

```
struct xycoord       /* Structure for pixel coordinates */
{
```

```
    short xcoord;     /* x-coordinate */
    short ycoord;     /* y-coordinate */
};
```

The return of *_getcurrentposition_w* is the current position in a *_wxycoord* structure. The structure is defined in *graph.h*.

SEE ALSO `_moveto` *To change the current graphics position*

`_lineto` *Uses and updates current position*

EXAMPLE Suppose you want to draw a line with a rectangle attached to the end point of the line. If you didn't know the coordinates of the end point, you could still draw the rectangle at the right place by calling *_getcurrentposition* after the line has been drawn. (The example program will also work with the *_getcurrentposition_w* version, adjusting the arguments from *struct xycoord* to *struct _wxycoord.*)

```
#include <stdio.h>
#include <graph.h>
/* Yellow is 14 in EGA's default palette */
#define YELLOW 14
main()
{
    char buffer[80];
    struct xycoord current;
/* Assume an EGA environment */
    if (_setvideomode(_ERESCOLOR) == 0)
    {
        printf("Not EGA environment\n");
        exit(0);
    }
    _settextposition(1,1);
    _outtext("Demonstrating _getcurrentposition");
    _setcolor(YELLOW);
/* Draw a line from (50,40) to (150,90) */
    _moveto(50,40);
    _lineto(150,90);
/* Now draw a 20 by 20 rectangle with the upper left
 * corner at the end of the line we just drew. Suppose
 * we don't know the coordinates of the end point.
 * Let's first get it.
 */
    current = _getcurrentposition();
/* Draw rectangle using coordinates just retrieved */
```

```
    _rectangle(_GBORDER,current.xcoord, current.ycoord,
                current.xcoord+20, current.ycoord+20);
/* Current graphics position will still be the end
 * point of the line
 */
    current = _getcurrentposition();
    sprintf(buffer,"Current graphics position = \
(%d,%d)", current.xcoord, current.ycoord);
    _settextposition(2,1);
    _outtext(buffer);
/* Wait for user to hit a key, then reset everything */
    _settextposition(25,1);
    _outtext("Hit any key to reset mode and exit:");
    getch();
    _setvideomode(_DEFAULTMODE);
}
```

_getimage, _getimage_w, _getimage_wxy

COMPATIBILITY

MSC 3	MSC 4	MSC 5	MSC 6	QC1	QC2	QC2.5	TC1	TC1.5	TC2	TC++	ANSI	UNIX V	XNX	OS2	DOS
		▲	1	▲	▲	▲		2	2	2					▲

PURPOSE Use the *_getimage* function to save a rectangular screen image in a buffer. You must allocate sufficient storage for the buffer and provide the buffer's address to *_getimage*. Use the *_getimage_w* or *_getimage_wxy* version when using the view or window coordinate systems.

SYNTAX

```
void _far _getimage(short x1, short y1, short x2, short y2,
                    char _far *image_buffer);

void _far _getimage_w (double wx1, double wy1, double wx2,
                       double wy2, char_huge *image_buffer);

void _far _getimage_wxy (struct _wxycoord _far *pwxy1,
                         struct_wxycoord _far *pwxy2, char _huge
*image_buffer);
```

`short x1, y1;` *Upper-left corner of rectangular boundary of screen image to be saved*

`short x2, y2;` *Lower-right corner of rectangular boundary of screen image to be saved*

`char _far *image_buffer;` *Buffer where image is to be stored*

`wx1, wy1`	*Upper-left corner of the bounding rectangle*
`wx2, wy2`	*Lower-right corner of the bounding rectangle*
`image_buffer`	*Storage buffer for the screen image*
`pwxy1`	*Upper-left corner of the bounding rectangle*
`pwxy2`	*Lower-right corner of the bounding rectangle*

EXAMPLE CALL

```
_getimage(50,50,100,100,image); /* Save the image */
```

INCLUDES `#include <graph.h>` *For function declaration*

DESCRIPTION The *_getimage* function saves the pixels corresponding to a rectangular region of the screen into the buffer whose address is provided in the argument *image_buffer*. The screen image to be saved is specified by the rectangle whose upper-left corner is (*x1, y1*) and lower-right corner is (*x2, y2*).

Enough storage must be allocated to hold the image. The minimum number of bytes necessary to save an image can be determined by calling the function *_imagesize*.

The screen image defined by a specified bounding rectangle is saved into the buffer argument (we called it *image_buffer* in the syntax example) by the *_getimage_w* macro. It defines the bounding rectangle with the window coordinates (*wx1, wy1*) and (*wx2, wy2*). It was introduced in version 6.0 and is a double float version of *_getimage*. See the tutorial for more information about double float functions.

The *_getimage_wxy* version (which is also implemented as a macro) also stores the screen image defined by a specified bounding rectangle into the buffer identified as *image_buffer* in the syntax example above. It uses the window coordinate pairs, *pwxy1* and *pwxy2*. It was also introduced in Microsoft C 6.0 and is a *_wxycoord* structure version of *_getimage*.

1. The *_getimage_w* and *_getimage_wxy* routines were introduced in Microsoft C 6.0. 2. The Turbo C and Turbo C++ version of these functions is *getimage*.

COMMON USES The *_getimage* function is used in conjunction with *_putimage* to save and restore screen images. You can, for example, use the *_getimage* function to draw an object once, save it, and reproduce it at several locations on the screen with *_putimage*. Additionally, erasing the old image before displaying the new one enables you to make an image appear to move on the screen.

RETURNS The *_getimage_w* and *_getimage_wxy* functions do not generate a return value, although you should check *_grstatus* to confirm the success of the call.

SEE ALSO

`_imagesize`	*To determine number of bytes necessary to save a screen image*
`_putimage`	*To display a stored image*
`_grstatus`	*To check results of a graphics call*

EXAMPLE In a graphics mode, draw some graphical objects and save them in memory by calling *_getimage*. Now clear the screen and use *_putimage* to reproduce the objects several times on the screen. (The example program will work equally well with the *_w* and the *_wxy* versions of the *_getimage* function. The declarations need to be changed to accommodate the different nature of the arguments, but the underlying operation of the *_getimage* functionality remains the same.)

```
#include <stdio.h>
#include <malloc.h>
#include <graph.h>
#define RED    4
#define YELLOW 14
main()
{
    char _far *image;
    char buffer[80];
    unsigned numbytes;
/* Assume EGA. Put it in high-res graphics mode */
    if (_setvideomode(_ERESCOLOR) == 0)
    {
/* Error setting mode */
        printf("Not EGA hardware\n");
        exit(0);
    }
/* Draw some graphical objects to save */
    _setcolor(RED);
    _rectangle(_GBORDER,50,50,90,90);
    _setcolor(YELLOW);
    _ellipse(_GFILLINTERIOR,60,60,100,100);
/* Determine storage needed for entire screen and
 * display result
 */
    numbytes = (unsigned int)_imagesize(50,50,100,100);
    sprintf(buffer, "To save 51 x 51 image using \
```

```
_getimage, we need %u bytes of memory.", numbytes);
    _settextposition(1,1);
    _outtext(buffer);

/* Allocate buffer for image */
    if ((image = (char _far *) malloc(numbytes)) ==
        (char far *)NULL)
    {
        _setvideomode(_DEFAULTMODE);
        printf("Not enough memory for image storage\n");
        exit(0);
    }
    _getimage(50,50,100,100,image); /* Save the image */
    _settextposition(2,2);
    _outtext("Image saved. Hit any key to continue");
    getch();
/* Now clear screen and draw saved image at several
 * screen locations
 */
    _clearscreen(_GCLEARSCREEN);
    _setbkcolor(_CYAN); /* Change the background color*/
    _settextposition(1,1);
    _outtext("Demonstrating _getimage and _putimage");

    _putimage(80,80,image,_GXOR);
    _putimage(150,20,image,_GPSET);
    _putimage(300,200,image,_GPRESET);
/* Once user hits any key, reset mode and exit */
    _settextposition(24,1);
    _outtext("Hit any key to exit:");
    getch();
    _setvideomode(_DEFAULTMODE);   /* Restore mode */
}
```

COMPATIBILITY

_getpixel, _getpixel_w

MSC 3	MSC 4	MSC 5	MSC 6	QC1	QC2	QC2.5	TC1	TC1.5	TC2	TC++	ANSI	UNIX V	XNX	OS2	DOS
		▲	1	▲	▲	▲		2	2	2					▲

PURPOSE Use the *_getpixel* function to retrieve the pixel value of a certain pixel whose location is specified in coordinates. The *_getpixel_w* routine is used to determine the pixel value at the location specified in the window coordinates.

SYNTAX

```
short _far _getpixel(short x, short y);

short _far _getpixel_w (double wx, double wy);
```

`short x, y;` *The logical* x *and* y *coordinates of the pixel whose value is returned*

`wx, wy` *Coordinates of the pixel whose value is returned*

EXAMPLE CALL

```
pix_value = _getpixel(100, 150);

if (_getpixel_w (old_wnd.wx, old_wnd.wy) == color)
colr_screen = TRUE;
```

INCLUDES `#include <graph.h>` *For function declaration*

DESCRIPTION The *_getpixel* function first checks to see if the pixel specified by the coordinates (*x,y*) lies within the current clipping region or viewport. If it does, *_getpixel* returns the *pixel value* contained in the video memory location corresponding to the pixel coordinate (*x,y*).

References to the logical coordinate system are presented to provide guidance for users of Microsoft C 5.0 and 5.1, but the logical system was dropped starting in Microsoft C 6.0 (and Quick C 2.0). The later versions of *_getpixel* use the view coordinate system.

Both *_getpixel* and *_getpixel_w* are restricted to a range of possible pixel values and color translations that are determined by the current video mode and palette, respectively.

The *_getpixel_w* routine, implemented as a macro, determines the pixel value at the location specified in the window coordinates.

1. The *getpixel_w* routine was introduced in version 6.0 and is a double float version of *_getpixel*. 2. The Turbo C and Turbo C++ version of these functions is *getpixel*.

COMMON USES The *_getpixel* function is used to perform operations such as turning all red pixels to blue. You can use *_setcolor* and *_setpixel* to go through the pixels, checking the value of each and changing those containing red to blue. (See the example below.)

RETURNS If the pixel is inside the clipping region, *_getpixel* returns the current pixel value. Otherwise, it returns a –1 to indicate failure. An error is also generated if the functions are called while the program is in text mode. Returns for the *_getpixel_w* version match those of *_getpixel*. The *_grstatus* values for the *_getpixel* group are _GRERROR and _GRNOTINPROPERMODE as errors and _GRPARAMETERALTERED for a warning.

Drawing and Animation

COMMENTS The term *pixel value* is often used interchangeably with the term *color index*, although the latter usage is considered to be more precise.

SEE ALSO

`_getcliprgn, _getviewport`	*To define a limited area of the screen as clipping region for graphics output*
`_setpixel`	*To set a pixel to current color*

EXAMPLE In a graphics mode, draw a small red rectangle. Examine a larger rectangular area and use *_getpixel* to find all the red pixels. Turn each red pixel to blue. Since a 0 value indicates a background pixel, you can also turn each pixel containing a 0 to another color. Using the *_getpixel_w* version in the example is a matter of changing the declarations and arguments from the *shorts* used by *_getpixel* to the *doubles* used by *_getpixel_w*. The underlying work of the *_getpixel* routine remains exactly the same.

```
#include <stdio.h>
#include <graph.h>
#define BLUE 1       /* Blue is color number 1 in EGA */
#define RED  4       /* Red is color number 4 in EGA  */
main()
{
    short x, y, color;
/* Assume an EGA environment */
    if (_setvideomode(_ERESCOLOR) == 0)
    {
        printf("Not EGA environment\n");
        exit(0);
    }
    _settextposition(1,1);
    _outtext("Changing colors using _getpixel with \
_setpixel");
/* Draw a red bordered rectangle */
    _setcolor(RED);
    _rectangle(_GBORDER, 70,50,130,80);
    _settextposition(2,1);
    _outtext("Hit any key to turn red into blue:");
    getch();
/* Go over a rectangular region and change red to blue*/
    for(x=50; x<150; x++)
    {
        for(y=40; y<90; y++)
        {
            if(_getpixel(x,y) == 0)
            {                     /* it's  background */
```

```
                _setcolor(RED);
                _setpixel(x,y);  /* turn pixel red   */
                continue;        /* skip next check..*/
            }
            if(_getpixel(x,y) == RED)
            {                    /* it's  a red pixel */
                _setcolor(BLUE);
                _setpixel(x,y);  /* turn pixel blue   */
            }
        }
    }
/* Wait for user to hit a key, then reset everything  */
        _settextposition(25,1);
        _outtext("Hit any key to reset mode and exit:");
        getch();
        _setvideomode(_DEFAULTMODE);
}
```

_getwritemode

COMPATIBILITY

MSC 3	MSC 4	MSC 5	MSC 6	QC1	QC2	QC2.5	TC1	TC1.5	TC2	TC++	ANSI	UNIX V	XNX	OS2	DOS
			▲			▲								▲	▲

PURPOSE Use the *_getwritemode* function to get the current logical write mode used by the *_lineto, _rectangle,* and *_polygon* function groups. This can be saved and later restored.

SYNTAX

```
short _far _getwritemode (void);
```

EXAMPLE CALL

```
sav_mode = _getwritemode ();  /* save the current */

_setwritemode (sav_mode);     /* restore it later */
```

INCLUDES `#include <graph.h>` *For function declaration*

DESCRIPTION The *_getwritemode* function returns the current logical write mode used by the *_lineto, _rectangle,* and *_polygon* function groups. There are five modes, each of which is identified as a short integer. The logical write modes are_GAND, which transfers the image over an existing one on the screen; _GOR, which superimposes the image onto an existing image; _GPRESET, which will transfer data point-by-point onto the screen; _GPSET, which also transfers data point-by-point onto the screen; and

_GXOR, which causes the points on the screen to be inverted where a point exists in the image buffer.

The default value is _GPSET, which causes lines to be drawn using the current graphics color.

RETURNS Success yields the logical write mode, either _GPSET, _GXOR,_GAND, _GOR, or _GPRESET. An error, such as not being in graphics mode, returns a –1. There is one possible *_grstatus* return, an error, of _GRNOTINPROPERMODE.

SEE ALSO _setwritemode *To set the write mode for subsequent graphics*

EXAMPLE The code fragment below elaborates on that shown in the EXAMPLE CALL section, and it shows how the values yielded and used by the *_getwritemode* function are used.

```
{

   int    oldmode, newmode;
   oldmode = _getwritemode();      /* save old mode */

   _setwritemode (newmode);

      /* perform processing */
   _setwritemode (oldmode);        /* restore original */

}
```

The following program displays the use of the *_getwritemode* function in a larger context.

```
#include <conio.h>
#include <graph.h>
#include <math.h>
#include <stdlib.h>

short wrt_mds[5]  = { _GPSET,   _GPRESET, _GXOR,    _GOR,
                      _GAND    };

char *wrt_str[10] = { "pset  ", "preset", "xor   ", "or    ","and   ","6
", "7     ", "8     ", "9     ", "10    " };

void draw_star (double centr_x, double centr_y, double radius,
        int writemode, int fill);  /* prototype */

void main(void)
```

```
{
   short cntr, txt_colr;
   double x, y;

   if (!_setvideomode (_MAXCOLORMODE)) exit (6);
   _setwindow (0, -60.0, -50.0, 60.0, 50.0);
   x = y = -10.0;

   draw_star (x, y, 25.0, _GPSET, _GFILLINTERIOR);
   getch();
   txt_colr = _getcolor();
   _setcolor (2);
   _floodfill_w (x, y, txt_colr);

   for (cntr = 0; cntr < 10; cntr++)
   {
      _settextposition (6, 6);
      _outtext (wrt_str[cntr]);
         _setcolor (cntr);
      draw_star (x += 2.0, y += 1.0, 25.0, wrt_mds[cntr],
                 _GBORDER);
      getch();
   }

   _setvideomode (_DEFAULTMODE);
}

void draw_star (double centr_x, double centr_y, double radius,
                int writemode, int fill)

{
   const float PI = 3.14159F;
   int    wrt_md, side;
   struct _wxycoord poly_side[5];
   double radians;

   /* save writemode, set new */
   wrt_md = _getwritemode();

   _setwritemode (writemode);
   /* calc the star points of star over 144 degrees - then
      connect */

   for (side = 0; side < 5; side++)
   {
```

```
        radians = 144 * PI / 180;
        poly_side [side].wx = centr_x + (cos (side * radians) *
                              radius);

        poly_side [side].wy = centr_y + (sin (side * radians) *
                              radius);

    }
    _polygon_wxy (fill, poly_side, 5);

    /* restore original mode */
    _setwritemode (wrt_md);
}
```

COMPATIBILITY

_grstatus

MSC 3	MSC 4	MSC 5	MSC 6	QC1	QC2	QC2.5	TC1	TC1.5	TC2	TC++	ANSI	UNIX V	XNX	OS2	DOS
			▲			▲								▲	▲

PURPOSE The *_grstatus* function is used to determine whether errors or warnings were generated by the most recently called graphics function. It should be used immediately after a graphics call in order to test for its success.

SYNTAX `short _far _grstatus (void);`

EXAMPLE CALL `if (_grstatus < _GROK);  /* then handle error */`

INCLUDES `#include <graph.h>` *For function declaration*

DESCRIPTION The *_grstatus* function yields a warning or an error message when it identifies a failure of a function call to a graphics routine. The tutorial presents a table which lists the functions with which *_grstatus* works and the values each of those functions may generate. The list is also available through the on-line Help files accompanying Microsoft C 6.0.

The *graph.h* file maintains a list of constants for use with *_grstatus*. The values are shown below:

Value	Constant	Interpretation
0	_GROK	A successful call.
–1	_GRERROR	A graphics error has happened.
–2	_GRMODENOTSUPPORTED	The requested video mode not supported.

Value	Constant	Interpretation
–3	_GRNOTINPROPERMODE	The requested routine works only in certain video modes.
–4	_GRINVALIDPARAMETER	One (or more) parameters was invalid.
–5	_GRFONTFILENOTFOUND	No matching font file was found.
–6	_GRINVALIDFONTFILE	One (or more) font file was invalid.
–7	_GRCORRUPTEDFONTFILE	One (or more) font file was inconsistent.
–8	_GRINSUFFICIENTMEMORY	Not enough memory to allocate buffer (or complete *_floodfill*).
–9	_GRINVALIDIMAGEBUFFER	Image buffer data was inconsistent.
1	_GRNOOUTPUT	No action was taken.
2	_GRCLIPPED	Output was clipped to the viewport.
3	_GRPARAMETERALTERED	One (or more) input parameter was changed to stay within range, or parameter pairs were swapped to put in the proper order.

The following functions cannot cannot give errors, and all set the *_grstatus* value to _GROK: *_displaycursor, _gettextposition, _outmem, _getactivepage, _gettextwindow, _outtext, _getgtextvector, _getvideoconfig, _unregisterfonts, _gettextcolor, _getvisualpage,* and *_wrapon.*

The *_grstatus* function currently yields values for the following functions and function groups: *_arc, _clearscreen, _ellipse, _getarcinfo, _getcurrentposition, _getfontinfo, _getgtextextent, _getimage, _getphyscoord, _getpixel, _gettextcursor, _getviewcoord, _getwindowcoord, _getwritemode, _imagesize, _lineto, _moveto, _outgtext, _pie, _polygon, _putimage, _rectangle, _registerfonts, _scrolltextwindow, _selectpalette, _setactivepage, _setbkcolor, _setcliprgn, _setcolor, _setfont, _setgtextvector, _settextcolor, _settextcursor, _settextposition, _settextrows, _settextwindow, _setvideomode, _setvideomoderows, _setvieworg, _setviewport, _setvisualpage, _setwindow,* and *_setwritemode.*

COMMON USES The *_grstatus* routine is useful in identifying problems with graphics calls as they are made. Certain of the graphics errors may not show up immediately, and when subsequently noticed, perhaps many statements later, debugging will have become unnecessarily complex. Appropriate use of *_grstatus* will help you identify problems quickly.

RETURNS The *_grstatus* routine returns the status of the most recently called graphics function.

EXAMPLE The example program on the reference page for *_getarcinfo* shows use of the *_grstatus* function.

Drawing and Animation

COMPATIBILITY

_imagesize, _imagesize_w, _imagesize_wxy

MSC 3	MSC 4	MSC 5	MSC 6	QC1	QC2	QC2.5	TC1	TC1.5	TC2	TC++	ANSI	UNIX V	XNX	OS2	DOS
		▲	1	▲	▲	▲		2	2	2					▲

PURPOSE Use the *_imagesize* function to determine the number of bytes necessary to store a rectangular region of the screen. Call *_imagesize* before allocating memory to store an image or before storing the image with *_getimage*. The function is also available in *_w* and *_wxy* versions.

SYNTAX

```
long _far _imagesize(short x1, short y1, short x2, short y2);

long _far _imagesize_w (double wx1, double wy1, double wx2,
                        double wy2);

long _far _imagesize_wxy (struct _wxycoord _far
                          *pwxy1, struct_wxycoord _far *pwxy2);
```

`short x1, y1;`	*Upper-left corner of rectangular boundary of image*
`short x2, y2;`	*Lower-right corner of rectangular boundary of image*
`wx1, wy1`	*Upper-left corner of bounding rectangle*
`wx2, wy2`	*Lower-right corner of bounding rectangle*
`pwxy1`	*Upper-left corner of bounding rectangle*
`pwxy2`	*Lower-right corner of bounding rectangle*

EXAMPLE CALL

```
bytes_needed = _imagesize(min_x, min_y, max_x, max_y);

bytes_needed = _imagesize_w (wx1, wy1, wx2, wy2);
```

INCLUDES `#include <graph.h>` *For function declaration*

DESCRIPTION The *_imagesize* function computes the number of bytes necessary to store the screen image within the rectangular region specified by the upper-left corner by (*x1, y1*) and the lower-right corner (*x2, y2*). This is the minimum amount of storage that the function *_getimage* needs in order to save that rectangular region of screen.

The *_imagesize_w* routine calculates the number of bytes needed to store the image as specified by the window coordinates (*wx1, wy1*) and (*wx2, wy2*). The *_imagesize_wxy* version calculates the number of bytes needed to store the image as specified by the window coordinate pairs, *pwxy1* and *pwxy2*.

1. The *_imagesize_w* and *_imagesize_wxy* variants were introduced in Microsoft C 6.0 and are the *_wcoord* and *_wxycoord* structure versions, respectively, of *_imagesize*. (See the tutorial for more information about coordinate systems.) 2. The Turbo C and Turbo C++ version of this function is *imagesize*.

The formula used to compute the number of bytes necessary to store the image is illustrated by the following C code fragment:

```
    long   imagesize;            /* Size in bytes      */
    struct videoconfig config;   /* For bits-per-pixel */
      .
      .
      .
    xwidth = abs(x1 - x2) + 1;   /* x width in pixels  */
    ywidth = abs(y1 - y2) + 1;   /* y width in pixels  */
    _getvideoconfig(&config);    /* get bits-per-pixel */
/* Storage in bytes needed to save image using _getimage
 */
    imagesize = 4 + ((long)((xwidth*config.bitsperpixel
                           + 7)/8) * (long)ywidth);
```

COMMON USES The *_getimage* and *_putimage* functions in Microsoft C 5.1 and later provide the capability to save and restore screen images enabling movement or animation of images on the screen.

When saving an image, you must provide a buffer of adequate size. The *_imagesize* function allows you to determine the buffer size, taking into account the number of bits of storage needed in the current video mode.

RETURNS The *_imagesize* function returns a long integer containing the number of bytes needed to store the specified rectangular screen image. The returns are the same for the *_w* and *_wxy* versions.

SEE ALSO

`_getimage` *To save an image in memory (needs storage buffer)*

`_putimage` *To display a stored image*

EXAMPLE If you have an EGA, set it in the 640×350, 16-color video mode. Then call *_imagesize* to determine the amount of storage *_getimage* will need to save the entire display area in memory. The only difference between the *_imagesize* generic function and the *_w* and *_wxy* versions is the type of the arguments and return values.

```
#include <stdio.h>
#include <graph.h>
```

```
main()
{
    struct videoconfig config;
    char buffer[80];
    long numbytes;
/* Assume EGA. Put it in high-res graphics mode */
    if (_setvideomode(_ERESCOLOR) == 0)
    {
/* Error setting mode */
        printf("Not EGA hardware\n");
        exit(0);
    }
/* Get the maximum number of pixel on screen   */
   _getvideoconfig(&config);
/* Determine storage needed for entire screen and
 * display result
 */
    numbytes = _imagesize(0, 0, config.numxpixels-1,
                             config.numypixels-1);
    sprintf(buffer, "To save %d x %d image using \
_getimage, we need %ld bytes of memory.",
     config.numxpixels, config.numypixels, numbytes);
     _settextposition(1,1);
    _outtext(buffer);
/* Once user hits any key, reset mode and exit */
    _settextposition(24,1);
    _outtext("Hit any key to exit:");
    getch();
    _setvideomode(_DEFAULTMODE);   /* Restore mode */
}
```

COMPATIBILITY

_lineto, _lineto_w

MSC 3	MSC 4	MSC 5	MSC 6	QC1	QC2	QC2.5	TC1	TC1.5	TC2	TC++	ANSI	UNIX V	XNX	OS2	DOS
		▲	1	▲	▲	▲		2	2	2					▲

PURPOSE Use *_lineto* to draw a line from the current position to a new point using the current color and the current line style. The *_lineto_w* function is used to draw a line to a window coordinate.

SYNTAX

```
short _far _lineto(short x, short y);

short _far _lineto_w (double wx, double wy);
```

```
short x, y;
```
Logical coordinates of point to which line is drawn

```
wx, wy
```
Coordinates of the point to which a line is drawn

EXAMPLE CALL `_lineto(next_x, next_y);`

INCLUDES `#include <graph.h>` *For function declaration*

DESCRIPTION The *_lineto* function joins the current position to the point whose logical coordinates are specified by the short integer arguments *x* and *y*. The line is drawn using the current color (set by *_setcolor*) and the current line style (defined by *_setlinestyle*). The end point of the line becomes the new current position. (See the tutorial section of Chapter 17 for an explanation of the physical and logical coordinate systems.)

The *_lineto_w* version draws a line from the current position up to and including the window coordinate (*wx, wy*).

Use of the term "logical coordinate" is provided for compatibility with Microsoft C 5.0 and 5.1.

1. The *_lineto_w* version was introduced in Microsoft C 6.0 and is a double float version of *_lineto*. 2. The Turbo C and Turbo C++ version of this function is *lineto*.

COMMON USES The *_lineto* function provides the basic capability, present in any graphics package, of drawing a line between two points. The *_lineto* function, together with *_moveto*, enables you to draw the most complex line drawings.

RETURNS The *_lineto* function returns a nonzero value if the line is drawn successfully. Otherwise it returns a 0. The *_lineto_w* routine returns a nonzero value if successful; 0 if not.

COMMENTS Microsoft C compiler versions after 5.1 (including Quick C 2.0) use three low-level graphics coordinate systems, two of which were not in 5.0 or 5.1. The three coordinates originally presented in Quick C 2.0 are called "physical," "viewport," and "window." The logical coordinate system is no longer in use.

The graphics functions without a *_w* or *_wxy* suffix use the view coordinate system and take short *ints* for coordinate arguments. Graphics functions with a *_w* suffix use window coordinates and take *doubles* for their coordinate arguments.

SEE ALSO `_moveto` *To move to a new point without drawing*

EXAMPLE Use *_lineto* with *_moveto* to draw a graph showing a *sin(x)* function against *x*. Except for the type of arguments, the two *_lineto* versions behave identically.

Drawing and Animation

```
#include <stdio.h>
#include <math.h>
#include <graph.h>

#define RED    4     /* Color number 4 is RED      */
#define TWOPI  6.283 /* Approximate value of 2 Pi  */
#define MAXPNT 100   /* Points on the sinusoid     */

main()
{
    struct videoconfig config;
    short i, x, y, oldx, oldy, midpoint;
    double xd, yd, ampl;
/* Enter hi-resolution graphics mode on EGA */
    if (_setvideomode(_ERESCOLOR) == 0)
    {
/* Error setting mode */
        printf("Mode not supported by hardware\n");
        exit(0);
    }
/* Get current configuration */
    _getvideoconfig(&config);
    midpoint = config.numypixels/2 - 1;
    ampl = (double)midpoint - 30.;
/* Let the logical origin be halfway down the screen */
    _setlogorg(0, midpoint);
/* Move to logical origin */
   _moveto(0,0);
   _settextposition(1,1);
   _outtext(
"Demonstrating _lineto with a plot of sin(x) vs x");
   _setcolor(RED);

    for (i=0; i<=MAXPNT; i++)
    {
        yd = ampl *
             sin(TWOPI * ((double)i)/((double)MAXPNT));
        xd = ((double)config.numxpixels/2.0 - 1.)*
             (double)i / (double)MAXPNT;
        x  = (short)xd;
/* Negate y so that y axis is positive upwards     */
        y  = - (short)yd;
/* Draw a line to the new point by calling _lineto */
       _lineto(x,y);
    }
```

```
/* Restore original mode */
/* Give user a chance to see the result          */
    _settextposition(40,1);
    _outtext("Hit any key to exit:");
    getch();
    _setvideomode(_DEFAULTMODE);
}
```

_moveto, moveto_w

COMPATIBILITY

MSC 3	MSC 4	MSC 5	MSC 6	QC1	QC2	QC2.5	TC1	TC1.5	TC2	TC++	ANSI	UNIX V	XNX	OS2	DOS
		▲	1	▲	▲	▲		2	2	2					▲

PURPOSE Use *_moveto* to change the current position maintained by the graphics routines. Use the *_moveto_w* routine when you wish to move the current graphics position while within a window coordinate system.

SYNTAX

```
struct xycoord _far _moveto(short x, short y);

struct _wxycoord _far _moveto_w (double wx, double wy);
```

`short x, y;` *New position in logical coordinates*

`wx, wy` *New position in window coordinates*

EXAMPLE CALL `_moveto(10, 20);`

INCLUDES `#include <graph.h>` *For function declaration and definition of the structure* xycoord

DESCRIPTION The *_moveto* function changes the current position that is maintained internally by the graphics routines. The current position is used by the *_lineto* routine as the starting point for any line it draws. The coordinates of this point are specified by the short integer arguments *x* and *y*. See the tutorial section of Chapter 17 for an explanation of the coordinate systems.

The *_moveto_w* routine moves the current graphics output position to the specified window coordinates. It is a double float version of *_moveto*. Use of the term "logical coordinates" is provided for compatibility with earlier versions of the Microsoft C compiler.

1. The *_moveto_w* routine was introduced in Microsoft C 6.0. 2. The Turbo C and Turbo C++ version of this function is *moveto*.

COMMON USES This function is one of the basic capabilities present in a graphics package. If you think in terms of drawing on a piece of paper with a pen, calling *_moveto* is analogous to lifting the pen and moving to a new point on the paper.

RETURNS The *_moveto* function returns the previous graphics position's *x* and *y* coordinates in a structure of type *xycoord*, defined in *graph.h* as shown below.

```
struct xycoord
{
    short xcoord;   /* x coordinate */
    short ycoord;   /* y coordinate */
};
```

The *_moveto_w* function returns the coordinates of the previous position in a *_xycoord* structure.

SEE ALSO `_lineto` *To draw a line to another point*

COMMENTS The logical coordinate system used in Microsoft C 5.0 and 5.1 has been replaced starting in Microsoft C 6.0.

Microsoft C compiler versions after 5.1 (including Quick C 2.0) use three low-level graphics coordinate systems, two of which were not in 5.0 or 5.1. The three coordinates originally presented in Quick C 2.0 are called "physical," "viewport," and "window." The logical coordinate system is no longer in use.

The graphics functions without a *_w* or *_wxy* suffix use the view coordinate system and take short *ints* for coordinate arguments. Graphics functions with a *_w* suffix use window coordinates and take *doubles* for their coordinate arguments.

EXAMPLE Use *_moveto* with *_lineto* to draw a few disjointed line segments. (The behavior of the *_moveto_w* functions is identical except for the size of the arguments.)

```
#include <stdio.h>
#include <graph.h>
#define RED  4      /* Color number 4 is red */

main()
{
    int i;
    char buffer[80];
    struct xycoord lastpos;
/* Enter hi-resolution graphics mode on EGA */
```

```
    if (_setvideomode(_ERESCOLOR) != 0)
    {
        _settextposition(1,1);
        _outtext("Demonstrating _moveto");
/* Set up red as the current color */
        _setcolor(RED);
/* Move to beginning of a line segment and draw a line*/
        _moveto(0,40);
        _lineto(100,40);
/* Now move to the beginning of next line segment. Show
 * how to use the returned structure
 */
        lastpos = _moveto(150,40);
        sprintf(buffer,"Last position was: (%d, %d)",
                lastpos.xcoord, lastpos.ycoord);
        _settextposition(5,1);
        _outtext(buffer);
/* Restore original mode */
/* Give user a chance to see the result */
        _settextposition(40,1);
        _outtext("Hit any key to exit:");
        getch();
        _setvideomode(_DEFAULTMODE);
    }
    else
    {
/* Error setting mode */
        printf("Mode not supported by hardware\n");
    }
}
```

_pg_analyzechart, _pg_analyzechartms

COMPATIBILITY

MSC 3	MSC 4	MSC 5	MSC 6	QC1	QC2	QC2.5	TC1	TC1.5	TC2	TC++	ANSI	UNIX V	XNX	OS2	DOS
			▲		▲	▲									▲

PURPOSE Use the *_pg_analyzechart* function to analyze (but not display) a single series of data and to fill the chart environment with default values for a single-series bar, column, or line chart. (The type of chart is identified in the arguments.) The *_pg_analyzechartms* function performs the same operations on a multiseries chart.

SYNTAX

```
short _far _pg_analyzechart (chartenv _far *chrt_env,
                char_far *_far *categories, float _far *values, short n);
```

```
short _far _pg_analyzechartms (chartenv _far *chrt_env,
        char_far *_far *categories, float _far *values, short
        nmof_series, short nmof_valus, short arry_dmn, char _far
        *_far *serieslabels);
```

`chrt_env`	*The chart environment variable*
`categories`	*An array of category variables*
`values`	*An array of data values*
`nmof_seres`	*The number of series to be charted*
`nmof_valus`	*The number of data values to chart*
`arry_dmn`	*Row dimension of data array*
`serieslabel`	*An array of labels for series*

EXAMPLE CALL

```
_pg_analyzechartms (&chrt_env, weeks, values, OFFICES, WEEKS, WEEKS,
                    staff);
```

INCLUDES `#include <pgchart.h>` *For function declaration*

DESCRIPTION The *_pg_analyzechart* and *_pg_analyzechartms* functions supply appropriate default values to the chart environment according to arguments specified in a call to *_pg_defaultchart.* The arguments *categories* and *values* provide data for calculating variables, and are the same as those used by the *_pg_chart* function.

The *analyze* functions shift the math workload to library routines and thus typically result in faster execution of your program.

RETURNS The *_pg_analyzechart* and *_pg_analyzechartms* functions return 0 if there were no errors. A value of nonzero indicates a failure.

COMMENTS The Boolean flags in the chart environment (such as legend) should be set to TRUE so that defaults are calculated.

SEE ALSO

`_pg_initchart`	*To initialize presentation graphics*
`_pg_defaultchart`	*To initialize the chart environment*

EXAMPLE Write a program to show how some of the members of the *_pg_analyze* family of functions work, including the multiseries version of *_pg_analyzechart,* by creating barcharts.

```
/* PGANLYZ.C show mechanics of the _pg_analyze function group  */

#include <conio.h>
#include <string.h>
#include <stdlib.h>
#include <graph.h>
#include <pgchart.h>

#define FALSE 0
#define TRUE  1
#define QRTR  4
#define REGNS 5

char  _far *time_prd[QRTR] = {"1st", "2nd", "3rd", "4th"};

char  _far *offices[REGNS] = {"Atlanta","Boston","Chicago","Dallas","San
Jose"};

float _far values[REGNS * QRTR] = { .703F, .529F, .627F, .628F,
                  .638F, .536F, .392F, .347F, .512F, .612F,
                  .473F, .404F, .232F, .339F, .401F, .224F,
                  .312F, .328F, .513F, .493F};

void main()

{

   chartenv chrt_env; /* init chrt_env as the chart environment
                      */

   if(!_setvideomode(_MAXRESMODE)) exit(1); /* exit on error */

   _pg_initchart();   /* init to defaults  */

   _pg_defaultchart(&chrt_env, _PG_BARCHART, _PG_PLAINBARS);

   strcpy(chrt_env.maintitle.title, "Sales of Christopher Corp.");

   chrt_env.chartwindow.x2 = 327;       /* right edge  */

   chrt_env.chartwindow.y2 = 284;       /* bottom      */

   _pg_chartms(&chrt_env, time_prd, values, REGNS, QRTR, QRTR,
            offices);
```

```
    getch();

    /* analyze a multiseries bar chart */
    _pg_defaultchart(&chrt_env, _PG_BARCHART, _PG_PLAINBARS);
    strcpy(chrt_env.maintitle.title, "Sales of Christopher
         Corp.");

    strcpy(chrt_env.subtitle.title, "after a call to
         _pg_analyzechartms");

    chrt_env.xaxis.autoscale = TRUE;

    _pg_analyzechartms(&chrt_env, time_prd, values, REGNS, QRTR,
                       QRTR, offices);

    /* axistype variables are covered in Chapter 18 */

    chrt_env.xaxis.grid = TRUE;
    chrt_env.xaxis.autoscale = FALSE;
    chrt_env.xaxis.ticinterval = 0.2F;
    chrt_env.xaxis.scalemax = 1.0F;
    strcpy(chrt_env.xaxis.scaletitle.title, "Performance Index");
    chrt_env.xaxis.scaletitle.justify = _PG_LEFT;

    /* windowtype variables are covered in Chapter 18 */

    chrt_env.chartwindow.y1 = 120;    /* top edge */
    chrt_env.chartwindow.x1 = 210;    /* left edge */

    _pg_chartms(&chrt_env, time_prd, values, REGNS, QRTR, QRTR,
            offices);

    getch();
    _setvideomode(_DEFAULTMODE);
}
```

The results of the program are presented in both Figures 18-5 and 18-6. Figure 18-6 shows that a subsequent chart may be displayed without erasing the first chart. The size of the second chart differs from the first, and it could have been made larger or smaller without major effort.

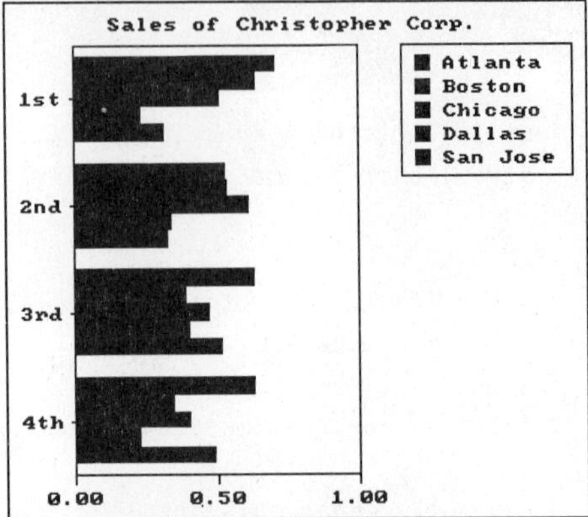

Figure 18-5. *Presentation bar chart*

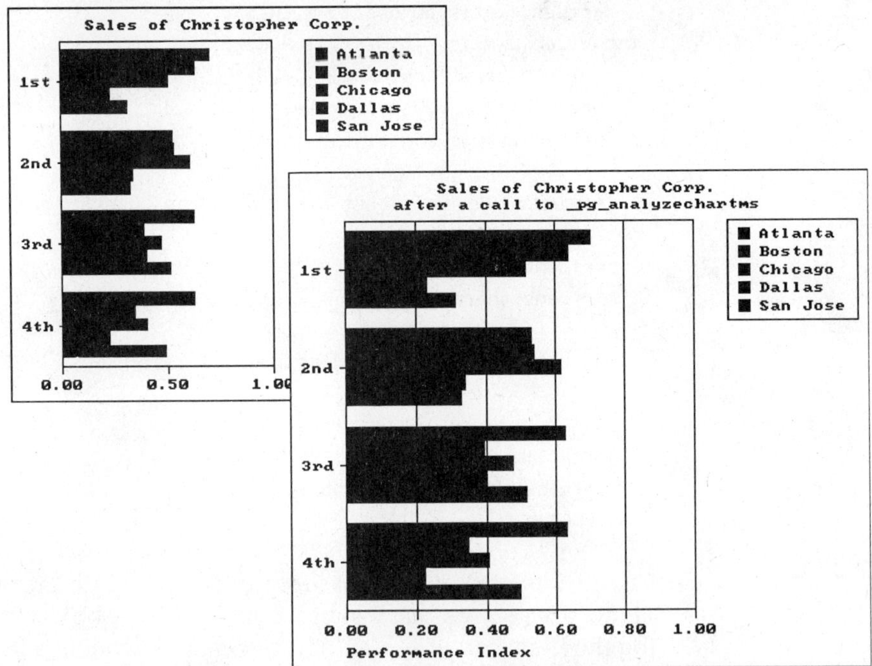

Figure 18-6. *Overlaid bar charts*

Drawing and Animation

COMPATIBILITY

_pg_analyzepie

MSC 3	MSC 4	MSC 5	MSC 6	QC1	QC2	QC2.5	TC1	TC1.5	TC2	TC++	ANSI	UNIX V	XNX	OS2	DOS
			▲		▲	▲									▲

PURPOSE Use the *_pg_analyzepie* function when you wish to analyze a single series of data and fill the chart environment for a pie chart.

SYNTAX

```
short _far _pg_analyzepie (chartenv _far *chrt_env, char
           _far *_far *categories, float _far *values, short _far
           *explode, short nmof_valus);
```

`chrt_env`	*The chart environment structure*
`categories`	*An array of category variables*
`values`	*An array of data values*
`explode`	*An array of explode flags*
`nmof_valus`	*The number of data values to chart*

EXAMPLE CALL `_pg_analyzepie (&chart_env, category, values, explode, FIRMS);`

INCLUDES `#include <pgchart>` *For function declaration*

DESCRIPTION The data for the chart is contained in the array named *values* in the syntax example above. The *_pg_analyzepie* function does not actually display the data; it fills the environment for a pie chart using information read from the *values* array. The arguments are the same as those used by the *_pg_chartpie* function.

The *analyze* functions shift the arithmetic workload to the library routines, and thus typically they improve the speed at which your program runs.

RETURNS The *_pg_analyzepie* function returns 0 if there were no errors and a nonzero value if the call failed.

SEE ALSO

`_pg_chartpie`	*To draw a pie chart*
`_pg_initchart`	*To initialize presentation graphics*
`_pg_defaultchart`	*To initialize the chart environment*

EXAMPLE The example program at the end of the tutorial shows the use of the *_pg_chartpie* function, which takes the exact same arguments as the *_pg_analyzepie* routine. A look at the *analyze* functions is provided in the example program accompanying the reference page for the *_pg_analyzechart* function.

_pg_analyzescatter, _pg_analyzescatterms

COMPATIBILITY

MSC 3	MSC 4	MSC 5	MSC 6	QC1	QC2	QC2.5	TC1	TC1.5	TC2	TC++	ANSI	UNIX V	XNX	OS2	DOS
			▲		▲	▲									▲

PURPOSE Use the *_pg_analyzescatter* function to analyze a single series of data, and to fill the chart environment, for a single-series scatter diagram. Use the *_pg_analyzescatterms* function to analyze data, and to fill the chart environment, for a multiseries scatter diagram.

SYNTAX

```
short _far _pg_analyzescatter (chartenv _far *chrt_env,
           float_far *x_values, float _far *y_values, short n);

short _far _pg_analyzescatterms (chartenv _far *chrt_env,
           float _far *x_values, float _far *y_values, short
           nmof_seres, short nmof_valus, short row_dimn, char _far
           *_far *serieslabels);
```

`chrt_env` *The chart environment structure*

`x_values` *An array of* x*-axis data values*

`y_values` *An array of* y*-axis data values*

`nmof_valus` *The number of data values to chart*

`nmof_seres` *The number of series to chart*

`row_dimn` *The row dimension of the data array*

`serieslabels` *An array of labels for the series*

EXAMPLE CALL

```
_pg_analyzescatter (&env, doctors[0], lawyers[0], ITEMS);

_pg_analyzescatterms (&env, (float _far *) staff, (float
                     _far *) expenses, SERIES, ITEMS, ITEMS, firms);
```

INCLUDES `#include <pgchart.h>` *For function declaration*

DESCRIPTION The *analyzescatter* functions fill the chart environment for a single series or multiseries scatter diagram. The variables calculated by the *_pg_analyzescatter* and *_pg_analyzescatterms* functions are built from data received in the *x_values* and *y_values* arguments. The arguments are the same as those used in *_pg_chartscatter* and its multiseries version, *_pg_chartscatterms.*

RETURNS The *_pg_analyzescatter* and *_pg_analyzescatterms* routines return a 0 if the call executes successfully and a nonzero if the call fails.

COMMENTS Set all chart environment Boolean flags.

SEE ALSO

`_pg_defaultchart`	*To initialize the chart environment*
`_pg_analyzechart`	*To analyze data for charting*
`_pg_chartscatter`	*To draw a scatter chart*
`_pg_chartscatterms`	*To draw a scatter chart for more than one series of data*

EXAMPLE Write a program to show the *_pg_analyzescatter* functions.

```
#include <conio.h>
#include <graph.h>
#include <pgchart.h>
#include <string.h>
#include <stdlib.h>

#define ITEMS  5
#define SERIES 2

float _far costs [SERIES][ITEMS] = {{21.3F, 53.2F, 26.1F, 37.8F,
                   58.9F}, {16.6F, 34.2F, 94.2F, 43.1F, 63.7F}};

float _far sales [SERIES][ITEMS] = {{573.F, 953.F, 892.F, 256.F,
                   572.F}, {232.F, 339.F, 439.F, 788.F, 627.F}};

char  _far *firms [SERIES] = {"Penn_Burg Corp.", "Silver Aries
                              Co."};

char  byte_storage [10]; /* for chardef */

void main (void)

{

   chartenv chrt_env;
```

```
     if (!_setvideomode (_MAXRESMODE)) exit (8);
    _pg_initchart();

      /* use chardefs to show _grstatus usage */
    _pg_getchardef (65, byte_storage);

      if (_grstatus < _GROK) exit (29);
      _pg_setchardef (65, byte_storage);

      if (_grstatus < _GROK) exit (211);
    /* single-series scatter chart */

    _pg_defaultchart (&chrt_env, _PG_SCATTERCHART, _PG_POINTONLY);

    strcpy (chrt_env.maintitle.title, "Penn_Burg Corp.");
    strcpy (chrt_env.subtitle.title, "calendar - not fiscal");
    strcpy (chrt_env.xaxis.axistitle.title, "costs");
    strcpy (chrt_env.yaxis.axistitle.title, "sales");

    _pg_chartscatter (&chrt_env, sales[0], costs[0], ITEMS);
    getch();

    _clearscreen (_GCLEARSCREEN);

    /* multiseries scatter chart */

    _pg_defaultchart (&chrt_env, _PG_SCATTERCHART,
                      _PG_POINTANDLINE);

    strcpy (chrt_env.subtitle.title, "per C. Avery");
    strcpy (chrt_env.xaxis.axistitle.title, "costs");
    strcpy (chrt_env.yaxis.axistitle.title, "sales");
    _pg_chartscatterms (&chrt_env, (float _far *)sales,
       (float _far *)costs, SERIES, ITEMS, ITEMS, firms);

    getch();

    _setvideomode (_DEFAULTMODE);
}
```

Drawing and Animation

COMPATIBILITY

_pg_chart, _pg_chartms

MSC 3	MSC 4	MSC 5	MSC 6	QC1	QC2	QC2.5	TC1	TC1.5	TC2	TC++	ANSI	UNIX V	XNX	OS2	DOS
			▲		▲	▲									▲

PURPOSE Use the *_pg_chart* function to display a single-series bar, column, or line chart, and use the *_pg_chartms* routine to display a multiseries bar, column, or line chart. (The multiseries nature of the function is identified by the "ms" suffix.)

SYNTAX

```
short _far _pg_chart (chartenv _far *chrt_env, char
      _far *_far *categories, float _far *values, short nmof_valus);

short _far _pg_chartms (chartenv _far *chrt_env, char
      _far *_far *categories, float _far *values, short nmof_seres,
      short nmof_valus, short aray_dmn, char _far *_far
      *serieslabels);
```

`chrt_env`	*The chart environment variable*
`categories`	*An array of category variables*
`values`	*An array of data values*
`nmof_valus`	*The number of values to chart*
`nmof_seres`	*The number of series to chart*
`aray_dmn`	*The row dimension of the data array*
`serieslabels`	*An array of labels for series*

EXAMPLE CALL `_pg_chart (chart_env, category, value, ARRESTS);`

INCLUDES `#include <pgchart.h>` *For function declaration*

DESCRIPTION The *_pg_chart* and *_pg_chartms* functions display a single-series or multiseries chart, respectively. The chart environment should be loaded with your desired values before a call is made to these functions.

All the series in the multiseries chart must have the same number of data points. That value is specified by the *aray_dmn* argument. Values for the multiseries chart are maintained in the two-dimensional array *values*. Each column of values represents a single series. The *nmof_valus* parameter is the integer value used to dimension rows in the array declaration for *values*.

The following fragment declares the identifier *chart_val* to be a two-dimensional floating-point array with 15 rows and 10 columns (the number of columns in an array cannot exceed 10, which is the maximum number of data series you can display on a single chart):

```
#define ARY_DMN 15
float chart_val [ARYDMN][10];
short aray_dmn = ARYDMN;
```

The *aray_dmn* value must be greater than or equal to the *nmof_valus* argument, and the column dimension in the array declaration must be greater than or equal to the *nmof_seres* argument. Setting *nmof_valus* and *nmof_seres* to values less than the full-dimensional size of the *chart_val* array will allow the plotting of only part of the data contained in *chart_val*.

The *serieslabel* character array holds the labels used in the chart legend. The legend is used to identify each series of data.

COMMON USES The example program CHART01.C at the end the tutorial shows *_pg_chart* being called twice (for both a column and a bar) with certain items in the chart environment being changed between calls. The *_pg_chart* function is the routine that actually builds the chart on the display device.

RETURNS The functions return a 0 if there are no errors and a nonzero value if there is trouble.

SEE ALSO

`_pg_defaultchart`	*To initialize the chart environment*
`_pg_initchart`	*To initialize presentation graphics*
`the _pg_analyzechart functions`	*To analyze data for charts*

EXAMPLE The example program at the end of the tutorial draws three charts, presented earlier as Figures 18-2 (a column chart), 18-3 (a pie chart), and 18-4 (a bar chart). All three charts were composed from the same data.

Drawing and Animation

COMPATIBILITY

_pg_chartpie

MSC 3	MSC 4	MSC 5	MSC 6	QC1	QC2	QC2.5	TC1	TC1.5	TC2	TC++	ANSI	UNIX V	XNX	OS2	DOS
			▲		▲	▲									▲

PURPOSE Use the *_pg_chartpie* function when you wish to display a pie chart for the data contained in the array values.

SYNTAX

```
short _far _pg_chartpie (chartenv _far *chrt_env, char
      _far *_far *categories, float _far *values, short _far
      *explode, short nmof_valus);
```

`chrt_env` *The chart environment structure*

`categories` *An array of category labels*

`values` *An array of data values*

`explode` *An array of explode flags*

`nmof_valus` *The number of data values to chart*

EXAMPLE CALL

```
_pg_chartpie (&chart_env, category, values, explode, FIRMS);
```

INCLUDES `#include <pgchart.h>` *For function declaration*

DESCRIPTION The *_pg_chartpie* function causes a pie chart to be displayed. The characteristics of the pie chart are determined by the arguments to the *_pg_chartpie* function. The *chartenv* structure type carries values for labels, colors, sizes, and the like. One characteristic of type *chartenv* structures with which you should take special care is the display coordinates you provide to set the size of a chart. There are some coordinate combinations that will generate an error message informing you that a chart is too small, but others will result in only a blank screen. The first diagnostic step if *_pg_chartpie* yields no display is to restore the default coordinate settings and repeat the call.

The explode flags (an array) tell the *_pg_chartpie* function which pieces of the pie should be immediately adjacent and which should be separated slightly from the rest of the pie in order to increase emphasis. The effect of the explode option is shown in the example program CHART01.C discussed at the end of the tutorial. An example of "explode" usage is

```
short explode[8] = {0, 1, 0, 0, 1, 0, 0, 0};
```

where the pie slices corresponding to the second and fifth entry of the *categories* array will be displayed "exploded" or slightly apart from the other six slices.

COMMON USES The *_pg_chartpie* function is called whenever you wish to display a pie chart.

RETURNS The *_pg_chartpie* function returns a 0 if the pie is displayed without errors. Any nonzero value indicates a failure.

SEE ALSO

`_pg_analyzepie` *To draw a pie chart*

`_pg_initchart` *To initialize presentation graphics*

COMMENTS Pie charts are formed from a single series of data, so there is no multiseries version of this function.

EXAMPLE See the example program at the end of the tutorial.

_pg_chartscatter, _pg_chartscatterms

COMPATIBILITY

MSC 3	MSC 4	MSC 5	MSC 6	QC1	QC2	QC2.5	TC1	TC1.5	TC2	TC++	ANSI	UNIX V	XNX	OS2	DOS
			▲		▲	▲									▲

PURPOSE Applications that require a scatter diagram for a single series of data use the *_pg_chartscatter* function. If you need to use a scatter diagram for more than one series of data (for example, a multiseries format) use the *_pg_chartscatterms* function.

SYNTAX

```
short _far _pg_chartscatter (chartenv _far *chrt_env,
          float_far *x_values, float _far *y_values, short
          nmof_valus);

short _far _pg_chartscatterms (chartenv _far *chrt_env,
          float_far *x_values, float _far *y_values, short
          nmof_seres, short nmof_valus, short aray_dimn, char _far
          *_far *serieslabels);
```

`chrt_env` *The chart environment structure*

`x_values` *An array of* x*-axis data values*

`y_values` *An array of* y*-axis data values*

`nmof_seres`	*The number of data series to chart*
`nmof_valus`	*The number of data values to chart*
`aray_dmn`	*The row dimension of the data array*
`serieslabels`	*An array of labels for series*

EXAMPLE CALL

```
_pg_chartscatter (&env, bats[0], members[0], ITEMS);

_pg_chartscatterms (&env, (float _far *) catalog, (float
                   _far*) expenses, SERIES, ITEMS, ITEMS, projects);
```

INCLUDES

`#include <pgchart.h>` *For function declaration*

DESCRIPTION

The *x* and *y* arguments are two-dimensional arrays that contain the data for the scatter chart axes. Each column in the array contains plot data for an individual series, so the *_pg_chartscatter* array (which has only one series) has only one column. The array in the multiseries version of the routine, *_pg_chartscatterms*, may have more than one column. Five series in the scatter chart means, for instance, five columns in the array.

All the series in the multiseries chart must have the same number of data points. That value is specified by the *aray_dmn* argument. Values for the multiseries chart are maintained in the two-dimensional array, *values*. Each column of values represents a single series. The *nmof_valus* parameter is the integer value used to dimension rows in the array declaration for *values*.

The following fragment declares the identifier *chart_val* to be a two-dimensional floating point array with 15 rows and 10 columns (the number of columns in an array cannot exceed 10, which is the maximum number of data series you can display on a single chart).

```
#define ARY_DMN 15
float chart_val [ARYDMN][10];
short aray_dmn = ARYDMN;
```

The *aray_dmn* value must be greater than or equal to the *nmof_valus* argument, and the column dimension in the array declaration must be greater than or equal to the *nmof_seres* argument. Setting *nmof_valus* and *nmof_seres* to values less than the full-dimensional size of the *chart_val* array will allow the plotting of only part of the data contained in *chart_val*.

The *serieslabel* character array holds the labels used in the chart legend. The legend is used to identify each series of data.

COMMON USES Scatter charts are useful when you have a lot of data to show.

RETURNS The *_pg_chartscatter* and *_pg_chartscatterms* functions return a 0 if there were no errors. Any nonzero value indicates that the call did not work.

SEE ALSO

`pg_analyzescatter functions`	*To analyze data for scatter charts*
`_pg_defaultchart`	*To initialize the chart environment*
`_pg_initchart`	*To initialize presentation graphics*

EXAMPLE See the program on the reference page for the *_pg_analyzescatter* function for an example of the *_pg_chartscatter* logic.

_pg_defaultchart

COMPATIBILITY

MSC 3	MSC 4	MSC 5	MSC 6	QC1	QC2	QC2.5	TC1	TC1.5	TC2	TC++	ANSI	UNIX V	XNX	OS2	DOS
			▲		▲	▲		1	1	1					▲

PURPOSE Use the *_pg_defaultchart* routine to initialize variables in the chart environment and thus generate a clean and predictable base on which to build your charts.

SYNTAX

```
short _far _pg_defaultchart (chartenv _far *chrt_env,
          short chrt_type, short chrt_style);
```

`chrt_env`	*The chart environment structure*
`chrt_type`	*_PG_BARCHART, _PG_COLUMNCHART, _PG_LINECHART, _PG_SCATTERCHART, _PG _PIECHART*
`chrt_style`	*Chart style 1 or 2*

EXAMPLE CALL

```
_pg_defaultchart (&chrt_env, _PG_BARCHART, _PG_PLAINBARS);
```

INCLUDES `#include <pgchart.h>` *For function declaration*

DESCRIPTION The *_pg_defaultchart* function initializes all variables in the chart environment that are appropriate to the type of chart specified by the *chrt_type* variable.

The title fields (maintitle and subtitle) are initialized, and you will need to give them a value if you wish to have titles on your chart.

The *chrt_type* argument may be set to one of the following:

_PG_BARCHART

_PG_PIECHART _PG_COLUMNCHART

_PG_SCATTERCHART _PG_LINECHART

The argument for *chrt_styl* may be set to one of two constants, as detailed below:

chrt_type	available *chrt_styl*
Pie	_PG_NOPERCENT, _PG_PERCENT
Bar	_PG_PLAINBARS, _PG_STACKEDBARS
Column	_PG_PLAINBARS, _PG_STACKEDBARS
Line	_PG_POINTANDLINE, _PG_POINTONLY
Scatter	_PG_POINTANDLINE, _PG_POINTONLY

1. The Turbo C and Turbo C++ version of this function is *graphdefaults.*

RETURNS The *_pg_defaultchart* routine returns a value of 0 if there were no errors. Any nonzero value indicates a failure in the operation of the function.

COMMENTS The *_pg_analyzechart* and *_pg_analyzechartms* functions fill the chart environment with the default values for either a single-series or multiseries (respectively) bar, column, or line chart, depending on the type specified by the call to the *_pg_defaultchart* function.

SEE ALSO

`_pg_getchartdef`	*To get the pixel map for a character*
`_pg_setpalette`	*To select a presentation graphics palette*
`_pg_resetstyleset`	*To reset the styleset to default values*
`_pg_getstyleset`	*To get the current styleset values*

EXAMPLE The program accompanying the reference page to *_pg_analyzechart* shows usage of the *_pg_defaultchart* function. This function is also shown in the *STYLSET.C* program on the reference page for *_pg_resetstyleset.*

_pg_getchardef

COMPATIBILITY

MSC 3	MSC 4	MSC 5	MSC 6	QC1	QC2	QC2.5	TC1	TC1.5	TC2	TC++	ANSI	UNIX V	XNX	OS2	DOS
			▲		▲	▲									▲

PURPOSE Your program may require a copy of the pixel bit map for a specified character, and the *_pg_getchardef* function will provide it for you.

SYNTAX

```
short _far _pg_getchardef (short byte_val, unsigned char
                                  _far*byte_def);
```

`byte_val` *The ASCII number of the desired byte value*

`byte_def` *A pointer to an 8x8 bit map array*

EXAMPLE CALL

```
_pg_getchardef (65, byte_storage);
```

INCLUDES `#include <pgchart.h>` *For function declaration*

DESCRIPTION The *_pg_getchardef* routine retrieves the current 8x8 pixel map for the character with the value that matches the ASCII number specified by *byte_val*. The *byte_def* array is used to store the bitmap.

RETURNS The *_pg_getchardef* function returns a value of 0 if there were no errors. Any nonzero value indicates trouble, and, therefore, is an error.

SEE ALSO

`_pg_initchart` *To initialize presentation graphics*

`_pg_setchardef` *To define a character*

COMMENTS The *_pg_getchardef* routine retrieves the bit map for the specified character of the default font, without regard to which font is currently registered. The function should be used only with the 8x8 bit raster fonts of the presentation graphics library and not with Windows (as in Microsoft Windows) fonts.

EXAMPLE See the program on the reference page for the *_pg_analyzescatter* function, for an example of the *_pg _getchardef* logic.

Drawing and Animation

COMPATIBILITY

_pg_getpalette

MSC 3	MSC 4	MSC 5	MSC 6	QC1	QC2	QC2.5	TC1	TC1.5	TC2	TC++	ANSI	UNIX V	XNX	OS2	DOS
			▲		▲	▲		1	1	1					▲

PURPOSE Use the *_pg_getpalette* function to retrieve presentation graphics palette colors, fill patterns, plot characters, and line styles for use by your application.

SYNTAX

```
short _far _pg_getpalette (paletteentry _far *prgf_palet);
```

`prgf_palet` *A pointer to first palette structure in the array*

EXAMPLE CALL

```
_pg_getpalette (pgfr_palet); /* get a palette */
```

INCLUDES `#include <pgchart.h>` *For function declaration*

DESCRIPTION The *_pg_getpalette* function retrieves palette colors, line styles, fill patterns, and plot characters for all of the presentation graphics palettes. The pointer *prgf_palet* points to an array of palette structures that will contain the desired palette values. Presentation graphics palettes are different from the palettes used by the low-level graphics routines.

1. The equivalent Turbo C and Turbo C++ function is *getpalette.*

RETURNS The *_pg_getpalette* version returns a 0 if there were no errors. It returns _BADSCREENMODE value if current palettes have not been initialized by a previous call to the *_pg_setpalette* function.

SEE ALSO

`_pg_defaultchart` *To initialize the chart environment*

`_pg_resetpalette` *To reset the presentation graphics palette*

`_pg_setpalette` *To select a presentation graphics palette*

EXAMPLE In the fragment below, a palette named *pgfr_palet* is interrogated using *_pg_getpalette.* This makes the palette variables available for changing. The process continues as some of the variables are amended with assignment statements and a *memcpy* and then set using the *_pg_setpalette* function. The changes become a part of the current chart environment, and a *_pg_getpalette* call at this point would yield the changed version of the palette.

The fragment then displays a multiseries chart, and it pauses through *getch* to allow the user to examine the chart. The final statement is a call to *_pg_resetpalette* which restores the default version of the presentation graphics palette.

```
_pg_getpalette (pgfr_palet);      /* get default palette    */

pgfr_palet[1].plotchar = 16;
memcpy (pgfr_palet[1].fill, fill1, 8); /* fill masks to palette */

pgfr_palet[1].color = 14;              /* change palette colors */

pgfr_palet[1].style = 0xfcfc;          /* change plt line styles */
_pg_setpalette (pgfr_palet);

_pg_chartms(&chrt_env, time_prd, values, REGNS, QRTR, QRTR,
                                    offices);

getch();
_pg_resetpalette();             /* restore defalt palette*/
```

A working example of the *_pg_getpalette* function may be seen in the program accompanying the reference page for the *_pg_resetstyleset* function.

_pg_getstyleset

COMPATIBILITY

MSC 3	MSC 4	MSC 5	MSC 6	QC1	QC2	QC2.5	TC1	TC1.5	TC2	TC++	ANSI	UNIX V	XNX	OS2	DOS
			▲		▲	▲									▲

PURPOSE The contents of the current styleset can be retrieved through a call to *_pg_getstyleset.*

SYNTAX `void _far _pg_getstyleset (unsigned short _far *styl_set);`

`styl_set` *A pointer to current styleset*

EXAMPLE CALL `_pg_getstyleset (styles);`

INCLUDES `#include <pgchart.h>` *For function declaration*

DESCRIPTION The *_pg_getstyleset* function retrieves the contents of the current styleset. A style set is created automatically to allow you to chart discernable values, with presentation graphics functions, after you have "run out of colors." As noted in the tutorial, a change of color is the first step the graphics functions take when switching between one data series and another. If you have more series than available colors, the functions change the style of the display. In the presentation graphics functions only, the set of available styles is maintained in a styleset, the first element of which is always the border style.

RETURNS There is no return value.

SEE ALSO

`_pg_resetstyleset`	*To reset styleset to default values*
`_pg_defaultchart`	*To initialize the chart environment*
`_pg_setstyleset`	*To select a styleset*

COMMENTS A styleset is valid only with the presentation graphics environment.

EXAMPLE See the program accompanying the reference page for the *_pg_reset-styleset* function.

_pg_hlabelchart

COMPATIBILITY

MSC 3	MSC 4	MSC 5	MSC 6	QC1	QC2	QC2.5	TC1	TC1.5	TC2	TC++	ANSI	UNIX V	XNX	OS2	DOS
			▲		▲	▲									▲

PURPOSE Use the *_pg_hlabelchart* function to write text horizontally on the screen.

SYNTAX

```
short _far _pg_hlabelchart (chartenv _far *chrt_env,
           short x_coord, short y_coord, short txt_colr, char _far
           *labl_txt);
```

`chrt_env`	*The chart environment structure*
`x_coord`	*The* x-*coordinate, expressed as a pixel, for text*
`y_coord`	*The* y-*coordinate, expressed as a pixel, for text*
`txt_colr`	*The code for the text you wish to display*
`labl_txt`	*The actual text for the label*

EXAMPLE CALL

```
_pg_hlabelchart(&chrt_env, 312, 220, 11, "assigned to Barbara");
```

INCLUDES `#include <pgchart.h>` *For function declaration*

DESCRIPTION The *_pg_hlabelchart* function writes text horizontally on the screen. The arguments are pixel coordinates, relative to the upper-left corner of the chart, for the beginning location of the desired text. The text is stored in the *labl_txt* variable.

COMMON USES The text labels displayed by *_h_labelchart* and the related *_v_labelchart* function are not reliant on the data being plotted. That makes them useful for adding notes and comments, such as author and creation date, to a chart. The comments can be written so that they respond to command-line arguments, or they can be #defined so that they may be kept out of the way when the final version of the program is compiled.

RETURNS The *_pg_hlabelchart* function returns a 0 if everything went well and a nonzero value if there was a failure.

SEE ALSO `_pg_defaultchart` *To initialize the charting environment*

`_pg_initchart` *To initialize presentation graphics*

EXAMPLE In the example below, the *y* coordinate is "hard coded" to pixel 220 while the *x* coordinate is written to be 50 percent from the left of the window area (note the cast on the *x* coordinate). The latter is the safer practice because the system will make the necessary adjustments to start it halfway across the chart no matter what kind of video adapter is in use. By contrast, the position of the hard-coded coordinate will not adjust.

```
_pg_hlabelchart(&chrt_env, (short)(chrt_env.chartwindow.x2
*.50F), 220, 11, "David will edit");
```

The example program for the reference entry for *_pg_resetstyleset* shows the *_pg_hlabelchart* function within the context of an operating program.

_pg_initchart

COMPATIBILITY

MSC 3	MSC 4	MSC 5	MSC 6	QC1	QC2	QC2.5	TC1	TC1.5	TC2	TC++	ANSI	UNIX V	XNX	OS2	DOS
			▲		▲	▲									▲

PURPOSE The first step to using presentation graphics in the Microsoft C compiler is to initialize the various variables which support these functions. The *_pg_initchart* routine accomplishes that task for you.

SYNTAX
```
short _far _pg_initchart (void);
```

EXAMPLE CALL
```
_pg_initchart();
```

INCLUDES `#include <pgchart.h>` *For function declaration*

DESCRIPTION The *_pg_initchart* function initializes the presentation graphics package. The variables include the color and style pools and the chartline styleset. The function also builds default palette modes and reads presentation graphics character-font definitions from the disk. This function is required in all programs that use presentation graphics.

RETURNS The return value is 0 if successful; nonzero if not.

SEE ALSO `_pg_setstyleset` *To select a style set*

`_pg_getpalette` *To get the presentation graphics palette*

EXAMPLE The example program accompanying the reference page to *_pg_resetstyleset* shows a use of the *_pg_initchart* function.

_pg_resetpalette

COMPATIBILITY

MSC 3	MSC 4	MSC 5	MSC 6	QC1	QC2	QC2.5	TC1	TC1.5	TC2	TC++	ANSI	UNIX V	XNX	OS2	DOS
			▲		▲	▲									▲

PURPOSE Use *_pg_resetpalette* to reset the presentation graphics palette.

SYNTAX
```
short _far _pg_resetpalette (void);
```

EXAMPLE CALL
```
_pg_resetpalette();  /* reset the palette */
```

INCLUDES `#include <pgchart.h>` *For function declaration*

DESCRIPTION The *_pg_resetpalette* function resets the palette colors, line styles, fill patterns, and plot characters for the presentation graphics palette to the default for the current screen mode. The presentation graphics palette is separate from the palette used by the low-level graphics functions.

RETURNS The return value is 0 if successful; _BADSCREENMODE if the screen mode is not valid.

SEE ALSO `_pg_defaultchart` *To initialize the chart environment*

`_pg_initchart` *To initialize presentation graphics*

EXAMPLE In the example fragment below, a palette named *pgfr_palet* is assessed using *_pg_getpalette*, amended with assignment statements and a *memcpy*, and then set using the *_pg_setpalette* functions. At that time the changes are a part of the current chart environment.

The fragment then displays a multiseries chart and pauses through *getch* to allow the user to examine the chart. The final statement is a call to *_pg_resetpalette* which restores the default version of the presentation graphics palette.

```
_pg_getpalette (pgfr_palet);        /* Get default palette*/

pgfr_palet[1].plotchar = 16;
memcpy (pgfr_palet[1].fill, fill1, 8); /* fill masks to palette*/

pgfr_palet[1].color = 14;           /* change palette colors*/

pgfr_palet[1].style = 0xfcfc;       /* change plt line styles*/

_pg_setpalette (pgfr_palet);

_pg_chartms (&chrt_env, time_prd, valus, RGNS, QTR, QTR, centers);

getch();

_pg_resetpalette();        /* restore default palette */
```

A complete example may be found in the example program that accompanies the *_pg_resetstyleset* function.

_pg_resetstyleset

COMPATIBILITY

MSC 3	MSC 4	MSC 5	MSC 6	QC1	QC2	QC2.5	TC1	TC1.5	TC2	TC++	ANSI	UNIX V	XNX	OS2	DOS
			▲		▲	▲									▲

PURPOSE Use the *_pg_resetstyleset* function to reinitialize the styleset to the default values for the current screen mode.

SYNTAX
```
void _far _pg_resetstyleset (void);
```

EXAMPLE CALL
```
_pg_resetstyleset ();
```

INCLUDES `#include <pgchart.h>` *For function declaration*

Drawing and Animation

DESCRIPTION The *_pg_resetstyleset* functions to reset or reinitialize the styleset within a presentation graphics program. A styleset has no utility outside of the presentation graphics environment. A styleset is created automatically to allow you to chart discernable values, with presentation graphics functions, after you have "run out of colors." As noted in the tutorial, a change of color is the first step the graphics functions take when switching from one data series to another. If you have more series than available colors, the functions change the style of the display. In the presentation graphics functions only, the set of available styles is maintained in a styleset, the first element of which is always the border style.

RETURNS There is no return value.

SEE ALSO

`_pg_getstyleset`	*To get information about current styleset*
`_pg_defaultchart`	*To initialize the chart environment*
`_pg_setstyleset`	*To set a styleset*

COMMENTS A styleset is valid only with the presentation graphics environment.

EXAMPLE This code fragment modifies a styleset, draws a chart, and resets the styleset.

```
_pg_getstyleset (styles);            /* get styles    */
styles[1] = 0x5555;                  /* change border */

_pg_setstyleset (styles);            /* set new       */
_pg_defaultchart (&chrt_env, _PG_BARCHART, _PG_PLAINBARS);
_pg_chartms(&chrt_env, time, vals, AREAS, WKLY, WKLY, losses);
getch();                              /* await response */

_pg_resetpalette();       /* restore default palette */
_pg_resetstyleset();      /* restore style set       */
```

A more complete treatment of the styleset is presented below. It is a modified version of the program accompanying the reference pages for the *_pg_analyzechart* function group. The changes to the styleset make the charts easier to read (especially in black and white) than they were in the earlier example. The results of the program are presented as Figures 18-7 and 18-8. Compare them with the charts shown earlier in Figures 18-5 and 18-6.

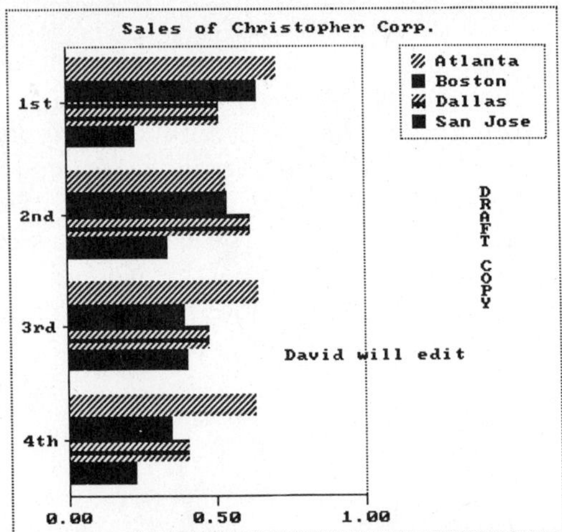

Figure 18-7. *Improved chart with styleset*

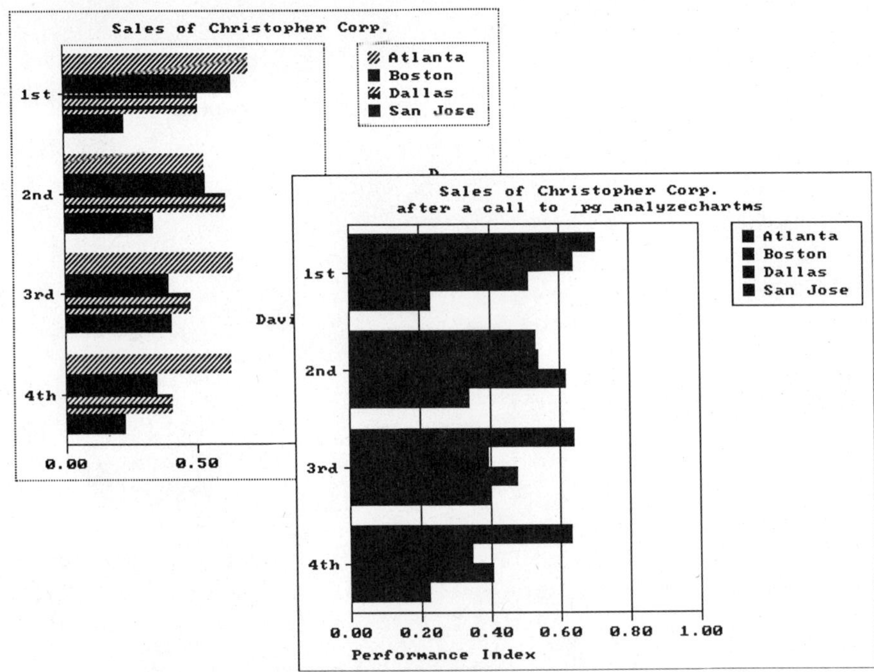

Figure 18-8. *Improved overlaid charts with styleset*

Drawing and Animation

```
include <conio.h>
#include <string.h>
#include <stdlib.h>
#include <graph.h>
#include <pgchart.h>

#define FALSE 0
#define TRUE  1
#define QRTR  4
#define REGNS 4

char  _far *time_prd[QRTR] = {"1st", "2nd", "3rd", "4th"};

char  _far *offices[REGNS] = {"Atlanta","Boston","Dallas","SanJose"};

float _far values[REGNS * QRTR] = { .703F, .529F, .637F, .628F, .638F,
.536F, .392F, .347F, .511F, .612F, .473F, .404F, .232F, .339F, .401F,
.224F};

/* build fill map and declare structures */

fillmap fill1 = { 0x99, 0x33, 0x66, 0xcc, 0x99, 0x33, 0x66, 0xcc};
fillmap fill2 = { 0x99, 0xcc, 0x66, 0x33, 0x99, 0xcc, 0x66, 0x33};

styleset styles;
palettetype pgfr_palet;

void main()

{
    chartenv chrt_env;          /* declare chart nvironment */

    if (!_setvideomode (_MAXRESMODE)) exit (1);
    _pg_initchart();            /* init pg chart system  */

    /* modify the style set.  It contains the global set of line
       styles used for borders, data connectors, and grids, and
       will be read by the next call to _pg_defaultchart. */

   _pg_getstyleset (styles);                  /* get styles    */

   styles[1] = 0x5555;                        /* change border */

   _pg_setstyleset (styles);                  /* set new       */
    _pg_defaultchart (&chrt_env, _PG_BARCHART, _PG_PLAINBARS);
```

```
/* Line styles are set in the palette, not in the the style
   set   */

_pg_getpalette (pgfr_palet);     /* Get default palette*/

pgfr_palet[1].plotchar = 16;

memcpy (pgfr_palet[1].fill, fill1, 8);  /* fill masks to
                                           palette  */

pgfr_palet[1].color = 14;               /* change palette
                                           colors  */

pgfr_palet[1].style = 0xfcfc;           /* change plt line
                                           styles */

pgfr_palet[3].plotchar = 9;
memcpy (pgfr_palet[3].fill, fill1, 5);
pgfr_palet[3].color = 12;
pgfr_palet[3].style = 0xfc02;
_pg_setpalette (pgfr_palet);

/* Multiseries bar chart */

_pg_defaultchart(&chrt_env, _PG_BARCHART, _PG_PLAINBARS);
strcpy(chrt_env.maintitle.title, "Sales of Christopher
       Corp.");

chrt_env.chartwindow.x2 = 364;      /* right edge */

chrt_env.chartwindow.y2 = 340;      /* bottom*/

_pg_chartms(&chrt_env, time_prd, values, REGNS, QRTR, QRTR,
            offices);

/* print labels indicating a DRAFT chart */

_pg_hlabelchart(&chrt_env, (short)(chrt_env.chartwindow.x2 *
                .50F), 220, 11, "David will edit");

_pg_vlabelchart(&chrt_env, 312,

(short)(chrt_env.chartwindow.y2 * .34F), 11, "DRAFT COPY");

getch();
```

Drawing and Animation

```
    _pg_resetpalette();          /* restore default palette */
    _pg_resetstyleset();         /* restore style set       */


   /* analyze a multiseries bar chart */
   _pg_defaultchart(&chrt_env, _PG_BARCHART, _PG_PLAINBARS);


   strcpy(chrt_env.maintitle.title, "Sales of Christopher
          Corp.");


   strcpy(chrt_env.subtitle.title, "after a call to
          _pg_analyzechartms");


   chrt_env.xaxis.autoscale = TRUE;


   _pg_analyzechartms(&chrt_env, time_prd, values, REGNS, QRTR,
                      QRTR, offices);


   /* edit some of the axistype variables */


   chrt_env.xaxis.grid = TRUE;
   chrt_env.xaxis.autoscale = FALSE;
   chrt_env.xaxis.ticinterval = 0.2F;
   chrt_env.xaxis.scalemax = 1.0F;
   strcpy(chrt_env.xaxis.scaletitle.title, "Performance Index");
   chrt_env.xaxis.scaletitle.justify = _PG_LEFT;

   chrt_env.chartwindow.y1 = 120;       /* top edge          */


   chrt_env.chartwindow.x1 = 210;       /* left edge         */


   _pg_chartms(&chrt_env, time_prd, values, REGNS, QRTR, QRTR,
             offices);


   getch();


   _setvideomode (_DEFAULTMODE);
}
```

_pg_setchardef

COMPATIBILITY

MSC 3	MSC 4	MSC 5	MSC 6	QC1	QC2	QC2.5	TC1	TC1.5	TC2	TC++	ANSI	UNIX V	XNX	OS2	DOS
			▲		▲	▲									▲

PURPOSE Use the *_pg_setchardef* function when you wish to set the 8x8 pixel bit map for a specific ASCII character.

SYNTAX

```
short _far _pg_setchardef (short byte_val, unsigned char
                                    _far*byte_def);
```

`byte_val` *ASCII number of character*

`byte_def` *A pointer to 8x8 bit map array*

EXAMPLE CALL

```
_pg_setchardef (66, byte_storage);
```

INCLUDES `#include <pgchart.h>` *For function declaration*

DESCRIPTION The *_pg_setchardef* function sets the 8x8 pixel bit map for the character with the ASCII number *byte_val*. The bit map is stored in the array named *byte_def*.

RETURNS The *_pg_setchardef* routine returns a 0 if there was no error. A returned value that is nonzero indicates an error.

COMMENTS The *_pg_setchardef* routine sets the bit map for the specified character of the default font, without regard to which font is currently registered. The function should be used only with the 8x8-bit raster fonts of the presentation graphics library and not with Windows (as in Microsoft Windows) fonts.

SEE ALSO `_pg_getchardef` *To get a character pixel map*

EXAMPLE See the program on the reference page for the *_pg_analyzescatter* function, for an example of the *_pg_setchardef* logic.

COMPATIBILITY

_pg_setpalette

MSC 3	MSC 4	MSC 5	MSC 6	QC1	QC2	QC2.5	TC1	TC1.5	TC2	TC++	ANSI	UNIX V	XNX	OS2	DOS
			▲		▲	▲									▲

PURPOSE Use the *_pg_setpalette* function to reset the presentation graphics palette.

SYNTAX

```
short _far _pg_setpalette (paletteentry _far *prgf_palet);
```

`prgf_palet` *A pointer to first palette structure in array*

EXAMPLE CALL

```
_pg_setpalette (presgrf_palet);    /* set the palette */
```

INCLUDES `#include <pgchart.h>` *For function declaration*

DESCRIPTION The *_pg_setpalette* routine sets the palette colors, line styles, fill patterns, and plot characters for all presentation graphics palettes. The pointer *prgf_palet* points to an array of palette structures that contains the desired palette values.

RETURNS The *_pg_setpalette* function returns a 0 when it executes without an error. The value _BADSCREENMODE is returned if the screen mode is not valid, for instance, when it is being set to text instead of graphics.

COMMENTS The palettes used in the presentation graphics routines are not the same as the palettes used by the low-level graphics routines.

SEE ALSO

`_pg_resetpalette` *To reset the presentation graphics palette*

`_pg_getpalette` *To get information on the current presentation graphics palette*

EXAMPLE The following example gets the default presentation graphics palette, modifies the line style, fill pattern, and color. The *_pg_setpalette* function then sets the changes.

```
_pg_getpalette (prsgf_plt);                /* get a default         */
prsgf_plt[1].style = 0xfcfc;               /* change line styles    */
memcpy(prsgf_plt[1].fill, filla, 8); /* fills to palette      */
prsgf_plt[1].color = 4;                    /* change colors         */
_pg_setpalette (prsgf_plt);                /* set the palette       */
```

The *_pg_setpalette* function also appears in the major example program which accompanies the reference page for the *_pg_resetstyleset* function.

_pg_setstyleset

COMPATIBILITY

MSC 3	MSC 4	MSC 5	MSC 6	QC1	QC2	QC2.5	TC1	TC1.5	TC2	TC++	ANSI	UNIX V	XNX	OS2	DOS
			▲		▲	▲									▲

PURPOSE Use the *_pg_setstyleset* function to set the current styleset.

SYNTAX

```
void _far _pg_setstyleset (unsigned short _far *styleset);
```

`styleset` *Pointer to the new styleset*

EXAMPLE CALL

```
_pg_setstyleset (new_styl);
```

INCLUDES `#include <pgchart.h>` *For function declaration*

DESCRIPTION The *_pg_setstyleset* function sets the new styleset. A styleset is created automatically to allow you to chart discernable values, with presentation graphics functions, after you have "run out of colors." As noted in the tutorial, a change of color is the first step the graphics functions take when switching between one data series and another. If you have more series than available colors, the functions change the style of the display. In the presentation graphics functions only, the set of available styles is maintained in a styleset, the first element of which is always the border style.

RETURNS The *_pg_setstyleset* function generates no return value.

COMMENTS A styleset is valid only with the presentation graphics environment.

SEE ALSO

`_pg_defaultchart` *To initialize the chart environment*

`_pg_getstyleset` *To get the current style set*

EXAMPLE This code fragment accesses the current styleset with a call to *_pg_getstyleset*, prepares a change for the style of the border in a chart using the assignment statement, and installs the change with a call to *_pg_setstyleset*. The variable *styl* is a styleset.

```
_pg_getstyleset (styl);       /* get current style set   */
 styles[1] = 0x5555;          /* change the border       */
_pg_setstyleset (styl);       /* install the change      */
```

Also, see the example program which accompanies the reference page for the *_pg_resetstyleset* function.

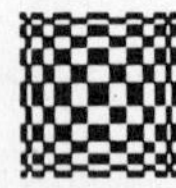

Drawing and Animation

COMPATIBILITY

_pg_vlabelchart

MSC 3	MSC 4	MSC 5	MSC 6	QC1	QC2	QC2.5	TC1	TC1.5	TC2	TC++	ANSI	UNIX V	XNX	OS2	DOS
			▲		▲	▲									▲

PURPOSE The *_pg_vlabelchart* function is used to generate vertical text on a presentation graphics chart.

SYNTAX

```
short _far _pg_vlabelchart (chartenv _far *chrt_env, short x, short y,
                            short txt_colr, char _far *labl_txt);
```

`chrt_env` *The chart environment structure*

`x` *The* x*-coordinate pixel for the text*

`y` *The* y*-coordinate pixel for the text*

`txt_colr` *The color of the text*

`labl_text` *The text of the label*

EXAMPLE CALL `_pg_vlabelchart (&chrt_env, 312, 122, 11, "for the Moose");`

INCLUDES `#include <pgchart.h>` *For function declaration*

DESCRIPTION The *_pg_vlabelchart* function writes text vertically on the screen. The arguments *x* and *y* are pixel coordinates, relative to the upper-left corner of the chart window, for the starting location of the text.

COMMON USES The text labels displayed by *_v_labelchart* and the related *_h_labelchart* function are not reliant on the data being plotted. That makes them useful for adding notes and comments, such as author and creation date, to a chart. The comments can be written so that they respond to command-line arguments, or they can be *#defined* so that they may be kept out of the way when the final version of the program is compiled.

RETURNS The *_pg_vlabelchart* function returns a 0 if there were no errors. Any nonzero value indicates a failure.

SEE ALSO `_pg_hlabelchart` *To write text horizontally on a chart*

EXAMPLE In the example below, the *x* coordinate is "hard coded" while the *y* coordinate is written to be down 20 percent from the top of the window area. The latter is the safer practice because the system will make the necessary adjustments to place it one-fifth the way down the chart, no matter what kind of video adapter is in use. By contrast, the position of the hard-coded coordinate will not adjust. The argument *11* is to set the color of the text. The phrase "DRAFT COPY" is the label that will actually appear.

```
_pg_vlabelchart(&chrt_env, 312, (short)(chrt
_env.chartwindow.y2 *.20F), 11, "DRAFT COPY");
```

A working example may be found in the program that accompanies the *_pg_resetstyleset* reference page.

_pie, _pie_w, _pie_wxy

COMPATIBILITY

MSC 3	MSC 4	MSC 5	MSC 6	QC1	QC2	QC2.5	TC1	TC1.5	TC2	TC++	ANSI	UNIX V	XNX	OS2	DOS
		▲	1	▲	▲	▲		2	2	2					▲

PURPOSE Use *_pie* to draw a filled or bordered wedge whose boundary consists of a segment of an ellipse and lines joining the center of the ellipse to the beginning and the end points of the segment. See below for information on specifying the shape of the *pie*. Use the *_pie_w* version to draw a pie shape in the view coordinate system. The *_pie_wxy* version uses the window coordinate system.

SYNTAX

```
short _far _pie(short flag, short x1, short y1, short x2,
                short y2, short xb, short yb, short xe, short ye);

short _far _pie_w (short flag, double x1, double y1, double x2,
               double y2, double x3, double y3, double x4, double y4);

short _far _pie_wxy (short flag, struct _wxycoord _far
                *a, struct _wxycoord far *b,struct _wxycoord _far
                *c,struct _wxycoord_far *d);
```

`short flag;` *Indicates whether to fill or just draw a border*

`short x1, y1;` *Coordinates of upper-left corner of bounding rectangle of the ellipse to which the curved edge of the pie belongs*

`short x2, y2;` *Coordinates of lower-right corner of bounding rectangle of the ellipse to which the curved edge of the pie belongs*

`short xb, yb;` *The curved edge of the pie begins at the point where a line drawn from the center of the bounding rectangle to* (xb, yb) *cuts the ellipse*

`short xe, ye;`	*The curved edge of the pie ends at the point where a line drawn from the center of the bounding rectangle to* (xe, ye) *cuts the ellipse*
`x1, y1`	*Upper-left corner of bounding rectangle*
`x2, y2`	*Lower-right corner of bounding rectangle*
`x3, y3`	*Start vector*
`x4, y4`	*End vectors*
`pwxy1, pwxy2`	*Upper-left/lower-right corner of bounding rectangle, respectively*
`pwxy3`	*Start vector*
`pwxy4`	*End vector*

EXAMPLE CALL

```
_pie(_GFILLINTERIOR, 0, 150, 150, 200, 0, 150, 0, 200);
```

INCLUDES `#include <graph.h>` *For function declaration*

DESCRIPTION The *_pie* function draws a segment of the ellipse defined in terms of a bounding rectangle whose upper-left corner is (*x1, y1*) and whose lower-right corner (*x2, y2*). Then it constructs a wedge by joining the end points of the segment to the center of the ellipse. Depending on the value of the argument *flag*, the pie is either filled with the current color using the current fill pattern or only a border is drawn in the current color. Use *_setcolor* to select the color and *_setfillmask* to choose a fill pattern.

The curved edge of the pie is drawn as follows (see Figure 18-1). A line is drawn from the center of the ellipse to the point (*xb, yb*). The *_pie* function begins drawing the curved edge at the point where that line intersects the ellipse. The function traces over the underlying ellipse, using the current color, in a counter-clockwise direction until it comes to the point where a line drawn from the center to (*xe, ye*) cuts the ellipse.

The argument *flag* indicates whether the ellipse pie is to be filled or drawn with a border. The value specified for *flag* can be either of the _GFILLINTERIOR or _GBORDER constants, defined in the include file *graph.h*, and listed in Table 18-13.

The *_pie_w* function draws a pie-shaped wedge through a process of drawing an elliptical arc, the center and two endpoints of which are joined by lines. The *_pie_wxy* version uses the window coordinate pairs, and it is thus a *_wxycoord* structure version of *_pie*. See the tutorial for more information about coordinate systems, remembering that the logical coordinate system was dropped from Microsoft C 6.0.

1. *_pie_w* was introduced in version 6.0 as a double float version of _pie. 2. The two Turbo C and Turbo C++ versions of these functions are *pieslice* and *sector.*

COMMON USES This function is useful in programs that prepare "pie charts" for business graphics.

RETURNS The return value is nonzero if everything went well, otherwise *_pie* returns a 0. The variant functions *_w* and *_wxy* perform the same way.

SEE ALSO

`_setcolor`	*To set the current color*
`_setfillmask`	*To set the current fill pattern*

EXAMPLE Write a C program to illustrate how a wedge is drawn with *_pie*. Draw two pieces of pie: one with a border only, the other filled using a fill pattern. (The *_w* and *_wxy* versions behave identically to *_pie*, except for the type of arguments. The program in the tutorial also shows an example of *_pie* usage.)

```
#include <stdio.h>
#include <graph.h>
#define BLUE 1    /* Color number 1 is blue */
#define RED  4    /* Color number 4 is red */
unsigned char fmask[8]=
{ 0xf0, 0xf0, 0xf0, 0xf0, 0xf, 0xf, 0xf, 0xf };

main()
{
/* Enter hi-resolution graphics mode on EGA */
    if (_setvideomode(_ERESCOLOR) != 0)
    {
/* Draw a bordered pie --
 * Note that line style does not affect border
 */
        _settextposition(1,1);
        _outtext("A bordered pie:");
        _setcolor(BLUE);
        _pie(_GBORDER, 0, 50, 150, 100, 0, 100, 0, 50);
/* Draw a filled pie-shaped wedge --
 * this one complements the earlier pie
 */
        _settextposition(10,1);
        _outtext("A filled piece to match:");
        _setcolor(RED);
```

```
        _setfillmask(fmask);
        _pie(_GFILLINTERIOR,
            0, 150, 150, 200, 0, 150, 0, 200);

/* Restore original mode */
/* Give user a chance to see the result */
        _settextposition(20,1);
        _outtext("Hit any key to exit:");

        getch();
        _setvideomode(_DEFAULTMODE);
    }
    else
    {
/* Error setting mode */
        printf("Mode not supported by hardware\n");
    }
}
```

COMPATIBILITY

_polygon, _polygon_w, _polygon_wxy

MSC 3	MSC 4	MSC 5	MSC 6	QC1	QC2	QC2.5	TC1	TC1.5	TC2	TC++	ANSI	UNIX V	XNX	OS2	DOS
			▲			▲		1	1	1					▲

PURPOSE Use the *_polygon* functions to draw or scan fill a polygon.

SYNTAX

```
short _far _polygon (short cntrl, struct xycoord _far *points,
                     short num_pnts);

short _polygon_w (short cntrl, double_far *points, short
                  num_pnts);

short _polygon_wxy (short cntrl, struct _wxycoord _far
                    *points, short num_pnts);
```

`cntrl` _GFILLINTERIOR, _GBORDER. *The* _GBORDER *value means that the figure will not be filled.* _GFILLINTERIOR *specifies that the figure will be filled using current color and fill mask.*

`points` *An array of* xycoord *or* xxycoord *structures specifying the polygon's vertices*

`num_pnts` *The number of vertices*

EXAMPLE CALL
```
_polygon_wxy (fill_list, poly_side, 5);
```

INCLUDES `#include <graph.h>` *For function declaration and definition of action constants*

DESCRIPTION Members of the *_polygon* function family are used to draw polygons. The border for each polygon you draw uses the current color and line style. The *_polygon* function uses view coordinates while the *_polygon_w* and *_polygon_wxy* functions use real valued window coordinates expressed in *_wxycoord* structures. See the tutorial for more detail about coordinate systems.

1. The Turbo C and Turbo C++ version of these functions is *fillpoly.*

RETURNS The *_polygon* functions return a nonzero value if anything is drawn. A value of 0 is returned if nothing is drawn.

COMMENTS Output from these functions is affected by *_setwritemode, _setlinestyle,* and *_setfillmask.*

SEE ALSO

`_setfillmask`	*To set pattern for filling figures*
`_setlinestyle`	*To set style for lines*
`_setwritemode`	*To specify how new and existing images will interact*

EXAMPLE The *_polygon_wxy* function is shown in the example program that accompanies the *_getwritemode* reference page.

_putimage, _putimage_w

COMPATIBILITY

MSC 3	MSC 4	MSC 5	MSC 6	QC1	QC2	QC2.5	TC1	TC1.5	TC2	TC++	ANSI	UNIX V	XNX	OS2	DOS
		▲	1	▲	▲	▲		2	2	2					▲

PURPOSE Use the *_putimage* function to display a rectangular screen image saved in a buffer by *_getimage.* The *_putimage_w* should be used to transfer a buffer image to the screen in the windows coordinate system.

SYNTAX
```
void _far _putimage(short x1, short y1, char _far *image_buffer,
                    short action);

void _far _putimage_w (double wx, double wy, char _huge
                       *buf_img, short action);
```

`short x1, y1;`	*Logical coordinates of point on screen where the upper-left corner of the rectangular image will be placed*
`char _far *image_buffer;`	*Buffer where image has been saved*
`short action;`	*Command to* _putimage *instructing it to redraw the saved image in a particular manner*

`wx, wy`	*Position of upper-left corner of image*
`buf_img`	*Stored image buffer*
`action`	*_GAND, _GOR, _GPRESET, _GPSET, _GXOR*

EXAMPLE CALL

```
_putimage(100, 200, image, _GXOR);

_putimage_w (wx, wy, buf_img, action);
```

INCLUDES

`#include <graph.h>` *For function declaration and definition of action constants*

DESCRIPTION

The *_putimage* function redraws the image of a rectangular region of the screen saved earlier by *_getimage* in the buffer whose address is specified in the argument *image_buffer*. The saved image is drawn with the upper-left corner at the point whose coordinates are (*x1, y1*). The size of the rectangular region need not be specified because this information is saved with the image.

The manner in which the image is redrawn depends on the value of the argument *action*. This argument should be one of the constants defined in the file *graph.h* and shown, along with their meanings, in Table 18-14.

The *_putimage_w* function transfers to the screen the image stored in the buffer *buf_img*. It places the upper-left corner of the image at the window coordinate (*wx, wy*). There is no *_wxycoord* structure version of this function.

The logical coordinate system was dropped from the Microsoft C compiler starting with version 6.0. See the tutorial for more information about coordinate systems.

1. Introduced in version 6.0, *_putimage_w* is the double float version of *_putimage*. 2. The Turbo C and Turbo C++ version of this function is *putimage*.

COMMON USES

The *_putimage* function is used to redraw screen images saved by *_getimage*. For example, you can draw an object, save it by calling *_getimage*, and move it around the screen with *_putimage*, in effect performing animation.

Table 18-14. *Interpreting Action Constants for* _putimage

Constants	Interpretation
_GAND	The image is drawn by performing a logical AND of the existing pixel value with the one from the saved image.
_GOR	The pixel values from the saved image are logically ORed with the existing pixel values in the area where the image is being drawn.
_GPRESET	Each bit in each pixel of the saved image is logically inverted, then these values are transferred to the screen, overwriting the existing image. For example, the areas of a saved EGA screen that were yellow (pixel value 14 = 1110 in binary) become blue (pixel value 1 = 0001 in binary).
_GPSET	The saved image is drawn at the specified area, overwriting any existing image.
_GXOR	Each pixel from the saved image is exclusive-ORed with the current pixels in the area where the image is being drawn. Very useful in animation because exclusive OR of an image with itself erases the image. Thus the background can be restored with this action command.

RETURNS The *_putimage* function does not generate a return value. You should call *_grstatus* immediately upon returning from *_putimage* to check for status.

COMMENTS As noted in greater detail in the tutorial, Microsoft C 6.0 employs three coordinate systems for the low-level graphics functions. (The logical coordinate system of version 5.1 was left out of the later versions; see the tutorial for more information.) They are the physical coordinate system, the viewport (or view) coordinate system, and the window coordinate system. The window coordinate system is also referred to as being "real valued." The graphics functions without a *_w* or *_wxy* suffix use the view coordinate system and take short *ints* for coordinate arguments. Graphics functions with a *_w* suffix use window coordinates and take *doubles* for their coordinate arguments. The graphics functions that end with a *_wxy* suffix take *_wxycoord* structures as arguments.

SEE ALSO

`_imagesize`	*To determine number of bytes necessary to save a screen image*
`_putimage`	*To display a stored image*

EXAMPLE In a graphics mode, draw some graphical objects and save them in memory by calling *_getimage*. Now clear the screen and use *_putimage* to animate the object on the screen. The *_putimage_w* version behaves identically to *_putimage*, except for the type of the arguments.

```
#include <stdio.h>
#include <malloc.h>
#include <graph.h>
#define YELLOW 14
```

```
main()
{
    char _far *image;
    char buffer[80];
    short x=0, y=0;
    unsigned numbytes, c = 0;
/* Assume EGA. Put it in high-resolution graphics mode */
    if (_setvideomode(_ERESCOLOR) == 0)
    {
/* Error setting mode */
        printf("Not EGA hardware\n");
        exit(0);
    }
/* Draw some graphical objects to save */
    _setcolor(YELLOW);
    _ellipse(_GFILLINTERIOR,0,0,10,10);
    _moveto(5,10);
    _lineto(5,20);
    _lineto(0,30);
    _moveto(10,30);
    _lineto(5,20);
    _moveto(0,15);
    _lineto(0,10);
    _lineto(10,15);
/* Determine storage needed for entire screen and
 * display result
 */
        numbytes = (unsigned int)_imagesize(0,0,10,30);
/* Allocate buffer for image */
        if ((image = (char _far *) malloc(numbytes)) ==
             (char _far *)NULL)
        {
            _setvideomode(_DEFAULTMODE);
            printf(
              "Not enough memory for image storage\n");
            exit(0);
        }
        _getimage(x,y,10,30,image); /* Save the image */
/* Now clear screen and draw saved image at several
 * screen locations
 */
        _clearscreen(_GCLEARSCREEN);
        _settextposition(1,1);
        _outtext(
          "Demonstrating animation with _putimage");
```

```
        _setlogorg(320,175);
        _putimage(x,y,image,_GXOR);
        _settextposition(24,1);
        _outtext(
          "q = exit, h=left, j=down, k=up, l=right");
/* Perform some animation */
        while(c != 'q')
        {
            c = getch();
/* First erase at last position */
            _putimage(x,y,image,_GXOR);
            switch(c)
            {
                case 'h': x -= 2; /* 2 pixels left */
                          break;
                case 'l': x += 2; /* 2 pixels right */
                          break;
                case 'j': y += 2; /* 2 pixels down */
                          break;
                case 'k': y -= ?; /* 2 pixels up   */
                          break;
            }
/* Redraw at new position */
            _putimage(x,y,image,_GXOR);
        }
/* Restore mode when done */
        _setvideomode(_DEFAULTMODE);
}
```

_rectangle, _rectangle_w, _rectangle_wxy

COMPATIBILITY

MSC 3	MSC 4	MSC 5	MSC 6	QC1	QC2	QC2.5	TC1	TC1.5	TC2	TC++	ANSI	UNIX V	XNX	OS2	DOS
		▲	1	▲	▲	▲		2	2	2					▲

PURPOSE Use *_rectangle* to draw a filled or a bordered rectangle (see the tutorial section on specifying coordinates). Before calling *_rectangle,* use *_setcolor* to select the fill color, *_setfillmask* to select a fill pattern, and *_setlinestyle* to select a solid or a dashed line for the border.

Use the *_rectangle_w* and *_rectangle_wxy* versions when you are employing the window coordinate system.

SYNTAX

```
short _far _rectangle(short flag, short x1, short y1,
                                  short x2, short y2);
```

```
short _far _rectangle_w (short control, double wx1, double wy1,
                         double wx2, double wy2);

short _far _rectangle_wxy (short control, struct_wxycoord
                           _far*pwxy1, struct _wxycoord _far *pwxy2);
```

`short flag;`	*To fill or to draw a border only*
`short x1, y1;`	*Coordinates of upper-left corner*
`short x2, y2;`	*Coordinates of lower-right corner*
`control`	*_GFILLINTERIOR, _GBORDER*
`wx1, wy1`	*Coordinates of upper-left corner*
`wx2, wy2`	*Coordinates of lower-right corner*
`pwxy1`	*Coordinates of upper-left corner*
`pwxy2`	*Coordinates of lower-right corner*

EXAMPLE CALL

```
_rectangle(_GBORDER, 100, 110, 250, 200);

_rectangle_w (_GBORDER, -4.0, -5.0, 4.0, 5.0);
```

INCLUDES `#include <graph.h>` *For function declaration and definition of fill flag constants*

DESCRIPTION The *_rectangle* function draws a rectangle specified by its upper-left corner (*x1, y1*) and its lower-right corner (*x2, y2*). The *x* coordinates go from left to right, and the *y* coordinates go from top to bottom with (0,0) at the upper-left corner of the screen.

The argument *flag* indicates whether the rectangle is filled or drawn with a border. The value specified for *flag* can be either of the _GFILLINTERIOR or _GBORDER constants, defined in the include file *graph.h*, and listed in Table 18-13.

The *_rectangle_w* function draws a rectangle with the current color, line style, and write mode, using the window coordinate system. It is a double float version of *_rectangle*. The *_rectangle_wxy* version draws a rectangle with the current color, line style, and write mode, using the window coordinate system, but is a *_wxycoord* structure version of *_rectangle*. See the tutorial for more information about the differences between the window coordinate systems.

1. Both *_rectangle_w* and *_rectangle_wxy* were introduced in

Microsoft C 6.0 and are implemented as macros. 2. The Turbo C and Turbo C++ version of this function is *rectangle*.

COMMON USES This function can be used as the basis of a graphics window program because filled or bordered rectangular regions are the building blocks for drawing "windows."

RETURNS The return value is nonzero if everything went well. If there is an error (for example, when the coordinates of the upper-left and lower-right corners do not define a rectangle), *_rectangle* returns a 0. The *_rectangle_w* and *_rectangle_wxy* both return a nonzero value if anything is drawn or a 0 if nothing is drawn.

COMMENTS If you want a rectangle with a border color different from that used to fill the interior, you can first draw the rectangle with a border, then select a new color, and fill it by calling the *_floodfill* function. When you use this approach, the line style for the border must be solid. If the border is a dashed line, *_floodfill* leaks colors through the holes in the border.

SEE ALSO

`_setcolor`	*To set the current color*
`_setlinestyle`	*To set the current line style*
`_setfillmask`	*To set the current fill mask*
`_floodfill`	*To fill a bordered rectangle with color*

EXAMPLE Using a graphics mode appropriate for your graphics hardware, write a C program to draw two rectangles, one bordered and one filled, on the screen. The *_rectangle_w* function is used in the program in the tutorial for Chapter 17. A modified version of that program appears in the reference page of *_ellipse*.

```
#include <stdio.h>
#include <graph.h>
#define BLUE 1    /* Color number 1 is blue */
#define RED  4     /* Color number 4 is red */
main()
{
/* Enter hi-resolution graphics mode on EGA */
    if (_setvideomode(_ERESCOLOR) == 0)
    {
/* Error setting mode */
        printf("Mode not supported by hardware\n");
        exit(0);
```

```
    }
/* Draw a filled rectangle */
    _settextposition(1,1);
    _outtext("A bordered rectangle:");
    _setcolor(BLUE);
    _rectangle(_GBORDER, 0, 50, 100, 100);
/* Draw a filled rectangle */
    _settextposition(10,1);
    _outtext("A filled rectangle:");
    _setcolor(RED);
    _rectangle(_GFILLINTERIOR, 0, 150, 100, 200);

/* Restore original mode */
/* Give user a chance to see the result */
     _settextposition(20,1);
     _outtext("Hit any key to exit:");
     getch();
     _setvideomode(_DEFAULTMODE);
}
```

COMPATIBILITY

_setpixel, _setpixel_w

MSC 3	MSC 4	MSC 5	MSC 6	QC1	QC2	QC2.5	TC1	TC1.5	TC2	TC++	ANSI	UNIX V	XNX	OS2	DOS
		▲	1	▲	▲	▲		2	2	2					▲

PURPOSE Use the *_setpixel* function to set a specific pixel to the current color. The location of the pixel is given in coordinates. The *_setpixel_w* function sets a pixel at the specified window coordinate location to the current color. Remember that logical coordinates are used only in Microsoft C 5.0 and Microsoft C 5.1.

SYNTAX `short _far _setpixel(short x, short y);`

`short _far _setpixel_w (double wx, double wy);`

`short x, y;` *The logical* x *and* y *coordinates of the pixel to be set to current color*

`wx, wy` *The coordinates of the pixel to be set to the current color*

EXAMPLE CALL `_setpixel(120, 95);`

INCLUDES `#include <graph.h>` *For function declaration*

DESCRIPTION The *_setpixel* function first checks to see if the pixel specified by the coordinates (*x,y*) lies within the current clipping region or viewport. If it does, *_setpixel* fills the pixel with the current color.

The *_setpixel_w* function sets a pixel at the specified window coordinate location to the current color. See the tutorial for more information about coordinate systems.

1. The *_setpixel_w* function was introduced in version 6.0 and is a double float version of *_setpixel*. 2. The Turbo C and Turbo C++ version of this function is *putpixel*.

COMMON USES The *_setpixel* function can be used for drawing complicated graphics images with multiple colors.

RETURNS If the pixel is inside the clipping region and *_setpixel* succeeds, it returns the previous pixel value. Otherwise, it returns a –1 to indicate failure. A call to *_setpixel_w* generates the previous value of the target pixel if successful; –1 if not.

COMMENTS The logical coordinate system used in Microsoft C 5.0 and 5.1 has been replaced starting in Microsoft C 6.0.

Microsoft C compiler versions after 5.1 (including Quick C 2.0 and 2.5) use three low-level graphics coordinate systems, two of which were not in 5.0 or 5.1. The three coordinates were originally presented in Quick C 2.0 and are called "physical," "viewport," and "window." The logical coordinate system is no longer in use.

The graphics functions without a *_w* or *_wxy* suffix use the view coordinate system and take short *ints* for coordinate arguments. Graphics functions with a *_w* suffix use window coordinates and take *doubles* for their coordinate arguments. The graphics functions that end with a *_wxy* suffix take *_wxycoord* structures as arguments.

SEE ALSO

`_setcliprgn, _setviewport`	*To define a limited area of the screen as the clipping region for graphics output*
`_getpixel`	*To determine the current value of a pixel*

EXAMPLE In a graphics mode appropriate for your hardware, use *_setpixel* to draw a rectangle filled with many different colored pixels. Except for the type of argument, the *_setpixel_w* version behaves identically to the *_setpixel* function.

```
#include <stdio.h>
#include <graph.h>

main()
{
```

```
    short x, y, color;
/* Assume an EGA environment */
    if (_setvideomode(_ERESCOLOR) == 0)
    {
        printf("Not EGA environment\n");
        exit(0);
    }
    _settextposition(1,1);
    _outtext("Multicolored rectangle using _setpixel");
/* Go over a rectangular region and fill pixels with
 * color
 */
    color = 0; /* Initialize to first color in palette*/
    for(x=50; x<150; x++)
    {
        for(y=40; y<90; y++)
        {
            _setcolor(color);
            _setpixel(x,y);      /* Set pixel to color*/
        }
        color++;                 /* Go to next color  */
       if(color > 15)
            color=0;               /* Color in 0-15  */
    }
/* Wait for user to hit a key, then reset everything  */
    _settextposition(25,1);
    _outtext("Hit any key to reset mode and exit:");
    getch();
    _setvideomode(_DEFAULTMODE);
}
```

COMPATIBILITY

_setwritemode

MSC 3	MSC 4	MSC 5	MSC 6	QC1	QC2	QC2.5	TC1	TC1.5	TC2	TC++	ANSI	UNIX V	XNX	OS2	DOS
			▲			▲									▲

PURPOSE Use the *_setwritemode* function to set the current logical write mode used when you draw lines with the *_lineto*, *_rectangle*, and *_polygon* functions.

SYNTAX `short _far _setwritemode (short action);`

`action` *_GPSET, _GPRESET, _GAND, _GOR, _GXOR*

EXAMPLE CALL `_setwritemode (new_mode);`

INCLUDES `#include <graph.h>` *For function declaration*

DESCRIPTION The *_setwritemode* sets the current logical write mode used by the *_lineto, _rectangle,* and *_polygon* function groups.

There are five modes, each identified as a short integer. The logical write modes are _GAND, which transfers the image over an existing one on the screen; _GOR, which superimposes the image onto an existing image; _GPRESET, which will transfer data point-by-point onto the screen; _GPSET, which also transfers data point-by-point onto the screen; and _GXOR, which causes the points on the screen to be inverted where a point exists in the image buffer.

RETURNS The previous write mode is returned by a successful call to the *_setwritemode* function. A value of a –1 identifies an error.

SEE ALSO `_getwritemode` *To get the current drawing mode*

`_setlinestyle` *To select a style for drawing lines*

EXAMPLE The code fragment below shows how the values yielded and used by the *_getwritemode* function are used.

```
{

   int    oldmode, newmode;
   oldmode = _getwritemode();      /* save old mode */
   _setwritemode (newmode);

      /* perform processing */

   _setwritemode (oldmode);        /* restore original */
}
```

Another example of *_setwritemode* may be found in the example program on the *_getwritemode* reference page.

Drawing and Animation

Chapter 19 Combining Graphics and Text

Introduction

Descriptive text is an essential part of effective graphics. If you prepare, for example, a bar graph or a pie chart, you have to annotate the graph so that the reader can understand the meaning of the plots. Version 5.1 of the Microsoft C compiler provided seven routines to control text output to graphs. Version 6.0 added functions, including several that allowed creation of fonts. You can use these routines, for instance, to position text anywhere on the screen, to select a text color, and to confine text within a window.

Notes on Mixing Graphics and Text

Table 19-1 lists the routines available for text output, for controlling the appearance of text on the screen, and for creating and managing fonts. Table 19-2 categorizes these routines by task. The text output routines work in both graphics and text modes.

TEXT OUTPUT The ANSI C library features such routines as *printf* and *cprintf* to print formatted text on the screen. These routines work in both text and graphics modes, but they will not pick up the current color from the Microsoft graphics model. The *_outtext* routine has been provided to remedy the current color problem. It works with both text and graphics modes.

The *_outtext* function does not have formatting capability, thus it must be sent data that has already been formatted. This is accomplished via the *sprintf* function, which is a string formatting routine. You prepare a formatted string and pass it to *outtext* for display. Here is an example:

```
char string[80]

double result;

     :
sprintf (string, "The result is: %.2f", result);
_outtext (string);
```

This prints the string in the current text color at the current text position, which is updated as each character is displayed.

Table 19-1. *Text Output Routines*

Routine	Description
_getfontinfo	Returns the current font characteristics in a *_fontinfo* structure defined in GRAPH.H. Introduced in Microsoft C 6.0.
_getgtextextent	Returns the width required to print the text string in the current font, using *_outgtext*. Introduced in Microsoft C 6.0.
_getgtextvector	Finds the orientation (horizontal or vertical) for font text output by *_setgtextvector*. Introduced in Microsoft C 6.0.
_gettextcolor	Returns current text color.
_gettextcursor	Determines the current cursor shape in text modes.
_gettextposition	Returns current text position.
_gettextwindow	Gets the boundaries of the current text window. Introduced in Microsoft C 6.0.
_outgtext	Outputs the null terminated string text using the current font and rotation on the screen at the current graphics-output position. Introduced in Microsoft C 6.0.
_outmem	Outputs the specified number of characters from a buffer. Introduced in Microsoft C 6.0.
_outtext	Outputs text to screen at current text position.
_registerfonts	Initializes the font-graphics system. Font files must be registered with the *_registerfonts* function before any other font-related library function can be used. Introduced in Microsoft C 6.0.
_scrolltextwindow	Scrolls the current text window. A positive value for lines scrolls the window up, and a negative value scrolls down. Introduced in Microsoft C 6.0.
_setfont	Finds a single font from the set of registered fonts that has the characteristics specified by the options string and returns the index of that font. Introduced in Microsoft C 6.0.
_setgtextvector	Sets the current orientation for font text output. (0,0) is ignored. Introduced in Microsoft C 6.0.
_settextcolor	Sets the text color to be used in future text output.
_settextcursor	Sets the BIOS cursor attribute (the shape) to a specified value, in text modes. Introduced in Microsoft C 6.0.
_settextposition	Sets the text position where subsequent text output will begin.
_settextrows	Requests the number of text rows to be used in the current video mode. Introduced in Microsoft C 6.0.

Table 19-1. ***(cont.)***

Routine	Description
_settextwindow	Defines a scrolling text display window.
_unregisterfonts	Frees memory previously allocated and used by the *_registerfonts* function. The *_unregisterfonts* routine removes the header information for all fonts and unloads the currently selected font data from memory. Introduced in Microsoft C 6.0.
_wrapon	Toggles an internal flag that enables or disables wrapping of a line of text that extends beyond the window. When disabled, the line is truncated at the boundary of the window.

Table 19-2. ***Text Output Routines by Task***

Task	Routines
Control text cursor.	_gettextcursor, _settextcursor
Control line wrapping.	_wrapon
Control text color.	_gettextcolor, _settextcolor, _settextrows
Management font.	_getfontinfo, _getgtextextent, _getgtextvector, _setgtextvector, _setfont, _registerfonts, _unregisterfonts
Output font.	_outgtext,
Output text.	_outmem, _outtext
Position text on the screen.	_gettextposition, _settextposition
Set up a window.	_gettextwindow, _scrolltextwindow, _settextwindow

TEXT COLOR

The current text color can be set with a call to *_settextcolor*. A companion function, *_gettextcolor*, lets you query the graphics package for the current text color so that it may be saved prior to setting a new one. This allows you to reset to the previous color once your display is complete. You specify the color with a color index. For example,

```
_settextcolor(14);     /* normally yellow */
_outtext (string);
```

prints the string in yellow. Two text modes, _TEXTC40 and _TEXTC80, allow the color numbers to go beyond the maximum allowed in the palette. As noted in Table 17-1, the CGA, EGA, and VGA offer a 16-color text mode. Colors from 0 through 15 are as defined in the palette (see Chapter 17), but color indexes 16 through 31 are also allowed. These generate blinking text using the same colors as found in the 0 through 15 range.

The *_getvideoconfig* function (see Chapter 17) allows you to select text colors and backgrounds that are appropriate for your adapter and monitor combination. A color combination that works well on CGA systems may not be visible on the MDA. (There is no color on the monochrome adapter, so the specified values map to text attributes such as underline, blink, and reverse.)

TEXT WINDOW AND POSITION

The text position parameter is maintained internally by the Microsoft C graphics library. Text positions are always specified in the (row, column) format presented in Chapter 17, even within graphics modes. The *_settextposition* function is used to set the text position and *_gettextposition* is used to find the current value.

All text positions are relative to the upper-left corner of a rectangular area called the "text window." The default text window encompasses the entire physical screen, but smaller windows may be defined with a call to *_settextwindow*. For example, the fragment

```
_settextwindow (10,10,15,70);    /* define a text window */
_clearscreen (_GWINDOW);         /* clear the text window */
_settextposition (2, 30);
_outtext ("Hello, world!");
```

defines a rectangular text window, 15 rows by 60 columns, with the upper-left corner as row and column coordinates (10,10). The *_clearscreen* call clears only the text window, leaving the rest of the physical screen intact. The call to *_settextposition* moves the current text position to the second row and the thirtieth column in the text window (which is the twelfth row and fortieth column of the physical screen) and *_outtext* prints the message.

Text windows can be used to implement pop-up menus or message windows.

LINE WRAP

A long line of text may not fit within the confines of the text window. You can set a flag using the *_wrapon* function which controls whether a line is truncated at the window boundary or is automatically wrapped around (down) to the next line. The call *_wrapon (_GWRAPON)* turns wrapping on. Conversely, substituting *_GWRAPOFF* as the argument turns it off.

FONTS

Video adapters (graphics cards) and monitors combine to display text and, in some cases, graphics. The set of shapes of the text characters of the screen is a "font," and there are dozens of generally recognized font styles. Specialized fonts (those that differ from the default fonts generated by your hardware) first appeared in the Microsoft C compiler in version 6.0. (They were available earlier in Quick C 2.0.)

Understandably, an in-depth discussion of fonts, typesizes, scales, and other elements of the typesetter's art is beyond the scope of this book. We will also not spend much time on vector graphics, bit-mapped graphics, and other terms common to computer graphics and font processing. Our goal is simply to discuss the font tools made available by Microsoft in their C compiler. Two terms you will need to be familiar with are "typeface" and "type size."

The *typeface* is the shape of the character. Microsoft included six font typefaces with the version 6.0 compiler, and they are listed in Table 19-3. The *type size* is the screen area, in pixels, occupied by the characters; it is not directly related to point sizes used in typography. Times Roman 12x6, for example, identifies a Times Roman typeface where characters occupy a screen area (pixel grid) 12 pixels high by 6 pixels wide. The "real" size of the character will depend on the size of each pixel and of the screen area between each pixel.

There are two principal methods of creating fonts, and Microsoft provides three typefaces for each. The first is "bit mapped," in which a character image is defined in a binary map corresponding to precise pixel locations. The second is "vector mapped," in which each character is represented in terms of arcs and lines and is drawn individually on the screen.

The bit-mapped characters tend to have fewer gaps than vector characters, but they are restricted to certain predefined sizes that vary from typeface to typeface. Vector characters, on the other hand, at some cost in appearance, may be scaled through a wide range of sizes.

Table 19-3. ***Typefaces and Charactertistics in Microsoft C 6.0***

Typeface	Mapping	Spacing	Size (in pixels)
Modern	Vector	Proportional	Scaled
Roman	Vector	Proportional	Scaled
Script	Vector	Proportional	Scaled
Courier	Bit	Fixed	13x8, 16x9, 20x12
Helv	Bit	Fixed	13x5, 16x7, 20x8, 13x15, 16x6, 19x8
Tms Rmn	Bit	Fixed	10x5, 12x6, 15x8, 16x9, 20x12, 26x16

USING FONTS

The data from which vector-mapped and bit-mapped fonts are built reside in disk files (extension ".FON") supplied with the compiler. The .FON files are the same as the .FNT files used with the Microsoft Windows product, which means that the utilities and extra fonts available for Windows development may be employed with the C compiler as well. Note that Windows refers to the Microsoft Windows product, and not to the generic types of windows discussed in the graphics chapters of this book.

Font use involves three steps: registering the font, setting the current font from the register, and displaying text using the current font.

FONT REGISTRY

Font registering is the process of organizing selected fonts into a list in memory. The register list contains various data about the fonts, and it is built with a call to the *_registerfonts* function. In this example call

```
short _far _registerfonts (unsigned char _far *font_nam);
```

**font_nam* points to the file name of a desired font. The file name may include wildcards, thus allowing several fonts to be registered with only one function call. A successful call to *_registerfonts* returns the number of fonts registered (failure returns a negative value).

CURRENT FONT The *_setfont* function establishes and returns the current font. It checks to see if the font has been registered, and then reads mapping data from the selected .FON source file. No font may be used unless it has been marked as current.

The definition of the *_setfont* function is:

```
short _far _setfont (unsigned char _far *);
```

It takes a pointer to a character string as the argument. Legal values for the string are presented in the reference pages.

DISPLAY The display step has two parts. The first is to select a screen position (use *_moveto*); the second is to display the text using *_outgtext*. These functions are described in the reference pages.

The following program shows the mechanics of font management and displays each of the six fonts available in Microsoft C 6.0. The output is shown in Figure 19-1. It looks for font files and asks the user for their location if they are not in the current directory. Once found, the fonts are displayed one at a time, after which two fonts are shown in a right-angle format. Notice that all the fonts may appear on the screen at one time. With just a slight shift in addressing and multiple calls to the *_outgtext* routine, a font may be made to appear as having great depth.

At the present time, font rotation may only be done in 90-degree increments.

```
#include <conio.h>
#include <graph.h>
#include <stdio.h>
#include <stdlib.h>
#include <string.h>

#define NUM_FONTS 6

unsigned char *styls[NUM_FONTS] =
{
      "Courier font - bit","Helvetica font - bit","Modern font -
      vector", "Roman font - vector","Script font -
      vector","Times Roman font - bit"
```

Courier font - bit

Helvetica font - bit

Modern font — vector

Roman font — vector

Script font — vector

Times Roman font - bit

Helvetica font - bit

Times Roman font - bit

Helvetica font - bit

Times Roman font - bit

Figure 19-1. ***Output of font program***

```
};

unsigned char *optns[NUM_FONTS] =

{
    "courier","helv","modern","roman","script","tms rmn"
};


void main(void)
{
    unsigned char font_lst[20];
    char fondir[_MAX_PATH];
    struct videoconfig vdocnfg;
    struct _fontinfo fnt_info;
```

```
short cntr, x, y;


/* read .FON files.  Query if not in current directory */

if (_registerfonts ("*.FON") <= 0)

{
     _outtext ("Where are the .FON files located? [path]:      ");

     gets (fondir);

     strcat(fondir, "\\*.FON");
     if (_registerfonts (fondir) <= 0)

     {
          _outtext ("Sorry, I cannot register the fonts");
          exit (1);
     }
}

/* set highest available video mode */

if (!_setvideomode (_MAXRESMODE) ) exit (1);
_getvideoconfig (&vdocnfg);


/* display font names */

for (cntr = 0; cntr < NUM_FONTS; cntr++)

{

     /* build option string in font_lst */
     strcat (strcat (strcpy (font_lst, "t'"), optns[cntr]),
               "'");
     strcat (font_lst, "h35w20b");

     if (_setfont (font_lst) >= 0)
     {
          x = (vdocnfg.numxpixels) /6;
          y = (vdocnfg.numypixels) /12;
          if (_getfontinfo (&fnt_info))
          {
```

```
                    _outtext ("Sorry, I cannot get font
                    information");
                    break;
                }


                _moveto ((cntr * 4), (y * cntr));


                if (vdocnfg.numcolors > 2) _setcolor (cntr + 2);
                /* display text from the array */


                    _setgtextvector (1, 0);
                    _outgtext (styls[cntr]);


                /* show two fonts in right angle format */


                if ((cntr == 1) || (cntr == 5))


                {
                    _moveto (166, (366 + (cntr * 12)) );
                    _setgtextvector( 1, 0 );
                    _outgtext(styls[cntr] );
                    _setgtextvector( 0, 1 );
                    _outgtext(styls[cntr] );
                }
            }
            else
            {
                _outtext ("Sorry, I cannot set the font: ");
                _outtext (font_lst);
            }
        }
        getch();
        _unregisterfonts();
        _setvideomode (_DEFAULTMODE);
}
```

_getfontinfo

COMPATIBILITY

MSC 3	MSC 4	MSC 5	MSC 6	QC1	QC2	QC2.5	TC1	TC1.5	TC2	TC++	ANSI	UNIX V	XNX	OS2	DOS
			▲		▲	▲									▲

PURPOSE Use the *_getfontinfo* routine to get the current font characteristics. They are stored in a structure of type *_fontinfo*, defined in *graph.h*.6.0.

SYNTAX

```
short _far _getfontinfo (struct _fontinfo _far *fnt_bufr);
```

The *_fontinfo* structure is composed of the following members:

`type` *An* int *where 0 = bit-map and 1 = vector*

`ascent` *An* int *specifying the pixel distance from the top to baseline*

`pixwidth` *An* int *measuring character width: 0 = proportional*

`pixheight` *An* int *identifying character height in pixels*

`avgwidth` *An* int *specifying the average width of the characters*

`filename` *An 80-character array to carry the file name and path*

`facename` *A 32-character array that specifies the font name*

EXAMPLE CALL

```
if( _getfontinfo (&fnt_inf))
{

   _outtext( "I cannot find any font information");
   break;

}
```

INCLUDES `#include <graph.h>` *For function declaration*

DESCRIPTION The *_getfontinfo* function gets the characteristics of the current font and stores them in a *_fontinfo* structure. That structure is defined in *graph.h*.

RETURNS The *_getfontinfo* routine returns a negative number if a font has not been loaded or registered. A non-negative number means that the call was successful.

SEE ALSO `_outgtext` *To print text using fonts in graphics mode*

Combining Graphics and Text

EXAMPLE This example program displays all of the fonts supplied with the Microsoft C 6.0 compiler.

```
#include <conio.h>
#include <graph.h>
#include <stdio.h>
#include <stdlib.h>
#include <string.h>

#define NUM_FONTS 6

unsigned char *styls[NUM_FONTS] =

{
     "Courier - bit","Helvetica - bit","Modern - vector",
     "Roman - vector","Script - vector","Times Roman - bit"
};

unsigned char *optns[NUM_FONTS] =
{
     "courier","helv","modern","roman","script","tms rmn"
};

void main(void)
{
     unsigned char font_lst[20];
     char fondir[_MAX_PATH];
     struct videoconfig vdocnfg;
     struct _fontinfo fnt_info;
     short cntr, x, y;

     /* read .FON files.  Query if not in current directory */

     if (_registerfonts ("*.FON") <= 0)

     {

               _outtext ("Where did you put the .FON files? [path]:");
          gets (fondir);
          strcat(fondir, "\\*.FON");

          if (_registerfonts (fondir) <= 0)
          {
               _outtext ("I cannot register the fonts");
               exit (6);
```

```
        }
    }

    /* set highest available mode */

    if (!_setvideomode (_MAXRESMODE) ) exit (1);
    _getvideoconfig (&vdocnfg);

    /* display font names */

    for (cntr = 0; cntr < NUM_FONTS; cntr++)
    {
    /* build option string in font_lst */

        strcat (strcat (strcpy (font_lst, "t'"), optns[cntr]),
             "'");
        strcat (font_lst, "h45w25b");

        if (_setfont (font_lst) >= 0)
        {
            x = (vdocnfg.numxpixels) /6;
            y = (vdocnfg.numypixels / 12) + (_getgtextextent
               (styls[cntr])/12); /* _getgtextextent use */

       /* alternate way to figure y coordinate is y =
          (vdocnfg.numypixels) /12;  */

            if (_getfontinfo (&fnt_info))
            {
                _outtext ("Sorry, I cannot get font
                         information");
                break;
            }

            _moveto ((cntr * 4), (y * cntr));
            if (vdocnfg.numcolors > 2) _setcolor (cntr + 2);

            /* display text from the array */

            _setgtextvector (1, 0);
            _outgtext (styls[cntr]);
        }
        else
        {
            _outtext ("I cannot set the font: ");
```

```
                _outtext (font_lst);
            }
        }
        getch();
        _unregisterfonts();
        _setvideomode (_DEFAULTMODE);
    }
```

COMPATIBILITY

_getgtextextent

MSC 3	MSC 4	MSC 5	MSC 6	QC1	QC2	QC2.5	TC1	TC1.5	TC2	TC++	ANSI	UNIX V	XNX	OS2	DOS
			▲		▲	▲									▲

PURPOSE Use the *_getgtextextent* function to find the width (in pixels) needed to print a given string.

SYNTAX

```
short _far _getgtextextent (unsigned char _far *text);
```

`text` *Text to be analyzed*

EXAMPLE CALL

```
x = (vc.numypx/2) + (_getgtextextent (fce[fontx])/2);
```

INCLUDES `#include <graph.h>` *For function declaration*

DESCRIPTION The *_getgtextextent* function tells you how many pixels are necessary for the *_outgtext* routine to print the text string in the current font.

COMMON USES Font management, particularly of scaleable fonts, includes figuring out whether the string you are about to display will fit on the screen. You can add the return value of *_getgtextextent* to the coordinate of the text start position and subtract that from the total number of available pixels. If your answer is positive you have room. If it is not, you can either scale the font to a smaller size (or choose a smaller bit-mapped font), reduce the length of the text, or some combination of the two.

RETURNS The *_getgtextextent* function returns the width, in pixels, if the call is a success. A value of –1 indicates that the font has not been registered.

SEE ALSO `_getfontinfo` *To get current font characteristics*

EXAMPLE See the example program on the reference page for *_getfontinfo*.

_getgtextvector

COMPATIBILITY

MSC 3	MSC 4	MSC 5	MSC 6	QC1	QC2	QC2.5	TC1	TC1.5	TC2	TC++	ANSI	UNIX V	XNX	OS2	DOS
			▲			▲									▲

PURPOSE Use the *_getgtextvector* function to identify in 90-degree increments the current vector of fonted-text output.

SYNTAX
```
short xycoord _far _getgtextvector (void);
```

EXAMPLE CALL
```
_getgtextvector (void);
```

INCLUDES `#include <graph.h>` *For function declaration*

DESCRIPTION The *_getgtextvector* function finds the orientation for fonted text that is output by the *_outgtext* function. The orientation of fonted text is determined by a two value (*x,y*) construction for which the following are legal values:

(0,0)	leave unchanged
(1,0)	horizontal text (the default)
(0,1)	rotate 90 degrees, counter-clockwise
(−1,0)	rotate 180 degrees
(0,−1)	rotate 270 degrees, counter-clockwise

RETURNS The *_getgtextvector* routine returns the vector determining the direction of font text rotation. It is in the form of an *xycoord* structure, as defined in *graph.h*, which contains two shorts. The declaration looks like this:

```
struct xycoord { short xcoord; short ycoord; };
```

The values identified in the DESCRIPTION section are returned in the structure.

SEE ALSO `_outgtext` *To display text using a font in graphics mode*

EXAMPLE This example program is a modified copy of the example program shown on the *_getfontinfo* reference page. A structure to return the *_getgtextvector* has been added to the declaration section, and an intentional error leading to a "goto" statement provides the context for the *_getgtextvector* statement.

```
#include <conio.h>
#include <graph.h>
```

```
#include <stdio.h>
#include <stdlib.h>
#include <string.h>

#define NUM_FONTS 6

unsigned char *styls[NUM_FONTS] =
{
     "Courier","Helvetica","Modern",
     "Roman","Script","Times Roman"
};

unsigned char *optns[NUM_FONTS] =

{
     "courier","helv","modern","roman","script","tms rmn"
};

void main(void)
{
     unsigned char font_lst[20];
     char fondir[_MAX_PATH];
     struct videoconfig vdocnfg;
     struct xycoord fnt_vctr;
     /* added for this sample program */

     struct _fontinfo fnt_info;

     short cntr, x, y;

     /* read .FON files.  Query if not in current directory */

     if (_registerfonts ("*.FON") <= 0)
     {
          outtext ("Where are the .FON files located? :
                  ");
          gets (fondir);
          strcat(fondir, "\*.FON");
          if (_registerfonts (fondir) <= 0)
          {
               _outtext ("Sorry, I cannot register the fonts");
               exit (1);
          }
     }
     /* set highest available mode */
```

```
if (!_setvideomode (_MAXRESMODE) ) exit (1);
_getvideoconfig (&vdocnfg);

/* display font names */

for (cntr = 0; cntr < NUM_FONTS; cntr++)
{
/* build option string in font_lst */

     strcat (strcat (strcpy (font_lst, "t'"), optns[cntr]),
          "'");
     strcat (font_lst, "h35w20b");
     if (_setfont (font_lst) >= 0)
     {
          x = (vdocnfg.numxpixels) /6;
          y = (vdocnfg.numypixels) /12;
          if (_getfontinfo (&fnt_info))
          {
               _outtext ("Sorry, I cannot get font
                         information");
               break;
          }
          /* show fonts in right angle format */

          if (cntr == 1)
          {
               _moveto (166, (150 + (cntr * 12)) );
               _setgtextvector (1, 0);
          _outgtext (styls [cntr]);
          _setgtextvector (0, 1);
          _outgtext (styls[cntr]);

     /* intended error in usage of _getgtextvector*/

          fnt_vctr = _getgtextvector ();
          if ((fnt_vctr.xcoord) > 200) goto BAD;

     /* end of intended error section */
          }
     }
     else
     {
          _outtext ("Sorry, I cannot set the font: ");
          _outtext (font_lst);
```

Combining Graphics and Text

```
        }
    }

    BAD: printf("Error in _getgtextvector: press any key");
    getch();  /* note the goto LABEL */
    _unregisterfonts();
    _setvideomode (_DEFAULTMODE);
}
```

COMPATIBILITY

_gettextcolor

MSC 3	MSC 4	MSC 5	MSC 6	QC1	QC2	QC2.5	TC1	TC1.5	TC2	TC++	ANSI	UNIX V	XNX	OS2	DOS
		▲	▲	▲	▲	▲		1	1	1				▲	▲

PURPOSE Use the *_gettextcolor* function to get the value of the current text color parameter (see *_settextcolor* for interpretation of the value). Also, note that only *_outtext* uses this text color value; other C routines such as *printf* are not affected.

SYNTAX `short _far _gettextcolor(void);`

EXAMPLE CALL `txt_color_now = _gettextcolor();`

INCLUDES #include <graph.h> *For function declaration*

DESCRIPTION The *_gettextcolor* function returns the value of the current text color parameter maintained internally by the graphics package. This color is only used by *_outtext* to determine the color of the text it displays. The standard C library routine for text output, *printf*, does not use this color.

1. The Turbo C and Turbo C++ function is *gettextinfo.*

COMMON USES The *_gettextcolor* function allows you to save the current text color before changing it. By doing so, you can restore the color to its original value before exiting from your routine.

RETURNS The *_gettextcolor* function returns a short integer containing the current value of the text color parameter.

SEE ALSO `_settextcolor` *To set the current text color to a new value*

EXAMPLE In text mode, set the color to a specific value by calling *_settextcolor.* Then call *_gettextcolor* to verify that the current color is what you expect it to be. Also display a string to show the color.

```
#include <stdio.h>
#include <graph.h>
#define RED 4       /* Text color 4 means red */
main()
{
    char buffer[80];
    short color;
/* Assume we are already in text mode */
    _clearscreen(_GCLEARSCREEN);        /* Clear screen */
    _gettextposition(1,1);    /* set up text position  */
    _settextcolor(RED);       /* Set text color to RED */
    color = _gettextcolor();      /* Get current color */
    sprintf(buffer,"_gettextcolor says: current color \
= %2d\n", color);         /* Display the current color */
    _outtext(buffer);
    _outtext("The value should be 4\n");
}
```

_gettextcursor

COMPATIBILITY

MSC 3	MSC 4	MSC 5	MSC 6	QC1	QC2	QC2.5	TC1	TC1.5	TC2	TC++	ANSI	UNIX V	XNX	OS2	DOS
			▲		▲	▲								▲	▲

PURPOSE Use the *_gettextcursor* function to find out the cursor shape in the text modes.

SYNTAX

```
short _far _gettextcursor (void);
```

EXAMPLE CALL

```
_gettextcursor();
```

INCLUDES `#include <graph.h>` *For function declaration*

DESCRIPTION The *_gettextcursor* function determines, while the system is in text modes, the current shape of the cursor. The legal values for the low-byte and high-byte (which correspond to the top and bottom line of the cursor) are a range from 0 through 7, of which three popular examples are:

0x0707 Underline

0x0007 Full block cursor

0x0607 Double underline

A value of 0x2000 means that no cursor is showing.

Combining Graphics and Text

RETURNS The *_gettextcursor* returns the current cursor attribute if the call is successful. A –1 value indicates that the call failed, typically because it was called from a graphics mode. The *_grstatus* value is *_GRNOTINPROPERMODE.*

EXAMPLE The example program preserves the current cursor with a call to the *_gettextcursor* function, walks the user through a display that shows seven different patterns for the cursor, and closes with a call to the *_settextcursor* function that restores the original cursor shape.

```
#include <conio.h>
#include <stdio.h>
#include <graph.h>

/* the CRSR_SHAPE macro helps prepare the argument for the
   _settextcursor function.                                   */

#define CRSR_SHAPE(top,crsr_btm) (((top) < 8) | (crsr_btm))

void main()
{
    short old_shape, new_shape;
    char  buffer[80];
    unsigned char crsr_top, crsr_btm;
    old_shape = _gettextcursor();     /* save current cursor */
    _clearscreen (_GCLEARSCREEN);
    _displaycursor (_GCURSORON);      /* turn cursor on      */
                                      /* change cursor shape */

    for (crsr_top = 7, crsr_btm = 7; crsr_top; crsr_top--)
    {
        _settextposition (1, 1);
        sprintf (buffer, "cursor top is at line %d ", crsr_top);
        _outtext (buffer);
        new_shape = CRSR_SHAPE (crsr_top, crsr_btm);
        _settextcursor (new_shape);
        getch();
    }

    _settextcursor (old_shape);
    _clearscreen (_GCLEARSCREEN);
}
```

_gettextposition

COMPATIBILITY

MSC 3	MSC 4	MSC 5	MSC 6	QC1	QC2	QC2.5	TC1	TC1.5	TC2	TC++	ANSI	UNIX V	XNX	OS2	DOS
		▲	1	▲	▲	▲		2	2	2				▲	▲

PURPOSE Use *_gettextposition* to retrieve the current text position in a structure of type *rccoord* that contains the current row and column where text output appears if you call the output function *_outtext* or any other standard C output routine such as *printf*.

SYNTAX

```
struct rccoord _far _gettextposition(void);
```

EXAMPLE CALL

```
row_col_pos = _gettextposition();
```

INCLUDES `#include <graph.h>` *For function declaration and definition of the structure* rccoord

DESCRIPTION The *_gettextposition* function returns the current text position which is maintained internally by the graphics package. The current row and column are returned in the structure *rccoord.* This is the position where text appears if you call the graphics library function *_outtext* or standard C I/O routines such as *printf.*

1. Changed in Microsoft C 6.0 to provide OS/2 capability. 2. The Turbo C and Turbo C++ functions are *wherex* and *wherey.*

COMMON USES The *_gettextposition* function can be used to save the current text position before changing it for the specific purposes of your routine. That way, the saved value can be used to reset the text position to its original value before exiting your routine.

RETURNS The *_gettextposition* function returns a structure of type *rccoord* containing the row and column defining the current text position. This structure, shown below, is declared in the include file *graph.h.*

```
struct rccoord      /* Structure for text position   */
{
    short row;      /* row number of text position    */
    short col;      /* column number of text position */
};
```

COMMENTS The *_settextposition* function also returns the last text position in the form of a *rccoord* structure, but you have to move to a new position (calling *_settextposition* implies this) to find out the current row and column posi-

tion. You can get this information in a more straightforward manner by calling *_gettextposition.*

SEE ALSO `_settextposition` *To change current text position*

EXAMPLE In a text mode, move to a specific text position by calling *_settextposition.* Verify that *_gettextposition* returns the same location. Display a sample text string showing the results obtained from *_gettextposition* at that location.

```
#include <stdio.h>
#include <graph.h>
main()
{
/* Assume we are already in text mode */
    struct rccoord curpos;
    short row = 1;
    char c=0, buffer[80];
    _clearscreen(_GCLEARSCREEN);    /* Clear screen */
    _settextposition(1,1);
    _outtext("1234567.. This is row 1");
    _settextposition(2,2);
    curpos = _gettextposition(); /* get new position */
    sprintf(buffer, "This string begins at (%d,%d)",
                curpos.row, curpos.col);
    _outtext(buffer);
}
```

COMPATIBILITY

_gettextwindow

MSC 3	MSC 4	MSC 5	MSC 6	QC1	QC2	QC2.5	TC1	TC1.5	TC2	TC++	ANSI	UNIX V	XNX	OS2	DOS
			▲			▲	1	1	1	1				▲	▲

PURPOSE Use the *_gettextwindow* to find the boundaries of the current text window.

SYNTAX

```
void _far _gettextwindow (short _far *r1, short _far *c1,
                          short _far *r2, short _far *c2);
```

`r1` *Top row of current text window*

`c1` *Leftmost column of current text window*

r2 *Bottom row of current text window*

c2 *Rightmost column of current text window*

EXAMPLE CALL `_gettextwindow (&top, &lft, &btm, &rgh);`

INCLUDES `#include <graph.h>` *For function declaration*

DESCRIPTION The *_gettextwindow* function is used to find the boundaries of the current text window. Four shorts are returned that give you the left, top, bottom, and right boundaries of the text window.

1. The Turbo C and Turbo C++ equivalent of this function is provided in the separate functions *wherex* and *wherey*.

RETURNS There is no return value.

SEE ALSO `_settextwindow`

COMMENTS The text window is the screen region to which output from *_outtext* and *_outmem* is limited. This is, by default, the entire screen—unless you redefine it with a call to the *_settextwindow* function.

A screen definition using the *_settextwindow* routine has no effect on *_outgtext* output. Displaying text via the *_outgtext* routine is limited to the current viewport.

EXAMPLE The example program (a modification of the program on the reference page for *_setvideomoderows* in Chapter 17) sets and gets a text window and uses the values to tell the user the top and left values for the text window.

```
   /*The purpose of this program is to give an example usage for
     the _settextwindow and _gettextwindow functions*/

#include <conio.h>
#include <stdio.h>
#include <graph.h>

short vd_mds[] = {_TEXTBW40,  _TEXTC40,  _TEXTBW80,  _TEXTC80};

char *vd_lbl[] = {"TEXTBW40", "TEXTC40", "TEXTBW80", "TEXTC80"};

short no_rows[]= { 43, 25 };  /* number of rows  */

void main()
```

```
{
   short cntr1, cntr2, row, y, w, x, num =
   sizeof(vd_mds)/sizeof(vd_mds[0]);
   struct videoconfig vdo_cfg;

   short top, lft, btm, rgh;     /* gettextwindow values */
   char scratch [512];           /* scratch buffer */
   _displaycursor (_GCURSOROFF);

   /* try each mode */
   for (cntr1 = 0; cntr1 <= num; cntr1++)
   {
      for (cntr2 = 0; cntr2 < 2; cntr2++)
      {
         /* try both row values */
         row = _setvideomoderows (vd_mds[cntr1], no_rows[cntr2]);
         if ((!row) || (no_rows[cntr2] != row))
            continue;
         else
         {
            _getvideoconfig (&vdo_cfg);
            x = (vdo_cfg.numtextcols - 25) / 2;
            y = (vdo_cfg.numtextrows - 12) / 2;
            /* orient output to the middle of the screen */
            _settextwindow( y, x,
            vdo_cfg.numtextrows - y, vdo_cfg.numtextcols - x );

            _gettextwindow (&top, &lft, &btm, &rgh);

            /* set data to a string */

            w  = sprintf (scratch,   "mode: %s\n",
                          vd_lbl[cntr1]);

            w += sprintf (scratch+w, "rows: %d\n",
                          vdo_cfg.numtextrows);

            w += sprintf (scratch+w, "mntr: %d\n",
                          vdo_cfg.monitor);

            w += sprintf (scratch+w, "mmry: %d\n",
                          vdo_cfg.memory);

            /* use values from _gettextwindow */
```

```
                w += sprintf (scratch+w, "top:  %d\n", top);
                w += sprintf (scratch+w, "lft:  %d",   lft);

                _outtext (scratch);      /* display string */
                getch();
            }
        }
    }

    _displaycursor (_GCURSORON);
    _setvideomode  (_DEFAULTMODE);
}
```

_outgtext

COMPATIBILITY

MSC 3	MSC 4	MSC 5	MSC 6	QC1	QC2	QC2.5	TC1	TC1.5	TC2	TC++	ANSI	UNIX V	XNX	OS2	DOS
			▲		▲	▲									▲

PURPOSE Use the *_outgtext* to output graphic text to the screen.

SYNTAX

```
void _far _outgtext (unsigned char _far *txt_strng);
```

`txt_strng` *The text to be displayed*

EXAMPLE CALL

```
_outgtext (styls [cntrl]);
```

INCLUDES `#include <graph.h>` *For function declaration*

DESCRIPTION The *_outgtext* function outputs the null-terminated string pointed to by the *txt_strng* argument. It uses both the current font and current rotation on the screen, at the current graphics output position.

The *_outgtext* function does not provide any formatting, unlike standard console I/O routines such as *printf*; however, the string can be formatted before printing by using the *sprintf* function.

The *_outgtext* routine updates the current graphics position after it completes its display task. It operates only in graphics video modes such as _MRES4COLOR, and the color of the text is set by the graphics function *_setcolor* and not the text-based *_settextcolor* routine.

RETURNS There is no return value.

SEE ALSO `_setfont` *To set current text font*

`_setcolor` *To set current text color*

Combining Graphics and Text

COMMENTS Use of *_outgtext* (or *_setfont*) after a call to *_unregisterfonts* will generate an error.

EXAMPLE See the example program for the entry for *_getfontinfo* and the font program at the end of the tutorial for examples of the use of *_outgtext.*

COMPATIBILITY

_outmem

MSC 3	MSC 4	MSC 5	MSC 6	QC1	QC2	QC2.5	TC1	TC1.5	TC2	TC++	ANSI	UNIX V	XNX	OS2	DOS
			▲			▲								▲	▲

PURPOSE Use the *_outmem* function to display text while your system is set to a graphics mode.

SYNTAX

```
void _far _outmem (unsigned char _far *text, short num_bytes);
```

`text` *The text to be displayed*

`num_bytes` *The number of characters you wish to display*

EXAMPLE CALL This code fragment shows the measurement of the output string so that an argument of accurate length can be passed to the *_outmem* function.

```
length = sprintf (out_bufr, "%4d %c", e, y);

_outmem (out_bufr, length);
```

INCLUDES `#include <graph.h>` *For function declaration*

DESCRIPTION The *outmem* function displays characters from a buffer. The number of characters it displays is set by the length argument, which is *num_bytes* in the syntax example above.

The *_outmem* function prints all characters literally, including 0x13, 0x00, and 0x00 as equivalent graphics characters. There is no formattting provided (a workaround is discussed below) and text is printed using current text color at the current text position. The function will not work with special fonts; for these you must use *_outgtext.*

COMMON USES Graphics modes do not allow the use of text functions such as *printf.* The *_outmem* function combined with *sprintf* provides partial relief. Values are sent to a buffer by *sprintf,* and the buffer is displayed by *_outmem.* This essentially gives you *printf* capability within the graphics modes, which is important for both the final application and debugging it along the way. It will not, however, let you get around the fact that newline characters and other similar byte values print as graphic values—just as they do in a hex dump of a screen.

Another way to deal with the problem of formatting is shown in the example program. It involves using the *textposition* functions to handle line feed (and potentially tab) operations.

RETURNS There is no return value.

SEE ALSO `_outtext` *To display text in graphics mode*

EXAMPLE This code fragment is similar to several other font programs within this chapter. It has been modified to use the *_outmem* function, and it shows how to use the *textposition* functions to work around the inability of *_outmem* to deal with formatting characters such as a newline.

```
#include <conio.h>
#include <graph.h>
#include <stdio.h>
#include <stdlib.h>
#include <string.h>

#define NUM_FONTS 6

unsigned char *styls[NUM_FONTS] =
{
     "Courier","Helvetica","Modern",
     "Roman","Script","Times Roman"
};

unsigned char *optns[NUM_FONTS] =
{
     "courier","helv","modern","roman","script","tms rmn"
};

void main(void)

{
     unsigned char font_lst[20];
     char fondir[_MAX_PATH];
     char scratch [200];     /* for use with _outmem() */
     struct rccoord txt_pos;
     struct videoconfig vdocnfg;
     struct _fontinfo fnt_info;
     short cntr, x, y, num_bytes;
```

```
        /* read .FON files.  Query if not in current directory */

        if (_registerfonts ("*.FON") <= 0)
        {
             _outtext ("Where are the .FON files located? [path]:");

             gets (fondir);
             strcat(fondir, "\*.FON");
             if (_registerfonts (fondir) <= 0)
             {
             /* this use of _outmem() will almost work - except that
                the newline character behaves as a graphic value
                and thus there is no newline on the screen
             */

                  _outmem ("\nSorry, I cannot register the fonts",
                              36);

             /* a more complete way of handling the display
            (assuming  you simply must use _outmem() in the first
             place) is to increment the current row value and then
             you can forget having to use a newline
             */

              /* adjust text position */

            txt_pos = _gettextposition();
            txt_pos.row = txt_pos.row + 1;
            _settextposition (txt_pos.row, 0);
            _outmem ("Sorry, I cannot register the fonts", 34);
             exit (9);

            }
        }
}
```

_outtext

COMPATIBILITY

MSC 3	MSC 4	MSC 5	MSC 6	QC1	QC2	QC2.5	TC1	TC1.5	TC2	TC++	ANSI	UNIX V	XNX	OS2	DOS
		▲	1	▲	▲	▲		2	2	2				▲	▲

PURPOSE Use the *_outtext* function to display null-terminated C strings (arrays of characters that end with a byte containing zero) at the current text position (see *_settextposition*) using the current text color (see *_settextcolor*). To display formatted strings, first prepare output in a buffer by calling *sprintf*, and then display the buffer by calling *_outtext* with the buffer address as the argument (see the example below).

SYNTAX

```
void _far _outtext(char _far *buffer);
```

`char _far *buffer;` *Pointer to character buffer that holds the null-terminated string to be printed by* _outtext

INCLUDES `#include <graph.h>` *For function declaration*

DESCRIPTION The *_outtext* function displays on the screen the string whose address is specified in the argument *buffer*. The text output begins at the current text position and uses the current text color. These parameters can be set by calling the graphics library routines *_settextposition* and *_settextcolor*. The text output always occurs in the current page (a portion of video memory that can hold one screenful of text), which is set by calling *_setactivepe*.

After displaying the string, *_outtext* updates the current text position to the screen location next to the last character printed. If a text window is defined by calling *_settextwindow*, text display is confined to this window. If a line spills beyond the window, it is either wrapped around or clipped according to an internal flag set by the function *_wrapon*.

1. Changed in Microsoft C 6.0 to provide OS/2 capability. 2. The Turbo C and Turbo C++ function is *outtext*.

COMMON USES The *_outtext* function is used extensively for displaying text in both text and graphics modes. Its ability to display text in various colors is especially handy in designing text-oriented user interfaces that use color to highlight output.

COMMENTS You will often want to display formatted text, for example, text that includes the ASCII representation of an integer value. Note that *_outtext* is not capable of any formatting. So, in these cases, you should first prepare the formatted string by calling *sprintf* and then display the string using *_outtext*.

Combining Graphics and Text

SEE ALSO

`_setactivepage`	*To set the block of video memory (page) where text is actually entered*
`_settextcolor`	*To change the current text color*
`_settextposition`	*To set the row and column coordinates where text output will begin*
`_settextwindow`	*To define a window within which text is output*
`_wrapon`	*Control whether text that extends beyond the display region gets wrapped or clipped*

EXAMPLE Suppose you are in a text mode. Define a window for text by calling *_settextwindow*. Make the window stand out by setting a new background color with *_setbkcolor* and calling *_clearscreen* to clear the text window and fill it with the new background color. Select an appropriate text color and display some text by using *_outtext*.

```
#include <stdio.h>
#include <graph.h>
/* Need a "long" constant for _setbkcolor  */
#define RED    4L
/* Text color number 14 is yellow          */
#define YELLOW 14
main()
{
    char buffer[80];        /* Buffer for text string */
/* Assume we are already in text mode                 */
    _clearscreen(_GCLEARSCREEN);   /* Clear screen    */
    _settextwindow(10,10,15,70);/* Define text window*/
    _setbkcolor(RED); /* Set background color to red */
    _clearscreen(_GWINDOW);      /* clear text window */

/* Once a text window is defined all text positions are
 * relative to upper-left corner of the window. Notice
 * that this can be used for pop-up menus
 */
    _settextposition(1,10); /* Set text position     */
    _settextcolor(YELLOW);  /* Set text color        */
    _outtext("_outtext in a text window\n");
/* We'll be in the next line because of the '\n'     */
/*  Prepare a formatted string and display it        */
    sprintf(buffer,
 "This line begins at = (%d,%d) and in color = %d\n",
```

```
(_gettextposition()).row,  /* position is  returned */
(_gettextposition()).col,  /* in a structure        */
_gettextcolor());
   _outtext(buffer);
}
```

_registerfonts

COMPATIBILITY

MSC 3	MSC 4	MSC 5	MSC 6	QC1	QC2	QC2.5	TC1	TC1.5	TC2	TC++	ANSI	UNIX V	XNX	OS2	DOS
			▲		▲	▲			1	1					▲

PURPOSE The first step to take when using the fonts graphics system is to initialize it. The *_registerfonts* function performs that task.

SYNTAX

```
short _far _registerfonts (unsigned char _far *pathname);
```

`pathname` *Pathname specifying the .FON files to be registered*

EXAMPLE CALL

```
if (_registerfonts ("*.FON") <= 0)
```

INCLUDES `#include <graph.h>` *For function declaration*

DESCRIPTION The *_registerfonts* function initializes the font graphics system. Font files must be registered with the *_registerfonts* function before any of the other font-related library functions can be used. Those functions are *_getgtextextent, _outgtext, _setfont,* and *_unregisterfonts.*

1. Equivalent Turbo C 2 and TC++ functions are *installuserfont, registerbgifont,* and *registerfarbgifont.*

RETURNS The *_registerfonts* routine returns the number of fonts registered if successful. A negative value means that the call failed.

SEE ALSO `_getfontinfo` *To get information about the current font*

EXAMPLE The code fragment below searches the current directory for fonts; the default extension is .FON. If no fonts are found, the user is queried for a path. This logic could be modified to read an environment variable, for instance, so that it could search several directories. This logic may also be seen in the font program in the tutorial.

Note that the user prompts use *_outtext* and not *_printf.* This is a graphics-mode program, and text-mode routines will not work. Additional

coverage for handling such prompts may be found in the program fragment that accompanies the *_outmem* reference page.

```
if (_registerfonts ("*.FON") <= 0)
{
     _outtext ("Where are the .FON files located? [path]:");
     gets (fondir);
     strcat(fondir, "\*.FON");
     if (_registerfonts (fondir) <= 0)
     {
          _outtext ("Sorry, I cannot register the fonts");
          exit (1);
     }
}
```

COMPATIBILITY

_scrolltextwindow

MSC 3	MSC 4	MSC 5	MSC 6	QC1	QC2	QC2.5	TC1	TC1.5	TC2	TC++	ANSI	UNIX V	XNX	OS2	DOS
			▲			▲								▲	▲

PURPOSE The *_scrolltextwindow* function is used when you want to scroll the text in a text window.

SYNTAX `void _far _scrolltextwindow (short scroll_lines);`

`scroll_lines` *Number of lines to scroll.*

EXAMPLE CALL `_scrolltextwindow (12);`

INCLUDES #include <graph.h> *For function declaration*

DESCRIPTION The *_scrolltextwindow* function scrolls the text in the current text window. Text windows are defined by the *_settextwindow* function. A positive value for the *scroll_lines* argument scrolls the window up, and a negative value scrolls it down.

COMMON USES A frequent use of the *_scrolltextwindow* capability is in Help screens. You typically do not want to obscure much of the display for which the user is asking for help, and scrolling allows your program to provide a lot of information from a small space.

RETURNS There is no return value.

COMMENTS A number that is larger than the height of the current text window is the equivalent of calling the *_clearscreen(_GWINDOW)* function. A value of 0 for the *scroll_lines* argument has no effect.

SEE ALSO `_settextwindow` *To establish a text window*

EXAMPLE The example program shows the *_scrolltextwindow* function in use, moving up and down.

```
#include <conio.h>
#include <graph.h>
#include <stdio.h>

void banner (char *sts_msg);    /* prototype */

void main(void)

{
   short row;
   char  scratch[66];
   /* set up for scroll - install text window */
   _settextrows (25);
   _clearscreen (_GCLEARSCREEN);
   for (row = 1; row <= 25; row++)
   {
      _settextposition (row, 1);
      sprintf (scratch, "Line %c     %2d", row + 'a' - 1, row);
      _outtext (scratch);
   }

   getch();
   _settextwindow (1, 1, 25, 10);
   /* scroll */

   _scrolltextwindow (-7);
   banner ("down 7 lines");

   _scrolltextwindow (6);
   banner ("up   6 lines");

   _setvideomode (_DEFAULTMODE);
}

void banner (char *sts_msg)
```

```
{
    short top, left, bottom, right;
    _gettextwindow (&top, &left, &bottom, &right);
    _settextwindow (1, 25, 8, 80 );
    _outtext (sts_msg);
    getch();
    _clearscreen (_GWINDOW );
    _settextwindow (top, left, bottom, right);
}
```

COMPATIBILITY

_setfont

MSC 3	MSC 4	MSC 5	MSC 6	QC1	QC2	QC2.5	TC1	TC1.5	TC2	TC++	ANSI	UNIX V	XNX	OS2	DOS
			▲		▲	▲			1	1					▲

PURPOSE The *_setfont* function is used to find a font.

SYNTAX

```
short _far _setfont (unsigned char _far *options);
```

The options string, some possible elements of which are in conflict with each other, includes one or more of the following:

`t'name`	*Typeface of the font*
`hx`	*Character height;* x *is the number of pixels*
`wy`	*Character width,* y *is the number of pixels*
`v`	*Find only a vector font; excludes* r, *below*
`r`	*Find only raster-mapped (bitmap) font; excludes* v, *above*
`b`	*Select a best-fit font*
`f`	*Find only a fixed-space font; excludes* p, *below*
`p`	*Find only proportional font; excludes* f, *above*
`nx`	*Select font number;* x *less than or equal to a value returned by* _registerfonts. *This allows you to step through an entire set of fonts.*

EXAMPLE CALL

```
if (_setfont (font_lst) >= 0)
```

INCLUDES `#include <graph.h>` *For function declaration*

DESCRIPTION The *_setfont* routine finds a single font from the set of registered fonts. The font is identified by matching the characteristics specified by the options string, and the function returns the index of that font.

1. The Turbo C 2, 2.5, and Turbo C++ functions are *installuserfont, registerbgifont,* and *registerfarbgifont.*

RETURNS A call to *_setfont* returns the index number, if successful. A negative number is returned if the call failed.

EXAMPLE The code fragment below shows two values being established for the string which serves as the argument in the *_setfont* function. A fully functional example may be found in the font program in the tutorial.

```
/* build option string in font_lst */

strcat (strcat (strcpy (font_lst, "t'"), optns[cntr]), "'");
strcat (font_lst, "h35w20b");

if (_setfont (font_lst) >= 0)
```

_setgtextvector

COMPATIBILITY

MSC 3	MSC 4	MSC 5	MSC 6	QC1	QC2	QC2.5	TC1	TC1.5	TC2	TC++	ANSI	UNIX V	XNX	OS2	DOS
			▲			▲									▲

PURPOSE Use the *_setgtextvector* routine to set the orientation for fonted text output.

SYNTAX

```
struct xycoord _far _setgtextvector (short x, short y);
```

`x, y` *Integer values defining the vector that determines the direction the font text will rotate*

EXAMPLE CALL

```
_setgtextvector (1, 0);
```

INCLUDES `#include <graph.h>` *For function declaration*

DESCRIPTION The *_setgtextvector* function sets the current orientation for font text output. (0,0) is ignored, leaving the font text unchanged; (1,0) generates horizontal text, (0,1) rotates 90 degrees counter-clockwise; (–1,0) rotates 180 degrees from the current position; and (0,–1) rotates the font text 270 degrees counterclockwise.

Combining Graphics and Text

Other values that may be supplied are ignored, although the function will keep the sign of such value. An argument of (0,–4) will yield a (0,–1) result.

RETURNS The previous vector is returned in an *xycoord* structure, as defined in *graph.h*. The values of the *xycoord* structure can be obtained by passing a (0,0) argument to *_setgtextvector*.

SEE ALSO

`_getfontinfo` *To get information about current font*

`_getgtextvector` *To get current text orientation*

EXAMPLE The code fragment below sets a value for *x* and *y* coordinates by interrogating the video configuration structure and then operating on those values. A call to *_getfontinfo* is used to detect the presence of the desired font (specified elsewhere in the program). This code section is from a longer program in the tutorial that displays a sample of whatever presentation graphics fonts are available on a given machine. Fonts numbered 2 and 5 were arbitrarily chosen for an additional display in a 90-degree left-triangle format.

```
{
    x = (vdocnfg.numxpixels) /6;
    y = (vdocnfg.numypixels) /12;
    if (_getfontinfo (&fnt_info))
    {
        _outtext ("Sorry, I cannot find font information");
        break;
    }
    _moveto ((cntr * 4), (y * cntr));
    if (vdocnfg.numcolors > 2) _setcolor (cntr + 2);
    /* display text from the array */

    _setgtextvector (1, 0);
    _outgtext (styls[cntr]);

    /* show two fonts in left angle format */

    if ((cntr == 1) || (cntr == 5))
    {
        _moveto (166, (366 + (cntr * 12)) );
        _setgtextvector (1, 0);
        _outgtext (styls[cntr]);
        _setgtextvector (0, 1);
        _outgtext (styls[cntr]);
    }
}
```

_settextcolor

COMPATIBILITY

MSC 3	MSC 4	MSC 5	MSC 6	QC1	QC2	QC2.5	TC1	TC1.5	TC2	TC++	ANSI	UNIX V	XNX	OS2	DOS
		▲	1	▲	▲	▲		2	2	2				▲	▲

PURPOSE Use the *_settextcolor* function to set the current text color parameter, a short integer value that is used as the attribute for each text character. The mapping of this "attribute value" to a specific color is determined by the current palette. The graphics library allows text color values in the range 0 to 31. The values 0 to 15 produce normal colors (see Table 17-3) while the rest (16 through 31) generate similar colors but with blinking text. As you can see, text color values are not restricted to the range of color numbers available in the current palette (current color and background color in text mode have this restriction). Note that only *_outtext* uses this text color value, other C routines such as *printf* are not affected.

SYNTAX

```
short _far _settextcolor(short color);

short color;        Text color parameter
```

EXAMPLE CALL

```
_settextcolor(1);
```

INCLUDES

```
#include <graph.h>        For function declaration
```

DESCRIPTION The *_settextcolor* function sets the current text color parameter maintained internally by the graphics package. In text mode, each character displayed requires 2 bytes of storage; one holds the ASCII value, the other has an attribute which is the color parameter specified in the argument *color.* This argument can take any value between 0 and 31. The first 16 numbers, 0 to 15, produce text with normal color. The mapping of the value to the color is shown in Table 17-3.

The last 16 values, 16 through 31, display text that is blinking with the color corresponding to the value obtained by subtracting 16. This is the color in which text will appear if you call the graphics library function *_outtext.*

1. Changed in Microsoft C 6.0 to provide OS/2 capability. **2**. The Turbo C and Turbo C++ similar function is *textcolor.*

COMMON USES The *_settextcolor* function enables you to use different text colors as a means of highlighting your output.

RETURNS The *_settextcolor* function returns the previous value of the text color parameter.

Combining Graphics and Text

SEE ALSO `_gettextcolor` *To retrieve the current text color*

EXAMPLE Assuming that the display environment is already in a text mode, generate a screenful of text showing each text color. Use *_settextcolor* to set the color and *_outtext* to display the strings. Show the first 16 colors on the left half of the screen and the corresponding blinking colors on the right half.

```
#include <stdio.h>
#include <graph.h>
main()
{
    char buffer[80];
    short i, color, lastcolor;
/* Assume we are already in text mode */
    _clearscreen(_GCLEARSCREEN);     /* Clear screen */
/* Set up initial text position */
    _settextposition(1,1);
/* Display the first 16 colors  */
    for (i=0; i<16; i++)
    {
/* Set a text color and show what the return value is*/
        lastcolor = _settextcolor(i);
        sprintf(buffer,"Current color = %2d, \
last value= %2d\n", i, lastcolor);
        _outtext(buffer);       /* Display the string */
    }
/* Display the next 16 colors on right half of screen */
    for (i=16; i<32; i++)
    {
/* Set a text color and show what the return value is */
        lastcolor = _settextcolor(i);
        sprintf(buffer,"Current color = %2d, \
last value= %2d\n", i, lastcolor);
        _settextposition(i-15, 40);
        _outtext(buffer);       /* Display the string */
    }
}
```

_settextcursor

COMPATIBILITY

MSC 3	MSC 4	MSC 5	MSC 6	QC1	QC2	QC2.5	TC1	TC1.5	TC2	TC++	ANSI	UNIX V	XNX	OS2	DOS
			▲		▲	▲				▲				▲	▲

PURPOSE Use the *_settextcursor* function to adjust the size of the cursor.

SYNTAX
```
short _far _settextcursor (short attr);
```

`attr` *0x0707, 0x0007, 0x0607, 0x2000, etc.*

EXAMPLE CALL
```
short new_crsr = 0x007;             /* solid block */

_settextcursor (new_crsr);
```

INCLUDES `#include <graph.h>` *For function declaration*

DESCRIPTION The shape of the BIOS cursor can, in text modes, be amended by passing a short as an argument to *_setttextcursor*. The short is a two-byte type. The low-order byte of the argument determines the bottom line of the cursor, and legal values are typically 0 through 7. The high-order byte determines the top line of the cursor, and the 0-through-7 range obtains there as well. A value of 0x2000 turns the cursor off.

A cursor attribute of 0x0707 generates an underlining cursor 1 pixel row high. Both the top and bottom of the cursor are on row 7. An attribute of 0x0007 generates a full cursor because the top and bottom values are 8-pixel rows apart.

1. The Turbo C++ function is *_setcursortype*.

COMMON USES Changing the shape of a cursor is one way to identify a mode shift in a program. A text editor, for example, may use an underlining cursor for normal text entry but switch to a full block cursor when certain tasks (such as delete or text move) are invoked. This helps alert the user to the fact that something important is happening.

RETURNS The previous cursor attribute if successful; –1 if not. Calling the function in a graphics mode will yield an error.

SEE ALSO `_gettextcursor` *To get current cursor shape*

EXAMPLE There is a sample program on the reference page for *_gettextcursor*.

Combining Graphics and Text

COMPATIBILITY

_settextposition

MSC 3	MSC 4	MSC 5	MSC 6	QC1	QC2	QC2.5	TC1	TC1.5	TC2	TC++	ANSI	UNIX V	XNX	OS2	DOS
		▲	1	▲	▲	▲		2	2	2				▲	▲

PURPOSE Use *_settextposition* to move the current text position to a specific row and column in both text and graphics modes. The text output function *_outtext* as well as standard C output routines such as *printf* begins displaying text from this position.

SYNTAX

```
struct rccoord _far _settextposition(short row, short column);
```

`short row, column;` *Row and column where new text output will begin*

EXAMPLE CALL

```
_settextposition(24, 1);
```

INCLUDES `#include <graph.h>` *For function declaration and definition of the structure* rccoord

DESCRIPTION The *_settextposition* function changes the current text position maintained internally by the graphics package to the row and column specified in the arguments *row, column*. This position becomes the starting point for all future text outputs from such routines as *_outtext*, *printf*, and other console I/O routines.

The upper-left corner of the screen in text mode corresponds to row 1 and column 1. The maximum row and column numbers allowable can be determined by calling *_getvideoconfig* in the text mode.

Text output can be limited to a smaller region by calling *_settextwindow* to define a window. After calling *_textwindow*, all row and column references are considered relative to the upper-left corner of the window (see *_settextwindow*).

1. Changed in Microsoft C 6.0 to provide OS/2 capability. 2. The Turbo C and Turbo C++ function is *gotoxy*.

COMMON USES The *_settextposition* function can position text output at arbitrary locations on the screen.

RETURNS The *_settextposition* function returns a structure of type *rccoord*, which contains the row and column of the last text position (the cursor's location before *_settextposition* was called). This structure is defined in the include file *graph.h* and is shown below.

```
struct rccoord    /* Structure for text position   */
{
```

```
    short row;     /* row number of text position    */
    short col;     /* column number of text position */
};
```

The last position returned in this structure can be used to save and restore the old text position.

SEE ALSO

`_gettextposition`	*To get current text position in a structure of type* rccoord
`_outtext`	*To display text starting at current text position*

EXAMPLE Suppose you are in a text mode on a color display. Define a position for text by calling *_settextposition.* Prepare a string containing the previous text position returned by *_settext* and display it by calling *_outtext.* When you hit a key, the program should advance to the next row and display the same information again. Exit when the user hits a 'q'.

```
#include <stdio.h>
#include <graph.h>
main()
{
    struct rccoord lastpos;
    short row = 1;
    char c=0, buffer[80];
    _clearscreen(_GCLEARSCREEN);       /* Clear screen */
/* Keep on displaying text until user hits 'q'        */
    while(1)
    {
/* Set new position */
        lastpos = _settextposition(row,1);
        sprintf(buffer, "Hit 'q' to exit. Last \
position = (%d,%d)", lastpos.row, lastpos.col);
        _outtext(buffer);
        c = getch();
        if(c == 'q' || c == 'Q')
        {
            _setvideomode(_DEFAULTMODE); /* reset mode*/
            exit(0);
        }
        row++;                    /* Advance to next row */
    }
}
```

Combining Graphics and Text

COMPATIBILITY

_settextrows

MSC 3	MSC 4	MSC 5	MSC 6	QC1	QC2	QC2.5	TC1	TC1.5	TC2	TC++	ANSI	UNIX V	XNX	OS2	DOS
			▲		▲	▲	▲							▲	▲

PURPOSE Use the *_settextrows* routine when you wish to specify the number of text rows to be used in a text-mode program.

SYNTAX

```
short _far _settextrows (short txt_rows);
```

`txt_rows` *The number of text rows you are requesting*

EXAMPLE CALL

```
_settextrows (25);
```

INCLUDES `#include <graph.h>` *For function declaration*

The *_settextrows* function requests the number of text rows to be used in the current video mode.

RETURNS The number of rows actually set is returned if the call is a success. An unexpected error returns a 0 for a value.

SEE ALSO `_getvideoconfig` *To set video settings information*

EXAMPLE The first code fragment sets up a 25-row scroll area. The second fragment uses a somewhat more portable construction by specifying the constant _MAXTEXTROWS as the argument to *_settextrows*. The _MAXTEXTROWS value will yield a 50-row display on a VGA system, 43 rows on EGA hardware, and 25 rows on other systems. There are graphics modes that support either 30 or 60 rows, and the _MAXTEXTROWS argument chooses the 60-row option in that case.

Another example may be found in the program that accompanies the reference page for the *_scrolltextwindow* function.

```
/* FRAGMENT ONE */

_settextrows (25);
_clearscreen (_GCLEARSCREEN);

for( row = 1; row <= 25; row++ )
{
     /* various processing steps */
}
getch();
```

```
/* FRAGMENT TWO */
_settextrows (_MAXTEXTROWS);
_clearscreen (_GCLEARSCREEN);
for( row = 1; row <= _MAXTEXTROWS; row++ )
{
     /* various processing steps */
}
getch();
```

_settextwindow

COMPATIBILITY

MSC 3	MSC 4	MSC 5	MSC 6	QC1	QC2	QC2.5	TC1	TC1.5	TC2	TC++	ANSI	UNIX V	XNX	OS2	DOS
		▲	▲	▲	▲	▲		1	1	1				▲	▲

PURPOSE Use *_settextwindow* to define a window in terms of row and column coordinates (see the tutorial section) for scrolled text output. You can define a new background color for text (see *_setbkcolor*) and clear the text window to give it a different background color from the rest. Similar windows for graphics can be defined by calling the *_setviewport* function.

SYNTAX

```
void _far _settextwindow(short r1, short c1, short r2, short c2);
```

`short r1, c1;` *Upper-left corner of text window in row and column coordinates*

`short r2, c2;` *Lower-right corner of text window in row and column coordinates*

EXAMPLE CALL

```
_settextwindow(10, 10, 16, 70);
```

INCLUDES #include <graph.h> *For function declaration*

DESCRIPTION The *_settextwindow* function defines an area of the screen (a text window) as the current display window for text output. The window is specified in terms of the row and column (row 1, column 1 corresponds to the upper-left corner of the screen) coordinates of the upper-left corner (*x1, y1*) and that of the lower-right corner (*x2, y2*).

Once the text window is defined, all row and column references are relative to the upper-left corner of the window (see the example below).

1. The Turbo C and Turbo C++ version of this function is *window*.

COMMON USES The *_settextwindow* function can be used to design pop-up menus.

Combining Graphics and Text

SEE ALSO `_setbkcolor` *To change the background color*

`_settextposition` *To set location where text is output next*

`_outtext` *To display text*

EXAMPLE Suppose you are in a text mode on a color display. Define a window for text by calling *_settextwindow*. Set a new background color by calling *_setbkcolor* and call *_clearscreen* to clear the text window and fill it with the new background color. Let the user type lines of text into the window to show the effect of scrolling in the window.

```
#include <stdio.h>
#include <graph.h>
/* Need a "long" constant for _setbkcolor   */
#define RED 4L
main()
{
    unsigned i=0;
    char c=0, buffer[80];
    _clearscreen(_GCLEARSCREEN); /* Clear screen */
    _settextwindow(10,10,15,70);
    _setbkcolor(RED);            /* Set background color to red */
    _clearscreen(_GWINDOW);      /* clear text window */

/* Once a text window is defined all text positions are
 * relative to upper-left corner of the window. This
 * can be used for pop-up menus
*/
    _settextposition(1,1);     /* Display a message  */
    _outtext("Scrolling in a text window\n");
/* Let user see the effect of scrolling */
    while(1)
    {
/* Notice the use of a buffer and sprintf to print a
 * formatted string with _outtext
 */
        sprintf(buffer,
            "Hit 'q' to exit. -- else scroll %d\n",i);
        _outtext(buffer);
        c = getch();
        if(c == 'q' || c == 'Q')
        {
            _setvideomode(_DEFAULTMODE); /* reset mode*/
            exit(0);
```

```
            }
            i++;
        }
    }
```

_unregisterfonts

COMPATIBILITY

MSC 3	MSC 4	MSC 5	MSC 6	QC1	QC2	QC2.5	TC1	TC1.5	TC2	TC++	ANSI	UNIX V	XNX	OS2	DOS
			▲		▲	▲									▲

PURPOSE The *_unregisterfonts* routine allows you to free the memory taken up by fonts that are no longer in use.

SYNTAX

```
void _far _unregisterfonts (void);
```

EXAMPLE CALL

```
_unregisterfonts();
```

INCLUDES `#include <graph.h>` *For function declaration*

DESCRIPTION The *_unregisterfonts* function frees memory previously allocated and used by the *_registerfonts* function. It removes the header information for all fonts but unloads only the currently selected font from memory.

COMMON USES Managing memory is an increasingly complex problem. This routine allows you to use several fonts in an application without consuming so much memory that other parts of the application cannot fit.

RETURNS There is no return value.

EXAMPLE The font program in the tutorial and the several variants found in other reference entries (such as for *_getfontinfo*) show usage of the *_unregisterfonts* routine.

Combining Graphics and Text

COMPATIBILITY

_wrapon

MSC 3	MSC 4	MSC 5	MSC 6	QC1	QC2	QC2.5	TC1	TC1.5	TC2	TC++	ANSI	UNIX V	XNX	OS2	DOS
		▲	1	▲	▲	▲								▲	▲

PURPOSE Use the *_wrapon* function to control whether text being output by *_outtext* is clipped or wrapped to the next line when the text string extends beyond the current text window. The default setting is to wrap long lines.

SYNTAX

```
short _far _wrapon(short flag);
```

`short flag;` *Turn wrapping on or off*

EXAMPLE CALL

```
_wrapon(_GWRAPOFF);
```

INCLUDES `#include <graph.h>` *For function declaration and definition of constants for the flag*

DESCRIPTION The *_wrapon* function copies the argument *flag* into an internal flag in the graphics package used by the text output routine *_outtext* to decide how to handle a line of text that extends beyond the edge of the current text window. The setting of the flag can take one of two defined values shown below. The interpretation of each value is also shown. Table 19-4 shows these constants, which are defined in the include file *graph.h*.

Table 19-4. *Constants Used by _wrapon*

Constant	Interpretation
_GWRAPOFF	Long lines are truncated at the edge of text window.
_GWRAPON	Lines extending beyond the text window get wrapped to a new line.

1. The *_wrapon* function was changed in Microsoft C 6.0 to provide OS/2 compatibility.

RETURNS The *_wrapon* function returns a short integer containing the value of the *flag* before the current call.

COMMENTS The wrapping is done by character, not by word. You have to write your own routines to break lines at word boundaries.

SEE ALSO

`_settextwindow` *To define a window within which text is output*

`_outtext` *To display a text string*

EXAMPLE In a text mode, define a window for text by calling *_settextwindow*. Fill the window with a new color to make it distinguishable from the rest by setting a new background color with *_setbkcolor* and calling *_clearscreen* to clear the text window. Select an appropriate text color and demonstrate the effects of calling *_wrapon*.

```
#include <stdio.h>
#include <graph.h>
/* Need a "long" constant for _setbkcolor  */
#define RED    4L
/* Text color number 14 is yellow          */
#define YELLOW 14
main()
{
/* Assume we are already in text mode                 */
    _clearscreen(_GCLEARSCREEN);     /* Clear screen */

    _settextwindow(5,30,20,50); /* Define text window*/
/* Set background color to red                        */
    _setbkcolor(RED);
    _clearscreen(_GWINDOW); /* clear out text window */

/* Once a text window is defined, all text positions
 * are relative to the upper-left corner of the window.
 */

    _settextposition(1,1);     /* Set text position  */
/* Show the effect of default setting first           */
    _outtext("As you can see, default is WRAP ON\n");

    _settextcolor(YELLOW);      /* Set text color   */
/* Turn wrapping off and show the results -- truncated
 * line
 */
    _wrapon(_GWRAPOFF);
    _outtext("This line extends beyond the edge.\n");
    _outtext("That was WRAP OFF.\n\n");
/* Turn wrapping back on and see line being wrapped  */
    _wrapon(_GWRAPON);
    _outtext("Now it's WRAP ON:\n");
    _outtext("This line extends beyond the edge.\n");
}
```

Combining Graphics and Text

Index

D

H

I

T

U

Microsoft C Functions Arranged by Chapter

3. Process Control

4. Variable-Length Argument Lists

5. Memory Allocation and Management

6. Buffer Manipulation

7. Data Conversion Routines

8. Math Routines

9. Character Classification and Conversion

10. String Comparison and Manipulation